STUDY GUIDE TO ACCOMPANY SAMUELSON-NORDHAUS

ECONOMICS

STUDY GUIDE TO ACCOMPANY SAMUELSON-NORDHAUS

ECONOMICS

Thirteenth Edition

GARY W. YOHE

Wesleyan University

McGRAW-HILL BOOK COMPANY

New York St. Louis San Francisco Auckland Bogotá Caracas Colorado Springs Hamburg Lisbon London Madrid Mexico Milan Montreal New Delhi Oklahoma City Panama Paris San Juan São Paulo Singapore Sydney Tokyo Toronto

STUDY GUIDE TO ACCOMPANY
SAMUELSON AND NORDHAUS: ECONOMICS

1 2 3 4 5 6 7 8 9 0 HES HES 8 9 4 3 2 1 0 9

ISBN 0-07-054799-8

This book was set in Times Roman with Helvetica by Publication Services.
The editors were Elisa Adams, Scott D. Stratford, and Peggy C. Rehberger;
the designer was Joan E. O'Connor;
the production supervisor was Diane Renda.
Cover illustration by Roy Wiemann.
New drawings were done by Fine Line Illustrations, Inc.
D. B. Hess was printer and binder.

FOR LINDA

CONTENTS

To the Student

This *Study Guide* has one specific objective: to help you master the fundamentals of economic analysis as presented in the thirteenth edition of *Economics* by Paul A. Samuelson and William D. Nordhaus. It has been prepared in close consultation with these authors to cover the material presented in the text and to involve you in deciphering that material. It is hoped that your work in the *Guide* will lead you to a deeper understanding of not only the content of each chapter of the text, but also of the rationale for anyone's ever worrying about such things. It will, however, accomplish this goal only if your reading of the *Guide* is an active process. If you simply read the pages of the *Guide* as you would any other text, you will see another presentation of the same material, but nothing more. Your passive reading will have caused you to lose most of the value of your supplementary purchase. If, however, you read the pages more slowly with pencil in hand and work through the various questions that they will pose, your active participation in exercising the fundamentals of economic analysis will generate a deeper understanding of what is going on and, I hope, a higher grade in your economics class.

Each chapter of the *Guide* begins with a list of learning objectives. These lists have been prepared to outline the major points of each chapter and appendix. After reading the text chapter, match them with a list that you draw up to see whether you (or I) have missed anything. You will, at that point, have a good idea of the material that the remainder of the chapter will exercise.

The second major part of each chapter in the *Guide* amounts to a collection of questions and problems designed to enhance your understanding of the learning objectives. Working through them one at a time (*before* looking at the answers provided in small print after each question) will test and extend your knowledge as you apply what the text has taught you. The process is much like the one by which you might learn a new language. You can go to class and read textbooks to be exposed to the fundamentals of a new language, but it sinks in and becomes part of you only if you practice. With enough practice, you begin to think in the new language, and further progress becomes easier. Working through the question section of the *Guide*, you will similarly practice what you have learned in class and in the text, and eventually you might even begin to think like an economist.

Each chapter in the *Guide* concludes with a series of multiple choice quiz questions, with the answers provided at the end of the book. These are designed to tell you whether or not you have really mastered the chapter's content. You should, as you work through the questions, select one of the five alternative answers. It should be the answer that makes the *most* sense in context. Some answers are correct statements but are irrelevant to the question being posed. Other answers are simply wrong. Still others are almost right, but nonetheless inferior to an alternative choice. The answer listed in the back represents the *best* selection, and is accompanied by a brief explanation of why. The multiple choice sections are as much a part of the *Guide* as other sections, and taking care in working through them should pay dividends.

One of the most successful ways of mastering the fundamentals of economic analysis is to try to summarize the material of each chapter or unit in successively shorter outlines. The prose that surrounds the questions in the middle of each *Guide* chapter represents a first cut at such an outline. The list of learning objectives can, perhaps, represent a final stage. In the process of synthesizing text material down to the lists of objectives, use the *Guide* to look for threads of common thought and rationalization. When you have reached the point of needing only the objectives lists to recall content, make sure that you have a firm understanding of their connection to each other. Having accomplished that understanding, you will be able to apply your knowledge to unfamiliar problems and contexts.

The real lessons of economics are ones of process—insights into the methods by which economists try to identify logically the essentials of a particular circumstance from a multitude of data. Equipped with insight into these processes and methods, you will be ready to proceed to subsequent economics courses and do well. Perhaps more importantly, though, you will be equipped with the mental skills necessary to deal with the myriad of economics-related issues and decisions that will face you all of your life. You may forget what marginal cost is, but you should continue to be able to identify essential tradeoffs and weigh them accordingly.

ACKNOWLEDGMENTS

Preparation of this *Guide* would not have been accomplished on schedule without the assistance of many people. I would like to formally recognize their contributions and express my gratitude.

My family, who missed another summer of my attention but supported my efforts anyway, certainly deserves a heartfelt "thanks." Their support certainly made the project worthwhile. Gerome Le Chat also contributed steadfast loyalty and moral support; N.W.W. d'Automne provided necessary comic relief.

The following reviewers, through their comments and constructive criticisms, helped to strengthen this study guide: Cecil Gouke, Ohio State University; Trellis Green, University of Southern Mississippi; Roger Hewett, Drake University; Steven J. Matusz, Michigan State University; James Rigterink, Polk Community College; Richard Robertson, Hinds Community College; James Scheib, Red Rocks Community College; and Jack Wimberly, University of Southern Mississippi.

Many people at McGraw-Hill also deserve grateful acknowledgment. Peggy Rehberger and Eileen Gualberto certainly fall into that category. A special thanks must, however, be extended to Elisa Adams. Her excellent work, good humor, and constant encouragement were above and beyond.

Finally, I express my gratitude for the opportunity, education, and friendship offered by Bill Nordhaus.

Gary W. Yohe

NOTE TO STUDENTS USING THE PAPERBACK
INTRODUCTION TO MICROECONOMICS
INTRODUCTION TO MACROECONOMICS

by Samuelson-Nordhaus

The following chapters in this Study Guide relate to your paperback text:

	TEXT	STUDY GUIDE
INTRODUCTION TO MICROECONOMICS	1–4	1–4
	5	18
	6	19
	7	20
	8	21
	9	22
	10	23
	11	24
	12	25
	13	26
	14	27
	15	28
	16	29
	17	30
	18	31
	19	32
	20	33
	21	34
	22	35
	23	36
	24	37
	25	38
	26	39
	27	40
INTRODUCTION TO MACROECONOMICS	1–17	1–17
	18	36
	19	37
	20	38
	21	39
	22	40

STUDY GUIDE TO ACCOMPANY SAMUELSON-NORDHAUS

ECONOMICS

CHAPTER 1
INTRODUCTION

This introductory chapter is, above all, one which should be read with a view toward perspective. It has been designed to provide a rough outline of what the discipline of economics is all about. You need not worry terribly about the few details that are presented. Try, instead, to get the "lay of the land." Try to get an idea of why people would ever want to concern themselves with the study of economics and how, in broad and general terms, such a study should be conducted. Having kept this in mind, you should be able to meet the following objectives after studying the text chapter and working through the *Study Guide* questions. (Each chapter in this guide will begin with a similar list of objectives. These lists should serve as both preliminary outlines of the material that you are about to cover and, once you have completed the chapter, review outlines of the points that you should have mastered. They will serve you best, therefore, if you read them at least twice—once as a preview of coming attractions and once again as a review of past material.)

LEARNING OBJECTIVES

1. Understand the breadth of the study of economics by understanding how all the topics mentioned in the specialized definitions of economics fit into the umbrella definition: *Economics is the study of how societies choose to use scarce resources that have alternative uses to produce commodities of various kinds and to distribute those commodities to various people.*

2. Distinguish between microeconomics and macroeconomics and between positive and normative economics.

3. Identify and describe the four major tools in the scientific approach to the study of economic issues.

4. Identify and explain the many potential pitfalls in the study of economics: the fallacy of composition, the fallacy of *post hoc, ergo propter hoc*, the fallacy of failing to hold other things constant, the danger of advancing individual subjective views of the world as generally valid descriptions of how the world operates, and the difficulties of coping with the enormous uncertainties of our economic lives. Explain how each might lead to faulty undersanding of an economic system.

5. Describe how the law of averages helps us uncover economic knowledge in the face of uncertainty.

The text provides a very brief historical perspective by citing three individuals whose contributions represent landmarks in the development of economics as a scholarly discipline. Adam Smith published *The Wealth of Nations* in 1776, Karl Marx published *Capital* (*Das Kapital*) in three installments from 1867 to 1894, and John Maynard Keynes published *The General Theory of Employment, Interest and Money* in 1936. You will become increasingly familiar with these men and their thinking as you progress through your study of economics. It is enough, at this point, to be familiar with the broadest descriptions of their work.

1. Indicate in the parentheses provided whether the following statements apply to the work of Adam Smith (S), Karl Marx (M), or John Maynard Keynes (K).

a. Capitalism is doomed, and its abuses will quickly be followed by business depressions, revolution, and socialism. ( )

b. Active fiscal and monetary management by federal governments can be used to avoid the worst downturns of the traditional business cycle. . . . . ( )

c. Markets can function quite well in the allocation of scarce resources if they are set free from heavy-handed governmental regulation and intervention. . . . . ( )

---

a. (M) **b.** (K) **c.** (S)

Five alternative definitions of economics are cited in the text. Paraphrased slightly, they are:

1. Economics is the study of activities that involve the production and/or the exchange of goods.
2. Economics is the analysis of trends in the variables that summarize the performance of the overall economy—prices, output, employment, etc.
3. Economics is the study of how people choose to use scarce resources to produce various goods and to distribute those goods across society.
4. Economics is the study of commerce, broadly defined.
5. Economics is the study of money, banking, capital, and wealth.

Economics is, of course, all of these things and much more. A single, umbrella definition is therefore provided to capture a common theme:

> Economics is the study of how societies use scarce resources to produce valuable commodities and distribute them among different groups of people.

2. Review the five more specialized definitions of economics cited above and try to see how each fits under the general umbrella. With all six notions in mind, which of the following seem to fall correctly (C) within the scope of economic investigation and which seem to fall outside (O) the general umbrella?

a. The first objective of economics as a science is to study the psychology of human performance in producing and selling goods in order to indicate to business how it can induce people to perform these activities more efficiently. . . . . . . *(C / O)*

b. Economics is closely associated with the particular activities in which money is involved—the purchase and sale of goods and of securities, the employment of labor, and so on. *(C / O)*

c. Economics is a study of the activities with which a nation acquires a high standard of income and of consumption. *(C / O)*

d. In economics, we look at the processes of producing, selling, buying, and consuming goods in order to develop some theory with respect to these behaviors. . . . . *(C / O)*

e. Economics is a study of how people in a society decide what commodities and services they are going to produce, now and in the future, and how those commodities and services are to be distributed among members of the population. . . . *(C / O)*

---

a. O **b.** C **c.** C **d.** C **e.** C

Within the general rubric of economics, a significant distinction is made between studying the behavior of individual components of an economy (individuals, households, firms, industries, etc.), on the one hand, and the functioning of the economy taken as a whole, on the other. The former, called **microeconomics**, looks at the small building blocks of a larger system. How are vegetable prices set? How do people negotiate their employment contracts? How should people negotiate those contracts? Will some people work less hard if they are forced to pay higher income taxes? Will some save more if they are forced to pay higher sales taxes? These are the types of questions that are asked in the study of microeconomics.

By way of contrast, **macroeconomics** focuses on broader sorts of questions. How is national income determined? What is the relationship (if any) between the rate of unemployment and the rate of inflation? How should we expect the economy to respond to an enlarged supply of money? What should we expect to see as a consequence of enormous budget deficits at the federal level? These are all macroeconomic issues.

3. To exercise your understanding of the distinction between microeconomics and macroeconomics, consider the following list of publications. Each will appear in a footnote somewhere later in the text. Indicate, simply on the basis of the content suggested by the titles, whether or not you expect to see each in Part Two or Three of the text, in which macroeconomics (MA) is covered, or in Part Four or Five, where microeconomics (MI) is covered.

a. Arthur Okun, *The Political Economy of Prosperity* . . . . *(MA / MI)*

b. Orley Ashenfelter, "Union Relative Wage Effects," in Stone and Petersen (eds.), *Econometric Contributions to Public Policy* . . . . *(MA / MI)*

c. Edward Denison, "Is U.S. Growth Understated because of the Underground Economy? Employment Ratios Suggest Not," *Review of Income and Wealth* . . . . *(MA / MI)*

d. R. J. Gordon, "Inflation, Flexible Exchange Rates and the Natural Rate of Unemployment," in M. N. Baily (ed.), *Workers, Jobs and Inflation* . . . . *(MA / MI)*

e. Joseph Pechman, *Who Bears the Tax Burden?* . *(MA / MI)*

f. A. A. Berle, Jr., and Gardner Means, *The Modern Corporation and Private Property* . . . . *(MA / MI)*

---

a. MA **b.** MI **c.** MA **d.** MA **e.** MI **f.** MI

4. Economic knowledge is generally the result of research conducted according to what has been dubbed the **scientific approach**. List the four major tools of the scientific approach:

a. ______________________

b. ______________________

c. ______________________

d. ______________________

Of the four tools noted above, ______________________

is the process by which a multitude of data and seemingly unrelated facts are shaped into a coherent view of reality. It is a process that depends upon ____________________ for the generation of some initial hypotheses. Without some careful review of what history tells us, we have no idea what to study. We have no hypotheses to investigate.

Validation of the hypotheses can be accomplished by one of at least two means. The most common is ______________________________, in which mathematical methods are used to test whether or not the relationships suggested either by a preliminary review of history or by the logical implications of a theory or hypothesis hold water. With what degree of confidence can we put forward a correlation of economic variables as an interesting, causal connection? The answer to this question depends upon, among other things, the strength and accuracy of the purported connection, the quality of the data, and the degree to which the connection can be isolated. In a few cases, though, ________ ______________________________ can be employed to serve the same function. Problems here involve designing and administering the exercise so that the data collected are useful, constructing and administering the control group so that statistical analysis of the data can be conducted "other things being held equal," and maintaining interest over the long time required to generate undistorted data.

---

a. observation **b.** analysis **c.** statistical analysis **d.** controlled experiments; analysis; observation; statistical analysis; controlled experiments

The distinction between microeconomics and macroeconomics can, to be sure, blur somewhat at their interface. When, for example, is an industry so large that an analysis of its response to a certain tax treatment is a question of macroeconomics and not microeconomics? When does a question of tax burden get so large that it has macroeconomic content? The list can be extended almost indefinitely. Recognizing this blurring is not, however, nearly as important as recognizing that macroeconomic and microeconomic views of how the world behaves must be consistent with each other. Sure, the economy taken as a whole is only a physical collection of individual economic agents operating in their own little environments. But how, in our study of economics, are we to add the actions of many agents to get a picture of an overall economy? The answer is, Very carefully.

The text includes a short section on potential pitfalls in economic reasoning; the **fallacy of composition** is a major concern of that section. This fallacy occurs when something that is known to be true for a part of an organization (or a microeconomy) is therefore assumed to be true for the whole organization (an overall macroeconomy). While our knowledge of how a macroeconomy works must be checked for consistency with our understanding of how its microeconomic components behave, it must also be developed in its own right if we are to make certain that we avoid this fallacy. The distinction between micro and macro is far more than a semantic one; you will see different tools and different modes of analysis presented as you pass from coverage of macroeconomics in Parts Two and Three of the text into coverage of microeconomics in Parts Four and Five.

Two other logical pitfalls are also identified in the text. The first of these, linked with **failing to keep "other things equal,"** notes that the interdependencies of economic systems frequently make it difficult to study the relationship in which you are interested. Failure to note these interdependencies can, however, prove fatal. Suppose, for example, that you noticed that sales of Japanese VCRs climbed throughout 1985 and 1986 even though a falling dollar made the machines increasingly expensive. You might conclude that more people wanted Japanese VCRs simply because the VCRs got more expensive, and you would be wrong. To draw such a conclusion, you would have to show that the increase in demand was not produced by other possible causes (e.g., higher incomes, an increase in the number of good movies available at video rental stores, reduced rental prices at those stores, an increase in the cost of hiring babysitters and going out to the movies, a perceived reduction in the quality of VCRs produced elsewhere in the world, etc.). Otherwise, we should expect that the normal relationship between price and demand held notwithstanding the experience of 1985 and 1986: all other things held constant, the observed higher prices for VCRs in 1985 and 1986 would have meant smaller demand.

The next fallacy, labelled *post hoc, ergo propter hoc*, is closely related to, but less subtle than, the "other things equal" pitfall. It warns that the fact that two events happen at the same time does not necessarily mean that one caused the other. People have noted that sunspot activity usually increases during times of recession in the United States. Do U.S. recessions cause sunspots? Hardly. Do sunspots cause recessions? Hard to swallow, too, unless you believe that increased sunspot activity increases some sort of radiation onto the earth's surface that somehow makes people less productive.

5. For each statement listed below, indicate whether the fallacy of composition (C), the fallacy of *post hoc, ergo propter hoc* (P), or the fallacy of failing to hold all other things equal (E) is involved. If none of the three applies, record (N).

a. The American economy remains essentially competitive as a result of diligent application of the antitrust laws. . . . . . *(   )*

b. All theories in social science are forced to simplify the real and complex world; because of this simplification, the conclusions of any such theory are inevitably distorted and inaccurate explanations. . . . . *(   )*

c. Workers in any single industry will benefit from higher wages; hence workers in all industries would benefit from a comparable wage increase. . . . . ( )

d. During the early stages of the energy-price shock of the late 1970s, lines at gasoline stations all across the United States typically extended well into the streets. It is clear, therefore, that the demand for gasoline increased dramatically as its price doubled. . . . . ( )

e. A recent report in the *New England Journal of Medicine* observed that gypsies in Boston all smoked too much but hardly ever died of lung cancer. Doubt is thus cast upon the purported link between excessive smoking and the incidence of lung cancer. . . . . ( )

f. The more the human brain masters a subject in social science, such as economics, the less room it has for comprehension of ny quite different subject, such as physics. . . . . ( )

g. If one firm in an industry benefits from a large-scale advertising campaign, this is an indication that if all firms in that industry were to advertise, they would all obtain comparable increases in sales. . . . . ( )

h. I can gain 15 minutes by driving my car to work instead of using public transportation; if everyone in my community were to follow my example, the total gain in time would run into hundreds of hours each day. ( )

---

a. P **b.** N **c.** C **d.** E **e.** P **f.** N **g.** C **h.** C

Two other pitfalls in the study of economics are cited in the text. Unlike the previous three, though, neither relates to the logical construction of an economic investigation. Both, instead, ask that we ponder how we interpret what we see. First, we are reminded that we all look at the world through glasses that are tinted by our own **subjective** impressions of how things are. Collecting the "facts" about a situation is thus not always an easy task. The raw elements of experience which our senses carry to the brain are meaningless until they are organized into a pattern. The brain's disposition in that process is to fit the material, if possible, into a familiar pattern even though, in the new situation, that pattern may be a false one.

When the ordinary business of living requires us to do so, we are forced to develop some workably valid interpretations of the behavior around us. In everyday experience, we can often discover quickly whether or not our conclusions are workably accurate. Interpret a person's behavior falsely, act on your conclusion, and you may soon learn that your interpretation was incorrect. There is, however, a broader range of human experience where this element of immediate verification is lacking, or where the degree of verification is uncertain. When the verification of a theory is difficult, the familiar theory may survive regardless of its veracity until it can be supplanted by a clearly superior theory. The risk involved in this process should be clear. If an unsatisfactory theory is used so frequently that it becomes entrenched in the canonical view of the world, then the development of a new, potentially superior theory will become highly unlikely—nobody will think to question an ingrained theory, so nobody will try to develop a new one.

The final pitfall, dealing with the **uncertainties** that pervade our economic lives, can compound the difficulties involved in validating our subjective views of the world. Economics is the study of extremely complicated decisions being made simultaneously by billions of people all across the world. The outcomes of these decisions frequently depend upon the decisions made by others, and the resulting interdependence compounds the confusion of linking cause to effect. Overall, therefore, economic laws hold only on the average.

For any given proposition showing how people should behave in a given circumstance, it is always possible to find someone or some firm that does perfectly well by doing something different. For any given proposition linking some action to a specific effect, there are historical episodes in which the causality did not hold. The general patterns of economic relationships may therefore be obscured by exceptions, and the truth of these propositions may be difficult to validate. Still, if the proposition is true and it really is in people's best interest to respond to the given circumstance as reported, then careful study should be able to find sufficient conformity to achieve validation. If the causality has been correctly described, then careful study should be able to uncover it despite the clutter of contradictory circumstances. Economics, as a profession, has been in the forefront in developing analytical and statistical tools to accomplish these sorts of tasks.

6. Consider Figure 1-1 (Figure 1-2 in the text). A straight line with a slope equal to *(0.50 / 0.95 / 1.2)* shows a general relationship for the United States between total consumption expenditure and total disposable income. It is based on the hypothesis that people tend to spend more when they have more income, but it is more specific than that. The slope of the indicated relationship means that *(all people / people on the average)* consistently spent *(50 / 95 / 120)* cents of the last dollar that they earned on consumption.

Figure 1-2 suggests one way in which Figure 1-1 might be correct even if many people spent more or less than 95 cents of the dollar. Notice that more than 10 percent of the people spent 97 cents of the dollar. Roughly the same percentage spent 93 cents. Five percent spent 91 cents, and less than 2 percent even spent 101 cents. (How? By dipping into their savings—perhaps because good times seemed to be on the way or perhaps in response to an emergency.) All that is required to support

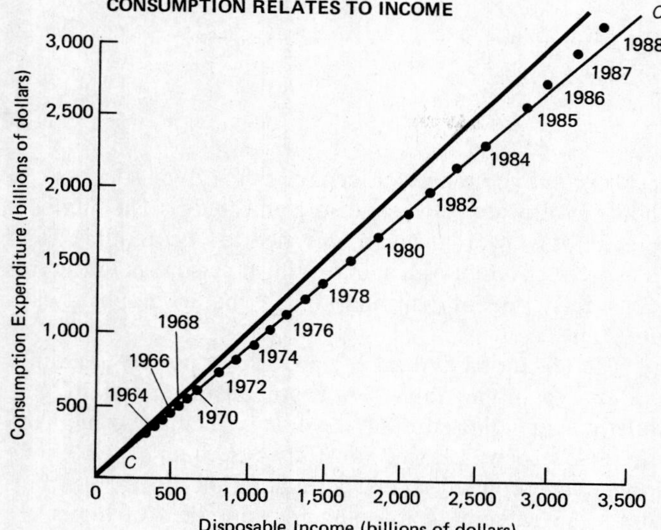

Figure 1-1

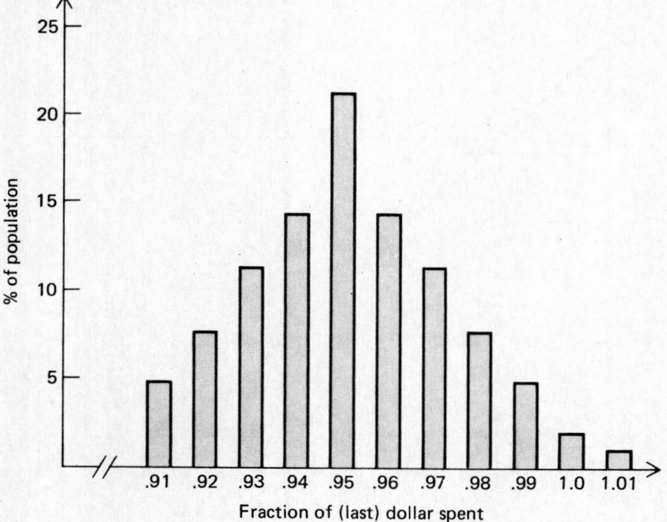

Figure 1-2

Figure 1-1 is that these fractions *(sum to 0.95 / converge to 0.95 / average 0.95)*. Given that support, Figure 1-1 tells us that people spent roughly 95 cents of the dollar *since the turn (of the century / most years after 1964 / only for those years where the point lies below the C line)*.

0.95; people on the average; 95; average 0.95; most years after 1964

7. A distinction is often raised between normative and positive economics. Positive economics is descriptive—a relating of facts and circumstance based upon observation. Normative economics is prescriptive—a relating of solutions and actions based upon ethics and value judgment. Economists disagree *(more / less / about the same)* on issues of positive economics than they do on issues of normative economics. Indicate which of the following are statements of normative (N) or positive (P) character.

a. Taxes should be progressive. . . . . *(N / P)*

b. Taxes discourage work effort. . . . . *(N / P)*

c. Inflation tends to be high when unemployment is low. . . . . *(N / P)*

d. Inflation is less harmful than unemployment. . . . *(N / P)*

e. Pollution restraints cost jobs. . . . . *(N / P)*

f. Pollution restrains are worth the cost. . . . . *(N / P)*

---

less **a.** N **b.** P **c.** P **d.** N **e.** P **f.** N

The above should not be construed as a statement that economists agree on all issues of positive economics. There could, for example, be considerable debate over whether periods of low inflation need to be accompanied by high unemployment. This would be a different debate from the one over whether or not inflation is as harmful to the economy at large as unemployment.

SUGGESTED ANSWERS TO QUESTIONS IN THE TEXT: Chapter 1

1. The study of how to cope with scarcity, expressed in many forms by many people with many perspectives.

2. **a.** Correlation does not necessarily imply causality.

b. To focus upon the relationship between two variables, everything else that might affect either of them is held constant.

c. Positive economics studies how things are.

d. Normative economics studies how things ought to be, according to some norm—Shea Stadium analysis: "Baseball the way it oughta' be!"

3. Normative: b and c; positive: a, d, and e.

4. Positive analysis lends itself to objectivity; normative analysis does not.

The fallacy of composition is not involved in the smoking-cancer debate because the correlation is being shown to be dependent upon human characteristics that are typical of all of us; there are therefore general explanations of why a higher frequency of cancer among smokers leads us to conclude that smoking would make any person more likely to contract cancer. The same explanation should rule out consideration of the *post hoc, ergo propter hoc* fallacy, but that is nonetheless the basis of the defense offered by the tobacco companies.

5. They should be available for consultation, not in charge. In evaluating this statement, remember that it is likely that your instructor is an economist (!).

6. Any answer is correct, if it is what you think and you think well. Well, what do you think?

APPENDIX: 1
How to Read Graphs

Economics makes extensive use of graphs and charts. They appear in nearly every chapter of the text, and the appendix to Chapter 1 is included to provide the reader with a basic review of their foundation. This associated appendix amplifies that review.

Graphs and charts are tools with which the fundamental notions of economic reasoning can be illustrated, exercised, and stretched. They provide an easy context within which to explore many economic phenomena that would otherwise require pages of prose. To proceed without a minimal understanding of graphs would be to proceed at a great disadvantage; it would be like fighting a championship fight with one arm tied behind your back. This appendix is designed to present both a brief review of the basics of graphical analysis and some small insight into its usefulness. Most fundamentally, a *graph* is simply an illustration picturing how two sets of numbers are related to each other.

First Example: Study Hours and Leisure Hours

Suppose that you decide to plan your working day. A considerable part of each 24 hours must be given over to sleep, meals, and class attendance. Suppose that these matters take up 14 hours per day. This leaves the remaining 10 hours to divide between study on the one hand, leisure and recreation on the other.

That 10 hours could be divided in an infinite number of ways. At one extreme would be 10 hours for leisure and 0 hours for study. This particular time allocation must be considered unsatisfactory in the sense that its pursuit tends to lead to unpleasant interviews with the dean of students or similar people of limited imagination. It is, nonetheless, a possible allocation of time.

At the other extreme would be 10 hours for study and 0 for leisure and recreation; i.e., the week-before-examinations allocation. Between the two extremes is a wide selection of alternatives. Among these choices are the allocations indicated in Table 1A-1.

Table 1A-1

	A	B	C	D	E	F	G
Leisure hours	10	8	7	6	4½	2½	0
Study hours	0	2	3	4	5½	7½	10

Table 1A-1 shows two sets of numbers. One set gives the number of possible study hours; the other gives the *corresponding* number of leisure hours (given a total of 10 hours to allocate between leisure and study). The numbers are, in other words, inexorably tied to one another; each study-hour number is paired with a leisure-hour figure. It is this type of pairing process that a graph always illustrates.

The leisure-study tradeoff provides a perfect example. All the pairs in Table 1A-1 are characterized by one relationship: the sum of the hours spent studying and the hours spent relaxing must always equal 10. All such points are captured somewhere along the line AG in Figure 1A-1 (assuming that negative numbers of hours are not allowed).

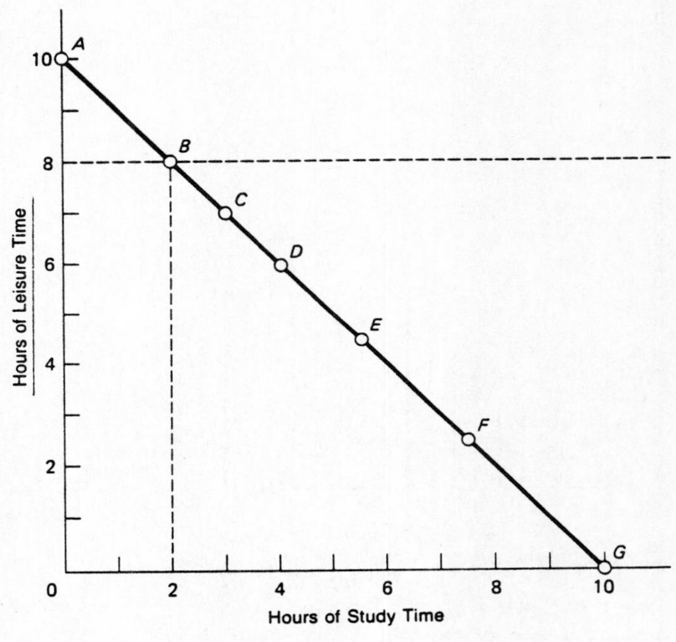

Figure 1A-1

To see how, notice that the vertical line at the left of Figure 1A-1 and the horizontal line at the bottom are the axes against which the pairwise linkage is to be charted. Each is divided off with a number scale, and the meaning of these numbers is indicated by the labels: "Hours of Study Time" (horizontally) and "Hours of Leisure Time" (vertically).

The slanting line carrying points labelled A through G has already been identified as the actual graph of the leisure-study relationship. Each point identified along that line corresponds to a pair in Table 1A-1. Take point *B*, for example. Point *B* in Table 1A-1 pairs 2 hours of study with 8 hours of leisure time. The dashed lines in Figure 1A-1 do the same thing. Passing down from point *B* to the study-time/horizontal axis, note that 2 hours is associated with point *B*; moving left to the leisure-time/vertical axis, similarly note that 8 hours is associated with point *B*. Table 1A-1 and Figure 1A-1 illustrate the same thing, for point *B* and every other point along the line.

1. In the horizontal or west-east dimensions, a figure of 0 would be recorded on the line at *(extreme left / extreme right / very bottom / very top / exact center)*. In the vertical dimension, 0 would be recorded on the line at *(extreme left / extreme right / very bottom / very top / exact center)*.

2. The measuring line used to position numbers in the west-east dimension is called the ____________________ or the ____________________. The south-north measuring line is the ____________________ or the ____________________.

3. In Figure 1A-1, point *B* stands for the combination of 2 *(study / leisure)* hours and 8 *(study / leisure)* hours. In Figure 1A-1, leisure hours are measured *(vertically / horizontally)* and study hours *(vertically / horizontally)*. Point *D* stands for ________ leisure hours and ________ study hours; 9 study hours and 1 leisure hour would be a pair indicated by a point between points *(A and B / D and E / F and G)*.

4. The rate at which study hours can be turned into leisure time is ________ hour(s) for every 1 hour of study time sacrificed.

1. extreme left; very bottom
2. horizontal axis; *X* axis; vertical axis; *Y* axis
3. study; leisure, vertically; horizontal; 6; 4; *F* and *G*
4. 1

Second Example: Money, Apples, and Oranges

Suppose that someone particularly interested in either apples or oranges were to decide that he would allocate $40 to the purchase of one, or the other, or both. Let apples cost $2 per bushel and let oranges cost $1 per dozen. Table 1A-2 records a few possible combinations of apples and oranges that this person might consider. Notice, for example, that devoting the entire $40 to apples would allow him to bring 20 bushels of apples home (point *A* in Table 1A-2). Devoting the entire $40 to oranges would allow him to bring 40 dozen oranges home (point *G* in Table 1A-2). Other intermediate combinations, designated elsewhere in Table 1A-2, would also be possible and should not be ignored. It is likely, in fact, that these intermediate points would be preferred to "specializing" exclusively in the consumption of one fruit or the other.

Table 1A-2

	A	B	C	D	E	F	G
Apples (bushels)	20	18	15	10	5	2	0
Oranges (dozens)	0	4	10	20	30	36	40

Figure 1A-2 is blank save for a series of vertical and horizontal "grid lines," used to help locate the point that matches up with any given pair of numbers. On Figure 1A-2, draw a graph that illustrates the points in Table 1A-2. First label your axis lines. Then pick a scale for each of the axes, i.e., choose how much distance you are going to use to represent 1 bushel of apples and 1 dozen oranges. With these scales in mind, plot the seven points of Table 1A-2 and label each with its letter identification. They should all lie along a straight line much like the one drawn in Figure 1A-1. After you have satisfied yourself that they do, draw the entire line by connecting the points. This "smoothing" allows the graph to reflect all the points that you could have marked off if you had had the time and patience—all combinations of oranges and apples (including fractions) that could be purchased with $40.

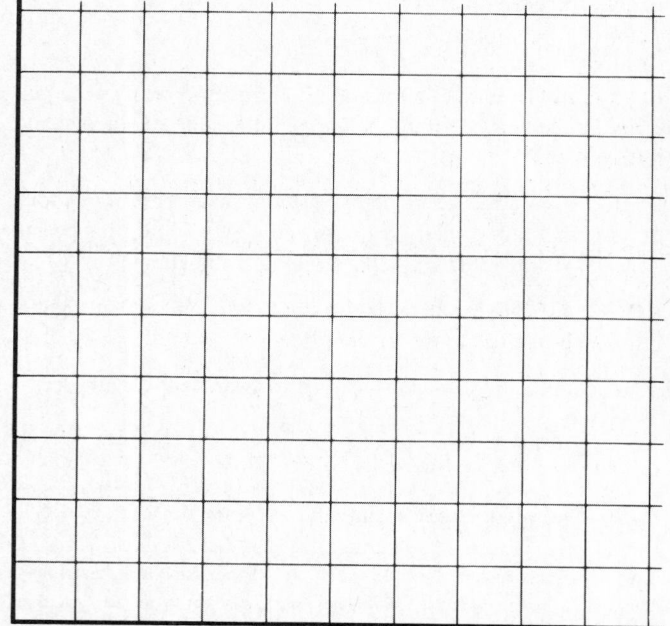

Figure 1A-2

This last idea bears repeating. You cannot, in Figure 1A-1, possibly find any add-up-to-10 combination of positive numbers that does not appear somewhere on *AG*. *AG* includes every possible pair that satisfies this linking rule. Moreover, *AG* can be trusted in another respect. It has no point that does not meet the linking rule. In other words, *AG* is an exact graphical representation of the add-up-to-10 rule in the sense that (1) it includes *all* points that satisfy this rule, and (2) it includes *only* points that satisfy this rule. Similarly, the line that you drew in Figure 1A-2 includes all combinations of apples and oranges that cost $40 and only combinations that cost $40.

5. In the apples-oranges example, our fruit lover would have loved to have purchased 20 dozen oranges and 20 bushels of apples. He *(could / could not)* do that because he had *(more than enough / not enough)* money. That combination would cost ________.

6. In the study-leisure example, the rate of exchange between study time and relaxation time was ________ hour studying for every 1 hour of forgone relaxation. In the apples-oranges example, the tradeoff was ________ dozen oranges for every bushel of forgone apples.

7. Take any point inside the triangle formed by the three lines of Figure 1A-1 (the *AG* line and the two axis lines). The pair of measurements for any such point:

a. must together total more than 10.

b. must together total less than 10.

c. must together total 10.

d. may total more than 10 or less than 10.

8. Which alternative in question 7 correctly describes the pair of measurements belonging to any point outside *AG* (above and to the right)? . . . . *(a / b / c / d)*

9. If we redid this example by assuming that there was a total of 11 hours rather than 10 to allocate, what would happen to *AG* (as the line indicating all possible combinations)?

a. It would move outward—i.e., upward and to the right—remaining parallel to the present line.

b. It would move inward—i.e., downward and to the left—remaining parallel to the present line.

c. Its position would not change.

d. It would pivot or rotate outward on point *A*.

---

5. could not; not enough; $60 **6.** 1; 2 **7.** b. (For example, take any point—other than *B*—on the vertical broken line running between *B* and the 2 mark on the horizontal axis. This is a typical point inside the triangle. That point must stand for 2 study hours and—because it is below *B*—less than 8 hours of leisure time, or a total of less than 10.) **8.** a. **9.** a.

Third Example: The Guns-or-Butter Diagram

One of the first graphical diagrams that you will encounter in the text is the guns-or-butter chart of Chapter 2. As the following table (reproduced from the text) shows, it involves pairs of figures once again.

Table 1A-3

	A	B	C	D	E	F
Butter (millions of pounds)	0	1	2	3	4	5
Guns (thousands)	15	14	12	9	5	0

The background of the guns-or-butter case is this: The economy has only a limited and fixed stock of machinery, labor, and all the other things needed to produce such items as guns or butter. Some of these resources can be used in the production of either commodity. Labor, for instance, can be transferred from the production of guns to the production of butter, or vice versa (with due allowance for the training time that might be required to make labor proficient in its new location). If labor were switched from, say, work on guns to work on butter, the result would be an increase in the output of butter and a corresponding reduction in the output of guns. If resources were fully employed, the inevitable cost of getting more of one commodity must, by extension of this example, always be a reduction in the supply of another.

(The "guns-or-butter" metaphor first arose in Nazi Germany. By the late 1930s, Hitler's government had turned so much of German industry toward rearmament that there were shortages of some civilian goods, butter among them. The late and generally unlamented Hermann Goering made a famous speech in which he sought to appease the public's complaints by declaring, "We must choose between guns and butter!")

As a further exercise in graph drawing, draw the guns-or-butter diagram for yourself in Figure 1A-3. Use the figures in the preceding table. As before, first label your two axes. Measure quantity of guns in the vertical dimension (as the text does) and quantity of butter horizontally. Ordinarily, you want to make use of all the space available on a graph. In Figure 1A-3, the maximum butter quality to be recorded is 5 (million pounds); so put 5 at the bottom right-hand corner. There are 15 little squares sitting on the horizontal axis line; if 5 goes below the end of the fifteenth square, then 1 must go below the end of the third one, 2 below the end of the sixth, and so on. As to guns, your maximum is 15 (thousand); so put 15 at top left, with the smaller numbers correspondingly below. Notice that (in the matter of graph distances) your two number scales can be different. Here, the same distance in inches which measures 5 million pounds of butter (horizontally) records 15,000 guns (vertically).

Having put labels and numbers on your axes, indicate on the graph the six points in the table. (This is known as *plotting* the points.) Identify them by letter and join them with a smooth curve. You have, at this point, completed

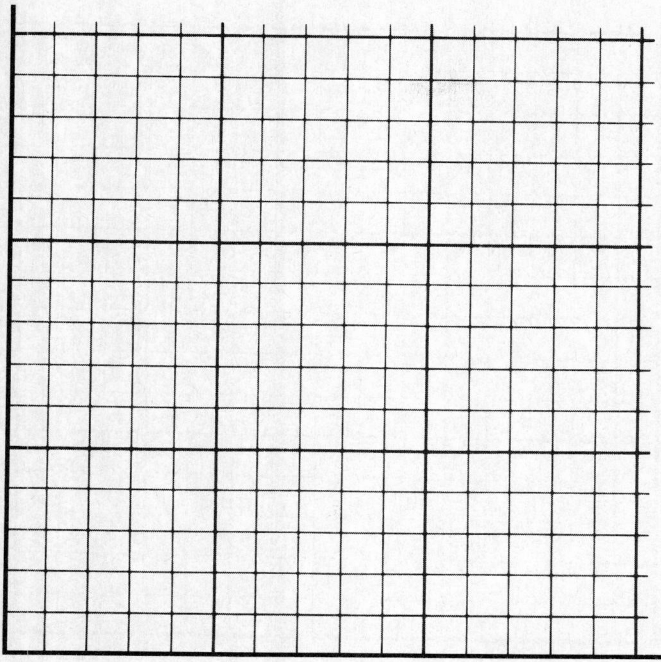

Figure 1A-3

a graph of the guns-butter *production-possibility frontier* (*PPF*). What can you learn from it? Why was it worth the trouble? Four different observations spring to mind.

1. The area of the graph above and to the right of the frontier (the *ABCDEF* line) represents more desirable but unattainable territory. Points in that region represent larger guns-butter combinations than those represented by *ABCDEF*, but they are unattainable unless or until the economy acquires more productive agents or develops better techniques for using what it has. The process of economic growth can be represented as a gradual outward shifting of the *ABCDEF* line.

2. The graph area below and to the left of the frontier is fully attainable. If the economy's actual guns-butter production were to be represented by a point in this area, it would signify (*a*) that the economy was not fully using all its available resources, or else (*b*) that although it was employing them, it was somehow failing to use them to the best advantage. We assume that the economy can reach any point on the frontier without disrupting its social order and without undue strain on its productive agents and that its people will want production to reach this line. Both of the two commodities are scarce relative to the desire for them.

3. If both the unattainable area above the curve and the undesirable area below the curve were removed from consideration, then only the frontier would remain. The decision which people in this economy (or their leaders) must somehow make about what to produce can thus be represented as the problem of deciding which point along line *ABCDEF* to choose. To describe this as a "guns-or-butter" decision can be a bit misleading; it suggests (all) guns or (all) butter. If both guns and butter were desirable, though, it is most likely that points *A* and *F* would both be rejected in lieu of some intermediate point such as *C* or *D*.

4. In actual life, decisions of what to produce have somehow been made for a long time; they are still being made. A decision of this nature is not something that need be made only once and can then be forgotten, for tastes change and so do productive conditions. It is a little more realistic, then, to think of an economy which is currently operating at some point such as *D*, and which might, for example, be disposed to move toward having a little more butter. This would mean a movement away from *D* toward *E*.

10. The figures in the guns-or-butter table represent *(maximum / minimum)* combinations of these two commodities which some imaginary community could produce per unit of time. The figures stand for *(money values / physical quantities)* of guns and butter.

11. If all available resources or inputs were devoted to butter production, butter output would be ________ million pounds and gun output would be ________ thousand guns. If the economy wished to have 9000 guns per period, butter output could not exceed ________ million pounds.

12. Suppose the community is producing a total of 1 million pounds of butter. It wants to increase this by a further 1 million pounds. The required decrease in gun production would be ________ thousand. If the community were producing 4 million pounds of butter and wanted to increase this by 1 million (to a total of 5 million), the required decrease in gun production would be ________ thousand.

13. Suppose the community is currently producing 15,000 guns and is considering a reduction to 14,000. The change would make possible a butter increase of ________ million pounds. Alternatively, if the community currently produces 9000 guns and decides on a reduction to 5000, a butter increase of ________ million pounds would be possible. If gun production were to be increased from 9000 to 10,000, this 1000 increase would call for a reduction in butter output of approximately ________ million pounds.

---

10. maximum; physical quantities **11.** 5; 0; 3 **12.** 2; 5 **13.** 1; 1; ⅓

Notice that your answers in question 12 varied with those at the starting point—the cost of butter in terms of guns changed as more butter was produced. This notion will be important later.

One essential distinction that pervades economic thought is the difference between movement along a curve and shifts in a curve. It has already been noted in the context of the guns-or-butter example of Table 1A-3 that a society disposed toward having a little more butter could move from a point like *D* toward a point like *E*, at which more butter means fewer guns. Note that point *D* represents 3 million pounds of butter and 9000 guns; point *E* represents 4 million pounds of butter but only 5000 guns. Without any increase in resources or advances in technology, this sort of movement along the *PPF* is society's only choice.

When the things that are held constant in the construction of a curve change, however, the entire curve can actually *shift*. Suppose, for example, that the economy whose guns vs. butter tradeoff was represented in Table 1A-3 were to discover a better way to make butter—a way that would use fewer resources that are applicable to the production of guns. Table 1A-4 reflects such a change.

Table 1A-4

	A′	B′	C′	D′	E′	F′
Butter (millions of pounds)	0	2	4	6	8	10
Guns (thousands)	15	14	12	9	5	0

For any given level of gun production (except the maximum), in fact, butter production doubles.

Graph the production-possibility frontier defined in Table 1A-4 on Figure 1A-4. Label the points and smooth the curve. Now replicate your graph of the production-possibility frontier from Table 1A-3 on Figure 1A-4. The frontier should have shifted out in moving from Table 1A-3 to Table 1A-4 for every level of gun production but one—the one in which no butter at all is produced so that 15,000 guns can be manufactured. That makes sense, though, because the technological advances in the production of butter increase the opportunities of the economy except in the case where it ignores the new butter technology and specializes entirely in the production of guns. Movement from *D* to *E* is no longer necessary. Shifting from *D* to *D′* increases butter production to 4 million pounds *even though* gun production holds at 9000.

Slope: Straight Lines One way that works in describing a straight-line relationship between some variable *X* and another variable *Y* is this: *X* and *Y* are linked so that *any* given change in *X* always generates exactly the same change in *Y*. That is how, in reality, problems and relationships are often presented. Starting with *X* and *Y* occupying some initial positions, we often ask, "What would happen to *Y* if *X* were to change its position (i.e., its value)?" Put a more useful way, perhaps we might ask, "What change in *Y* would be forthcoming if *X* were to increase by 1 unit?"

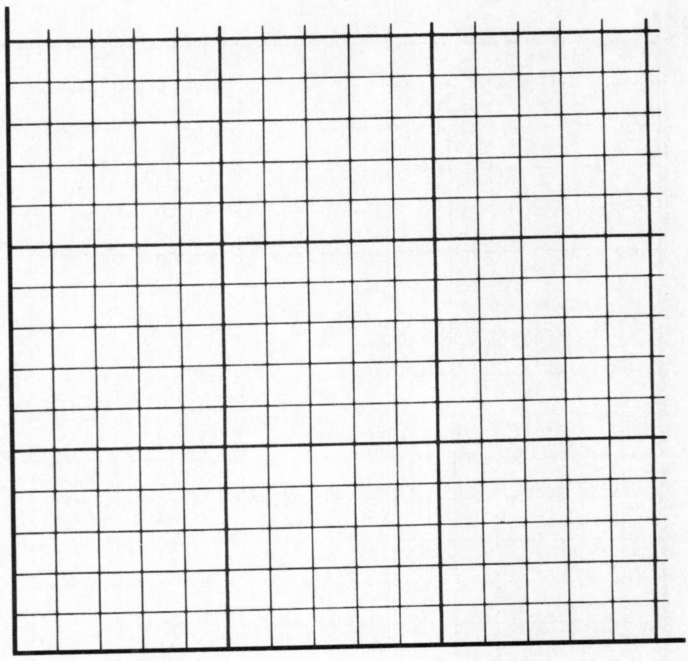

Figure 1A-4

To get a picture of what is going on, think of starting somewhere on a straight-line graph and making little movements to the right in two stages. Think, in particular, first about making a strictly horizontal movement of sufficient length to indicate a 1-unit increase in the *X* value. Since the move was horizontal, the *Y* value will not have changed. Then think about a vertical movement up or down to signify a change in *Y* of a very special dimension: a vertical distance precisely equal to the amount of movement required to return to the straight line. For example, in either of the two little diagrams composing Figure 1A-5, the true path traced out is *ABDE*, but the movement from *B* to *D* can be considered in two parts. First, there is a probing movement from *B* to *C* (the 1-unit change in *X* which takes the point momentarily off its true path). Then, there is a second correcting movement from *C* to *D* (the required matching change in *Y*). If *BC*'s length indicates a 1-unit increase in *X*, then *CD*'s length must indicate the rate at which *Y* must change in response to *X* to stay on the straight line. On the graph, this vertical measure of the change is called the slope of the line *ABDE*.

Several points about the slope of a line should now be clear:

1. Slope is always a number that measures change. It is the amount by which *Y* must change in response to a

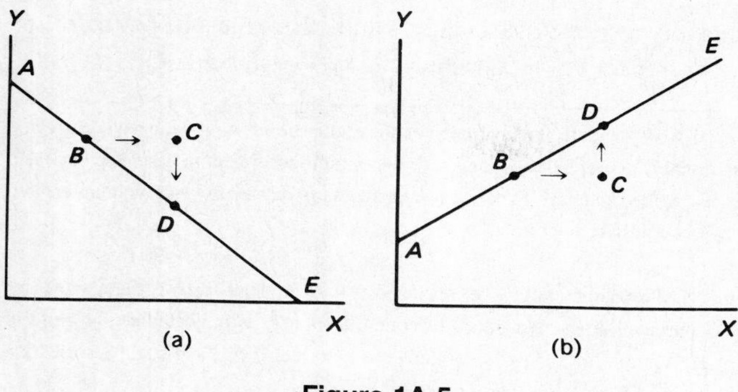

Figure 1A-5

1-unit change in X if we are to stay on the same straight line.

2. If the graph line is straight, one single number measures its slope at any and all points thereon. This is just another way of saying that a straight line is one whose direction does not change.

3. The slope always assumes a negative value if the X-Y relation is an *inverse one*—one in which a positive increase in X requires a reduction in Y. Both the study-leisure and the apples-oranges examples qualify, and both straight lines drawn above to reflect them have negative slopes. In terms of what we draw, therefore, the slope is negative if the graph falls down to the right. The slope is, conversely, positive if the line climbs up toward the right. A linkage with a positive slope is called *direct*.

Now consider a little more fully the technique for measuring or illustrating graphically the slope of a straight line. We have said that the slope of the graph line *ABDE* in Figure 1A-5 is measured by the length of *CD*. This assumes that *BC* is of a length equal to 1 X unit. We could equally well have said that slope is measured by the fraction *CD/BC*, with the lengths of *CD* and *BC* representing the numbers for which they stand. Since *BC* corresponds to the number 1, *CD/BC* reduces to *CD* anyhow. The only objection to naming slope as *CD/BC* is that at first it seems needlessly clumsy; but measuring slope as *CD/BC* is a reminder that the Y movement (*CD*) can be considered only relative to the amount of X movement (*BC*).

Some people find it helpful to think of slope as "the rise over the run." "The rise" is the vertical distance involved; in Figure 1A-5 terms, the rise is *CD*. "The run" is the horizontal distance; it is *BC* in Figure 1A-5 terms. So the rise over the run would in this instance be *CD* over *BC*.

It is tempting to associate the measure of slope with the steepness with which the graph line rises or falls, so that a steeply tilted line is taken as one with a high slope value, positive or negative. Sometimes this conclusion is valid, but don't overlook the fact that the steepness with which a graph line rises or falls depends in part on the scale chosen for the graph. Diagrams (a) and (b) in Figure 1A-6 both portray exactly the same relationship, and either is a perfectly respectable illustration. Notice in (b), however, that the horizontal scale has been stretched out in comparison with that used in (a). The slope of the line in both parts of Figure 1A-6 is $+\frac{1}{2}$. The trick is that relative steepness accurately reflects relative slope only when the scales are the same. When you have two lines on the same graph, therefore, you can certainly say that the steeper line has the larger slope, in absolute value—more negative if the two lines are negatively sloped and downward-sloping or more positive if the two lines are positively sloped and upward-sloping. In Figure 1A-6(c), for example, line I has a slope of 4, line II has a slope of 2, 4 is greater than 2, and I is clearly steeper than II. In Figure 1A-6(d), line I has a slope of -4, line II has a slope of -2, 4 is still greater then 2, -4 is more negative than -2, and I is again steeper than II.

Figure 1A-7 contains six different graphs. In each, X signifies the magnitude being measured horizontally, and Y the magnitude being measured vertically. Circle the correct letter or letters below.

14. Diagrams *(a / b / c / d / e / f)* illustrate an inverse relation (positive change in one accompanied by negative change in the other) between X and Y.

15. In one case, Y's response to a change in X is zero, namely, in diagram *(a / b / c / d / e / f)*.

16. The X-Y relation is positive rather than inverse (i.e., plus

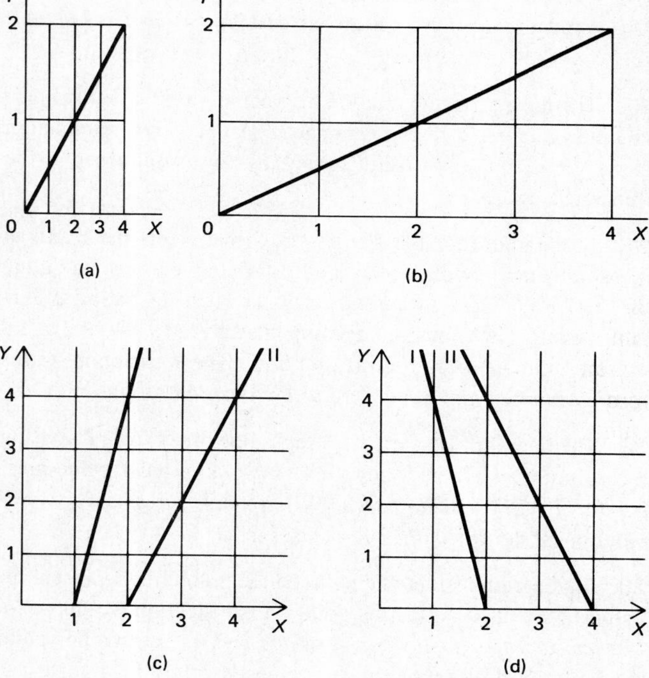

Figure 1A-6

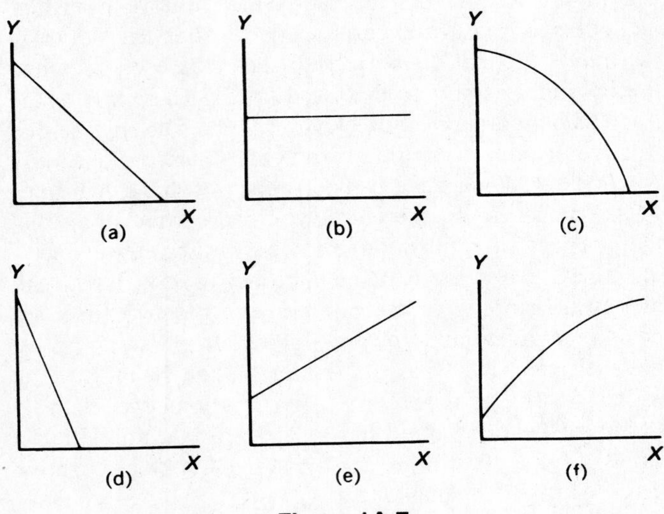

Figure 1A-7

change is accompanied by plus change) in diagram(s) *(a / b / c / d / e / f).*

17. Among the diagrams illustrating an inverse relation such as study-leisure or butter-guns, the terms of trade are constant in diagram(s) *(a / b / c / d / e / f)* and they vary in diagram(s) *(a / b / c / d / e / f).*

18. To illustrate the relation between an adult's daily food intake in calories (measured along *X* axis) and his or her weight (measured along *Y* axis), the diagram best suited would be (either of two) *(a / b / c / d / e / f).*

19. The relationship between one's age (*X*) and one's height (*Y*) would probably be illustrated best by *(a / b / c / d / e / f).*

20. The most probable relation between number of study hours you put in before a given examination (*X* axis) and examination grade earned (*Y* axis) is illustrated by (or is supposed to be illustrated by) *(a / b / c / d / e / f).*

21. In diagram (d), assume the graph line meets the *Y* axis at measurement 10 and the *X* axis at 5. (Write these figures on the diagram.) The *X-Y* swapping terms are then as follows: A 1-unit increase in *X* must be accompanied by a *(0 / $\frac{1}{2}$ / 1 / 2 / 4 / 10)* unit *(increase / decrease)* in *Y*. These swapping terms *(are constant / vary according to the position on the line).*

22. In diagram (b), let the graph line meet the *Y* axis at measurement 4. Then, when the *X* value is 0, the *Y* value must be *(0 / 1 / 2 / 4 / can't tell).* When the *X* value is 10, the *Y* value must be *(0 / 1 / 2 / 4 / can't tell).*

23. In diagram (e), let one point on the graph line represent the values $X = 0$, $Y = 4$. This point on the diagram would be *(at extreme left near center / at extreme right).* Let another point on the graph line represent the values $X = 3$, $Y = 5$. These two points indicate an underlying linking rule as follows: for every increase of 1 in the *X* value, there must be *(an increase / a decrease)* in the *Y* value of *($\frac{1}{4}$ / $\frac{1}{3}$ / 1 / 3 / 4).*

If you find yourself stuck on any of these questions, or if you have answered incorrectly, do not be too concerned: the unfamiliar is seldom easy. Go back and review earlier material if necessary, until you are reasonably sure you understand why each answer is correct.

14. a, c, d **15.** b **16.** e. f **17.** a and d; c **18.** e or f **19.** f
20. f [Although e would be reasonably correct, presumably the payoff for continued investment in study hours tapers off, as indicated by the bend in (f)'s graph line. If you thought (a) was correct, you have some justification to provide in this semester's examinations!]
21. 2; decrease; are constant [Start with the point at the *Y* axis, where $X = 0$, $Y = 10$. From here, a 5-unit increase in *X* (from 0 to 5) would have to be matched by a 10-unit decrease in *Y* (from 10 to 0). Swapping terms are constant because the line is straight; and 5 for 10 is equivalent to 1 for 2.]
22. 4; 4 (A horizontal line means that the *Y* value stays the same, no matter what the *X* value is.)
23. at extreme left; an increase; $\frac{1}{3}$ (A 3-unit measure in *X*, from 0 to 3, is matched by a 1-unit increase in *Y*, from 4 to 5; 3 to 1 is equivalent to 1 to $\frac{1}{3}$.)

24. Slope is a measure of the rate at which the *Y* value changes for each change of *(0 units / 1 unit / the same number of units)* in the *X* value.

25. A graph line has the same slope value throughout when that line is *(curved / rising / straight / falling).*

26. Graphically, we can illustrate or measure slope in terms of a right-angled triangle below the graph line. Slope is the fraction or ratio obtained by putting the length of the *(vertical / horizontal)* side of the triangle over the length of the *(vertical / horizontal)* side.

27. When the *X-Y* relation is an inverse one, then its graphical illustration can be considered the path of a point which *(falls / rises)* as it moves to the right. The slope value of such a relation is *(positive / zero / negative).*

28. In diagram (b) of Figure 1A-7, the slope of the line illustrated is *(positive / negative / zero / impossible to tell).*

29. Two positions of *X* on a straight graph line are 5 and 7. What is the value of slope if the corresponding *Y* positions are:

a. 5 and 7? . . . . . *(−3 / −2 / −1 / 0 / 1 / 2 / 3 / infinity)*

b. 4 and 2? . . . . . *(−3 / −2 / −1 / 0 / 1 / 2 / 3 / infinity)*

c. 2 and −2? . . . *(−3 / −2 / −1 / 0 / 1 / 2 / 3 / infinity)*

d. 4 and 4? . . . . . *(−3 / −2 / −1 / 0 / 1 / 2 / 3 / infinity)*

e. −2 and −8? . . *(−3 / −2 / −1 / 0 / 1 / 2 / 3 / infinity)*

f. −8 and −2? . . *(−3 / −2 / −1 / 0 / 1 / 2 / 3 / infinity)*

---

24. 1 unit **25.** straight **26.** vertical; horizontal **27.** falls; negative
28. zero **29. a.** 1 **b.** −1 **c.** −2 **d.** 0 **e.** −3 **f.** 3

The Slope of Curved Lines A curved line is one whose slope continually changes; i.e., the amount of *Y* change required to accommodate a 1-unit *X* change varies according to the position from which this change begins.

Consider the curved line *ABCDEF* in Figure 1A-8. Suppose we are at point *B*. If we know the exact *X* and *Y* values associated with every point on this line, then we should have no difficulty in learning what the changes in both *X* and *Y* would be as a result of moving from *B* to *E*. Moreover, we could put the usual right-angled triangle underneath, with corners at *B* and *E*, and from it develop a slope value—a value called the *arc slope from B to E*. The arc slope would not, however, be the slope of the curved line itself; it would really measure the slope of the straight line running between *B* and *E*. We would get a different and somewhat higher slope figure if we dealt similarly with a change from *B* to *D*, and a still different figure for a change from *B* to *C*.

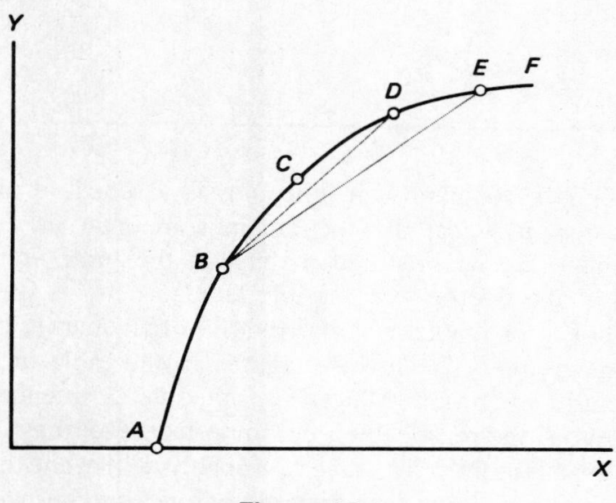

Figure 1A-8

For some purposes, it is quite sufficient to know the arc slope from *B* to *E*, or to *D*, or to *C*. But for other problems it is useful or even necessary to ask: What is the slope of the curved line exactly at some point, such as *B*?

To ask this question is to pose another one: Does it make sense to speak of the slope of a line precisely at a single point?

Certainly point *B*, considered in isolation, has no slope, no direction. Point *B* considered as part of the line *ABCDEF* is, however, another matter. The slope of the line is a measure of the direction in which it runs, computed in terms of the scales on the two axes. Think for the moment of *ABCDEF* as the path traced by a moving automobile. The direction of movement of that automobile changes continually, since it follows a curved path, but we can say that the automobile is headed in a specific direction at the exact moment when it passes over point *B*. We can certainly do so in the sense that a compass mounted on the car's dashboard at that exact moment would give an exact reading.

But how is this direction at *B* to be indicated on a piece of graph paper? The accepted answer is this: by a tangent drawn to the curved line at point *B*. The tangent to a curved line is itself by definition a straight line; it does not cross the curved line, and it touches it at only one point. By inspection of Figure 1A-9(a), it is easy to see how the slope of the tangent line *FJ* is considered as measuring the slope of the curved line at point *B*; and *GH* does the same for point *D*. To each such straight line we can apply our usual right-angle measuring technique for slope.

What does this slope mean? Figure 1A-9(b) redraws the guns-or-butter production-possibility frontier from

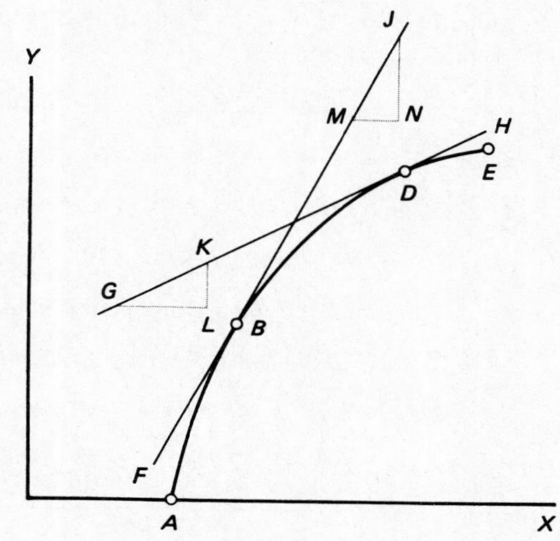

Figure 1A-9(a)

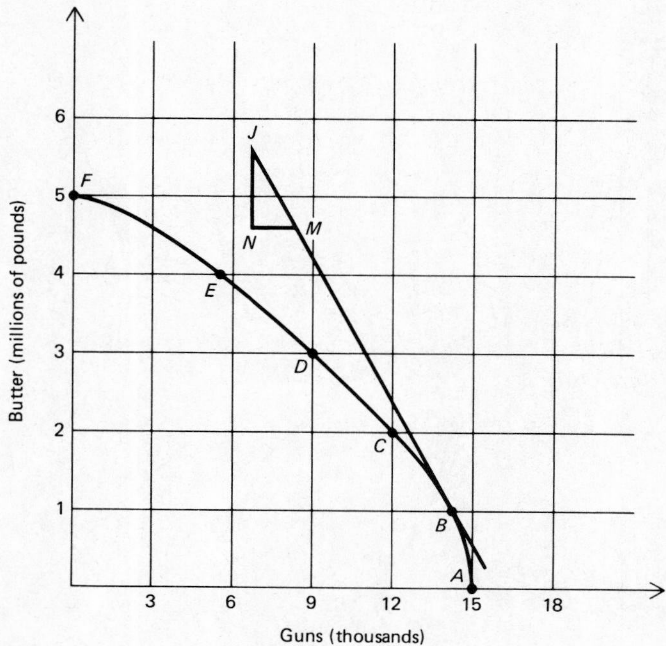

Figure 1A-9(b)

Table 1A-4. At point B, a tangent line is drawn, and its slope, $-(JN/MN)$, represents the slope of the guns-or-butter schedule at point B. It is, intuitively, a reflection of how many guns need to be sacrificed to increase the production of butter not by 1 million pounds, but by 1 pound—a much smaller number. In reality, the slope of line B is the sacrifice in guns required to finance a minuscule change in butter production; and after all, 1 pound is a small quantity when it is compared to 1 million pounds.

Circle each correct alternative below.

30. Figure 1A-10 consists of eight separate diagrams, each illustrating a small segment of a graph line. In each, the numbers indicate the length of the adjacent straight-line segment. What is the slope of each AB line? Where AB is curved, it is the slope at point C that is desired.

a. *(−4 / −3 / −2 / −1 / 0 / 1 / 2 / 3 / 4 / 10 / infinity)*

b. *(−4 / −3 / −2 / −1 / 0 / 1 / 2 / 3 / 4 / 10 / infinity)*

c. *(−4 / −3 / −2 / −1 / 0 / 1 / 2 / 3 / 4 / 10 / infinity)*

d. *(−4 / −3 / −2 / −1 / 0 / 1 / 2 / 3 / 4 / 10 / infinity)*

e. *(−4 / −3 / −2 / −1 / 0 / 1 / 2 / 3 / 4 / 10 / infinity)*

f. *(−4 / −3 / −2 / −1 / 0 / 1 / 2 / 3 / 4 / 10 / infinity)*

g. *(−4 / −3 / −2 / −1 / 0 / 1 / 2 / 3 / 4 / 10 / infinity)*

h. *(−4 / −3 / −2 / −1 / 0 / 1 / 2 / 3 / 4 / 10 / infinity)*

---

a. −4 **b.** 3 **c.** 10 **d.** 2 **e.** 0 **f.** −2 **g.** −2 **h.** −1

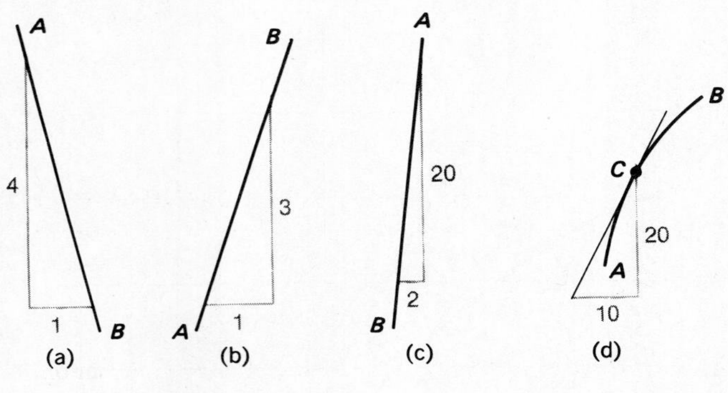

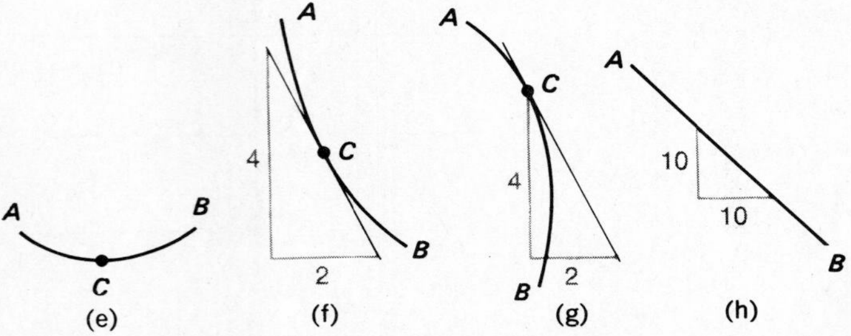

Figure 1A-10

Two or More Lines on a Graph So far our discussion has run in terms of the interpretation of a single line on a graph. But most text diagrams include two lines, usually intersecting at one point on the graph. Some students will even joke about the "fundamental theorem of economics": whenever two lines intersect, it is more likely than not that the economics instructor will spend two class periods describing something "essential."

The supply-and-demand diagram of Chapter 4 is a good example. The demand line, or demand curve, is drawn as usual—from two sets of figures paired together. Here is one example of a demand curve:

	Price of Wheat (per bu)	Quantity Demanded (million bu per month)
A	$5	9
B	4	10
C	3	12
D	2	15
E	1	20

This is a "demand schedule." It is a schedule of the quantities of wheat that buyers in some market would demand (i.e., be prepared to buy) if the price were to stand at any one of five possible levels.

It does not matter whether this is a real market or an imaginary one. The precise figures in the table are not especially important. What this schedule is intended to illustrate is the reasonable (and important) fact that as the price of anything falls, buyers probably will want to buy a larger total amount than they did before. In other words, quantity of wheat bought is *inversely* related to the price of wheat.

It is also possible to prepare another schedule, indicating what sellers of wheat (the producers of wheat, the suppliers of wheat) are prepared to do. In this case, it seems reasonable to assume that if the price were to go up, then suppliers would try to supply a larger quantity because the higher price would generate a higher return on their efforts. Alternatively, if the price were to fall, then they would choose to supply less. Below is a representative supply schedule. Note that it illustrates what has

	Price of Wheat (per bu)	Quantity Demanded (million bu per month)
A	$5	18
B	4	16
C	3	12
D	2	7
E	1	0

just been said—the quantity of wheat supplied is directly related to the price of wheat.

At this stage, it is not particularly essential that you fully understand the ideas conveyed by the demand and/or supply schedules. What matters for the moment is that you recognize something familiar in the construction: the demand curve consists of two sets of inversely related figures, neatly paired one with the other; the supply curve consists of two sets of positively related figures, equally neatly paired with each other. This means that either can be depicted as a line on a graph—even together on the same graph.

Why? Despite their differences, there is a fundamental similarity between the two schedules. Although they represent the attitudes or the intentions of two entirely different groups of people, the two schedules match one another in that one column refers to price and the other to quantity. It is only because they match in this respect that both can be depicted on the same graph. If we are to make any sense out of two or more lines on the same graph, these lines must refer to the same kinds of things, measured in the same kinds of units.

In Figure 1A-11, draw the lines corresponding to these two schedules. (Plot the five points for each schedule and join them with a smooth curve.) Label your demand curve *DD* and your supply curve *SS*.

Your two lines should cross at one point, and one point only. That is the point signifying a price of $3 and a quantity of 12 million bushels. Its significance is that at this level of price, and no other, the intentions of buyers and the intentions of sellers match. In these circumstances, the price of $3 will be called an "equilibrium price," and the quantity of 12 million bushels an "equilibrium quantity." At a price of $3, buyers want to purchase exactly the 12 million bushels that suppliers are willing to deliver.

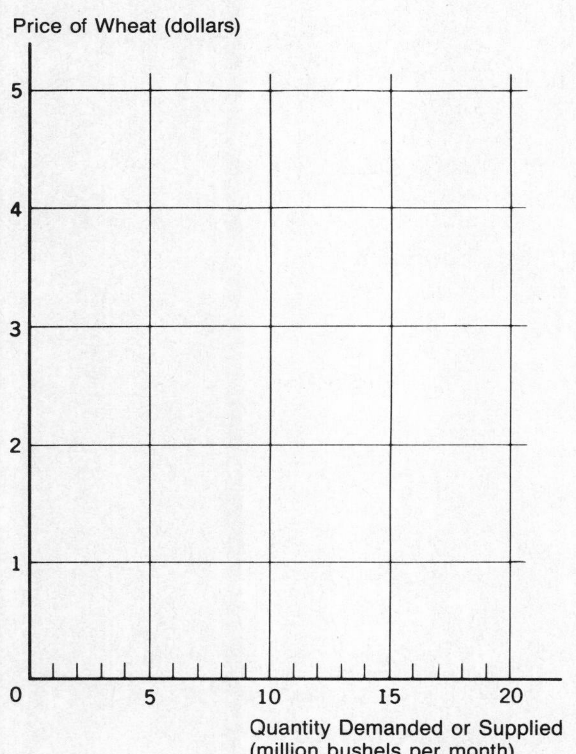

Figure 1A-11

Conclusion Graphs were made to help people grasp ideas with as little expenditure of time and effort as possible; but if you want to take advantage of this device, you must learn the rules and you must ask the right questions:

1. What does the graph measure on each axis? What are the labels on the axes? Each line on a graph indicates some kind of relation or linking rule between these two sets of numbers.

2. Which way does the line run? Does it fall to the right or rise to the right? If it falls, then the relation between the two sets of numbers is an inverse one—as one rises, the other falls. If it rises to the right, then the two sets of numbers move in the same direction and they represent a direct relationship.

3. Is the line straight or curved? If it is straight, the ratio of change in Y to change in X is constant. If the line curves, this ratio varies.

4. If there are two or more lines on a graph, then there are two or more schedules in the background. What kind of relationship is involved in each schedule, and why is it important to bring them together on the same graph? Usually the two lines cross one another at some point, and usually this intersection is important because at this point the two schedules match one another. Why is this matching important?

Review Complete as before.

31. One point on a graph indicates an X value of 4, a Y value of 10. Another point indicates an X value of 5, a Y value of 8. If these two points are joined by a straight line, the slope of that line is ________.

32. The slope of a straight line is −3. If movement from one point to another along that line results in an increase in Y from 10 to 16, what change in X must have taken place? It will have *(risen / fallen)* by *(6 / 3 / 2 / 1 / ½)*.

33. A line on a graph appears as the upper half of a circle: it starts out at the origin of the graph, rises, and then falls, until finally it drops to the horizontal axis from which it started. Which of the following correctly describes the slope value of this line?

a. It will have a changing slope value, but a figure which is positive throughout.

b. It will at first have a negative slope-value figure (toward the left-hand side) and this slope value will grow larger; then, as the line proceeds to the right, the slope-value figure will become positive.

c. It will at first have a positive slope-value figure (toward the left-hand side) and this slope value will grow larger as the line proceeds to the right; then the slope-value figure will become negative.

d. It will at first have a positive slope-value figure (toward the left-hand side), but this slope value will diminish in value as the line proceeds to the right; it will reach a value of zero, and then become a negative figure.

34. In Figure 1A-11, the *DD* curve has a *(negative / positive)* slope value. This figure is a *(constant / changing)* one. The SS curve in this figure has a *(negative / positive)* slope value. This figure is a *(constant / changing)* one.

---

31. −2 **32.** fallen; 2 **33. d.** **34.** negative; changing; positive; changing

SUGGESTED ANSWERS TO QUESTIONS IN THE TEXT: Appendix to Chapter 1

1. The idea is that the sum of leisure time (X) and study time (Y) is 16 hours, so $X + Y = 16$. So, graph $Y = 16 - X$.

2. It *is* a straight line with slope $= -1$.

3. Six hours of leisure leaves 10 hours of study; plot (6,10).

4. Graph $X + Y = 18$ or $Y = 18 - X$. This new line is out further from the origin, but parallel.

5. Do *not* send the scatter graph home!

6. Plot money supply measured along one axis against GNP measured along the other. The scatter suggests correlation, but cannot indicate causality.

CHAPTER 2
BASIC PROBLEMS OF ECONOMIC ORGANIZATION

Most of this chapter is organized around a series of fundamental ideas and concepts. They are all related, but they are all distinct. They are important as a group because they define the essence of the economic problem. They are important individually because they introduce tools for and methods of thinking about the world that will be carried throughout the text. It is essential, therefore, that you grasp each of them before you proceed.

When you have finished, you should be able to meet the following objectives.

LEARNING OBJECTIVES

1. State (*a*) the three basic economic problems that confront *all* societies regardless of their political organization and (*b*) the single underlying fact that gives rise to these problems.

2. Distinguish between several alternative economic systems and understand how mixed economies display characteristics of the extreme alternatives.

3. Differentiate between inputs and outputs; list the three major types of inputs.

4. Show how a production-possibility frontier illustrates the three basic economic questions as well as the underlying truth from which they grow. Explain, as well, how the *PPF* illustrates (*a*) efficiency and (*b*) opportunity cost.

5. Explain (*a*) why it is impossible for an economy to move outside its given frontier; (*b*) how it is nonetheless possible for the frontier to shift out over time; and (*c*) the undesirable circumstances under which an economy might operate beneath its frontier.

6. Understand the definition and the importance of the law of diminishing returns.

The real productive inputs for any economy are the items genuinely needed to satisfy life's material demands. Money plays a crucial part in the production process; it will be considered at length in due course. Money is not, however, one of the basic real inputs upon which an economy is built. It is something else—special, but different. It is the device with which the cooperative employment of real inputs can be effectively arranged. It is a kind of lubricating oil that allows the machinery of an economy to operate with a minimum of friction.

▶ The basic inputs from which our material wants for goods and services are satisfied are labor, capital goods, and natural resources. The output that we produce comes from the labor effort of men and women, using tools and machinery, mainly to process raw materials obtained from our natural resources. Every society has only a finite supply of productive inputs—the real sources of economic value. There is, as a result, a physically imposed limit on the total output of goods and services which any one society can produce. Goods of economic value are, in other words, scarce.

It is impossible to produce enough to satisfy everybody's desire for everything even in rich societies. Today, many poor economies are still hard pressed to turn out enough in the way of elemental food and shelter for their populations. The richer societies are easily capable of covering life's basic necessities for all their members, but our interest here is not with necessities alone. It is with consumers' *total* demands. Once necessities have been met, consumer wants pass quickly to comforts and to luxuries. In this sense, even rich societies face the *law of scarcity*: total consumer demands outrun total productive capacity defined by the limited supplies of productive inputs.

1. a. Three basic social problems arise from the law of scarcity; they are ____________________, ____________________, and ____________________ goods are to be produced.

b. The total stock of inputs available to any economy is limited. If the proportion of stock devoted to the production of some good A were to increase, then there would remain fewer inputs for the production of other goods B, C, D, etc. The output of *(at least one / all / none)* of these other goods would therefore have to *(rise / fall)*. Questions of how much to produce of A (of B, of C, etc.) are all part and parcel of the *(what / how / for whom)* problem.

c. Output restricted by limited input availability must somehow be shared by any society's members. This is the *(what / how / for whom)* problem.

---

a. what; how; for whom **b.** at least one; fall; what **c.** for whom

The problem of *how* goods should be produced is a little trickier. It is the problem of the exact mix of resources to be used in the manufacture of any given commodity.

It may strengthen your grasp of both *what* and *how* problems to consider instances in which they would not arise at all. The *what* problem emerges because resources are versatile, i.e., because they have more than one possible use or occupation. To see why this is so, suppose, for the sake of illustration, that resources are not versatile. Suppose, in particular, that the types of machines and labor and raw materials that are useful in the production of some good A are totally useless in the production of any other goods. Suppose, in fact, that all resources are specialized in this way so that they can be used in the production of only a single, specific good. Were that the case, then there would be no opportunity to swap less of A for more of B (for example). There would be no problem of what to produce because there would be only one combination of goods that could be produced.

The question of *how* similarly arises because there are usually many ways of producing any particular good. Were there only one "recipe" for producing A, though, then there would be no way of substituting a little more of one input for a little less of another. And if this single-recipe condition held throughout the economy, then there would be no problem in determining how things should be produced—if they are to be produced at all (i.e., if they are to be included in the answer to the *what* question), then they must be produced according to the one and only formula.

The more general situation, of course, is one in which there is more than one known productive technique (e.g., workers can be substituted for machines, and vice versa). If so, then *how* exists as a social problem.

2. Several alternative economic systems are all capable of answering the three economic questions of *what, how,* and *for whom*. The most primitive relies on ________ to provide the decision-making apparatus. Answers to the fundamental questions come simply from the traditions that dictate how things have always been done.

An economy in which the government makes all of the decisions about production and distribution is called a ________________ economy. It *(would have to be dictatorial to / would have to be democratic to / could be democratic, dictatorial, or anything in between and still)* qualify under the definition, but it would give enormous powers to the government.

A third approach, labelled the ________________ economy, uses a system of prices, markets, profits and losses, incentives, and rewards to answer the questions almost automatically. What is produced? Goods that generate the ________________. How are they produced? By the process that is ________________. For the people with ________________ earnings generated from their provision of labor services and/or their ownership of capital and resources.

Mixed economies are the *(most / least)* common across the world today. They include aspects of *(market and command / command and custom / market, command, and custom)* in the mechanisms that they have established to handle economic scarcity.

---

custom; command; could be democratic, dictatorial, or anything in between and still; market; largest profit; least costly; wealth (or money); most; market, command and custom.

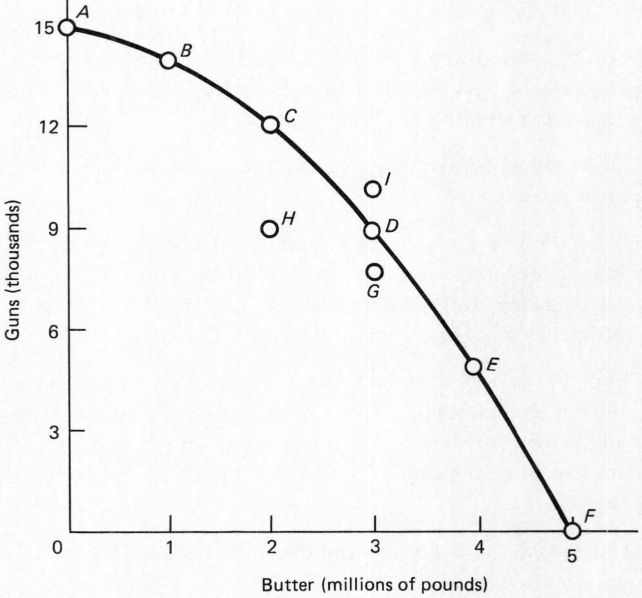

Figure 2-1

The nature of all three of the fundamental questions can be explored by using a **production-possibility frontier** (denoted *PPF*). Figure 2-1 here duplicates Figure 2-2 in the text and serves as an illustration. Recall that a *PPF* reflects all of the combinations of goods that an economy can produce given its fixed supply of inputs. Where? On and under (downward and/or below) the curve. Point *D* in Figure 2-1, for example, makes it clear that the economy could afford to produce 9000 guns and 3 million pounds of butter. It could, just as well, produce 8000 guns and 3 million pounds of butter (point *G*) or 9000 guns and 2 million pounds of butter (point *H*). It could not, though, produce 10,000 guns and 3 million pounds of butter (point *I*). It does not have the input stock to be able to do that, and that combination lies outside (upward and/or to the right) of the frontier.

Because a graph has only two dimensions, the *what* problem must be described against a graphed *PPF* as a choice between only two goods—guns and butter in Figure 2-1. The principles would be the same if there were 20 or 20,000 goods, though. The problem of *what* is ultimately a choice between a little more of this and a little less of that. The slope of the *PPF* shows this most dramatically because it is always negative.

The *how* question is subsumed in the definition of the frontier itself. If new technology or clever insight were to bring forth a new production technique for butter, e.g., then the frontier itself would change because the economy could produce more butter using fewer inputs. Output of *both* guns and butter could then increase *simultaneously* from a point on the old frontier. It follows, then, that the existing frontier captures all of the combinations of gun production and butter production that are the best the economy can do. If it could produce more of either with no cost, then it would. So, *how* does the economy produce its goods? With the most efficient techniques available. **Efficiency** is, in fact, defined as having achieved a point on the *PPF*:

> An economy is producing efficiently when it cannot produce more of one good without producing less of another.

Insight into the *for whom* question can also be gleaned from a production-possibility frontier, but only indirectly. The answer to the question of distribution does not show up in the construction of the schedule; it is, instead, picked up as an inference of the point that a society actually selects. If the economy picks a point that indicates a strong concentration in the type of good that only a particular group of people favors, e.g., then we need not look very far to find out "for whom the bell tolls." It tolls for them.

3. a. Which of the following are measured along the axes of a *PPF* graph?

(1) Quantities of productive inputs or resources.

(2) Quantities of finished commodities.

(3) Values of finished commodities.

b. Each and every point on such a graph (whether on the curve or off it) stands for some combination of the two goods involved (e.g., so many guns produced and so much butter produced per unit of time). With a given input stock, some of these points would be attainable, others would not. Specifically, with respect to production, the economy could operate:

(1) anywhere on the curve, and only on the curve.

(2) anywhere on the curve or anywhere inside it (below and to the left).

(3) anywhere on the curve, inside it, or outside it.

c. In order to operate outside the curve (above and to the right of it), the economy would have to (pick one or more):

(1) somehow increase its stock of inputs.

(2) discovery some new production techniques enabling any given input stock to produce more output than before.

(3) remove some incompetent bureaucrats from their jobs.

(4) eliminate the sources of significant abuse of monopoly power.

d. If the economy did somehow add to its input stock, or if it did discover new production techniques, then the production-possibility curve would:

(1) remain unchanged.

(2) move appropriately inward and to the left.

(3) move appropriately outward and to the right.

e. If there is a law of scarcity, then the economy will want to make good use of its limited input supply; that is, it will want to operate *on* the production-possibility frontier and not inside it. Should the economy be operating inside the curve, this would be attributable to some inefficiency or breakdown in economic organization. Specifically (pick one or both):

(1) some part of the input supply must be unemployed.

(2) the input supply, if fully employed, is somehow being used improperly. The best available production techniques are not being used, or some inputs are in the wrong jobs.

---

a. (2) b. (2) c. (1) and **(2) d. (3) e. (1)** and **(2)**

The production-possibility frontier drawn in Figure 2-1 is curved. It is, more specifically, concave (bowed away from the origin). Increasing the production of butter by million-pound increments results in increasingly larger reductions in the number of guns that can be simultaneously produced. To move from 1 million pounds of butter to 2 million pounds (from point *B* to point *C*) would, for example, require a 2000-unit reduction (14,000 − 12,000) in the production of guns. To move from 2 million pounds of butter to 3 million would require a 3000-unit reduction (12,000 − 9,000). And so on. A full accounting of the possible reasons behind this shape would be complicated and inappropriate at this early stage. Still, one background factor deserves some careful attention even now—the **law of diminishing returns**.

The nature of this law is most easily illustrated by assuming that only two inputs, say, A and B, are needed for production of some commodity X. Input A (which in the text example is land) is available in some fixed and limited quantity only. Input B (labor, in the text example) can be varied in quantity employed. The question with which the diminishing-returns law deals is this: We would like to have more of X. The supply of input A, which is essential for X production, is limited. To what extent can we get more X by adding more of input B to the fixed A quantity?

4. The diminishing-returns law gives the following answer: Up to a point, more B will yield more X, but the cost of getting additional X, in terms of the additional B quantity required, will steadily *(increase / decrease)*. To say the same thing differently, the "payoff" from each extra unit of B employed, in terms of the number of extra units of X resulting, will *(increase / decrease)*. In fact, a point will ultimately be reached at which, because of the restricted supply of A, the payoff from an extra unit of B employed would be *(zero / infinity)*.

Notice that this law is expressed in terms of physical quantities of A, B, and X; that is, it is expressed in *(money / "real")* terms.

For illustrative purposes, it is convenient to use an example involving two inputs only. Most actual productive processes involve more than two (e.g., tools, equipment, and seed grain in addition to labor and land). Where more than two inputs are involved, then, for the diminishing-returns law to apply, *(all the inputs / at least one input, but not all inputs / one input and one only)* must be fixed in available supply.

---

increase; decrease; zero; "real"; at least one input, but not all inputs

5. This question uses a specific, illustrative example to develop more fully the relation between the production-possibility frontier, the shape of that frontier, and the diminishing-returns law.

A certain economy produces only two consumer goods, X and Y. For manufacture of these goods, it has three kinds of resources: (1) a fixed stock of resources useful only in the production of X; (2) a similarly fixed stock of different resources useful only in the production of Y; and (3) a fixed labor force of 100 workers capable of working in either occupation. Table 2-1 indicates the amounts of X and Y producible daily when various quantities of labor work with the specialized resources.

Since we are interested in looking at the production-possibility frontier, we must consider how much it can produce of both goods when it is operating efficiently. Table 2-1 defines efficiency in the production of either good; i.e., the table indicates the *maximum* amount of output that can be produced employed various amounts of labor. To be efficient, the economy must make sure that the production of each good is proceeding at the pace indicated in Table 2-1. That is, however, not enough. To guarantee that the output of one good cannot be increased without reducing the output of the other, the economy also must make certain that the entire labor force is fully employed.

There are 100 workers in the labor force. If all 100 are employed in the production of X, then the economy will produce 600 units of X and 0 units of Y. Why? Because Table 2-1 shows that while 100 workers can produce 600 units of X, devoting all of the workers to the production of X leaves nobody to help in the production of Y; Table 2-1 also shows that 0 workers produce 0 units of Y. Suppose there are 40 workers employed in the production of X. ______ units of X would be produced and ______ units of Y would be produced employing ______ workers.

Table 2-1

Number of Workers	Daily X Production	Number of Workers	Daily Y Production	Corresponding X Production
0	0	0	0	600
10	40	10	5	______
20	105	20	12	______
30	200	30	20	______
40	300	40	28	______
50	390	50	36	______
60	450	60	43	______
70	500	70	49	______
80	550	80	54	______
90	580	90	58	______
100	600	100	60	______

Fill in the blanks in the extreme right-hand column of Table 2-1 with the proper levels of maximum production of X. Draw the resulting *PPF* on the graph scales provided in Figure 2-2.

300; 43; 60; table column: 580, 550, 500, etc. [The figures in the "Daily X Production" column are inverted; the *PPF* should be concave and anchored by points (X = 600; Y = 0) and (X = 0; Y = 60).]

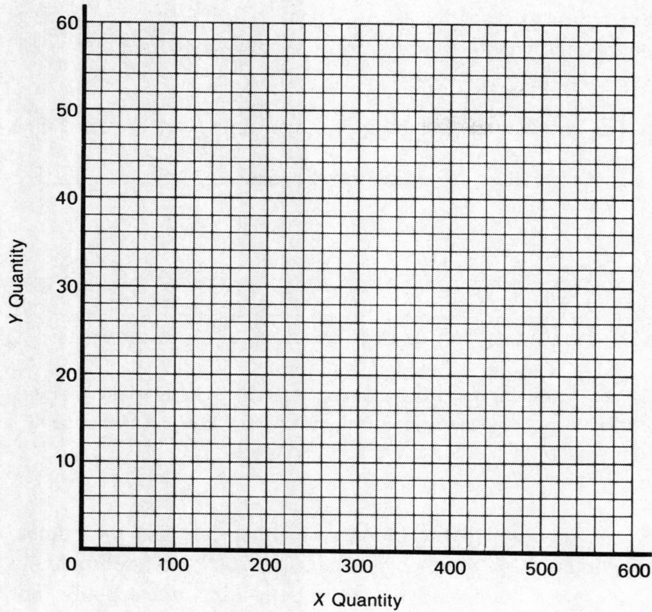

Figure 2-2

6. a. According to Table 2-1, diminishing returns first appears in X production when the total of workers employed rises to *(10 / 20 / 30 / 40 / 50 / 60 / 70 / 80 / 90 / 100).*

b. The corresponding diminishing-returns point in Y production is at *(10 / 20 / 30 / 40 / 50 / 60 / 70 / 80 / 90 / 100).*

c. This diminishing-returns phenomenon occurs because, as output and employment are increased:

(1) the competence or skill of the workers later employed is less than that of the workers first employed.

(2) each worker has proportionately less of the fixed or specialized resource to work with.

(3) the product must sell for a lower price.

---

a. 50 **b.** 60 **c.** (2)

One of the more fundamental concepts of economics that is most easily demonstrated in terms of a production-possibility frontier is the notion of **opportunity cost**. Most actions have a cost; everyone who has ever had to manage a personal budget knows that. The problem is that monetary costs do not necessarily reflect "true economic costs"—the value of the opportunity forgone. Opportunity costs are those true costs.

7. To get some practice in computing opportunity costs from production frontiers, return to the data of Table 2-1. Suppose that production is 600 X units daily and zero Y. If it were instead decided to produce 5 Y units daily, a sacrifice of *(zero / 5 / 20 / 40 / 600)* X units would be required. Each of the 5 Y units would cost *(zero / 4 / 5 / 10 / 20)* X units. Suppose now that X output is 500 units, so that Y output can be *(zero / 4 / 5 / 10 / 20)* units daily. To raise this Y quantity to 28 would require reduction of X output to *(zero / 100 / 250 / 400 / 450)*—a drop of *(zero / 10 / 20 / 50 / 100)* units. Each extra Y unit would thus cost *(1 / $5\frac{1}{2}$ / $6\frac{1}{4}$ / 8 / 10)* X units.

The greater the amount that total Y output happens to be, the *(higher / lower)* would be the cost of obtaining further Y output, measured in terms of X given up.

Whenever a production-possibility frontier is concave, as it is (or should be) in Figure 2-2, each additional unit of either good costs slightly more (in terms of sacrifice of the other good) than its predecessor. Each 1-unit increase in Y means a small, vertical, upward movement on the graph. To stay on the curve, this requires a *(leftward / rightward)* movement to compensate—a *(decrease / increase)* in X. If we want further increases in Y, these compensating *(leftward / rightward)* movements (the required decreases in X) grow larger.

20; 4; 20; 450; 50; $6\frac{1}{4}$; higher; leftward; decrease; leftward

8. In a model in which there exists only one discretionary input (i.e., one input that can be employed in the production of either X or Y), it is easy to get the idea that the law of diminishing returns is the only thing operating to produce the concave, outward bending of the production-possibility curve. This problem will present an example for investigation in which the *PPF* is a straight line despite the existence of diminishing returns in both X and Y for two distinct inputs.

Table 2-2 summarizes the production of either X or Y for various combinations of capital (K) and labor (L). It shows, for example, that 30 units of X (or Y) would be produced if 10 units of capital and 10 units of labor were employed. If 10 units of labor were combined with 30 units of capital, 48 units of X (or Y) would be produced. And so on. Suppose throughout this exercise that the economy is endowed with 30 units of capital and 15 units of labor. Both inputs can be employed in either industry. Fill in the blanks in Table 2-3 on the basis of Table 2-2 and the endowment constraints; assume full employment of

Table 2-2
Production Schedule for Either Good X or Good Y

Labor Employment (units of X or Y)	Capital Employment 0	10	20	30
0	0	0	0	0
5	0	20	30	32
10	0	30	40	48
15	0	32	48	60

Table 2-3

	X Production			Y Production		
Case	**Capital**	**Labor**	**Output**	**Capital**	**Labor**	**Output**
A	0	0	0	30	15	60
B	___	___	___	0	0	0
C	10	___	___	___	10	___
D	10	10	___	___	___	30
E	20	___	40	___	___	___
F	20	___	___	___	___	30
G	___	___	___	10	15	___

both capital and labor. Plot points A through G on Figure 2-3 and draw the production-possibility frontier.

a. For any level of employment of labor, X and Y *(do / do not)* display diminishing returns. For 10 units of labor, for example, the output of X increases by ________ as capital employment increases from 0 to 10 units, by ________ as capital employment increases from 10 units to 20, and by ________ as capital employment rises from 20 units to 30. Per unit of capital, the return to the employment of capital is therefore ________, ________, and ________, respectively, for the three increments just noted.

b. For any level of employment of capital, X and Y *(do / do not)* display diminishing returns. For 30 units of capital, the per

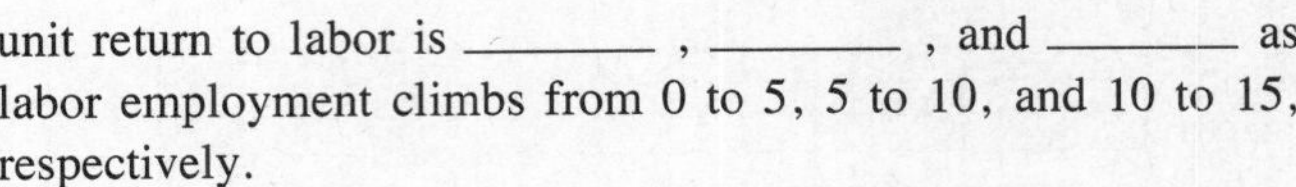
unit return to labor is ________, ________, and ________ as labor employment climbs from 0 to 5, 5 to 10, and 10 to 15, respectively.

c. The production-possibility frontier drawn in Figure 2-3 is *(concave, convex, a straight line)* because ________________
____
____
____

B: 30, 15, 60; C: 5, 20, 20, 40; D: 30, 20, 5; E: 10, 10, 5, 20; F: 5, 30, 10, 10; g: 20, 0, 0, 32 **a.** do; 30; 10; 8; 3.0; 1.0; 0.8 **b.** do; 6.4; 3.2; 2.4 **c.** a straight line; inputs are always used in the same proportion regardless of whether they are employed in the production of X or the production of Y (This is a difficult question to which we will return.)

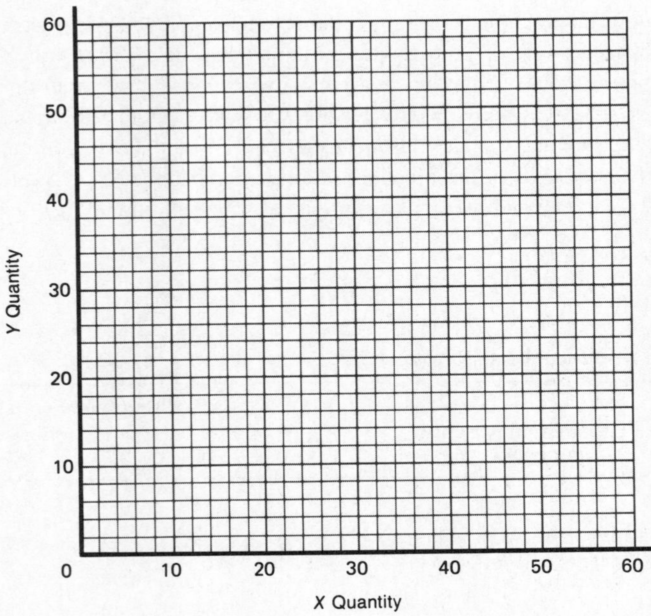

Figure 2-3

9. a. Suppose, given the data of Table 2-1, that the number of workers is to increase from 100 to 200 (the fixed amounts of X resources and Y resources remaining unchanged). The production-possibility curve would then move outward (pick one):

(1) until its end points indicated 1200 units of X, and 120 units of Y.

(2) by a greater amount than stated in alternative (1).

(3) by a much lesser amount than indicated in (1).

(4) not at all.

b. Suppose X is a necessity (say, food) and Y is a luxury. Every worker (or family) must have at least 3½ units of X daily in order to live. The population still consists of only 100 workers, and they choose to produce 450 of X, 28 of Y. (Mark this point on Figure 2-2.) If output is equally distributed, this means each worker gets daily 4½ X units and a little more than ¼ Y unit.

Now let the number of workers rise from 100 to 200. An extended X-production table indicates that 200 workers can produce 700 X. If all workers are to remain alive, what quantities of X and Y will be produced?

(1) 700 X plus about the same amount of Y per worker as before.

(2) 700 X and no Y at all.

(3) More than 700 X and about the same amount of Y per worker as before.

(4) Impossible to tell from information given.

The answer to the *for whom* question is thus provided.

a. (3) **b.** (2)

10. The following questions will investigate your understanding of "Pictures in an Exhibition."

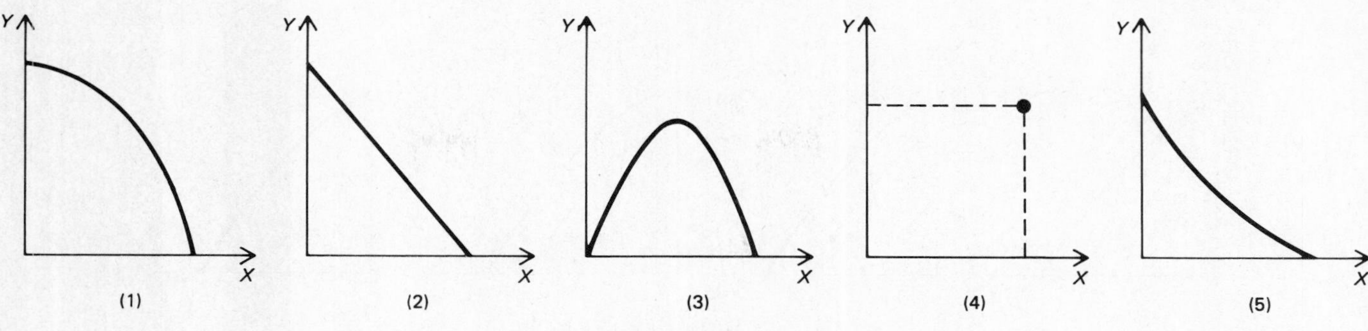

Figure 2-4

a. Consider the production-possibility curves drawn in Figure 2-4.

(1) An economy produces only two goods, and employs all inputs in exactly the same proportion. Which of the alternatives drawn in Figure 2-4 most accurately reflects this circumstance?

(2) An economy produces only two goods, and one of those goods displays increasing returns to scale. Which panel in Figure 2-4 most accurately reflects this circumstance?

(3) An economy produces only two goods. All of the inputs are entirely specialized for the production of one good or the other; i.e., the X inputs would be useless in the production of Y and the Y inputs would be useless in the production of X. Which alternative most accurately reflects this circumstance?

b. Consider the production-possibility curves drawn in Figure 2-5. In each, the lighter schedule represents an original curve; darker schedule represents what happens to the frontier after something has changed the economy.

(1) Suppose that scientific invention increased the productivity of resources used only in the production of X. Which panel most accurately reflects this development?

(2) Many scientists believe that we are exhausting our natural resources. Assume that there are two inputs, labor and natural resources, used to produce one of two goods, X and Y, but assume that resources are employed only in the production of Y. Which of the alternatives in Figure 2-5 most accurately reflects what would happen if the scientists were correct and there were no improvement in the technology involved in producing Y?

(3) Now assume that technology improves the efficiency of resources in the production of Y in (2). Which alternative might then be appropriate?

c. Let X represent consumption goods and Y represent investment goods. Suppose that an economy is in full employment and operating at point A in Figure 2-6. Which panel in Figure 2-6 represents the growth result most accurately? Now suppose that the economy is suffering through a period of unemployment that discouraged investment (high unemployment corresponds to low demand, excess capacity, and thus no need to invest in new equipment or technology). Which panel would now be most appropriate?

---

a. (1) 2 **(2)** 5 **(3)** 4 **b. (1)** 3 **(2)** 2 **(3)** 5 **c.** 4; 2

QUIZ: Multiple Choice

(These quizzes are provided at the end of chapters in this *Guide* to test your understanding of the material. Answers are found, with brief explanations, at the end of the *Guide*.)

1. When production is subject to the influence of the law of diminishing returns then, in order to obtain successive increases in output of 1 extra unit:

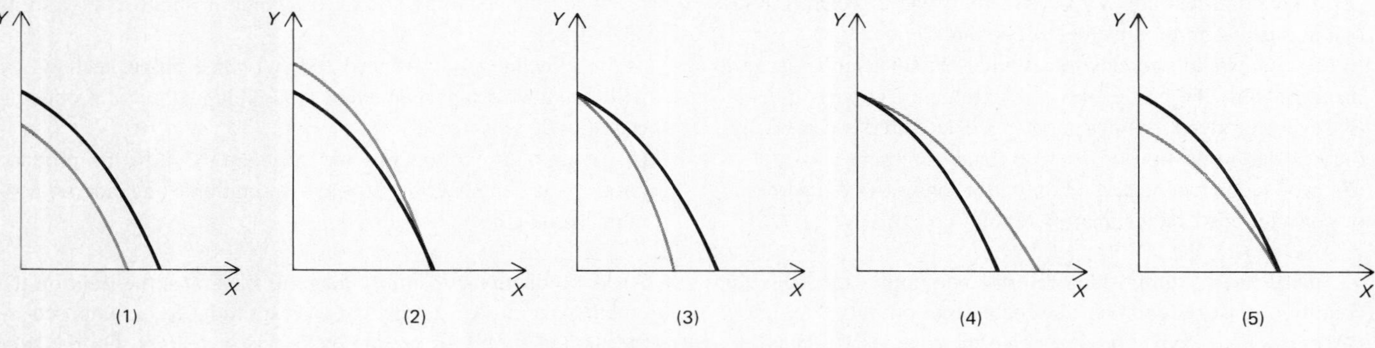

Figure 2-5

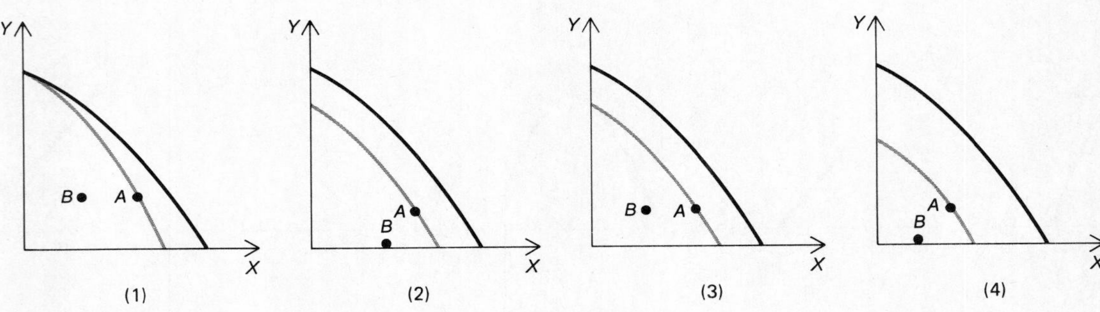

Figure 2-6

(1) smaller and smaller amounts of the variable input will be needed.
(2) adding more of the variable input will do more harm than good, because it must diminish total output instead of increasing it.
(3) the cost of hiring each additional unit of the variable input must steadily increase.
(4) greater and greater amounts of the variable input will be needed.
(5) none of the above is necessarily true.

2. The three economic problems of *what*, *how*, and *for whom* goods shall be produced apply:
(1) mainly to totalitarian or centrally planned societies, wherein the problem of planning arises directly.
(2) only or principally to free enterprise or capitalist societies, wherein the problem of choice is most acute.
(3) only or almost entirely to the less developed societies, since development is largely a question of meeting these three problems.
(4) to all societies, regardless of stage of development or form of political organization.
(5) to none of the above necessarily, since they are problems for the individual business firm or family, not for society.

3. There cannot be a problem of *what* goods shall be produced if:
(1) the supply of productive resources is small so that it must be devoted to the production of necessities.
(2) production has not yet reached the stage at which the law of diminishing returns begins to operate.
(3) the supply of productive resources is sufficiently large to make possible the production of some luxury goods.
(4) every productive input is so specialized that it can be used only in the production of one good and no other.
(5) production can be carried on under conditions of decreasing or constant cost, rather than increasing cost.

4. If the law of diminishing returns is to apply, the following condition must be satisfied: the increase in output:
(1) must come from a proportionate increase in all inputs.
(2) comes from an increase in some inputs, but at least one input must remain fixed in quantity.
(3) must come from an increase in one input only, all others remaining fixed in quantity.
(4) must grow less because of a decline in the competence or skills of inputs later applied.
(5) may be proportionate in physical quantity to the increase in inputs, but the *value* of that extra output must decline.

5. The economic problem of *what* goods shall be produced:
(1) may be a problem for any individual firm seeking to make a profit, but is not in any sense a problem for society as a whole.
(2) can be illustrated as the problem of choosing a point on the production-possibility curve.
(3) is a problem whose nature is illustrated by the law of diminishing returns.
(4) arises only when the stock of productive resources is very small, so that it must be devoted to the production of necessities.
(5) arises only when all productive inputs are so specialized that each can be used only in the production of one good and no other.

6. The economic problem of *how* to produce goods does not exist:
(1) if the required proportions of inputs are fixed for all commodities, so that substitution of input B to replace part of input A in production is impossible.
(2) only if production has not been carried to the point where the law of diminishing returns has begun to set in.
(3) when the economy's stock of capital is small relative to its labor force.
(4) in a technically advanced society, since proper technology will then have established the best possible method of producing each good.
(5) in any circumstances—the problem of how to produce goods is an engineering problem throughout and not an economic problem.

7. A production-possibility diagram illustrates the limit on the amount of finished goods that can be produced, as imposed by the limited supply of productive inputs or factors. On the axes

of this diagram are measured:
(1) quantities of productive inputs.
(2) prices of productive inputs.
(3) the quantity of inputs on one axis; the value of finished goods on the other.
(4) the money value of finished goods.
(5) quantities of finished goods.

8. On the heavy production frontier drawn in Figure 2-7, which point corresponds to the economy's valuing food most heavily?

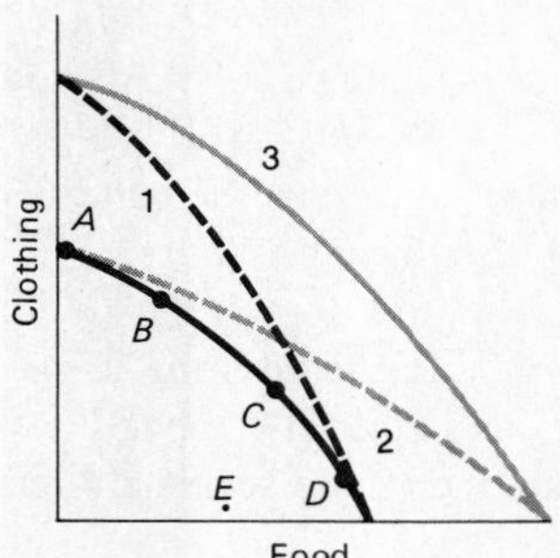

Figure 2-7

(1) *A*.
(2) *B*.
(3) *C*.
(4) *D*.
(5) *E*.

9. The heavy curved line in Figure 2-7 illustrates a country's production-possibility curve. A shift in this curve to the position indicated by the line marked 1 would be appropriate to illustrate:
(1) a change in the tastes of the population whereby its members want more food produced and less clothing.
(2) the appearance of some new resources useful only in the clothing industry.
(3) an improvement in technology applicable to both occupations.
(4) a change in the production mix involving an increase in clothing output and a decrease in food output.
(5) the development of a better technology in the food industry.

10. Which alternative in question 9 would apply had the heavy curve shifted to position 2?
(1).
(2).
(3).
(4).
(5).

11. Which alternative in question 9 would apply had the heavy curve shifted to position 3?
(1).
(2).
(3).
(4).
(5).

12. Figure 2-8 shows outputs of wheat obtainable on a fixed plot of land by varying the input of labor. The curve that correctly illustrates the law of diminishing returns is:

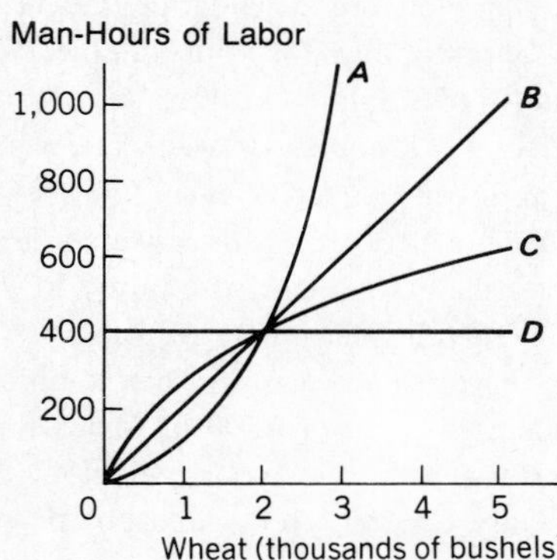

Figure 2-8

(1) *A*.
(2) *B*.
(3) *C*.
(4) *D*.
(5) either *A* or *C*.

13. A production-possibility frontier is intended to show:
(1) the exact amounts of two goods that an economy will decide to produce.
(2) the most valuable combination of two goods that an economy can produce.
(3) the alternative combinations of products available from a given quantity of resources.
(4) when the law of diminishing returns first begins to take effect.
(5) none of the above.

14. Suppose that actual output is marked by a point inside a guns-and-butter production-possibility frontier. This would signify that:
(1) it is impossible to produce more guns without the sacrifice of some butter output.
(2) either all available resources are not being fully employed or they are not being employed to the best advantage.
(3) the law of diminishing returns cannot be in operation.
(4) the diagram illustrates something which could not possibly happen.
(5) the law of diminishing returns must be in operation.

15. An economy can produce 200 of good X and 300 of good Y—i.e., this is one point on its production-possibility frontier. Another point on this frontier is 240 of X and 290 of Y. Which of the following points would also be on the frontier if it displayed the usual concave shape?
(1) 280 of X, 270 of Y.
(2) 160 of X, 310 of Y.
(3) 280 of X, 280 of Y.
(4) 160 of X, 315 of Y.
(5) 280 of X, 285 of Y.

16. Suppose that you are considering the relative financial merits of two opportunities for your summer vacation. In the first, you would live at home (for free but not necessarily with freedom) and work 40 hours per week at $5 per hour for 10 weeks. You would also need a car. Your neighbor will sell you a "junker" for $100; it will consume $100 in gas and $150 in oil over the 10 weeks if used only to get to and from work. Then it will fall totally and irreparably apart. The other opportunity is to work at a camp in the south of France. You will receive the equivalent of $500 in francs, but will have to purchase round-trip airfare on your own. It will cost $450 on Fly-by-Night-Only Charter. Room and board will be provided by your French employer. The fun of going to the sun of France has an opportunity cost of:
(1) $2000.
(2) $1750.
(3) $1700.
(4) $2050.
(5) $50.

SUGGESTED ANSWERS TO QUESTIONS IN THE TEXT: Chapter 2

1. Definitions.

2. Operating on the frontier means that the economy cannot simultaneously increase the production of two (or more) goods. It can be inside the frontier (unemployment, e.g.) but not outside; to go outside would allow for the possibility of simultaneous expansion of two industries that is disallowed by the definition and construction of the frontier.

3. The maximum number of haircuts possible is $[1000/(\frac{1}{2})] = 2000$. No shirts can be made with 2000 haircuts, so (0,2000) is on the frontier. To make one shirt always requires the release of 5 hours of time; i.e., the sacrifice of $[5/(\frac{1}{2})] = 10$ haircuts; the slope of the frontier is thus -10. So, graph $H = 2000 - 10S$.

4. Plot the following points: $A' =$ (0 butter, 15 guns) $= A$; $B' = (2,14)$; $C' = (4,12)$; $D' = (6,9)$; $E' = (8,5)$; $F' = (10,0)$. Connect the points. Notice that the butter intercept doubles but the guns intercept is unchanged.

5. The voluntary army should bring its pay into line with the true opportunity cost; otherwise, nobody would join. The cost of the army would then more accurately reflect its social cost.

6. Depletion causes the frontier to contract gradually. Invention and technological change could slow the rate of that contraction.

7. If each can take advantage of all production technology, then the *PPF* would be the same for all. If, e.g., custom precludes the adoption of certain technologies, then its frontier would be smaller (inside).

8. Food—market; army—command; family—custom (?); college—who knows?

9. 1984 frontier higher; 1984 point closer to the 1984 frontier.

CHAPTER 3

MARKETS AND COMMAND IN A MODERN ECONOMY

The three sections of this chapter provide a three-step introduction to the workings of a price system in an advanced mixed economy. In the first, the means by which markets solve the three fundamental problems of economics are presented in general terms. The specifics of their operation are the topics of Parts Four and Five of the text, so be patient. Section B develops a broad list of reasons by a government might choose to intervene in a functioning market system; it outlines how the innate efficiency of such a system could break down or lead to an undesirable outcome. The third and final section provides some temporal context by delineating three primary features of advanced industrial economies that are absolutely necessary if they are to function as vibrant, modern, mixed economies.

When you have covered the material in the text and this *Guide*, you should be able to satisfy the following objectives.

LEARNING OBJECTIVES

1. Describe what Adam Smith meant by the invisible hand. Indicate the particular system of political and economic organization that Smith was advocating when he introduced this phrase.

2. State the requirement that must be satisfied if the invisible hand is really to function just as Smith said it would.

3. Describe briefly how a market system (system of money and prices) settles the three basic problems of *what*, *for whom*, and *how* goods shall be produced. Explain as fully as you can (recognizing that the approach here is an introductory one) what economists mean in saying that the resolution of these problems is an interdependent process, or that the system is a "general-equilibrium" one.

4. Outline what economists mean by a "mixed economy," indicating the major elements of a free enterprise system present therein, and those of a communist (socialist) system.

5. Describe three roles that government might play in a mixed economy and indicate how each might influence the economy's answers to the fundamental questions of *what*, *how*, and *for whom*. Indicate the market system failures that would suggest each role.

6. Explain carefully what is meant by "capital," as the word is used in this chapter. Explain why, in discussing capital, economists speak of "time-consuming indirect methods," and of "the need to forgo present consumption."

7. Define or explain briefly the significance of (*a*) monopoly (imperfect competitor), (*b*) externality, (*c*) public good, (*d*) capitalism, (*e*) specialization (division of labor), (*f*) interest rate, (*g*) interdependence.

A pure **market economy**, sometimes labelled "free enterprise" or "competitive capitalism," permits individual ownership of capital goods and land. Why? Because it is believed that this private ownership encourages initiative and productivity. A market system will tolerate inequality since the lure of higher income encourages the introduction of new and better commodities as well as new and better production techniques. The fundamental rationale behind this faith in the efficiency of the market system is perhaps best described in terms of Adam Smith's notion of the **invisible hand**. In his words, cited even before the text chapter begins, "Every individual endeavors to employ his capital [physical and human] so that its produce may be of greatest value. . .[intends] only his own security, only his own gain. . .being led by an invisible hand to promote an end which was no part of his intention. . .that of society more effectually than when he really intends to promote it [society's]." The present author added the brackets to, in part, emphasize that people contribute all their assets—their possessions and their skills—to a degree that they alone control in the pursuit of their own individual well-being. The market mechanism functions so that the interaction of all such people solves the three central problems of economies—*what*, *how*, and *for whom*.

A **command economy**, by way of extreme contrast, is one in which these questions of resource allocation are solved by the government and by individuals doing exactly what they are told to do. A command economy forbids, for the most part, the very private ownership that is the cornerstone of the market system. Why? Perhaps on the claim that private ownership leads to unfair distributions of income. Perhaps on the grounds that an individual's control over economic resources can never lead to the production of precisely the output mix that the government feels is best. For whatever reason, a pure command economy is the polar opposite of a market economy.

Neither of these extremes represents the reality of the American economic system. Most, if not all, advanced industrial economies of the world are **mixed economies** in which both private and public institutions exercise control over economic resources. Private institutions exert their control through markets; public institutions, through regulations and fiscal incentives. It is, therefore, necessary to study both to understand how they can "coexist" in a mixed economy like the one we observe in the United States.

The market system is essentially one of exchange. Each person specializes (usually in cooperation with others) in producing some commodity or service. Each good or service produced is then sold for a money price. These money proceeds are shared among those who helped in the production. Each person's money share is his or her claim on the commodities and services that have been produced.

1. a. One vital part of the pricing system is *the market for consumer goods*. The text speaks of the *two* market fronts on which consuming families face business enterprises. There is a second vital part of the pricing system, a second market with which families must deal. This is the market for ______________________________.

b. In the market for finished goods, the individual consumer (or family) is a *(buyer / seller)*. In the market for productive inputs, the individual consumer is a *(buyer / seller)*. By contrast, the business firm whose task it is to manufacture consumer goods or to ready them for sale is a *(buyer / seller)* in the consumer-goods market, and a *(buyer / seller)* in the productive-input market.

---

a. productive inputs (notably labor) **b.** buyer; seller; seller; buyer

The workings of the market system are best understood in the context of a perfectly competitive **laissez-faire** economy. To that end, consider an economy for which the government exists only to provide an inner framework of law and order. Assume, in addition, that there are no monopolies. Assume, in other words, that no buyer or seller is sufficiently large to be able to affect the market price at which any good is being bought or sold. Prices are, nonetheless, extremely flexible in their response to collective changes on either the demand (buying) or the supply (selling) side of the market.

2. This question will lead you through a description of how such an economy solves our three fundamental economic questions.

a. Consumers use their "dollar votes" (the money incomes that they have available for purchasing commodities) to buy the goods that they want the most. If enough of them want some of these goods badly enough, then their collective bidding might push the prices of those goods up relative to the prices of others.

It is important to note, however, that *(any / no)* single individual can influence a market price. To see why, suppose that you feel a sudden urge to purchase a small collection of wall posters—say, enough to cover one wall in your room. Your going to the store and buying these posters will *(spur a large increase in / have no effect on)* the price that distributors and retailers charge for posters. Your increment in demand would simply *(be noticed and exploited / go unnoticed)* by the retailer. An increase in the demand for posters by all college students could, *(however, do the trick / in fact, cause an excessive and exaggerated price increase)*.

So, prices can rise in response to widespread changes in the desirability of particular items. Suppliers observe market conditions and pay special attention to prices. They will move to produce commodities whose prices are high (relative to production costs), and to reduce or cut down entirely on production of goods whose prices are similarly low. In this way, the problem of *(what / how / for whom)* goods shall be produced is settled. Producers are consciously trying to *(earn profits / satisfy consumer preferences)*. In so doing, though, they are also *(earning profits / satisfying consumer preferences)*.

b. The same perfectly competitive market system can operate effectively to settle the question of *for whom* goods will be produced. Productive inputs such as labor (be it skilled or unskilled), land, and capital carry prices just like consumer goods and services. These prices *(are certainly / are not)* part of the pricing structure of a market system. Since individuals supply inputs for the system, the resulting money incomes of all individuals are governed by (pick one):

(1) the market prices of inputs and the input quantities that they own.

(2) only the prices of the inputs that they own.

(3) only the input quantities that they own.

The *for whom* problem is one of distributing (whether fairly or unfairly) the available consumer-goods supply among society's members. The relative size of an individual's money income settles this question in a laissez-faire market system. It all comes down to (1) "Who owns what?" and (2) "What is it worth?"—two questions relating to (1) the distribution of the ownership of productive inputs and (2) the relative prices of those inputs.

c. Now turn to the question of *how* goods are to be produced. Consider the following example. Suppose that a given quantity of some consumer good of some value can be made with either (*a*) 2 units of capital and 10 units of labor or (*b*) 10 units of capital and 2 units of labor. Suppose further, but only for simplicity, that (*a*) and (*b*) are the only two combinations that will produce this good.

The *how* problem is now easily illustrated as one of choosing between these two methods. To make the choice properly, producers must know *(the price of the finished good / which of them is more efficient / the prices of labor and capital)*. "The most efficient method" is that method which costs *(less / more)* than any other method. The *how* question persists until *(input / finished-good)* prices are known, and it is settled by reference to these prices. For example, if capital costs $2 per unit and labor costs $3, the method *(a / b)* above is preferable. If capital costs $3 and labor $2, then method *(a / b)* is preferable.

---

a. no; have no effect on; go unnoticed; however, do the trick; what; earn profits; satisfying consumer preferences **b.** are certainly; **(1)** **c.** the prices of labor and capital; less; input; b; a

Perfectly competitive market economies are sometimes conceptualized as mazes of interdependencies. You will, through Parts Four and Five of the text, build toward an understanding of how these interdependencies work. Many of their implications are, however, quite intuitive. Try to see if you can see through the linkages to answer the following questions—not by reading more in the text or the *Guide*, but by thinking about the structure that is described.

3. Consider five types of people, labelled A through E, whose relevant attributes are described below:

A: Owns a coal mine; likes ice cream; hates fancy dessert yogurt

B: Works in a coal mine; likes yogurt and ice cream

C: Owns fancy yogurt company; hates dessert

D: Works at yogurt factory; hates dessert

E: Works at ice cream plant; hates dessert

Assume that there are enough of each type of person so that changes in their economic condition could affect a market price.

a. If an oil embargo increased the demand for coal, would the following *(increase / decrease / stay the same / you can't tell from the information given)?* (Write your answer in the blanks provided.)

(1) A's earnings . . . . ________________

(2) B's wages . . . . ________________

(3) C's earnings . . . . ________________

(4) D's wage . . . . ________________

(5) E's wage . . . . ________________

b. If a nationwide mine workers settlement increased B's wage without extending A's market, would the following *(increase / decrease / stay the same / you can't tell from the information given)*?

(1) A's earnings . . . . ________________

(2) C's earnings . . . . ________________

(3) D's wage . . . . ________________

(4) E's wage . . . . ________________

---

a. All increase. [A higher demand for coal should increase the earnings of A—the coal-mine owner. He will increase his demand for ice cream and (perhaps eventually) pay his labor (B) a higher wage. Higher demand for ice cream increases the earnings of the owner of the ice cream plant (C), who will pay the people who work for him (E) more. The higher income for coal miners increases the demand for yogurt, so eventually produces a higher wage for the people who work in the yogurt plant (D).]

b. **(1)** decrease [Paying labor more means less income for the owner (A).] **(2)** increase **(3)** increase [Richer coal miners mean more demand for both ice cream and yogurt, so the wages paid to people working in the yogurt plants (D) and the earnings of the owners of the yogurt plants (C) should increase.] **(4)** cannot tell [The demand for ice cream may fall or rise depending upon whether or not the reduced demand from the coal-mine owners is larger or smaller in magnitude than the increased demand from the coal miners. The wages paid to people working in the ice cream plants (E) may therefore fall or rise.]

Section B of the chapter introduces the various roles that government might play in very broad terms. These roles are catalogued according to the equity, efficiency, and stability difficulties that typically plague an economy left to its own devices. The existence of monopolies, or other forms of significant market imperfection, creates inefficiency that government might try to ameliorate. So do externalities, good or bad, and public goods that need societal support to be financially viable. Competitive laissez-faire solutions do not necessarily produce fair or just distributions of income, and governments sometimes try to use devices like progressive income taxation and social safety nets to diminish inequities. Fiscal and monetary policies have, since the 1930s, been used to try to shave off the peaks of economic boom and fill in the troughs of economic bust. The experience of the

1930s is, in fact, strong historical evidence that we cannot rely on laissez-faire policy to avoid dramatic turns in the long-term business cycle.

It should be noted, however, that government intervention need not be the best solution. Many times, the medicine of government policy is worse than the economic disease that it was intended to cure. We should, in short, avoid the error of the monarch who awarded a medal for singing talent to the second of two contestants after hearing only the first contestant sing.

4. This question will explore the potential roles of government in a mixed economy.

a. If monopoly power allowed the owner of a firm to produce too little, to charge too high a price, to earn an extraordinary rate of profit, and to ignore competitive pressures of potential competitors, would it alter society's answers to the three fundamental questions?

(1) Would the answer to *what* change? *(yes / no / probably)* Why? ______

______

______

(2) Would the answer to *how* change? ______

Why? ______

______

(3) Would the answer to *for whom* change? ______

Why? ______

______

b. If freedom to dump pollution into the air allowed a polluter to produce too much and charge too little regardless of competitive pressures, would answers to the questions change?

(1) Would the answer to *what* change? ______

Why? ______

______

(2) Would the answer to *how* change? ______

Why? ______

______

(3) Would the answer to *for whom* change? ______

Why? ______

______

c. If instability in the business cycle increased risk so that the price charged for a given good had to be higher than otherwise would have been appropriate and production were therefore smaller than appropriate, would answers to the questions change?

(1) Would the answer to *what* change? ______

Why? ______

______

(2) Would the answer to *how* change? ______

Why? ______

______

(3) Would the answer to *for whom* change? ______

Why? ______

______

d. If policy were enacted to redistribute income, would answers to the questions change?

(1) Would the answer to *what* change? ______

Why? ______

______

(2) Would the answer to *how* change? ______

Why? ______

______

(3) Would the answer to *for whom* change? ______

Why? ______

______

e. Listed below are three policy options that a government might consider:

1. Enact a minimum-wage law that prohibits the payment of any hourly wage rate below $3.35.
2. Construct a new toll-free highway.
3. Enact progressive taxes on incomes that reduce the spending power of rich citizens.

Item *(1 / 2 / 3)* illustrates an influence directly exerted on the decision as to *what* goods shall be produced. Item *(1 / 2 / 3)* illustrates a similar influence on *how*, and item(s) *(1 / 2 / 3)* on *for whom*.

---

a. (1) yes; Too little of one good also means too much of another. **(2)** probably; The most efficient process is probably not used. **(3)** yes; The monopolist is earning relatively more than otherwise. **b. (1)** yes; Too much of one good also means too little of another. **(2)** yes; The process chosen makes more pollution than it would if the polluter had to pay to pollute. **(3)** probably; Never say never in general equilibrium. **c.** The answers of **a** apply except that the income distortion would probably not weigh heavily in **(3)**. **d. (1)** probably; The people receiving the income would probably want different things than the wealthier people, and giving them more dollar "votes" would cause the market system to accommodate. **(2)** probably; The scales of various industries might change and thereby change the most appropriate production process. **(3)** yes; This is the point of the policy. **e.** 2; 1; 1 and/or 3 (*Note:* Indirect effects on answers to all three questions can be expected from each alternative.)

5. Listed below are several examples of how a government might try to modify the workings of an automatic price system:

a. pure food and drug laws . . . . . . ________________

b. minimum-wage laws . . . . ________________

c. pollution limitations . . . . ________________

d. free penicillin . . . . ________________

e. rent controls . . . . ________________

f. military draft . . . . ________________

g. unemployment compensation . . . ________________

Write in the blanks which of the three motives for government action—efficiency concerns, equity concerns, and stability concerns—is closest to the rationale that might underlie each policy.

---

a. efficiency **b.** equity **c.** efficiency d.equity **e.** equity **f.** equity and/or efficiency **e.** equity (and stabilization—you will see why in Parts Two and Three)

6. When the invisible hand breaks down because it cannot bring a monopoly to produce the correct output, government might *(intervene in the market / subsidize a more worthwhile activity / redistribute income)* to try to correct the inefficiency created. In the face of an externality, government might *(intervene in the market / subsidize a more worthwhile activity / stabilize the macroeconomy)* to try to ameliorate the resulting inefficiency. When society notices that an unacceptably large proportion of its citizens are impoverished, its government might *(subsidize a worthwhile activity / redistribute income / stabilize the macroeconomy)* to try to reduce the inequities derived from the distribution of inputs and their relative prices. Faced with many people driven to poverty because they cannot find work, a government might *(intervene in the marketplace / subsidize a worthwhile activity / stabilize the macroeconomy)* to try to diminish the associated economic and social losses.

Indicate in the spaces provided below whether the listed policies are designed to intervene in a market (I), subsidize a worthwhile activity (SU), redistribute income (R), or stabilize the macroeconomy (ST). Some policies may work in more than one area, so record two or three answers when necessary.

a. antitrust laws . . . . (________)

b. the Clean Air Act . . . . (________)

c. an arranged increase in the interest rate . . . . . (________)

d. the food-stamp program . . . . (________)

e. federal support of public education . . . . (________)

f. Food and drug regulations . . . . (________)

g. more public-works projects during recession . . (________)

---

intervene in the market; intervene in the market; redistribute income; stabilize the macroeconomy

a. I (prohibiting certain types of behavior by suppliers of certain goods) **b.** I (limiting emissions by setting clean air standards that must be met by enforcing a set of regulations) **c.** ST (This is monetary policy.) **d.** R (tax revenue collected from society at large to underwrite the food purchases of needs-qualified individuals and families) **e.** SU and R (Education is a public good, but federal support directed at needy students and/or school districts is a form of redistribution.) **f.** I (prohibiting the marketing of drugs and foods that do not meet certain standards) **g.** SU and ST (Public-works projects are generally focused on providing public goods, and if they are increased during recession, it is stabilizing fiscal policy.)

Section C of the chapter discusses the subject of *capital*. "Capital" is a word with too many meanings; you must understand the particular meaning here involved. Capital here does not mean money. It means manufactured productive inputs. It includes durable items like blast furnaces, factory buildings, machine tools, electric drills, tack hammers, etc. It includes stocks of semifinished goods; such goods are on the way to becoming consumer goods, but they are still manufactured inputs to be used in later stages of the production process.

Capital is important only because it "pushes back" the law of scarcity; it makes possible the production of more consumer goods. Every nation would like to become "capitalist" in the sense of having a large stock of capital relative to its population. However, there is a cost involved in the production of capital goods. The same resources that make these goods also make consumer goods; there is a choice to be made between capital and consumer goods. Recall the production-possibility frontiers drawn in text Chapter 2 between consumption goods and investment goods. Countries that climbed farther on the frontier away from the consumption axis found themselves on a higher curve the next year, but enjoyed less consumption in the current year.

7. As essential as capital is to the modern economy, heavy reliance on capital is but one characteristics of successful advanced economies in the world today. List two others in the spaces provided below.

a. ____

b. ____

---

a. an elaborate use of specialization; an intricate division of labor **b.** an extensive use of money

8. Specialization (or division of labor) is rampant in a modern economy because it increases the output obtainable from a given resource supply. The consequences of specialization include (circle as many as are correct):

a. exchange of goods.

b. use of money.

c. social interdependence.

d. an intensified law of scarcity.

e. possibly a sense of alienation on the part of members of the society involved.

---

a, b, c, and **e**

9. a. Circle all the following that qualify as capital.

(1) An oil refinery

(2) An issue of General Motors stock

(3) Cash in a business owner's safe

(4) A screwdriver

(5) Money borrowed by a business firm from a bank to expand its operations

(6) A steel-ingot inventory held by a steel company

(7) Unsold automobiles held by an auto manufacturer

(8) An inventory of groceries held by a supermarket

b. Money *(is / is not)* counted as part of capital because (pick one):

(1) it is essential to production.

(2) it has no part to play in production.

(3) it is not actually useful in production, although it is essential to have money in order to buy the real inputs that are needed for production.

c. To qualify as capital, the item in question *(must be / need not necessarily be)* an input that is useful or necessary at some stage of production, and the item must be *(of a type found only in highly developed economies / a primary factor of production / manufactured).*

---

a. (1), (4), (6), (7), and **(8)** **b.** is not; **(3)** **c.** must be; manufactured

10. a. Remember two elementary but essential things about capital, or "capital goods":

1. In the final reckoning, only consumer goods are important. Capital goods have no merit in themselves. They are produced only because they are roundabout ways of producing consumer goods.

2. Because any item of capital takes time to make, the effort devoted to making it is production for tomorrow's consumption use. The resources employed in constructing that item of capital could have been used to satisfy today's consumption demands.

Any developed nation, whether "capitalist" or not, possesses a large stock of capital, and much of each day's productive effort goes into maintenance and expansion of that stock. Consequently, in such nations today's productive effort is largely going to satisfy *(yesterday's / today's / tomorrow's)* needs, while the consumer goods actually enjoyed today result from *(yesterday's / today's / tomorrow's)* effort.

b. Circle as many of the following as are correct:

(1) The larger the available stock of capital, the larger the output of consumer goods that is possible.

(2) In terms of a production-possibility frontier, additions to the stock of capital can push the frontier upward and outward.

(3) A decision to produce or not produce more capital goods is not part of the decision of *what* goods to produce.

(4) In a fully employed economy, a decision to produce more capital goods is a decision to produce fewer consumer goods in the immediate future.

c. When reference is made to "a capitalist economy," the speaker is probably contemplating an economy (pick one or more):

(1) in which most capital goods are privately owned.

(2) in which the stock of capital is large relative to the population of that economy.

(3) not under communist or socialist direction, so property rights to the capital do not flow to the government.

---

a. tomorrow's; yesterday's **b. (1), (2),** and **(4)** **c. (1), (2),** and **(3)** [*Note:* There is room for dispute concerning properties **(2)** and **(3)**. A dictionary definition of capitalism may not specify that the stock of capital must be large relative to the country's size or population; nevertheless, the "capitalist" countries are typically those in which the stock is large. However, even a communist country may be "capitalist" in the sense of having a large capital stock relative to its population, and wanting to have an even larger stock.]

11. Consider the three investment projects described below:

A: Cost = \$150 in current consumption
Future gain = \$ per year in extra consumption

B: Cost = \$150 in current consumption
Future gain = \$15 per year in extra consumption

C: Cost = \$1000 in current consumption
Future gain = \$75 per year in extra consumption

a. Compute the percentage return for each project.

A: ________%

B: ________%

C: ________%

b. Indicate in the table below whether or not you would favor undertaking the project if the interest rate were equal to the values at the top of each column.

Project	5%	7%	9%	11%
A	_____	_____	_____	_____
B	_____	_____	_____	_____
C	_____	_____	_____	_____

c. The general insight that is suggested by the table in part **b** is that the number of attractive new capital projects tends to *(increase / decrease)* as the interest rate goes up; i.e., demand for new capital *(rises / falls)* as its price climbs.

a. A: 6%; B: 10%; C: 7.5% **b.** For project A, the decision is yes until the interest rate exceeds 6%; the first row reads yes, no, no, and no. For project B, the second row therefore reads yes, yes, yes, and no. For project C, the third row reads yes, yes, no, and no. **c.** decreases; falls

QUIZ: Multiple Choice

1. Capital (considered as a factor of production, or as one of the three major inputs of "land, labor, and capital") means:
(1) manufactured productive inputs.
(2) undeveloped natural resources, such as iron ore not yet mined.
(3) the financial assets of producing businesses.
(4) the same thing as the nation's total money stock.
(5) none of these things.

2. One vital reason why indirect, or "capital-using," methods of production have not displaced direct methods in economically less developed nations is that:
(1) the governments of such nations have not issued enough money to finance indirect production methods.
(2) people do not realize that indirect methods would produce more consumption goods.
(3) there are no indirect methods that would actually produce more consumption goods.
(4) such areas lack a properly functioning price system.
(5) the introduction of such indirect methods would involve a sacrifice of present consumption.

3. The economic problem of *how* goods shall be produced is solved in market economies:
(1) through the decisions of consumers in the marketplace, as these appear in the form of finished-good prices.
(2) by means of the profit motive impelling producers, which prompts them to try to keep their costs of production at a minimum.
(3) by means of extensive use of capital goods.
(4) by means of extensive specialization, which may or may not involve large-scale use of capital goods.
(5) in none of the above ways, since *how* to produce goods is not a basic problem in market economies.

4. The economic problem of deciding *what* goods to produce includes, among other things:
(1) the necessity of deciding the degree to which specialization is to be employed in the manufacture of goods.
(2) a decision as to the quantity of advertising that should be used to encourage the sale of whatever has been produced.
(3) the choice between the production of consumer goods and the production of capital goods.
(4) the establishment of a central government, since all decisions on *what* are ultimately made by such governments.
(5) the establishment of a system of pure (or perfect) competition.

5. We speak of "land, labor, and capital" as the basic grouping of the factors of production. Which of the following is correct with respect to whether or not money, stocks, and/or bonds should be counted as "capital"?
(1) All three (money, stocks, and bonds) count.
(2) Stocks and bonds count, but money does not.
(3) Money counts, but stocks and bonds do not.
(4) Money and stocks count, but bonds do not.
(5) None of the three counts.

6. A major social problem to which specialization and division of labor give rise is:
(1) the need to use paper money.
(2) the need to use capital.
(3) interdependence.
(4) the need to learn economics.
(5) none of these.

7. In economics, the term "imperfect competitor" is applied to a seller who:
(1) operates outside the system of specialization and money pricing.
(2) supplies a sufficiently large quantity of the good involved to be able to affect its price.
(3) seeks to distort the pattern of consumer tastes (through advertising campaigns and the like).
(4) knowingly or unknowingly uses inferior production methods.
(5) is not correctly described by any of these descriptions.

8. Figure 3-1 depicts a production-possibility frontier involving capital goods and consumer goods. What is the significance of points *A* and *B*?

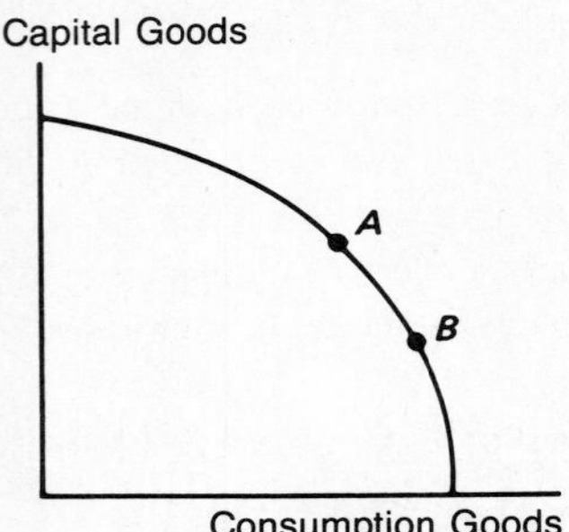

Figure 3-1

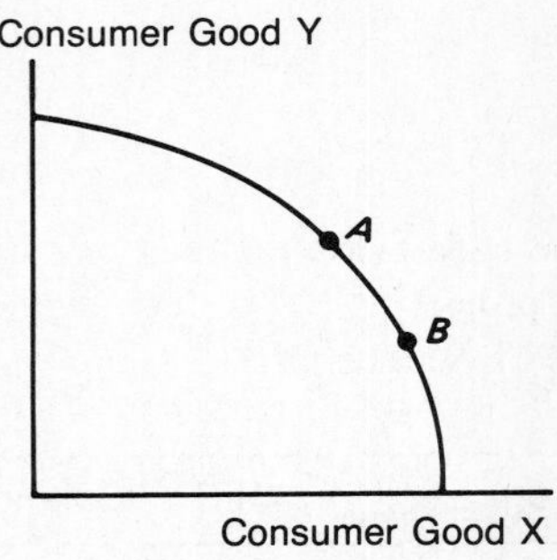

Figure 3-2

(1) They indicate possible demands for capital goods and consumer goods—*A* representing capital-good demand and *B* consumer-good demand.
(2) They represent possible and alternative combinations of maximum output which the economy in question could produce.
(3) They indicate the maximum possible quantities of capital goods and consumer goods which could be produced—*A* indicating maximum possible capital-good output and *B* maximum possible consumer-good output.
(4) Movement from *A* to *B* would indicate the growth of output resulting from the use of capital goods.
(5) There is no significance at all, since production-possibility diagrams refer to consumer goods only, not to capital goods.

9. In Figure 3-1, operation at a point such as *A* indicates production of some capital goods. Assuming this is more than sufficient to replace capital goods currently being worn out, then continued operation at *A* should result in:
(1) an inward movement of the whole curve.
(2) no change in the curve, but a move from *A* to *B*.
(3) no change necessarily either in the position of the curve or in the operation of the economy at *A*.
(4) no change in the curve, but a move from *A* to a point inside the curve.
(5) an outward movement of the frontier.

10. Figure 3-2 depicts a production-possibility frontier with respect to consumer goods X and Y. The economy involved makes full use of a money pricing system. The significance of such points as *A* and *B* is that:
(1) either is a possible operating point, and if selected, it indicates a verdict on *what* to produce with respect to X and Y, settled by consumer preferences as expressed through the price system.
(2) either is a possible operating point, but it will have been reached quite independently of the operation of the price system, since the curve in question refers to production, not prices.
(3) if either is chosen as an operating point, it will indicate the combination of X and Y having maximum money value, but it is not necessarily a point in any way related to consumer preferences.
(4) each is a typical point on the curve, and the position of the entire curve (all points thereon) is established by consumer preferences as expressed through the price system.
(5) either is a possible operating point, but a money pricing system is bound to show that *A* is a point preferable to *B*.

11. In a money-using, capitalist society, the economic problem of *for whom* goods shall be produced is primarily settled as follows:
(1) each producer looks for the type of consumer or market most likely to be interested in the product offered, then tries to tailor that product so that it is particularly appealing to the consumer or market.
(2) consumers bid up the prices of those goods they most want to have, and refuse to bid, or bid only a low price, for goods they find less attractive.
(3) business firms bid for the services of productive inputs according to their usefulness in production, thus giving each input supplier a money income that can be used to buy goods.
(4) competition operates so as to keep down profits, hence to keep prices at a level which consumers can afford to pay.
(5) income is distributed in keeping with the needs of individual consumers.

12. Which alternative in question 11 best describes the process by which the problem of *what* goods shall be produced is primarily settled, in a society which relies on the mechanism of money and prices?
(1).
(2).
(3).
(4).
(5).

13. If it is true that most of the goods a certain society consumed today were produced in the past, and that most of its production today is intended for future consumption, then from these facts it must be true that this society makes extensive use of:
(1) specialization and division of labor.
(2) money.

(3) a money pricing system.
(4) advertising.
(5) capital.

14. In a decentralized, capitalist society, the reliance on a market pricing system is not expected to help settle which of the following economic problems?
(1) Distributing money incomes among the members of the society.
(2) Helping a consumer with given tastes and a limited income to decide how best to spend that income.
(3) Deciding how much of the available resource supply is to be occupied in making any given consumer good.
(4) Choosing the particular kinds of inputs (factors of production) that should be used for the manufacture of any given consumer good.
(5) Determining the particular output of goods and services which the society really needs, regardless of the tastes of any or all individual consumers therein.

15. The government role that significantly affects the question *for whom* is:
(1) promotion of equity.
(2) promotion of efficiency.
(3) promotion of stabilization.
(4) all the above.

SUGGESTED ANSWERS TO QUESTIONS IN THE TEXT: Chapter 3

1. Produce corn, using all productive labor and land for the farmers.

2. Pollution limitations—improving efficiency (public "bad"); defense spending—improving efficiency (public good); food stamps—equity; ATT regulation—efficiency; monetary policy—stability.

3. Different jobs in an assembly line, etc. Firemen on trains.

4. Defer consumption.

5. Slaves were human capital; owning slaves was literally investing in that capital.

6. Price reflects (relative) scarcity; people who can afford things get the things.

7. Money goes in the opposite direction.

8. Smith did not think highly of the ability of government to intervene successfully in a market.

9. Yes, there are lots of potential government failures. Name one at your own peril—your failure may be someone else's necessity and success story.

CHAPTER 4
THE ELEMENTS OF SUPPLY AND DEMAND

There is a common expression among people who think about economic issues: "It's all a matter of supply and demand." For the most part, this expression is exactly correct. Properly framed, the essence of almost any economic question can be approached from a supply-demand perspective; properly interpreted, the answer to almost any economic question can be explained in terms of supply-demand intuition. This chapter will provide you with your first systematic exposure to these two most powerful tools of economic analysis. By the end of your work here, the following objectives should be within easy reach.

LEARNING OBJECTIVES

1. Define demand and supply; understand their graphical representations.

2. Describe the law of downward-sloping demand, and provide three economic forces that contribute to the resulting negative slope of a typical demand curve.

3. Explain why a supply curve is normally positively sloped.

4. Describe and define the market-clearing price. Explain how a competitive market operates to move toward that price.

5. Explain what is meant by "other things being equal" in the context of a demand curve. Discuss the significance of the five factors that are held constant in the construction of a demand curve.

6. Explain what is meant by "other things being equal" in the context of a supply curve. Discuss the significance of the four factors that are held constant in the construction of a supply curve.

7. Explain precisely how changes in the factors identified in objectives 5 and 6 work to change market equilibrium. Be clear about how to graph the effects of each. Be equally clear that the factors that influence demand are different from the factors that influence supply.

8. Understand three sources of confusion in analyzing changes in markets: (*a*) the meaning of "other things equal," (*b*) the difference between shifting curves and movement along curves, and (*c*) the critical word "willingly" in the definition of supply and demand.

Many forces can operate to push the price of any given commodity higher or lower: changes in people's tastes, changes in their incomes, changes in the costs of production, changes in the prices of substitute products, etc. The list is nearly endless. If we are to explain the price that a commodity actually takes in the marketplace, therefore, we will need to have a firm grasp on several essential, fundamental points. First and foremost, the forces that can influence price can be divided into two distinct groups:

▶ One group of forces operates through its influence on the behavior of buyers of the commodity. We sum up what buyers want to do through the device of a demand schedule, or demand curve. The demand curve is concerned exclusively with buyer attitudes—not with sellers.

▶ The second group of forces operates through its influence on the behavior of sellers. This we represent by means of the supply schedule, or supply curve. The supply curve reflects solely seller (not buyer) attitudes.

The division between these two groups of people is nearly absolute. Its importance in correctly analyzing the workings of even the simplest of markets cannot be overstated. In all but a very few exceptional cases, economic forces *directly* influence either the demand side of a market or the supply side of a market, but not both.

1. This question will explore the forces that play on the demand side.

a. The text notes that the demand curve is, typically, downward-sloping. To explain why the slope is negative, list three reasons why the quantity demanded should increase as the price of some good falls:

(1) ______________________

(2) ______________________

(3) ______________________

b. The text also identifies five economic forces that determine precisely where a demand curve must be located; i.e., five factors other than price are identified as determinants of the quantity demanded. Changes in these factors shift the entire demand curve. List them:

(1) ______________________

(2) ______________________

(3) ______________________

(4) ______________________

(5) ______________________

---

a. (1) New buyers enter. **(2)** More is purchased by existing consumers. **(3)** New uses might become economical. **b. (1)** income **(2)** size of the market **(3)** prices of substitute or complementary goods **(4)** tastes **(5)** particular commodity-specific factors

2. We will now explore the forces that play on the supply side.

a. The text notes that the supply curve is, typically, upward-sloping. To support this slope, list one important reason why suppliers must be paid a steadily increasing price to increase the quantity that they are willing to sell; explain how it works.

____

____

____

____

b. The text also identifies four economic forces that determine precisely where a supply curve must be located; i.e., four factors other than price are identified as determinants of the quantity supplied. Changes in these factors shift the entire supply curve. List them:

(1) ______________________

(2) ______________________

(3) ______________________

(4) ______________________

---

a. Law of diminishing returns; To increase output, more and more of some variable inputs will have to be added to work with relatively fixed supplies of other inputs; they become increasingly less productive. **b. (1)** costs of production **(2)** technology **(3)** taxes and/or subsidies **(4)** market structure

3. Each of the 10 prices (*P*) below is associated with a particular quantity (*Q*). In Figure 4-1, mark the 10 points corresponding to these *PQ* pairs. Join them with a smooth curve.

P:	$10	$ 9	$ 8	$ 7	$ 6	$ 5	$ 4	$ 3	$2	$1
Q:	1	2	3	5	8	12	15	20	25	40

a. In this schedule, the lower the price, the *(lower / higher)* the quantity. These figures therefore suggest a *(supply / demand)* curve.

b. Also record the following 10 pairs in Figure 4-1. Join them with a smooth curve.

P:	$10	$ 9	$ 8	$ 7	$ 6	$ 5	$ 4	$ 3	$2	$1
Q:	26	25	24	22	20	18	15	10	0	0

This would represent a *(supply / demand)* curve.

---

a. higher; demand **b.** supply

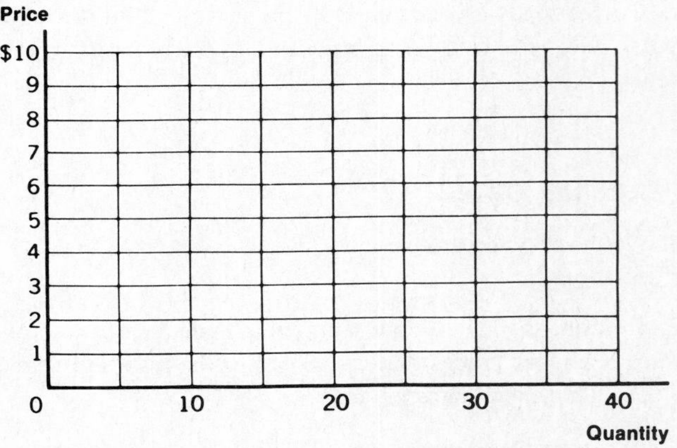

Figure 4-1

4. Given the data of question 3, what would be the market-clearing price? . . . . *($10 / 9 / 8 / 7 / 6 / 5 / 4 / 3 / 2 / 1)*

b. Why would this be the market-clearing price? (Pick one.)

(1) It is about midway in the total schedule of prices.

(2) It is the price that sellers have decided should be charged for this commodity.

(3) It is the only price at which the quantity buyers want to purchase just equals the quantity sellers want to supply.

---

a. 4 **b. (3)**

5. a. If (still using question 3 data) price stood temporarily at a level of $6, what would be the situation? (Pick one.)

(1) Quantity offered for sale would exceed quantity demanded. Competition among sellers would drive price higher.

(2) Quantity demanded would exceed quantity offered for sale. Competition among buyers plus seller awareness of shortages would drive price higher.

(3) Quantity demanded would exceed quantity offered for sale. Competition among sellers plus buyer awareness of shortages would drive price lower.

(4) Quantity demanded would be less than quantity offered for sale. Competition among sellers would drive price lower.

b. If price stood temporarily at a level of $3, which alternative in part **a** would apply? . . . . *(1 / 2 / 3 / 4)*

---

a. (4) **b.** 2

6. When economists refer to the **law of downward-sloping demand**, they are speaking of a particular kind of behavior among buyers that is observed with so few exceptions that it can be designated a "law" of behavior. Circle as many of the following as correctly describe or illustrate this law.

a. If the price of X falls, at least some X buyers will increase the quantity they purchase by at least some small amount.

b. When people have more income to spend, they normally increase their purchases of any commodity.

c. Demand curves normally slope downward as they run to the right.

d. The quantity of any commodity bought ultimately tends to decline as it goes out of style or is superseded by something of better quality.

e. When the price of X rises significantly, people tend to reduce the quantity of X that they purchase.

f. If the price of butter falls considerably, the drop will tend to reduce purchases of oleomargarine.

---

a, c, e (The law of downward-sloping demand has to do with the influence of price on quantity demanded. Item **b** does not illustrate this law because it refers to an income change; changes in income shift the entire demand curve in or out for all prices. In item **d**, the change in purchases is not set off by a price change; tastes change, to be sure, but the entire curve shifts when they do, regardless of the price. Item **f** does refer to a price change, but it is a change in the price of another commodity. Like items **d** and **b**, this change generates a shift in the entire curve for each and every price.)

7. If the price of any good falls, the quantity buyers want to purchase will rise because (*a*) new buyers are attracted, and/or (*b*) existing buyers increase their purchases. The text cites two background reasons for such increases: The **substitution effect** and the **income effect.**

a. First, if X's price were to fall, buyers may substitute X for Y. Even though the price of Y remains unchanged, Y would now be relatively more expensive. This would be *(an income / a substitution)* effect, and would apply to *(only old / only new / both old and new)* buyers. Similarly, if X's price were to rise, *(only old / only new / both old and new)* buyers may substitute Y for X because Y would now be relatively *(more / less)* expensive.

b. A fall in X's price resembles an increase in income, because the same amount of X can now be bought with money left over. With this "increase in income," buyers may want to purchase more of various goods—including good X. This is *(a substitution / an income)* effect, and it applies *(only to old / only to new / to both old and new)* buyers.

c. These two effects apply *(only for price reduction / only for price increases / for both price reductions and increases)*.

---

a. a substitution; both old and new; only old; less (only current consumers can substitute away from a commodity) **b.** an income; only to old **c.** for both price reductions and increases

8. Put (S) in the space below if the description suggests the substitution effect; put (I) if the income effect is indicated; put (N) of neither is appropriate.

a. A family decides its guests cannot tell the difference between butter and margarine; consequently it switches some of its purchases from butter to margarine. . . . . ( )

b. A sharp increase in rents forces the family to move to a smaller apartment. . . . . ( )

c. Butter prices go up, and the family switches more of its purchases from butter to margarine. . . . . ( )

d. The family receives a considerable increase in income and therefore buys, among other things, more butter and more apartment space. . . . . ( )

---

a. N **b.** I **c.** S **d.** N (These two "effects" are intended to apply to the consequences of a price change only. In cases **a** and **d**, the behavior change was not set off by a price change. There would also be an income effect in case **c**, but it would be *very* small since the proportion of income devoted to purchasing either margarine or butter must be minuscule.)

It is essential to keep in mind that a demand curve is a conditional schedule; it answers an "if this, then that" type of question. It shows, in particular, that if the price of some good were to stand at some specified level, then consumers would be willing to purchase the indicated quantity.

In Figure 4-2, the demand curve indicates that if the price were equal to *AO*, then consumers would want to buy a quantity *AF* (or *OC*). Should the price fall to *BO*, then the quantity demanded (willingly) by consumers would rise to *BG* (or *OE*).

When equilibrium in the marketplace has been worked out, there will be just one price for which the quantity *willingly* demanded will equal the quantity *willingly* supplied. The quantity read from the curve does not depend at all upon whether or not that quantity is feasible to supply at the given price. It reflects only the desires of consumers who worry only about their own preferences and what they can afford.

Remember, too, that price is not the only factor that influences consumers' decisions to buy. The income that they receive, the prices of other goods, and their own tastes also have an effect. Rather than try to capture all these effects in one curve, economists have historically favored charting the price effect on the quantity demanded under the assumption that the other factors do not change. Buyer behavior for one good is thus insulated against disturbances arising from other sources, and we can indicate how this behavior changes solely in response to changes in the price of the good in question. This is the "other things equal" or "other things constant" assumption.

These other "nonprice" determinants of demand do, of course, change. These changes are recognized by a shift in the entire demand curve to an appropriate new position; *each price* is, in other words, *associated with a new quantity demanded.*

In Figure 4-3, for example, the *dd* demand curve is shown as shifting to an entirely new position, *d'd'*—because, say, buyer incomes have increased. Demand curves are always drawn on an *other things equal* assumption. These "other things" include consumers' incomes; if this factor changes, then the demand curve must change position accordingly. If good X's price had been *AO*, then the consumers would have been buying quantity *OC*. Now, with higher incomes, they want to increase their purchases to *OE*. This doesn't mean they will succeed in buying quantity *OE* at price

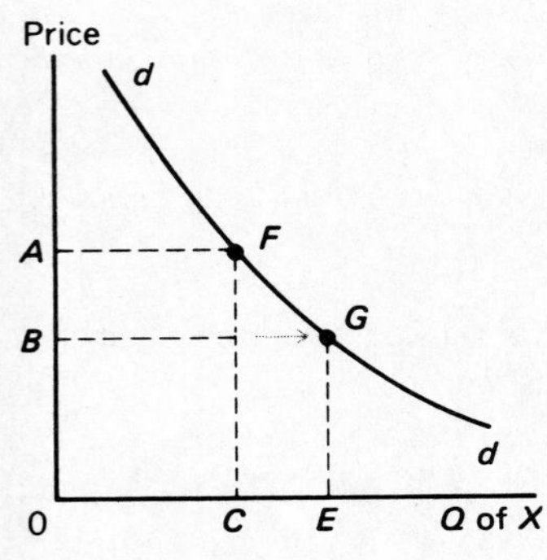

Figure 4-2

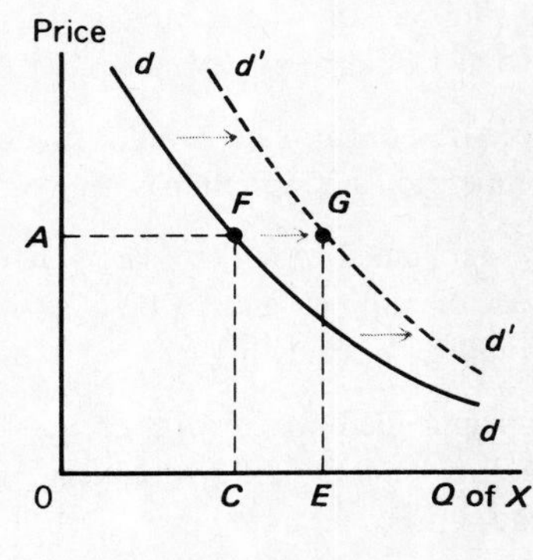

Figure 4-3

AO. The supply curve will have an influence on that. Our concern for the moment is with demand, not supply, and it is with what buyers *want* to do. The point is that at each and any price, because of the income rise, consumers will *want* to buy a larger quantity than they would previously have wanted.

The same notions apply equally well to supply curves. A supply curve is also a conditional schedule; it shows that if the price of some good were to stand at some specified level, then suppliers would be *willing* and able to deliver the indicated quantity to market.

Figure 4-4 illustrates this point. If, for example, price were equal to *AO*, then quantity *AF* (or *OC*) would be *willingly* supplied. If the price fell to *OB*, then the quantity supplied would fall to *BG* (or *OE*). These quantities depend only upon the parameters of the suppliers' decisions; they do not indicate in any way, shape, or form the willingness of consumers to purchase the indicated quantities at the indicated prices.

Price is, of course, not the only factor that influences the disposition of suppliers to sell. If the costs of pro-

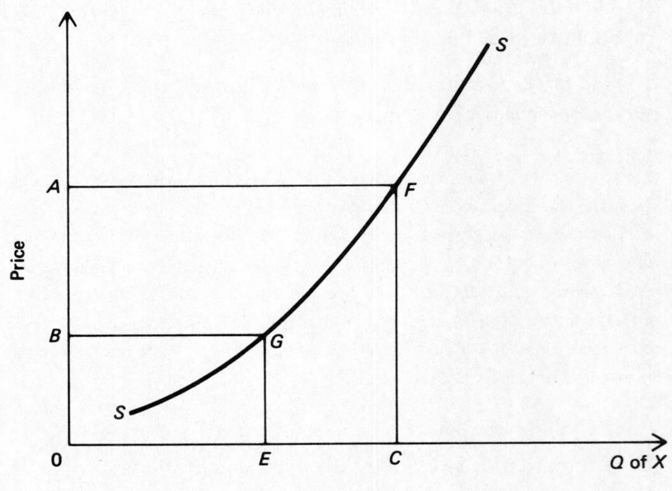

Figure 4-4

duction climb, then suppliers will want to produce and sell fewer units. If costs climb high enough, in fact, they may shut down entirely. Technological advances in the production process would, meanwhile, have the opposite effect. Taxes, market structure, production costs, etc., all influence the supply response to any specific price. A supply curve is, therefore, an "other things equal" curve just like a demand curve. It assumes that all of the factors, other than the price of output, which influence suppliers' decisions are fixed. If any one of these "other things" changes, then the entire supply curve must shift to a new position to be appropriate.

The next set of questions will exercise your understanding of changes in demand and supply (i.e., shifts in demand and supply curves).

9. The four panels of Figure 4-5 illustrate these ideas. In each, one curve, either demand or supply, has shifted position because of a change in some influencing factor other than price. The solid lines indicate an initial position; the broken lines, a new position. In panel (a), for example, the notion is that demand has shifted from curve *dd* to *d′d′*.

a. Indicate in the table below whether the market-clearing price and quantity would increase or decrease in response to the changes portrayed in the indicated figures.

	Price	Quantity
Panel (a)	______	______
Panel (b)	______	______
Panel (c)	______	______
Panel (d)	______	______

b. Each of the following events could reasonably be expected to change the position of a demand or supply curve for some commodity X. For each, indicate which panel in Figure 4-5 best illustrates its likely effect on a supply-demand representation of the market for X.

(1) The costs of manufacturing good X increase. . . ( )

(2) Consumer tastes shift away form X in favor of some other good. . . . . ( )

(3) The demand for some good Y, another commodity that can readily be produced by the suppliers of X in the place of X, increases. . . . . ( )

(4) A recession reduces the incomes of the people who demand X. . . . . ( )

(5) The price of a substitute commodity increases. . ( )

(6) The government removes a heavy tariff on imports of X from abroad. . . . . ( )

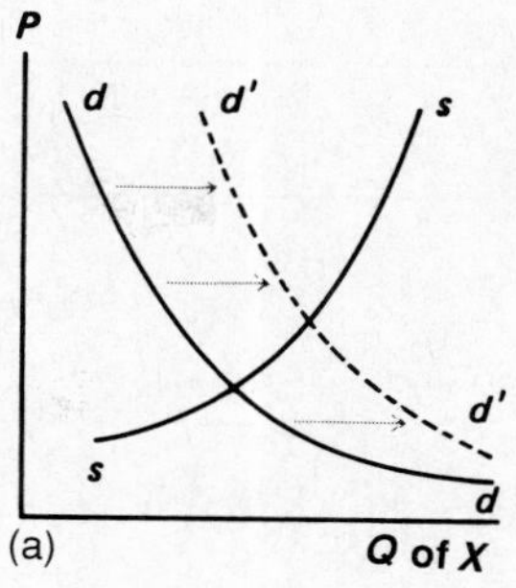

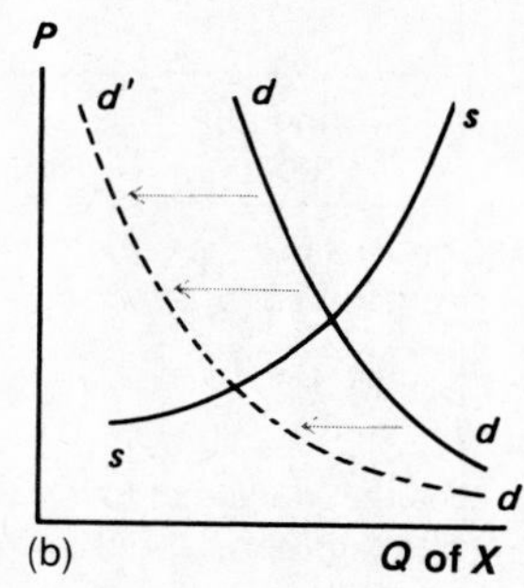

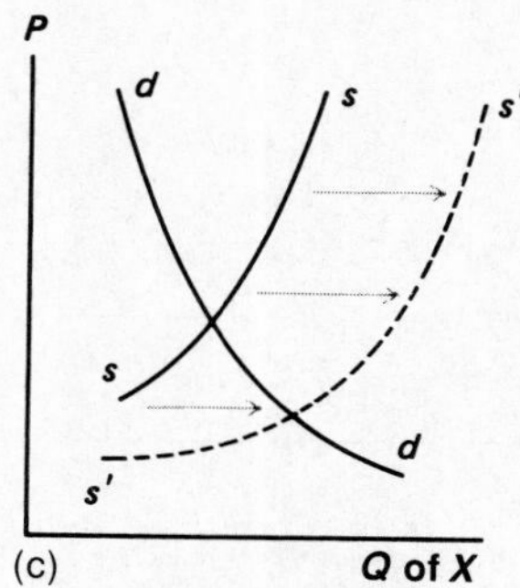

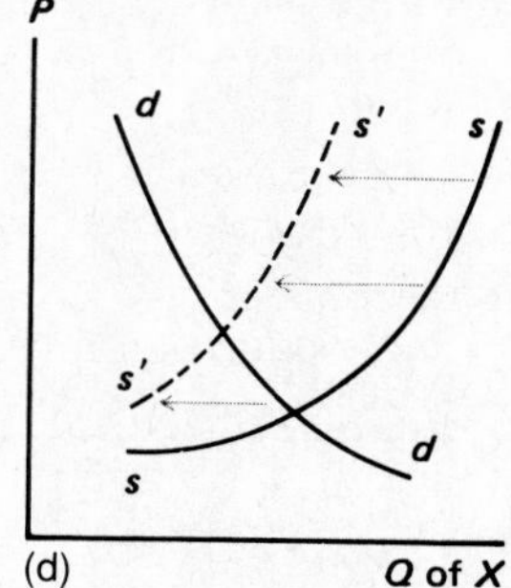

Figure 4-5

(7) The price of an input essential in the production of X increases dramatically. . . . . ( )

(8) Emigration produces a sudden reduction in the number of people demanding X. . . . . ( )

(9) The government increases the fines that must be paid by the producers of X for the pollution that they must emit. ( )

---

a. Panel (a): Price and quantity both increase as demand climbs. Panel (b): Price and quantity both fall as demand falls. Panel (c): Price falls and quantity climbs as supply increases. Panel (d): Price climbs and quantity falls as supply contracts.

b. (1) supply contracts, panel (d) **(2)** demand falls, panel (b) **(3)** supply contracts, panel (d) **(4)** demand falls, panel (d) **(5)** demand expands, panel (a) **(6)** supply expands, panel (c) **(7)** supply contracts, panel (d) **(8)** demand shrinks, panel (b) **(9)** supply contracts, panel (d)

10. a. Fill in the blanks in Table 4-1 with:

(1) the most appropriate graphical representation from panels (a) through (d) in Figure 4-5.

(2) an explanation of your answer to part (1).

(3) the direction that the equilibrium price would move (+ = up and − = down).

(4) the direction that the equilibrium quantity would move (same convention).

Table 4-1

Change in Condition	(1) Figure	(2) Rationale	(3) Price	(4) Quantity
A. Good X is clothing that has gone out of style.	b	change in taste shifts *did* in...	—	—
B. Pollution tax on supplier.	___	___	___	___
C. Opening of market to foreign buyers.	___	___	___	___
D. Price of substitute good falls.	___	___	___	___
E. Market structure requires more advertising.	___	___	___	___
F. A 10% across-the-board income-tax cut.	___	___	___	___
G. Robot makes production more efficient.	___	___	___	___

The first row of the table is filled in to help elucidate the directions.

b. In general, an increase in supply will *(lower / raise)* the price and *(lower / raise)* the market-clearing quantity. A decrease in supply will *(lower / raise)* the price and *(lower / raise)* the quantity.

c. In general, an increase in demand will *(lower / raise)* the price and *(lower / raise)* the market-clearing quantity. A decrease in demand will *(lower / raise)* the price and *(lower / raise)* the quantity.

---

a. B: panel (d), production more expensive, +, −; C: panel (a), market size increased, +, +; D: panel (b), substitute out of X, −, −; E: panel (d), cost of production increased, +, −; F: panel (a), income increased, +, +; G: cost of production diminished, −, + **b.** lower, raise, raise, lower **c.** raise, raise, lower, lower

11. When either the demand or the supply curve shifts in position, things are thrown "out of equilibrium," and a new market-clearing price and quantity must be established. It is easy to draw supply and demand curves upon a page or blackboard, but the market does not have such pretty little diagrams laid out for its inspection. The market has to fumble its way toward its new equilibrium. Without knowing the curves, how does it get there? Question 5 has already touched upon this matter; now it is examined in a little more detail.

a. Figure 4-6 reproduces panel (a) of Figure 4-5; i.e., it depicts one possible shift in one of the two curves. Specifically, note the arrow and the new broken-line position. It shows *(an increase / a decrease)* in *(supply / demand)*.

Before this change, the market-clearing price was *AO*, and the quantity bought and sold was *OE*. Now demand has increased—again, let's say, because of an increase in consumer incomes. At the *AO* price, buyers would now like to buy the larger quantity *(OE / OF / OG)*. But this buyer wish does not match the supplier wish. To furnish this larger quantity in full, suppliers would require the price *(CO / BO / AO)*. This in turn does not match consumer wishes. The new equilibrium must ultimately be a compromise in which price is *(CO / BO / AO)* and quantity bought and sold is *(OE / OF / OG)*.

b. How is this new equilibrium reached? What the market can discern, without the provision of supply and demand curves, is that at the old *AO* price, quantity demanded now *(exceeds / falls*

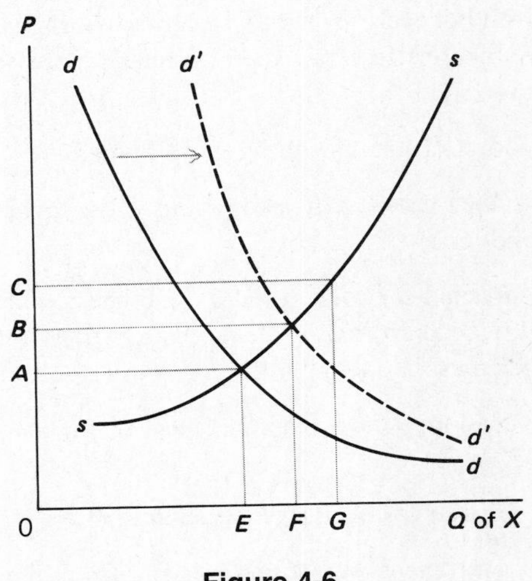

Figure 4-6

short of) quantity supplied. Buyers find it *(difficult / easy)* to buy all they want to buy; suppliers find it *(difficult / easy)* to sell what they want to sell at the *AO* price. Thus, on both buying and selling sides, the pressure is toward a *(higher / lower)* price. This pressure persists so long as the price holds at any level at which quantity demanded exceeds quantity supplied. This disequilibrium pressure ends when—with the demand curve at its *d′d′* position—price reaches the level of *(CO / BO / AO)*.

In the opposite situation—a decrease in demand or an increase in supply—the mechanism just outlined works in reverse.

---

a. an increase; demand; *OG; CO; BO; OF* **b.** exceeds; difficult; easy; higher; *BO*

12. The two panels of Figure 4-7 show special cases of possible demand or supply curves: a horizontal line in panel (a), a vertical line in panel (b). As a demand or as a supply curve, what would such a line mean? (Never mind whether such a curve would be reasonable or not. The question is: What is the information which such a line would convey?)

a. A demand curve indicating desire to buy some fixed quantity at any price (at least within the range of prices indicated by the length of the line drawn), with no intention of ever buying any greater quantity would be illustrated by panel *(a / b)*.

b. A supply curve indicating that any quantity (at least up to the quantity indicated by the length of the line drawn) would be supplied at the indicated price, but no quantity at all at any lower price, would be illustrated by panel *(a / b)*.

c. A demand curve indicating willingness to buy any quantity (at least up to the quantity indicated by the length of the line drawn) at the indicated price, but refusal to buy any quantity at any higher price, would be illustrated by panel *(a / b)*.

d. A supply curve indicating willingness to supply some fixed quantity, regardless of price (even at zero price), but refusal to supply any greater quantity, no matter how high the price (at least within the range of prices indicated by the length of the line drawn), would be illustrated by panel *(a / b)*.

a. b **b.** a **c.** a **d.** b

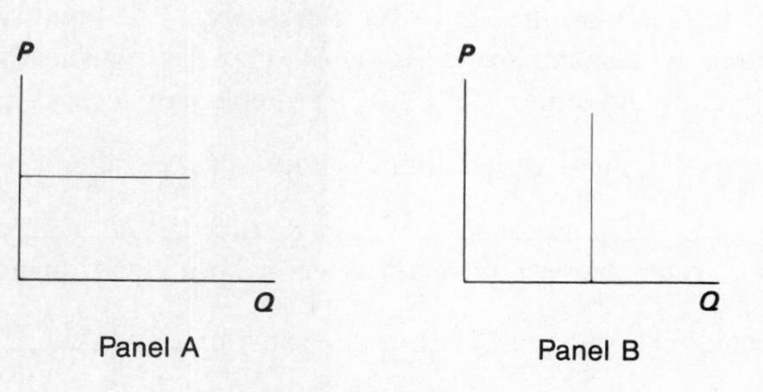

Figure 4-7

13. Identify whether each of the following involves a shift in the demand curve or a change in the quantity demanded:

a. Auto sales rise as consumer incomes rise. *(shift / change)*

b. Fish prices fall after the Pope allows Catholics to eat meat on Friday. . . . . *(shift / change)*

c. A gasoline tax lowers the consumption of gasoline. . . . . *(shift / change)*

d. A disastrous wheat blight causes bread sales to fall. . . . . *(shift / change)*

e. The wheat blight causes peanut butter and jelly sales to fall. . . . . *(shift / change)*

---

a. shift [The demand curve shifts out as income rises. This is panel (a) of Figure 4-5, with X measuring auto sales.] **b.** change [You might think, at first, that this must be a shift in demand as people can eat fish more often, but that would suggest an increase in price. Since the price fell, it must be the result of an exaggerated supply response (increase) to the Pope's announcement causing the market-clearing price to *move down* a demand curve. This is, therefore, panel (c) of Figure 4-5, with X measuring fish sales.] **c.** change [The quantity demanded falls as the after-tax price of gasoline climbs along a fixed demand curve. This is panel (d) of Figure 4-5, with X measuring the consumption of gasoline.] **d.** change [The quantity demanded falls as the blight shifts the supply curve in (up) and moves the price of bread up along a fixed demand curve. This is also panel (d) of Figure 4-5, with X measuring the consumption of bread.] **e.** shift [The demand curves for peanut butter and jelly shift in as the price of a complement good rises; the market-clearing quantity falls against a fixed *supply* curve. This is panel (b) of Figure 4-5, with X measuring either peanut butter or jelly sales.]

14. For parts **a, c, d,** and **e** of question 13, indicate below whether the indicated changes in market-clearing quantity should be expected to be associated with a higher or lower market-clearing price.

a. Part **a** . . . . ____________

b. Part **b** . . . . ____________

c. Part **d** . . . . ____________

d. Part **e** . . . . ____________

---

a. higher [The upward shift in the demand curve portends a higher market-clearing price—again, panel (a) of Figure 4-5.] **b.** higher [The upward shift in the supply curve portends a higher market-clearing price—panel (d).] **c.** higher [The upward shift in the supply curve still portends a higher market-clearing price—panel (d).] **d.** lower [The downward shift in the demand curve portends a lower market-clearing price—panel (b).]

15. Indicate whether the following statements are true or false, and explain why in terms of the four panels of Figure 4-5.

______ **a.** Failure of Brazil's coffee crop will lower the prices of coffee, tea, lemon, and cream.

____

____

____

_______ **b.** A fad for long skirts will lower the price of wool and raise the price of salt.

____

____

____

_______ **c.** A new yen for meat will lower the prices of grain and raise the prices of hide and horn.

____

____

____

_______ **d.** Development of the sugar beet raised the rents paid on tropical cane lands.

____

____

____

---

a. false; Failure of the coffee crop means that coffee will be in short supply; panel (d) tells us to expect the price of coffee to climb. Demand for substitutes of coffee (like tea) will shift up [Panel (a)], so their prices will rise. So, too, will the prices of the complements of tea (lemon). Only the price of cream might fall, but some people do take cream with their tea.

b. false; Longer skirts will mean higher demand for wool (more wool per skirt); panel (a) tells us to expect the price of wool to increase. There should be no effect on the price of salt unless an income effect contracts demand; then the price might fall as shown in panel (b).

c. false; Higher demand for meat will increase the demand for cows and what they eat. They eat grain, so panel (a) tells us to expect higher grain prices. The supply of hides should increase, meanwhile, so panel (c) suggests that their price should fall.

d. false; Sugar beets lowered the demand for cane, and thus the land it is grown on. Panel (b) tells us that the rent on that land should have fallen.

You will, by now, have noticed that you have been asked repeatedly to consult the four panels of Figure 4-5, and you might be wondering why. There are two answers. First of all, remember the dichotomy that was noted very early in this chapter. Things that affect demand affect demand; things that affect supply affect supply. It is the rare exception when some change in circumstance directly affects both demand and supply. The answer to "What happens to market equilibrium if. . .?" is thus found in one of the four panels of Figure 4-5. How do you know which one? Does the change you are considering affect demand? If so, then panels (a) and (b) apply. If not, then panels (c) and (d) apply. Does it make demand (supply) expand? Then panel (a) [panel (c)] applies. If not, then it is panel (b) [panel (d)] that shows what happens. That's it; you're done. And if most of economics is nothing but supply and demand, then you already know a lot!

Secondly, you will not always have Figure 4-5 handy. During an exam, for example, your instructor might not appreciate your referring to a picture from your *Study Guide*. Not to worry, though. If you have consulted Figure 4-5 with sufficient frequency and attention, then you can easily reproduce any of its four panels when you need to. The easiest way to answer "What if?" sorts of questions is, in fact, to draw your own versions of Figure 4-5. How? Start with some initial supply and demand curves; show the usual slopes unless told otherwise. Then decide whether the effect that you are considering affects the demand side or the supply side. Demand side? Draw a higher or lower demand curve, depending upon whether demand expands or contracts in response to the change in circumstance that you are considering. There, you have your own version of panel (a) or panel (b). Compare market-clearing quantity-price pairs, and read the answer. Supply side? Draw a new supply curve above or below the original. Look at your own version of panel (c) or panel (d), compare the equilibria, and read the answer. Simple? Good!

The text identifies three pitfalls of incorrect logic that must be avoided when we conduct supply-and-demand analysis of various markets. The first two are closely related: (1) care must be taken to remember what is being assumed constant, and (2) care must be taken to determine whether the market adjustment to be studied shifts a demand or a supply curve, or does something else. If the adjustment occurs in one of the forces that is normally assumed to be held constant (income, tastes, other prices, etc., on the demand side and costs, technology, market structure, taxes, etc., on the supply side), then a shift in one schedule or the other is appropriate. The final pitfall warns us to remember that demand and supply curves reflect quantities that people are willing to purchase and supply, respectively, at any given price. Equilibrium will involve a single price, but demand and supply curves cover the entire domain of possible prices.

16. a. Consider the following statement: "A simultaneous increase of demand and decrease of supply is statistically and logically impossible. Demand and supply are identically the same thing." Into which pitfall has the speaker fallen? _______

____

What would happen to market-clearing price and quantity if demand rose and supply fell at the same time? _______

____

b. Now consider Figure 4-8. What is the market-clearing

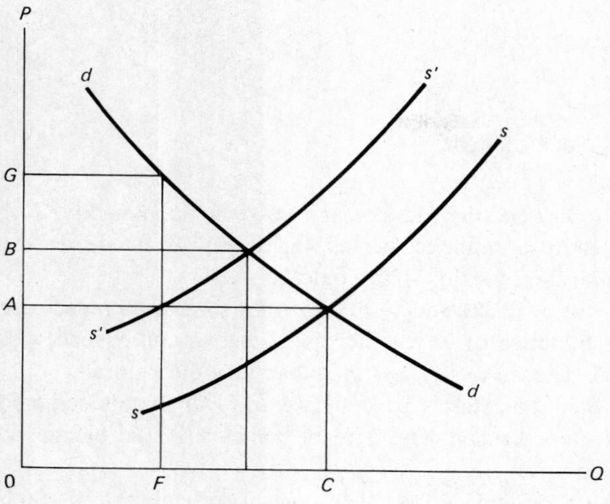

Figure 4-8

price if *dd* and *ss* represent demand and supply schedules, respectively? ________ Now let supply move to *s′s′*. This represents a *(contraction / expansion)* of supply. Suppose that the government was to impose a price ceiling at *OA* so that the price could not climb. The market-clearing quantity would be ________ read from *(supply curve ss / supply curve s′s′ / demand curve dd)*. There would be a *(shortage / surplus)* equal to ________ because the quantity demanded would be ________ read from *(supply curve ss / supply curve s′s′ / demand curve dd)*. If a black market arose for X in which people who possessed some of the good could sell it at an illegally high price, what price would clear the market? ________ What price would clear the market if the government had not interfered? ________ What would be the effect of the government's action?

____

____

____

____

a. all three. The speaker missed the interpretation that things normally held fixed must have changed requiring shifts in the demand and supply curves. The speaker also presumed that equilibrium always exists when price questions are answered by quantities along supply and demand curves. **b.** *OA*; contraction; *OF*; supply curve *s′s′*; *FC*; *OC*; demand curve *dd*; *OG*; *OB*; a larger contraction in the quantity supplied than necessary, and a higher than necessary market-clearing price

QUIZ: Multiple Choice

1. Which of the following statements is a complete and correct definition of the demand curve for commodity X? "The demand curve for some good X shows:
(1) how much of X would be bought at the equilibrium price."
(2) how, as people's incomes rise and they have more money to spend, their purchases of X would increase and by how much."
(3) how the amount of money people spend to purchase X changes as the price they must pay for it changes."
(4) the amount of X that would be bought each period, at each and any price, assuming other factors influencing demand (income, tastes, etc.) remain constant."
(5) the amounts of X to be supplied in each period, at each and any price, assuming other factors influencing sale remain constant."

2. The law of downward-sloping demand holds that:
(1) an excess supply over demand will cause a reduction in price.
(2) as people's incomes increase, they normally buy more of a commodity.
(3) when a demand schedule is illustrated graphically, it generally runs from northeast to southwest.
(4) when price falls, the quantity willingly purchased normally increases.
(5) the quantity bought of any good will ultimately decline as it goes out of style or is replaced by something of better quality.

3. One reason frequently given to explain the law of downward-sloping demand is that:
(1) when the price of something we buy falls, we are slightly better off; it is as though our incomes have risen slightly, and so we buy a little more.
(2) most commodities, over a sufficiently long period of time, tend to lose their markets in favor of newer and more attractive goods.
(3) the law of scarcity permits us to consume only so much of a commodity, no matter how much of it we may wish to have.
(4) in the case of many commodities, a fall in price will bring in very few new buyers, or none at all.
(5) the producers of a given commodity will not offer any quantity for sale at all if its price falls below some critical level.

4. The government declares that it is prepared to purchase any and all gold supplied to it by domestic gold mines at a price of $500 an ounce. Which, if any, of the four panels of Figure 4-9 would illustrate this demand situation? (The labels *P* and *Q* on the axis lines refer respectively to price and to quantity.)
(1) a.
(2) b.
(3) c.
(4) d.
(5) None of them.

5. A patient must purchase some given quantity of a given drug (but not more than that quantity) and will pay any price, if necessary, in order to obtain it. Which, if any, of the four panels of Figure 4-9 could be used to illustrate this situation?
(1) a.

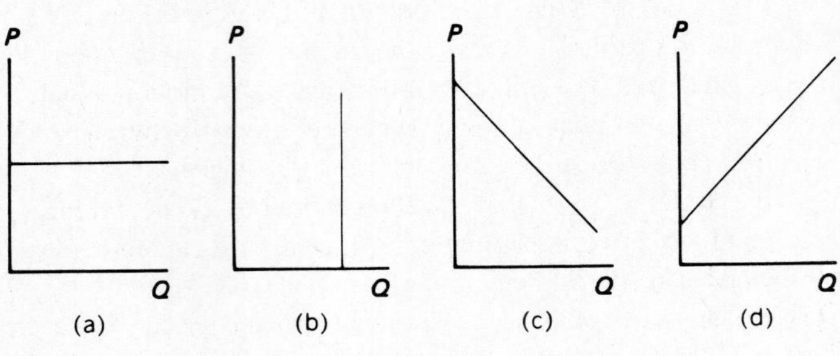

Figure 4-9

(2) b.
(3) c.
(4) d.
(5) None of them.

6. I can buy sugar in a supermarket at a fixed price of 40 cents per pound. This price applies to any quantity—1 pound, 5 pounds, 100 pounds. The store is so obliging that it will even sell me fractions of a pound at the same price per pound—e.g., 20 cents for a half-pound. Which, if any, of the four panels of Figure 4-9 can be used to illustrate this supply situation?
(1) a.
(2) b.
(3) c.
(4) d.
(5) None of them.

7. An increase in consumers' money incomes prompts them to demand a greater quantity of consumer good X. Which, if any, of the four panels of Figure 4-9 could be used to illustrate the demand side of this situation?
(1) a.
(2) b.
(3) c.
(4) d.
(5) None of them.

8. At any given price, the producers of commodity X are willing to supply some given quantity. If they are to supply a larger quantity, they must be persuaded to do so through the offer of a higher price. Which, if any, of the four panels of Figure 4-9 can be used as shown to illustrate this situation?
(1) a.
(2) b.
(3) c.
(4) d.
(5) None of them.

9. Which, if any, of the four panels of Figure 4-9 could illustrate the law of downward-sloping demand?
(1) a.
(2) b.
(3) c.
(4) d.
(5) None of them.

10. Suppose that the demand curve for commodity X shifts its entire position to the left (or downward). One reasonable explanation for this shift would be:
(1) the available supply of X has for some reason decreased.
(2) the price of X has increased, and in consequence people have decided to buy less of it than they did before.
(3) consumer tastes have shifted in favor of this commodity, and they want to buy more of it than they did before at any given price.
(4) the price of X has fallen, and in consequence people have decided to buy more of it than they did before.
(5) none of these events.

11. Four of the five events described below might reasonably be expected to shift the demand curve for beef to a new position. One would not shift that demand curve. The single exception is:
(1) a rise in the price of some good which consumers regard as a substitute for beef.
(2) a fall in the price of beef.
(3) an increase in the money incomes of beef consumers.
(4) a widespread advertising campaign undertaken by the producers of a product competitive with beef (e.g., pork).
(5) a change in people's tastes with respect to beef.

12. The phrase "other things equal," or "others things constant" when applied to the demand for commodity X, means:
(1) the price of X is held constant.
(2) both buyer incomes and the price of X are held constant.
(3) buyer incomes, tastes, and the price of X are held constant.
(4) all factors that might influence the demand for X, including the price of X, are held constant.
(5) none of the above.

13. An increase in the cost of materials needed to produce commodity X causes:
(1) the demand curve to move upward (or to the right).
(2) the supply curve to move upward (or to the left).
(3) both the demand curve and supply curve to move upward.
(4) the supply curve to move downward (or to the right).
(5) none of the above—no reason why this change need occasion a shift of either curve.

14. In prosperous times, the price of commodity X may go up, and consumption of X may go up also. This situation:
(1) is one of the few recognized exceptions to the law of downward-sloping demand.

(2) is precisely what the law of downward-sloping demand says can be expected.
(3) is the consequence of a demand curve running from southwest to northeast.
(4) cannot be explained by means of ordinary supply-curve and demand-curve analysis.
(5) is not correctly described by any of the preceding.

15. Beef supplies are sharply reduced because of drought in the beef-raising states, and consumers turn to pork as a substitute for beef. In the beef market, this would be described, in supply-and-demand terms, as:
(1) a leftward (or downward) shift in the demand curve.
(2) a leftward (or upward) shift in the supply curve.
(3) a rightward (or upward) shift in the demand curve.
(4) a rightward (or downward) shift in the demand curve
(5) both a leftward (or downward) shift in the supply curve and a leftward (or upward) shift in the supply curve.

16. Which alternative in question 15 would be correct with respect to the events described, had that question referred to the pork market?
(1).
(2).
(3).
(4).
(5).

17. If the price of a good is $5 (in a competitive market), and if at that price buyers wish to purchase 4000 units weekly and sellers wish to sell 5000 units weekly, then:
(1) price will tend to fall below $5 and suppliers will tend to offer less than 5000 units.
(2) price will tend to rise above $5 and suppliers will tend to offer more than 5000 units.
(3) price will tend to fall below $5 and buyers will tend to buy less than 4000 units.
(4) price will tend to rise above $5 and suppliers will tend to offer less than 5000 units.
(5) something is wrong—this could not occur in a competitive market.

18. Supply curves are typically "positively sloped." The meaning conveyed by any such curve is that:
(1) any increase in costs of production will result in a higher price.
(2) the lower the price, the larger the supply that consumers are prepared to buy.
(3) the higher the price, the larger the quantity suppliers will wish to sell.
(4) the larger the quantity suppliers have to sell, the lower the price they will have to quote in order to dispose of it.
(5) none of the preceding.

SUGGESTED ANSWERS TO QUESTIONS IN THE TEXT: Chapter 4

1. **a.** Crop failure restricts supply (shifts curve in), so equilibrium quantity (Q^*) falls and price (P^*) increases along a fixed demand curve.
b. Even if short skirts are made of wool, less is needed per skirt, so demand falls (shifts in); P^* and Q^* both fall along a fixed supply curve.
c. Meat demand moving up means that the demand for feed should increase (shift out with P^* and Q^* moving up) and the supply of ancillary products should increase (shift out with P^* moving down and Q^* moving up).
d. Sugar beet development means that the demand for cane and the land on which it is grown declines (shifts in); rent (price) should fall.

2. Definition.

3. Supply increasing means that the quantity supplied increases *for any price*. When drawn, this looks like a shift to the right (and down, since supply curves have positive slopes). Demand increasing means that the quantity demanded increases *for any price*. When drawn, this again looks like a shift to the right (but up, since demand curves have negative slopes).

4. Changes in prices of substitutes, income, etc., can change the demand for corn. Changes in the price of land, farm technology, etc., can change the supply for corn. Cheap oil should increase the supply of gas (increase quantity supplied for any price). The price of coal and the quantity of coal burned should fall as the demand for coal falls (coal is a substitute fuel); downward pressure on the wages paid to coal miners should therefore be felt as the demand for miners falls.

5. Price too high means that the quantity supplied exceeds the quantity demanded. Inventories build, and the prices called out by suppliers fall. If the price is too low, the opposite happens.

6. Move the curves around. An increase in supply, e.g., shifts the curve out to the right, and equilibrium moves down along a fixed demand curve. Price falls and quantity goes up.

7. (*a*) Demand change; (*b*) demand change; (*c*) change in the quantity demanded; (*d*) change in the quantity demanded; (*e*) demand change; (*f*) change in the quantity demanded.

8. Both curves shift when demand and supply both change.

9. $P^* = \$6$; $Q^* = 20$. Tripling demand means that $P^* = \$8$ and $Q^* = 30$. With a price of $4, there is excess demand.

10. **a.** Restricting the supply from competitors effectively raises demand with supply fixed. Quantity and price should both climb along the fixed supply curve.
b. Tax reduction lowers the cost of producing any level of output, so supply shifts down (out). Quantity should climb as price falls along a fixed demand curve.
c. Effective demand increases; refer to **a**.
d. Diminished regulation lowers cost; refer to **b**.
e. Lower wages mean lower costs; refer again to **b**.

CHAPTER 5
OVERVIEW OF MACROECONOMICS

The study of macroeconomics is the study of the "big picture." It is the study of how entire economies move through time. It ponders the sources of growth, inflation, unemployment, and business cycles. It ponders the ability of governments to help (or hinder) their economies by manipulating a wide variety of macroeconomic policy instruments. It wonders why some policies work and why some fail. It wonders how to assess this success, and it is frustrated that many policy objectives seem to be mutually incompatible—objectives that are admirable when considered on their face value, but which are damaging to other objectives of debatably equal importance when pursued too strenuously. Policies which produce low unemployment rates can, for example, also generate increased inflation.

Having completed your work on this overview, you will not have many answers. You will, instead, have collected a multitude of questions whose answers will be addressed over the course of the next 13 chapters. Your working through this list of questions without answers will not, however, be an exercise in futility. In noting the significance and the context of each, you will have accomplished the following objectives even without the answers.

LEARNING OBJECTIVES

1. Explain the difference between microeconomics and macroeconomics.

2. Identify the major goals of macroeconomic policy: (*a*) output (high level and rapid growth), (*b*) employment (high employment and low involuntary unemployment), (*c*) price stability, and (*d*) foreign balance (export-import equilibrium and exchange-rate stability).

3. Identify the major macroeconomic policy instruments: (*a*) fiscal policy (government spending and taxation), (*b*) monetary policy (from interest rates to the money supply), (*c*) foreign economics (trade policies and exchange-rate intervention), and (*d*) incomes policies (from voluntary wage-price guidelines to mandatory controls).

4. Tell the stories of two or three major events in the history of active governmental macroeconomic policy.

5. Recognize the potential for tradeoffs between two or more policy objectives (e.g., price stability versus high employment, rapid growth versus high current consumption).

6. Distinguish between policy variables, and external variables.

7. Delineate the difference between the long run and the short run in the context of determining actual and potential GNP.

8. Develop the fundamentals of aggregate supply, aggregate demand, and macroeconomic equilibrium; further delineate the difference between the long run and the short run.

9. Use aggregate supply-and-demand analysis to illustrate how inflation can be created by either the demand or the supply side of the macroeconomy; also demonstrate the likely effects of high interest rates caused by tight monetary policy.

There are four major goals of economic policy: high output, high employment, price stability, and foreign balance. The first four questions will deal with each one in turn.

1. Output is usually denoted by gross national product, its most comprehensive measure. GNP is the (*market / discounted / stable*) value of all goods and services produced during any given year. When measured at current prices, this measure is termed (*nominal / real / potential*) GNP. When measured after correcting for inflation, it is termed (*nominal / real / potential*) GNP. When measured in terms of maximum sustainable output, it is termed (*nominal / real / potential*) GNP. The correct measure for the target for high employment upon which this last measure is based (*is / is not*) 0 percent unemployment. During the 1970s, periods of high inflation caused real GNP to (*match potential GNP / exceed nominal GNP / fall short of nominal GNP*).

Periods of high unemployment during the early 1980s caused nominal GNP to (*exceed potential GNP / fall short of potential GNP / fall short of real GNP*).

---

market; nominal; real; potential; is not; fall short of nominal GNP; fall short of potential GNP (Study Figure 5-1 to answer this question.)

2. The objective of high employment is usually conceptualized from the other side of the coin: the objective of a low rate of unemployment. The rate of unemployment has, on average since 1950, (*climbed from / fallen from / remained steady at*) roughly ________ percent. From 1950 to 1970, this pattern persisted despite a (*falling / growing / fairly constant*) rate of labor-force participation (*at roughly 60 percent / through 70 percent by 1970*). Since 1970, this picture (*has / has not*) changed. In the 1970s and 1980s, participation rates (*fell / rose / remained steady*).

---

climbed from; 3 to 4; fairly constant; at roughly 60 percent; has; rose (to 65 percent in 1988) (Consult Figure 5-2 to answer this question.)

3. Price stability, as a goal of macroeconomic policy, does not mean absolute stability of all prices. Absolute stability would eliminate the natural role of changes in relative prices in allocating goods and services. Price stability is, instead, an objective stated in terms of a price index like the (*DAR / CIA / CPI*) that (*ignores price movement across goods and services / averages price movement across goods and services / includes only price increases across goods and services*). Inflation, then, is measured as (*the rate of change in the index / the absolute value of the price index / the absolute price levels of a representative number of goods*). In the last 20 years, inflation peaked in (*1973 and 1979 / 1972 and 1973 / 1973 and 1976*). Between 1929 and 1988, the average rate of inflation measured by the CPI was (*8.7% / 1.2% / 3.4%*).

CPI; averages price movements across goods and services; the rate of change in the index; 1973 and 1979; 3.4% (Consult Figure 5-3.)

4. Stability in external economic affairs is the last major goal. It is important because disruptions in import and export markets disrupt not only mutually beneficial international markets but also domestic, internal markets. A highly valued dollar in the early 1980s caused a higher rate of (*inflation / unemployment / growth*) and a lower rate of (*inflation / unemployment / growth*) in the United States than would have otherwise been observed. The source of these changes was a (*decline / expansion / explosion*) in the U.S. exporting sector; the high dollar made U.S. goods more expensive abroad (costing jobs in the United States) and foreign goods cheaper at home, (holding U.S. inflation down).

---

unemployment; inflation and growth; decline

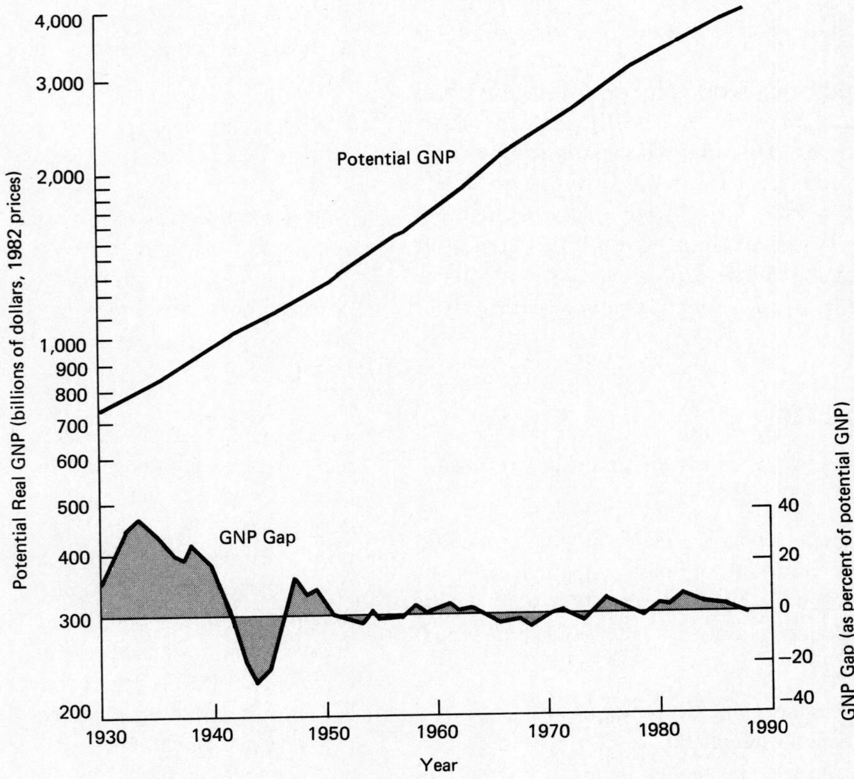

Figure 5-1

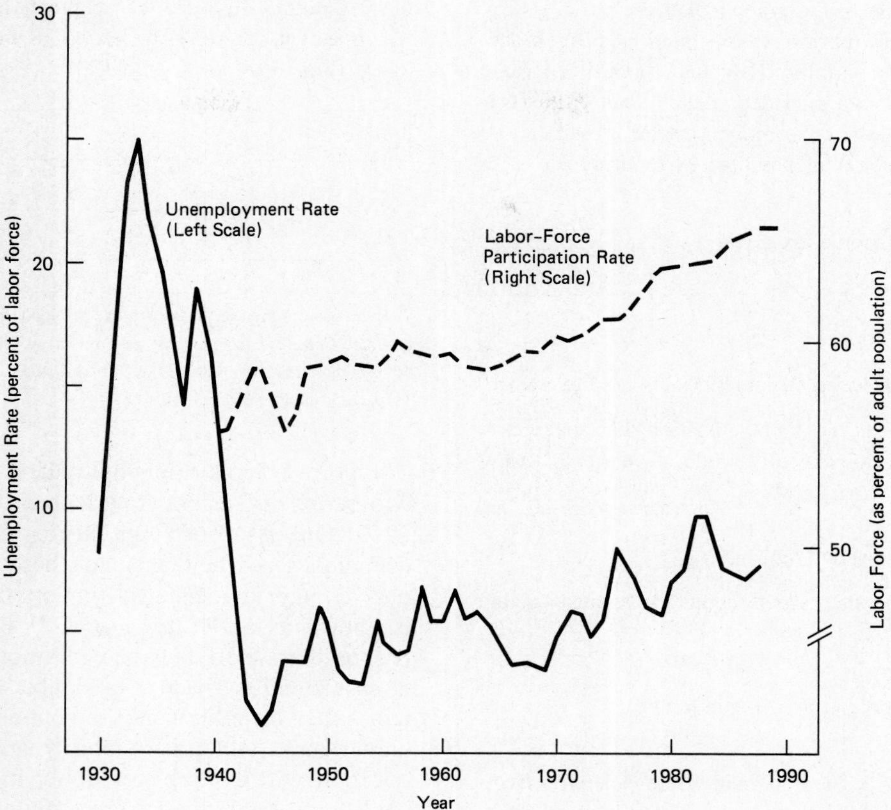

Figure 5-2

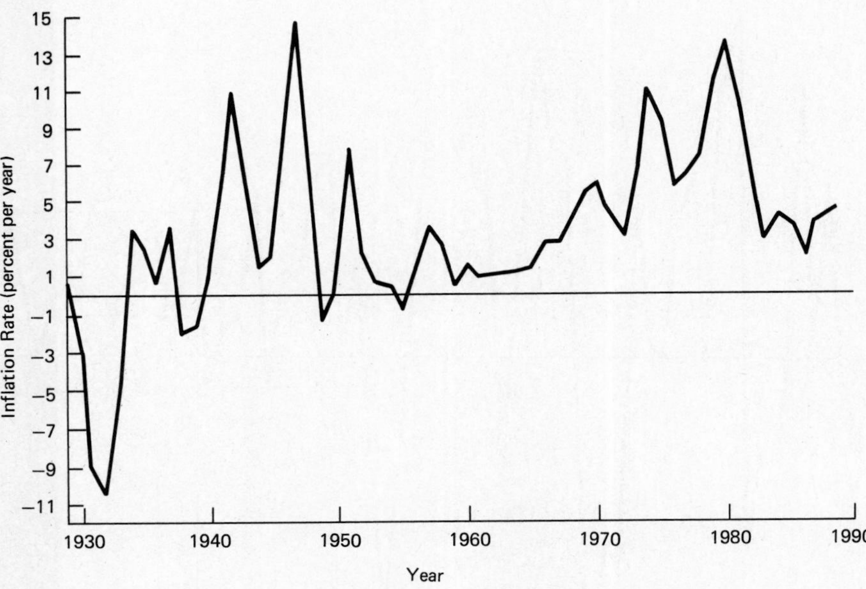

Figure 5-3

5. Policy tools available to the policymaker are varied. They fall under four general rubrics: fiscal policy (FP), monetary policy (MP), incomes policy (IP), and foreign economic policy (FEP). In the spaces provided, match each of the following more specific policies with its general classification; use the abbreviations noted in parentheses to designate your answer.

a. a change in federal income-tax rates . . . . . . (________)

b. an increase in the money supply . . . . (________)

c. a tariff on German cars . . . . (________)

d. a tax penalty on high wage settlements . . . . . (________)

e. the passage of domestic content legislation that specifies a minimum percentage of domestically produced inputs that must be used in production . . . . (________)

f. an increase in defense spending . . . . (________)

g. the elimination of the interest-rate deduction against taxable income . . . . (________)

a. FP **b.** MP **c.** FEP **d.** IP **e.** FEP **f.** FP **g.** FP

6. The Employment Act of 1946 had some positive effects on the ability of the United States to achieve stability in its macroeconomic circumstance, but the Humphrey-Hawkins Bill of 1978 did not. Explain this statement in light of Figure 5-4, in which annual rates of growth in GNP are plotted for the United States from 1901 to the mid-1980s.

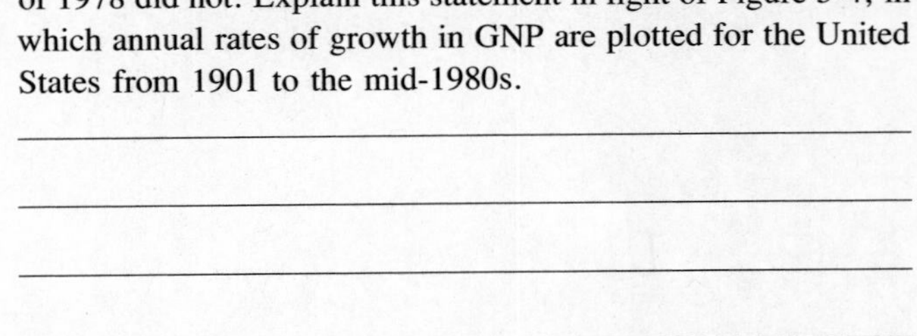

The variation in the rate of growth has declined markedly since 1946—the year in which Congress declared that government would take an active role in trying to steer the macroeconomy of the United States. Unemployment peaked at over 11 percent in early 1983.

Figure 5-5 plots unemployment against inflation for two periods of recent experience: 1960–1969 and 1976–1979. One issue of some current debate among macroeconomists is whether or not these and other points display enough evidence to support the existence of what is known as a *Phillips curve*. If they do not, then the proposed tradeoff between inflation and unemployment is cast under a shadow of doubt. If they do, then certain issues of policy and the contradictory nature of high employment and price stability are clarified. The next question will explore this doubt by suggesting the possibility of two tradeoff curves among the points of Figure 5-5.

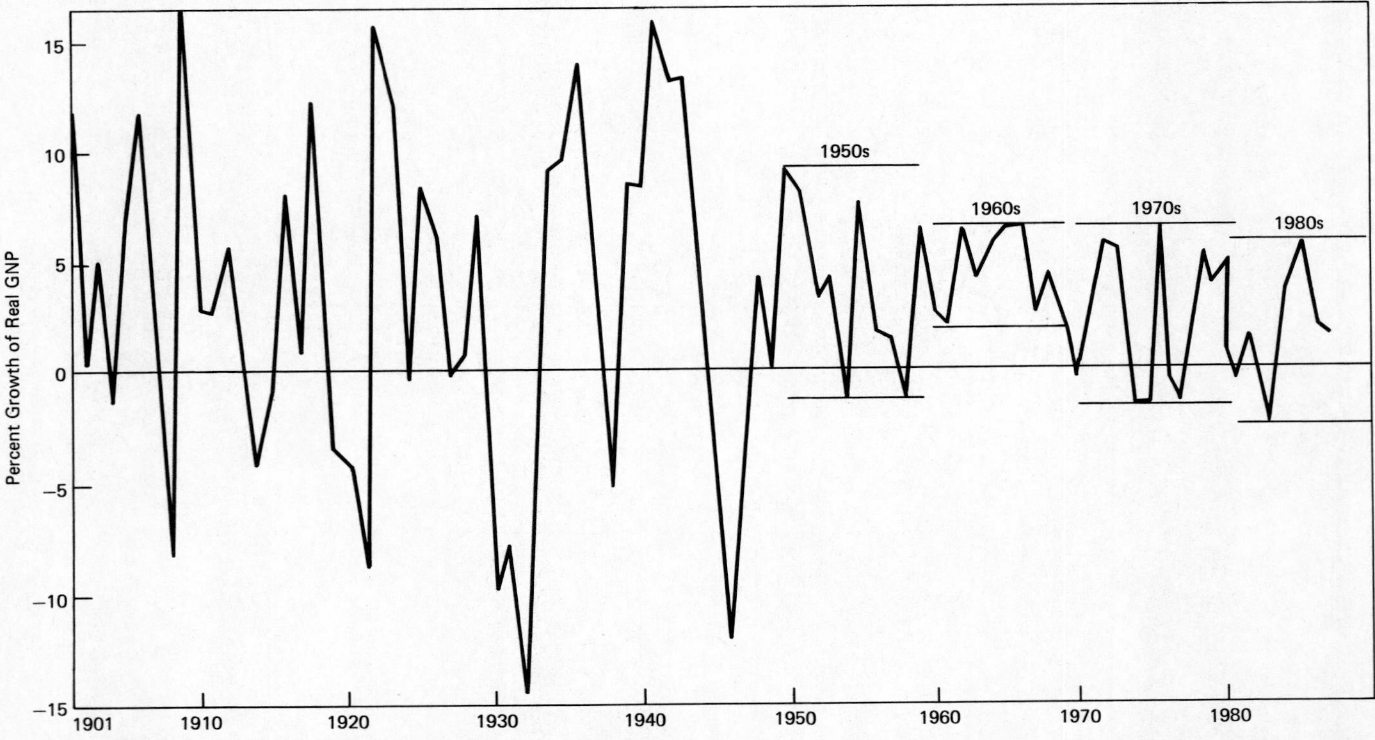

Figure 5-4 (*Source*: M.N. Baily: "Stabilization Policy and Private Economic Behavior," *Brookings Papers on Economic Activity*, vol. 1, 1978. Updated by author.)

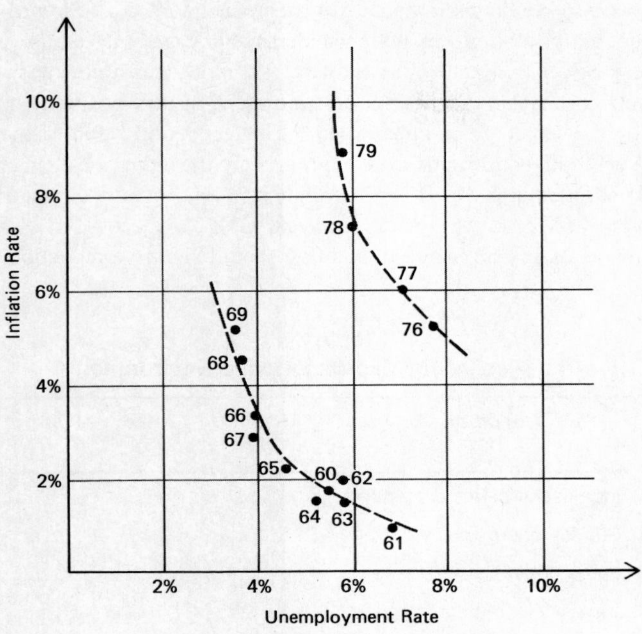

Figure 5-5

7. Draw a *smooth* (not necessarily straight) line running through the points labeled 1960 through 1969. Your line indicates that each 1-percentage-point increase in the unemployment rate above 4 percent seems to be associated with (*a reduction / an increase*) in the rate of inflation of (*5 / 0.5 / 0*) percentage points. By way of contrast, each 1-percentage-point reduction in the unemployment rate below 4 percent seems to be associated with (*a reduction / an increase*) in the rate of inflation of (*5 / 0.5 / 0*) percentage points. The "terms of tradeoff" between unemployment and inflation seem to have depended upon whether or not the rate of unemployment was higher or lower than 4 percent.

Now draw a second smooth line through the points labeled 1976 through 1979. Inflation rates that were associated with unemployment rates in the neighborhood of 3.5 percent in the 1960s were, in the late 1970s, associated with unemployment rates in the neighborhood of (*3.5 / 8 / 10*) percent. The tradeoff between unemployment and inflation (*had / had not*) worsened. Moreover, this curve (*is steeper / has roughly the same slope / is flatter*) for unemployment rates in excess of 4 percent than the curve for the 1960s. Increases in unemployment through the higher ranges had, apparently, (*become more / remained equally / become less*) effective in slowing inflation. Then again, they were starting from higher levels. Much of the discussion of macroeconomic policy contained in subsequent chapters will focus on the meaning of these preliminary insights.

---

a reduction; 0.5; an increase; 5; 8; had; is steeper; become more

8. Which of the following are policy variables (P), and which are external variables (EX) that may shock the economy from beyond its confines? Identify each by recording the appropriate abbreviation in the spaces provided.

a. money supply . . . . (________)

b. wars . . . . (________)

c. canceling a grain sale to the Soviet Union . . . (________)

d. government spending . . . . (________)

e. sunspots . . . . (________)

f. population growth . . . . (________)

g. import tariffs . . . . (________)

h. tax deductions . . . . (________)

i. changes in the weather . . . . (________)

j. public employment programs . . . . (________)

---

a. P **b.** EX **c.** P **d.** P **e.** none of the choices (sunspots do not affect economies.) **f.** EX **g.** P **h.** P **i.** EX **j.** P

9. Economists make a careful distinction between the long run and the short run. In the long run, the performance of the economy is determined *primarily* by the sources of growth in (*nominal / real / potential*) GNP. In the short run, the economy is determined *primarily* by (*imports / spending / external variables*). Identify each of the following variable as determinants primarily of either the short run (SR) of the long run (LR) by recording the appropriate abbreviation in the spaces provided.

a. labor growth . . . . (________)

b. oil prices . . . . (________)

c. availability of resources . . . . (________)

d. fiscal policy . . . . (________)

e. rate of growth of technology . . . . (________)

f. monetary policy . . . . (________)

Short-run performance is measured in terms of (*actual GNP / unemployment / inflation*).

---

potential; spending (though external shocks do play some role) **a.** LR **b.** SR **c.** LR **d.** SR **e.** LR **f.** SR; all three (each of the variables recorded in the numbered list has impacts in both the long and the short runs; the answers indicate the arena of the larger effect.)

Aggregate supply and demand curves might appear, to the casual reader, to suggest a loose application of the tools of Chapter 4 to the workings of the macroeconomy. They have the familiar axes of price and quantity, to be sure, but the careful reader will have noted that these terms take on new meaning in a macro setting. The quantity measured is not the quantity of some particular good; it is, instead, the total quantity of goods and services produced across the economy. It is, in short, GNP. The price is not the unit cost of purchasing some particular good; it is, instead, a price index reflecting the overall level of prices across the economy. It is, in short, something like the CPI.

These changes in the interpretations of the axes mean that the curves, while they have familiar shapes, assume those shapes for different reasons. The aggregate demand (*AD*) curve is, on the one hand, downward-sloping not because of tastes and budget constraints but because of an asymmetry in the effect of lower prices on goods and assets. As prices fall, financial assets become more valuable, people feel wealthier, and they therefore want to buy more stuff—they demand more.

The aggregate supply (*AS*) curve, on the other hand, is upward-sloping in the short run only because higher prices for final products make increasing output a profitable enterprise (at least until input prices catch up). When input prices eventually climb in the long run to keep up with output prices, however, that enterprise loses its appeal, output is contracted, and the curve becomes vertical at the level of potential output. The following two questions will explore the application of *AS* and *AD* to questions of policy and implication.

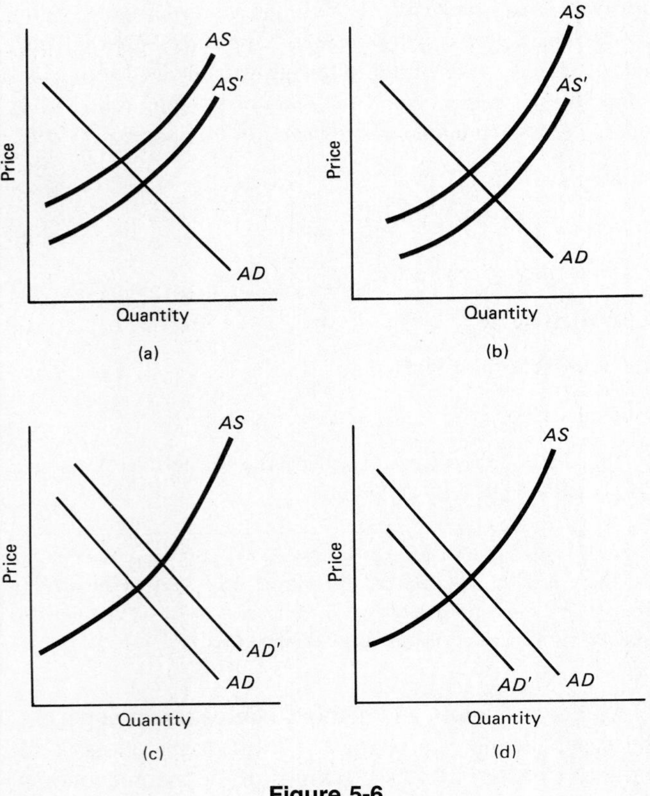

Figure 5-6

10. Figure 5-6 uses aggregate supply and demand to illustrate four possible reactions, in the short run, to changes in the macroeconomic environment. In each panel, *AD* and *AS* represent initial positions of aggregate demand and aggregate supply, respectively. In panels (**a**) and (**b**), *AS'* represents a new position; in panels (**c**) and (**d**), *AD'* represents a new position. In Table 5-1, record in column (2) the letter identification of the panel in Figure 5-6 that most appropriately illustrates the change noted in column (1). Note in columns (3) and (4) the direction of the effect on the price level and GNP, respectively; (+) should signify an increase, and (−) should signify a reduction.

Table 5-1
Changes in the Macroeconomic Environment

Condition (1)	Panel (2)	Price (3)	Output (4)
A. Increase in defense spending	______	______	______
B. Sudden energy crisis	______	______	______
C. Large cut in personal taxes	______	______	______
D. Increase in interest rates	______	______	______
E. Large reduction in government taxation of inputs	______	______	______

For the changes indicated in rows A, C, and D, passing to the long run would cause (*the price effect / the output effect / neither effect*) just noted for the short run to be exaggerated.

Reading across the rows of the table: A: c, +, +; B: b, +, −; C: c, +, +; D: d, −, −,; E: a, −, +; the price effect (because the long-run supply curve is vertical)

11. Suppose that Figure 5-7 illustrates the short-run effect of a sudden energy shock. *AD* would represent the preshock aggregate demand curve, (AS_1 / AS_2) would represent the preshock aggregate supply curve, and (AS_1 / AS_2) would represent the

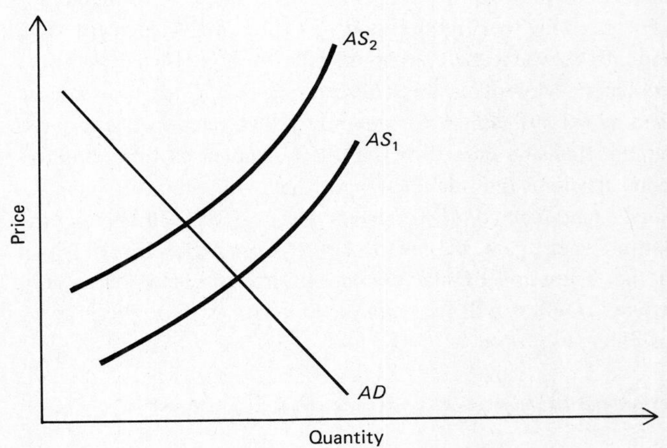

Figure 5-7

postshock aggregate supply curve. (*An increase / A decrease / No change*) in aggregate demand would be required in the short run to accommodate the shock and keep output at its preshock level. If this accommodation were kept in place in the long run, however, the appropriate shift in the aggregate supply curve would be to (*leave a vertical supply curve unchanged / shift a short-run supply curve back down*), and the accommodation just prescribed would produce the (*increase / reduction*) in prices that it was intended to avoid.

AS_1; AS_2; An increase; leave a vertical supply curve unchanged; increase

QUIZ: Multiple Choice

1. The study of macroeconomics includes, among other topics, which of the following?
(1) The sources of inflation, unemployment, and growth.
(2) The microeconomic foundations of aggregate behavior.
(3) Reasons why some economies succeed and some fail.
(4) Policies that can be enacted to improve the likelihood of success in achieving macroeconomic objectives.
(5) All of the above.

2. The practice of directing policy to support the macroeconomic health of the United States was initiated formally in:
(1) the Humphrey-Hawkins Act of 1978.
(2) the Tax Reform Act of 1986.
(3) the Full Employment and Balanced Growth Act of 1946.
(4) the Balanced Budget Act of 1985.
(5) none of the above.

3. The objective of stable prices can, in the view of at least some of the world's economists, be tackled by adjustments in:
(1) fiscal policy.
(2) monetary policy.
(3) incomes policies.
(4) all of the above.
(5) none of the above.

4. Policies directed at stimulating exports can influence:
(1) the employment picture.
(2) price stability.
(3) growth of actual GNP relative to potential GNP.
(4) the foreign-trade balance.
(5) all of the above.

5. Which of the following pairs of objectives seem to be mutually contradictory?
(1) Low inflation and low unemployment.
(2) Low unemployment and high rates of growth in actual GNP.
(3) High rates of growth in actual GNP and balance in the foreign-trade balance.
(4) Price stability and balance in the foreign-trade balance.
(5) Price stability and rapid growth in potential GNP.

6. The aggregate supply curve is positively sloped in the short run because of:
(1) increasing costs of production.
(2) decreasing returns to scale.
(3) uneven short-run distributions of high output prices and high input prices.
(4) the potential for high unemployment.
(5) none of the above.

7. The aggregate supply curve is vertical in the long run because:
(1) wealth effects in the quantity demanded cancel out.
(2) it is determined by potential output.
(3) of decreasing returns to scale in the extreme.
(4) of policy adjustments that constrain total output below a certain level.
(5) of the Phillips-curve tradeoff.

8. Unemployment, inflation, and the rate of growth of actual GNP are all examples of
(1) policy variables.
(2) external variables.
(3) international variables.
(4) variables determined by the economy.
(5) none of the above.

9. Which of the following is a determinant of potential output in the long run?
(1) Taxes.
(2) Money.
(3) Technology.
(4) Tax penalties for excessive wage demands.
(5) Defense spending.

10. The short-run effect of increased defense spending that is not accommodated by increased taxation could be:
(1) higher prices and higher GNP.
(2) higher prices and lower GNP.
(3) lower prices and lower GNP.
(4) lower prices and higher GNP.
(5) lower prices and the same GNP.

11. Accommodation of the OPEC oil shock would have:
(1) preserved prices and GNP.
(2) preserved output with higher prices.
(3) increased output with lower prices.
(4) lowered domestic oil prices.
(5) none of the above.

12. The effect of the orchestrated increase in interest rates in the United States in the early 1980s can be illustrated in an *AS-AD* graph by:
(1) a shift upward of the *AS* curve.
(2) a shift downward in the *AS* curve.
(3) a shift upward in the *AD* curve.

(4) a shift downward in the *AD* curve.
(5) no shift in either the *AD* or the *AS* curve.

SUGGESTED ANSWERS TO QUESTIONS IN THE TEXT: Chapter 5

1. Consult the summary to section A, item 2, if you need the list. When you consider why each is important, write one paragraph for each for the nation as a whole [e.g., high growth means larger incomes, larger consumption, larger saving (perhaps), more jobs, etc., for the entire economy]. Consider some of the negative ramifications, as well (e.g., high growth means greater resource depletion, etc.). Finally, write a short paragraph about why the macro objective might be important to you. These are macro objectives, to be sure, but they are objectives because they help people. How about you?

2. Note that relative prices reflect relative scarcity, and a market economy rations on the basis of those prices. The economy can have low inflation and still allow relative prices to move around to reflect that scarcity (and thus efficiently allocate resources) if some move down while others move up. To fix all prices is to disallow this sort of efficient rationing.

3. $[(315 - 300)/300] \times 100\% = (15/300) \times 100\% = 5\%$.

4. **a.** Higher oil prices would increase the cost of doing business, so they would cause the short-run *AS* curve to shift up.
b. Reduced defense spending (with no accompanying reduction in taxes and/or increase in other government spending) would reduce aggregate demand at any price level, so it would cause the *AD* curve to shift to the left.
c. A blight would contract output at any price level, so it would cause the *AS* curve to shift to the left.
d. Lower interest rates would increase investment and consumption (a simple reason why: making it cheaper to borrow makes borrowing more likely) at any price level, so it would cause the *AD* curve to shift to the right.

5. **a.** *AS* up means prices climb and output falls along *AD*.
b. *AD* left means prices and output fall along short-run *AS*.
c. *AS* left is the same as up.
d. *AD* right means prices and output climb along short-run *AS*.

6. Shifting *AD* up and to the right moves prices and output up along the short-run *AS* curve; employment climbs. In the long run, though, *AS* is determined by potential GNP; the *AS* curve is vertical over potential GNP. As a result, an increase in *AD* can increase prices in the long run only if the economy starts at potential GNP.

7. *AD* slopes down because lower prices make people wealthier (assets worth more), so they spend more. Short-run *AS* slopes up because higher prices inspire increased production until the cost of inputs has time to adjust; when that adjustment is complete, though, output will have fallen back to the original level. Were everything auctioned all the time, then all prices—even input prices—would be immediately responsive, and the intermediate expansion would not be possible. Even the short-run *AS* curve would be vertical in that case.

8. **a.** Cut government spending an equal amount; output and price would be maintained.
b. Cut government spending to restrict *AD* so that *AD* intersects the now-higher *AS* at the same price level; output would fall.
c. Cut government spending to restrict *AD* so that *AD* intersects the now-leftward vertical *AS* at the same price level; output would fall.
d. Increase spending elsewhere or cut taxes to increase consumption to maintain *AD*; output and price would be maintained.
e. A fall in net exports means *AD* is down. Do something to increase it by (e.g.) intervening in the exchange markets to increase the value of the dollar or increase domestic expenditures. Output and price would be maintained.

9. Tax cut increases *AD* by increasing consumption. Higher government spending increases *AD* directly. Combined, the two might increase output and prices in the short run, and just prices in the long run. That did not happen because the economy was operating so far below potential in 1982. The resulting federal deficits increased interest rates, and that reduced *AD* some by stifling investment.

CHAPTER 6
MEASUREMENT OF NATIONAL OUTPUT AND INCOME

This chapter is important. It must be approached carefully and patiently. You will, however, discover that there is really only one basic idea being presented here. It is surrounded by complication, to be sure, but the point of this chapter is singular: the accounting procedure with which a nation measures its total output in any one year simply adds up the market value of all the goods and services that it produces. Every nation uses its limited stock of labor, machines, and materials to produce commodities and services. The money value of the resulting mix of total output valued at the market price for which each component is sold (or would have been sold) constitutes the national product for the period—the year in question. You should ignore the difficulties that are certainly involved in a computational exercise of this magnitude. Your job is not to do the counting. Your job, instead, is to understand the rules that govern the counting. Having completed your work in this chapter, you will have achieved the objectives listed below. Without this achievement, you will find it almost impossible to understand what economists mean when they talk about growth, unemployment, and inflation.

LEARNING OBJECTIVES

1. Describe briefly what each of the following concepts is designed to measure: (*a*) gross national product (GNP), (*b*) net national product (NNP), (*c*) depreciation, and (*d*) disposable income (*DI*).

2. Explain the difference between nominal GNP and real GNP, paying close attention to the role of the GNP deflator.

3. Define the flow-of-product approach and the earnings-cost approach to computing GNP. Explain the residual cost interpretation of profit and its role in equating the two.

4. Explain how focusing on either final product in the product approach or value added in the earnings approach helps statisticians avoid double counting in the computation of GNP.

5. Divide GNP into its major component parts in the flow-of-product approach: consumption (*C*), gross private domestic investment (*I*), government purchases of goods and services (*G*), and net exports (*X*). That is, explain why GNP $= C + I + G + X$, or GNP $= C + I^n + G$, where $I^n = I + X$, representing total national investment.

6. Relate disposable income (*DI*) to personal income (*PI*) and personal taxes (*PT*) according to $DI = PI - PT$.

7. Argue why, in general, total national investment must equal the sum of net private saving (*NPS*), gross business saving including depreciation (*NBS*) and net government saving (*NGS*).

8. Define net economic welfare, and explain why it is different from net national product.

There are two fundamental measures of national income. **Gross national product** (GNP) is the sum of the total output of final goods and services produced by any economy in a given year. Each good and service is valued at its market price in this summation, and no allowance is made for depreciation of the underlying capital stock. **Net national product** (NNP) for the same year is GNP minus a suitable allowance for depreciation.

1. Suppose, for example, that the national output consists of only two commodities: X, a consumer good, and Y, a capital good (some form of machine or tool needed in production). In 1989, just 500 units of X were produced and sold to consumers at a price of \$2 each. Twenty units of Y were produced and sold to business firms, at a price of \$10 each. Then the national product for 1989 would be (*500 / 800 / 1000 / 1200 / 1500 / 2000*).

1200

2. The figure computed in question 1 was the *gross* national product. To produce this total output, however, the nation's existing stock of capital goods must have been, to some extent, used up or worn out; that is to say, the capital stock must have depreciated. Suppose that the nation began the year with a stock of 100 Y machines (assuming, for simplicity, that there is just one kind of capital good involved). By the year's end, a few of these machines, the oldest, will have become completely worn out, and all the others will have moved just a little closer to the scrap heap.

Suppose, now, that the best possible estimate of this 1989 depreciation (still using the question 1 examples) is $50. There is no cash expenditure in a depreciation figure; it is just an estimate of the extent of "wearing out" during the year. With the price of a new Y machine being $10, it is *as though* five Y machines, brand new at the year's beginning, had been completely worn out by the year's end in the production of 1989's national product.

The 1989 gross national product figure of $1200 included the value of the 20 new Y machines produced. But to make these machines, and to make also the 500 units of consumer good X, the equivalent of five new Y machines was totally used up. So the nation was not "better off" at the year's end by 20 machines. Its capital stock had increased by only (*5 / 10 / 15*) machines.

With "gross" meaning "no allowance for depreciation," and "net" meaning "after allowance for depreciation," then this nation's gross national product for 1980 was $1200, and its *net national product* was $(*1000 / 1050 / 1100 / 1150 / 1200*).

(In the statistics for national product and national income, the *capital consumption allowance* may be used instead of the word "deprecation.")

15;1150

3. There are certain distinctions that are made among the goods that comprise either GNP or NNP. The most basic of these distinctions is the division between (*a*) goods that were produced to be consumed during the year in questions and (*b*) goods that were produced during the year not to be consumed but to be additions to the existing stock of capital. This is precisely the difference noted in question 1, with X representing a consumption good and Y representing an investment good.

The consumption-goods total is the same figure in both GNP and NNP. The investment-goods figure in GNP is gross investment: total production of new capital goods without depreciation allowance. The investment figure in NNP is net investment: value of new capital goods produced after a deduction for depreciation. In the example above, the GNP of $1200 would divide between consumption of $(*200 / 800 / 1000 / 1150 / 1200*) and gross investment of $(*0 / 100 / 150 / 200 / 250 / 300*). The NNP of $1150 would divide between consumption of $(*200 / 800 / 1000 / 1500 / 1200*) and net investment of $(*0 / 100 / 150 / 200 / 250 / 300*).

1000; 200; 1000; 150

Like all developed nations, the United States relies overwhelmingly on the price-and-market mechanism. The commodities and services produced normally reach consumers by being sold for a market price. Indeed, that is what makes possible single dollar-value totals for GNP and NNP. In less developed countries, though, many goods do not pass through a market pricing mechanism. The value of these goods must be estimated, therefore, and the money figures for GNP and NNP in these countries are necessarily subject to more uncertainty; they are simply made less precise by the absence of markets. Even in developed economies, precise measurement is impossible. Why? Because even in developed countries like the United States there are many goods and services that do not pass through a pricing mechanism.

Two notable examples of this type of good or service come to mind easily:

1. "Social" or "public" goods purchased or produced by an agency of the government and provided to the population are frequently not sold in the marketplace. People pay for them, instead, by paying their taxes, and it is hard to measure their value. How much is a submarine worth? In terms of its contribution to national defense, who knows? We know only how much it costs to build and operate.
2. A housewife supplies her family members with goods and services of great value; but ordinarily, even on her more difficult days, she does not think of charging a market price for each service that she furnishes.

To master the basics of national-income accounting, though, it is best to set these and other exceptions aside and to concentrate instead on the easy cases—the cases in which each and every good and service supplied is given a money price in a market and supplied through that market according to that price.

The price of any item is the exact amount of money available for distribution among all the people who helped to produce and sell it. Because incomes are earned by making some contribution to production, the total value of what is produced ought to equal the total value of the incomes earned. There should, therefore, be two ways of computing national product. The first, already defined, is the sum of the value of all final goods and services produced in a year; this is the **product-flow** approach. The second, now suggested to be equivalent, is the sum of the earnings of all the factors involved in production and sales, this is the **earnings-cost** approach.

Figure 6-1 demonstrates this equivalence. The product flow approach is illustrated in columns 1 and 2 as the sum of government purchases (*G*), consumption expenditures (*C*), net exports (*X*), and investment (*I*). The difference between NNP and GNP is clearly shown as depreciation. Total national investment (investment plus net exports) appears at the top of both—gross in column 1 and net of depreciation in column 2. Notice that there are essentially five fundamental categories in the earnings approach represented in column 3:

1. Wages and salaries
2. Interest earned (by people lending money to firms)
3. Rentals and other property income (paid to people who supply property)
4. Corporate and unincorporated profits
5. Indirect business taxes (levied on businesses)

The profits noted in number 4 above are, by definition, the difference between the value of ouputs and the costs of inputs. They are, in other words, the residual values that guarantee that the earnings-cost approach generates the same result as the product-flow approach.

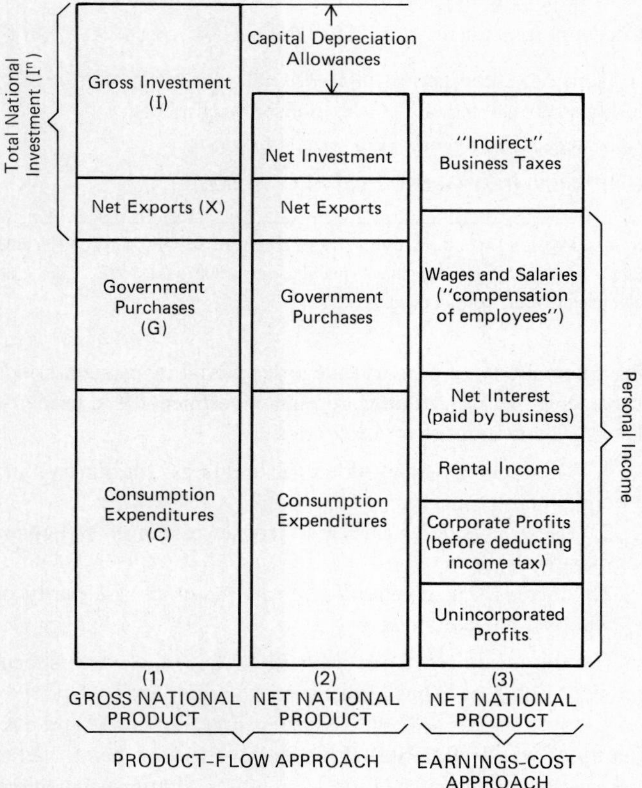

Figure 6-1

4. a. A firm's income statement begins with the value of its sales for a given period—say, for the year 1990 sales amount to $800. All costs incurred in making and selling these goods are then listed: depreciation, wages, interest paid, rents paid. Suppose depreciation was $25, and the total of the other three items $650. What's left after deducting all such costs from the sales total would be profit—in this instance, $(*0 / 25 / 50 / 75 / 100 / 125 / 150*).

The initial sales figure of $800 would be this firm's contribution to the product-flow computation of GNP. Deduct depreciation, and its NNP contribution would be $(*700 / 725 / 750 / 775*). Its earnings-cost figure would meanwhile equal the total of wages, interest paid, and profit remaining: $(*700 / 725 / 750 / 775*). Hence (*less than / equal to / greater than*) the product-flow figure.

b. Notice that profit is the residual item which makes things come out even. Had our firm paid out wages, interest, and rents totaling $775, its profit (allowing for depreciation) would have been $(*0 / 25 / 50 / 70 / 100*). The earnings figure would (*still / no longer*) be $775, so it would (*still / no longer*) match the product-flow estimate.

---

a. 125; 755; 775; equal to **b.** 0; still; still

5. a. All goods and services purchased for the public through the agency of government (federal, state, or local) count in GNP and NNP—assuming that they were produced within the year in question. Many such goods will have gone through the market system in that they were produced by a private firm and sold to a government. Except for a few items like (*national defense / post office services*)—they are not sold to the public for a price per unit. They are "social goods"; the public (*gets them entirely free / pays for them via taxation*).

b. All these goods and services enter the GNP and NNP totals valued at the price the government pays for them. A judge's legal services are valued at the salary paid that judge; the production of a new typewriter is valued at the price the government paid the typewriter-manufacturing firm.

Incomes earned via production of such government-purchased goods and services are (*counted / not counted*) in the earning's approach; as the GNP and NNP columns grow because government purchases expand, the earnings column of Figure 6-1 (*grows / does not grow*).

You can well argue that GNP and NNP do not need this third component, since every cent of "government purchases" should count either as consumption (e.g., services furnished by a police officer in protecting the public) or as investment (e.g., construction and purchase of some long-lived item like a new highway). The "government purchases" category is kept separate because government statistics are not kept in a way that makes a meaningful division between consumption and investment within this category possible.

c. For inclusion in GNP and NNP, there must be a good or a service currently produced. Hence, one important category of federal expenditure (and to a lesser degree, of state and local expenditure) is not included: payments under the social security program and other "transfer payments" through which the government takes money from some people and gives it to others. The recipient of such a transfer payment, by definition (*must give something / does not give anything*) concurrently in return.

d. Suppose that, in addition to the $1200 in private purchases of question 1, we had to recognize government expenditure on goods and services totaling $400 and health and welfare expenditures (payments made to social security beneficiaries) of $100. If depreciation were still $50, then GNP would now be $(*1200 / 1250 / 1550 / 1600 / 1700*), and NNP would be $(*1200 / 1250 / 1550 / 1600 / 1650*). The required increase (from the original GNP of $1200) would be (*GNP only / GNP and NNP, not national income / all of GNP, NNP, and national income*), and the amount of this increase would be $(*100 / 400 / 500*).

---

a. post office services; pays for them via taxation **b.** counted; grows as well **c.** does not give anything **d.** 1600 (only government spending, not transfer, added); 1550; all of GNP, NNP, and national income; 400

National income, technically the result of subtracting indirect taxes from the earnings approach computation of NNP (again, see Figure 6-1), is a useful concept. For example, the figures within it will give you at least a rough comparison between the total of incomes earned through personal effort and the total of those obtained through ownership of property. For many purposes, though, national income is less interesting than **disposable income**, i.e., income over which individuals have discretionary power to spend or save. **Personal income**, meanwhile, is the sum of disposable income and personal taxes paid to the government at any level.

6. One critical statistical problem deserves some attention: how is the dividing line between consumption and investment drawn? What goes into the "consumption expenditures" category of GNP and NNP, and what into "gross (or net) investment"?

Ideally, the consumption figure should measure the goods and services not only produced during that year but also actually consumed during the year (so that they were gone by the year's end), but there is no possible way of measuring this "true consumption." The statisticians must content themselves with recording what consumers bought. Items consumed immediately or almost immediately after purchase (bread, for example) pose no problem. For items like clothing, which last, say, 2 or 3 years, the interpretation of consumer purchases as "true consumption" still works fairly well, assuming that what is bought is pretty much a replacement for what is worn out through use. Items like housing, which last longer, demand different treatment. A house is far and away the longest-lived item a consumer ordinarily buys; it is typically the biggest purchase a person ever makes. It would be ridiculous to say that a house built in 1990 is fully "consumed" by the end of 1990. The statisticians handle this by saying that building a house is producing an investment good, not a consumer good. It is a kind of machine for providing consumer services. What *should* be counted as consumption in 1990 GNP and NNP is the service which the house supplies—and indeed, it the house is rented, there is a market price measure of the value of this service.[1]

With every house treated as a service-producing machine, the services supplied by that house are thus counted as consumption with GNP and NNP, valued at the market price of such services (rental value) for each year of its life that it is occupied. In the year it was built, the full construction value of the house is counted, but as an investment item, not as consumption.[2]

a. Suppose a house is built in the first half of 1990 and sold for $90,000. It is rented for the remainder of the year, total rental for the 6 months being $6000. Depreciation for this same period is estimated at $600. In the 1990 statistics, the proper entries for this house would be:

Gross investment, $(*0 / 600 / 6000 / 89,400 / 90,000*)

Net investment, $(*0 / 600 / 6000 / 89,400 / 90,000*)

Consumption expenditures, $(*0 / 600 / 6000 / 89,400 / 90,000*)

b. Hence the total entries in 1990 GNP and NNP, with respect to construction and use of this house, would be:

GNP: $(*89,400 / 90,000 / 95,400 / 96,000*)

NNP: $(*89,400 / 90,000 / 95,400 / 96,000*)

---

a. 90,000 (the price of the house); 89,400; 6000 **b.** 96.000; 95,400 (The GNP figure must be "gross investment" plus "consumption"; the NNP figure, "net investment" plus "consumption.")

7. There are three primary categories within investment goods considered here. A fourth, foreign investment, is considered later.[3] The three primary categories are:

1. New business and industrial buildings, machinery, and equipment produced
2. New housing constructed (private residences and apartment houses)
3. Increases in inventories of raw materials and partly or wholly finished goods

Category 1 is what we ordinarily think of as "investment goods." Category 2 has been covered in question 6.

If any firm has a bigger physical inventory of its product (partly or wholly finished) at the end of the year than it had at the year's beginning, then the value of its additional inventory must count as part of investment for the year.

Suppose a shirt manufacturer had a $3000 inventory of shirts on hand at the start of 1989 and a $4000 inventory at its close. (No problem of style or price change is involved; the firm just has more shirts on hand, as yet unsold, than it had a year ago.)

[1] If the house is owner-occupied, the rental value of its services must be estimated. (This is another exception to the general rule that goods and services go through the market mechanism.) Such an estimate of the total value of housing services for owner-occupied houses goes into each year's "consumption expenditures" for GNP and NNP.

[2] Is it double counting to include in the figures both the original purchase value of the new house and the value of the services that it supplies? Yes and no. The same is true of any other investment—a machine or a factory building. (The rent of a factory building works its way into the market price of the item produced therein. The use of a machine inside the factory does the same thing.) The key factor here is depreciation. Gross national product, which makes no allowance for depreciation, does double-count. However, in net national product, the original value of the house is gradually subtracted from the national product, year by year, using depreciation, until (at the end of its life) the entire original purchase value of the house has been deducted. All that remains is the total value of the services which that house supplied.

[3] The Commerce Department treats foreign investment as a separate (and fourth) block within GNP and NNP, calling it "net exports of goods and services," or "net foreign investment."

The fact that its inventory is up by $1000 means that this firm must have (*sold more than it manufactured / manufactured more than it sold*). (In the extreme case, you could think of the firm as, in 1989, making shirts worth $1000 and not selling one.)

The essence of investment in all its various forms is that it is production for future benefit. A newly finished machine tool yields no direct consumer satisfaction whatsoever. It is built to yield future benefit; it is expected to contribute toward consumer-goods production in the future, throughout its coming 5-year or 10-year life. A new house counts within investment for the same reason.

Our shirt firm's additional inventory must receive the same treatment. The firm made $1000 worth of shirts in 1989 which it has not yet sold. The shirts it did sell count as part of consumption in the regular way. The shirts it made but didn't sell must also go into GNP and NNP (because they were made in 1989), but (because they weren't sold) they do not go into consumption. They are included in investment because they will be consumed in the future, presumably *next* year.

This inventory rule must work both ways. Had this firm's beginning inventory been $4000 and its closing inventory $3000, then we would include a figure of (*minus / plus*) $(*1000 / 3000 / 4000*) within (*consumption / investment*).

---

manufactured more than it sold; minus; 1000; investment

8. a. Could a country's net investment for any given period ever turn out to be a negative figure? If you can think of any reason why it could, don't write down the reason; just check the "Yes" box below. If you cannot think of any reason, check the "No" box . . . . Yes( ) No( )

b. Could a country's gross investment ever turn out to be a negative figure? . . . . Yes( ) No( )

Answers are given in question 10's answers. Do 9 and 10 before checking your response to this one.

9. You are given the following data for a certain country:

	Year 1	Year 2
New buildings produced	5	5
New equipment produced	10	10
Consumer goods produced	110	90
Consumer goods consumed	90	110
Estimated depreciation on existing buildings during year	10	10
Estimated depreciation on existing equipment during year	10	10
Inventories of consumer goods at beginning of year	30	50
Inventories of consumer goods at close of year . .	50	30

These figures are complete; there is no government sector of GNP or NNP.

a. The difference, in year 1, between 110 consumer goods produced and 90 consumer goods consumed is explained by (*an increase / a decrease*) in inventories on hand at the (*beginning / end*) of the year.

The difference, in year 2, between 90 consumer goods produced and 110 consumer goods consumed is explained by (*an increase / a decrease*) in inventories on hand at the (*beginning / end*) of the year.

b. Compute the following for the 2 years:

	Year 1	Year 2
Gross national product	(1) ______	(7) ______
Breakup of GNP into:		
Consumption	(2) ______	(8) ______
Gross investment	(3) ______	(9) ______
Net national product	(4) ______	(10) ______
Breakup of NNP into:		
Consumption	(5) ______	(11) ______
Net investment	(6) ______	(12) ______

---

a. an increase; end; a decrease; end **b.** (1) consumption + buildings + equipment + change in inventories = 90 + 5 + 10 + (50 − 30) = 125 (2) 90 (3) 35 (4) GNP − building depreciation − machinery depreciation = 125 − 10 − 10 = 105 (5) 90 (6) 15 (7) 105 (8) 110 (9) −5 (10) 85 (11) 110 (12) −25

10. To summarize question 9: In the national product statistics, a negative net investment figure (*could / could not*) appear if total depreciation exceeded the total value of new buildings and equipment produced. A negative net investment figure (*could / could not*) appear if the value of inventory reduction exceeded the total value of new buildings and equipment produced.

A negative gross investment figure (*could / could not*) appear if total depreciation exceeded the total value of new buildings and equipment produced. A negative gross investment figure (*could / could not*) appear if (leaving depreciation aside) the value of inventory reduction during the year exceeded the total value of new buildings and equipment.

---

could; could; could not [Hence the answer to both parts of questions 8 is Yes (if you were fooled by the gross investment part, console yourself with the fact that you have plenty of good company.)]; could

11. A common use of national product figures is to compare total real output between 2 years. If prices have changed in the interim, however, the comparison is meaningless unless a proper price adjustment is made.

a. Consider this problem: NNP (in billions) was $500 in 1985 and $650 in 1990. The price index was 100 in 1985 and 125 in 1990—i.e., prices had risen by 25 percent since 1985. Was 1990's real output higher than 1985's and if so, by how much?

For the moment, set aside completely the question just posed. We'll start with an easier problem and then use it to answer the actual problem. Suppose, instead, that 1990's real output was exactly the same as that of 1985 ($500). That 1990 real output would, in 1985 prices of course, have to be $500. But again, the 1985 and 1990 price indexes were 100 and 125, respectively, showing that prices rose by 25 percent over that period. Allowing for this inflation, the 1990 NNP, expressed in 1990 prices, would have to be

$$\$500 \times \frac{125}{100}$$

That would make the nominal 1990 NNP $(*500 / 550 / 575 / 625*) in 1990 prices.

If we wanted to *deflate* this 1990 NNP to get it back to 1985 prices (to make it comparable with nominal 1980 NNP), we would reverse the process. That is, we would start with the $625 NNP and multiply it by a deflating factor of $^{100}/_{125}$. The result would be $500.

Still assuming, for convenience, a 25 percent price increase, we can apply this deflating factor of $^{100}/_{125}$ to bring any 1990 NNP down to a 1985 price level. Suppose, for example, that real output in 1990 was twice the 1985 NNP of $500. That 1990 real NNP would accordingly have to be twice $500, or $1000—measured in 1985 prices. Since prices were up by 25 percent, though, nominal 1990 NNP would be $1250.

To get finally to the problem posed at the start of this question (i.e., to get the nominal 1990 NNP of $650 expressed in terms of 1985 prices), we multiply by $^{100}/_{125}$. The resulting deflated figure is (*500 / 520 / 580 / 625*)—i.e., real output in 1990 was (*4 / 8 / 12 / 100*) percent (*higher / lower*) than in 1985.

Another way of making a proper comparison would be to inflate the 1985 NNP of $500 by 25 percent, thus making it comparable with 1990. That is, the real 1985 NNP expressed in 1990 prices would be $625 . Comparing this with the actual 1990 NNP of $650, we get (*a lower increase than / the same 4 percent increase as / a higher increase than*) before.

b. Sometimes this kind of problem is complicated by asking: What happened to per capita income (income per person, total income divided by total population)? Suppose, for example, that with the same pair of NNPs as before, total population fell by 5 percent between 1985 and 1990. What was the rise in per capita income?

Real NNPs, in 1985 prices, were $500 in 1985 and $520 in 1990. But the latter total was shared among a smaller population. Suppose the 1985 population was 100 people. If so, then given a 5 percent drop, it must have been 95 in 1990. If these were the two population figures, then real income per person was $5 in 1985 ($500 divided by 100), whereas in 1990 ($520 divided by 95) it was approximately $(*5.0 / 5.5 / 6.0 / 6.5*). Comparing $5 per person in 1985 with about $5.5 in 1990, you will find that real per capita income was about 10 percent higher in 1990 than it was in 1985. (To compute the percentage change in per capita income, it doesn't make any difference what pair of population figures you use, as long as they are in the proper ratio. Try it with 200 people and 190, or with 1000 and 950; you get exactly the same percentage increase.)

---

a. 625 [= 5 × 125]; 520; 4; higher; the same 4 percent increase as **b.** 5.5

12. One implication of the national-income accounting identity that GNP equals the sum of consumption, investment, government spending, and net exports should be emphasized: actual saving always equals actual investment. This does not, however, mean that actual saving always equals *intended* investment. This question will explore the implications of this distinction.

In question 9, there is no government and no foreign sector. In that question, therefore,

GNP = ________________ + ________________.

If the difference between GNP and consumption represents saving (that part of income which is not spent), then this equation can be rewritten as

________________ = investment.

This is the purported accounting identity. When government and foreign sectors are added, this identity requires that investment *plus net exports* (i.e., total national investment) equal the sum of *all* saving (net private saving plus gross business saving plus government saving). More on this later.

Continuing now with question 9, suppose that, in each year, business wanted to maintain inventories at the beginning of the year level throughout the year; that is, assume that intended inventories were 30 for the end of year 1 and 50 for the end of year 2. Another way of stating this assumption is to say that the intended level of investment in inventories in both years was zero. Suppose, additionally, that investment on building and machinery proceeded as intended in both years. Fill in the blanks of the table below with numbers drawn from question 9.

	Year 1	Year 2
Intended building investment	____	____
Intended equipment investment	____	____
Intended inventory investment	____	____
Total intended investment	____	____
Actual building investment	____	____
Actual equipment investment	____	____
Actual inventory investment	____	____
Actual saving (= **actual investment**)	____	____

From the table, it is clear that, in year 1, actual saving (*exceeded / equaled / fell short of*) intended investment by ________. Inventories were (*increasing / decreasing*) faster than intended, and the likely response of the firm owner would be to (*speed up / slow down / leave unchanged*) the level of his her production and employment. By the same token, actual saving (*exceeded / equaled / fell short of*) intended investment by ________ in year 2. Inventories were, in the second year, (*increasing / decreasing*) faster than intended, and the likely response of the owner would be to (*speed up / slow down / leave unchanged*) the level of his or her production and employment.

---

consumption; investment; saving; Table entries by column: Year 1: 5, 10, 0, 15, 5, 10, 20, 35; Year 2: 10, 0, 15, 5, 10, −20, −5; exceeded; 20; increasing; slow down; fell short of; 20; decreasing; speed up

13. A nation's GNP was $260 billion in 1980 and $325 billion in 1990. Both figures were computed as usual in terms of market prices for the year involved. The index prices rose from 100 in 1980 to 130 in 1990.

a. Did real output increase or decrease from 1980 through 1990?

b. In terms of 1990 prices, what would the 1980 GNP be?

c. In terms of 1980 prices, what would the 1990 GNP be?

---

decrease; $338 billion [= 260 × 130/100]; $250 billion [= 325 × 100/130]

14. A house is built and sold in the first 6 months of 1970 for a price of $50,000. It is rented for the next 20 years, beginning July 1, 1970. Annual rent is $3000 per year ($1500 for the last half of 1970, $1500 for the first half of 1990). The house lasts for exactly 20 years. Depreciation is charged at the rate of $2500 per year ($1250 for each of the 2 half-years involved, 1970 and 1990).

What figures enter the national product accounts with respect to the building and rental of this house? Answer by completing the columns below.

	1970	1971 or Any Later Year through 1989	1990	Total of All Years Combined
Gross investment	________	________	________	________
Net investment	________	________	________	________
Consumption	________	________	________	________

By column: 1970: $50,000, $48,750, $1500; 1971–1989: 0, −$2500, $3000; 1990: 0, −$1250, $1500; Total: $50,000, 0, $60,000 (Remember, there are 19 years between Jan. 1, 1971, and Dec. 31, 1989.)

15. a. In complex, interdependent societies such as ours, there has always been a steady demand for information on "how well the economy is doing." In major part, this demand asks: What is happening to total output? Is business improving, or not? In pre-GNP days, such questions had to be answered by piecing together data on total steel production, total freight-car loadings, and other bits of available information. The task of devising methods by means of which a reliable one-figure estimate of total production could be obtained was not easy. But once developed, the GNP measure was a vast improvement.

A single GNP figure is meaningless. (Does it enlighten you greatly to learn that GNP in the United States for 1987 is estimated at around $2,928 billion?) But things are different if you have two or more GNP figures for comparison. Year-to-year figures (properly adjusted for price changes) (*will / cannot*) indicate whether or not real output is increasing and, if increasing, at what rate. You (*can / cannot*) use GNP figures to compare (at least roughly) the sizes (economic sizes, not geographical) of the United States and the Soviet Union, and how those sizes are changing. You (*can / cannot*) use trends in GNP figures to assess the general employment outlook of an economy—how difficult or easy it will be for an individual of certain characteristics to find a job. You (*can / cannot*) even try to use recent movement in GNP to predict what will happen in the near future.

b. The gross national product idea was so useful that, after it had become part of everyday economic language, some people began to interpret it as conveying information it was never intended to carry. The rate of increase in GNP was taken as a measure of the improvement in human welfare, even of the increase in "happiness." This distortion set off, as might have been expected, a counterattitude which denounced even the computation of GNP as crass materialism at its worst. In point of fact, the gross national product should be regarded simply as a measure that is useful for specific purposes and is subject to particular limitations.

In response to this debate, James Tobin and William Nordhaus have produced a second, derivative measure. Its construction begins with the notion of GNP, but tries to adjust that notion to correct for the positive and negative influences of various parts of reality that are not captured in the GNP calculation. It tries, in that way, to be a more accurate indicator of genuine changes in the well-being of human beings. It does not purport to measure happiness, though; even economists agree that the measurement of happiness lies beyond the competence of economists, sociologists, philosophers, and New York City cabbies. Its name is ________________.

The GNP figure (simplifying it slightly) for any year is in principle an adding up of everything produced during that year, each item valued at the money price at which it sold. (Thus there is an underlying assumption that the "money worth" of any good is the market price that people do pay in order to buy it. If you dislike this assumption—and there are at least occasional instances that prompt one to wonder about it—remember that the world awaits your better, but workable, definition of worth.) The Tobin-Nordhaus NEW measure tries to take account of factors that do affect material welfare but are not caught within the GNP's market price net. One example would be (*atmospheric and other pollution / changes in market prices*). Another would be (*the appearance of new commodities / shorter working hours, hence more leisure time*).

Like GNP, the NEW measure is a single money figure. So it must place a money value (minus or plus) on each correction of GNP it deems necessary. In most instances, there is no market price measure of this adjustment. So its money size must be estimated. That makes the computation of NEW, in principle, much more difficult than the computation of GNP.

c. Ponder, for a moment, why NEW should exceed GNP during the Great Depression of the 1930s and fall so short of GNP during the past few decades.

---

a. will; can; can; can **b.** new economic welfare, atmospheric and other pollution; shorter working hours, hence more leisure time **c.** Recall that the cost of pollution is substracted from GNP and the value of leisure time is added to GNP in the NEW computation. The Great Depression provided many people with lots of leisure time—is that an appropriate addition? Recent experience has produced many pollution problems and shortened workweeks.

QUIZ: Multiple Choice

1. In GNP and NNP statistics, "investment" includes:
(1) any product produced through the agency of government.
(2) any purchase of a new common-stock issue.
(3) any increase in the amount of year-end inventories over their year-beginning amount.
(4) any commodity bought by a consumer but not fully consumed by the year-end.
(5) none of these items.

2. In GNP and NNP statistics, the value of housing services, where the houses are occupied by their owners, is:
(1) not counted, since property services are not considered "production."
(2) not counted, since such property services are included in the value of the house itself.
(3) not counted in GNP and NNP, using an arbitrary estimate of rental value.
(4) counted in both GNP and NNP, using an arbitrary estimate of rental value.
(5) counted in GNP, but not in NNP, using an arbitrary estimate of rental value.

3. To compute a firm's contribution to GNP on a value-added basis, we must deduct from the value at market price of the goods it has produced:
(1) all indirect business taxes paid.
(2) any undistributed profits.
(3) depreciation.
(4) all sales to other business firms.
(5) none of the above.

4. In GNP and NNP statistics, a negative gross investment figure:
(1) could never occur.
(2) could appear if the total of depreciation on buildings and equipment was sufficiently large.
(3) would automatically occur if there were no production of buildings or equipment during the year.
(4) could be caused by a sufficiently large reduction in inventories during the year.
(5) means simply that the economy has produced more than it has consumed.

5. There would be double counting in either GNP or NNP computations if statisticians were to add together:
(1) net value added by the iron-mining industry and net value added by the steel-manufacturing industry.
(2) net increase in inventories of flour mills and net increase in inventories of bakeries.
(3) total output of iron ore and total output of iron.
(4) value added by bakers and value of the baker's salespeople's services.
(5) total consumer services purchased and total of investment goods produced.

6. Subtract (*a*) corporation income taxes and (*b*) undistributed corporation profit from the total of corporation profit before taxes, and the remainder must equal:
(1) indirect business taxes.
(2) addition to retained earnings.
(3) dividends.
(4) bond interest.
(5) disposable income.

7. Among the five items listed below, one is not in the same class as the other four for purposes of national-income accounting, namely:
(1) corporation income (or profits).
(2) government transfer payments.
(3) net interest payments by business.
(4) rental income.
(5) wages and salaries.

8. If you know the NNP figure, and from it want to compute disposable personal income, one thing you must not do is:
(1) deduct depreciation.
(2) add government transfer payments.
(3) deduct indirect business taxes.
(4) deduct social security levies.
(5) deduct undistributed corporation profits.

9. In computing the "government" sector of GNP for a particular period:

(1) all governmental expenditures on commodities and services are counted.
(2) all governmental expenditures on commodities are counted; those on services are not.
(3) all governmental expenditures on final commodities and services are counted; those on intermediate items are not.
(4) all governmental expenditures on consumption items are counted, whether commodities or services; others are not.
(5) none of the above is correct.

10. "National income" (*NI*), as this term is used in the national product and national income statistics, means specifically:
(1) NNP (net national product) plus all taxes not considered taxes paid out of income—i.e., NNP plus indirect business taxes.
(2) NNP minus all taxes that are considered taxes paid out of income, such as the personal and corporation income taxes.
(3) NNP plus all taxes that are considered taxes paid out of income, such as the personal and corporation income taxes.
(4) NNP minus all taxes not considered taxes paid out of income—i.e., NNP minus indirect business taxes.
(5) none of the preceding.

11. If nominal NNP were $360 (billion) in 1990 and if the price level had risen by 20 percent from 1985 to 1990, then 1990 NNP, measured in 1985 prices, would be (in billions):
(1) $300.
(2) $320.
(3) $340.
(4) $360.
(5) $432.

12. In computing the national income and national product accounts, it would be incorrect to add together the following two items:
(1) consumption expenditures and personal saving.
(2) net investment and consumption expenditures.
(3) corporate profits and net interest paid by business.
(4) government purchases and consumption expenditures.
(5) government purchases and wages and salaries.

SUGGESTED ANSWERS TO QUESTIONS IN THE TEXT: Chapter 6

1. Cite the definitions. Examples:

Consumption—the purchase of a hamburger and some fries

Gross investment—the purchase of a computer

Government purchase—the purchase of a B-2 bomber

Transfer payment—receipt of a social security check

Export—sale of a U.S.-made computer to OPEC

2. GNP (apples, oranges) = price of apples × quantity of apples + price of oranges × quantity of oranges

3. Real GNP (1986) = (100/206.9) × $3073 billion
= $1485 billion (1982$)

Real GNP (1987) = (100/215.3) × $3305 billion
= $1535 billion (1982$)

Rate of growth of nominal GNP = [(3305 − 3073)/3073] × 100%
= 7.5%

Rate of growth of real GNP = [(1535 − 1485)/1485] × 100%
= 3.4%

Rate of inflation = [(215.3 − 206.9)/206.9] × 100%
= 4.1%

(Note that the rate of growth of nominal GNP equals the rate of growth of real GNP plus the rate of inflation.)

4. Profit must be $50 to match the upper-loop total of $1000. C = $750 means that I = $250. The earnings approach sums wages ($750), interest ($125), rent ($75), and profit ($50).

5. Some goods are not market-evaluated, but they still offer benefits and/or impose costs.

6. Remember that goods must be produced in the given year to count. There should also be some sort of compensation. Some services are missed because they are not compensated. That is part of the point of NEW.

7. Product-flow approach:

Personal consumption ($5 × 87)	$435
Gross private investment ($5 × 6)	30
Government expenditure ($5 × 10)	50
Net exports ($5 × −3)	−15
Total	$500

8. Earnings-cost approach:

Wages (¾ × $500)	$375
Indirect taxes	50
Rent	75
Total	$500

CHAPTER 7
CONSUMPTION AND INVESTMENT

This chapter begins a two-chapter coverage of the intellectual core of "Keynesian economics." The tools described in these pages were outlined by Keynes more than 50 years ago; they first appeared in print in *The General Theory*, published in 1936. Even though their application in contemporary thought about macroeconomic issues has changed over the intervening years, the impact of their development is still felt today. It is, therefore, useful to study the basic Keynesian construction of aggregate demand for at least two reasons.

First, a careful review of the Keynesian foundations builds an understanding of the antecedents of modern macroeconomic theory. Without such an understanding, modern students can find much of contemporary theory isolated and virtually impenetrable; they cannot understand why certain questions are raised, much less fathom their proposed answers.

Second, it is equally important to view the evolutionary process which brought us to our current state of economic awareness. To do this, particularly in macroeconomic analysis, we need a point of departure—a historical benchmark against which the reasons behind changes in viewpoint can be cast. The original Keynesian construction is an excellent starting point in this effort, and the integration of monetary policy into that model is an equally good example of the type of change that has occurred.

This initial chapter on investment and consumption begins to define the Keynesian benchmark. In addition to starting the process of understanding that benchmark, your work here should allow you to accomplish the following objectives.

LEARNING OBJECTIVES

1. Understand the deterministic relationship between income and consumption (household spending on food, clothing, etc.). Saving, the mirror image of consumption, is also determined in large part by income.

2. Define (*a*) consumption function, (*b*) the savings schedule, and (*c*) the marginal propensity to consume.

3. Follow the aggregation of individual consumption functions into a national consumption function determined by disposable income, wealth, and expectations about future income.

4. Recognize investment (in housing, plants, equipment, etc.) as a second major component of total spending. Understand that the level of investment spending in an economy depends on anticipated revenues, cost, and expectations about the future.

5. Formalize the relationship between the real interest rate and the level of investment in an investment demand schedule. The real rate of interest is equal to the nominal rate of interest minus the rate of inflation.

6. Recognize that the U.S. savings rate has declined sharply over the last 10 years. Suggested reasons behind the decline include large federal deficits (most importantly, in the view of many economists), social security pension programs, capital market changes, and changes in attitudes about debt.

Two factors typically determine the level of consumption undertaken by a family in any given period of time:

1. The amount of disposable income (*DI*) received (and, to a lesser degree, anticipated)
2. The allocation of that income between consumption (*C*) and savings (*S*)

The relationship between consumption spending and disposable income can be formalized by an **individual consumption function**; it matches any level of disposable income with its corresponding level of consumption. A corresponding savings schedule can be constructed by subtracting consumption from disposable income.

1. Suppose that a certain family's weekly expenditure on consumption is governed by this rule: spend $100 plus one-half of weekly *DI*. Hence its *C* spending and its saving at various income levels would be (fill in the blanks):

DI	*C*	*S*	*DI*	*C*	*S*
$ 0	$ ______	$ ______	$300	$ ______	$ ______
100	______	______	400	______	______
200	______	______	500	______	______

(Remember that *S* must be the difference between *DI* and *C*. So at low income levels, *S* will be a negative amount.)

C: 100, 150, 200, 250, 300, 350; S: -100, -50, 0, 50, 100, 150

2. a. In Figure 7-1 plot the points relating to consumption and disposable income for the six *DI* values of question 1. Joint these points with an appropriate line.

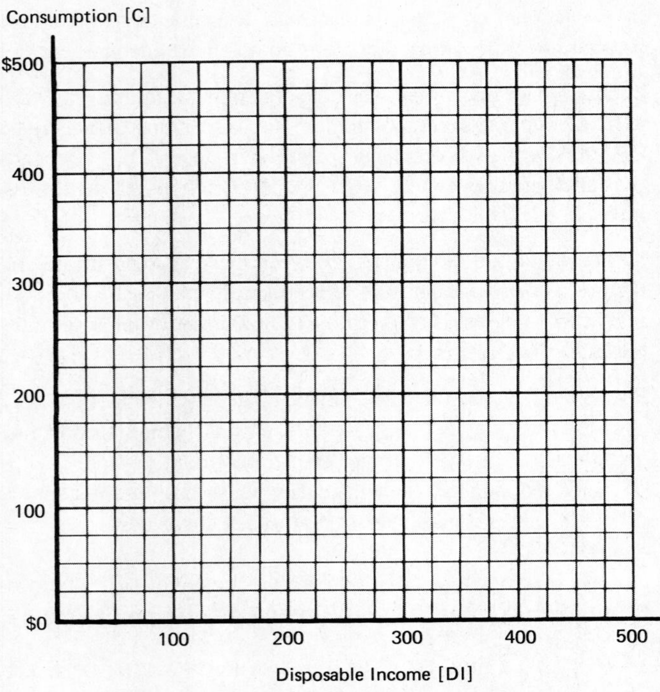

Figure 7-1

The figures you calculated in question 1 illustrate a consumption function. So does the graph you have just drawn. Notice that although the detail of the figures is different, the line you have drawn corresponds in general shape and direction to a consumption function. Some consumption curves display some curvature, but that is not essential. The case developed here is sufficient to illustrate the fundamental points of a basic macroeconomic tool.

b. Now draw a diagonal line from the bottom left corner to the top right corner of Figure 7-1. (Use, if possible, a different color to distinguish this line from the consumption function.) You have just drawn a 45° line running through all the equal-value combinations of *C* and *DI*. For example, the line you have just drawn on Figure 7-1 runs through the point marking off $100 of *DI* and $100 of *C*; through the point marking $200 *DI* and $200 *C*; through $300 *DI* and $300 *C*; and so on. *All* the points where *DI* and *C* are equal are found on this line, and all points on this line have *DI* and *C* equal. In fact, the 45° line can be represented algebraically by $C = DI$ (consumption equals disposable income).

One thing that the 45° line tells us, then, is the particular *DI* level at which the family just "breaks even"—spends on *C* an amount just equal to its *DI*. This is where the 45° line and the propensity to consume intersect: in our Figure 7-1 it is at a *DI* of $(*100 / 200 / 300 / 400*).

To the *left* of this intersection point, the consumption function lies (*above / below*) the 45° line. The significance of this is that within this range of incomes—from $0 to $200—the family spends on *C* (*more / less*) than its *DI*.

To the *right* of the intersection point, the consumption function lies (*above / below*) the 45° line. In this income range, the family would spend (*more / less*) than its *DI*; that is, it would save part of its *DI*.

b. 200; above; more; below; less

The point made immediately above is a simple one, but be sure you have grasped it: to the left of the intersection between the two lines, the family spends more than its income; at the intersection, it just "breaks even"; to the right it spends less than its income (and saves the remainder). Moreover, the vertical distance from the consumption function to the 45° line indicates the amount of saving.

3. a. For example, at $400 *DI* (at the 400 mark on the horizontal axis of Figure 7-1), the vertical distance up to the 45° line is $(*500 / 400 / 300*). The vertical distance up to the consumption function is $(*500 / 400 / 300*); this is the amount of *C* spending. The difference of $100—the vertical distance between the two lines—is the amount of saving (*S*).

b. Similarly, Figure 7-1 indicates, with the aid of the 45° line, that at *DI* of $300 the family would (*save / "dissave"*) an amount of $(*0 / 50 / 100 / 150*). At *DI* of $100, the family would (*save / "dissave"*) an amount of $(*0 / 50 / 100 / 150*). When the consumption function is above the 45° line, there is "dissaving," or "negative saving." This means simply that if the family's income should happen to be temporarily at a low level such as $100, it would draw on past savings, or borrow, in order to supplement *DI* currently received for *C* spending.

c. The amount of saving can of course be plotted directly on a saving-*DI* graph. Record the same six points of question 1 in Figure 7-2, and join them.

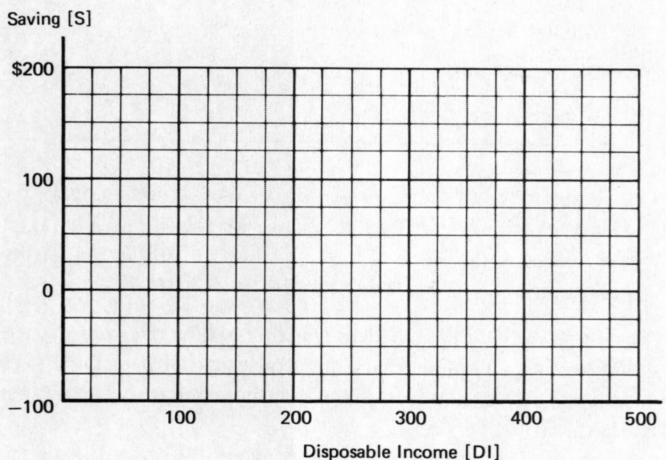

Figure 7-2

What you have drawn in Figure 7-2 is a graph of the savings schedule. If you are given a family's consumption function (*then you know / this does not necessarily tell you*) its savings schedule: $S = DI - C$.

a. 400; 300 **b.** save; 50; "dissave"; 50 **c.** then you know

To review, the idea behind the consumption function is this: income governs spending (and saving). If you know a family's income, you can estimate reasonably well what its total expenditure on consumer goods will be. Not precisely, of course, because families differ. Out of the same income, one family will spend more than another. Some are more freehanded with money; some have more children to support. There are many families, and many possible reasons for different spending patterns, so income is by no means the only factor to influence consumer spending. It is, however, the primary control. Consumption functions might vary among families, but they will show the same general construction.

We can also speak of a **national consumption function**—a nation being the aggregate of its individual members. There are one or two analytic problems in aggregating individual consumption functions into a national consumption function, but they turn out to be fairly unimportant. Despite differences in spending patterns from family to family, the statistical evidence indicates a remarkably consistent pattern between total community *DI* and total *C* spending. Figure 7-3 shows that over the years, in the United States, the actual relationship between total disposable income and total consumer expenditures has matched the "fitted consumption schedule" fairly well.

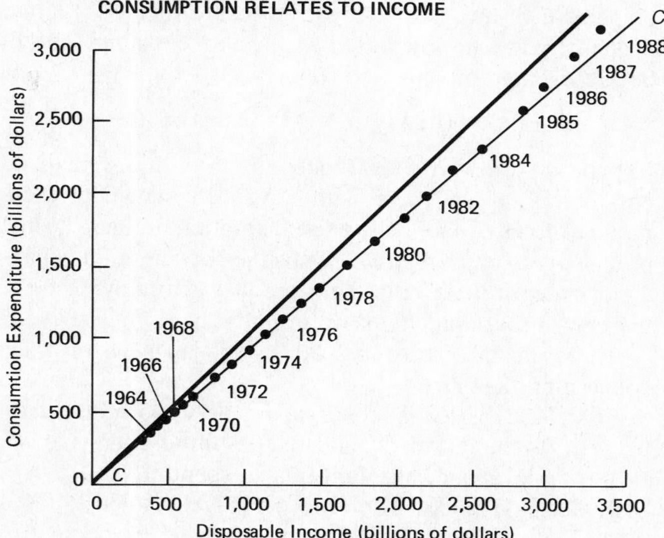

Figure 7-3

It follows from the very construction of a consumption function that *any* change in *DI* is likely to produce some change in *C* spending. In noting this connection, we are reaching for an extremely important concept—the idea of the **marginal propensity to consume** (MPC). The MPC is the ratio between extra consumption spending and extra disposable income.

To approach the marginal propensity idea slowly, consider first the individual consumption function defined by the following table:

Yearly *DI*	Yearly *C*	Increase in *C*
$12,000	$11,600	
		$640
13,000	12,240	
		590
14,000	12,830	

These figures indicate that a $1000 increase in *DI* from $12,000 to $13,000 would support an increase in consumption expenditure from $11,600 to $12,240—an increase of $640 (an amount much less than $1000), with the remaining $360 going into saving. The *MPC* for this change would be

$$\$640/\$1000 = 0.64$$

The next $1000 increase would inspire a second increase in consumption of only $590 (=$12,830 − $12,240), so the *MPC* would have fallen to 0.59.

Passing once again from individual to national consumption functions, the key now lies in the careful aggregation (summation) of individual behavior over the entire population. If the community were, for instance, composed of two families who earned $12,000 and $13,000, respectively, then an aggregate measure of the marginal propensity to consume based on the above example might be the average of 0.64 and 0.59:

$$0.5 \times 0.64 + 0.5 \times 0.59 = 0.615$$

Expanding this type of procedure to a more realistic community of any size with advanced statistical techniques allows economists to use the notion of the marginal propensity to consume to describe the consumption behavior of an entire nation in the same way that they describe the consumption behavior of an individual.

There are three essential facts that you need to grasp concerning the *MPC*:

First, the *MPC* is concerned solely with the ratio between a change in *DI* and the resulting change in *C*. In the table above, the family's *C* spending at a *DI* of $12,000 is $11,600. The ratio of $11,600 to $12,000 is 0.9667—that is, the family is spending 96.67 percent of its total income on consumption at this level. This might indicate the average propensity to consume, but it is *not* the *MPC*. The *MPC* tells what extra consumption spending will go with any extra income (i.e., any increase or decrease in income), and the *MPC* in the vicinity of *DI* = $12,000 is about 0.64.

Second, the *MPC* is the slope of the consumption function. If you have had any training in calculus, it is now clear that the *MPC* is really the derivative of the consumption function; if you have not, understanding the notion of *MPC* might help you when you do take calculus. Finally, there is also a **marginal propensity to save** (*MPS*). We know already that a family must always decide to allocate any increase in *DI* (positive or negative) between extra *C* and extra *S*. If the *MPC* stands for the fraction of an extra dollar of income devoted to *C*, then the remaining fraction (*MPS*) must go to saving; that is,

$$MPC + MPS = 1$$

by definition.

4. Question 1 reflected the following consumption function: spend on *C* one-half of weekly *DI* plus $100. Given this consumption function, complete the blanks in the table at the top of the next column to indicate the change in *C* spending resulting from the indicated change in *DI*. Complete also the *MPC* column (ratio of extra *C* to extra *DI*).

Change in *C*: +50¢, +50¢, +50¢, +$5, −$5, −50¢; *MPC*: ½ throughout

5. a. What is the slope of the consumption function of Figure 7-1? ______

Change in *DI*	Change in C	*MPC*
From $0 to $1 (+$1)	______	______
From $399 to $400 (+$1)	______	______
From $400 to $401 (+$1)	______	______
From $400 to $410 (+$10)	______	______
From $410 to $400 (−$10)	______	______
From $400 to $399 (−$1)	______	______

Slope, as measured by the rule above, would indicate the ratio of change in (*DI / C / S*) to change in (*DI / C / S*). That is, it would measure the value of the (*marginal / average*) propensity to consume.

b. The *MPC*, in this instance, (*falls / remains constant / rises*) as *DI* rises. Graphically, the consumption function is a (*straight / curved*) line. Its slope does not change; hence neither does the *MPC*.

By contrast, the propensity to consume illustrated in Figure 7-4 "bends over." Its slope (*increases / remains constant / decreases*) as the *DI* level increases. Correspondingly, the *MPC* involved (*increases / remains constant / decreases*) as *DI* increases.

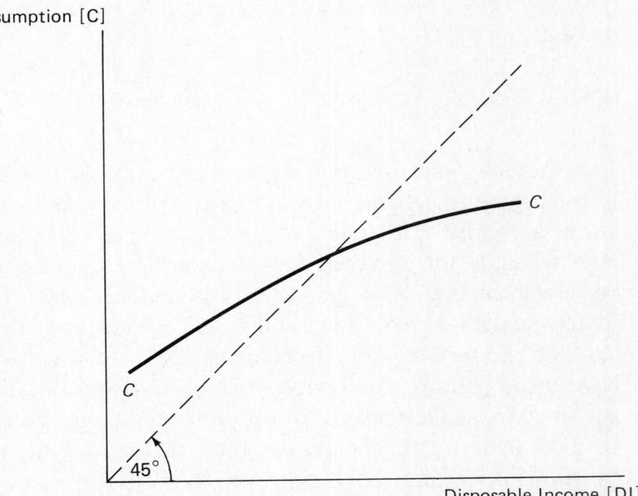

Figure 7-4

a. ½; *C*; *DI*; marginal **b.** remains constant; straight; decreases; decreases

6. Show, for the income levels given, the fraction of total income spent on consumption, and the marginal propensity to consume, for the family in questions 1 through 5.

The figures you have entered in the middle column above represent a series of (*marginal / average*) propensities to consume. They deal with total *DI* and total *C*, whereas the *MPC* deals with extra or additional amounts.

DI	Fraction of DI Spent on C	MPC
$100	____	____
200	____	____
300	____	____
400	____	____
400	____	____
500	____	____

DI fractions: 3/2, 1, 5/6, 3/4, 7/10; *MPC*: 1/2 throughout; average

Now consider one final point regarding the consumption function. If a family increases its *C* spending, a likely explanation—but not the only possible one—is that its *DI* has increased. If the imaginary family of the preceding questions were to increase its *C* spending from $300 to $350 weekly, the increase could well be attributable to a rise in *DI* from $400 to $500, but this change could occur for other reasons. The family might (with an unchanged *DI*) be changing the distribution of its *DI* between *C* and *S*. It might have decided that its saving for future needs was close to sufficient; or it might be increasing its *C* spending because of greater optimism about the level of its future income. There are plenty of conceivable explanations. In any case, if the amount of money habitually spent on consumption changes for any reason other than a change in *DI*, then the consumption function has shifted to a new position. To put the same idea in different words, any nontransitory change in the distribution of *DI* between *C* and *S* means a change in the position of the consumption function.

The situation is precisely analogous to the demand-curve analysis of Chapter 4. A demand curve shows how quantity purchased will increase if price falls. But price is not the only factor influencing quantity of purchases. Purchases may change because of a change in tastes or a rise in the price of substitute goods or for other reasons. If some factor such as this—anything other than a change in the price of the good involved—is responsible, then we must show the demand curve as moving to a brand-new position.

The same reasoning applies to the consumption function. It shows how *C* expenditure will change with any change in *DI* —other factors held constant. If one of these other factors changes (thus producing a change in *C* for some reason other than a change in *DI*), then we must show the whole consumption function having moved to an appropriate new position.

7. a. The family of earlier questions has a *DI* of $450 weekly (so that its *C* expenditure is $325). One family member now leaves home to get married, so the consumption function changes. It now becomes one-half of *DI*, plus $75.

If family *DI* is unaltered, its weekly *C* spending will henceforth be $(*300 / 325 / 350 / 375*). On a consumption function graph such as Figure 7-4, this change would be represented as (pick one):

(1) a movement downward along the existing curve.

(2) a movement upward along the existing curve.

(3) a shift of the entire consumption function upward to a new position.

(4) a shift of the entire consumption function downward to a new position.

Is the value of the marginal propensity to consume changed? (*No / Yes, it has risen / Yes, it has fallen*)

b. Suppose the new consumption function had been: spend two-fifths of *DI*, plus $75. If so, as compared with the previous schedule, the value of the *MPC* would (*fall / remain unchanged / rise*).

a. 300 (=225 + 75); **(4)**; No **b.** fall (*Note:* When the consumption function changes, the *MPC* may or may not change. The *MPC* is strictly concerned with a given propensity to consume, and with the ratio between extra *C* and extra *DI*, given that propensity to consume. Here it falls from .5 in part **a** to .4 in part **b**.)

8. a. The solid line *CC* in Figure 7-5 illustrates a community's consumption function. One possible level of total *DI* is indicated by the horizontal measure *OA*, and total consumption expenditure out of that particular *DI* by the vertical measure *DO*.

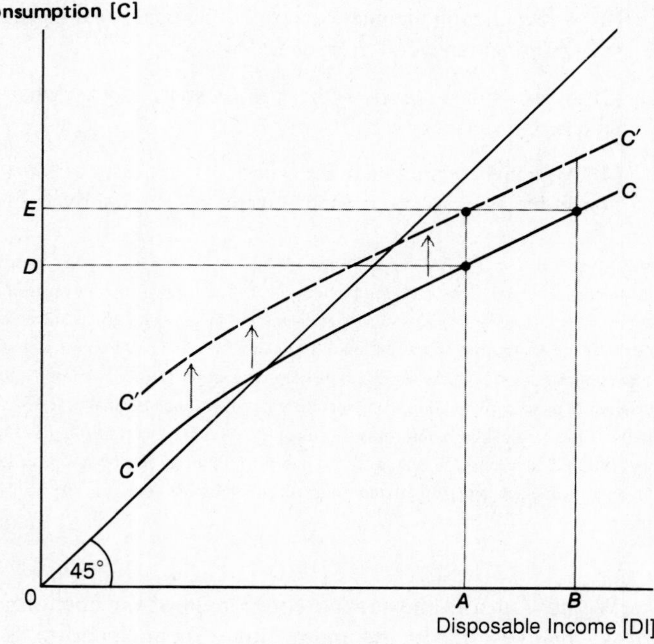

Figure 7-5

The community's total C expenditure now rises from DO to EO. This increase could be the consequence of (pick one):

(1) only an increase in DI from level OA to level OB.

(2) only some factor other than a DI increase—a factor causing the consumption function to shift upward to a new position indicated by the broken line $C'C'$.

(3) either **(1)** of **(2)**—an increase in DI, or else a decision to spend more prompted by some factor other than an increase in DI.

b. A respected economic authority predicts a coming recession. His prediction is influential, and people decide that they should spend less and save more as a precaution against coming hard times (even though DI has not fallen—not yet, at any rate). If this decision were to be illustrated in Figure 7-5 terms, it would imply (pick one):

(1) a movement downward and to the left *along* a given consumption function, say, the solid CC one, to indicate the reduced C spending caused by reduced disposable income.

(2) an upward movement of the entire consumption function, say, from the position indicated by the solid CC line upward to the broken $C'C'$ line.

(3) a downward movement of the entire consumption function, say, from the position indicated by the broken $C'C'$ line downward to the solid CC line.

c. Which of the following would cause the consumption function to shift up? ________ To shift down? ________

(1) An anticipated downturn in business conditions that leads people to worry that they might lose their jobs.

(2) A reduction in the interest rate paid by banks that makes saving less attractive to everyone.

(3) A reduction in taxes so that people retain more of their income after taxes.

(4) An actual contraction in the economy that causes a reduction in the availability of outside or overtime employment.

---

a. (3) **b. (3)** **c. (1)** [Answers **(3)** and **(4)** are incorrect because they imply movement along the consumption function rather than shifts in the curve itself. Answer **(3)**, e.g., implies an increase in disposable income and not an increase in the marginal propensity to consume. The careful reader might object to this because there could be some sensitivity in the marginal propensity to consume to changes in income. When things are aggregated, though, the marginal propensity to consume is remarkably insensitive to income. The key, therefore, is that **(1)** and **(2)** produce changes in the level of consumption at any level of disposable income, while **(3)** and **(4)** produce only changes in the level of disposable income.]

We now turn to the second component of the spending flow: *investment*. In the main, investment spending is spending by business firms for the purchase of new capital goods—new buildings, new machinery, and so on. Changes in the levels of inventories count, too.

We cannot isolate any one factor that dominates in explaining the flow of investment. Investment spending is undertaken in the hope of making some profit relative to the cost. It is, therefore, influenced by a wide range of economic and psychological variables. First, of course, is the cost of the investment, both for the physical equipment of material involved and for the money required to finance the expenditure. The real rate of interest charged by the financing institution is thus critical. This is true whether or not the business is borrowing to finance the investment or using its own money. Why? When the investing firm is considering what to do with its money, it has no particular allegiance to anything. It will put its money where it will earn the highest real return. If that highest return is earned by putting the money in a bank or some government bond, then so be it. The proposed physical investment project will go by the boards.

The second determinant of the flow of investment is the anticipated stream of income that the investment would generate. Would the project pay off quickly, or would it take a long time? Can business conditions in the future be expected to support the increased activity that the project would generate, or would the project appeal to a market that is already saturated by competition? Critical here, of course, is the anticipated health of the entire economy. If a weak economy were anticipated, then an investment project that would try to sell a new product or more of an old product would not be as attractive as it would be if a vigorous, growing economy were forecast.

The result of all this anticipation is that investment spending is extremely volatile and extremely hard to predict. It is, in fact, much harder to predict than the consumption flow. Investment is, nonetheless, one of the keys to disturbances in the growth of GNP and NNP. Its full significance will be revealed in subsequent chapters.

9. Investment, as the term is used in economics (e.g., a firm purchases a new machine tool or an addition to its existing plant), generates employment while the investment item in question is being built, and results in income earned for those so employed. It is a flow of money expenditure to the firms which produce such investment goods. In this sense, do the following constitute investment?

a. having a contractor build a new house for you . . *(Yes / No)*

b. buying a house built a year ago . . . . *(Yes / No)*

c. buying du Pont stock on the stock market . . . . . *(Yes / No)*

d. buying stock in a newly formed corporation, where the money proceeds from the stock sale are to be used to build a new factory building . . . . *(Yes / No)*

e. using money obtained from the bond or stock issue of item **d** to build a new factory building . . . . *(Yes / No)*

a. Yes **b., c., d.,** No **e.** Yes (*Note:* The answer cannot be Yes for both **d** and **e**, or else there would be double counting. The sale of stock may be a necessary prerequisite to investment, but it is only a transfer payment from the stock buyers to the new corporation. Actual investment takes place only when money is in fact spent for the purpose defined as investment.)

10. a. A firm is considering building a new plant to add to its output capacity. To do this sensibly, it must try to evaluate the future market for its product to be sure there is likely to be sufficient demand to justify that plant. This requires that the firm estimate, among other things, the likely degree of competition from rival firms and the coming "general business conditions"—i.e., probable future course of GNP. True or False? *(T / F)*

b. This means, then, that the flow of investment expenditure is governed by many considerations frequently having to do with forecasts about the future. . . . . *(T / F)*

c. A large corporation which has been steadily adding new plant and equipment may stop doing so because it feels it has "caught up" with probable demand for its product for the time being. If it stops, the investment flow will be correspondingly reduced even though the stock of capital is maintained net of depreciation. . . . . *(T / F)*

d. Such investment plans may be postponed or canceled because the firm is fearful of a recession—a drop or pause in GNP. This would again mean a drop in the flow of investment spending. . . . . *(T / F)*

e. If any such reduction in the investment-spending flow occurs, it is reasonable to assume that there will at once be a matching reduction in the flow of personal saving. . . . . *(T / F)*

f. The economy goes through a period of high interest rates caused by a variety of internal and external factors. The result should be a reduction in both the investment financed through borrowing *and* the investment financed through retained earnings. . . . . *(T / F)*

g. After a period in which every economist in the country had a different forecast of future economic activity, the nation enters a period during which there is rough consensus among major forecasters (there will *never* be absolute consensus about the past, much less the future) that a period of reasonable and sustainable growth should be expected to pull an economy out of its current slump. The result should be an immediate increase in investment activity. *(T / F)*

All true except **e** and **g**. (Plans to save are, in general, made quite independently of plans to invest; **e** is, therefore, false. After a recession, investment does not increase even with the expectation of recovery until capacity idled by the recession is more fully utilized and the need for investment to increase or improve capacity is more completely known. The result; **g** is also false.)

11. a. Money saved by a family and hidden in the family mattress is money withdrawn from the income stream; it creates no income or jobs for anyone as long as it remains in the mattress. . . . . *(T / F)*

b. Money saved by a family and promptly used to buy a new house is money put right back into the income stream. Because (by the definitions in Chapter 6) any consumer expenditure for the construction of a new house counts as investment expenditure, these actions would count as both saving and investment. . . . . *(T / F)*

c. Money saved by a family and promptly used to buy General Motors stock would count as both saving and investment. . . . . *(T / F)*

d. Money saved and deposited in a savings account in a bank counts as saving. This is not investment in the national income sense. So long as this money stays deposited, it can be used for investment spending only if the bank lends it to some borrower or if the bank uses the money itself. . . . . *(T / F)*

e. Much investment spending is financed by use of other people's money, i.e., financed by borrowing from a bank or by sale of bond or stock issues. . . . . *(T / F)*

f. Those who are in a position to lend money must consider (1) the honesty of the would-be borrower and (2) his or her ability to repay the borrowed money, i.e., the prospects for profitable use of such money. . . . . *(T / F)*

g. If business conditions seem particularly uncertain, people with money to spare may hesitate to lend it, feeling that would-be borrowers are likely to get into trouble and be unable to make repayment. Thus, even though there are mechanisms for converting saving into investment, this does not mean that all saved money is automatically transformed into investment. . . . . *(T / F)*

All true except **c** [*Note 1:* Money spent to buy a stock or a bond does not count as investment; see parts **(3)** and **(4)** of question 9. *Note 2:* When a family spends money to have a new house built, we must think of this money, in terms of Figures 7-6 and 7-7, as passing through the "savings drain," going at once through the saved-money resevoir, and up through the "investment-spending intake." It would be easier to think of it as simply passing through the consumption loop, like any other consumer expenditure; but we can't do that

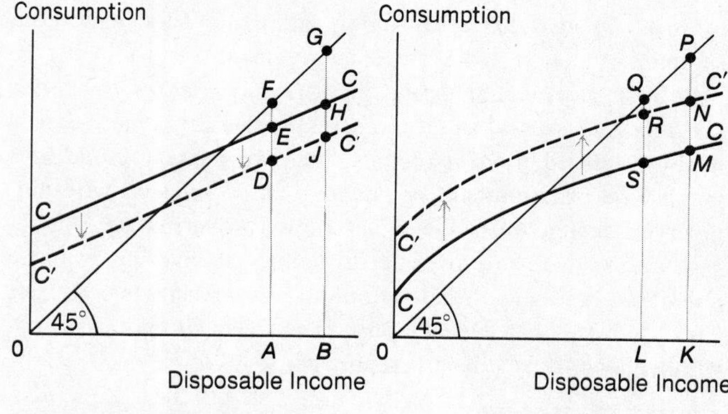

Figure 7-6 **Figure 7-7**

because the national product definitions say that any new housing purchase is the one consumer expenditure item which must be classified as investment. No great analytic issue is involved; it's just a matter of respecting the definitions.]

Having spent the effort in exploring the reasons why saving might not match investment, it seems reasonable to spend a little extra effort in anticipating the answer to the "So what? " question that will be addressed over the next several chapters. The key lies in the fact that spending flows generate business activity and thus employment. Suppose, for the sake of illustration, that actual and intended *S* were to exceed intended *I*. The flow of spending generating business activity would, therefore, necessarily shrink, thereby supporting fewer jobs. Unemployment should, as a result, be expected to rise.

What of the accounting identity that demands that actual investment always equal actual saving. How can the measured investment be brought up to the level of saving in the example just described? The answer lies in inventory investment. Less business, fewer jobs, and more unemployed workers mean lower-than-expected demand for products in the real economy. Unsold products therefore accumulate on shelves and create higher-than-expected accumulation of final product inventories. Since these accumulations are part of actual investment, they swell actual investment beyond the intended level and up to the level of actual saving. More on this will be provided later.

12. Suppose that there are 100 families in an economy. Half have an *MPC* of ½; half have an *MPC* of ¾. if this economy's disposable income rises by $10,000, and all this goes to the first group, then *C* spending will rise by $(*0 / 2500 / 5000 / 7500 / 10,000*). If, instead, all the additional *DI* goes to the second group, the *C* spending will rise by $(*0 / 2500 / 5000 / 7500 / 10,000*).

Thus, even if we know the exact propensity to consume of each family, we (*cannot / can*) predict the exact *C* increase that would follow any given *DI* increase. If different families have different marginal propensities, then for such a prediction, we would have to know how the *DI* increase was distributed—i.e., which families got the extra *DI*.

Now suppose that every family has exactly the same consumption function, with some curvature as shown in Figure 7-4. Such a curvature means that *MPC* (*increases / remains constant / decreases*) as *DI* increases. If there is some inequality in the distribution of income, then we (*could / could not*) predict the exact amount of change in *C* associated with any given *DI* change unless we again know its distribution.

In sum, there are analytic difficulties in moving from an individual-family to a whole-community propensity to consume. Note, though, that the relationship between *DI* and *C* for the whole economy is still remarkably consistent.

5000; 7500; cannot; decreases; could not

13. Assume that there are 200 families in a community. Each of these families spends exactly $100 plus one-half its income each week on consumption. Half (100) these families are "poor"; they each receive weekly incomes of $200. The other 100 families are "rich"; they receive $400 apiece weekly.

It is desired to increase total consumption spending in this community. (Reasons for wishing such an increase can be disregarded.) It is proposed to increase total spending by taxing rich families $100 apiece weekly, giving the tax proceeds to poor families to spend. Thus, each and every family would have a net weekly income of $300.

This proposal is justified as follows: Poor families spend 100 percent of their incomes on consumption; they receive $200, and they spend $200. Rich families spend only 75 percent of their income; they receive $400, but they spend only $300. So the total of consumption spending would be increased by redistribution of income.

a. Would such a proposal, if adopted, increase total consumption spending? Explain your answer in terms of the marginal propensity to consume. ______________________

____

____

b. Are there any different circumstances in which such a redistribution-of-income proposal would increase consumption spending? Again answer in terms of the *MPC*. ____________

____

____

c. Explain two circumstances in which a redistribution of income through this tax scheme might actually lower consumption spending. (This is a hard question; think beyond the *MPC* notion that was sufficient to answer part **b.**) ____________

____

____

____

____

---

a. No; their *MPCs* are identical **b.** Yes, if the *MPC* for the lower-income people were higher than the *MPC* for the upper-income people. **c.** One clearly is the opposite case of the one described in **b**. A second takes note of how hard people work. If the wealthier people worked less in response to the tax and were therefore paid correspondingly less, total spending might fall because total output fell regardless of the poor people's *MPC*.

QUIZ: Multiple Choice

1. The marginal propensity to consume is:
(1) at any income level, the ratio of total consumption to total income.

(2) at any income level, the change in consumption spending caused by an income change (increase or decrease).
(3) for each and all income levels, a schedule showing the amount of consumption spending at that level.
(4) at any income level, the ratio of a change in consumption to a change in income level.
(5) none of these things.

2. The volume, or magnitude, of investment opportunities in the American economy is governed primarily by:
(1) the total amount of saving available for investment users.
(2) the level of prevailing interest rates.
(3) the state of the stock market.
(4) the rate at which new and commercially exploitable inventions are appearing from laboratories.
(5) none of the above, there being no such single dominant factor.

3. The relation between the marginal propensities to consume and to save is that:
(1) their total must equal 1, since some fraction of extra income must go to extra consumption spending, and the remaining fraction to extra saving.
(2) the ratio between them must indicate the average propensity to consume.
(3) their total must indicate the current total of disposable income received, since *DI* must divide between consumption and saving.
(4) the point at which they are equal must be the breakeven level of income.
(5) their total must equal zero.

4. "Personal saving," as the term is used in connection with national income and national product analysis, means explicitly:
(1) the total of all assets held by families.
(2) income received within the period in question and not spent on consumption.
(3) the total of all assets held by families minus the total of their liabilities.
(4) income received within the period in question but used only to buy a security or deposited in a bank.
(5) income received within the period in question, not spent on consumption and not used to buy a security or deposited in a bank.

5. If people do not consume all their income and put the unspent amount into a bank, they are, in national income and product terms:
(1) saving but not investing.
(2) investing but not saving.
(3) both saving and investing.
(4) neither saving nor investing.
(5) saving, but investing only to the extent that they buy securities.

6. Which of the following would be regarded as investment by economists concerned with national product and income?
(1) Any purchase of a corporation bond.
(2) Any amount saved out of income and not hoarded.
(3) Any purchase of a new corporation bond.
(4) Any productive activity resulting in present consumption.
(5) None of the preceding.

7. The breakeven point on a family's consumption function is the point at which:
(1) its saving equals its income.
(2) its income equals its consumption.
(3) its saving equals its consumption.
(4) its consumption equals its investment.
(5) the marginal propensity to consume equals 1.

8. In Figure 7-6, the solid line *CC* is the consumption function for some family or community. If the total amount of consumption expenditure is *EA*, then the amount of disposable income must be:
(1) *AB*.
(2) *FD*.
(3) *FA*.
(4) *DA*.
(5) none of the preceding.

9. Alternatively, given the total amount of consumption expenditure *FA* in Figure 7-6, then the amount of disposable income must be:
(1) *EA*.
(2) *GB*.
(3) *ED*.
(4) *OA*.
(5) none of the preceding.

10. In Figure 7-7, if the solid consumption function *CC* were to shift upward to the broken-line position *C′C′*, this would be appropriate to illustrate:
(1) an increase in consumption expenditure resulting from a rise in disposable income.
(2) a decision on the part of the family or community involved to consume more and save less out of any given disposable income.
(3) a decrease in consumption expenditure resulting from a fall in disposable income.
(4) a decision on the part of the family or community involved to consume less and save more out of any given disposable income.
(5) none of these events.

11. The difference between Figures 7-6 and 7-7, both consumption function diagrams, is that:
(1) in Figure 7-6, the *MPC* (marginal propensity to consume) is constant; in Figure 7-7, the *MPC* decreases as income increases.

(2) in Figure 7-6, the *MPC* decreases as income increases in Figure 7-7, the *MPC* is constant.
(3) in Figure 7-6, the *MPC* increases as income increases; in Figure 7-7, the *MPC* is constant.
(4) in Figure 7-6, the *MPC* is constant; in Figure 7-7, the *MPC* increases as income increases.
(5) in both instances, the *MPC* falls as income increases, but it falls more rapidly in the case of Figure 7-7.

12. In Figure 7-7, if the consumption function is the solid line *CC* and the amount of disposable income if *OK*, then the amount of saving out of that disposable income *OK* must be:
(1) *PK*.
(2) *MK*.
(3) *PM*.
(4) *NM*.
(5) none of the preceding.

13. If, again in Figure 7-7, the amount of disposable income were to change from *OK* to *OL*—the solid *CC* line still indicating the consumption function—the amount of saving out of income would become:
(1) *SM*.
(2) *QR*.
(3) *PQ*.
(4) *RS*.
(5) *QS*.

14. In Figure 7-6, a change in consumption expenditure from *HB* to *EA* could be the result of:
(1) a decision to spend more and save less at each level of income.
(2) a decrease in disposable income from *OB* to *OA*.
(3) a decision to spend less and save more at each level of income.
(4) an increase in disposable income from *OA* to *OB*.
(5) none of the preceding.

15. The consumption function refers to:
(1) the level of income at which consumption spending just equals income.
(2) the inclination on the part of some consumers to "keep up with the Joneses" in their consumer spending.
(3) the fraction of extra income that will be spent on consumption.
(4) a schedule showing the amount a family (or community) will spend on consumption at different levels of income.
(5) the fact that, at low incomes, families spend more on consumption than the amount of their incomes.

16. According to the statistical evidence, which of the following characterizes the typical American family's behavior with respect to spending out of income?
(1) An increasing proportion of income is spent on consumption as income increases.
(2) The same proportion of income is spent on consumption at all except very low income levels.
(3) The same proportion of income is spent on consumption at all income levels.
(4) A decreasing proportion of income is spent on consumption as income increases.
(5) The same proportion of income is spent on consumption at all except very high income levels.

17. A family spends $2000 on consumption when its income is zero, and $6000 on consumption when its income is $6000. Graphically, its consumption function is a straight line, as in Figure 7-6. At this family's $6000 income level, its marginal propensity to consume is:
(1) $2/3$.
(2) $3/4$.
(3) $4/5$.
(4) 1.
(5) greater than 1.

18. "Investment" and "consumption," as these terms are used in national income and product analysis, have which feature in common?
(1) Both activities are undertaken by the same group (i.e., households), although not always for the same reasons.
(2) Both are demands calling for the current use, or employment, of the economy's stock of productive inputs.
(3) Both are components of disposable income.
(4) In both instances, the only factor of major consequence which governs them is the level of national product or disposable income.
(5) None of the preceding.

SUGGESTED ANSWERS TO QUESTIONS IN THE TEXT: Chapter 7

1. As disposable income rises, the percentage expended on food and clothing falls, and the percentage expended on luxury goods and devoted to saving rises.

2. Motives for saving include (*a*) precaution against possible bad times, (*b*) the desire to leave a large bequest, (*c*) the need for a large sum for some transaction, and (*d*) preparation for a comfortable retirement. Reasons for the decline in the U.S. savings rate in the 1980s include (*a*) deficit spending, which encourages consumption, (*b*) increased and more secure social security benefits, which reduce the retirement motive, (*c*) high inflation, which reduces the real rate of return, (*d*) a reduction in borrowing opportunities for certain expenditures (e.g., college, housing), (*e*) an increase in household wealth (particularly homes), (*f*) a change in work-save ethics. Many more reasons could be cited.

3. By definition,

$$MPC = \text{change in } C/\text{change in } DI$$

while

$$MPS = \text{change in } S/\text{change in } DI$$

Since the change in C plus the change in S exhausts any change in DI, $MPC + MPS$ = change in DI/change in $DI = 1$.

4. $MPC = 1$; $MPS = 0$; consumption function is $C = DI$; i.e., the 45° line.

5. After-tax return to investment falls for any pre-tax real rate of interest, so the demand for investment must fall.

6. You are on your own; the degree of my dissaving is classified.

7. $MPC < 1$; $MPS > 0$.

8. **a.** Demand shifts out for all r.
b. Define a new point on the demand curve; quantity smaller.
c. Demand shifts out for all r such that project J is profitable.
d. Demand shifts in for all r.

9. MPC = slope = ⅔. $DI = C + S = 450 + (2/3)DI + S$, so that subtraction reveals that $S = -450 + (1/3)DI$. MPS therefore equals ⅓. Also, $MPC + MPS = 1$.

10. A total of $100,000 must be consumed in equal lumps for each of 5 years (no interest paid on saving means that accrual is not relevant). So $20,000 must be consumed each year. With no tax, the table should look like this:

	(3)	(4)	(5)
Year 1	$20,000	$10,000	$10,000
Year 2	20,000	10,000	20,000
Year 3	20,000	5,000	25,000
Year 4	20,000	−5,000	20,000
Year 5	20,000	−20,000	0

With the tax and benefit program the table looks like this:

	(3)	(4)	(5)
Year 1	$20,000	$ 8,000	$ 8,000
Year 2	20,000	8,000	16,000
Year 3	20,000	3,000	19,000
Year 4	20,000	−7,000	12,000
Year 5	20,000	−12,000	0

Note that consumption is unaffected by the tax and benefit but private saving falls. Why? The government is doing part of it.

CHAPTER 8
THE THEORY OF OUTPUT DETERMINATION

Previous chapters have introduced you to many of the fundamental concepts of macroeconomic analysis: aggregate supply, aggregate demand, GNP, price indexes, consumption, saving, and investment. It is now time to begin to learn how to use these concepts to develop an understanding of how a macroeconomy works. What, in particular, can an understanding of how these concepts interact teach us about our ability to manipulate a large economy? Can we learn what sort of policies might help us to avoid overheated periods of unacceptably high inflation? Or sluggish times of unacceptably high unemployment? Or stagnant times marked by unacceptably high levels of both? Or is the die cast somewhere beyond our control?

Chapter 8 will begin your investigation into these questions, and it will quickly lead you into an area of enormous controversy. The first part of the chapter will use the simple notions of aggregate supply and demand to contrast two fundamentally different schools of thought. On the one hand will be the classical view of the world that will be summarized, in an oversimplified way, by drawing a vertical aggregate supply curve. Classicists believe that prices and wages adjust so quickly and completely that output and employment are determined only by the potential of an economy. There will not, for any significant length of time (in the absence of artificial interference by the government), exist any involuntary unemployment of any productive resources. Changes in aggregate demand, classicists believe, do nothing but create changes in prices and wages, and so there is neither the need nor the ability for policies to be written to move aggregate demand one way or the other in the hopes of influencing GNP.

Keynesians take a different approach. They note many reasons why wages and prices do not always respond to periods of either excess demand or (more importantly) excess supply. Wages do not, the Keynesians argue for example, fall very quickly when the supply of labor exceeds the demand for labor (as in a recession or depression). Their simplified aggregate supply curve is therefore horizontal at least for levels of economic activity below potential GNP, and the equilibria that they envision can occur anywhere in that range with any level of employment. Equilibrium can, in particular, occur well below the potential output of the economy in question and persist there for a long time. Keynesians also believe, however, that the manipulation of aggregate demand can be used to move equilibrium up toward potential GNP when it is required to reduce unemployment.

The second part of the chapter presents the simplest version of the Keynesian model and shows how equilibrium is computed. Embedded in this computation is the observation that a given change in consumption or investment expenditure will cause a greater change in the equilibrium level of GNP. This amplification is known as the **multiplier effect**, and it will serve as a focal point of the discussion of fiscal policy to be conducted in Chapter 9. The concluding section to Chapter 8 will, however, emphasize that this multiplier result depends critically upon the Keynesian assumption about wages and prices. A reduction in aggregate demand must not be associated with lower wages and prices if GNP is to fall by the full amount predicted by the multiplier. An enlarged aggregate demand must, similarly, be accommodated by employing resources that had been idled by an existing equilibrium falling well below potential GNP; otherwise, the stimulus of higher demand will simply generate higher prices.

It will serve you well to remember when the full multiplier effect is applicable as you proceed through the coming chapters on macroeconomic policy. Having completed even this first chapter in output determination, though, you will have accomplished the following objectives.

LEARNING OBJECTIVES

1. Recall that aggregate demand is the sum of consumption expenditures (C), investment expenditures (I), government expenditures (*G*), and net exports (*X*). When drawn against a price index, it is generally downward-sloping because (e.g.) increases in prices diminish the real value of personal wealth and thereby cause them to spend less.

2. Note that the determinants of aggregate demand are somewhat in dispute. Some economists emphasize the role of money in determining aggregate demand; others emphasize the roles of autonomous spending (*I*, *G*, and/or *X*). The eclectic view mixes these two emphases.

3. Recall that aggregate supply is a measure of potential GNP in the long run, but assumes different shapes in the short run depending upon perspective. Complete wage and price flexibility produces a vertical short-run aggregate supply curve at potential GNP. Significant wage and price stickiness produces a horizontal short-run aggregate supply curve below potential GNP at least. Intermediate cases produce positively sloped short-run aggregate supply curves.

4. Understand that the classical view of the world envisions wages and prices responding so quickly that an economy's performance is determined almost exclusively by its potential GNP. In the simplified arena of aggregate supply and demand, this view is represented by a vertical aggregate supply curve at potential GNP.

5. Understand that the Keynesian view of the world envisions wages and prices responding so slowly that an economy can be in equilibrium well below its potential. In terms of aggregate supply and demand, this view is represented by a horizontal aggregate supply curve to the left of potential GNP.

6. Derive the classicists' results that (*a*) there can exist no involuntary unemployment and (*b*) there exists no policy which can affect either GNP or employment by manipulating aggregate demand.

7. Derive the Keynesian results that (*a*) there can exist involuntary unemployment in equilibrium, at least in the short run, and (*b*) there do exist policies which can affect both GNP and employment by manipulating aggregate demand when actual GNP falls below potential GNP.

8. Explain why an equilibrium level of GNP is reached in the Keynesian model when the amount of intended investment just equals the amount of saving indicated by the savings schedule.

9. Explain why the same equilibrium level of GNP can be characterized in the Keynesian model by the equality of GNP and the sum of intended consumption and investment.

10. Describe what happens in the Keynesian model (*a*) when the total dollar value of intended investment falls short of saving and (*b*) when the total dollar value of intended investment exceeds saving.

11. Describe precisely why the Keynesian view of the world can be considered only when there exist unemployed resources in an economy operating below its full potential.

12. Draw and explain graphs to illustrate objectives 6 through 11 listed above.

This list of objectives is uncommonly long. Its length speaks graphically to the importance of this chapter, though, so it is presented in its entirety without apology. Chapter 8 is simply a critical juncture in your journey through the foundations of modern macroeconomics—critical for two very good reasons. First, the tools and concepts developed here will prove to be the essential building blocks for what follows. You will be using the tools presented in Chapter 8 to contemplate answers to questions of policy and practice for the next 10 chapters. Without a thorough understanding of the foundation laid in Chapter 8, you will be lost. Second, the very heart of the policy controversy that rages throughout the free world today is accurately identified in this chapter in the simplest possible terms. As you work through the various parts of this chapter, the bare essentials of the debate will be laid before you. You will, as you begin to study the debate, be laying your own groundwork for understanding the sources of the controversy, perceiving the relative merits of both sides, and making up your own mind about which view is more reasonable. You will use the simplicity of this chapter later to see and assess the need for the theoretical middle ground that is so elusive. The time that you spend here will, quite assuredly, pay large dividends later.

1. List, in the spaces provided below, the four major components of aggregate demand.

a. ____________________

b. ____________________

c. ____________________

d. ____________________

Circle the letters corresponding to those components whose value you would expect to see decline as prices increased. It is these components that contribute to the negative slope of a representative aggregate demand curve drawn with aggregate quantity measured along the horizontal axis and a price index measured along the vertical axis.

---

a. consumption **b.** investment **c.** government spending **d.** net exports; the letters corresponding to all four components [Higher prices should reduce consumption because they diminish the real value of personal assets and make individuals feel poorer. Higher prices increase the cost of investment projects and thereby reduce the projects that are profitable at any given interest rate (they move the demand for investment in unless expected returns are correspondingly inflated). Higher prices reduce the quantity of goods and services that a government can afford with any expected collection of tax revenue. Higher prices make domestic goods more expensive relative to world prices and reduce the demand for exports.]

2. The first column of Table 8-1 records a series of changes in economic circumstance. Indicate the component of aggregate demand that would be most directly affected in the second column and the direction of that effect in the third column; use (+) to designate an increase and (−) to signify a reduction. The first row is completed for your reference.

Table 8-1
Exercises in Changing Aggregate Demand

(1)	(2)	(3)
a. Increased population	Consumption	(+)
b. Reduced money supply	______	______
c. Increased personal income taxes	______	______
d. Severe recession abroad	______	______
e. Anticipated recession at home	______	______
f. Anticipated recession abroad	______	______
g. Rapid escalation in house prices	______	______
h. An October stock market crash	______	______
i. Diminished defense spending in the wake of the INF treaty	______	______
j. Higher prices abroad	______	______

b. investment; (−) (through higher interest rates) **c.** consumption; (−) (through reduced disposable income) **d.** net exports; (−) (through less foreign demand for domestic goods) **e.** investment; (−) (Through the fear of lower profits) **f.** investment; (−) (through the fear of lower profits in the export markets) **g.** consumption; (+) (through increased consumer wealth) **h.** consumption; (−) (through reduced consumer wealth) and/or investment; (−) (through increased cost of raising funds and reduced wealth) **i.** government; (−) (through reduced government spending) **j.** net exports; (+) (through reduced imports that are now relatively more expensive)

3. Consult Figures 8-1 and 8-2. On both are depicted aggregate supply schedules based upon a potential output of $1000 (billion). Identify the indicated figure with either the classical or the Keynesian view of the economic world in the spaces provided below:

a. Figure 8-1: ______________________

b. Figure 8-2: ______________________

The (*Keynesian / classical*) view holds that a reduction in aggregate demand will cause no significant change in GNP because there will be (*an immediate / no significant*) change in prices. The appropriate representation of the aggregate supply curve is therefore (*a horizontal line up to / a vertical line directly above*) potential output. The (*Keynesian / classical*) view meanwhile holds that a reduction in aggregate demand will cause GNP to fall by more than the initial reduction in demand because there will be (*an immediate / no significant*) change in prices. The appropriate representation of the aggregate supply curve is therefore (*a horizontal line up to / a vertical line directly above*) potential output.

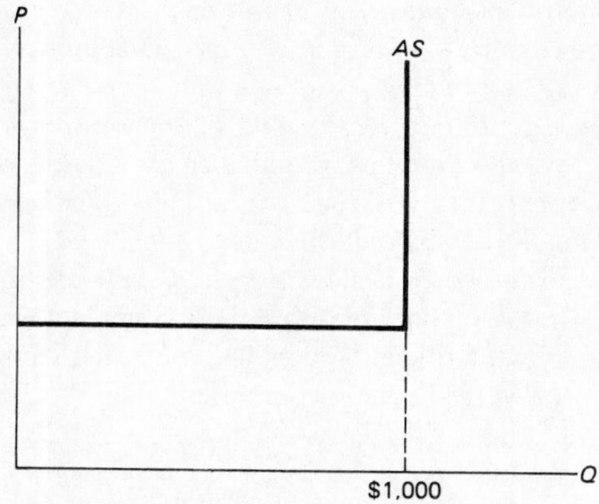

Figure 8-1

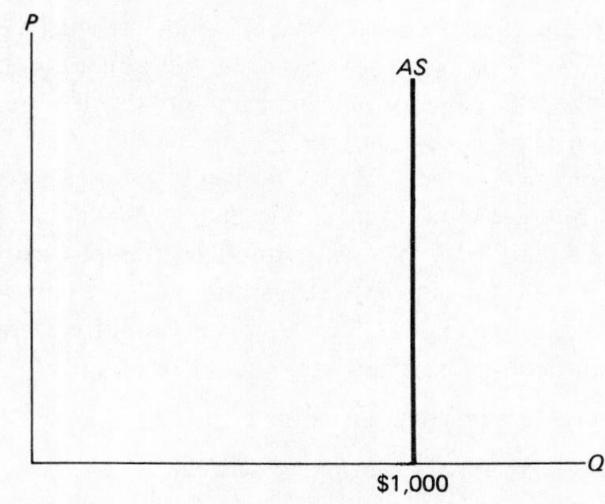

Figure 8-2

a. Keynesian **b.** classical; classical; an immediate; a vertical line directly above; Keynesian; no significant; a horizontal line up to

4. The classical view of the economic world is based upon the immediate responsiveness of wages and prices to disequilibrium. Belief in the this responsiveness was dealt a severe blow by (*World War II / the stock market crash of 1929 / the Great Depression*). A persistent unemployment rate of about (*8 percent / 25 percent / 34 percent*) during the early 1930s cast serious doubt on the ability of wages to fall in response to excess supply of labor. Even today, many reasons why wages appear to be sticky, at least "sticky-down," can be advanced; list at least four:

a. ______________________

b. ______________________

c. ______________________________

d. ______________________________

If you accept the stickiness of wages, as the Keynesians do, then it (*is / is not*) possible for an equilibrium to persist with a high rate of unemployment of not only labor but also other productive resources. In response to this situation, a Keynesian would prescribe (*nothing, because nothing would work / some kind of increase in aggregate demand / some kind of reduction in aggregate demand*) that would increase equilibrium GNP and thus employment. A classicist would prescribe (*nothing, because nothing is required / some sort of increase in aggregate demand / some sort of reduction in aggregate supply*); he or she would remark either that the existing unemployment was voluntary or that artificial barriers had prevented the necessary movement of wages down to equilibrium.

---

the Great Depression; 25 percent **a.** multiyear (3) labor contracts **b.** cost-of-living clauses **c.** regulated prices **d.** the price-setting inertia of large corporations; is; some kind of increase in aggregate demand; nothing, because nothing is required

5. In the spaces provided in Table 8-2, indicate what a Keynesian and a classicist would expect to be the effect on GNP and prices of the following events. Indicate only the direction of the expected effect by recording a (+) for "up," (−) for "down," and (0) for "no change." It may be useful (as it always seems to be) to represent the event on the graph with the appropriate aggregate supply curve drawn beforehand. Graphs hardly ever generate any news, but they frequently make it easier to apply something that we already know. Assume no effect other than the direct effect of the event noted on one curve.

A: An increase in potential output

B: A large increase in aggregate demand

C: An increase in interest rates that depresses aggregate demand

D: An increase in OPEC oil prices that depresses the demand for other goods and services

E: A major catastrophe that reduces potential output by 25 percent

Table 8-2

	Keynesian		Classicist	
Case	**Price**	**Output**	**Price**	**Output**
A	____	____	____	____
B	____	____	____	____
C	____	____	____	____
D	____	____	____	____
E	____	____	____	____

Reading across rows: A; (0), (0), (−), (+); B: (+), (+), (+), (0); C: (−), (−), (−), (0); D: (−), (−), (−), (0); E: (0) though perhaps (+) if potential output is now less than demand, (0) though perhaps (−) if potential output is now lower than the old equilibrium, (+), (−)

We now turn to a more thorough development of the simple Keynesian multiplier model of output determination. The critical concept underlying the Keynesian construction is one of equilibrium. Although it might look different in the geometry of consumption, investment, and GNP, the Keynesian equilibrium notion to be developed here is really the very same as the one presented earlier in terms of aggregate supply and aggregate demand. Even in its simplest form, though, the Keynesian equilibrium is much more than an intersection of two lines in the geometry of price indexes and aggregate quantity measures. From a Keynesian perspective, an equilibrium level of GNP is one from which actual GNP has no tendency to move. Why? Because none of its components has any disposition to move. Moreover, actual GNP need not be in equilibrium. If it is out of equilibrium, it must be rising or falling in value toward equilibrium over time; and it must continue to rise or fall until it reaches equilibrium. Finally, even equilibrium GNP does not necessarily guarantee full employment.

To emphasize that final point, Keynesians hold that equilibrium GNP and full-employment GNP are two different things and that they need not match. While it is possible, in the Keynesian view, for GNP to be in equilibrium with resources fully employed, it is also possible for GNP to be in equilibrium at a level well below full employment—in a serious recession or depression like that of the 1930s. On the other side of the coin, Keynesians see the possibility that actual GNP may be at full employment and be out of equilibrium if the economy is trying to reach an unattainable point beyond full employment. In sum, the fundamental Keynesian insight is that there is no automatic tendency for GNP to gravitate toward a level that is warranted or desired. It is the task of the remainder of this chapter to show how that might be so.

To simplify matters, Chapter 8 presents a closed economy (i.e., no exports or imports) in which government spending and taxation are negligible. Before you start laughing too hard, you should be warned that this is an assumption which will soon lapse—in the very next chapter. For the time being, though, no government sector means that NNP and disposable income are virtually identical. Depreciation is also taken to be negligible, so GNP and NNP also match. This stripping-down process, while it clears away a lot of important detail, greatly simplifies the analysis that follows. It does not, however, significantly distort the fundamental reasoning behind its applicability.

Chapter 7 noted that consumption expenditure is determined primarily by disposable income. In Figure 8-3, though, C is shown varying with GNP rather than DI.

Why do we do that? Because it is the level of GNP that we want to explain, and the simplification process just outlined has assured us that GNP = NNP = *DI*. Notice, too, that the consumption function drawn in Figure 8-3 is a straight line. Giving the function a little real-life curvature would not alter the conclusions significantly, but it would seriously complicate the analysis. The point here is to understand how consumption, as a part of aggregate demand, helps to determine equilibrium GNP. For that purpose, adding curvature to the consumption function has no utility.

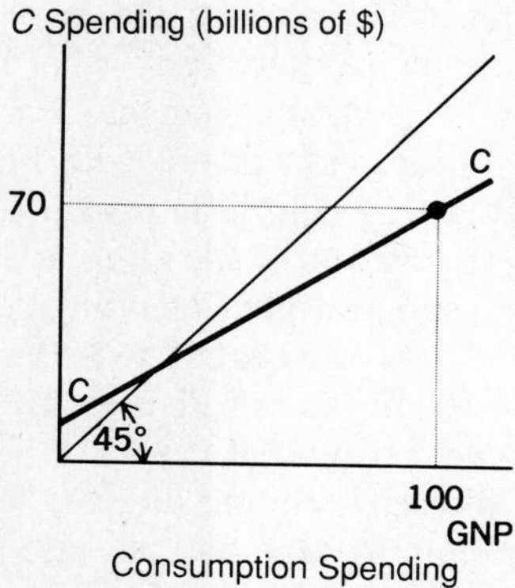

Figure 8-3

Figure 8-4 depicts a simple picture of investment spending. The solid *I* line, for example, shows investment fixed at $30 (billion) regardless of the level of GNP. This is unrealistic, as well, because any change in GNP is likely to affect investment. Again, we start with the simplest case so that we can focus attention on the determination of GNP and not the complications of investment's dependence on GNP. Note in passing, though, that the effects of changes in other economic and/or psychological factors can be captured even in this simple framework. Investment might drop to, e.g., $20 (billion) if people get pessimistic; the broken *I′* line would then apply. Interest rates might fall, on the other hand, so investment might climb to, again e.g., $40 (billion); the dotted *I″* line would then apply.

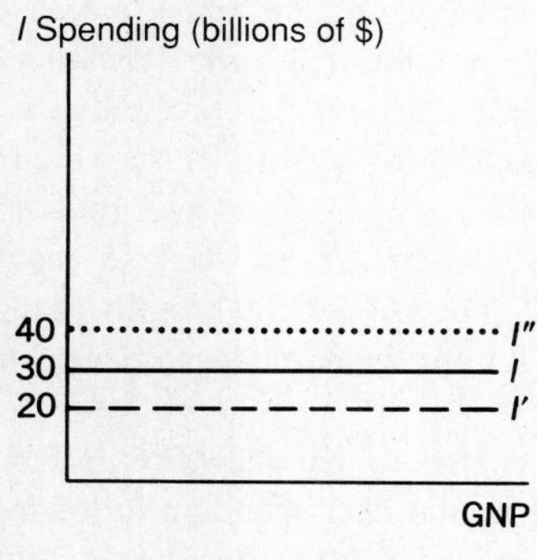

Figure 8-4

We begin working within the simple model of Figures 8-3 and 8-4 by considering, quite deliberately, an equilibrium economy with I = $30, C = $70, and GNP = $100 (in billions). Saving, therefore, is $30 billion and matches investment. There are various ways to grasp the notion of equilibrium, and the equality of saving and investment is certainly a good one. So, too, is the equality between total income earned and total expenditure on goods and services; in this case, total income is GNP and equals $100 billion, which is a value that is matched by the sum of the two nonzero components of aggregate demand: C = $70 billion and I = $30 billion.

With equilibrium firmly established as a concept, the next set of questions focuses on shocks to that equilibrium. What can make it change? In the simple model which we are presently considering, only two things could throw an economy out of equilibrium: (1) a decision to change the level of investment up or down and/or (2) a decision to change the level of consumption up or down. In terms of Figures 8-3 and 8-4, either the *I* line must shift or the *C* line must shift. Without one or the other of these shifts, a Keynesian equilibrium is, in this simple model, eternally durable.

Investment is, of course, inherently volatile. That was one of the lessons of Chapter 7. Disturbances to equilibria in simple models like ours are therefore usually cast in terms of sudden, unanticipated changes in *I*, and that is the tact to be taken here. The consumption function can also shift, to be sure, but the effects of such a shift are similar to the effects of a change in investment, and their coverage is postponed until later.

6. Figures 8-5 (consumption) and 8-6 (investment) are similar in construction to Figures 8-3 and 8-4.

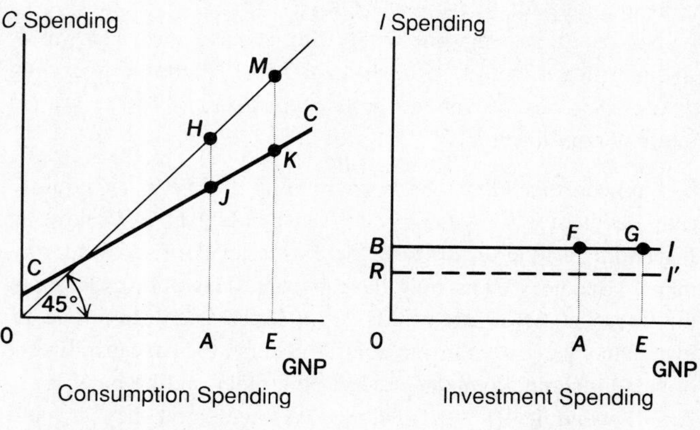

Figure 8-5 **Figure 8-6**

a. Consider Figure 8-6. (Disregard for the moment the broken *I′* line at height *RO*.) The solid *I* line at height *BO* is horizontal. To draw this line horizontally is to say that if the level of GNP were to rise, the amount of investment spending would (*rise / remain unchanged / fall*); if the level of GNP were to fall, *I* spending would (*rise / remain unchanged / fall*).

b. Consider Figure 8-5. It says that if the amount of GNP were to be *OE*, the amount of consumption spending would be (*HA / JA / ME / KE*). With GNP at *OE*, the amount of saving would be (*HA / JA / MK / KE*).

If, however, GNP were to be at the lower level *OA*, then *C* spending would be (*HA / JA / ME / KE*), and *S* would be (*HJ / JA / MK / KE*).

---

a. remain unchanged; remain unchanged **b.** *KE; MK; JA; HJ*

7. If GNP is to be "in equilibrium," the amount of *S* and *I* must be equal. Measure the two *S* amounts indicated on Figure 8-5 (*HJ* and *MK*), and compare them with the investment amount indicated by the solid *I* line (*BO, FA,* or *GE*) in Figure 8-6. The *S* value that would match this *I* value would be (*HJ / MK*). That is to say, *S* and *I* will be equal when *S* has climbed to level *MK*. This would call for a GNP level of (*OA / OE*).

Given the *I* level *BO* (or *FA* or *GE*) and the consumption function of Figure 8-5, the equilibrium GNP level must be *OE*. This is the only GNP value at which *C*-spending plans and *I*-spending plans "fit together" properly. Equilibrium is characterized either by

$$S = I \qquad \text{(i.e., } MK = GE\text{)}$$

or by

$$GNP = C + I \qquad \text{(i.e., } OE = KE + GE\text{)}$$

MK; OE

8. a. Alternatively, suppose that the total of investment spending is indicated in Figure 8-6 by level *RO* and not by *BO*. What would the equilibrium value of GNP then be? Again measuring *S* against *I*, it follows that saving would have to be (*HJ / MK*). Saving would be this amount only if GNP were at the corresponding level, namely, (*OA / OE*).

Notice in passing one interesting consequence: if the *I*-spending level were to drop from *BO* to *RO*, then *C* spending would (*also have dropped / remain unchanged / have risen*) in the new equilibrium.

b. Suppose that GNP has been holding steady at an equilibrium level of *OE*, with investment spending at *BO*. Now let *I* spending suddenly drop to the lower level of *RO* and stay there. (Business firms may have become less optimistic about the future.) The impact of this cut in *I* spending does not occur instantaneously. At the moment it occurs, the last installment of GNP income payments made at the older and higher *I* level is still wending its way toward consumers, and they are still spending accordingly. So we have a situation in which GNP (*OE*) is not equal to the sum of *C* spending (*KE*) and *I* spending (*RO*). GNP is out of equilibrium. Because of the drop in *I* spending, it is going to (*fall / rise*).

c. The following table shows three sets of values based on Figures 8-5 and 8-6. In at least one, the situation is "out of equilibrium." Which one, or ones?

Case	GNP	C	I	S
(1)	*OA*	*JA*	*RO*	*HJ*
(2)	*OA*	*JA*	*BO*	*HJ*
(3)	*OE*	*KE*	*BO*	*MK*

---

a. *HJ*; OA; also have dropped **b.** fall **c.** **(2)** [$BO \neq HJ$ and $OA \neq (JA + BO)$]

It should be clear, by now, that investment spending can call the tune in determining the level of GNP. We must, therefore, explore more fully what happens when the level of this *I* spending changes. For this, we use the figures (in billions) associated with Figures 8-3 and 8-4. GNP has been in equilibrium at a level of $100, with *I* spending at $30 and *C* spending at $70. But, as in question 5 above, suppose that *I* spending drops. Suppose, in particular, that it drops from $30 to $20 and that it stays at $20. The horizontal *I* line of Figures 8-4 and 8-6 drops to a new and lower position at *I′*.

The flow of money spending directed toward producers has dropped from $100 to $90 because the *I*-spending component of this flow has dropped. It will take a little time before consumers begin to feel the impact of this. When business was paying out $100 in wages and salaries, interest and dividend payments, it was simply passing on money it received from the buyers of consumption goods and of investment goods. When (because of the drop in investment spending) this incoming flow drops to $90, then the earnings flow (wages and salaries, dividend payments, etc.) *must* also drop correspondingly. There is no alternative source which could maintain the sum of those payments at the old $100 level. Some workers will be laid off, or required to work short time, and total profits earned by incorporated and unincorporated businesses will fall. Specifically, the flow of earned income reaching consumers must likewise drop from $100 to $90. Not great news, to be sure, but the story is not over; the news gets worse.

9. a. When income (which here we are measuring in the form of GNP) drops, *C* spending will (*drop / remain constant / rise*); this is what the consumption function tells us. The question is, "By how much?" To answer this, we must know the (*average / marginal*) propensity to consume. [Now you can begin to understand why we lavished so much time on the *MPC* in Chapter 7. The *MPC* will tell us the change (rise or fall) in *C* that goes with any given change (rise or fall) in income received.]

Suppose, for example, that the *MPC* is 0.6, or 6/10. This means that the reduction in *C* spending following a $10 reduction in income will be $(*0 / 6 / 10*). That is, with income now at $90 rather than $100, *C* spending, instead of being $70, will be $(*10 / 64 / 70 / 90 / 100*). And the amount saved out of this income of \$90, rather than being \$30, will be \$(*0 / 6 / 10 / 26 / 30 / 36*).

b. Investment spending, remember, has dropped to \$20 and stays at \$20. After the cut in C just reviewed, is $S = I$? (*Yes / No*). Is GNP at an equilibrium level? (*Yes / No*)

---

a. drop as well; marginal; 6; 64; 26 **b.** No; No

We now reach the point in the analysis at which the notion of "multiplier" must be confronted. Although C spending has fallen from \$70 to \$64 in response to the \$10 drop in GNP, we are still nowhere near a new equilibrium GNP level. The fact that GNP is still out of equilibrium is evident from the fact that S (\$26) is still not equal to I (\$20).

The all-important point is that any drop in consumption spending has exactly the same effect on production and on incomes earned as a drop in investment spending. Consumption spending has fallen from \$70 to \$64. To producers, this means that the demand for consumer goods has fallen off; and a smaller volume of such goods produced and sold means a smaller total of incomes earned.

10. a. If the total of incomes earned by producing and selling consumer goods drops by \$6, this means a drop of \$(*3 / 6 / 10*) in GNP. Note that this is in addition to the initial drop of \$10 set off by the reduction in I spending. So GNP, which first fell from \$100 to \$90, drops further to \$(*60 / 80 / 84 / 88*).

b. To review the sequence of events thus far, and to extend it:

Event 1: Investment spending falls from \$30 to \$20. GNP consequently falls from \$100 to \$90. This means a drop in employment, and a \$10 drop in incomes earned, for the firms and the individuals producing investment goods.

Event 2: With lower incomes, the people in these investment-goods industries must reduce their consumption spending—specifically, the income drop of \$10 with a marginal propensity to consume of 0.6 causes consumption to fall by \$6. That is, total consumption drops from \$70 to \$64. Saving (which had been \$30) drops by 0.4 times \$10, to \$26. GNP falls again, this time from \$90 to \$84. [Note exactly what we did in event 2: we recognized the immediate (not full) consequences of event 1, the \$10 drop in I spending. These consequences were C spending down \$6, GNP down \$6, S down by \$4.]

Event 3: This reduction of \$6 in investment-worker spending (event 2) means a drop of \$6 in incomes for the business firms and individuals engaged in producing consumer goods. A different group is hit, but the overall effects are similar: a further drop in employment and incomes. The second income reduction is \$6, the consumption spending cut is 0.6 times \$6, or \$3.6. Adding this to the initial drop of \$6, total C spending is now down from its original level of \$70 to \$(*50.6 / 56.4 / 58.6 / 60.4 / 64.0*). Saving is correspondingly down. Its original level was \$30; it dropped first by \$4, and has now fallen by 0.4 times \$6 or \$2.4. So its level is now \$(*20.0 / 21.6 / 22.4 / 23.0 / 23.6*). GNP has fallen again; its level is now \$(*80.4 / 80.6 / 82.0 / 86.4 / 90.0*).

What we have done in event 3 is recognize the immediate (not full) consequences of event 2, a reduction in C spending and in GNP of \$6. (Event 3 will in turn set off event 4.)

Notice the roles played by the fall in C and by the fall in S in this around-and-around process. It is the drop in consumer spending that precipitates another drop in incomes earned (since what you call expenditure is really income on the other side) and hence a further (but smaller) drop in such consumer buying. It is the drop in saving that indicates we are drawing closer to a new equilibrium. We assume (for simplicity; this is not necessarily indicative of how it would behave in real life) that investment spending, once having dropped from \$30, holds steady at \$20. By the close of event 3 (and by comparison with its original level), total saving has moved (and is moving) (*closer to / farther away from*) this new and lower investment-spending level.

Event 4: This of course repeats event 3, but on a still smaller scale. It concerns the results of a drop in GNP and C spending of \$3.6—i.e., still another reduction in such spending, this time of 0.6 times \$3.6, and a corresponding reduction in saving, this time of 0.4 times \$3.6.

We need hardly pursue this sequence through events 5, 6, 7, ... The process will gradually peter out, ending when (with investment at \$20) (*GNP has fallen to zero / saving has fallen to zero / saving has fallen to \$20*).

---

a. 6; 84 **b.** 60.4; 23.6; 80.4; closer to; saving has fallen to \$20

Question 10 had two points. First, it exercised your understanding of equilibrium. Throughout the "events" of question 10, GNP was, in fact, out of equilibrium. To cement your grasp of why, recall what happened when GNP first fell to \$90 before consumption spending had begun to drop from its initial level of \$70. By the $S = I$ test, of course, C = \$70 and I = \$20 could not have been equilibrium because saving was \$30. But what of the consumption side of the analysis; did total spending match supply? Does not, in particular, a \$90 GNP conform with consumption of \$70 and investment of \$20? Sure, but only if consumption is really \$70 when GNP is \$90, and this is not the case. We can expect C to be \$70 if and only if GNP is \$100. It was precisely because GNP fell to \$90 that we had to move to event 2, reducing C from \$70 to \$64. Thus if you are using the GNP $= C + I$ test, make sure that the C figure on the right-hand side of this equation matches up with the GNP figure on the left; i.e., make certain that the C figure is what it should be, according to the propensity to consume, given that particular GNP.

The second point of question 10 was an initial elaboration of the multiplier sequence. Mathematically, this kind of sequence is known as a convergent geometric progression—an elegant phrase, useful for impressing your friends (or some of them) on social occasions, if you can manage to work it into the conversation. All you need to know about such a progression is the its sum has a finite limit.[1] That is, GNP does not keep dropping until it collapses to zero or below. The sequence here involved is as follows: $10 + 6 + 3.6 + \cdots$ etc. The sum of this sequence, fully extended, is 25, not infinity. The full GNP drop will be \$25, and GNP, upon dropping from its original value of \$100, will stop when it reaches a new equilibrium at \$75.

How do we know that? A straight-line consumption function with an *MPC* of 0.6 (i.e., a slope of 0.6) which matches a GNP value of \$100 with a consumption value of \$70 (the original equilibrium position) must have the following equation:

$$C = \$10 + 0.6(\text{GNP})$$

Try it! GNP = \$100 means that C = \$10 + \$60 = \$70. So what happens when GNP = \$75? C = \$10 + \$45 = \$55 and S = \$75 − \$55 = \$20. Since I = \$20, now, this *must* be equilibrium. Also, $C + I$ = \$55 + \$20 = \$75 = GNP.

11. In equilibrium, saving equals investment, so we must be able to use a saving-investment diagram to illustrate equilibrium GNP. If we know the consumption function, then Chapter 7 tells us that we can derive the savings schedule according to S = GNP − C. In Figure 8-7, the *SS* line is such a savings schedule; it corresponds to Figure 8-3's consumption function. The solid *I* line in this figure repeats that of Figure 8-4. The intersection of *SS* and *I* curves, at GNP = \$100, indicates the equilibrium GNP level, because it is the only GNP level at which *S* and *I* are equal.

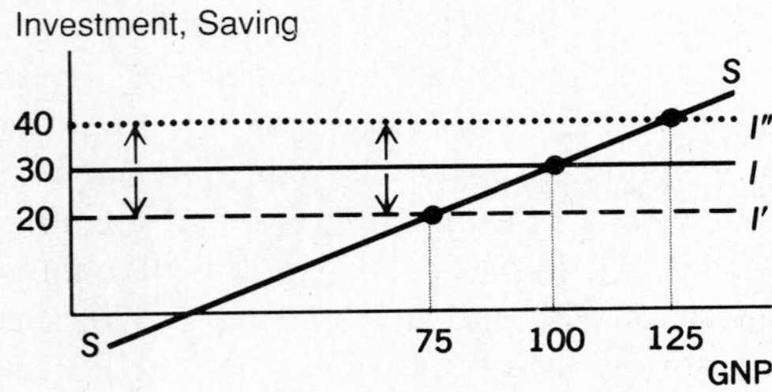

Figure 8-7

a. The broken I' line shows what happens if *I* spending drops from \$30 to \$20. The new equilibrium GNP must be \$(*20 / 30 / 60 / 75 / 90 / 100*), for the same reason as before. If *I* spending is to be \$20, then *S* must be \$20 also; \$75 is the only GNP level at which *S* is \$20.

b. Also shown in Figure 8-7 is a dotted I'' line, at level \$40. If *I* spending were to rise to this level, the diagram indicates that the resulting GNP equilibrium level would be \$(*75 / 100 / 110 / 125 / 150*). (CAUTION: Should full-employment GNP happen to be in the vicinity of \$100, the applicability of the Keynesian model lapses and this equilibrium GNP might be unattainable.)

a. 75 **b.** 125

12. As question 7 noted, there are two possible algebraic statements of the equilibrium requirement: $S = I$, and GNP = $C + I$. Each has its corresponding diagram. Make sure that you understand that the two diagrams are simply two alternative ways of illustrating exactly the same set of relationships. The figure corresponding to GNP = $C + I$ is the now-familiar 45° diagram, already used in this chapter as Figures 8-3 and 8-5.

a. In Figure 8-8, the line *CC* is the same consumption function we have already used in Figures 8-3 and 8-5. Remember: the amount of *C* spending, for any given GNP level, is measured vertically. At the GNP level indicated by *OG* in Figure 8-8, *C* spending would be *DG*. If the GNP level were *OH*, then *C* spending would be (*KD / DG / LM / MH*).

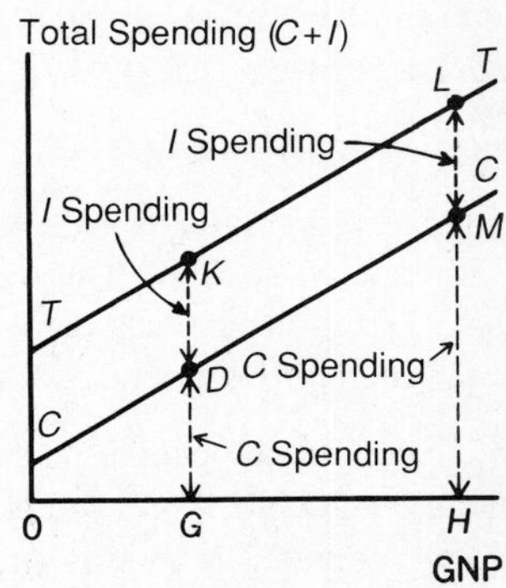

Figure 8-8

For GNP purposes, our interest is in total spending—in *C* spending plus *I* spending. There is no reason why we cannot add *I* spending on this diagram, thus showing total spending. We draw the line *TT* above *CC*, and we make the vertical distance between these two lines the amount of *I* spending. The *TT* line thus reflects aggregate demand for any level of GNP.

b. This means that the vertical distance from any point on *TT* down to the axis line now measures total spending, $C + I$. At GNP level *OG*, the *I* spending would be *KD*, the *C* spending would be *DG*, and total spending, $I + C$, would be *KG*—i.e., *KD* plus *DG*.

Similarly, if the GNP level were *OH*, the amount of *I* spending would be indicated by (*LM / DG / MH*). *C* spending would

[1] Algebra says the formula for an infinite geometric progression is

$$1 + r + r^2 + r^3 + \cdots + r^n \cdots + = \frac{1}{1 - r}$$

as long as r is less than 1.

be measure by (*LM / DG / MH*). Total spending would be measured by (*LM / KG / MH / LH*).

c. Figure 8-9 is basically the same as Figure 8-8. The same *CC* and *TT* lines appear. We have simply added a 45° line. The fundamental issue, now, is this: pick any level of GNP at random. Given a consumption function and a level of investment, would that GNP represent an equilibrium?

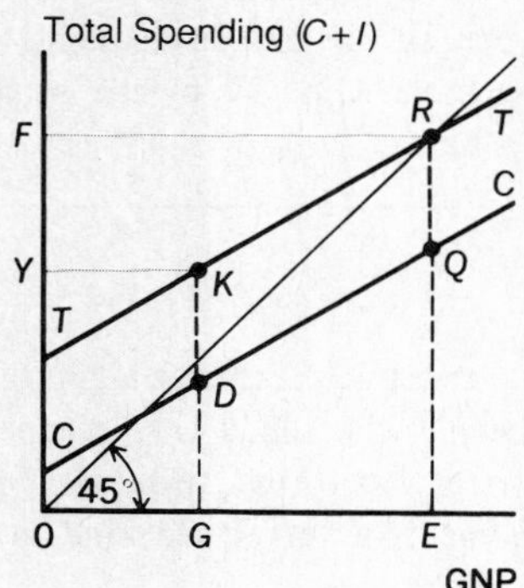

Figure 8-9

For example, take a GNP of *OG* in Figure 8-9. Total spending, $C + I$, would then be *KG*. But point *K* is off the 45° line. So *KG* is not equal to *OG*. That is, GNP would *not* be equal to $C + I$. In fact, an equilibrium GNP level can only occur at the point where the total-spending line, *TT*, cuts across the 45° line. This is at point *R*, indicating a GNP of *OE*. Here, total spending of *RE* (*is / is not*) just equal to GNP of *OE*.

d. If the two equilibrium conditions come to one and the same thing, then it ought to be true that the equilibrium GNP of *OE* depicted in Figure 8-9 marks an $S = I$ position, and it does. Saving at any GNP level is the vertical distance from the consumption function up to the 45° line. Hence at GNP of *OE*, saving must be *RQ*. This (*is / is not*) the same as investment.

At any GNP lower than (to the left of) *OE*, *S* would be (*less than / equal to / greater than*) *I*. At any GNP higher than (to the right of) *OE*, *S* would be (*less than / equal to / greater than*) *I*.

a. *MH* **b.** *LM; MH; LH* **c.** is **d.** is; less than; greater than

13. Suppose there is a sudden and drastic drop in the level of *I* spending: it falls, say, from $30 (billion) per period to $10. In terms of Figure 8-9, this would mean a (*rise / drop*) in the total-spending line *TT*.

Figure 8-10 shows this event. The *TT* line drops from its former position (the solid black line) to the level *T′T′* (the broken line). The new total-spending line will cut the 45° line at point (*X / R / D / Q*), and the new equilibrium level of GNP indicated will be (*OG / OE*). That is, the drastic drop in investment spending has produced an even more drastic reduction in incomes and thus employment.

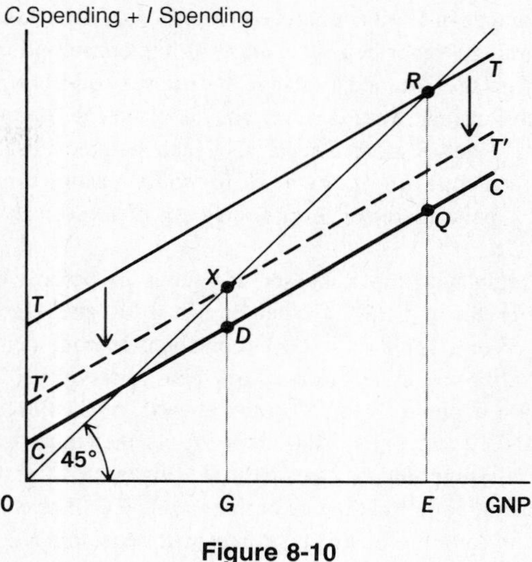

Figure 8-10

drop; *X; OG*

14. a. Remember that any such change in *I* spending has a magnified, or "multiplied," effect on the GNP level because it sets off a series of *C* changes (as earlier outlined).

If the multiplier figure is 3, and *I* spending rises by $10 billion, then GNP will (*rise / fall*) by $(*10 / 20 / 30 / 40 / 50*) billion. If *I* spending rises by $10 billion with a multiplier of 4, then GNP will (*rise / fall*) by $(*10 / 20 / 30 / 40 / 50*) billion.

The multiplier formula is

$$\frac{1}{1 - MPC} \quad \text{or} \quad \frac{1}{MPS}$$

This means that if the *MPC* is 0.6, the multiplier is (*1 / 2 / 2½ / 3 / 3½ / 4*). If the MPC is 0.8, the multiplier is (*1 / 2 / 2½ / 3½ / 4 / 5*).

b. Suppose there is a change in investment (either rise or fall) of $10. If the *MPC* is 0.6, the resulting change in GNP (rise or fall) will be $(*10 / 20 / 25 / 30 / 50*). If the *MPC* is 0.8, the resulting change in GNP (rise or fall) will be $(*10 / 20 / 25 / 30 / 50*).

(NOTE: The multiplier formula given above holds only in the simplified conditions used in this chapter. In Chapter 9, we will incorporate some complications, and the multiplier formula will be changed accordingly.)

a. rise; 30; rise; 40; 2½; 5 **b.** 25; 50

15. An equilibrium GNP will not be disturbed unless either the *II* line or the *CC* line shifts to a new position. (That is, it will not be disturbed unless there is some change either in investment-spending plans or in consumer-spending plans. We are of course still assuming the influence of government spending and taxation to be entirely absent.) Thus far, we have considered only disturbances in equilibrium GNP produced by a change in investment spending (a shift in the *II* line of Figure

8-4). Changes in GNP are most commonly attributed to changes in *I* spending. Nevertheless, changes in the consumption function can occur. Any such change will upset equilibrium GNP just as an *I* change would. Here, you should recall *Study Guide* questions 7 and 8 from Chapter 7 which pointed out that the *CC* line can shift up (or down) if, for some reason, consumers decide to spend more (or less) money out of a given *DI* (here, a given GNP).

We begin with the same set of figures as before: GNP is in equilibrium at $100, *C* spending is $70, and *I* spending is $30. Saving is likewise $30. For some reason, consumers decide to become more thrifty. They plan to spend $10 less on consumption, and to save $10 more, at each and any GNP level. Since GNP is currently $100, this means they plan to spend $60 on consumption and to save $40. Figure 8-11 shows the same consumption function as before in line *CC*. The consumer decision to save more and spend less will cause the *CC* line to shift downward to the position *C′C′* (the broken line). The total-spending line, *TT* in Figure 8-12, is the sum of *C* + *I*. If *CC* is displaced vertically downward by $10 as in Figure 8-11, the same must hold for *TT*. It must shift downward to position *T′T′* (also a broken line).

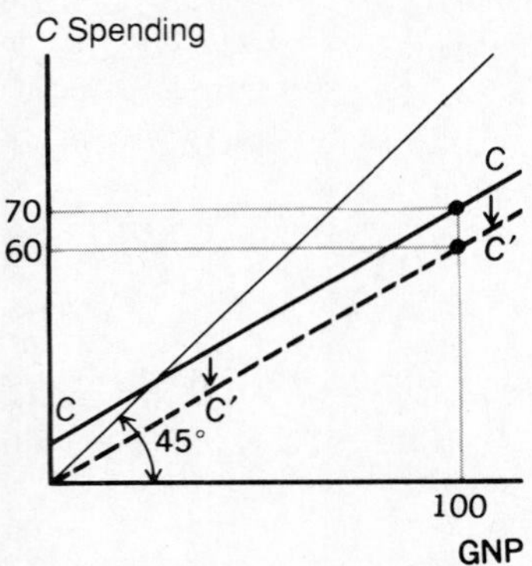

Figure 8-11

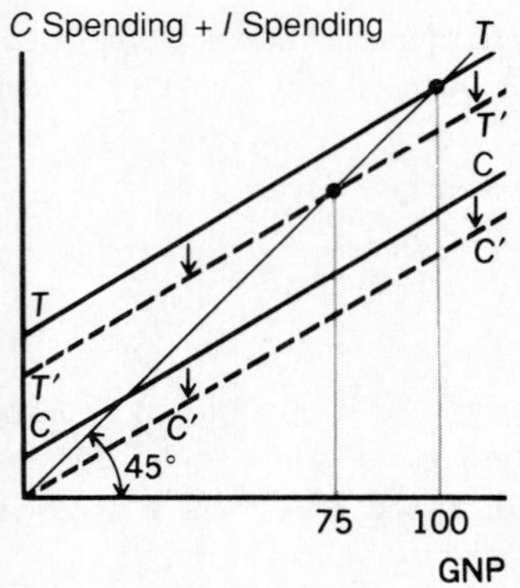

Figure 8-12

This (*affects / does not affect*) equilibrium GNP. GNP will (*fall / rise*). The resulting new equilibrium level of GNP indicated in Figure 8-12 is $_______ .

(Notice that this initial change in *C* spending has the same multiplier effect as a change in *I* spending would have: an initial change of $10 causes equilibrium GNP to change by $25. This follows directly, and only, from the fact that a $10 reduction in investment and a $10 increase in saving cause the same $10 discrepancy between saving and investment. On the 45° line graph, both changes shift line *TT* by the *same* amount in the *same* direction.

---

affects; fall; 75

16. The level of investment indicated throughout these exercises by *II* has been "scheduled," or "planned," investment. It is possible also to have "unscheduled," or "unintended," investment. Investment of this latter kind is symptomatic of disequilibrium in GNP.

Consider question 15's reduction in *C* spending. When this first occurs, department stores and other firms involved in retail trade may be taken by surprise. Their inventories pile up as a consequence of reduced consumer buying. Chapter 7 told us that any increase in inventories counts as investment. So, temporarily, the drop in *C* spending is matched by a rise in *I*. This makes it appear as if GNP were still in equilibrium because the total of *C* plus *I* is unchanged. In fact it is not, because the inventory pile-up (the increase in *I*) was unintended and unwanted. The stores will proceed to work down their inventories by canceling or reducing their orders to their suppliers. That is how the impact of reduced buying spreads to other firms; that is how the drop in incomes begins. When the new equilibrium is finally reached, there is (*still some / no longer any*) unscheduled, unintended, investment.

---

no longer any

17. You are given the following consumption function for some economic community: consumption spending for each and any level of GNP will be $20 (billion) plus three-fifths of that GNP.

a. What will consumption be if GNP is $40? _______

If GNP is $60? _______ If GNP is $100? _______

b. Draw this consumption function in Figure 8-13.

c. Suppose that investment spending will be $20, at each and every level of GNP. Draw in Figure 8-13 a total-spending line (assuming government spending to be zero). What will be the resulting equilibrium value of GNP? _______

---

a. $44; $56; $80 **c.** $100

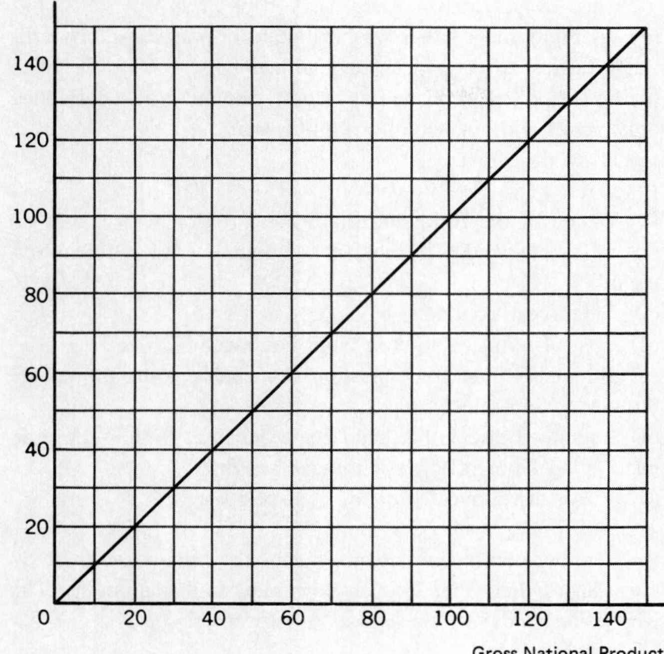

Figure 8-13

18. You are given the following information:

1. The full-employment level of GNP in a certain economy is estimated at $100 billion.
2. The amount of consumption spending to be expected at this full-employment GNP level is $80 billion.
3. The marginal propensity to consume is 0.8.
4. The amount of planned investment spending will be $10 billion, regardless of the GNP level.

a. Assuming that all government items (spending and taxation) are equal to zero, then the equilibrium level of GNP will be (pick one):

(1) $100 billion.

(2) $90 billion.

(3) less than $90 billion.

b. The increase in investment spending, if any, needed to bring GNP up to its full-employment, $100 billion level would be (pick one):

(1) zero.

(2) $10 billion.

(3) $20 billion.

(4) more than $20 billion.

---

a. (3) (Since the *MPC* is constant, the consumption function is a straight line. Since C = $80 when GNP = $100 and the *MPC* = 0.8, the equation for that line is $C = 0.8$ GNP. The savings schedule is therefore $S = 0.2$ GNP and $S = I$ at equilbrium when GNP = 50; there, too, $C + I$ = $40 + $10 = $50 = GNP.) **b. (2)** (New equilibrium at $100 must be supported by S = $20 = I, so I must climb by $10 from its original level. Note, alternatively, that the multiplier is (1/0.2) = 5, so a $10 increase in I will raise GNP by 5 × $10 = $50; i.e., from $50 to $100.)

19. The following figures (billions of dollars) indicate an economy's consumption function:

GNP:	130	150	170	190	210	230	250	270	290	310
C:	112	126	140	154	168	182	196	210	224	238

a. If the amount of investment spending is 60, and if government spending of all types is zero, what is the equilibrium level of GNP? . . . . ________

b. If the total of this investment spending should drop by 30, what would be the new resulting equilibrium level of GNP?

. . . . ________

---

a. $270 (where S = (GNP − C) = $60 = I) **b.** $170 (where S = $30)

20. Consult Figure 8-14. The top panel there will present equilibrium in the consumption-investment geometry of the Keynesian model; the bottom panel will present equilibrium in the aggregate supply-aggregate demand geometry of earlier chapters. Note that the shape of the aggregate supply curve drawn there conforms to the shape identified with the Keynesian view in the first part of the chapter.

Draw, first of all, an aggregate demand curve in the lower panel that would support the same equilibrium level as curve *TT* in the upper panel.

Now let investment increase to I' so that $T'T'$ becomes the appropriate representation of total spending. Draw a second aggregate demand curve in the bottom panel to illustrate the same new equilibrium. Reading from the vertical and horizontal axes, it would appear that a $10 increase in investment has produced a $(*5 / 10 / 15 / 30*) increase in GNP; the multiplier would, therefore, appear to be ________ .

Now consider $T''T''$ in the upper panel. It would appear, given the geometry of the upper panel, that the second $10 increase in investment should, by producing $T''T''$, cause GNP to increase by another $________ . This will, however, not be the case because $T''T''$ had already brought GNP up to its maximum potential. The second increase in I will simply cause (*prices / employment / output*) to rise. Show this by drawing a third aggregate demand curve on the lower panel.

---

downward sloping through E; downward sloping through E'; 30; 3; 30; prices; *downward sloping through E''* (*Note:* Italicized phrases give descriptions of demand curves to be drawn on the bottom panel of Figure 8-14.)

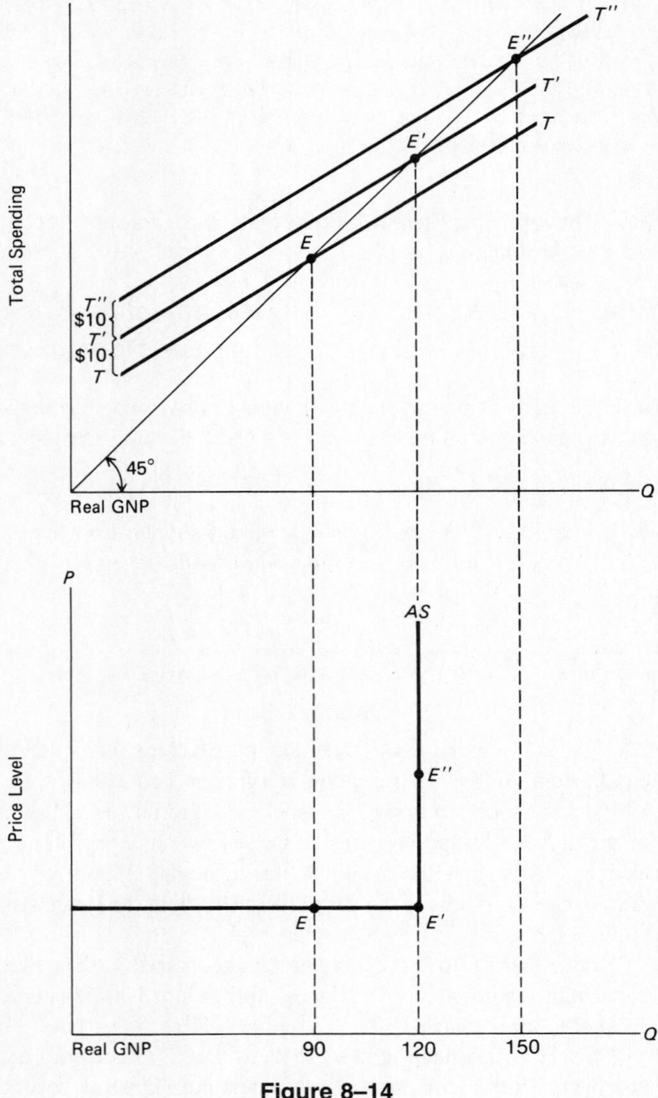

Figure 8–14

QUIZ: Multiple Choice

1. Keynes, in the "general theory," suggested:
(1) that wages and prices were unresponsive to disequilibrium in economic markets.
(2) a structure that can be summarized in its simplest form as a horizontal aggregate supply curve.
(3) that macroequilibrium could include massive numbers of unemployed workers.
(4) that active policy to manipulate aggregate demand could influence output and employment.
(5) all of the above.

2. By way of contrast, the classical view of macroeconomics is that:
(1) wages and prices are always responsive to disequilibrium.
(2) the aggregate supply curve is vertical at a level of GNP indicated by potential output.
(3) unemployment either was voluntary or was caused by artificial barriers to wage-necessary adjustments.
(4) active policy to change aggregate demand would influence only prices and not output or employment.
(5) all of the above.

3. Which of the following might be a reason why wages do not fall very rapidly in the face of high levels of unemployment?
(1) Three-year contracts.
(2) Cost-of-living clauses in labor contracts.
(3) Unemployment compensation that cushions the immediate blow of losing a job.
(4) Regulated prices that keep wage demands high among the negotiating labor officials who have seniority.
(5) All of the above.

4. Suppose that business firms change their plans and increase the total of their spending on new plant and equipment. The Keynesian model would lead us to expect:
(1) no change in GNP.
(2) GNP and consumer spending to rise.
(3) GNP to rise, but consumer spending to be unaffected.
(4) GNP to rise, but consumer spending to fall.
(5) GNP to fall, but consumer spending to rise.

5. If, on a graph of the consumption function, the entire curve were to shift to a new and different position above its previous position, this would mean that consumers decided:
(1) to increase the amount of their saving *S* because of an increase in income.
(2) to increase *S* because of some factor other than an increase in income.
(3) to reduce *S* because of a reduction in income.
(4) to reduce *S* because of some factor other than a reduction in income.
(5) to do none of the above necessarily, since a shift in the consumption function affects consumption, not saving.

6. In the simplest Keynesian model with only consumption and investment contributing to aggregate demand, if the value of the marginal propensity to consume is 0.8, then the value of the multiplier must be:
(1) 1.6.
(2) 2.5.
(3) 2.8.
(4) 4.
(5) 5.

7. If the amount of investment (*I*) spending should suddenly fall, then the Keynesian model predicts that:
(1) GNP will fall slowly, but the ultimate reduction in GNP will be less than the original decline in *I*.

(2) GNP will fall by an amount equal to the original decline in *I*.
(3) GNP will fall immediately by an amount less than the original decline in *I*, and it will show no tendency to fall further.
(4) it is more likely that GNP will rise rather than fall.
(5) GNP will fall until it has fallen by an amount considerably greater than the original decline in *I*.

8. A change in the total of consumer spending can have the same effect upon GNP (throwing it from equilibrium into disequilibrium, and so changing the GNP value by a multiplied amount) that a change in the total of investment spending would have:
(1) only if that *C*-spending change is set off by some factor other than a change in GNP.
(2) only if that *C*-spending change is itself set off by a change in GNP.
(3) regardless of the circumstances that set off the *C*-spending change.
(4) with respect to increases in *C*-spending only, not with respect to decreases.
(5) in no circumstances, since disequilibrium GNP results only from changes in *I* spending.

9. If an equilibrium level of GNP is altered by a reduction in planned investment spending, then we would expect to see:
(1) GNP fall but saving (*S*) rise.
(2) GNP fall but no change in *S*.
(3) GNP fall and *S* fall also.
(4) GNP remain unchanged but *S* fall.
(5) none of the preceding.

10. Assume that government spending and net exports are both zero. On a graph that plots spending against GNP, the intersection of the consumption function and a 45° line drawn up from the origin necessarily indicates:
(1) the GNP level at which net investment spending (*I*) first rises above zero.
(2) equality of consumption (*C*) and *I*.
(3) equilibrium GNP.
(4) equality of *C* and saving.
(5) none of the above, unless *I* happens to be zero.

11. Consider an economy with government spending and net exports both fixed at zero. Actual GNP would then be above its equilibrium level if:
(1) the amount that consumers planned to save exceeded the amount that businesses and others planned to invest.
(2) the total of planned consumption spending (*C*) exceeded the total of planned *I*.
(3) there were no unscheduled or unplanned *I*.
(4) GNP had moved temporarily above the breakeven point on the consumption function.
(5) the total of planned *I* plus the total of planned *C* exceeded the current level of GNP.

12. Which alternative in question 11 would be correct had that question referred to a GNP below its equilibrium level?
(1).
(2).
(3).
(4).
(5).

13. Before a particular Christmas, shoppers decide to spend considerably less than retail stores anticipated, leaving those stores with considerable unsold inventories of goods. This situation is an example of:
(1) planned investment.
(2) unscheduled saving.
(3) a rise in GNP.
(4) unscheduled investment.
(5) none of the preceding.

14. If GNP were to fall because of a decline in investment spending, we would expect to see:
(1) both consumption (*C*) and saving (*S*) rise.
(2) both *C* and *S* fall.
(3) *C* rise but *S* fall.
(4) *C* fall but *S* rise.
(5) neither *C* nor *S* change in value.

15. Without government spending and net exports, one way of specifying the requirement that must be satisfied if a given level of GNP is to be judged an equilibrium level is to assert that:
(1) the total of incomes earned must just equal the total that consumers are planning to spend out of that income plus the total they are planning to save.
(2) the total of consumer spending must be just equal to the breakeven level of income.
(3) the total of GNP must be just equal to the total of planned saving plus the total of planned investment.
(4) the total of incomes earned must just equal the total consumers are planning to spend out of that income plus the total of planned investment.
(5) the total of spending must be just enough to bring production to its full-employment level.

16. Suppose that the current level of GNP is $500 (billion) and that consumers wish to spend $390 (billion) of that $500 (billion) on consumption. Let the total amount of investment spending planned be $120 (billion). These figures indicate:
(1) that GNP is out of equilibrium and will fall in value.
(2) that GNP is out of equilibrium and will rise in value.
(3) that NP is out of equilibrium, although whether it will rise, fall, or remain at its present level is indeterminate.
(4) that GNP is in equilibrium.
(5) none of the above necessarily, since from the information given, GNP may be in equilibrium or out of it.

17. If the marginal propensity to save is 0.3 (i.e., 3/10), and investment spending rises by \$6 billion, then the simple Keynesian model with $G = X = 0$ would lead us to expect that the equilibrium level of GNP will increase by:
(1) \$2 billion.
(2) \$6 billion.
(3) \$18 billion.
(4) \$20 billion.
(5) \$60 billion.

18. In a certain country, (*a*) full employment implies a GNP of \$200 billion; (*b*) consumption expenditure at this full-employment level of GNP would be \$170 billion; (*c*) total investment expenditure will be \$20 billion regardless of the level of GNP; and (*d*) the country's *MPC* is 3/4. Given these facts and without any government spending or net exports, the equilibrium level of GNP will be:
(1) more than \$200 billion.
(2) \$200 billion.
(3) \$190 billion.
(4) less than \$190 billion.
(5) impossible to compute from information given.

19. With respect to the preceding question, the increase in investment spending needed to restore the economy to full employment would be:
(1) more than \$10 billion.
(2) \$10 billion.
(3) less than \$10 billion but a positive amount.
(4) zero.
(5) impossible to compute from information given.

20. The pure Keynesian multiplier applies:
(1) whenever investment increases.
(2) only when investment increases in any economy in which there exist unemployed resources.
(3) only when some economic variables like investment change in either direction, thereby either creating or putting to work unemployed resources.
(4) only to changes in government finance.
(5) none of the above.

SUGGESTED ANSWERS TO QUESTIONS IN THE TEXT: Chapter 8

1. In the context of this chapter, GNP $= CC + SS$ because there is no government sector and no foreign trade. In general, though, $DI = C + S$, by definition. It follows that any change in *DI* must be distributed between a change in *C* and a change in *S*. So,

$$\text{Change in } DI = \text{change in } C + \text{change in } S$$

Dividing both sides by the change in *DI*, then,

$$1 = MPC + MPS$$

Returning to this chapter's 45° graph, GNP $= C + S$. At the breakeven point, GNP $= C$, so *S* must equal 0.

2. Equilibrium is defined by $S = I$. If $I = 0$, then *S* must equal 0 in equilibrium; i.e., equilibrium must occur at the breakeven point where $C =$ GNP. If $I > 0$, then $S = I > 0$ in equilibrium, so $C <$ GNP.

3. Their equilvalence follows directly from GNP $= C + S$. In equilibrium, GNP $= C + I$, so $S = I$.

4. With $I =$ \$300, \$3900 is equilibrium; contraction is the result only for \$4200; expansion applies for listed values of \$3600 and below. With $I =$ \$400, \$4200 is equilibrium. Every \$100 change in *I* causes a \$300 change in GNP. The multiplier is equal to 3.

5. The common sense of the multiplier follows from the tracing of successively smaller changes in consumption caused by (e.g) a change in investment. The arithmetic follows from adding up the successively smaller changes in GNP according to the formula for a geometric series (footnote 1 in the *Guide*, 3 in the text). The geometry is shown in either the saving-investment graph or the 45° graph. The multiplier equals $1/(1 - MPC)$ or $1/MPS$.

6. $MPC = 2$ creates successively larger changes in consumption and thus GNP.

7. Consult the following table. It indicates the effects on GNP and price of the cases listed. A positive change is indicated by (+), a negative change by (−), and no change by (0).

	Keynesian		Classicist	
Case	**Price**	**GNP**	**Price**	**GNP**
(**a**)	(0)	(0)	(−)	(+)
(**b** small)	(0)	(+)	(+)	(0)
(**b** large)	(+)	(+)	(+ +)	(0)

8. The economy starts in equilibrium. The multiplier is (1/0.5) =2, so GNP increases by \$20. Producers of (and workers for) computers get the first \$10 increase in aggregate demand; the rest goes to the producers of (and workers for) consumer goods.

9. Equilibrium GNP (GNP*) solves $C + I =$ GNP*. With all the restrictions, GNP $= DI$, so $C + I =$ GNP* is really

$$(100 + 0.8\text{GNP}^*) + (50 + 0.1\text{GNP}^*) = \text{GNP}^*$$

Collecting terms, then,

$$150 = (1 - 0.9)\text{GNP}^*$$

so GNP* $= 1500$. If investment were to increase by 10, equilibrium would solve

$$160 = (1 - 0.9)\text{GNP}^{**}$$

so GNP** = 1600. The multiplier would appear to be 10. That is, in fact, correct, because aggregate demand is given by

$$C + I = (100 + 0.8\text{GNP}) + (50 + 0.1\text{GNP})$$

$$= 150 + 0.9\text{GNP};$$

the marginal propensity to spend is thus 0.9, and the multiplier is 1/(1 - 0.9) = 1/0.1 = 10.

CHAPTER 9

THE MULTIPLIER EXTENDED: FISCAL POLICY AND INTERNATIONAL TRADE

Chapter 8 presented all the essential elements of the Keynesian theory of output determination. It was also noted explicitly that the Keynesian view of the world represents only one polar vision of the workings of an economy that should always be tempered by a recognition of the contrasting, classical picture. Chapter 9 applies the fundamentals of that chapter to the study of fiscal policy—the expenditure of public funds and the collection of government taxes. It should be no surprise to discover that one's expectations about the effects of fiscal policy will depend critically upon one's sympathies in the Keynesian-classical controversy, and your understanding of this point will plant the seeds of understanding the synthesis of "modern mainstream theory."

Chapter 9 also explores what has become known as the "paradox of saving"—the counterintuitive notion that an increase in saving by everyone in an economy can actually reduce that economy's level of output and thus its source of well-being. The Keynesian-classical controversy will be seen to be important here, as well. You will, in fact, begin to see why macroeconomists with different feelings vis à vis the shape of the aggregate supply curve hardly ever agree on anything. When the chapter closes with a review of empirical estimates of the multiplier, you should, therefore, not be surprised by the wide range of disagreement. Economists who estimate multipliers face not only the uncertainties of dealing with an enormously complex economy but also the ramifications of different academic and philosophical traditions.

In between, you will also be introduced to the complication of opening the economy, i.e., of adding a foreign-trade sector to the construction of aggregate demand. You will see the fiscal policy and investment multipliers change if imports are sensitive to changes in domestic GNP, but that is the easy part. Adding a foreign sector brings questions of exchange-rate effects and international policy coordination to the fore, and they will be discussed, as well.

Having worked through this chapter, then, you will have not only accomplished the following objectives but also begun to understand both the wide-ranging implications of the Keynesian-classical debate and the complex interdependencies that frame the contemporary world economy.

LEARNING OBJECTIVES

1. Modify the simple Keynesian model of Chapter 8 to include a government sector by defining aggregate demand as the sum of consumption (C), investment (I), and government spending (G), i.e., GNP $= C + I + G$.

2. Describe the potential, in the Keynesian macroeconomic model, for changes in fiscal policy to counter inflation on the one hand and unemployment on the other.

3. Within the Keynesian model, outline the multiplier effect of a change in government spending and the smaller multiplier effect of a change in taxes. Explain explicitly why the spending multiplier ($= 1/MPS$) is numerically larger than the tax multiplier [$= (MPC/MPS) < (1/MPS)$], i.e., why changes in spending have a greater effect on GNP than do changes in taxes.

4. Describe carefully the ability of changes in government spending and taxes to adjust the level of GNP when the classical model applies.

5. Show why the paradox of thrift is a perfect example of the fallacy of composition; but be clear that it is a paradox which (*a*) is most clearly demonstrated in the Keynesian model and (*b*) disappears in the classical model.

6. Describe the history of net exports in the United States, being particularly clear that the decade of the 1980s was a time of enormous deficit.

7. Modify the Keynesian model to include a foreign sector by defining net exports (X) as the difference between exports (e)

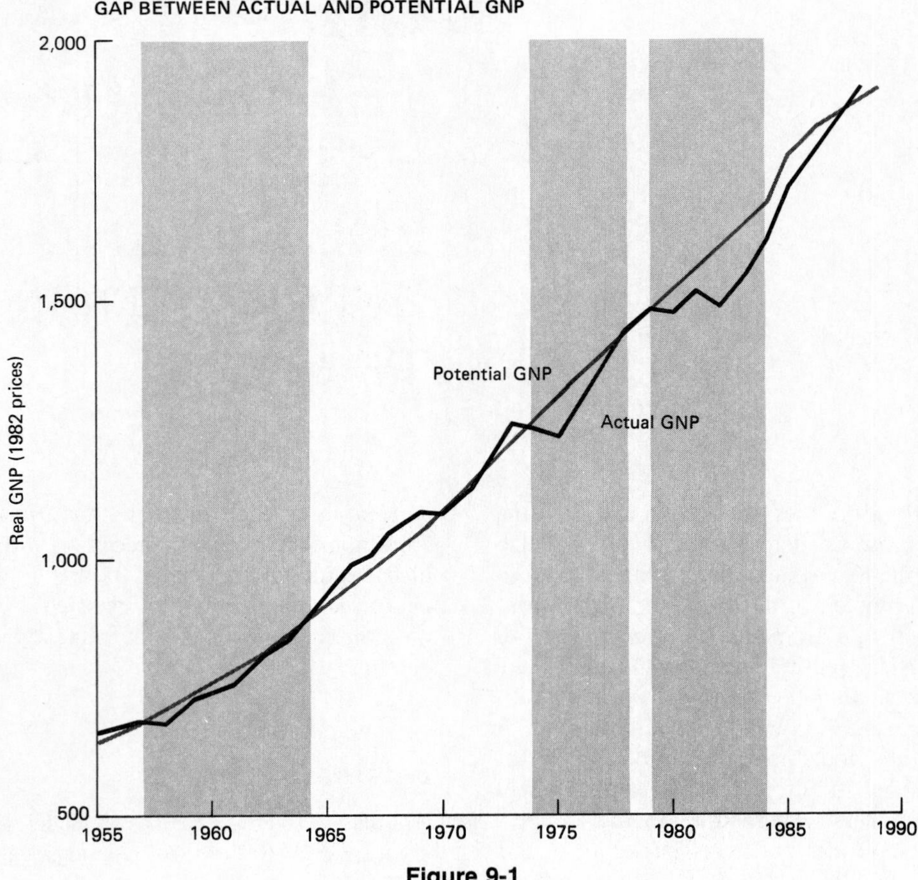

Figure 9-1

and imports (m); i.e., $X = e - m$, and GNP $= C + I + G + X$.

8. Show that the open-economy multiplier for (e.g.) government spending is smaller [$= 1/(MPS + MPm)$] than the closed-economy multiplier when the level of imports increases with GNP (MPm is the marginal propensity of import).

9. Understand (*a*) how import restrictions can "export" unemployment, (*b*) how changes in exchange rates can have effects on domestic aggregate demand, and (*c*) the potential value of coordinating macroeconomic policy across international borders.

10. Understand why there is so much disagreement among economists over the size of the fiscal-policy multiplier; link the discord to the Keynesian-classical debate.

This is, to be sure, another long list of objectives, but this is another important chapter. Chapter 8 described how fluctuation in aggregate demand could be translated into fluctuation in GNP. Chapter 9 suggests how that translation might be harnessed by policymakers to diminish aggregate demand during periods of inflation (contractionary policy) or increase aggregate demand during periods of unemployment (stimulative policy).

1. Refer to Figure 9-1 for enough information to be able to record in the following table whether you would expect unemployment or inflation to have been the dominant economic illness during the periods noted. Also record, in the spaces provided, whether a policy response should have been stimulative or contractionary.

Time Period	Unemployment or Inflation	Policy Prescription
1958–1962	______	______
1965–1970	______	______
1973–1975	______	______
1975–1977	______	______
1981–1983	______	______

1958–1962: unemployment, stimulative; 1965–1970: inflation, contractionary; 1973–1975: inflation, contractionary (responding to the first OPEC oil shock); 1975–1977: unemployment, stimulative; 1981–1983: unemployment, stimulative

There is, of course, more to the design of fiscal policy than the simple comparison of actual and potential

Table 9-1

Case	Keynesian View		Classical View		Intermediate	
	Price	Output	Price	Output	Price	Output
A. Increase in taxes	______	______	______	______	______	______
B. Increase in government spending	______	______	______	______	______	______
C. Reduction in taxes	______	______	______	______	______	______
D. Reduction in government spending	______	______	______	______	______	______

GNP. There are issues of monetary policy; these will be discussed in future chapters. There are issues of outside shocks and the need to fight unemployment and inflation at the same time; these, too, will be addressed later. The point of question 1 was not, therefore, to provide an illustration of a methodology for setting fiscal policy. It was, instead, included only to provide some insight into how one determines (1) when a policy response might be a good idea and (2) what direction it should take.

Chapter 8 recorded two equivalent characterizations of equilibrium in the Keynesian model:

1. $S = I$ (as shown in a saving-investment graph)
2. $GNP = C + I$ (as shown in a 45° diagram)

They were both valid only in the absence of both a government sector and a foreign sector. How we have added a government sector with a level of expenditure G and a level of personal taxation T. What does equilibrium look like now?

In the context of aggregate demand equalling aggregate supply on the 45° graph, the addition of a government sector means that equilibrium is specified by

$$GNP = C + I + G$$

The role of taxes is subsumed in C through its effect on disposable income. Framing the equivalent condition for the saving-investment graph requires only that one rewrite this equation as

$$\begin{aligned} I &= GNP - C - G \\ &= (DI + T) - C - G \\ &= (DI - C) + (T - G) \end{aligned}$$

Since $DI - C$ is simply private saving and $T - G$ is government (public) saving (literally the government surplus, defined as the amount of tax revenue collected minus the amount of money spent), we have once again the fact that investment must equal saving. The only difference now is that total saving is the sum of private saving and public saving.

2. The pure Keynesian model envisions a (*vertical / horizontal*) aggregate supply curve at least for GNP less than potential. As a result, any adjustment in aggregate demand created in that region by an adjustment in either taxes or government spending produces (*no / a dollar-for-dollar / a multiplied)* effect on GNP and (*no / a dollar-for-dollar / a multiplied)* effect on prices. At the other extreme, the classical view holds that fiscal policy will produce (*no / a dollar-for-dollar / a multiplied*) effect on GNP and (*a significant / absolutely no*) effect on prices. In between these two extremes, changes in fiscal policy can be expected to affect (*both prices and GNP / only GNP / only prices*).

Record in the spaces provided in Table 9-1 the expected effects of the policy changes indicated. Denote "up" by (+), "down" by (−), and "no change" by (0). Take care to note that you must answer according to the specified philosophy.

---

horizontal; a multiplied; no; no; a significant; both prices and GNP. Reading across rows: A: (0), (−), (−), (0), (−), (−); B: (0), (+), (+), (0), (+), (+); C: (0), (+), (+), (0), (+), (+); D: (0), (−), (−), (0), (−), (−)

3. With respect to its effect on employment and income, government spending (G) on goods and services (*is / is not*) in the same category as I spending. Figures in Chapter 8 showed how, on a 45° diagram, I spending could be added to C spending to produce a total-spending line. G spending is handled in precisely the same way: it is added vertically above $I + C$ so that the total-spending line is now a $G + I + C$ line.

An increase in G would (*push up / pull down*) (vertically) the total-spending line. A decrease in G would (*push it up / pull it down*) (vertically). A change in G spending (*would / would not*) have multiplier effects similar to any change in I spending.

---

is; push up; pull it down; would

4. Thus far in Chapters 8 and 9, we have been able to work entirely in terms of GNP, using this figure as a measure both of total production and of total income earned from production. Once we get into the matter of taxes, and the effect of taxes on income and spending, though, we must reintroduce some of the more refined measures employed in Chapter 6. Specifically, we must bring back (*a*) national income, which is the measure of total income earned in producing the GNP and NNP, before any taxes and (*b*) disposable income, which is income earned after taxes.

a. Suppose that the government suddenly imposes a personal income tax. The immediate effect of this tax will be that national income (*NI*) is (*unchanged / lowered*). However, disposable income (*DI*) will be (*unchanged / lowered*).

b. When *DI* is reduced, we must expect consumption spending to (*rise / remain unchanged / fall*). If *C* spending is reduced, then production and the incomes earned thereby are likewise reduced. That is, GNP and *NI* will (*rise / remain unchanged / fall*).

---

a. unchanged; lowered **b.** fall; fall

At least to a first approximation, then, government spending and taxation tend to cancel one another in their effects upon GNP. Any increase in *G* tends to raise GNP; any increase in taxation, to lower GNP. Strangely enough, however, *equal* increases in spending and taxes may not cancel each other exactly. To see why this might be so, suppose that spending and personal taxes were both increased by the same amount. One's inclination is to say that these two increases would "net out" to zero, leaving GNP unchanged. That expectation is wrong. A given amount of extra *G* has slightly more upward leverage on GNP than the same amount of extra personal taxation has by way of downward leverage.

5. The crucial point involves the exact amount by which such a personal tax increase "pulls down" the consumption function on a 45° diagram showing *C* spending at various GNP levels. It turns out that the tax pulls the *CC* line down by an amount less than the tax increase.

a. Assume that personal taxes are increased by a flat $30 billion.[1] As an immediate result, GNP (*is unchanged / falls by $30*). (GNP changes only when *C*, *I*, or *G* changes. GNP is going to fall in a moment, to be sure, because higher personal taxes cut the public's disposable income. That will reduce *C* spending, but by how much? That is the real question.) What *does* happen when the extra $30 (billion) in personal taxes is imposed is that *DI* (disposable income, after-tax income) will (*remain unchanged / at once fall by $30*).

Now suppose the community's *MPC* is ⅔, or 0.67. If so, then consumption spending is going to (*remain unchanged / fall by $20 / rise by $20*) because *DI* is $30 lower. Planned consumption drops not because GNP has fallen, but because consumers are being hit by higher taxes. Even at the old, as-yet-unchanged level of GNP, they feel they must cut their spending by $20.

[1] For simplicity, we assume the dollar amount of the tax increase to be fixed and not to change with any change in incomes.

Finally, we recognize that when *C* is cut (by $20), GNP will begin to fall because aggregate demand has contracted. The consumption cut of $20 will have the usual multiplier effects on GNP, but note carefully that this multiplier process is going to begin working from a base of $20 and not $30. The tax increase was $30, but consumers adjusted to this increase by cutting their consumption by only $20. (The other $10 was made up by a reduction in saving.)

b. In sum, the initial *C* reduction which starts off the multiplier reduction in the level of GNP will be (*less than / the same as / greater than*) the amount of the tax increase. That is, the public is most likely to adjust to any increase in personal taxes by cutting its *C* spending (pick one):

(1) by the full tax amount.

(2) by less than the full tax amount, the balance of the adjustment being made by a reduction in saving.

(3) not at all, the entire adjustment being made in *S*.

The *CC* line's downward displacement is illustrated in Figure 9-2. Note that the amount by which consumers cut their spending, with an unchanged GNP, equals the amount of the tax cut multiplied by the ________ .

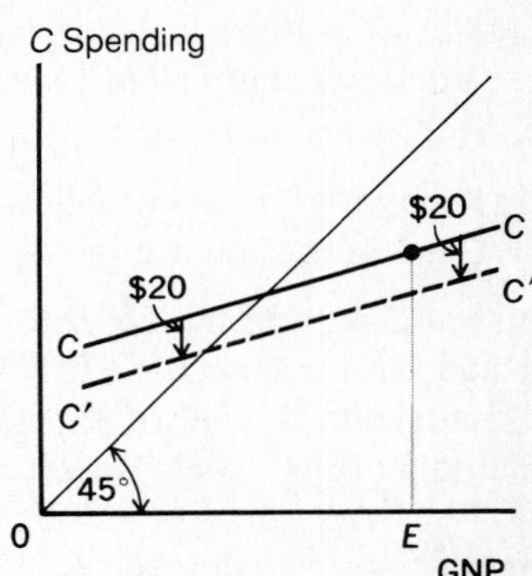

$30 Increase in Personal Taxation

Figure 9-2

---

a. is unchanged; at once fall by $30; fall by $20 **b.** less than; **(2)**; *MPC*

6. a. Now consider what happens if the government spends the full $30 (billion) of its additional tax proceeds for the purchase of goods and services. This will push up the total-spending line, as shown in Figure 9-3, by $(*10 / 20 / 30 / 40*).

b. Finally, combine the two effects: (*a*) levying the tax, resulting in a downward shift of the *C* component of the total-spending line, and (*b*) spending the tax proceeds, resulting in an upward shift of the *G* component of the total-spending line. The overall effect on this total-spending line will be (pick one):

(1) to push it up somewhat higher than before.

(2) to push it down somewhat lower than before.

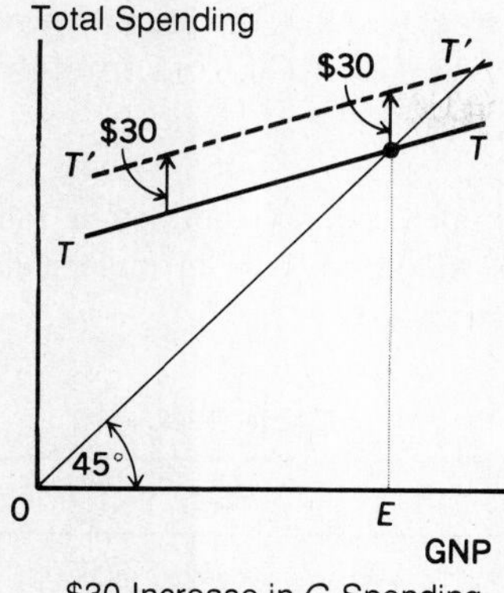

$30 Increase in *G* Spending

Figure 9-3

(3) to leave it in its original position.

The net effect is (*an increase / no change / a reduction*) in aggregate demand.

---

a. 30 **b.** **(1)**; an increase

To put the entire issue into an analytical context, the simple Keynesian multiplier for a change in either investment or government spending is

$$1/(1 - MPC)$$

The corresponding multiplier for a change in taxes is

$$MPC/(1 - MPC) = MPC \times \text{the spending multiplier}$$

The reason for the difference lies entirely in the first round of spending. When government expenditures increase by, say, $10 billion, the first-round increase in aggregate demand is $10 billion; the multiplier therefore works on the full amount. When taxes are cut by $10 billion, though, the first-round increase in aggregate demand is not the full $10 billion; it is, instead, equal to the (MPC x $10 billion) increase in consumption that the tax cut inspires.[2]

[2] Starting with a $10 (billion) increment in government spending, subsequent rounds of spending increases are

Second round: $MPC \times \$10$

Third round: $MPC \times MPC \times \$10$

Fourth round: $MPC \times MPC \times MPC \times \$10$ and so on.

When taxes are cut by $10 (billion), the first-round increment in aggregate demand is not the full $10; it is equal to the second-round increment identified above—the increase in consumption ($MPC \times \$10$) that the tax cut inspires. Compared with the government-spending exercise, therefore, the tax-cut effect simply misses the first $10 billion increment. So it the government-spending effect is

$$\$10 \times [1/(1 - MPC)]$$

then the total tax effect is

$$\{\$10 \times [1/(1 - MPC)]\} - \$10 = \$10 \times \{[1/(1 - MPC)] - 1\}$$
$$= \$10 \times \{[1 - (1 - MPC)]/(1 - MPC)\}$$
$$= \$10 \times MPC \times [1/(1 - MPC)]$$

7. The **paradox of thrift** is a fancy name for the observation that while increased saving might make an individual wealthier in the long run, higher saving can actually make an economy poorer. It is a classic example of the (*fallacy of correlation, not causality / fallacy of composition / application of irrelevant alternatives*).

One place to illustrate the paradox is the usual Keynesian graph that plots total spending against GNP. Figure 9-4 provides such a graph. As it stands, equilibrium GNP is $1000 (billion). Now suppose that everyone saves more so that, for any level of GNP, total saving is always $10 higher than before. Draw the new total-spending curve), it shows a new equilibrium GNP that is (*higher than / exactly equal to / lower than*) the original. If the marginal propensity to consume were 0.6, government spending and taxes were fixed, and investment did not change, then the new equilibrium would, in fact, be $______ . To maintain equilibrium at $1000, an increase in government spending of $______ or a reduction in tax collections of $______ would be required.

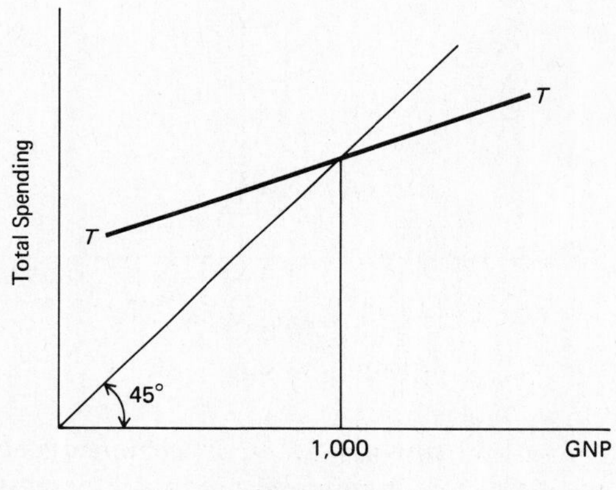

Figure 9-4

The paradox is decidedly a (*Keynesian / classical*) phenomenon. Show, in both panels of Figure 9-5, aggregate demand curves that would support equilibrium at $1000 (note that $1000 is potential GNP). Now draw new aggregate demand curves to reflect an increase in saving. On the Keynesian panel, GNP (*rises / stays the same / falls*) while prices (*rise / stay the same / fall*). On the classical panel, meanwhile, GNP (*rises / stays the same / falls*) while prices (*rise / stay the same / fall*). For an intermediate view somewhere between the Keynesian and classical extremes, we should expect that higher saving would cause GNP to (*rise / stay the same / fall*) and prices to (*rise / stay the same / fall*).

---

fallacy of composition; lower than; 975; 10; 16.67; Keynesian; *downward sloping, cutting AS above $1000; downward sloping, cutting AS to the left of $1000;* falls; stay the same; stays the same; fall; fall; fall (*Note:* Italicized answers describe schedules to be drawn in Figure 9-5.)

We now open the economy to the world marketplace by adding a simple foreign sector to the model. Denoting

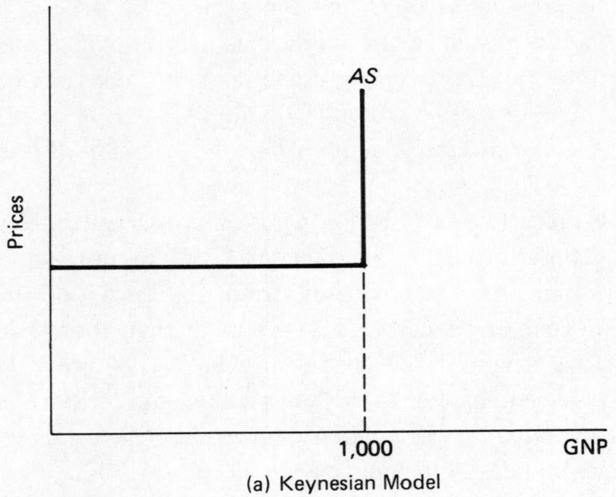

(a) Keynesian Model

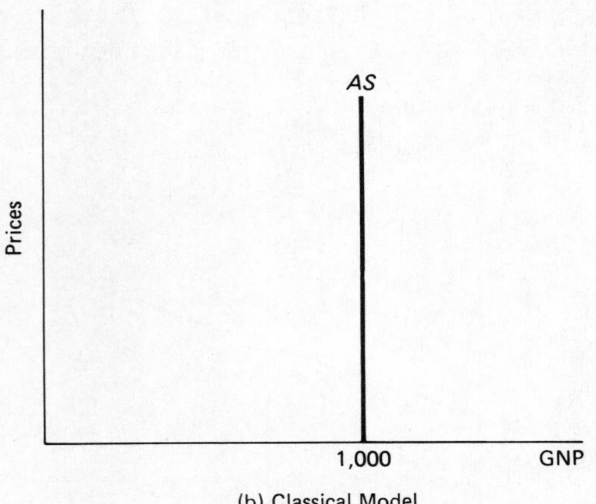

(b) Classical Model

Figure 9-5

exports by x and imports by m, it is immediately clear that domestic expenditures need not match domestic production in an open economy. Goods produced at home may be sold abroad, creating a flow of exports to consumers in other countries. Goods produced abroad may be purchased at home, creating a flow of imports into the domestic economy. The values of these need not match, so a model of an open economy must keep track of the net effect of both.

Letting X denote net exports (i.e., define $X = x - m$), aggregate demand in an open economy has a fourth component, and equilibrium sets aggregate demand equal to aggregate supply according to

$$\text{GNP} = C + I + G + X$$

In the usual 45° diagram, therefore, the addition of an international trade sector simply adds X to the previously drawn $C + I + G$ line. In the investment-saving context, equilibrium continues to be defined by the equality of saving and investment, but in a more complicated manner. Algebraically, equilibrium is characterized by

$$I = S + (T - G) - X$$

in words, investment equals the sum of private saving (S), government saving ($T - G$), and foreign saving [$(m - x) = -X$].

8. Consider the open economy defined in Table 9-2. The following questions will exercise your understanding of equilibrium in an open economy.

Table 9-2

GNP	C	I	G	T	x	m
900	340	200	500	500	250	90
950	370	200	500	500	250	95
1,000	400	200	500	500	250	100
1,050	430	200	500	500	250	115
1,100	460	200	500	500	250	110
1,150	490	200	500	500	250	115
1,200	520	200	500	500	250	120
1,250	550	200	500	500	250	125
1,300	580	200	500	500	250	130
1,350	610	200	500	500	250	135
1,400	640	200	500	500	250	140
1,450	670	200	500	500	250	145
1,500	700	200	500	500	250	150
1,550	730	200	500	500	250	155
1,600	760	200	500	500	250	160
1,650	790	200	500	500	250	165
1,700	820	200	500	500	250	170
1,750	850	200	500	500	250	175
1,800	880	200	500	500	250	180
1,850	910	200	500	500	250	185
1,900	940	200	500	500	250	190
1,950	970	200	500	500	250	195
2,000	1,000	200	500	500	250	200
2,050	1,030	200	500	500	250	205

a. Solve GNP $= C + I + G + X$ to compute the equilibrium level of GNP for the open economy of Table 9-2. GNP* = $________ .

b. Confirm that you have selected the equilibrium by recording the values assumed by the following variables at your G*:

(1) $I =$ $________

(2) $S =$ $________

(3) $T - G =$ $________

(4) $m - x =$ $________

At the G* that you computed, the sum of private saving, government saving, and foreign saving is $_______ ; it (*matches / falls short of / exceeds*) investment at G*.

c. If the economy were closed, so that exports and imports were both zero, then equilibrium GNP would be G* = $_______ ; opening the economy according to the date provided in Table 9-2 therefore (*increases / has no effect on / decreases*) GNP by _______ percent.

---

a. 1500 **b.** **(1)** 200 **(2)** 300 [$DI - C =$ (GNP $- T) - C =$ (\$1500 − \$500) − \$700] **(3)** 0 **(4)** −100(\$150 − \$250); 200(\$300 − \$100); matches **c.** 1250; [(\$250/\$1250) × 100%]

9. Opening an economy can distort the Keynesian multipliers because the level of imports can change with the level of domestic economic activity; and if imports change while exports hold constant, then net exports must change.

One measure of the sensitivity of imports to GNP is the **marginal propensity to import** (*MPm*). Given any change in GNP, the *MPm* is defined as the ratio of the resulting change in imports to the change in GNP. If imports increase by $2 billion every time GNP climbs by $10 billion, the *MPm* = _______ . A $10 billion increase in GNP would therefore be expected to cause net exports to (*increase by $_______ billion / hold steady at current levels / decrease by $_______ billion*). The import schedule displayed in Table 9-2 exhibits a marginal propensity to import of _______ .

Given any marginal propensity to import, the Keynesian multiplier for a change in government spending and/or a change in domestic investment is no longer 1/*MPS*. It is, instead,

$$1/(MPS + MPm)$$

As long as the *MPm* is greater than zero, therefore, the open-economy multiplier is (*larger than / equal to / smaller than*) the closed-economy multiplier. Changes in either therefore have a smaller effect on GNP in an open economy than in a closed economy. Why? Because any stimulus, e.g., that might be created by an increase in investment or government spending in an open economy is partially vented abroad. Some of the increased consumption spending fostered by the stimulus is therefore separated geographically from the domestic economy and contributes to subsequent rounds of domestic consumption.

Compute the marginal propensity to consume exhibited by the consumption function in Table 9-2; *MPC* = _______ . The closed-economy multiplier would then be _______ , but the open-economy multiplier is _______ .

0.2; increase by $2 billion; 0.1; smaller than; 0.6; 2.5 [= 1/0.4]; 2 [= 1/(0.4 + 0.1)]

10. Return now to Table 9-2 to answer the following questions.

a. Suppose that investment was to increase by $250 billion. If the economy were closed, you would expect GNP to (*increase by $_______ / stay the same / fall by $_______*). In the open economy illustrated there, though, GNP should (*increase by $_______ / stay the same / fall by $_______*). Verify your second calculation using the saving-investment approach:

(1) GNP** = $_______

(2) I = $_______

(3) S = $_______

(4) $T - G$ = $_______

(5) $m - x$ = $_______

b. Suppose that the trading partner of the economy depicted in Table 9-2 was to follow "beggar-thy-neighbor" trade policy by prohibiting our economy's exporting any product; i.e., let x fall to $0. Equilibrium would (*rise / fall*) to $_______ . The dimension of this change (*would / would not*) still hold to the open-economy multiplier, this time applied to a $250 reduction in X. Why? Because the import schedule still shows an *MPm* of 0.1.

c. Now suppose that a change in the exchange rate made imports more expensive, so exports rose by $100 and the import schedule fell by $30 for every level of GNP. Our economy's currency must, therefore, have (*appreciated / depreciated*). The new equilibrium would be $_______ .

---

a. increase by \$625; increase by \$500 **(1)** 2000 **(2)** 450 **(3)** 500 (\$2000 − \$500 − \$1000) **(4)** 0 **(5)** −50; 450(= I) **b.** fall; 1000; would (at GNP = \$1000, C = \$400, I = \$200, G = \$500, and X = −\$100) **c.** depreciated; 1750

11. Estimates of the dynamic multiplier for non-defense government expenditure differ widely. Consulting Figure 9-6, it is apparent that most models compute a multiplier in the range of (*0.5 / 1 / 2*) after about 4 to 6 months. The Wharton model climbs above (*2 / 3 / 4*) and never falls; the **DRI** model reaches a peak of about (*0.5 / 1.2 / 1.8*) after about 12 months and then declines; and the St. Louis Federal Reserve model falls to (*0 / 0.2 / 0.4*) in a little over a year's time. One reason behind the declines is (*that all the money leaves the country by the end of 2 years / the effect of monetary accommodation of the lack thereof / that no investment is created by non-defense spending*). The reasons behind the differences of opinion include (*the inherent uncertainties in predicting economic behavior / the different economic philosophies of various researchers that dictate different models / the innate desire of researchers to differentiate their product / differences in the assumed type of non-defense expenditure*).

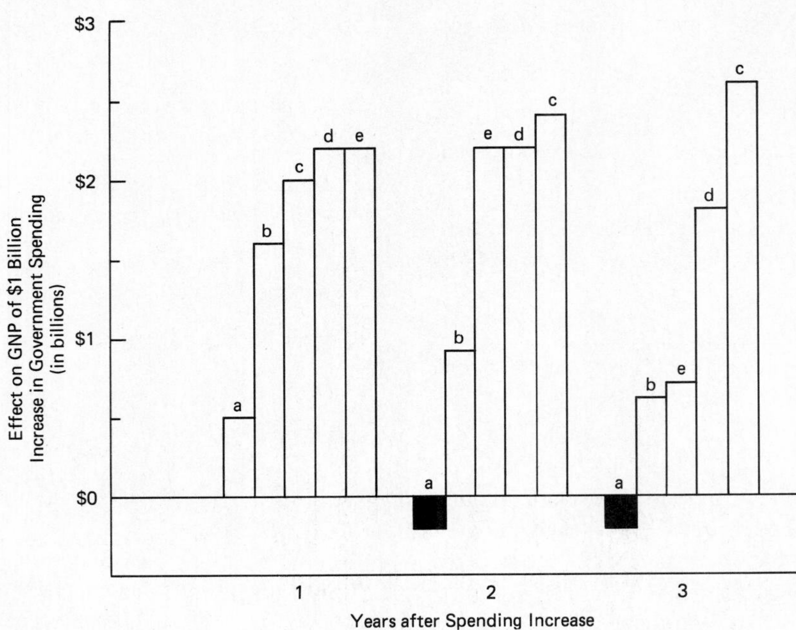

Figure 9-6 Multipliers in five macroeconomic models

The figure shows the government-expenditure multipliers at 1, 2, and 3 years as estimated for five models. In each, the experiments were the same: a hypothetical permanent increase in non-defense government spending by $1 billion above what it would otherwise have been.

Note that the multipliers start small, grow to a peak of between 1 and 2.5, then generally decline after a year or two.

Models:

(*a*) Andersen-Jordan St. Louis Federal Reserve model
(*b*) Data Resources, Inc.
(*c*) Wharton model, University of Pennsylvania
(*d*) Bureau of Economic Analysis, Department of Commerce
(*e*) MIT-Penn-SSRC economic model

(*Source*: Gary Fromm and Lawrence R. Klein: "A Comparison of Eleven Econometric Models of the United States," *American Economic Review*, May, 1973.)

1; 2; 1.8; 0; the effect of monetary accommodation or the lack thereof; the inherent uncertainties in predicting economic behavior (and) the different economic philosophies of various researchers that dictate different models

QUIZ: Multiple Choice

1. The difference between actual and potential GNP was:
(1) positive (i.e., actual exceeded potential) in 1982.
(2) negative in 1965.
(3) positive in 1961.
(4) negative in 1973.
(5) positive in 1968.

2. In the pure Keynesian view of the world:
(1) prices and wages are assumed to be sticky.
(2) the aggregate supply curve is assumed to be flat.
(3) changes in the level of government spending can influence GNP.
(4) changes in tax policy can influence GNP.
(5) all of the above.

3. If the Keynesian prescription for correcting recession is applied but the aggregate supply curve has some finite slope to it, then:
(1) GNP should climb while prices fall.
(2) GNP should climb while prices hold steady.
(3) prices should climb along with real GNP.
(4) real GNP should not change while prices soar.
(5) none of the above.

4. If people suddenly decide to spend less at every level of income, then the total-spending line on the usual Keynesian graph should be drawn:
(1) higher and to the right.
(2) lower and to the right.
(3) higher and to the left.

(4) lower and to the left.
(5) none of the above.

5. If (*a*) GNP is initially in equlibrium, (*b*) the government then increases its total expenditure on goods and services by \$2 billion, (*c*) there is no increase at all in tax collection, (*d*) the marginal propensity to consume is 0.75 and (*e*) the marginal propensity to import is zero, then (assuming no price-inflationary consequences) in the new equilibrium thus produced, GNP will have:
(1) fallen by \$4 billion.
(2) risen by \$2 billion.
(3) risen by \$6 billion.
(4) risen by \$8 billion.
(5) risen by \$4 billion.

6. Which alternative in question 5 would be correct had that question referred to a total reduction of \$2 billion in the government's income-tax collections, with its expenditure on goods and services not being increased at all?
(1).
(2).
(3).
(4).
(5).

7. Which answer to question 5 would have been correct if the marginal propensity to import had been 0.25?
(1).
(2).
(3).
(4).
(5).

8. Which answer to question 5 would have been correct if the *MPm* had been 0.25 and exports had responded to depreciation in the value of the home currency?
(1).
(2).
(3).
(4).
(5).

9. In the Keynesian model with investment fixed autonomously, the result of an increase in saving is:
(1) no change in real GNP, consumption (*C*), or saving (*S*).
(2) higher levels of real GNP, *C*, and *S*.
(3) no change in real GNP and *C* but a decrease in real *S*.
(4) no change in real GNP and *S* but an increase in real *C*.
(5) lower levels of real GNP, *C*, and *S*.

10. Which answer to question 9 would have been correct if it had appealed to the classical model?
(1).
(2).
(3).
(4).
(5).

11. The moral of the paradox of thrift is that:
(1) reduction in saving during low-employment periods may temporarily increase consumption, but only at the cost of lower GNP later on.
(2) an increase in the amount of saving is always a desirable thing in terms of increasing real GNP.
(3) a decrease in the amount of saving is always a desirable thing in terms of increasing real GNP, even in the classical model.
(4) attempts to increase saving may actually increase consumption also, since saving provides the funds to finance investment.
(5) none of the above.

12. If GNP is in equilibrium, then:
(1) consumption must be just equal to investment.
(2) business receipts from consumption spending must just equal national income.
(3) any increase in spending must result in an inflationary gap.
(4) the overall budgets of federal, state, and local governments must be just balanced.
(5) none of the above is necessarily correct.

13. GNP is in equlibrium at its full-employment level. The federal government finds it necessary to increase its expenditures on goods and services by \$10 billion. It wants to increase taxes sufficiently so that there will be no more serious threat of inflation—i.e., it wants the net change in the equilibrium level of GNP to be zero. The probable increase in tax collections needed will be:
(1) more than \$10 billion.
(2) \$10 billion.
(3) less than \$10 billion, although not zero.
(4) zero.
(5) less than zero—i.e., tax collections can be reduced.

14. An equilibrium level of GNP (below full employment) is disturbed by an autonomous rise in planned investment spending of \$10 billion. The marginal propensity to consume is 0.6. Imports are completely insensitive to changes in GNP. In the new equilibrium, GNP will have risen (in billions) by:
(1) \$10.
(2) \$25.
(3) \$60.
(4) \$80.
(5) \$100.

15. There is a small but significant difference between the multiplier effect of an increase of, say, \$10 (billion) in government spending and that of a decrease of \$10 in personal taxes

levied. This is because:
(1) government spending, by increasing income earned, increases consumption spending.
(2) a $10 reduction in taxation has a significantly greater effect on the government surplus or deficit than has a $10 increase in government spending.
(3) a tax reduction affects consumer income and spending directly, whereas the effect of an increase in government spending on consumers is only indirect.
(4) a $10 reduction in personal taxes does not produce a $10 increase in consumer spending, since part of this reduction goes into extra saving.
(5) none of the above reasons.

16. Whenever total planned investment exceeds the total of planned saving, then
(1) GNP will fall below potential GNP.
(2) GNP will rise above potential GNP.
(3) GNP will rise if initially below potential GNP.
(4) GNP will fall only if initially at potential GNP.
(5) there is no reason to expect any change in GNP, either up or down, or to expect, as a necessary result, any change in potential GNP.

17. The paradox is a perfect example of the fallacy of composition if you accept:
(1) the pure Keynesian model.
(2) the pure classical model.
(3) a model somewhere in between the Keynesian and the classical models.
(4) items 1 and 2 only.
(5) items 1 and 3 only.

18. According to the classical model, an increase in saving should:
(1) lower real GNP.
(2) lower potential GNP.
(3) affect only the rate of growth of future potential GNP.
(4) leave nominal GNP unaffected.
(5) none of the above.

19. Estimates of the non-defense spending multiplier vary significantly from researcher to researcher because:
(1) of inherent uncertainties and philosophical differences.
(2) different researchers use different data to make their estimates.
(3) different researchers want to make certain that readers distinguish their work from the work of others.
(4) the estimation procedures are so complex that errors necessarily distort the results beyond belief.
(5) none of the above.

SUGGESTED ANSWERS TO QUESTIONS IN THE TEXT: Chapter 9

1. Definitions.

2. The first-round effect on aggregate demand of a spending increment (e.g.) is that spending increment. It then feeds into consumption patterns in which each successive addition to aggregate demand is smaller than the last by some amount (the *MPC* or the *MPC* minus the *MPm*). An equal tax reduction starts with consumption, so the first round is *MPC* times the reduction. Since it misses the first full round of a spending change, its total effect must be smaller by that amount.

3. This is the paradox-of-thrift business; think about the differences under the Keynesian model and the classical model. In between, a little price reduction happens, but so does a little GNP reduction.

4. Early in the 1980s, during severe recession, the likely effect of smaller deficits should have been deeper recession. Later in the decade, as the economy approached its potential, the effect could have been less concern about inflation. Alas, though, the balanced-budget amendment president of the 1980s had a great deal of trouble bringing deficits down with enormous defense spending programs accompanying large tax cuts.

5. Fiscal policy gives governments a lever with which to manipulate aggregate demand. In a Keynesian world, that can alter real GNP; in a classical world, it cannot.

6. Note in Table 9-2 that imports increase with GNP.
a. Higher investment increases GNP and imports; net exports fall.
b. Lower government spending does the opposite.
c. Higher exports are stimulative, increasing GNP and imports. Net exports should, though, increase.
d. Stimulus greater than in part *c*.

7. The spending multiplier equals

$$1/(MPS + MPm) = 1/(1 - MPC + MPm)$$

The multiplier could fall short of unity if

$$1 > [1/(1 - MPC + MPm)]$$

i.e., if

$$(1 - MPC + MPm) > 1$$

This could happen, then, if $MPm > MPC$; i.e., if the last dollar made increased imports faster than it did domestic consumption.

8. A depreciation in the dollar should increase American exports and reduce American imports; U.S. exports would be cheaper abroad and European imports would be more expensive at home. The result would be an increase in U.S. aggregate demand that would have to be matched by a reduction in U.S. government spending if U.S. equilibrium is to be unaffected. Meanwhile, European countries would see a fiscal stimulus through, for them, higher exports and lower imports.

9. Different government spending programs have different employment implications and social spin-offs. Do not judge something as complicated as social value on the basis of only one parameter without thinking about opportunity cost. Could the money have had a greater effect being spent elsewhere?

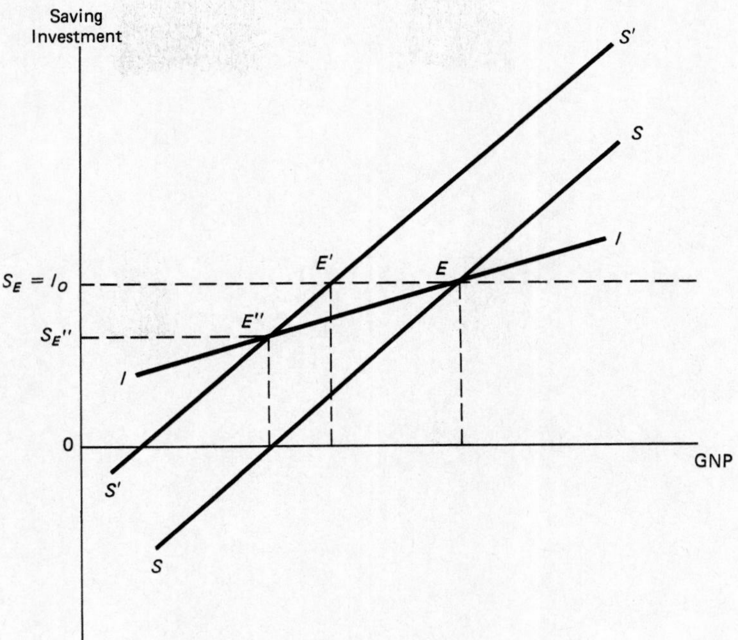

Figure TQ9-1

10. The fallacy of composition, the Keynesian-classical debate, and the applicability of these models in different circumstances must be considered. In depression, e.g., the Keynesian simple model applies; in an inflationary time, it does not.

11. Net exports rise (m down). Domestic GNP should rise (some consumption spending stays home that would have otherwise left the country). Foreign GNP should fall with a reduction in their aggregate demand (unless already overheated with equilibrium above potential).

12. Matching increase in other programs to maintain G; lower taxes to maintain aggregate demand; etc.

13. Consumption shifts up by less than government spending shifts down. The net effect should be contractionary; the pure Keynesian multiplier is unity.

14. Refer to Figure TQ9-1. There, an increase in the savings function would move equilibrium from E to E' if investment were constant at I_o, and to $E'' < E'$ if investment were positively correlated with GNP as in schedule II. GNP, saving, and investment all fall. The desire to increase saving (a shift from schedule SS to schedule $S'S'$) moves saving down from $S_E = I_o$ to S_E''.

CHAPTER 10
AGGREGATE SUPPLY AND BUSINESS CYCLES

Previous chapters have stressed the determinants of aggregate demand. It is now time to turn our attention to a careful examination of the supply side of a macroeconomy. What, in particular, are the determinants of aggregate supply? What are the sources of growth of potential GNP? What are "supply-side" policies, and how are they supposed to work? What is the connection between the interaction of aggregate supply and demand, on the one hand, and the level of unemployment, on the other? How, in short, are we going to close the macroeconomic loop, and why will it matter when we have done so?

These are theoretical issues, to be sure, and they occupy our full attention in the first part of Chapter 10. They would, however, be empty theory if their importance were not supported by empirical evidence, recent observation, and practical relevance. Relevance is provided at the end of section A by a critical discussion of the supply-side policy experiment of the Reagan administration; empirical evidence is presented in the second section. It all leads to questions of designing policies which can be used to help us avoid the ups and downs of the business cycle. Can we do that? Probably not perfectly. We should, however, be able to design policies that reduce the size of business-cycle swings.

Having completed your work in this chapter, then, you should have accomplished the following objectives.

LEARNING OBJECTIVES

1. Identify the sources of growth of potential GNP (growth in the labor supply, the capital stock, technological parameters, etc.), growth which has averaged between 2.5 and 4 percent per year in the United States over the last half-century.

2. Clearly delineate the role of potential GNP in defining the hinge point between two distinct regions in an aggregate supply curve—one nearly horizontal and one nearly vertical.

3. Explain how growth in potential GNP shifts an aggregate supply curve out to the right, while increasing costs shift it up.

4. Understand the meaning, significance, and empirical validation of Okun's Law, relating each percentage point of GNP gap (difference between actual and potential GNP) to 1/2 percentage point of unemployment.

5. Explain the three major components of supply-side economic policy, and discuss the results of the Reagan experiment in its implementation. Discuss, theoretically, the circumstances under which it is and is not likely to be effective.

6. Distinguish between internal and external theories of business cycles, including in your consideration the political business cycle.

7. Explain the operation of the acceleration principle in explaining the business cycle.

8. Understand, at least intuitively, why economists who do reasonably well in forecasting real GNP have a difficult time in accurately forecasting inflation.

This list of objectives is a bit shorter than the lists in the last two chapters, but these objectives should focus your attention on one of the critical issues of the economics profession: Can economic policy be designed to adequately control the adverse effects of the business cycle? Design is a matter for economic analysis—answers to questions like "If this happens, should we do that?" The notion of defining "adequately" is, however, subjective. Different people have different ideas. What do you think should be the criteria for adequacy? You have, even now, more economic education than many who publicly argue for one criteria or another, so you are at least as qualified to form an opinion as they are. So what are your expectations? Should the designers of economic policy be able to insulate from the business cycle, or is simply dampening the amplitude enough?

Evidence of the existence of the business cycle can be found in the periodic fluctuation of almost all the major macroeconomic variables that we study: prices, employment, output, interest rates, etc. To understand where the cycle might come from, though, we cannot simply jump into the cycle and look around; we need first to understand why potential GNP grows and what that growth does to the aggregate supply curve.

1. From 1948 through 1988, potential GNP grew at an annual rate of approximately *(1.2 / 2.9 / 4.5)* percent. Of that growth, *(0.5 / 0.7 / 1.4)* percentage points have been attributed to growth in the labor force, *(0.4 / 1.6 / 2.1)* percentage points have been attributed to growth in the capital stock, *(0.3 / 0.7 / 0.9)* point has been attributed to technological advancement, and the rest is unexplained. It is, however, estimated that the rate of growth of potential output fell to 2.7 percent during the recession period from 1981 to 1984.

Now consult Figure 10-1. It shows that growth in potential GNP shifts the aggregate supply curve *(up / down)* and to the *(right / left)* because wages and other costs of production tend to *(climb / fall)* over time. The figure also shows curvature *(only below / in a small neighborhood on both sides of / only above)* estimated potential GNP. Prices appear to be sticky through potential GNP until they begin to become "unstuck." When the curves turn up, though, they turn up quickly.

Could equilibrium have moved from point *A* in Figure 10-1 to point *B* without an increase in aggregate demand? ________ . If aggregate demand had decreased between 1981 and 1984, potential output would have *(still grown / fallen)*, actual GNP would have *(grown / fallen)*, and prices would have *(climbed / fallen)*.

2.9; 0.7; 0.4; 0.9; up; right; climb; in a small neighborhood on both sides of; no (For *A* and *B* both to lie on the same *AD* curve, it would have a positive slope.); still grown; fallen; climbed (*AS'* is higher in the region below potential GNP than *AS*.)

2. Figure 10-2 shows, in two separate panels, shifts in aggregate demand from *AD* to *AD'*. Panel (a) illustrates a shift that would cause *(recession / expansion)* because equilibrium GNP would *(fall / climb)* and price inflation would *(accelerate / slow)*. Panel (b) shows the opposite, of course—*(a recession / an expansion)* with *(accelerating / braking)* prices and *(expanding / contracting)* GNP. Formally, a recession is an economic downturn during which *(real / nominal)* GNP declines for *(1 / 2 / 3)* successive calendar quarters. To the first people to be laid off, however, the technical definition is not important; it is a recession as soon as they lose their jobs.

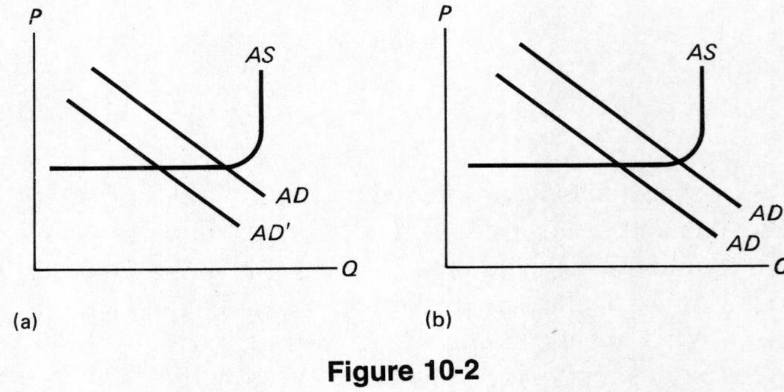

Figure 10-2

---

recession; fall; slow; an expansion; accelerating; expanding; real; 2

3. Okun's Law is one of those miracles of statistics—a simple rule that fits reality extremely well. Okun's empirics tell us that every time that actual GNP falls 2 percent relative to potential GNP, unemployment *(increases / decreases)* by *(1 / 2 / 3 / 4)* percentage point(s). In application of this result, we now know that if potential GNP is growing at *X* percent per year, then real

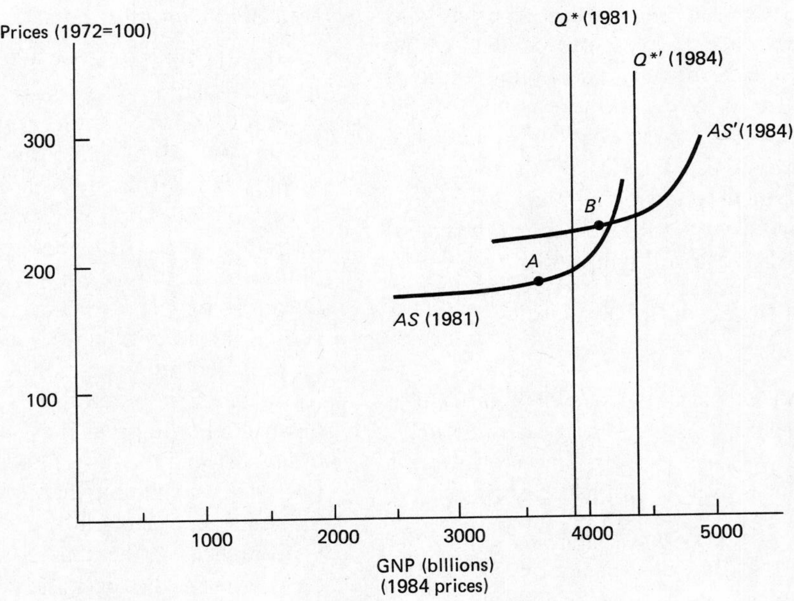

Figure 10-1

GNP will have to grow at *(less than X percent / X percent / more than X percent)* to keep unemployment from climbing.

Other computations are also possible. In completing the following table, you will not only practice those computations but also confirm the accuracy of the law by comparing your answers with observed unemployment rates. Record, in particular, your prediction for the actual unemployment rate for the years indicated by applying Okun's Law to the data provided. The actual rates, listed down the column, were 6.7 percent, 3.8 percent, 4.9 percent, 8.5 percent, 9.8 percent.

		Rate of Growth of:		Unemployment Rate	
Starting Year	Ending Year	Potential GNP, %	Actual GNP, %	Initial, %	Predicted
1960	1961	3.3	2.2	5.5	______
1965	1961	3.3	6.0	4.8	______
1970	1971	3.3	−0.2	3.5	______
1975	1976	3.3	−1.1	5.6	______
1981	1982	2.7	−1.3	7.5	______

increases; 1; X percent
1960: $5.5 + 0.5[3.3 - 2.2] = 6.05 \approx 6.7$ actual
1965: $4.8 + 0.5[3.3 - 6.0] = 3.45 \approx 3.8$ actual
1970: $3.5 + 0.5[3.3 - (-0.2)] = 5.25 \approx 4.9$ actual
1975: $5.6 + 0.5[3.3 - (-1.1)] = 7.80 \approx 8.5$ actual
1981: $7.5 + 0.5[2.7 - (-1.3)] = 9.50 \approx 9.8$ actual

4. There were three components of the **supply-side** recovery packages enacted in the early 1980s by the Reagan administration in the United States and the Thatcher administration in the United Kingdom. The first was a retreat from the short-run stabilization prescriptions of the Keynesian model, turning attention instead to the medium run. This retreat was supported by a view that the aggregate supply curve was *(nearly vertical / nearly horizontal)* so that any recession that might be forthcoming would be short and mild. Prices and wages would, in particular, *(quickly / slowly)* adjust to any excess supply in the labor market, and changes in aggregate demand would have *(large / little)* effect on GNP.

The second was a set of tax incentives designed to move the aggregate supply curve up and (mostly) out by boosting potential GNP, as shown in Figure 10-3 by the shift from *AS* to *AS'*. The effectiveness of this policy also depends upon the shape of the aggregate supply curve. If the curve were vertical (or if the economy were represented by AD_1 on the vertical portion of the *AS* supply curve), then the shift would be effective in *(increasing / reducing)* actual GNP and *(lowering / increasing)* prices. If the curve were horizontal (or the economy represented by AD_2 on the flat portion of *AS'*), though, the supply shift would *(increase actual GNP slightly / reduce actual GNP slightly / still be effective in increasing GNP substantially)* and actually *(increase / reduce)* prices. Again, support for the program was based upon a rejection of the horizontal *AS* curve of the Keynesian model.

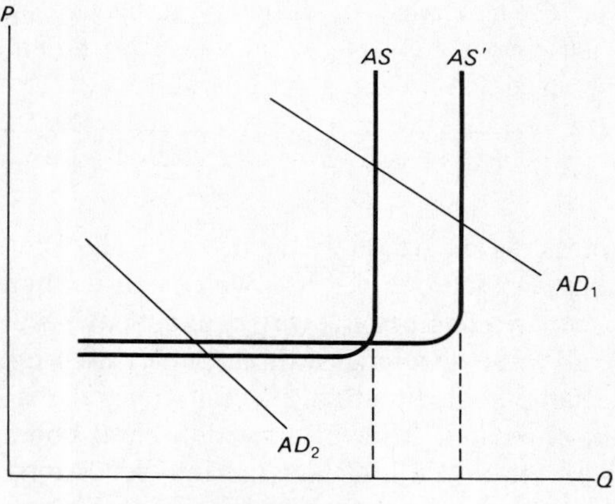

Figure 10-3

The third arm of the program was a substantial reduction in personal income taxes. The effect of this reduction would, of course, influence *(aggregate demand / aggregate supply)*. As such, one should have expected that it would increase actual GNP with stable prices only if the aggregate supply schedule were *(nearly vertical / nearly horizontal)*. Otherwise, the increase in aggregate demand would be vented almost exclusively in *(prices / potential GNP / output)*. In supporting this final component of the program, it would appear that the architects of the program were not ready to discard Keynes entirely. Indeed, the Reagan people campaigned for the program by comparing it favorably with the Kennedy round of tax cuts of the early 1960s—the beginning of the high point for Keynesians in making federal policy.

nearly vertical; quickly; little; increasing; lowering; reduce actual GNP slightly; increase; aggregate demand; nearly horizontal; prices

5. The record of the supply-side experiment in the United States has run its course over two presidential terms. The 1981 Economic Recovery Program forecast annual growth rates for real GNP averaging 4.8 percent into the middle of the 1980s; actual experience showed growth *(significantly greater than / roughly equal to / significantly lower than)* the forecast. The program aimed to support this growth by significant increases in saving, investment, and productivity. Over the course of the 1980s, in fact, the national savings rate *(rose significantly / held roughly constant / fell significantly)*. Investment was *(down / stable / up)*, and productivity growth *(increased / held steady / declined)*.

The record was not what was hoped. Would it have mattered? Edward Denison calculated that a 2-point increase in the savings rate (from 6 percent at the beginning of the 1980s to 8 percent) channeled entirely into investment would translate into a 1 percent higher real GNP in 1990 than would otherwise be enjoyed; the growth rate of potential GNP would have climbed from 3 to 3.1 percent. There *(would / would not)* have been further benefits through the 1990s, but the lesson is simple: It would have been enormously difficult to achieve a significant change in the rate of growth of potential GNP even if the supply-side experiment had worked as advertised.

---

significantly lower than; fell significantly; down; declined; would

Business cycles are, at the same time, all different and all the same. Each one has its own cause, its own length of time, its own degree of severity, and its own trajectory. Despite all these differences, though, they all seem to follow the same general pattern: decline into recession; bottom out; climb into recovery; continue into boom; peak; fall toward price stability; decline into recession; and so on. The differences are confounding, but the similarities suggest the possibility that some equally general pattern of policy might reduce the severity of the cycle.

6. Record in the blanks provided the phase of a business cycle during which you would expect to observe the indicated events; denote recession by (R) and boom by (B).

a. business investment increasing . . . . (________)

b. profits falling . . . . (________)

c. tax receipts climbing . . . . (________)

d. demand for labor rising . . . . (________)

e. stock prices falling . . . . (________)

f. accelerating inflation . . . . (________)

g. unemployment insurance payments increasing . . . . (________)

h. interest rates falling . . . . (________)

---

a. B **b.** R **c.** B **d.** B **e.** R **f.** B **g.** R **h.** R

7. Recessions (or depressions) most commonly arise from a *(drop / rise)* in *(consumption / investment / government)* spending. Because of the "multiplier effect," this initial *(drop / rise)* has magnified consequences—i.e., total spending drops *(even more / somewhat less)* than the initial drop in *(C / I / G)* spending.

Among the following economic variables, the greatest cyclical fluctuation is typically found in *(wholesale prices / production of capital goods / production of basic materials such as petroleum / expenditures on consumer goods)*.

---

drop; investment; drop; even more; *I*; production of capital goods

8. Play a "what if" game test your understanding of a few definitions. If you were to believe that changes in the population were never caused by changes in economic circumstance, then a theory that held that changes in total population caused the business cycle would be *(an external / an internal / a political)* theory of the cycle.

Were you to go to the other extreme, holding that changes in population were exclusively the result of changes in economic circumstance (e.g., you might think that depression increases the number of poor people who cannot have children because they cannot support them), then a theory that proposed a causal relationship between changes in total population and the business cycle would be *(an external / an internal / a political)* theory of the cycle.

The notion that incumbent political parties the policy tools at their disposal to time recovery and boom for election years and recession and trough for off-election years is *(an external / an internal / a political)* business-cycle theory.

---

an external; an internal; a political

The **acceleration principle** is one theory of investment that applies directly to a descriptive theory of the origins of the business cycle. Simply put, the acceleration principle states that an economy's need for capital is driven by its level of production, so additions to the capital stock (read net investment) are made only when an economy is growing. As a result, a period of prosperity may be undermined not because total sales fall but simply because total sales have stabilized—even at a very high level.

The logic behind the acceleration principle is quite simple. Net investment spending (gross investment net of depreciation) adds to an economy's total capital stock. To produce a level of GNP equal to, say, \$3.8 trillion, a certain capital stock, say, K_0, is required. If you had less than K_0, then you couldn't produce \$3.8 trillion worth of goods and services; if you had more than K_0, then stopping at \$3.8 trillion would be wasteful. Similarly, there is a second capital stock, say, K_1, that is the correct amount for \$4 trillion. Assuming stable prices, in fact, it must be so that $K_1 > K_0$.

Once the economy has reached equilibrium at \$3.8 trillion, then, no further net investment is required. As long as equilibrium GNP holds at \$3.8 trillion, the capital stock is correctly maintained if it is held constant at K_0. Similarly, maintaining equilibrium at \$4 trillion simply means maintaining the stock of capital at K_1. Only if an economy starts to grow (e.g., from \$3.8 trillion to \$4 trillion) is there a need for positive net investment.

9. a. You are a sales representative for a machine-tool firm. One of your customers is a firm which has 10 machines, identical except for age. Each machine has a 10-year life, and the machines are nicely staggered in age, so that each year one machine is ready for the scrap heap. If you visit the firm, you will find one machine 9 years old, one 8 years old, and so on. The plant has just enough business to keep its 10 machines steadily occupied.

As seller of these machines, you visit the plant once yearly, expecting an order for one machine to replace the machine currently wearing out. Assuming, for simplicity, that each new machine costs $10, your order each year will be $10. In national product terms, gross investment will be $*(100 / 10 / 0)*, and net investment will be $*(100 / 10 / 0)*.

Suddenly, the demand for this firm's product jumps. Sales rise by 30 percent and stay at this higher level. The firm must expand its equipment (its capital-goods stock) to allow for this extra production. On your annual visit (which is happily timed to coincide with the sales jump), you receive an order for *(5 / 4 / 3 / 2 / 1 / 0)* machine(s). That is, gross investment (at the $10 price) is $*(50 / 40 / 30 / 20 / 10)*, and net investment is $*(40 / 30 / 20 / 10 / 0)*.

One year passes. Again you visit the plant, knowing in advance that the firm's sales are still holding at their 30 percent–higher level. The firm expects them to remain steady at that level. What will your order be this time? It will be for *(5 / 4 / 3 / 2 / 1 / 0)* machine(s). That is, gross investment is $*(40 / 30 / 20 / 10 / 0)*.

This is a small-scale example of the acceleration-principle idea. Net investment is not a matter of the absolute level of output. It takes place when output is rising.

b. Suppose that the level of GNP for 4 successive years is summarized as follows: year 1, $500; year 2, $600; year 3, $650; year 4, $650. The acceleration principle would say that net *I* spending would be (pick one):

(1) a positive but different amount in each of the 4 years.

(2) positive between years 1 and 3, zero in year 4.

(3) zero in the first 2 years, but positive and increasing in the last 2 years.

c. It is hard to say how far the acceleration-principle idea has been verified in experience. Even its most zealous proponents would hardly argue that this principle affords a complete account of net *I* spending, but many economists think it carries an important element of truth.

Its critics point out that most *I* spending is undertaken by business firms in the hope of profit. Even if GNP is presently in equilibrium at a certain level, but if business firms think (rightly or wrongly) that the GNP is going to rise, so that there will be an increased demand for output, they *(will / will not)* be encouraged to undertake new investment spending. Conversely, if GNP is presently rising but if firms are inclined to believe that this rise will be small and of short duration, they *(will / will not)* be encouraged to undertake *I* spending.

---

a. 10; 0; 4; 30; 1 (Only the 10-year-old machine has worn out.); 10; 0 **b.** **(2)** (GNP increases in first 3 years, remains steady in fourth.) **c.** will; will not

10. Both the following statements should recall ideas with which you are now familiar.

1. The level of consumption spending is influenced by the level of investment spending, because *C* spending depends considerably on the level of GNP, and the level of GNP depends considerably on the level of *I* spending.
2. The level of *I* spending is influenced by *C* spending—specifically, by the rate at which the level of *C* spending is increasing.

a. Which of the above is a statement of the acceleration principle? . . . . *(1 / 2 / neither)*

b. Which is a statement of the Keynesian theory of income determination? . . . . *(1 / 2 / neither)*

In other words, *I* spending and *C* spending can be thought to interact with one another, each influenced by the other, so that both may be changing as they seek out mutually compatible levels. In the process, GNP (which includes the sum of *C* and *I* spending) must change also. That is, the ups and downs of GNP that we call the business cycle are to at least some degree the result of this interaction.

---

a. 2 **b.** 1

When the acceleration-principle idea is introduced, the interaction becomes a complicated one. You should understand the acceleration-principle idea. You should understand that there is an interaction between *C* and *I*; you should grasp its general nature. But an introductory course cannot outline in full detail how *I*, *C*, and GNP would interact in an acceleration-principle world.

QUIZ: Multiple Choice

1. Compared with the experience of the United States between 1948 and 1975, the rate of growth of real GNP has, through the 1980s:
(1) climbed dramatically by more than 50 percent.
(2) climbed slightly by about 18 percent.
(3) remained at the historical level.
(4) fallen by about 18 percent.
(5) fallen by more than 25 percent.

2. Business cycles seem to be caused:
(1) exclusively by external factors.
(2) exclusively by internal factors.
(3) by factors of any type that mostly influence aggregate demand.
(4) by factors that mostly influence aggregate supply.
(5) entirely by the vagaries of the political seasons.

3. According to Okun's Law, if potential GNP rose by 9 percent between 1979 and 1982 but actual GNP did not change,

then unemployment should have climbed from 5.8 percent in 1979 to:
(1) 6.1 percent.
(2) 10.3 percent.
(3) 11.2 percent.
(4) 8.8 percent.
(5) 9.7 percent.

4. Which of the following statements is (are) true about the supply-side program for economic recovery offered by the Reagan administration in 1981?
(1) It represented a retreat from belief in the Keynesian model of macroeconomic behavior.
(2) It represented a belief that price and wage adjustments would keep any recession short.
(3) It included a prescription to increase potential output that depended upon a nearly vertical aggregate supply curve to be most effective.
(4) It included a prescription to increase aggregate demand by cutting personal taxes, which depended upon a nearly horizontal aggregate supply curve to be most effective.
(5) All of the above.

5. Which of the following would you *not* expect to see during a period of recession?
(1) Lower business investment on durable equipment.
(2) Lower stock prices; lower demand for labor.
(3) Lower tax receipts.
(4) Lower corporate profits.
(5) Lower unemployment compensation payments.

6. Which of the following time frames was marked by the most severe period of recession?
(1) 1969–1970.
(2) 1982–1983.
(3) 1974–1975.
(4) 1960–1961.
(5) 1953–1954.

7. Which of the following time frames was marked by the most energetic period of economic boom?
(1) 1983–1984.
(2) 1973–1974.
(3) 1938–1939.
(4) 1955–1956.
(5) 1967–1968.

8. The implication of the theory of political business cycles is that:
(1) anti-inflationary medicine is generally administered early in an administration.
(2) the year after an election is frequently a year of austerity.
(3) the year of an election is frequently a year of growth and prosperity.
(4) the timing of elections can dictate the timing of the business cycle.
(5) all of the above.

9. In the United States, the major business cycle:
(1) has been much less pronounced than in European economies, with the single exception of the 1930s.
(2) strikes very sharply at certain limited sectors of the economy, but leaves major sectors almost totally unaffected.
(3) shows a remarkably uniform and symmetrical pattern in the sequence of prosperity, peak, slump, and depression, once "random" elements have been removed.
(4) has been more intense than in European economies, at least with respect to the degree of variation in total employment.
(5) is not correctly described by any of these statements.

10. If we look to any particular kind of spending as a key factor in accounting for the major business cycle, we find it in:
(1) net investment spending, specifically spending on inventories.
(2) net investment spending, specifically spending on durable goods.
(3) consumer spending.
(4) variations in spending by state and local governments.
(5) none of the above, the point stressed being that no single type of spending plays any key role.

11. The multiplier and the acceleration principle are related in what way?
(1) They both seek to explain how changes in the level of investment spending come about.
(2) The multiplier seeks to explain how a condition of full-employment GNP can be maintained, and the acceleration principle seeks to explain how a condition of depression may come about and may persist despite efforts to increase spending.
(3) The multiplier shows how a change in the level of GNP, particularly an upward change, may give rise to net investment, and the acceleration principle shows how a given change in spending (e.g., in investment) can result in a larger change in the level of GNP.
(4) The multiplier shows how a given change in spending (e.g., in investment) can result in a larger change in the level of GNP, and the acceleration principle shows how a change in the level of GNP, particularly an upward change, may give rise to net investment.
(5) In none of the ways described above.

12. The role of consumer spending in the business cycle, according to U.S. experience, is best understood by noting that:
(1) changes in consumer durable purchases may occasionally set off an upswing or downturn, and changes in consumer spending will intensify the effect of any disturbance originating outside the consumer sphere, via the multiplier.

(2) consumer spending and investment spending seem to have approximately equal parts to play in the cycle, although the two are so intermixed that it is difficult to separate one from the other and to analyze the role of either.
(3) changes in consumer spending on nondurables most commonly initiate the downturn in a major business cycle, whereas increases in consumer durable purchases are most likely to start the upturn, as replacement of worn-out durable items becomes necessary.
(4) changes in consumer spending are most often the initial disturbing factor, and the impact then spreads to investment spending, thus intensifying the original disturbance.
(5) consumer spending has no part to play in the cycle, which (except for wartime disturbances) is almost entirely due to investment-spending changes.

13. In economics, "capital formation" means specifically:
(1) the purchase of any new commodity.
(2) net investment.
(3) the borrowing of money.
(4) the sale of any new stock issue.
(5) none of these activities.

14. According to the acceleration principle, spending on net investment will take place:
(1) when GNP or consumption is at a high level.
(2) when GNP or consumption is at a low level.
(3) when GNP or consumption is rising.
(4) when GNP or consumption is falling.
(5) perhaps in any of the above situations, since no such link with GNP or consumption is assumed.

15. Statistically, the widest swings between peak and bottom of the major business cycle are to be found in:
(1) the supply of consumer services.
(2) the production of inventories.
(3) the production of durables—i.e., capital goods.
(4) wholesale rather than retail goods.
(5) export and import goods.

SUGGESTED ANSWERS TO QUESTIONS IN THE TEXT: Chapter 10

1. Depends on where you are and what you are doing. For example, employees of firms in the consumer durable industries (housing, cars, appliances, etc.) do not do well in recessions, especially recent hires.

2. Definitions of trough, expansion, peak, recession. What is going on now depends on when it is; your newspapers should be able to tell you and should provide coverage of what experts expect will happen next.

3. Let potential GNP be defined by a natural rate of unemployment of around 6 percent (e.g.). Unemployment 2 percentage points below that means, by Okun's Law, that GNP is 4 points below potential (Y^*). Solve for Y^* such that $(1 - 0.04) \times Y^* = \$4000$; $Y^* = \$4167$. Annual growth at 3 percent per year leads to potential GNP of \$4421 in 2 years ($= 1.03 \times 1.03 \times \$4167$); annual growth in actual GNP of slightly more than 5 percent per year gets you there.

4. The large tax cut, if in the personal income tax, would increase *AD*, increasing prices and having no effect on GNP if the economy were at its potential; it would increase GNP and have a smaller effect on prices if the economy were below its potential. This is a Keynesian answer, though. The supply-side focus of tax incentives might simultaneously increase investment and enlarge potential GNP. Then the output effect would be enlarged, and the price effect would be dampened somewhat.

5. Planning for the future is better than crisis management. You should forecast by reading what experts say and by critically evaluating their forecasts through application of the intuition of macroeconomic reasoning that you are learning in this course. Accept, though, a range of expected outcomes, and plan for various scenarios consistent with that range. It is all the better if you can understand what might drive you to the high, low, or middle part of that range; knowing this, you can monitor some critical variables and narrow the range of expectations as the future unfolds.

6. It is both an art and a science. Overreliance on one or the other (the tendency with computer models is to rely too heavily on the quantitative results of models at the expense of intuition) is a mistake.

7. **a.** Government-spending splurge (demand side) tends to push prices and/or actual GNP up; higher oil-price shock (supply side) tends to push prices up and actual GNP down. Draw the *AD-AS* graphs.
b. Defense-spending increase—*AD* shifts up.
Bombing damage—*AS* shifts in.
Net exports down—*AD* shifts in.
Oil-price jump—*AS* shifts up.
Productivity growth slowdown—*AS* shifts right over time more slowly, making higher *AD* more likely to be inflationary.

8. Apply Okun's Law. Starting at 7 percent unemployment, the Reagan estimates had actual GNP growing 0.5 percent per year faster than potential GNP, so unemployment should have declined over the 4-year period by $4 \times (0.5\%/2) = 1$ percentage point to 6 percent. If potential GNP grew at only 3 percent per year, then actual GNP would have increased 2 percent per year faster than potential. Full employment would then have been reached in 1 year (6 percent unemployment), and inflation would have followed. With potential GNP growing by 3 percent per year and actual GNP stagnant for 2 years, unemployment should have started at 7 percent and grown by $2 \times (3\%/2) = 3$ percentage points to 10 percent. It did, roughly.

9. **a.** Surely yes, because sudden general price increases look like personal price increases for a while and inspire expansion by the very definition of the model.
b. It should not allow for persistent downturns, because it can be consistent with a vertical *AS* curve. After a downturn, prices adjust down, relative prices adjust to the previous equilibrium, and the businesses should go back to where they started in terms of output and employment.

10. You are on your own. Does your graph look like a chart of stock prices from the financial pages? A chart of the Dow-Jones Average?

CHAPTER 11
MONEY AND COMMERCIAL BANKING

Up until now, the determination of national output has been described with little or no reference to money. It is now time to correct this omission; money is perhaps the most powerful tool of modern stabilization policy, and to continue to ignore its potential would be an enormous mistake. As you progress through the next chapters, though, it will become clear to you that the omission was a matter of exposition—a recognition that we could not do everything at once. The models that were constructed in earlier chapters can easily be expanded to include the monetary side of an economy. It therefore made sense to develop them fully before adding a second, financial dimension to their stories.

Chapter 11 begins with a discussion of the evolution of money and its associated financial institutions. It is perhaps surprising to note here at the beginning that there is no single, functional definition of money. There are, quite simply, so many "near-money" financial instruments available from across a wide spectrum of contemporary financial institutions that one definitive definition is impossible to write. Economists offer, instead, a list of definitions, each one applying to a slightly different notion and/or application of "money" or "credit."

Chapter 11 also introduces both the demand for money (a concept rooted in two motives for holding money that are themselves derived from three distinct functions that money can fulfill) and the supply of money (a potential policy tool whose effects are determined by the behavior of a fractional-reserve system of banking). Noting also a quick mention of a price of money (an interest-rate opportunity cost of holding money), you should begin to suspect that you will shortly see a money market evolve; and you would be right. Before that happens, though, you should master the following preliminary learning objectives.

LEARNING OBJECTIVES

1. Outline the highlights of the evolution of the monetary system from barter, through commodity money, and into today's system of fiat money. Note particularly the definition of fiat money and the contemporary roles of paper and bank monies.

2. Relate the differences among the various definitions of the money supply, starting with M_1 (transactions money, including cash, currency, and checking accounts), M_2 (M_1 plus close substitutes like savings accounts, mutual funds, etc.), L (M_2 plus all liquid accounts, including short-term Treasury notes, etc.), and D (total domestic debt). Understand that there is no single correct definition.

3. Describe the three functions of money (medium of exchange, unit of account, and store of value), and relate their role in supporting a transactions demand for money and an assets demand for money.

4. Note that the transactions demand for money depends upon nominal GNP and that the assets demand for money is sensitive to changes in the interest rate. The interest rate is thus the opportunity cost of holding money, reflecting the "price" of money in a demand context.

5. Outline briefly the evolution of the banking system from a collection of simple goldsmith depositories of wealth into an interconnected array of banks and other financial intermediaries.

6. Describe the process by which a banking system built on fractional reserves can create money. Understand the mathematics behind the resulting "money multiplier," and define the two qualifications upon which its precise computation is dependent.

In primitive times when people were nearly self-sufficient, there was, by definition, almost no need for any exchange of goods or services. As soon as specialization in production began, though, a system of exchange was required. Barter worked at first, but it was quickly overwhelmed by the complication of many people with many goods to exchange for their own specific needs. Even before thinking about the terms of trade, any individual owning some good A and wanting good B first had to find someone possessing good B and wanting good A. This requisite "double coincidence of wants" rendered barter clumsy and inefficient.

1. Money evolved because it was essential for large systems of exchange. It began as *(fiat money / commodity money / metal money)* when people started to measure the values of various goods and services in terms of so many units of one particular commodity. Today, all U.S. money is *(fiat money / commodity money / gold-based money)*—legal tender which must be accepted for *(all private and some public / some private and all public / some private and some public / all private and all public)* debts.

---

commodity money; fiat money; all private and all public

Today, virtually all money is **fiat money**; the government decrees that it is money, so it is. People accept it and conduct business with it, but what is it, really? The answer that applies to the strict M_1 definition associates money with anything that, by convention, is immediately spendable. A store will readily give you merchandise in exchange for part of your checking bank account. (If you propose to pay by check, the only thing the store will want to make sure of is that you really have a bank account of at least the required amount; if you pay by coins or bills, this problem does not arise.)

Anything not immediately spendable is never part of the money supply, strictly defined. However, there are certain classes of assets which are very close to being money; their owners think of them as money because conversion is ordinarily such a quick and simple process. An example is a savings deposit with a commercial bank. You cannot spend such a deposit, under normal circumstances, but the bank will ordinarily exchange your deposit for money in a matter of minutes.

2. a. It has become conventional, in tables listing the money supply, to make the distinction between "M_1" and "M_2." Items within M_1 are exclusively the three strictly defined money items. The M_2 category takes account of the "very close to being money" items. It consists of the total of *(these "very close" items alone / the "very close" items plus the M_1 items)*.

A basic problem with the "very close to being money" idea is, How close is very close? The "official" definition of M_2 includes only time deposits in commercial banks and money market funds. Why not federal government bonds? The market for such bonds is so well organized that ordinarily they can be converted into money very rapidly indeed. However, if such bonds are included, then why not other easily marketed securities?

As in all such cases, the decision is necessarily an arbitrary one. The M_2 category consists of M_1 plus commercial-bank time deposits and money market funds. Other time deposits, and government bonds, are lumped into a category called *(convertible money / non-money / near-money / high-grade money)*. In brief, the boundary around M_1 is logical. It's money if you can readily make payments with it. This excludes time deposits on which you cannot write checks. The boundary around M_2 is arbitrary. Just what truly constitutes "near-money" is a topic you can debate endlessly, if you have the time and inclination.

b. Consider the following list of financial "items," for want of a better term:

1. Any deposit in a commercial bank on which checks may be issued
2. Any deposit in a commercial bank, regardless of whether or not checks may be issued against it
3. A deposit in a mutual savings account or in a credit union
4. A high-grade corporation bond
5. A check drawn on a commercial-bank checking account

List the numbers of those items which would be included in M_1: ________________. Now list those items which would be included in M_2: ________________.

---

a. The "very close" items plus the M_1 items; near money **b.** 1 (Note for item 5: For many students, the temptation to argue that a check drawn on a bank account is money is almost overwhelming. You can hand a $10 bill across a store counter, or you can use a $10 check. But consider: if the total in your deposit at the bank has been counted in the money supply, you can't count any check drawn on that account in addition. To do so would involve double counting. The check is just an order to your bank, instructing it to transfer part of your account to someone else.); 1, 2, and 3

3. Table 11-1 in the text (page 229) records the various components of three major measures of the money supply. Referring to that table, determine whether the statistical importance of the specified component fell significantly (FS), fell slightly (F), held exactly stable (HS), rose slightly (R), or rose significantly (RS) from 1959 through January 1988.

a. currency as a component of M_1 . . . . (________)

b. NOW and checkable accounts as a component of M_1 . . . . (________)

c. M_1 as a component M_2 . . . . (________)

d. M_2 as a component of total domestic debt . . . (________)

---

a. R (from 21 percent to 24 percent) **b.** RS (from 0.3 percent to 35 percent) **c.** FS (From 47 percent to 28 percent) **d.** F (from 43 percent to 37 percent)

Money has three functions: (1) a medium of exchange, (2) a store of value, and (3) a unit of account. The first and the third functions are easily understood. As a medium of exchange, money is a device to avoid the inconvenience of barter. As a unit of account, money is simply a yardstick with which people measure how much things cost and how much things are worth. The second function, though, is a bit more complicated and deserves more than cursory mention.

In January 1988, the total money stock in the United States (the M_1 measure of coins, bills, and demand-deposit bank accounts) was over $843 billion. Each dollar of that stock had, and still has, an owner: an individual, a business, a financial institution. Why was this money being held?

At first this may seem a foolish question. Who wouldn't want to hold money? You can buy things with it! Nevertheless, there are alternatives to holding money as an asset. If you hold any significant amount of money, you could buy a security with it. Most securities pay an interest or dividend return; money does not. If you reject the idea of buying any security, then you must have some reason for holding onto money instead. If you buy the security, then you pass your money on to someone else and the recipient must have some reason for wanting to hold it.

What are the reasons, then, for holding money in preference to other assets that would yield some income return? Essentially, there are two. The first is simple. You need some money on hand because income does not arrive in a minute-by-minute flow. Instead, it comes at discontinuous intervals; wage or salary payments come each week, half-month, or month. Hence, you hold a cash balance which is gradually spent, until the next installment of income arrives. This is your **transactions demand** for money.

The second reason is a bit more complex, and its origins are varied. It is the desire to hold money as an asset, over and above the ordinary amount needed to tide you over until the next wage or salary payment reaches you. Why? Well, (1) you may want to keep some surplus cash against the possibility of some unexpected and cash-demanding emergency. Or, (2) having acquired your cash illegally, you may be shy about doing anything that would reveal you have it. Or, (3) you may be strongly convinced that security prices are going to fall so that the immediate purchase of any such security would be a bad idea. Any or all of these notions contribute to your **assets demand** for money.

4. The result of adding these two components together to compute the demand for money is significant. The first, the transactions demand for money, means that the demand for money will *(increase / be unaffected / decrease)* as income climbs. The more income that is available, the more people want to spend and the more money they will have to keep around to pay for those purchases. The second, the assets demand for money, emerges from portfolio theory to give the demand for money some (arguably, monetarists would say) sensitivity to the nominal interest rate. Why? Because the interest rate is the price of holding wealth in money instead of in some interest-bearing asset. The interest rate is, in fact, the opportunity cost of holding money. Thus, as the interest rate falls, the demand for money should, through its assets demand component, *(fall / remain the same / climb)*.

In Figure 11-1, four panels show the quantity of money demanded changing from M to M'. Record in the spaces below which panel illustrates the indicated change in economic conditions.

a. an increase in nominal GNP that leaves interest rates fixed . . . . (________)

b. an increase in the rate of interest . . . . (________)

c. a reduction in prices that is not yet reflected in interest rates . . . . (________)

d. a reduction in interest rates that is not yet reflected in a change in aggregate demand . . . . (________)

increase; climb **a.** a **b.** c **c.** d (Nominal GNP falls with price reductions.) **d.** b

5. Banks and other firms that offer banklike services are engaged in "financial intermediation." They are in the business of making money by facilitating the flow of your money to those people, businesses, and governments who are willing to pay higher interest rates to borrow it. You could do the same thing, but you would quickly wind up with the barter problem of coincidence. Moreover, unless you have a lot of money to lend, you could not spread the risk of bad loans across many borrowers with the same efficiency that these financial intermediaries achieve.

In the spaces below, list five major types of firms that engage in financial intermediation.

a. ____________________

b. ____________________

c. ____________________

d. ____________________

e. ____________________

a. commercial banks **b.** savings and loans **c.** life-insurance companies **d.** pension funds **e.** money market funds

The questions which follow begin with a situation in which there is no "bank money." They trace the development of such money through lending activity on the part of banks.

These questions concern an isolated community which uses initially only gold coins as money. The local goldsmith has a storage vault for gold. He is prepared to store money for others in this vault, charging a small fee. He chooses to list such deposits as an asset on his balance

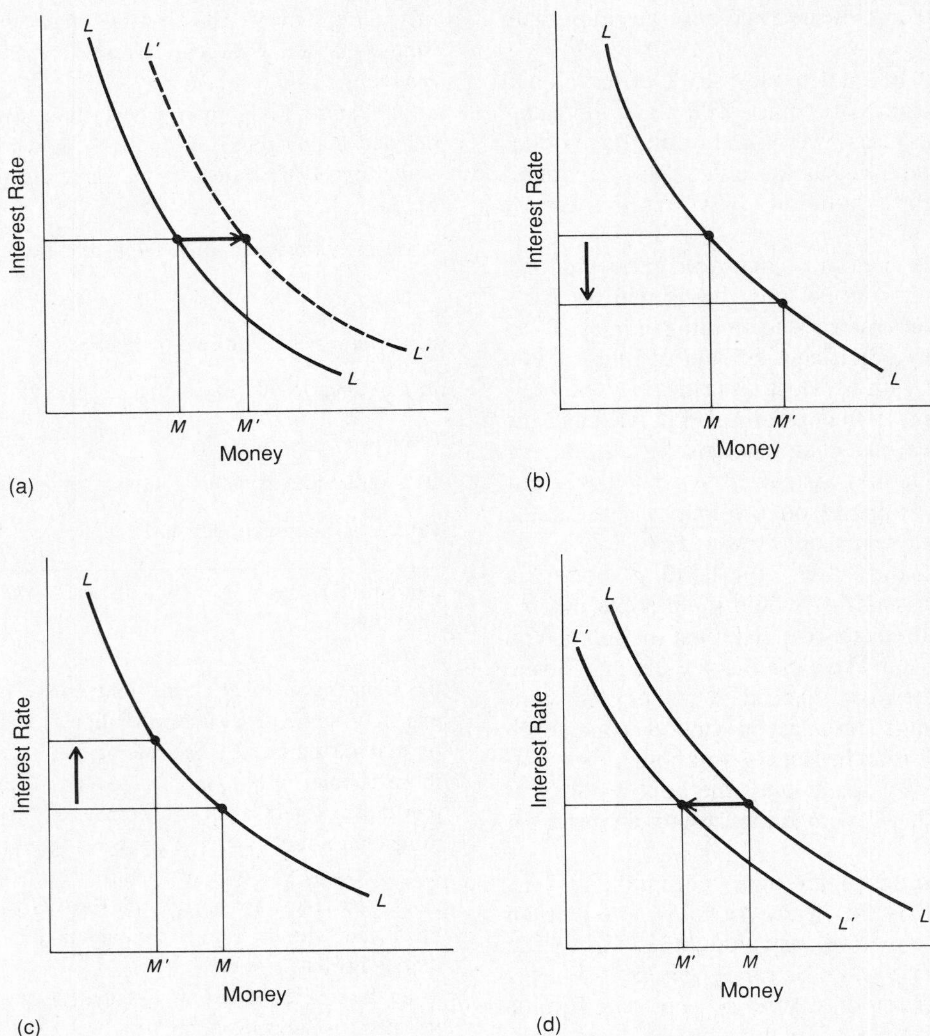

Figure 11-1

sheet, matched by a "deposit liability" of equal amount. His balance sheet, with respect to such deposits, reads:

Assets		Liabilities	
Gold coins in vault	$10,000	Deposits—payable to customers on demand	$10,000

6. a. A. Pennywise, a customer of the goldsmith, is asked for payment by one of his creditors. The goldsmith's shop having already closed for the day, Pennywise gives his creditor a note reading as follows:

To: Ye Gold Shoppe. Pay B. Poundfoolish $5
from my deposit. (Signed) A. Pennywise

What is the name given to such a note? __________

b. Poundfoolish presents the note the next morning, but instead of taking coins, he asks the goldsmith to keep the money stored in his name. Is any change necessary in the goldsmith's balance sheet? If so, explain.

____

____

____

____

a. check **b.** total of deposits unchanged; only ownership of deposits need be changed

7. Observing how convenient it was to settle an account by check, the townspeople adjust their behavior so that many transactions are now handled by check. Occasionally a depositor withdraws gold to make a payment, but the person receiving payment usually deposits it once again, since the vault is the safest place for gold storage and checks can always be drawn against such deposits.

A responsible merchant now asks the goldsmith for a loan

of $2000. The goldsmith has no gold free of deposit claims, only the $10,000 deposited with him. Is there any reason why he should nonetheless consider making the loan?

no, because most of the $10,000 in gold is not being used

8. The loan is made. The merchant is given $2000 in gold. The goldsmith's balance sheet (insofar as these transactions are concerned) now reads:

Assets		Liabilities	
Gold	$8,000	Demand deposits . . .	$10,000
Loans	2,000		

a. If the person receiving the loan redeposits it with the goldsmith, how will his balance sheet then appear?

Assets		Liabilities	
Gold	$______	Demand deposits . .	$______
Loans	______		

b. Has the money supply (the total of "spendable stuff") increased? *(yes / no)*. By how much? ______

a. Gold: $10,000; Loans: $2000; Demand deposits: $12,000 **b.** yes; $2000

9. Now suppose that the borrower, instead of taking $2000 in gold, simply asks for a $2000 deposit account against which he can draw checks. How will the balance sheet appear before the loan is spent? (NOTE: In actual practice, this is how bank loans are normally handled.)

Assets		Liabilities	
Gold	$______	Demand deposits . .	$______
Loans	______		

same answer as in question 8**a**

10. After the borrower has spent his $2000 loan (making payment to people whose custom is to keep a deposit with the goldsmith), how will the balance sheet look?

Assets		Liabilities	
Gold	$______	Demand deposits . .	$______
Loans	______		

same answer as in question 8**a** (The borrower's deposit account is $2000 smaller, but other accounts are a total of $2000 larger.)

11. We now change the situation slightly. The community holds $2000 in gold for transactions. If the goldsmith has made $20,000 in loans, then his balance sheet looks like:

Assets		Liabilities	
Gold	$ 8,000	Demand deposits	$28,000
Loans	20,000		

a. The total money supply (M_1) is now $______, consisting of $______ in bank money (demand deposits) and $______ in gold held in circulation.

b. Should the $8000 in gold in the vault count as part of M_1? ______. Why or why not? ______

a. $30,000; $28,000; $2000 **b.** no; It must be withdrawn before it is "spendable"; withdrawal will reduce bank money by the same amount.

Imagine, now, a swift passage of time so that we can add three aspects of contemporary realism to the scenario. First, imagine that the institution of goldsmith has evolved into the institution of banker. The balance sheets that will be considered in the questions which follow therefore apply to banks. Second, suppose that the gold-based currency system of the previous questions has evolved into a system of fiat money—dollars that reflect wealth because the government says they do and people accept that as fact. Finally, presume that a central financial authority of the government requires that banks maintain reserve stores of currency equal to at least 20 percent of their total demand deposits. Banks are, in other words, expected to restrain their total lending so that their demand deposits are never greater than 5 times the quantity of currency that they hold in reserve. For the time being, though, there is still only one bank (bank A, grown up from Ye Gold Shoppe) in town.

12. a. Show bank A's balance sheet if it has $8000 in reserve currency on deposit and is fully "loaned out" against the 20 percent legal reserve requirement. A full $2000 in cash and currency is held across the community in transactions demand.

Assets		Liabilities	
Reserves . . .	$______	Demand deposits . . .	$______
Loans	______		______

b. Given only one bank, the community's total M_1 is, at this point, $______, consisting of $______ in bank money (again, demand deposits) and $______ in transactions currency.

____

____

a. Reserves: $8000; Loans: $32,000; Demand deposits: $40,000 **b.** $42,000; $40,000; $2000

13. a. A storekeeper brings $500 in cash into the bank for deposit. The resulting balance sheet, before any new loans are issued, should be:

Assets		Liabilities	
Reserves . . .	$______	Demand deposits . . .	$______
Loans	______		

b. With this deposit, the storekeeper has enough money on deposit to repay a $1000 loan. His deposit is reduced by $1000, and he is given back his note. Disregarding any interest on the loan, what does the balance sheet look like now?

Assets		Liabilities	
Reserves . .	$______	Demand deposits . . .	$______
Loans	______		

c. When the loan is paid off, is the community's M_1 affected? ______. If so, how? If not, why not? ____________

____

____

____

a. Reserves: $8500; Loans: $32,000; Demand deposits: $40,500 **b.** Reserves: $8500; Loans: $31,000; Demand deposits: $39,500 **c.** yes; M_1, the sum of demand deposits and currency held, falls by $1000. M_1 can recover if a new $1000 is issued to someone else.

We have assumed thus far that there is just one bank in town; i.e., that there is just one bank. Suppose, instead, there are two, the original (call it A) and a new one (call it B). Considering this case will illustrate two fundamental points about a modern, multifaceted banking system. First, neither (no) bank (or financial institution) will have as much freedom to increase loans as the monopoly bank of the previous questions. If either (any) bank has sufficient reserves to issue a loan, it must allow for the fact that any such loan will cause some of its reserves to "spill over" into the other bank(s). Second, though, the "banking system" as a whole *does* have the same power to expand loans as the monopoly bank. Taken together, they function *as the monopoly bank*. The next set of questions will explore these points.

14. The new bank (B, remember) is willing to store cash and handle some checks as a means of transferring deposits from one customer's account to another. Suppose B receives checks drawn on A for $4000. Before offering any loans, the balance sheet for bank B should look like:

Assets		Liabilities	
______ . .	$______	______ . . .	$______

Assets: Checks (drawn on A). . .$4000; Liabilities: Demand deposits. . .$4000

15. Things finally shake out so that each bank has $4000 in reserves; $2000 in currency is held by the townspeople for transactions. Each bank, fully "loaned up" against a 20 percent required reserve ratio, would now have a balance sheet that looks like:

Assets		Liabilities	
Reserves . . .	$______	Demand deposits . .	$______
Loans	______		

Taking the two banks together, the balance sheet for the banking system as a whole would meanwhile look like:

Assets		Liabilities	
Reserves . . .	$______	Demand deposits . .	$______
Loans	______		

This *(does / does not)* match the balance sheet for the monopoly bank in the same situation (question 11). The community's total M_1 is $______, with $______ in bank money and $______ in circulation.

For either A or B: Reserves: $4000; Loans: $16,000; Demand deposits: $20,000 For A and B together: Reserves: $8000; Loans: $32,000; Demand deposits: $40,000 does; $42,000; $40,000; $2000

16. Now suppose that a local girl who has made good abroad returns with $3000 new currency. She deposits the cash entirely with B. Question 14 defines the starting point.

a. Before B has a chance to issue new loans, the revised balance sheet should look like:

Assets		Liabilities	
Reserves	$______	Demand deposits . .	$______
Loans	______		

b. Now assume that B extends loans to the maximum extent allowed by the 20 percent required reserve ratio. If *all* the loans result in demand deposits in B, then the fully extended balance sheet for B should be:

Assets		Liabilities	
Reserves	$______	Demand deposits . .	$______
Loans	______		

The corresponding balance sheet for A should be:

Assets		Liabilities	
Reserves	$______	Demand deposits . .	$______
Loans	______		

The resulting cumulative balance sheet for the banking system as a whole should meanwhile be:

Assets		Liabilities	
Reserves	$______	Demand deposits . .	$______
Loans	______		

c. Assume, instead, that any loan issued by either A or B results in 50 percent of the money finding its way into a demand deposit in A and 50 percent of the money findings its way into a demand deposit in B. Assume, again, that B is fully "loaned out." The resulting balance sheet for B should be:

Assets		Liabilities	
Reserves	$______	Demand deposits . .	$______
Loans	______		

The corresponding balance sheet for A should be:

Assets		Liabilities	
Reserves	$______	Demand deposits . .	$______
Loans	______		

The cumulative balance sheet for the banking system as a whole should be:

Assets		Liabilities	
Reserves . . .	$______	Demand deposits . . .	$______
Loans	______		

d. Notice that M_1 is *(different / the same)* for the two cases listed in parts **b** and **c**. Total M_1 is $______ in part **b** and $______ in part **c**, with currency holdings of $______ in both and bank money of $______ in part **b** and $______ in part **c**.

a. Reserves: $7000; Loans: $16,000; Demand deposits: $23,000
b. For B: Reserves: $7000; Loans: $28,000; Demand deposits: $35,000 For A: Reserves: $4000; Loans: $16,000; Demand deposits: $20,000 Together: Reserves: $11,000; Loans: $44,000; Demand deposits: $55,000
c. For B: Reserves: $5800; Loans: $23,200; Demand deposits: $29,000 For A: Reserves: $5200; Loans: $20,800; Demand deposits: $26,000 Together: Reserves: $11,000; Loans: $44,000; Demand deposits: $55,000
d. the same; $57,000; $57,000; $2000; $55,000; $55,000 [*Note:* To compute part **c**, observe that the initial $3000 goes to B. Bank B then lends 0.8 × $3000 = $2400, and both banks get an influx of $1200. Since the subsequent-round loans are identical for both banks and the resulting deposits are split equally, the result for A is just like a "monopoly-bank" influx of $1200; it results in a $6000 (= 5 × $1200) increase in demand deposits covered by $1200 in additional reserves and $4800 in loans. For B this monopoly-bank influx is added to the original $3000 deposit that is covered by $0.2 × $3000 = $600 in reserves and the first-round $2400 loan.]

The previous questions show that any increase in reserves can be expected to increase the M_1 money supply by 5 times that increase when the required reserve ratio is 20 percent. The general formula for the **money multiplier** is $1/rrr$, where *rrr* represents the required reserve ratio (expressed as a fraction). For the 20 percent required reserve ratio quoted above, therefore, the multiplier is $1/0.2 = 5$. Question 16 explores two caveats to this computation.

17. Complete Table 11-2 by recording the money multipliers in column (1) that correspond to the required reserve ratios listed in the left-hand column. Notice that each of the two required ratios indicated by an asterisk corresponds to the requirements currently set by the Federal Reserve for time deposits up to 1.5 years in maturity and for checking accounts (3 percent for accounts up to $37 million and 12 percent above $37 million).

Now complete column (2) under the assumption that banks hedge against the reserve requirement by holding 2 percentage points above and beyond the requirement in "extra reserve." The notion here is that bank hedging against being short can turn a required reserve ratio set by the monetary authorities into a functionally stricter requirement and that the actual money multiplier can fall as a result. Required reserve ratios are, in practice, set higher than necessary so that banks are discouraged from doing too much of this sort of hedging. Why? Because it adds an element of unpredictability to the computation of the money multiplier that the monetary authorities would prefer to live without.

Table 11-2

Required Reserve Ratio, %	Money Multipliers		
	(1)	(2)	(3)
3*	______	______	______
5	______	______	______
10	______	______	______
12*	______	______	______
16	______	______	______

*Corresponds to current Federal Reserve requirements for checking accounts and time deposits.

Finally, complete column (3) under the additional assumption that 2 percent of the money that moves into circulation through loans stays there. Functionally, this leakage looks just like a second, behavioral increase in the reserve requirement that also reduces the money multiplier and makes its precise value uncertain.

Reading down column (1): 33.33, 20, 10, 8.33, 6.25 Reading down column (2): 20, 14.29, 8.33, 7.14, 5.56 Reading down column (3): 14.39, 11.11, 7.14, 6.25, 5

18. a. The combined balance sheet (billions of dollars) of all the commercial banks in some economy appears below. The legal reserve requirement is 10 percent of deposits. The banks thus have excess reserves of $*(0 / 5 / 10 / 15 / 20 / 30)* billion.

Assets		Liabilities	
Reserves (deposits with Federal Reserve and cash in vaults) . . .	$30	Demand deposits	$100
Loans	70		

b. Show their balance sheet after they have taken full advantage of excess reserves to expand loans. All new money remains as demand deposits.

Assets		Liabilities	
Reserves . . .	$______	Demand deposits . . .	$______
Loans	______		

---

a. 20 b.Reserves: $30; Loans: $270; Deposits: $300 (When there are many banks, the reasoning can be the same as in the monopoly-bank case.)

19. The process of bank-money creation is most easily explained in terms of deposit of cash in a bank. Bear in mind, though, that once the credit expansion process is completed and banks are fully loaned up, most deposits made with banks do not permit any further loan expansion at all.

In the two cases following, assume the banking system to be fully loaned up. The reserve requirement is 10 percent.

a. I deposit $1000 in cash in my bank. Which description is more correct?

(1) This $1000 will permit the banking system to expand loans by $4000.

(2) Unless the $1000 was a net addition to reserves, no loan expansion by the banking system is possible. The money may have been withdrawn from another bank (or even my bank) a day or two earlier.

b. I deposit a $1000 salary check in my bank. Again, pick the better description.

(1) This $1000 will permit the banking system to expand loans by $4000.

(2) My bank's reserves are increased, but at the cost of the reserves of some other bank. There has been no net addition to the entire banking system's reserves.

---

a. (2) b. (2)

20. Consider the following sequence of events:

1. A single small bank receives a deposit of $1000 in coins and bills, money which hitherto had been hidden in a mattress.
2. Out of this deposit it makes a loan of $800 by giving the borrower credit for a deposit (checking) account of $800. (The remaining $200 is retained as a reserve against the original deposit.)
3. The borrower issues checks in order to spend his $800 loan. The deposit thus passes (via those to whom the checks are made payable) from the original bank to other banks.

a. Did event 1 change (increase or decrease) M_1? ______.

Explain. ______________________________

b. Did event 2 change M_1? ______. Explain. ______

____

c. Did event 3 change M_1? ______.

d. If your answer to **b** was yes, how can you reconcile it with the argument that no single bank can create money, since it only lends out part of what was deposited with it? If your answer to **b** was no, how can you reconcile it with the fact that the bank's demand deposits rose by $800? ______

______

e. Suppose the bank had given the borrower $800 in cash instead of a deposit account. How, if at all, would this change your answers to the preceding questions? ______

______

______

______

a. no; Coin-and-bill money is down; bank money is up. **b.** yes; Bank money is up by $800; no change in coin-and-bill money. **c.** no **d.** The single bank can create money. You cannot reconcile a "no" answer; it is wrong. **e.** M_1 would again be up by $800, just as in part **b**; but it would be an increase in coin-and-bill money, not in bank money.

QUIZ: Multiple Choice

1. Barter, the first step in the evolution of a monetary system above self-sufficiency, gave way to commodity money because:
(1) barter was an inefficient transaction mechanism involving high transaction cost incurred by the necessity of finding someone willing to trade what you have for what you want.
(2) it was inconvenient at best.
(3) barter stood in the way of efficient division of labor unless the output was divisible.
(4) barter depended upon a double coincidence of wants that became increasingly unlikely as economies grew more diverse.
(5) all of the above.

2. Commodity money was a step toward efficiency, but was undermined frequently by:
(1) frequent relapse into barter.
(2) the vagaries of supply and demand for the commodity that altered the value of the money.
(3) the inability of communities to agree to one commodity.
(4) the inability of communities to find a commodity that was not perishable.
(5) none of the above.

3. The strictest definition of money, M_1, includes:
(1) coins, currency, and demand deposits.
(2) coins, currency, and time deposits.
(3) coins, currency, and all deposits in a bank.
(4) all currencies and near-monies.
(5) none of the above.

4. Financial intermediaries are institutions that:
(1) buy and sell all types of goods, including merchandise.
(2) include only international corporations that must have large holdings of various types of currency.
(3) accept the deposits of some people and institutions and use that money to support the borrowing needs of others.
(4) are not really necessary in the United States because of the size of the federal debt.
(5) all of the above.

5. Commercial banks are the largest category of financial intermediaries; others include:
(1) life-insurance companies.
(2) pension funds.
(3) savings and loan institutions.
(4) money market funds.
(5) all of the above.

6. The essential difference between "money" and "near-money" is that:
(1) money is directly spendable, whereas near-money is not.
(2) near-money includes all deposits in bank accounts, whereas money includes none of these.
(3) the velocity of circulation of money is rapid, while that of near-money is slow.
(4) near-money is fiat money, whereas money is not.
(5) near-money is made up of any and all items that can be marketed for a money price.

7. If you write a check on your bank account, that check:
(1) counts as part of M_1 provided it is a valid check, i.e., there are funds in the bank to support it.
(2) counts as part of M_1 whether valid or not, provided the person to whom it is given accepts it.
(3) counts as part of M_1 if used to buy goods and services, but not otherwise.
(4) does not count as part of M_1, since no bank account is considered part of the money supply.
(5) does not count as part of M_1; to count both it and the deposit account on which it is drawn would be double counting.

8. When money has been deposited in any private financial institution (e.g., a commercial bank, a savings and loan association, etc.), the critical factor in deciding whether that deposit should count as part of the money supply (M_1, or "money narrowly defined") is that:
(1) checks can be freely written against the deposit by its owner.
(2) the deposit has insurance or backing by the government or some public institution.
(3) the institution maintains 100 percent backing or reserve for the deposit—whether the backing is provided by the government or not.
(4) the institution has a legal franchise which permits its deposits to be counted as money.
(5) so long as the money deposited consists of genuine bills or coins, then the deposit within any such institution must be counted as part of the money supply.

9. Money serves:
(1) as a medium of exchange.
(2) as a store of value.

(3) as a unit of exchange.
(4) all of the above.
(5) none of the above.

10. On the basis of the transactions demand component of the demand for money:
(1) the demand for money climbs as the interest rate climbs.
(2) the demand for money climbs as the interest rate falls.
(3) the demand for money falls as nominal income rises.
(4) the demand for money falls as nominal income falls.
(5) none of the above.

11. Which answer to question 10 would have been correct if it had referred to the assets demand component of the demand for money?
(1).
(2).
(3).
(4).
(5).

12. The "demand for money" means:
(1) the desire to hold securities which can readily be converted into money at a fixed or near-fixed price if necessary.
(2) the amount which businesses will wish to borrow at any given interest rate.
(3) the desire to save more money out of income as protection against the uncertainties of the future.
(4) the same thing as "asset demand for money."
(5) the same thing as the sum of "assets and transactions demand for money."

13. In a fractional-reserve banking system, such as that of the United States, the required reserve ratios imposed on commercial banks:
(1) are primarily intended to set a limit on the total money supply rather than to serve as adequate protection against bank runs.
(2) are in excess of what is normally required, but are sufficient to cover what would be needed if for any reason people became uneasy over the safety of bank deposits.
(3) are essentially an average of the amounts needed to meet the public's demands in good times and bad.
(4) are now obsolete, according to the text, and will shortly be replaced by a 100 percent reserve requirement.
(5) are not correctly described by any of the above.

14. The commercial banking system (all banks taken together) lends money to business firms and consumers, normally by setting up demand deposits which the borrowers may spend. As a result, the money supply:
(1) decreases by the total amount of all coins and bills deposited with the banking system for safekeeping.
(2) neither increases nor decreases.
(3) increases by an amount somewhat less than the system's total coin-and-bill deposits, owing to the fraction it holds as reserves.
(4) increases by an amount just equal to the system's total coin-and-bill deposits.
(5) increases by an amount considerably greater than the system's total coin-and-bill deposits.

15. The economy's total money supply will increase whenever commercial banks:
(1) increase their deposits with a Federal Reserve Bank.
(2) increase their total loans to the public.
(3) increase their demand-deposit liabilities by receiving coins or bills from the public as a deposit.
(4) withdraw part of their deposits from a Federal Reserve Bank.
(5) reduce their demand-deposit liabilities by paying out part of these accounts in the form of coins or paper bills.

16. I deposit, in Bank X, $10,000 in paper currency which has for a long time been hidden and out of circulation. The legal minimum reserve requirement for banks is 25 percent of deposits. Bank X is one among many banks. Unless bank X is already short on reserves, this deposit would enable the bank, if it wished, to increase its loans by at least:
(1) an undetermined amount.
(2) $7500.
(3) $10,000.
(4) $30,000.
(5) more than $30,000.

17. Assuming that the loan increase does not set off any increase of coins and paper currency in hand-to-hand circulation, the deposit described in question 16 would enable the banking system to increase its loans by a maximum of:
(1) zero.
(2) $7500.
(3) $10,000.
(4) $30,000.
(5) more than $30,000.

18. In the circumstances of questions 16 and 17, if consideration is given to some small increase of coins and paper currency in hand-to-hand circulation, the most probable maximum amount (among the five alternatives listed below) by which the banking system as a whole could increase loans would be:
(1) zero.
(2) less than $5000.
(3) between $20,000 and $30,000.
(4) between $30,000 and $40,000.
(5) more than $40,000.

19. Had bank X been a monopoly bank with all other circumstances as in question 16 (including zero hand-to-hand circula-

tion leakage), then the maximum amount by which this deposit would have enabled bank X to increase its loans, if so disposed, would be:
(1) zero.
(2) $7500.
(3) $10,000.
(4) $30,000.
(5) more than $30,000.

20. If the required reserve ratio had been 20 rather than 25 percent, but with all other circumstances as in question 16, the deposit would have enabled bank X to increase its loans, if so disposed, by:
(1) zero.
(2) $2000.
(3) $8000.
(4) $10,000.
(5) $40,000.

21. If the deposit of question 16 had been a $10,000 check drawn on bank Y, then this deposit (considered in isolation from all other deposits or withdrawals) would have enabled bank X to increase its loans, if so disposed, by:
(1) zero.
(2) $7500.
(3) $10,000.
(4) $30,000.
(5) more than $30,000.

22. The deposit of question 21 would enable the entire banking system to increase loans, if so disposed, by:
(1) zero.
(2) $7500.
(3) $10,000.
(4) $30,000.
(5) more than $30,000.

23. If the legal required reserve ratio is a minimum of 30 percent of the amount of demand deposits, and if the banking system now has excess reserves of $15 million, then (disregarding any resulting increase in hand-to-hand circulation) the banking system could increase demand deposits by a maximum of:
(1) zero.
(2) $10.5 million.
(3) $15 million.
(4) $35 million.
(5) $50 million.

24. The "excess reserves" of a commercial bank consist of:
(1) assets which, although not money, can be quickly converted into money by the bank should the need arise.
(2) money and near-money assets possessed by the bank in excess of 100 percent of the amount of its demand deposits.
(3) cash which must be kept on hand, not because everyday bank needs require it, but because of a legal requirement.
(4) money held by the bank in excess of that fraction of its deposits required by law.
(5) the difference between the amount of its money assets and the amount of its demand deposits.

25. The money multiplier is the multiplicative inverse of the required reserve ratio as long as:
(1) currency leakages into circulation and/or foreign markets do not occur.
(2) banks do not maintain excess reserves.
(3) the required reserve ratio is far in excess of the reserves that banks think are prudent given the deposits that they hold.
(4) all the above.
(5) none of the above.

SUGGESTED ANSWERS TO QUESTIONS IN THE TEXT: Chapter 11

1. M_1 is currency and demand deposits; M_2 adds savings accounts, small time deposits, and money market funds to M_1. M_1 is labeled transactions money and reflects a good deal of transactions demand. The opportunity cost of holding M_1 is the interest rate (or the difference between low rates paid on NOW accounts and higher rates that can be earned elsewhere). The things that are added in the computation of M_2 pay some return, but not as much as elsewhere, either. They therefore reflect, imprecisely, the image of assets demand.

2. Refer to the history in the text.

3. Table 11-5a:

Assets		Liabilities	
Reserves	$1,000	Demand deposits	$1,000
Total	$1,000	Total	$1,000

Table 11-7:

Assets		Liabilities	
Reserves	$1,000	Demand deposits	$1,000
Loans	0		
Total	$1,000	Total	$1,000

No money is created by the bank with a 100 percent required or functional reserve requirement.

4. Table 11-5a would show [−$2,000] for all four entries. Table 11-7 would show Reserves. . . −$2,000; Loans. . . −$8,000 and Demand deposits. . . −$10,000. Both totals would be [−$10,000]. The multiples would be [1/.2] = 5.

5. a. Demand for money increases through transactions demand.
b. Demand for money falls with nominal GNP through transactions demand.
c. Demand for money falls through assets demand.
d. Demand for money increases through assets demand; the opportunity cost for demand deposits (part of M_1) fell.
e. No change.

6. Interest rates reflect earnings on loans; they are thus the opportunity cost of excess reserves.

7. It might increase the level of excess reserves, making bank behavior less predictable and making the money multiplier less stable.

8. Yes: traveler's checks. Everything else fits the intuition of "near-money" with varying degrees of "proximity." Other opinions can be supported in the never-never land border between the definitions of monetary aggregates.

9. Reserves would fall. The multiplier would rise, but it would be hard to predict accurately.

10. No. The monopoly-bank multiplier is the same as the bank-system multiplier.

11. The FED follows all monetary aggregates at different times. The line is arbitrary and means different things at different times. There is no uniformly correct answer.

12. The multiplier formula $(1/rrr) > 10$ if $rrr < 0$.

13. Consider increasing reserves by $\$R$. Loans increase by $\$(0.9)R$, and $\$(20/21)(0.9)R$ in new deposits are created. In the second round, then, loans are increased by $\$(0.9)(20/21)(0.9)R$ and deposits increase by $\$(0.9)^2(20/21)_2R$. Creating the geometric series (footnote 6) by $\$R\{1+(0.9)(20/21)+[0.9(20/21)]_2+\ldots\}$, the multiplier is $1/[1-0.9(20/21)]=7$. The money supply for $\$R$ must therefore equal $\$7R$. Deposits equal 20/21 of that total [$\$(6\frac{2}{3})R$] and currency held equals 1/21 of that total [$\$(1/3)R$].

14. People demanding gold against a fixed supply could cause a shortage. If the value of currency were tied to its being convertible into gold, then this shortage could be a crisis. The solution is to simply devalue the currency so that each dollar is worth less gold. Or, as was done, remove the convertibility provision and create fiat money backed only by faith.

APPENDIX: 11

Stock Market Fluctuations

The main part of Chapter 11 examined the nature of money and credit. The appendix focuses on the common-stock holdings that many Americans find so attractive. These are assets that, while they fall outside the technical definitions of M_1 and M_2, are nonetheless held in great quantity by thousands of households across the United States. The share of wealth held in M_1 has declined slightly since 1960, but the shares of pension funds and savings accounts have climbed.

In working through the appendix, you will not only review the size of these holdings but also gain some insight into the workings of the stock market. Upon completing your work, therefore, you will have accomplished the following objectives.

LEARNING OBJECTIVES

1. Relate the distribution of wealth across the myriad of financial assets available to the individual and the distribution of holdings of common stock across the population.

2. Understand the basis of the "efficient-market" hypothesis and how it translates into a "random-walk" theory of stock market prices.

3. Glean some notion of what the efficiency of the stock market means to investment strategies in the market and your ability to "beat the market" by being very clever.

Holdings of common stock were very popular as late as the 1960s, but their popularity has declined dramatically since then. Nonetheless, they are still the form in which almost 25 percent of the wealth of the American population is held, and they gained renewed, if perhaps short-lived, popularity during the market boom that began in August 1982. Fallout from the "crash" of October 19, 1987 is still being felt in the stock market, but not, apparently, in the "real" economy.

1. In 1985, corporate equities represented a higher proportion of the total assets of American households than (circle as many as apply) *(currency / savings accounts / pension funds / government securities)*. Measured in dollars, holdings were up from nearly *($200 / $300 / $400)* billion in 1960 despite the decline in the relative popularity of stocks. Over *(35 million / 50 million / 75 million)* people own stock, with at least *(1 million / 2 million / 3 million)* of those earning less than $10,000 a year holding at least one share. For those low-income people, the average dividend payment is approximately $80 per year. On the other side of the distribution, more than *(25 percent / 35 percent / 50 percent)* of the outstanding corpo-

rate stock in the United States is owned by the wealthiest 1 percent of the population.

---

currency, pension funds, government securities; $400; 35 million; 3 million; 50 percent

2. a. *Margin buying* on the stock market works as follows: You want to buy XYZ stock, currently selling at $40 per share; you think XYZ will rise to $50 or higher. You have only $1000 in cash; this will buy only 25 shares (disregarding the broker's commission and other incidental buying costs). But with a margin requirement of 25 percent, you can buy a larger number of shares. You do this by borrowing $3000 from your broker or, via the broker, from a bank or other lending agency. The loan proceeds plus your own cash will buy *(25 / 50 / 100 / 200)* shares. Of course you must put up some security against your loan. But you have this; you can furnish XYZ stock worth $*(1000 / 3000 / 4000)*. This is accepted as adequate security for your $3000 loan.

b. If XYZ goes to 50, you sell your stock, pay off principal and interest on your loan, and pocket the rest of your profit, happy at having taken an economics course. But if, instead, XYZ should drop below 40—say, to 35 or 34—you will get a call from your broker to report that the bank "wants more margin," for the value of the asset you have supplied as collateral is falling. You must put up some more security or else pay off part of the loan. If you fail to come across, the bank will sell your XYZ stock. If it sells at close to 30, the entire sale proceeds go to to cover your loan, leaving you with the sad reminder that you should first have read beyond Chapter 4 in the text.

Note the unstable quality of a market heavily involved with margin buying. If prices begin to fall, this sets off a *(further wave of selling / wave of buying)*, as borrowers cannot furnish more margin and lenders sell to protect their loans. This pushes stock prices down even more.

---

a. 100; 4000 **b.** further wave of selling

3. a. A "bull" market is one in which most expectations are that stock prices are going to *(rise / fall)*. Most people with cash are accordingly inclined to *(buy / refrain from buying)* stocks. Most people holding stocks are inclined to *(continue to hold / sell)* them. The consequence of such expectations is that stock prices generally *(rise / fall)*.

b. A "bear" market is one in which most expectations are that stock prices are going to *(rise / fall)*. Most people with cash are accordingly inclined to *(buy / refrain from buying)* stocks. Most people holding stocks are inclined to *(continue to hold / sell)* them. The consequence of such expectations is that stock prices generally *(rise / fall)*.

---

a. rise; buy; continue to hold; rise **b.** fall; refrain from buying; sell; fall

4. If you buy stock through your broker and through the New York Stock Exchange, the seller of that stock (pick one):

a. may have been some private holder, or may have been the corporation whose stock it is (i.e., it may have been stock newly issued by that corporation).

b. must have been the corporation whose stock it is.

c. must have been some private holder—i.e., it cannot normally have been the corporation whose stock it is.

(The NYSE, like other exchanges, is a place where "used" securities are exchanged. A corporation cannot use it to "float" a new issue of stock.)

5. When you buy a stock, you do so either because you think its price will rise or else because you think the dividend yield is sufficiently high to make it worth buying. But remember: someone holds just the opposite opinion from yours—namely, whoever it was that sold you that stock. (In the stock market, you cannot know the identity of that "whoever it was." All transactions are anonymous.) This need not stop you from buying. Your judgment may be better than that of the anonymous somebody on the other side of your buying (or for that matter, selling) transaction.

This leads us into two topics discussed in the text: (*a*) the idea of an "efficient market," and (*b*) the "random-walk" hypothesis of stock market prices.

Today there are thousands of professionals whose job it is to scrutinize the background of all stocks listed on the New York, American, and lesser stock exchanges. (They look into "over-the-counter" stocks as well—stocks of smaller companies that are unlisted but do trade through less formal channels.) They have probed into everything that is to be known about all the companies involved; their balance sheet positions, the competence of their managers, their future sales and earning prospects, and so on. All this information has been passed on to stock buyers and sellers. This yields—in principle, at any rate—an **efficient market**, one in which there are no underpriced stocks, and none overpriced.

Why? Because accurate information is quickly absorbed into the price. Suppose, for the sake of illustration, that you decide that you want to buy a few shares of stock in a firm that has suddenly become more profitable. The firm has just marketed a new product for which demand is unexpectedly high, or just developed a new technology that will dramatically lower its costs and improve its competitive position, or has just discovered an enormous oil deposit under its Texas plant. In any case, you are attracted to the stock because future earnings by that firm should be significantly *(higher / lower)* than had originally been expected. You and other investors will want to *(buy / sell)* stock in that firm. People who already own stock in that firm will, on the other hand, want to *(sell / hold onto)* those issues in the expectation that they will soon be worth *(less / more)*. The result will be an immediate *(increase / reduction)* in the price of that stock in response to *(higher / lower)* demand and *(higher / lower)* supply at the original market-clearing price. By the time you get to the market and find someone who will be willing to sell you the shares that you want, therefore, the price will already include the increment in value of the newly announced profitability that you had hoped to cash in on.

The problem is that the efficient-market hypothesis means that the effects of foreseeable events are already included in the prices of stocks before you can get to them. You are therefore left with trying to predict unforeseeable events in your effort to "beat the market." As a result, if you invest in the stock market and accept the hypothesis, then you should (pick one or more):

a. concentrate your purchases on a small number of stocks.

b. buy a widely diversified collection of stocks.

c. keep altering your portfolio—i.e., trade frequently.

d. stick to your portfolio—i.e., trade infrequently.

---

higher; buy; hold onto; more; increase; higher; lower; **b** and **d**

Table 11A-1

(1) The Sum of Two Dice	(2) Sequence	(3) Column (1) Plus Column (2)
______	1	______
______	2	______
______	3	______
______	4	______
______	5	______
______	6	______
______	7	______
______	8	______
______	9	______
______	10	______
______	11	______
______	12	______
______	13	______
______	14	______
______	15	______
______	16	______
______	17	______
______	18	______
______	19	______
______	20	______

6. Find a pair of dice. Roll them 20 times in succession and record the sum of each roll in column (1) of Table 11A-1. Record in column (3) the sums of your entries in column (1) and the sequence of numbers provided in column (2). Plot the numbers recorded in column (3) on Figure 11A-1 and connect the points. Does the pattern of the resulting graph look like Figure 11A-1 in the text? ______

It should, at least vaguely.

QUIZ: Multiple Choice

1. Holdings in common stock:
(1) amount to about 10 percent of the assets held by American households.
(2) amount to about 50 percent of the assets held by American households.
(3) have fallen proportionally in the portfolios of American households but have risen absolutely since 1960.
(4) have risen proportionally in the portfolios of American households since the crash of 1975.
(5) have held remarkably steady as a proportion of the assets of the American household.

2. Holdings of common stock:
(1) are distributed over a wide range of income levels but are concentrated in the wealthiest 1 percent of the American population.
(2) are held exclusively by the wealthy.
(3) are confined to pension funds and insurance companies.
(4) are considerable, but less than holdings of currency.
(5) are dwarfed only by holdings of government securities needed to finance the federal debt.

3. The efficient-market theory:
(1) states that all public information is reflected almost immediately in the price of a share of common stock.
(2) implies that "beating the market" involves predicting unforeseeable events.
(3) implies that stock market prices move in the short run as if they were random numbers.
(4) implies diversification is a reasonable strategy for investing in the stock market.
(5) all of the above.

4. The essential property of margin buying of a stock is:
(1) participation in stock buying during a period of price rise by inexperienced investors.
(2) trading in a stock in quantities that do not really exist.
(3) any purchase of a stock in anticipation of a rise in its price, provided the stock is held for a short period only.
(4) a stock purchase financed in part by use of borrowed money.
(5) none of the above.

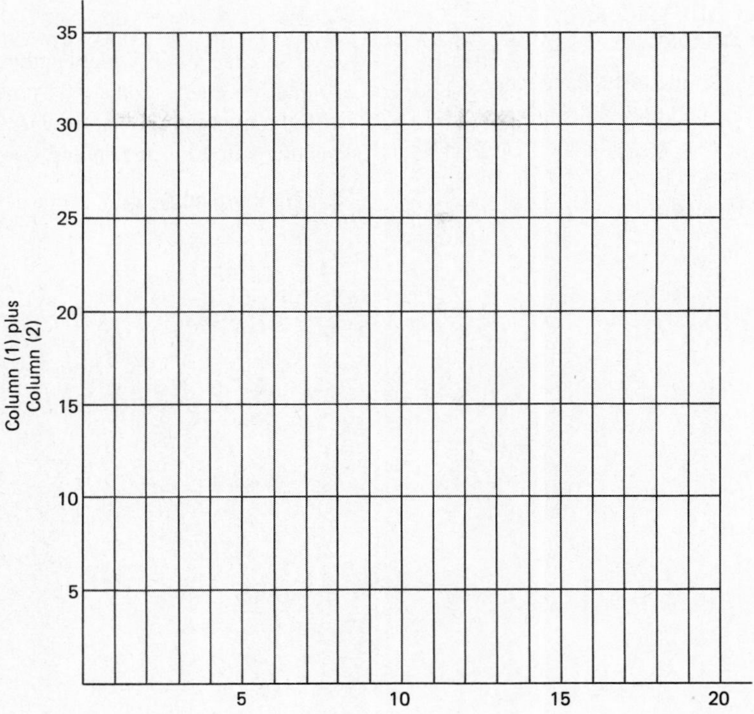

Figure 11A-1

5. As the result of some favorable news regarding a company, the price of its stock rises. If we were to use supply and demand curves to illustrate the nature of that price rise, we would say that it resulted from:
(1) solely a rightward or upward shift of the demand curve.
(2) solely a leftward or upward shift of the supply curve.
(3) both a rightward demand-curve shift and a leftward supply-curve shift.
(4) principally a rightward (or downward) shift of the supply curve.
(5) principally a rightward shift of both demand and supply curves.

6. Some profitable and well-regarded companies whose stocks are listed on the New York exchange pay no dividends at all; profits are used entirely for expansion of plant and operations. A shrewd investor:
(1) might buy such stock in hope of capital gains, but not otherwise.
(2) might buy such stock in expectation of a "stock split," but not otherwise.
(3) might buy such stock in expectation of a dividend being declared in the near future, but not otherwise.
(4) might buy such stock when expecting stock prices to fall.
(5) would not buy it at all.

7. One group of stock market investors buys and holds for the long pull, disregarding short-term price fluctuations. This type of investor has the following overall effect on the market. He or she:
(1) destabilizes it in that his or her purchases keep tending to push price upward.
(2) stabilizes it by refusing to sell on price declines, but destabilizes it by making the market "thinner."
(3) stabilizes it by making it "thinner."
(4) destabilizes it by selling at times which have no relation to the current price of the stock.
(5) does none of these things, since his or her group is not of sufficient importance to have any impact.

8. The contribution of margin buying to the great stock market crash of 1929 was which of the following?
(1) Owners of stock were forced to sell that stock in order to raise the cash needed to buy the further stock which their margin commitment required them to buy.
(2) The small or marginal stock buyers grew panicky and dumped their stock for whatever price they could get.
(3) Margin buying had increased the volume of stock trading and thus intensified the fall in prices, but otherwise it played no special part in the crash.
(4) The lenders of money sold the stock they were holding as collateral security when stock prices began to fall substantially.
(5) Margin buyers made an unsuccessful attempt to stop the decline in stock prices by increasing the amount of their buying.

SUGGESTED ANSWERS TO QUESTIONS IN THE TEXT: Appendix to Chapter 11

1. **a.** Price down; the surprise factor causes the change.
   b. No change; already anticipated and built into the price.
   c. Price up; GM should be able to do better with protection—at least in terms of profits, if not employment.
   d. No change; already anticipated.

2. How did you all do?

3. The changes in variables that everyone sees could explain a small fraction of the 509-point decline; that is consistent with the hypothesis. The rest is supposed to be noise, but was misinterpreted by people and computers.

4. They probably did.

CHAPTER 12

THE FEDERAL RESERVE AND CENTRAL BANK MONETARY POLICY

Having come to understand how fractional reserves allow a banking system to create "bank money," it is time to ponder the next logical question: "So what?" The present chapter will begin to answer that query by providing an initial discussion of how changes in the money supply can influence real economic variables. It will be seen to be an indirect influence, operating from a change in reserves through the resulting change in the money supply to effect a change in the interest rate and thus aggregate demand. Once aggregate demand changes, of course, the old stories that translate those changes into changes in real GNP, prices, and employment apply immediately, and we are done.

After covering that long chain of indirect influences, Chapter 12 turns directly to the nature of the primary moving variable—the interest rate. Macroeconomists tend to speak of *the* interest rate, but there are, of course, many interest *rates*. Fortunately, they all tend to move roughly in sync, so we need not keep track of them all. It is, nonetheless, important to understand why there are so many and how they differ.

Those questions are answered in section A. Section B occupies the remainder of the chapter, considering carefully how a central banking system actually works in an international environment. With particular reference to the Federal Reserve System of the United States, you will see how a variety of policies can be used to adjust monetary policy. Since monetary policy is arguably the most important factor in modern macroeconomic stabilization policy, especially in the short and medium runs, it is essential that you understand precisely not only how each control mechanism works in theory but also how each is managed in the real world of policymaking.

Once you have completed your work in this chapter, therefore, you should have accomplished the following learning objectives.

LEARNING OBJECTIVES

1. Outline the five-step chain of events that translates a change in the quantity of reserves available to banks into a change in GNP, prices, and/or employment. It runs through the level of checking deposits, the availability of credit and its price (the interest rate), the level of private wealth and public spending (particularly investment), all the way to aggregate demand.

2. Understand how the interest rate charged or earned on a particular asset depends upon term (maturity), risk, liquidity, and administrative costs. Review the difference between a nominal rate of interest and its corresponding real rate.

3. Describe the history of interest rates in the United States over the past two decades or so.

4. Describe the operating structure of the Federal Reserve System of the United States (the Fed), paying close attention to the role of the Board of Governors and the Federal Open Market Committee.

5. Explain precisely how open-market operations (purchases or sales), changes in the discount rate, and changes in the reserve ratio requirements work. These are the major policy instruments available to the Fed; relate how they are manipulated in practice in setting monetary policy.

6. Explain the "backstop" role of the Fed (or any central bank) in times of financial crisis.

7. Describe the differences between variables of monetary policy, intermediate target variables for that policy, and objective variables that help define the intermediate targets. Outline the changes in targets that occurred in October 1979 and after August 1982; show the evolution through those changes to the current policy philosophy of the Fed.

8. Understand the nature of the deregulation of financial institutions accomplished in the United States by the Banking Acts of 1980 and 1982. Describe their effects on (*a*) the independence of the Fed and (*b*) the ability of the Fed to control the money supply.

9. Define "sterilization" of international capital movement, and explain why it is necessary.

We begin with a chronicle of the path that leads from some sort of adjustment in bank reserves to a corresponding change in GNP and employment; it harbors the answer to the "So what?" question.

1. Suppose, for the sake of illustration, that an open-market operation designed to lower inflation is orchestrated by reducing the level of reserves available to the entire banking system. The result would be *(an expansion / a contraction)* in the quantity of bank money supplied to the economy. It should be expected, therefore, that interest rates would *(climb / fall)* and the supply of credit would *(contract / expand)*. Businesses would therefore find it *(easier / more difficult)* to finance new investment. Individuals would feel *(richer / poorer)* and would therefore *(increase / reduce)* their consumption expenditures. And so on. Aggregate demand would, in general, *(climb / fall)* and thus put pressure on GNP to *(climb / fall)*, prices to *(climb / fall)*, and/or unemployment to *(climb / fall)*.

---

a contraction; climb; contract; more difficult; poorer; reduce; fall; fall; fall; climb

2. The critical link between changes in reserves and changes in aggregate demand is accomplished by interest rates—the prices paid for borrowing money measured in dollars per year paid back per dollar borrowed and expressed in percent per year. People are willing to pay interest because the borrowed funds allow them to satisfy consumption needs and/or make profitable investments. When rates rise, the amount of borrowing *(rises / stays the same / falls)*.

The time trends for the interest rates associated with various debt instruments are shown in Figure 12-1. Use it to indicate

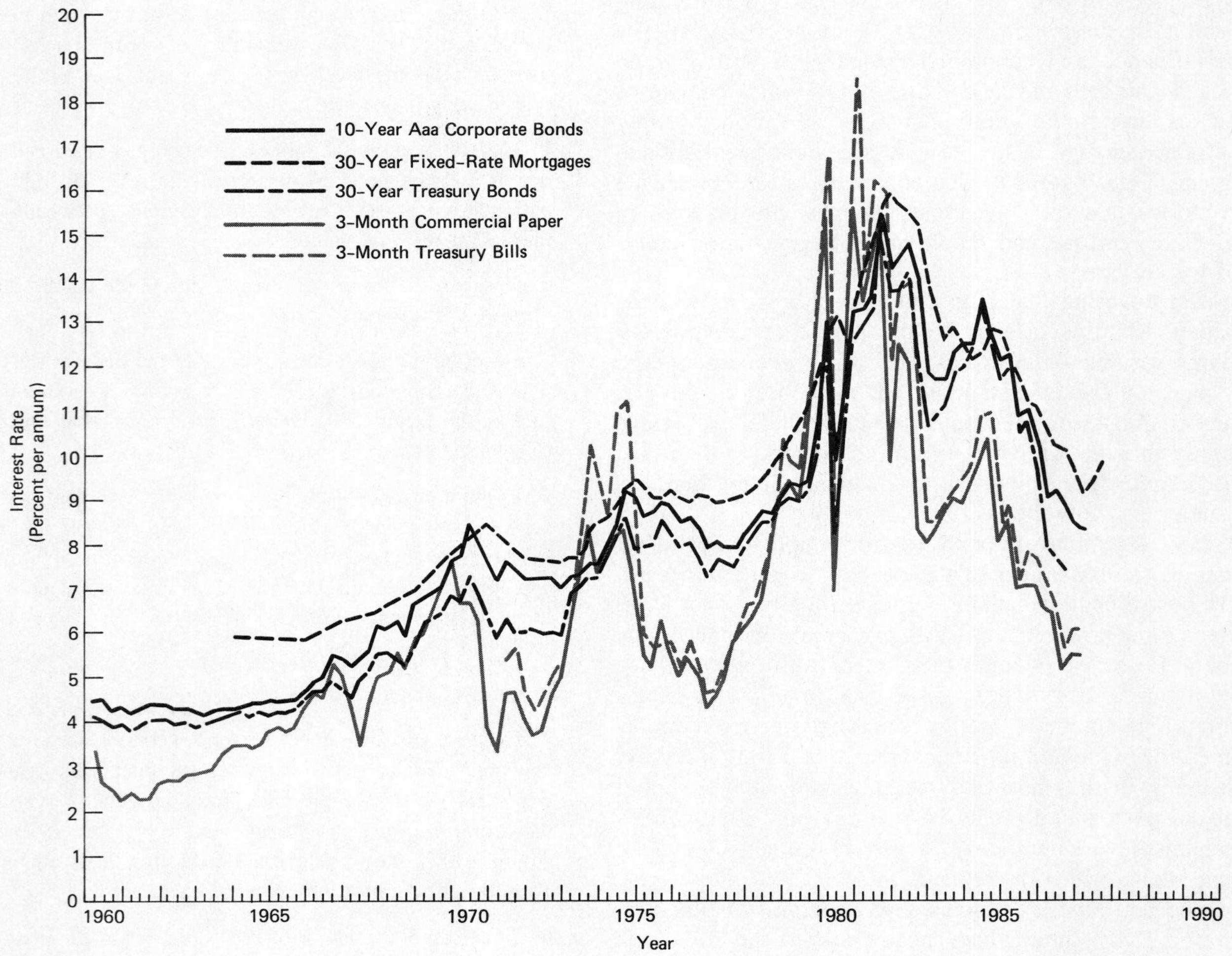

Figure 12-1

in the spaces provided whether the changes listed below should cause the rate of interest paid to rise (R), fall (F), or stay the same (S).

a. an increase in the term of the debt . . . . (________)

b. a reduction in the risk associated with the debt (________)

c. an increase in the degree of liquidity . . . . . . (________)

d. a reduction in the cost of administering the debt (________)

Longer-term debt tends to have a *(higher / lower)* interest cost. We can see this by comparing ____________________

and ____________________

in Figure 12-1. Why does the gap exist? ____________________

____

____

Riskier debt tends to have a *(higher / lower)* interest cost. We can see this by comparing ____________________

and ____________________

in Figure 12-1. Why does this gap exist? ____________________

____

____

The greater the liquidity of a debt, the *(higher / lower)* the interest cost. Why does this final gap exist? ____________________

____

____

The higher the rate of inflation, the *(larger / smaller)* the difference between the real rate of interest and the nominal rate of interest. Why? ____________________

____

____

falls **a.** R **b.** F **c.** F **d.** F
higher; 3-month Treasury bills; 30-year Treasury bonds; People are willing to take lower return for quicker access to their money.
higher; 30-year Treasury bonds; 30-year fixed-rate mortgages (or 3-month Treasury bills and 3-month commercial paper); People need to be compensated with higher return to assume an increase in the risk of default.
lower (cannot really see this in Figure 12-1); Greater access to their money brings people to accept lower return.
larger; The nominal rate of interest equals the real rate plus the rate of inflation

Monetary policy, in essence, is policy designed to make the borrowing of money easier or more difficult, as conditions require. Those who borrow money do so in order to spend it. Consequently, if the amount of borrowing can be increased or decreased, so too can the total volume of spending; and as spending goes, so goes GNP. The total of borrowing can be manipulated by the Federal Reserve System—the central bank of the United States. The Fed can significantly influence the borrowing total because of the power it can exercise over the reserves of the commercial banks.

3. a. To understand how monetary policy is conducted, it is necessary to have some familiarity with the various accounts on the Federal Reserve balance sheet. Begin by writing down the names of the three asset accounts (omitting miscellaneous assets) of the Fed.

(1) ____________________

(2) ____________________

(3) ____________________

b. Omitting miscellaneous liabilities and capital accounts, write down the five items on the liabilities and net worth side of the Fed's balance sheet.

(1) ____________________

(2) ____________________

(3) ____________________

(4) ____________________

(5) ____________________

a. (1) gold certificates and other cash **(2)** U.S. government securities **(3)** loans and acceptances **b. (1)** Federal Reserve notes **(2)** bank reserve deposits **(3)** U.S. Treasury deposits **(4)** foreign and other deposits **(5)** capital accounts

4. The Federal Reserve can operate monetary policy primarily because it is "a bank for bankers." Commercial banks keep most of their cash on deposit with the Fed. This means that on the balance sheet for the commercial banks (combined) there is *(an asset / a liability)* deposit with the Federal Reserve. On the Fed's balance sheet, there is a matching *(asset / liability)* account called ____________________ .

This relationship between a commercial bank and the Federal Reserve corresponds exactly to the relation you have with your own (commercial) bank. You count as an asset whatever money you have on deposit there. Disregarding any checks you may have written but which have not yet worked their way back to your bank, exactly the same figure shows up on your bank's balance sheet as *(an asset / a liability)*. To the bank, it is money owed to you.

an asset; liability; bank reserve deposits; a liability

Commercial banks do not keep a deposit with the Fed just to demonstrate their faith in the banking principle.

They do so because they are legally required to keep a reserve against their own customer deposit accounts, and a deposit with the Fed is the most convenient way of keeping most of it. This is particularly true because there are continually accounts to be settled with other banks. Cash on the bank's own premises—"vault cash," or "till money"—may also be counted as part of this reserve, but the reserve must take one of these two forms: either a deposit with the Fed or cash on hand.

If a bank is deficient in its reserve requirement (i.e., if its total reserve is less than the legally required percentage of its total customer deposits), then it must do one of two things: increase its reserve, or decrease its customer deposits. Usually a bank can temporarily increase its reserve by borrowing funds from another bank which happens to have excess reserves. (There is an active market in such transfers. It is the **Federal Funds market**, and the interest rate charged is the "Federal Funds rate." These loans are made strictly on an overnight basis.) Alternatively, the deficient bank might sell some of its security holdings to another bank with reserves in excess, or it might borrow from the Federal Reserve. As will be noted shortly, though, this is simply one more short-term option of limited expedience.

If the reserve situation is tight throughout the entire banking system, and some banks are deficient in reserves, then the remedy will almost certainly have to be a reduction in demand deposits. For reasons indicated in Chapter 11, banks accomplish this demand-deposit reduction by reducing their lending to customers.

5. a. A bank's reduction in loans works to remedy a reserve deficiency because it is the opposite of the loan-expansion process examined in detail in Chapter 11. It was noted there that a bank which increases it loans loses reserves to other banks. Now we deal with the same process in reverse. A business firm accumulates the money needed to pay off its bank loan by means of sales to customers. The checks received from customers, which the borrowing firm deposits in its bank, ordinarily come from other banks; and the receiving bank collects funds in settlement from these other banks. Hence, as funds for loan repayment accumulate, reserve funds tend to flow *(away from / toward)* the bank which earlier made this loan.

In sum, when a bank is deficient in reserve, it can remedy the deficiency by cutting its loans. This transfers the deficiency to other banks, and they too must curtail loans, unless they have excess reserves. A reduction in loans means *(a reduction / an increase)* in total deposits. So when the banking system reduces total loans, it is reducing deposits to the level which the specified reserve total will support.

b. If total reserves, in Federal Reserve deposits and cash on hand, were $20 (billion), total demand deposits owned by the public were $110, and the required reserve ratio were 20 percent, then reserves would be *(in excess / deficient)*. The amount of reserve *(deficiency / excess)* would be $*(2 / 10)* billion.

c. In such a case, the banks may be able to supplement reserves by borrowing from the Fed, but there are limitations on this method. Banks are usually reluctant to borrow from the very gency which polices their overall activities; and even if the banks are prepared to borrow, there is no automatic guarantee that the Fed will lend. The Fed's ordinary policy is to grant loans to deficient banks only for enough time to permit the adjustment to be made by other means without disrupting the economy. Ultimately, the banking system must *(increase / decrease)* its loans unless the Fed decides that a credit expansion is desirable and increases the reserve base by one of the methods outlined in this chapter.

Such a loan reduction would *(reduce / increase)* the demand-deposit total. It may also perhaps bring in some coins and bills hitherto in hand-to-hand circulation, which can be added to reserves.

d. In the situation described in **b** above, assuming no change in coins or bills in circulation, loans and deposits would have to be *(increased / decreased)* by $*(1 / 2 / 5 / 10 / 20)* billion.

---

a. toward; a reduction **b.** deficient; deficiency; 2 **c.** decrease; reduce **d.** decreased; 10 (the money multiplier, 5 = 1/0.2, times the reserve deficiency)

6. Consider the $153.8 billion liability that appears on the March 1984 Federal Reserve balance sheet record in Table 12-1 under "Federal Reserve notes." Circle the letters identifying which of the following statements are correct.

a. This liability represents the bulk of the paper money circulating in the United States. It is, in fact, all such money except for a few bills of various types (silver certificates, U.S. notes) which date back to earlier generations. They are still held in small amounts by the public, but they are withdrawn whenever they come out of hiding and reappear in circulation.

b. This figure of $153.8 billion represents the total of all such Federal Reserve paper money existing outside the Fed itself, i.e., held by commercial banks and by the public.

c. This total of paper money is listed as a liability by the Federal Reserve because, in the last analysis, such bills are simply IOUs of the Fed and must be listed on its balance sheet, as any such IOU must be.

d. If any member commercial bank deposits a $10 Federal Reserve note with the Fed, then on the Fed's balance sheet the liability bank reserves rise by $10 and the liability Federal Reserve notes fall by $10 (since this particular IOU is no longer outstanding).

e. If a Federal Reserve employee receives a brand-new $10 Federal Reserve note as part of his or her salary, the Fed's liability Federal Reserve notes must rise by $10.

f. If any commercial bank withdraws $10 from its deposit with its Federal Reserve Bank, and takes this withdrawal in the form of a $10 Federal Reserve note, then the Fed's liability bank

Table 12-1
Federal Reserve notes and deposits underlie our money supply
Combined Balance Sheet of 12 Federal Reserve Banks, March 1984 (in billions of dollars)

Assets		Liabilities and Net Worth	
Gold certificates and other cash	$ 16.2	Capital accounts	$ 3.5
U.S. government securities	159.4	Federal Reserve notes	153.8
Loans and acceptances	0.9	Deposits:	
Miscellaneous other assets (including "uncollected items")	16.8	Bank reserves	22.2
		U.S. Treasury	3.7
		Foreign and other	0.8
		Miscellaneous liabilities	9.3
Total	$193.3	Total	$193.3

reserves must fall by $10, and its liability Federal Reserve notes must rise by $10.

g. Federal Reserve notes held by a commercial bank in its own vaults may be counted as part of its legal reserve.

h. The public can increase its holding of Federal Reserve notes simply by withdrawing part of its demand-deposit accounts. This action would decrease the deposit-money total and increase the total of paper money held by the public.

All statements are correct. [*Note:* Some students have difficulty accepting the fact that any piece of paper money such as a $10 bill is really an IOU. It is; it is an IOU of the Federal Reserve. Like any other IOU, it must appear on the Fed's balance sheet as a liability. Any new Federal Reserve notes which the Fed pays out must increase that liability; any notes returned to the Fed (e.g., deposited by a bank for credit to its reserve) reduce that liability.]

The questions that follow deal with the operation of monetary policy in terms of Federal Reserve and commercial bank balance sheets. In these questions, assume that each bank is required to keep a *bank reserve* of at least 10 percent of its own total demand deposits (owned by its customers). Assume, as well, that the bank tries to keep this reserve as follows: 7.5 percent as a deposit with the Fed, and 2.5 percent as cash on its own premises—vault cash.

We start with the following balance sheets (in billions of dollars) for the Federal Reserve and the combined commercial banks.

Federal Reserve

Assets		Liabilities	
Gold certificates	$10	Federal Reserve notes	$15
Gov't. securities	35	Deposits:	
Loans	5	U.S. Treasury	5
		Bank reserves	30

Combined Commerical Banks

Assets		Liabilities	
Federal Reserve deposits	$ 30	Demand deposits	$400
Vault cash	10		
Loans	360		

7. This question outlines the working of the principal instrument which the Federal Reserve uses in conducting its monetary policy: **open-market operations**. Suppose that the Fed decides (for reasons that will shortly be evident) to buy government securities from the public. It enters the bond market and buys $10 (billion) of short-term government securities (bidding up the prices of these securities somewhat, if necessary, in order to obtain them). With rare exceptions, the Federal Reserve conducts its open-market operations by buying or selling short-term federal government IOUs: Treasury bills, Treasury certificates, Treasury notes. Bonds are much longer-term government IOUs, and ordinarily the Fed does not deal in them for its open-market activities. The Fed pays for these bonds by means of checks drawn on itself. These checks pass through the following sequence:

1. Those who sold the securities—financial institutions, business corporations, individuals—and to whom the Fed's checks are payable, deposit these checks in their accounts in commercial banks.
2. The banks, to whom these claims on the Fed have now passed, return them to the Fed as increases in their reserve account deposits.

Hence, as a consequence of this bond purchase by the Fed, two significant account totals have increased:

1. The public now has an additional $10 in its total demand deposits with commercial banks.
2. The commercial banks likewise have an additional $10 in their deposits with the Federal Reserve.

Write out new balance sheets for the Fed and the banks, corresponding to those immediately preceding this question, but showing the changes just described. (As yet, the banks have changed neither their vault cash nor their loans.)

Federal Reserve

Assets		Liabilities	
Gold certs.	$______	FR notes	$______
		Deposits:	
Gov't. securities .	______	U.S. Treasury .	______
Loans	______	Bank reserves .	______

Combined Commerical Banks

Assets		Liabilities	
FR deposits	$______	Demand deposits .	$______
Vault cash	______		
Loans	______		

For the Fed: Gold certs.: 10; Govt. securities: 45; Loans: 5; FR notes: 15; U.S. Treasury deposits: 5; Bank reserve deposits: 40 For the banks: FR deposits: 40; Vault cash: 10; Loans: 360; Demand deposits: 410

8. The position of the commercial banks is now that they *(have excess reserves / are just fully loaned up / are deficient in their total reserve requirement)*. This means that they *(will want to increase / must decrease)* their total loans in order to increase their earnings. Specifically, their total reserves are now $*(10 / 20 / 30 / 40 / 50)*, and this is sufficient to maintain demand deposits totaling a maximum of $*(150 / 200 / 250 / 275 / 300 / 350 / 400 / 450 / 500 / 550 / 600)*.

have excess reserves; will want to increase; 50; 500 (required reserve ratio = 10 percent)

9. Show balance sheets for both the Fed and the combined banks, after the banks have taken full advantage of this opportunity to increase their loans.[1]

Remember that both Fed deposits and vault cash count as reserves and that, by assumption, banks want to keep them in a 3-to-1 ratio. Vault cash is increased by withdrawing part of their Fed deposit. Assume that withdrawal is made in Federal Reserve notes.

Federal Reserve

Assets		Liabilities	
Gold certs.	$______	FR notes	$______
		Deposits:	
Gov't. securities .	______	U.S. Treasury . .	______
Loans	______	Bank reserves .	______

Combined Commerical Banks

Assets		Liabilities	
FR deposits . . .	$______	Demand deposits .	$______
Vault cash	______		
Loans	______		

For the Fed: Gold certs.: 10; Gov't. securities: 45; Loans: 5; FR notes: 17.5; U.S. Treasury deposits: 37.5; Bank reserves deposits: 5 For the banks: FR deposits: 37.5; Vault cash: 12.5; Loans: 450; Demand deposits: 500

10. a. Assuming that the banks do so increase their loans, then the money supply has *(increased / decreased)*, altogether, by $*(0 / 20 / 40 / 60 / 80 / 100)*.

Would you expect this to affect the level of GNP? Why?

____

____

b. In sum, if the Federal Reserve enters the securities market as a buyer (and remember, its purchase of securities set off the process explored in the previous questions), its objective would be to *(raise / restrain)* the GNP level by making credit *(easier / more difficult)* to obtain. This would be an **easy-money policy**. Interest rates, those on bank loans in particular, should *(rise / fall)*.

a. increased; 100; yes, because increased lending by banks means increased spending by borrowers **b.** raise; easier; fall

11. a. Would the increase in the money supply indicated in the previous questions happen automatically or inevitably? What would stop it from happening?

____

____

____

b. If banks should refuse to increase their loans at all, will this open-market operation have increased the money supply at all?

[1] At the close of Chapter 11, it was pointed out that if the banks create a considerable amount of new "bank-account money," as in this case, the public may want to convert some of it into coins and bills. If this happens, the banks must provide the public with such coin-and-bill money by getting it from the Fed. This of course reduces their own deposits (reserves) with the Fed. Consequently, this reduces somewhat bank power to increase deposits on the basis of a given amount of new and excess reserves. For simplicity assume (in this and subsequent questions) that the deposit increase causes no increase in the quantity of coins and bills held by the public. Assume, as well, that banks do *not* maintain excess reserves as a hedge against falling short of the required reserve ratio.

If so, how, and by how much?

____

____

____

a. no, if banks cannot find satisfactory borrowers or want to keep excess reserves because they are uneasy about expanding loans **b.** yes, by the $10 created when the Fed bought securities

12. If the Federal Reserve wanted to reduce credit and to restrain the GNP level, then it would pursue a **tight-money policy**. It would work the open-market process of the previous questions in reverse.

a. That is, the Fed would enter the securities markets as a *(buyer / seller)*. If necessary, it would accept a price somewhat *(higher / lower)* than the previously existing market level in order to bring about its *(purchases / sales)* of government securities. The buyers of these securities (insurance companies, other financial institutions, business corporations, even individuals) would pay for them by means of checks drawn on their commercial bank accounts. The Fed would return these checks to the banks involved and require settlement by *(increasing / reducing)* the reserve deposit which these banks kept at the Fed.

b. When the reserves of commercial banks decline, then (unless they have excess reserves) they must *(increase / decrease)* their loans to customers. The effect of this tighter-money open-market operation is that the totals of commercial bank loans and demand deposits go *(up / down)*.

(If you wish, you can work all this out in detail, starting with the same pair of balance sheets provided above and with a sale by the Fed of $10 of its government securities. Remember that if a bank has more Federal Reserve notes than needed to cover the 2.5 percent vault-cash requirement, it can return the excess to the Fed, thereby increasing the amount of its reserve deposit.)

c. Because money loaned by banks is ordinarily spent by the borrowers, and because so much of this spending goes to maintain or increase GNP, the overall effect of this tight-money operations is to *(restrain / increase)* the GNP level.

a. seller; lower; sales; reducing **b.** decrease; down **c.** restrain

13. Should the commercial banks happen to have excess reserves when the Fed begins a tighter-money open-market operation, then all this operation does is soak up part of the excess. The banks are not under pressure to reduce their loans and deposits because of a shortage of reserves. The Fed must continue its operation until the banks do come under pressure. The point of specifying high reserve requirements is to guarantee that this won't happen. The Fed can, in other words, assume that banks will operate close to the reserve requirement.

Notice a difference between easy- and tight-money policies. When an easy-money policy gives them more reserves, the banks *(must / may or may not)* then increase their loans to the fullest possible extent. If they don't like the credit prospects of the would-be borrowers standing in line, they may decide not to become fully loaned up. Nothing the Fed can do can force them to change this decision. Conversely, the Fed can always push a tight-money operation until any excess reserves have been mopped up. Thereafter, the banks *(do not have any / still have some)* choice. They *(need not necessarily / must)* reduce their loans outstanding.

may or may not; do not have any; must

14. In a tight-money period, interest rates are generally going *(up / down)*. In such a period (pick the best alternative):

a. borrowed money is hard to obtain because the total of loans granted is going down.

b. the total supply of borrowable money is small.

c. the total of loans granted may actually be increasing, but not so fast as the demand for such loans; to any borrower, money therefore seems hard to obtain.

up; **c**

15. a. The **discount rate** means the interest rate charged by the *(commercial banks / Federal Reserve)* for loans made to the *(the public / commercial banks / Federal Reserve)*.

b. As indicated earlier, commercial banks can and do borrow from the Fed. But such borrowing is limited in amount and in scope. The Fed reserves the right to refuse the loan, and it will not permit a bank to maintain continuously part of its loans on the strength of reserves borrowed from the Fed. Such borrowing is intended primarily to tide the bank over a period of adjustment, since it cannot reduce its loans to customers overnight. Banks themselves are often reluctant to borrow from the Fed; there is a feeling among many banks that such borrowing is unwise or undesirable.

If banks did borrow continuously from the Fed as a means of obtaining reserves to increase their own loan total (which they do not), then an increase or decrease in the discount rate charged by the Fed could reasonably be expected *(to affect / not to affect)* the amount so borrowed. But since such borrowing is limited, a discount-rate change has little immediate effect. Such a change is really a kind of flag raised by the Fed to signal that it is continuing to move toward easier or tighter money and that its open-market operations will be conducted accordingly. Thus, an increase in the discount rate is most likely to indicate continued, or even increased, *(selling / buying)* of bonds by the Fed in the open market; a decrease in the discount rate, greater *(selling / buying)* of bonds.

a. Federal Reserve; commercial banks **b.** to affect; selling; buying

In a brief summary of earlier material, the money supply can change as business firms and families seek to borrow more or to borrow less. The Federal Reserve seeks to control this money supply (and interest rates), having as its goal the maintenance of a reasonably stable price level and avoidance of recession.

The money supply can change also as a consequence of international reserve movements. The transactions here involved can be exceedingly complex, but the elements that need to be grasped for present purposes are simple.

The U.S. dollar has become something of an international currency. It is widely held by foreign central banks, financial institutions, and business firms. Any flow of these foreign-held dollars back to the United States may increase commercial bank reserves—and hence, the U.S. domestic money supply. An outflow of dollars (caused, say, by an excess of U.S. imports over U.S. exports) may have the reverse effect.

16. a. Consider how an inflow of foreign-held dollars increases U.S. commercial bank reserves. The effect is the same as if the Federal Reserve had conducted an open-market *(purchase / sale)* of securities. However, the Fed did not initiate this action, and it *can* undertake offsetting action; i.e., it can sterilize the increase in reserves by means of an open-market *(purchase / sale)*.

b. To illustrate this matter of international reserve movements more fully, consider an altogether different example, one arising out of foreign trade. Suppose that the Bavarian Motor Works and Audi-Volkswagen have sold $100 million worth of their automobiles in the United States. These sales are not matched by U.S. sales abroad, so the United States has imported $100 million more than it has exported. The two German companies accordingly have $100 million in deposits in U.S. commercial banks. (For simplicity, assume that the entire sales amount accrues to them, disregarding the fact that some part would actually go to U.S.–owned automobile agencies.) These companies, being German-based, want to convert their dollars into deutsche marks. So they sell their dollar accounts to the West German central bank, the Bundesbank, receiving the marks that they want in exchange.

The Bundesbank in turn sells these dollar accounts to the Federal Reserve. It doesn't matter here how the Fed makes payment to the Bundesbank; that is a matter of international settlements, a topic discussed later in the text. The point is that the Fed now owns the U.S. commercial-bank deposit accounts. In this respect, it is in exactly the same position as if it had conducted an open-market operation, *(buying / selling)* U.S. government securities. It has an increased claim on these banks.

If the Fed wishes, it can ask the banks to settle up. This will cause them to *(lose / gain)* reserves. In effect, the Fed would have conducted a *(tight- / easy-)*money operation. Of course, if the Fed considers that policy undesirable in the light of domestic conditions, it can keep the commercial-bank deposit accounts, or it can conduct a sterilizing *(tight- / easy-)*money operation.

---

a. purchase; sale **b.** selling; lose; "tight-"; "easy-"

Decisions about the direction of monetary policy are routed through the Federal Open Market Committee (FOMC). Comprised of 12 members—the Federal Reserve Chairman, six other members of the Board of Governors, the president of the Federal Reserve Bank of New York, and the presidents of four other Federal Reserve Banks—the FOMC meets eight times a year to construct "policy directives" and to deliver them to the New York Fed. Each directive is divided into two sections: (1) a general assessment of economic conditions and (2) a description of the objectives of monetary policy given those conditions. The latter concludes with specific instructions about precisely what the New York Fed should do.

17. a. Prior to the 1970s, those instructions were vague; they were interpreted operationally as instructions (pick one of the following):

(1) to try to "keep the bond market orderly" by keeping interest rates stable.

(2) to use a combination of variables, such as interest rates, exchange rates, commodity prices, as signals for the need for policy adjustment.

(3) to set explicit target growth rates for major monetary aggregates like M_1 and/or M_2.

b. Late in the 1970s, partially in response to changes in philosophy and partially in response to the passage by Congress of a concurrent resolution in 1975 and the Humphrey-Hawkins Act in 1978, FOMC directives began (pick one of the above):

________.

c. Having been roundly criticized for the major role that restrictive monetary policy played in creating and prolonging the worldwide recession of the early 1980s, the tone of FOMC directives changed again. The committee was persuaded to (pick one of the above): ________.

---

a. (1) **b.** (3) **c.** (2)

18. The political independence of the Federal Reserve is an issue of enormous importance. As it stands now, the Fed belongs to the *(administrative / legislative / judicial / no single)* branch of government. It reports directly to *(Congress / the President)*, hears advice and criticism from *(Congress / the*

President / everyone), but makes up its own mind. The major movement in future years will probably be to open up the process to more public scrutiny, but a strong desire to preserve the ability of the Fed to resist contributing more to the political business cycle will probably preserve its independence.

---

no single; Congress; everyone

19. A second current issue of potentially extreme consequence is the effect of recent deregulation on the ability of the Fed to control the money supply. Two significant acts of Congress in ________________ and ________________ greatly diminished the Fed's power. Nontransactions accounts were *(totally / partially)* deregulated so that, by 1986, there will be *(no / higher / lower)* interest-rate ceilings and *(higher and substantial / lower and minimal)* reserve requirements applied to those accounts. These accounts include *(savings / checking / store-based credit)* accounts. Transactions accounts were *(totally / partially)* deregulated, as well, with interest-rate ceilings *(lapsing / being raised / being lowered)* by 1986, but with substantial reserve requirements remaining. The effects of these provisions are, as yet, still unknown.

In addition, deregulation has allowed a variety of institutions beyond the traditional sphere of the Federal Reserve System to offer banklike services. Because these institutions face *(large / small / no)* reserve requirements, the current ability of the Fed to control their contributions to bank money is *(high / small / zero)*. The one source of consolation is that all this is the product of legislation, and legislation can be changed if it is harmful.

1980; 1982; totally; no; lower and minimal; savings; partially; lapsing; no; zero

Today, central banks everywhere seem to be acutely sensitive to the charge that they have caused (or contributed significantly to) past inflation by excessive expansion of the money supply. Central bank presidents and monetary officials from around the world have responded to this sensitivity by becoming strongly inclined toward tight money. In 1980, the remarkably high levels of interest rates began to reflect this attitude. Blame for the subsequent worldwide recession of 1982 has been laid by many observers squarely on those interest rates. Although interest rates have fallen, in nominal terms, they still approximate historical highs in real terms; they continue to reflect a sensitivity to the potential of loose monetary policy to spark renewed inflation. It is especially revealing to note that most policy officials at the Western economic summit conferences have called on the United States to lower its interest rates not by expanding the money supply but by reducing the size of the federal deficit. But that is a story for another chapter.

QUIZ: Multiple Choice

1. "Open-market operations" means specifically:
(1) the activity of commercial banks in lending to business firms and to consumers.
(2) the activity of the Federal Reserve in making loans to commercial banks.
(3) the effect on the level of interest rates caused by an increase or a decrease in the total of commercial bank loans.
(4) the total operations of the Federal Reserve designed to increase or to decrease the total of member-bank demand deposits.
(5) the activity of the Federal Reserve in buying or selling government securities.

2. The principal assets on a Federal Reserve balance sheet are:
(1) gold certificates and cash, deposits by banks, and deposits by government.
(2) Federal Reserve notes, government securities, and loans.
(3) gold certificates and cash, bank deposits, and loans.
(4) gold certificates and cash, loans, and government securities.
(5) Federal Reserve notes, gold certificates and cash, and member-bank deposits.

3. If the Fed seeks to increase GNP, which of the following is *not* among the steps that link the Fed's action to GNP?
(1) Increase investment spending so as to raise the level of total spending.
(2) Increase interest rates to make lending more attractive to holders of cash.
(3) Increase bank reserves so as to encourage the banks to increase their noncash assets.
(4) Increase demand deposits.
(5) Increase the availability of credit.

4. Which among the following five combinations constitutes the tools of monetary policy used by the Federal Reserve in its routine operations (i.e., excluding tools that might be employed in exceptional situations)?
(1) Discount-rate policy, control over stock-buying margin requirements, and moral suasion.
(2) Moral suasion and legal reserve-requirement changes.
(3) Open-market operations and discount-rate changes.
(4) Discount-rate policy and legal reserve-requirement changes.
(5) Open-market operations, legal reserve-requirement changes, and selective controls over consumer and mortgage credit.

5. The total of Federal Reserve notes held by business and the public appears on the Federal Reserve balance sheet:
(1) as a liability, because these notes are IOUs of the Fed.

(2) as an asset, since these notes constitute part of the money supply; i.e., they are cash.
(3) as a liability, because these notes are part of reserves; i.e., they represent deposits made by commercial banks.
(4) within the capital accounts section, since this represents the money by means of which the Federal Reserve is financed.
(5) not at all—only notes not held by business or the public appear on this balance sheet.

6. If the Federal Reserve System raises the discount rate, this act should be interpreted as part of a general policy intended, among other things, primarily to:
(1) reduce the total of commercial bank reserves.
(2) increase the amount saved out of income by the public.
(3) encourage increased borrowing from the Fed by commercial banks.
(4) increase the total of commercial bank reserves.
(5) do none of the preceding.

7. Suppose the Federal Reserve System conducts a large-scale open-market purchase of government securities from the public. Which alternative in question 6 would be correct as the primary objective of this act?
(1).
(2).
(3).
(4).
(5).

8. If a commercial bank deposits a $20 Federal Reserve note with the Federal Reserve, how will the Federal Reserve balance sheet be affected?
(1) The asset discounts and loans will rise.
(2) The liability commercial bank demand deposits will fall.
(3) The asset U.S. government securities will rise.
(4) The liability Federal Reserve notes will rise.
(5) None of the preceding is correct.

9. One reason why a reduction in the discount rate might have limited effectiveness as a tool of monetary policy is the fact that:
(1) the Fed, although it can increase the quantity of money held by the public, cannot force the public to spend that money, which is what is needed to increase GNP.
(2) the Fed no longer has the same statutory power it once had to change the discount rate.
(3) the Fed cannot control the quantity of discount borrowing, since banks borrow only in whatever amounts they choose.
(4) such a reduction is likely to be offset (have its effect canceled out) by an increase in member-bank reserves.
(5) such a reduction is likely to drive down the prices of stocks and bonds.

10. If the Federal Reserve sells a large quantity of U.S. government securities to the public, it would be reasonable to conclude that this action is intended to:
(1) increase the total of personal saving.
(2) decrease the total of loans made by commercial banks to their customers.
(3) increase the total of deposits of member banks with the Federal Reserve.
(4) decrease the general level of interest rates.
(5) increase the volume of Federal Reserve notes in circulation.

11. If the Federal Reserve buys a large quantity of U.S. government securities from the public, then:
(1) the Federal Reserve liability in the form of bank reserve deposits will go up.
(2) the commercial bank liability demand deposits will go down.
(3) the total quantity of money held by the public will go down.
(4) the Federal Reserve asset discounts, loans, and acceptances will go up.
(5) the commercial bank asset loans and discounts will go down.

12. If the Federal Reserve wants to restrict the growth of the total money supply, its task is made more difficult if:
(1) it lacks legal power to reduce the reserve requirements of commercial banks.
(2) commercial banks are holding large excess reserves.
(3) the amount of personal saving out of income is very high.
(4) gold is being exported to other countries in large quantities.
(5) business firms and the public are anxious to buy more government bonds than they now hold.

13. The "discount rate," as this term is used in monetary-policy discussion, means:
(1) the degree of reduction in price required by the Federal Reserve when it purchases any government security.
(2) the degree of pressure exerted by the Federal Reserve upon commercial banks to reduce their loans to customers.
(3) the interest rate charged by the Federal Reserve on loans made to commercial banks.
(4) the extent to which the Federal Reserve is acting so as to increase the money supply and the level of GNP.
(5) none of the preceding.

14. A large-scale "easier-credit" operation conducted by the Federal Reserve through open-market operations will:
(1) raise the price of government securities.
(2) reduce the total of commercial bank reserves.
(3) lower the level of prices generally.
(4) lower the price of government securities.
(5) raise the legal reserve requirements imposed upon commercial banks.

15. If the Federal Reserve sells a large quantity of government securities in the open market, one of its purposes is normally to:

(1) make credit generally more easily available.
(2) discourage the public from buying government securities.
(3) increase the level of investment spending.
(4) decrease the discount rate.
(5) decrease the total quantity of money in circulation.

16. An increase in the discount rate will ordinarily:
(1) cause both stock and bond prices to rise in value.
(2) cause stock prices to rise but bond prices to fall in value.
(3) cause stock prices to fall but bond prices to rise in value.
(4) cause both stock and bond prices to fall in value.
(5) have none of these results.

17. The Federal Reserve System of the United States:
(1) is part of the judicial branch of government.
(2) is part of the administrative branch of government.
(3) is part of the legislative branch of government.
(4) is part of the regulative branch of government.
(5) none of the above.

18. The bank deregulation of the early 1980s has:
(1) reduced the ability of the Fed to control the money supply.
(2) begun a process to lift interest-rate ceilings from accounts in financial institutions.
(3) preserved the reserve requirement on transactions accounts.
(4) done nothing to undermine the legislative mandate to the Fed that it announce its policy objectives.
(5) all of the above.

SUGGESTED ANSWERS TO QUESTIONS IN THE TEXT: Chapter 12

1. Tools: open-market sales and purchases, changes in the discount rate, changes in the required reserve ratio, plus some other more minor mechanisms. Open-market operations are used most frequently and directly affect reserves. Changes in the discount rate are mostly signals and affect reserves through the anticipation of future complementary open-market operations. Changes in the required reserve ratios are most drastic and are hardly contemplated as a tool to change the money supply (a tool with which to make the linkages tighter, perhaps, but not an operational tool; too heavy, like a sledgehammer after a penny nail).

2. Purchase: $1 billion in new reserves makes the banks want to lend more. Interest rates fall; investment and consumption climb. Higher aggregate demand means more jobs and output. A sale does the opposite, by withdrawing $1 billion in existing reserves.

3. Doubling the reserve requirement halves the money supply that can be supported by any quantity of reserves; halving the requirement doubles the money supply. Changes in the reserve requirement, because they change the profitability of every dollar of reserve, affect bank profits more.

4. **a.** For the Fed (only changes noted in billions of dollars):

Assets		Liabilities	
U.S. securities	−$1	Bank reserves	−$1

For the banks:

Assets		Liabilities	
Reserves	−$1	Checking deposits . .	−$10
Loans, etc.	− 9		

b. No change at the Fed; banks show checking deposits down 50 percent and loans down so that reserves plus loans add to checking deposits.
c. For the Fed:

Assets		Liabilities	
Loans	+$1	Bank reserves	+$1

For the Banks:

Assets		Liabilities	
Reserves	+$1	Account at Fed	+$1

The Fed does not allow banks to use loans from the discount window to support increased loans.

5. The precise effects of these depend upon the type of account created when people come back to the bank at each iteration. The 10 percent reserve-requirement multiplier is thus a lower bound to M_1 expansion in **a**. The borrowing in **b** cannot multiply into increased bank money. The higher reserve requirement in **c** contracts bank money and demand deposits. Moving from uncontrolled saving to checking in **d** should shrink the money supply as more deposits fall under the 10 percent reserve requirement.

6. Expansionary monetary policy is connected to real economic variables only through individual behavior that can be expected, but not guaranteed and thus not exactly predicted.

7. **a.** The opportunity cost climbs.
b. No effect if the rates are less than the NOW maximum; higher cost if the rates are higher than the NOW maximum.
c. No effect in either case, since NOW account interest should move in sync with market rates to maintain their relative attractiveness.

You should expect a change in the demand for money only when the opportunity cost changes.

8. **a.** $2134.32 compounded continuously.

b. $13,310 = $10,000 × 1.1^3.

c. Nominally, a dollar increases to

$$1.07 \times 1.1 \times 1.115 \times 1.14 = \$1.49$$

over the 4 years, an annual nominal return of roughly 10 percent. Discounting to real terms, though, the dollar is worth $0.9988 after 4 years, a real return of 0 percent.

d. Setting 90 days at roughly 0.25 years, $9836.35 grows to $10,000 in 90 days at an annual rate of 6.6 percent.

9. Tying monetary policy to gold (1) reduces discretion over the money supply, (2) ties the money supply to the rate of discovery and mining of gold, (3) allocates the creation of money to countries which have gold deposits (U.S., U.S.S.R., The Republic of South Africa, etc.), (4) reduces exchange-rate flexibility, and (5) reverts to a commodity money whose price would naturally vary with supply, etc.

10. Your thoughts. Remember that Fed governors are appointed by the President for 14-year terms and that the Fed regularly reports to Congress.

11. A bank run would cause the money supply to fall as reserves fell (below a reserve requirement), loans were contracted, and the quantity of bank money fell. The Fed can insure deposits to prevent crises and provide liquidity for reserve replenishment during crises.

CHAPTER 13
UNEMPLOYMENT

Unemployment is, to some, the major macroeconomic issue of the past two or three decades; to others, it is simply a measure of how many people do not want to work at the going wage. Chapter 13 explores both these points of view, as well as the multitude of opinions that fall somewhere in between. A precise definition of unemployment will be presented, in terms of both economic content and statistical expedience. Interpretation of the scope and the texture of the problem of involuntary unemployment will also command some of our attention. In closing, though, the discussion will not turn to the macro policies that might help reduce unemployment by pushing output higher; those are the topics of past and future chapters. We will, instead, mention briefly the types of employment-focused micro-based policies that might be designed specifically to alleviate the problem, on the one hand, and the social safety net programs that might actually aggravate it, on the other.

Having worked your way through the chapter, therefore, you will have accomplished the following objectives.

LEARNING OBJECTIVES

1. Understand the dimension of the economic and social consequences of unemployment: foregone GNP, foregone investment, increased stress, heightened illness, and lost skills.

2. Explain how the unemployment rate (the percentage of people in the labor force who are without jobs of any kind) is estimated (people with jobs are employed; people without jobs but looking for jobs are unemployed; and people without jobs who are not looking are not in the labor force). Discuss the problems associated with the measurement procedure and definitions.

3. Differentiate between frictional (moving between jobs), structural (looking for jobs in industries or sectors in persistent slumps), and cyclical (business cycle induced) unemployment.

4. Differentiate between voluntary (qualified people unwilling to work for the going wage) and involuntary (qualified people looking unsuccessfully for work) unemployment. Outline the logical necessity of Keynesian-styled wage stickiness in explaining the existence of involuntary unemployment, and relate that stickiness to the cost of administering flexible compensation processes.

5. Recognize that unemployment is distributed unevenly over different classifications of workers, but that recessions are remarkably "equitable" in their impact.

6. Understand that the natural rate of unemployment is not an optimal rate; it is, instead, simply a rate consistent with stable prices. Explain why it has been growing over the past few decades, and use the notions of frictional and structural unemployment to support the widely held view that the natural rate stood at approximately 6 percent in the 1980s.

7. Explore the role of policy and other changes in the economic environment in explaining the recent, protracted increase in the natural rate. Suggest some micro-based policies that might reverse that trend.

Economists are quick to recall Okun's Law when they are asked to evaluate the economic costs of unemployment. The joblessness that plagued the United States from 1975 through 1984 cost as much as $1333 billion in (e.g.) 1982—roughly 35 percent of 1982 GNP. These losses are astronomical when they are compared with the efficiency costs of monopoly and other forms of imperfect competition, the costs of strict environmental controls, or even the Grace Commission's estimate of waste in government. Nonetheless, it misses the human cost: the homes that are broken by the strain; the kids who decide on their own to sell their bikes to buy milk for their baby sisters; the anguish of 10,000 unemployed workers that show up to interview for 40 openings at a tanning factory. Unemployment is one of those topics that brings the dismal science out of its tower of numbers and makes it a social science.

1. When the unemployment rate is measured every month, *(10,000 / 30,000 / 60,000)* households are sampled to determine their employment status. There are three categories: employed, unemployed, and not in the labor force. Indicate the category into which people who find themselves in the following circumstances would be classified; designate employed by (E), unemployed by (U), and not in the labor force by (N).

a. a laid-off autoworker . . . . (______)

b. a laid-off autoworker employed part-time at Wendy's . . . . (______)

c. a lawyer too sick to work . . . . (______)

d. an unemployed steelworker too discouraged to look for a job . . . . (______)

e. a full-time college student . . . . (______)

f. a car mechanic going to college at night . . . . . (______)

g. an executive on leave to go to law school . . . . (______)

h. a housewife who works full-time at home . . . (______)

i. a housewife who works part-time at the library . (______)

j. a housewife who volunteers part-time at the library . . . . (______)

60,000 **a.** U **b.** E **c.** N **d.** N **e.** N **f.** E **g.** N **h.** N **i.** E **j.** N

Many of the entries in the list recorded in question 1 were constructed to illustrate one problem or another with the unemployment-rate measurement procedure. It is a procedure which does *not*, for example, count a person who works full-time as a homemaker as employed. Were that person working for the telephone company on his or her computer at home, however, that person *would* be employed. People who can find only part-time work, even if they are used to full-time employment at a much higher wage or salary, *are* employed. People who are so discouraged that they are no longer even looking for work are *not* unemployed—they are not even members of the labor force, even if they were gainfully employed just 1 year ago, or 6 months ago, or 4 weeks ago.

These issues and questions are not simply academic curiosities designed to interest the scholar and confound the bureaucrat. In December 1982 when the unemployed rate rose above 10 percent for the first time since the 1930s, the unemployed rate reflected over 11 million people who were officially out of work. At the same time, though, there were nearly 2 million discouraged workers who were officially "out of the labor force" and another 2 million underemployed workers who were officially "employed." Certainly not a "curiosity" for their families. The procedure can even produce anomalies like recording lower unemployment rates even as the number of people officially counted as employed declines. Question 2 produces a quick illustration of how that might happen.

2. The formula for the unemployment rate is simply:

$$\text{Unemployment rate} = \frac{U}{U + E} \times 100\%$$

where U and E represent the number of people counted as unemployed and employed, respectively. Suppose, to begin with, that U = 10 million and E = 90 million; in that case, the unemployment rate would be ______ percent. Now let 1 month pass during which 0.5 million of the 90 million who had jobs were laid off and 1 million of the 10 million who had been officially unemployed get discouraged and officially leave the labor force. One month later, in other words, E = ______ million, U = ______, and the unemployment rate has *(risen / fallen)* to ______ percent.

10; 89.5; 9.5; fallen; 9.6

Economists have, after decades of study, identified three different sources of unemployment. **Frictional unemployment**, caused by the usual turnover of some workers, reentry of others, and migration by still others, is the first major category. It is generally viewed as a lubricant for the overall labor market because it improves that market's economic efficiency. It can, however, be driven to an extreme. Teenage unemployment, driven statistically by changing jobs, is among the highest in the country.

Structural unemployment meanwhile arises from the contraction of some industries whose time has come and is now going; even in a growing economy, some industries contract as the demand for their products contracts and they must therefore lay workers off. Finally, **cyclical unemployment** is the natural manifestation of the business cycle in the labor market; an overall contraction in business activity means that fewer people are required to produce the desired level of output, and employment must therefore fall.

The distinction between the three categories is critical because their different sources indicate different degrees of concern and different policy prescriptions. If frictional unemployment improves efficiency, for example, then we need not worry terribly about it. If structural unemployment can be associated with a particular industry or group of industries, then specific policies targeted at the people who used to work for them may be appropriate. If cyclical unemployment is most troublesome, finally, then policies targeted at macro stabilization may be most appropriate.

3. Identify each of the following scenarios with the type of unemployment that it most closely exemplifies. Denote structural employment by (S), frictional unemployment by (F), and cyclical unemployment by (C).

a. a graduating senior who cannot find a job . . . (_______)

b. a steelworker who loses his job because of permanent foreign competition . . . . (_______)

c. an autoworker who loses her job in a recession. . . . . (_______)

d. an executive who loses her job because higher oil prices cause aggregate demand to fall . . . . (_______)

e. an executive who loses his job because higher oil prices cause the demand for oil burners to fall . . . . (_______)

f. a spouse who quits a job because the family had to move . . . . (_______)

g. a member of the garment union who loses his job because U.S. wages cannot fall in the face of inexpensive foreign labor . . . . (_______)

---

a. F **b.** S **c.** C **d.** C **e.** S **f.** F **g.** S

Entirely separate from the statistical characterization of worker status and the frictional/structural/cyclical distinction, economists differentiate between voluntary and involuntary unemployment. People are *voluntarily* unemployed if they choose not to work at the offered wage; people are *involuntarily* unemployed if they would like to work at the going wage but cannot find work.

4. To explore this second distinction, consult Figure 13-1. Curve *SS* there represents a typical supply schedule for labor, with *LL* indicating the size of the available labor force. Curve *DD* meanwhile reflects the (derived) demand for labor. Accordingly, the equilibrium wage is $_______, with _______ people desiring and finding employment and _______ people choosing not to work. The number of people voluntarily unemployed is therefore _______; the number of people involuntarily unemployed is _______.

Now suppose that demand conditions deteriorate so that *D′D′* represents the demand for labor. If the wage could fall, then the new equilibrium wage would be $_______, total employment would be _______, total involuntary unemployment would be _______, and total voluntary unemployment would be _______. If the wage could not fall, though, then

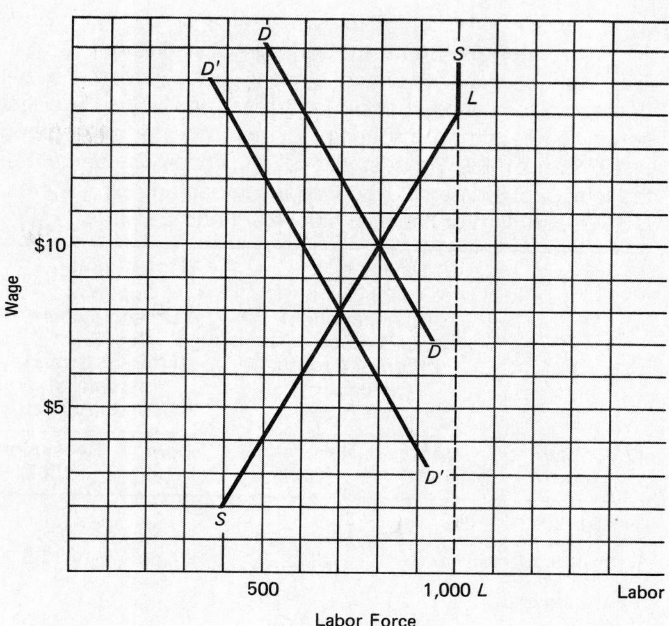

Figure 13-1

total employment would be _______, total involuntary unemployment would be _______, and total voluntary unemployment would be _______.

The important point to note from this exercise is that the existence of involuntary unemployment depends critically upon the inability of the wage to fall in response to excess supply in the labor market. Quite simply, no one who wanted to work at the going wage would be unable to do so if wages were sufficiently flexible. This *(is / is not)* to say that total employment would not fall if the demand for labor were to fall; it is simply a statement about the ability of people who want to work even at the lower wage to find a job.

10; 800; 200; 200; 0; 8; 700; 0; 300; 600; 200; 200; is not

5. Table 13-1 records unemployment rates for various demographic groups for 1973, a boom year, and 1982, a year of severe recession. Several points can be gleaned by studying the numbers recorded in this table. It is clear, first of all, that unemployment hits *(all / most / only some)* demographic groups *(in exactly the same degree / differently)*. Nonetheless, comparing the experience of the United States in 1973 and 1982 suggests that recession *(is / is not)* fairly even-handed in its effect on unemployment rates. While the overall unemployment rate in 1982 was roughly twice as large as it was in 1972, teenage unemployment *(more than / almost exactly / less than)* doubled; black unemployment *(more than / almost exactly / less than)* doubled; white unemployment *(more than / almost exactly / less than)* doubled; and so on. The only real exception was male unemployment. The numbers recorded in

Table 13-1
Unemployment by Demographic Group

This table shows how unemployment varies across different demographic groups in boom and recession years. The first set of figures shows the unemployment rate for each group in 1973 and 1982. The last two columns show the percent of the total pool of unemployed that lies in each group. (Source: U.S. Department of Labor, *Employment and Earnings.*)

	Unemployment Rate of Different Groups (percent of labor force)		Distribution of Total Unemployment across Different Groups (percent of total unemployed)	
Labor Market Group	**Boom (1973)**	**Recession (1982)**	**Boom (1973)**	**Recession (1982)**
By age:				
16–19 years	14.5	23.2	28.5	18.5
20 years and older	3.8	8.6	71.5	81.5
By race:				
White	4.3	8.6	79.2	77.2
Black and other	8.9	17.3	20.8	22.8
By sex (adults only)				
Male	3.3	8.8	51.8	58.5
Female	4.8	8.3	48.2	41.5
All workers	**4.9**	**9.7**	**100.0**	**100.0**

the table prompted Senator Kennedy of Massachusetts to quip that the recession of 1982 advanced the cause of equal rights for women because it brought the male unemployment rate up to the level of the female unemployment rate.

The effect of recession on the duration of unemployment is also noted in Figure 13-2. Glancing at the picture, we see clearly that recession tends to *(increase / decrease)* the average duration of unemployment by *(reducing / increasing)* the proportion of unemployed who are out of work for less than 5 weeks and *(increasing / decreasing)* the proportion who are out of work for more than 15 weeks.

Finally, Figure 13-3 shows us that recession tends to increase the unemployment rate by increasing the percent of the labor force that is unemployed because it has *(reentered the labor market / lost its job / left its job voluntarily / entered the labor market for the first time)*.

---

all; differently; is; almost exactly; almost exactly; almost exactly; increase; reducing; increasing; lost its job

6. The natural rate of unemployment has a variety of nearly equivalent definitions. One of the most operative is the lowest rate consistent with stable prices. At the natural rate, therefore, upward and downward pressures on prices would be exactly balanced across the various sectors of an economy. It is greater than zero primarily because of the contribution of *(frictional / structural / cyclical)* unemployment to the overall rate. From Figure 13-3, in fact, it can be seen that new entrants and reentrants into the labor force typically account for *(1 to 2 / 2 to 3 / 4 to 5)* percentage points of unemployment. Quits account for another *(1 / 2 / 3)* point(s), so that the unemployment rate

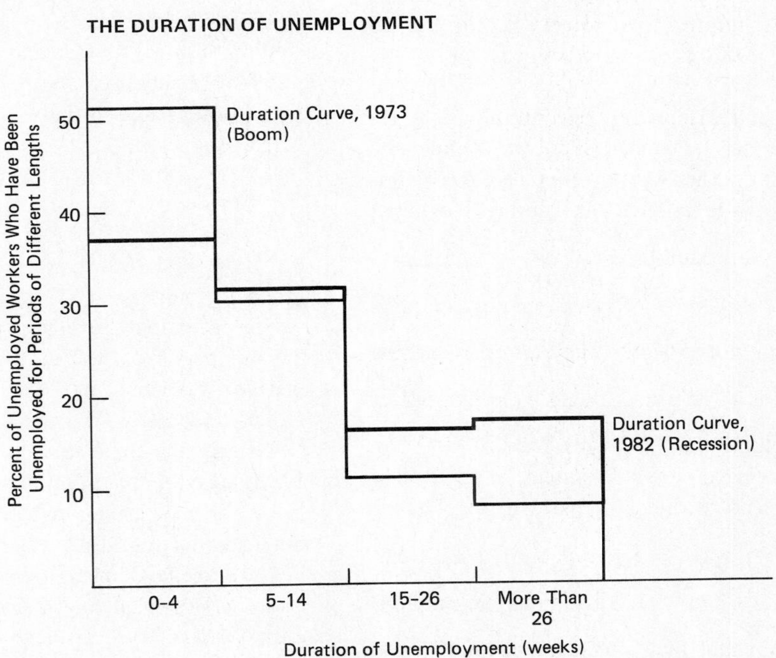

Figure 13-2

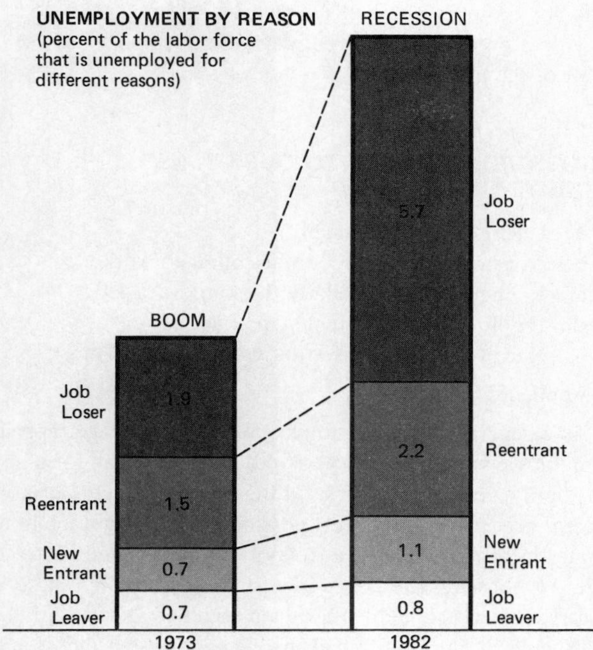

Figure 13-3

would hover around *(2 to 3 percent / 3 to 4 percent / 4 to 5 percent)* even without anyone forceably losing a job.

Most scholars put the natural rate around *(5 percent / 6 percent / 8 percent)* in the 1980s, though, so there must be more to it than efficient frictional components. The natural rate *(is / is not)*, therefore, an optimal rate. There has, in particular, been a growing structural component over the past few decades. Additionally, the labor force has accumulated a larger proportion of teenage and female participants over the past few decades, and their underlying rates of unemployment seem to be *(higher / the same / lower)* than the rate associated with the historical composition.

Finally, some have blamed social policies for the growing natural rate. The growth of unemployment compensation can, for example, be blamed for easing the pain of being unemployed. Unemployed workers might, therefore, search for a new job with *(less / greater)* urgency and stay unemployed for a *(longer / shorter)* period of time. The minimum wage has, in addition, been blamed for making it *(more / less)* difficult for new entrants to find work.

---

frictional (although structural unemployment does play a role, and business cycle downturns can accelerate the decline of industries contributing to structural unemployment); 2 to 3; 1; 3 to 4 percent; 6 percent; is not; higher; less; longer; more

7. Many different types of micro-based employment policies have been suggested to reduce the level of structural unemployment and thus reverse the upward trend in the natural rate. List four of them below.

a. ______________________

b. ______________________

c. ______________________

d. ______________________

---

a. job matching; **b.** training; **c.** public employment; **d.** removal of governmental obstacles

QUIZ: Multiple Choice

1. A computation based on Okun's Law would put the cost in forgone output of the 1975–1984 period of high unemployment at:
(1) $2100 billion.
(2) $40 billion.
(3) $1333 billion.
(4) $3000 billion.
(5) an amount roughly comparable to the deadweight loss created by the abuse of market power.

2. Based on the research of Dr. Harvey Brenner, unemployment caused by the loss of a job:
(1) ranks among the top five items in a list of most stressful events in one's life.
(2) ranks below getting married as a stressful event in one's life.
(3) ranks above the death of a spouse as a stressful event.
(4) has no effect on one's life expectancy.
(5) all of the above.

3. A person who is waiting to be recalled to a job would be classified as:
(1) employed.
(2) unemployed.
(3) not in the labor force.
(4) underemployed.
(5) a discouraged worker.

4. Which answer to question 3 would have been correct if it had asked for the classification of a person who was too sick to work?
(1).
(2).
(3).
(4).
(5).

5. Because of the treatment of discouraged workers, the official unemployment statistics:
(1) overestimate the proportion of the labor force that is out of work.
(2) can actually climb even as the number of people with jobs falls.
(3) can actually fall even as the number of people with jobs falls.

(4) are not at all controversial.
(5) none of the above.

6. The existence of involuntary unemployment:
(1) depends critically on the Keynesian assumption that wages do not rise in response to excess demand in the labor market.
(2) depends critically upon the Keynesian assumption that wages do not fall in response to excess supply in the labor market.
(3) is accepted even by classical economists.
(4) plays a small role in the overall unemployment statistics.
(5) none of the above.

7. Which of the following statements is most accurate?
(1) Unemployment rates are generally different for different demographic categories of people.
(2) Unemployment rates tend to move in parallel as the economy proceeds through the business cycle.
(3) The duration of unemployment tends to increase during recession.
(4) Unemployment does not increase during recession because the number of reentrants rises.
(5) All of the above are accurate.

8. Someone who loses his or her job because of a recession would fall into the category of:
(1) frictionally unemployed.
(2) structurally unemployed.
(3) cyclically unemployed.
(4) permanently unemployed.
(5) none of the above.

9. Which of the answers to question 8 would have been correct if the person in question had lost employment because of the decline of the U.S. steel industry?
(1).
(2).
(3).
(4).
(5).

10. Which of the answers to question 8 would have been correct if the person in question had just entered the labor force but had not yet found a job?
(1).
(2).
(3).
(4).
(5).

11. The natural rate of unemployment:
(1) has been growing over the past few decades.
(2) has a base of 3 to 4 percent because of frictional components.
(3) is not an optimal rate of unemployment.
(4) is the lowest rate that is consistent with stable prices.
(5) all of the above.

SUGGESTED ANSWERS TO QUESTIONS IN THE TEXT: Chapter 13

1. **a.** Unemployed (frictionally).
b. Not in the labor force (a discouraged worker).
c. Unemployed (frictionally; looking for a job).
d. Employed (even if underemployed).
e. Not in the labor force (not working or looking).

2. Applied definitions.

3. As a generality, the economic stress for a teenager appears (from the viewpoint of a 40-year-old) to be less than for a head of a family; and that suggests different policy approaches to different needs. It is, however, possible that getting a job in the summer means going back to school (and thus a lot of stress), while the household leader is independently wealthy and does not care. Policies should be designed with enough flexibility to handle both the generality and the exception—but that is hard to do in practice.

4. The natural rate of unemployment is, by definition, the lowest rate consistent with stable prices. It is high in the United States because frictional unemployment is so high (such as a large turnover of people in different jobs) and structural unemployment has been growing. In Japan, with "lifetime employment" implicit in contracts, the rate of frictional unemployment should be lower, so the natural rate should be correspondingly lower.

5. Yes, but at the risk of inflation—and the longer the time period during which unemployment is below the natural rate, the larger that threat.

6. Higher unemployment compensation means (1) less hardship for the unemployed and thus less stress and social/psychological damage *and* (2) increases in the likelihood of unemployment and the duration of unemployment. The second set of (negative) effects should cause the natural rate to increase and, through a sort of moving application of Okun's Law, cost significant fractions of GNP.

7. **a.** The natural rate should fall in response to a lower real minimum wage because it should make it easier for new entrants to find work. (A lower real wage increases demand for labor at the entry level.)
b. The natural rate should fall when unemployment compensation is newly taxed because the personal cost of being unemployed should increase.
c. The natural rate should increase as training funds are cut back because the match of labor to demanded skills should be reduced.
d. The natural rate should increase as on-the-job training falls for the same reason as in **c**.

e. The natural rate should fall with shorter (on the average) collective bargaining contracts because there should be less wage stickiness and thus less involuntary unemployment.

f. The natural rate could easily increase with an increase in the severity of macroeconomic shocks because average cyclical unemployment should rise. (The unemployment rate would be less likely to return to a low boom level before the next shock hit if each shock causes a larger increase in cyclical unemployment.)

CHAPTER 14
INFLATION: DEFINITIONS AND COSTS

Earlier chapters have concentrated your attention on how changes in economic conditions can move real GNP up or down. They have conducted the analyses of these changes in the context of both the fundamental aggregate supply-and-demand model of macroeconomics and the total-spending construction of the rudimentary Keynesian model. Simple application of Okun's law has, subsequently, been used to translate these changes in actual real GNP (relative to potential real GNP) to changes in employment. It is now time to extend your field of vision to include changes in price level. It is time, more specifically, to ponder the sources of inflation and costs of inflation.

Extending the analysis to include price effects is not necessarily a straightforward process. In the recession year of 1982, for example, prices increased at a rate of 6 percent per year even though real GNP fell at an annual rate of 2 percent. Previous analysis suggests that an increase in aggregate demand in that environment could have easily increased nominal GNP, but it is not a simple matter to determine whether that increase would have been created by an increase in real output or simply a further increase in prices.

Chapter 14 begins your progress toward bringing changes in prices explicitly into the analysis. As you work through this material, and the material that follows, you will be confronting some of the fundamental economic issues of today (and yesterday and tomorrow). Why has history recorded an occasional episode of hyperinflation, and what can be done to guard against its recurrence? What are the costs of inflation, and how are those costs dependent upon economic circumstance? Are there different strains of inflation that are more or less costly than others?

Having completed your work in this chapter, you will have begun to achieve some understanding of not only the answers to these questions but also the following more specific learning objectives.

LEARNING OBJECTIVES

1. Describe precisely the means by which inflation is measured, and understand the distinction between inflation (an increase in a price index), deflation (a reduction in a price index), and disinflation (a reduction in the rate of increase in a price increase).

2. Articulate the conceptual and economic difficulties involved in constructing the price indices with which inflation, deflation, and disinflation are measured.

3. Outline the history of inflation for the United States (and, to some degree, for other countries such as the United Kingdom).

4. Delineate the differences between moderate inflation, galloping inflation, and hyperinflation, and cite the incidence of each through history and throughout today's world economy.

5. Relate how inflation imposes economic cost: "shoe leather" costs, distortionary costs, and the cost of any reduction in the informational content of prices.

6. Decipher the distinction between anticipated and unanticipated inflation, on the one hand, and balanced and unbalanced inflation, on the other. Note how the impact and costs of inflation depend critically on these distinctions.

7. Relate recent inflationary episodes in the United States to the distinctions identified in objective 6.

8. Explain how one major cost of inflation can be the expense associated with anti-inflationary macroeconomic policies that might create a gap between actual GNP and potential GNP.

Inflation is measured as a rate of change in a price index from one period (e.g., 1 year) to the next. If $P(t)$ represents the price index recorded in period t and $P(t + 1)$ represents the index recorded in period $(t + 1)$, then inflation between period t and period $(t + 1)$ would be

$$\frac{P(t + 1) - P(t)}{P(t)} \times 100\%$$

A major issue, therefore, must be how the price indices are constructed. Questions 1 and 2 will focus your attention on that construction.

1. *Inflation* is not an increase in all prices. It is, instead, an increase in the general level of prices and costs. *Deflation* is exactly the opposite, and *disinflation* is a reduction in the rate of inflation. One commonly quoted price index, based on the prices of the things that the typical individual buys, is the *(DRI / CPI / CIA)*. It is based on the cost of a market basket of goods computed across 285 major groups in 85 cities. Rank, according to your own experience and that of your family and friends, the following major categories of goods in the order of their importance in computing this index. (Indicate your perception of their relative importance by recording integers from 1 through 5 in the blanks provided; their actual ranking is given in the answer.)

Food . . . . ______

Shelter . . . . ______

Transportation . . . . ______

Medical expenses . . . . ______

Clothing . . . . ______

The weights given to these categories in the consumer price index represent *(the share of income devoted to purchases in the indicated category / the ratio of prices across the indicated categories / selected likelihoods of high inflation in the indicated categories)* observed in a survey conducted *(between 1971 and 1973 / in 1977 / between 1982 and 1984)*.

A second index that is widely used is the producer price index (the PPI). It is based upon the *(retail / world / wholesale)* prices of *(1000 / 3400 / 6200)* products. The GNP deflator is a third index. It has the advantage of being based on *(a sample of the current product mix of the economy / all of the goods and services produced in the economy / a weighted average of the production of the world's industrial economies)*, but it is difficult to compute contemporaneously.

CPI; Ranking in order from most important to least important: shelter, food, transportation, clothing, medical expenses (If your ranking does not match, you have discovered one of the problems with applying a general price index to individual circumstances.); the share of income devoted to purchases in the indicated category; between 1982 and 1984; wholesale; 3400; a large fraction of the goods and services produced in the economy.

2. Price indices can easily suffer from two major deficiencies. They do not, for one thing, take *(quantity / quality / the rest of the world)* into account. Better products that cost more cause any price index to *(fall if the improvement is worth more than the higher price / rise in response to the higher price regardless of the improvement)*.

Price indices with fixed weights do not, moreover, reflect the substitution out of more expensive items that we might usually expect to diminish the impact of product-specific inflation. Columns (1) and (2) in Table 14-1 below record hypothetical price indices for the five major categories of goods noted in 2 successive years. Columns (3) and (4) indicate the proportions of income allocated to the five categories in the 2 years in response to those prices. Based upon the CPI formula using year 1 weights, the price index for year 1 would be ______. Based on upon the CPI formula using year 1 weights, again, the price index for year 2 would be ______; an inflation rate of ______ percent would therefore be announced on the basis of this calculation. Now suppose that the year 2 price index is computed on the basis of year 2 weights. The index would then be ______, with the resulting inflation rate *(rising / falling)* to ______ percent. If year 2 weights were used to compute the index for year 1, moreover, then the year 1 index would be ______, and the quoted rate of inflation would again be ______percent.

The point of this exercise is not that one index is correct and the others are wrong. It is, instead, that the selection of weights can be critical in the computation of inflation. Based on the substitution that occurred, though, it can be said that the computation that used year 1 weights for both years probably *(overestimated / underestimated / correctly estimated)* the effect of inflation on the real well-being of the population.

---

quality; rise in response to the higher price regardless of the improvement; 100 $(= 0.2 \times 100 + \ldots + 0.2 \times 100 = 1 \times 100)$; 115$(= 0.2 \times 110 + 0.2 \times 150 + 0.2 \times 100 + 0.2 \times 110 + 0.2 \times 105)$; 15; 107.25$(= 0.2 \times 110 + 0.05 \times 150 + 0.35 \times 10 + 0.15 \times 110 + 0.25 \times 105)$; *falling*; 7.25; 100$[= 100 \times (0.2 + 0.05 + 0.35 + 0.15 + 0.25) = 100 \times 1]$; 7.25; overestimated

3. Figures 14-1 and 14-2 trace the inflationary experiences of the United States and the United Kingdom. Several lessons can be gleaned from the trends that they portray even without getting into the specifics of the numbers recorded there. First of all, it is clear from plotting wages and prices against time that inflation *(necessarily implies / does not necessarily imply)* a reduction in real income. Wages have, over the long term of history, risen *(faster than / slower than / at the same rate as)* prices. In England, for example, a 350-fold increase in the cost of a market basket of grain, meat, dairy products, drink, fuel, and cloth since the year 1300 has been supported by a *(100-fold / 3000-fold / 5000-fold)* increase in wages. Real wages have, as a result, *(fallen 250-fold / increased 2650-fold / increased 4650-fold)* over the course of seven centuries. (Note that Figures 14-1 and 14-2 use a logarithmic scale on the vertical axis; be careful how you read them.)

Second, the U.S. experience includes a marked increase in the *(rate of increase of / stickiness of / rate of reduction of)* prices since World War II. If prices rise in good times and remain stable in bad times, then prices can never fall.

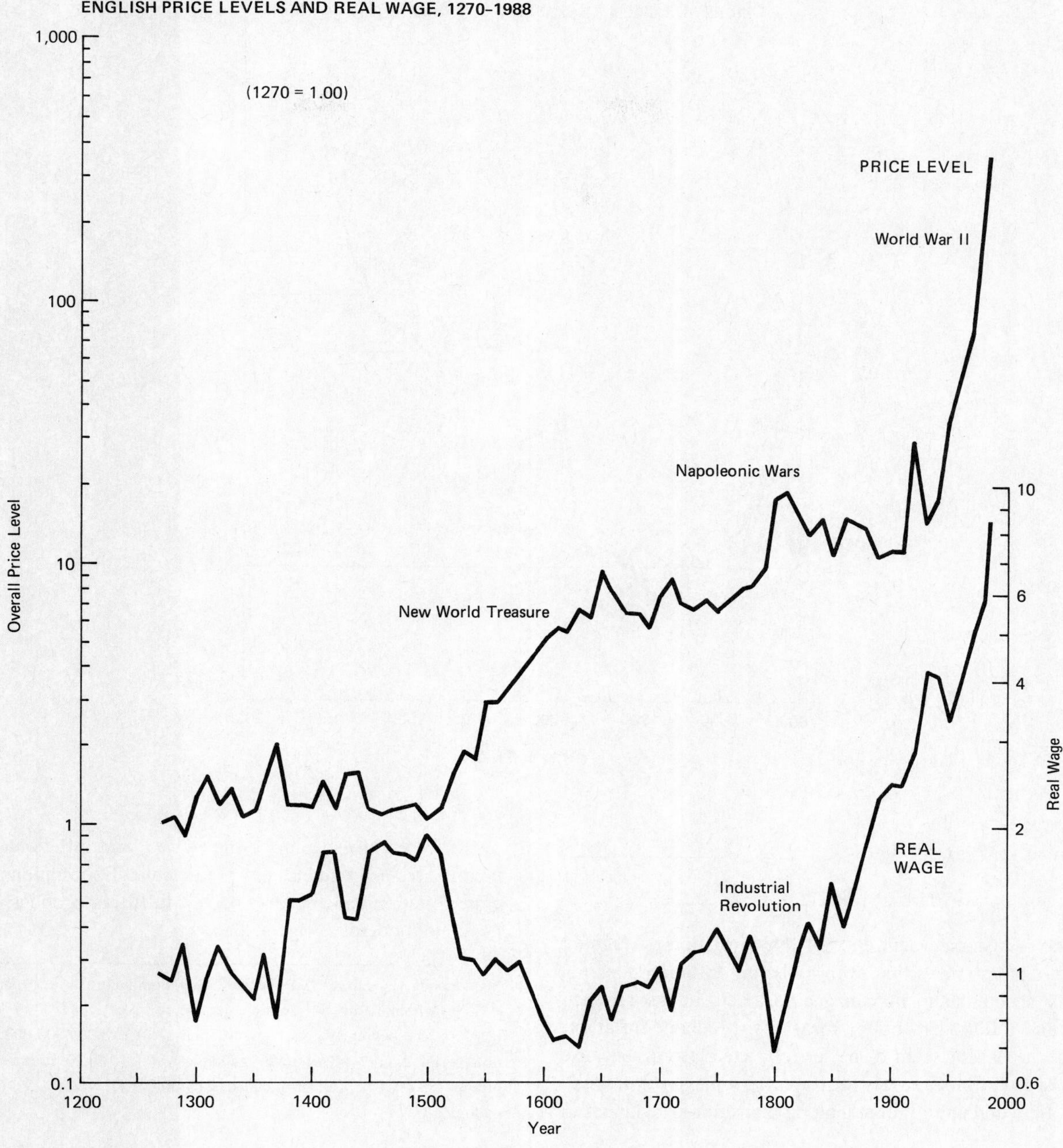

Figure 14-1

---

does not necessarily imply; faster than; 3000-fold; increased 2650-fold; stickiness of

4. Three "strains" of inflation, distinguished by their virulence, have been identified; they are:

a. ____________________

b. ____________________

c. ____________________

Use Figure 14-3 to diagnose the strain infecting each of the following countries for the years indicated. Record the approximate rate of inflation for each country in the smaller spaces.

(1) United States (1970s) ______% ______

(2) Germany (1922) ______% ______

(3) Germany (1923) ______% ______

(4) Israel (1970s) ______% ______

(5) United Kingdom (1980) ______% ______

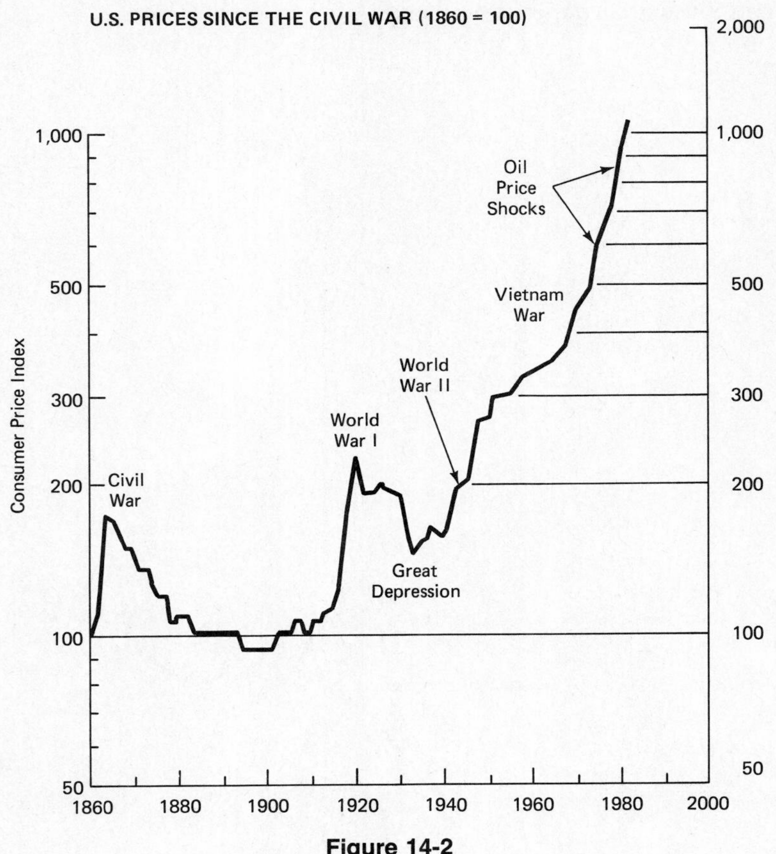

Figure 14-2

(6) Brazil (1970s) ________% ____________

(7) Argentina (1970s) ________% ____________

Despite the occasional occurrence of hyperinflation throughout history, it is happy news that even galloping inflation does not necessarily accelerate to unmanageable levels in the absence of heroic anti-inflationary policy measures. Moderate inflation, meanwhile, does not seem to be terribly troublesome because relative prices are not terribly distorted, people do not spend too much time and energy in managing their money balances to avoid losses in real purchasing power, and inflationary expectations are fairly stable and predictable. Expectations of moderate inflation can, in fact, be self-fulfilling prophesies if they generate moderate wage settlements.

---

a. moderate (less than 10 percent) **b.** galloping (up to 150 percent or so) **c.** hyperinflation (up to 1 million percent per year) **(1)** 7 to 9; moderate **(2)** 500; (the beginnings of) hyperinflation **(3)** over 20,000,000; the throws of hyperinflation! **(4)** 90 to 95; galloping **(5)** 15 to 20; (the border of) galloping **(6)** 120 to 150; (maintained) galloping **(7)** 120 to 150; (maintained) galloping

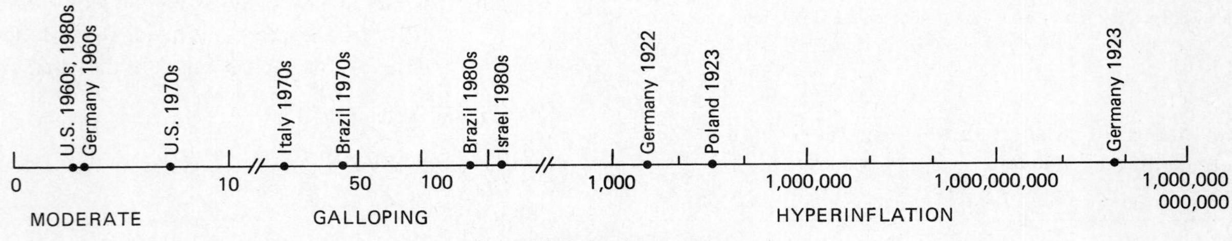

Figure 14-3

Chapter 13 has taught you that the costs of unemployment are easily identified and documented. They are costs that can be seen in the faces of unemployed workers standing in long lines to apply for new jobs. They can be seen in the faces of the children of unemployed workers who worry about their younger brothers and sisters. They can be computed in terms of forgone GNP. They can even be seen in the pattern of government expenditure and the magnitude of federal tax revenues. Given the aversion that most people, politicians, and governments have to inflation, you might expect that the same type of clear documentation would be possible when we now turn to consider the costs of inflation. That is, however, not the case. The remaining questions will consider that documentation.

5. Consider, first of all, the impact of inflation on GNP. In the first three panels of Figure 14-4, draw a new aggregate demand curve that would illustrate the potential that higher demand (caused by, for example, higher government spending or a tax cut) might cause inflation. In each case, *AS* indicates the aggregate supply curve, and *AD* represents aggregate demand before the increase. It is clear from this analysis that higher aggregate demand is most likely to produce higher prices when equilibrium GNP is *(nearly equal to / far above / far below)* potential GNP. Moreover, GNP can be expected to *(rise / fall / hold roughly constant)* when inflation is most likely. When an intermediate increase in prices is expected, though, real GNP might actually *(fall / rise)*.

Now record in the remaining three panels of Figure 14-4 the change in aggregate supply that might produce inflation as the result of an outside price shock that leaves potential GNP fixed. In each case, GNP can be expected to *(fall / rise)*. Contrasting the six possible cases, therefore, an inflationary episode can be associated with *(an unambiguous increase in GNP / an ambiguous increase or reduction in GNP depending upon the source of the inflation / an unambiguous reduction in GNP)*. [Recall that aggregate supply and demand were developed fully in Chapter 5.]

Draw higher AD curves in the first three panels; nearly equal to; hold roughly constant; rise; *Draw higher AS curves turning vertical at the same potential GNP but at a higher price level;* fall; an ambiguous increase or reduction in GNP depending upon the source of the inflation. (*Note*: Italicized answers indicate instructions for drawing new *AD* and/or *AS* curves in Figure 14-4.)

6. Inflation can cause two general types of effects. The first surrounds the distribution of wealth and income; the second concerns the efficiency of relative prices and the information that they contain. The incidence of these effects can be expected to depend critically upon whether or not the inflation is *(a)* anticipated or unanticipated and *(b)* balanced or unbalanced.

If all prices were to increase at the same rate, for example, then the resulting inflation would be ________________.

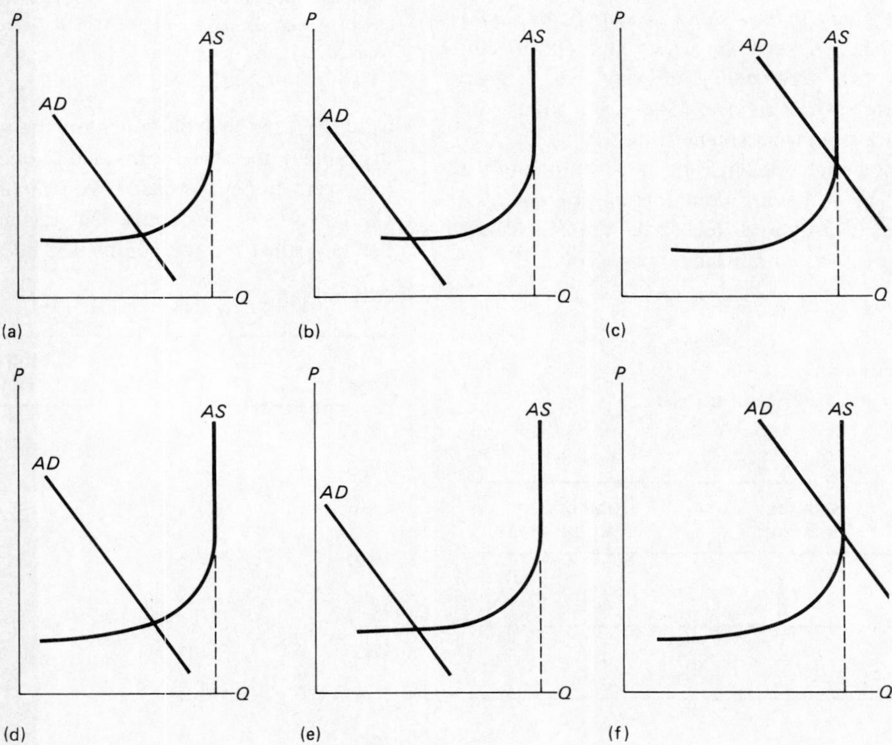

Figure 14-4

If it were anticipated, then it *(would / would not)* be expected to produce "winners and losers" depending upon what types of goods and services individuals and institutions purchased or produced. There *(would / would not)*, in other words, be troublesome efficiency losses created by the inflation. If the prices of some goods rose disproportionately, though, some people could win at the expense of others. People might therefore spend *(more / less)* time managing their money to avoid becoming locked into a disadvantageous financial position. The information contained in relative prices could, meanwhile, be *(increased / decreased)* in extreme cases because they would change so quickly that nobody could keep up.

If balanced inflation were fully anticipated, there would be *(almost no / surely a significant)* cost. The inflation would look like a situation of stable prices to all those people who could insulate themselves from the rising prices. This insulation would, in particular, include such things as the indexing of transfer payments like social security and the adjustment of nominal interest rates to preserve the desired real rate. If 10 percent inflation were expected, for example, then banks that wanted a 3 percent real return would charge ________ percent.

If the inflation were unanticipated, though, then *(distribution al/ governmental)* effects would be expected even if it were balanced. Borrowers would, for instance, be *(worse off / better off / unaffected)* because they could pay off their debt with currency that was *(worth more / worth less)*. Lenders would experience the opposite effect. Under conditions of high inflationary risk, therefore, lenders can be expected to hedge against unanticipated inflation by charging *(higher / lower / exactly the same)* interest rates on new loans. Alternatively, they might try to shift the risk to the borrower through *(policy lobbying / offering no loans / offering adjustable-rate loans)*. [These are points you should be able to deduce from what you now know.]

Summarize these potential costs in Table 14-2 by noting the correlations between the following combinations of potential costs and the character of inflation. Record the number identifying the appropriate cost structure in the boxes provided.

1. Virtually no cost
2. Efficiency losses
3. Distribution losses
4. Both efficiency and distribution losses

Table 14-2

	Balanced Inflation	Unbalanced Inflation
Anticipated inflation		
Unanticipated inflation		

The general conclusion to be reached is that the costs of inflation may or may not appear, they may or may not be associated with lower GNP, and they can be expected to be randomly distributed across an economy even if higher GNP results. It all depends upon where people are economically and how flexible their situation is when unanticipated inflation strikes.

---

balanced; would not; would not; more; decreased; almost no; 13; distributional; better off; worth less; higher; offering adjustable-rate loans; Reading across the rows: 1, 2; 3, 4

7. The following statements have been made about inflation. Indicate by (T) those that are true and by (F) those that are false.

a. "Inflation is just big oil companies ripping off the little people." . . . . (________)

b. "Inflation is theft. Government can increase the taxes without passing tax bill." . . . . (________)

c. "Inflation lowers our living standards by raising the cost of living." . . . . (________)

d. "The only cost of inflation is the unemployment that follows as government tries to lower inflation." . . . . (________)

---

a. F (Even if oil companies try to rip people off, oil prices are not the only source of inflation; they helped keep inflation down in the 1980s. **b.** F (theft presumes intent, and governments do not create inflation to increase taxes.) **c.** F (Wages might increase with prices.) **d.** F (The total cost of inflation depends up on its character, but one major cost of inflation is certainly the unemployment cost of reducing it.)

8. Fill in the inflation rates for the years noted in the following table in the spaces provided. Notice that high rates of inflation seem to be associated with *(high / low)* rates of interest. Do you see any evidence that recent interest rates include a hedge against the possibility that inflation might be unexpectedly rekindled? ________

Year	CPI (1967 = 100)	Inflation Rate, %	Nominal Rate of Interest, %
1977	181.5		5.5
1978	195.4	________	7.6
1979	217.4	________	10.0
1980	246.8	________	11.4
1981	272.4	________	13.8
1982	289.1	________	11.1
1983	298.4	________	8.8
1984	312.7	________	9.8

---

high; yes; Reading down the column: 7.7, 11.3, 13.5, 10.4, 6.1, 3.2, 4.8

QUIZ: Multiple Choice

1. The consumer price index is in part based upon the share of income devoted to which of the following major categories?
(1) Shelter.
(2) Food.
(3) Medical expenses.
(4) Transportation expenses.
(5) All of the above.

2. Inflation measured in terms of annual changes in the CPI using a single year's spending weights might overestimate the impact of inflation on individual purchasing power because:
(1) it ignores the likely substitution out of expensive categories.
(2) it ignores the depressing effect of world prices on American goods.
(3) it ignores the effects of unemployment on aggregate demand.
(4) it inaccurately includes the price effects of improved production technology.
(5) all of the above.

3. Since the 1983 index price for medical care was 357, it is true that the 1983 value for the CPI:
(1) must have been greater than 357.
(2) must have been less than 357.
(3) must have been exactly equal to 357.
(4) could have been anything because medical expenses are not included in the CPI.
(5) none of the above.

4. Prices in the United States:
(1) became less volatile after World War II.
(2) have stabilized since World War II.
(3) have increased faster than wages since World War II.
(4) have increased since World War II only because of the Vietnam War and the OPEC oil shock.
(5) none of the above.

5. Moderate inflation:
(1) is characterized by less than double-digit rates.
(2) is characterized by relatively stable *relative* prices.
(3) does not seem to cause people to spend excessive amounts of time and energy managing their account balances.
(4) creates fairly stable inflationary expectations.
(5) all of the above.

6. Inflation in Brazil in the 1980s was lower than the rate experienced by:
(1) the United States in the 1980s.
(2) Germany in the 1960s
(3) Israel in the 1980s
(4) Italy in the 1970s.
(5) all of the above.

7. Inflation can to be associated with:
(1) only increasing GNP.
(2) increasing or decreasing GNP, depending upon its source.
(3) only decreasing GNP.
(4) increasing GNP only when the economy is operating at its full potential.
(5) none of the above.

8. One of the potential costs of unanticipated inflation is:
(1) the redistribution of wealth from lenders to debtors.
(2) the redistribution of wealth from debtors to lenders.
(3) the redistribution of wealth from the government to those who have helped finance its debt.
(4) the indexing of transfer payments to inflation.
(5) the elimination of variable-rate mortgages.

9. In response to increased risk of unanticipated inflation, you should expect:
(1) that banks will charge a risk premium on loans that they write.
(2) that the government will try to index transfer payments to people on fixed incomes.
(3) that banks will try to sell variable-rate mortgages to homebuyers.
(4) that people will look for assets whose value is insulated from inflation.
(5) all of the above.

10. Unbalanced and unanticipated inflation usually causes:
(1) no harm.
(2) efficiency losses.
(3) the redistribution of income and wealth.
(4) efficiency losses accompanied by the redistribution of income and wealth.
(5) none of the above.

11. One potential cost of anticipated and balanced inflation is:
(1) the economic cost of overmanagement of money.
(2) the loss of employment required to lower the inflation rate for political reasons.
(3) the excessive inflation of real-estate prices.
(4) a reduction in the flow of imports into the country.
(5) none of the above.

12. Which of the following is a hedge that you might expect to see an individual pursue in an effort to protect only himself or herself from the risk of unanticipated inflation?
(1) Negotiate a cost-of-living clause in a long-term wage contract.
(2) Accept an adjustable-rate mortgage whose rate of interest would be expected to climb with inflation.
(3) Offer a friend a loan at a rate of interest lower than that charged by a hedging bank.
(4) Start a new business whose cash needs would be covered by borrowing from a bank.
(5) All of the above.

SUGGESTED ANSWERS TO QUESTIONS IN THE TEXT: Chapter 14

1. The answer depends on who you are. Consider lots of things, including, for example, the potential that an anti-inflationary recession will be arranged for the spring of your senior year, making it difficult for you to get a job (arrange a job now through careful selection of summer employers). Tuition should also be expected to increase as faculty, staff, and even administration push to receive compensation increases sufficient to keep up with the anticipated inflation. If everyone is expecting inflation (not just you), then all prices and wages might increase in sync; the damage might then be slight, except for seriously eroding the standard of living of those on fixed incomes. If you have saved a fixed amount to pay for college, that might include you (try to line up better-paying employment or more financial aid). Think of some more!

2. **a.** Inflation is not oil company theft; prices might be too high; but inflation implies a high *rate of change in prices*. In fact, stable energy prices kept inflation low in the 1980s.
b. Inflation is not government theft, either. Inflation may increase government tax revenue (less now with the personal income tax having only three brackets), but governments do not create inflation to increase tax collections.
c. This is redundancy in definitions.
d. Future recession is *one* potential cost, but it is not necessarily the *major* cost of all inflations.

3. **a.** Postal clerk comment: Confuses general inflation with higher prices for one given service, and attributes inflation there to one component of cost—wages. Anticipated (predicted and attributed) and unbalanced.
b. Grocery price comment: More to the point of inflation (food is a major category of the CPI), but misunderstands how the CPI is measured. One category of the CPI can easily have a larger (or smaller) rate of inflation than the index as a whole. Continuing to argue "with no reason" confuses the index number issue and the sources of price movement in agriculture. Probably unanticipated ("no reason" again) and definitely unbalanced.
c. Deficit problem: This could be a legitimate inflation concern; deficits can create excessive aggregate demand. If inflation results, it should be anticipated and *could* be balanced (but might not be, depending upon how the government spends its money).
d. Strauss's salary: Even then, $66,000 is a small offering to people with the talent to offer potential employers that Robert Strauss brought to the job market.
e. The balloon analogy: Not bad in the extreme, but moderate inflation can continue indefinitely.

4. Things would move faster. As balanced and anticipated inflation, though, quicker adjustments in prices, wages, and salaries could alleviate many problems. Indexing the incomes of those on "fixed incomes" could be accomplished, as well. Orchestrated correctly, 10 percent per month of balanced, anticipated inflation looks just like 0 percent per month inflation.

5. Reading down the column from 1979–1980, the inflation rates are 14, 10, 6, 3, 4, 4, 2, and 0 percent. The corresponding real rates of interest are, starting with 1979, −4 (10 − 14), 1.4, 7.8, 8.1, 4.8, 5.8, 5.7, and 6 percent. The trend is up, over the 8-year period. It peaked in 1982, but it did not recover to the usual 3 percent range until 1987.

6. **a.** Balanced (across individuals); unbalanced (between goods and labor cost) and (naively) anticipated.
b. Balanced (across goods) and unanticipated.
c. Balanced and anticipated.

7. **a.** The farmers' incomes were (if farm prices and general prices moved down in balance) fixed in real terms, but their mortgage obligations were fixed in nominal terms. That is to say, they had fixed monthly payments on their mortgages that were more expensive in terms of purchasing power, and they received less income to cover those payments. Many of them lost their farms because they could not make their payments. (Deflation is not necessary to play out this scenario. The same thing happened in the 1980s when farm prices fell relative to other prices during a period of low inflation.)
b. The same thing would happen. The loans, usually contracted with fixed nominal monthly payments, would become more expensive in real terms.

CHAPTER 15

INFLATION AND UNEMPLOYMENT

Chapter 14 probed the measurement and history of inflation in the United States and elsewhere. It is now time to explore the potential of an economy to enjoy the simultaneous blessings of low inflation and low unemployment. We need, more specifically, to explore the purported tradeoff between unemployment and inflation. Is an economy forever doomed to endure high levels of one or the other, or can fiscal and monetary policies be employed to reduce the severity of the tradeoff? If not, are there other policy options that might help? Can, in particular, some type of incomes policies be exploited to, for example, lower inflation without creating intolerable levels of unemployment? And finally, can the cost of reducing inflation by enduring high levels of unemployment be assessed in either the short run or the long run?

Having worked through this chapter, you will have achieved some preliminary insight into not only these fundamental questions but also the following more specific learning objectives.

LEARNING OBJECTIVES

1. Differentiate between inertial inflation (expected and built into contracts and agreements), demand-pull inflation (caused by too much spending and too few goods), and cost-push inflation (caused by higher production costs without excess demand). Relate how shocks to an economy can contribute to increases in the inertial rate of inflation.

2. Illustrate each type of inflation in the context of graphs of aggregate supply and demand. Demand-pull is shown by upward shifts in *AD*; cost-push is shown by upward shifts in *AS*; and inertial is illustrated by upward shifts in both.

3. Understand the dimensions and significance of the modern Phillips curve in illustrating inertial inflation and how price shocks affect an economy. Note particularly the distinction made between the short run and the long run as well as the instability of the Phillips-curve relationship.

4. Outline precisely the roles of the natural rate of unemployment and the inertial rate of inflation in short- and long-run Phillips curves; i.e., unemployment rates lower than the natural rate are associated with inflation above the inertial rate.

5. Use both the short-run and the long-run Phillips-curve constructions to derive the spiral patterns of unemployment and inflation combinations that describe the U.S. experience of the 1970s and 1980s.

6. Understand, based on the Phillips-curve construction, the cost of reducing inflation by enduring high rates of unemployment; a second Okun relationship links each point of year-long unemployment above the nature rate to reductions in inflation of ½ point.

7. Understand how indexing to inflation can lead to greater instability in prices.

8. Define the general rubric of incomes policies, outline the range of potential structures that they might assume (from strict controls to "moral" guidelines), and discuss their potential utility in reducing inflation.

The "rate of inertial inflation" is a bit of a misnomer. The rate itself has some inertia—a tendency not to move unless pushed—only because prices have a consistent momentum that translates into a stable rate of increase. **Inertial inflation** therefore reflects an internal rate of inflation with which an economy seems to be comfortable. Individuals expect it, and those expectations tend to become self-fulfilling prophesies. Policies are written in acceptance of those expectations. Interest rates include premiums to accommodate those expectations. Transfer payments are amended to keep up. And so on. Inertial inflation has the potential to be both balanced and anticipated, but only because prices display a clear, well-defined momentum. Question 1 explores how that can happen in a very simple example.

1. Suppose that labor is the only productive factor available to an economy, so it has only one type of production cost—the wage paid to the labor that it employs. Let the rate of growth of labor productivity be zero and assume that labor expects prices to climb over the next year at a rate of 5 percent. When the workers negotiate their contracts for that year, therefore, they demand and receive a 5 percent raise. The result must be a ________ percent increase in the average cost of production, a ________ percent increase in the price of output, and thus a ________ percent rate of inflation. Labor's inflationary expectations are thereby *(exceeded / met exactly / found to be excessive).*

Reinforced by this experience, labor should be expected to demand a second-year raise that would be *(higher than / identical to / lower than)* the first-year raise that initiated the process. *(Declining / Stable / Increasing)* price and wage inflation could therefore be perpetuated in the absence of any outside shocks.

Now suppose that the economy suffers an outside shock that produces an additional 5 percent increase in prices so that the overall rate of inflation in year 2 is 10 percent. If labor expects that year 2 inflation to continue into year 3, then labor will demand a *(5 percent / 10 percent / 15 percent)* raise for year 3 that would support a *(5 percent / 10 percent / 15 percent)* wage-based inflation rate in year 3 even without another outside shock. Once again, labors' expectations would be *(exceeded / met exactly / found to be excessive)*, and the inertial rate of inflation would have *(increased / remained the same / decreased).*

5; 5; 5; met exactly; identical to; Stable; 10 percent; 10 percent; met exactly; increased

Notice two things about question 1. First, the pattern that you discovered in question 1 would, if it were graphed against time, look a lot like the pattern for the inertial rate of inflation for the 1960s and 1970s that is depicted in Figure 15-1. The inertial rate "ratcheted" up during that period because the outside shocks suffered by the U.S. economy all pushed prices up. The Vietnam War spending of the late 1960s, the OPEC oil shock of 1973–1974, and the onset of the Iran-Iraq war of 1978 all produced inflationary pressures that were reflected not only in wage negotiations that were settled shortly thereafter but also in wage negotiations that were conducted well into the future.

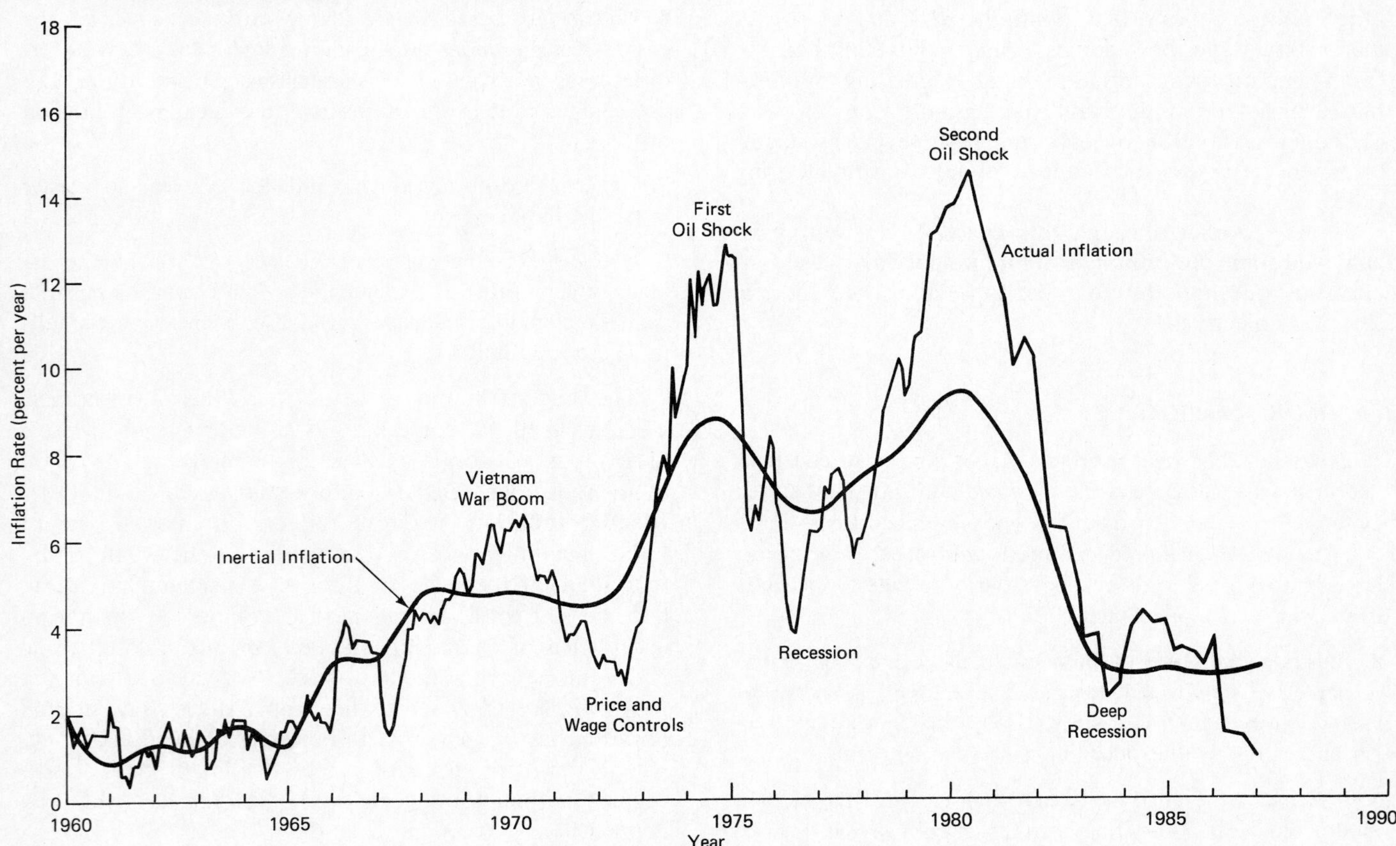

Figure 15-1

Second, it should be clear that the expectations story need not be followed down to the last letter to produce this "ratchet" effect. Cost-of-living clauses in existing contracts can produce the same effect even without active wage negotiation based upon inflationary expectations. Those expectations can probably be identified as the source of the cost-of-living clause designed to protect wage earners from inflation, but the clauses themselves can produce the identical pattern.

2. Label each of the three panels of Figure 15-2 according to the type of inflation that it illustrates. On the basis of that labeling, notice one fundamental difference between cost-push inflation and demand-pull inflation. **Demand-pull inflation** occurs, in particular, only when the economy is operating *(at or above its potential / below its potential)* and usually produces *(an increase / almost no change / a reduction)* in real GNP. **Cost-push inflation**, on the other hand, can occur when the economy is operating *(above / at / below)* its potential and produces *(an increase / no change / a reduction)* in real GNP. *(Cost-push / Demand-pull)* inflation can, therefore, be identified as one source of "stagflation"—the simultaneous occurrence of rising prices and rising unemployment.

Turning now to the specific sources of cost-push and demand-pull inflation, indicate in the spaces provided which type of inflation each of the following is more likely to create. Denote cost-push with a (C) and demand-pull with a (D).

a. a dramatic increase in oil prices . . . . (________)

b. a dramatic increase in government expenditure to finance a war . . . . (________)

c. an automatic wage increase produced by a cost-of-living clause . . . . (________)

d. a sudden reduction in the saving of an entire population . . . . (________)

e. a wage settlement that increases the cost of steel (________)

f. a sudden and large reduction in personal income taxes . . . . (________)

Panel (**a**): cost-push; panel (**b**): inertial; panel (**c**): demand-pull; at or above its potential; almost no change; below; a reduction; Cost-push **a.** C **b.** D **c.** C **d.** D **e.** C **f.** D

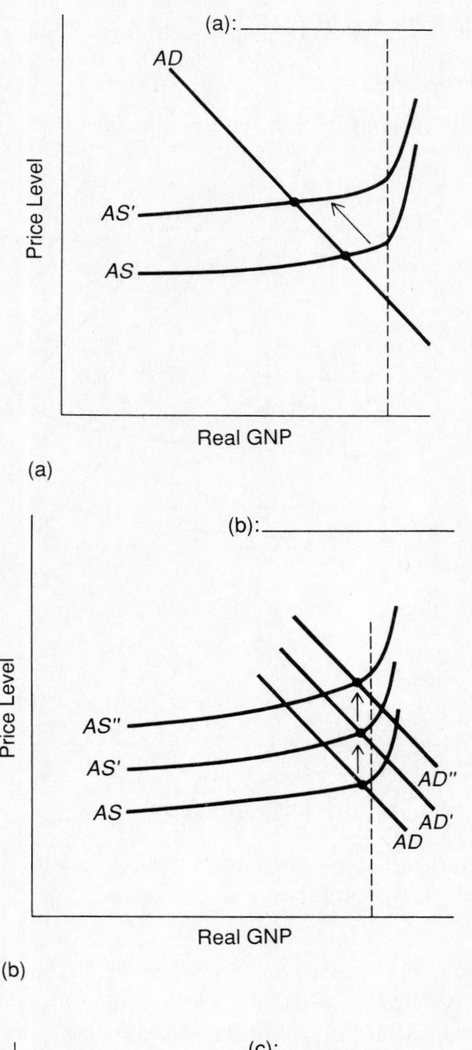

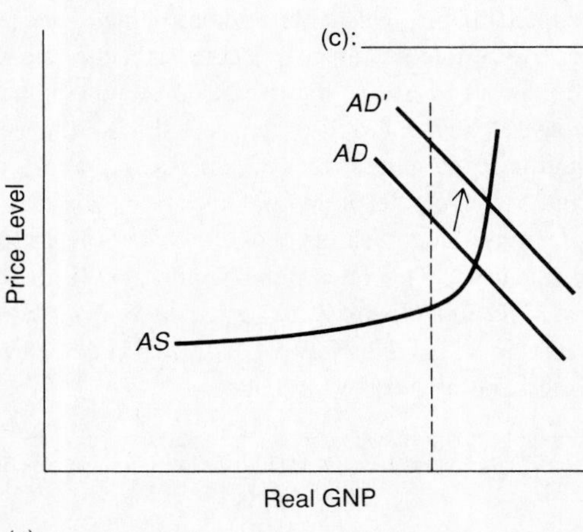

Figure 15-2

3. Refer now to Figure 15-3. Three aggregate supply curves are drawn there. AS_1 represents aggregate supply at the beginning of year 1; AS_2 represents aggregate supply at the beginning of year 2 (the end of year 1); and AS_3 represents aggregate supply at the beginning of year 3 (the end of year 2). The corresponding aggregate demand curves are indicated by AD_1, AD_2, and AD_3. The rate of inflation during year 1 was, therefore, ________ percent, while the rate of inflation during year 2 was ________ percent. If potential GNP were growing at 4 percent per year throughout this 2-year period, then an initial unemployment rate of 6 percent would, by application of Okun's Law, *(grow / fall)* to ______ percent by the end of year 1 and ______ percent by the end of year 2.

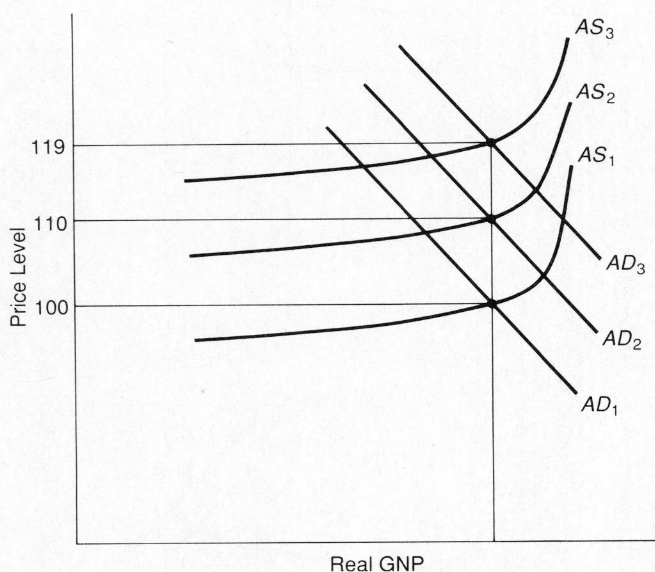

Figure 15-3

10 (The price index rose from 100 to 110.); 8 (The price index rose from 110 to 119); grow; 8; 10 (Apply Okun's Law from Chapter 13.)

4. Question 3 produced some numbers that would lie along a *(short-run / long-run)* Phillips curve. Because the experience illustrated there pushed the unemployment rate *(above / below)* the nature rate, it can be expected that the rate of inertial inflation would *(rise / fall)* in year 3 to put the economy onto a *(lower / higher)* Phillips curve. Should the economy then expand past the natural rate in subsequent years, it would be expected that the rate of inertial inflation would then *(increase / decrease)* and push the economy back toward the original Phillips curve. The time trend would thus look like the *(vertical straight line / nearly horizontal curved line turning at the natural rate / spiral pattern around the natural rate)* that has characterized the past two decades.

short-run; above; fall; lower; increase; spiral pattern around the natural rate

5. The geometry of the Phillips curve can be displayed with either price inflation or wage inflation on the vertical axis. This arithmetic equivalence can be supported by a markup theory of pricing that equates the difference between the rate of wage inflation and the rate of price inflation with *(a constant 2.45 percent / the rate of growth of labor productivity / the rate of conservation of scarce energy resources)*. On the basis of this equality, complete the following table.

Rate of Wage Inflation, %	Rate of Price Inflation, %	Rate of Productivity Growth, %
10	______	3
10	______	0
3	5	______
______	7	2
______	150	0

the rate of growth of labor productivity; Reading across each row of the table in sequence: 7, 10, −2, 9, 150

6. Assume that labor has a long-term contract guaranteeing that wages will climb by 80 percent of the rate of increase of prices during the previous year. Using the equation that you employed in question 5 (namely, the rate of inflation equals the rate of wage increase *minus* the rate of productivity growth), complete the following table given a constant rate of growth of labor productivity of 2 percent per year and an initial rate of price inflation of 20 percent.

Year	Rate of Wage Inflation, %	Rate of Price Inflation, %
1	______	______
2	______	______
3	______	______
4	______	______

For year 1: Wage inflation equals 0.8 × 20 percent = 16 percent and price inflation equals 16 − 2 percent = 14 percent. Continuing down the columns: Wage inflation would be 11.2, 7.4, 4.3; price inflation would be 9.2, 5.4, 2.3.

7. Repeat the process in question 6 with the additional assumption that a price shock adds 10 percent to the inflation rate that occurs in year 2.

Year	Rate of Wage Inflation, %	Rate of Price Inflation, %
1	______	______
2	______	______
3	______	______
4	______	______

The numbers are identical for year 1; in year 2, wage inflation based on 80 percent of year 1 price inflation is still 11.2 percent, but price inflation combines the 9.2 percent wage-based increase with the 10 percent shock for a total of 19.2 percent; in year 3, then, wages climb by 0.8 × 19.2 percent = 15.4 percent and prices climb by 15.4 percent − 2 percent = 13.4 percent; year 4 thus has wage inflation at 10.7 percent and price inflation at 8.7 percent. Over 6 percentage points of the price shock still remain after year 4 (8.7 percent here versus 2.3 percent in question 6).

8. Now repeat question 7 under an assumption that the outside price shock causes productivity growth to fall to 0 percent per year in year 2 and beyond.

Year	Rate of Wage Inflation, %	Rate of Price Inflation, %
1	______	______
2	______	______
3	______	______
4	______	______

The experience of year 1 is unchanged; the 19.2 percent price inflation of year 2 produces a 15.4 percent rate of price and wage inflation in year 3, and a 0.8 × 15.4 percent = 12.3 percent rate of price and wage inflation in year 4. All 10 percentage points of the price shock now remain after year 4.

There are two points to questions 6, 7, and 8. First, the rate of growth of labor productivity is a buffer between wage and price inflation that can serve to reduce inertial inflation over periods of time in which an economy is insulated from outside shocks. Question 6 shows this with an 80 percent cost-of-living clause, but the decline in inflation would have proceeded at a rate of 2 percentage points per year even with a 100 percent cost-of-living clause. Second, no indexation scheme in the world will allow the standard of living to increase faster than real output—the rate of growth of labor productivity in these questions.

9. Figure 15-4 shows four panels. Each panel corresponds to either a boom cycle, an austerity cycle, an inflationary supply

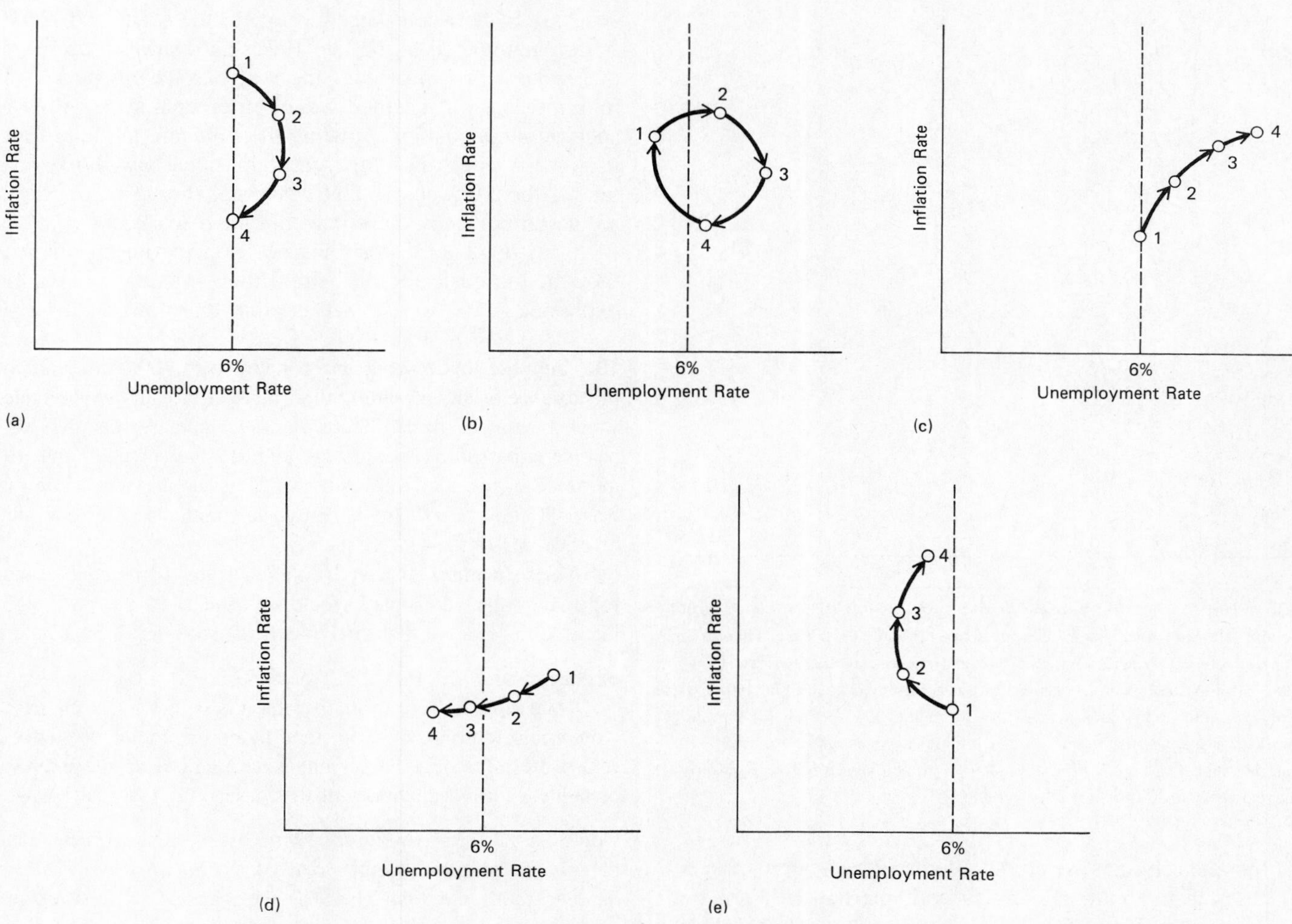

Figure 15-4

shock, or a complete political business cycle. The 6 percent level indicates the natural rate of unemployment, and the dots along the schedules indicate years (dot 1 for year 1, dot 2 for year 2, etc.).

Identify each panel with its most appropriate cycle in the spaces provided in the upper right-hand corners of the graphs. Record a brief chronicle of what each panel portrays in the spaces of the table below. Also record on the table a period in the past two decades whose pattern exemplifies the experience illustrated by the indicated panel. For example, panel (e) shows rapid expansion past potential GNP causing demand-pull inflation—the experience of the Vietnam War buildup from 1965 through 1968.

Panel	Description of Events Portrayed	Sample Period
(a)	______________	______
	______________	
	______________	
	______________	
(b)	______________	______
	______________	
	______________	
	______________	
(c)	______________	______
	______________	
	______________	
	______________	
(d)	______________	______
	______________	
	______________	
	______________	

(a): austerity cycle **(b):** political business cycle **(c):** supply shock **(d):** boom cycle **(a):** unemployment rising above the natural rate along a short-run Phillips curve until inertial inflation falls and employment can recover; 1981–1983 **(b):** expansion during election year, austerity to reduce resulting inflation, employment recovery and postering for next election: 1980–1984 **(c):** upward shock to aggregate supply curve producing higher prices and lower real GNP and thus higher unemployment; 1978–1979 **(d):** prolonged recovery gingerly moving below the natural rate; 1985–1988.

Incomes policies are devices whose very design reflects an attempt by policymakers to curb inertial inflation by reducing the effect of inflationary expectations on future rates of inflation. The idea is to try to avoid the severe costs associated with dramatically higher unemployment. That is, of course, an enormously difficult task to accomplish, and it must be stated that this difficulty has led to a widespread reluctance to give incomes policies a try.

One attempt was made to employ an extreme form of incomes policies, but the results were not very encouraging. The Nixon administration enacted strict wage-and-price controls in the early 1970s, but they did not work. Pressure against the rigidity of these strict controls caused the system to collapse before it could convince anyone that anything substantive had happened. Everyone thought that the controls were temporary and that inflation would return to its old rate as soon as they were lifted. The controls *were* temporary, they *were* lifted quickly, and inflation *did return* to its former level of virulence. This experience is clearly shown in Figure 15-1. Note that *inertial* inflation dipped ever so slightly before heading dramatically higher even though *actual* inflation declined noticeably.

The other extreme, voluntary wage-and-price guideposts, has also been attempted, but with only limited success. In between these extremes, the Carter administration announced in the late 1970s an insurance program that would have protected the real purchasing power of individuals who accepted wage settlements at or below a specific guidepost by adjusting their income-tax liabilities in April of the following year. This idea was, however, one of those proposals that never got through Congress, so we do not know how it would have worked.

As difficult as history has been on incomes policies, though, the basic notion behind their operation is easily explained. Question 10 will explore that notion.

10. Suppose that there is an economy with 1000 workers. In the absence of any growth in their productivity and any outside shocks, suppose further that any wage increase that they all receive is passed on, percentage point for percentage point, to the price of the economy's output. Thus, an X percent rate of wage inflation would always be translated into an X percent rate of price inflation.

If these workers expected inflation to be 10 percent in the following year, then they would demand a 10 percent wage increase to preserve their real standards of living. That would, of course, produce a ________ percent rate of inflation.

If one worker were to realize that his or her wage increase would contribute to inflation, then he or she could, of course, refuse the offer of a 10 percent wage increase in the interest of being a "good citizen." In that case, his or her real wage would *(rise / fall / remain the same)* by ________ percent, but the rate of inflation would *(rise / fall dramatically / remain almost exactly the same)* because the increase in the average cost of production would *(rise / fall dramatically / fall ever so slightly)*.

If, by way of contrast, everyone were to realize that his or her wage settlement contributed to inflation and were to demand only a 5 percent wage increase, then inflation would *(rise / fall)* to ______ percent. If all the workers agreed to no wage increase, in fact, then inflation in this simple economy would *(rise / fall)* to ______ percent.

The key, therefore, is to get everyone to adjust his or her wage demand at the same time. Nobody would want to be alone in taking a lower wage settlement, but something that would encourage everyone to react in the same moderating way could have a moderating effect on price inflation. It would be the purpose of an incomes policy to provide the incentive for everyone to behave in that way.

10; fall; (very nearly) 10; remain almost exactly the same; fall ever so slightly; fall; 5; fall; 0

QUIZ: Multiple Choice

1. Inertial inflation:
(1) can usually be traced to some sort of supply-side price shock.
(2) can usually be traced to some sort of increase in aggregate demand.
(3) reflects an expected rate of inflation to which the major institutions of an economy have adjusted.
(4) is highly volatile and unpredictable at best.
(5) none of the above.

2. Which answer to question 1 would have been correct if it had referred to cost-push inflation?
(1).
(2).
(3).
(4).
(5).

3. Which answer to question 1 would have been correct if it had referred to demand-pull inflation?
(1).
(2).
(3).
(4).
(5).

4. The inertial rate of inflation is reflected in:
(1) interest rates.
(2) wage settlements.
(3) long-term price specifications.
(4) federal macroeconomic-policy specifications.
(5) all the above.

5. Consult Figure 15-5. AS_1 and AS_2 depicted there represent aggregate supply curves for 2 successive years; AD_1 and AD_2 depict the corresponding aggregate demand curves. In moving from year 1 to year 2:
(1) prices climb in classic illustration of cost-push inflation.
(2) prices climb, illustrating inertial inflation.
(3) prices are stable but GNP falls.
(4) prices climb in illustration of demand-pull inflation.
(5) prices are stable, but real GNP falls in response to lower aggregate demand.

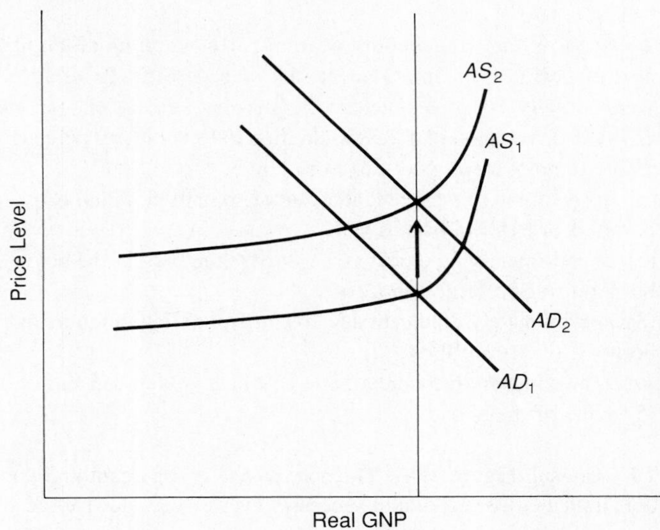

Figure 15-5

6. The occurrence of stagflation can be explained as a consequence of:
(1) a cost-push inflationary episode caused by a supply shock.
(2) inertial inflation that lowers the rate of growth of actual GNP below the rate of growth of potential GNP.
(3) a demand-push inflationary episode caused by an increase in aggregate demand.
(4) answers (1) and (3).
(5) answers (1) and (2).

7. The short-run Phillips-curve tradeoff might be made favorable by:
(1) a policy that lowers export competition.
(2) an incomes policy that reduces inertial inflation.
(3) a trade policy that deflects inflationary price shocks from abroad.
(4) a constitutional amendment that mandates that the fraction of GNP supported by government spending cannot climb.
(5) none of the above.

8. Which of the following correctly states the correlation between the natural rate of unemployment and the rate of inertial inflation?

(1) Any inertial rate of inflation can be maintained at the natural rate of unemployment as long as nonlabor costs increase at the same rate as labor costs.
(2) If the rate of unemployment falls below the natural rate, then the inertial rate of inflation can be expected to climb, and vice versa.
(3) If the rate of unemployment is driven above the natural rate, then the inertial rate of inflation can be expected to climb, and vice versa.
(4) Answers (1) and (2).
(5) Answers (1) and (3).

9. Suppose that an economy were initially operating at its full potential with an unemployment rate of 6 percent. If inflation were initially 10 percent and policymakers were to choose to engineer a recession of 1 year's duration to lower it to 9 percent, then unemployment would have to climb:
(1) approximately 8 percent at a cost of something in the neighborhood of $160 billion in GNP.
(2) approximately 8 percent at a cost of something in the neighborhood of $80 billion in GNP.
(3) approximately 7 percent at a cost of something in the neighborhood of $160 billion.
(4) approximately 6.5 percent at a cost of less than $45 billion.
(5) none of the above.

10. Consult Figure 15-6. The natural rate is 6 percent and the dots indicated correspond to successive years (i.e., dot 1 to year 1, dot 2 to year 2, etc.). Figure 15-6 reflects:
(1) an austerity cycle.
(2) a boom cycle.
(3) a complete business cycle.
(4) a supply-side price shock.
(5) none of the above.

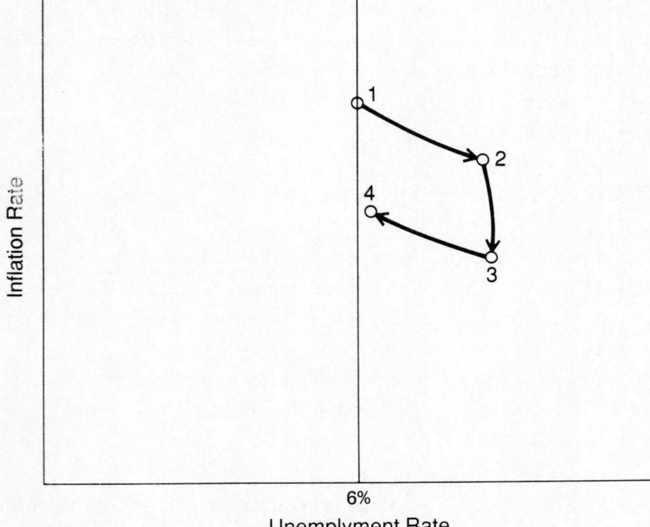

Figure 15-6

11. In Figure 15-6, movement from dot 1 to dot 2 represents:
(1) movement along a short-run Phillips curve toward higher levels of unemployment
(2) a shift in Phillips curves caused by increased supplies
(3) a shift in Phillips curves caused by a reduction in the rate of inertial inflation
(4) movement along a short-term Phillips curve toward lower levels of unemployment.
(5) movement along a long-run Phillips curve.

12. Which answer to question 11 would have been correct if it had referred to movement from dot 2 to dot 3?
(1).
(2).
(3).
(4).
(5).

13. Which answer to question 11 would have been correct if it had referred to movement from dot 3 to dot 4?
(1).
(2).
(3).
(4).
(5).

14. The point of an incomes policy would be to:
(1) lower inertial inflation without the country suffering a period of high unemployment.
(2) simultaneously moderate the wage demands of as many workers as possible.
(3) lower the inflationary expectations of bankers so that the inflationary premiums built into interest rates might fall.
(4) facilitate a monetary policy designed to support a lower rate of inflation without creating unemployment.
(5) all of the above.

15. One of the paradoxes of the study of inflation is that:
(1) lower unemployment is sometimes associated with higher inflation and sometimes not.
(2) indexing an economy to protect it from inflation tends to make inflation worse.
(3) inflationary expectations are sometimes more important than anything going on in a contemporaneous market.
(4) foreign trade is entirely unaffected by rates of domestic inflation.
(5) all of the above.

SUGGESTED ANSWERS TO QUESTIONS IN THE TEXT: Chapter 15

1. The phenomenon can be explained in terms of things like long-term contracts with specified wage increases and cost-of-living clauses. It could be broken by renegotiating contracts, but

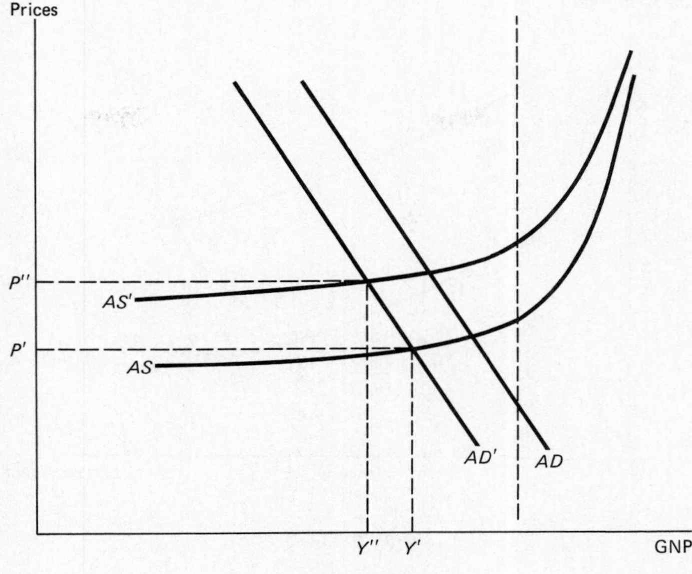

Figure TQ15-1

that can be expensive and not very popular among steelworkers (e.g.) with seniority. Their jobs are not in much jeopardy, and maintaining their real standard of living depends on keeping up with inflation.

Figure TQ15-1 illustrates the scenario with a downward shift in aggregate demand from *AD* to *AD'* (unemployed workers demand less) and an upward shift in aggregate supply from *AS* to *AS'* (the cost of production increasing with the higher wages). Note that GNP falls further than it would without the supply response $Y'' < Y'$), and prices rise further ($P'' > P'$).

2. This simply refers to definitions and the ability of changes in the rate of inertial inflation to move the short-run Phillips curve up or down along a vertical long-run curve. The inflation rate is measured along the vertical axis, and the unemployment rate is measured along the horizontal axis.

3. Refer to Figure TQ15-2. The inflation-unemployment pairs are plotted there with some suggested short-run Phillips curves shown in contrast to a vertical long-run Phillips curve at the natural rate of approximately 6 percent. Inertial inflation declined over the 9 years, and there was an absence of outside price shocks (e.g., oil prices did not jump at any time as they did in the 1970s).

4. The issue is the width of the spirals around the long-run Phillips curve and the effect of inflationary episodes on the iner-

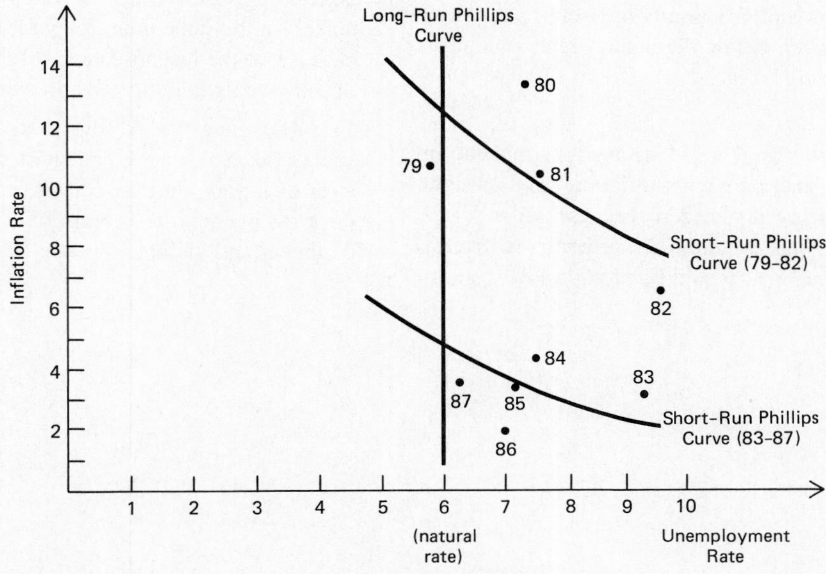

Figure TQ15-2

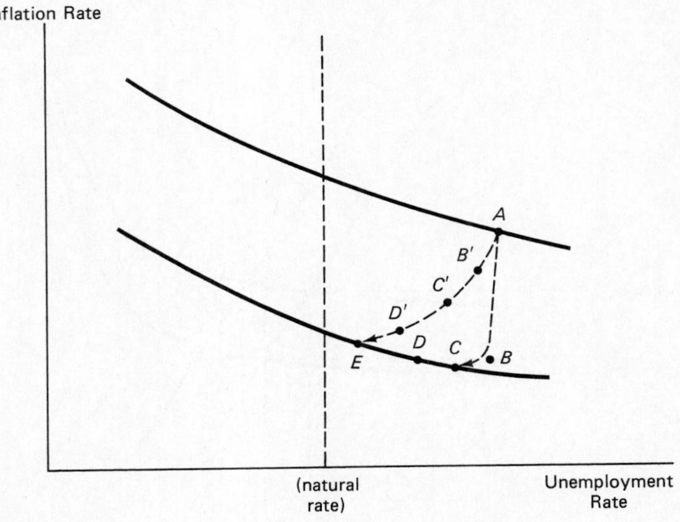

Figure TQ15-3

tial rate of inflation. A short-run tradeoff along a lower short-run Phillips curve should be preferred to a similar tradeoff along a higher short-run Phillips curve; and the recession expense of shifting down can be enormous.

5. The answer depends on where the rate is right now. Remember the costs of unemployment that is away from the natural rate; they are not symmetric.

6. Your thoughts are beckoned, but couch your answers in what you have learned over the past three chapters, and not in how you feel about it. Your answers should also depend upon the likely policy response that may, or may not, be employed to fight inflation or unemployment.

7. Reading from left to right, from top to bottom: austerity cycle (unemployment rose to combat inflation); political business cycle (the election should be timed to occur at 4); supply shock (unemployment and inflation both rising); and boom cycle (unemployment driven below the natural rate, accompanied by increased inflation).

8. See Figure TQ15-2.

9. Strict wage-and-price controls, if deemed permanent in effect, would move the unemployment-inflation point straight down quickly, but probably not to zero because some prices would probably be allowed to climb in response to excess demand. Subsequent movement would be along a lower short-run Phillips curve. This could be illustrated by movement from point A to point E through points B, C, and D in Figure TQ15-3. A series of successively lower inflation targets would move inflation down more slowly, with simultaneous reductions in unemployment as the economy converged to the lower curve; movement from A to E through points B', C', and D' in Figure TQ15-3.

10. Again, your thoughts. Recall the costs and likely effectiveness of all the options. For example, high unemployment works, but it is very expensive. Strict wage-and-price controls have an immediate effect on prices, but it is seldom permanent because people think of the controls as temporary and do not adjust their expectations. Voluntary guidelines work sometimes, but only in less serious circumstances of inflation where the personal cost of "volunteering" is relatively small. Tax-based policies provide incentives which try to get everyone to "volunteer" at the same time. They are more likely to get a response because (a) the incentives and (b) the relative standards of living of individuals tend to move in sync.

11. The long-run Phillips curves shift left, if they are successful. So, too, do the short-run curves, because the same rates of inflation are associated with lower rates of unemployment (to maintain the comparable gaps between quoted unemployment and the natural rate).

CHAPTER 16
THE EFFECTS OF MONEY ON OUTPUT AND PRICES

Chapters 11 and 12 provided a detailed description of how banks and the Fed work to determine the money supply. It is now time to look to the other side of the money market to ponder how the sources of the demand for money work against the supply side of the money market to influence real economic variables. Recall that two underlying motives, the demand for money to facilitate transactions and the demand for money to round out a diversified financial portfolio, were identified in Chapter 11. Together with the supply of money, they will determine an equilibrium interest rate, a corresponding level of investment, a resulting level of aggregate demand, and finally, a supportable level of nominal GNP.

With that mechanism in place, a thorough discussion of monetarism will occupy the second part of the chapter. You will be introduced not only to the historical antecedents of modern monetarism (the crude quantity theory of money) but also to the power of its present incarnation. An appendix will, in fact, bring you up to date with an exploration of the hypothesis of rational expectations. Even before you read the appendix, though, you will be able to understand the crux of the recent monetarist-mainstream (or neo-Keynesian) policy debate by referring once more to the aggregate supply-and-demand geometry. The major tenets of modern monetarism can be represented there (in a way that you have already seen and which will now be reinforced) and contrasted with the current incarnation of mainstream thinking. The resulting policy differences will become clear in the process, as will the basis for the general conservative political view of monetarist economists. Finally, recent experience in the United States will be reviewed with an eye toward bringing the debate into practical, not overstated academic, focus. The monetarist experiment conducted in the United States between October 1979 and August 1982 will be of particular interest.

Chapter 16 covers a lot of material, and understanding what it says is essential if you are to be able to apply what you have learned in the macro section of the text to events that you will see happening and that will be discussed in today's world. Your general learning objective here is, therefore, to develop sufficient feel for the various schools of thought to be able to sort through all their similarities and differences in practical as well as academic contexts. In addition, a long list of more specific learning objectives should be mastered.

LEARNING OBJECTIVES

1. Recall the composition of the demand for money from Chapter 11: the sum of transactions demand (depending upon nominal GNP) and assets demand (depending inversely upon nominal interest rates).

2. Describe the link between changes in the supply of money and changes in the nominal interest rate within a money market supply-and-demand construction that identifies the nominal rate of interest as the price of holding money.

3. Describe the link between changes in the money supply (M) and changes in nominal GNP [a price index (P) times real GNP] that works through the nominal interest rate (i), its effect on investment (I) and other spending, and resulting changes in aggregate demand (AD). In summary,

$$M \text{ up} \rightarrow i \text{ down} \rightarrow I \text{ up} \rightarrow AD \text{ up} \rightarrow \text{ real GNP \& } P \text{ up}$$

$$M \text{ down} \rightarrow i \text{ up} \rightarrow I \text{ down} \rightarrow AD \text{ down} \rightarrow \text{ real GNP \& } P \text{ down}$$

4. Understand that the interest-rate effect on aggregate demand is not confined to changes in investment; the list of affected sectors includes housing, business investment, consumer durables, state and local capital spending, and net exports (through changes in exchange rates).

5. Explain how (e.g.) a reduction in the supply of money might cause nominal interest rates to climb in the short run but fall in the (very) long run; correspondingly, the long-run effect on real interest rates may be ambiguous.

6. Define the velocity of money and explain its role in (*a*) the classical quantity theory and (*b*) the modern monetarist view of macroeconomic policy. Relate both to an assumed stability in the velocity of money.

7. Understand how modern monetarism rests on three major propositions: (*a*) growth in the money supply is the primary determinant of growth in nominal GNP; (*b*) prices and wages are quite flexible in response to excess supply and/or demand; and (*c*) the private economy is very stable. Derived from these propositions are beliefs that (*a*) macroeconomic fluctuation is caused by erratic money-supply growth; (*b*) active government intervention into economies should be avoided; and (*c*) stable money growth at 3 to 4 percent per year should painlessly produce stable prices and steady growth.

8. Relate the lessons of the monetarist experiment in the United States during the early 1980s: (*a*) money *is* a powerful determinant of aggregate demand; (*b*) most short-run effects of money changes are felt in output and not prices; (*c*) the cost of lowering inflation with firm monetary control is not appreciably smaller than the costs of employing other methods; and (*d*) the velocity of money is quite unstable when firm monetary controls are in place.

9. Identify issues of current debate. How effective is monetary policy? Should monetary policy be set according to rules, or should the Fed exercise its discretion? What are the appropriate targets for monetary policy? How is monetary policy affected by an open economy with flexible exchange rates?

There has been, throughout the macro chapters of the text, an almost unstated differentiation between nominal and real variables. The distinction is always important, but it has not been emphasized—at least, not until now. Your work in Chapter 16 will be much easier if you take a great deal of care to see if the paragraph that you are reading is discussing real or nominal levels of interest rates, GNP, etc.

Recall from Chapter 11 that money has three functions: (1) a medium of exchange, (2) a store of value, and (3) a unit of account. The first and the third functions are easily understood. As a medium of exchange, money is a device to avoid the inconvenience of barter. As a unit of account, money is simply a yardstick with which people measure how much things cost and how much things are worth. The second function, though, is a bit more complicated and deserves more than cursory mention.

In the early part of 1988, the total money stock in the United States (the M_1 measure of coins, bills, and demand-deposit bank accounts) was over $843 billion. Each dollar of that stock had, and still has, an owner: an individual, a business, a financial institution. Why was this money being held? There are, after all, alternatives to holding money as an asset. If you hold any significant amount of money, you could buy a security with it. Most securities pay an interest or dividend return; money does not. If you reject the idea of buying any security, then you must have some reason for holding onto money instead.

What are the reasons, then, for holding money in preference to other assets that would yield some income return? We previously identified two. First of all, people generally need some money on hand because income does not arrive in a minute-by-minute flow. Instead, it comes at discontinuous intervals; wage or salary payments come each week, half-month, or month. Hence, people hold a cash balance which is gradually spent, until the next installment of income arrives; this is the *transactions demand* for money.

The second reason is derived from a desire to hold money as an asset, over and above the ordinary amount needed to tide you over until the next wage or salary payment is collected. Why? People sometimes want to keep some surplus cash against the possibility of some unexpected and cash-demanding emergency; alternatively, people may be strongly convinced that security prices are going to fall so that the immediate purchase of any such security would be a bad idea. In either case, an *assets demand* for money is generated.

1. (Repeated from Chapter 11) The result of adding assets and transactions demands together to compute the demand for money is significant. Transactions demand for money will *(increase / be unaffected /decrease)* as income climbs. The more income that is available, the more people want to spend and the more money they will have to keep around to pay for these purchases. Assets demand for money gives the total demand for money some (arguable, monetarists would say) sensitivity to the nominal interest rate. Why? Because the nominal interest rate is the price of holding wealth in money instead of in some interest-bearing asset. Thus, as the interest rate falls, the demand for money, through its assets demand component, should *(fall / remain the same / climb)*.

In Figure 16-1, four panels shows the quantity of money demanded changing from M to M'. Record in the spaces below which panel illustrates the indicated change in economic conditions.

a. an increase in nominal GNP that leaves interest rates fixed . . . . (_______)

b. an increase in the nominal rate of interest . . . (_______)

c. an increase in the proportion of wealth held in savings accounts . . . . (_______)

d. a reduction in real interest rates that is not yet reflected in a change in aggregate demand . . . . (_______)

---

increase; climb **a.** a **b.** c **c.** c, or d (At any interest rate, there is a greater desire to hold savings accounts-d; a rise in interest rates makes savings accounts more attractive-c) **d.** b

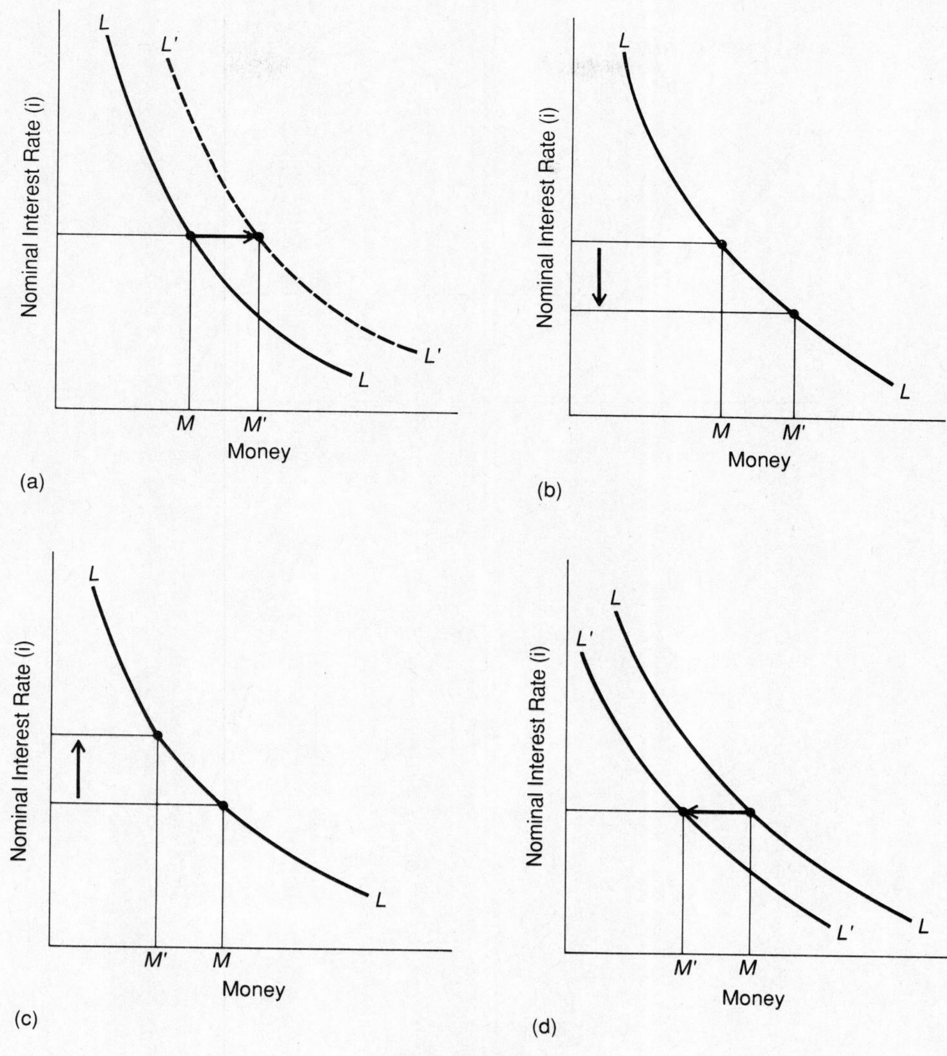

Figure 16-1

It is especially important that you understand the link between changes in the money supply and changes in nominal GNP. Consult Figure 16-2. It shows, in particular, that monetary policy can be expected to work as follows:

1. The quantity of money in an economy affects the nominal interest rate and thus the availability of credit. Specifically, the greater the quantity of money available, the lower the interest rate. This relationship is portrayed in panel **(a)** of Figure 16-2 by movement along curve LL—the demand-for-money curve—as the money supply climbs from S_AS_A to S_BS_B.

2. The interest rate influences investment spending in a similar fashion. The lower the interest rate, the more attractive is physical investment in, say, plant and equipment. This is one of the lessons of Chapter 7, and is portrayed in panel **(b)** of Figure 16-2 by movement along D_1D_1—the demand-for-investment curve—from A' to B' as the interest rate falls from 8 percent to 4 percent.

3. The level of investment is one of the major determinants of GNP. The saving-investment equality that characterized equilibrium GNP in Chapter 8 is portrayed in panel **(c)** of Figure 16-2. The change in the money supply moves equilibrium out along curve SS from A'' to B''.

The effect of changing the money supply can now be illustrated in this simple framework. Should the money supply climb from S_AS_A to S_BS_B, the interest rate would fall from 8 percent to 4 percent, investment would climb from \$100 to \$200, and nominal GNP would climb from \$3000 to \$3300. This is a change in nominal GNP because the increase would be felt entirely in the price level if \$3000 were equal to potential GNP.

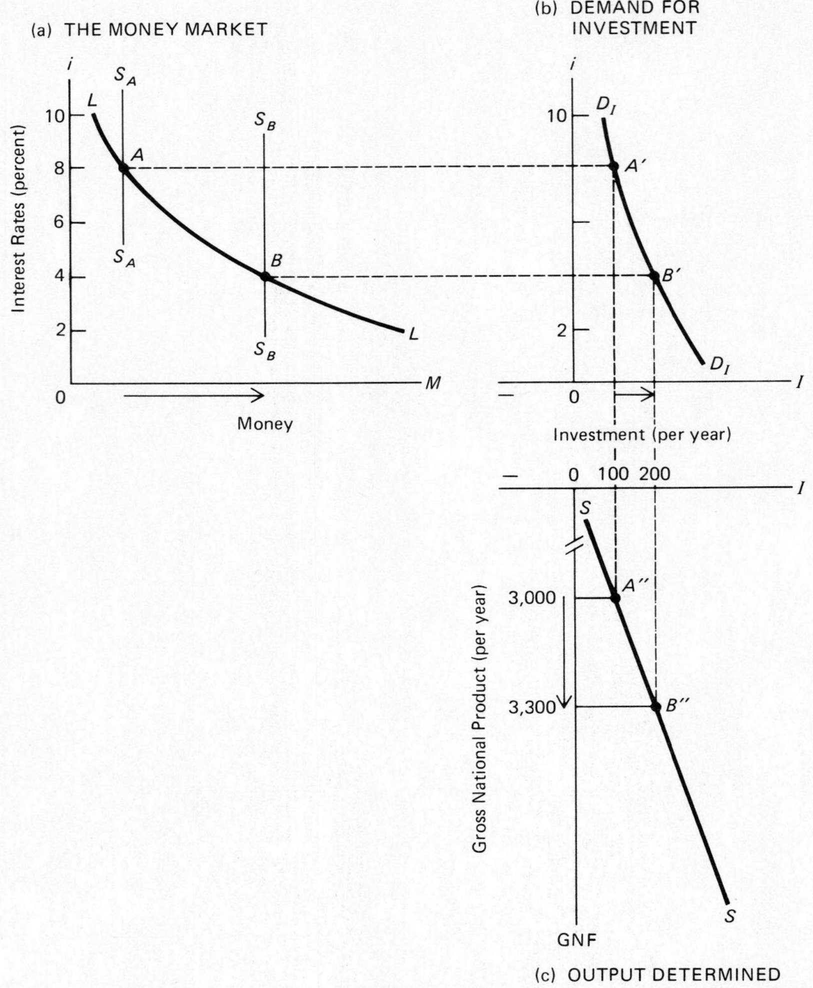

Figure 16-2

2. With the *LL* curve drawn as it is, this diagram says that if the interest rate were to go up, some people would decide that they ought to *(use some of their "idle" money to buy securities / sell some of their securities and hold money as an asset instead)*. Alternatively, if the interest rate were to fall, then the total quantity of money which people would want to hold as an asset would *(increase / decrease)*.

In sum, interest is the reward paid to you for parting with money (parting with liquidity). If the interest rate falls, that reward is less, and the attractiveness of parting with money decreases; i.e., the demand to hold money becomes a stronger force.

---

use some of their "idle" money to buy securities; increase

3. Figure 16-2 shows how the Fed would try to use an increase in the money supply to push an economy out of a recession; i.e., the ultimate policy goal here is to increase nominal GNP. Start at point *A*. The policy step is to increase the money supply from S_AS_A to S_BS_B; it can be accomplished by a large open-market operation. The Fed would simply enter the securities market and *(buy / sell)* government securities—bidding *(up / down)* their prices to the extent necessary to make supply and demand match. Equilibrium in the money market therefore moves from point *A* to point *B*, with the nominal rate of interest lower than before.

How is this reduction accomplished? Recall that the Fed is *(buying / selling)* government issues. This action bids their prices *(up / down)* and sends their effective returns *(up / down)*; i.e., the interest that these issues pay to their holders *(climbs / falls)*. The sellers of these issues also look for other securities to buy with their newly acquired cash. This sends the prices of such securities *(up / down)* and their effective interest yields *(up / down)*. With *(lower / higher)* interest rates and easier credit conditions, borrowers with real investment projects in mind are *(discouraged / encouraged)* to undertake them.

---

buy; up; buying; up; down; falls; up; down; lower; encouraged

4. Look once again at the *LL* curve in Figure 16-2. Suppose it were much steeper (closer to being vertical). Such a steeper curve (as compared with the one drawn) would mean that any given change in interest rates—say, the reduction from 8 percent to 4 percent indicated—would produce a *(larger / smaller)* change in the demand for money. That is, starting from point *A*, but with a steeper *LL* curve than that shown, the Federal Reserve would have to pump a *(smaller / larger)* amount of extra money into the economy to get the interest rate down from 8 to 4 percent.

Conversely, if the *LL* curve were flatter (closer to being horizontal) than shown, then the Fed's task (for any desired reduction in interest rates) would be *(easier / more difficult)*. If the *LL* curve were flatter, it would mean that asset holders were highly sensitive to interest-rate changes. Even a fairly modest reduction in interest rates would "turn them off" to securities; they would want to sell securities in large quantities and to hold money instead.

Should the *LL* curve be very close to horizontal (i.e., highly elastic with respect to interest-rate changes), monetary policy may prove ineffective for we then have what some early Keynesians described as "the depression model." In depression conditions, people are fearful of the risk which security holding involves; they dread the possibility of a calamitous price drop. (And when buyers are few, security prices quite naturally do drop.) In seeking to produce easier-money conditions, the Fed must always battle against preference for cash holdings, but this struggle is at its worst when the *LL* schedule is higher elastic. In such conditions, when the Fed raises the price of government securities, the public sells them readily; but people then hold their cash proceeds as cash. They do not look for other securities to buy, because they are uneasy about the entire securities market. As a result, the extra money pumped into the economy does no good. The Fed wants to see this money move out of the hands of asset holders and into the hands of borrowers who will spend it. In the depression model, the cash remains with the asset holders; it is idle, inactive money.

---

smaller; smaller; more difficult

5. All the preceding discussion of "assets demand for money" has dealt with the attitudes and behavior of lenders of money (the buyers of securities). That is, we have been considering people and financial institutions holding money saved out of income who would be interested in exchanging this money for securities (bonds or stocks) if the terms seemed sufficiently attractive.

We now pass to the other side of the market—to the attitudes and behavior of sellers of securities. Some of these sellers may be people wanting to dispose of securities they bought earlier. Perhaps they want to sell because they need cash for some expenditure. Or perhaps their assets demand for money has risen because they think security prices are likely to fall.

The sellers also consist of business firms wanting to borrow money (to sell new IOUs) because they need financing for new investment projects, and this brings us to the demand for investment. Any sensible firm contemplating a new investment project—say, the building of a new plant—must do its best to estimate (1) what it would cost to build that plant, and (2) what this plant would yield in the way of net income (income over and above operating costs) if built. Such estimates or forecasts, being clouded with uncertainty, are exceedingly difficult, but an intelligent decision requires that the firm make the best estimate it can.

This topic is discussed much later in the text. All you need know at this stage is that such an estimate can be summed up in the form of an interest rate. The firm must be able to say: "We think the cost of building and establishing this projected new plant would be approximately *X* dollars. By a conservative estimate of the net income it would bring in, if and when built, the plant would yield us, say, 15 percent on the *X* dollars that would be tied up in it." If money could be borrowed at 12 percent, and if the firm has been conservative in its cost and revenue estimates, then the plant *(would / would not)* be worth building. Even after paying the interest charges on borrowed money, there would be income left over. If money could be borrowed only at 20 percent, that plant *(still would / would not)* be worth building.

Suppose that the market interest rate had been 20 percent; the plant was not built. Now let the market rate drop to 12 percent. It will now be worth borrowing the money to build this plant. It is a "marginal" investment project, worth building only if and when the market interest rate falls significantly below 15 percent. Similarly, it can be expected that there will be other new investment projects to be tackled if—but only if—the market interest rate drops from 12 percent to 10 percent, or from 8 percent to 6 percent.

In sum, if the market interest rate decreases, some investment projects hitherto considered unprofitable will become *(more / less)* attractive to business firms, since their financing will have become *(cheaper / more expensive)*. Conversely, if the market rate rises, some planned investment projects will be *(undertaken / canceled)*.

---

would; would not; more; cheaper; canceled

6. In a few instances, supplying firms can make fairly close estimates of the likely "efficiency" of a proposed investment project. (For example, a power company can often make pretty good estimates of the likely increase in demand for electricity in its community over the next 10 years.) More commonly, there are so many uncertainties over future marketing conditions and the like that these "efficiency" estimates are very rough even at best. The firm will therefore include a big "safety factor" in its estimate before it goes ahead with an investment project.

Because precise estimates are difficult or impossible, some economists argue that the investment demand schedule will not show much responsiveness to any moderate change in interest rates. That is, a small change in the market rate will product *(a very large / only a very small)* change in the total of investment spending. Insofar as this is true, it would make the D_ID_I curve of Figure 16-2(b) very *(steep / flat)*. And it would make the Fed's task of altering the GNP level via changes in the money supply *(easier / more difficult)*.

There are, of course, sectors besides the business investment sector where demand is sensitive to changes in the nominal interest rate. Higher interest rates should, in fact, cause (1) the demand for housing to *(fall / climb)*, (2) the demand for consumer durables to *(fall / climb)*, (3) public investment at the state and local levels to *(fall / climb)*, and (4) net exports to *(fall / climb)*. If any of these sectors are more interest-sensitive than business investment, then including them in the D_ID_I curve should make it *(more / less)* interest elastic.

---

only a very small; steep, more difficult; fall (Mortgage rates effect monthly payments.); fall (many people borrow to finance major durables expenditures); fall (Most public investment projects are financed by selling bonds and paying the going rate of interest.); fall (Higher interest rates make domestic securities more attractive to foreigners, increase the demand for dollars, increase the international value of the dollar, and thus increase the cost of U.S. exports.); more

7. Figure 16-2 depends, in its final panel, on the Keynesian construction that determines GNP by the equality of saving and investment (in the absence of government spending and taxes). That dependence is not, however, critical in comparing the Keynesian model to the modern mainstream construction. Figure 16-3 portrays the increase in investment that was depicted in panel **(b)** of Figure 16-2 as an increase in aggregate demand. In panel **(a)** of Figure 16-3, the story told by Figure 16-2 is repeated; the higher investment causes real GNP to climb because output was initially *(well below / almost equal to / far above)* potential GNP. In panel **(b)**, though, the higher investment causes only nominal GNP to climb because *(real GNP / only prices)* climb. The key here, of course, is that GNP was initially *(far below / almost equal to / well above)* potential.

---

well below; only prices, almost equal to (Actually, the same result would apply if GNP were initially well above potential, too.)

8. The algebraic difference between the real interest rate and the nominal interest rate is the ____________. The demand for money depends on the *(nominal / real)* interest rate; the demand for investment depends upon the *(nominal / real)* interest rate. As a result, a reduction in the money supply can cause nominal interest rates to *(fall / climb)* in the long run even though they *(fall / climb)* in the short run. As the money supply contracts, in particular, *(the nominal / the real / both)* interest rate(s) climbs, causing investment to fall, aggregate demand to fall, and eventually, price inflation to slow down. As a direct result of the slowdown in inflation, though, the *(nominal / real)* rate falls; it is supported by the slower growth in nominal GNP that causes the demand for money to shift *(to the right / nowhere / to the left)* where it can intersect even a smaller money supply at a lower nominal rate of interest. The problem with this scenario is, though, that *(it may happen too fast for people to keep up / it may happen too slowly to avoid the costs of high unemployment)*.

---

rate of inflation; nominal; real; fall; climb; both; nominal; to the left; it may happen too slowly to avoid the costs of high unemployment

The point of question 8 is illustrated in Figure 16-4. Initial conditions in the money market are given by demand (curve LL), supply (curve SS), and equilibrium (point E with nominal interest rate i^*). When the Fed contracts the money supply, its graphical representation shifts to the left, to something like $S'S'$. In the short run, then, the nominal interest rate climbs to i'; and since prices have not yet changed, the corresponding real interest rate must also be higher. Now suppose, in the

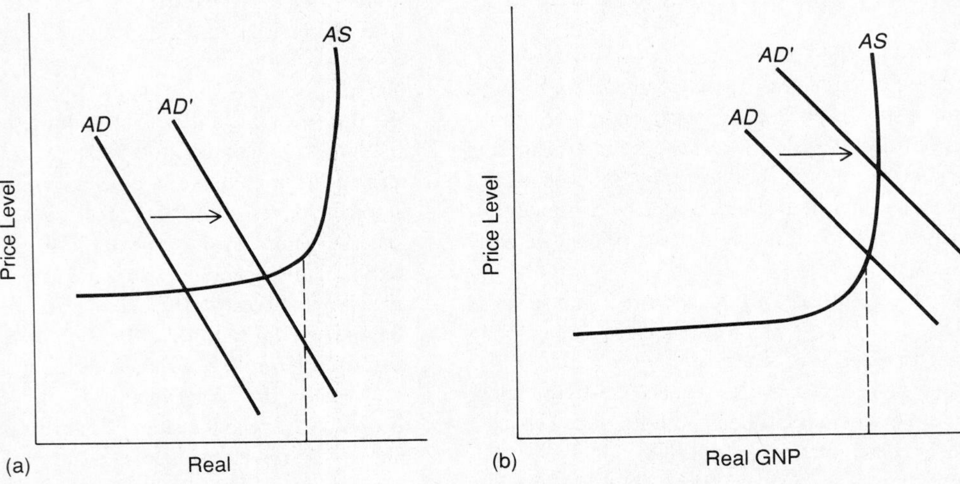

Figure 16-3

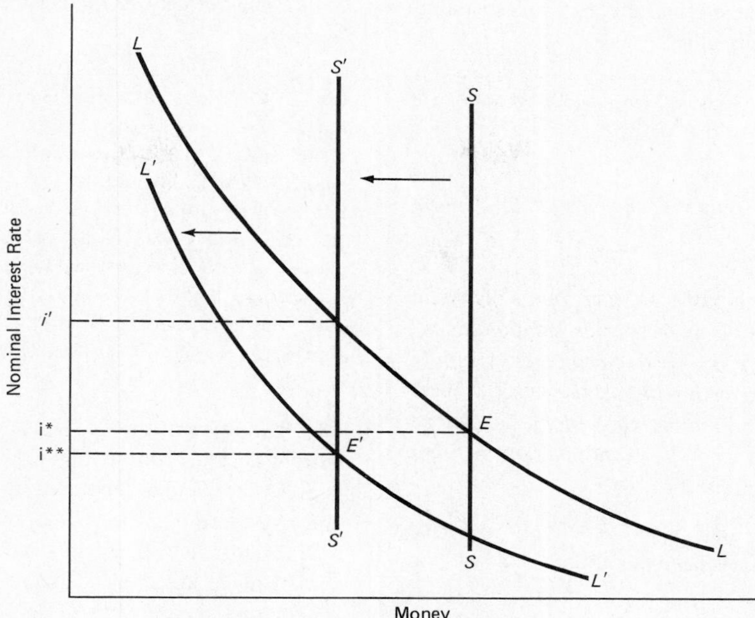

Figure 16-4

long run, that the monetary contraction works and slows growth in nominal GNP. If that supports a lower demand for money such as $L'L'$, long-run equilibrium could be established at point E' with $i^{**} < i^{*}$.

Modern monetarism, based on the evolution of the quantity theory of money among other things, has generated several propositions that impact directly upon policy. Monetarists believe, first of all, that the money supply is the major determinant of nominal GNP in the short run. They believe, moreover, that the money supply is also the major determinant of prices in the long run. Finally, they support maximum reliance on the market. These propositions lead them to espouse (1) the advisability of fixed policy rules for the sake of predictability, (2) the advisablity of minimum government intervention into the marketplace, and (3) a firm belief that the macroeconomic fluctuations are caused by erratic money-supply growth. The expectations is that stable growth in the money supply between 3 and 4 percent per year should produce steady growth in real GNP with stable prices.

9. In the space provided, record the quantity exchange equation.

According to the crude quantity theory, velocity and real GNP are assumed to *(vary proportionately / be fixed / be wildly variable)*. The result is, according to the crude theory, that any change in the money supply will be immediately reflected in *(prices / output / investment)*. While this is a reasonable explanation of *(recession / hyperinflation / hyperventilation)*, it is not very satisfactory in a world where the velocity of money has been *(climbing / falling)* for the past three decades and was quite variable during the monetarist experiment of 1980, 1981, and much of 1982.

$MV = PQ$ (i.e., the money supply multiplied by the velocity of money always equals nominal GNP); be fixed; prices; hyperinflation; climbing

10. The problems with the crude theory aside, modern monetarists use a fairly stable velocity and the quantity theory of money to make their points. Rough stability in V is all that they need. They first proposition is that the money supply determines nominal GNP in the short run. If V is fixed in the short run, then any change in the money supply will, by application of the quantity equation, be *(proportionately / progressively)* reflected in *(nominal / real)* GNP.

Their second proposition is that the money supply determines prices in the long run. This follows from the quantity theory and their *(conservative political views / belief in the market responsiveness of wages and prices / belief in the proportional variation of velocity)*. In particular, market clearing sets real GNP at its *(potential / nominal level / second-best optimum)* so that the quantity equation has, in effect, *(one / two / three)* constants, namely: ______

Any change in the money supply is therefore translated directly and proportionately into changes in prices.

As an aside, the quantity theory of modern monetarism still precludes the effectiveness of fiscal policy to move GNP around. There is, quite simply, no place in the quantity equation for either government spending or taxes to appear. The only role for fiscal policy is to determine the mix of spending between the public and private sectors.

---

proportionately; nominal; belief in the market responsiveness of wages and prices; potential; two; potential real GNP and velocity

11. The Fed conducted a monetarist experiment in the United States from ______________ through ______________; under the leadership of Chairman Paul Volcker, it stopped trying to *(maintain stable interest rates / maintain stable exchange rates / keep bank reserves and the money supply moving along predetermined growth paths)* and focused instead on *(smoothing interest rates / maintaining stable exchange rates / keeping bank reserves and the money supply moving along predetermined growth paths)*.

a. Which of the following statements accurately describe lessons that were learned from the experiment? (Circle the accurate statements.)

(1) The velocity of money proved to be quite stable in the context of firm monetary policy.

(2) The short-run effects of tight money are felt more in prices than they are in output.

(3) Money proved to be relatively impotent in determining aggregate demand.

(4) Firm monetary policy proved to be a relatively inexpensive way to curb high rates of inflation.

b. These lessons were gleaned from the experience of those 35 months. Which of the following statements accurately describe that experience? (Again, circle the accurate statements.)

(1) Interest rates were stable and held firm at moderate levels.

(2) Interest-sensitive spending was remarkably constant throughout the period.

(3) The value of the dollar rose sharply, causing net exports to climb dramatically. This was the dominant link to aggregate demand.

(4) The debt burdens of many countries rose appreciably, causing severe recessions and foreign-trade contractions in much of the third world.

(5) Real GNP rose in the United States at a brisk 2.5 percent per year.

(6) Unemployment rose from 6 percent in 1979 to a peak of 10.5 percent in late 1982.

(7) Inflation fell a bit, from 7 percent in 1980 to 4 percent in 1983.

(8) Long-term bonds continued to be safe investments because of consistently stable interest rates.

(9) The velocity of money was extremely stable during the period.

October 1979; August 1982; maintain stable interest rates; keeping bank reserves and the money supply moving along predetermined growth paths

a. All the purported lessons listed are inaccurate; they state, in fact, exactly the opposite of what was learned.

b. **(4)** and **(6)** [For the other statements, the actual lessons learned are: **(1)** Interest rates were volatile and high. **(2)** Interest-sensitive spending plunged. **(3)** Net exports plunged with the higher dollar. **(5)** Real GNP stagnated in the United States. **(7)** Inflation fell from 13 percent in 1980. **(8)** Long-term bonds became risky with variable interest rates. **(9)** The velocity of money proved to be unstable.]

12. The effectiveness of monetary policy is still an issue of current debate. Consult Figure 16-5. There, initial equilibrium is given by E and is supported by long-run aggregate supply AS and aggregate demand AD. Short-run aggregate supply below equilibrium is shown by AS'. A contraction in the money supply should move aggregate demand to *(AD' / AD'')*. In the short run, output should fall to *(OB / OC / OF / OG)*. In the long run, prices should fall to *(OB / OC / OF / OG)*. Figure 16-5 can therefore be used to explain why the effect of monetary policy seems to be felt more in *(output / prices)* in the short run and more in *(output / prices)* in the long run. Because potential GNP determines GNP in the long run, contractionary monetary policy eventually produces lower price (inflation); it does not, however, avoid the cost of recession required to initiate the process.

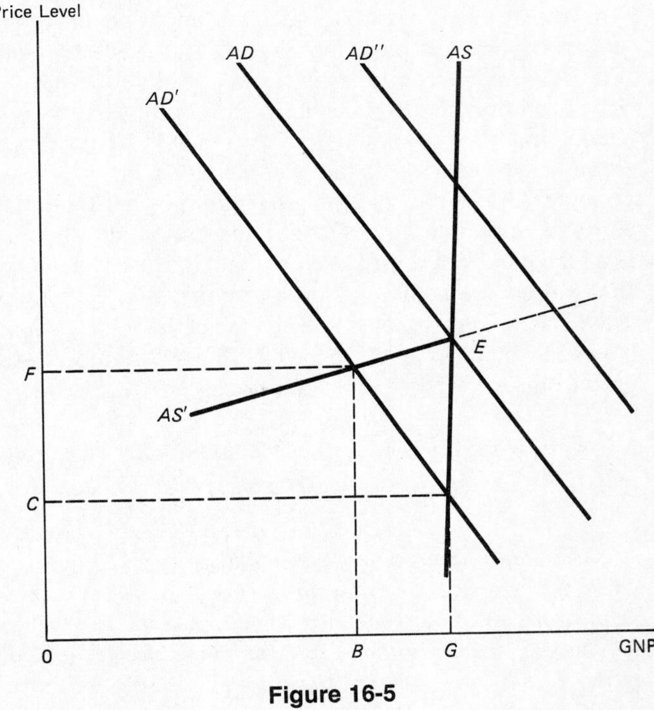

Figure 16-5

AD'; OB; OC; output; prices

There are, of course, many open issues. Should monetary policy be set according to predetermined rules so that everyone will know what to expect, or should the Fed be allowed to use its discretion to change policy as conditions warrant? In either case, what are the appropriate targets for monetary policy, and upon what should its specification depend? How does the international sector influence the answers to these questions? You should be able to see these issues discussed on almost a daily basis with a careful eye and some time to devote to reading current newspapers.

QUIZ: Multiple Choice

1. On the basis of the transactions demand component of the demand for money:
(1) the demand for money climbs as the nominal interest rate climbs.
(2) the demand for money climbs as the nominal interest rate falls.
(3) the demand for money falls as nominal income rises.
(4) the demand for money falls as nominal income falls.
(5) none of the above.

2. Which answer to question 2 would have been correct if it had referred to the assets demand component of the demand for money?
(1).
(2).
(3).
(4).
(5).

3. The demand curve for investment:
(1) parallels the demand curve for money in that high interest rates reduce demand.
(2) most precisely plots the real rate of interest against quantity demanded.
(3) is negatively sloped because high real interest rates cause marginal investment projects to be rejected.
(4) is a vital link between changes in the money supply and nominal GNP.
(5) all of the above.

4. A reduction in interest rates engineered by the Federal Reserve can reasonably be expected to:
(1) encourage investment (*I*) spending because it makes lending of money more attractive.
(2) discourage *I* spending because it makes borrowing of money less attractive.
(3) have little or no effect on *I* spending, since that is not its purpose—interest-rate changes are intended to alter security prices, not *I* spending.
(4) discourage *I* spending because it makes lending of money less attractive.
(5) encourage *I* spending because it makes borrowing of money more attractive.

5. According to a monetarist, monetary policy and fiscal policy differ in what way?
(1) Monetary policy should be deliberately operated in the short run in an effort to keep GNP in the full-employment region, whereas fiscal policy cannot have anything but minor effects on the GNP level.
(2) Monetary policy deals with the amounts of money spent and collected by the government, whereas fiscal policy deals with interest rates.
(3) Monetary policy seeks to encourage or discourage investment (*I*) spending and consumption (*C*) spending by business firms and private citizens by influencing interest rates and credit availability, whereas fiscal policy operates directly upon the level of public spending through spending and taxation.
(4) Fiscal policy works principally through changes in the level of *I* spending, whereas monetary policy affects *I* spending little or not at all.
(5) There is no essential difference between them at all, since both objectives and techniques of operation are the same—they differ only in that they are administered by two different agencies.

6. Monetary policy is made somewhat less effective in restraining a period of excessive spending whenever:
(1) the demand-for-investment schedule is highly elastic.
(2) dollars held abroad are attracted to higher interest rates.
(3) the money demand schedule is highly inelastic.
(4) changes in interest rates tend to bring with them changes in the market value of securities.
(5) investment spending responds more to changes in credit availability than to changes in interest rates.

7. In terms of the saving-investment diagram used extensively in Chapters 7 and 8, the introduction of a tight-money policy by the Federal Reserve would be intended to:
(1) lower both the investment (*I*) and savings (*S*) schedules, hence lower GNP.
(2) raise the *I* schedule, hence lower GNP.
(3) raise the *I* schedule, hence raise GNP.
(4) lower the *S* schedule, hence raise GNP.
(5) lower the *I* schedule, hence lower GNP.

8. If the Federal Reserve conducts a large-scale easy-money open-market operation:
(1) government security prices will rise and interest rates will fall.
(2) interest rates will fall, but government security prices need not be affected.
(3) both government security prices and interest rates will fall.
(4) government security prices will fall and interest rates will rise.

(5) interest rates will rise, but government security prices may or may not change.

9. The Federal Reserve should slow down or halt a tight-money policy:
(1) as soon as interest rates have reached a sufficiently low level.
(2) when investment spending has been sufficiently increased.
(3) whenever the equilibrium level of GNP has been reached.
(4) when prices begin to rise sharply.
(5) in none of these situations.

10. The effectiveness of monetary policy in a recession will be reduced or destroyed if:
(1) interest rates cannot be forced down much because the level of borrowing is highly responsive to small changes in the level of the interest rate.
(2) the Fed finds that security prices start to go up as soon as it begins its easy-money operation.
(3) interest rates cannot be forced down much because money holders prefer to retain money rather than buy securities at any lower rate.
(4) the asset demand or liquidity demand for money is very low.
(5.) the value of the multiplier is very high.

11. The effectiveness of monetary policy in a recession will be reduced or destroyed if:
(1) the public is principally interested in holding securities rather than money as assets.
(2) the Federal Reserve does not wish the prices of government securities to fall below their maturity value.
(3) the Federal Reserve is determined to maintain an easy-money rather than a tight-money policy.
(4) the current level of interest rates is very high.
(5) potential borrowers do not respond to reductions in the interest rate or to greater availability of credit.

12. If the Federal Reserve conducts a large-scale open-market sale of government securities, then we would expect:
(1) the demand for investment to increase.
(2) the federal government's budget to move into surplus or at least into balance.
(3) the total quantity of money in circulation to increase.
(4) the assets demand for money to decrease.
(5) none of the preceding to occur.

13. When fiscal policy and monetary policy are being operated in concert in order to combat a recession, we are likely to observe the combination of a:
(1) budget deficit and open-market security purchases.
(2) budget surplus and open-market security purchases.
(3) budget deficit and open-market security sales.
(4) budget surplus and open-market security sales.
(5) balanced budget and open-market security sales.

14. What will be the impact, if any, of the bond price change described in question 14 on new bonds being offered for sale by the federal government and corporations?
(1) Both new government and new corporation bonds must be offered for sale at a somewhat higher interest rate.
(2) New government bonds can be offered for sale at a lower interest rate, but new corporation bonds must be offered at a higher rate.
(3) Both new government and new corporation bonds can be offered for sale at a somewhat lower interest rate.
(4) New government bonds can be offered for sale at a somewhat lower interest rate, but new corporation bonds will not be affected at all.
(5) There is no reason why the sale of either new government or new corporation bonds should be affected at all.

15. Because the difference between real and nominal interest rates is the rate of inflation:
(1) nominal rates can fall, in the long run, in response to tight monetary policy.
(2) nominal rates must rise, in both the short and the long runs, in response to tight monetary policy.
(3) there is no difference between the demand for money and the demand for investment.
(4) the quantity theory of money is unquestionably true.
(5) none of the above.

16. The crude quantity theory of money:
(1) assumed that both V and nominal GNP were fixed.
(2) assumed that both V and real GNP were fixed.
(3) assumed that only V was fixed.
(4) assumed that V and the price level were fixed.
(5) none of the above.

17. Monetarists believe:
(1) the money supply determines nominal GNP in the short run.
(2) the money supply determines prices in the long run.
(3) fiscal policy is essentially ineffective.
(4) market forces will maintain potential GNP in the long run.
(5) all of the above.

18. The lessons of the past decade or so include which of the following?
(1) Strict adherence to money-supply growth targets can cause substantial unemployment.
(2) The Keynesian view is entirely wrong.
(3) There is nothing to the monetarist view of the world that should be accepted in constructing policy.
(4) Money matters, but so does fiscal policy.
(5) Answers (1) and (4).

SUGGESTED ANSWERS TO QUESTIONS IN THE TEXT: Chapter 16

1. Velocity equals the ratio of nominal GNP to the stock of money. For 1981, therefore, $V(81) = 3053/416.6 = 7.33$; in 1982, $V(82) = 3166/443.2 = 7.14$. Velocity therefore fell at an annual rate of roughly 2.6 percent through 1981. The other years' statistics are similarly computed.

2. Read Figure 16-4 backward; i.e., move the supply of money from S_BS_B to S_AS_A so that interest rates climb. Investment therefore falls, aggregate demand falls, and macro-equilibrium moves down along a fairly horizontal short-run aggregate supply curve.

3. Higher interest rates would mean that the assets demand for money is smaller; for a given level of nominal GNP, this is reflected by movement *along* a given *DD* curve like the one drawn in Figure 16-2 with transactions demand holding steady. To maintain equilibrium in the money market, therefore, the money supply must be diminished, so the velocity of money must be increased ($V = \text{GNP}/M$, and GNP is constant). Interest sensitivity in the demand for money thereby undermines the assumption that the velocity of money is constant.

4. Military expenditures are part of government spending, and thus part of aggregate demand; higher military spending can therefore be expansionary. So can increased domestic spending. So can increases in investment and other interest-sensitive spending encouraged by loosened monetary policy.

5. Refer to the quantity theory of money, and the wage-price flexibility assumptions of the monetarist school. If wages and/or prices are not flexible in the short run, then changes in aggregate demand created by either fiscal or monetary means can adjust equilibrium. In the long run, though, with aggregate supply determined by potential GNP, changes in aggregate demand are much less effective. Monetary policy must then be set to sustain growth at the rate of growth of potential GNP without leaking excessively into price inflation.

6. Nominal rates include an inflation factor which can be (and was in the 1980s) reduced so much over the long run by tight money that nominal rates fall even though real rates hold steady. In the short run, before nominal GNP is affected, tight money starts to work by moving up a given demand curve for money toward higher nominal and real rates. Refer to Figure 16-4 in the *Study Guide*.

7. The net export curve would have the same shape as the D_ID_I curve in Figure 16-4. Why? Because higher interest rates increase the value of the dollar and thus diminish net exports. The *SS* line in panel **(c)** then maps levels of GNP against net exports such that saving equals investment (now fixed) plus net exports. Any change in monetary policy therefore looks the same on the graph. A contradiction, e.g., increases interest rates, lowers net exports, and must therefore call forth a lower level of GNP to support the necessary lower level of saving.

8. **a.** Expanding the money supply moves the money supply curve out to the right and moves equilibrium down a fixed *DD* curve.

b. A falling exchange rate with correspondingly higher net exports and GNP increases transactions demand; the entire *DD* curve shifts out.

c. The supply curve stays fixed; the demand curve moves in, so interest rates climb.

9. Prices would climb dramatically; the crude theory of money applies to some degree, especially in boom times when actual GNP is close to or slightly above potential. A 1 percent increase in the money supply in a depression might have no effect if *(a)* people held the cash or *(b)* the resulting reduction in interest rates had no effect on investment (things being that bad, and all, there may not exist any attractive investment projects).

10. No, because we may want discretion over the rules. Rules may have to be changed, from time to time, and still provide some stability in expectations in the shorter run.

11. Think also in terms of long run versus short run. Things that are not stable in the short run may, over the long haul, be more stable and predictable.

12. Consult the table shown at the top of the following page.

	Monetarist	Keynesian: GNP < Potential	Keynesian: GNP Near Potential
a[1]	Prices up Output unchanged Employment unchanged	Prices stable Output up Employment up	Prices up Output unchanged Employment unchanged
b[2]	Prices down Output unchanged Employment unchanged	Prices stable (SR); Prices down (LR) Output down (SR); Output restored (LR) Employment moves with output	Prices stable (SR); Prices down (LR) Output down (SR); Output restored (LR) Employment moves with output
c[3]	Prices up Output unchanged Employment unchanged	Prices up Output down Employment moves with output	Prices up Output down (less?) Employment moves with output
d[4]	Prices down Output up Employment unchanged	Prices stable Output unchanged Employment unchanged	Prices stable Output unchanged Employment unchanged
e[1]	Prices up Output unchanged Employment unchanged	Prices stable Output up Employment up	Prices up Output unchanged Employment unchanged

[1] In terms of aggregate demand and supply, a large tax cut (or more exports) moves aggregate demand out. Against the monetarist vertical *AS*, it causes only a price increase. For the Keynesian, it would be expansionary unless output were close to potential.

[2] For the monetarist, there would be only pressure to move prices—down. For the Keynesian, the short-run effect would be felt in output and employment (down); the long-run effect, in prices.

[3] An increase in the price of oil shifts the *AS* schedule up. For the monetarist, this increases prices at potential GNP; for the Keynesian, this can cause stagflation.

[4] Innovation increases potential GNP. For the monetarist, this reduces pressure on prices; for the Keynesian, it does nothing unless aggregate demand moves, as well.

APPENDIX: 16

The Rational-Expectations Approach

The mainstream neo-Keynesian policies that called upon governments to manipulate aggregate demand to smooth out business cycles were moderately successful in countries like the United States, Japan, and West Germany from 1950 through the early 1970s. Starting in 1973, though, a combination of outside shocks and "stop-and-go" policy adjustments worked to accelerate what had, until then, been a gradual worsening of the Phillips-curve tradeoff between unemployment and inflation. The latter half of the 1970s and the early 1980s were, in fact, marked by unacceptably high levels of both inflation and unemployment that were lowered only at the cost of a severe recession. Throughout this painful period, the natural-rate theories of Milton Friedman and Edmund Phelps that were so bitterly resisted in the 1960s gradually worked themselves into the mainstream of economic thought. They appeared, in fact, in the form of a vertical long-run Phillips curve and the resulting cycle pattern of unemployment and inflation noted in earlier chapters.

This acceptance does not, however, mean the end of debate. Monetarists and mainstream theorists still debate the effectiveness of fiscal policy. Beyond the mainstream, though, there is a new school of thought that debates the effectiveness of any policy. The "rational-expectations macroeconomics" of people like Lucas, Barro, Sargent, and Wallace question the ability of even monetary policy to affect a short-run change in GNP. These economists conclude, in fact, that the short-run Phillips curve is, in effect, just as vertical as the long-run Phillips curve. They hold that any slope which may be observed in the short run tradeoff between inflation and unemployment *cannot* be exploited by macroeconomic policy. This appendix is devoted to their contribution.

Having completed this appendix, therefore, you will have accomplished the following objectives.

LEARNING OBJECTIVES

1. Understand the two fundamental assumptions of the rational-expectations macroeconomics: (*a*) people's expectations are efficiently and rationally formed, and (*b*) prices and wages are extremely flexible.

2. Relate the reasoning that leads from the assumptions listed in objective 1 to the conclusion that predictable policy cannot move the unemployment rate from its natural level even in the short run.

3. Relate the criticisms leveled against the rational-expectations macroeconomics, and explain the responses of its proponents to the criticisms.

4. Recall the "Lucas critique" (i.e., the velocity of money will not remain constant if monetary policy maintains a steady money growth posture), and relate it to the experience of the United States during the monetarist experiment of the early 1980s.

The **rational-expectations theory** holds that people make the best use of their limited information and their understanding of economic theory to undo any policy adjustment that the government might attempt. It follows that policy cannot fool anyone. If, for example, the government were to lower taxes in an attempt to increase aggregate demand, people would see that their taxes would have to increase later to pay for the current reduction. They would therefore save their tax savings in anticipation of that future increase in tax liability so that increased consumption would not provide the desired increase in aggregate demand.

The second assumption of the rational-expectations school is familiar; it presumes that wages and prices are sufficiently flexible to clear all markets in response to any outside shock. Prices and wages are, therefore, always in equilibrium (or at the very least, moving rapidly toward equilibrium).

1. It follows from the second assumption that most unemployment that is observed during a recession is *(voluntary / involuntary)*. Consider the supply and demand curves representing a labor market in Figure 16A-1; *SS* represents the supply curve and *DD* represents an initial demand curve. The initial equilibrium wage is $_______ with _______ people voluntarily unemployed; i.e., they *(are / are not)* willing to work for the going wage because *(it is too small / they cannot find a job)*. If the demand curve were to fall to *D′D′*, the rational-expectations theory would predict *(an immediate / a slow and tortured)* decline in wage to $_______ with _______ people in voluntary unemployment and _______ in involuntary unemployment. If the wage did not fall, though, _______ would be employed

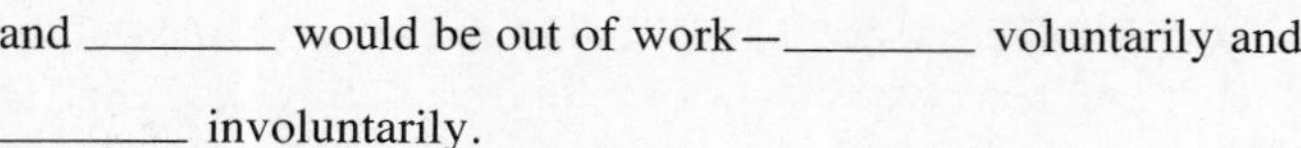

and _______ would be out of work—_______ voluntarily and _______ involuntarily.

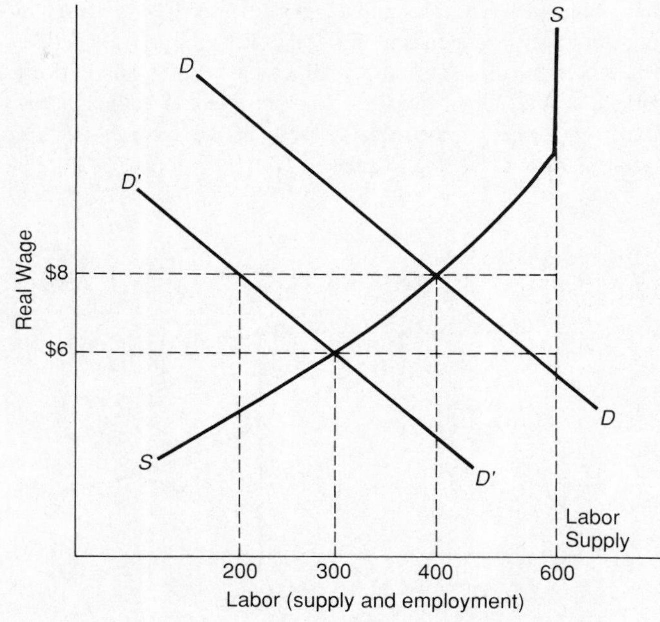

Figure 16A-1

voluntary; 8; 200 (600 − 400); are not; it is too small; an immediate; 6; 300; 0; 200; 400; 200; 200

2. The proponents of rational-expectations macroeconomics hold that the observed slope in the short-run Phillips curve is a source of confusion and misperception. Consult Figure 16A-2. Beginning at point *A*, wage inflation would be running at _______ percent with unemployment holding at the natural rate of 6 percent.

Suppose, now, that government policy is initiated to try to stimulate employment and to move the economy along the short-run Phillips curve to a point like *B*. Rational-expectations theory states that unemployed workers would *(have to be offered higher real wage increases / have to be tricked into thinking that higher nominal wage increases were higher real wage increases)* to accomplish that move. Only if labor thought that the *(nominal / real)* wage were rising would the workers be attracted to work (remember, the 6 percent natural rate includes a significant number of voluntarily unemployed workers) so that the unemployment rate would fall. The _______ percent wage increase noted at point *B* would, according to the theory, be exhausted by price inflation so that the real wage increase would be *(the expected positive increment / zero / actually negative)* and those who were voluntarily unemployed at point *A* would again leave the labor force. As a result, the economy would have moved to point *(C / D / E)* instead of *B*. Even in the short run, because labor would not have been so fooled in the first place, the policy stimulus would have been vented entirely in price and wage inflation and not in the intended reduction in the rate of unemployment. Notice that it *(does / does not)* matter whether or not the stimulus was the result of a change in monetary policy or a change in fiscal policy; the result *(would / would not)* be the same in either case—a short-run Phillips curve that is unstable and, for policy purposes, effectively *(vertical / horizontal)* in the region directly above the *(current rate / natural rate)* of unemployment.

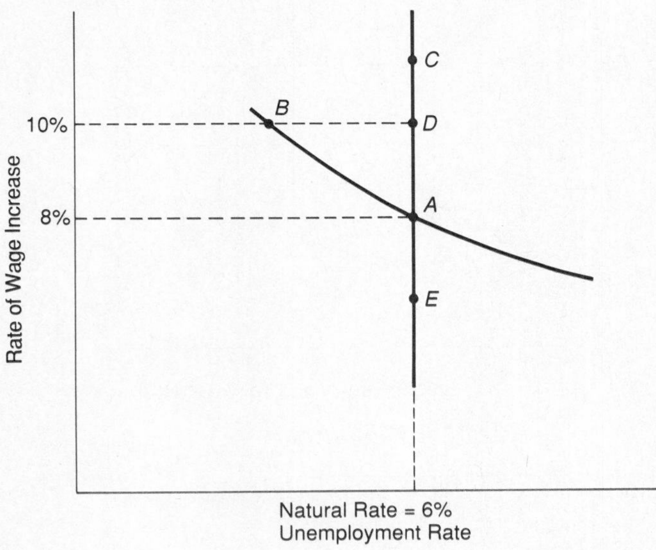

Figure 16A-2

8; have to be tricked into thinking that higher nominal wage increases were higher real wage increases; real; 10; zero; *D*; does not; would; vertical; natural rate

3. If employment policy can (*a*) always be immediately undone and (*b*) create bad things like inflation, then it follows that discretionary changes in policy *(should nonetheless be allowed because they are currently expected / should be discontinued because they are only harmful)*. The money supply should increase at a *(targeted / variable)* rate with the clear understanding that the velocity of money will *(be fixed / vary to preserve potential GNP)*.

should be discontinued because they are only harmful; targeted; vary to preserve potential GNP

4. Mainstream economists have attacked both of the assumptions that form the basis of the rational-expectations macroeconomics. In reviewing these countercriticisms, it is important to note that the policy conclusions derived from the rational-expectations theory depend upon both assumptions. If, for example, people form rational expectations about the future but markets do not clear immediately, then policy can still make a dent in the short run. There can, in particular, still exist involuntary unemployment that *(can / cannot)* be reduced by stimulus. If the 6 percent initial level of unemployment noted in Figure 16A-2 were *(above / below)* the natural rate, for example, then the stimulus might have achieved a reduction in the rate of unemployment. Inflation would have *(increased / decreased)*, to be sure, but the short-run Phillips curve *(would / would not)* have some slope to exploit.

On the other hand, disallowing the formation of rational expectations on the part of labor would, even in the presence of rapidly clearing markets, make the misperception story of the rational-expectations theorists right on target. Since that *(is / is not)* their explanation for the observed slope to the short-run Phillips curve, their conclusions about a vertical Phillips curve would not hold.

Prolonged periods of high unemployment do damage to *(both assumptions / only the expectations assumption / only the flexibility assumption / neither assumption)*, but they are "explained" to some degree by the practitioners of rational expectations in terms of *(a)* artificial impediments to market clearing and *(b)* confusing "stop-and-go" policies by the federal government.

can; above; increased; would; is; both assumptions

QUIZ: Multiple Choice

1. The basic assumptions of the rational-expectations macroeconomics include:
(1) a presumption that people form their expectations about the future efficiently and rationally.
(2) a presumption that prices are extremely flexible in both directions.
(3) a presumption that wages are extremely flexible in both directions.
(4) all of the above.
(5) answers (1) and (3) only.

2. It follows from the assumptions that:
(1) most unemployment is voluntary.
(2) monetary policy can work in the short run and not the long run.
(3) fiscal policy can affect the long term but not the short term because of delays in Congress.
(4) any policy might work depending upon the circumstance.
(5) none of the above.

3. It follows from the assumptions that a reduction in taxes to stimulate consumption:
(1) would work as advertised.
(2) would not work unless accompanied by accommodating monetary policy.

(3) would not work because people would save their tax break in anticipation of future higher taxes.
(4) might work unless there were substantial leakages into foreign markets.
(5) none of the above.

4. According to the rational-expectations macroeconomics, the short-run Phillips curve is effectively:
(1) horizontal.
(2) positively sloped.
(3) vertical.
(4) negatively sloped.
(5) sloped in either direction depending upon conditions.

5. The observed slope in the short-run Phillips curve is explained by the rational-expectations macroeconomics in terms of:
(1) cost-of-living contracts.
(2) inherent instability.
(3) the effects of monetary policy only.
(4) the vagaries of the uncertain international market.
(5) all of the above.

6. Should an economy attempt to move up its short-run Phillips curve to reduce unemployment below the natural rate, the rational-expectations macroeconomist would expect that:
(1) people would not be fooled and only inflation would result.
(2) people would gradually find out that real wages had climbed, turning the curve vertical in the long run.
(3) the economy would be successful in the short term, but successful in the long term only if there were substantial economic growth.
(4) the natural rate would indeed fall as potential output grew.
(5) none of the above.

7. The policy prescription of the rational-expectations macroeconomics includes:
(1) a notion that stable monetary-policy rules should be constructed and followed so that changes in velocity can maintain equilibrium at potential GNP.
(2) a notion that discretionary policy should be avoided.
(3) a notion that no policy adjustment would be required to help an economy over an oil crisis like the one that occurred in 1973.
(4) a notion that fiscal policy should determine the mix of public and private spending once and for all and then leave it alone.
(5) all of the above.

8. The existence of periods of prolonged unemployment in our history does damage to:
(1) the expectations assumption only.
(2) the flexibility assumption only.
(3) both assumptions of the rational-expectations theory.
(4) either assumption depending upon conditions.
(5) neither assumption in any circumstance.

9. Without the flexibility assumption:
(1) periods of unemployment could exist.
(2) the short-run Phillips curve would have some slope.
(3) policy could be used to exploit the short-run tradeoff.
(4) the expectations hypothesis would be damaged but not necessarily destroyed.
(5) all of the above.

SUGGESTED ANSWERS TO QUESTIONS IN THE TEXT: Appendix to Chapter 16

1. The key here is that people will know that the Fed will have to contract the money supply over the course of the next few weeks, and they will respond in anticipation of that policy by selling assets. Why? Because they want to be liquid when the higher rates come with the tighter money supply. Selling the assets lowers their prices and thus increases their returns in advance of the tighter money.

2. Instead of taking the price as given, they expect prices to rise with excess demand and to fall with excess supply. This tightens the cobweb.

3. Rational expectations diminish the consumption effect of the tax cut, and thus its effectiveness (through any multiplier).

CHAPTER 17
FISCAL POLICY, DEFICITS, AND THE GOVERNMENT DEBT

You have nearly completed your introduction to macroeconomics. You have seen how the business cycle can produce periods of high inflation and low unemployment, periods of high unemployment and low inflation, and periods during which both inflation and unemployment are high or low. You have seen how monetary policy and fiscal policy can be used to combat these macroeconomic ills, and you have seen that there is a difference of opinion about the likely success of these policies in achieving their objectives. It is now time to look at fiscal policy and monetary policy together and to ponder their appropriate mix. Part of this chapter will explore that question.

It is also time for you to confront one of the most controversial political and economic issues of our time: what to do about the federal deficit and the resulting federal debt. Are deficits recession- or policy-induced? Do their dimensions depend upon the fiscal-monetary policy mix? Are there burdens associated with deficits that should cause us to avoid them at all cost? These and other questions are also topics to be covered in Chapter 17.

Having completed your work in this chapter, therefore, you will have achieved the culmination of your study of macroeconomics. In addition to "putting it all together" in an exploration of these general questions about policy interaction and the federal debt, you will have accomplished the following more specific objectives.

LEARNING OBJECTIVES

1. Differentiate between the old (classical) view of the federal debt that the budget should be balanced every year and the new (modern) view that allows the budget to be used as a fiscal-policy tool subject to evaluating the costs of running in the red.

2. Differentiate between the structural deficit (surplus), reflecting what the government would collect and spend if it were operating at full potential, and the cyclical deficit (surplus), reflecting the effect of the business cycle on what the government spends and collects. The impact of fiscal policy is derived from the structural deficit; changes in the cyclical deficit are the result of movement through the business cycle.

3. Differentiate between demand-management decisions and policy-mix decisions undertaken in any one year, and apply this distinction to hypothetical and realistic policy deliberations.

4. Understand why a policy mix that directs monetary policy at controlling inflation and fiscal policy at controlling unemployment is likely to produce a low-investment, high-consumption, high-deficit economy. Explain why, conversely, switching the targets might produce the opposite result: a high-investment, low-consumption, budget-surplus economy.

5. Explain why the crowding out of investment is an issue when considering the structural component of a deficit. Show why monetarists always worry about complete crowding out even in the short run, while others expect little crowding out in the short run, particularly during recessions, and complete crowding out only in the long run.

6. Outline a brief chronicle of the federal debt of the United States, paying special attention to its recent, unprecedented peacetime growth.

7. Explain why each of the following views is a myth: (*a*) people cannot run deficits forever, and neither can governments; and (*b*) private debt is growing without concern, so there is no reason to worry about public debt, either.

8. Explain the potential sources of true concern over the burden of debt: (*a*) the servicing of external debt, (*b*) the tax distortions created by servicing even internal debt, and (*c*) the potential displacement of capital.

Old public finance policies were based on the belief that the federal budget should always balance, that debt of any size imposes a burden on future generations, and that public finance and private finance are one and the same. Modern public finance has turned each of these conclusions into a question. Budgets do not seem to balance, so why not? Does the policy mix have anything to do with it? What is the true burden of the debt? How is public finance different from private finance? Chapter 17 explores each of these questions in turn.

1. Two distinct components of the federal deficit have been identified. One component, the ________ deficit, reflects active or discretionary changes in fiscal policy; the second, the ________ deficit, reflects automatic changes caused by the business cycle. Automatic stabilizers built into our country's tax structure and social infrastructure can thus contribute to the ________ deficit. For example, every point of unemployment above the natural rate that lasts a full year causes the deficit to *(increase / decrease)* by approximately $35 billion because tax revenues *(fall/ rise)* and expenditures *(fall / rise)*. Because these cyclical changes happen automatically to help to ward off recession or slow inflation, it is essential to look at the ________ deficit when you are trying to tell whether discretionary fiscal policy is stimulative or contractionary.

In the spaces provided, record whether or not the indicated policy would affect the structural deficit (S), the cyclical deficit (C), or neither (N).

a. a reduction in tax rates of 25 percent . . . . (________)

b. an increase in unemployment compensation during recession . . . . (________)

c. an increase in defense spending of $50 billion . (________)

d. a reduction in social security tax rates . . . . . (________)

e. an expansion of the money supply . . . . (________)

f. an expansion in tax receipts during an economic upswing . . . . (________)

g. a reduction in funding for Head Start and other welfare programs . . . . (________)

structural; cyclical; cyclical; increase; fall; rise; structural **a.** S **b.** C **c.** S **d.** S **e.** N **f.** C **g.** S

2. In the spaces provided in Table 17-1, indicate the likely short-term effects on the structural and cyclical deficits of the indicated changes in economic condition. Denote a reduction with a (−), and increase with a (+), and no change with a (0). Differentiate only on the basis of the active or passive character of an indicated policy change and on the basis of the short-run effect of a non-policy change.

Table 17-1

Change in Condition or Policy	Structural Deficit	Cyclical Deficit
A A permanent tax cut	(________)	(________)
B A sharp increase in private investment	(________)	(________)
C Tighter monetary policy	(________)	(________)
D A corn blight	(________)	(________)
E An increase in welfare payments	(________)	(________)
F An increase in tax evasion	(________)	(________)

Reading across the rows: A: +, −, (or 0, depending upon the stimulus of the cut); B: 0, −; C: 0, +; D: 0, +; E: +, − (or 0, depending upon the stimulus of the spending); F: +, + (because lower tax revenues increase both) [*Note:* If an increase in evasion works like a tax cut, it could reduce the cyclical deficit while increasing the structural deficit.]

3. From 1979 through 1982, the actual deficit *(fell / rose)* in response to *(active fiscal policy / passive fiscal policy)*. The result was actually a(n) *(increase / reduction)* in the *(structural / cyclical)* deficit that signaled *(more stimulative / no change in the degree of stimulus applied by / less stimulative)* fiscal policy.

In 1982, though, the supply-side tax cuts and the massive defense buildup of the Reagan administration came on line. The result was fiscal *(stimulus / contraction)* reflected by a dramatic increase in the *(structural / cyclical)* deficit. In fact, from 1982 through 1986 the cyclical deficit *(fell / rose)* while the structural deficit *(fell / rose)*.

Numbers supporting your answers to these questions can be found in Table 17-2. Note that the federal government ran an actual deficit of $________ in 1986. This was up $________ from 1979 and $________ from 1982. A deep recession in 1982 increased the cyclical deficit by $________ from 1979, but that increase fell to $________ by 1986. The structural deficit, meanwhile, climbed by only $________ through 1982, but by $________ through 1986. It is clear, therefore, that fiscal policy was *(stimulative / contractionary)* over the second period.

Under contributing factors, it is important to note that higher interest payments added $________ to the actual deficit from 1979 through 1986. Why? Certainly because the government borrowed a lot more money, but that is not the only reason. The federal government turns over the equivalent of its entire debt every 3 or 4 years; large increases in current interest rates can therefore have large effects on the cyclical deficit. Also notice that the combined effect of the listed contributing factors sums to more than the increase in the actual deficit (i.e.,

$206 billion > $188 billion). How is that possible? Other items in the spending budget were slashed by the difference ($18 billion).

Table 17-2
The Source of Rising Federal Deficits

Deficit or Contributing Factor	Year 1979	1982	1986
A. Budget deficit			
Actual	$16	$146	$204
Cyclical	0	91	26
Structural	16	55	178
B. Increase in budget deficit from 1979			
Actual	0	130	188
Cyclical	0	91	26
Structural	0	39	162
C. Contributing factor			
Decreased share of taxes	0	5	26
Increased share of defense	0	40	72
Increased transfer payments	0	58	44
Increased interest payments	0	31	64
Total, Contributing Factors	0	134	206

(Source: U.S. Department of Commerce.)

rose; passive fiscal policy; increase; cyclical; no change in the degree of stimulus applied by; stimulus; structural; fell; rose; 204; 188; 58; 91; 26; 39; 162; stimulative; 64

4. Suppose, in the face of "secular stagnation," that the President wants to stimulate recovery without adjusting monetary policy. You would, as adviser to the President, recommend a policy that would *(increase / decrease)* government spending and/or *(increase / decrease)* federal taxes. The immediate result of your recommendation would be a(n) *(reduction / increase)* in the size of the *(structural / cyclical)* deficit. If your policies were implemented and worked to stimulate recovery, the ultimate result would be a(n) *(reduction / increase)* in the *(structural / cyclical)* deficit. To bring the actual deficit down, though you would have to also recommend *(the eventual cancellation of the active policy / no further change)*.

Facing the opposite problem, of course, you would recommend the opposite policies. If you were free to suggest changes in monetary policy to support the stimulus package that you proposed above, though, you would recommend *a reduction / an increase* in the money supply, probably instituted by *(an open-market operation / a reduction in the reserve requirement / an increase in the discount rate)*. The desired result would be a(n) *(increase / decrease)* in investment because of *(higher / lower)* interest rates and perhaps induced investment (crowding in).

increase; decrease; increase; structural; reduction; cyclical; the eventual cancellation of the active policy; an increase; an open-market operation; increase; lower

5. The Reagan Economic Recovery Program instituted in January 1981 called for *(a)* substantial cuts in personal taxes, *(b)* substantial cuts in business taxes, *(c)* substantial increases in defense spending, and *(d)* moderate cuts in social spending. President Reagan also asked the Fed to pursue fairly tight monetary policy. The ultimate result was *(stimulative / contractionary)* fiscal policy reflected halfway through his first term by an increase in the *(cyclical / structural)* deficit but lower investment caused by high interest rates. Some contend that the recession of 1982 was caused in large part by the high interest rates.

The Carter administration tried to stimulate investment in the late 1970s by *(a)* increasing taxes, *(b)* maintaining government spending, and *(c)* encouraging expansionary monetary policy. The idea was to *(increase / reduce)* the structural deficit and thereby *(increase / decrease)* public saving, lower interest rates, and promote investment. Monetary policy turned out to be too tight, though, and investment did not climb. Combined with the oil shock of the Iran-Iraq war, a recession developed because the change in the *(structural / cyclical)* deficit actually signaled a move toward more *(contractionary / expansionary)* fiscal policy.

stimulative; structural; reduce; increase; structural; contractionary

6. Actual experience in the United States, as illustrated in the preceding examples, has tended to target monetary policy at *(inflation / unemployment)* and fiscal policy at *(inflation / unemployment)*. Each successive recession has, therefore, produced employment-targeted spending and tax programs that have increased the structural deficit in ways that *(have seldom been / have generally been)* erased during the subsequent recovery. As a result, the actual deficit has been *(growing / falling)* over time, and monetary policy has had to become increasingly *(more / less)* contractionary. The overall trend in interest rates has thus been *(up / down)*, and the federal debt has been growing *(faster / slower)* than GNP. We have had, in short, a *(high- / low-)*investment, *(high- / low-)*spending, *(high- / low-)*deficit experience over the past several decades.

One way to turn that around would be to target monetary policy at *(inflation / unemployment)* and fiscal policy at *(inflation / unemployment)*. Running structural surpluses over time would keep *(inflation / unemployment)* down, and quick adjustments in monetary policy could be left to deal with the business cycle. The cyclical component of the deficit would, of course, continue to help through the operation of its built-in stabilizers.

inflation; unemployment; have seldom been; growing; more; up; faster; low-; high-; high-; unemployment; inflation; inflation

7. The basic mechanism behind the concern that increased government spending "crowds out" private investment can be traced through expected changes in interest rates. An increase in government spending initially causes GNP to *(rise / fall)*. As a result, the transactions demand for money *(rises / falls)* so that interest rates must *(rise / fall)* to engineer the change in the assets demand for money required to cancel the change in transactions demand. And because interest rates respond, investment must decline. The problem is particularly acute in the monetarist view of the world in which GNP does not increase with G because government spending replaces investment spending dollar for dollar. The economy is, by assumption, at its potential, and further increases in GNP are impossible. An increase in aggregate demand caused by an increase in government spending must, therefore, be matched by an equal reduction in investment.

The evidence on crowding out is mixed. The expansionary fiscal policy of the early 1960s did not cause any substantial crowding out, but that was not really a fair test. Why? Because during the 1960s, *(the natural rate of unemployment was lower / the Fed accommodated fiscal policy to keep interest rates constant / the Keynesian model was widely accepted)*. Recent evidence suggests that *(25 percent / 50 percent / 75 percent)* of the stimulative effects of increases in government spending are canceled in the short term, and that *(75 percent / 90 percent / 100 percent)* of the effects may disappear in the long term. That is because the *long-run* aggregate supply curve is *(horizontal / vertical)* over potential GNP.

Even in the long term, though, crowding out appears to be a problem associated only with the *(cyclical / structural)* deficit. There is reason to believe that an increase in government spending caused by automatic stabilizers during a recession might actually increase investment. How? If the spending does in fact promote recovery, then GNP will begin to rise, and *(higher / lower)* investment might be induced by the prospect of a more vigorous economy. By the time the potential for crowding out appears (i.e., by the time the economy approaches its level of potential GNP), the cyclical spending will have *(disappeared / accelerated)* and there will be *(nothing left / even more spending)* to do the crowding.

---

rise; rises; rise; the Fed accommodated fiscal policy to keep interest rates constant; 50 percent; 100 percent; vertical; structural; higher; disappeared; nothing left

8. Indicate which of the following arguments for or against large deficit spending are valid (V) and which are invalid (I).

a. I can't run a deficit forever, so neither can the government. . . . . (______)

b. The debt is internally held, so there is no problem. . . . . (______)

c. There are efficiency losses associated with the taxes required to pay the interest. (______)

d. Private debt is high, too, and that is not a source of concern. . . . . (______)

e. There is a significant likelihood that large deficits displace capital from private borrowers to public ones. . . . (______)

f. If interest payments grow faster than GNP, then increasingly large proportions of GNP will have to be taxed away to pay for the debt service. . . . . (______)

---

a. I **b.** I **c.** V **d.** I **e.** V **f.** V

9. The basic trend over much of recent experience, particularly the early 1980s, has been for the size of the debt measured as a proportion of nominal GNP to *(rise / fall)*. More alarmingly, the proportion of GNP required to pay the interest on the debt has *(risen / fallen)*, as well. To see why this is so alarming, consider the following exercise.

Let the budget be balanced except for interest payments and denote the rate of growth of nominal GNP and the nominal rate of interest by g and i, respectively. Starting in 1989, then, GNP produced t years into the future will be

$$(1 + g)^t$$

times larger than it was in 1989. With no further deficit spending, the federal debt will grow at a rate i over the foreseeable future because borrowing will have to proceed to pay for the interest due each year. The debt will, therefore, be

$$(1 + i)^t$$

times larger t years into the future than it was in 1989. The ratio of the debt to nominal GNP will therefore change at a rate given by the ratio of these two rates of change; i.e., it will change by $(1 + i)/(1 + g)$ each year, and it will be

$$\left(\frac{1 + i}{1 + g}\right)^t$$

times bigger or smaller t years into the future. Now, if i is bigger than g, as it has been recently, then this fraction climbs to infinity as t gets larger. It passes through 1, therefore, the point at which all of the year's GNP would have to go to paying off the interest on the debt.

---

rise; risen

QUIZ: Multiple Choice

1. Structural deficits:
(1) vary in size with changes in discretionary fiscal policy.
(2) vary in size with the sensitivity of the tax revenues to upswings in the economy.

(3) vary in size depending upon the latitude of welfare entitlement programs during economic downturns.
(4) are reflections of the degree of stimulus embodied in monetary policy.
(5) none of the above.

2. Cyclical deficits:
(1) are the products of discretionary fiscal policy.
(2) are the appropriate reflection of the stimulative character of fiscal policy.
(3) are dependent in part on the automatic stabilizers built into the macroeconomy.
(4) are never considered until strict monetary control raises the specter of crowding out.
(5) none of the above.

3. A $50 billion increase in defense spending is an example of:
(1) monetary policy directed at reducing inflation.
(2) fiscal policy directed at reducing inflation.
(3) fiscal policy that would contribute directly to increasing the structural deficit.
(4) fiscal policy that would contribute directly to increasing the cyclical deficit.
(5) none of the above.

4. Which answer to question 3 would have been correct if it had asked about an increase in tax revenues caused by a growing economy and a progressive income tax?
(1).
(2).
(3).
(4).
(5).

5. Which answer to question 3 would have been correct if it had asked about an open-market operation that purchased bonds?
(1).
(2).
(3).
(4).
(5).

6. Deficits in the early 1980s were enormous, in part, because the Reagan administration:
(1) pursued expansionary fiscal policy with high structural deficits.
(2) received the tight monetary policy that it wanted.
(3) suffered a recession that enlarged the cyclical deficit.
(4) all of the above.
(5) none of the above.

7. In the face of a stagnant economy, a government should:
(1) spend more, tax less, and/or pursue a contractionary monetary policy.
(2) spend less, tax less, and/or pursue and expansionary monetary policy.
(3) spend more, tax less, and/or pursue an expansionary monetary policy.
(4) tax more, spend less, and/or pursue an expansionary monetary policy.
(5) do nothing and rely on the ability of the economy to rapidly return to potential GNP just as it did in the 1983 recovery.

8. Which of the following characterizes the Carter policy to stimulate investment that was tried in the late 1970s?
(1) Faster monetary growth, spending growth, and lower taxes.
(2) Lower spending, slower monetary growth, and lower taxes.
(3) Faster money growth, stable spending, and higher taxes.
(4) Faster money growth, lower spending, and lower taxes.
(5) None of the above.

9. A policy mix that targets monetary policy at inflation and fiscal policy at unemployment seems to produce high-consumption, low-investment, high-deficit economies because:
(1) monetary policy is ineffectual against inflation.
(2) fiscal stimulus during recession is never turned off so monetary policy must become increasingly contractionary over time.
(3) Congress never writes fiscal policy fast enough to avoid a recession.
(4) fiscal policy is ineffective in stimulating an economy past its potential GNP.
(5) none of the above.

10. Examples of the "ratcheting" of fiscal stimulus that was never fully repealed include:
(1) the temporary tax surcharge of 1968 which followed and did not match the 1962–1964 tax cuts.
(2) the tax increases of 1983 which followed and did not match the supply-side cuts in 1981–1983.
(3) the continuation of foreign-trade job benefits in 1984 well after the recovery of the automobile industry.
(4) the continuation of investment tax credits through 1984 even after they did not stimulate investment.
(5) all of the above.

11. The linkage between government spending that could lead to the crowding out of private investment is best outlined by a causal connection from spending growth to:
(1) output growth to an increase in the assets demand for money to higher interest rates to lower investment.
(2) output contraction to an increase in the transactions demand for money to a lower assets demand for money to lower interest rates to higher investment.
(3) output growth to an increase in the transactions demand for money to lower assets demand for money and higher interest rates that cause lower investment.

(4) output growth to higher investment with higher transactions and assets demands for money.
(5) none of the above.

12. Monetarists believe that the vertical aggregate supply schedule mandates that, for every dollar increase in government spending, private investment will fall:
(1) 50 cents.
(2) 75 cents.
(3) 90 cents.
(4) $1.
(5) none of the above.

13. Which answer to question 12 would have been correct if it had referred to the mainstream view of crowding out in the short run?
(1).
(2).
(3).
(4).
(5).

14. Which answer to question 12 would have been correct if it had referred to the mainstream view of crowding out in the long run?
(1).
(2).
(3).
(4).
(5).

15. Which of the following is a valid reason to be concerned about the size of the federal debt?
(1) It has grown, in the recent past, as a proportion of GNP.
(2) It has grown, in the recent past, so much that interest payments are growing faster than GNP.
(3) High deficits may displace capital by distorting the financial markets.
(4) The taxes required to pay the interest are inefficient, as are most taxes.
(5) All of the above.

16. If federal budgets in the future were all balanced except for borrowing needed to pay the interest on the current debt and if GNP were growing at a rate that was smaller than the rate of interest, then:
(1) the interest payments required to keep the debt afloat would eventually grow larger than GNP itself.
(2) the debt would remain at a constant proportion of GNP.
(3) the debt would gradually decline to a negligible fraction of GNP.
(4) the debt would remain at substantial levels, but fall as a fraction of GNP.
(5) none of the above.

SUGGESTED ANSWERS TO QUESTIONS IN THE TEXT: Chapter 17

1. Cite definitions and generate a list on the basis of the degree to which tools are (automatically) sensitive to changes in economic conditions. Evaluate your preferences on the basis of timing, effectiveness, fiscal-monetary mix, and likely output, growth, and consumption outcomes. States your philosophical bent, as well; your answers in a monetarist framework should not match your answers in a more mainstream framework.

2. Outline some demand stimulus for the 1870s and some demand contraction of the early 1900s.

3. **a.** A permanent tax cut should increase the structural deficit (discretionary policy choice), but the resulting stimulus should reduce the cyclical deficit (unless the economy was operating at potential before the cut).
b. A decrease in *I* should have no effect on the structural deficit (no policy involved), but the resulting reduction in aggregate demand should increase the cyclical component.
c. Tighter money has no effect on the structural deficit (no fiscal policy involved), but the resulting reduction in aggregate demand should increase the cyclical component.
d. An increase in exports increases aggregate demand with no change in fiscal policy; the effect is the opposite of **b**.
e. Higher welfare benefits have the same effect as in **a**; they just operate on the other side of the government budget ledger—expenditure rather than revenue.
f. An increase in tax evasion should increase both deficits because a revenue shortfall would be exaggerated, and increasingly so through the business cycle.

4. A change in taxes works to change aggregate demand only through consumption, and thus is diminished by the marginal propensity to consume. If the *MPC* is 0.9, then, a $1 reduction in taxes would increase consumption by $0.90, and that would crowd out $0.90 in investment.

5. At potential GNP, the cyclical deficit is zero. The $20 stimulus leaves real GNP at potential, but it increases nominal GNP by $2 \times \$20 = \$40$ (prices climb). Without any adjustment in tax revenue, though, the structural deficit would match the $20 increase in the actual deficit from $50 to $70. The cyclical deficit would stay at zero.

If taxes change with income, though, tax revenue climbs by $8. The structural deficit is still $70, but the actual deficit is only $62. The cyclical component must therefore be in surplus by $8.

6. Look it all up in the newspapers. Your answer will likely be incomplete unless you have been reading the paper throughout your introduction to macro.

7. The Keynes idea takes the notion of fiscal stimulus to its logical extreme—payment for nothing useful simply to increase disposable income, consumption, and thus aggregate demand. Think of better ways to spend the "taxpayers' money."

8. Yes, they could feel richer, spend a larger fraction of their disposable incomes, save less, and thereby support less investment. Slower growth could result. In Figure 17-7 in the text, this would be illustrated by the same shift from SS to $S'S'$ as government debt.

9. The key difference is where the money goes. Does it go directly into consumption, or does it support future consumption by going into capital. The parable about giving people fish or teaching them *to* fish applies.

10. If 50 percent of any increase in government spending crowds out investment, then any reduction in spending might stimulate investment by lowering interest rates. If, however, it causes contraction in the economy so that profitable investment projects cannot be found, then that stimulus will turn into retardation.

11. Trace the effect through the interest rate; smaller government borrowing and looser money should bring interest rates down, investment up, and growth up.

12. No one policy, alone, would be enough. Any reduction in fiscal stimulus would have to be balanced by monetary stimulus to preserve aggregate demand. That would, though, achieve **c** as a favorable side effect. International trade issues, and the fact that all fiscal spending is tied to some project with other social value, complicate things.

13. Figure 17-5 in the text is not an encouraging picture. The arithmetic follows. Interest on the debt in 1989 is $i \times D(1989)$, so the debt ratio in 1990 is

$$d(1989 + 1) = \frac{D(1989) + i \times D(1989)}{\text{GNP}(1989) + q \times \text{GNP}(1989)}$$

$$= \frac{(1 + i) \times D(1989)}{(1 + q) \times \text{GNP}(1989)}$$

In 1991, it is

$$d(1989 + 2) = \frac{(1 + i)^2 \times D(1989)}{(1 + q)^2 \times \text{GNP}(1989)}$$

For some year t years past 1989, then, it is

$$d(1989 + t) = \frac{(1 + i)^t \times D(1989)}{(1 + q)^t \times \text{GNP}(1989)}$$

This blows up if $i > q$; it converges to 0 if $i < q$.

APPENDIX: 17

Advanced Treatment of Monetary and Fiscal Policy

The classical view of the macroeconomic world was based upon a firm belief in Say's Law. Say's Law depended, in turn, on a strong analogy between a barter economy and a monetary economy to conclude that workers would always be around to buy whatever was produced. How so? That analogy supported the notion that prices and wages would always adjust immediately to any disequilibrium so that the income that the workers earned would just exhaust the output of the economy. Overproduction would be impossible, therefore, and so would underproduction. There would, in other words expressed in terms that should now be familiar, be a vertical aggregate supply curve directly over potential GNP. Classical economists would write at the height of the Great Depression that whatever involuntary unemployment happened to exist was the result of "frictional resistance" to market forces. Maybe barter economies did not record their bouts with depression!

Modern macroeconomic theory has come a long way since that characterization of 25 percent unemployment was advanced, of course, and you have been introduced to much of that progress in the preceding 10 chapters. Now that you have worked through that material, your introduction closes by presenting a more succinct analytical framework within which the workings of today's mainstream macroeconomic theory can be explored. This appendix outlines this framework with an eye toward not only its construction, but also its application to the policy debates that you have studied. Having worked through this appendix, therefore, you will have accomplished the following objectives.

LEARNING OBJECTIVES

1. Understand the process by which an IS schedule is constructed to indicate along a downward-sloping curve the combinations of real GNP and real interest rates that support equilibrium in the goods markets (i.e., equality of aggregate supply and aggregate demand).

2. Understand the process by which an LM schedule is constructed to indicate along an upward-sloping curve the combinations of real GNP and real interest rates that support equilibrium in the money market (i.e., equality of the demand for money and the supply money).

3. Explain how intersections of LM and IS curves indicate macroeconomic equilibria; i.e., both the goods markets and the money market clear simultaneously.

4. Explain why a monetarist view of the world implies a vertical

LM curve and why a mainstream view of the world allows some slope in both the *IS* and the *LM* curves.

5. Describe precisely how changes in fiscal policy move the *IS* curve, how changes in monetary policy move the *LM* curve, and how *IS-LM* analysis can therefore be used to investigate the ramifications of changes in a single policy or a combination of policies.

We begin with a review of Say's Law and build toward more sophisticated notions of modern theory.

1. A simple statement of Say's Law is that "__________ __________ creates its own ____________________." If that were the case, then GNP would always converge quickly to *(actual / potential / real)* GNP and unemployment would correspondingly converge to its *(natural / actual / potential)* rate. The inflation rate, meanwhile, *(could proceed at any moderate rate / would have to fall to zero / would be expected to accelerate into hyperinflation if not controlled)*, and the aggregate *(supply / demand)* curve would be vertical.

---

supply; demand; potential; natural; could proceed at any moderate rate; supply

2. Consult Figure 17A-1 to construct an *IS* curve from the familiar geometry of aggregate supply and demand. Panel **(a)** of Figure 17A-1 shows one aggregate supply curve *AS* and three aggregate demand curves AD_1, AD_2, and AD_3. Each successively higher demand curve corresponds to higher investment and thus *(higher / lower)* aggregate demand at every price; it is higher investment that must be caused by *(higher / lower)* interest rates. Judging from the rates identified along the vertical axis of panel **(b)**, r_1 must therefore be associated with (AD_1 / AD_2 / AD_3) and thus an equilibrium level of real GNP given by (Q_1 / Q_2 / Q_3). Similarly r_2 must be associated with (Q_1 / Q_2 / Q_3) and r_3 must be associated with (Q_1 / Q_2 / Q_3). Connect these points in panel **(b)** and observe an *IS* curve with its usual *(negative / vertical / horizontal / positive)* slope.

---

higher; lower; AD_1; Q_1; Q_2; Q_3; negative [passing through points (Q_1, r_1), (Q_2, r_2), and (Q_3, r_3)]

3. Figure 17A-2 will accomplish a similar construction of an *LM* curve from the familiar confines of supply and demand in the money market. Panel **(a)** of Figure 17A-2 shows one money supply curve denoted *MS* and three money demand curves denoted MD_1, MD_2, and MD_3. Each successively higher demand curve corresponds to successively *(higher / lower)* levels of GNP so that *(higher / lower)* transactions demand for money can be canceled by *(higher / lower)* assets demand—lower assets demand caused by *(higher / lower)* equilibrium real interest rates. Given the three levels of GNP denoted on the horizontal axes of panel **(b)**, MD_1 must correspond to Q_1 / Q_2 / Q_3 and (r_1 / r_2 / r_3), MD_2 must correspond to (Q_1 / Q_2 / Q_3) and (r_1 / r_2 / r_3), and MD_3 must correspond to (Q_1 / Q_2 / Q_3) and (r_1 / r_2 / r_3). Plot these combinations on panel **(b)**, connect them, and observe an *LM* curve with the usual *(vertical / negative / horizontal / positive)* slope.

---

higher; higher; lower; higher; Q_3; r_1; Q_2; r_2; Q_1; r_3; positive [passing through points (Q_1, r_3), (Q_2, r_2), and (Q_3, r_1)]

4. Now consider an economy initially in equilibrium at r^* and Q^* as shown in Figure 17A-3. In the spaces provided in Table 17A-1, indicate whether the specified policy change(s) would cause the *IS* curve or the *LM* curve or both to move. Record your answers by signifying a shift to the right in either curve

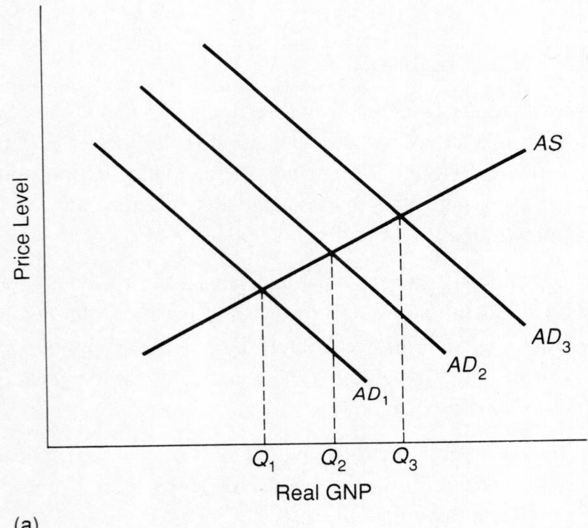

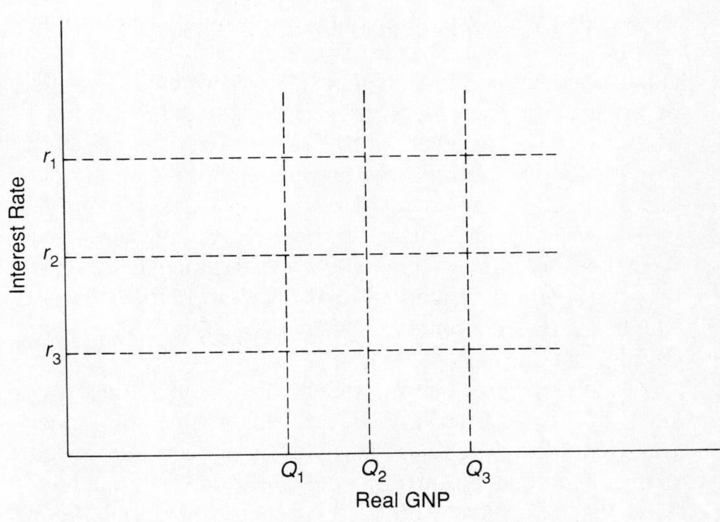

Figure 17A-1

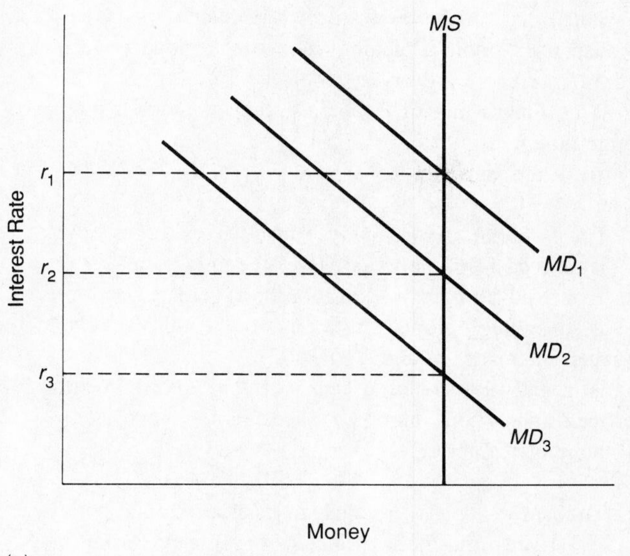

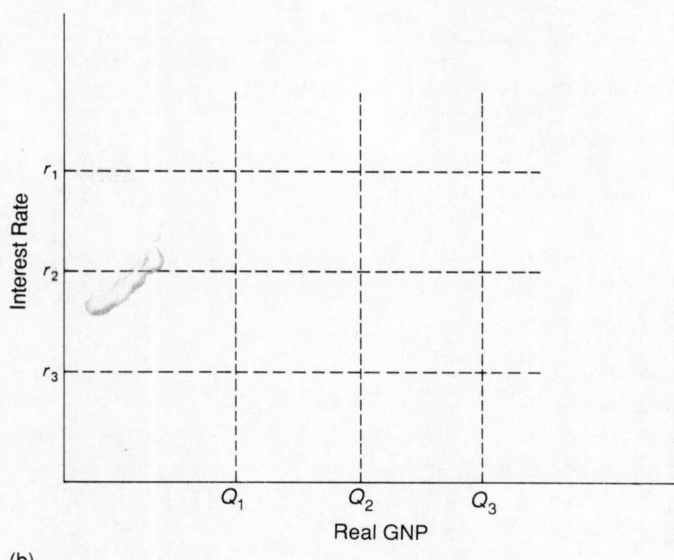

Figure 17A-2

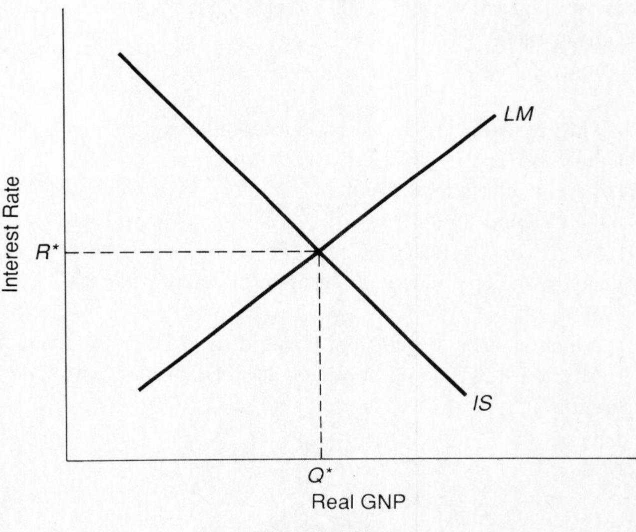

Figure 17A-3

Table 17A-1

	Policy Change	Effect on *IS* Curve	Effect on *LM* Curve	Effect on r^*	Effect on Q^*
A	An increase in government spending	_____	_____	_____	_____
B	An increase in the money supply	_____	_____	_____	_____
C	A reduction in the money supply	_____	_____	_____	_____
D	A reduction in federal taxes	_____	_____	_____	_____
E	An open-market operation that buys bonds plus a tax cut	_____	_____	_____	_____
F	A reduction in the money supply and an increase in government spending	_____	_____	_____	_____

by (+), a shift to the left in either by (−), and no shift at all by (0). Also indicate with the same notation the direction of the resulting movement in the equilibrium levels of real interest rates and GNP. [Use (+) for an increase, (−) for a decrease, and (?) to denote an ambiguous effect when policies collide and cancel each other.]

Reading across the rows: A: (+), (0), (+), (+); B: (0), (+), (−), (+); C: (0), (−), (+), (−); D: (+), (0), (+), (+); E: (+), (+), (?), (+); F: (+), (−), (+), (?)

---

5. The monetarist view of the world postulates a *(vertical / horizontal) LM* curve. That assumption is based on the quantity theory of money in which the demand for money is *(infinitely sensitive / totally insensitive)* to changes in the interest rate; i.e., potential GNP is associated with *(any / only one)* price level and *(any / only one)* interest rate.

In Table 17A-2, redo the exercise of question 4 under the monetarist assumption. Be sure to note any changes in the predicted changes in GNP and interest rates that are the result of that assumption.

Table 17A-2

Policy Change	Effect on *IS* Curve	Effect on *LM* Curve	Effect on *r**	Effect on *Q**
A An increase in government spending	______	______	______	______
B An increase in the money supply	______	______	______	______
C A reduction in the money supply	______	______	______	______
D A reduction in federal taxes	______	______	______	______
E An open-market operation that buys bonds plus a tax cut	______	______	______	______
F A reduction in the money supply and an increase in government spending	______	______	______	______

vertical; totally insensitive; any; any

Reading across the rows: A: (+), (0), (+), (0); B: (0), (+), (−), (+); C: (0), (−), (+), (−); D: (+), (0), (+), (0); E: (+), (+), (?), (+); F: (+), (−), (+), (−)

6. Crowding out is the circumstance in which government spending, whether for investment or not, replaces private investment in aggregate demand. Why? Because higher aggregate demand can cause interest rates to *(fall / climb)* and thus cause investment to fall. This effect is complete along the *(vertical / horizontal) LM* curve of the monetarists; interest rates climb so far that equilibrium GNP is maintained at potential GNP.

If the *LM* curve were *(horizontal / vertical)*, to assume the opposite Keynesian extreme, then there would *(still be some / be no / still be substantial)* crowding out because interest rates *(would / would not)* climb with the stimulated aggregate demand. Thus, one more distinction between the Keynesians and the monetarists: the ______________ worry about crowding out, and the ______________ do not. (Actually, mainstream theorists do too, to a lesser degree—unless deficits climb to unacceptably high levels.)

climb; vertical; horizontal; be no; would not; monetarists; Keynesians

QUIZ: Multiple Choice

1. Say's Law:
(1) formed the foundation of classical macroeconomics.
(2) stated that supply creates it own demand.
(3) depended upon an analogy between a monetary economy and a barter economy for its proof.
(4) is no longer part of the mainstream of modern macroeconomic thought.
(5) all of the above.

2. The *IS* curve used to analyze macroeconomic policy:
(1) is derived from the workings of the money market.
(2) is derived from the workings of the aggregate goods market.
(3) is positively sloped because of the direct correlation between interest rates and GNP.
(4) is negatively sloped because of the inverse relationship between transactions and assets demands for money.
(5) none of the above.

3. The *LM* curve used to analyze macroeconomic policy:
(1) is derived from the workings of the money market.
(2) works with the representation of the goods market to illustrate macroeconomic equilibrium.
(3) is positively sloped because of the negative correlation between transactions and assets demands for money.
(4) all of the above.
(5) none of the above.

4. An increase in the money supply would cause:
(1) the *LM* curve to shift in.
(2) the *LM* curve to shift out.
(3) the *IS* curve to shift in.
(4) the *IS* curve to shift out.
(5) any of the above depending upon the circumstances.

5. Which answer to question 4 would have been correct if it had referred to a sale of bonds by the Fed in an open-market operation?
(1).
(2).
(3).
(4).
(5).

6. Which answer to question 4 would have been correct if it had referred to a reduction in the federal income tax?
(1).
(2).
(3).
(4).
(5).

7. Which answer to question 4 would have been correct if it had referred to a reduction in the discount rate charged by the Fed to borrowing banks?
(1).
(2).

(3).
(4).
(5).

8. Suppose that there is a sudden increase in the tax rates built into the federal income tax. You should expect, based on *IS* and *LM* curves with some appropriate slope, that:
(1) GNP and interest rates will both climb.
(2) GNP and interest rates will both fall.
(3) interest rates will climb, but the effect on GNP will be ambiguous.
(4) GNP will climb and interest rates will fall.
(5) GNP will fall but the effect on interest rates will be ambiguous.

9. Which answer to question 8 would have been correct if it had referred to a purchase of bonds by the Fed in an open-market operation?
(1).
(2).
(3).
(4).
(5).

10. Which answer to question 8 would have been correct if it had referred to a simultaneous contraction of the money supply and expansion of government spending?
(1).
(2).
(3).
(4).
(5).

11. In the monetarist model:
(1) the *IS* curve is horizontal.
(2) the *LM* curve is horizontal.
(3) the *IS* curve is vertical.
(4) the *LM* curve is vertical.
(5) answers (3) and (4).

12. If you were to analyze an increase in government spending from a monetarist perspective, you would expect the result to be:
(1) an increase in both interest rates and GNP.
(2) an increase in GNP and a reduction in interest rates.
(3) an increase in interest rates and no change in GNP.
(4) an increase in interest rates and an ambiguous effect on GNP.
(5) an ambiguous effect on interest rates and an increase in prices.

13. If you were a monetarist and you noted that an increase in government spending accompanied by an increase in the money supply produced a higher level of GNP, then you would conclude that:
(1) the fiscal policy did not really work; the result was due to the effect of the increase in the money supply.
(2) both policies worked to reinforce each other.
(3) the monetary policy helped bring down the inflation that would have been the result of the fiscal policy.
(4) crowding out was not a problem and the monetary policy was unnecessary.
(5) none of the above.

14. If you were a mainstream theorist and observed the happenings of question 13, which answer would have been correct?
(1).
(2).
(3).
(4).
(5).

SUGGESTED ANSWERS TO QUESTIONS IN THE TEXT: Appendix to Chapter 17

1. Contemplate holding the interest rate constant at any given level; its effect on aggregate demand is thus fixed. An increase in *G* or a reduction in taxes then increases aggregate demand. For aggregate demand to equal aggregate supply at the given interest rate, GNP must therefore increase. Since this is true for any interest rate, the entire *IS* schedule shifts to the right. The intersection of the *LM* curve must therefore occur at a higher level of GNP; since the *LM* curve is upward-sloping, the real interest rate must climb.

A contraction in the money supply moves the *LM* curve to the left. Why? For any interest rate, and thus any level of assets demand, transactions demand must be smaller if their sum is to match the now smaller money supply. The only way for this to happen is for the level of GNP associated with the interest rate to be smaller. Since this is true for any interest rate, the entire *LM* curve shifts to the left. Equilibrium is thus indicated by an intersection that occurs at a lower GNP; since the *IS* curve is downward-sloping, the real interest rate must climb.

2. High deficits move the *IS* curve to the right; tight money moves the *LM* curve to the left. Either change makes their intersections occur at higher interest rates; both together amplify the effect.

3. The first simply moves the *IS* curve to the right and moves equilibrium along a positively sloped *LM* curve to a higher interest rate; investment must therefore fall. The second reestablishes equilibrium at the original point by canceling the initial contraction in investment. It is a matter of what came first and why.

4. **a.** Move the *LM* curve to the left and the *IS* curve to the right.
b. Cutting defense spending moves the *IS* curve to the left, causing output and interest rates to fall to some degree.

In a deep recession, the *LM* curve is nearly horizontal and most of the contraction would be felt in output . . . and employment. Not a great idea.

c. Move the *LM* curve to the right so that intersection occurs above the original equilibrium. The interest rate falls further.

d. Compare interest rates, investment, growth, etc., for two equilibria achieved by the two combinations. Expansionary monetary policy and contractionary fiscal policy seem to be a better mix.

5. Fiscal policy moves only the *IS* curve; equilibrium GNP stays at the same level. Monetary policy moves the *LM* curve right (expansionary) or left. An increase (e.g.) in the structural deficit causes the *IS* curve to shift to the right. GNP stays where it is, unless the money supply is moved. Interest rates climb, and investment (and other interest-sensitive components of aggregate demand) contracts by the exact amount of the deficit increase so that aggregate demand continues to equal aggregate supply at the same (real) level.

6. The dollar rises, net exports fall, and the *IS* curve shifts to the left (aggregate demand falls for any *r*). GNP falls, and so do interest rates.

CHAPTER 18

SUPPLY AND DEMAND IN INDIVIDUAL MARKETS

Before you concentrate on the new material to be presented in Chapter 18, you should make certain that you are in firm command of the material covered in Chapter 4. The foundation upon which almost all of microeconomics is built was laid in that final chapter of the introduction. Unless you have mastered the basic ideas of supply and demand that were advanced there, you will have a great deal of trouble making any progress here. We begin, then, with a quick review of the learning objectives that were assigned in Chapter 4 of this *Guide*. Read through them carefully to determine if you have picked up enough baggage to be able to move on; they should all be more than familiar.

Paraphrased slightly, the *Learning Objectives* of Chapter 4 included:

1. Define supply and demand; represent each graphically.

2. Explain three forces that contribute to the usual negative slope of a demand curve; explain why the supply curve is usually positively sloped.

3. Define market-clearing price and quantity and explain why competitive markets tend to clear.

4. Understand why the construction of a demand curve assumes "other things being equal": income, tastes, market size, prices of other goods, and commodity-specific factors.

5. Understand why the construction of a supply curve assumes a *different* set of "other things being equal": production costs and technology, taxes and/or subsidies, and market structure.

6. Explain how changes in these "other things" work to change market equilibrium; show each graphically.

Should any of these notions appear foreign to you, return to Chapter 4 for some further review.

The study of microeconomics is the study of relative prices. Why are cars so expensive? Why is sand so cheap? Why is gasoline now so expensive when it used to be so cheap? Why do doctors earn so much money? Why are some athletes paid even more? Are there really 150 taxes buried in the price of a suit (as one presidential candidate claimed in 1980)? The answers to these and other questions will be found in pitting individual tastes against the scarcity of resources. They are interesting to economists in their own right, but they also contribute to our understanding of macroeconomics, our understanding of the distribution of income, our understanding of the sources of judgmental tradeoffs between, for example, equity and efficiency, and much more. These understandings are the goals of our study of microeconomics.

Chapter 18 begins that study by covering two major topics: (1) the effects of changes in supply and demand and (2) the price elasticities of supply and demand. Applications of both are presented through a set of examples ranging from simple supply shocks to the equity-efficiency tradeoff in designing a tax structure. When you have completed this chapter, you should have mastered the following new objectives.

LEARNING OBJECTIVES

1. Define the price elasticity of demand, and indicate how to compute its numerical coefficient.

2. Relate difference in the value of the price elasticity of demand to (1) differences in the character of various goods (necessities vs. luxuries, e.g.) and (2) differences in the direction of change in total revenue as quantity increases along a demand curve. Define elastic demand, inelastic demand, and unitary elasticity in terms of both distinctions.

3. Define cross and income elasticities of demand.

4. Define the price elasticity of supply. Relate the Marshallian notions of momentary equilibrium, short-run equilibrium, and long-run equilibrium to the price elasticity of supply.

5. Explain the difference between changes in demand and changes in the quantity demanded. Tell what causes each.

6. Delineate with the help of graphs the effect on market equilibrium of changes in supply demand, and/or both. Understand how to apply this skill in analyzing changes in market conditions, changes in government policy, the effects of alternate policies, etc.

7. Relate the concept of time to both the price elasticity of demand and the price elasticity of supply.

The first major topic in this chapter is one that was introduced in Chapter 4: changes in demand or supply. Price is one important factor influencing the quantity of good X that will be bought, but it is by no means the only influencing factor. Others include the level of consumer incomes, consumer tastes or preferences for X, and the prices at which goods competing with X are selling.

The demand curve for X does not ignore these other factors; it assumes them held constant. If any other such factor changes, then the demand curve must be redrawn in an appropriate new position. If consumer incomes rise, for example, it is likely that the demand curve for X will shift to the right (or upward), as in Figure 18-1. This is just a particular way of saying that if consumers have more spendable income, they will want to buy more of X, at every price, than they did previously. And what happens? For the circumstance depicted in Figure 18-1, the market-clearing quantity bought and sold rises from *OA* to *OB*, and the price goes up.

Now here is a point you must watch carefully. In Figure 18-2, alongside Figure 18-1, there has also been a change in the equilibrium position. Purchases have again risen from *OA* to *OB*—but price has fallen, not risen. This change was initiated by a shift of the supply curve.

▶ Figure 18-1 illustrates an *increase in demand*—a shift of the entire demand curve to a new position.

▶ Figure 18-2 illustrates an *increase in quantity demanded*—a movement along a demand curve from one point thereon to another. The position of the demand curve has not changed.

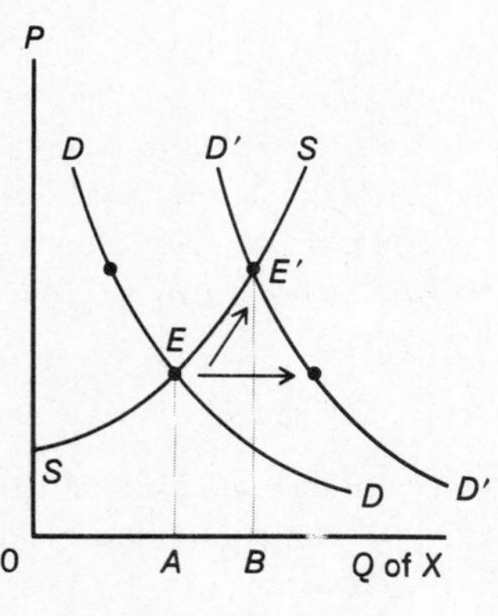

Figure 18-1

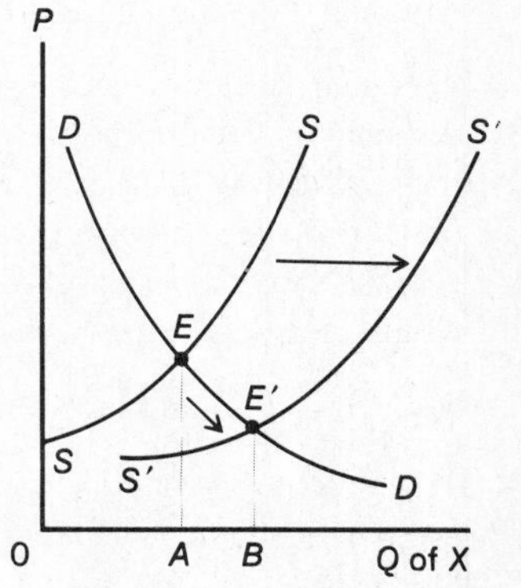

Figure 18-2

The phrases "increase in demand" and "increase in quantity demanded" have significantly different meanings. An increase in demand (Figure 18-1) occurs when some factor other than the price of good X changes, causing buyers to change their decisions; the entire demand curve shifts. An increase in quantity demanded (Figure 18-2) occurs when more of X is bought because its price fell. (Price fell because some background factor caused the supply curve to shift in position.)

1. a. A change in quantity demanded means precisely (pick one):

(1) a change in the schedule of quantities that producers will offer for sale at each and any possible price caused by some change in background conditions such as an increase in production costs.

(2) a change in the particular quantity which producers offer for sale caused by a change in market price.

(3) a change in the particular quantity which consumers buy caused by a change in market price.

(4) a change in the schedule of quantities that consumers will buy at each and any possible market price caused by some change in background conditions such as a change in tastes or consumer incomes.

b. Which alternative properly describes a change in supply? . . . . *(1 / 2 / 3 / 4)*

c. Which alternative properly describes a change in demand? . . . . *(1 / 2 / 3 / 4)*

d. Which alternative properly describes a change in quantity supplied? . . . . *(1 / 2 / 3 / 4)*

---

a. (3) b. (1) c. (4) d. (2)

2. a. As already noted, Figure 18-1 illustrates an increase in demand. This figure also illustrates an *(increase in supply / increase in quantity supplied)*.

Barring the exceptional case of a perfectly flat supply curve, this increase in demand will *(always / sometimes / never)* set off a price increase.

Notice that the increase in quantity supplied in Figure 18-1 does not bring about any price reduction. It is just the supplier response to a higher price. All we can say is that insofar as there is some slope to the supply curve (i.e., insofar as a higher price elicits a larger supply quantity), it makes the price increase set off by the increase in demand less than it would otherwise have been.

Thus an increase in quantity supplied will *(always / sometimes / never)* result in a price reduction.

b. In contrast, Figure 18-2 depicts an increase in quantity demanded. This increase came about only because of an *(increase in supply / increase in quantity supplied)*. Such an increase in quantity demanded *(will always / might / would never)* be the reason for a price increase. It is simply the buyer response to a lower price.

This difference in the effect upon price in large part explains why all the tedious distinction between the two kinds of increases and decreases is necessary.

c. An example framed in terms of quantity reduction can cement this distinction. Suppose for the sake of illustration that the production of good X is disrupted by lengthy strikes. The supply quantity available is much reduced, and price rises in consequence. This would be an instance of *(a decrease / an increase)* in *(quantity supplied / supply)*, followed by *(a decrease / an increase)* in *(quantity demanded / demand)*. The price rise was set off by the decrease in *(demand / supply)*, and not by the decrease in quantity *(demanded / supplied)*.

---

a. increase in quantity supplied; always; never **b.** Increase in supply; would never **c.** a decrease; supply; a decrease; quantity demanded; supply; demanded

The concept of **price elasticity** was devised to indicate the degree to which quantity demanded (or supplied) would respond to any price change. Compare the two demand curves D_1 and D_2 drawn *to the same scale* in Figure 18-3; they are drawn there to reflect two potential demand curves for the same good X. Both curves satisfy the ordinary "law of demand" that any price reduction should produce an increase in the quantity demanded and purchased. D_2 is the more elastic of the two, though, because the quantity demanded is more responsive to any change in price. Why? Notice that if the price were to fall from p_a to p_b, for example, then the quantity demanded would grow by a larger amount along the D_2 curve; if the price were to rise from p_a to p_c, on the other hand, the quantity would shrink further along D_2. Quantity is more responsive to changes in price—more *price elastic*—along D_2.

3. a. If we say that "demand in this situation is highly price elastic," we mean that any price reduction would produce a

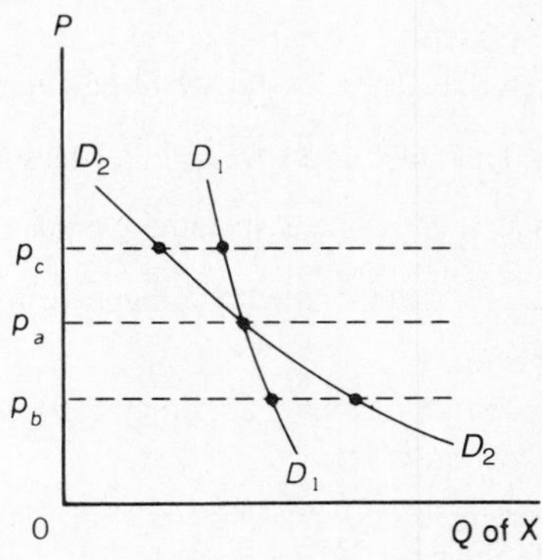

Figure 18-3

(large / small) (decrease / increase) in purchases, and that a price rise would yield a *(large / small) (decrease / increase)* in buying.

b. To describe supply as "decidedly price inelastic" would mean that any price increase would call out a *(large / small) (increase / decrease)* in quantity offered for sale, and that any price reduction would produce a *(large / small) (increase / decrease)*.

---

a. large; increase; large; decrease **b.** small; increase; small; decrease

Terms like "highly elastic" or "decidedly inelastic" are imprecise. The task now is to give a more exact meaning to elasticity. The text defines the price elasticity of demand as

$$E_D = \frac{\%\text{ change in quantity demanded}}{\%\text{ change in price}}$$

The sign of this expression is assumed to be positive by convention. Given this numerical expression, three different possibilities emerge:

$E_D > 1$, representing elastic demand
$E_D = 1$, representing unitary elasticity
$E_D < 1$, representing inelastic demand

The importance of the distinction between these three cases will become increasingly clear as you progress through your study of economics. Your first introduction to this importance comes in the linkage between the price elasticity of demand and the sensitivity of revenue to changes in the price. If the price of some good were to increase by 10 percent, revenue generated by its sale could go up, remain the same, or go down depending upon the price elasticity. To see why, take each case one at a time:

1. If demand were price elastic, then the 10 percent increase in the price would have to be associated with a reduction in the quantity demanded of more than 10 percent to get a number greater than 1 out of the elasticity formula. That would mean that quantity would be falling faster than price was rising, and revenue would fall (recall that revenue is simply price times quantity).
2. If demand displayed unitary price elasticity, then the 10 percent increase in the price would be matched by a 10 percent reduction in the quantity demanded to get 1 out of the elasticity formula. That would mean that revenue would remain exactly the same.
3. If demand were price inelastic, then the 10 percent increase in the price would have to be associated with a reduction in the quantity demanded of less than 10 percent to get a number less than 1 out of the elasticity formula. That would mean that revenue would actually rise with the price.

The text also defines the price elasticity of supply in a like manner:

$$E_S = \frac{\text{\% change in quantity supplied}}{\text{\% change in price}}$$

No adjustment in sign is required, in this case, because increases in prices are always matched with increases in quantities supplied along the usual upward-sloping supply curve. The same differentiation between elastic, unitary, and inelastic supply is made, but the demand-side connection to revenue is not valid.

The next set of questions will explore and illustrate these points.

4. The table below shows demand for some commodity at prices from $10 to $1. Use these figures to draw a demand curve in the upper part of Figure 18-4.

Price	Quantity	Revenue	Price	Quantity	Revenue
$10	0	____	$5	20	____
9	4	____	4	24	____
8	8	____	3	28	____
7	12	____	2	32	____
6	16	____	1	36	____

Associated with each possible quantity bought (and hence with each possible price) will be a certain amount of revenue received by sellers (i.e., expenditure by buyers). If price is $9, so that 4 units are bought, revenue will be $36. Show the proper revenue amounts in the 10 blanks above. Then complete the lower part of Figure 18-4 to show the quantity-revenue relation (e.g., with quantity 4, revenue is $36, etc.).

$0; $36 (= $9 × 4); $64; $84; $96; $100; $96; $84; $64; $36 [The demand curve is straight line from ($Q = 0$; $P = 10$) through ($Q = 40$; $P = 0$); the revenue cure is parabola peaking at ($Q = 20$; Rev $= 100$) and equalling zero at both $Q = 0$ and $Q = 40$.]

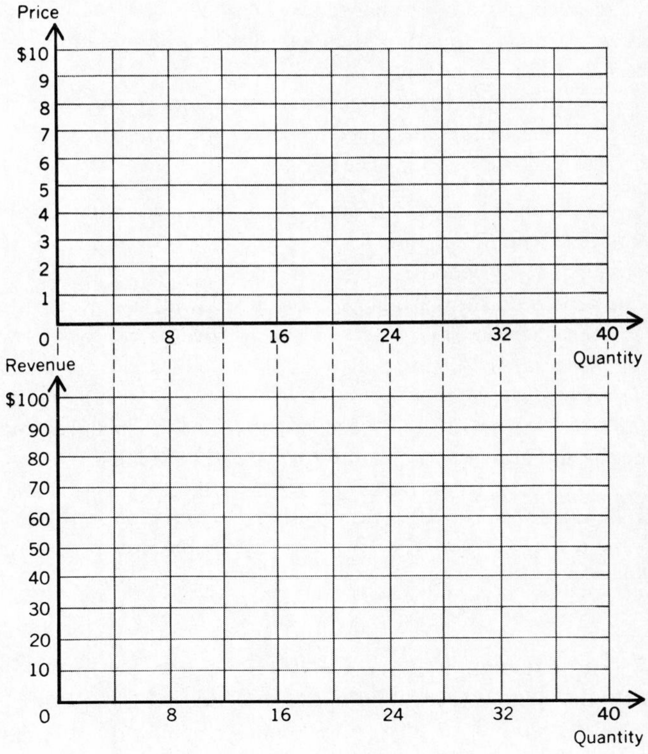

Figure 18-4

5. a. Notice the interesting behavior of the revenue curve as you move down the length of the straight-line demand curve that you should have drawn on the top panel of Figure 18-4. As price falls, revenue (pick one):

(1) remains the same at all quantities.

(2) falls throughout the entire price range.

(3) rises first, reaches a peak, and then falls.

(4) falls first, reaches a minimum, and then climbs.

b. If the price falls from $7 to $6, then total revenue (*rises / stays the same / falls*). How is this possible when the lower price means that each unit that was purchased at $7 is now purchased at $6? For the 12 units demanded at $7, in fact, lowering the price by $1 results in $12 less revenue being collected.

The key to the mystery is, of course, found in the observation that the lower price means that a larger quantity is demanded and thus sold. Only one question remains: Is the revenue collected from the sale of these extra units enough to overcome the initial loss just noted? Sixteen units are demanded when the price is $6—an increase in the quantity demanded of ________ units bringing in an additional $________ in revenue. In this case, the increase in revenue generated by selling more units (*is / is not*) enough to offset the initial loss.

Now suppose that the price falls from $4 to $3. Selling the ________ units demanded at $4 for a dollar less results in a revenue loss of $________. The associated increase in the quantity demanded of ________ units meanwhile means a counterbalancing revenue gain of $________. The loss (*outweighs / exactly balances / falls short of*) the gain, and total revenue (*falls / stays the same / increases*).

a. (3) b. rises; 4; 24 (= 4 × $6); is; 24; 24 (= 1 × $1); 4 (= 28 − 24); 12 (= 4 × $3); outweighs; falls

6. "Price elasticity" means the responsiveness, or "stretch," of quantity to any given price change. We can reach a more explicit statement of what demand elasticity means with respect to price just by using the phenomenon noted in question 4—that revenue may, for a given price change, go up, go down, or remain constant.

If there is enough "stretch" in quantity demanded when price goes down to cause revenue to go up, then we designate this section of the demand curve as *elastic* (or as price elastic). If revenue stays constant, it is *unit-elastic*. If revenue falls, it is *inelastic*. This means the demand curve of question 4 is elastic for prices from $_______ to $_______, and inelastic for prices from $_______ to $_______.

10; 5; 5; 0

7. Put (E) for price elastic, (U) for unitary elastic, or (I) for price inelastic in each blank below according to which most accurately describes each demand situation.

a. Price falls from \$6 to \$5 and revenue falls from \$60 to \$55. . . . . (_______)

b. Price falls from \$6 to \$5 and revenue stays the same. . . . . (_______)

c. Price climbs from \$5 to \$6 and quantity purchased falls from 80 to 60. . . . . (_______)

d. Price drops from \$6 to \$5 and there is no increase in quantity demanded. . . . . (_______)

e. Price climbs from \$300 to \$301 and there is no reduction in quantity demanded. (_______)

f. Price climbs and revenue climbs by \$10. . . . (_______)

g. Price climbs from \$5.00 to \$5.10 and people stop buying the stuff completely. . . . . (_______)

---

a. I (The price reduction does not create enough of a quantity increase to keep revenue from falling.) **b.** U (The price reduction creates just enough of a quantity increase to maintain revenue.) **c.** E (Revenue falls from \$400 to \$360; the quantity reduction must have been larger, in percentage terms, than the price increase.) **d.** I (This is perfectly inelastic demand.) **e.** I (same) **f.** I (Price increase, quantity reduction, and still revenue climbs.) **g.** E (This is perhaps perfectly elastic demand.)

8. Instructors in economics always illustrate inelastic demand on the blackboard by means of a steeply sloping (near-vertical) line. Question 6 shows that this method of illustration can be quite deceptive. No straight-line demand curve has a uniform elasticity. It is here that the demand curve constructed in question 4 always reported the same "responsiveness" to each \$1 price change: an increase (or decrease) of 4 in quantity demanded. But in percentage terms, the drop in price from \$10 to \$9 was *(far more / much less)* drastic than the drop from \$2 to \$1, for the latter reduction cut the price in half. That is why the elasticity of this demand curve is different in different regions. It is, in fact, different at every point.

This means that if you take any straight-line demand curve with some slope to it, no matter how steep, you can always find a section along that curve in which the quantity demanded is elastic with respect to price (i.e., $E_D > 1$). All you need to do is move *(up / down)* the curve to a price that is sufficiently *(high / low)*. You can always find a region that is inelastic, too. Finally, there is always one point where the price elasticity of demand is unity. (Can you convince yourself that the point of unitary elasticity is always the midpoint of the line?)

---

much less; up; high

We can compute the **price elasticity coefficient** by (*a*) putting the quantity change in percentage terms, (*b*) putting the price change in percentage terms, and (*c*) forming the quotient of these two changes. When we do this between two points on a demand or supply curve, however, the denominator of the percentage-change calculations is ambiguous. The text suggests using averages as the basis of the computations of percentage changes. Suppose, for example, that you are interested in the price elasticity of demand between two points on a demand curve: (Q_1, P_1) and (Q_2, P_2). The price elasticity of demand could then be computed according to

$$E_D = \frac{(Q_2 - Q_1)/[(Q_2 + Q_1)/2]}{(P_2 - P_1)/[(P_2 + P_1)/2]}$$

9. a. Using question 4 data, compute price elasticity coefficients between the prices indicated below.

(1) Between price \$8 and price \$7 _______________

(2) Between price \$5 and price \$4 _______________

(3) Between price \$3 and price \$2 _______________

b. This elasticity-coefficient idea is just an extension of the three-way system of division outlined in the section preceding question 4. For example, in the unit-elastic case, the two percentage changes just cancel one another out—they are equal. This makes the elasticity-coefficient figure *(1 / greater than 1 / less than 1)*. In the price elastic case, that figure must be *(1 / greater than 1 / less than 1)*. In the inelastic case, it must be *(1 / greater than 1 / less than 1)*.

---

a. (1) $\frac{(12-8)/[(12+8)/2]}{-(7-8)/[(7+8)/2]} = \frac{4/10}{1/7.5} = \frac{4 \times 7.5}{10} = 3$

(2) $\frac{4/18}{1/4.5} = \frac{4 \times 4.5}{18} = 1$

(3) $\frac{4/30}{1/2.5} = \frac{4 \times 2.5}{30} = .33$

b. 1; greater than 1; less than 1

10. a. A *perfectly elastic* demand curve is illustrated as a horizontal line. Such a line illustrates the ultimate in elasticity (i.e., "infinite elasticity") because it means (pick one):

(1) no matter what the change in price might be, within the range of prices indicated by length of this line, there would be no response in quantity purchased.

(2) The slightest increase in price above the level at which this horizontal line runs would cause purchases to respond—i.e., to decrease—to the point of falling to zero.

b. *Perfectly inelastic* demand signifies a vertical line, or zero elasticity. Which alternative above correctly indicates why such a demand curve would represent the ultimate in inelasticity? . . . . *(1 / 2 / neither)*

Notice that the two extreme cases of perfectly elastic and perfectly inelastic demand constitute exceptions to the point made in question 8. When a demand curve is illustrated as perfectly horizontal or perfectly vertical, the slope of that line does tell you what the elasticity of the demand curve is.

c. A demand curve with unitary elasticity everywhere along its length *(can / cannot)* be a straight line. It is characterized instead in terms of revenue linking price and quantity numbers such that total revenue must be *(always rising as the price climbs / always constant regardless of price / always falling as the price climbs)*.

---

a. (2) b. (1) c. cannot; always constant regardless of price

11. The idea of responsiveness to a price change applies just as easily to supply as it does to demand. In dealing with supply, however, we cannot use the association of elasticity to revenue. Why? Because the revenue asked by suppliers moving along a supply curve almost never has the "either-direction" character of the revenue paid by consumers moving along a demand curve. Along a conventional supply schedule, a higher price always means a higher quantity and thus more revenue. Nevertheless, we can use for supply exactly the same elasticity-coefficient ("responsiveness") measure already developed for demand:

$$E_s = \frac{\text{percentage change in quantity supplied}}{\text{percentage change in price}}$$

a. In this sense, perfectly inelastic supply would be represented by a *(vertical / horizontal)* line, and perfectly elastic supply by a *(vertical / horizontal)* line.

b. Perfectly elastic supply appears as a *(vertical / horizontal)* line because that indicates the "ultimate" in responsiveness. It indicates simply a particular price; it says that any desired quantity is available at that price; it says that if price were to drop even slightly below this level, quantity supplied would *(fall to zero / become infinitely large)*.

When you enter a supermarket and find you can buy as little or as much as you wish of any given item at its fixed price, in effect you are facing a perfectly elastic supply curve.

---

a. vertical; horizontal **b.** horizontal; fall to zero

If there should be an increase in demand, price will rise, and suppliers will want to increase their supply offers. The extent to which they can do so depends on the amount of time they are given in which to increase production. This is the basis for Alfred Marshall's *distinction between time periods*, on the supply side.

12. a. If an increase in demand is sudden and suppliers have no reserve inventories on hand, it may be that no greater quantity can be offered immediately, despite the price rise. If so, the supply curve must be shown as *(perfectly elastic / perfectly inelastic)*. This is what the text refers to as the new *(long-run / short-run / momentary)* equilibrium.

b. Given a little time, suppliers can adjust to a demand surge by working their plant and equipment harder (e.g., by adding an extra shift of workers). The result of this increase in supply quantity is the new *(long-run / short-run / momentary)* equilibrium.

c. If the shift in demand were sustained, then existing and potential new suppliers would have even more time to build new plant and install new equipment. There would be a further increase in the quantity offered in supply. Finally, therefore, an equilibrium price that indicates *(long-run / momentary / short-run)* equilibrium may be reached.

d. Note carefully that all this is just a statement about price elasticity of supply. It says that the degree of responsiveness of supply to a price change will depend on the amount of adjustment time suppliers can have. The longer this time period, the *(higher / lower)* will be the price elasticity (the elasticity coefficient) of supply. The same kind of dependence of elasticity on time *(can / cannot)* be made for the demand side.

---

a. perfectly inelastic; momentary **b.** short-run **c.** long-run **d.** higher; can

The concept of market equilibrium was introduced in Chapter 4. A price-quantity pair represents an equilibrium situation if the quantity supplied at the specified price exactly matches the quantity demanded at that price. Markets tend to move toward these equilibria all by themselves. Excess supplies caused by excessively high prices tend to lead suppliers to cut their prices in an effort to liquidate their surpluses; this tendency constitutes automatic pressure on the prices to move down toward an equilibrium when they are too high. Shortages caused by bargain prices tend to lead suppliers to hike their prices to take advantage of the high levels of demand; this tendency constitutes the opposite pressure on prices to move up toward equilibrium when they are too low.

Comparisons of market equilibria are therefore appropriate analytical tools with which to trace the effects of various changes in any given market. If markets tend toward equilibrium all by themselves, then we can get a fair idea of the impact of some change in, say, the demand schedule by tracing what happens to market equilibrium. If, to continue the example, higher demand means that the equilibrium price climbs, then we can conclude that higher demand will begin to push the price upward as soon as demand conditions change.

A methodology based on this type of reasoning has a name; it is called **comparative statics**. It is the method through which many economic investigations are conducted; it is, in fact, the method employed in applications of supply-and-demand analysis that occupy the latter portion of Chapter 18.

When you are asked to trace the effect of some sort of demand or supply adjustment, you are being asked to do some comparative statics of your own. You should not, in this effort, hesitate to use the graphical tools that you know. First draw a typical supply-and-demand graph and identify the equilibrium intersection. Then ask yourself whether the adjustment to be studied affects the demand side or the supply side of the market. Few factors affect both sides simultaneously, so there should be one answer to this question. Decide whether or not the required adjustment is out (up) or in (down), and draw a new schedule in the appropriate position. Now you are finished. Comparing the new equilibrium with the old, you can read directly from the graph the direction of the effect you were asked to analyze. Playing around with the shapes of the supply and demand curves that you drew, you can even uncover the sensitivity of the result to supply-and-demand elasticities.

13. a. Record the following supply schedule in the upper part of Figure 18-4 (question 4), using the Q_1 supply figures. (The Q_2 fill-in blanks are for part **b** of this question.)

P	\$1.00	\$2.00	\$3.00	\$4.00	\$5.00
Q_1	0	12	20	24	26
Q_2	____	____	____	____	____
P	\$6.00	\$7.00	\$8.00	\$9.00	\$10.00
Q_1	28	29	30	31	32
Q_2	____	____	____	____	____

With the demand curve previously drawn, the equilibrium price indicated is \$*(3 / 4 / 5 / 6)*.

b. A tax of \$1 per unit sold is now levied on the suppliers of this commodity. *Note:* Such a tax is an increase in cost per unit of \$1; so the suppliers will now sell only at \$5 the particular quantity they were formerly willing to sell at \$4.) In the Q_2 line above, enter the new supply-schedule figures. Then graph the new supply curve in Figure 18-4. Make it a broken or dotted line, to distinguish this after-tax supply schedule from the pre-tax schedule previously drawn.

The new equilibrium price will be approximately \$*(3.00 / 3.10 / 3.60 / 4.00 / 4.50)*. The price received by suppliers is \$*(2.00 / 3.10 / 3.50 / 4.50)*.

---

a. 4 **b.** 0, 0, 12, 20, 24, 26, 28, 29, 30, 31; 4.50; 3.50 (= price − tax = \$4.50 − \$1.00)

The question of the incidence of a tax like the one posed in question 13 is interesting because it shows that the greater portion of a tax may be paid by either buyers or sellers. The first thing to recognize in your study of such taxes is that their imposition can be modeled as a simple change in supply. A sales or production tax can be seen to reduce the quantity that suppliers willingly offer at any given price (assuming some nonzero price elasticity of supply)—a leftward shift in the supply curve like the one you just drew. [For the \$1 tax of question 13, you produced the Q_2 values by picking a price (say, \$3), noting that the supplier would receive \$1.00 less than that price after the tax was paid (say, \$2.00), recording the quantity that the supplier would deliver at that *after-tax* price (12 units for \$2 = \$3 − \$1). The point (12, \$3) is thus on the after-tax supply curve.

Alternatively, the tax may be viewed as increasing the price required to induce suppliers to produce the same quantity—an equivalent upward shift in the supply curve. [Before the tax, the supplier in question 13 facing a \$2 price would willingly produce 12 units. To continue to produce 12 units after the \$1 tax, the supplier must continue to receive \$2. The price paid by consumers must, in other words, be \$3 if the supplier is to maintain output. The point (12, \$3) is still on the after-tax supply curve.] In either view, the intuition behind the shift in the supply schedule is simple: if suppliers don't get the full price that they require for their product, then they won't produce the full amount.

14. a. In the case of a per-unit commodity tax of the sort imposed on the market in question 13, the degree to which the price paid by consumers increases in response to the tax depends upon the shapes of the supply and demand curves. Which of the following circumstances (circle one or more) would make it likely that the price paid by consumers would increase by almost the full amount of the tax?

(1) Highly price elastic demand.

(2) Highly price inelastic demand.

(3) Highly price elastic supply.

(4) Highly price inelastic supply.

The price received by suppliers in this case would *(fall significantly / fall slightly / necessarily remain the same)*.

b. Which alternative(s) in part **a** [select one or more, and note your selection(s) in the space provided] would leave the after-tax price paid by consumers almost the same as the pre-tax price? ______________ The price received by suppliers would *(fall by almost the full value of the tax / fall slightly / necessarily remain the same).*

---

a. (2) and **(3)**; fall slightly (Draw some graphs with, e.g., identical supply shifts measured against price elastic demand on the one hand and price inelastic demand on the other. The market-clearing price will increase more with the inelastic demand. Repeat the process with price elastic and inelastic supply.)
b. (1) and **(4)**; fall by almost the full value of the tax

15. The various panels of Figure 18-5 display some possible illustrations of comparative static exercises in the market for apartments. In each case, *DD* represents an initial demand curve, *SS* represents an initial supply curve, *E* represents an initial equilibrium, and *E′* represents a new equilibrium supported by either a new supply curve *S′ S′* or a new demand curve *D′ D′*. For each of the following, indicate in the blank provided which panel most accurately reflects the indicated change in the market for apartments.

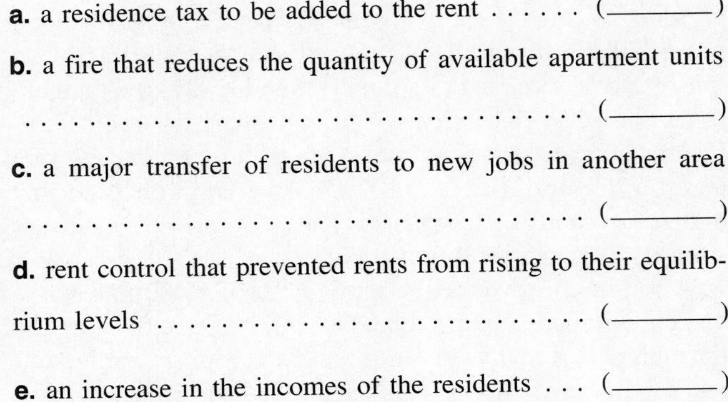

a. a residence tax to be added to the rent . . . . . . (______)

b. a fire that reduces the quantity of available apartment units . . . . (______)

c. a major transfer of residents to new jobs in another area . . . . (______)

d. rent control that prevented rents from rising to their equilibrium levels . . . . (______)

e. an increase in the incomes of the residents . . . (______)

---

a. c (See incidence coverage above.) **b.** c (simple reduction in supply) **c.** b (simple reduction in demand) **d.** d (equilibrium read from supply curve) **e.** a (simple reduction in demand)

16. Necessities tend to be the types of goods that are relatively price inelastically demanded; they are needed regardless of the price (within reason), and so the quantity demanded *(is / is not)*

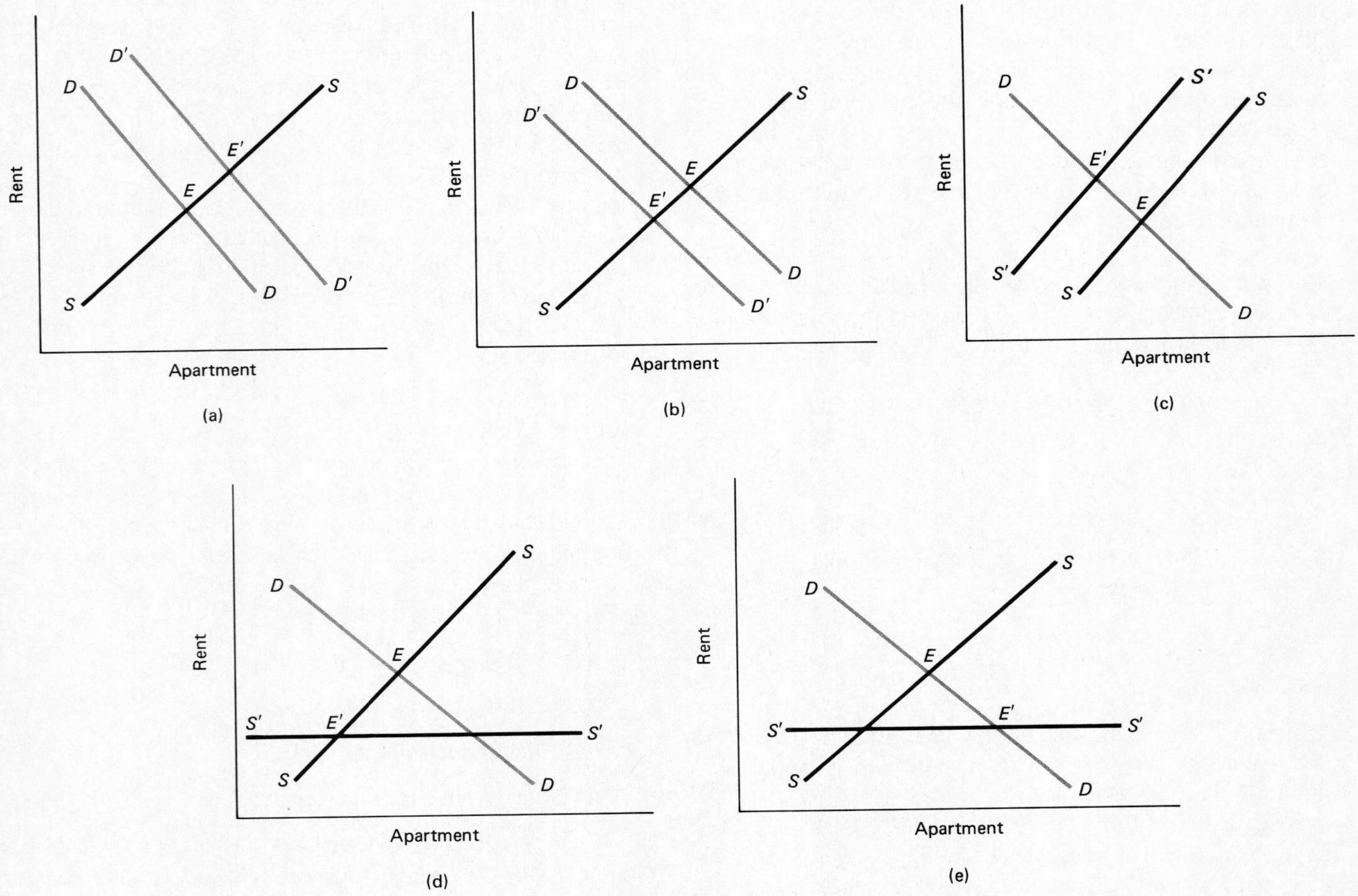

Figure 18-5

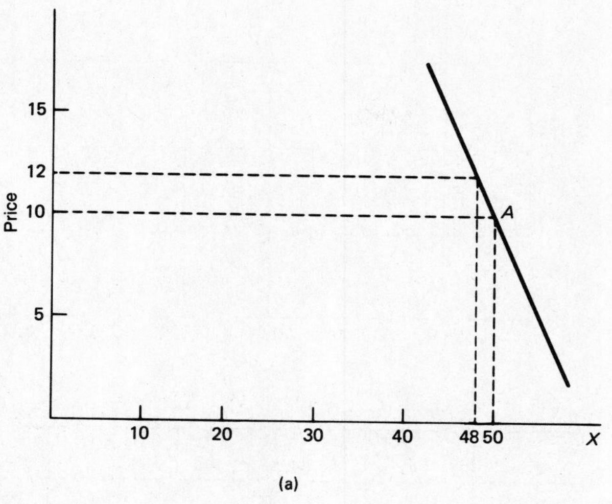

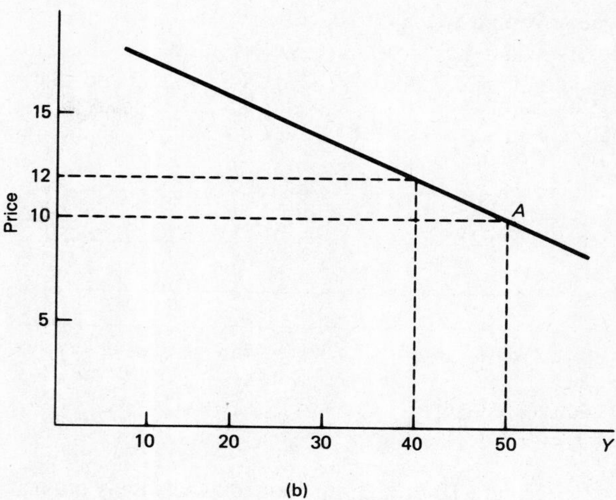

Figure 18-6

terribly sensitive to changes in the price. The purchase of necessities also tends to exhaust a higher percentage of the income earned by families on the lower end of the income scale. Luxury goods tend to be the opposite; they can be foregone easily if the price climbs and are therefore usually *(elastically / inelastically)* demanded. Look at the two demand curves in Figure 18-6; the curve in panel *(a / b)* portrays a demand schedule that shows that good *(X / Y)* should be thought of as a necessity in the vicinity of a $10 price. Let supply be perfectly elastic at a price of $10. Draw the appropriate supply curve in both panels of Figure 18-6; it should be *(horizontal at P = $10 / sloped upward through point A / sloped downward through point A)*. Now suppose that the government wants to raise as much money as possible by placing a $2 tax on one of the two goods. The tax would raise $________ in tax revenue if it were applied to good X and $________ in revenue if it were applied to good Y. This is because *(X / Y)* is more inelastically demanded at P = $10 and the $2 increase in the price causes a *(smaller / larger)* reduction in the quantity demanded. Were the government to pursue a program of taxing X instead of Y, would this be the more equitable policy? ________. Why or why not? ____________

____

____

____

____

is not; elastically; a; X; horizontal at P = $10; 96 [48 units of X still demanded with $2 tax means that tax revenue = (48 × $2 = $96.]; $80 [40 units of Y demanded after the tax means that tax revenue = (40 × $2) = $80.]; X; smaller; no; The efficiency of taxing necessities with low price elasticities causes low-income families to spend a higher proportion of their incomes paying the tax than high-income families would spend.

17. Consider Figure 18-7. The equilibrium price for X is $________ and the equilibrium quantity is ________ units. Were the government to want to restrict consumption to 500 units, it could exercise a number of policy options. It could, first of all, impose a price *(ceiling / floor)* of $________; the quantity demanded would then be ________ units, but the quantity supplied would be ________ units. A *(shortage / surplus)* of ________ units would result in the short run, but suppliers would quickly catch on that the production level was unsustainable. They would, therefore, lower their output to 500 units, where the price they received would exceed the price required to get them to supply 500 units by $________. Alternatively, the government could set a production quota at 500 units, and suppliers

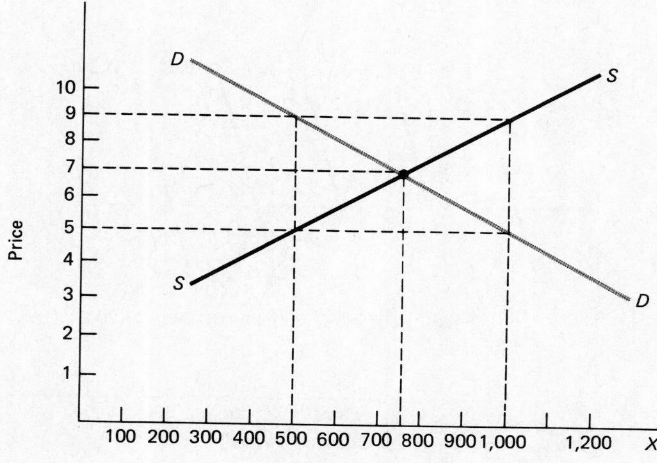

Figure 18-7

would receive a price of $______ for every unit that they sold. Finally, the government could issue ration tickets and announce that one ticket and no more than $5 would be required to purchase one unit of X. If the tickets could be bought and sold, they would command a price of $______. Why? ______

7; 750; floor; 9; 500; 1000; surplus; 500; 4; 9; 4; They would assume a value equal to the difference between what people would be willing to pay for X and what they were allowed to pay.

18. Examine Figure 18-8. It shows demand and supply curves for wheat for different years. Fill in the table accompanying Figure 18-9 with the required price and quantity data as well as the identification of the supporting supply and demand curves; row 1 is completed to illustrate the procedure. Plot the price and quantity data that you recorded in the table on Figure 18-9, label the points by year, and connect them. You have plotted a line that *(slopes upward / is horizontal / slopes downward).*

Is it a supply curve or a demand curve? ______. Why? ______

Recording data by row: $2, 1000, *DD*(1985), *SS*(1985); $2, 1500, *DD*(1990), *SS*(1990); $2, 2000, *DD*(1995), *SS*(1995); $2, 2500, *DD*(2000), *SS*(2000); is horizontal; neither; It collects the intersection of many different supply and demand curves, not points along any one supply or demand curve. (Note your identification of demand and supply curves in the two rightmost columns of the table in Figure 18-9.) The intersections would have represented a supply curve

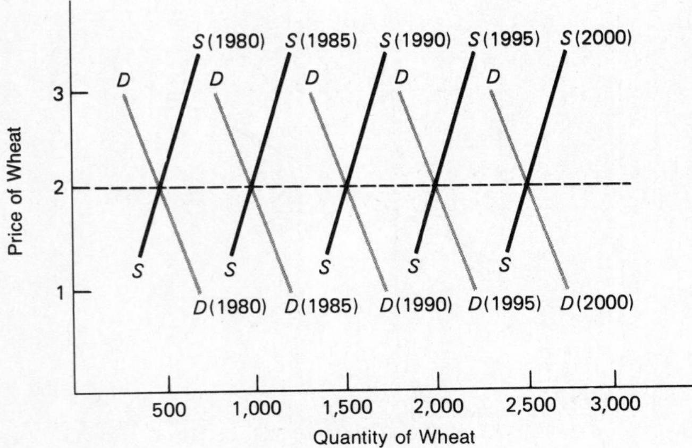

Figure 18-8

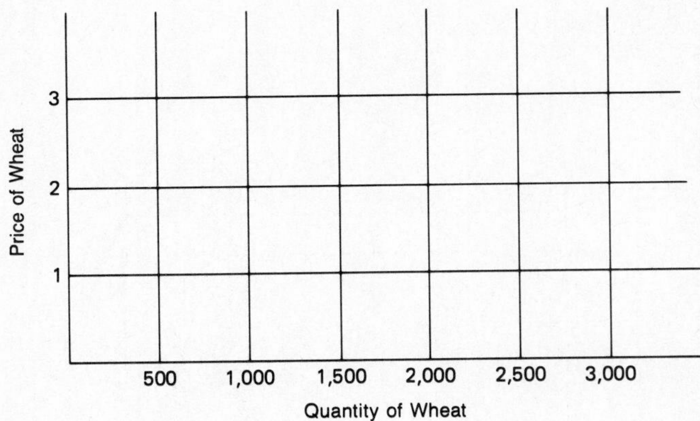

Year	Price	Quantity	Demand Curve	Supply Curve
1980	$2	500	*DD*(1980)	*SS*(1980)
1985				
1990				
1995				
2000				

Figure 18-9

only if the supply schedule had remained fixed from 1980 through 2000; they would have represented a demand curve only if demand had been unchanged. They would have been one point if both had been constant

QUIZ: Multiple Choice

1. Consumers have budgeted a fixed money amount to buy a certain commodity. Within a certain range of prices, they will spend neither more nor less than this amount on it. Their demand in this price range would properly be designated as:
(1) in equilibrium.
(2) perfectly elastic.
(3) perfectly inelastic.
(4) highly inelastic but not perfectly so.
(5) unit-elastic.

2. The price elasticity coefficient of demand equals:
(1) amount of price decrease divided by amount of quantity increase.
(2) percentage change in revenue divided by percentage decrease in price.
(3) percentage change in revenue divided by percentage increase in quantity demanded.
(4) percentage change in quantity demanded divided by percentage change in price.
(5) none of the above.

3. When the words "total revenue" are used in any discussion of demand curves, their meaning is:

(1) the profit, after deduction of costs, which the suppliers of the commodity involved earn from selling it to consumers.
(2) the total amount of money consumers will spend on the commodity at any particular price.
(3) the income suppliers will receive from sales if they sell the quantity they hope to sell.
(4) the quantity of the commodity that is associated with any particular price.
(5) null; the words "total revenue" cannot have any meaning in relation to demand curves.

4. Alfred Marshall's concepts of "momentary," "short-run," and "long-run" supply curves were intended to bring out which fact?
(1) Over a long period of time, gradual increases in skill and improvements in the art of production tend to bring down the price of any commodity.
(2) Price increases as cost of transport to any given market increases.
(3) The extent to which quantity supplied will respond to a given price or demand change depends on the amount of time given producers to adjust their operations to this change.
(4) In order to make the supply-curve idea meaningful, it is necessary to speak of the quantity that will be supplied per period of time.
(5) Although demand may exert some short-run influence, ultimately the price of any commodity must be determined by the cost of its production.

5. As the result of an increase in family incomes in a certain community, purchases of butter rise from 1000 pounds daily to 1500 pounds daily. As a further result, the price of butter per pound rises from $1.25 to $1.50. This behavior:
(1) cannot be explained by the demand-curve-and-supply-curve analysis of price determination.
(2) represents a movement by consumers upward along their demand curve to a point of higher price and greater quantity.
(3) must be explained as a shift in the supply curve.
(4) represents a movement of price and quantity to a position above the equilibrium level.
(5) must be represented by a shift in the demand curve to a different position from that formerly occupied.

6. If a 10 percent reduction in price brings a 5 percent increase in the amount of money people spend to buy that commodity, then in this region of the demand curve, demand is (with respect to price):
(1) elastic.
(2) unit-elastic.
(3) inelastic, although not perfectly so.
(4) perfectly inelastic.
(5) perhaps any of these—information given is insufficient to determine elasticity.

7. Which alternative in question 6 would have been correct if the 10 percent reduction in price had caused a 5 percent increase in the quantity of the commodity that people buy?
(1).
(2).
(3).
(4).
(5).

8. If I can buy any quantity I please of a commodity at a fixed price, this means that the supply curve which confronts me is:
(1) perfectly inelastic.
(2) perfectly elastic.
(3) unit-elastic.
(4) elastic, but not necessarily perfectly elastic.
(5) none of these things, necessarily.

9. The government levies an excise tax of 5 cents per unit sold on the sellers in a competitive industry. Both supply and demand curves have some elasticity with respect to price. When this tax is represented on the supply-and-demand diagram:
(1) the entire supply curve shifts leftward by an amount indicating 5 cents, but (unless demand is perfectly elastic) price will not rise.
(2) the entire supply curve shifts upward by an amount indicating less than 5 cents, but (unless demand is highly elastic) price will rise by the full 5 cents.
(3) the entire supply curve shifts leftward by an amount indicating less than 5 cents.
(4) the entire supply curve shifts upward by an amount indicating 5 cents, but (unless supply is perfectly elastic) any price rise will be less than 5 cents.
(5) the entire demand curve shifts upward by an amount indicating 5 cents, and price will rise by 5 cents.

10. The change brought about by the tax levy described in question 9 would be designated as:
(1) a decrease in supply followed by a decrease in quantity demanded.
(2) a decrease in quantity supplied followed by a decrease in quantity demanded.
(3) a decrease in supply followed by a decrease in demand.
(4) a decrease in quantity supplied followed by a decrease in demand.
(5) none of the above.

11. A perfectly inelastic supply curve would be shown in the ordinary supply-and-demand graph as:
(1) a vertical line.
(2) a horizontal line.
(3) a straight line, but neither horizontal nor vertical.
(4) a curved line.
(5) perhaps any of the above.

12. Which alternative in question 11 would be correct for the graphical portrayal of a perfectly inelastic demand curve?

(1).
(2).
(3).
(4).
(5).

13. A change in quantity demanded, as distinct from a change in demand, means:
(1) that buyers have decided to buy more (or less) than they did before, at the existing price.
(2) that the elasticity of demand with respect to price has increased or decreased.
(3) simply that the quantity of purchases has changed, regardless of the factor which brought about this change in buying.
(4) that the market price has fallen or risen, and buyers have changed their total purchases accordingly.
(5) an increase in total purchases, but not a decrease.

14. Which alternative in question 13 would be correct for a change in demand, as distinct from a change in quantity demanded?
(1).
(2).
(3).
(4).
(5).

15. Following the OPEC price rise, consumers of gasoline and oil products reduced their purchases—but not by very much. This means that their demand curve for such products:
(1) was price elastic.
(2) shifted slightly to the right.
(3) was price inelastic.
(4) shifted slightly to the left.
(5) was unit-elastic with respect to price.

16. If a demand curve is unit-elastic throughout its entire length, this means, with respect to (*a*) graphical appearance of the demand curve and (*b*) total expenditure by buyers to purchase the commodity, that:
(1) the demand curve is a straight line, and total expenditure by buyers is the same at all prices.
(2) the demand curve is not a straight line, and total expenditure by buyers falls as price falls.
(3) the demand curve is a straight line, and as price falls total expenditure by buyers first increases and later decreases.
(4) the demand curve is not a straight line, and total expenditure by buyers rises as price falls.
(5) none of the above is correct.

17. An increase in demand for a certain product occurs. In Alfred Marshall's analysis, a new short-run and a new long-run equilibrium price will emerge. In the normal case, these would be related to the original price as follows: long-run equilibrium price would be:
(1) higher than both the short-run and original prices.
(2) lower than the short-run price but could be higher than the original price.
(3) lower than both the short-run and original prices.
(4) related to short-run and original prices in a manner not indicated by any of the above.

18. Suppose that the demand curve for wheat is perfectly inelastic with respect to price. A tax of 50 cents per bushel sold is imposed on suppliers. Then:
(1) price will rise, but by less than 50 cents, and there will probably be some reduction in the quantity bought and sold.
(2) price will rise by the full 50 cents, but there will be no reduction in the quantity bought and sold.
(3) price will rise, but by less than 50 cents, and there will be no reduction in the quantity bought and sold.
(4) price will rise by the full 50 cents, and there will definitely be a reduction in the quantity bought and sold.
(5) none of the above is correct.

19. A crop failure reduces the amount of wheat available, and so the price rises. In precise terms, this is:
(1) a decrease in quantity supplied followed by a decrease in demand.
(2) a decrease in supply followed by a decrease in demand.
(3) a decrease in quantity supplied followed by a decrease in quantity demanded.
(4) a decrease in supply followed by a decrease in quantity demanded.
(5) none of these things.

20. Early in the 1970s, OPEC raised oil prices very sharply by forming a cartel. In elementary supply-and-demand-curve terms, OPEC's action of restricting world trade in oil could be described as:
(1) a leftward shift of the supply curve.
(2) a leftward shift of the demand curve.
(3) a rightward shift of the supply curve.
(4) a rightward shift of the demand curve.
(5) an increase in equilibrium price, but with no change in either demand curve or supply curve.

21. Which of the following observations would tend to make you expect that some good would display a price inelastic demand curve even if you did not know exactly what good it was?
(1) The good in question is more of a necessity than a luxury for most people.
(2) There do not exist substitutes for the consumption of this good.
(3) The time period allowed to respond to a change in price is very small.
(4) All or any of the above.
(5) None of the above.

22. Which of the following describes a supply curve of unitary elasticity drawn in the usual price-quantity quadrant?

(1) A straight line drawn from the origin with a constant and positive slope.
(2) A rectangular hyperbola bowed out from the origin.
(3) A straight line drawn from any "price intercept" with a constant and positive slope.
(4) A horizontal line drawn at the market-clearing price.
(5) A vertical line drawn at the market-clearing quantity.

SUGGESTED ANSWERS TO QUESTIONS IN THE TEXT: Chapter 18

1. Demand factors: (e.g.) higher income, more radio play, larger concert-age population—and you know who you are. Supply factors: (e.g.) number of good bands, number of good halls and stadiums.

2. More price elastic: perfume, ice cream, and (optional) reading books, because they are closer to luxuries than necessities in the pairs; chocolate ice cream, because there exist more substitutes than for ice cream in general.

3. Higher price (smaller quantity) will cause revenue to increase, stay the same, and decrease as demand is price inelastic, displays unit price elasticity, and is price elastic, respectively. Larger quantity does the opposite.

4. Demand would be inelastic, with $E_D < 1$.

5. Assume that demand and supply both show some price elasticity.

a. Output and price up along supply curve (demand-curve shift).

b. Output down and price (paid by renters) up.

c. \$200/month greater than market-clearing rent: no change.

\$200/month less than market-clearing rent: output and quantity down along supply curve (horizontal effective demand with excess real demand).

d. Output up and price down along demand curve (supply shift).

e. Output down and price up along demand curve (supply shift).

6. Rent regulation breeds excess demand at the regulated rent.

7. Good harvest shifts a fairly inelastic supply curve out. Equilibrium moves down along an inelastic demand curve to support a (much) lower price and lower revenue.

8. Available substitutes generate elastic demand, especially outside the range of transportation cost; Washington is small.

9. Maintains demand and prices during periods of high supply; encourages high supply.

10. **a.** Elasticity between (e.g.) \$5 and \$10 is 0.5. The move from \$10 to \$5 represents a 50 percent reduction. Quantity must therefore climb by 25 percent so that the ratio of the percentage change in quantity to the percentage change in price equals 0.5. Do the others in like fashion.

b. Supply down by 50 percent means that price must increase by 500 percent to keep the price elasticity equal to 0.1. Crime should increase if addicts steal to feed their habits.

c. Supply down by 5 percent with elasticity of 0.05 means that price must increase by 100 percent.

d. Elasticity is a ratio of percentages; it is thus unitless.

11. The relevant intersections move along *SS* from 1985 through 1995, but then skip to *S'S'*. The first three equilibrium points therefore trace out *SS*, but not all four. The identification problem is really one of not knowing when the skips occur.

12. Triangle *Oba* is similar to triangle *apc*. Therefore, $OP/Pa = Cb/Ca$. Note, as well, that $OP/Pa = P/(a - P)$.

13. In the shorthand of calculus:

$$\begin{aligned} E_D &= d[\log f(P)]/d\log P \\ &= [df(P)/fP]/(dP/P) \\ &= P[df(P)/dP]/fP \end{aligned}$$

CHAPTER 19

DEMAND, UTILITY, AND CONSUMER BEHAVIOR

Demand theory provides the framework within which we study the economic factors that produce and affect demand curves. The power of demand curves as tools for economic investigation has already been noted—showing that power was one of the fundamental points of Chapters 4 and 18. This chapter explores their sensitivity to changes in income, prices, and tastes by postulating and manipulating a model of consumer behavior. Having completed the chapter, you will have met the following objectives.

LEARNING OBJECTIVES

1. Define total utility and marginal utility; distinguish between the two.

2. Explain the law of diminishing marginal utility and its importance in economic analysis.

3. Explain why an individual's utility is maximized subject to an income constraint if the marginal utility derived from the last dollar spent is the same for all the goods purchased.

4. Express the utility-maximizing rule mathematically, and show how it combines with the law of diminishing marginal utility to produce downward-sloping demand curves.

5. Define substitution and income effects (terms first appearing in Chapter 4); explain how they work to produce downward-sloping demand curves.

6. Explain how market demand curves are derived from the horizontal summation of individual demand curves.

7. Describe the paradox of value, and resolve it through application of the utility-maximizing rule.

8. Define consumer surplus; explain how it is used.

Consumers, like you for example, ordinarily have only a limited amount of money to spend in any given period of time on the things that they need or want. Each good has a market price which usually cannot be altered by bargaining or bickering. You must decide which goods to buy and how much of each good to buy, knowing from the quoted prices that each purchase will exhaust part of your limited income or budget.

If your budget were so large that you could buy all you wanted of all the goods that interested you, then there would be no problem of choice and the study of economics would not be a story about you and your life. Unless I miss my guess, though, that is not the case. You must choose. You must decide, for example, whether to buy 2 more units of one good (call it good A) at a price of $1 per unit or 1 more unit of a different good (call it good B) at a price of $2. Either purchase would entail the same $2 outlay, but your limited budget tells you that you can't have both. You must, therefore, carry inside your head some personal measuring scale which says that buying the 1 unit of B would yield you more satisfaction than would purchase of the 2 units of A (or vice versa). Tastes differ, of course. The individual next to you, with the same income, might well make the opposite choice.

This small A-or-B choice illustrates the more general problem of how to make the best use of a limited income. There are literally thousands of different assortments of goods, each one a little different from the next, which could be bought with a given income (and at given prices). Which among them is the "best" choice? The answer lies in weighing personal tastes against price-income-determined budget constraints, but that is perhaps easier said than analyzed formally.

Prices and incomes are objective, easily understood concepts, but tastes are more difficult. We have to devise some analytic concept to represent what we mean by personal "tastes," "preferences," or "needs."

Economists have developed the notion of **utility** to accomplish this representation. Each consumer is envisioned to evaluate commodities on the basis of his or her personal quantitative standard of satisfaction or utility.

A certain buyer may reckon, for example, that buying 1 unit of A would yield 70 utility units ("utils"); 2 units would yield a total of 120 utils; and a third A unit would raise the satisfaction meter to 150 utils.

In real life, nobody is conscious of putting exact numerical values on each quantity of each good consumed. The utility notion represents consumers as being a lot more precise than buyers actually are, but don't be too impatient with the utility idea on this account. It says that consumers must do something at least approximating this, even if only intuitively, if they want to make the best possible use of a limited income. This quantitative utility idea is employed because it is a way of showing how a consumer will go about "maximizing satisfaction," i.e., making the best possible use of a limited income in the light of his or her own set of preferences.

The very first step is to distinguish carefully between **total utility** and **marginal utility**. In the example above, the buyer derived a total utility of 70 utils from consuming 1 unit of A, 120 utils from 2 units, and 150 utils from 3 units. Marginal utility is the extra utility contributed by the last unit consumed (the unit that is just at the edge or margin of consumption, so to speak). The marginal utility of the first unit of A must be 70 (because its consumption raised total utility from 0 to 70); that of the second unit, 50 (because total utils rose from 70 to 120); that of the third unit, 30 (from 120 to 150).

The second step is to note the **principle of diminishing marginal utility**. This principle says that as consumption of any single good increases, the total utility derived from that consumption will increase at a decreasing rate; i.e., marginal utility gradually decreases. The third ice-cream cone (or the third martini) may add to your satisfaction, but not so much as the first one did; the fifth one may add still a little more satisfaction, but not so much as the third one did. In these circumstances, your total satisfaction is still rising, but the payoff from each additional (marginal) unit consumed is becoming less and less.

1. a. If the total utilities associated with the consumption of 1, 2, and 3 units of B were to be, respectively, 100, 160, and 200, then the corresponding marginal utilities would be ______, ______, and ______.

b. Which of the following sets of total utility figures (designated for 1, 2, 3, and 4 units consumed) illustrates the idea of diminishing marginal utility? *(200, 300, 400, 500 / 200, 450, 750, 1100 / 200, 400, 1600, 9600 / 200, 250, 270, 280)*?

c. Which of the following sets of marginal utility figures (once again defined for 1, 2, 3, and 4 units consumed) would likewise illustrate the diminishing-marginal-utility principle? *(200, 150, 100, 50 / 200, 300, 400, 500 / 200, 200, 200, 200 / 200, 250, 270, 280)*?

---

a. 100; 60; 40 **b.** 200, 250, 270, 280 **c.** 200, 150, 100, 50

Now we use the ideas of total and marginal utility to illustrate the idea of maximizing satisfaction, or making the best possible use of a given income. Suppose that your fixed weekly budget will allow consideration of only three goods: A, B, and C. Table 19-1 shows your personal schedule of total utility for these three goods.

You want to spend your fixed income so as to obtain that particular A-B-C combination yielding the maximum number of utility units. The utility units for A are of the same kind as those for B and C. For example, if you buy 2 units each of A, B, and C, your total satisfaction would be 950 utility units (120 plus 700 plus 130).

In this table, the three sets of utility values are assumed to be independent of one another. That is, the amount of utility you get for any given quantity of A is not affected by the amount you happen to be consuming of B or of C. This is not necessarily true in real life; A and B might, for example, be close substitutes. The assumption of independence is made here only for the sake of simplicity and clarity.

2. Use the information in Table 19-1 to record, in Table 19-2, marginal utilities of A, B, and C. To speed things up, a few of the marginal utility figures are already entered.

A: 10, 7, 5, 5, 4, 4, 3; B: 20, 10, 8, 6, 4, 2, 1, 1; C: 45, 40, 35, 28, 20, 12, 6

Suppose that you, as the consumer whose preferences are reflected by the utility function described in question 2, had $52 per week to spend on commodities A, B, and

Table 19-1
Total Satisfaction, Measured in Utility Units, Derived from Consumption of:

	1 Unit	2 Units	3 Units	4 Units	5 Units	6 Units	7 Units	8 Units	9 Units	10 Units	11 Units	12 Units
A	95	165	210	240	258	268	275	280	285	289	293	296
B	400	700	900	1,000	1,020	1,030	1,038	1,044	1,048	1,050	1,051	1,052
C	70	130	180	225	265	300	328	348	360	366	370	373

Table 19-2
Marginal Satisfaction or Utility, Measured in Utility Units, when Consumption Is:

	1 Unit	2 Units	3 Units	4 Units	5 Units	6 Units	7 Units	8 Units	9 Units	10 Units	11 Units	12 Units
A	95	70	45	30	18							
B	400	300	200	100								
C	70	60	50									

C. These are the only goods available, or at least the only goods in which you have any interest. Let the price of good A be $1, the price of B be $2, and the price of C be $4. How much of A, B, and C should you purchase for maximum satisfaction? There are plenty of combinations of A, B, and C that you could afford with $52, but which one buys the maximum total utility?

One possible combination is 12 units of A, 10 of B, and 5 of C; it would yield a total of 1161 utility units. Is this best? No. If you reduced your purchases of A by 4 units and used the surplus money to purchase an extra unit of C, your utility would increase by 19 utility units. The utility lost by reducing your consumption of A would be more than compensated by the utility gained from consuming 1 more unit of C.

Marginal utility is the critical factor in measuring losses and gains, but it is not the only critical factor in evaluating utility-maximizing equilibrium. In the example above, the last units of A purchased were not the utility bargains when compared with C that they might have looked like if only price were considered, but looking at marginal utility numbers alone would have been equally misleading. What must be asked to check to see if utility is maximized is really this: Are the three commodities offering equally good utility returns per dollar spent? Is, in other words, the marginal value of the dollar the same regardless of what good it is spent on? If it is—if the three goods are contributing equally to utility per dollar expended—then utility is maximized.

The method with which to check whether or not this is happening is simple. The ratios of marginal utility to price must be computed for each good. (An old physics trick can provide some insight here. The units of evaluation should be units of utility per dollar spent. If marginal utility is measured in units of utility per units of consumption and prices are measured in dollars per unit of consumption, then marginal utility divided by price must be in units of utility per dollar—the units of consumption cancel.) If the marginal-utility-to-price ratios are equal, then utility is maximized. If they are not, then there exists some adjustment in consumption that will increase utility—an increase in the consumption of the good with the high utility payoff per dollar and a reduction in the consumption of the good with the low utility payoff per dollar.

3. a. Use the data of Table 19-2 to compute the marginal-utility-to-price ratios indicated in Table 19-3 given A's price of $1, B's of $2, and C's of $4.

b. Table 19-3 has several combinations of goods A, B, and C generating equal marginal utilities per dollar. Circle the *MU*-per-dollar figures in this table for three of them, namely:

1. 6 of A, 5 of B, 5 of C (common *MU*/$: 10)
2. 8 of A, 6 of B, 8 of C (common *MU*/$: 5)
3. 12 of A, 8 of B, 9 of C (common *MU*/$: 3)

Among these three "shopping baskets," only one can be bought for $52, namely ________.

c. Given your income constraint and the prices quoted by the market, the best possible expenditure of $52 is 8 of A, 6 of B, and 8 of C. Table 19-1 indicates that the total number of utility units attained from this A-B-C combination is *(1030 / 1658 / 3050)* units.

Table 19-3
Marginal Utility Units per Dollar of Outlay (*MU* Divided by Price of the Commodity), when Consumption Is:

	1 Unit	2 Units	3 Units	4 Units	5 Units	6 Units	7 Units	8 Units	9 Units	10 Units	11 Units	12 Units
A	95	70	45	30	18							
B	200	150	100	50								
C	17.5	15	12.5									

To check that this combination really maximizes utility, experiment with a change. Reduce your C purchases from 8 units to 7. This saves you $4, which you use to buy 2 extra units of good B. Combining the reduction in total utility from lower C purchases with the increase from higher B purchases, the net change in total utility would be *(an increase / a decrease)* of *(8 / 7 / 6 / 5 / 4)* units.

---

a. A: same as Table 19-3; B: 10, 5, 4, 3, 2, 1, 0.5, 0.5; C: 11.25, 10, 8.75, 7, 5, 3, 1.5, 1, 0.75 **b.** 2 **c.** 1658; a decrease; 6

4. a. Referring still to Tables 19-1 through 19-3, suppose that your spendable income has just been cut from $52 to $36 per week. In the following table, show the details of your new equilibrium (utility-maximizing) position.

Quantity Purchased (units)	Price	Expenditure	Marginal Utility	*MU/$*
A ____	$1	____	____	____
B ____	2	____	____	____
C ____	4	____	____	____

b. To compensate you for the pain that you suffered in part **a**, suppose finally that your budget is back to $52 and that the price of commodity C has been reduced from $4 to $3. Again show the details of your resulting equilibrium position.

Quantity Purchased (units)	Price	Expenditure	Marginal Utility	*MU/$*
A ____	$1	____	____	____
B ____	2	____	____	____
C ____	3	____	____	____

---

a. A: 6, $6, 10, 10; B: 5, $10, 20, 10; C: 5, $20, 40, 10 **b.** A: 11, $11, 4, 4; B: 7, $14, 8, 4; C: 9, $27, 12, 4

5. a. Both Chapters 4 and 18 stressed the distinction between an *increase (or decrease) in demand* and an *increase (or decrease) in quantity demanded*. Question 4**a** illustrates this: There was a leftward shift of the consumer demand curve caused by an income drop. Formerly you bought ________ units of A. After the income drop, even though A's price was unchanged, your purchases were only ________ units. In Chapter 18 language, this is a decrease in *(demand / quantity demanded)*.

b. The reduction in C's price in question 4**b** illustrates, with respect to C, an increase in *(demand / quantity demanded)*.

That is, out of the utility background, we can identify consumer demand curves. For example, with a budget of $52, and with A's and B's prices $1 and $2, respectively, you would buy ________ units of C if its price were $4, and ________ units if its price were $3. Other points on the C demand curve would be derived by taking other C prices.

---

a. 8; 6; demand **b.** quantity demanded; 8; 9

In summary, then, the problem of consumer behavior is choosing the combination of goods one can afford (given income and prices) that maximizes total utility (given individual tastes and preferences). The rule for solving this problem sets the ratios of marginal utilities to prices equal for all goods; i.e., for all goods I and J with prices P_I and P_J, utility will be maximized if

$$\frac{MU_I}{P_I} = \frac{MU_J}{P_J} = \text{marginal utility per dollar of income}$$

Satisfying this condition guarantees that the utility derived from spending the last dollar of income (the marginal dollar) will be the same regardless of where it is spent. There exist, therefore, no affordable rearrangements of consumption that can increase utility.

To see why this last interpretation holds, suppose that your common marginal utility of a dollar is K units of utility; K can be any number. Now consider reducing your purchases of some good A by $1. Your utility would fall by K units. What to do with the extra dollar? What would happen if you devoted it to increasing the purchase of *any* other good B? That would generate an increase in utility of K units for a net change in total utility of zero. No change in your consumption pattern will increase your total utility.

6. a. Back in Chapter 4, the text spoke of the two "effects" which explain why, if the price of a commodity falls, more of it is bought (or why less is bought if price rises). These effects are introduced once again in this chapter. Specifically, they are (1) the *(substitution / institutional)* effect and (2) the *(envy / income)* effect.

In this question and the one following, we use the idea of marginal utility to examine in more detail the nature of these two effects. Table 19-4 at the top of the next page is similar in general construction to Tables 19-1 and 19-2. It shows the levels of marginal utility (*MU*) and total utility (*TU*) associated with different quantities of commodities X and Y, measured in satisfaction units. (Commodities X and Y are the only ones you can buy, or the only ones in which you are interested.)

b. Suppose that the prices of X and of Y are $2.40 and $1.00, respectively, and that you have just $20 per period to spend. What will be your equilibrium or maximum-satisfaction X-Y combination? In this situation, you will buy ________ units of X and ________ units of Y. The total satisfaction units you obtain, from X and Y combined, will be ________.

Table 19-4

No. Units Consumed	*MU* of X	*TU* of X	*MU* of Y	*TU* of Y
3	32	348	20	130
4	28	376	18	148
5	24	400	16	164
6	20	420	14	178
7	16	436	12	190
8	12	448	10	200
9	8	456	8	208
10	5	461	5	213
11	3	464	3	216

c. Now let the price of X drop from $2.40 to $1.00. The price of Y is still $1, and you still have $20 to spend. What will be your new equilibrium position? (Since the prices of X and Y are now equal, look for an X-Y combination with equal *MU*'s, purchasable for just $20.) You will now buy ________ units of X, as compared with 5 previously, and will now buy ________ units of Y, as compared with 8 previously.

In the new situation, the X quantity has *(increased / decreased)*. This is not surprising, since X's price has fallen. The Y quantity has *(increased / decreased)*. Why this should happen is not immediately obvious. Y's price has not fallen; indeed in relative terms—relative to the price of X—that price has risen.

d. What has happened is that you were spending considerably more than half your income on X. Thus a reduction in X's price had an effect similar to a substantial rise in your income—as witness to the rise in your total satisfaction level, from the original total of 600 units to *(620 / 664 / 670 / 674)* units. With what is equivalent to a larger income, you buy more of X—and more of Y.

When X's price falls, there are thus two resulting effects which operate upon Y purchases. Insofar as X and Y are substitutes, you will be disposed to buy *(more / less)* of Y. But countering this is the income effect just discussed, which inclined you to buy *(more / less)*. In this case, the income effect won out over the substitution effect. Had X and Y been to a greater extent substitutes, the Y quantity would have fallen instead of rising.

a. substitution; income **b.** 5; 8; 600 (*Note*: At X = 5 and Y = 8, MU_X/P_X = 24/$2.40 = 10, while MU_Y/P_Y = 10/$1 = 10.) **c.** 10; 10; increased; increased **d.** 674; less; more

7. Question 6 was based upon the notion that X and Y were substitutes. We should therefore have expected that any reduction in the price of X would reduce purchases of Y. This substitution effect can, as in question 6, be blurred or concealed by an income effect—the effect of the increase in real income caused by the price reduction that inspires the typical consumer to buy more of everything, including Y. To get a measure of the "pure substitution effect," which is uncluttered by the income effect, some type of economic benchmark was needed to establish a constant basis of comparison. Economists have found such a benchmark—the level of utility or satisfaction. This question is designed to show you how this helps us isolate the substitution effect. It asks you to consider how you would respond to the lower price of X if your money income were simultaneously reduced just enough to permit you to achieve at best only your original level of satisfaction.

a. Let the price of X fall from $2.40 to $1.00 while your budget income simultaneously falls from $20 to $12. Assume that the price of Y is $1 throughout.

The top and bottom lines in the table below summarize the two situations discussed in question 9. In the blank spaces in the middle line, fill in the details of the equilibrium situation required by the conditions just outlined.

Budget	X Price	Y Price	X Quantity	Y Quantity	Satisfaction Units
$20	$2.40	$1.00	5	8	600
12	1.00	1.00	______	______	______
20	1.00	1.00	10	10	674

Compare the top line with the one you have just completed. X's price has fallen, but so has income. You adjust your purchases as best you can to the new conditions. When you have done so, your satisfaction level *(has risen / is unchanged / has fallen)*. There is no income effect arising from the lower X price, because your money income is deliberately (if temporarily) squeezed by just enough to keep your satisfaction constant.

Compare purchases in these two situations. Purchases of X *(rise / fall)* from 5 to *(3 / 7 / 10)*. This is the pure substitution effect (of the reduction in X's price) upon X purchases. Purchases of Y *(rise / fall)* from 8 to *(5 / 7 / 10)*. This is the pure substitution effect on Y purchases. We get what we would expect if X and Y were substitutes and X's price fell: *(an increase / a reduction)* in Y purchases.

b. Now we return you to your $20 income (with the reduced price of X still in effect). This means we compare the middle line in the table with the third line. Purchases of X rise further from 7 to 10; those of Y, from 5 to 10. These are the income effects of the reduction in X's price. All we have done is to "break apart" the price reduction of question 6. First we observe the results of the pure substitution effect (comparing the top line with the middle one) and then the results of the income effect alone (comparing the middle line with the bottom one). In question 6, we went straight from the top to the bottom line (the two effects combined) without any intermediate pause.

To summarize, with matters still put in terms of a reduction in the price of X: given such an X-price reduction, the substitution effect tends to *(increase / leave unchanged / decrease)* X purchases, and to *(increase / leave unchanged / decrease)* Y purchases. The income effect of such a price reduction (with a small qualification noted below) tends to *(increase / leave unchanged / decrease)* X purchases, and to *(increase / leave unchanged / decrease)* Y purchases.

a. 7; 5; 600; is unchanged; rise; 7; fall; 5; a reduction **b.** increase; decrease; increase; increase

8. A consumer has $50 per week to exhaust on either commodity X (price $5) or commodity Y (price $4).

For each of the four cases below, indicate, if you can, whether or not this consumer is "at equilibrium," i.e., deriving the maximum-attainable satisfaction. If you lack sufficient information to answer, explain why. If you know the consumer is not at equilibrium, indicate the required direction of movement, e.g., buy more of X and less of Y, less of X and more of Y, more of both, etc.

a. Purchases are now 2 of X and 10 of Y. Total utility of X at this level is considered to be 500 utility units; total utility of Y, 400 units. ______

b. Purchases are now 6 of X and 5 of Y. Total utility of X at this level is considered to be 400 utility units; marginal utility (*MU*) of X, 60 units; total utility of Y, 800 units; *MU* of Y, 30 units. ______

c. Purchases are now 6 of X and 5 of Y. *MU* of X at this level is considered to be 25 units; *MU* of Y, 20 units. ______

d. Purchases are now 6 of X and 4 of Y. *MU* of X at this level is considered to be 25 units; *MU* of Y, 20 units. ______

a. Impossible to tell; *MU*s are not given. **b.** Buy more of X, less of Y. (*Note:* $MU_X/P_X = 60/\$5 = 12 > MU_Y/P_Y = 30/\$4 = 7.5$.) **c.** now at equilibrium (*Note:* $MU_X/P_X = 25/\$5 = 5 = MU_Y/P_Y = 20/\$4 = 5$.) **d.** Buy more of both. *MU*s are balanced with prices, but not all income is spent.

The text notes that a market demand curve can be produced by the "horizontal" addition of individual demand curves—i.e., the summation, for every price, of the quantities demanded by all the individuals participating in the market.

9. Table 19-5 records the quantities of some good X that each of three people would demand for a variety of prices. Fill in the column indicated for the market demand schedule if these three people were the only people interested in X at any price. If individual A's income were to increase, *(higher / identical / lower)* quantities would be entered in the Market Demand column for *(the equilibrium price only / all prices / all prices below $5)*. If X were considered a close substitute to Y by individual B only and the price of Y were to fall, then *(higher / identical / lower)* quantities would be entered in the Market Demand column for *(the equilibrium price only / all prices / all prices below $5)*.

Table 19-5

Price	Individual A	Individual B	Individual C	Market Demand
$8	2	0	0	____
7	3	0	1	____
6	4	0	3	____
5	5	0	5	____
4	6	1	7	____
3	7	3	10	____
2	8	5	14	____

Reading down the column: 2, 4, 7, 10, 14, 20, 27; higher; all prices; lower; all prices below $5

10. The relation between the utilities of commodities B and C in Table 19-1 illustrates something of Adam Smith's **paradox of value**. Smith was puzzled by the fact that commodity prices often are poor indicators of the true relative usefulness of commodities. Water, which is essential for life, is cheap. Diamonds, which have no such necessity status, are expensive.

In the equilibrium of question 3, you were buying ______ units of B and ______ units of C. In this position, the total utility of B is ______ units, and the total utility of C is ______ units. Measured in terms of total utility furnished, B is the more useful or desirable of the two commodities. Yet the market sets a higher price per unit on C.

The explanation is that market prices are influenced by *(marginal / total)* utility. The *(marginal / total)* utility of extra units of a commodity such as B declines sharply after a certain total quantity is consumed. If the supply offered is sufficiently large, consumers will bid a price for extra units of B reckoned only in terms of its low *(marginal / total)* utility, and this price will hold for the entire supply. If B's supply were sufficiently reduced, its price *(would rise very sharply / would rise a little but not much / would fall)*. The "utility bargain" consumers get from purchasing a commodity with high total utility at a low price is termed: ______

When the price of C fell from $4 per unit to $3, total utility *(rose / fell / stayed the same)*. At the same time, consumer surplus *(rose / fell / stayed the same)*. If Figure 19-1 were to illustrate the demand curve for C in the $2 to $5 price range, then the change in consumer surplus caused by the price reduction from $4 to $3 would be *(area EDF / area KFIL / area EGIF / area FHI)*.

If the government were to stick a tax onto the $3 price of C so that $4 became the after-tax price, then the government would collect revenue equal to *(area DGHK / area EGHF / area OGIL)*, and consumer surplus would fall by *(area EDF / area KFIL / area EGIF / area FHI)*. The amount of consumer surplus not extracted by the government in tax revenue—the deadweight loss of the tax—would be *(area EDF / area ILM / area FHI)*.

6; 8; 1030; 348; marginal; marginal; marginal; would rise very sharply; consumer surplus; rose; rose; area *EGIF*; area *EGHF*; area *EGIF*; area *FHI*

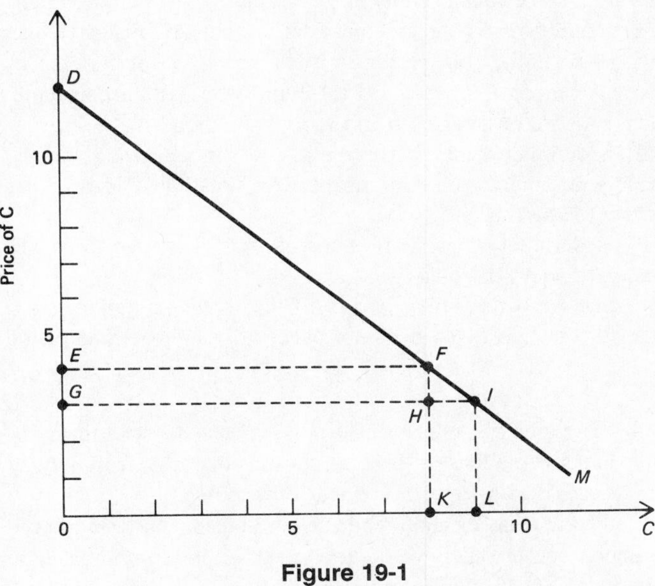

Figure 19-1

QUIZ: Multiple Choice

1. The marginal utility of a commodity is:
(1) an indication of the last use to which the commodity has been put, or the use to which it would next be put if more were available.
(2) the same thing as the price of that commodity.
(3) the relationship that the total utility generated by consuming that commodity bears to the total utility of all other commodities that are consumed.
(4) the extra utility yielded by consuming each successive unit of that commodity.
(5) the same thing as the total utility derived from consuming that commodity.

2. The paradox of value refers to which of the following?
(1) Prices of commodities are not always proportional to the total satisfaction that they give us; witness the fact that some of the absolute necessities of life are inexpensive.
(2) It is impossible to explain the price of a commodity in terms of either demand factors alone or supply factors alone.
(3) It is impossible to explain why people's tastes are what they are, or why they vary from one person to the next.
(4) Some consumers tend to value commodities according to their price, even to the point of buying more if price goes up.
(5) None of the above.

3. The income effect captures which of the following economic phenomena?
(1) If people's money incomes fall, they will normally purchase less of any given commodity.
(2) Any fall in price of a major purchase has an effect similar to a small rise in people's incomes, and this may prompt them to buy even a little more of that good.
(3) The amount purchased of certain goods may actually decrease as people's incomes rise.
(4) As people's incomes rise, they save proportionately more out of income; hence they actually spend a smaller fraction of their incomes.
(5) If the price of a good drops, it is as though the prices of all other goods have risen, in relative terms; hence slightly less of those other goods will tend to be bought.

4. When a consumer is maximizing his or her utility subject to the constraint of income and given prices, then:
(1) the total satisfaction derived from each commodity must equal the total satisfaction derived from every other commodity.
(2) the ratio between total satisfaction derived from any commodity and the price of that commodity must be equal for all commodities.
(3) the satisfaction derived from the last tiny unit of each commodity bought must be equal among all commodities.
(4) the ratio between total satisfaction derived from any commodity and the total expenditure on that commodity must be equal for all commodities.
(5) none of the preceding descriptions is necessarily correct.

5. A consumer's demand curve for any given commodity is most likely to shift to the right (or upward) with:
(1) a rise in the price of substitutes, or a fall in the price of complements.
(2) a rise in the price of either substitutes or complements.
(3) a fall in the price of substitutes, or a rise in the price of complements.
(4) a fall in the price of either substitues or complements.
(5) none of these cases.

6. You have $20 per week available to spend as you wish on commodities A and B. The prices of these commodities, the quantities you now buy, and your evaluation of the utility provided by these quantities are as follows:

	Price	Units Bought	Total Utility	Marginal Utility
A	70¢	20	500	30
B	50	12	1,000	20

For maximum satisfaction, you should:
(1) buy less of A, more of B.
(2) buy the same quantity of A, more of B.
(3) buy more of A, less of B.
(4) buy more of A, the same quantity of B.
(5) remain in your present position, since that position is the best-attainable one.

7. You regard goods X and Y as substitutes. If the price of X rises and there is some income effect from this price rise, then this *income* effect should induce you to:
(1) purchase more of good Y only if the price of X falls short of the price of Y.
(2) purchase less of good Y.
(3) purchase the same amount of Y.
(4) purchase more Y only if the price of X exceeds that of Y.
(5) do none of the above.

8. Which alternative in question 7 would have been correct if it had referred to the *substitution* effect and not to the income effect?
(1).
(2).
(3).
(4).
(5).

9. The price of good X is $1.50 and that of good Y is $1.00. If a consumer considers the marginal utility of Y to be 30 units, and is maximizing utility with respect to purchases of X and Y, then he or she must consider the marginal utility of X to be:
(1) 15 units.
(2) 20 units.
(3) 30 units.
(4) 45 units.
(5) none of the above necessarily; information given is insufficient to tell.

10. If, in question 9, the figure of 30 units had been the total (rather than marginal) utility of Y, which alternative would be correct with respect to the total utility of X?
(1).
(2).
(3).
(4).
(5).

11. The price of good X falls. The income effect (if any) of this price change:
(1) will normally cause X purchases to be increased.
(2) will normally cause X purchases to be decreased.
(3) may cause X purchases either to increase or to decrease, there being no "normal" consequence.
(4) by definition, neither increases nor decreases X purchases.
(5) will not apply, since income effects refer to changes in spendable income, not to price changes.

12. If the marginal utility of a commodity is zero, then:
(1) total utility for this commodity has reached a maximum.
(2) the commodity in question has no utility; i.e., it is not one that consumers want to use.
(3) the paradox of value must be involved.
(4) the consumer has reached his or her equilibrium position with respect to purchase of this commodity.
(5) total utility for this commodity must be zero also.

13. A consumer moves to a new equilibrium position as a result of some change either in market price or in income. In this new equilibrium situation, marginal utilities are all lower than they were in the old equilibrium situation. Tastes or preferences are unchanged. This means that (in utility terms) this consumer:
(1) is definitely worse off in the new situation.
(2) is definitely better off in the new situation.
(3) is definitely worse off in the new situation if income has changed, but not otherwise.
(4) is definitely better off in the new situation is price has changed, but not otherwise.
(5) may be better off or worse off in the new situation, since the information given does not necessarily indicate one or the other.

14. The idea of "consumer surplus" reflects the fact that:
(1) in some purchases, the gain consumers obtain from buying exceeds the gain suppliers obtain from selling.
(2) the purchase of many goods is an immense bargain to consumers, because they would have been willing to pay far more than they actually do in order to get them.
(3) the marginal utility of the first units of a product consumed may considerably exceed the total utility which this product supplies.
(4) total utility increases either when consumer incomes rise or when the prices they must pay for goods fall.
(5) when demand is price inelastic, buyers can obtain a larger quantity for the expenditure of less money.

SUGGESTED ANSWERS TO QUESTIONS IN THE TEXT: Chapter 19

1. Definitions

2. $MU(\text{hamburger})/\$2.00 = MU(\text{coke})/\$0.50$
$= MU(\text{pizza})/\$1.00$
$= MU(\text{hot dog})/\$1.50$

3. Substitutes: beef, lamb, and pork; gum and cigarettes (?); etc.

Complements: beef and ketchup (?); cigarettes and air travel (?); etc.

Independent: beef, etc., and paperbacks.

4. This holds only if the prices of all goods are constant. It is the ratio of marginal utility to price that is constant over all goods in equilibrium.

5. As the price of a good increases, you tend to substitute out of it into a now relatively cheaper good that will provide nearly the same utility; i.e., you reduce the quantity demanded of the good whose price just increased. Meanwhile, the higher price makes your real income smaller and provides a second reason to reduce consumption. With this sort of normal goods story, an increase in the price of a good should be expected to cause the quantity demanded to fall.

6. Now that we have a VCR, . . .

7. Consult the following table for marginal utility numbers.

Days Skied	Marginal Utility
1st	30 − 0 = 30
2d	25
3d	18
4th	15
5th	10
6th	5
7th	0
8th	−3

The demand for skiing, given 1 million skiers with this utility function, would be as follows:

Price	Quantity Demanded
$30	1,000,000 × 1 = 1,000,000
25	2,000,000
18	3,000,000
15	4,000,000
10	5,000,000
5	6,000,000

The reason that marginal utility gives the demand curve is that total utility is cardinal and given in dollar values. Slightly less than 3,000,000 ski days should be expected for a price of $20 per day.

8. Recall the definition of price elasticity and solve for the missing piece of information.

9. The demand curve becomes flatter and flatter, but the percentage changes stay the same. To see why, consider the following simple example. Suppose that a 10 percent increase in price caused two people to reduce their consumption 10 percent from 10 units to 9 units. Together, they would reduce their total consumption from 20 units to 18 units—a 10 percent reduction.

10. If they are all free, then the marginal utilities of all the activities would be the same. If they all had a price, then the ratio of their marginal utilities to their prices would be the same.

APPENDIX: 19

Geometrical Analysis of Consumer Equilibrium

The purpose of this appendix is the same as that of Chapter 19: to explain how consumers can use their fixed incomes to their own best advantage, given their own personal tastes, in the face of universal prices. It begins with the same stylized description of the consumer's dilemma, and it reaches the same results. In fact, only the method of description is different; the whole problem of maximizing satisfaction subject to a budget constraint is illustrated on a single graph.

So why bother? To be sure, the graph deals with a very simple case in which only two goods are involved, but the geometry will nonetheless reveal with increased clarity the general nature of making choices among many times that number of goods in the face of scarcity. The content of the analysis is not, in other words, confined to the two cases that can be drawn on a piece of graph paper.

More important, though, the geometric approach frees us from the assumption that consumers put numerical values onto the satisfaction derived from consuming each unit of a commodity—an assumption which many economists dislike, with good reason. The geometry assumes, instead, that people can display their preferences simply by ranking possible combinations of goods. Constructing the geometry of consumer decision making requires only that consumers are able to express a preference between two or more alternative combinations of any number of goods; ie., they are able to say which combination of goods they want. An approach that features consumers' ranking of preferences as the driving force of demand theory is far easier to swallow than one that relies on consumers' ability to quantitatively evaluate consumption bundles.

Having worked through this appendix, you should accomplish the following learning objectives.

LEARNING OBJECTIVES

1. Define (*a*) indifference curve; (*b*) indifference map.

2. Explain why indifference curves may vary from one individual to the next.

3. Show that it would be impossible for an indifference curve representing normal preferences to run in the southwest-to-northeast direction.

4. Draw a line at any angle across an indifference-map graph, starting at the origin. Move northeast along that line, crossing indifference curves as you do so. Explain whether, in this movement, you are reaching lower levels of utility, are reaching higher levels, or are not changing the utility level at all.

5. Describe what is meant by a budget (or consumption-possibility) line.

6. Explain how the budget line shifts with a price increase (reduction) for one of the two goods involved. Explain how it would move for an income increase (decline).

1. a. Indifference curves are intended to depict a consumer's tastes. Any single indifference-curve line, such as the ones in Figure 19A-1, is made up of a series of points. Each point on such a line stands for a different *amount of money / level of satisfaction / combination of two commodities*. What these points—all the points on any one indifference curve—have in common is that they all represent the same *(amount of money / level of satisfaction / combination of two commodities)* in the eyes of this consumer.

b. We can represent a consumer's **indifference map** by drawing any one or two of *(several / an infinite number of)* indifference lines or curves. Given any two such indifference curves, the one lying farther from the graph's origin—i.e., farther to the northeast—must stand for the *(higher / same / lower)* level of satisfaction. On Figure 19A-1, draw a 45° line from the origin (bottom left-hand corner) of the graph. The four points at which this line crosses the four indifference curves mark four different clothing-food combinations. The farther out the indifference curve from the origin, the larger is the indicated level of consumption of both food and clothing and thus the higher the level of utility (recall that marginal utility is always positive, so supplements in the consumption of any good without some sacrifice of another must improve utility).

c. If two different clothing-food combinations lie on the same indifference curve, then the second must represent more food and less clothing (or vice versa) than the first. (You cannot be

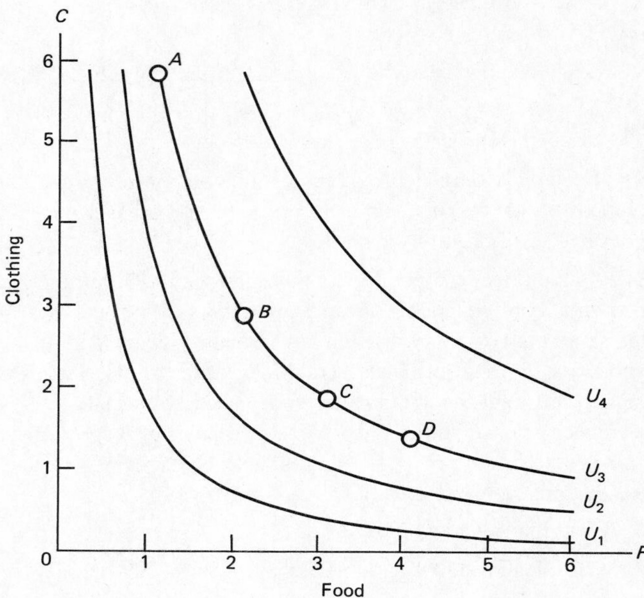

Figure 19A-1

at the same level of satisfaction as before if you have more food and more clothing, or if you have less food and less clothing.) This is indicated by the fact that any single indifference curve runs in a generally *(northeast-to-southwest / northwest-to-southeast)* direction.

---

a. combination of two commodities; level of satisfaction **b.** an infinite number of; higher **c.** northwest-to-southeast

2. a. Now set aside for a moment the indifference-curve idea. Turn, instead, to what you could buy (regardless of your tastes) if blessed with a given income and faced with a particular set of prices.

In the simple two-good case here discussed, all the possible combinations purchasable can be represented by a straight line on a graph—the **budget line** or **consumption-possibility line** in Figure 19A-2.

Be sure you understand the information which this budget or consumption-possibility line is intended to convey. Each and any point on this line stands for a different *(amount of money income / level of satisfaction / combination of the two commodities)*. The combinations are all different, but they all have one thing in common, namely that, given the prices specified, they all *(are purchasable for the same money-income amount / stand for the same level of satisfaction)*.

b. You can move up or down this budget line as you wish; all points thereon are equal so far as the expenditure of money income is concerned. Which point should you choose? That is a matter of your tastes. In the matter of the satisfaction they yield, the various food-clothing combinations on the budget line are

THE BUDGET LINE

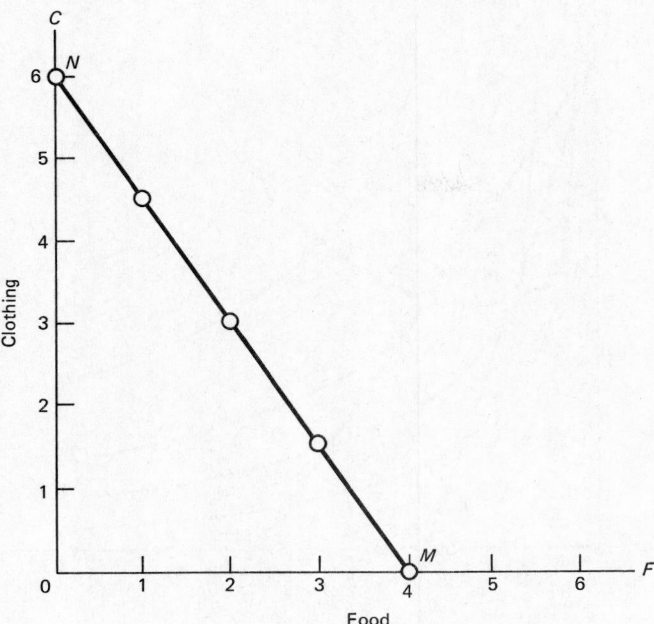

Figure 19A-2

CONSUMER'S EQUILIBRIUM

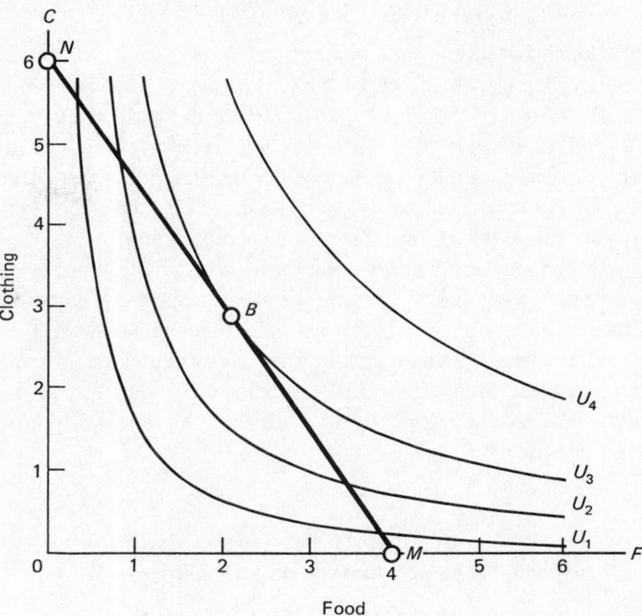

Figure 19A-3

not equal. You should pick the combinations which you like most—the combination which "maximizes your satisfaction."

The mention of tastes pulls us back to indifference curves again. The task of moving back and forth along the budget line, seeking the maximum-satisfaction food-clothing combination, is just a matter of finding the point on this budget line which reaches the *(highest- / lowest-)* attainable indifference curve. This is illustrated in Figure 19A-3. The highest-attainable indifference curve is always the one which lies farthest to the *(northeast / southwest)* on an ordinary graph.

---

a. combination of the two commodities; are purchasable for the same money income amount **b.** highest-; northeast

It is important to note that the division of tastes and budget concerns that is apparent in the organization of question 1 and 2 is more than an accident. It is a division that is, in economic terms, equally clear and well defined. Factors that influence preferences are reflected only in indifference curves; factors that influence what you can afford are reflected only in the budget line.

3. Studying Figure 19A-3, you will see that point *B*, the equilibrium or maximum-satisfaction point, is one at which the indifference curve is just tangent to the budget or consumption-possibility line. That is, equilibrium is a situation where the slope of the one line matches the slope of the other.

It happens that the slope of the budget line is a matter of the prices of the two commodities involved. This question explores the matter more fully.

The slope of the line in Figure 19A-3 (neglecting its negative sign) is 6/4, or 1½. At the two extreme positions, you could have either 6 of *C* and zero *F* (point *N*), or 4 of *F* and zero *C* (point *M*). If you move any distance down the line from point *N*, you find that this 6/4 (or 3/2) swapping ratio applies. If you move from *N* to the middle dot on *NM*, you must give up 3 units of *C*, but you gain 2 units of *F*.

The prices of *F* and *C* govern this swapping ratio. Giving up 3 units of *C* (price $1) recovers $3 of your budget. This you can use to buy 2 units of *F* (price $1.50). So, whether measured at 6/4, 3/2, or $1.50/$1.00, the slope measures market swapping terms. (But note that when we switch from quantities to prices, *C* and *F* change places. You can buy the commodity with the lower price in greater quantity.)

To exercise your understanding of this part, suppose that a budget limits combined expenditure on clothing (*C*) and food (*F*) to $40. With the prices for *C* and *F* as indicated below, compute the slope of the consumption-possibility line (the budget line) first as a ratio of *C*/*F* and then compare that slope to the ratio P_F/P_C. *F* is the commodity measured along the horizontal axis. Assume that all slope values are preceded by an unrecorded minus sign.

	Ratio *C/F*	Ratio P_F/P_C
A P_C = $1, P_F = $4	____/____	____/____
B P_C = $5, P_F = $2	____/____	____/____
C P_C = $2, P_F = $10	____/____	____/____

A: 40, 10; $4, $1; B: 8, 20; $2, $5; C: 20, 4; $10, $2

4. We conclude with a brief survey of the effects of a change in income or in price upon the equilibrium position.

a. Consider income changes first. If your income is halved, then you must cut down on your purchases. The income cut means—look at Figure 19A-4—a shift of the budget line to the *(northeast / southwest)*. The new half-the-income budget line *(is / is not)* parallel to the old one because the prices that define the slope *(have / have not)* changed (see question 3 again if you do not know what prices have to do with anything).

In this new and painful income situation, you will not necessarily buy food and clothing in the same proportions as before. You must cut your purchases, and may indeed cut each of them by 50 percent, but you may not. The point you pick on your new budget line will be governed, as before, by your tastes. You may wind up buying relatively more food and less clothing, or vice versa.

EFFECT OF INCOME CHANGE ON EQUILIBRIUM

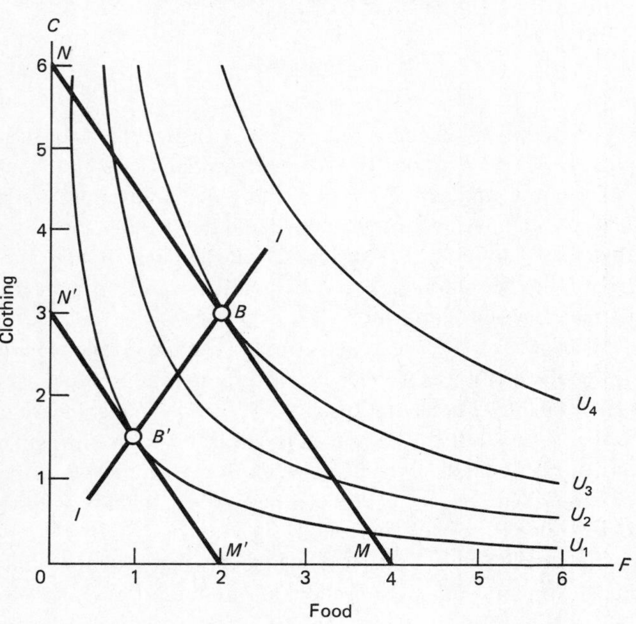

Figure 19A-4

b. An increase in the price of food or of clothing works somewhat like an income reduction: it pulls you down to a lower satisfaction level. But compare Figure 19A-5 (illustrating an increase in food price) with Figure 19A-4 (income reduction). In both instances, the budget line shifts in position. In Figure 19A-5, the new budget line *(is / is not)* parallel with the old one. The point is that if you wanted to spend all your income on clothing, a food-price increase would not affect you. Point N (Figure 19A-5) is still attainable. At the other extreme, if you

EFFECT OF PRICE CHANGE ON EQUILIBRIUM

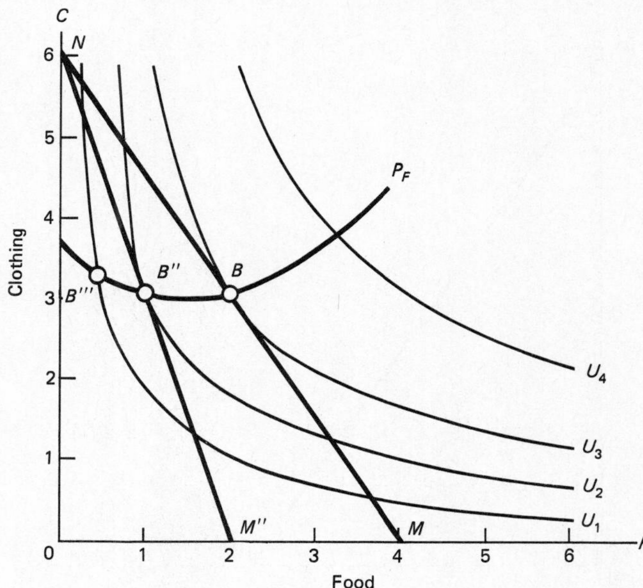

Figure 19A-5

spend all your income on food, a doubling of its price would *(leave you unaffected / require you to halve your purchases)*.

That is why the budget line shifts as it does. As before, you pick the best-attainable position on your new budget line, as your personal tastes dictate. There is more to be said on these topics, but it must be left for more advanced texts.

---

a. southwest; is; have not **b.** is not; require you to halve your purchases

5. In the upper part of Figure 19A-6, the line AB_0 is a consumer's initial budget line, and E_0 is his or her equilibrium point thereon. The curved line is an indifference curve for this consumer, and it is tangent to the budget line at this E_0 point. (The two other curved lines are also indifference curves.) The price of good X is \$4.

a. The consumer's income or budget must be:

(1) \$50.

(2) \$20.

(3) \$10.

(4) \$5.

(5) \$2.

(6) impossible to tell.

b. The price of good Y must be:

(1) \$1.

(2) \$2.

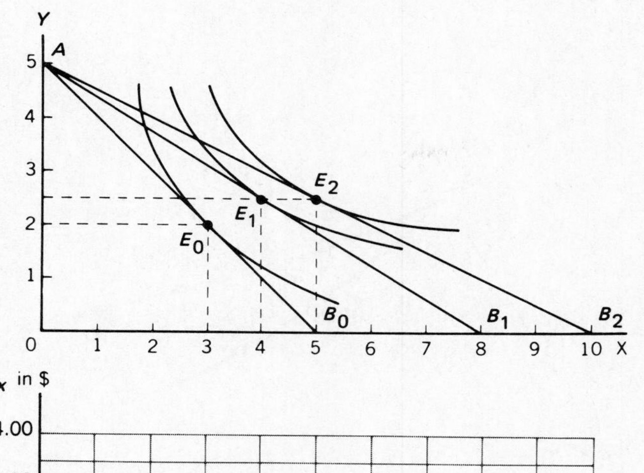

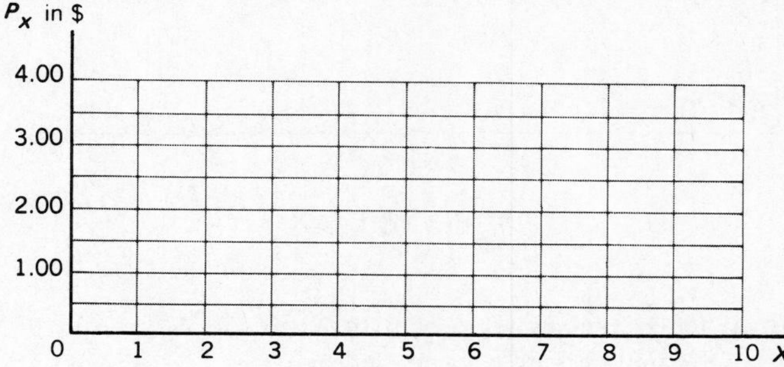

Figure 19A-6

(3) \$3.

(4) \$4.

(5) \$5.

(6) impossible to tell from diagram.

c. The budget or consumption-possibility line shifts from position AB_0 to position AB_1. Such a shift could be caused only by:

(1) a fall in the price of X.

(2) a rise in the price of X.

(3) a rise in the price of Y.

(4) a fall in the price of Y.

(5) an increase in income.

d. Quantitatively, what change is indicated by the shift from AB_0 to AB_1? That is, whether it is price of X, price of Y, or income that has changed, what is its new value?

(1) \$50.

(2) \$20.

(3) \$10.

(4) \$5.

(5) \$2.50.

(6) \$2.

(7) \$1.

e. If a further shift in the *AB* line occurs, from AB_1 to AB_2, which alternative in part **c** explains it? . . . *(1 / 2 / 3 / 4 / 5)*

f. Which alternative in part **d** indicates the new value of the magnitude which has changed? . . *(1 / 2 / 3 / 4 / 5 / 6 / 7)*

g. Use the lower part of Figure 19A-6 to show the demand curve of the consumer in the preceding questions for commodity X. This demand curve is to be drawn given the particular level of income and price of good Y indicated by the preceding questions. Plot three points on this curve, correctly indicating the consumer's demand for X in these circumstances. (*Hint*: What price or prices of X must go with the three consumption-possibility lines illustrated? What quantity or quantities of X will be bought? Join these three points with a smooth curve.)

---

a. (2) b. (4) c. (1) d. (5) (\$2.50 = P_X) **e. (1)** (another fall in the price of X) **f. (6)** (\$2 = P_X) **g.** There are three combinations of price and quantity that can be gleaned from the top of Figure 19A-6: (P_X = \$4, X = 3), (P_X = \$2.50, X = 4), and (P_X = \$2, X = 5), from budget lines AB_0, AB_1, and AB_2, respectively.

QUIZ: Multiple Choice

1. The position and shape of any indifference curve for any particular consumer are governed:
(1) by his or her tastes and by the amount of the income or budget.
(2) solely by the prices of the goods bought.
(3) by tastes, by the amount of income, and by the prices of the goods bought.
(4) by the prices of the goods bought and by the amount of income, not by tastes.
(5) solely by his or her tastes.

2. Which alternative in question 1 correctly names the factor or factors governing the budget line?
(1).
(2).
(3).
(4).
(5).

3. On an indifference-curve map, a consumer's approach to the equilibrium position is properly described as follows. The consumer:
(1) moves to that point on the budget line representing the combination of goods having the highest money value.
(2) moves to that point on the budget line whose slope equals the ratio of the two prices.
(3) moves along the budget line until the extra utility supplied by one good is just equal to the extra utility supplied by the other.

(4) picks the highest-valued indifference curve which the budget line makes attainable.
(5) picks the highest-valued budget line which the indifference curve makes attainable.

4. Among the following five statements describing indifference-curve analysis, one is incorrect. Which one?
(1) Each point on an indifference curve stands for a different combination of two goods.
(2) Each point on a budget line stands for a different combination of two goods.
(3) All points on an indifference curve stand for the same level of real income in the sense of satisfaction.
(4) All points on a budget line stand for the same level of money income.
(5) All points on an indifference curve stand for the same level of money income.

5. You are told that an indifference curve involving goods X and Y runs from southwest to northeast. Your response to this statement is that this:
(1) must indicate an increase in the consumer's income.
(2) is impossible because it would indicate that the consumer gets no satisfaction at all from X, or else none from Y.
(3) must indicate a change in the consumer's tastes.
(4) must indicate a change in the price of either X or Y.
(5) is impossible because larger quantities of both X and Y cannot indicate the same satisfaction level as lesser quantities thereof, unless the consumer wants no more of either of these two goods.

SUGGESTED ANSWERS TO QUESTIONS IN THE TEXT: Appendix to Chapter 19

1. Using ">" to denote "preferred to" and "≈" to denote "indifferent to," consider Figure TQ19A-1. There, indifference curves I and II cross at point *A*. Because moving from point

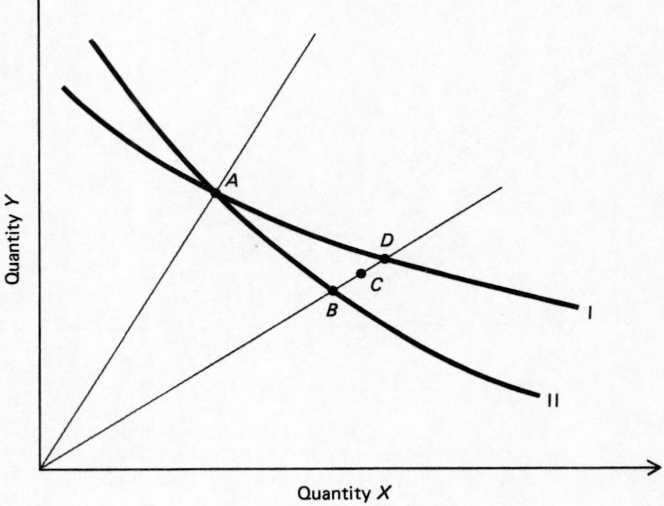

Figure TQ 19A-1

B to *C* to *D* involves more of both X and Y, $D > C > B$. Because *B* and *A* are on the same indifference curve (curve II), $B \approx A$. Because *D* and *A* are on the same indifference curve (curve I), $D \approx A$. So it must be that $D \approx B$, but $D > B$. This contradiction was caused by the intersection of curves I and II.

2. Move along the budget constraint in the direction of the interior of the area that is (*a*) above the indifference curve *and* (*b*) below the budget constraint.

3. As the price of food increases from $1.50 to $3.00 and finally to $6.00 per unit, the quantity demanded falls from 2 units to 1 unit and finally to 0.5 unit. Downward sloping for reasons of substitution and income effects.

4. As long as the number always increases as the curve gets further from the origin, the tangency of the curve indicating the highest utility is unaffected.

5. Figure TQ19A-2.

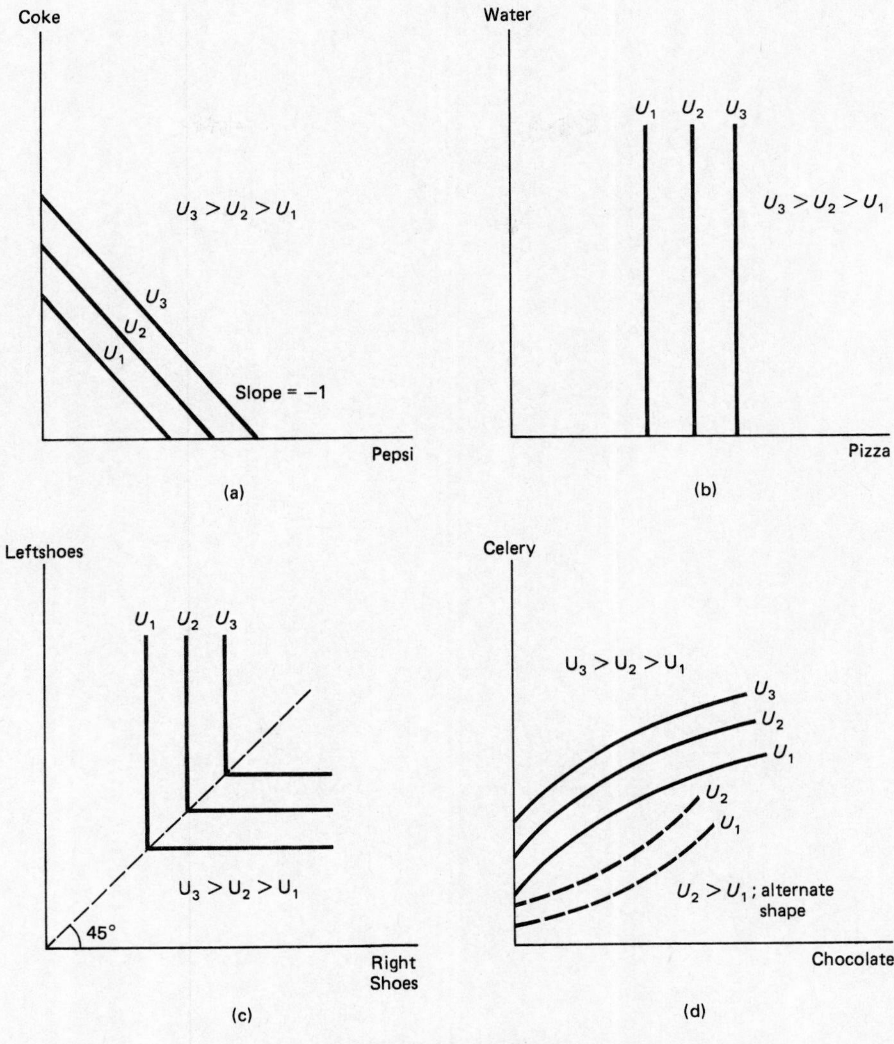

Figure TQ 19A-2

CHAPTER 20
BUSINESS ORGANIZATION

There are, late in the 1980s, more than 17 billion businesses in the United States. The largest preponderance of these businesses are independent proprietorships, but these forms of business are hardly ever very large. For average annual sales of less than $40,000, proprietors work long and hard (50 to 60 hours per week). They typically face chronic cash flow problems, but they find bankers reluctant to lend them money without assessing high-risk premiums. Help in these matters is sometimes available from the Small Business Administration and/or small-business investment companies, but not always. Proprietors own their own businesses and are thus their own bosses, of course, but they face personal income taxation if they are unusually successful and unlimited liability if they are not. It is not life on Easy Street.

The least popular form of business organization is the partnership. Partnerships are typically larger than an individual proprietorship, with average annual sales in the neighborhood of $200,000, but the good news might stop there. Partners face the personal income tax, risk, unlimited liability, and experience cash flow problems just like the proprietor. In addition, partners share decision-making authority with other people. Partnerships may, therefore, appear to some to capture all the bad characteristics of proprietorships without garnering any of the advantages of incorporation.

Corporations represent the third and last major form of business organization. They tend to be large and powerful. Their average annual sales hover around $2 million, but over 250 corporations sell more than $1 billion in goods and services annually. Owners typically forfeit decision-making authority to professional managers, but they are rewarded for this sacrifice with liability limited to the amount of their investment. Corporations can last forever, too, so that a voluntary or involuntary decision of one owner to leave the corporation is hardly ever noticed—his or her stock is simply sold in the market or bequested in a will to someone else. Corporate income is subject to the corporate income (profits) tax, and dividends are awarded out of the remaining after-tax income to individual stockholders. These dividends are, of course, subject themselves to the personal income tax. The system therefore effectively sets up a sort of double taxation that has made the corporate income tax one of this country's most controversial.

Having worked through the story of the computer-software company in the text and the problems recorded here, the reader should have met the following objectives.

LEARNING OBJECTIVES

1. Explain the differences between the three major forms of business organization: proprietorship, partnership, and corporation.

2. Explain the three roles that firms play in a modern economy.

3. Explain the meaning of unlimited liability as its applies to each of the three forms.

4. Explain why any growing business is likely to find itself in potentially acute need of more capital financing.

5. Explain the propensity of large businesses to be incorporated.

6. List the advantages and/or disadvantages to any individual with money to invest across the three business forms.

7. Distinguish between (*a*) bonds, (*b*) common stock, (*c*) bank loans, and (*d*) retained earnings as mechanisms for raising new capital. Note the advantages and disadvantages of each in the context of the corporate income tax.

8. Outline what is meant by the "divorce of ownership and control" in large corporations. List social problems that this divorce might create.

9. Define and explain the following sources of growth: (*a*) knowledge, (*b*) sales personnel, (*c*) economies of scale, (*d*) vertical integration, (*e*) horizontal integration, and (*f*) diversification.

10. Understand the basic objectives of and defenses against corporate takeovers.

Much of this chapter concentrates on a single theme: the form that a business takes—be it proprietorship, partnership, or corporation—is almost always dictated by the amount of money needed to operate in the chosen line of work. In many industries, in fact, there is simply no room for choice, and only large corporations are found. If large quantities of money are required for successful operation in some line of work, then no individual proprietorship or small partnership will be found. In other areas of business, there are choices, and other forms can flourish (or at least hope to).

The need for money—financial capital—can be explained in terms of two distinct phenomena. First of all, firms typically find it necessary to buy expensive, long-lasting machinery, tools, equipment, buildings, etc.; i.e., firms usually find it impossible to operate without making substantial investments in procuring and maintaining physical capital. They have to pay for this capital before it earns enough return to pay for itself, so they need some money "up front." Second, there is an inevitable lag between the money expenditure (for labor, raw materials, transportation costs, etc.) and money receipts (from the sale of product). A growing and vital business therefore needs **working capital** even when it is not buying more physical capital. Both needs work constantly to make just about every business feel "cash poor."

Incorporation is, above all else, a device that makes it easier to raise large quantities of money. Ownership shares in a corporation can be sold to a small number of people or to a large number of people at a price which reflects the value of the ownership claims that they represent. People will buy these shares because they can be attractive financial assets. They can be bought in almost any quantity. They release the shareholder from any concern about running the business; professional managers are hired to do that. The limited liability that they carry guarantees that, even in the very worst of circumstances, shareholder losses will be no larger than the purchase price of the stock. They can be sold at any time without the corporation's consent (though perhaps not without a spousal consent or needle). And it is *incorporation* that opens the door to this form of money harvest.

The text illustrates these points by showing how the need for money might inspire a fictitious software company to grow from a small proprietorship into a successful corporation. The following questions emphasize the lessons of that story.

1. Five people own equal shares in a partnership. For any one of the five, **unlimited liability** holds that any person is responsible for *(20 percent of the partnership's debts, up to the amount he or she has invested in the business / 20 percent of the partnership debts, no matter how large the amount / 100 percent of the partnership debts, if necessary, in the event that other partners cannot pay their shares, no matter how large the amount).*

---

100 percent of the partnership debts, if necessary, in the event the other partners cannot pay their shares, no matter how large the amount

2. Note that in this chapter the word "capital" has a meaning quite different from that given it in Chapter 3. "Capital" in the physical sense of that earlier chapter means *(money used to finance a business / money loaned with a strong element of risk involved / manufactured production inputs, not money).*

"Capital" in this present chapter means money.

---

manufactured productive inputs, not money

3. a. A corporation *(must / may or may not)* have common stock. The law which created the corporate form says that a corporation must have owners—and the stockholders are its owners.

This stock *(must / may or may not)* be listed on an exchange, such as the New York Stock Exchange. (Actually, only a surprisingly small number of giant corporations have their stock so listed. Many corporations are "private," in the sense that their stock is not publicly listed for trading. Often this stock is held entirely or almost entirely by members of a single family, only rarely changing hands.)

b. A corporation *(must / may or may not)* have bonds outstanding. The vital difference between stocks and bonds is that bonds are *(certificates of ownership / IOUs).* The corporation is free to borrow (i.e., issue such IOUs) or not to borrow, as it sees fit.

---

a. must; may or may not **b.** may or may not; IOUs

4. Put a check in the spaces below if the description properly applies to a bond (B), a common stock (S) and/or a stock option (O); you may want to check more than one box on a few of the lines.

	B	O	S
a. Income generated is called interest.			
b. Income generated is called a dividend. . .			
c. Does not pay more than a fixed and stated amount of income to owner.			
d. No specified dollar amount of income implied in ownership.			
e. Represents a share of ownership in corporation.			

	B	O	S
f. Represents corporation's IOU, not a share of ownership.			
g. Offers complete assurance of steady annual income for owner.			
h. Annual payment to purchaser is a fixed obligation of corporation.			
i. Offers a chance for capital gain.			
j. May be sold or canceled at any time by purchaser without consulting corporation.			
k. Among these three types, offers greatest assurance of steady annual income.			
l. Corporation will buy it back for stated amount at specified future date.			
m. Must be issued by every business corporation.			
n. Has limited liability feature for owner.			
o. Income anticipated is essentially a capital gain if executed.			
p. Income must be paid to owner in all circumstances short of bankruptcy.			
q. Represents a purchase agreement contracted on a contingency basis.			
r. Income paid to owner only when board of directors decides it should be paid.			
s. Income received therefrom is subject to personal income tax.			
t. Is equity capital for corporation.			
u. Is a fixed charge for corporation.			

Bond: a, c, f, h, i, j, k, l, n, p, s, u
Option: d, i, j, n, o, p, q, r, s, t
Common: b, d, e, i, j, m, n, r, s, t
None: g (Not even interest is *completely* ensured.)

5. a. Two businesses are identical with one another with respect to size, machinery, competence of working force, cash on hand, etc. They differ only in that No. 1 is a newly organized concern and No. 2 has established a good reputation over 20 years. If you could buy either of these for the same price, the better buy would be *(No. 1 / No. 2)*. In fact, the worth of *(No. 1 / No. 2)* would exceed that of the other company. The best possible estimate of the extra worth of this company in dollars is called its *(fixed assets / net worth / monopoly power / goodwill / equity capital)*.

b. Suppose promoters buy such an established company. They then sell stock to the public, and in the process they deliberately exaggerate the money worth of such *(fixed assets / net worth / monopoly power / goodwill)*, or the worth of other assets, in order to sell the stock at a higher price. This process is called *(watering the stock / incurring fixed charges / obtaining inequity capital / making a capital gain)*.

a. No. 2; No. 2; goodwill **b.** goodwill; watering the stock

6. In each blank below, put (H) if the act in question represents *horizontal integration*; put (V) if *vertical integration*; put (N) if neither.

a. An aluminum-manufacturing company buys a bauxite mine. (Bauxite is the ore from which aluminum is made.) (_______)

b. The same company buys a competing aluminum-manufacturing concern. . . . . (_______)

c. It builds a fabricating plant to process aluminum sheeting into finished aluminum consumer goods. . . . . . . (_______)

d. It buys a chain of retail hardware stores in order to market its aluminum products more effectively. . . . . . (_______)

e. It buys a second chain of retail stores to expand its market still further. . . . . (_______)

a. V **b.** H **c.** V **d.** V **e.** H

7. a. The function of an investment banking firm is to (pick one):

(1) accept money deposits from its customers or clientele and to lend out this money to corporations.

(2) act as intermediary between corporations wishing to raise money by a bond or stock issue and people with money available to purchase such securities.

b. When an investment banking firm underwrites a stock or bond issue, this means it gives its assurance to (pick one):

(1) the buyers of the issue that it is of good quality, at the risk of incurring liability to those buyers should trouble later develop.

(2) the sellers of the issue that they will receive a specified price, the bank taking the risk that it may itself have to buy some part of the issue at that price, then sell it later at a lower price.

a. (2) **b.** (2)

QUIZ: Multiple Choice

1. The term "limited liability" is frequently used in enumerating the characteristics of a corporation. It means that:

(1) any officer of the corporation is strictly limited in his or her ability to speak for the corporation and commit it to any liability.
(2) once shareholders have paid for their stock, they have no further financial obligation, regardless of how much trouble the corporation gets into.
(3) the corporation's liability to pay dividends to its stockholders is a limited one, since it need pay them only if it has earned a profit.
(4) there are certain obligations which a corporation can legally refuse to pay.
(5) the corporation has only a limited obligation to meet claims made by any single person or firm against it (provided it has acted within the scope of its charter), so that there is some protection for its assets and financial position.

2. A corporation's obligation to pay interest on bonds it has issued is properly described by which of the following statements?
(1) Interest *must* be paid regardless of whether a profit has been earned or not.
(2) Interest *must* be paid only when a profit has been earned.
(3) Interest need not be paid even if a profit has been earned, but it *must* be paid before any dividend is paid.
(4) Normally, interest ranks ahead of dividends, but there are some circumstances in which a dividend can be paid without payment of bond interest.
(5) Interest ranks behind dividends, and is paid only after dividends have been paid in full.

3. In considering the order or ranking in which a corporation is obligated to pay out various sums of money, payment of dividends on common stock takes precedence over:
(1) corporation income taxes.
(2) local property taxes.
(3) the salaries of management.
(4) bond interest.
(5) none of these obligations.

4. The primary business of an investment banking firm is to:
(1) make loans to small businesses.
(2) sell corporation securities.
(3) accept money deposits from its customers.
(4) own the shares of a number of corporations—i.e., act as a "holding company."
(5) sell its own securities, using the proceeds to buy stock in other corporations.

5. A preferred stock is like a:
(1) bond, because the dividend must always be paid by the corporation.
(2) bond, because the holder of such stock is legally a creditor of the corporation rather than a part owner.
(3) bond, since both bond interest and preferred-stock dividend payments are considered operating costs rather than distributions of profit.
(4) common stock, because dividends on both stock types ordinarily increase when company profits increase.
(5) common stock, since no dividend need be paid on either stock if the board of directors decides it is inappropriate to pay one.

6. The term "goodwill" refers to:
(1) a valuation placed on the personal integrity of those who own or operate the business.
(2) a fictitious increase in the company's net worth position, created by inflating the value of one or more assets to an exaggerated figure.
(3) the earning power of the business.
(4) the extra earning power of the business resulting from its established position.
(5) providing working capital for established customers by allowing them extra time for settlement of their accounts.

7. A corporation that is considering debt financing (financing via a bond issue) must recognize that:
(1) bonds always involve a fixed annual charge to be paid to debt holders whether the corporation has earned profits or not.
(2) the issuance of debt gives the debt holders a voice in the management of the corporation's affairs, so that they may usurp some part of management's authority.
(3) the new debt holders are not necessarily the same group as the original stockholders, so that the ownership shares of those stockholders are diluted by debt financing.
(4) it does not actually bring in any additional cash to the corporation.
(5) this method of financing first requires an amendment to the corporation's charter.

8. If a steel-producing company merges with two other companies, one a producer of iron ore, the other a company which fabricates steel into finished or semifinished steel products, this would be an example of:
(1) vertical integration.
(2) establishing a holding company.
(3) the acquisition of venture capital.
(4) the development of goodwill.
(5) none of the preceding.

9. Today's most common ownership and control arrangement for large American corporations is best described by which of the following statements?
(1) The professional managers are also the group owning a majority or near-majority of stock, so that they can make all major decisions without real consideration of the wishes of minority stockholders.
(2) The professional managers make all the major decisions, and the board of directors does not intervene unless it is losing confidence in those managers.
(3) The professional managers control the company on all matters of importance except for basic decisions on such matters as

production, new plants, and new products, these being left to the board of directors as stockholder representatives.
(4) The board of directors makes the decisions on all matters of real importance, the role of the professional managers being confined to routine matters.
(5) The stockholders rather than the board of directors are increasingly making major decisions, through voting-power control exercised at stockholder meetings.

10. If an investment banking house underwrites a stock or a bond issue for some corporation, it:
(1) gives its personal guarantee that the interest or dividend promised in this issue will be paid as specified.
(2) lends the corporation an amount of money equal to the value of that issue, to be repaid when the issue in question has been fully sold to the public.
(3) sells the issue to its customers, with the assurance that, upon request and within a specified time period, it will buy back any part thereof, at a specified minimum price.
(4) acts as agent for the corporation, but without any firm guarantee as to the amount of the issue it will sell or the price it can obtain.
(5) guarantees the corporation full sale of that issue at a fixed price, even if the bank has to buy part of the issue itself.

11. A corporation's obligation with respect to payment of interest on loans (B) and dividends on common stock (CS) is correctly described as follows. It:
(1) must pay its bond interest if it has earned sufficient profit to do so, but pays a CS dividend only if the board of directors so decides.
(2) must pay both if profits are sufficient to do so.
(3) must pay its interest regardless of profit earned or loss incurred, but pays its CS dividend only if the board of directors so decides.
(4) must pay both regardless of profit earned or loss incurred, unless so doing would force it into bankruptcy.
(5) need pay neither regardless of the amount of profit earned, unless the board of directors decides on such dividend payment, although the bond interest must have priority.

12. The usual progression through business forms is:
(1) partnership, proprietorship, corporation.
(2) proprietorship, partnership, corporation.
(3) partnership, corporation, proprietorship.
(4) nonexistent because there does not exist a typical evolution.

13. Which of the following sources of investment capital comes from internal sources?
(1) Stock sales.
(2) Bank loans.
(3) Depreciation.
(4) Bond sales.
(5) None of the above.

14. The personal income tax of the United States is, through the personal returns of stockholders, applied:
(1) in full to any corporation's entire income regardless of whether or not it is distributed in the form of dividends.
(2) only to that part of profits that is actually distributed as dividends.
(3) only to that part of income not paid out as dividends but held instead as retained earnings.
(4) neither to dividends nor to retained earnings.
(5) both to dividends and to retained earnings, but with dividends getting preferential treatment.

15. If question 14 had referred to the U.S. corporate income tax, then the correct answer would have been:
(1).
(2).
(3).
(4).
(5).

SUGGESTED ANSWERS TO QUESTIONS IN THE TEXT: Chapter 20

1. Economies of scale account for most large corporations—at least concentrated portions of large corporations that today tend to be conglomerates. Piecework of all kinds, consulting services, a variety of personal services (haircuts, etc.), garden vegetables, etc., may be produced simply by individuals and not by business firms.

2. Appeal to the definitions; focus on liability and availability of financial capital.

3. Focus on the evolution of a firm from proprietorship through corporation, using its need for financial capital as a unifying thread; the evolution leads from using personal funds and loans through floating all sorts of stock issues.

4. The financial decision depends upon relative cost and risk; remember that interest *must* be paid, while dividends need not be paid.

5. The key is constructing the appropriate incentives so that rewards and/or penalties for management depend upon efficiency, or the lack thereof—pecuniary (cash, stock options, etc.) and nonpecuniary (ridicule, honoraria, etc.) rewards and penalties can both work.

6. Business run by people hired by the owners, not the owners themselves. Corporations are typically run by such management staffs.

7. Almost anything can generate conflict at shareholder meetings. There is harmony only when the perceived goals of management jive with the articulated goals of the shareholders.

APPENDIX: 20

Elements of Accounting

Accounting concepts are among the realities of life in the economic age. This appendix provides an introduction to two of the basics: the balance sheet and the income statement. The **balance sheet** is a snapshot of financial health; it reflects the economic condition of an economic entity at some prescribed point in time. The **income statement** is, by way of contrast, a motion picture—it reflects growth or problems over a given period of time; it clarifies the blur between two different snapshots. Having completed work on this appendix, you will have met the following objectives.

LEARNING OBJECTIVES

1. Explain carefully the information which a balance sheet is intended to convey. List the major categories appearing on the two sides of a balance sheet, and indicate the meaning (or definition) of each of those categories.

2. List the major items appearing on an income statement. Indicate the information which an income statement is intended to convey. (Include the beginning inventory and closing inventory items in your listing, and explain the need for their appearance.)

3. Explain why some cash expenditures by a firm do not appear on its income statement, and why some items that are not cash expenditures do appear.

4. Distinguish between (*a*) straight-line depreciation, declining-balance depreciation, and accelerated depreciation; (*b*) depreciation charges on the income statement and allowance for depreciation on the balance sheet; (*c*) addition to earnings retained on the income statement and earnings retained on the balance sheet.

The principal lesson of this appendix concerns the kinds of information that two accounting forms are intended to convey: the balance sheet and the income (or profit-and-loss) statement.

The balance sheet is a point-in-time statement. Its primary function is to record what the company is "worth," as closely as can be estimated, at some point in time.

The balance sheet begins by listing the firm's assets: everything it owns—cash, buildings, equipment, inventory and so on. Each item is given a money value, the best possible estimate of its money worth at that point in time. Sometimes the estimating job isn't easy. There is no problem in figuring the worth of a given amount of cash, but reckoning the true present worth of a factory building or of an elderly machine may be a tough job. Among these assets, the company can and should include legitimate money claims on others (e.g., money owed by its customers). Sometimes, "intangible" assets are included; but you should disregard these for now.

The firm's "worth" is not likely to be the same figure as the total of its assets. Any debts owed to others—its liabilities–must be deducted. The resulting figure is its net worth. Note carefully:

Net worth, by definition, is assets minus liabilities.

Accordingly, it must also be true that

Total assets = total liabilities + net worth.

Balance sheets are ordinarily drawn up in precisely this manner: assets in one column; liabilities in an adjoining column; net worth below liabilities. To say that "the balance sheet always balances" is just to say that the Assets column total must be the same as the Liabilities plus Net Worth column total. This must be true, because net worth is defined to be whatever figure is needed to make things come out even; that's how it is computed.

Turning now to the income (or profit-and-loss) statement:

The income statement is a period-of-time statement. Its primary function is to record how much profit the company earned from its sales during that period (e.g., 1 year).

The income statement begins by listing the total of goods sold during the period in question, at their sale price. From this sales total are deducted all the expenses that ought properly to be charged as part of the cost of making and selling the goods in question, but only the expenses that ought to be so charged. What's left after deduction of these expenses is the company's profit for the period in question.

Watch out for the most common of income-statement mistakes: do not assume that income statements record only cash transactions. It is true that the sales total is likely to be matched by a cash inflow of approximately the same amount; but some of the "expenses" listed on an income statement need not entail any cash outputment during the period involved, and some cash outpayments that were made during the period will not show up on the income statement at all.

If some items shown on an income statement do not stand for cash transactions, and if some cash transactions during the period aren't shown on that statement, then net profit (at the bottom of the income statement) is certainly not going to be an accurate record of the change in the company's cash position. It isn't intended to be. Every item on an income statement, or on a balance sheet, has a money figure appended. But in almost all instances, this is using "money" in its abstract, "estimate-of-value" sense, and not in the sense of "cash on hand." If you want to know how much cash a company has, its balance sheet is a very good place to look. But don't look for it under esoteric categories like net worth or retained earnings. Just look under cash on hand.

1. In December 1988, the Utter Confusion Manufacturing Company was formed, with sale for cash of 5000 shares of common stock at $10 apiece.

Table 20A-1

Assets		Liabilities and Net Worth	
Cash	$____	Liabilities	$____
		Net worth:	
		Capital	$____

On Table 20A-1, show this firm's balance sheet as of December 31, 1988. Assume that the proceeds from the entire $50,000 stock sale are still held in cash and that no other transactions have yet taken place. Note that Table 20A-1 is set up in the conventional way: a column headed Assets at the left, a column headed Liabilities and Net Worth on the right.

Assets		Liabilities and Net Worth	
Cash	$50,000	Liabilities	$ 0
		Net worth:	
		Capital	50,000

2. During 1989 the firm's operations were as follows:

1. Money received (all in cash):
   A. Sales of merchandise manufactured ... $115,000
   B. Bonds sold (100 bonds @ $1,000) 100,000
2. Money paid out (all in cash):
   A. Machinery purchased $170,000
   B. Raw materials purchased for use 50,000
   C. Wages paid to labor 24,000
   D. Interest paid on bond issue 10,000
3. Other factors (not involving cash received or paid):

All raw materials purchased were fully used up in manufacturing before the year-end (i.e., closing inventory of raw materials was zero).

All finished goods manufactured were sold (i.e., zero finished-goods closing inventory).

Depreciation on machinery was estimated at $17,000. (i.e., the machinery that was worth $170,000 when bought—say, on January 1—was estimated as being worth only $153,000 on December 31, having been partly "used up" or worn out by use during the year; it does not mean a cash outlay of $17,000.)

The interest rate paid on the bonds is 10 percent. Note that item 2D shows interest paid as $10,000; assume the bonds were floated on January 1, 1989.

a. How much cash did Utter Confusion have on December 31, 1989? (Start with the cash it had when the year began; you have this figure from question 1. Add the money received from sales of merchandise and bonds, listed above; then deduct the various cash outlays also listed.) $__________

b. On Table 20A-2, draw up the firm's balance sheet as of December 31, in three steps:

1. Run through the information above for assets held at the year-end, to be listed at their proper value on that date. (*Hint*: You have already dealt with cash; you should find only one other asset.)
2. Do the same for liabilities. (*Hint*: You should find only one.)

Table 20A-2

Assets (thousands)			Liabilities and Net Worth (thousands)		
Current: Cash		$____	Current Liabilities		$____
Fixed			Long-term liabilities:		
Machinery	$____		Bonds		$____
Less: dep'n allowance			Net worth		
			Capital	$____	
	$____	$____	Retained Earnings	$____	$____
		$____			$____

3. Repeat for net worth. Remember that net worth must be whatever figure is needed to prop the balance sheet into balance. Follow the convention of dividing net worth between capital and retained earnings. Leave capital at $50,000 (because no more stock was sold during the year). Let retained earnings be the line within net worth to perform the balancing act.

---

a. 11,000

b. (To save space, the final three zeros have been dropped—e.g., $11,000 is written $11.)

[Note that the assets have been divided between current and fixed, and liabilities between current and long-term. The original value of machinery ($170) is shown; then accumulated depreciation is deducted, in order to reach its proper current value of $153. These are simply accounting conventions.]

Assets			Liabilities and Net Worth		
Current: Cash		$ 11	Current Liabilities		$ 0
			Long-term liabilities:		
Fixed:			Bonds		100
Machinery	$170		Net worth:		
Less: Dep'n.			Capital	$50	
allowance	17	153	Retained earnings	14	64
		$164			$164

3. In this and the three questions following, we develop the firm's income (or profit-and-loss) statement for 1989, using the information already furnished in question 2.

Remember that this income statement (*a*) records revenue earned from sales in 1989, (*b*) deducts from this revenue the costs of making and selling the goods in question, and (*c*) shows the income (or profit) remaining after that deduction. It indicates also the disposition of that profit (paid out as a dividend, or retained within the business).

The sales figure is obviously $115,000. Raw materials purchases and wages are clearly expense items to be subtracted from sales revenue. Are there other items? Ought the machinery expenditure of $170,000 be included as a cost to be deducted on the income statement? . . . . *(Yes / No)*

no (Deduct only costs that should be applied against the goods sold. The $170,000 did not go into the making of those goods, as witness the fact that at the close of the period, the firm still has something worth $153,000 left out of its initial $170,000 outlay.)

4. **a.** Is there any "machinery cost" associated with 1980 production? ______

b. This depreciation *(was / was not)* a cash outlay. It *(should / should not)* be recorded as an expense on the 1980 income statement *(despite / because of)* this fact.

a. yes, depreciation, $17,000 (This is an estimate, in money terms, of the extent to which the machinery was "used up" or worn out as a result of its work in 1980.) **b.** was not; should; despite (For comment on this point, see the introductory discussion immediately preceding question 1.)

5. The 1989 bond sale of $100,000 *(ought / ought not)* to appear on the income statement. What must be recorded on that statement, however, is ______

ought not; bond interest (The fact that the company borrowed $100,000 to buy machinery and the like has nothing to do with the income statement, but the interest it must pay on borrowed money is a cost of doing business. As such, it must be recorded as an expense.)

6. On Table 20A-3, draw up the income statement.

Table 20A-3

Sales		$ ______
Less manfacturing cost of goods sold:		
Raw materials bought	$ ______	
Labor cost (wages)	$ ______	
Dep'n. on machinery	$ ______	$ ______
Gross profit		$ ______
Deduct bond interest		$ ______
Net profit and addition to retained earnings		$ ______

Sales		$115
Less manfacturing cost of goods sold:		
Raw materials bought	$50	
Labor cost (wages)	24	
Dep'n. on machinery	17	91
Gross profit		$ 24
Deduct bond interest		10
Net profit and addition to retained earnings		$ 14

(Note the convention of deducting bond interest after manufacturing costs.)

7. The addition to retained earnings figure on this income statement is *(the same as / different from)* the retained earnings figure on the year-end balance sheet. This *(is / is not)* a coincidence. The earnings retained in the business figure on the balance sheet is the total of all income (profit) earned, for all years since incorporation, minus all dividends paid out throughout that period.

For example, if Utter Confusion's income statement for the following year (1990) ended with an addition to retained earnings of $18,000, the retained earnings on the end-of-1990 balance sheet would be $*(14,000 / 18,000 / 28,000 / 32,000)*.

the same as; is not; 32,000

8. Suppose, now, that in addition to everything listed in questions 1 through 7, Utter Confusion had ended 1989 with an inventory of unsold finished goods of $6000. (Its sales were $115,000, as before.) Note carefully that this $6000 is an "at-cost" valuation, based on the raw materials, labor, and depreciation that went into those unsold goods. Utter Confusion expects to sell them next year, and for more than $6000. But until finished goods are sold, they are always valued at cost.[1]

Thus in 1989, Utter Confusion *(sold more goods than it made / made more goods than it sold)*. Its total manufacturing

[1] More precisely, the valuation rule is "at the lower of cost or market price." Its purpose is to cover the unhappy situation in which market price has fallen so much (or the goods are so unattractive to customers) that the merchandise cannot be sold even for the basic costs of its manufacture. This complication can be disregarded in an introductory survey.

expenses for materials, labor, and depreciation were (as before) $91,000. A small part of these expenses went into the making of these unsold goods. In fact, since the $6000 is an at-cost figure, the cost amount attributable to these unsold goods is *(less than $6000 / $6000 / more than $6000)*.

The general rule that we have been following bears repeating: Do not load costs onto merchandise if those costs are really attributable to the manufacture of other goods. With total manufacturing costs of $91,000, and with $6000 of that total attributable to the unsold goods, the manufacturing cost of goods sold in 1989 ought to be $*(80,000 / 85,000 / 90,000 / 91,000 / 97,000)*. This *(is / is not)* the correct manufacturing cost of goods sold.

The introduction of this $6000 closing inventory *(will / will not)* change Utter Confusion's 1989 net profit. Specifically, this profit will *(remain at / be changed to)* $*(6000 / 12,000 / 14,000 / 20,000)*. This is true only because prices have been assumed to be stable. Profit will typically be altered during periods of inflation (or deflation for that matter).

---

made more goods than it sold; $6000; 85,000; is; will; be changed to; 20,000

9. Table 20A-4 lists accounts for Company Z, Inc. All figures are in millions of dollars.

In the space provided in Table 20A-5 on the next page, construct:

a. a balance sheet for December 31, 1988.

b. an income statement for the year 1989.

c. a balance sheet for December 31, 1989.

QUIZ: Multiple Choice

1. In the preparation of an income statement for a certain period (in particular, the manufacturing cost section):

(1) all expenses listed therein must represent cash actually paid out during that period, and all such cash outpayments (pertaining to manufacturing) must be listed.
(2) every cash outlay (pertaining to manufacturing) during the period must be listed, and in addition some expenses which did not involve an outlay of cash may appear.
(3) some expenses listed may not represent cash outlays during the period, and some cash outlays during the period (pertaining to manufacturing) may not be listed.
(4) all expenses listed must represent cash actually paid out during the period, but not all such cash outpayments (pertaining to manufacturing) need to be listed.
(5) none of the preceding statements is a correct description.

2. If a manufacturing corporation sells an issue of long-term bonds, then on its income (profit-and-loss) statement for the period in which the bonds were sold:
(1) both the bond sale and any interest paid thereon during the period will be recorded.
(2) the bond sale will be recorded, but not any interest paid thereon.
(3) the bond sale will not be recorded, but any interest paid thereon will be.
(4) neither the bond sale nor any interest paid thereon will be recorded.
(5) only that fraction of the bond sale chargeable to that period will be recorded.

Table 20A-4

December 31, 1988		For the Year 1989		December 31, 1989	
Bonds payable	250	Materials	200	Accounts payable	100
Cash	100	Labor cost	250	Accounts receivable	200
Plant and equipment	800	Sales	600	Inventories	600
Depreciation allowance	200	Selling cost	30	Depreciation allowance	300
Accounts payable	50	Dividends	100		
Accounts receivable	300	Bond interest	20		
Inventory	500				
Common stock	1,000				
Retained earnings	?				

a.

Table 20A-5
Balance Sheet
December 31, 1989

Assets	Liabilities and Net Worth

b.

Income Statement
Year Ended December 31, 1989

c.

Balance Sheet
December 31, 1989

Assets	Liabilities and Net Worth

a.

Balance Sheet
December 31, 1988

Assets			Liabilities and Net Worth		
Current:			Current:		
Cash	100		Accts. payable	50	
Accts. rec.	300		Bonds	250	
Inventories	500		Total		300
Total		900			
Fixed			Net worth		1,200
P & E	800				
Depreciation	−200				
Total		600			
Total assets		1,500	Total liabilities and net worth		1,500

b.

Income Statement
Year Ended December 31, 1989

Sales		600
Less:		
Materials	200	
Labor	250	
Total		−450
		150
Add: Beginning inventory	500	
Less: End inventory	−600	
Total		−100
Less:		
Selling cost	30	
Bond interest	20	
Total		−50
Net profit		0
Dividends paid	100	
Addition to retained earnings		−100

c.

Balance Sheet
December 31, 1989

Assets			Liabilities and Net Worth		
Current:			Current:		
Cash	200		Accts. payable	100	
Accts. rec.	400		Bonds	250	
Inventories	600		Total		350
Total		1,100			
Fixed			Net worth		1,050
P & E	600				
Depreciation	300				
Total		−300			
Total assets		1,400	Total liabilities and net worth		1,400

3. If an income statement records no depreciation expense for particular machinery, even though that machinery was used for production during the year, a reasonable explanation from the accounting viewpoint would be that:
(1) the company did not find it necessary to spend money on maintenance or repair of the machines during the year.
(2) depreciation entries equal in total to the original cost of the machines had already been made on earlier income statements.
(3) because sales for the year have been below normal, the company has decided not to charge any depreciation cost for this year.
(4) because of an increase in market prices, it is estimated that the money worth of the machinery is unchanged even though it has undergone some depreciation through use during the year.
(5) no explanation is needed, since depreciation entries are properly made on the balance sheet, not the income statement.

4. When an allowance for depreciation figure is entered in the fixed-asset section of a company's balance sheet, its purpose is:
(1) to prevent an overstatement of net profit.
(2) to reduce the original cost of some asset to an estimate of its true present worth, as closely as can be estimated.
(3) to ensure that there will be sufficient cash on hand to replace assets when they are worn out.
(4) to record the money actually spent in keeping some asset or group of assets in working condition.
(5) to record the total amount of money spent on purchase of new assets during the period in question.

5. Which alternative in question 4 would be correct as to the purpose of listing depreciation as an expense on a company's income statement?
(1).
(2).
(3).
(4).
(5).

6. "A balance sheet must always balance" specifically because:
(1) total assets, properly specified, equal total liabilities, properly specified.
(2) net profit is defined as total revenue earned minus total expenses incurred.
(3) the definition of net worth is total assets minus total liabilities.
(4) current assets plus fixed assets must equal current liabilities plus long-term liabilities.
(5) the definition of net worth is capital stock plus retained earnings.

7. A company's total assets at the end of 1988 were $100,000, and its total liabilities, $70,000. At the end of 1989, its total assets were $115,000, and its total liabilities, $75,000. It paid dividends totaling $15,000 in 1989. Assuming no change in its capital stock, its net profit after taxes for 1989 must have been:
(1) $10,000.
(2) $15,000.
(3) $20,000.
(4) $25,000.
(5) $30,000.

8. A "sinking fund" is:
(1) another name for the depreciation account.
(2) a liability reserve set up to cover future commitments of fairly certain amount.
(3) a special type of surplus reserve.
(4) a "pool of liquid assets" found on the assets side of some firms' balance sheets.
(5) the special account used to value a firm's goodwill.

9. A company's 1988 income statement shows a net profit earned (after taxes) of $200,000. This means that on its end-of-1988 balance sheet, as compared with its end-of-1987 balance sheet:
(1) the total of assets will be up by $200,000, and so will the total of liabilities plus net worth.
(2) retained earnings will be up by $200,00 minus the total of dividends paid.
(3) current assets minus current liabilities will be up by $200,000.
(4) cash on hand minus expenditures for new fixed assets will be up by $200,000.
(5) net worth will be up by $200,000 minus the total of any bond interest paid.

10. If the term "retained earnings" appears on a firm's balance sheet, it reflects:
(1) an account on the assets side having no connection with cash on hand.
(2) an account on the assets side indicating cash on hand.
(3) an account on the liabilities and net worth side having no connection with cash on hand.
(4) an account on the liabilities and net worth side indicating cash on hand.
(5) "retained earnings" is not ordinarily a term used in connection with balance sheets.

11. The use of accelerated depreciation, or "fast write-off," has, during the period of write-off, the effect of:
(1) increasing stated profits but decreasing taxes paid.
(2) decreasing stated profits but increasing taxes paid.
(3) increasing both stated profits and taxes paid.
(4) decreasing both stated profits and taxes paid.
(5) none of these.

12. A company's total assets were $600,000, and its total liabilities, $400,000, at the end of 1987. At the end of 1988, its total assets were $550,000, and its total liabilities, $200,000.

During 1988, it (*a*) paid a dividend of $50,000 and (*b*) sold additional shares of its own stock for $100,000. With these figures, its net profit after taxes for 1988 must have been:
(1) zero.
(2) $50,000.
(3) $100,000.
(4) $150,000.
(5) $200,000.

SUGGESTED ANSWERS TO QUESTIONS IN THE TEXT: Appendix to Chapter 20

1. Right-hand side: Liabilities (current—accounts payable, notes payable, taxes payable, etc.; long-term—bonds payable) and net worth—common stock, retained earnings, etc.
Left-hand side: Assets (current—cash, inventory, etc.; fixed—equipment less depreciation, buildings less depreciation; intangible—patents, goodwill, etc.).
The totals on both sides must match—the definition of net worth.

2. Depends in some part on the length of the loan and its productivity. At a minimum, though, you might want to lend $200,000 for 1 year taking note of net worth of $220,000 that could cover the interest and the principle.

3. Definitions of the item listed in answer 1.

4.

Net sales		$10 million
Less: Costs	−$9 million	
Net income		1 million
Less: Dividends	0	
Addition to retained earnings		$1 million

5. Assets climb to $51 million; net worth climbs from $50 million to $51 million.

6. On the income statement, subtract depreciation costs of $2 million, so net income is a negative $1 million. The balance sheet would show a left-hand side like:

Current assets		$51 million
Fixed assets:		
Building	$20 million	
Less: Depreciation	2 million	18 million
Total		$69 million

and a right-hand side like:

Long-term liabilities	
Bonds payable	$20 million
Net worth	49 million
Total	$69 million

7. A $1000 deduction means tax liability falls $500. The first $500 would earn interest for 10 years, the second $500 (year 2's tax saving) for 9 years, etc. Given the $5000 tax saving of expensing (which matches the total allowed under the straight-line option of 10 percent per year for 10 years), total interest earnings would be higher. Writing things off quicker always makes them more valuable.

CHAPTER 21

THEORY OF PRODUCTION AND MARGINAL PRODUCTS

Having been introduced to the workings of supply and demand in the product markets, it is now time to consider the various decisions that businesses must make in servicing those markets. Scarcity and need determine why it costs more to purchase some goods than others, but what determines wages and salaries? Why are some occupations more highly paid than others? If all inputs are employed to work together to produce a specific output, how are their respective contributions assessed in the computation of their appropriate rates of compensation? How is it that the return to capital has held steady over the past *80* years despite an increase in the size of the capital stock compared with the size of the labor force? After all, a lot has happened since Teddy Roosevelt was in the White House.

The answers to these and other questions will again be found in the workings of supply and demand—this time in the markets for inputs. In a product market, for example, you have seen that demand for any good arises from the utility that the good provides to the consumer. In an input market, demand arises from the productivity that the good can offer the employer in the production of some other good that people are willing to buy. The demand for an input is, therefore, a derived demand based not upon the immediate, innate value of that input to the firm but upon the ultimate value of the final good being produced. Still, we will see that the basic principles of supply and demand hold in this input arena just as they do in the output arena.

This chapter, the first of five chapters covering the behavior of firms, presents an analysis of production. How do economists conceptualize the relationship between inputs and outputs, and what do they do with that picture? Subsequent chapters will relate this conception of production to costs and then will relate those costs to supply in a variety of market structures. For the moment, though, focus on production. You should accomplish the following objectives as you complete your work in this chapter.

LEARNING OBJECTIVES

1. Define a production function and relate it to the notions of (*a*) total product, (*b*) marginal product, and (*c*) average product.

2. Explain the law of diminishing marginal returns.

3. Define constant, increasing, and decreasing returns to scale, and relate each to the law of diminishing marginal returns.

4. Compare and contrast measures of total productivity and the productivity of a particular input. Relate both to technological change and the law of diminishing marginal returns.

5. Distinguish between momentary run, short run, and long run in the context of production.

6. State and explain the stylized facts that describe the growth of the aggregate U.S. economy since the turn of the century. Describe why it can be said that the experience of the United States over the past two decades has not been as profitable as the century taken as a whole.

The first concept to grasp is the notion of a production function. Suppose that engineers and scientists defined a process through which certain types of inputs could be employed to produce a certain type of output. A **production function** representing that process would record the maximum output that could be produced from various (all possible) combinations of inputs, *given the specific state of technology defined by the engineers*. Conversely, the production function would also identify all the various combinations of inputs that could be combined to produce a particular level of output.

1. a. The total amount of output measured in physical units of production is called ______________________. Average product is the ratio of *(the change in total product / total product)* to *(the change in the employment of one input / the change in the employment of all inputs / the total employment of all inputs / the total employment of one input)*; it is *(an input-*

specific concept / defined for a production process as a whole). Marginal product is *(also input-specific / also defined for a process at large)*. Marginal product is the ratio of *(the change in total product / total product)* to *(the change in the employment of all inputs / the change in the employment of one input / the total employment of all inputs / the total employment of one input)*.

b. Consider a production function that relates the quantity of some good produced (X) with the quantities of capital (K), labor (L), and material (M) employed. Indicate in the spaces provided whether each stated formula applies to the total product, the marginal product, or the average product of capital, labor, or material. Use MP_K, for example, to indicate the marginal product of capital; AP_L, the average product of labor; etc. If the stated definition applies to none of the possible combinations, write "n/a."

(1) change in K / change in X = ... (________)

(2) change in X / quantity of L = ... (________)

(3) quantity of X / quantity of K = ... (________)

(4) change in X / change in L = ... (________)

(5) quantity of X = ... (________)

(6) quantity of K / quantity of M = ... (________)

(7) change in X / change in K = ... (________)

(8) quantity of K / quantity of X = ... (________)

a. total product; total product; the total employment of one input; an input-specific concept; also input-specific; the change in total product; the change in the employment of one input **b. (1)** n/a **(2)** n/a **(3)** AP_K **(4)** MP_L **(5)** $TP_K = TP_L = TP_M$ **(6)** n/a **(7)** MP_K **(8)** n/a

2. Table 21-1 provides the data for a production function that relates the employment of capital (K) and labor (L) to maximum output levels of some good Y. Fill in the blanks for the average and marginal products of labor given capital employment of 4 units and 8 units.

Graph the total product curves for both levels of capital employment in the top panel of Figure 21-1 (use different-colored pencils or pens to differentiate the two cases); graph

Table 21-1

4 Units of Capital Employed				8 Units of Capital Employed			
Labor	***TP***	***MP_L***	***AP_L***	**Labor**	***TP***	***MP_L***	***AP_L***
0	0		undefined	0	0		undefined
		22				____	
1	22		____	1	22.5		____
		20				____	
2	42		____	2	44		____
		____				____	
3	60		____	3	64.5		____
		____				____	
4	76		____	4	84		____
		____				____	
5	90		____	5	102.5		____
		____				____	
6	102		____	6	120		____
		____				____	
7	112		____	7	136.5		____
		____				____	
8	120		____	8	152		____
		____				____	
9	126		____	9	166.5		____
		____				____	
10	130		____	10	180		____

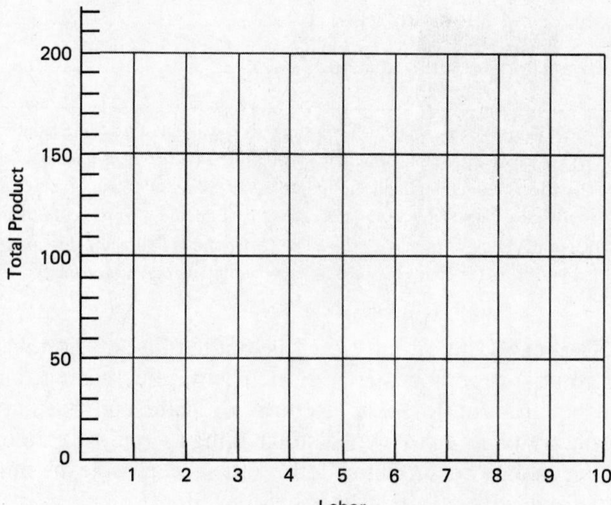

Panel (a)

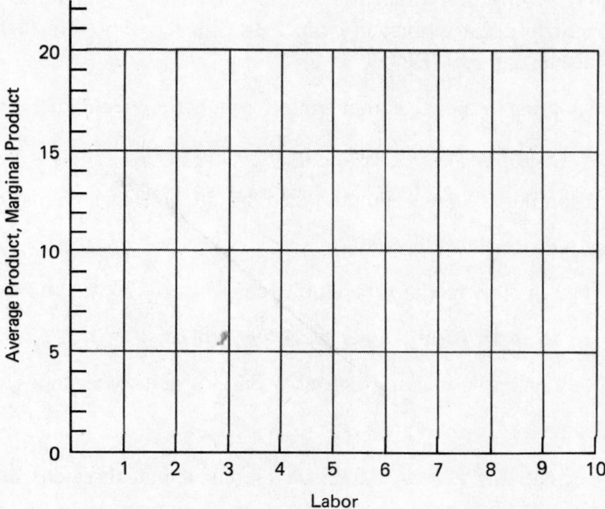

Panel (b)

Figure 21-1

the marginal and average product curves for both cases in the bottom panel of Figure 21-1 (use the same colors).

[When drawing the marginal product curves, use the convention of plotting the value against the halfway points of labor employment. The marginal product of the second unit of labor with 4 units of capital is, for example, given as 20; plot the point (1.5,20) on the marginal product curve.]

Reading down the MP_L column for 4 units of capital: 18, 16, 14, 12, 10, 8, 6, 4 Reading down the corresponding AP_L column: 22, 21, 20, 19, 18, 17, 16, 15, 14, 13 Reading down the MP_L column for 8 units of capital: 22.5, 21.5, 20.5, 19.5, 18.5, 17.5, 16.5, 15.5, 14.5, 13.5 Reading down the corresponding AP_L column: 22.5, 22, 21.5, 21, 20.5, 20, 19.5, 19, 18.5, 18

Notice from the table and perhaps more vividly from the graphs that doubling the capital stock from 4 units to 8 units increases (1) total product, (2) average product, and (3) marginal product for each level of labor employment. Working with more capital, labor is, quite simply, more *productive*.

3. Refer again to the data of Table 21-1. Suppose that 3 units of labor are employed and that the capital stock increases from 4 units to 8 units. Labor productivity, measured in terms of output per unit of labor, should increase from ______ to ______; an increase of ______ percent. If 8 units of labor had been employed, the growth in labor productivity would have been from ______ to ______ for a ______ percent increase.

20; 21.5; 7.5; 15; 19; 26.67

The increase in productivity might have been the result of technological change instead of capital deepening. For example, some new invention might have made each piece of capital listed on the left-hand side of Table 21-1 work like two pieces. If that were so, then the matching of labor employment to total product recorded on the right-hand side would apply *even with 4 units of capital employed*. The productivity gains that you just noted would have been the result of new technology and not of an increase in the capital stock.

4. The law of diminishing returns is a widely observed empirical regularity which holds that the marginal product of any input should (eventually) decline as the employment of that input *(climbs / falls)*. In Table 21-1, *(both / only the right-hand / only the left-hand / neither)* total product schedule(*s*) generates (*generate*) marginal product curves for labor that *(obey / contradict)* this law. Because the law of diminishing returns is defined in terms of the marginal product of some input, it applies when the *(employments of all inputs are being changed simultaneously / employments of all inputs are being changed simultaneously and proportionately / employment of only one input is being changed while all other levels are held fixed)*. The law also applies *(when technology is unaltered / even if the technology changes as employment changes)*. Why? Because marginal product is defined for a given production function and thus for a specific production technology.

---

climbs; both; obey; employment of only one input is being changed while all other levels are held fixed; when technology is unaltered

The notion of marginal product is input-specific; it measures the response in total product of a change in the employment of any input under the assumption that the employment of *all other inputs is constant*. Returns to scale are a measure of the response in total product when all inputs move together—not arbitrarily in a cacophony of simultaneous change, but proportionately.

The term **constant returns to scale** refers to the circumstance in which multiplying the employment of *all* inputs by the same factor results in the multiplication of output by the same factor. Double all inputs and you get twice the output. Quadruple all inputs and you get 4 times the output. Multiply all inputs by some number k, and you get k *times* the output. (The best visual image for constant returns to scale is replicating a production plant. Everything else being equal, you can always double the output of any plant by building its twin next door.)

A situation characterized by **decreasing returns to scale** is the poor cousin: double all inputs and get less than twice the output; multiply all inputs by k and get less than k *times* the output. The opposite occurs with **increasing returns to scale**: double all inputs and get more than twice the output. If decreasing returns are the scourge of size, then increasing returns are the blessing of size. Firms requiring the use of a specific natural resource sometimes display the former; industries having a "volume technology" to exploit, the latter.

Table 21-2

Labor	Alt B	Alt C	Alt D	Alt E
0	0	0	0	0
1	24.5	20.5	18.5	25.5
2	48.0	40.0	36.0	50.0
3	70.5	58.5	52.5	73.5
4	92.0	76.0	68.0	96.0
5	112.5	92.5	82.5	117.5
6	132.0	108.0	96.0	138.0
7	150.5	122.5	108.5	157.5
8	168.0	136.0	120.0	176.0
9	184.5	148.5	130.5	193.5
10	200.0	160.0	140.0	210.0

5. The right-hand side of Table 21-1 shows one possible production response to increasing the capital stock from 4 units to 8 units; call it Schedule A. Table 21-2 shows four alternative schedules for $K = 8$ units, labeled B, C, D, and E. On the basis of the inferences that you can make by comparing the left-hand side of Table 21-1 with these various alternatives, indicate in the spaces provided below the schedules which, when linked with the left-hand side of Table 21-1, conform to the specified characteristic.

a. increasing returns to scale . . . . (__________)

b. constant returns to scale . . . . . (__________)

c. decreasing returns to scale . . . (__________)

d. diminishing returns to labor . . (__________)

---

a. B and E (The five cases in which you can trace the effect of doubling inputs all produce more than a doubling of output.) **b.** A (The five cases in which you can trace the effect of doubling inputs all produce a doubling of output.) **c.** C and D (The five cases in which you can trace the effect of doubling inputs all produce less than a doubling of output.) **d.** A, B, C, D, and E (All show diminishing returns right from the start. To see this, compute the marginal products.)

The real point of question 5 is that the law of diminishing returns is compatible with increasing, decreasing, and constant returns to scale. Returns to scale and marginal productivity refer to two distinct things—one, a proportional change in *all* inputs; the other, a change in only *one* input with all the others held fixed.

6. Indicate in the spaces provided which of the following would be reactions that you would expect to see undertaken by a firm in the momentary run (MR), in the short run (SR), or in the long run (LR).

a. Adopting a new, computerized production technique that involves reworking the assembly line . . . . (_____)

b. Adopting a new, computerized production technique that improves inventory control . . . . (_____)

c. Having 50 percent of the employees work overtime, amounting to an extra 10 hours per week per worker . . . (_____)

d. Reopening an existing assembly line located closer to a new and developing market . . . . (_____)

e. Recognizing a new market development that threatens half the firm's existing market share . . . . (_____)

f. Reworking the technology of the assembly technique to reduce material waste by 50 percent . . . . (_____)

g. Increasing the work force by 10 percent to increase capacity utilization by 5 percent . . . . (_____)

h. Doubling the work force to take advantage of increasing returns to scale . . . . (_____)

---

a. LR **b.** SR **c.** SR **d.** LR **e.** MR **f.** LR **g.** SR **h.** LR

7. Which of the following empirical statements accurately describes the recent experience of the aggregate U.S. economy?

a. Total productivity has risen in the United States by an average rate of 1.5 percent per year throughout the twentieth century. . . . . *(T / F)*

b. On average, labor productivity grew faster than the 1.5 percent annual rate of growth of total productivity throughout the twentieth century. . . . . *(T / F)*

c. The return to capital has held remarkably steady in the United States since the turn of the twentieth century. . . . . . *(T / F)*

d. There has, since 1970, been a decline in the rate of growth of the real wages that support the American standard of living. . . . . *(T / F)*

All the statements are true.

8. Since all the statements recorded in question 7 are true, there must be an economic justification for each that is consistent with the fundamentals of production. Match each of the following with the empirical statement that it helps explain.

a. The rate of technological progress nearly matched the rate at which diminishing returns affected capital. . . . *(a / b / c / d)*

b. Sustained technological progress accounted for sustained growth in overall productivity. . . . . *(a / b / c / d)*

c. The capital stock of the United States grew faster than the number of hours of labor supplied throughout most of the twentieth century. . . . . *(a / b / c / d)*

d. The rate of growth of total productivity has declined against historical trends. . . . . *(a / b / c / d)*

---

a. c **b.** a **c.** b **d.** d

9. Which of the following represent substitution of one factor of production for another with an unchanged technology (S), which represent technological change (T), and which represent neither?

a. A firm replaces an oil-fired boiler with a regenerative heat capture system. . . . . *(S / T / N)*

b. Following a successful unionization drive by clerical workers, a university buys personal computers for its faculty and thereby reduces its secretarial work force. . . . . . *(S / T / N)*

c. A publishing firm reduces its employment of staff editors and increases its reliance on computer typesetting with a spelling/-grammar check program. . . . . *(S / T / N)*

d. A manufacturing firm improves its quality guarantee by replacing human quality control with an optic surveillance system. . . . . *(S / T / N)*

e. A manufacturing firm improves its quality guarantee because it determines that it must ensure its customers that it can match the quality of its foreign competition. . . . . *(S / T / N)*

---

a. T **b.** S **c.** S **d.** S or T (depending upon whether or not the optic system was an alternative all the while) **e.** N

10. Assume that the law of diminishing returns always holds. Which of the following statements is true? Why?

a. If average product exceeds marginal product, then average product must be climbing. . . . . *(T / F)*

Why? ____

____

____

____

b. Average product is, in fact, always above marginal product. . . . . *(T / F)*

Why? ____

____

____

____

---

a. F [$AP > MP$ means that the incremental increase in total product is smaller than the average; the average must therefore fall. (Think about a .300 hitter going 1 for 10 in a doubleheader. What happens to his batting average with a "marginal" batting contribution of .100? It falls!)]
b. T (except perhaps for the first unit of employment) [For the first unit of employment, MP and AP essentially match; for the second, with MP falling, AP falls only half as far; and so on. For example, let $AP(1) = MP(1) = 20$, and $MP(2) = 10$; then $AP(2) = (20 + 10)/2 = 15 > 10$. AP always falls slower from a higher point, so it must always exceed MP.]

QUIZ: Multiple Choice

1. The law of diminishing returns holds that:
(1) the total product of any input must eventually reach a maximum and turn downward as the employment of that input increases.
(2) the average product of any input must eventually reach a minimum and turn upward as the employment of all inputs increases proportionately.
(3) the marginal product of any input should eventually begin to decline as the employment of that input increases.
(4) the marginal product of any input should eventually begin to decline as the employment of all inputs increases proportionately.
(5) the average product of any input should rise before it falls as the employment of that input increases.

2. If a production process displays diminishing returns for all inputs, then:
(1) it cannot display constant returns to scale.
(2) it must display decreasing returns to scale.
(3) it cannot display increasing returns to scale.
(4) all of the above are true.
(5) none of the above is true.

3. If the average product of some input is observed running higher than its marginal product, then:
(1) the marginal product must be increasing with the employment of that input.
(2) marginal product must be converging toward the average product.
(3) average product must be increasing with the employment of that input.
(4) average product must be falling with the employment of that input.
(5) total product must be falling with the employment of that input.

4. Let production be defined by the function described in Table 21-3. With 3 units of capital on site, the average product of the fourth unit of labor is:
(1) 13.
(2) 11.
(3) 10.
(4) 18.
(5) 16.

Table 21-3
Total Product

Labor	Capital Stock		
	$K = 2$	$K = 3$	$K = 4$
0	0	0	0
1	10	16	20
2	19	29	38
3	27	41	54
4	34	52	68
5	40	62	80
6	45	71	90

5. Let production be defined by the function described in Table 21-3. With 5 units of labor employed, the marginal product of the third unit of capital is:
(1) 12.4.
(2) 10.
(3) 9.
(4) 22.
(5) 18.

6. Let production be defined by the function described in Table 21-3. Which of the following statements is true?
(1) Production conforms to the law of diminishing returns with respect to K only when L is greater than 3 units.
(2) Production conforms to the law of diminishing returns with respect to L only when K is equal to 4.
(3) Production conforms to the law of diminishing returns with respect to L only.
(4) Production conforms to the law of diminishing returns with respect to K only.
(5) None of the above is true.

7. Let production be defined by the function described in Table 21-3. Given the information provided, it would appear that production displays:
(1) decreasing returns to scale.
(2) constant returns to scale.
(3) increasing returns to scale.
(4) tendencies to exploit labor.
(5) tendencies to exploit capital.

8. Let production be defined by the function described in Table 21-3. If the function were to display constant returns to scale given the total products recorded there for $K=2$, then the output associated with $K = 4$ and $L = 6$ would have to equal:
(1) 20 units.
(2) 27 units.
(3) 38 units.
(4) 54 units.
(5) 90 units.

9. Which of the following adjustments to economic circumstance might the firm be able to accomplish in the long run?
(1) Adoption of a new computer-based production technology that replaced 50 percent of the labor working the assembly lines.
(2) Increased capacity utilization accomplished by hiring a third shift of workers.
(3) Reduction of the work force by 30 percent in the face of stiff foreign competition.
(4) Adoption of cost-cutting measures throughout middle management.
(5) All of the above are possible in the long run.

10. As a matter of historical record, it is widely agreed that:
(1) total productivity in the United States has risen, on average, by nearly 0.5 percent per year since the turn of the twentieth century.
(2) labor productivity has increased in the United States faster than total productivity over the past nine decades even though the ratio of capital stock to labor force has remained remarkably constant.
(3) the rate of growth of total productivity in the United States over the past 20 years has been nearly 1 percentage point smaller than the average over the past 80 years.
(4) the return to capital has increased dramatically in the United States since the turn of the twentieth century—an increase due in large part to a deepening of the U.S. capital stock relative to that of the rest of the world.
(5) none of the above statements is true.

11. A total product curve has been drawn on a piece of graph paper. If a second curve is drawn to reflect technological progress, this second curve will:

(1) appear everywhere below the original curve and be flatter.
(2) appear everywhere above the original curve and be flatter.
(3) appear everywhere below the original curve and be steeper.
(4) appear everywhere above the original curve and be steeper.
(5) appear above the original curve until diminishing returns set in.

SUGGESTED ANSWERS TO QUESTIONS IN THE TEXT: Chapter 21

1. Definition.

2. Reading down the *MP* column: $(114K - 86K)/(20K - 10K) = 28/10 = 2.8, 2, 1.6, 1.4$. Reading down the *AP* column: $86K/10K = 8.6, 5.7, 4.47, 3.75, 3.28$.

3. Graph the points.

4. Each point should be 20 percent higher against the vertical axis.

5. Pick any of a wide variety in, e.g., transportation, food processing, communication.

6. The size of the flower pot defines the fixed factor against which the diminishing returns of seed and fertilizer must be measured.

7. Definition across the table.

8. Plug in the numbers to show that the formula applies. Marginal products are given by

$$MP_H = 17.2(H/10,000)^{-.6}(P/12)^{1.7}$$

and

$$MP_P = 6,080(H/10,000)^{.4}(P/12)^{.7}$$

9. Short run—cut back on overtime; capacity utilization (number of assembly lines in operation at any one time, number of shifts per day); etc. Long run—close a plant; adopt new technology to lower cost; move plant to lower costs; etc.

10. (*a*) substitution; (*b*) new technology; (*c*) substitution; (*d*) new technology.

11. Diminishing returns can coexist with any returns-to-scale parameter.

12. Marginal product decreasing means that the increase in output is always smaller for successive increments of employment. Thus, the next increase in output is always smaller than the last, which was smaller than all of the previous; the next increase is thus always smaller than the average of the previous increases. Including this smaller number in the average must, therefore, reduce the average.

13. The marginal products are both ½; every 1-unit increase of either L or A increases Q by ½ unit. For the given Cobb-Douglas function, MP_A equals $\frac{1}{2}(L/A)^{.5}$, which falls with A; $MP_L = \frac{1}{2}(A/L)^{.5}$, which falls with L.

CHAPTER 22

ANALYSIS OF COSTS

This chapter explores the nature of costs. *Minimum* production costs of a firm are represented along a total cost schedule that depends on the level of output. Inputs used in their least-cost combination are the link between output and cost, and it is the ability to adjust (or not to adjust) their employment that provides the distinction between the two components of total cost: variable cost and fixed cost. The major objective here is for you to obtain a solid understanding of an economist's perspective of cost accounting so that subsequent descriptions of market structure will make sense. By the end of the chapter, you should have mastered the following objectives.

LEARNING OBJECTIVES

1. Define and describe total cost, fixed cost, variable cost, marginal cost, and average cost. Understand what these measures of cost are designed to reflect, and understand how they are related to one another. Derive, in particular, average and marginal cost from total, fixed, and/or variable cost.

2. Explain the link between productivity and cost: when the law of diminishing returns applies (does not apply), marginal cost increases (falls or remains fixed) with output.

3. Demonstrate why constant input prices and constant returns to scale imply a horizontal marginal cost curve in the long run.

4. Demonstrate precisely why marginal cost *always* intersects average cost at the minimum of any U-shaped average cost curve.

5. Construct the long-run cost envelope from short-run average cost curves, and explain its significance.

6. Demonstrate why production costs are minimized when inputs are hired in combinations such that the ratios of their marginal products to their prices are all equal. Explain what this "least-cost rule" implies about substitution within production processes as the prices of inputs change.

7. Understand opportunity cost, and apply it to management decisions of firms and individuals.

Total costs include all the costs incurred in producing and selling a product. In the markets of our everyday experience, every firm incurs production costs; production costs are like death and taxes—unavoidable (if you want to make anything). Selling costs are, however, different. They may or may not be important components of a given firm's cost picture, depending upon the nature of its product and the structure of its market. Wheat farmers, for example, do not advertise their product; they take the price as given and sell as much as they can. For them, selling costs are exclusively delivery costs. Automobile manufacturers, by way of contrast, spend millions of dollars every week on advertising of all types—everything from television commercials during coverage of the Winter Olympics to small-print ads in narrowly distributed weekly newspapers. Be they foreign or domestic manufacturers, their selling operations include trying to manipulate buyers by changing tastes and adjusting prices. Why the difference? The market faced by the auto giants is entirely different from the market faced by the wheat farmer.

To avoid confusing these two sources of cost, this chapter concentrates exclusively on production costs. Selling costs depend so critically upon market structure that discussion of their contribution to total cost is postponed until later.

Total cost has two parts and one important derivative:

1. **Variable costs** are those costs whose total amount varies with the amount of output produced. For example, direct labor cost is a cost whose total amount will rise as the amount of output rises; this is a variable cost.

2. **Fixed costs** are those costs which are fixed in amount regardless of the level of output and which would accordingly have to be paid by the firm even if

its output were zero. Interest on a bond issue is a cost the firm must pay whether it is operating at zero output or at maximum capacity; this is a fixed cost.

3. **Marginal cost** is a measure of the increase in total cost resulting from a 1-unit increase in output. Since it depends only on costs that change with output, marginal cost can also be defined in terms of the increase in variable cost resulting from a 1-unit expansion in output.

The distinction between fixed and variable costs turns out to be important and interesting. Sometimes you cannot understand a firm's situation and the problems that it faces until you have grasped the distinction between these two kinds of costs. Marginal cost, though, depends only upon variable costs. Why? Because fixed costs do not, by their very definition, change as output is increased or reduced.

1. In each space below, put (V) if you think the item would contribute to variable cost; put (F) if you think that it would be part of fixed cost.

a. The cost of purchasing raw materials . . . . . . (________)

b. Depreciation on machinery, when quantity of output produced is considered to be the factor responsible for the amount of this cost . . . . (________)

c. The annual fire-insurance premium on plant buildings . . . . (________)

d. A sales tax levied on the firm for each unit of an input employed . . . . (________)

e. Depreciation on machinery, when time rather than quantity of output produced is considered to be the factor principally responsible for the amount of this cost . . . . (________)

f. Salaries paid to supervisors on an annual basis . (________)

g. Local property taxes on buildings . . . . (________)

h. The cost of purchasing electric power for machines . . . . (________)

i. The cost of maintaining an active research and development department . . . . (________)

j. A royalty paid for the use of certain machines according to number of units produced . . . . (________)

k. Extra pay for overtime work by labor . . . . . . (________)

a. V **b.** V **c.** F **d.** V **e.** F **f.** F **g.** F **h.** V **i.** F **j.** V **k.** V

2. In Table 22-1, the figures in columns (1) and (2) indicate the estimated total cost incurred in producing quantities of output from 0 to 20 units weekly for a particular firm.

Table 22-1

(1) Output	(2) Total Cost	(3) Average Cost	(4) Average Variable Cost	(5) Increase in Total Cost	(6) Marginal Cost
0	$50.00	undefined	undefined		
				$14.00	$7.00
2	64.00	$ _____	$7.00		
				7.00	3.50
4	71.00	17.75	$ _____		
				9.00	4.50
6	80.00	13.33	5.00		
				_____	_____
8	90.00	_____	_____		
				10.50	5.25
10	100.50	10.05	5.05		
				11.00	_____
12	111.50	_____	_____		
				13.00	6.50
14	124.50	8.89	5.32		
				_____	_____
16	140.50	8.78	5.66		
				_____	11.00
18	162.50	_____	6.25		
				40.00	_____
20	202.50	10.13	7.63		

a. In column (3), complete the missing figures for *average cost*—the cost per unit of output, or total cost divided by number of units produced.

b. Table 22-1 indicates that, for this firm and this product, average cost reaches its minimum level at an output in the vicinity of *(10 / 12 / 14 / 16 / 18 / 20)* units.

c. In column (5), complete the missing figures for increases in total cost; i.e., indicate the rise in cost resulting from an increase from 0 to 2 units, from 2 to 4, etc. Notice that these figures are not lined up opposite 0, 2, 4 units, etc. Instead, they are set between 0 and 2, between 2 and 4, etc., to indicate that each figure marks the cost of moving from one output figure to the adjacent one. If output is increased from 2 units to 4, total cost rises by $10; if it is reduced from 4 units to 2, total cost falls by $10.

d. To obtain marginal cost, the figures in column (4) must be divided by 2. Marginal cost is, more precisely, the ratio of a change in total cost divided by a change in output. If that output change equals 1, then the change in total cost is marginal cost. If it is some number other than 1, however, then the change in total cost must be adjusted to a "per-unit" level by dividing by that number. Complete, then, the missing marginal cost figures in column (6).

Note carefully that marginal cost, even though it is also a per-unit cost measure, is not the same thing at all as average cost. Marginal cost measures *only* the change in total cost resulting from the last unit produced.

Because this table deals with 2-unit output changes, column (5) is not precisely accurate as a measure of marginal cost. If the table were enlarged to show unit-by-unit (rather than 2-unit) changes, then, for example, the 8-to-9 marginal cost figure in column (5) would be a little below $5.25, and the 9-to-10 figure a little above. But $5.25 is a reasonably close estimate for both.

a. $37; $11.25; $9.29; $9.03 **b.** 16 **c.** $10; $16; $22 **d.** $5; $5.50; $8; $20

3. **a.** In Figure 22-1, plot the total cost curve, using columns (1) and (2) of Table 22-1 (i.e., plot the several points indicated by these columns; then join them with a smooth curve).

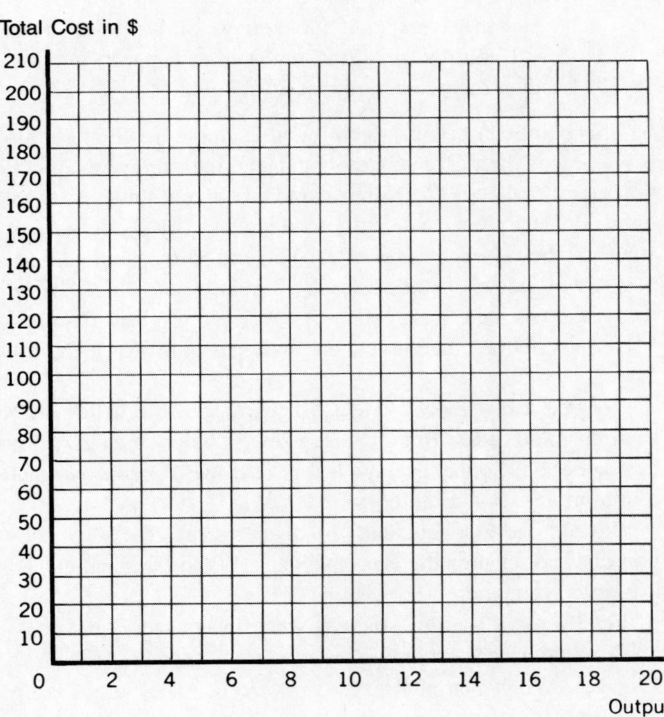

Figure 22-1

b. In Figure 22-2, use columns (1) and (3) of Table 22-1 to plot the average cost (AC) curve. Also in Figure 22-2, use columns (1) and (6) to plot the marginal cost (*MC*) curve. (Because the *MC* values are in-between points, record them opposite odd-numbered quantities of output—1, 3, 5, 7, etc.) Mark your two curves on Figure 22-2 as *AC* and *MC*, respectively.

c. Figure 22-2 indicates that (pick one or more):

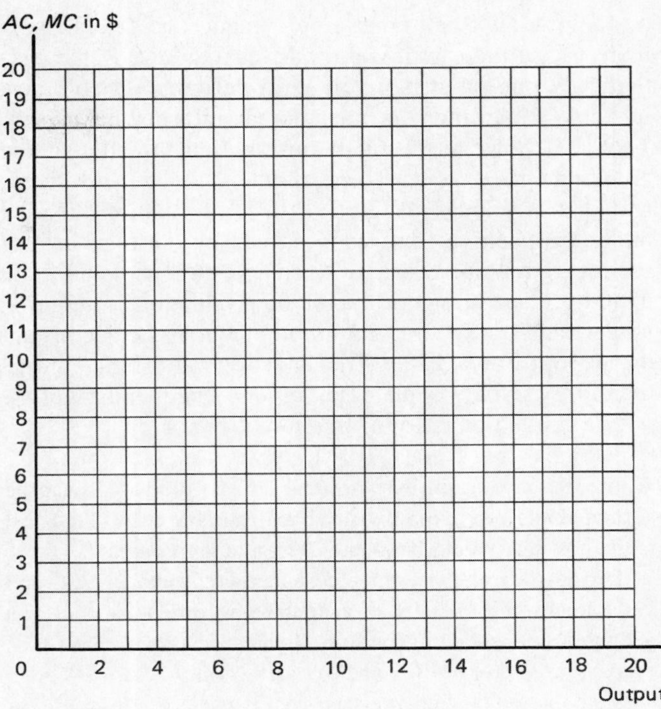

Figure 22-2

(1) the *AC* curve cuts through the bottom point of the *MC* curve as it moves to the right through higher output levels.

(2) the *MC* curve cuts through the bottom point of the *AC* curve as it moves to the right through higher output levels.

(3) the *MC* curve eventually begins to climb as it continues to move to the right through higher output levels.

(4) the *MC* curve eventually begins to fall as it continues to move to the right through higher output levels.

c. (2) and (3)

It is important to note that the eventual climbing of the marginal cost curve just noted and displayed in your version of Figure 22-2 can be attributed directly to the law of diminishing returns. How can this linkage be seen in Table 22-1? Notice that the increase in total cost required to increase output by 2 units falls through 6 units of total production, but then begins to climb. Since this increase in cost is driven entirely by the costs of purchasing productive inputs, it must be the case that increasing quantities of inputs are required for each successive increment in output beyond 6 units. The law of diminishing returns must therefore be ravaging the marginal productivity of the inputs whose purchase defines variable cost.

For the purists who remember that the law of diminishing returns is defined in terms of marginal products that are in turn defined in terms of increases in the employment of one input with all other employment levels held fixed, there is one more wrinkle to add. It may not be the case that only one input is involved in defining variable cost in Table 22-1; there is not enough information to tell. There is, however, enough information to tell that the employment of at least one input is being held fixed, and that is enough. Where is that information? Buried under the positive fixed cost defined by the total cost of producing nothing. Positive fixed costs tell us that a fixed quantity of at least one factor of production is required to get under way, and its employment is held constant throughout Table 22-1. The law of diminishing returns therefore applies to all other inputs which must get by with a limited quantity of this initial factor.

4. Recall once again that the total cost of production can be separated into two parts: fixed cost and variable cost. Fixed cost is the cost that would be incurred even at zero output.

Divide each of these three cost measures (total, fixed, and variable) by the quantity of output being produced, and you get three corresponding per-unit figures: *average cost (AC)*, *average fixed cost (AFC)*, and *average variable cost (AVC)*.

Note one point: Because total cost is made up of fixed cost and variable cost, it must be true that *(AC = AFC − AVC / AC = AFC + AVC / AFC = AC + AVC)*.

AC = AFC + AVC

5. a. Now compute a few average fixed cost values for Table 22-1. When output is 4, *AFC* would be $______; when output is 8, *AFC* would be $______; when output is 12, *AFC* would be $______.

Notice that the mathematical computation involved is not overwhelmingly complicated. As we move to higher outputs, we are just dividing $50 by successively larger figures. On a graph which shows what happens to per-unit costs as output is increased, *AFC* would *(rise / stay the same / fall)* continuously. *AFC*, in fact, falls along a rectangular hyperbola as a fixed money cost is spread out over more and more output.

b. To compute average variable cost for any output, you must first establish (total) variable cost by subtracting *(marginal / fixed / variable)* cost from total cost. In the case of Table 22-1, for example, you must subtract $______ from total cost. Complete column (4) of Table 22-1 by writing in the three missing *AVC* figures—those for outputs of 4, 8, and 12 units.

Using the *AFC* and *AVC* figures that you have already computed, check to make certain that $AFC + AVC = AC$. This rule must hold because total cost is the sum of variable cost and fixed cost. Graph both *AFC* and *AVC* on Figure 22-2.

---

a. 12.50; 6.25; 4.17; fall **b.** fixed; 50; $5.25; $5.00; $5.12

6. a. Suppose that in constructing Table 22-1 we had used a case in which *AVC* initially fell. Note that *AVC* is nothing more than the average of all the previous marginal costs. Why? Because the marginal cost (*MC*) schedule traces the increase in cost caused by producing each unit of output in sequence (first, second, etc.), and *AVC* is simply the average of these cost increments. So if *AVC* fell as output moved from (e.g.) 2 units to 3 units, from 3 to 4 units, and from 4 to 5 units, then *MC* for the third, fourth, and fifth units of output would have to be *(greater than / equal to / smaller than)* the corresponding *AVC* figures. Only then could the inclusion of each extra *MC* figure pull the average down as specified. In sum, therefore, if *AVC* is falling as output climbs, then *MC* must be *(less than / equal to / greater than) AVC*.

What if *AVC* were rising with output? In that case, each increment in cost would have to be *(greater than / equal to / smaller than)* the previous average to push the average higher. *MC* in other words, would have to be *(greater than / equal to / smaller than) AVC*.

Finally, if *AVC* and *MC* were equal, then adding the cost of 1 more unit of output would *(increase / have no effect on / decrease)* the average. If the average of 116 numbers is 10.73342 and you add a 117th number that happens to equal 10.73342, then the average remains 10.73342.

b. This point can be illustrated by an example involving classroom grades. In a given class of students, the average examination grade is always 70. Now we add a few new students (some extra, or "marginal," students) to this class. They are weaker students; they always score between 50 and 55 on examinations. So, when added to the class, they *increase / pull down* the class average from 70 to, say, 65. (When marginal value is below average level, the marginal pulls down the average.)

We add a few more students. They are a little better; they score from 60 to 63. But they are likewise below the new class average of 65. So that average is *(pulled down / increased)* just a little more—say, from 65 to *(64 / 66)*.

We add one more student who always scores 64. This addition does not change the class average. (When marginal equals average, average does not change.)

Finally we add a few students who always score above 64. Their addition will accordingly *(increase / decrease)* the class average. (When marginal exceeds average, marginal pulls up average.)

---

a. smaller than; less than; greater than; greater than; have no effect on **b.** pull down; pulled down; 64; increase

It follows from question 6 that marginal cost always intersects average variable cost at the minimum of the average variable cost curve. How so? Question 6 tells us that *MC* must be running below *AVC* if *AVC* is falling. If, on the other hand, *AVC* is climbing, then question 6 tells us that *MC* must be running above *AVC*. As average variable costs stop falling and start to climb (i.e., as the *AVC* curve reaches its lowest point), therefore, the *MC* curve must somehow pass from being underneath *AVC* to being on top of *AVC*. The *MC* curve must, in other words, cut through *AVC* precisely where *AVC* stops falling and starts to climb—its minimum point.

7. The implications of question 6 go beyond average variable costs. To grasp them fully, consult Figure 22-3. Notice that it shows a U-shaped *AVC* curve intersecting the *MC* curve at the minimum of the *AVC* curve. Notice, too, that the average cost (*AC*) curve is also U-shaped. As output gradually expands from the zero level, it shows that *AC* will initially *(rise / fall)*, because fixed cost is being spread over increasingly *(larger / smaller)* outputs. However, as plant capacity is approached, *AC* must ultimately *(rise / fall)* because of the influence of *(fixed cost / the law of diminishing returns)*.

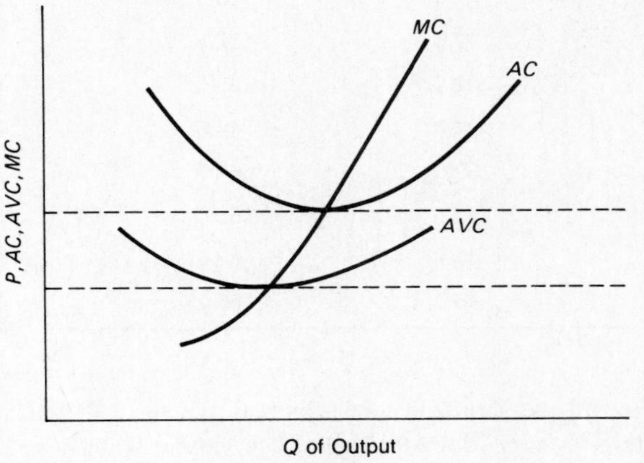

Figure 22-3

In these circumstances, the *MC* curve must also cut through the exact minimum of the *AC* curve. Why? For exactly the same reasons as those developed in question 6. Notice, finally, that the intersection of *MC* with *AC* will *(always occur at a higher level of output / usually occur at a higher level of output / always occur at a lower level of output)* than its intersection with *AVC*.

fall; larger; rise; the law of diminishing returns; usually occur at a higher level of output (as long as fixed costs are greater than zero)

Figure 22-3 therefore illustrates the general relationship that must exist between the three most important per-unit cost measures. Given the law of diminishing returns, *AC* must be, at least approximately, U-shaped, and *MC* must cut through its bottom point. *AVC* may or may not be U-shaped, but it most certainly will rise as plant capacity is approached. If it *is* U-shaped, and if it has a unique bottom point, then *MC* will cut through that point.

Short-run cost curves of the type illustrated in Figure 22-3 answer one type of question: Given the plant that we now own and assuming fixed input prices, what would be the average and marginal cost of producing any particular level of output? That is not, however, the only question in town. The firm can ask a different question with a different time frame: What would be the lowest cost of producing any given level of output, no matter how small, if we had complete freedom over the size of the plant? Put another way, what size plant would produce some (any) given output at the lowest possible cost given the current state of technology and the current level of input prices?

When a firm asks this second question, it is moving beyond the limitation of its present fixed plant size. It is thinking in terms of freedom in the matter of plant size, and looking for the output that (with such freedom) would yield maximum profit. For this purpose, it needs a *long-run average cost curve* (*LRAC*, or *LAC*). Such a curve is unlike the *AC* curve of Figure 22-3, which refers to a plant of given size. In building the *LRAC* curve, you ask: For each and every output, what is the lowest-attainable *AC* (given present input prices and technology), no matter what the plant size needed to obtain that *AC*? (The firm is assumed to have complete and reliable information as to the *AC* curve that goes with each and every plant that could possibly be built.)

The graph illustrating *LRAC* for a firm is structurally the same as that for the short-run situation; i.e., cost is measured on the vertical axis and the quantity of output is measured horizontally. But on the long-run diagram, Figure 22-4, for example, we show a number of possible short-run *AC* curves. There is one such short-run *AC* curve for each possible plant size. The "bottom edge" resulting from this accumulation of short-run curves is the

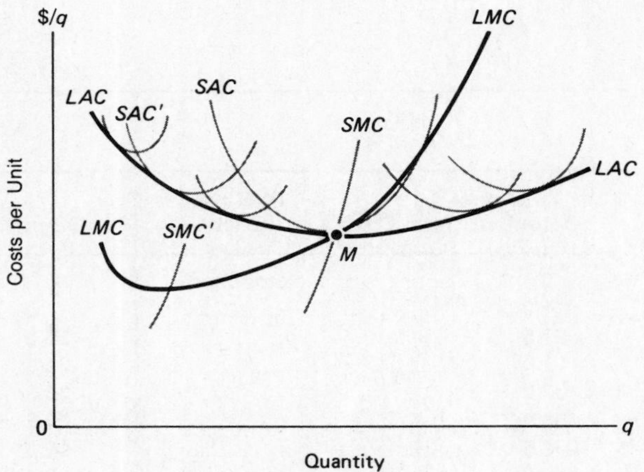

Figure 22-4

long-run curve. This long-run curve is sometimes called (borrowing a mathematicians' term) the "lower envelope curve," or the "planning curve."

8. a. The firm's long-run *AC* curve for commodity X could be used to indicate (pick one or more):

(1) the lowest possible *AC* at which any quantity of X could be produced, and the particular size of plant needed in order to obtain that *AC*.

(2) the level of output at which it would be most profitable to produce X.

(3) the particular quantity (or quantities) of X at which the very lowest per-unit cost (*AC*) of all would be possible, and the plant size (or range of plant sizes) required for that minimum *AC*.

(4) the price the firm ought to charge in order to obtain the maximum profit from the sale of X.

b. The long-run *AC* is usually depicted as a saucer-shaped, U-shaped curve—first falling, then flat, and finally rising. Sometimes the bottom is flat over a region; sometimes the bottom is simply a single point.

The falling region is that of *increasing returns to scale*, where, as the size of plant is increased and the scale of operations expanded, the result is a *(higher / lower)* short-run *AC*. The flat region (or the bottom point) represents minimum-attainable *AC* (given present technology and input prices).

At some level of output (perhaps very large), presumably some inefficiencies of too-large size set in, so that the *LRAC* curve will ultimately begin to turn up, even if only slightly. This is a region of *(increasing / constant / decreasing)* returns to scale. In light of recent developments in communication and record-keeping methods, such as computers, it is clear that a firm can often become very large indeed without incurring inefficiencies of large size that are of sufficient importance to offset the economies of large-scale operation.

---

a. (1) and **(3)** **b.** lower; decreasing

9. This question investigates the link between the production function developed in Chapter 21 and the cost curves developed in the present chapter in the context of short- and long-run production decisions. To that end, consider the production function recorded in Table 22-2; it indicates the level of output associated with various levels of labor employment (*L*) for 1, 2, and 3 units of capital (*K*). In the long run, the firm in question will have discretion over its employment decisions concerning both capital and labor. In the short run, however, the chosen capital stock is fixed and only the quantity of labor employed can be adjusted. Assume throughout the problem that the unit price of capital is $5 and that the unit price of labor is $10.

Table 22-2

L	*K* = 1	*K* = 2	*K* = 3
0	0	0	0
2	15.0	17.0	17.5
3	21.5	25.0	24.5
4	27.0	32.5	31.5
5	32.0	38.5	38.5
6	36.0	44.5	45.0
7	39.5	51.0	51.5
8	42.0	56.0	58.0
9	44.0	62.0	64.5
10	45.0	66.0	70.0

a. Record the short-run total cost and average cost values for all three possible levels of capital employment in Table 22-3. Graph all three short-run *AC* curves in Figure 22-5. Sketch the long-run *AC* curve.

b. Movement from 1 unit of capital to 2 units of capital captures a region of *(increasing / constant / decreasing)* returns to scale. We know this for two reasons. First, doubling inputs causes output to increase by *(more than / exactly / less than)*

Table 22-3

(a) *K* = 1			(b) *K* = 2			(c) *K* = 3		
Output	Total Cost	Average Cost	Output	Total Cost	Average Cost	Output	Total Cost	Average Cost
0	______	undefined	0	______	undefined	0	______	undefined
15.0	______	______	17.0	______	______	17.5	______	______
21.5	______	______	25.0	______	______	24.5	______	______
27.0	______	______	32.5	______	______	31.5	______	______
32.0	______	______	38.5	______	______	38.5	______	______
36.0	______	______	44.5	______	______	45.0	______	______
39.5	______	______	51.0	______	______	51.5	______	______
42.0	______	______	56.0	______	______	58.0	______	______
44.0	______	______	62.0	______	______	64.5	______	______
45.0	______	______	66.0	______	______	70	______	______

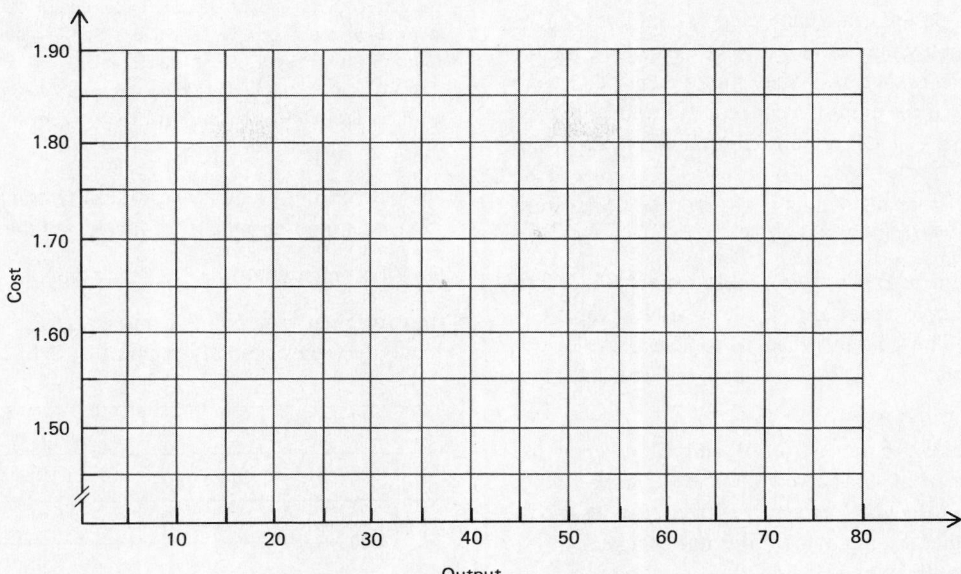

Figure 22-5

100 percent. Second, the minimum of the short-run *AC* curve for $K = 2$ is *(higher than / exactly equal to / lower than)* the minimum for $K = 1$. For $K = 1$, the minimum short-run average cost is $______; for $K = 2$, it is $______.

c. Movement from 2 units of capital to 3 units of capital reflects a region of *(increasing / constant / decreasing)* returns to scale. The minimum of the short-run *AC* curve for $K = 3$ is $______, which is *(higher than / exactly equal to / less than)* the corresponding minimum for $K = 2$.

d. Were the firm to consider moving from $K = 1$ to $K = 3$, the production numbers indicate *(increasing / constant / decreasing)* returns to scale. Multiplying inputs by a factor of 3 causes output to *(less than / exactly / more than)* triple. The corresponding minima of the short-run *AC* curves are identical.

e. Suppose that you are working for the firm and are asked how much labor and capital should be employed to produce output at the smallest possible average cost. You would recommend that ______ units of capital be operated by ______ units of labor to produce ______ units of output.

---

a. Reading down the columns: For $K = 1$, total cost: $5, 25, 35, etc., in increments of $10; average cost: $1.67, 1.63, 1.67, 1.72, 1.81, 1.90, 2.02, 2.16, 2.33. For $K = 2$ total cost: $10, 30, 40, etc., in increments of $10; average cost: $1.76, 1.60, 1.54, 1.56, 1.57, 1.57, 1.61, 1.61, 1.67. For $K = 3$, total cost: $15, 35, 45, etc., in increments of $10; average cost: $2.00, 1.83, 1.75, 1.69, 1.67, 1.65, 1.64, 1.63, 1.64

b. increasing; more than; lower than; 1.63; 1.54

c. decreasing; 1.63; higher than

d. constant; exactly

e. 2; 4; 32.5

The long-run *AC* curve provides a wealth of information. Most importantly, it identifies the smallest average expenditure on inputs that can support any given level of output. Since it is constructed assuming discretion over the employment of *all* factors, the input combination that produces this smallest average cost *must* satisfy the least-cost rule. That is to say, the combination of inputs associated with any output-cost pair located on the long-run *AC* curve is characterized by the equality of the marginal product to price ratios of *all* inputs.

10. a. Suppose that 200 units of some good X are being produced using inputs A, B, and C. The quantities employed, prices, and *MPs* of inputs A, B, and C are shown in Table 22-4.

Table 22-4

	A	B	C
Quantity employed	10	30	20
Price	$2	$1	$3
MP	2	3	1

Total cost incurred for the 200-unit output is $*(90 / 100 / 110 / 120 / 130)*. The least-cost rule *(is / is not)* being satisfied.

Leave input A to one side in order to compare B and C. The last unit of B employed added *(1 / 2 / 3 / 4)* unit(s) of X to output. Since B's price is $1, each of these units costs approximately *(10 / 25 / 33 / 39 / 75)* cents. In contrast, the last unit of C employed added *(1 / 2 / 3 / 4)* unit(s) of X. Since C's price is $3, that unit cost $*(1 / 2 / 3 / 4)*.

b. The conditions of part **a** mean that total cost could be reduced by increasing the employment of *(B / C)* and decreasing that of *(B / C)*. What would output be if the employment of C were reduced by 3 units and the employment of B were increased by 1 unit? Assuming that C's *MP* remains constant over the 3-unit change, it would be *(196 / 197 / 200 / 201 / 203)* units of X. Total cost would, as a result of this change, *(rise / fall)* from $110 to $*(100 / 102 / 106 / 108 / 112)*.

c. As the employment of B rose, we should expect B's *MP* to *(rise / fall)*; as the employment of C fell, we would expect C's *MP* to *(rise / fall)*. Thus, as the changes indicated are made, we would be *(approaching / moving away from)* the least-cost position.

d. Now reverse the *MP* numbers for B and C given at the beginning of this question; make them 1 and 3, respectively. This revised situation *(would / would not)* then be a least-cost position, assuming that A employment did not change.

Suppose, for one final example in this question, that the *MPs* of A, B, and C were 4, 2, and 6, respectively. Let their prices remain as before. This *(would / would not)* be a least-cost position.

---

a. 110; is not; 3; 33; 1; 3 **b.** B; C; 200; fall; 102 **c.** fall; rise; approaching **d.** would; would

11. Elements of opportunity cost should always be included in a firm's cost calculations. Suppose, for example, that you run your own firm. You should, therefore, include the cost of your own labor—$5 per hour—in reckoning costs. Suddenly, you learn that you could get a job down the street at $10 per hour. The fact of this opportunity means that you should include in costs your labor at *(zero / $5 / $7.50 / $10)* per hour. (Of course, you may prefer to run your own business. If so, you may be happy to continue to run it, even though conceivably it might seem to be running at a slight loss when this full opportunity cost is counted.)

$10

12. Suppose that you are considering whether to fly from Boston to Washington or to take the bus. The airfare is $100 and the flight takes 1 hour. The bus fare is only $50, but the drive takes 6 hours. How much would the two options cost:

a. if you are a businessperson whose time costs $40 per hour?

____

____

b. if you are a student whose time is worth $4 per hour? ______

____

c. to you? ________________

____

---

a. Including the cost of time, airfare is $100 + $40 = $140 and bus fare is $50 + 6($40) = $290. **b.** Airfare is $100 + $4 = $104 and bus fare is $50 + 6($4) = $74. **c.** I do not know the cost of your time, but if it exceeds $10 per hour, then the plane is the better deal.

13. Given the production-possibility frontier shown in Figure 22-6, the opportunity cost of increasing the production of wheat by 1000 units would be ______ units of corn if the economy were originally at point *A* and ______ units of corn if the economy were originally at point *B*. Why?

____

____

____

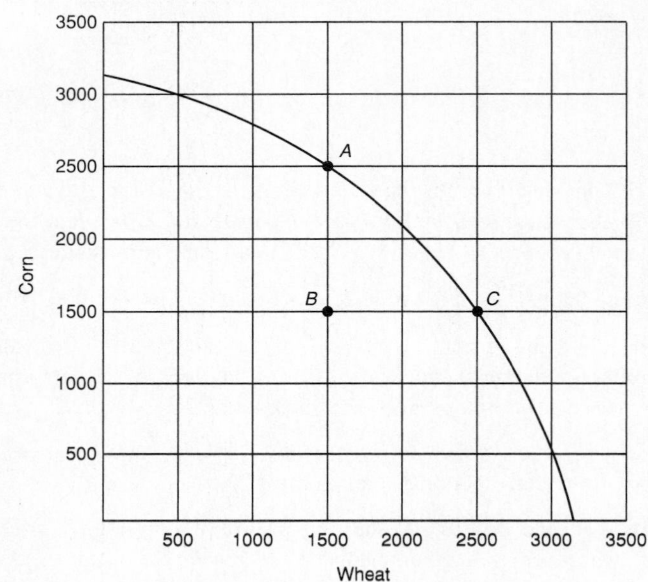

Figure 22-6

1000; 0; Opportunity cost involves transferring utilized resources from one activity to another, and movement from *B* to *C* simply employs resources that were otherwise unemployed.

14. Consider the data recorded in Table 22-5. Assume that land is the input whose employment can be adjusted only in the long run.

a. Plot the short-run *MC* and *AC* curves in Figure 22-7.

b. Now assume that the price of labor doubles. Plot the resulting revised *MC* and *AC* curves in Figure 22-7 using a different color this time. Which of the following statements accurately describes the result of this price increase? ______

(1) Both marginal cost and average cost shift down.

(2) Both marginal cost and average cost shift up.

Table 22-5

(1) Output (tons of wheat)	(2) Land Inputs (acres)	(3) Labor Inputs (workers)	(4) Land Rent (dollars per acre)	(5) Labor Wage (dollars per worker)
0	15	0	12	5
1	15	6	12	5
2	15	11	12	5
3	15	15	12	5
4	15	21	12	5
5	15	31	12	5
6	15	45	12	5
7	15	63	12	5

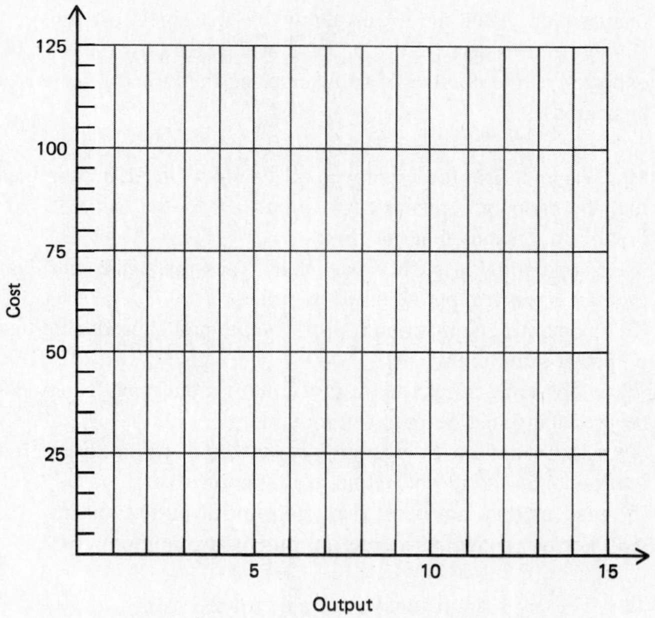

Figure 22-7

(3) Marginal cost shifts up, but average cost is left where it is.

(4) Average cost shifts up, but marginal cost is left where it is.

(5) Average cost shifts up or down depending upon the elasticity of demand, but marginal cost definitely shifts up.

c. Suppose that part **b** had referred to a doubling of the cost of land. Which of the statements there would then have been correct? ________

d. Finally, assume that overall productivity doubles. Which of the statements listed in part **b** would now apply? ________

---

a. For *AC*, plot (1,$210.00), (2,$117.50), (3,$85.00), (4,$71.25), (5,$67.00), (6,$67.50), and (7,$70.78). For *MC*, plot (1.5,$25.00), (2.5,$20.00), (3.5, $30.000), (4.5,$50.00), (5.5,$70.00), and (6.5,$90.00).
b. For AC, plot (1,$240.00), (2,$145.00), (3,$110.00), (4,$97.50), (5,$98.00), (6,$105.00), and (7,$115.78). For *MC*, plot (1.5,$50.00), (2.5,$40.00), (3.5,$60.00), (4.5,$100.00), (5.5,$140.00), and (6.5,$180.00). Statement **(2)** is accurate.
c. (4) (Changes in fixed cost do not affect marginal cost; they affect average cost, though, through average fixed cost.)
d. (1)

---

15. Which of the following statements are true (T) or false (F)?

a. Average costs are minimized when marginal costs are at their lowest point. . . . . *(T / F)*

b. Because fixed costs never change, average fixed cost is a constant for each level of output. . . . . *(T / F)*

c. Average cost is rising whenever marginal cost is rising. . . . . *(T / F)*

d. The opportunity cost of spilling oil in the Atlantic Ocean is zero because no one pays to sail or swim there. . . . . *(T / F)*

e. A firm minimizes costs when it spends the same amount on each input. . . . . *(T / F)*

All are false.

QUIZ: Multiple Choice

1. Fixed cost for a firm's operating plant means:
(1) any cost whose amount is established at the time the input is purchased.
(2) the minimum cost of producing any given quantity of output under the most favorable operating conditions.
(3) any cost whose per-unit amount has been settled for some considerably future period, such as a long-term wage contract with a labor union.
(4) the amount of cost that must be incurred even if zero output is produced.
(5) none of these things.

2. Marginal cost for a firm's operating plant means:
(1) the increase over normal cost that must sometimes be paid to obtain output, such as the extra amount of overtime pay.
(2) the cost incurred even if the firm produces zero output.
(3) the difference between the amount of total cost actually incurred to produce any given output and what is considered to be the minimum possible total cost of producing that output.
(4) the increase in total cost that accrues from a 1-unit increase in quantity produced.
(5) the increase in total cost that accrues from any increase in quantity produced, whether 1 unit or more.

3. The property taxes a firm must pay on its plant are increased; i.e., its fixed cost is increased. On a graph illustrating this firm's cost curves, the marginal cost curve would be affected by this fixed cost increase as follows. It would:
(1) move to the right.
(2) move to the left.
(3) move upward.
(4) move downward.
(5) not move at all.

4. Total cost in a certain plant, at an output level of 1000 units daily, is $4900. If production were to be reduced by 1 unit (to a total of 999 units), total cost would becomes $4890. Within this output range:
(1) average cost (*AC*) would exceed marginal cost (*MC*).
(2) *AC* and *MC* would be approximately equal.
(3) *MC* would exceed *AC*.
(4) no comparison between *MC* and *AC* is possible, since the information given is not sufficient to determine *MC*.
(5) no comparison between *MC* and *AC* is possible, since the information given is not sufficient to determine *AC*.

5. If the term "opportunity cost" is used with respect to any of a firm's costs, it means:
(1) including as the cost of any input the market price or return that input is offered in any other occupation.
(2) certain nonrecurring or once-and-for-all costs involved in getting production under way.
(3) costs which would be incurred even at zero output but which do not increase in amount as output is increased.
(4) any cost incurred which does not involve an actual outlay of cash.
(5) nothing at all, since the term would not be used with respect to production costs.

6. At the quantity of output where average cost has reached its minimum level:
(1) average variable cost will equal fixed cost.
(2) profit must be at its maximum level for the firm.
(3) marginal cost will equal average variable cost.
(4) marginal cost will equal average cost.
(5) none of the above is necessarily true.

7. If marginal cost exceeds average cost (*AC*) within a certain range of plant outputs, then, with respect to any increase in output within that range:
(1) *AC* must rise.
(2) *AC* must fall.
(3) *AC* must either rise or fall.
(4) *AC* must remain constant.
(5) *AC* may rise, fall, or remain constant.

8. In a certain plant, marginal cost is $2.00 at 400 units of output weekly, and it is $2.50 at 500 units of output. Referring to output increases within this 400-to-500 range, average cost:
(1) must rise.
(2) must fall.
(3) must remain constant.
(4) may rise, may fall, or both, but cannot remain constant throughout this output range.

9. The long-run average cost curve is intended to show (referring to given conditions of technology):
(1) the minimum cost of producing any given output quantity, if the firm can select, for each such output, the plant most economical for producing that quantity.
(2) the minimum cost for the profit-maximizing output, using the particular plant best suited for that particular output.
(3) the minimum cost of producing any given output quantity, using a plant of one given size only for all such outputs, but the plant which yields the lowest-attainable average cost figure.
(4) the minimum cost of producing any given output quantity, using a plant of one given size only for all such outputs, but the plant which yields the lowest-attainable marginal cost figure.
(5) the future increase or decrease in average cost that can be expected as the number of firms entering the industry increases or decreases.

10. When a firm has employed all its inputs in such quantities that the ratio of input price to input *MP* is the same for all inputs, this means that the firm:
(1) is operating in such a way that it has made the marginal product of each input equal to its price.
(2) is operating at maximum-profit output and is producing that output at minimum cost.
(3) is operating at maximum-profit output, but may or may not be producing that output at minimum cost.
(4) may or may not be operating at maximum-profit output, but is producing its present output at minimum cost.
(5) may or may not be at maximum-profit output and may or may not be producing its present output at minimum cost.

11. The production function alone will tell a firm:
(1) what it will cost to produce any given quantity of output.
(2) the maximum-profit level of output.
(3) the various combinations of inputs that should be used in order to produce any given quantity of output most efficiently, i.e., at least money cost.
(4) the various combinations of inputs that could be used in order to produce any given quantity of output.
(5) none of these.

12. A, B, and C are inputs employed to produce good X. If the quantity of A used is increased, we would ordinarily expect A's marginal product to:
(1) increase, in all circumstances.
(2) increase if the quantities of B and C are left unchanged, but not necessarily to increase if B and C quantities are increased in the same proportion.
(3) decrease, in all circumstances.

(4) decrease if the quantities of B and C are left unchanged, but not necessarily to decrease if B and C quantities are increased in the same proportion.
(5) decrease if B and C quantities are increased in the same proportion, increase if B and C quantities are left unchanged.

13. When a firm has satisfied the least-cost rule for input employment, then it:
(1) cannot be at its maximum-profit position.
(2) may or may not be at its maximum-profit position, but must be operating at the particular output level which yields lowest-attainable average cost.
(3) must be at its maximum-profit position.
(4) may or may not be at its maximum-profit position, but will have equated the marginal product of each input with marginal revenue.
(5) may or may not be at its maximum-profit position—the information furnished is insufficient to be able to tell.

14. One of the following is not a correct statement of the relationship between the total product of an input or factor and the marginal product (*MP*) of that factor. Which one?
(1) Total product at any output level equals the sum of all *MPs* up to that level.
(2) *MP* at any output level multiplied by that output quantity equals total product.
(3) Graphically, the slope of the total product curve at any output level equals *MP* at that level.
(4) Graphically, the area under the *MP* curve for any quantity of the input equals the total product associated with that input quantity.
(5) *MP* is defined as the increment in total product resulting from a 1-unit increase in the factor (other factor quantities being held constant).

15. A firm employs such quantities of inputs A and B that the marginal product of A is 60 units, and that of B is 40 units. Prices of A and B are $4 and $2, respectively. Assuming A and B to be the only inputs involved, this firm is:
(1) producing its present output at minimum cost, but definitely is not earning maximum possible profit.
(2) not producing its present output at minimum cost, and is not earning maximum possible profit.
(3) producing its present output at minimum cost, but may or may not be earning maximum possible profit.
(4) not producing its present output at minimum cost, but nevertheless is earning maximum possible profit.
(5) possibly in any of the positions just described—information furnished is insufficient to tell.

16. In question 15, change the price of input A from $4 to $3, all other information remaining as before. Which alternative in that question is then correct?
(1).
(2).
(3).
(4).
(5).

SUGGESTED ANSWERS TO QUESTIONS IN THE TEXT: Chapter 22

1. Remember that the categorization should depend upon the time frame; in the long run, everything is a variable cost.

2. Definitions. Recall that *MC*, since it reflects how costs change as output is altered, depends only upon variable cost.

3. *MC* and *AVC* do not change; *TC*, *AC*, and *AFC* shift up. Minimum occurs where *MC* = *AC* = $60 at 5 units.

4. *AC* above (below) *MC* means that the next increment lowers (increases) the average; i.e., *AC* is falling (climbing). Only when *MC* = *AC* is the *AC* neither rising nor falling; i.e., it is at its minimum.

5. Going from a few to a continuous pattern makes the envelope smooth.

6. Diminishing returns means that successive increases in employment (costing the same, say $*C*) generate smaller and smaller increases in output. *MC*, as the change in cost divided by the change in output, must therefore climb because the denominator climbs against a constant numerator (=$*C*). The falling part relates the "eventually" clause in the definition of diminishing returns.

7. **a.** Fixed cost equals 15 × $12 = $180. *MC* is the cost of the labor required for each unit increase in output: $30, $25, $20, $30, $50, $70, $90. Variable cost is total labor times the wage: $30, $55, $65, $105, $155, $225, $315.
b. Doubling the wage increases *AC* and *MC* (doubles, in fact, *MC* but not *AC*).
c. Doubling productivity cuts *MC* and *AC* in half. Factor prices and productivity both influence cost curves.)

8. **a.** Average costs are minimized when marginal cost equals average cost; *AC* is falling where *MC* is minimized.
b. *AFC* = *FC*/output; *FC* may be fixed, but output changes with output.
c. *AC* is rising whenever *MC* > *AC*, but *AC* falls with *MC* rising where *MC* < *AC*.
d. The absence of a market does not imply the absence of value.
e. The least-cost rule collapses to this only in *very* special circumstances.

9. **a.** Airplane costs $100 + (1 × $40) = $140, including the opportunity cost of the travel time; the bus costs $50 + (6 × $40) = $290.
b. Airplane: $100 + (1 × $4) = $104; bus, $50 + (6 × $4) = $74.

c. How much is your time worth? More than \$10 per hour? Then take the plane!

10. **a.** See answer 4 above.

b. AC a straight line means that $AC = \$TC/X = a + bX$ for parameters a and b. For panel **(a)** of the figure, for example both $a > 0$ and $b > 0$; for panel **(b)** $a > 0$ and $b < 0$; for panel **(c)**, $a > 0$ and $b = 0$. So $\$TC = aX + bX^2$ and $MC = a + 2bX$. MC is a straight line with the same intercept and twice the slope.

APPENDIX: 22

Production, Cost Theory, and Decisions of the Firm

This appendix deals with one of the topics that the chapter discusses: how to choose among input combinations so as to obtain that particular alternative which costs the least. If we limit the number of inputs to two (e.g., labor and land), the idea of the "production function" can be illustrated by a series of *equal-product lines*. On the same diagram, we may easily draw any number of *equal-cost lines*. Taken in combination, equal-product and equal-cost lines readily outline the whole business of cost minimization.

Having worked through the appendix in this simplified two-input case, you should be able to meet the following objectives.

LEARNING OBJECTIVES

1. Define (in terms of the graphical illustration of the production function) (*a*) an equal-cost line, (*b*) an equal-product line.

2. Explain why the minimum-cost point for any given output is found at the point of tangency between an equal-cost line and the equal-product line for that particular output.

3. Show how it is possible to develop a firm's total cost curve by reference to a series of these tangency points.

1. From Table 22A-1, show in Figure 22A-1 the various land-labor combinations that will produce an output of 346 units. Join these points with a smooth curve. Repeat the process for outputs of 490 and 282. For identification, label the three curves $q = 282$, $q = 346$, and $q = 490$.

Each of the three resulting curves in Figure 22A-1 is an equal-product line. It is correctly described as follows (pick one):

a. Each and every point on the curve stands for a different combination of labor and land quantities; these combinations all have the common property that they can be bought for the same total dollar outlay.

b. Each and every point on the curve stands for a different quantity of output; these quantities all have the common property that they can be bought for the same dollar outlay on labor and land.

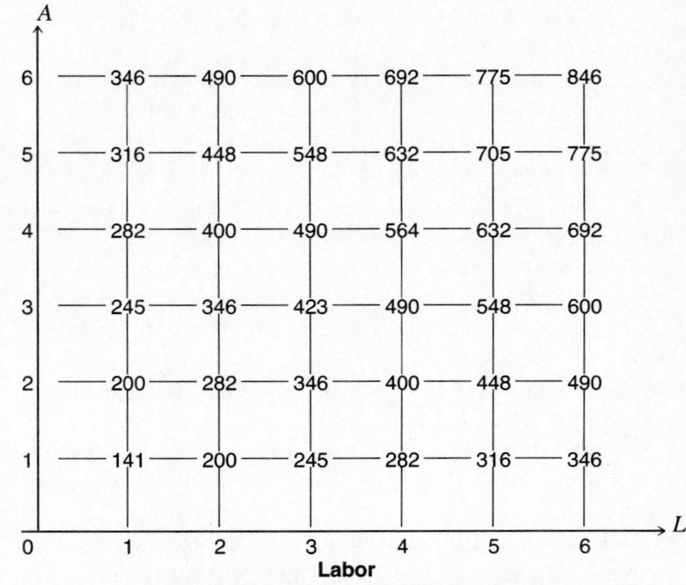

A \ L	1	2	3	4	5	6
6	346	490	600	692	775	846
5	316	448	548	632	705	775
4	282	400	490	564	632	692
3	245	346	423	490	548	600
2	200	282	346	400	448	490
1	141	200	245	282	316	346

Labor

Table 22A-1 A tabular picture of a production function relating amount of output to varying combinations of labor and land inputs

When you have 3 land units and 2 labor units available, the engineer tells you your maximum attainable output is 346 units. Note the different ways to produce 346. Do the same for 490. (The production function shown in the table is a special case of the "Cobb-Douglas production function," one given by the formula $Q = 100\sqrt{2LA}$)

c. Each and every point on the curve stands for a different combination of labor and land quantities; these combinations all have the common property that they can produce some given quantity of output.

---

c

2. **a.** Equal-cost lines may also be drawn in Figure 22A-1. Suppose that labor costs \$2 per unit, and that the rental of a unit of land costs \$3. Pick, at random, any dollar amount that would be sufficient to buy a few units of land and labor at these prices—say, \$12. Now you must draw a line which shows all the possible combinations of land units and labor units which (given these prices) \$12 would just buy.

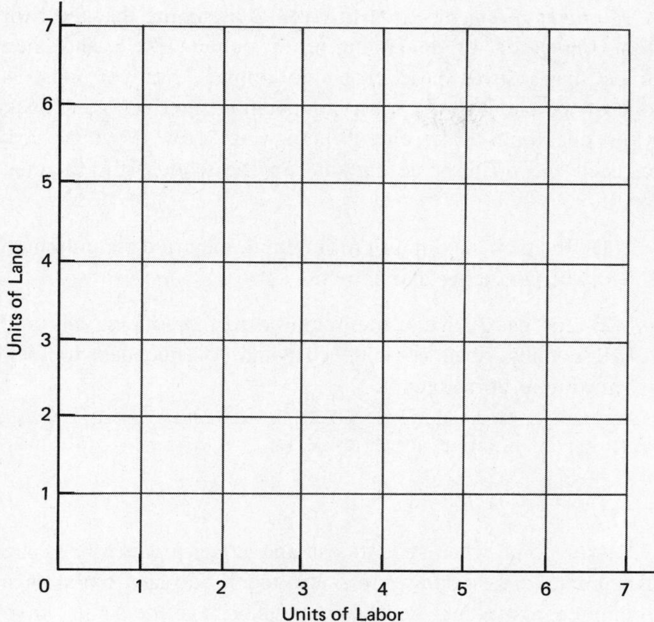

Figure 22A-1

If, for example, the entire $12 were spent on land, it would buy *(1 / 2 / 3 / 4 / 5 / 6)* units. So one point on the $12 equal-cost line would, in Figure 22A-1, fall on the *(vertical / horizontal)* axis—the one measuring land units.

Another possibility would be to spend all the $12 on labor units. If so, it would buy *(1 / 2 / 3 / 4 / 5 / 6)* units; and another point on the $12 equal-cost line would be on the *(vertical / horizontal)* axis.

The full $12 equal-cost line is a straight-line joining these two end points. (Draw this line in Figure 22A-1.) Take *any* and-labor combinations that $12 will just buy (given the two prices specified)—for example, 2 land units and 3 labor units. The point on the diagram corresponding to these two values falls on the line just drawn. That is, this line sums up all the possible land-labor combinations which $12 will just buy.

b. Which of the equal-product curves drawn earlier does this $12 equal-cost line barely touch at a point of tangency? *(the 282 line / the 346 line / the 490 line / none of them)*

---

a. 4; vertical; 6; horizontal **b.** The 346 line

3. One point on this equal-cost line is 1½ labor and 3 land. The output which this combination would produce, according to Figure 22A-1 would be *(less than 282—probably about 250 / between 282 and 346—probably about 300 / between 346 and 490—probably about 420 / more than 490—probably about 530)*. In the given circumstances, and with the goal of minimizing cost, it *(would / would not)* be sensible to spend $12 to buy this particular combination of inputs.

---

between 282 and 346—probably about 300; would not

4. a. Which alternative in question 1 correctly describes the equal-cost line you have drawn? . . . . *(1 / 2 / 3)*

b. Remember that the cost figure of $12 was picked at random. There is nothing to indicate that it is the amount of cost the firm would actually incur, or should incur; it is just some figure convenient for illustration. (There are plenty of other cost figures that could be used, and plenty of other equal-cost lines that could be drawn; we'll come to this in a moment.) But suppose we assume arbitrarily that the firm did have just $12 to spend, and wanted to spend it to the best advantage. Expressing this $12 as an equal-cost line, what would the firm seek to do? (Pick one.)

(1) Move up or down that line seeking the highest-attainable equal-product curve the line encounters.

(2) Find the point on the equal-cost line which represents the lowest dollar outlay for the labor and land inputs.

(3) Move up or down that line seeking the lowest-attainable equal-product curve the line encounters.

c. Still assuming land and labor prices of $3 and $2, respectively, draw in Figure 22A-1 the equal-cost line signifying total expenditure of $6—another cost figure picked at random. Now note the properties of the two equal-cost lines. They are *(parallel / not parallel)*. The line for $12 cost lies *(below and to the left / above and to the right)* of the $6 cost line.

Thus, given a fixed pair of input prices, the higher the cost figure selected, the *(higher and farther to the right / lower and farther to the left)* the corresponding equal-cost line will be. If the input prices are the same for any two or more such lines, then they will be parallel; i.e., they will have the same slope. Given such fixed input prices, the swapping terms between land and labor (the rate at which you could exchange a little less of one for a little more of the other) are fixed, regardless of the amount available to be spent.

---

a. (1) b. (1) c. parallel; above and to the right; higher and to the right

5. Draw a third equal-cost line parallel to the previous two, but this time draw it so that it just touches your 282 equal-product curve. Drawing this line parallel to the other two implies that (pick one):

a. The dollar expenditure on each of the inputs is the same.

b. It touches the same equal-product curve as did the other two.

c. The prices of land and labor are again $3 and $2.

The equal-cost line you have just drawn stands for a dollar outlay of approximately $*(5 / 10 / 12 / 15 / 18)*. (HINT: Use the same device employed in question 2a. Go to either one of the line's two end points, where all the money is spent on one of the two inputs. How much does it cost to buy that particular quantity?)

---

c; 10

6. a. As you study these equal-product and equal-cost curves, it becomes evident that the points of tangency between them—the points where an equal-cost curve just touches an equal-product curve—are important. Why is that so? (More than one of the alternatives may be correct.)

(1) Because for any given level of output it indicates the lowest possible equal-cost line that can be reached—i.e., it indicates minimum cost for that output.

(2) Because for any given level of outlay on factors it indicates the highest possible equal-product line that can be reached—i.e., it indicates the maximum output that can be obtained for that dollar outlay.

(3) Because it indicates maximum-profit output level.

(4) Because it indicates the minimum possible level of output that can be attained for any given dollar outlay.

b. You now have drawn three equal-cost curves, and two of them are tangent to equal-product curves. (An equal-product curve indicating somewhere around 140 units of output, had you drawn it, would be tangent to the third equal-cost curve, that was identified with cost $6.)

Studying carefully these tangency points, you will notice that each such point defines a pair of numbers. For the two tangency points involved here, therefore, there are two pairs of numbers corresponding to cost and output. Which of the following accurately describes these pairs?

(1) Output 282, cost $12; output 346, cost about $10.

(2) Output 282, cost about $10; output 346, cost $12.

(3) Output 346, cost $12; output 490, cost $15.

(4) Output 282, cost $12; output 490, cost $15.

c. You must think through the significance of these pairs of figures. Given the specified prices of land and labor, an output of 282 units cannot be produced for less than $*(6 / 10 / 12 / 15 / 20)*, and an output of 346 units cannot be produced for less than $*(6 / 10 / 12 / 15 / 20)*. The significance of these two pairs of figures, then, is that (pick one):

(1) one of them is maximum-profit output.

(2) they are two points on the total cost curve.

(3) they discourage anyone from studying economics.

d. Thus, given the production function and input prices, the firm can develop its total cost curve; that is, the minimum cost of production, in the given circumstances of technology and input prices, for each and any level of output. (We have here developed the minimum cost for two levels of output. The cost for the many other possible levels would be obtained by consulting other tangency points between equal-cost and equal-product curves.)

Students often make the mistake of assuming that the firm first settles on its maximum-profit output level, and then finds the cost of producing that output. Not so: cost is one of the elements in profit computation, and you can't pick your maximum-profit output until you know the total cost of each and all possible outputs. So the sequence is to (pick one):

(1) first pick maximum-profit output, then find the minimum cost of producing that output.

(2) first establish the minimum cost of producing any and all outputs, then combine cost and revenue data to pick maximum-profit output.

---

a. (1) and **(2)** **b. (2)** **c.** 10; 12; **(2)** **d. (2)**

7. Any point where equal-cost and equal-product lines are tangent to one another (i.e., just touch, do not cross) is a minimum-cost point. At this point, they have the same slope. Using *A* and *L* as symbols for land and labor, respectively, then the slope of the equal-*(cost / product)* line is always $-P_L/P_A$. Slope of the equal-*(cost / product)* line is always $-MP_L/MP_A$. A point at which the two slope values are equal is always a minimum-cost point.

---

cost; product

Do not be too disturbed if these matters of slope cause you difficulty. The essential point, which is not too hard to grasp, is that a least-cost point must be one where an equal-product line is just tangent to an equal-cost line. When we go on to express this tangency point in terms of the slopes of these two lines, we are just trying to state the nature of this least-cost position in more precise (and mathematical) form.

In particular, you may have trouble understanding why the slope of any equal-product line must be $-MP_L/MP_A$. Here is a rough explanation: Slope is always the ratio of the two changes needed to move from one point on the line to another point very close by. Suppose land is reduced by 1 tiny unit and that labor must be increased by 2 tiny units to compensate (stay on the equal-product line). That would make the slope of the equal-product line $-\frac{1}{2}$.

When land was reduced, output fell—by an amount dictated by MP_A. The amount of labor needed to make up that output loss was dictated by MP_L. Since it took the addition of 2 *L* units to compensate for the removal of 1 *A* unit, labor's *MP* must be only one-half that of land. So slope can be measured by the ratio of *MP*s as well as by the ratio of input quantity changes.

8. a. If the conditions of production are such that for any given output level there is only one possible input combination, then (pick one):

(1) there is no production function.

(2) there are no equal-product curves.

(3) this is a case of fixed proportions.

Figure 22A-2 contrasts this case, the "fixed-coefficients case," with that assumed up to this point. Both curved and right angled lines illustrate equal-product curves for some given output quantity. (You can of course draw as many of these equal-product curves as you wish, one for each possible output level. Figure 22A-2 shows only one illustrative curve for each situation.) A curved line implies that *(different input combinations are / only one input combination is)* possible for the output in question. A right-angled line implies that substitution of one input for another (thus producing a different input combination) *(is / is not)* possible.

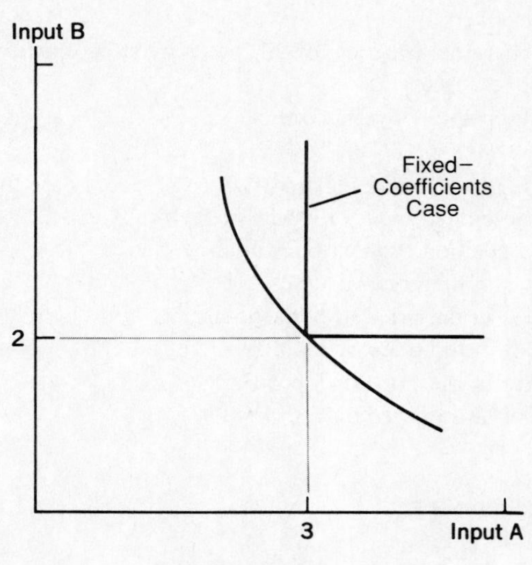

Figure 22A-2

b. In Figure 22A-2, the inputs are A and B, and in the fixed-proportions case, the required "mix" has (arbitrarily) been made 3 to 2. If B inputs were to be increased from 2 to 3 (with A inputs at 3), this would mean *(a rightward / an upward)* movement away from the "corner" on the right-angled equal-product line. With B inputs increased to 3, total output would be *(increased / unchanged / decreased)*, for we would still be on the same equal-product line.

This means that in the fixed-proportions case, the marginal product (*MP*) of each input must be *(positive / zero / negative)*. The least-cost marginal product rule set out in the chapter cannot be applied in this case, but then there is no need for it, either; there is no longer any problem of choice. Given any set of positive input prices, there is only one possible cost figure associated with each possible output level, assuming the inputs are used to the best advantage.

There is considerable dispute over the extent to which the fixed-proportions case is found in reality. In part, it may be a question of what you mean by "input" or "factor." If you speak in general terms of "labor" or "capital," substitution is certainly possible. The more specific you become about the *type* of labor or capital, though, the more likely fixed proportions seem to become.

---

a. (3); different input combinations are; is not **b.** an upward; unchanged; zero

9. Figure 22A-3 illustrates a production function involving the employment of inputs X and Y. The two curved lines are equal-product lines for outputs of 300 and 420 units. *AB* and *CD* are equal-cost lines. *AB* marks a cost outlay of $36.

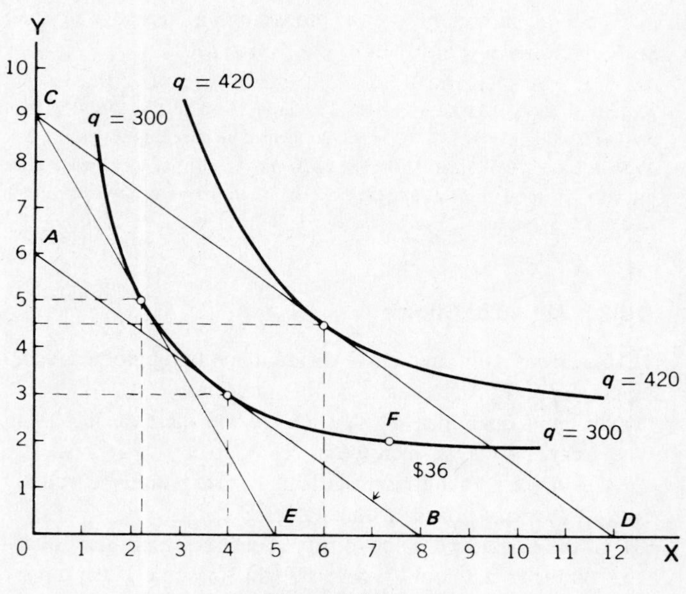

Figure 22A-3

a. From examination of *AB*, the price of X must be $*(2.50 / 4.50 / 5.50 / 6.00 / 8.00)*, and the price of Y must be $*(2.50 / 4.50 / 5.50 / 6.00 / 8.00)*. The minimum total cost of producing 300 units of output is $*(36 / 45 / 54 / 100 / 160)*. Average cost is *(5 / 10 / 12 / 15 / 60)* cents.

The quantities of X and Y used to produce 300 units of output at minimum cost could be *(2¼ of X, 5 of Y / 4 of X, 3 of Y / 5 of X, 9 of Y / 8 of X, 6 of Y)*.

Given the above prices of X and Y, equal-cost line *CD* must indicate a total outlay of $*(36 / 45 / 54 / 100 / 160)*.

b. Suppose the firm is operating at point *F*. This *(is / is not)* a minimum-cost point. Operating at *F*, the quantity of output produced would be *(100 / 300 / 360 / 400 / 420)*. Total cost of that output would be (approximately) $*(36 / 45 / 54 / 100 / 160)*. Average cost would be (approximately) *(5 / 10 / 12 / 15 / 60)* cents. For this expenditure amount, the maximum output quantity that *could* be produced would be (approximately) *(100 / 300 / 360 / 420 / 500.)*

c. Suppose equal-cost line *CD* (still signifying the same total cost amount as before) were to shift to position *CE*. This would indicate *(a decrease / an increase)* in the *(price of X / price of Y / quantity of output produced)*.

Specifically, the price of *(X / Y)* would have *(risen / fallen)* to $*(3.50 / 4.00 / 6.00 / 7.80 / 10.80)*.

This shift in *CD (would / would not)* require a comparable shift in line *AB*.

d. Given part **c**'s price change, the minimum cost of producing 300 units of output would become $*(36 / 45 / 54 / 100 / 160)*. The X and Y quantities needed to produce that 300-unit output would be *($2\frac{1}{4}$ of X, 5 of Y / 4 of X, 3 of Y / 5 of X, 9 of Y / 8 of X, 6 of Y)*.

The total (minimum) cost of producing 420 units would then be (approximately) $*(36 / 45 / 54 / 86 / 150)*.

---

a. 4.50(= \$36/8); 6.00 (= \$36/6); 36 (tangency); 0.12 (= \$36/300); 4 of X, 3 of Y (tangency); \$36 **b.** is not; 300 (equal-product curve); 45 ($\approx$ 7.5 $\times$ \$4.50 + 2 $\times$ \$6.00); 15; 360 (must be $<$ 420 and $>$ 300) **c.** an increase; price of X (Y intercept fixed means the price of Y unchanged); X; risen; 10.80; would **d.** 54; $2\frac{1}{4}$ of X, 5 of Y (tangency); 86

QUIZ: Multiple Choice

1. On an equal-product-curve diagram involving product X and inputs A and B, any equal-cost line indicates:
(1) different quantities of X, showing the increase in X that would entail an equal increase in cost.
(2) the various quantities of A and B that would be equally costly at various prices of either A or B.
(3) all the various combinations of A and B (in physical quantities of each) that could just be bought for some given money outlay.
(4) different combinations of A and B (in physical quantities of each), all having the common property that they could just produce some given quantity of X.
(5) none of the above, there being no such line on an equal-product-curve diagram.

2. Which alternative in question 1 correctly describes any equal-product line?
(1).
(2).
(3).
(4).
(5).

3. The equal-product-curve diagram illustrates:
(1) the total cost curve.
(2) the separate marginal products of the inputs involved.
(3) the point of maximum profit.
(4) the production function.
(5) different quantities of the product involved that would be equally profitable to produce.

4. The slope of an equal-cost line is a measure of:
(1) the ratio of the price of the factor on the vertical axis to the price of the factor on the horizontal axis.
(2) the ratio of the price of the factor on the horizontal axis to the price of the factor on the vertical axis.
(3) the various outputs which may be produced at a given cost.
(4) the total cost of producing a given output.
(5) the marginal productivity of one of the factors.

5. If factor or input proportions are fixed, then:
(1) all marginal products must be zero.
(2) all marginal products will be higher than if proportions were not fixed.
(3) all marginal products will be the same as if proportions were not fixed.
(4) all marginal products of all inputs must be equal, but they will not be zero.
(5) none of the above is correct.

6. In Figure 22A-4, the line *GH* is an equal-cost line, with respect to employment of inputs of factors A and B. A shift of *GH* to a position such as *GJ* would be caused by:
(1) a fall in the price of input A.
(2) a rise in the price of both inputs.
(3) a fall in the price of input B.
(4) a rise in the price of input B.
(5) a fall in the price of both inputs.

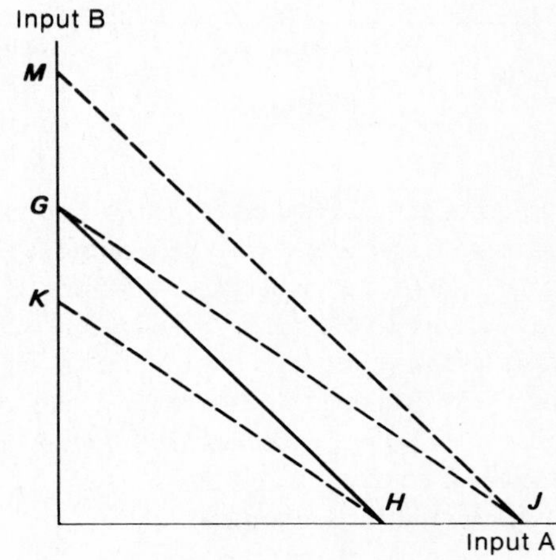

Figure 22A-4

7. Suppose, in Figure 22A-4, that the equal-cost line *GH* had instead shifted to position *MJ* (there being no change in the total

cost figure assumed). Which alternative in question 6 would correctly explain this shift?
(1).
(2).
(3).
(4).
(5).

8. Suppose, in Figure 22A-4, that the equal-cost line *GH* had instead shifted to position *KH*. Which alternative in question 6 would correctly explain this shift?
(1).
(2).
(3).
(4).
(5).

9. When an equal-cost line such as *GH* in Figure 22A-4 is drawn, it is assumed that which of the following is given or held constant. The:
(1) total expenditure on input A.
(2) total expenditure on input B.
(3) quantity of the product produced.
(4) total expenditure on either A or B, but not both.
(5) total expenditure on the two inputs combined.

10. Had question 9 referred to an equal-product rather than an equal-cost line, which alternative in that question would then be correct?
(1).
(2).
(3).
(4).
(5).

11. Equal-product lines and equal-cost lines have this property in common: any point on either of these two lines is intended to mark some:
(1) quantity of finished product output.
(2) figure of total revenue in dollars.
(3) combination of physical quantities of inputs.
(4) pair of input prices.
(5) figure of total cost in dollars.

12. When the difference between the "fixed-proportions" (*FP*) and "variable-proportions" (*VP*) cases (with respect to the use of inputs in production) is illustrated by means of equal-product curves or lines, it shows up as follows. The:
(1) *FP* case is a straight line, the *VP* case is a right angle.
(2) *FP* case is a right angle, the *VP* case is a curved line.
(3) *FP* case is a curved line, the *VP* case is a right angle.
(4) *FP* case is a right angle, the *VP* case is a straight line.
(5) *FP* case is a curved line, the *VP* case is a straight line.

SUGGESTED ANSWERS TO QUESTIONS IN THE TEXT: Appendix to Chapter 22

1. Given a wage (w) paid to labor (L) and rent (r) paid to land (A), equal-cost lines have the formula

$$\$C = rA + wL$$

In terms of slope and intercept with land measured up the vertical axis, that formula translates into

$$A = (\$C/r) - (w/r)L$$

As the wage w climbs, therefore, the line gets steeper, so tangencies must occur further up the equal-product curves, showing more land employed per unit of labor.

2. Land = 3 and labor = 2. Output doubling is accomplished by doubling all inputs if input prices are fixed; land = 6 and labor = 4 thus conforms with $q = 692$.

Let L^* and A^* minimize the cost of producing q^* for any q^*; let that cost equal $C^*(q^*)$. Now suppose that you are considering producing kq^*, where k is any number; let $C_k(kq^*)$ represent the minimum cost of producing kq^*. Constant returns to scale imply that

$$C_k(kq^*) = kC(q^*)$$

because you can produce kq^* by employing k times each input. As a result, though, $C_k(kq^*)$ can be smallest only if $C(q^*)$ is the lowest cost involved in producing q^*; i.e., $C(q^*)$ must equal $C^*(q^*)$. Since this can only be accomplished by employing L^* and A^*, kq^* can only be produced at minimum cost if kL^* and kA^* are employed. Since factor intensity was A^*/L^*, it remains $kA^*/kL^* = A^*/L^*$.

3. Do the calculus that the question instructs; notice that the definition of marginal product—ratio of the change in output for a change in the employment of an input *with other inputs (variables) and technology (function) held constant*—is *the* definition of the partial derivative of a production function with respect to an input.

4. $WMP_L/PQ = 0.75$ means that

$$MP_L L = 0.75PQ$$

$MP_K K/PQ = 0.25$ means that

$$MP_K K = 0.25PQ$$

As a result,

$$MP_L L + MP_K K = 0.75PQ + 0.25PQ = PQ$$

CHAPTER 23

COMPETITIVE SUPPLY AND COMPETITIVE MARKETS

Chapter 22 presented the litany of cost concepts that occupy the economist's mind (at least some of the time). We are now ready to apply those concepts to an analysis of how a competitive firm decides how much it wants to produce when confronted by the market that "calls out" some arbitrary price over which it has no control. The link between cost and the output decision will be based upon an assumption that firms are motivated primarily by a desire to maximize their profits. It will, in particular, be assumed that every firm chooses its desired level of output for any price by maximizing the difference between the revenue that it can earn by selling the targeted output at the given price and the *minimum* cost required to produce that output. Our study will provide insight into not only the firms' individual and market supply curves but also the structural and efficiency properties of competitive markets.

Having completed your work in this chapter, you should have accomplished the following objectives.

LEARNING OBJECTIVES

1. Describe the notion of perfect competition in terms of structure and in terms of how it limits the sphere of economic variables over which a competitive firm has influence.

2. Identify the profit-maximizing goal of each firm and indicate decision rules through which each firm can achieve that goal.

3. Review clearly the notions of total cost, fixed cost, variable cost, average cost, and marginal cost.

4. Develop the supply curve of a competitive firm in terms of marginal cost.

5. Explain breakeven ($p =$ minimum AC) and shutdown ($p <$ minum AVC) conditions and their relevance to the competitive marketplace.

6. Explain the long-run and short-run equilibrium conditions for the competitive firm and the competitive market.

7. Understand more fully why decreasing costs lead to monopolistic and oligopolistic market structures.

8. Explain the efficiency of perfect competition in terms of (*a*) marginal cost and marginal utility, (*b*) consumer surplus and net social welfare, and (*c*) a utility-possibility frontier.

This is, to be sure, a long list of learning objectives, but this is a chapter of unusual importance. There are not very many purely competitive markets in the world, but an understanding of their implications and workings is essential in understanding the significance of the imperfections that we find throughout most of reality. Perfect competition is, in short, another one of those benchmark notions against which a wide variety of other concepts can be cast and thereby more easily understood.

Perfect competition can be characterized in terms of three simple conditions. In a perfectly competitive market, the firm (1) is faced with a market price for its output over which it has no control (it is too small relative to the market to be able to affect the price), (2) can sell as much or as little as it wants to at the given price without incurring selling costs of any kind, and (3) selects its desired level of output and sales for any given price by maximizing profits.

1. a. Economists refer to both *the firm* and *the industry*; the difference between these terms is important. The individual unit producing and selling output in the hope of making a profit is the *(firm / industry)*, and its supply curve shows what this unit would offer for sale at each possible price. The total of all individual units together is the *(firm / industry)*, and the supply curve of this aggregate shows total quantity that will be offered for sale by all these units combined at each possible price.

b. A "competitive firm" is one operating under the special conditions of perfect competition. Remember carefully what was said above: *in these conditions, the firm can choose the* *quantity of output it is going to produce and sell, and it is assumed to choose the quantity which (given the market price offered) yields it the highest-attainable profit.*

"Profit" here means (pick one):

(1) total cost incurred in producing output minus total revenue or income from selling that output.

(2) total revenue or income from selling output, without regard to costs incurred.

(3) total revenue or income from selling output, minus total cost incurred in producing that output.

Profit means, then, the revenue that you take in from sales of your product, minus the costs incurred in producing that product.

c. Under conditions of perfect competition, the short-run industry supply curve can be derived from the supply curves of the individual firms *(by adding the price received by each firm for a given output to determine a market price / by adding the quantity produced by each firm for a given price to determine a market quantity supplied / only by a trained statistician)*. The short-run market supply curve therefore depends critically upon *(the number of firms in the market / the output of each firm at each price / the number of consumers in the market)*.

---

a. firm; industry **b.** **(3)** **c.** by adding the quantity produced by each firm for a given price to determine market quantity supplied; the number of firms in the market *and* the output of each firm at each price

The terms "revenue" and "cost" are used extensively in the next few chapters. They need careful review.

Revenue, or *total revenue*, is equal to total number of units sold multiplied by market price at which they sold.

Total cost captures all costs incurred in producing and selling that output. This chapter deals with the special situation of pure (or perfect) competition, however, so there are no selling costs; there are only production costs.

Recall, as well, that total cost can be divided into two distinct parts:

1. *Variable costs* reflect those costs whose total amount varies with the amount of output produced.
2. *Fixed costs* are costs which are constant regardless of the level of output and which would accordingly have to be paid by the firm even if its output were zero.

In addition, two other derivative cost notions are important:

3. *Marginal cost* measures the extra cost that would be incurred if the firm were to produce 1 more unit of output.
4. *Average cost* equals the ratio of total cost to total output.

Table 23-1

Quantity	Cost Data			Revenue Data			
				Price = $11.20		Price = $8.80	
	Total Cost	Average Cost	Marginal Cost	Revenue	Profit	Revenue	Profit
10	$100.50	____		____	$11.50	____	____
12	111.50	____	____	$134.40	____	____	____
14	124.50	____	____	$156.80	32.30	____	____
16	140.50	____	____	$179.20	____	____	____
18	162.50	____	____	____	____	____	____
20	202.50	____	____	____	____	____	____

2. Table 23-1 records a wide variety of cost and revenue information for various levels of output and two possible price specifications. It shows the total revenue obtained for each price for various quantities of output from 10 to 20 as well as the profit to be earned for each of these outputs. Complete the blanks in this table.

a. From Table 23-1, it is clear that the profit-maximizing output for a price of $11.20 would be *(12 / 14 / 16 / 18 / 20)* units. At this output, average cost would be $______ and marginal cost would approximate $______.

b. At a price of $8.80, profit-maximizing output would be *(12 / 14 / 16 / 18 / 20)*, with average cost equalling $______ and marginal cost approximating $______.

Reading down the columns: *AC*: $10.05, $9.29, $8.89, $8.78, $9.02, $10.13 *MC*: $5.50, $6.50, $8.00, $11.00, $20.00 Revenue: $112.00, $201.60, $224.00 Profit: $22.90, $38.70, $39.10, $21.50 Revenue: $88.00, $105.60, $123.20, $140.80, $158.40, $176.00 Profit: −$12.50, −$5.90, −$1.30, $0.30, −$4.10, −$26.50 **a.** 18; 9.02; 11 **b.** 16; 8.78; 8

3. **a.** At maximum-profit output, price (*P*) and *(average / marginal)* cost are equal. Think of the firm as expanding weekly output from 10 units to 11, from 11 to 12, and so on. As output quantity changes, the *AC* figure changes, and so does the *MC* figure. For maximum profit, the firm should halt output expansion when *(MC has fallen / AC has fallen / MC has risen / AC has risen)* to a level equal to price. To go further would be to produce goods whose incremental (marginal) cost exceeded the price that would be received, and profit *would fall*.

b. Refer once again to Table 23-1. Notice that it does not pay to produce and sell the 17th and 18th units at a price of $8.80 even though they could be sold profitably at $11.20. This is so because the firm has a plant of fixed size, and when its capacity output is approached, per-unit costs begin to rise. Specifically, total cost will rise by $*(6.50 / 8 / 11 / 20)* for each of the 17th and 18th units. The simple but basic point involved is this: In profit terms, it pays to produce and sell an extra unit of output only if the extra revenue that unit brings in (here, the price of that unit) exceeds the extra cost (marginal cost, the rise in total cost) which was incurred in producing and selling that extra output unit.

a. marginal: *MC* has risen **b.** 11

4. The relation between revenue, costs, and profit can be directly illustrated by a diagram. In Figure 23-1, draw the total revenue line for a price of $11.20. (Just show the point that would indicate revenue from 2 units sold at $11.20 each, from 4 units so sold, etc. Then join your points.) Now plot total cost.

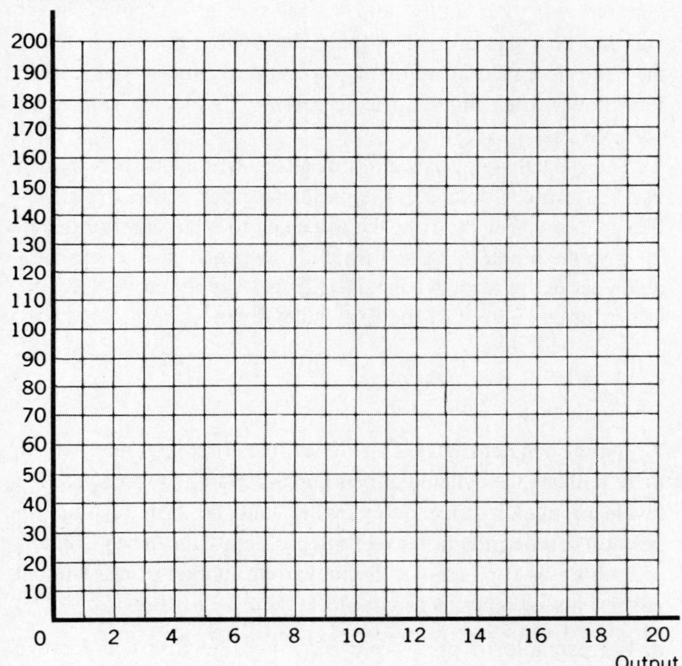

Figure 23-1

Total profit for any output is the distance measured vertically down from the total revenue (*TR*) line to the total cost (*TC*) line. The search for maximum-profit output is the search for the output level at which this distance is greatest.

Draw a similar *TR* line for price $8.80 in a different color and note that at most outputs, *TC* is higher than *TR*; at any such output, a loss would be incurred. For identification, mark your first line $11.20 and your second $8.80.

Finally, draw two more lines for prices of $7 and $4 in still different colors if possible. Completing the missing figures in Table 23-2 will help with this last bit of graphing.

Table 23-2

Quantity	Price: $7			Price: $4		
	Revenue	Total Cost	Profit	Revenue	Total Cost	Profit
10	$ 70.00	$110.50	−$30.50	$40.00	$100.50	−$ 60.50
12	84.00	111.50	______	48.00	111.50	______
14	98.00	124.50	−26.50	56.00	124.50	−68.50
16	112.00	140.50	______	64.00	140.50	______
18	126.00	162.50	−36.50	72.00	162.50	−90.50
20	140.00	202.50	−62.50	80.00	202.50	−122.50

Your four *TR* lines should be four straight lines radiating out from the origin, with $11.20 the highest and $4 the lowest; neither the $7 nor the $4 line should intersect *TC*. For Table 23-2, the profit numbers for $7 are −$27.50 and −$28.50; for $4, they are −$63.50 and −$76.50.

There will clearly be no output at which the firm of Tables 23-1 and 23-2 can even break even if the price falls much below $8.80. Were that to happen, should the firm continue to operate, or should it shut down completely (supplying 0 units of output even while incurring fixed costs)? To answer that question correctly, the point to be stressed is easily articulated. No firm can totally escape loss just by shutting down. The firm of Tables 23-1 and 23-2 has fixed costs of $50 that must be paid regardless of its chosen level of output (e.g., interest on some debt, taxes on some property), and it is stuck with these costs unless it declares bankruptcy. Given this constraint, it must simply do the best it can in difficult times. It must pick the output that maximizes profit; and if the price is so low that no output yields a positive profit, then this decision rule translates directly into one of minimizing its losses. In the worst of all situations, though, it can limit its losses to its fixed cost by shutting down. Short of that circumstance, it might be able to produce an output for which there is economic loss that is smaller than fixed cost.

5. a. To continue with our specific example, suppose that the market price facing the firm of Tables 23-1 and 23-2 is $7. Application of this rule would mean that the firm should (pick one):

(1) shut down.

(2) operate at output 10, since a loss of $30.50 is preferable to a loss of $50.00.

(3) operate at output 14, since loss at that output ($26.50) is lowest among the figures listed in Table 23-1, and is preferable to a $50.00 loss.

b. If market price were to be $4, then the firm should *(operate at output 10 / operate at output 14 / shut down).*

c. The general rule which emerges out of these considerations is (pick one):

(1) if there is some output at which loss would be less than the amount of fixed cost, produce and sell that output; shut down operations if loss exceeds fixed cost at all (nonzero) outputs.

(2) Shut down whenever there is no output at which it is possible to earn a profit or at least to break even.

(3) If there is some output at which loss would be greater than the amount of fixed cost, produce and sell that output; shut down operations if loss is less than fixed cost at all (nonzero) outputs.

---

a. (3) **b.** shut down (because $50.00 is less than any operating loss) **c.** (1)

In summary, the preceding questions have illustrated a two-part rule for profit-maximizing output decisions:

Pick the output at which $MC = P$. This is the best possible (nonzero) operating point.

If this best possible (nonzero) output yields a loss, compare this loss with fixed cost. If loss is less than fixed cost, then operate at that output. If loss exceeds fixed cost, then disregard the $MC = P$ rule, and shut down.

WARNING: The first of the two rules stated above applies only in the special case of pure (or perfect) competition treated in this chapter. It is a special instance of a more general rule. When we turn to imperfect competition, in Chapters 24 and 25, the same general reasoning will apply, but the profit-maximizing rule will be restated in a different and more general form.

6. An example may illustrate more fully the nature of the *shutdown rule*—the second of the two rules just noted. Figure 23-2 depicts two different situations. The height of each block indicates the dollar value of revenue or of cost, when the firm is at its best possible operating position. The two situations are exactly alike with respect to total revenue, total cost, and operating loss incurred. They differ only in the distribution of costs as between fixed and variable. The fixed cost is larger, and variable cost is smaller, in situation *(1 / 2)*.

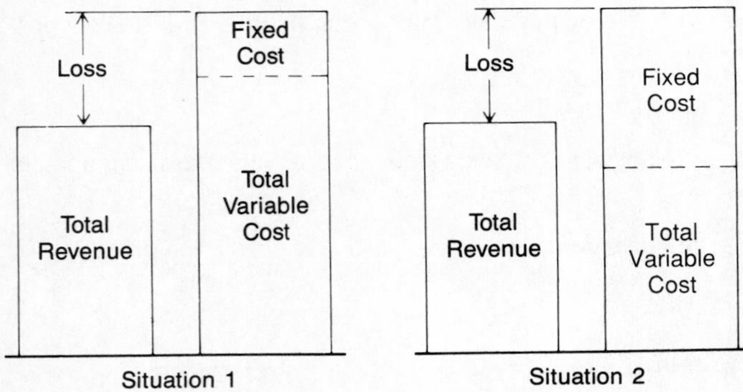

Figure 23-2

The shutdown rule says the firm should cease production in situation *(1 / 2)*, and continue to operate despite loss in situation *(1 / 2)*. The reasoning behind this rule is just that set out in question 5. You are stuck with a loss no matter what you do. The worst that can happen is that you incur a loss equal to fixed cost. If you can find an operating level at which the revenue earned from sales more than covers your variable cost, then some part of that revenue remains to be applied against fixed cost and your loss can then be smaller than fixed cost. The $P = MC$ rule is then *(still / not)* useful, because it *(will / will not)* indicate the minimum-loss operating level.

Figure 23-2 also suggests an alternative statement of the shutdown rule: Shut down when total revenue (at the best possible operating position) is *(less / greater)* than total *variable* cost. How is that? Notice that the blocks in Figure 23-2 stand for *TR* and *TC* at some particular quantity of output (the one indicated by the $P = MC$ rule). Divide *TR* by that quantity of output, and we get price (since TR = price × quantity). Divide total variable cost by quantity, and we get average variable cost, or variable cost per unit of output. We could, therefore, frame the shutdown rule in terms of price and average variable cost: Shut down when market price *(exceeds / is less than)* average variable cost.

The special significance of this alternative is that it is framed in price terms. It indicates the particular price which is just sufficiently low that the firm then decides to stop supplying anything to the market. A price which is just equal to average variable cost is the razor's edge. The firm's supply curve "breaks" at this price. Below it, the firm shuts down.

2; 1; 2; still; will; less; is less than

7. Now consider Figure 23-3. The three horizontal lines shown there indicate the demand curves corresponding to three possible levels of market price. [Remember that the firm in pure (or perfect) competition has no selling problems. It can sell as much or as little as it pleases at the prevailing market price, without advertising or other sales cost.]

a. For example, if price were *HO*, then the firm could move anywhere along d_1d_1. The point at which *MC* has risen to equality with *that* market price is *N*; i.e., if *HO* were the market price, the firm would produce and sell quantity *(OF / OE / OG)*. Note carefully that in this position, price is above *AC* so that the firm would be *(earning a profit / just breaking even / incurring a loss)*.

b. If price happened to be *JO*, then the firm's demand curve would be *(d_1d_1 / d_2d_2 / d_3d_3)*, and its maximum-profit output would be *(OF / OE / OG)*. It would then be *(earning a profit / just breaking even / incurring a loss)*.

c. If price were *KO*, the firm's best possible position would be to produce *(nothing / output OF / output OE)*. In this position, its loss would be *(less than / equal to / greater than)* the amount of its fixed cost.

d. If price fell so low that it did not even cover average variable

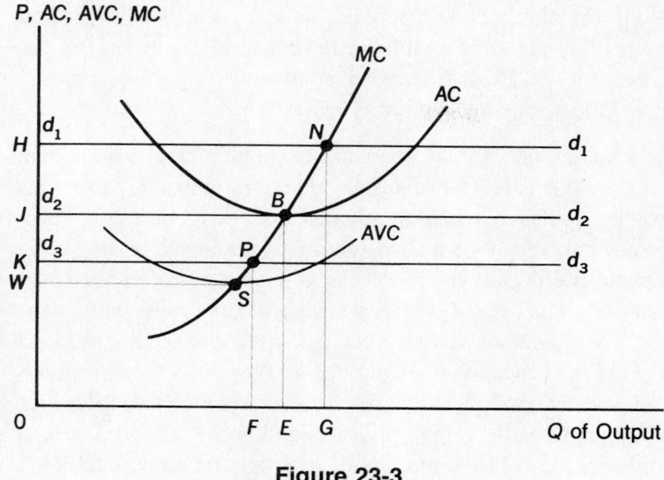

Figure 23-3

cost, then the firm would do better to cease operations entirely. (REMEMBER: If price does not cover average variable cost, then operating loss exceeds fixed cost.) On Figure 23-3, the boundary of this shutdown price zone is marked by price *(HO / JO / KO / WO)*. This price is *(greater than / just equal to / less than)* the minimum level of *(average variable / average fixed)* cost.

a. *OG*; earning a profit **b.** d_2d_2; *OE*; just breaking even **c.** output *OF*; less than **d.** *WO*; just equal to; average variable

All of the preceding work has concentrated on the short-run notion of equilibrium from the competitive, profit-maximizing firms' perspective. We now turn to consider the long run.

8. The market price which each firm in pure (or perfect) competition must accept is the price resulting from the intersection of industry demand and supply curves. At any moment of time, it could, for example, be any of the prices highlighted in Figure 23-3: *HO*, *JO*, *KO*, or even *WO*. However, it is argued that there is a long-run tendency for price to gravitate toward level *JO*, the *(breakeven / shutdown)* price.

The reasoning behind this argument is not difficult to grasp. Suppose that the market price is below *JO*. This would mean that all supplying firms are losing money. (For convenience, suppose that every firm operates along the cost curves shown in Figure 23-3—all producing the same product with the same technology and paying the same input prices.) If the price persists below *JO* for a long period of time, some firms will eventually leave the market. Either they would go voluntarily when some of their fixed-cost obligations came up for renewal and offered them an opportunity to exit, or they would be forced out by the bankruptcy courts. In any case, when they leave the market, the market supply curve will *(shift in / stay in the same place / shift out)* and the market price will *(rise / stay the same / fall)*.

If, on the other hand, the market price were higher than *OJ*, then existing firms would be making extraordinary profits. These surplus profits would attract other firms to the industry because the typical firm is earning a "normal" return on its invested capital even at the breakeven price. As these new firms enter, though, the market supply curve will *(shift in / stay in the same place / shift out)* and cause the market price to *(rise / stay the same / fall)*.

Notice that a firm bent on profit maximization has no special incentive to try to produce the output defined by the minimum of its average cost curve. With the technology that supports Figure 23-3, the lowest average cost that can be attained is *BE*. It is consistent only with output *(OF / OE / OG)*, but the firm will produce that output *only* if the market price happens to be *(HO / JO / KO / WO)*. For prices higher than that, output should be *(higher than / exactly equal to / smaller than) OE* with average costs *(higher than / exactly equal to / smaller than) BE*. For prices smaller than *JO*, output should be *(higher than / exactly equal to / smaller than) OE* with average costs *(higher than / exactly equal to / smaller than) BE*.

breakeven; shift in; rise; shift out; fall; OE; JO; higher than; higher than; smaller than; higher than

In sum, then, there is a tendency for the market price to fall if it is higher than the breakeven price and to rise if it is *above* the breakeven price. In the long run, therefore, we expect equilibrium to be characterized by the equality of price and the minimum of the average cost curve. By combining that with the short-run profit-maximizing condition that price equals marginal cost (anything possible in the short run is possible in the long run), the complete description of long-run equilibrium is obtained:

$$P = MC = \text{minimum } AC = \text{breakeven price}$$

9. It follows from this long-run tendency of price to converge to the minimum of the average cost curve that we *(must / need not)* know the market demand curve to determine the market-clearing long-run equilibrium price. That price is, always, given by *(the minimum of the average cost curve of the typical firm / the intersection of demand and short-run supply / the intersection of the marginal cost curve of the typical firm and its average variable cost)*.

need not; the minimum of the average cost curve of the typical firm (Equilibrium always occurs at the breakeven point because of adjustments in the number of firms of the type just noted.)

10. To see why the individual firm has no power over the price of its output, consider the following mental exercise. Suppose that one firm tries to increase its price above an established equilibrium. The result would be *(a collapse / an explosion)* of its market share and the *(entry / exit)* of a competitor to take its place. No help there! Now suppose that the wary firm tries the opposite strategy—a lower price. The result would be *(an increase / a decrease)* in the number of consumers wanting to buy its output, *(an increase / a decrease)* in its desired level of output, and *(a reduction / an increase)* in its pure economic profit below zero (meaning subpar return on its investment). Another bad idea!

The analytical implication of this exercise is that even though market demand curves for competitive markets are usually *(upward-sloping / horizontal / downward-sloping)*, the effective demand curve facing an individual competitive firm is *(upward- / horizontally / downward-)* sloped *(through / at)* the established price. Any attempt to move from that curve would be disastrous.

---

a collapse; entry; an increase; a decrease (because the lower price would move the firm down and in along its positively sloped *MC* curve); a reduction; downward-sloping; horizontally; through

11. We are now ready for a more thorough exploration of the long run. Recall that the long run allows enough time for firms to exit or enter a market or industry at will. It allows firms to adjust their plant size if economical. It allows, in the broadest of terms, the maximum possible supply adjustment to any change in market or industry demand. The question is: What will happen to prices?

a. Let us start with a competitive industry consisting of identical firms that finds itself initially in full long-run equilibrium. For each and every firm, therefore, price (*P*) must equal minimum long-run average cost (*LAC*), which in turn must equal long-run marginal cost (*LMC*). Panel **(a)** of Figure 23-4 shows this for the typical firm with equilibrium price equal to *OJ*; the typical firm (each firm, since they are all identical) produces output

_______. There must be enough of these firms to support an industry supply curve *ss* that intersects market demand at price *OJ*; i.e., the total quantity supplied must equal the total quantity demanded at price *OJ*. This is shown in panel **(b)** of Figure 23-4. Since *OA* is this market-clearing quantity and each firm produces *Oa* given *OJ*, there must be enough firms (say, *n* firms) so that $n \times Oa = OA$.

Now suppose that there is a sudden increase in demand to something like *d'd'*—the broken-line demand curve in panel **(b)**. The fundamentals of supply and demand tell us that price

must increase from *JO* to _______ in the short run. Why? Because the *ss* curve drawn in panel **(b)** is a short-run curve for a fixed number of firms, all of whom respond to the higher price

by increasing their own outputs from *Oa* to _______ in panel **(a)**. They are all employing their given plant and equipment more intensively in this short-run response to the higher output price.

Because the output price has risen, all firms are now making profit above and beyond the normal return that was expected on their investment in physical capital. These excess profits attract new firms, and the *ss* curve begins to shift to the *(right / left)*. Industry output will then have risen for two reasons. First of all, each of the firms already operating in the market before the influx of higher demand will be producing more (movement along the old *ss* curve); second, new firms will have entered the market (creating a shift in the *ss* curve). Both reasons (or either one) will call for greater employment of *all* inputs, and their prices may or may not climb as a result.

b. Assume, only for the moment, that input prices do not climb. (Maybe this is a small industry relative to the supply of inputs so that a pulse in demand generated from this industry is inconsequential; maybe there are lots of unemployed inputs sitting around waiting to be hired at the going price; it doesn't matter why.) In this case, the long-run supply curve must be *(a positively sloped / a horizontal / a negatively sloped)* line through point *E* in panel **(a)** of Figure 23-4. Why? Because the long-run cost curves depicted in panel **(a)** are not affected. Price *(JO / KO)* must still be the long-run equilibrium price because it still represents the minimum average cost possible. The long-run supply curve is supported, then, by an increase in the number of firms until their combined *s's'* curve intersects the *d'd'* curve in panel **(b)** at a point like E_1'' / E_2'' / E_3''. Total output will have increased because *(there are more firms, each producing more output than before / there are more firms, each producing the same output as before / there are more firms, each producing less output than before)*.

c. Now suppose, by way of contrast, that input prices *are* affected as the demand for input increases. We should expect to see input prices *(rise / fall)*, and we should also expect to see this change reflected in the final price of output.

We now have two effects working on the price of this finished good. Entry of new firms, by increasing industry supply, is pushing price *(down / up)* from its new short-run level *KO*. But higher input cost is tending to push price *(down / up)*. Referring again to panel **(b)** of Figure 23-4, we see that the long-run outcome should be one in which the price has *(fallen / risen)* somewhat from the *KO* level, but has *(fallen / risen)* somewhat from its original *JO* level.

---

a. *Oa*; *KO*; *Ob*; right **b.** a horizontal; *JO*; E_2''; there are more firms, each producing the same output as before **c.** rise; down; up; fallen; risen

12. This is a more difficult problem. You are employed as a consultant in profit maximization. Each row of Table 23-3 provides you with some information about the operation of a different competitive firm. You are to sort through the information provided in each to make a recommendation of what the firm should do given its own particular circumstance. Answer for each case by recording *one* of the numbers 1 through 7 in the last column according to the following code:

1. Firm is now at correct position.
2. Firm should increase price.
3. Firm should decrease price.
4. Firm should increase quantity of output and sales.
5. Firm should decrease quantity of output and sales.
6. Firm should shut down operations.
7. A nonsense case—figures supplied are inconsistent and could not all be correct.

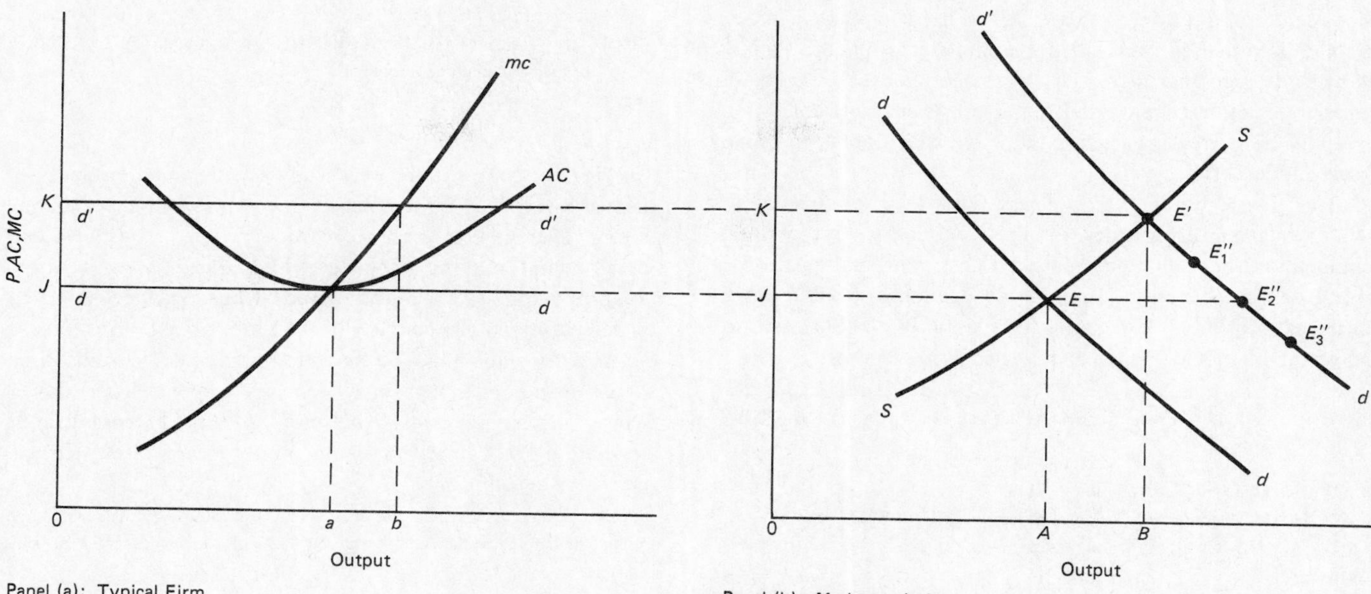

Panel (a): Typical Firm

Panel (b): Market or Industry

Figure 23-4

Table 23-3

Case	Price	*Q* of Output	Total Revenue	Total Cost	Total Fixed Cost	Total Variable Cost	Average Cost	Average Variable Cost	Marginal Cost	With Increase in Output, *MC* Would	Answer
a.	$2.00	10,000		$16,000			At minimum level			rise	
b.			$10,000		$2,000		$4.00	$3.00	$6.00	rise	
c.	$2.00	$2,000			2,000	$5,000			2.00	fall	
d.			6,000	6,000		4,500	At minimum level	0.75		rise	
e.	5.00	2,000						5.25	5.00	rise	
f.			20,000	18,000			3.60		4.00	rise	
g.		4,000	16,000	16,000			At minimum level	5.00	3.00	fall	
h.	4.50				9,000	12,000	5.25	At minimum level		rise	
i.		3,000	9,000					3.25	3.00	rise	
j.		2,000	16,000		3,000			7.00	8.00	rise	

The same number may, of course, be used more than once. Enough information is provided in each case despite the blanks. Notice, though, that there is at least one "nonsense" case, in which the numbers provided are inconsistent and could not possibly be correct; in such cases, tell your clients to come back later!

Note: These problems are not easy. They require you to know the profit-maximizing rules for the firm in pure (or perfect) competition (price to equal marginal cost; marginal cost to be rising with any increase in output; production to be shut down in the even of a loss exceeding the fixed-cost amount), and to know the relationship among the various cost curves.

Listed here are lines of reasoning that produce answers to the 10 cases of Table 23-3.

a. **(1)** Get *AC* from *Q* and *TC:AC* = \$1.60.
(2) Get *MC* from fact that *AC* is at minimum: *MC* = \$1.60.
(3) *P* > *MC*, therefore increase output.
Answer: 4

b. **(1)** Get *AFC* from *AC* and *AVC:AFC* = \$1.
(2) Get *Q* from *AFC* and *TFC:Q* = 2000.
(3) Get *P* from *Q* and *TR:P* = \$5.
(4) *P* < *MC*, therefore decrease output.
Answer: 5

c. *P* = *MC*, but *MC* is falling. Therefore output should be increased.
Answer: 4

d. **(1)** Get *Q* from *TVC* and *AVC:Q* = 6000.
(2) Get *P* from *Q* and *TR:P* = \$1.
(3) Get *AC* from *Q* and *TC:AC* = \$1.
(4) Get *MC* from the fact that *AC* is at minimum: *MC* = \$1.
(5) *P* = *MC*, and there is no loss, therefore position okay.
Answer: 1

e. **(1)** *P* = *MC*, but check for possible loss.
(2) *P* < *AVC*, therefore loss exceeds *TFC*; shut down.
Answer: 6

f. **(1)** Get *Q* from *TC* and *AC:Q* = 5000.
(2) Get *P* from *Q* and *TR:P* = \$4.
(3) *P* = *MC*, and there is no loss, therefore position okay.
Answer: 1

g. *MC* is said to be falling, therefore output should be increased. But *AC* is said to be at its minimum level—at which *MC* should be rising. This alone indicates an impossible case. Moreover, at that minimum *AC* level, *AC* = *MC*. This must mean that *AC* = \$3. But *AVC* alone is specified as \$5—which further makes this an impossible case.
Answer: 7

h. **(1)** Get *TC* from *TFC* and *TVC:TC* = \$21,000.
(2) Get *Q* from *TC* and *AC:Q* = 4000.
(3) Get *AVC* from *Q* and *TVC:AVC* = \$3.
(4) Get *MC* from fact that *AVC* is at minimum: *MC* = \$3.
(5) *P* > *MC*, therefore increase output.
Answer: 4

i. **(1)** Get *P* from *Q* and *TR:P* = \$3.
(2) *P* = *MC*, and *MC* is rising, but check for possible loss.
(3) Compare *P* and *AVC*. The fact that *P* < *AVC* indicates not only that there is a loss, but one of such magnitude that the firm should shut down.
Answer: 6

j. **(1)** Get *P* from *Q* and *TR:P* = \$8.
(2) *P* = *MC*, and *MC* is rising, but check for possible loss.
(3) Get *TVC* from *Q* and *AVC:TVC* = \$14,000.
(4) Get *TC* from *TVC* and *TFC:TC* = \$17,000.
(5) Since *TR* is \$16,000, loss is \$1000. This is less than *TFC* of \$3000, so firm should continue to operate.
Answer: 1

13. Perfect competition breaks down under circumstances of decreasing costs. When marginal cost is falling as output climbs, average cost must be *(rising / falling / constant)*, and higher outputs must be associated with *(higher / lower / identical)* profits for any price. The first few firms to achieve this type of decreasing-cost situation will therefore be able to *(increase / decrease)* output and *(raise / cut)* prices at the same time to *(drive out / complement / minimally compete with)* slower firms with higher costs. The result of this process can be *(monopoly / a few sellers of the same good / price warfare among large suppliers)*.

---

falling; higher; increase; cut; drive out; any of the choices is a possible outcome

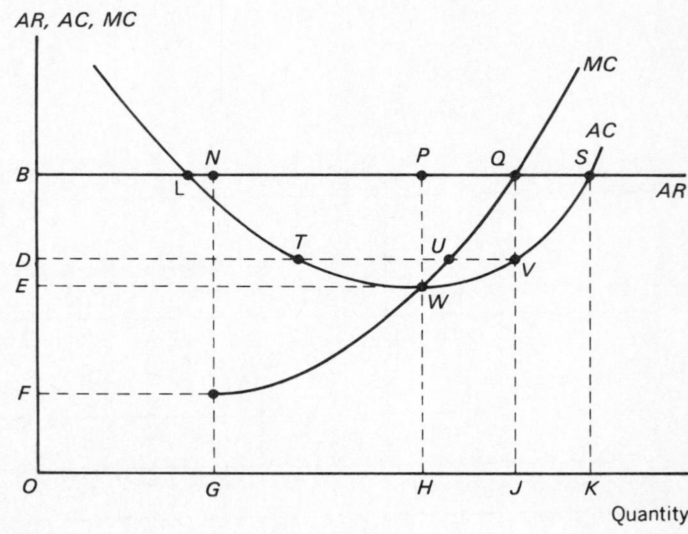

Figure 23-5

14. Figure 23-5 shows a production-possibility frontier for an economy that can produce only two goods: X and Y. Point *(A / B / C)* represents a point of allocational efficiency in the "Pareto" sense *if all people value X and Y equally*. Point A *(is / is not)* efficient because ______________________

____

____

Point B *(is / is not)* efficient because ______________________

____

____

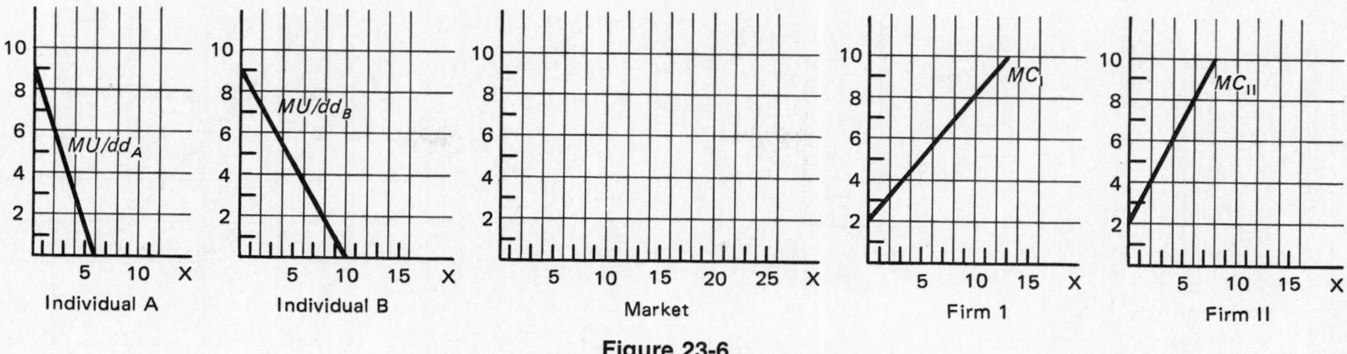

Figure 23-6

Point C *(is / is not)* efficient because ______________________

____

____

In particular, social welfare can be improved by moving from point *B* to *C* because the 100 fewer units of X can release sufficient resources to produce ________ more units of Y, of which ________ units can be used to compensate those who sacrificed their units of X and ________ units represent a surplus.

C; is not; *A* reflects unemployed resources so that increases in the supplies of both X and Y can increase the welfare of anyone without sacrifice; is not; *B* is on the frontier, but does not reflect the equal value preferences of the people (too much X and too little Y is produced); is; *C* is on the frontier and reflects prices accurately; 200; 100; 100

15. Figure 23-6 depicts demand/marginal (cardinal) utility curves for some good X for two different people (A and B) on its left side and supply/marginal cost curves for X for two different firms (I and II) on the right. Assume that these two people and two firms represent the entire market for X and that the market is competitive. Carefully draw the market supply and demand curves for X on the middle graph and fill in the blanks in Table 23-4 for the resulting equilibrium. Notice in Table 23-4 that the efficiency conditions that $MU = MC = P$ *(is / is not)* satisfied for both firms and both individuals. Total consumer surplus at equilibrium is $________.

Now suppose that the two firms are, in fact, the two individuals (A = I and B = II) who produce X entirely from their own labor. In that case, the individual marginal cost curves would reflect *(input costs other than labor / the marginal disutility of work / the wage rate)*. If the two people were to cooperate in a way that would maximize their joint consumer surplus, A would make ________ units of X and consume ________ units; B would make ________ units and consume ________ units. This allocation would be achieved by the payment of $________ per unit of X for each of the ________ units that A would *(sell to / buy from)* B.

Table 23-4

	Price	Quantity Demanded (units)	Quantity Supplied (units)	Marginal Utility/ Marginal Cost
Market	$______	______	______	$MU = MC =$ $______
Individual A		______		$MU =$ ______
Individual B		______		$MU =$ ______
Firm I			______	$MC =$ ______
Firm II			______	$MC =$ ______

Finally suppose that an economic planner wanted to call out a single price for X that would generate an allocation of consumption and work effort that would maximize total consumer surplus in the X market. What price would be specified? $________

The demand curve should be a straight line connecting (X = 0; price = $9) and (X = 16; price = $0); the supply curve should be a straight line from (X = 0; price = $2) and continuing through (X = 8; price = $5).
Reading across the table in rows: $5, 8, 8, $5; 3, $5; 5, $5; 5, $5; 3, $5
is; The consumer-surplus triangle is given by its corners: (0,$9), (0,$5), and (8,$5); its area is $\frac{1}{2} \times (\$9 - \$5) \times (8 - 0) = \$16$ = consumer surplus.
the marginal disutility of work; 5; 3; 3; 5; 5; 2; sell to; $5 (The key here is that the planner would mimic the market.)

16. Consult Figure 23-7. Panel **(a)** shows the marginal cost schedule for a power generator; marginal cost is constant at $2 up to 100,000 units, but 100,000 units is an absolute capacity constraint. Panel **(b)** shows a similar schedule for an older generator. Draw, in panel **(c)**, the marginal cost schedule for the firm owning these two generators. What price should, from a social perspective, be charged in off-peak times when dd_1 represents the market demand curve? $________. What price should be charged during the peak period when dd_2 is the demand curve? $________. Is the old generator ever used during an off-peak time? ________. What price should be

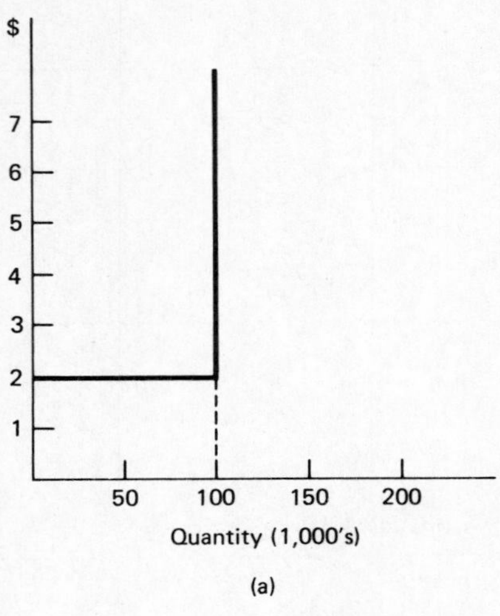

(a)

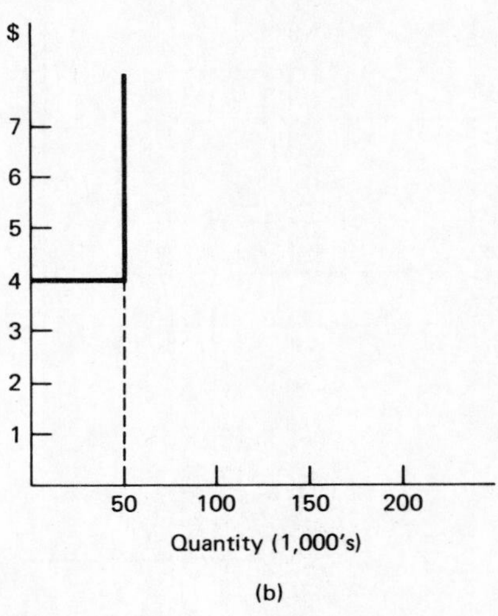

(b)

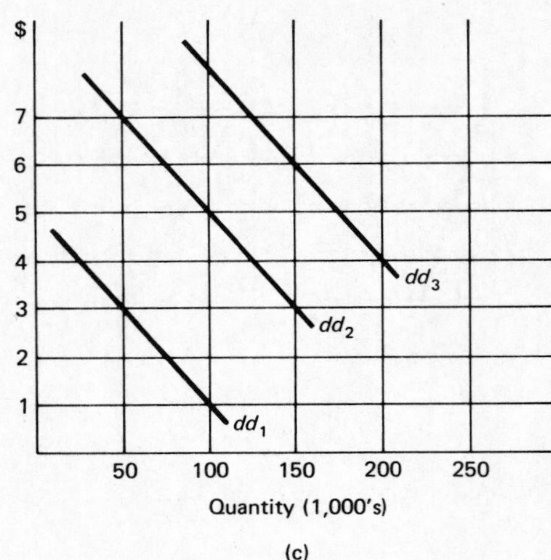

(c)

Figure 23-7

charged during the peak time if dd_3 were the demand curve?

$______

Your combined curve should be their horizontal sum: flat at $2 from 0 to 100 (× 1000) units of output; vertical at 100 from $2 to $4; flat at $4 from 100 to 150 units of output; vertical at 150 above $4.
2; 5; no; 6

QUIZ: Multiple Choice

1. The profit-maximizing rule for a firm in pure (or perfect) competition is "price to equal marginal cost." This rule means that a firm should:
(1) keep increasing output quantity *(Q)* until price *(P)* has risen to equality with marginal cost *(MC)*.
(2) keep increasing *Q* until *P* has fallen to equality with *MC*.
(3) keep increasing *Q* until *MC* has fallen to equality with *P*.
(4) keep increasing *Q* until *MC* has risen to equality with *P*.
(5) keep decreasing *P* until *P* reaches equality with *MC*.

2. The supply curve of a firm in pure (or perfect) competition is the same thing as:
(1) its entire marginal cost curve.
(2) a part of its marginal cost curve.
(3) its average cost curve.
(4) that entire part of its average cost curve in which *AC* rises or remains constant as output increases.
(5) none of these.

3. A firm operating in circumstances of pure (or perfect) competition faces a market price of $10. It is producing 2000 units of output daily, at a total cost of $19,000. This firm:
(1) to improve its profit position, should increase the amount of its output.
(2) to improve its profit position, should reduce the amount of its output.
(3) to minimize its loss, should shut down.
(4) although making some profit, may or may not be at the output level yielding maximum profit—the information furnished is not sufficient to cover this point.
(5) from the information given, is apparently now at its maximum-profit position.

4. If the firm described in question 3 were to increase its output to 2001 units, total cost would thereupon become $19,010. Would this additional information change your answer to that question? The correct alternative would then (or still) be:
(1).
(2).
(3).
(4).
(5).

5. A firm operating in circumstances of pure (or perfect) competition finds that, at its best possible operating position (for any nonzero output), its total revenue does not cover its total cost, although this revenue is more than sufficient to cover fixed cost. This firm:
(1) is incurring a loss, and would improve its position by shutting down.
(2) is incurring a loss, but minimizes that loss by continuing to operate at its present position.
(3) is incurring a loss, but could reduce or perhaps remove it by increasing its production and sales.
(4) is incurring a loss, but the information given is not sufficient to indicate whether it would minimize that loss by continuing to operate or by shutting down.
(5) may be incurring a loss or earning a profit—the information furnished is insufficient to tell.

6. Which alternative in question 5 would be correct had that question specified that the firm's total revenue (although still insufficient to cover total cost) was more than sufficient to cover its total variable cost?

(1).
(2).
(3).
(4).
(5).

7. A firm which operates in short-run conditions of pure (or perfect) competition, and wants to earn as much profit as the situation will allow, must:
(1) try to set a price equal to average cost.
(2) try to produce an output at which its average cost is at the lowest-attainable level.
(3) try to produce an output at which average cost is just equal to market price.
(4) try to make its total revenue just equal to its fixed cost.
(5) take none of these actions, necessarily.

8. The "long-run" equilibrium condition, "price equal to minimum per-unit (average) cost," used in pure (or perfect) competition theory:
(1) is a rule which the firm need not consider in the short run, but must obey in the long run if it wants to choose the output level that will maximize its profit.
(2) is a rule the firm must obey in the short run only if it wants to choose the output level that will maximize its profit.
(3) is not a rule any profit-maximizing firm need consider either in the short or the long run, but indicates a situation toward which it is said all firms will be pushed in the long run.
(4) is a rule any profit-maximizing firm must respect in both the short and the long run.
(5) has no status either as a profit-maximizing rule or as a situation toward which firms will tend to be pushed, whether in the short or the long run.

9. A firm is operating in circumstances of pure (or perfect) competition. It is producing that quantity of output at which average cost is at its minimum level. This firm:
(1) must be at its maximum-profit output level, but may or may not be charging the best price it could get for that output.
(2) must be at its maximum-profit output level and need not reconsider its price, since this is a market price over which it has no control.
(3) is not at its maximum-profit position, and should increase its output.
(4) is not at its maximum-profit position and should decrease output.
(5) may or may not be at its maximum-profit position—information furnished is insufficient to tell.

10. Given the usual downward-sloping shape of a market demand curve, what should be the effect of a tax that affects only the fixed cost of every firm in a competitive market on the price received by and the quantity supplied by each competitive firm?
(1) Price up and quantity up.
(2) Price up and quantity down.
(3) Price down and quantity up.
(4) Price down and quantity down.
(5) Cannot tell from the information provided.

11. A firm operates under conditions of pure (or perfect) competition. At its present level of output, all the following have a value of $1: price it is charging, marginal cost, average cost. Marginal cost would rise with any increase in output. This firm:
(1) definitely is at its maximum-profit position.
(2) definitely is not at its maximum-profit position.
(3) may or may not be at maximum-profit position; average variable cost would have to be known before answering.
(4) may or may not be at maximum-profit position; total cost and total revenue would have to be known before answering.
(5) may or may not be at maximum-profit position; total fixed cost would have to be known before answering.

12. A firm operating in conditions of perfect competition is producing a daily output such that its total revenue is $5000. That output is its profit-maximizing output. The firm's average cost is $8, its marginal cost is $10, and its average variable cost is $5. Its daily output is:
(1) 200 units.
(2) 500 units.
(3) 625 units.
(4) 1000 units.
(5) impossible to tell from the information furnished.

13. The fixed cost for the firm described in question 12 is:
(1) $10.
(2) $100.
(3) $500.
(4) $1500.
(5) impossible to tell from the information furnished.

14. The daily profit earned, or loss incurred, by the firm in question 12 must be:
(1) a loss of $500.
(2) neither profit nor loss, for the firm just "breaks even."
(3) a profit of $500.
(4) a profit of $1000.
(5) impossible to tell from the information furnished.

15. Economists refer to the "breakeven point" for a firm in pure (or perfect) competition. This breakeven point occurs at the output level where two cost magnitudes are just equal, namely:
(1) marginal cost *(MC)* and average cost *(AC)*.
(2) average variable cost *(AVC)* and average fixed cost *(AFC)*.
(3) *MC* and *AVC*.
(4) *AC* and *AVC*.
(5) *MC* and *AFC*.

16. A firm operating in circumstances of perfect competition produces and sells 200 units of output daily at a price of $7. Its average cost is $4.99. If it were to increase output and sales to 201 units daily, average cost would rise to $5. To maximize its profit, and from the information supplied, this firm should:
(1) increase its output, since marginal cost (*MC*) is approximately $6.
(2) reduce its output, since *MC* is approximately $6.
(3) remain at its present output, since *MC* is approximately $7.
(4) certainly not reduce its output, and probably increase it, since average cost is approximately $5.
(5) increase its output, since *MC* is approximately $5.01

17. A firm must sell its product at a market price of $1.90. Its present operating figures are as follows: average cost, $2.00; marginal cost, $1.50; average variable cost, $1.50; total fixed cost, $500 per period. By the rules of maximum profit (or minimum loss) for a competitive firm, this firm would:
(1) definitely increase its present output level.
(2) definitely reduce its present output level.
(3) remain at its present output position.
(4) shut down.
(5) perhaps increase, perhaps decrease its output—the one critical figure needed to make this decision is lacking.

18. If the short-run marginal cost curve of a typical firm in a competitive industry should fall continuously over a substantial range of increasing outputs, the consequence indicated by the text chapter is that:
(1) new firms must enter that industry.
(2) the profit earned by that typical firm can be expected to rise.
(3) the marginal cost of that firm will exceed its average cost through the output range in question.
(4) the total amount of fixed cost which this firm must pay will fall.
(5) pure (or perfect) competition is likely to give way to imperfect competition.

19. Because of a city tax reduction, the total fixed cost a firm must pay is reduced by $500 monthly. The firm operates in conditions of pure (or perfect) competition. If the firm seeks to maximize its profit, this cost reduction should (at least in the short run) result in:
(1) a reduction in price.
(2) an increase in output.
(3) an increase in price.
(4) a reduction in output.
(5) no change in output or in price.

20. Given the usual downward-sloping shape of a market demand curve, what should be the effect of a tax on inputs that increases the marginal cost schedule (at every output) of each firm in a competitive industry on the market price and output?
(1) Price up and quantity up.
(2) Price up and quantity down.
(3) Price down and quantity up.
(4) Price down and quantity down.
(5) Cannot tell from the information given.

21. Which of the following is a characteristic of allocational efficiency of the Pareto sort?
(1) The allocation can be represented by a point on the economy's utility frontier.
(2) The allocation can be supported by a point on the economy's production-possibility frontier.
(3) The allocation maximizes the economy's total consumer surplus.
(4) The allocation achieves the quality of marginal utility, price, and marginal cost for every good produced.
(5) All of the above.

22. A firm operates in circumstances of pure (or perfect) competition. The market price at which it can sell its product is $5. At its present level of output and sales, average cost (total cost per unit of output) is $4. This firm:
(1) could increase its profit by increasing its output.
(2) could increase its profit by reducing its output.
(3) is making a profit, but the information furnished is insufficient to indicate whether that profit would be increased by any increase or decrease in output.
(4) is not making any profit, and should shut down operations.
(5) is not making any profit, but is nevertheless doing better than it would do if it were to shut down.

23. Which alternative in question 22 would be correct, had the figure of $4 referred to marginal cost, not average cost?
(1).
(2).
(3).
(4).
(5).

24. Given the situation of question 22, if both *AC* and *MC* were $4, then we would expect (in the long run with the usual downward-sloping demand assumption):
(1) the market price to fall and the quantity to fall.
(2) the market price to rise and the quantity to fall.
(3) the market price to fall and the quantity to rise.
(4) the market price to rise and the quantity to rise.
(5) nothing because we haven't sufficient information.

25. Monopoly is most likely to emerge when:
(1) average cost is declining over some range of initial levels of production.
(2) average cost is declining until it equals marginal cost.
(3) average cost is constant over all levels of output.
(4) average cost is declining over the range of output that might be demanded by the entire market.
(5) none of the above.

SUGGESTED ANSWERS TO QUESTIONS IN THE TEXT: Chapter 23

1. **a.** "A competitive firm . . . price equals *marginal cost*," if it is to maximize profits.
b. "A firm's shutdown point . . . minimum of average *variable* cost," so that price equals marginal cost equals *AVC*.
c. "A competitive firm's supply curve depends only on its *MC above the shutdown price where* $MC = AVC$," specifies the appropriate context and range.
d. Not for downward-sloping *MC*. Given diminishing returns, *MC* eventually turns up; $P = MC$ on downward slope is a profit minimum, not maximum. To see why, consider increasing output by 1 unit from downward intersection; profits climb!

2. If covering *VC*, then making up at least some fraction of *FC*. This is fine for a while, but only for a while.

3. 4000 units in all cases, although maximum profits are positive for $FC = \$0$, $55,000, and $-\$30,000$ and negative for $FC = \$100,000$ and $1,000,000. What you paid for the house is irrelevant.

4. Price $= \$21$: $Q^* = 3000$; profits $= \$63,000 - \$130,000 < \$0$; firms should exit.
Price $= \$40$; $Q^* = 4000$; profits $= \$160,000 - \$160,000 = \$0$; stable long-run equilibrium.
Price $= \$60$; $Q^* = 5000$; profits $= \$300,000 - \$210,000 > \$0$; firms should enter.

5. $E_s = [(4001 - 4000)/4000]/(40.02 - 40.00)/40.00] = 0.5$. For the industry supply, multiply the single-firm quantity by 2000 for *each price*. The supply elasticity does not change. Both the numerator and the denominator of the "percentage change in quantity" part of the elasticity ratio are multiplied by 2000; the 2000s therefore cancel and do not change the elasticity estimate.

6. For the same reason as for market economy. Unless $P = MC = MU$, a change in output mix can improve the welfare of at least one person without hurting someone else.

7. At competitive equilibrium, the price that people are willing to pay for output is less than the smallest *MC* for firm C. If C produced 1 unit more and B 1 unit less, total industry cost would increase by $MC_C(1) - MC_B(\text{last})$.

Economies of scale drive "Mom and Pop" stores out of business, except for locational advantages (convenience, etc.). The legislation would increase food prices because equal shares would not achieve total cost minimization that only occurs when *MC*s are equal across firms.

8. The definition of pure economic profit that includes the opportunity cost of owners' labor and capital investment is the key; it is driven to zero in perfect competition so there is no excess.

9. The combined supply curve is *MC* for the first plant up to the lowest *MC* for the second; then it is the horizontal sum of the two. If low demand intersects the combined curve at a price below value where plant number 2 cuts in, then the off-peak price should be that intersection, and the second plant should lie idle. If peak demand intersects the combined curve above the second plant's minimum *MC*, then the price should still be defined by that intersection; only this time, both plants operate where the price equals their respective *MC*s.

10. If labor is the only input, then all product is attributable to labor. A labor theory of value thus applies. For the given example, each deer costs two beaver, so the *PPF* has a slope of -2 and a height determined by the number of hours available for hunting.

When there is a second input, even in the production of only one good, then that good's product must be divided between factors in the determination of compensation. A labor theory of value thus breaks down. Moreover, the productivity of labor depends upon the quantity of (e.g.) land available, and diminishing returns sets in. Thus, the bow shape of the *PPF*.

APPENDIX: 23

Special Cases of Competitive Markets: Supply and Demand at Work

Chapters 18 through 23 have led you through the development of applying the fundamental notions of supply-and-demand analysis to competitive markets. Before you go on to the study of imperfect competition, though, it is useful to note that much of that analysis can be summarized in terms of two general propositions. There are exceptions to each, but applying a few usual results to specific problems will make these exceptions less unexpected. They are not the economic equivalent of irregular verbs, which must be memorized; they are, instead, special cases of a conventional world, which are perhaps more easily understood in that context. By the time you have finished your work in this brief appendix, then, you should not only understand why the propositions are valid representations of the norm but also recognize the potential for exception when it occurs. Completing this appendix should enable you to meet the following objectives.

LEARNING OBJECTIVES

1. Explain why, in general, an increase (a reduction) in the demand for a commodity tends to increase (reduce) the price of that commodity if supply does not change. At the same time, the quantity demanded *usually* increases (declines).

2. Explain why, in general, an increase (a reduction) in the supply of a commodity tends to lower (raise) the price of that commodity if demand does not change. At the same time, the quantity bought and sold *usually* increases (declines).

Proposition 1(*a*) in this appendix is, "As a general rule an increase in demand—supply being constant—will raise price." Be very clear on this: this is a proposition about movement along fixed supply curves. An "increase in demand" means a shift of the whole demand curve to the right, as in Figure 23A-1. If the supply curve does not shift (i.e., "supply being constant"), and if the outcome is that price is raised (e.g., from *CO* to *FO* in Figure 23A-1), then there is a strong likelihood that the supply curve must slope upward as illustrated by *SS* in Figure 23A-1.

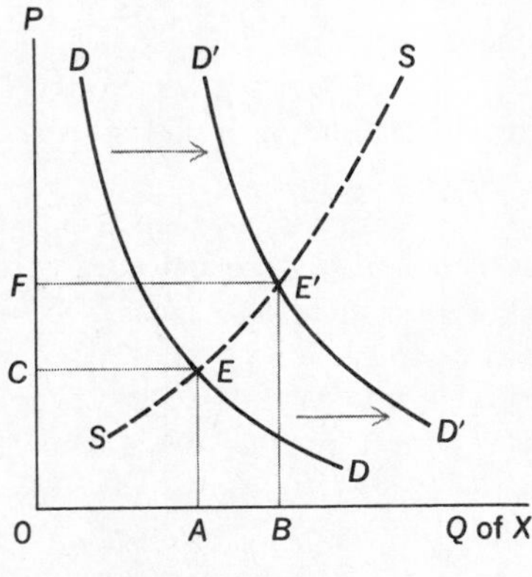

Figure 23A-1

Of course, price would also increase if *SS* were vertical or perhaps even backward-bending. So what happens to the quantity bought and sold in equilibrium? Note that part (*b*) of Proposition 1 reads, "For *most* commodities, an increase in demand will increase the quantity demanded, as well." If quantity is to increase with price, though (as it does in Figure 23A-1, going from *OA* to *OB*), the *SS* supply curve must be upward-sloping. Proposition 1 could therefore be reworded to say, "In general, supply curves are positively sloped." The way to discover the nature of the supply curve in a competitive market is to change the position of demand and see where the new equilibrium quantity-price pair lies.

1. a. The significance of a supply curve which is positively sloped is that, in the event of an increase in demand, we would expect quantity bought and sold to (*increase / remain unchanged / decrease*) and price to (*increase / remain unchanged / decrease*).

b. There are numerous exceptions to this general rule. Supply curves can be flat or vertical, for example. There can also be "backward-bending," or falling, supply curves (i.e., the supply line points downward rather than upward if you run your eye along it from left to right). Most of this appendix is taken up with the reasons behind the general rule for supply curves and the reasons for the exceptions.

Figure 23A-2 shows three different supply-curve situations: i, ii, and iii. Its parts illustrate different "cases" discussed in the text. Panel (i) shows Case 2, panel (ii) shows Case 1, and panel (iii) shows Case 3.

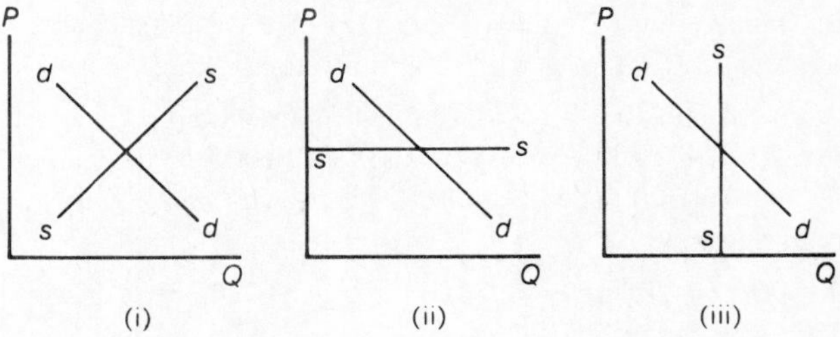

Figure 23A-2

(1) The *constant-cost* case is illustrated by (*i / ii / iii*).

(2) The perfectly inelastic supply case is (*i / ii / iii*).

(3) The *increasing-cost* case is (*i / ii / iii*).

(4) The perfectly elastic supply case is (*i / ii / iii*).

(5) The *economic-rent* case is (*i / ii / iii*).

(6) The case in which quantity supplied would respond neither to a price rise by increasing nor to a price fall by decreasing is (*i / ii / iii*).

(7) The case in which suppliers are ready to sell, at the prevailing price, a greater quantity or a smaller quantity than they now sell is (*i / ii / iii*).

c. Suppose an increase in buyer incomes pushes each of the demand curves of Figure 23A-2 to the right. The result will be a change in price and/or quantity bought and sold. Circle one or more letters, as appropriate. "N" signifies that the outcome described fits none of the three panels of Figure 23A-2. Given this increase in demand:

(1) price will rise in case(s) illustrated in panel (*i / ii / iii / N*).

(2) quantity bought and sold will increase in panel(s) (*i / ii / iii / N*).

(3) Both price and quantity will increase in panel(s) (*i / ii / iii / N*).

(4) price will not rise in panel(s) (*i / ii / iii / N*).

(5) quantity will not increase in panel(s) *i / ii / iii / N*.

(6) neither price nor quantity will increase in panel(s) *i / ii / iii / N.*

(7) price will rise and quantity will fall in panel(s) *i / ii / iii / N.*

---

a. increase; increase **b. (1)** ii **(2)** iii **(3)** i **(4)** ii **(5)** iii **(6)** iii **(7)** ii **c. (1)** i; iii **(2)** i; ii **(3)** i **(4)** ii **(5)** iii **(6)** N **(7)** N (the backward-bending case is not illustrated in Figure 23A-2.)

2. The term "economic rent" of case 3 in the text was first used because it was thought the rental of undeveloped land illustrated the case involved. The owners of such land might receive a high rent if the demand were sufficiently high; but they would have been willing to rent the same amount of land for a low rent if necessary. The supply curve to illustrate this situation would be *(perfectly elastic / perfectly inelastic / neither perfectly elastic nor perfectly inelastic / backward-bending).*

---

perfectly inelastic

3. a. In one case, case 4 in the text, an increase in price might decrease the amount suppliers offer for sale. This is the *(backward-bending supply / economic-rent / increasing-cost / inelastic-supply)* case. The commodity or service most commonly associated with this case is *(farm goods / labor service / manufactured goods / monopoly supply).*

b. The explanation for the *backward-bending case* is that with a higher price (pick one):

(1) it will be impossible for the supplier to furnish the same amount of the service as before.

(2) fewer people want to supply this service.

(3) the supplier can enjoy the same or more income and more leisure time.

(4) the supplier wants to reduce the amount of income obtained from supplying this service.

(Note that there is normally a limit on the degree of backward bend. Supply is unlikely to be cut back to such an extent that the supplier's money receipts are actually reduced.)

---

a. backward-bending supply; labor service **b.** (3)

4. Economists blithely recognize rising supply curves, horizontal supply curves, vertical supply curves, even some special backward-bending curves (as in the case of labor supply). But they suddenly become cautious if falling supply curves are suggested—i.e., any supply curve which goes beyond the perfectly horizontal into the northwest-to-southeast region.

Given such a supply curve, then, an increase in demand would lower price, not raise it. Economists caution against accepting this case without explanation on the basis of the law of scarcity. If resources are scarce, then an increased pressure of demand on any part of those resources should, if anything, raise price, not lower it.

The thought that springs to mind to justify a falling supply curve involves "economies of scale" or mass-production opportunities. Opportunities for lower per-unit costs at larger outputs arise from time to time, and firms will try to exploit them for as long as they exist. The firm that fails to seize such an opportunity could easily be driven out of business. Henry Ford, the founder of mass-production techniques, drove many small carriage builders into the ground when they did not follow his lead. To expand beyond the point where economies of scale disappear could, however, be equally disastrous. Occasionally, though, expansion that exploits lower per-unit costs can continue until one large firm covers the total quantity demanded in its market at almost any price. Such a firm is called a ____________________. Putting this story into the supply-and-demand context, many cases of economies of scale which look to the untrained eye like falling-supply-curve cases are really cases of ____

---

monopoly; shifts of short-run supply curve to the right

Proposition 2 in this appendix is, "An increase in supply—demand being constant—will almost certainly lower price and increase the quantity bought and sold." This is an assertion about demand curves (just as Proposition 1 was an assertion about supply curves). It is illustrated by Figure 23A-3: an increase in supply (a shift of *SS* to position *S′S′*) produces a lower price and a larger quantity bought and sold because the demand curve is negatively sloped.

Notice that Proposition 2 is much firmer about the probable consequences than was Proposition 1; hence the appendix spends little time discussing exceptions to this general characteristic of demand.

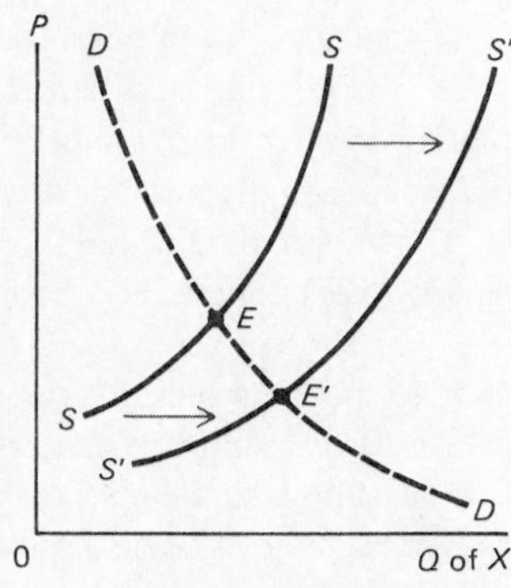

Figure 23A-3

5. a. Proposition 2 is just a restatement of (pick one):

(1) the law of supply and demand.

(2) the law of downward-sloping demand.

(3) the principle of demand elasticity.

b. The text does pause for a moment to note that the extent to which price will fall with any given supply increase (or rise with any given supply decrease) will be governed by demand elasticity with respect to price.

Figure 23A-4 illustrates this point. It shows two different demand curves: D_2 is more elastic than D_1. If supply were to increase in the manner indicated by the shift of SS to position $S'S'$, the price fall would be greater if the demand curve were *(D_1 / D_2)* than if it were *(D_1 / D_2)*. [REMEMBER: It is dangerous to associate price elasticity with the slope of the demand curve. It is, however, safe to say that if two demand curves are drawn on the same diagram (i.e., with the same scale used for both curves), then at the point where they intersect, the flatter curve is the more elastic of the two.]

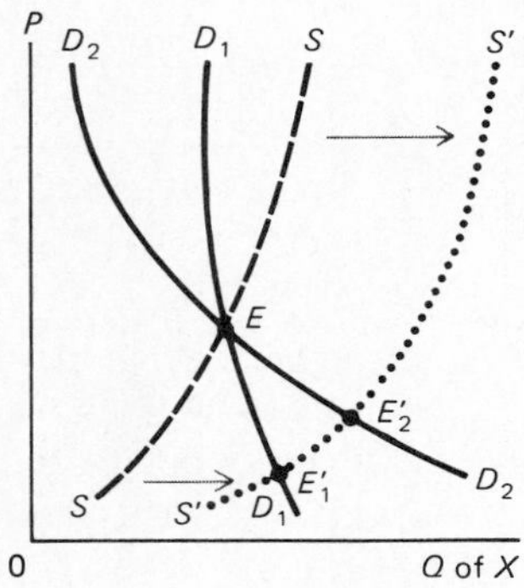

Figure 23A-4

In terms of a decrease in supply, the price rise associated with such a supply decrease will be greater the more *(elastic / inelastic)* demand is with respect to price.

---

a. (2) **b.** D_1; D_2; inelastic

6. Throughout most of your work in microeconomics thus far, it has been taken for granted that market forces will automatically push a competitive price to its equilibrium level at the intersection of demand and supply curves. A change in demand or supply will, of course, produce a period of disequilibrium during which the market seeks out its new equilibrium, but that period is presumed to be short.

The *dynamic-cobweb* theory argues that in particular circumstances these conclusions oversimplify matters. If equilibrium price is disturbed by a supply or demand change, the consequences may be a series of oscillations, with price swinging first above, then below, the equilibrium level.

The cobweb theory really involves two supply curves. First, there is the "true" supply curve—the schedule of quantities producers would want to supply, given various possible prices. It is a conventional supply curve, running approximately from southwest to northeast; i.e., the higher the market price, the more they will wish to sell. In elasticity terms, this curve *(is perfectly price elastic / has some price elasticity / is perfectly price inelastic)*.

What complicates matters is that producers are assumed to have to make their decision on quantity to be shipped to market before that market opens, and consequently before they know what the market price is going to be. In the cobweb case, their forecasts generally prove to be wrong.

In the text's example, it is assumed that all suppliers estimate that the coming period's price will be the same as last period's price. So they produce the quantity they would like to sell at that price (according to their "true" supply curve) and ship that quantity to the market.

The assumption is that there is no holding back on any part of this supply quantity, once shipped. It must sell—all of it—for whatever price the market establishes. This means we have a second supply curve, one different from the "true" curve. This supply curve *(is perfectly price elastic / has some price elasticity / is perfectly price inelastic)*.

When this supply reaches the market, things work out just as they are supposed to, in competitive conditions. Given a certain demand, an equilibrium price is quickly reached. But if demand conditions happen to have changed since the previous period, it will not be the same price as that earlier-period one, and consequently not the price that suppliers had anticipated. This is when they learn that their forecasts were wrong. For illustrative purposes, suppose this most recent price is (due to a decrease in demand) lower than the earlier-period price.

Next time around, suppliers must again guess what the price is going to be. Again (in the simplest version of the cobweb) they assume it will be what it was in the most recent period—the lower price. So (consulting their "true" supply curve) they ship a smaller quantity. Again the market works out an equilibrium: this time, smaller quantity, higher price. Another wrong forecast!

If suppliers stick rigidly to their belief that the next-period price will be the same as the previous-period price, the consequence will be a series of prices that swing from high to low to high. In extreme cases, these oscillations might even grow wider and wider. Of course, suppliers are unlikely to be so stupid as to cling to a forecasting method that proves to be consistently incorrect. Nevertheless, the cobweb theory does help to explain cyclical price swings in markets for some farm products.

---

has some price elasticity; is perfectly price inelastic

QUIZ: Multiple Choice

1. An increase in supply will lower price unless:
(1) supply is perfectly inelastic.
(2) demand is perfectly elastic.
(3) it is followed by an increase in quantity demanded.
(4) demand is highly inelastic.
(5) both demand and supply are highly inelastic.

2. An increase in demand will not raise price if:
(1) the case is that of pure economic rent.
(2) demand is highly elastic.
(3) supply is perfectly elastic.
(4) it is followed by an increase in quantity supplied.
(5) demand is perfectly inelastic.

3. Which panel in Figure 23A-5, if any, depicts the pure-economic-rent case?
(1) a.
(2) b.
(3) c.
(4) d.
(5) None of them.

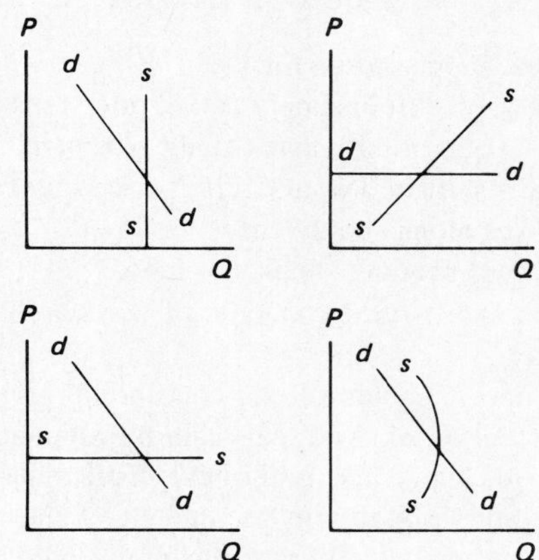

Figure 23A-5

4. Which panel in Figure 23A-5, if any, depicts the perfectly inelastic supply case?
(1) a.
(2) b.
(3) c.
(4) d.
(5) None of them.

5. Which panel in Figure 23A-5, if any, depicts the constant-cost case?
(1) a.
(2) b.
(3) c.
(4) d.
(5) None of them.

6. If a good is produced under constant-cost conditions, the effect of a $1 tax on each unit sold would normally be:
(1) to raise price to consumers by $1.
(2) to raise price to consumers by less than $1, if demand is elastic.
(3) to require the entire tax to be paid by producers, unless demand is perfectly elastic.
(4) to raise price to consumers by less than $1, if demand is inelastic.
(5) none of these.

7. The dynamic-cobweb supply-and-demand case refers to which of the following?
(1) A situation in which there is an interaction between supply and demand curves, so that a shift in one curve may set off a shift in the other, thus making it difficult for a stable equilibrium price to develop.
(2) The tendency of price to be pulled toward the critical point at which supply and demand curves diverge.
(3) A situation in which any disturbance of equilibrium price may set off a series of price oscillations, possibly with the swings growing wider as they continue.
(4) The case in which consideration is given to the quantity that will be demanded and the supply offered per period of time, instead of the time factor being disregarded, as it is in ordinary supply-and-demand analysis.
(5) A situation in which both demand curve and supply curve are highly elastic, so that any price fluctuations caused by a movement of either curve tend to be extremely wide.

8. The results observed in the dynamic-cobweb supply-and-demand case depend in large part on the assumption that:
(1) the supply curve for the commodity is inelastic.
(2) the commodity involved can be stored and kept in inventory, so that sellers can withdraw part of their supply from the market if they do not like the price that prevails.
(3) the demand and supply curves intersect at a price that is satisfactory neither to suppliers nor to buyers.
(4) suppliers decide on the quantity they will send to market in this period on the basis of an earlier-period price.
(5) both demand curve and supply curve are highly inelastic, so that any shift in either curve results in a large change in price.

9. "Increasing costs" means:
(1) the same thing as perfectly inelastic supply.
(2) that at any higher price a larger quantity will be supplied.
(3) any upward shift in a supply curve due to an increase in input prices.
(4) any leftward shift of the supply curve following an increase in demand.
(5) none of the above, necessarily.

10. If the revenue received by a factor of production is classed as a pure economic rent, and if the demand for this factor declines, then:
(1) the price of this factor will fall, but the quantity bought and sold will remain unchanged.
(2) the price of this factor will fall, and the quantity bought and sold will decline.
(3) the price of this factor will remain unchanged, but the quantity bought and sold will decline.

(4) both the price of this factor and the quantity bought and sold will remain unchanged.
(5) none of these is true.

11. Perfectly elastic supply indicates:
(1) constant cost.
(2) increasing cost.
(3) decreasing cost.
(4) that revenue received by suppliers is designated as economic rent.
(5) that a certain fixed supply will be offered no matter what price may be.

12. If a commodity's return is in the nature of a pure economic rent and a tax is imposed on the commodity, then:
(1) the incidence of the tax is borne wholly by the suppliers, and price to the buyers will not change.
(2) the incidence is borne wholly by the buyers.
(3) the incidence will be shared between the suppliers and the buyers.
(4) the output of the commodity will fall and its price will rise.
(5) the output of the commodity will not fall but its price will rise.

13. The law of diminishing returns plays which of the following background roles in demand and/or supply curves?
(1) It explains, at least in part, the increasing-cost case.
(2) It explains why an increase in supply will almost certainly lower price.
(3) It accounts, in part, for the fact that price must be lowered if a greater quantity is to be sold.
(4) It explains, at least in part, the backward-bending supply-curve case.
(5) Its part is not correctly indicated by any of these statements.

14. If the land suited for growing wheat is fixed in quantity, the supply curve for wheat:
(1) should still have some price elasticity to indicate that as price rises, supply quantity offered would increase.
(2) must rise vertically, i.e., be perfectly inelastic.
(3) may in consequence be backward-bending.
(4) might be perfectly horizontal, since the supply of wheat and the supply of wheat-growing land are two different things.
(5) will not be influenced by the price offered for wheat.

SUGGESTED ANSWERS TO QUESTIONS IN THE TEXT: Appendix to Chapter 23

1. **a.** Vertical supply curve for labor.
b. Downward shift in supply curve; price falls and quantity climbs as equilibrium moves along a demand curve.
c. Upward shift in demand curve; price climbs as equilibrium moves along supply curve.
d. Backward-bending supply for labor.

2. Case 1: *SS* shifts up by amount of tax; equilibrium up by amount of tax.

Case 2: up by amount of tax; equilibrium price up by less than 100 percent of tax, with part paid by suppliers.

Case 3: No change in equilibrium; suppliers pay all the tax.

Case 4: Supply shifts up by amount of the tax, with an indeterminant effect; equilibrium quantity could rise or fall. Draw it to see.

CHAPTER 24

MONOPOLY: ANALYSIS AND REGULATION

Perfect competition was defined in Chapter 23 to be the market structure that incorporates many small firms selling identical products. It has been studied extensively, as was noted there, not because of its wide application to reality, but because of its analytical properties. Perfect competition, for example, was seen to support allocational efficiency characterized by the inability to adjust a competitive equilibrium to make one person better off without hurting someone else. Perfect competition is, as a result, a standard against which the inefficiencies of other market forms can be measured. Additionally, the workings of perfect competition are easy to understand and easy to work with; there is a certain methodological convenience in examining certain economic issues first in the context of competitive markets. The list of reasons for concentrating on perfect competition can, of course, be extended, but that is not the point of Chapter 24. It is, instead, to turn to different types of market organization spawned by the failures of the competitive model—the rampant forms of imperfect competition.

This chapter presents the sources, patterns, and costs of imperfect competition, a theoretical discussion of monopoly (the exact opposite of perfect competition) based upon the notions of marginal cost and marginal revenue (a concept defined here), and a review of the regulatory alternatives open to a society that would like either to curb or to control the deficiencies that monopolies can generate. The germ of the content of the entire chapter is found in the quotation from Adam Smith's *Wealth of Nations* that precedes the text chapter: "The monopolists, by keeping the market constantly understocked, . . . sell their commodities much above the natural price, and raise their emoluments, whether they consist of wages or profit. . . ." Having worked through the chapter, you will have achieved an understanding of not only precisely where the truth in that statement lies but also the following objectives.

LEARNING OBJECTIVES

1. Prepare a general overview of the patterns of imperfect competition and the sources of that imperfection (cost conditions and barriers to competition).

2. Understand the functional and definitional distinctions among the various forms of imperfect competition.

3. Develop insight into the notion of marginal revenue and its role in determining the profit-maximizing level of output (output such that marginal cost equals marginal revenue).

4. Recognize that the profit-maximizing rule for perfect competition, price equals marginal cost, is simply a special case of the more general rule that marginal revenue equals marginal cost.

5. Understand the inefficiencies of monopoly markets that produce too little and charge too much, and demonstrate the cost of those inefficiencies in terms of lost consumer surplus (i.e., deadweight loss).

6. Be familiar with the various tools available to curb the inefficiencies of monopoly distortions of price and output.

7. Understand thoroughly the economic regulation of imperfect competitors, paying particular attention to the circumstances under which regulation can improve or reduce general welfare.

The intuition behind the sources of imperfect competition is easy to understand. Imperfect competition can arise whenever firms face a demand curve with some measure of negative slope; that slope gives firms some degree of power over not only the quantity that they choose to produce but also the price at which they will sell that output.

1. Figure 24-1 starts on the left-hand side with monopoly and proceeds to the right along two branches. Along the top branch, the number of firms selling the same product increases from 1 (the monopoly box) to a few (in box A) to an arbitrarily

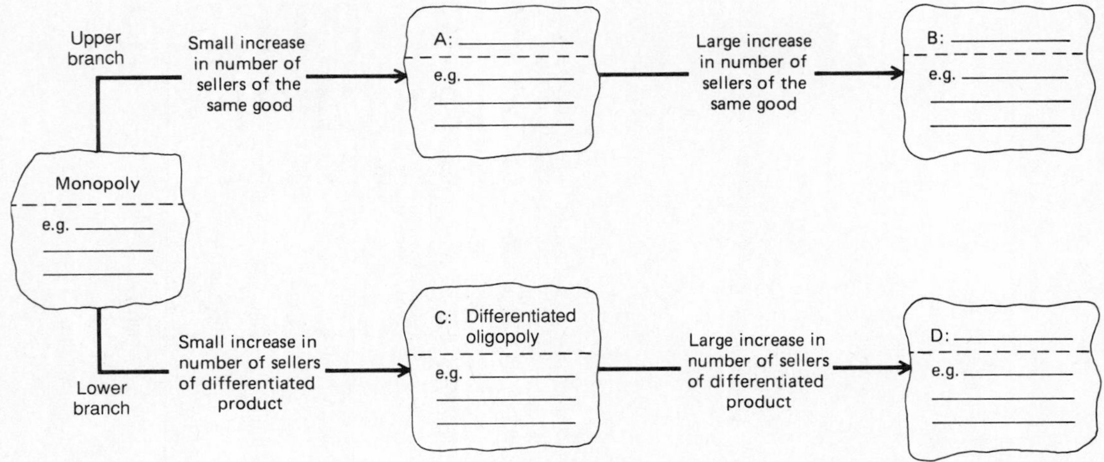

Figure 24-1

large number (in box B). Along the bottom branch, the number of firms producing differentiated but nearly identical products increases from 1 to a few (in box C) to an arbitrarily large number (in box D). Label each box by the market structure suggested by the process just noted (box C is already labeled "differentiated oligopoly"), and record an example of each type of structure from your knowledge of the American economy (consult Table 24-1 in the text). Along which branch would you expect advertising total expenditure to grow with the number of firms? ________________ . Provide a list of industries that display monopoly structures.

____

____

____

The figure: Upper branch: A—oligopoly; steel, chemical, etc.; B—perfect competition; farm products (wheat, corn, etc.) Lower branch: C—"differentiated" oligopoly; autos, computers, etc.; D—monopolistic competition; retail trade (gasoline, food products, etc)
lower; lower; local telephone, electricity, gas utilities, cable TV, etc.

2. There are two major sources of market imperfection. One, listed under the general rubric of "cost conditions," can be represented graphically. Which of the panels of Figure 24-2 illustrate relative cost circumstances that might lead to imperfectly competitive market structures? ________________ . The existence of "natural monopoly" (*does / does not*) fall under this classification; if so, which panel illustrates "natural monopoly"? ________ . What name should be attached to the structure suggested by panel **(b)**? ________________ .

The second rubric is entitled "barriers to entry" and incorporates a variety of situations. Indicate with **(B)** in the spaces provided those items in the following list that can reasonably be included in this second category.

a. 17-year patents for new products . . . . (________)

b. regulated entry into an industry . . . . (________)

c. tariff protection from foreign competitors . . . (________)

d. artificial product differentiation . . . . (________)

e. deliberate overinvestment in capacity to threaten new entrants with impossibly low price competition . . . . (________)

In the case of product differentiation, the distinction between products (whether real or perceived) generates market power by moving the demand curve that the firm faces (*in / nowhere / out*) relative to the market demand curve for the general class of product. The result is that panel (*a / b / c*) of Figure 24-2 can become an appropriate representation of the firm's individual market situation.

(a) and **(b)**; does; **(a)**; oligopoly; all items qualify as a "barrier"; in; **(a)** and/or **(b)**

3. One measure of the control (or potential control) over price is the **concentration ratio**. The four-firm ratio is, for example, the percentage of the total industry output produced by the largest four firms in an industry. In perfectly competitive markets, we should expect that this ratio would be nearly equal to (*0 / 25 / 50 / 75*) percent. From 1947 through 1972, this ratio (*rose dramatically / rose slightly / remained constant / fell slightly / fell significantly*) within the United States from 37 percent to (*45 / 38 / 37 / 36 / 25*) percent. It is likely that this trend (*overestimates / accurately estimates / underestimates*) the change in concentration because ________________ .

A second measure, the Herfindahl index, has been designed to capture size differences even within the largest four firms of an industry. If S_i represents the market share of *i*th firm, then the Herfindahl index for the top four firms would be

$H =$ ________________

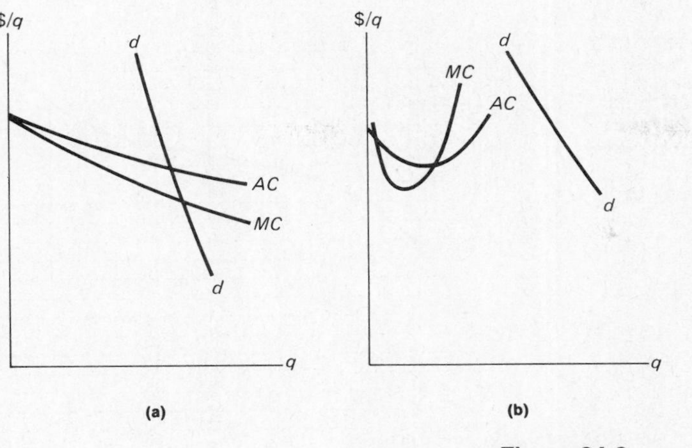

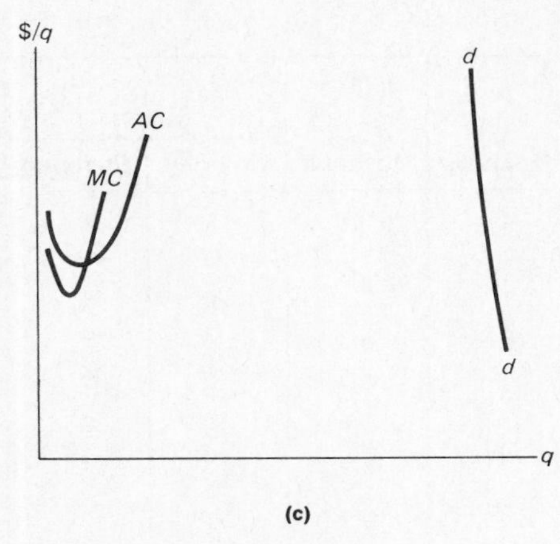

Figure 24-2

Suppose that the top four firms of industry X controled 80 percent of a market equally (with each capturing 20 percent of the total). Its Herfindahl index would equal ________ . A second industry, Y, with the top four firms capturing 40, 20, 10, and 10 percent, respectively, would display a (*higher* / *identical* / *lower*) index; specifically, it would register an index of ________ . If industry Z were perfectly competitive, its index should be approximately equal to ________ .

0; rose slightly; 38; overestimates; it ignores the recent influx of foreign competition; $S_1^2 + S_2^2 + S_3^2 + S_4^2$; 1600; higher; 2200; 0.

We turn now to an examination of the profit-maximizing behavior of a monopoly firm. Analytically, this monopoly case is decidedly easier than the so-called intermediate cases—those not perfectly competitive, and yet not completely monopolistic. It would be unwise to tackle these more intricate cases before having mastered the elementary ideas of monopoly pricing.

The terms and diagrams involved in a description of monopoly pricing may seem complicated at first. Yet the basic idea involved is simple. The monopoly firm is assumed to be motivated by profit in exactly the same way that the perfect competitor was motivated in Chapter 23. The results will be different only because the monopolist has power over price as well as quantity.

To review the basic ideas of profit maximization:

1. "Maximizing profit" means earning as much revenue net of costs as market and production conditions will permit.
2. To be able to maximize profit, there must be something the firm can do that will influence its profit. There must be some variable which the firm can control and which changes profit.
3. This chapter assumes that the monopoly firm can control the quantity it sells, just as the firm in pure (or perfect) competition can do. It looks, quite simply, for the particular quantity that will maximize its profit. In this respect, the monopoly firm is exactly like the perfectly competitive firm.
4. The monopoly firm is also assumed to know the price which that profit maximizing quantity will fetch. More generally, it knows the demand schedule for its product; it know the price which goes with each possible quantity sold.
5. From this demand schedule, it is easy to develop a revenue schedule (total revenue being quantity sold multiplied by price per unit)—a schedule showing revenue associated with each possible quantity sold.
6. The firm must also know the total cost of each and every level of output. By bringing together the revenue and cost schedules, it can identify that output at which the excess of revenue over cost (profit) is greatest. It can determine, as well, the price to charge for this maximum-profit output just by going back to its demand schedule. Again, this is just what the firm in pure (or perfect) competition did. The only difference is that that firm faced different demand conditions. The perfect competitor faced a perfectly elastic demand curve so the price was taken as given. The monopoly firm we are now considering faces a "tilted" demand curve so it can exercise some influence over its value.

The next seven questions will lead you through an illustrative example of precisely how this process works for a pure monopolist.

4. Columns (1) and (2) in Table 24-1 represent a demand schedule. We assume that a firm has done its market research homework accurately and that it has developed this schedule to indicate the quantities that it can sell at various prices.

This firm must operate under conditions of (*perfect* / *imperfect*) competition, since as the output to be sold increases, price (*remains constant* / *must be reduced*). We assume, in fact, that this firm has monopoly power over the market represented by the demand schedule in Table 24-1.

Table 24-1

(1) Price	(2) Quantity	(3) Total Revenue	(4) Extra: Quantity	(5) Extra: Revenue	(6) Marginal Revenue
$14.00	10	$140			
			7	$64	$9.14
12.00	17	204			
			8	46	5.75
10.00	25	____			
			____	29	____
9.00	31	279			
			8	33	4.13
8.00	39	312			
			11	____	3.45
7.00	50	____			
			____	14	____
6.50	56	364			
			7	14	2.00
6.00	63	378			
			8	13	1.63
5.50	71	391			
			____	____	____
5.00	80	____			
			10	5	0.50
4.50	90	405			
			11	____	−0.09
4.00	101	____			
			____	−5	−0.38
3.50	114	399			

imperfect; must be reduced

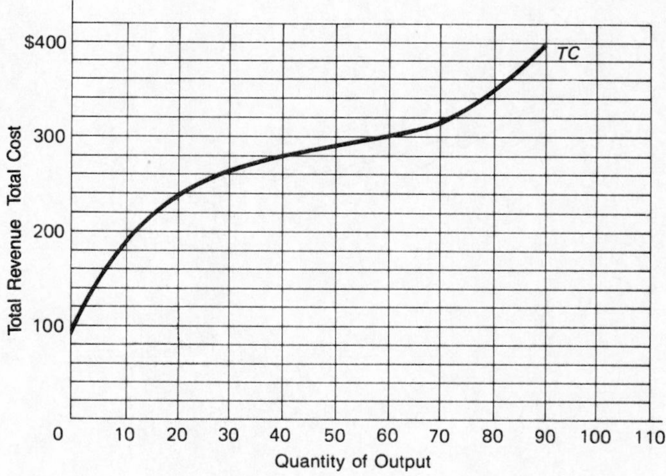

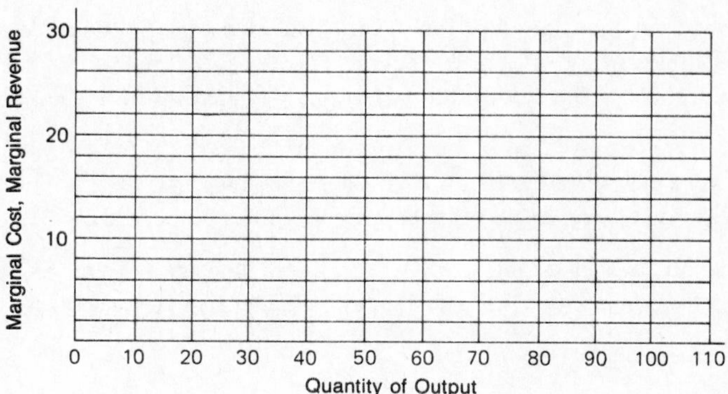

Figure 24-3

5. We now turn to the determination of profit-maximizing output and price.

a. Column (3) of Table 24-1 shows total revenue—price times quantity. As a small exercise, complete the four blanks in this column.

Use the figures in columns (2) and (3) to illustrate total revenue on the upper panel of Figure 24-3; i.e., show the total revenue associated with various output quantities. Join the points with a smooth curve.

b. Notice, incidentally, that this demand schedule becomes price inelastic when price is sufficiently low—specifically, when price falls below $(*8 / 7 / 6 / 5 / 4*).

a. $250; $350; $400; $404 **b.** 4 (Marginal revenue turns negative.)

6. a. Table 24-2 shows the firm's total cost and marginal cost for production of the commodity whose demand curve is detailed in Table 24-1. Table 24-2 is similar in construction to tables presented in previous chapters, but just to refresh your memory on the process of computing extra cost, complete the four blanks in columns (3) and (4) of Table 24-2 with the proper figures.

The graph of columns (1) and (2) of Table 24-2 is already drawn on the top panel of Figure 24-3 as a total cost curve (*TC*). Mark the curve that you drew earlier with *TR* to distinguish it from the cost curve. Now plot the marginal cost curve (denote it *MC*) in the bottom panel of Figure 24-3.

b. It is now possible to see at once why the profit-maximizing process outlined here is a simple one. The firm is doing nothing more than searching for the output at which the vertical distance between *TR* and *TC* is greatest. This distance, for any output, is (*fixed cost / price / profit or loss*). (If *TR* is above *TC*, it is profit; if *TC* is above, it is loss. It is thus prefereable to look for "greatest vertical distance" with *TR* above *TC*. The greatest distance with *TC* on top marks the maximum possible loss—somewhat less desirable as an operating position.)

a. $20; $4; $8; $1.60 **b.** profit or loss

7. a. Figure 24-3 is too small to indicate quickly the precise maximum-profit position, but even a glance is sufficient to indicate that this best possible position is approximately (*45 / 65 / 85*) units of output.

The firm can be thought of as gradually increasing its output and sales, pausing at each increase to see if its profit position is improved. Each extra unit of output brings in a little more revenue (unless demand has reached its price inelastic range); each extra unit incurs a little more cost. The profit

Table 24-2

(1) Output	(2) Total Cost	(3) Extra Cost	(4) *MC* per Unit
0	$90		
		$60	$12.00
5	150		
		35	7.00
10	185		
		30	6.00
15	215		
		______	______
20	235		
		15	3.00
25	250		
		12	2.40
30	262		
		10	2.00
35	272		
		8	1.60
40	280		
		6	1.20
45	286		
		5	1.00
50	291		
		4	0.80
55	295		
		5	1.00
60	300		
		______	______
65	308		
		10	2.00
70	318		
		12	2.40
75	330		
		15	3.00
80	345		
		20	4.00
85	365		
		35	7.00
90	400		

position is improved if this small amount of extra revenue (*exceeds / is equal to / is less than*) the small amount of extra cost.

b. In more precise terms, the extra revenue brought in from the sale of *1* extra unit of output is **marginal revenue (MR)**. It is the increase in total revenue resulting from the sale of that 1 further unit. For maximum profit, the firm should increase its output and sales if this *MR* exceeds marginal cost (*MC*)—the increase in total cost occasioned by that 1 extra unit. Total profit increases, with each unit increase in output, by an amount equal to the difference between *MR* and *MC*.

If the firm finds its operating level is such that *MR* is less than *MC*, it should (*increase / decrease*) the quantity it produces and sells. The "in balance" position is where *MR* is (*less than / equal to / greater than*) *MC*.

c. Column (4) in Table 24-1 shows the extra number of units sold if price is reduced. Column (5) shows the extra revenue (positive or negative) accruing from that price reduction. Complete the blanks in these two columns.

a. 65; exceeds **b.** decrease; equal to **c.** Col. (4): 6, 6, 9, 13; col. (5): $38, $9, −$1

8. Although column (5) in Table 24-1 carries "extra revenue" figures, these are not *marginal* revenue figures, since *MR* is a per-unit concept. The top figure in column (5) is, for example, $64, but it came from an increase of 7 units sold. The $64 must be divided by 7 to get the *MR* figure of $9.14 in column (6). [For a reason to be discussed in a moment, even the column (6) figures are not precisely accurate *MR* figures; they are, however, reasonable approximations.]

Complete the missing *MR* figures in column (6). Plot the marginal revenue curve (denote it *MR*) in the lower panel of Figure 24-3.

Marginal revenue is a concept of sufficient importance that you should pause for a moment, to make sure you have it straight. Note, in particular, three specific points.

a. First, marginal revenue is precisely analogous to marginal cost. Marginal cost is the extra cost resulting from the last unit of output produced. Similarly, marginal revenue is the extra revenue yielded by the last unit of output produced and sold.

b. Second, *MR* falls as quantity of sales is increased. It can even become a negative figure (and will, if demand becomes price inelastic so that revenue falls as sales increase).

c. Finally, the *MR*s of column (6) in Table 24-1 are not precisely accurate since that table records only price changes of $1 or 50 cents. A true *MR* table would show extra revenue from each separate extra unit, not from an average of anywhere from 6 to 11 extra units. The table would have to be greatly enlarged to show *MR's* precise unit-by-unit performance.

$4.83; $2.33; $1

9. The general profit-maximizing rule is expand your output until you reach the output level at which $MR = MC$—and stop at that point.

Chapter 23 gives a profit-maximizing rule for the firm in perfect competition: $P = MC$. This is nothing but a particular instance of the $MR = MC$ rule. It is assumed in perfect competition that the demand curve facing the individual firm is perfectly horizontal, or perfectly price (*elastic / inelastic*). That is, if market price is $2, then the firm receives (*less than $2 / exactly $2 / more than $2*) for each extra unit that it sells. In this special case, *MR* (extra revenue per unit) is (*greater than / the same thing as / less than*) price per unit (which could be called average revenue, or revenue per unit). In cases of perfect competition, therefore, $P = MC$ and $MR = MC$ are two ways of saying the same thing.

elastic; exactly $2; the same thing as

10. a. In imperfect competition, the firm's demand curve is (*tilted / flat*). From inspection of the figures in Table 24-1 [compare columns (1) and (6)], it is evident that with such a demand curve, *MR* at any particular output is *(greater than / the same thing as / less than)* for that output.

b. Why is this so? Suppose, at price $7, you can sell 4 units; at price $6, 5 units. Revenues associated with these two prices are, respectively, $28 and $30. Marginal revenue from selling the fifth unit is accordingly $*(2 / 5 / 6 / 7 / 28 / 30)*. It is the difference in revenue obtained as a result of selling the 1 extra unit. Why only $2 when the price at which that fifth unit sold was $6? Because to sell that fifth unit, price had to be reduced, and that lowered price applies to all 5 units. The first 4, which formerly sold at $7, now bring only $6 each and revenue takes a beating of $4. You must subtract this $4 from the $6 which the fifth unit brings in to compute the net change in total revenue. In this case, the net gain in revenue is $2—marginal revenue.

c. Notice also that *MR* and price elasticity are related. Recall that demand is price inelastic if, when price is reduced, revenue goes *(down / up)*. This means that when demand is inelastic with respect to price, *MR* is *(negative / zero / positive)*. At elasticity of unity, *MR* is *(negative / zero / positive)*. When demand is price elastic, *MR* is *(negative / zero / positive)*. Check to make sure that the *MR* and *TR* curves that you drew in Figure 24-3 conform to the results of this question.

---

a. tilted; less than **b.** 2 **c.** down; negative; zero; positive

11. Now return to the fortunes of the monopoly firm represented in Tables 24-1 and 24-2. The tables do not provide sufficient unit-by-unit detail to show the exact maximum-profit output level. But Table 24-1 does indicate that between sales outputs of 63 and 71, *MR* is $1.63. The *MR* figures fall as sales are expanded, so that the $1.63 would apply near the midpoint of this range, say, at output 67. *MR* would be somewhat higher between 63 and 66; somewhat lower between 68 and 71.

Similarly, *MC* (Table 24-2) would be about $1.65 at output of 67 units. So the maximum-profit position would fall very close to 67 units produced and sold per period. Check to make sure that the *MR* and *MC* curves that you drew in the bottom panel of Figure 24-3 intersect at roughly 67 units.

To sell this output, the firm would charge a price (see Table 24-1) of about $*(7 / 5.75 / 4 / 1.60)*. Its total revenue [look for nearby figures in column (3)] would be roughly $*(380 / 580 / 780)*. Total cost (Table 24-2) would be roughly $*(310 / 510 / 710)*, leaving profit per period of about $70.

5.75; 380; 310

12. In the section of the text labeled "Let Bygones Be Bygones," it is emphasized that a firm, in setting output and price according to *MR* = *MC*, will disregard fixed cost. This does not mean that fixed cost can be ignored completely; maximum profits could be negative, for example, if fixed costs were too large. Nonetheless, in the determination of the profit-maximizing production/sales point, marginal revenue and marginal cost are the critical parameters.

a. Suppose a firm's fixed cost was to increase (e.g., by a flat tax levied on a monopolist). Would the effect of this tax be to raise the firm's *AC* curve? . . . . *(Yes / No)*

b. Would the tax affect the monopolist's variable cost, or the *AVC* curve? . . . . *(Yes / No)*

c. Would the tax affect the monopolist's marginal cost curve? . . . . *(Yes / No)*

d. If the *MC* curve were unaffected, would such a flat tax change the maximum-profit output? (Presumably the tax will not affect demand for the product, so it will not affect marginal revenue.) . . . . *(Yes / No)*

e. If the tax did not affect *MC*, *MR*, or maximum-profit output, would the price be changed? . . . . *(Yes / No)*

---

a. Yes **b.** No (because the tax affects only fixed cost and the *AFC* curve) **c.** No (*MC* depends only on variable cost.) **d.** No (unless it drove profits below zero) **e.** No (again, not unless profits turned negative and production ceased)

13. Figure 24-4 Shows the per-unit cost and revenue measures confronting a monopolist. The *DD* line is the market demand curve. *MR* is the corresponding market marginal revenue curve. *AC* is the firm's average cost curve, and *MC* represents the corresponding marginal cost schedule.

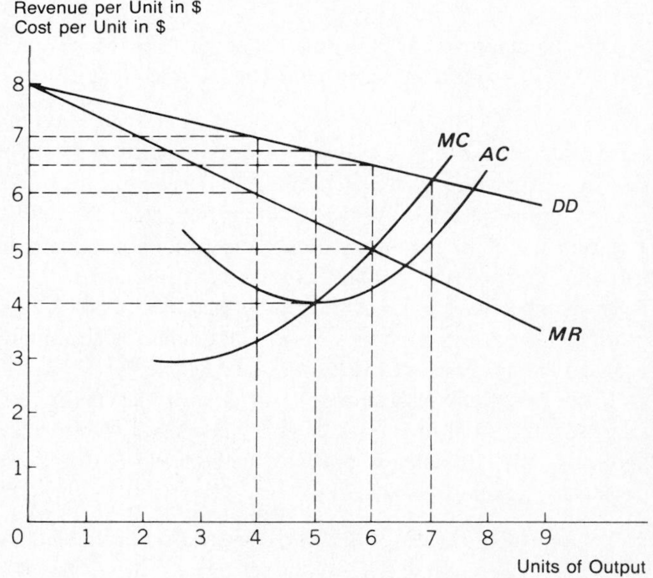

Figure 24-4

a. Which line indicates the demand curve facing the monopolist firm? . . . . (________)

b. If output is 4, what must price be? . . . . (________)

c. What is marginal revenue with output 4? . . . (________)

d. At what level of output does average cost fall to its minimum level? . . . . (________)

e. What would price be with output at this minimum *AC* level? . . . . (________)

f. What would total cost be (at this level)? . . . . (________)

g. What would total revenue be? . . . . (________)

h. What would profit be? . . . . (________)

i. At what output would profit be maximized? . . (________)

j. What is marginal revenue at this output? . . . . (________)

k. What is marginal cost at this output? . . . . . . (________)

l. What is average cost at this output? (Assume it is 20 cents above minimum level.) . . . . (________)

m. What is price at this output? . . . . (________)

n. What is total profit at this output? . . . . (________)

---

a. *DD* **b.** \$7 **c.** \$6 **d.** 5 **e.** \$6.75 **f.** \$20 **g.** \$33.75 **h.** \$13.75 **i.** 6 **j.** \$5 **k.** \$5 **l.** \$4.20 (roughly) **m.** \$6.50 **n.** \$13.80

14. This is another one of those profit-maximizing-consultant problems. It is more difficult than the straightforward computational questions that preceded it, but it is designed to test whether or not you have a thorough understanding of the concepts. What would you recommend in each of the seven cases listed in Table 24-3? In each case, the firm in question monopoly and wants to maximize its profits (or minimize its losses). Enough information is supplied in each case, though you may have to fill in some of the blank spaces in the table to do your job; that is, presumably, why you were hired. Note that there is at least one "nonsense case" in which the figures are inconsistent and cannot be correct. Ferreting out such a circumstance could lead you to tell your client to do a better job in picturing either his or her market or cost structure.

Answer for each case by putting one of the numbers 1 through 5 from the code below into the extreme right-hand column of the table. (The same number may of course be used for more than one question.)

1. Firm is now at correct position.
2. Firm should increase price and reduce quantity produced and sold.
3. Firm should reduce price and increase quantity produced and sold.
4. Firm should shut down operations because loss at best possible operating position exceeds fixed cost.
5. A nonsense case—figures supplied are inconsistent and could not all be correct.

---

a. 3 ($MR > MC$ means output should be increased; price will have to be reduced.) **b.** 1 (*AC* at the minimum means that $AC = MC$; in this case, $AC = \$4000/1000 = \$4$, and that matches *MR*) **c.** 2 (Price $= TR/Q = \$8000/4000 = \$2$. Since $MR < P$, $MR < \$2 = MC$ and output should be reduced to bring *MR* up to equality with *MC*.) **d.** 2 ($MC > MR$, so output should be reduced. This firm is now maximizing revenue, not profit.) **e.** 5 (*MR* cannot exceed price.) **f.** 2 ($AC = TC/Q = \$6000/2000 = \$3$. Since $\$3 = P > MR$, it must be that $MR < MC$.) **g.** 4 ($MR = MC$, so profit is highest, but it is negative. $TR = \$2.50 \times 10{,}000 = \$25{,}000 < TC = AC \times Q = \$3 \times 10{,}000 = \$30{,}000$.)

Table 24-3

Case	Price	Marginal Revenue	Quantity of Output	Total Revenue	Total Cost	Fixed Cost	Average Cost	Marginal Cost	Answer
a.	\$8.00	\$4.00	2,000			\$2,000	\$4.00	\$3.00	
b.	5.00	4.00	1,000		\$4,000	1,000	At minimum level		
c.			4,000	\$ 8,000			1.80	2.00	
d.	8.00	zero		32,000		5,000		4.00	
e.	1.00	2.00	10,000			2,000	2.00	2.00	
f.	3.00		2,000		6,000		At minimum level		
g.	2.50	2.00	10,000			4,000	3.00	2.00	

15. a. Imperfect competition (of which, remember, monopoly is an extreme example) is undesirable from an economic standpoint mainly because (*of the excess profits generated by the exploitation of price and quantity / of the distortions that it produces in the allocation of resources*).

Chapter 23 noted that all perfectly competitive, profit-maximizing firms operate so that marginal cost is (*lower than / equal to / higher than*) the going market price. Since price reflects marginal utility, competitive equilibria thereby achieve maximum efficiency because the marginal cost of producing any good by any competitive firm is necessarily maintained at a level that is (*lower than / equal to / greater than*) the marginal utility that its consumption produces. Total utility (*cannot / can*) be made higher by rearranging resources even though each firm acts only to maximize its own profits.

For a monopolist (e.g.), though, the equality of marginal utility and marginal cost is not obtained by self-motivated profit maximization. Since price is always (*greater than / equal to / less than*) marginal revenue along a sloped market demand curve, profit maximization requires that marginal cost be maintained at a level that is (*higher than / equal to / lower than*) the going price. Why? Because profits are maximized where marginal cost equals marginal revenue, and marginal revenue is less than price ($MC = MR < P$). Price still reflects marginal utility, though, so monopoly power brings marginal cost in (*higher than / equal to / lower than*) marginal utility. Total utility (*cannot / can*) then be improved by rearranging resources. In what way? In a way that (*brings resources into / moves resources out of*) the monopolists' markets to (*increase / decrease*) output.

b. Suppose, for example, that the monopoly firm sets its price at $2, with marginal revenue at $1. This means (by the profit-maximizing rule) that marginal cost must be $(*1 / 2*). The consumer pays $2 for each unit bought, including the last unit. Yet that last unit added only $1 to total production cost. It would cost only another $1 (or just over $1) to produce 1 further unit. Why shouldn't consumers be able to buy that unit for what it would cost to produce it? A resource is not being used to its best advantage if consumers, reckoning in terms of the price they must pay for an additional unit, halt their purchases at a point where the extra cost of using the resource to produce that additional unit is significantly less than price. Overall, resources are not being allocated properly.

---

a. of the distortions that it produces in the allocation of resources; equal to; equal to; cannot; greater than; lower than; lower than; can; brings resources into; increase. **b.** 1.

16. As was just noted, it follows from $P > MR = MC$ that the price which a monopolist charges is (*too high / too low / just right*) relative to the competitive price. Since monopoly firms face downward-sloping demand curves (otherwise they would have no monopoly power, right?), the monopolist must therefore produce (*less output than / more output than / the same output as*) the competitive firm. On the basis of the efficiency properties of the perfectly competitive market, it is thus clear that the marginal utility derived from consuming the monopolist's product is (*greater than/ less than / equal to*) the marginal cost of producing the good in question.

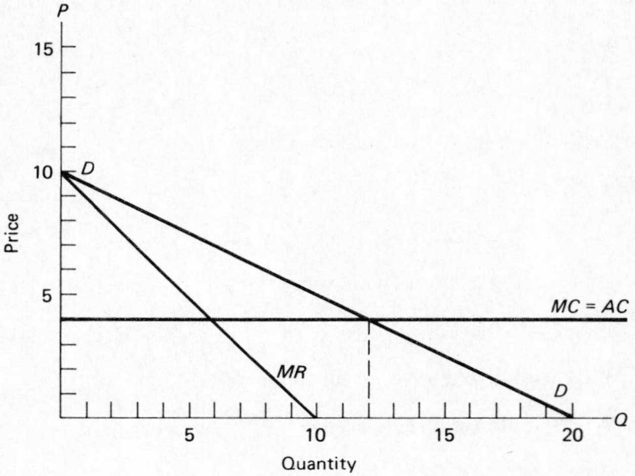

Figure 24-5

Consult Figure 24-5. The long-run competitive output and price for a market with the indicated cost structure must equal ________ units and $________ , respectively. A profit-maximizing monopolist would, meanwhile, sell ________ units at a price of $________ . The result would be a reduction in consumer surplus from $________ to $________ . Of that reduction, $________ would go to the monopolist in the form of excess economic profit and $________ would represent lost welfare that would disappear (deadweight loss).

The dimension of actual deadweight loss caused by imperfect competition across the United States appears to be (*less than / about equal to / more than*) what might be expected. The loss has been estimated by Arnold Harberger to be in the neighborhood of (*0.1 percent / 5.0 percent / over 10.0 percent*) of GNP. To conclude, in light of these numbers, that monopoly power should not be a major concern would, however, be to ignore the distortion in the distribution of income that excessive monopoly profits can create. More study is required to conclude that imperfect competition is a "non-problem."

---

too high; less output than; greater than; 12; 4; 6; 7; 36; 9; 18; 9; less than; 0.1 percent

There are at least five mechanisms that come to mind when society considers trying to curtail the abuses of monopoly power: taxation, price control, government ownership, antitrust policy, and regulation. Regulation is the subject of section C of this chapter, and we will turn to that topic shortly. Antitrust policy will be covered in Chapter 25. The first three possibilities are, however, more problematical and less popular in the United States. They are therefore reviewed only briefly before a more detailed consideration of regulation is presented. The next two questions cover the points raised in that review.

17. Suppose that the monopolist depicted in Figure 24-5 faces a lump-sum tax on profits of $18. The profit-maximizing monopolist would then (*increase / decrease / maintain*) the quoted price to support a (*larger / smaller / constant*) level of production and sales.

Suppose, instead, that government taxes the monopolist's implicit return to capital so that the effective (constant) marginal cost of production increases from $4 to $6 per unit. Output would (*fall to / rise to / continue to remain fixed at*) ______ units; price would (*climb to / fall to / stay put at*) $______, representing an increase in price (*equal to / less than / greater than*) the $______ increase in unit costs.

maintain; constant; fall to; 6; climb to; 8; less than; 2 (Neither option worked very well, did it?

18. Price controls are mentioned in the text as a second possible means of controlling the potential abuses of monopoly power. It is argued there that pervasive use of price controls to control the occasional monopolist can be expected to cause a plethora of economic problems. In the spaces provided, note with (Y) those effects that might be expected to appear in a list of these possible difficulties.

a. alienation of business and government . . . . . (______)

b. international trade problems . . . . (______)

c. shortages and surpluses . . . . (______)

d. absence of necessary flexibility in relative prices (______)

e. increased unemployment . . . . (______)

Government ownership is also an option, but it is seldom exercised in the United States. It is, though, a bit more popular in Japan and Western Europe. It would appear, then, that the choice between regulation and government ownership is more a matter of ______________ and ______________ than it is a matter of economic advantage.

all Y (Enforced price specifications are likely to cause problems in every economic sphere where adjustment to unpredictable events is required.); history; institutions

Regulation is, in the United States, the most popular mechanism with which governments at all levels protect their citizens from potential abuses of market power, particularly when a natural monopoly is under scrutiny. Regulation, in its broadest context, includes all rules and laws designed to change or control the operation of an economic enterprise. There are, in fact, two major categories within that context: social and economic.

19. Place (E) or (S) in the blanks provided to indicate whether each of the following regulatory activities is an example of an economic regulation or a social regulation.

a. restraints on price-setting practices among firms (______)

b. clean air policy . . . . (______)

c. limits on the rates of return earned by utilities (______)

d. drug testing by the FDA . . . . (______)

e. requirement to provide electricity to everyone who asks for it . . . . (______)

f. constraints on entry into and exit from given markets . . . . (______)

E; S; E; S; E or S; E

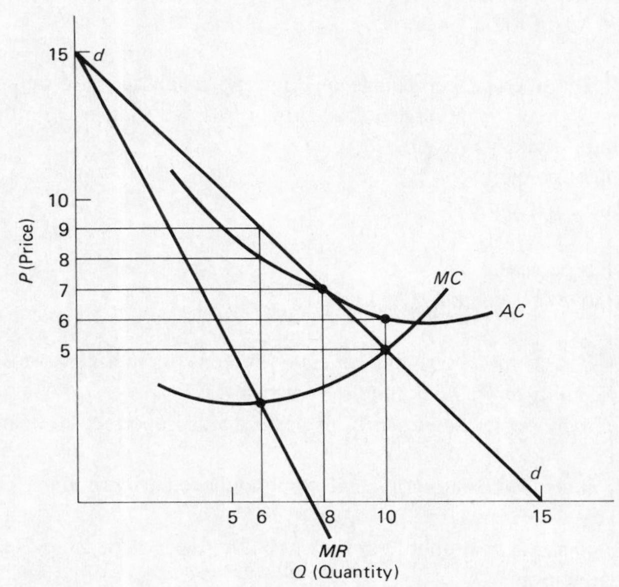

Figure 24-6

20. Consult Figure 24-6. For the indicated demand and cost curves, it is clear that the unregulated monopolist would produce ______ units of output for sale at a price of $______. Excess pure economic profits of $______ would then be earned. Regulation to the point of zero profits would require a price specification of $_____ at which _____ units of output would be expected. Consumer surplus would, in that case, increase from the unregulated monopoly level of $18 to $_____ . Regulation to the point where the efficiency conditions of $MR = MC$ were satisfied would, meanwhile, requre a price specification of $_____ , with _____ units of output expected only if the monopolist's losses in the amount of $_____ were covered. Consumer surplus would rise further to $_____ , but would actually equal $_____ if the subsidy to cover the losses just noted was deducted. This (*would / would not*) represent an improvement over the average cost pricing alternative.

6; 9; 6; 7; 8; 32; 5; 10; 10; 50; 40; would

QUIZ: Multiple Choice

1. Which of the following are possible sources of imperfectly competitive markets?
(1) Declining average costs over the range of possible quantities demanded.
(2) Legal barriers to entry.
(3) Perceived product differentiation.
(4) Tariff protection from foreign competition.
(5) All of the above.

2. The average percentage of domestic manufacturing output contributed by the largest four firms across all industries in the United States is about:
(1) 50 percent.
(2) 12 percent.
(3) 38 percent.
(4) 5 percent.
(5) over 60 percent.

3. If a firm's marginal revenue exceeds its marginal cost, maximum-profit rules require that firm to:
(1) increase its output in both perfect and imperfect competition.
(2) increase its output in perfect but not necessarily in imperfect competition.
(3) increase its output in imperfect but not necessarily in perfect competition.
(4) decrease its output in both perfect and imperfect competition.
(5) increase price, not output, in both perfect and imperfect competition.

4. Whenever a firm's demand curve is horizontal, or "perfectly elastic":
(1) the firm cannot be operating under conditions of perfect competition.
(2) the profit-maximizing rule of *MR*-equal-to-*MC* does not apply.
(3) price and marginal revenue must be one and the same.
(4) price and marginal cost must be one and the same.
(5) none of these conclusions is necessarily correct.

5. A basic difference between the firm in pure (or perfect) competition (the PC-firm) and the monopoly firm (the M-firm), according to economic analysis, is that:
(1) the PC-firm can sell as much as it wishes at some given price, whereas the M-firm must lower its price if it wishes to increase the volume of its sales by any significant amount.
(2) the M-firm can always charge a price yielding a significant profit, whereas the PC-firm can never earn such a profit.
(3) the price elasticity of supply offered by the M-firm is higher than that facing the PC-firm.
(4) The M-firm seeks to maximize profit, whereas the PC-firm's rule is to equate price and average cost.
(5) the M-firm deliberately seeks to operate at the minimum level of average cost, whereas the PC-firm does not.

6. "Oligopoly" means:
(1) the same thing as imperfect competition.
(2) a situation in which the number of competing firms is large but the products differ slightly.
(3) a situation in which the number of competing firms is small, but greater than 1.
(4) that particular condition of imperfect competition which is just removed from monopoly, regardless of the number of firms or type of product.
(5) none of these.

7. When a monopoly firm seeking to maximize its profits has reached its equilibrium position, then:
(1) price must be less than marginal cost.
(2) price must be equal to marginal cost.
(3) price must be greater than marginal cost.
(4) price may be equal to or below marginal cost, but not above it.
(5) none of the above is necessarily correct since equilibrium does not requre any particular relation between price and marginal cost.

8. "Marginal revenue" means:
(1) the price that can be obtained for the very last unit sold.
(2) total revenue divided by quantity of units sold.
(3) total revenue minus the price received for the very last unit sold.
(4) the amount of increase in total revenue brought in by the very last unit sold minus the increase in total cost which that unit occasioned.
(5) the amount of increase in total revenue brought in by the very last unit sold.

9. "Monopoly" exists, according to the economist's definition of this term:

(1) whenever there is only one seller of a particular product.
(2) whenever the seller has at least some degree of control over the price she or he can charge.
(3) whenever profit earned by the seller exceeds the amount that should properly be earned as interest on money invested, plus an allowance for risk undertaken.
(4) whenever a seller manages to maintain his or her position through successful advertising.
(5) in none of these situations, necessarily.

10. Marginal revenue could exceed price:
(1) in circumstances of oligopoly.
(2) and does, in all genuine monopoly situations.
(3) if, somehow, increased sales would bring about a higher price.
(4) in the circumstances of "differentiated" products.
(5) in no conceivable circumstances whatsoever.

11. A firm operating in a situation of imperfect competition finds that at its present output level, marginal revenue is $2.00 and average cost is $1.75, this being the minimum or lowest-attainable value of average cost. For maximum profit, this firm should:
(1) increase price.
(2) decrease price.
(3) decrease output and sales.
(4) leave price and output unchanged.
(5) perhaps do any of these things—information given is insufficient to tell.

12. Which alternative in question 11 would be correct had it specified that price rather than marginal revenue is $2?
(1).
(2).
(3).
(4).
(5).

13. The essential characteristic of imperfect competition is that the single firm's:
(1) demand curve has a downward tilt.
(2) marginal revenue exceeds the price it charges.
(3) average cost curve falls over a substantial or large range of outputs.
(4) product is differentiated from one firm to the next.
(5) average cost curve rises over a substantial or large range of outputs.

14. If the price a firm obtains for its output exceeds the marginal cost associated with that particular output, maximum-profit rules would require that firm to:
(1) increase its output in both perfect and imperfect competition.
(2) increase its output in perfect but not necessarily in imperfect competition.
(3) increase its output in imperfect but not necessarily in perfect competition.
(4) decrease its output in both perfect and imperfect competition.
(5) increase price, not output, in both perfect and imperfect competition.

15. Which alternative in question 14 would be correct had that question said that price is less than marginal cost?
(1).
(2).
(3).
(4).
(5).

16. To explain why imperfect competition is far more prevalent than perfect competition, economists lay considerable emphasis upon the fact that, for the firms in many industries:
(1) advertising has now become more powerful than price as a sales weapon.
(2) marginal revenue tends to equal or even to exceed price.
(3) average cost continues to fall until a large output has been reached.
(4) a high price charged to consumers has become the most effective method of maximizing profits.
(5) marginal revenue tends to fall significantly below price.

17. A correct statement of the relationship between marginal revenue (*MR*) and elasticity of demand (with respect to price) is this. When *MR* is:
(1) negative, demand must be inelastic.
(2) zero, demand must be inelastic.
(3) positive, demand must be inelastic.
(4) negative, demand must be unit-elastic.
(5) positive, demand must be perfectly elastic.

18. Among the five statements below, one is false with respect to any firm operating under conditions of imperfect competition. Which one?
(1) The number of competing sellers offering similar (although differentiated) products can be large.
(2) Other firms may sell products which are identical or almost identical with this firm's product.
(3) The number of competing sellers offering similar (although differentiated) products can be small.
(4) The firm's marginal revenue will be less than the price it obtains.
(5) The demand curve facing the firm can be perfectly horizontal.

SUGGESTED ANSWERS TO QUESTIONS IN THE TEXT: Chapter 24

1. Consult the definitions. General Motors—oligopoly in the United States, monopolistic competition worldwide (?); local telephone—local monopoly; Sears—monopolistic competitor; Farmer Jones—perfect competition; your college—(?).

2. If a corporation can pick its price, then maximizing profit puts it at a price where $MC = MR$—nothing more and certainly nothing less.

3. Constant TR means $MR = 0$.

4. Slopes of TC and TR are equal at $q = 4$; i.e., $MR = MC$.

5. Four-firm index = 70 percent; eight-firm index = 95 percent; Herfindahl index = 1550.

6. $MC = \$1000$. Demand: $P = 3000 - 0.01Q$; $MR = 3000 - 0.02Q$. MC equals MC at $Q = 100{,}000$.

7. Monopolist operates such that $MC = MR < P = MU$. Extrapolate.

8. Extrapolate by fiddling with the diagram.

9. Because it does not have a unified model that can be tested empirically for all circumstances.

10. Let your experience in the world lead the way.

11. $0 < MC = MR$ for the monopolist, so $MR > 0$, and demand is price elastic. AC or MC could cut demand in the inelastic region. Higher price should produce higher profits in all cases, since if the regulation is binding, the monopolist wants a higher price.

12. Use calculus and algebra. Even if you do not know calculus, take the MR and MC curves as given and do the algebra.

APPENDIX: 24

Economics of Risk and Uncertainty

The self-motivated actions of speculators and arbitragers tend to moderate price and consumption instability in a wide variety of markets. Acting in their individual interest, these people thereby generate a welfare improvement for society as a whole above and beyond their individual gains. The source of this improvement can be found in the principle of diminishing marginal utility, and it provides the same sort of benefit as insurance. Not all risk can be eliminated by either insurance or the actions of speculators—at least that much is certain. Having completed your quick work in this appendix, though, you will have come to understand precisely how diminished risk provides welfare gain. More specifically, you will have achieved the following learning objectives.

LEARNING OBJECTIVES

1. Explain why, given diminishing marginal utility, uncertainty diminishes economic welfare; the greater the uncertainty, the larger the social cost.

2. Understand the role of insurance in reducing the social cost of uncertainty.

It is the principle of diminishing marginal utility that leads us to the conclusion that stability in consumption is economically beneficial. Insurance offers stability at a cost; people can reduce fluctuation in consumption by purchasing protection against various losses. Speculators and arbitragers lower cost by reducing risk; by buying low and selling high, they shave off the peaks of high price periods and fill in the valleys of low price periods.

1. Consult Figure 24A-1. A cardinal utility schedule is drawn there dependent upon the level of income; it displays a (*diminishing / constant / increasing*) marginal utility of income.

a. Suppose that income is $50,000 per year; in terms of utility measured on the vertical axis in utils, this $50,000 would produce utility equal to ________ units.

b. Now suppose that we consider a "lottery" which has an expected payoff of $0 but which will return a gain of $10,000 with a probability of 50 percent or a loss of $10,000 with a probability of 50 percent. Would taking this lottery improve welfare? ________ . To see why or why not, notice that $60,000 would produce ________ units of utility—a gain of ________ units over

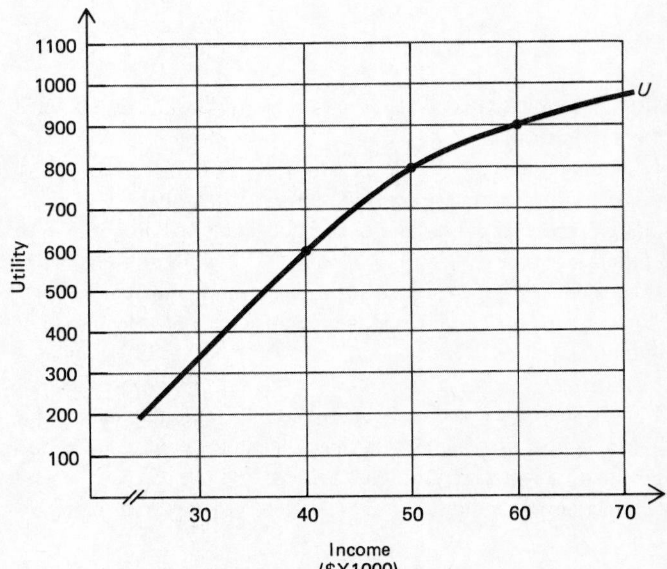

Figure 24A-1

$50,000. Meanwhile, $40,000 would produce ________ units of utility—a reduction of ________ units from $50,000. Losing $10,000 produces a (*larger / equal / smaller*), change in utility than gaining an extra $10,000 because marginal utility is (*increasing, constant, decreasing*).

c. To put this another way, the average level of utility that could be expected if the lottery were taken would be ________ . This level could be achieved with a fixed income of $________ . The risk involved in the lottery therefore costs, in terms of constant income alternatives, $________ —the difference between $50,000 without the lottery and the $________ value of taking the lottery.

d. Finally, assume that the lottery is not optional. Assume, instead, that it necessarily faces an individual with the utility schedule graphed in Figure 24A-1. How much would this person pay to get out of the uncertainty of receiving $40,000 with a 50 percent probability or $60,000 with a 50 percent probability? The lottery yields the same average utility as a constant income of $________ . The person would, therefore, pay $________ for an insurance policy that would remove the risk of the lottery—thereby guaranteeing an income of $________ even though the lottery produces an average income of $________ .

---

diminishing **a.** 800 **b.** no; 900; 100; 600; 200; larger; decreasing **c.** 750; 46,500 (roughly; subsequent answers based on this estimate); 3500; 46,500 **d.** 46,500; 3500; 46,500; 50,000

2. Suppose that the utility schedule was given by the straight line drawn in Figure 24A-2. To avoid any lottery (e.g., the case in question 1 with $10,000 on either side of $50,000) with an expected return of $0, an individual with this schedule would be willing to pay $________ . Why? ________________

____

____

____

$0; Figure 24A-2 shows constant marginal utility.

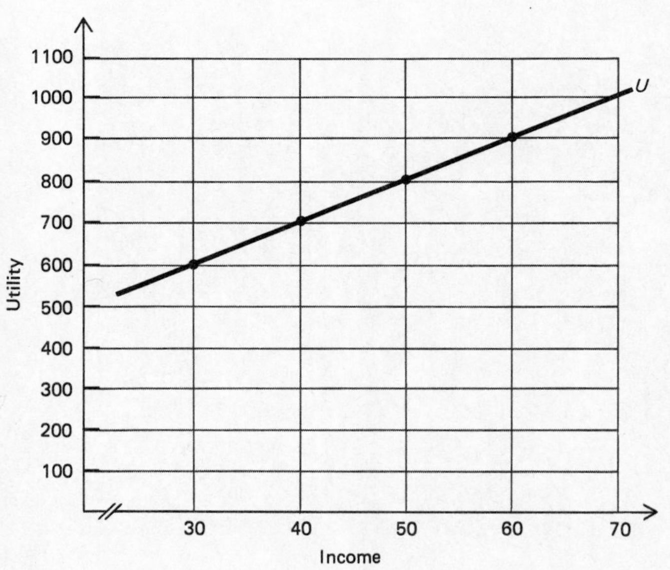

Figure 24A-2

SUGGESTED ANSWERS TO QUESTIONS IN THE TEXT: Appendix to Chapter 24

1. Speculators try to buy low and sell high. When they see a downturn (an upturn) in prices, therefore, they are tempted to buy (to sell); if they do, they stabilize prices. Their actions tend to reduce the amplitude of price swings.

2. Taking $1 from the rich and giving it to the less well-off increases total welfare because the marginal utility of the $1 for the rich (*MU* reflecting a loss) is smaller than the marginal utility of the $1 for the less well-off (*MU* reflecting a gain). If all people are the same, *MUs* are different and allow this sort of transfer to improve welfare unless incomes are identical.

3. Think about the difference between mandatory and voluntary.

4. Expect large variations because there was little geographical area over which to average fluctuations in demand or supply.

5. Each person owns a small share of the risk and has a variety of other sources of income over which to average.

6. $\text{Var}(kX) = k\text{var}(X)$, so $\text{var}(X/4) = (1/16)\text{var}(X)$. Applying this to the problem, the standard deviation of the shared risk is $[(1/16)\text{var}(X) + (1/16)\text{var}(X) + (1/16)\text{var}(X) + (1/16)\text{var}(x)]^{1/2} = SD/2$.

a. Straight application.

b. Let the probability of peak demand be p for both systems. The likelihood that both will be in peak is p^2. The likelihood that one will be in peak and the other will not is $2p(1 - p)$. Planning against those odds might make the utilities cut back on their maintained excess capacity.

c. Let the cost of holding inventory against demand per unit of time D be given by $C_HQ/2$, where C_H is the unit cost and Q is the quantity in any given order. The total cost C_HQ is divided by 2 because demand is assumed to be continuous, and half of any given order is sold by the midpoint of the order period. Let the cost of ordering during the period defining D be $C_O(D/Q)$, where C_O is the unit cost of an order and (D/Q) is the number of orders made in each period. The total cost of sales is thus

$$C_O(D/Q) + C_HQ/2$$

Differentiating with respect to Q to determine the optimal order and thus inventory shows that

$$Q^* = (2DC/C_H)^{1/2}$$

Increasing D by a factor of 4 therefore doubles Q^*.

CHAPTER 25

IMPERFECT COMPETITION AND ANTITRUST POLICY

Chapter 24 explored the various sources of monopoly power as well as the potential consequences of exploiting that power in a mixed economy. Based upon the results of that chapter, it is perhaps surprising that the profitability of supplying a market in the United States appears to increase only slightly as the concentration of market power in the hands of a few suppliers climbs. Perhaps even more surprising are the observed high advertising budgets for firms servicing concentrated American industries. If these firms were exploiting a truly strong market position of the type considered in the previous chapter, one might expect just the opposite—high profits and little advertising. If you have that kind of power, why not use it? And why advertise if you have no competition? In addition, empirical studies have found that concentrated industries have typically produced large research and development budgets. This is perhaps reassuring (suggesting that large firms are not necessarily lazy firms), but it is a third observation that is not explained very well by our models of monopoly behavior. Concentrated industries have, finally, displayed little in the way of flexibility in the pricing of their products. This is a troublesome reminder that size itself can breed potential for laziness—concentrated industries might be the homes of firms too big to bother constructing procedures with which to maintain efficient prices.

The theoretical basis for understanding these observations cannot, quite clearly, rest entirely on the pure monopoly modeling of Chapter 24. It will rest, instead, on modelings of intermediate forms of imperfect competition—market structures that lie somewhere between the efficiencies of perfect competition and the potential perversities of monopoly. Chapter 25 begins with an overview of a few of these models. Subsequent sections provide a little more insight into not only what actually goes on in the boardrooms of large American corporations that enjoy some market power, but also how the U.S. judicial system responds to that behavior. Upon completion of your work in this area, you will have accomplished the following objectives.

LEARNING OBJECTIVES

1. Review the determinants of market power, and understand how cost structure, barriers to entry, and the potential for collusion influence the translation of that market power into a particular market structure of imperfect competition. Be comfortable with the spectrum of imperfect competition stretching from perfect competition on one extreme to monopoly on the other. Identify examples of industries which appear at various spots along the length of this spectrum.

2. Understand the potential risks and gains involved in collusion between a few firms on price and/or quantity.

3. Reproduce and manipulate a few simple models of noncollusive behavior in imperfectly competitive markets: the dominant-firm model and monopolisitic competition.

4. Conceptualize how the profit-maximizing behavior that is hypothesized by economists can be perceived even within the constraints of bounded rationality that corporate management usually displays. Understand, for example, the profit motivations behind rule-of-thumb pricing behaviors like markup pricing.

5. Evaluate to your own satisfaction the Schumpeterian hypothesis that significant market power leads to extensive and socially desirable programs of research and development that would otherwise not be forthcoming. Do you think the hypothesis correct? How do you think it should it affect policy reaction to firms' exploiting market power?

6. Familiarize yourself with the major events in the history of antitrust activity in the United States. Trace the evolution of antitrust activity to its modern formulation: focus on improving efficiency and not just on preventing bigness itself. Explain how existing case law and legislation are being interpreted to achieve this focus.

Antitrust policy is, of course, written with full knowledge that imperfect competition has both a good and a bad side. Unbridled exploitation of market power can, on the one hand, depress output and generate excessive prices and profits. But, on the other hand, there *do* exist economies of scale that should not be sacrificed simply for the sake of having many firms instead of a few. There is, moreover, a demonstrable correlation between market concentration and research into discovery and development of new products and new processes. In light of this dichotomy of properties, it is the primary lesson of this chapter that antitrust activity should (1) keep the barriers to competition low, (2) tolerate bigness when size is determined by technology, and (3) be vigilant against anticompetitive practices whenever they occur.

Oligopoly, the circumstance in which there exist only a few sellers of the same good, is conceptually the simplest intermediate case of imperfect competition. It can emerge as the prevailing market structure for many reasons. Oligopoly can, first of all, appear whenever average costs decline through levels of output equaling 20 percent to 40 percent of market demand. These situations are, to some degree, "natural oligopolies" in the same sense that "natural monopolies" display declining costs across the demand of the entire market. They reflect economies of scale that should be exploited. Other, more artificial and sometimes less desirable conditions can, however, also produce oligopolistic markets. These include both legal and illegal barriers to entry; for example, tariffs, patents, and tacit or explicit price collusion to threaten potential entrants all fall under the general rubric of artificial constraints on competition. The first few questions will examine your understanding of oligopoly models.

1. Empirical research has uncovered patterns of correlation between the degree of concentration displayed by various industries and non-production activities such as research and development, advertising, and price administration. Indicate whether the following descriptions most likely apply to a high-concentration industry (H) like motor vehicles, a moderate-concentration industry (M) like chemicals, a low-concentration industry (L) like printing, or a perfectly competitive industry (P).

a. Industry A shows negligible expenditure on research and development (measured as a percentage of total sales), negligible expenditure on advertising, and no price administration. . . . . (______)

b. Industry B shows a normal rate of profit, small expenditure on research and development as well as advertising (each less than 1 percent of total sales), but the highest level of price administration. . . . . (______)

c. Industry C shows a normal rate of profit, high expenditure on research and development as well as advertising (each around 1.7 percent of total sales), and a moderate level of price administration. . . . . (______)

d. Industry D shows a normal profit rate, the highest expenditure on research and development, expenditure on advertising that is nearly comparable, and a high degree of price administration. . . . . (______)

From Table 25-1 in the text: **a.** P **b.** L **c.** H **d.** M

2. The case of **pure oligopoly** illustrates with special clarity the problems confronting the firm in imperfect competition. In this situation, the number of firms engaged in close competition is (*large / small, or comparatively small*), while the products they sell are (*uniform / differentiated*).

The important consequence of this uniformity, or "homogeneity," of product is that all firms must charge the same price. If any one company tries to raise its price and the others do not follow suit, that company will most probably (*gain / lose some of its / lose all or practically all of its*) customers. On the other hand, if this company reduces price, it is most likely that all rivals will be forced to follow suit. Thus, each firm has some influence over the price buyers must pay, particularly because of its ability to reduce price.

---

small, or comparatively small; uniform; lose all or practically all of its

The knowledge that "we're all in the same boat" may produce a tacit agreement among the firms to abide by some given price. (Economic theory still has a long way to go in describing how oligopoly members reach agreement as to the level of that price.) With price established by agreement or, perhaps, by a dominant firm and accepted by other industry members, the participants then use competitive weapons other than price (notably advertising or, more generally, selling effort) to secure business. There is rivalry among the member firms; there is a struggle for business; there is competition; but there is rarely any price competition. In the event of a serious downturn in business, though, this sort of convention against using price as a competitive weapon may weaken.

One interesting consequence of this method of competition is that even though the competing products can be essentially uniform (i.e., no one firm's product is really worth much more than any other firm's product), each supplier may try hard in its advertising to persuade the buying public that its product is "different" as part of the attempt to retain and to expand its share of the market. Thus on the surface the competing products may seem to be "differentiated." Yet if you examine the advertised differences carefully, you may find that they are trivial, and that for analytic purposes the products are really homogeneous, or uniform (think of toothpaste).

To review, then, oligopolistic firms in the same industry must recognize that they are mutually interdependent. The actions of one firm always affect the circumstances facing the others. This point is most clearly illustrated in a careful consideration of the profitability of collusion and the temptation to cheat. Cheating, it can be shown, can pay dividends, but it can also produce significant losses.

3. To see why all this is true, consider Figure 25-1. On that graph, *DD* represents the effective demand curve facing some oligopolist who abides by a colluding agreement with a few competitors. It could, for example, be the result of a consistent 30 percent share of total sales for any price along a market demand curve. Notice that every reduction of $1 in the price produces, for the firm when all other firms conform, an increase in sales of 10 units. Marginal revenue is given by *MR*. Average cost and marginal cost are assumed, for simplicity only, to be constant at $4 per unit regardless of output level.

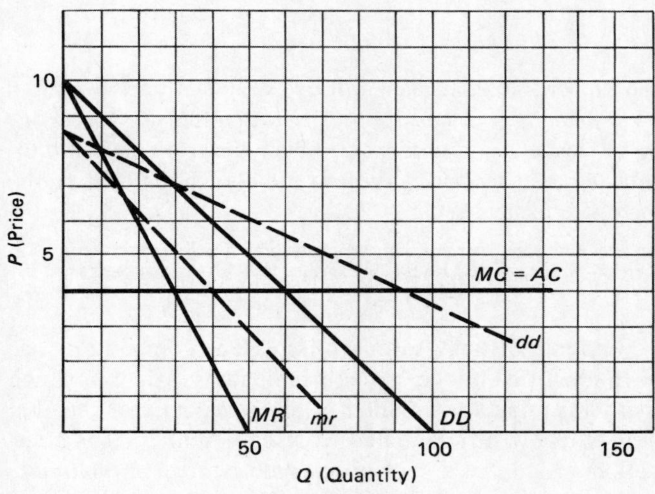

Figure 25-1

Based on the assumption of perfect collusion, the firm will maximize profits along *DD* by agreeing to a price of $________, therefore selling ________ units and earning excess profits of $________.

Now suppose that the firm could, by lowering its price relative to its colluding partners (i.e., by cheating on its colluding agreement), pick up an extra 20 units of sales for every $1 reduction in price. It could, in other words, increase its market share at the expense of other firms by lowering its price alone. The resulting demand and marginal revenue curves are represented in Figure 25-1 by *dd* and *mr*, respectively. The firm could, in this case, move to a new profit-maximizing position by (*reducing / maintaining / increasing*) its price to $________ and selling ________ units. The result would be $________ in excess profits.

It is, of course, highly unlikely that the other firms would not catch on. Suppose, in response to the cheating of the first firm, that all the other firms changed their prices to the cheater's new price. *DD* would again be relevant, and the cheating firm's profits would fall to $________ as sales declined to ________ units.

It is clear, therefore, that successful cheating is better for a single firm than successful collusion, but runs the risk of reducing profitability if all the firms catch on and follow to protect themselves. Were the process to continue, in fact, the firms would, collectively, end up producing the (*competitive / monopoly / duopoly*) output and selling it at the (*competitive / monopoly / duopoly*) price. In terms of Figure 25-1, price would converge to $________, output would converge to ________ units, and profits would converge to $________.

7; 30; 90; reducing: 6.50; 40; 100; 87.50; 35 (A price of $6.50 translates into sales of 35 units along *DD* and a profit of $2.50 per unit sold.); competitive; competitive; 4; 60; 0

4. Now consult Figure 25-2. Panel **(a)** there represents the *MC* schedule of one of two oligopolistic firms facing the demand curve of panel **(b)**. Remember the text's argument that colluding firms tend to share the monopoly output between themselves. Draw the combined *MC* curve of the two firms in panel **(b)**. Acting as a monopolist, profit-maximizing colluders equipped with knowledge of this joint *MC* curve could agree to charge a price of $________ for an expected ________ units of sales. Each firm would, under the agreement, expect to sell ________ units.

The joint *MC* curve is a straight line from ($Q = 10$; $P = \$2$) with half the slope of the *MC* curve of panel **(a)**. 7; 30; 15

5. Figure 25-3 illustrates a situation that might face a typical dominant firm. Curve *DD* represents the market demand curve for the industry in question, and *MR* traces the "market marginal revenue curve" corresponding to *DD*. Curve *dd*, meanwhile, represents the dominant firm's effective demand curve after the competitive fringe has been factored out of its market; the corresponding effective marginal revenue is indicated by curve *mr*. For simplicity, it is assumed that $MC = AC = \$5$, i.e., that variable costs are proportional to output and fixed costs are zero.

Given *dd*, the dominant firm would produce ________ units of output with the expectation of supporting a price of $________. In that circumstance, the competitive fringe would produce ________ units, and the total quantity demanded and actually produced by the dominant firm *and* the competitive fringe combined would equal ________ units.

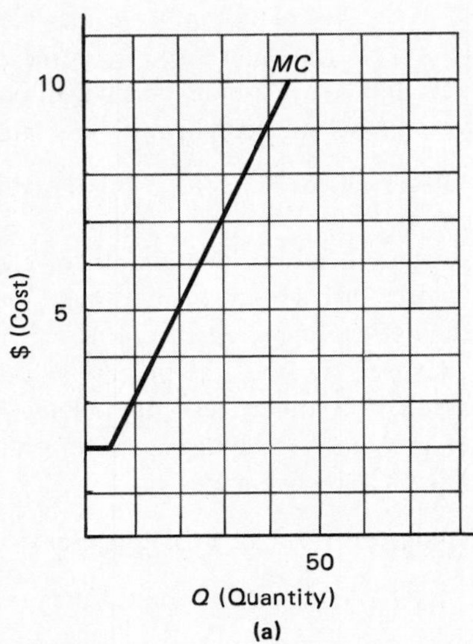

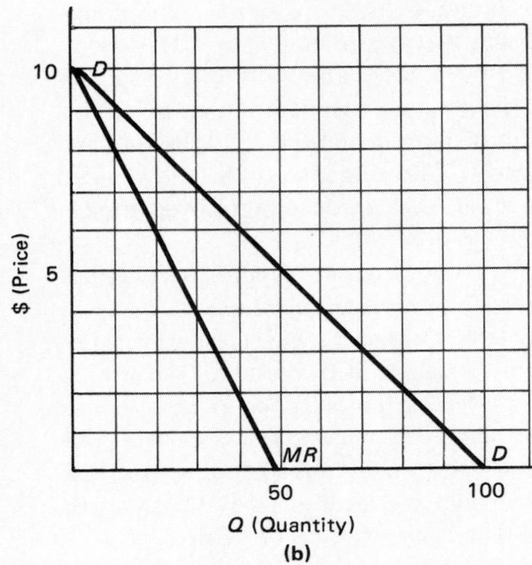

Figure 25-2

Now contrast this equilibrium with one in which the dominant firm is, in fact, a firm exploiting monopoly power derived from facing *DD* alone. Total output would then be (*higher / the same / lower*) than the total output of the dominant-firm case, equaling ________ units and supporting a profit-maximizing price of $________ . The competitive solution would, meanwhile, include total production of ________ units for a price of $________ .

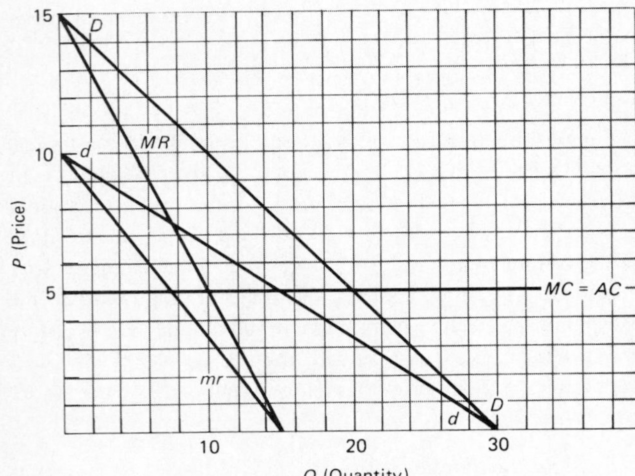

Figure 25-3

It is clear, from this example, that the dominant-firm market structure outlined in the text allows the same types of inefficiencies as the monopoly: price (*greater than / equal to / less than*) marginal cost, output therefore suboptimally (*low / high*), and supportable economic profit (*in excess of / exactly equal to / substantially less than*) zero. The only difference appears to be in degree; the distortions permitted under a dominant-firm structure are (*smaller / larger*) than those created by a profit-motivated monopolist.

7.5; 7.50; 7.5; 15; lower; 10; 10; 20; 5; greater than; low; in excess of; smaller

Another distinct form of imperfect competition has been identified by the economics literature—one in which many manufacturers market nearly identical products that are somehow differentiated from one another. It is a situation which gives each firm some degree of *monopoly* power over its own version of the product in question (i.e., some power to set its own price), but which does not remove the firm effectively from the pervasive *competition* offered by the many other producers of many slightly different items—items which are, in reality, all very close substitutes. Thus, this form of market structure has been dubbed *monopolistic competition*.

6. The fact that there are many sellers of similar goods suggests that it is fairly easy for new firms to enter a monopolistically competitive industry and for old firms to leave. New (existing) firms will be tempted to enter (leave), in fact, whenever existing firms are making excess pure economic profit (earning, at best, negative pure economic profit). This potential for entry and exit is, clearly, a second (long-run) parallel between monopolistic competition and the perfectly competitive market structure studied in Chapter 23.

a. Insofar as new firms *do* enter, they take over some part of the market of already-operating firms. This means that the demand curve facing any one of these existing firms tends to be pushed (*to the right or upward / to the left or downward*), and thereby (*reduces / increases*) the profit of the existing firm. If the entry tendency persists, every firm's demand curve will wind up just touching, or tangent to, the average cost curve. Such a tangency situation means that the firm in question can (*still earn a profit / just break even / operate only at a loss*). When this tangency point is reached for the typical firm—i.e., for most, if not all, firms—the profit feature which attracted new entrants (*still / no longer*) exists.

b. In this differentiated seller model, each firm's demand curve is assumed to be (*tilted / flat*) because product differentiation supposedly (*gives some / does not give any*) degree of monopoly power to that firm. If the demand curve is tilted, though, and if things wind up with this demand curve just touching the average cost curve, then the tangency point (*must / cannot*) occur at the very bottom of the *AC* curve. (A *tangency point* is one at which the two curves involved have the same slope. If the demand curve is tilted at the point in question, so must be the *AC* curve.)

c. The hypothetical monopolistically competitive firm therefore winds up earning no profit, yet operating at an output level which is (*less than / equal to / greater than*) its minimum-*AC* output. In the sense that a larger output would reduce its *AC*, this firm has "excess capacity." Economists were much taken with these ideas when Edward H. Chamberlin introduced them. They suggested that "differentiated competition" might not work quite as perfect-competition theory had suggested it would. In squeezing out profits, it might not, in particular, achieve minimum average cost. The argument of pure-competition theory had been that—if only in the long run—we would get the best of all the worlds: minimum average cost of production and zero profits with price equal to average cost.

Chamberlin would have insisted that any comparison between the supposed "long-run" results of perfect and monopolistic competition must not be used to condemn monopolistic competition. He was convinced that monopolistic competition was the near-universal and inevitable situation. Perfect-competition theory might point to an "ideal" situation; but he was certain that this ideal was unattainable in real-life circumstances.

---

a. to the left or downward; reduces; just break even; no longer **b.** tilted; gives some; cannot **c.** less than

7. For an industry structure that satisfies the characterization of monopolistic competition, long-run equilibrium is represented by a tangency between a firm's average cost curve and the effective demand curve for its differentiated product. It is, as a result, necessary that ($P > MC$ / $P = MC$ / $P < MC$) in equilibrium because the effective demand curve is (*negatively sloped / positively sloped / horizontal*). Furthermore, the properties of cost curves therefore require that ($MC > AC$ / $MC = AC$ / $MC < AC$) at the equilibrium level of output. Compared with the perfectly competitive equilibrium, the monopolistic competitor produces (*too much / too little / just the correct amount*).

Now consider the plight of a monopolistic competitor in an industry whose production costs have suddenly increased. In the short run, economic profits for this firm would be (*less than zero / equal to zero / still slightly positive*). In the long run, though, firms would (*enter / exit / proceed as before*) so that the effective demand curve facing our firm would (*shift in for every price / shift out for every price / do nothing*). The result, ultimately, would be (*lower / higher / identical*) prices and (*negative / zero / positive*) economic profits.

It was observed in Chapter 24 that a lump-sum tax would affect neither the price decision nor the output decision of a profit-maximizing monopolist. We can now see that this conclusion (*applies equally well / does not apply at all*) to the monopolistic competitor; even a change in AC with no change in MC can affect the output of a monopolistic competitor.

$P > MC$; negatively sloped; $MC < AC$; too little; less than zero; exit; shift out for every price; higher; zero; does not apply at all (Refer to Figure 25-4 in answering these questions. In fact, drawing pictures is usually a good idea when confronted with unfamiliar comparative statics questions.)

8. Compared with perfect competitors, imperfect competitors probably pay, in practice, (*more / the same / less*) attention to maximizing profits. This should be expected, in part, because most earn (*positive / zero / negative*) economic profits and (*are / are not*) on the same knife-edge of economic viability as their perfect competitor colleagues. "Bounded rationality" is given as one reason for this behavior; it is a notion that focuses attention on the expense and difficulty involved in collecting and processing the information required to set marginal cost precisely equal to marginal revenue. Instead of making the effort to accomplish that task, it is argued, "rules of thumb" emerge in boardrooms all across the country to help guide executives in making their pricing and output decisions without detailed knowledge of the underlying marginal schedules.

Markup pricing is the most popular of these rules, but the dimension of that markup is not a number that executives agree upon without some market analysis. It is, of course, this analysis that, in the long run, can make the search for a pricing rule look like a procedure that implicitly tries to maximize profits. Executives may not compute marginal cost and marginal revenue schedules, but they might still behave as if they did. This question is designed to illustrate how this "deception" might be achieved.

For a monopoly firm facing demand curve *DD* in Figure 25-3, we already know that profits would be maximized by setting

a price equal to $________ and expecting to sell ________ units.

Relative to average cost, that price amounts to a ________ percent markup over cost. Complete, now, Table 25-1 to convince yourself that a sequence of trial markup percentages could lead a careful manager to the profit-maximizing intersection of *MR* and *MC* without computing either schedule.

---

less; positive; are not; 10; 10; 100

Reading across the rows: 60%:$8, 14, $42; 80%: $9, 12, $48; 100%: $10, 10,

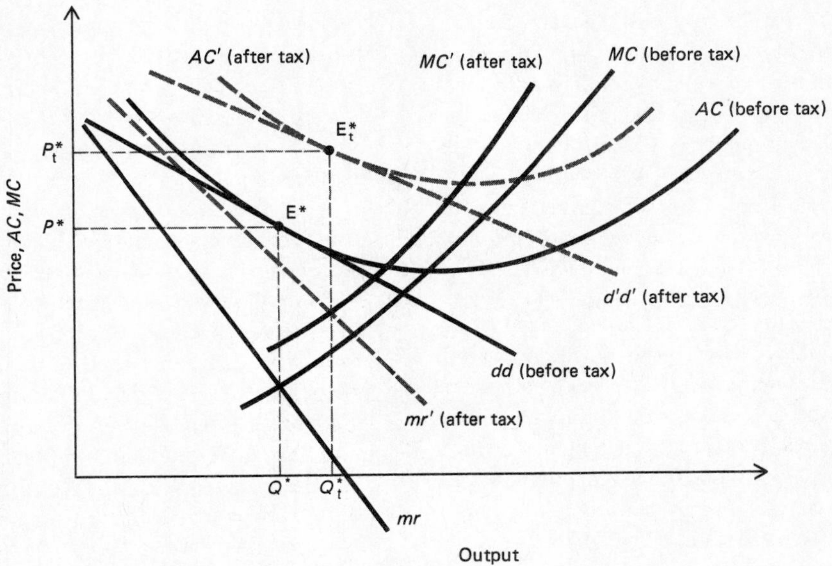

Figure 25-4

$50; 120%: $12, 8, $48; 110%: $10.50, 9, $49.50; 105%: $10.25, 9.5; $49.88 (The manager might, after noting that markup increases generated higher profits until 120 percent, begin to back up until the peak at 100 percent was discovered.)

9. The Schumpeterian hypothesis about the large firms that dominate imperfectly competitive markets postulates that "big business may have had more to do with creating our (high) standard of life than (with) keeping it down." This hypothesis is based, at least in part, upon the notion that (*research and development expenditure / purchasing power / real competition*) seems to be concentrated most heavily in the largest firms on the American scene. Since Mansfield has argued that the social return to invention is (*3 / 0.5 / 5*) times the private gain, it can certainly be argued that research and development is (*overfunded / properly funded / underfunded*). Moreover, the private gain to invention is (*larger / smaller*) for large firms than it is for small firms. A case can be made, therefore, that if big business conducts a large proportion of this country's research into new products and new production processes, then we should tolerate its bigness. The effect on our total expenditure on research and development of any policy or circumstance that reduces industrial concentration, like the breakup of AT&T, may thus be a source of major concern. Nonetheless, small success stories, like Apple Computers, sometimes turn into big success stories. Policy designed to foster research should therefore be the product of a balanced approach; it should not, in particular, concentrate its efforts exclusively on fostering big business research at the expense of other sources of ingenuity and invention.

research and development expenditure; 3; underfunded; larger

Table 25-1

Markup Percentage	Price	Output (units)	Profit
60%	______	______	______
80%	______	______	______
100%	______	______	______
120%	______	______	______
110%	______	______	______
105%	______	______	______

10. One of the most significant changes in the way that the legal system of the United States deals with the potential problems of imperfect competition is the recent focusing of judicial attention on how business is actually conducted. It is, according to this new view of how the law should be enforced, far more important to attack types of behavior that signify the abuse of market power than it is to concentrate simply on markets that display offensive types of industrial organization. These abusive methods of conducting business, including (*a*) price fixing, (*b*) output restraint, (*c*) market division, (*d*) predatory pricing, (*e*) resale agreements, and (*f*) price discrimination, (*are / are not*) necessarily confined to the concentrated industries with extreme and potentially profitable market power. They can appear in competitive markets just as easily.

The following list of behaviors contains examples of the six types of conduct just noted. Identify each with the conduct that it represents, and record your answer in the space provided.

a. Agreement between retailers and the manufacturer not to sell a certain doll for less than $25 . . . .

b. The pricing of computers below production costs to prevent entry by potential competitors . . . .

____

c. An agreement among suppliers of oil not to sell more than 1 million barrels per day . . . .

____

d. One firm selling hammers to hardware stores for $8.99 and to the Defense Department for $410.22 . . . .

____

e. An agreement among sugar retailers to sell only in specified geographical regions of the United States . . . .

____

f. An agreement among airlines to increase fares 20 percent over the weekend . . . .

____

g. The destruction of thousands of pounds of coffee beans before they get to market . . . .

____

The notion behind this focus on conduct is that research and development into new products and into new cost-reducing technologies will continue in any market with any structure as long as collusion, tacit or overt, does not undermine competitive pressures (actual or potential). Based upon this notion, concern about mergers should proceed on a case-by-case basis. General prescriptions should therefore be difficult to come by, but one is apparent: of the three types of merger activity— ________________, ________________, and ________________ —the one most likely to be troublesome is the ________________ type, which may lower competitive pressures by increasing the market concentration of the largest firms.

are not **a.** resale agreements **b.** predatory pricing **c.** output restraint **d.** price discrimination **e.** market division **f.** price fixing **g.** output restraint; vertical; horizontal; conglomerate; horizontal

QUIZ: Multiple Choice

1. Which of the following characteristics tends to prevail in highly concentrated markets?
(1) Slightly higher than normal profits.
(2) Above average advertising expenditures.
(3) Above average research and development expenditure.
(4) Below average price flexibility.
(5) All of the above.

2. Which of the following represents a legal barrier to entry that might support an oligopolistic market structure?
(1) Price setting below the lowest price a new entrant could afford to charge.
(2) A tariff that kept all but a trickle of foreign products off the domestic market.
(3) Product differentiation among a few producers.
(4) Average cost curves that reach their minima at roughly 30 percent of market demand.
(5) All of the above.

3. Which alternative to question 2 would have been correct if the barrier to entry were a cost barrier?
(1).
(2).
(3).
(4).
(5).

4. Which alternative to question 2 represents an illegal barrier to entry that might support an oligopolistic structure?
(1).
(2).
(3).
(4).
(5).

5. OPEC presents to the world a market structure most accurately represented by:
(1) the bounded-rationality model.
(2) the dominant-firm model.
(3) the monopolistic competition model.
(4) the "collusive oligopoly acting like a monopolist" model.
(5) perfect competition.

6. Which alternative to question 5 would have been correct if the market in question had been the breakfast cereal market in the United States?
(1).
(2).
(3).
(4).
(5).

7. Which alternative to question 5 would have been correct if the market in question had been the market for soybeans?
(1).
(2).
(3).
(4).
(5).

8. To earn positive economic profits over the long run, the dominant firm must have captured, by virtue of its size, a cost advantage over the competitive fringe. Otherwise:
(1) the fringe would be profitable enough to attract new firms.
(2) the fringe would be able to maintain short-run positive profits even as it undercut the dominant firm's price.

(3) the positive profits would continue until sufficient new suppliers drove them to zero.
(4) the ultimate long-run equilibrium would be the perfectly competitive solution, with the dominant firm either closing down or making zero economic profit along with everyone else at the market-determined price.
(5) all of the above.

9. If we consider an industry of many sellers of differentiated products, and if entry into this industry is free, then we should expect the long-run equilibrium position of the typical firm in this industry to have which of the following properties?
(1) Average cost (*AC*) will be at its minimum possible level, and price charged (*P*) will be equal to that *AC*.
(2) *AC* will be at its minimum level, and *P* will be above that *AC*.
(3) *AC* will be above its minimum level, and *P* will be above that *AC*.
(4) *AC* will be above its minimum level, and *P* will be equal to that *AC*.
(5) *AC* will be above its minimum level, but *P* will equal that minimum.

10. One reason why a firm operating under conditions of imperfect competition is likely to want to use an administered or markup price is:
(1) a lack of sufficient knowledge of marginal revenue at various levels of output.
(2) a lack of sufficient knowledge of marginal cost at various levels of output.
(3) the desire to have a breakeven point occurring at a high level of output.
(4) the fear that charging a higher price would attract new competition into the field.
(5) the notion that this price corresponds to the most efficient plant output level.

11. The Schumpeter hypothesis is that:
(1) big business is not necessarily bad business.
(2) firms never really have the power over price and output that economists attribute to them.
(3) research and development is more than sufficiently supported by a consortium of government, small business, and big business.
(4) innovation would be accelerated if managers of large firms were required to be owners of large firms.
(5) all of the above.

12. In light of the pros and cons of imperfect competition, policy should probably be directed at:
(1) keeping the barriers to competition low.
(2) attacking anticompetitive business conduct.
(3) tolerating bigness if it is founded in technology.
(4) encouraging the research and development efforts of large and small firms.
(5) all of the above.

13. The merger of United Technologies, a high-tech company, and Otis Elevator is an example of:
(1) a vertical merger.
(2) a horizontal merger.
(3) a conglomerate merger.
(4) a tax bailout.
(5) none of the above.

14. Which alternative to question 13 would have been correct if the merger in question had been the union of Standard Oil of Indiana and the Gulf Oil Corporation?
(1).
(2).
(3).
(4).
(5).

15. Which of the alternatives listed in question 13 is most likely to be the source of concern for those who worry about the conduct of antitrust policy in the United States?
(1).
(2).
(3).
(4).
(5).

16. Which of the following major contributions to the antitrust laws of the United States includes, in its amended state, a provision preventing the acquisition of a major share of the common stock of one company by another if it will substantially lessen competition?
(1) The Sherman Antitrust Act.
(2) The Clayton Antitrust Act.
(3) The Humphrey-Hawkins Bill.
(4) The Federal Trade Commission Act.
(5) The General Agreement on Tariffs and Trade.

17. Which alternative in question 16 would have been correct if the provision in question had prohibited unfair and deceptive methods of competition?
(1).
(2).
(3).
(4).
(5).

18. Which alternative in question 16 would have been correct if the provision in question had prohibited conspiracy to monopolize trade with foreign nations?
(1).
(2).
(3).
(4).
(5).

SUGGESTED ANSWERS TO QUESTIONS IN THE TEXT: Chapter 25

1. A rough table might look like this:

	Perfect Competition	Monopoly	Colluding Oligopoly	Dominant Firm	Monopolistic Competition
Number of firms	Many	1	Few	1 large, many others	Many
Collusion	None	None	Yes	None	None
Price vs. *MC*	$P = MC$	$P >> MC$	$P >> MC$	$P > MC$ for large; $P = MC$ for others	$P > MC$
Price vs. *LAC*	$P = LAC$	$P >> LAC$	$P >> LAC$	$P \geq LAC$	$P \geq LAC$
Efficiency	Efficient	Large loss	Large loss	Moderate loss	Moderate to small loss

2. The question is one of information. The choice depends upon how easy it is to get and manipulate the *MR* and *MC* information versus the potential profits lost by choosing the wrong markup fraction and thus both the wrong price and the wrong quantity.

3. Equilibrium in monopolistically competitive markets occurs to the left of the minimum of the average cost curve, so output is too small and price is too high and does not match marginal cost. The resulting deadweight loss is the cost of diversity. Is it worth it? Depends upon the quality of the diversification, . .

4. Decreasing costs may or may not cover the scope of the market. A few competitors may be enough, but only if watched carefully to prevent explicit and implicit collusion. What about R&D? One competitor, or a couple, could find real advantage in bringing a new product to market if a large fraction of its value could be appropriated. Some of that incentive may be lost when there is only one producer.

5. R&D, growth, spin-offs, security in pensions heavily invested in IBM stock, etc. Pick a side and defend it with fact and observation.

6. **a.** Locationally defined monopolistic competition.
b. It is expensive to change prices.
c. In fact and in spirit.

7. As the tariff rose, the demand curve facing the dominant firm would climb toward the market demand curve; the result could be a domestic monopolist with reduced total sales and a higher price.

8. Generally, newer statutes and rules look to conduct rather than structure. The Sherman Act, e.g., focused on monopolizing; the Federal Trade Commission Act, on unfair and deceptive practices. Structure suggests when the potential for abuse exists. It is therefore an important signal. Conduct is the source of welfare loss.

9. No, personally; people can go to jail for attempted murder.

10. The portion of the market demand curve above P_L would disappear, and the effective demand curve would be horizontal at P_L over to *DD*. Marginal revenue would then match the horizontal section until Q_L, and then it would jump down to the market *MR* curve. $P_L = MC$ would characterize the profit-maximizing price, or perhaps just below P_L so that potential entrants turn aside. The limit price is P_L. See Figure TQ25-1. The heavy line is effective demand; the heavy dotted line is corresponding marginal revenue.

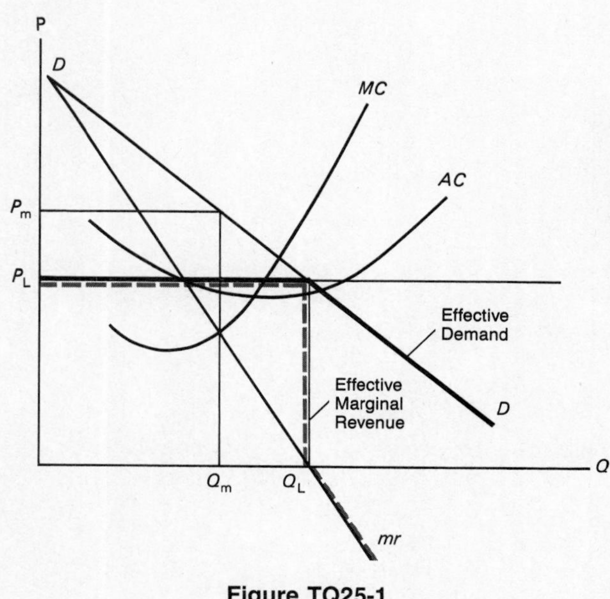

Figure TQ25-1

11. **a.** Price elasticity not infinity for monopolistic competitor.
b. $P = MC$ for perfect competitor; $P > MC$ for the monopolistic competitor.

c. Profits are zero for both.

d. Part **b** shows inefficiency for monopolistic competition as demand becomes more inelastic.

12. American and United would reduce the index by $400 + 100 = 20^2 + 10^2 = 500$; it would increase the index by $900 = 30^2$. The net effect would be an increase of 400 points. Bad news in any league. Do the other combinations in like manner. Continental and Piddly would not be noticed.

CHAPTER 26
INCOMES AND INEQUALITY

Chapter 26 is the first in a series of chapters that focus our attention on the distribution of income. Together, these chapters will bring the fundamentals of supply-and-demand analysis to bear on questions of how individual incomes are determined. Critical in this determination must be, of course, the ownership of the factors of production and the prices that they command, but there is more to it than that. Chapter 26 defines what economists mean when they speak of income, wealth, and equality (or inequality, as the case may be). Chapter 26 also explores the sources of wealth in a modern economy. Subsequent chapters will build on these concepts to develop a theory of income distribution and to apply that theory to an understanding of the employment of land, labor, other natural resources, and capital in a productive enterprise.

Having completed your work in this chapter, you will have accomplished the following objectives.

LEARNING OBJECTIVES

1. Become familiar with the questions that are posed by the economists who work to understand the distribution of income—questions about the determination of income (the *flow* of money to an individual during a given period of time) and wealth (the net value of the *stock* of accumulated economic assets).

2. Recognize the major sources of income and the major reservoirs of wealth in the United States.

3. Review critically, in the light of the experience of much of the industrialized world over the past half-century or so, the Marx-Engels notion that industrialization will ultimately make the rich richer and the poor poorer.

4. Recognize the Lorenz curve as a tool used to investigate relative (in)equality in the distribution of income and/or wealth. Outline (*a*) the information that these curves are intended to convey, (*b*) the link between that intention and their construction, and (*c*) the interpretation of the bulges that they usually portray.

5. Come to grips with the distributions of income and wealth within the United States—their relative (in)equality in historical and international contexts.

6. Explain the observed differences between typical distributions of ability and their corresponding distributions of income.

7. Outline and explain at least seven potential sources of inequality in the distribution of income both across the United States and elsewhere around the globe.

In the wake of the Industrial Revolution a significant dichotomy developed between the people who owned the machinery and the people who worked the machinery—the capitalists and the workers. Cities became both foci of industrialization and pockets of enormous poverty. The distribution of income evolved quickly into a question of dividing the riches earned by the machines between owner and laborer. People making decisions about where to hold their wealth had to include a tangible asset other than land in their considerations. Economics became more difficult to understand, but not impossibly so.

1. a. Income is defined as the amount of money received from all sources during a given period of time (a year, a month, etc.). In the spaces provided below, list the major sources of income in the United States, labor income, rent, dividends, interest and transfer payments, in the order of their importance.

(1) ____________________

(2) ____________________

(3) ____________________

(4) ____________________

(5) ____________________

b. Wealth consists of the net dollar value of assets owned at any particular time. In the spaces provided below, list the four major tangible assets and the four major financial assets that comprise wealth in the United States in the order of their importance.

Tangible assets:

(1) ____________________

(2) ____________________

(3) ____________________

(4) ____________________

Financial assets:

(1) ____________________

(2) ____________________

(3) ____________________

(4) ____________________

a. (Percentages are drawn from 1988 data for the average household.) **(1)** labor income (70%) [including wages and supplements (56%), other labor income like pension contributions (6%), and proprietors' income (8%)] **(2)** transfer payments (15%) **(3)** interest income (13%) **(4)** dividends (2%) **(5)** rent (less than 1%)

b. (Percentages of total wealth are from 1984.) Tangible assets: **(1)** own home (41%) **(2)** rental property (9%) **(3)** motor vehicle (6%) **(4)** other real estate (4%) Intangible assets: **(1)** interest-earning accounts (17%) **(2)** equity in business (10%) **(3)** stocks and mutual funds (7%) **(4)** checking accounts (1%)

2. a. Consider a group consisting of 10 individuals. The first receives a weekly income of $1, the second $2, and so on, with the tenth receiving $10. The first individual is low man on the income totem pole, representing the bottom 10 percent (ranked in terms of income) of this particular population. The $1 received by this poverty-stricken person is about 2 percent of the total weekly income received by all, which totals $55. Complete the remaining figures below. For example, the lowest 20 percent of the population consists of the $1 individual plus the $2 individual. Their combined income total of $3 is about 5 ½ percent of the combined incomes of all 10; i.e., $3 is about 5 ½ percent of $55. So 5 ½ should go in the first blank below.

Percent of Income Received by Lowest:

10%	20%	30%	40%	50%	60%	70%	80%	90%	100%
2%									100%

b. In Figure 26-1 draw the Lorenz curve illustrating this distribution of income. (Note that the Lorenz-curve chart is by nature a square. Most diagrams found in the text are not bounded on all four sides in this way.)

c. If the distribution of income were more unequal than that indicated at the beginning of this question, then the Lorenz curve would *(bulge closer to the lower right-hand corner / be drawn nearer to the 45° diagonal)*; if it were less unequal, the curve would *(bulge closer to the lower right-hand corner / be drawn nearer to the 45° diagonal)*.

a. 5 1/2%; 11%; 18%; 27 1/4%; 38%; 51%; 65 1/2%; 81 3/4% **c.** bulge closer to the right-hand corner; be drawn nearer to the 45° diagonal

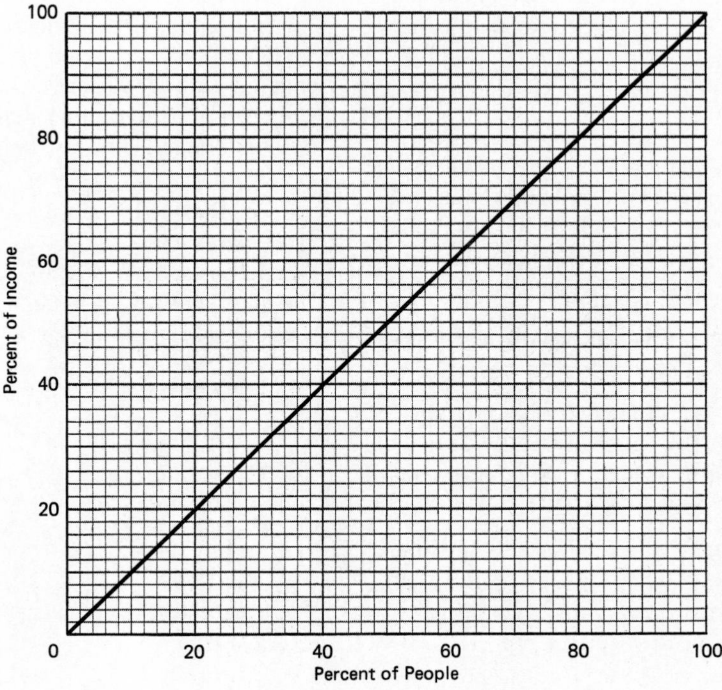

Figure 26-1

Table 26-1

Person	10%	20%	30%	40%	50%	60%	70%	80%	90%	100%
Income	$1.00	$2	$3	$4	$5	$6	$7	$8	$9	$10
Taxes paid	$0.20	______	______	______	______	______	______	______	______	______
Income after taxes	$0.80	______	______	______	______	______	______	______	______	______
Income after taxes and payment	$1.80	______	______	______	______	______	______	______	______	______
Percent of total income after the program received by the lowest indicated %	3.3%	______	______	______	______	______	______	______	______	100%

3. Suppose, using the data provided in question 2, that a 20 percent income tax is imposed by the government. Such a tax would collect, assuming no disincentive effects, $11 in revenue. Assume that the administration of the tax costs $1 that is not returned to the people, but that the remaining $10 is distributed to everyone as equal $1 "social" payments. Fill in the blanks in Table 26-1 and draw a new Lorenz curve to illustrate the resulting after-tax and payment distribution of income on Figure 26-1; use a different color pencil or pen for clarity.

Reading across the rows: taxes paid: $0.40, $0.60, $0.80, $1.00, $1.20, $1.40, $1.60, $1.80, $2.00; income after taxes: $1.60, $2.40, $3.20, $4.00, $4.80, $5.60, $6.40, $7.20, $8.00; income after payment: $2.60, $3.40, $4.20, $5.00, $5.80, $6.60, $7.40, $8.20, $9.00; percentage: 8.1%, 14.4%, 22.2%, 31.5%, 42.2%, 54.4%, 68.1%, 83.3%
The Lorenz curve should be closer to the 45° line—a more equal distribution of income achieved by a redistributive tax-subsidy scheme.

4. The following list records changes in a Lorenz curve that might be expected in response to some change in economic circumstance:

1. Movement up toward the 45° line
2. Movement away from the 45° line
3. No movement at all

In the spaces provided, indicate the likely effect of the following changes in economic condition on a Lorenz curve illustrating a distribution of income.

a. a 5 percent proportional income tax whose revenues are not redistributed . . . . (______)

b. a 5 percent proportional income tax whose revenues are redistributed equally to everyone . . . . (______)

c. a progressive income tax (which taxes higher incomes at a higher rate) whose revenues are not redistributed . (______)

d. a progressive income tax (which taxes higher incomes at a higher rate) whose revenues are redistributed equally to everyone . . . . (______)

e. a 5 percent sales tax whose revenues are not redistributed . . . . (______)

f. a deep recession that reduces employment for the working-class poor . . . . (______)

a. 3 (Everyone loses 5 percent, so the total loses 5 percent and the percentage of disposable income received by any one person is therefore unchanged.) **b.** 1 (See, e.g., question 3; people with the higher incomes pay more in tax than they receive in reimbursement.) **c.** 1 (Taking a larger tax bite from those with the higher incomes reduces their share of the total pie.) **d.** 1 (Even more strongly, for the same reason as in part **b.**) **e.** 2 (Lower-income classes spend a higher proportion of their incomes and thus would sacrifice a higher proportion of their incomes to a sales tax on those expenditures.) **f.** 2 (Prolonged unemployment certainly lowers income, especially at the lower end of the income distribution.)

5. Table 26-2 records data that describe the distribution of income in the United States in 1984. Plot the corresponding Lorenz curve in Figure 26-2. For each of the following, record in the spaces provided whether the corresponding Lorenz curve would be much further away from the 45° line (MA), slightly further away from the 45° line (SA), slightly closer to the 45° line (SC), or much closer to the 45° line (MC) than the curve you just drew.

Table 26-2

Cumulative Percentage of People	Cumulative Percentage of Income
20%	4.7%
40%	15.7%
60%	32.7%
80%	57.1%
100%	100.0%

a. a Lorenz curve depicting the distribution of income in the United States in 1972 . . . . (______)

b. a Lorenz curve depicting the distribution of income in the United States in 1929 . . . . (______)

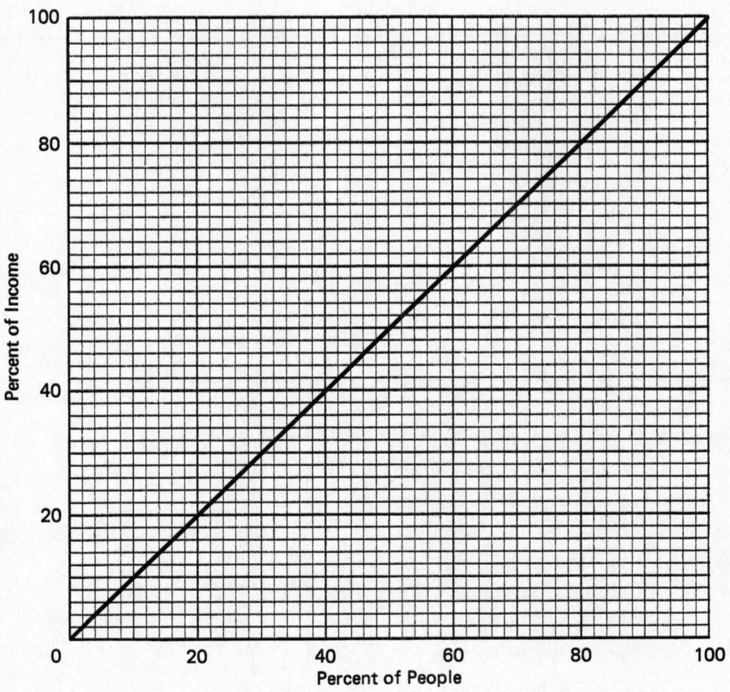

Figure 26-2

c. a Lorenz curve depicting the distribution of income in an "industrializing" nation in 1984 . . . . (________)

d. a Lorenz curve depicting the distribution of wealth in the United States in 1984 . . . . (________)

e. a Lorenz curve depicting the distribution of income in the United Kingdom in 1988 . . . . (________)

a. SC **b.** SA **c.** MA **d.** MA (Remember that the top 0.5 percent holds 14 percent of the nation's wealth.) **e.** SC (or MC depending upon your perspective.)

The data show, as reflected in the answers to question 5, that the distribution of income in the United States has grown slightly more equal over the past 60 years. The lowest 20 percent of the population received roughly 3.8 percent of the income in the late 1920s and 4.2 percent in the late 1980s. The trend has not, however, been entirely in one direction. The distribution was slightly more equal in the middle of the 1970s, with the lowest 20 percent of the population then receiving their highest percentage ever—roughly 4.7 percent of total income.

The notion that industrialization would help only the rich has not been borne out by experience. Enormous inequality *is* displayed by the industrializing countries (where Dickens might still apply), and the distribution of wealth throughout most of the world *is* extremely concentrated at the top. Nonetheless, most of the economies in the industrialized world display distributions of income *without* a large, thoroughly impoverished underclass.

6. The very concept of equality is at best a slippery and controversial issue. Most people would agree that equal opportunity, equal access to adequate education, and equal access to the electoral process are essential elements of the American experiment in democracy. But what about a (more) equal distribution of income? Should, more specifically, a progressive income-tax system be used to redistribute income? There is no definitive response to this question with which everyone would agree. The text, instead, identifies seven potential sources of inequity in the distribution of income that would exist regardless of the economic policy of the U.S. government. List them in the spaces provided below.

a. ______________________________________

b. ______________________________________

c. ______________________________________

d. ______________________________________

e. ______________________________________

f. ______________________________________

g. ______________________________________

a. ability **b.** occupation **c.** education **d.** work effort **e.** property **f.** risk taking **g.** inheritance

7. Figure 26-3 plots the distributions of ability and income in the United States. Label the two curves correctly. The importance of the discrepancy between the two distributions is that differences in ability cannot entirely explain observed differences in earnings across the American population.

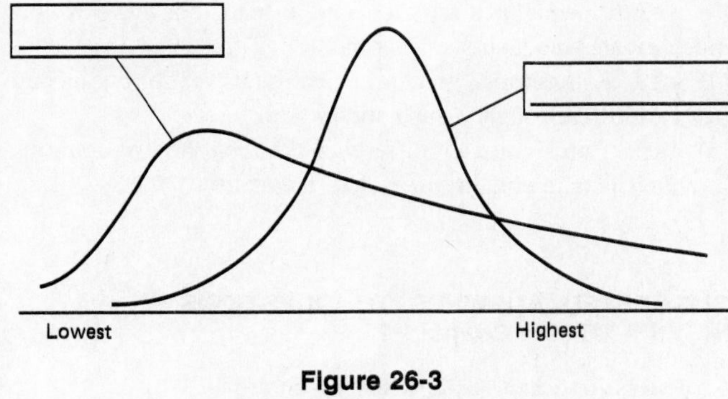

Figure 26-3

The curve that peaks first is income (the left box).

QUIZ: Multiple Choice

1. Karl Marx and Friedrich Engels expected that capitalism would make the rich richer and the poor poorer. That did not happen, at least not everywhere as predicted. Which of the following statements is an accurate statement of the actual experience of the past few years?
(1) Average working hours in the United States have declined steadily since the turn of the century.
(2) Per capita real incomes have risen steadily since the turn of the century.
(3) The distributions of wealth in the United Kingdom and the United States are less equitable than the corresponding distributions of income.
(4) The top 1 percent of the population in the United States currently holds title to 19 percent of the wealth.
(5) All of the above.

2. A Lorenz-curve chart is a graph on whose axes the following things are measured:
(1) amount of income in dollars on one axis, total number of individuals or families receiving that income or a lower one on the other.
(2) percent of people (10 percent, 20 percent, etc.) on one axis, percentage of total income received by the lowest 10 percent, the lowest 20 percent, etc., on the other.
(3) number of individuals or families receiving a certain income on one axis, percentage of total population represented by that number on the other.
(4) number of individuals or families in different occupations on one axis, mean or median amount of income received in that occupation on the other.
(5) income classes (e.g., $0 to $1999 and $2000 to $3999) on one axis, number or percentage of individuals or families in each such income class on the other.

3. On a Lorenz-curve chart, absolute or total equality in income distribution would appear as:
(1) a curved line well bowed out from the diagonal.
(2) a curved line close to the diagonal.
(3) a right-angled line.
(4) a 45° diagonal line.
(5) none of the preceding.

4. Which alternative in question 3 would be correct had that question referred to absolute inequality in income—i.e., a situation in which one individual or family gets all the income and the others receive no income at all?

(1).
(2).
(3).
(4).
(5).

5. The trend in the United States from the mid-1970s to the late 1980s was for the:
(1) lowest 20 percent of the income distribution to become poorer and the highest 20 percent of the income distribution to also become poorer relative to the middle 60 percent.
(2) the highest 20 percent to become relatively poorer and the lowest 20 percent to become relatively richer.
(3) the highest 20 percent to become relatively richer and the lowest 20 percent to become relatively poorer.
(4) both the highest and the lowest 20 percent of the income distribution to become richer at the expense of the middle class.
(5) none of the above.

6. The average income of American families in 1988 was approximately:
(1) $32,000.
(2) $44,400.
(3) $72,300.
(4) $54,600.
(5) $22,800.

7. The average per capita weekly income in the United States in 1988 was:
(1) between $100 and $130.
(2) between $130 and $175.
(3) between $175 and $240.
(4) between $240 and $275.
(5) over $275.

8. Which of the following statements is an accurate description of the distribution of income in the United States?
(1) The mean is higher than the median, due to the presence of a large number of relatively low incomes.
(2) The median is higher than the mean, due to the presence of a small number of exceptionally high incomes.
(3) The mean is higher than the median, due to the presence of a small number of exceptionally high incomes.

(4) The median is higher than the mean, due to the presence of a large number of relatively low incomes.
(5) The median, which used to be lower than the mean, has recently become somewhat higher, due to the influence of progressive income taxation.

9. The "median" family income is:
(1) the figure obtained by listing all incomes from lowest to highest and taking the one exactly in the middle of the ranking.
(2) the income figure that would result if the total incomes received by all families were divided equally among those families.
(3) the income it is estimated a family must have in order to reach the "minimum-comfort" level of consumption.
(4) the level of income found at the exact midpoint of a Lorenz curve.
(5) none of the preceding.

10. Which alternative in question 11 would be correct had that question referred to the "mean" rather than to the "median" family income?
(1).
(2).
(3).
(4).
(5).

11. If there is any inequality at all in the distribution of income, then which of the following will be true of the group making up the lowest 20 percent in the income ranking?
(1) It is just as likely as not that it will receive more than 20 percent of this total income.
(2) It must receive exactly 20 percent of this total income.
(3) It will usually, but not always, receive less than 20 percent of this total income.
(4) It must have received less than 20 percent of the total income of all groups together.
(5) None of the above is necessarily true.

12. Differences in ability are commonly cited to explain differences in income. This explanation:
(1) is only partial because there are so many more instances of skewness in ability than in income distribution.
(2) is only partial because the shape of the income frequency-distribution curve is significantly different from that of the ability distribution curve.
(3) is only partial because the measured range of individual ability differences is much wider than the range of income distribution.
(4) gives a reasonably accurate interpretation of income differences.
(5) is almost meaningless because there is no suitable way of comparing ability differences against income differences.

13. If inequalities of income and of wealth in the United Kingdom (U.K.) and the United States (U.S.) are compared:
(1) the U.K. has much greater inequality in both income and wealth.
(2) the U.S. has much greater inequality in both income and wealth.
(3) wealth inequalities are the same in both, but the U.K. has much greater inequality of income.
(4) the U.K. has much greater inequality of wealth, but income inequalities are roughly the same in both.
(5) there is no significant difference between the two countries in either income equality or wealth inequality.

SUGGESTED ANSWERS TO QUESTIONS IN THE TEXT: Chapter 26

1. Guess first, and see how close you are.

2. There is a large literature on the redistribution of income that takes work (dis)incentives into account. To make the income distribution more even, some people who work hard will have to pay higher taxes to subsidize the incomes of the less well-off. They may choose to work less, reduce the "pie" of total income, and make everyone worse off. This question goes to the heart of the tradeoff between equity and efficiency, and there is no right answer. It depends upon your "social objective function"; i.e., what you want for society.

3. **a.** No change; the tax reduces everyone's income at the same rate as the total.
b. Moves in toward the 45° line; larger chunks taken from the higher incomes mean their share of the pie shrinks.
c. Moves away from the 45° line; lower-income classes spend a larger proportion of their incomes, thus pay more tax as a fraction of their incomes.
d. Moves away from the 45° line; recessions are hardest on the lower middle classes whose jobs may be put in jeopardy.

4. Makes it difficult; comparisons should be cone in terms of locally defined real values (i.e., corrected by locally specific price indices).

5. Cash is generally more efficient (expands the utility possibilities of the recipients), but there is no guarantee that cash given to help pay for, e.g., food goes for food. Categorized benefits have such a guarantee (at least according to the law), but they are less efficient and spawn expensive bureaucracies.

6. Absolute equality; Gini = 0.
Absolute inequality; Gini = 10,000.
For Figure 26-3, Gini for U.S. income is roughly 3200; Gini for U.S. wealth, roughly 8000.

7. Listing the people in order of income, they receive \$1, \$2, \$3, \$4, \$5, \$5, \$6, \$7, \$8, \$9. Their total income is \$50. The 10-percentile intervals for population therefore collect, cumulatively, 2, 6, 12, 20, 30, 40, 52, 66, 82, and 100 percent of the income, respectively. (For the first two people, e.g., total income is \$3, or 6 percent of \$50.) Gini $\approx$ 740 $\times$ 2 = 1480.

8. The procedure is this: Get the population numbers; compute per capita incomes; rank the people according to per capita income; compute percentage of total population covered and income recorded for each per capita income cohort; and graph the resulting numbers in the cumulative fashion required in a Lorenz curve. The inequality should be enormous.

CHAPTER 27 PRICING OF FACTORS OF PRODUCTION

Now that you have studied how pricing and production decisions are made in product markets, it is time to consider how pricing and employment decisions are made in input markets. You will recall that relative scarcity and need were seen to determine why it costs more to buy some goods than it does to buy others; but what accounts for the large differences that one observes in the wages and salaries offered to people engaged in various occupations. Scarcity? Need? Or something else? Also, if all inputs work *interdependently* to produce any given product or service, how can one compute levels of compensation that reflect accurately the importance of their respective contributions. How, more specifically, are wage rates determined? And interest rates? And land rents? And so on?

The answers to all these questions can be found by searching in familiar territory—the workings of supply and demand. The only fundamental difference between product markets and input markets lies in the sources of their supply and demand sides. In a goods market, for example, demand materializes because the good being produced and sold generates some utility for the consumer; the consumer is willing to pay some positive price for the privilege of owning the good in question. In an input market, by way of contrast, factors of production are demanded only because they can be employed to produce such an item of value. The demand for inputs is a "derived demand" based not upon the immediate, innate value of the input to a firm, but upon the value of some other good that it can be employed to produce.

The first part of this chapter concentrates on the demand side of an input market. Because a producing firm must hire labor, buy raw materials, and invest in machinery, it is the **demander** of productive inputs. Its demand is not, however, unlimited. It makes its employment decisions on the basis of least-cost combinations of inputs defined by its production function and the prices of those inputs. The derived demand for any input will therefore be seen to result from (1) the cost-minimizing behavior of profit-maximizing firms and (2) a marginal-productivity theory of income distribution.

The second part of the chapter will show how this notion of derived demand can be used in a market context. It will, in particular, play derived demand against perfectly inelastic input supply curves—a supply characterization most accurately describing land and other natural resources of fixed quantity. Because their supply is perfectly inelastic, resources like these should earn rents which may or may not reflect true social cost. Opportunity cost will, as a result, once again be raised as an issue. So, too, will be issues surrounding instances in which economic rents are not collected: e.g., the indiscriminate pollution of our air and water; the exploitation of forests, fisheries, and village greens; the congestion that clogs some of our highways, bridges, and phone lines at certain times, etc.

Having completed your work in this chapter, you should have accomplished the following learning objectives.

LEARNING OBJECTIVES

1. Understand that the theory of distribution of income is concerned with the determination of different people's incomes as well as with the allocation of the value of total product among the various factors that are employed to produce that product.

2. Explain how the distribution of income is the result of the workings of supply and demand in an economy's input markets.

3. Define the notion of derived demand for a factor of production, and explain why it is algebraically represented by its marginal revenue product, i.e., by a schedule derived by multiplying the marginal product of an input by marginal revenue of an output.

4. Show precisely why, in cases of perfect competition, the marginal revenue product of any input, and thus its derived demand, is equal to the price of the output that it is employed to produce multiplied by its marginal product.

5. Demonstrate why a firm that hires all inputs up to the point at which their prices equal their marginal revenue products will guarantee that (1) they are producing the profit-maximizing output at (2) they are incurring the least cost; i.e., *MR* will equal *MC*, and the least-cost rule will be satisfied.

6. Show how the market derived demand curve for any factor of production is equal to the horizontal sum of the marginal revenue product curves of all firms demanding that product.

7. Explain the Clark marginal-productivity theory of income distribution. In light of that theory, define the "exhaustion of product" property for constant-returns-to-scale production.

8. Explain the notion of economic rent, the circumstances under which it applies, and the inferences that can be drawn from those circumstances regarding the theory of efficient taxation (i.e., Ramsey taxes).

9. Explain how economic rent can be considered a legitimate production cost that does not carry with it a matching social cost; explore the role of opportunity cost in this context.

10. Understand the role of economic rent in developing a theory of externalities. Explain why appropriate rents might not be charged for certain of our natural resources.

The key to factor pricing is the marginal-productivity theory of a firm. To recall the fundamentals of this theory (see Chapter 20 for a thorough review), let some product X be produced from various combinations of inputs A, B C, etc. Remember that any of the various production processes embodied in these combinations can be reflected by a mathematical production function—a systematic record of the maximum output of good X that can be produced from all possible combinations of inputs A, B, C, etc. *given a specific state of technology*. For the purposes of derived demand, though, it is the derivative concept of **marginal product** that is most important. The marginal product (*MP*) of any input is the ratio of the change in total product to the change in the employment of that input, *with the employment of* all *other factors held constant*. The *MP* of factor A can, then, be thought of as the change in the output of X caused by a 1-unit change in the employment of *only* factor A.

1. Suppose that X is produced from inputs A, B, and C; a very small portion of the production function is recorded below:

	Employment Levels		
Output	**A**	**B**	**C**
200	10	30	20
203	10	31	20

a. You can infer from the table that *(the MP of X is 3 units / the MP of A is 3 units / the MP of B is 3 units / the MP of C is 3 units)*.

b. If the employment of some input such as B were gradually to increase, with the employment of all other inputs such as A and C held constant, then we should expect that the marginal product of B would gradually *(increase / decline)* because of the *(law of diminishing returns / relative scarcity of B that would result)*. Similarly, if the quantity of B employed were to decline, with the employment of A and C held constant again, then we should expect that the marginal product of B would *(increase / decline)* because of the *(law of diminishing returns / relative scarcity of B that would result)*.

c. If the employment of some input such as B were gradually to increase, with the employment of inputs A and C held constant, then we should expect to see the marginal product of A *(increase / decrease)* along with the marginal product of C because of the *(law of diminishing returns / relative scarcity of A and C that would result)*.

a. the *MP* of B is 3 units **b.** decline; law of diminishing returns; increase; relative scarcity of B that would result **c.** increase; relative scarcity of A and C that would result

The point of question 1 is that the value of the marginal product of an input depends upon the level of employment of all inputs even though it is defined in terms of changes in the employment of one input. The more of input A (e.g.) that is employed, all other things equal, the higher should be the marginal products of inputs B and C.

2. If a firm wants to maximize profits, it will attempt to produce the output that sets marginal revenue equal to marginal cost; and in defining marginal revenue, it will be employing inputs at levels that satisfy the least-cost rule:

$$MP_A/P_A = MP_B/P_B = MP_C/P_C = \ldots$$

Steps in achieving that goal are listed below, but they do not appear there in the correct chronological order. Indicate their proper order by writing the corresponding numbers in the correct sequence in the space provided.

1. Pick the output where marginal cost equals marginal revenue.
2. Compute the least-cost combination of inputs for output levels in the anticipated range.
3. Compute marginal revenue for various levels of sales in the anticipated range from information about the demand side of the market.
4. Compute marginal cost for various levels of sales in the anticipated range from the least-cost data.
5. Collect information about input prices and the technology that defines how inputs can be utilized to produce various levels of output.

Correct order: ______________________________

Step 5; step 2; step 3 (*Note*: Step 3 could fall anywhere between steps 5 and 4.) step 4; step 1

3. With the link between the least-cost rule, total cost, and profit maximization established, the link between profit maximization and derived demand can be explored more fully.

a. If we say that A is an input, X is the product produced, and the *MP* of input A is 2, then the 2 refers to *(units of A / units of X / dollars)*. This *MP* is, so to speak, the "payoff" in X output resulting from the employment of the last unit of A. The payoff is, however, more commonly thought of in money terms. To know what this *MP* payoff is worth in dollars, we must know what revenue the sale of the additional X units will bring in—i.e., we need to know the *(price of A / marginal revenue accruing from sale of X)*.

b. If the marginal revenue accruing from sale of 1 additional X unit is $3 (the *MP* of input A being 2), then the dollar payoff resulting from hiring the last unit of A is $*(2 / 3 / 5 / 6 / 10 / 12)*. (We disregard the slight drop in *MR* that might come from selling the second of these 2 X units.)

c. The technical name for this dollar payoff is the **marginal revenue product** (*MRP*). That is, the *MRP* of, say, factor input A is specifically (pick one):

(1) *MP* of A multiplied by marginal revenue accruing from sale of X, or *MP* of A multiplied by *MR*.

(2) *MP* of A multiplied by price of A.

(3) *MP* of A not multiplied by anything.

d. In the special case of pure (or perfect) competition—but only in that case—this *MRP* of A could be defined as the *MP* of A multiplied by the price of X, but "marginal revenue from X" is more general. It takes in all the cases, pure competition included.

Barring the special case of pure (or perfect) competition, as the firm increases its output and sales, the marginal revenue from sale of X will *(rise / remain constant / fall)*. As a result, the marginal revenue product of each and every input will, as employment increases, *(rise / remain constant / fall)* for two reasons; they are:

(1) ____________________

(2) ____________________

a. units of X; marginal revenue accruing from sale of X **b.** 6 **c. (1)** **d.** fall; fall **(1)** diminishing marginal revenue **(2)** diminishing marginal product

4. Suppose our firm is satisfying the least-cost rule with respect to inputs A, B, and C. Now it wants to find out if it is at its maximum-profit output level.

To do this, it can look at any one of its inputs—say, input A. A's price is, say, $4 per unit. A's *MP* is 3. The marginal revenue from sale of X is $1.

a. This means that A's *MRP*—the dollar payoff from employing the last unit of A—is $*(1 / 2 / 3 / 4 / 7 / 12)*. It cost $*(1 / 2 / 3 / 4 / 7 / 12)* to buy that last unit of A services. So its employment *(added $1 to / subtracted $1 from / did not change)* total profit.

Our firm, remember, is satisfying the least-cost rule in making its employment decisions. It follows, therefore, that the same conclusion would have been reached had we looked at input B or input C. Hence, in the given circumstances, the firm *(definitely is / definitely is not / may or may not be)* earning maximum possible profit. In order for it to move toward that maximum, it should *(reduce / increase)* its output—i.e., *(reduce / increase)* its employment of all inputs.

b. Try, now, a different example to illustrate the point more fully. Suppose that the *MP*s of A, B, and C are, respectively, 12, 8, and 2. Their prices are, respectively, $6, $4, and $1. The firm *(is / is not)*, therefore, producing its current output at minimum cost.

The marginal revenue from sale of X is $1. Thus input A's *MRP* is $*(12 / 10 / 8 / 6 / 4 / 2)*. Input B's *MRP* is $*(12 / 10 / 8 / 6 / 4 / 2)*. Input C's *MRP* is $*(12 / 10 / 8 / 6 / 4 / 2)*.

This firm *(is / is not)* operating a maximum-profit output. For such a maximum, it should *(increase / decrease)* its output by *(increasing / decreasing)* the employment of *(input A only / B only / C only / all inputs)*.

c. As employment is so changed, input *MRP*s will *(fall / rise)*. The increase in input employment should be halted when each *MRP* has *(fallen below / reached equality with / risen above)* the price of the *(input / finished product)*.

a. 3; 4; subtracted $1 from; definitely is not; reduce; reduce **b.** is (The ratios of marginal product to price are 12/6 = 8/4 = 2/1 = 2.); 12; 8; 2; is not; increase; increasing; all inputs (*MRP* > *P* for *all* inputs.) **c.** fall; reached equality with; input

The process just described is nothing more than an elaboration of the *MR* = *MC* maximum-profit rule set out in earlier chapters. Think of the firm (as we did in those earlier chapters) as gradually approaching this *MR* = *MC* output level, starting from an output at which *MR* exceeds *MC*. As output is expanded, *MR* gradually falls [unless the situation is one of pure (or perfect) competition], and *MC* gradually rises.

The output increases needed to reach this *MR* = *MC* equality are obtained by increasing the employment of A, B, and C. However, as this increase is undertaken, the least-cost rule must be satisfied constantly. If it is not, the output in question could be produced at lower cost, and the firm would be "above" its true total cost curve rather than "on" it.

With cost minimization maintained, expanding output moves toward the *MR* = *MC* maximum-profit position. That position can be described in *MRP* terms, as well as *MR* = *MC* terms. As output is increased, *MRP*s fall. When they have fallen to equality with input prices, for all inputs employed, (*a*) the least-cost rule is automatically satisfied, and (*b*) so is the $MR = MC$ maximum-profit rule.

5. a. Take the *MP*s for inputs A, B, and C to be 12, 8, and 2, respectively. If you knew that the prices of A, B, and C were $6, $4, and $1, respectively, and that the firm had reached its maximum-profit output, what must have been the *MR* from the sale of the last X units? *($8 / $6 / $2 / $1 / 50 cents)*

b. Change to different figures. If *MR* were $2, if the prices of A, B, and C were $8, $4, and $10, and if the firm were at maximum-profit output, A's *MP* must have been *(1 / 2 / 3 / 4 / 5)* units of X, that of B must have been *(1 / 2 / 3 / 4 / 5)* units, and C's must have been *(1 / 2 / 3 / 4 / 5)* units.

c. Suppose that the firm is employing inputs A, B, and C according to the rule which states that each factor must be hired up to the point at which its marginal revenue product equals its price. Show in a few steps of algebra that this firm is automatically satisfying the least-cost rule. ________

____

____

____

____

____

a. 50 cents ($0.50 × 12 = $6; $0.50 × 8 = $4; $0.50 × 2 = $1)
b. 4 ($2 × 4 = $8); 2 ($2 × 2 = $4); 5 ($2 × 5 = $10)
c. Start with $MRP_A = MP_A \times MR = P_A$; $MRP_B = MP_B \times MR = P_B$; and $MRP_C = MP_C \times MR = P_C$. Rearranging each, notice immediately that $MR = MP_A/P_A = MP_B/P_B = MP_C/P_C$—the least-cost rule.

6. In everyday terms, the explanation of the maximum-profit rule for input employment (namely, equate the *MRP* of that input with its price) is (pick one):

(1) the price of the factor input should equal the price of the output X.

(2) the marginal product of each and all inputs should be the same amount.

(3) any extra unit of an input is worth hiring or buying so long as the extra revenue it brings in (via extra production and extra sales) exceeds what it costs to hire or buy it; the buying process should be halted only when the extra revenue has fallen to equality with the extra cost.

(4) the price of each factor input should be equal to marginal revenue from the last unit of X sold.

____

(3)

7. Consult Table 27-1, in which the outputs of identical fields of corn are recorded for a variety of levels of employment of labor. Let there be 10 workers in an economy defined by the two cornfields, and let the world determine the price of corn at $2. Fill in the Marginal Product and Marginal Revenue Product columns of the table. The numbers that you record there will be used to demonstrate that paying labor (the input, here) its marginal revenue product will result in a level of output that maximizes the value of the corn crop, i.e., an output that represents a point on the production-possibility frontier of this ridiculously simple economy.

Table 27-1

Labor Employed	Corn Output (bushels)	Marginal Product of Labor	Marginal Revenue Product of Labor
0	0	n/a	n/a
1	10	____	____
2	19	____	____
3	27	____	____
4	34	____	____
5	40	____	____
6	45	____	____
7	49	____	____
8	52	____	____
9	54	____	____
10	55	____	____

Suppose, initially, that seven workers toiled in the first field (field A) and three toiled in the second (field B). Output of field A would be ____ bushels worth $____; each worker, if paid his or her marginal revenue product, would receive $____. Output of field B would meanwhile be ____ bushels worth $____; each worker there would receive $____. In response to the wages that you computed, you should expect that workers would want to move *(from A to B / from B to A)*.

Suppose that happened, and four workers remained to work field A and six worked field B. Output of field A would fall to ____ bushels with a value of $____, and output of field B would climb to ____ units worth $____ on the world market. The total value of output would, in fact, have climbed from $____ to $____.

To equalize the wages paid to workers in both fields so that there would be no incentive for workers to want to switch from one to the other, however, ____ workers would have to work each field. Were that the case, total output would climb to ____ bushels worth $____ and each worker would earn

$\_\_\_\_\_\_$. There *(exists / does not exist)* any other distribution of workers that would increase the output of corn and thus increase the value of the economy's production on the world market.

The Marginal Product column; 10, 9, 8, 7, 6, 5, 4, 3, 2, 1; Marginal Revenue Product column: \$20, \$18, \$16, \$14, \$12, \$10, \$8, \$6, \$4, \$2; 49; 98; 8 $(= \$2 \times MP = \$2 \times 4)$; 27; 54; 16 $(= \$2 \times MP = \$2 \times 8)$; from A to B; 34; 68; 45; 90; 152; 158; 5; 80; 160; 12; does not exist

8. You are a consultant on cost minimization and profit maximization. What do you recommend with respect to each of the five cases listed in Table 27-2?

Table 27-2

Case	*MR* from X Sale	*P* of A	*P* of B	At Maximum Profit?	Answer
1	\$1	\$2	\$10	______	______
2	2	6	18	______	______
3	3	12	18	______	______
4	4	9	18	______	______
5	5	21	54	______	______

In all of them, product X is made through the employment of inputs A and B (and there are no other inputs involved). In all of them—note carefully—A's marginal product is 3 units of X, and B's marginal product is 9 units of X. "*MR* from X Sale" in the table means marginal revenue at the current output and sales level. "*P* of A" and "*P* of B" indicate the prices the firm must pay for these two inputs.

a. For each case, indicate whether or not the firm is at its maximum-profit position. Write "yes" or "no" in the column indicated.

b. What, if anything, is wrong with the firm's present position? Answer by putting *one* of the numbers 1 through 5 in the right-hand column, according to the following code:

1. Present position is the correct one.
2. For present output, employment of A is too high, employment of B too low.
3. For present output, employment of A is too low, employment of B too high.
4. Reduce output by employing less of both A and B.
5. Increase output by employing more of both A and B.

Case 1: no; 3 (*MRP*s are not equal to prices, so profits are not maximized; $MRP_A = \$1 \times 3 > P_A = \$2$, but $MRP_B = \$9 < P_B = \$10$, so we do not know if output is too high or too low; $MP_A/P_A = 3/2 > MP_B/P_B = 10/9$, so the firm needs to hire more A and less B to increase MP_A and reduce MP_B.)
Case 2: yes; 1 (*MRP*s are equal to prices, so profits are maximized; note that \$2 $\times$ 3 = \$6 for input A and \$2 $\times$ 9 = \$18 for input B.)
Case 3: no; 2 (*MRP*s are not equal to prices, so profits are not maximized; $MRP_A = \$3 \times 3 < P_A = \$12$, but $MRP_B = \$27 > P_B = \$18$, so we do not know if output is too high or too low; $MP_A/P_A = 3/12 < MP_B/P_B = 9/18$, so the firm needs to hire more B and less A to increase MP_B and reduce MP_A.)
Case 4: no; 5 (*MRP*s are greater than prices for both inputs, so the firm should increase employment of both to bring *MRP*s down.)
Case 5: no; 4 (*MRP*s are less than prices for both inputs, so the firm should reduce employment of both to increase *MRP*s.)

The preceding questions have tried to indicate the considerations that are most important to a firm in deciding how much of any input it will want to buy, given some set of prices. If A's price were, for example, to rise or to fall, the calculations would have to be redone. In sum, we are trying to isolate the considerations that lie behind a firm's demand for any input at various possible prices of that input.

The demand for any input is sometimes called a **derived demand**. People want a finished good, such as X, for the satisfaction it provides them. Nobody wants an input such as A for *that* reason. Nevertheless, A is in demand because it is useful in the production of X. The demand for A is "derived from" the demand for X.

We now turn briefly to the puzzling and difficult question with which the chapter began: that of income distribution. What are the forces which settle the manner of division of a cooperatively produced output? How much can any one contributing input expect to receive?

Clearly, the demand for the input is important in settling this question. Demand (together with available supply) determines the price per unit of input services; and if you know relative input prices, you know something about how those inputs are likely to share in the total value of goods produced.

The "marginal-productivity" analysis outlined in this chapter first began to emerge late in the nineteenth century. Economist John B. Clark, who did much to develop it, felt that this analysis pointed strongly toward the underlying laws which governed the distribution of real income (goods and services) among the inputs which had cooperated in the production of those goods and services.

Clark pointed out that if each input is paid a price just equal to the market value of its *MP*, there will—in the right circumstances (this we'll get to in a moment)—be just enough to pay off all the inputs, with no deficit, and nothing left over.

9. Suppose that total output is 200 units of X, produced with a 10-30-20 combination of inputs A, B, and C. Suppose further than the *MP*s of A, B, and C are 9 of X, 3 of X, and 1 of X, respectively. Finally, let X be a product to be sold in a competitive market at a price of \$1. Complete the following table in light of this information.

Quantity of Input	MRP of Input	Total Payment of Input
_______ units of A ×	$ _______	= $ _______
_______ units of B ×	$ _______	= $ _______
_______ units of C ×	$ _______	= $ _______
	Total payment	= $ _______

It is assumed that A, B, and C are the *only* inputs contributing to X's production. When each is paid according to its *MRP*, the total payments *(are less than / just equal / exceed)* the total value of the total amount of X produced; i.e., \$1 × 200 units = \$200.

Reading across rows: 10, 9, 90; 30, 3, 90; 20, 1, 20; 200; just equal

This approach had two seemingly attractive features. Payment according to *MRP*s just "exhausts the product"; i.e., there is just enough to go around. Moreover, payment according to (marginal) productivities carries with it some suggestion that the distribution is "fair" or "just."

Today it is conceded that income distribution is too complicated a business to be handled in such simple terms. Opinions differ sharply as to the meaningful content of the marginal-productivity approach. Moreover, Clark's treatment works as outlined above only with a *constant-returns-to-scale* production function, i.e., when doubling or tripling all input quantities just doubles or triples output quantity and when halving all input quantities just halves output quantity. There is no necessary reason why production functions should display this property; many clearly do not. If they do not, payment by marginal productivities will not "just exhaust the product."

10. The market demand for any input is the *(vertical / geometric / horizontal)* sum across all firms interested in employing that input of their individual demand schedules; i.e., their *(marginal product / marginal revenue product / marginal utility)* schedules. More specifically, suppose that there are only three firms interested in employing some input X, and let their demands be 3, 4, and 5 units, respectively, given a price of \$3 per unit. Market demand for \$3 would, in this case, be _______ units. At a price of \$4, though, we would expect, in general, that the quantity demanded by the market would *(increase / fall)* because the individual demands of the three firms would probably *(rise / fall)*.

horizontal; marginal revenue product; 12; fall; fall

11. **a.** Consider Figures 27-1 and 27-2. The one which illustrates the perfectly price inelastic situation is *(27-1 / 27-2)*. A supply curve such as Figure 27-1 implies that if price should drop, say, from p_1 to p_0, the quantity offered for sale would *(increase / decrease / remain the same as before)*. Sketch in Figure 27-1 a demand curve passing through the point on SS corresponding to p_1. Then sketch another to indicate a leftward shift of demand reducing the equilibrium price to p_0.

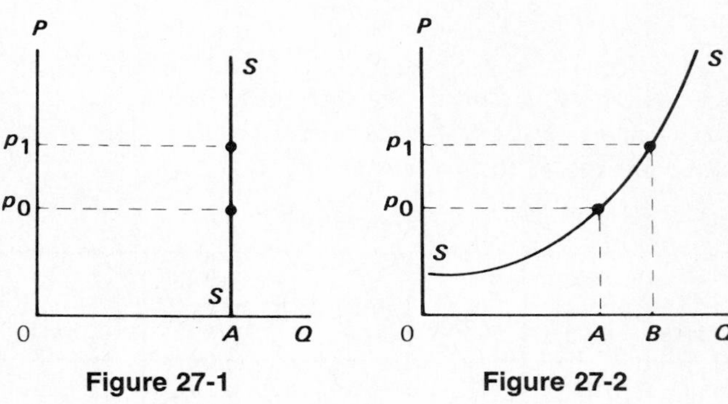

Figure 27-1 Figure 27-2

b. The significance of economic rent is best understood by considering an input supply curve having the more customary shape, as in Figure 27-2. Here, if price drops from p_1 to p_0, quantity offered for sale will *(increase / decrease / remain the same as before)*. Sketch two corresponding demand curves in Figure 27-2.

c. Implicit in Figure 27-2 is an essential question: Why does a drop in demand cause part (or all, if the drop is large enough) of supply to be withdrawn? What happens to the quantity of input services *AB* if they disappear from supply offered?

To answer this question, we need to spell out more carefully the nature of the supply curve we are discussing. Suppose it is specifically the land supply offered for rental to farmers who want it for growing corn. In these circumstances, a fall in price from p_1 to p_0 will persuade the landowners to rent part (or all) of their land to other demanders (for example, farmers who want land for barley growing). This would explain why, in the corn market, there is the reduction in supply quantity *AB* in Figure 27-2. If the demand of corn growers for land decreases, thereby reducing the land-rental price from p_1 to p_0, the *AB* quantity is transferred to farmers who want more land for barley production. Note carefully that this assumes the land in question has at least one alternative use; i.e., it can be used for barley production as well as for corn production.

If, however, the land has no alternative use, so that it is literally useful only in corn production, then any decrease in demand for land by corn growers will reduce only its price. The quantity of land supplied will *(increase / decrease / remain the same as before)*, so that Figure 27-1 is the relevant illustration. The landowners would not be happy about the price reduction, but they could not do anything about it.

a. 27-1; remain the same as before **b.** decrease **c.** remain the same as before

It is now possible to present a precise definition of **economic rent**. Economic rent, strictly interpreted, is the return paid to an input which has just one single occupation; it is useful in production of one single commodity only. Because its employment is so limited, the input's supply curve with respect to that occupation is perfectly price inelastic.

The problem here is, of course, the precise meaning of "one single occupation." Land suited for corn production could almost certainly be used for other grain crops. The idea of economic rent was developed by nineteenth-century British economists like David Ricardo. When these economists spoke of "corn production," they really meant "grain production" or "food production"; i.e., they interpreted the words "occupation" and "commodity" rather broadly. And we can speak of Iowa farmland in the same broad sense: if we say it has only a single occupation, we mean that its effective usefulness is pretty much limited to grain or food production, so that the only effective demand of significance is that of farmers who want to use it for this purpose.

12. a. When an input has only a single employment, the supply curve facing demanders who want to use it in that employment will be perfectly inelastic with respect to price because the suppliers have no alternative to which to turn should price be low. They must supply the same quantity, if necessary, even at a very low price. If the market for this input is competitive, *will* the price be low? (Pick one.)

(1) Yes, if competitive forces are operating.

(2) It is impossible to tell. Price will be set where the demand curve crosses this perfectly inelastic supply curve; this may be a very high price, if the demand for this limited supply is sufficiently great.

b. The single-occupation case illustrates how fallacious a "cost of production" theory of price can be. Suppose that the input is cows, and that cows are useful only for giving milk. Demand for milk has driven up its price to a high level. The resulting derived demand for cows has driven up *their* price to a high level. Here, it is incorrect to say that (pick one):

(1) the price of cows is high because the price of milk is high.

(2) the price of milk is high because the price of cows is high.

In short, you *(can / cannot)* in this case give a meaningful explanation of the price of milk in terms of the costs involved in producing milk.

c. The cows-and-milk example illustrates the more general issue which produced the term "economic rent." It arose from David Ricardo's exploration of changes in the prices of food and of land in early-nineteenth-century England. As in the cows-and-milk instance, a higher demand for food had driven up the rental price of land. Analytically, the proper conclusion was simple: the increased price of food cannot be blamed on the higher rental price of land; land's price has risen because the demand for food has increased.

Remember that this conclusion holds only for a single-occupation, perfectly inelastic supply input. Suppose that land has many uses other than food production. Demand in some of those other uses has driven up the rental price of land. Food producers must now pay a higher price for that part of the total land supply which they use, even though this price rise has nothing to do with the demand for food. Here, the higher price of food *(could / could not)* legitimately be blamed on the higher cost of inputs required to produce food.

---

a. (2) b. (2); cannot **c.** could

13. Economists' interest in the case of the single-occupation, perfectly inelastic supply input led them to ask another question: Does the payment made to such an input constitute a cost of production?

At first, this may seem an odd question. Each separate user of that input must pay the money price, high or low, for the quantity of that input which he or she buys, and to that buyer his or her outlay most certainly *is* a cost of production.

On the other side of the coin, though, money cost is supposed to be only the surface manifestation of real cost to society. The text's Chapter 2 pointed out that you can look at real cost in terms of opportunity cost—the cost of getting more guns is the sacrifice of butter which (when resources are fully employed) is necessary if more guns are to be produced. The way to get more guns is to switch some of those inputs which are useful in either occupation from butter production to gun production.

Economic-rent inputs, by definition, are those which have only one occupation and so cannot be switched. In terms of opportunity cost, their employment *(still entails / does not entail)* a cost to society. When such inputs are put to work, their employment does not entail any sacrifice of an alternative commodity.

---

does not entail

14. From the perspective of a single farmer, one among many such farmers, the supply curve of single-occupation land will not be perfectly inelastic. If the rental market for land is a competitive one, each farmer sees only the market price of land at which price he or she can rent as much or as little as he or she wishes. To the farmer, land supply appears *(perfectly elastic / somewhat elastic / perfectly inelastic)* with respect to price.

Consider now the case of an input which happens to have several widely differing possible occupations, and whose total supply curve (the supply quantity offered to all buyers taken together) is perfectly price inelastic. To any one class of buyers, though, the supply curve of this input will not be perfectly inelastic.

To illustrate: Suppose the input in question can be used for making any of goods X, Y, or Z, so that there are three classes of buyers. For some reason, the demand for this input on the part of those who use it for making X declines sharply. Because this demand is part of total demand, the input's price should *(fall / rise)*. Consequently, the producers who use it for making Y and Z will be disposed to buy *(more / less)*. That is, the input's total fixed supply will be redistributed: more goes toward Y and Z, and less toward X. Thus, to X producers, supply *(will / will not)* be perfectly inelastic, for when their demand decreases (and the input's price consequently falls), the quantity supplied to them decreases.

---

perfectly elastic; fall; more; will not

15. Henry George's **single-tax** movement drew on the idea of perfectly inelastic supply. In his book *Progress and Poverty*, George argued that the primary explanation for continuing poverty in the midst of economic progress was high land rent. Landlords were exacting large incomes from land which they (or their ancestors) had been shrewd (or lucky) enough to acquire before the present need for such land had evolved. Land's price was high because (*a*) the demand for it was now exceedingly high, and (*b*) supply, being fixed, had not expanded to match the increase in demand. Hence the single-tax movement—the single tax proposed being, of course, a tax on land.

Regardless of the merits or demerits of Henry George's single-tax movement, instances of perfectly inelastic input supply—if they can be found—have interesting implications for taxation policy.

As illustration, consider the case in which supply is not perfectly price inelastic. Figure 27-2, for example, might illustrate the fact that labor will work longer hours only if it is offered a higher price (for all hours supplied) for so doing. If an increased demand for labor were to push the price up from p_0 to p_1, then that higher price would accomplish two things: (*a*) it would coax out the additional quantity supplied *AB*, which would not have been forthcoming at price p_0; and (*b*) it would ration out the total available supply *OB* to those willing to pay the higher price.

Suppose now, with price at p_1, a tax is levied on the sale of this input. Its effect would be to reduce the after-tax return received by labor to, say, p_0. As a consequence, market quantity supplied would be reduced from *OB* to *OA*. The tax would have the unfortunate effect of "distorting production incentives"; i.e., people would decide to supply somewhat less labor in order to escape paying part of the tax.

By contrast, consider the case of perfectly inelastic supply—Figure 27-1. Here, a price rise from p_0 to p_1 (brought about by an increase in demand) would accomplish *(neither / only one / both)* of the results in the Figure 27-2 case. It *(would / would not)* coax out an additional supply quantity. It *(would / would not)* ration that available supply.

Moreover, if a tax were to be levied on the sale of this input, results would be different in the inelastic-supply case. The important thing is that if such a tax were to reduce the after-tax return of suppliers from p_1 to p_0, this would produce *(a large / a small / no)* reduction in supply quantity. Imposition of this tax *(would / would not)* cause any reduction in total real output, since there would be no reduction in quantity of work hours supplied.

---

only one; would not; would; no; would not

16. Modern tax theory has generalized the notion of taxing inputs whose supply is perfectly inelastic into what are called "Ramsey taxes." The observation behind this generalization is that taxes are more efficient in (*a*) raising revenue and (*b*) minimizing the loss in consumer surplus if they are imposed on goods with either (relatively) inelastic demand or inelastic supply. Figure 27-3 will help you explore the rationale behind this result.

In panel (**a**), a demand curve *DD* is drawn though point *E* to indicate, given supply curve *SS*, an equilibrium price and quantity pair of (price = \$5; quantity = 9). Demand curve *D'D'* had also been drawn to reflect the effect of a \$2-per-unit tax on the sale of good X. Since \$5 is required by suppliers to produce X, the new, after-tax equilibrium quantity would be ________ units for which people would spend \$________ per unit and suppliers would receive \$________ per unit. Before the tax, consumer surplus was \$________; after the tax it will have *(risen / fallen)* to \$________, a reduction of ________ percent. Tax revenue would, moreover, equal \$________.

Panel (**b**) repeats the process for a demand curve *DD* that, through the (price = \$5; quantity = 9) equilibrium, is *(more elastic / more inelastic)*. *D'D'* again represents effective demand after a \$2-per-unit tax has been imposed. The after-tax equilibrium would, in this second case, be ________ units selling at a price of \$________, of which \$________ per unit would show up in the hands of the supplier. Consumer surplus would, in this case, *(rise / fall)* from \$________ before the tax to \$________ after the tax—a reduction of ________ percent; total revenue generated by the tax would, meanwhile, equal \$________.

3; 7; 5; 13.5 (= area of triangle *aEb* = $\frac{1}{2} \times 3 \times 9$); fallen; 1.5 (= area of triangle *aEb'*); 89; 6 (= \$2 × 3 units); more inelastic; 7; 7; 5; fall; 40.5 (= area of triangle *aEb* = $\frac{1}{2} \times 9 \times 9$); 24.5 (= area of triangle *aEb'*); 40; 14 (= \$2 × 7 units)

17. The inability of an economy to charge rents for the utilization of resources of fixed supply produces an *(over / under)* utilization of those resources. Three reasons have been advanced to explain this inability. They are:

a. ________________________________

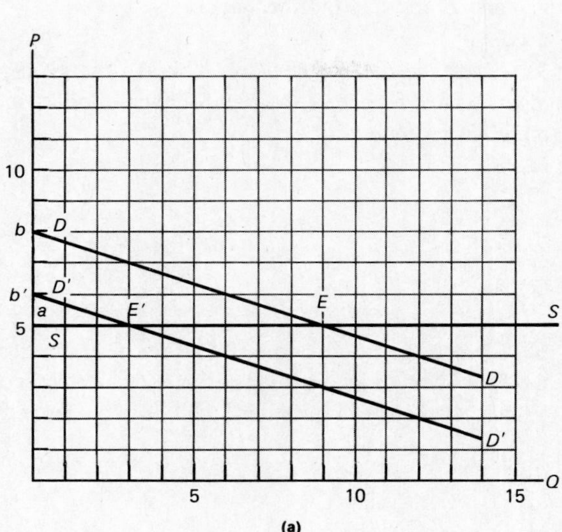

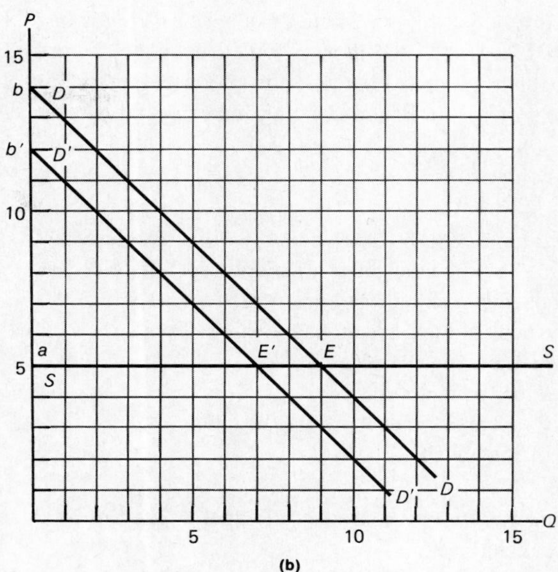

Figure 27-3

b. ______

c. ______

Now give an example from reality that illustrates each reason:

(1) ______

(2) ______

(3) ______

over **a.** no ownership **b.** owner does not charge for use. **c.** monitoring costs excessive **(1)** grazing on common land (no ownership) **(2)** hazardous dumping (monitoring costs) **(3)** carbon emissions (owner doesn't charge)

18. Consult Figure 27-4; *DD* there represents a demand curve for rental housing; *SS* represents a short run supply curve. The equilibrium rent for housing would, in this case, be $______. Suppose that the rent control authorities have determined that rents should be lowered and have imposed a ceiling equal to 80 percent of the equilibrium price. The quantity of rental housing provided would, in the short run illustrated in Figure 27-4, *(increase / remain the same / decline)* while the quantity demanded would *(increase / remain the same / decline)*. Additionally, the ceiling would *(provide incentives for / remove all incentives for)* landlords to increase the supply.

Now consider a 20 percent tax on rents collected by landlords. This policy would produce *(the same / a different)* equilibrium in the rental market in terms of quantity supplied in the short run. The rent paid would, meanwhile, *(climb / remain the same / fall)*, and a shortage of rental housing *(would / would not)* materialize. In the long run, though, with a sloped supply curve, the quantity supplied could fall and a shortage therefore materialize.

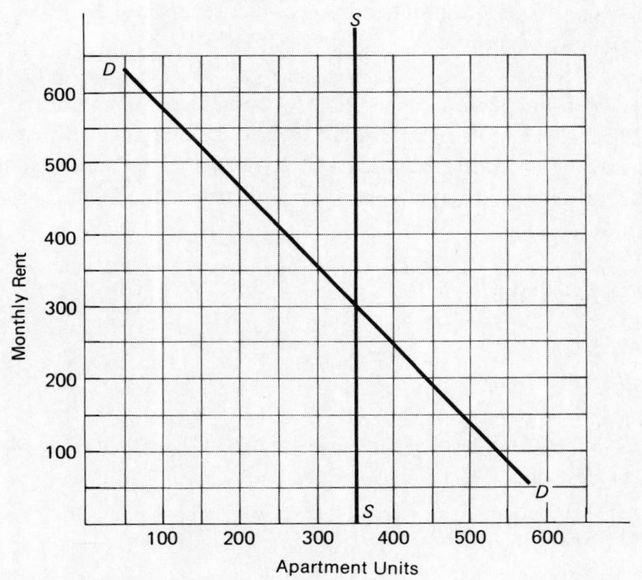

Figure 27-4

300; remain the same; increase; remove all incentives for; the same; remain the same; would not

QUIZ: Multiple Choice

1. If inputs A, B, and C together produce product X, the marginal product of input A is defined as:

(1) the extra output of X resulting from the employment of 1 extra unit of A, inputs B and C being increased proportionately.

(2) the amount of input A required to produce 1 extra unit of X, amounts of inputs B and C being held constant.

(3) the extra output of X resulting from the employment of 1 extra unit of A, amounts of inputs B and C being held constant.
(4) the amount of input A required to produce 1 extra unit of X, amounts of inputs B and C being increased proportionately.
(5) none of the above.

2. According to John B. Clark's theory of income distribution, if 10 units of a particular input are employed, the price paid to each of those units should be equal to the value of:
(1) the average of the *MP*s of each of the 10 units.
(2) its own *MP*.
(3) the *MP* of the tenth unit.
(4) the *AP* (average product) of the 10 units.
(5) none of the above.

3. The marginal revenue product of input A used to produce product X is defined as:
(1) the marginal product (*MP*) of A multiplied by the price of A.
(2) the average product (*AP*) of A multiplied by price of X.
(3) the *MP* of A multiplied by quantity of X.
(4) the *AP* of A multiplied by marginal revenue of X.
(5) none of the above.

4. A firm operates in conditions of imperfect competition. The price of one of its inputs, A is $10, and the marginal product of A is 5 units of finished product X. If this firm is at its maximum-profit output position, then the marginal revenue from sale of X must be:
(1) $1.
(2) $1.50.
(3) $2.
(4) $5.
(5) $10.

5. Input A's marginal revenue product, in question 4 circumstances, must be:
(1) $1.
(2) $1.50.
(3) $2.
(4) $5.
(5) $10.

6. Consider a monopoly. The price of one of its inputs, A, is $10, and the marginal product of A is 5 units of finished product X. The price of X is $2. The firm has satisfied the least-cost rule for input employment. This firm:
(1) cannot be at its maximum-profit position and to reach that position should decrease its output.
(2) cannot be at its maximum-profit position and to reach that position should increase its output.
(3) is at its profit-maximizing position.
(4) is at its maximum-profit position but should employ less of input A and more of other inputs.
(5) is at its maximum profit position but should employ more of input A and less of other inputs.

7. Given the data of question 6, if the marginal revenue of input A must be one of the five following dollar amounts, that marginal revenue is:
(1) $1.
(2) $2.
(3) $3.
(4) $4.
(5) $5.

8. Change the information of question 6 in one respect only: the firm operates in conditions of pure (or perfect) competition. Which alternative in question 6 will now be correct?
(1).
(2).
(3).
(4).
(5).

9. In a simple, one-good economy the demand curve for labor is really:
(1) labor's total revenue curve.
(2) the residual left after rent has been paid.
(3) labor's total product curve.
(4) labor's marginal product curve.
(5) labor's average product curve.

10. In a simple, one-good economy with two factors of production—one of fixed supply and one of variable supply—and constant returns to scale:
(1) each factor should earn a return based on average productivity.
(2) the returns to both factors are economic rents.
(3) the sum of the factor shares equals total product.
(4) the area under the total product curve is total output.
(5) both factors should receive the same return.

11. One characteristic of an economic-rent situation is that:
(1) price will increase with an increase in demand but will not decrease with a decrease in demand.
(2) total quantity supplied will increase with an increase in demand but will not decrease with a decrease in demand.
(3) total quantity supplied will not change if price falls.
(4) price will not change with an increase in supply.
(5) none of the above.

12. If land is fixed in total supply but has *many* alternative uses (one of which is tobacco production), then normally a 50 percent tax on rental price of any land used for tobacco production will result in:
(1) a 50 percent increase in the rent which tobacco producers must pay.
(2) a 50 percent decrease in the rent paid by users of such land.

(3) a 50 percent decrease in the rent received (net) by owners of such land.
(4) no change in amount of rent paid or received.
(5) none of these consequences.

13. If supply is perfectly inelastic with respect to price, and if there should be a decrease in total demand, then:
(1) quantity supplied will not be reduced, thus causing price to fall more than it otherwise would.
(2) quantity supplied will not be reduced, thus causing price to fall less than it otherwise would.
(3) quantity supplied will fall, thus causing price to fall more than it otherwise would.
(4) quantity supplied will fall, thus causing price to fall less than it otherwise would.
(5) none of these results will occur.

14. If a productive input has just one single employment (i.e., there is only one commodity it can help to produce), then the price paid to it:
(1) will tend to fall below the normal competitive level, because of the absence of competitive bidding.
(2) will be a cost to each of its separate users, but not a cost to the whole community or society.
(3) should not be counted as a cost by each of its separate users, although it will still be a cost to the whole community or society.
(4) will be a cost both to its separate users and to the whole community or society.
(5) will not be a cost either to its separate users or to the whole community.

15. It would be correct to say that economic rent is not a cost of production because:
(1) it is not a payment to a factor of production that actually makes a contribution to the output of finished goods.
(2) the suppliers of the input in question can receive the same price for employment in one occupation as they can in another.
(3) the rent payment in question is really a payment for buildings or improvements to the land, not for the use of the land itself.
(4) when this factor is used for the production of good A (e.g.), its employment does not entail any sacrifice of any other good B.
(5) competition among the suppliers will continually tend to push the price of this factor toward zero.

16. Henry George's explanation of the prevalence of poverty:
(1) assumes that the land supply curve is perfectly or almost perfectly inelastic with respect to price.
(2) finds the explanation of poverty in the multiplicity of taxes imposed on the poor by the capitalist class through the agency of government.
(3) is essentially the same as the Marxist analysis of the exploitation of workers by capitalist manufacturers.
(4) is based on the assumption that supply curves for many scarce inputs are backward-bending, so that increased quantities of these inputs will be supplied if prices are lowered, not raised.
(5) is not correctly described by any of these statements.

17. The verdict of economic analysis on rent payments is (in part) that:
(1) unless competitive rent payments are made, society's resources cannot be allocated properly into employment.
(2) the more elastic with respect to price an input's supply is, the more its rental payments should be taxed.
(3) it still is correct, broadly speaking, to say that rent does not enter into the cost of production.
(4) the allocation of resources tends to be distorted by the fact that certain input supplies are inelastic with respect to price.
(5) the more inelastic with respect to price an input's supply is, the more its rental payments should be taxed.

18. If we say that "the supply curve of input A is perfectly inelastic with respect to price," we are most likely to mean, if speaking correctly, that its supply curve will be perfectly inelastic when set against the demand curve of:
(1) any single user only.
(2) any single class of users (i.e., any single industry) only.
(3) all its users combined only.
(4) any single user or any single class of users, but not when set against the demand curve of all users combined.
(5) any of the above—i.e., it will be perfectly price inelastic no matter what demand curve it is set against.

19. Ramsey taxes:
(1) are higher the more inelastic demand happens to be.
(2) frequently run into the notion of equity because necessities tend to be inelastically demanded.
(3) are lower the more elastic supply happens to be.
(4) are computed to minimize the loss in consumer surplus and maximize tax revenue.
(5) all of the above.

20. The "tragedy of the commons" is, among the following list of examples, best illustrated by:
(1) the proliferation of fast-food hamburger joints.
(2) the overfishing of the Georges Bank.
(3) the development of a shopping center on the town commons.
(4) the poisoning of Harvard students on the "Commons."
(5) the overpricing of sweatshirts at the Yale "Co-op."

SUGGESTED ANSWER TO QUESTIONS IN THE TEXT: Chapter 27

1. Marginal product [in units of corn per (e.g.) hour of labor on the farm] is the increased yield that was generated by the last hour worked; marginal revenue product is the dollar value of that last increment. *MRP* should be set equal to price because profits could be increased by adjusting employment if it is not. If $MRP >$ price, e.g., then increasing employment by 1 unit would raise more extra revenue than it would cost. If $MRP <$ price, then decreasing employment by 1 unit would save more expense than it would sacrifice in revenue. In either case, when MRP is not equal to price, profits can be improved.

2. Grain, transportation, etc.
3. See Figure TQ27-1.

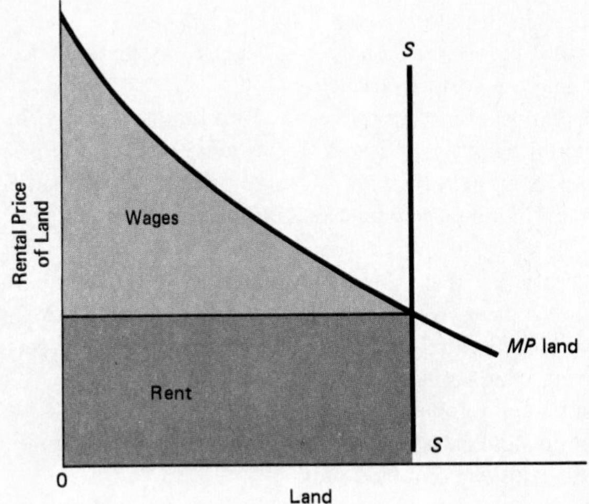

Figure TQ 27-1

4. **a.** Average product is output per worker; for *MP*, see answer 1.
   b. Input contributions to production are interdependent.
   c. Should pay according to marginal product; the *total* share paid to labor could be total product less the cost of raw material if that exhausts the lists of inputs, but this does *not* tell how to distribute the share among individuals.
   d. Only in perfect competition is $P = MR$; $MRP = MR \times MP$.
5. Average real wages equal TP/L. If TP increases at a rate g_{TP} and labor supply increases at a rate g_L, then average real wages increase at a rate $(g_{TP} - g_L) > 0$.
6. Inelastic supply means that the price is determined where demand matches that supply. If the price of some product (X) employing a factor (A) of fixed supply is high (because of high demand X), then the derived demand for A is high; its price is thus high, determined by the price of X. Should the supply of A increase, though, its price should fall along the given derived demand curve, reducing the cost of employing A in the production of X, and thereby allowing the price of X to fall.
7. They would pay it—after swearing at the referees.
8. Pay marginal (revenue) products—that is the point. Given constant returns to scale, total product is exhausted.
9. Question 18 of the *Study Guide* should help here.
10. Distance *CB* represents overuse—traffic jams, excessive automobile emissions, etc. There is a social cost to this congestion. The appropriate toll during the congested period is \$0.10 per vehicle-mile (distance *CE*). The cost of using the highway during the peak period would then reflect its scarcity. People who have to use the highway during the peak time for reasons worth, on the margin, more than \$0.10 per vehicle-mile would be helped; others would be hurt—overpaying to use the highway or adjusting the timing of their travel.
11. See question 16 in the *Study Guide*.

CHAPTER 28

WAGES AND THE LABOR MARKET

Wages are, perhaps, the most important prices determined by the operation of a mixed economy. Total payments for wages and salaries account for over 75 percent of the national income of the United States, and that percentage is typical of developed, Western economies. Despite their importance, though, wages are just prices—prices determined by the interaction of supply and demand schedules in very special markets, to be sure, but simple prices nonetheless. It is the variation in economic structure across these markets that piques an economist's interest.

Chapter 28 introduces you to the scope of this variability. Why? To explain why real wages are so much higher in the United States and Western Europe than they are elsewhere around the world. To explain why wages and salaries differ so much across the populations of individual countries. And to explain the contribution of discrimination to that intracountry variation.

Completing your work on this chapter, therefore, you will have not only gained some insight into these fundamental issues of wage determination but also achieved the following more specific objectives.

LEARNING OBJECTIVES

1. Use a simple homogeneous model of a labor market to explain why wages can differ so dramatically from one country to another.

2. Explain the determinants of both the supply of labor and the demand for labor, noting in particular the reasons why the curve for labor might actually bend backward toward lower supplies as the real wage climbs above some critical value.

3. Understand the various economic reasons why wages can differ so dramatically from one type of occupation to another: compensating wage differentials, quality differences, elements of economic rent, the existence of noncompeting groups, and discrimination.

4. Present and evaluate critically the "iron law of wages" advanced by both Malthus and Marx (for different reasons), as well as the "lump-of-labor" fallacy embraced by some labor unions in time of trouble.

5. Relate the scope of discrimination in the United States and the empirical evidence of its manifestation in wage differentials. Provide a brief overview of the implications of the Equal Pay Act of 1963 and the Civil Rights Act of 1964.

6. Construct a model of discrimination based on noncompeting markets, and trace the effect of eliminating the discrimination on real wages and total income (GNP).

7. Understand the notion of comparable worth, and explain how imposing a system of mandatory comparable worth might affect the efficient operation of labor markets.

Although wages vary across the populations of most countries, the general wage level in the United States has risen markedly over the past century. This growth in real purchasing power has been supported by increases in the real wages paid to virtually every category of labor. Question 1 refreshes your memory about the meaning of the difference between the real wage and the nominal wage.

1. a. Real wages are (pick one):

(1) the same thing as nominal wages.

(2) nominal wages after allowing for tax and other withholdings deducted from such wages.

(3) nominal wages in relation to the consumer price level—i.e., what nominal wages can buy in real goods.

b. Between 1965 and 1985 in a certain country, (1) money wages tripled and (2) the consumer-goods price index rose from 400 to 600. It follows that real wages *(did not rise at all / rose by a factor of 1½ / doubled / tripled / more than tripled).*

c. We say that, other things equal, an increase in population would lower wage rates because of the diminishing-returns law.

COMPARATIVE WAGE RATES

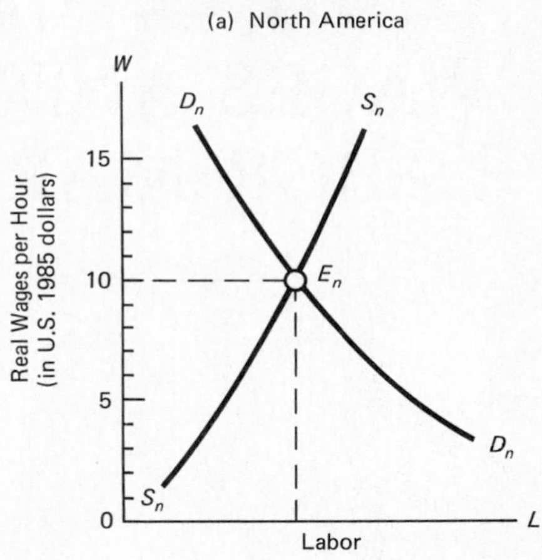

Figure 28-1

We mean by this that an increase in the labor force would lower wage rates (pick one):

(1) even if there were a corresponding increase in the available supply of other inputs such as raw materials and capital goods.

(2) with the supply of other inputs and technology held constant.

---

a. **(3)** **b.** doubled **c.** **(2)**

2. **a.** Figure 28-1 provides some insight into why real wages in North America are so much higher than they are in South America. From the units on the graph, in fact, it would appear that the real wage in North America is *(2 / 2 1/2 / 3)* times larger. One key to this difference is that *(the supply-of-labor curve is so much higher in the South American panel / the demand-for-labor curve is so much higher in the North America panel / the demand-for-labor curve is so much higher in the South America panel)*. Inasmuch as the demand-for-labor curve is a *(potential / derived / product)* demand curve, there are at least three reasons why it should be so positioned in panel **(a)** relative to panel **(b)**. List them below:

(1) ______________________

(2) ______________________

(3) ______________________

b. Each of these has the effect of raising the productivity of North American labor and thus the wage that employers are willing to pay. The demand curve is, nonetheless, downward-sloping because *(the marginal product of labor declines as employment increases / the price of output declines as output and thus employment increases)*.

---

a. 2 ½; the demand-for-labor curve is so much higher in the North America panel; derived **(1)** more resources in North America **(2)** more advanced technology in North America **(3)** more skilled labor force in North America **b.** Both of the answers given contribute to the downward slope of the derived demand curve.

3. The supply of labor has at least three major determinants. List them below:

(a.) ______________________

(b.) ______________________

(c.) ______________________

Based upon the supply and demand curves depicted in Figure 28-2, indicate in the spaces provided the likely effect on the real wage of each of the following economic adjustments. Denote an increase by (+), a reduction by (−), and no change by (0).

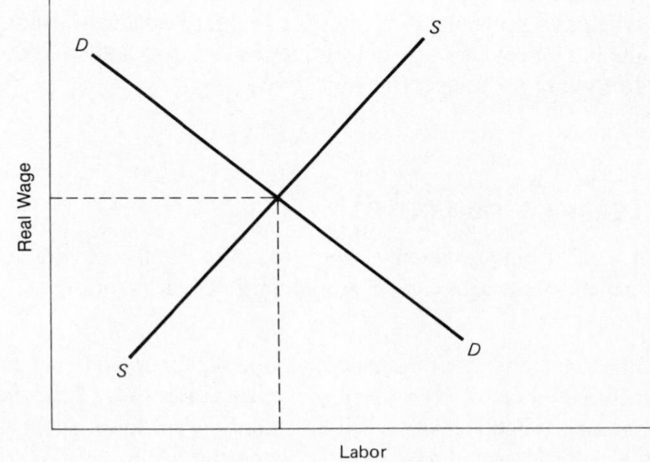

Figure 28-2

(1) an increase in the working population . . . (________)

(2) a move toward shorter workweeks . . . . . . (________)

(3) An increase in labor-force participation by women . . . . (______)

(4) passage of stronger child labor laws . . . . (______)

(5) restriction of certain types of people from employment . . . . (______)

(6) a large wave of immigrants who all want to work . . . . (______)

Buried in your answers to these wage questions are the answers to questions like: *(a)* Why do labor unions push for shorter workweeks? *(b)* Why does labor fear opening U.S. borders to anyone who wants to come? *(c)* Why do some drag their feet in the fight against discrimination on personal economic grounds?

---

a. population **b.** labor-force participation **c.** hours worked per week **(1)** – (because supply curve would shift right) **(2)** + (because supply curve would shift left) **(3)** – (because supply curve would shift right) **(4)** + (because supply curve would shift left) **(5)** + (because supply curve would shift left) **(6)** – (because supply curve would shift right)

4. a. Suppose that the hourly wage offered to you rises. You have some freedom of choice as to the number of hours you may work per day or week. In these circumstances, you could, if you wished, work (pick one or more):

(1) the same number of hours and earn more daily or weekly income.

(2) more hours and earn more income.

(3) fewer hours and earn the same income.

(4) fewer hours and earn more income.

b. The fact that you may choose any one of the four alternatives of part **a** indicates the opposite and conflicting pulls of *substitution effect* and *income effect*.

When you are offered a higher wage for each hour worked, you are then sacrificing more money income than before for each hour you do *not* work; i.e., the opportunity cost of leisure is climbing. The higher hourly wage is an inducement to work *(more / fewer)* hours per day or week because "leisure (not working) has become more expensive." This by itself is the substitution effect. It inclines a worker to give up some *(working hours in favor of leisure / leisure hours in favor of work).*

c. However, leisure time is (for most people) a desirable thing: as real incomes rise, they want more of it. The offer of a higher hourly wage makes more leisure possible *(with / without)* the sacrifice of any income. The pull of the income effect is toward *(fewer / more)* working hours and correspondingly *(fewer / more)* hours of leisure.

d. For example, suppose that you decide to work 40 hours weekly given a $6 hourly wage, for a weekly income of $240. With a $10 wage, though, you could choose to earn $350 per week by working *(35 / 40 / 45)* hours. Were that the case, the *(substitution / income)* effect would have dominated.

---

a. All four are possible. **b.** more; leisure hours in favor of work **c.** without; fewer; more **d.** 35; income

The opposing pulls of income and substitution effects on labor supply give rise to the possibility of a backward-bending supply curve (of the sort illustrated later in Figure 28-6). As wages climb, the supply curve will display its usual positive slope (and positive wage elasticity) only if the substitution effect (which pushes people toward working more) dominates the income effect (which tempts people to work less). If the income effect dominates, as it may for high wages, then an increase in wages might actually inspire a reduction in the quantity of labor supplied.

This possibility raises the obvious empirical question: "Well, which is it? Is the slope positive or negative?" As usual, the answer is, "It depends." The evidence for adult males in the United States suggests a wage elasticity in the range of −0.1 to −0.2; i.e., a 10 percent increase in the real wage should be expected to cause a 1 to 2 percent *reduction* in the quantity of labor supplied. For adult females and teenagers in the United States, though, widely varied estimates suggest a positive correlation between wages and labor supply. Taking an average of these disparate values over the entire U.S. economy, most economists expect a wage elasticity for the over-16-year-old working population to lie somewhere between 0.0 (a vertical supply curve) and +0.2.

5. The term "economic rent" is not usually applied to labor. But in instances like Babe Ruth in the good old days of baseball and "Dr. J" in the good old days of the Philadelphia 76ers, it applies. Babe Ruth was paid the fantastic sum (for the 1920s) of $80,000 annually for playing baseball. Had diminished competition among baseball-club owners forced him to do so, he would probably have played for $10,000 annually. His unique skill seems to have been in baseball alone, so it is unlikely that any alternative employment open to him would have paid anything like $80,000. (If the Babe played today, he could earn substantial supplementary income by extolling the benefits of (e.g.) certain types of underwear in commercials, but that fact does not alter the reasoning. He would be paid this *only because of* his status as a baseball player earning a king's ransom every year.)

This means that Babe Ruth's labor supply curve to baseball clubs would be perfectly inelastic with respect to wage or salary prices (pick one):

(1) from $80,000 annually to zero annually.

(2) from $80,000 annually to some figure such as $8000 annually.

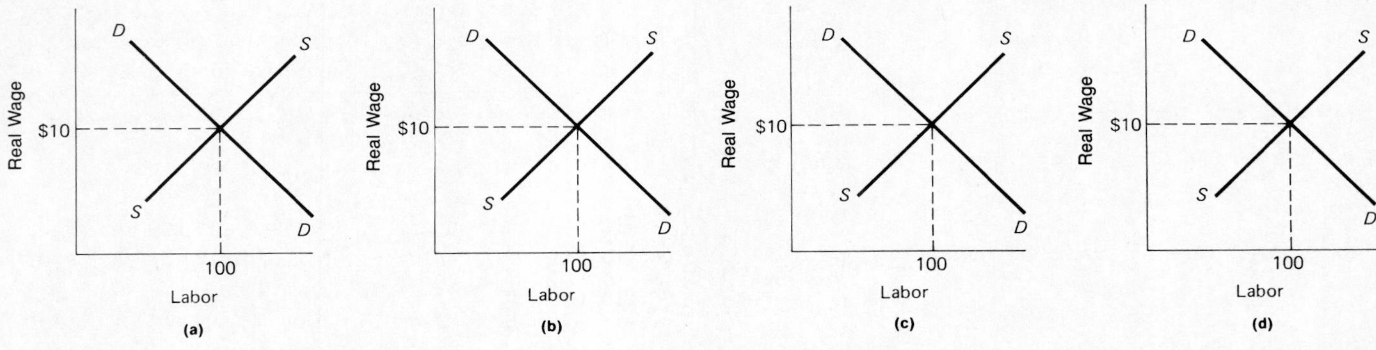

Figure 28-3

(3) only at $80,000 annually; it would be less than perfectly elastic at *any* lower figure.

---

(2) (It would cut to the vertical axes at the opportunity cost of not doing something else and playing amateur ball only in the evenings and on the weekends.)

6. There are four panels in Figure 28-3, one each for the four parts to this question listed below. In each part, draw a new supply and/or demand curve in the corresponding panel to represent the effect of the change indicated, and predict the direction that the change will push the real wage and employment. For example, if one of the parts asked you to consider an increase in the supply of labor, then you would draw a new supply curve to the right of the existing one and predict that wages would fall (−) and employment would climb (+). Record your predictions on the table provided below.

a. The job in question becomes more onerous than usual, and people demand compensation for its additional burdens.

b. The job becomes really very specialized, and only 10 people can accomplish the task that it requires.

c. Education and training improve the quality of the labor employed.

d. The job market is suddenly cut in half because of noncompeting discrimination.

Part	Effect on Employment	Effect on Wages
a	________	________
b	________	________
c	________	________
d	________	________

a. Draw the new supply curve above and to the left of *SS* because people are demanding more money to provide this type of labor service. Quantity of labor falls (−) and wages increase (+)—an example of compensating differential in the making.

b. Draw the new supply curve vertical at 10. Quantity of labor falls to 50 (−) and wages increase (+)—an example of collecting rent.

c. Draw the new demand curve above and to the right of *DD* because education and training have increased the marginal (revenue) product of labor and thus its derived demand. Quantity of labor and wages both increase (+ and +).

d. Same answer as for part **a**, but exaggerated—now an example of discrimination creating noncompeting groups.

7. The **iron law of wages** idea evolved in the arguments of both Thomas Robert Malthus and Karl Marx (although for quite different reasons). The essence of the iron-law idea is that wages tend to be pushed to the *(competitive / minimum-subsistence / marginal product)* level. (Malthus' argument rested on the belief that population would increase until this level was reached; Marx's, on the belief that this outcome was part of capitalist exploitation of the labor force.)

Both theory and experience have led most economists to *(agreement / qualified agreement / disagreement)* with the idea. Figure 28-4 shows why. With the wage set at w^*, unemployment *(would / would not)* exist, and the operation of the labor market might eventually push the wage *(up / down)* to equilibrium at *(*w^* */* w_E */* w_M*)*. There would, however, be no way for the market to push the wage down to the subsistence

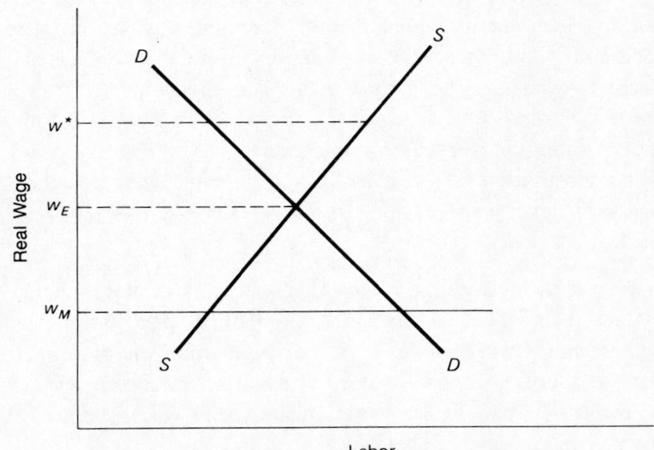

Figure 28-4

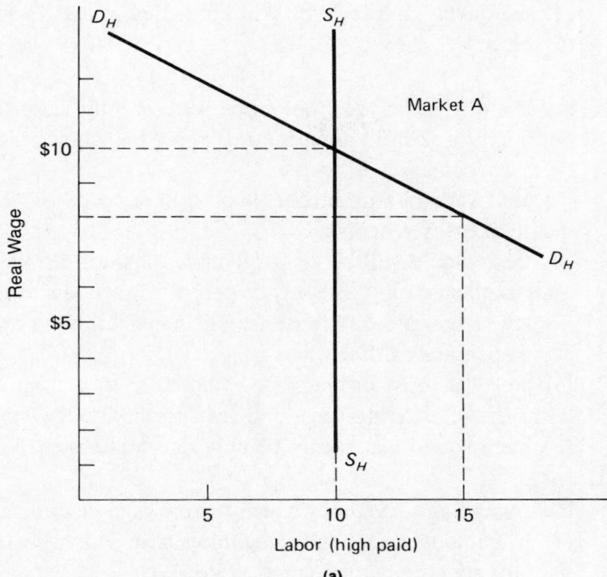

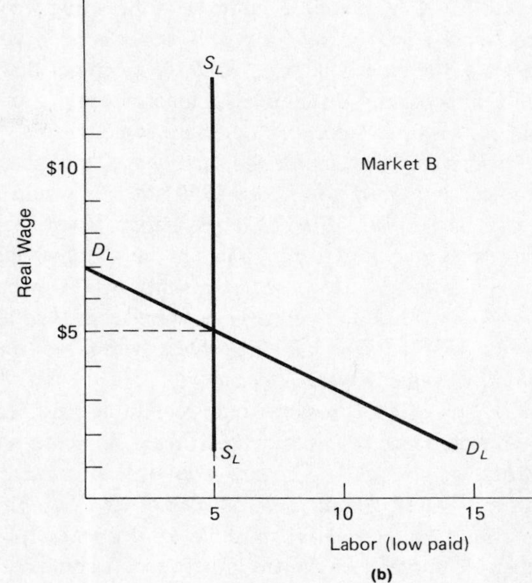

Figure 28-5

level because, while employers would love to see that happen, there would be *(excess supply / excess demand)* for labor at w_M that would push the wage back up.

---

minimum-subsistence; disagreement; would; down; w_E; excess demand

8. a. Consult Figure 28-5. It shows two labor markets separated by discrimination. Demand curves in both are indicated with *DD* notation; both have the same slopes. The supply curves are vertical at 10 and 5, respectively. If that discrimination were to lapse, then the demand curve in panel **(a)** would apply to everyone. The result would be *(an increase / a reduction)* in the wage paid to those initially alone in market A from

$______ to $______. This change would be caused by *(diminishing marginal productivity / diminishing labor utility / increasing productivity)*. At the same time, those who were initially confined to market B would see their wage *(climb / fall)*

from $______ to $______, a change that can be attributed to *(diminishing marginal productivity / increased productivity / increased labor utility)*. The net effect would be an increase in the dollar value of output (GNP, if this were a macro model) of $*(10 / 15 / 20)*.

b. If the derived demand curve in market A were extremely inelastic, how would your answers to the qualitative parts of the above paragraph change?

---

a. a reduction; 10; 8; diminishing marginal productivity; climb; 5; 8; increased productivity; 15 [Superimpose the trapezoid under D_LD_L in panel **(b)** over the D_HD_H trapezoid from $L = 10$ to $L = 15$; there remains a rectangle 5 units of labor wide and $3 high that reflects GNP gain.] **b.** If the curve D_HD_H were sufficiently inelastic [sufficiently vertical through (10, $10)], then the addition of five workers from market B could lower the wage below $5. All five would not move, if that were the case, and the equilibrium wage in both markets would still exceed $5.

Notice, in passing, that the analysis of question 8 applies to all types of discrimination—discrimination caused by geography (wage differentials across countries), discrimination caused by sex or race, discrimination caused by noncompeting groupings within the larger labor market.

9. The notion of **comparable worth**—that people with similar value to a company should receive equal pay despite the conditions of their respective labor markets—has been advanced by some as a solution to the sorts of discrimination that are not covered well by either the Equal Pay Act of 1963 (stipulating that men and women doing the same job should get the same pay) or the Civil Rights Act of 1964 (outlawing discrimination in hiring, firing, and employment). Comparable worth is fine in theory, but it runs into some problems even on theoretical grounds when placed in the context of operating labor markets.

To see this, suppose that company XYZ employs two different types of labor, A and B, who perform services of comparable worth for XYZ. Suppose further that the going weekly wage in the local labor market for type-A labor is $250 while the going wage for type-B labor is $350. Why might that be the case? Compensating differentials, noncompeting groups, discrimination, historical precedent, etc. are some reasons.

If XYZ wants to pay A and B the same wage, then it must make a choice. If it were to choose $250, then it would see no change in its *(A-type / B-type)* labor market but it would experience *(excess supply / excess demand)* in its other labor market; it would (*not be able to hire as many type-A workers as / not be able to hire as many type-B workers as / be able to hire more type-A workers than / be able to hire more type-B workers than*) it wanted. Were it to choose $350, though, then its *(A-type / B-type)* labor market would remain in equilibrium and it would experience *(excess supply / excess demand)* in the other. It would *(not be able to hire as many type-A workers as / not be able to hire as many type-B workers as / be able to hire more type-A workers than / be able to hire more type-B workers than)* it wanted. Anywhere in between, a combination of both circumstances would occur.

A-type; excess demand; not be able to hire as many type-B workers as; B-type; excess supply; be able to hire more type-A workers than

QUIZ: Multiple Choice

1. The concept of "noncompeting groups in the labor market" is considered useful in explaining:
(1) structural unemployment.
(2) wage differentials among different categories of labor.
(3) the lack of mobility among older workers.
(4) the impact of wage increases in unionized sectors of the economy upon nonunionized sectors.
(5) why wage rates in certain industries have risen faster than the average.

2. Imperfect competition in a labor market could be indicated by a situation in which:
(1) one firm makes wage determinations for an entire industry.
(2) different wages are paid for different jobs in order to compensate for differences in risk.
(3) different wages are paid for different jobs because the jobs have different requirements.
(4) the wages paid for certain jobs fall into the category of economic-rent payments.
(5) the excess of one wage rate over another is a compensating differential.

3. Determinants of the supply of labor for a given economy include:
(1) the size of its population.
(2) the rate of participation of its population in the labor force.
(3) the standard or legislated length of the workweek.
(4) the quality and level of skill embodied in the work force.
(5) all of the above.

4. If everyone in the labor force were exactly alike (i.e., no difference in skills or competence), and if the labor market were perfectly competitive, then:
(1) any wage-rate differences would have to be explained as qualitative differentials.
(2) there would still be a considerable range of different wage rates explained only in terms of perceived differences in skill.
(3) any wage-rate differences could nonetheless be explained as compensating differentials.
(4) any wage-rate differences would have to be explained in terms of the differing wage policies adopted by different firms.
(5) there would necessarily be only one wage rate.

5. According to Malthus's analysis of wage determination:
(1) it is impossible for either employers or unions to fix wage rates at anything but the competitive level.
(2) employers will be able to force wages down to the equilibrium level by maintaining a high degree of unemployment.
(3) the long-run supply-of-labor curve is a horizontal line at the wage level at which workers will just be able to maintain and reproduce themselves.
(4) the money wage received by workers must always equal the real wage.
(5) employers will be able to force wages down to the subsistence level by maintaining a high degree of unemployment.

6. A trade union which wants simultaneously to raise wages for its members and to maintain as much employment as possible for them will be helped most by:
(1) an elastic derived demand for labor.
(2) an elastic supply of labor.
(3) an inelastic demand for the finished product.
(4) a perfectly competitive labor market.
(5) a perfectly competitive product market.

7. The substitution effect, applied to a worker's decision to change or not change the number of hours worked daily when offered a different hourly wage, refers specifically to which of the following statements?
(1) If the price offered labor rises, then the worker's disposition is to buy better but more costly goods, hence to work longer hours.
(2) A general increase in wages tends to produce a general rise in consumer prices, which cancels out the worker's real-income gain.
(3) Leisure (nonwork) time is desirable, so a worker's normal inclination is to choose more leisure in response to any rise in real income.
(4) The cost of working is leisure (nonwork) time sacrificed; hence, if the wage offered labor falls, leisure becomes relatively less expensive.

(5) Any labor cost increase prompts employers to try to substitute capital for labor in production.

8. Which alternative in question 7 would be correct had that question referred to the income effect, not to the substitution effect?
(1).
(2).
(3).
(4).
(5).

9. The "lump-of-labor" viewpoint is essentially a belief that:
(1) the quality of a hand-crafted product is inherently superior to that of a machine-made product.
(2) the supply of labor will not vary significantly with the price that is offered for it; i.e., the labor supply curve is almost perfectly inelastic.
(3) labor effort is the ultimate measure of value, and the prices of goods should reflect the amount of labor effort that went into making those goods.
(4) any commodity embodies a fixed quantity of labor (direct or indirect) in its manufacture, regardless of the production technique used.
(5) there is only a finite and fixed amount of useful work to be done.

10. The viewpoint referred to in question 9 arose principally out of:
(1) the experience of workers in the depression periods.
(2) the clash between income effects and substitution effects.
(3) the experience of workers in inflationary periods.
(4) the fact that the total labor supply curve is highly inelastic with respect to price.
(5) the belief that the total fund of money out of which wages must be paid is essentially fixed in amount even in a growing economy.

11. Figure 28-6 illustrates a backward-bending, or backward-rising, labor supply curve and four possible demand curves. If the demand curve were to change from position 1 to position 2:
(1) the substitution effect would dominate over the income effect.
(2) the substitution effect and income effect would cancel one another out.
(3) the income effect would dominate over the substitution effect.
(4) the income effect and the substitution effect would work in the same direction.
(5) none of these statements would be correct.

12. Referring to the same figure, if the demand curve were to move from position 2 to position 3, which alternative in question 11 would be correct?

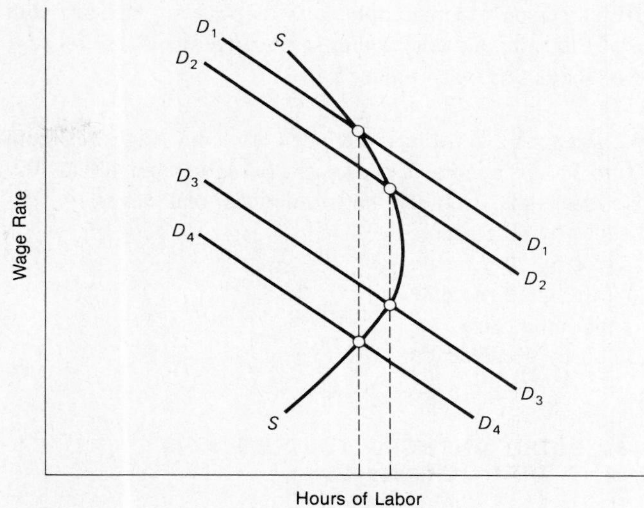

Figure 28-6

(1).
(2).
(3).
(4).
(5).

13. Again referring to this figure, if the demand curve were to move from position 3 to position 4, which alternative would be correct?
(1).
(2).
(3).
(4).
(5).

14. Still referring to this figure, if the demand curve were to move from position 4 to position 3, which alternative would be correct?
(1).
(2).
(3).
(4).
(5).

15. To say that there is an economic-rent element in a person's income means that:
(1) this income comes at least in part from property ownership rather than from the labor supply.
(2) this income exceeds what it would be were the labor market perfectly competitive.
(3) if the price offered for this person's labor were increased, he or she would want to reduce the number of daily hours worked.
(4) this income is much above average, but is the result of some relatively unique natural talent.

(5) this person's labor supply curve is perfectly inelastic with respect to price, at least within some range of prices, because he or she is somewhat unique.

16. Between two periods, the index of money wages fell from 600 to 540. The index of consumer prices fell from 400 to 300. This means that, between the two periods, real wages:
(1) rose by 50 percent.
(2) rose by 20 percent.
(3) rose by 10 percent.
(4) did not change.
(5) fell by 20 percent.

SUGGESTED ANSWERS TO QUESTIONS IN THE TEXT: Chapter 28

1. Review the definitions. Examples: compensating differentials—high-altitude steel welders make more than "on-the-ground" welders; economic rent (applied to labor)—Don Mattingly and soon David Cone; noncompeting groups—college professors and auto mechanics; etc.

2. Relative size of supply; relative size of markets; relative productivity of labor. India should try to invest in technology that improves labor productivity in the production of items the world wants and allows, perhaps, for economies of scale.

3. Less imperfect competition should mean smaller differentials. So should mobility that breaks down the geographical barriers to entry into high-paying labor markets. More equal opportunity for education should make the distribution of productivity more equal and thus diminish wage differentials. Less demand for "star product" should lower their rent.

4. Increased supply means wage should fall and the quantity supplied should climb along a sloping derived demand curve. Number of hours worked is a determinant of labor supply, just like population size.

5. They all serve as barriers either to the markets or to the places and connections of business transactions (clubs).

6. A number of examples can be listed, such as education paths by which women can secure the entry qualifications needed for high-paying jobs. There are lots of possible answers here; one is probably discussed in today's newspaper.

7. Lump of labor. It would lower real wage (measured, e.g., by the week) of some unit that reflects less work supplied by each worker even if the hourly wage were maintained.

8. Fairness versus the efficiency of markets. Fairness would probably work through comparable worth to bring the high-paying male compensations down as the lower-paying compensations rose. Thus, the potential division in support.

9. Consult Figure TQ28-1. Add S_b to S_w in panel **(a)** and see that the real wage falls along D_wD_w from E_w to A; the real wage for whites therefore falls, but the real wage for blacks climbs because their productivity is higher when they are hired along derived demand D_wD_w. Superimposing the total product of blacks in panel **(b)**—area OcE_ba—onto panel **(a)** starting at point C, it is clear that their increased total product against D_wD_w—are $CcAE_w$—exceeds their total product D_bD_b by the shaded area.

10. If the supply of people who are indifferent to certain risks is large compared with the demand for people willing to assume those risks, then the wage differential can be small and still attract enough people. Panel **(a)** of Figure TQ28-2 shows this against a "usual" wage of w_u; the differential appears to be in the order of 10 percent. If the supply of risk takers is small for some occupations of particularly large hazard, though, then those few will be able to demand very high compensation and produce a large differential. Panel **(b)** shows this, with a differential of nearly 100 percent.

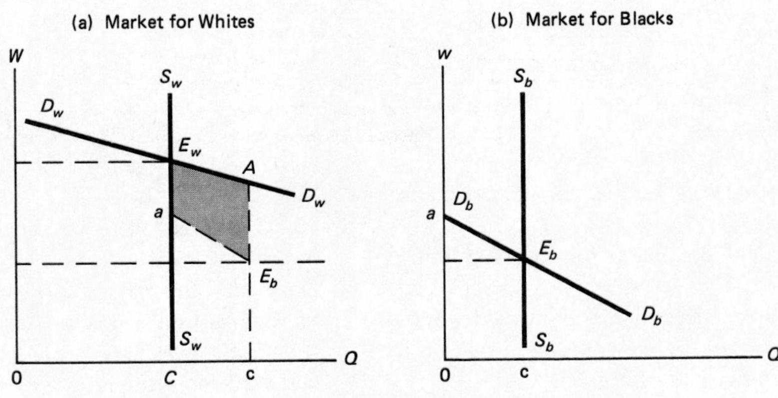

Figure TQ28-1

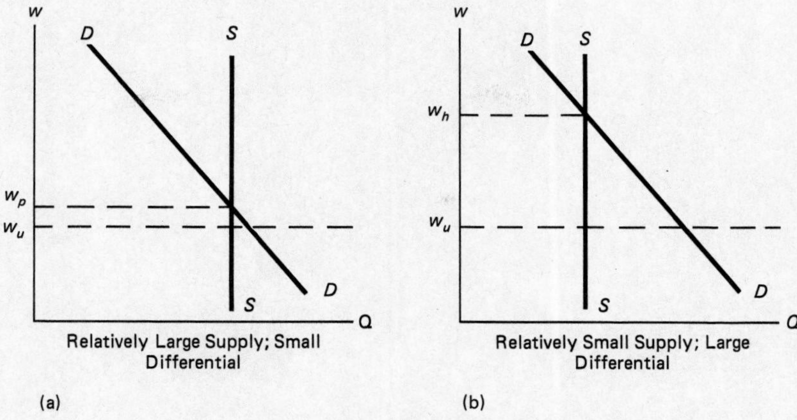

Figure TQ28-2

CHAPTER 29

LABOR UNIONS AND COLLECTIVE BARGAINING

Labor is not owned; it is "rented." This was one of the implications of the Civil War in the United States, and it is an implication that has had far-reaching effects on the labor markets of this country. Because labor is "rented," there must exist, between management and labor, some sort of contract outlining compensation schedules, work rules, procedures, and avenues for voicing grievances in both directions. The first part of Chapter 29 conducts a review of the role of labor unions in the process of forming these contracts. Their history is briefly chronicled, as is the role of government in shaping that history. So is their overall organization. The result is a thorough introduction into the issues surrounding unions before a cursory analysis of how unions try to increase wages is conducted in section B.

Having completed your work in this chapter, you will have accomplished the following objectives.

LEARNING OBJECTIVES

1. Review the history of the labor movement in the United States. Understand the roles played by industrial unions and craft unions in that history. Describe the extent of union power in the 1980s in terms of both the size of membership and its influence beyond that membership.

2. List the three layers of structure that mark contemporary unionism, and discuss the evolution of each.

3. Outline the changing mood of the federal government in its treatment of unions. Cite the major pieces of legislation that were either applied to unions or written for unions [Sherman Antitrust Act (1890), Clayton Antitrust Act (1914), Railway Labor Act (1926), Norris-LaGuardia Act (1932), Wagner Act (NLRA, 1935), Fair Labor Standards Act (1938), Taft-Hartley Act (1947), etc.]. Characterize the current governmental view of unions.

4. Understand why collective bargaining (including negotiation about the economic package, work rules, union security, etc.), strikes, deregulation, foreign competition, and productivity restraint are issues of enormous concern among both scholars of the labor movement and members of the labor movement.

5. Explain how wage stickiness can be attributed to the actions of both sides of contemporary labor markets.

6. Explain how unions might try to increase wages by (1) restricting supply, (2) increasing demand, (3) negotiating higher wages explicitly, and (4) fighting monopsony power.

7. Summarize the aggregate effect of 60 years of union activity on (1) the relative wage of union members, (2) the share of GNP paid to labor, and (3) unemployment.

Nineteen million Americans belong to unions—about one-sixth of the adult labor force. The employment arrangements of many millions more nonunion members are dictated by union agreements about wages, hours, and work conditions. Even though the union share of the labor force has been in decline for nearly four decades (from more than 25 percent in 1950 to the current 16 percent), these data clearly show that union power is still a major economic force in the United States—it is a force that must be recognized.

1. If all or most workers within a large plant belong to the same union, this would most probably be classified as *(a craft / an industrial)* union. If all or most union members have the same occupation, or closely allied occupations, this would most probably be classed as *(a craft / an industrial)* union.

---

an industrial; a craft

2. Note in the blanks provided whether the indicated efforts should cause union power (reflected specifically in the ability to maintain or increase high wages) to increase (I), decrease (D), or remain unchanged (U). When a particular industry is identified, presume that the question pertains to the union employed in that industry.

a. deregulation in the airline industry . . . . (________)

b. imposition of quotas to limit the importing of Japanese automobiles . . . . (________)

c. increase in auto sales . . . . (________)

d. elimination of import quotas . . . . (________)

e. increase in unemployment as part of the business cycle . . . . (________)

f. election of conservatives to the National Labor Relations Board . . . . (________)

g. repeal of the National Labor Relations Act . . (________)

h. doubling of OPEC oil prices . . . . (________)

i. eradication of the air-traffic controllers' union by the President . . . . (________)

j. widespread adoption of robot technology . . . . (________)

---

a. D (More competition in the product market tends to reduce prices and thus the derived demand for labor; it is therefore harder for a union to maintain high wages and wage increases.) **b.** I (The opposite of **a**: unions can exploit the market power of the employer even if it is artificially created by government intervention.) **c.** I (success in a unionized industry) **d.** D (the opposite of **b**) **e.** D (Excess supply of labor means that the threat of the layoffs that could accompany high wage settlements is more severe and less attractive to union members.) **f.** D (Conservatives tend to want to diminish union power.) **g.** D (The National Labor Relations Act helped solidify union power; repeal would do the opposite.) **h.** D (Doubling oil prices would weaken the economy, create recession, and make **e** apply.) **i.** D (Successful threats by government to the existence of unions weaken the power of others simply by changing the bargaining climate.) **j.** D (Weakened demand for labor undermines the ability of unions to demand high compensation.)

Several points can be made in light of the answers to question 2. First of all, much of recent history has worked against the power of unions, at least at the source of its traditional power. From the intervention of the President of the United States in the PATCO strike to the composition of the NLRB, the lot of the traditional labor union has declined. Second, general equilibrium effects are rampant in the labor market, so "no change" was the answer to none of the parts of question 2. You are hereby challenged to come up with one significant change in economic circumstances that will not influence the power of some labor union to some degree. Let me know care of Wesleyan University, Middletown, Connecticut.

3. In 1890, a federal act was passed which, for the next 20 years, was used as a weapon against union formation and activity even though the framers of this legislation never envisioned its application to labor markets. In 1914, another bill was passed specifically excluding labor unions from application of the first act. The first of these laws was the ________________ Act, and the second was the ________________ Act.

Sherman; Clayton (perhaps a reality only after the Norris-LaGuardia Act of 1932, given court interpretation)

4. Are the following statements concerning the National Labor Relations Board true or false?

a. On petition from a union claiming to represent a majority of workers, the NLRB can take a secret ballot of the workers to determine if this claim is valid. . . . . *(T / F)*

b. If a majority vote upholds the union claim in part **a**, then the NLRB can require that the employer recognize the union as a collective bargaining agent and deal with it. . . . . . *(T / F)*

c. The NLRB can enter a union-management dispute and seek to mediate the differences. . . . . *(T / F)*

d. If the dispute persists, the NLRB can, on petition to the courts, act as an arbitrator to settle it. . . . . *(T / F)*

e. The NLRB can designate an "unfair labor practice" and, if necessary, take the employer to court to enforce a cease-and-desist order against such practice. . . . . *(T / F)*

---

a. T **b.** T **c.** F **d.** F **e.** T

5. Insert the appropriate number to indicate the federal act which contains the provision or prohibition described. The same number may be used more than once.

1. Clayton Antitrust Act (1914).
2. Fair Labor Standards Act (1938).
3. Railway Labor Act (1926).
4. Norris-La Guardia Act (1932).
5. Sherman Antitrust Act (1890).
6. Taft-Hartley Act (1947).
7. Wagner (National Labor Relations) Act (1935).
8. No federal act contains this provision.

a. Explicitly stated that workers have the right to form unions, to bargain collectively, and to engage in concerted activities for purposes of collective bargaining; set up machinery to protect exercise of these rights by workers . . . . (________)

b. Explicitly accepted the basic promise of collective bargaining . . . . (________)

c. Prohibited the administration of major unions by salaried managers . . . . (________)

d. Prohibited individuals from being members of more than one union . . . . (________)

e. Provided that the attorney general may secure a court injunction to suspend strikes in a "national emergency dispute" (______)

f. Established the National Labor Relations Board to act as watchdog against "unfair labor practices" on the part of employers . . . . (______)

g. Vastly reduced the employer's power to obtain federal court injunctions to break strikes or harass unions . . . . (______)

h. Stated that union activities were *not* to be considered a "conspiracy in restraint of trade" such as would violate the Sherman Antitrust Act . . . . (______)

i. Sharply restricted the closed shop . . . . (______)

j. Established an hourly minimum wage for most workers in occupations involving interstate commerce . . . . . (______)

k. Defined "unfair labor practices" on the part of unions . . . . (______)

l. Prohibited unions from making loans to union officials . . . . (______)

---

a. 7 **b.** 3 **c.** 8 **d.** 8 **e.** 6 **f.** 7 **g.** 4 **h.** 7 **i.** 6 **j.** 2 **k.** 6 **l.** 6

6. Deregulation and foreign competition can diminish the ability of unions to maintain high wages because both *(increase / decrease)* the market power of employers. As long as employers have market power, they can price their products *(above / at / below)* average cost, i.e., *(above / at / below)* the competitive price. Since the wage offered to labor in the competitive labor market model is the multiplicative product of *(the price of output and the marginal utility of labor / the price of output and the marginal product of labor / the price of capital and the marginal product of labor)*, labor can receive a wage that is *(higher than / equal to / lower than)* the competitive wage. If deregulation and foreign competition make the output market more competitive, therefore, they *(increase / reduce)* the ability of labor to derive a higher wage.

---

decrease; above; above; the price of output and the marginal product of labor; higher than; reduce

7. One of the four methods by which a trade union can try to raise wages involves a direct attempt to increase the wage rate. If this path is followed, the most desirable situation from the union's standpoint (to minimize any unemployment arising out of the wage increase) would be to have the derived demand for labor *(elastic / inelastic)* with respect to the wage, and the supply of labor *(elastic / inelastic)*.

---

inelastic; inelastic

8. Which of the following union practices operates primarily by shifting the labor supply curve to the left, and which by moving the derived demand curve for labor to the right? After each, put (S) for supply curve or (D) for demand curve.

a. putting featherbedding rules in local building codes . . . . (______)

b. setting long apprenticeship periods for entrants into the occupation . . . . (______)

c. asking consumers to buy only union-made goods . . . . (______)

d. imposing high initiation fees upon entrants into the occupation . . . . (______)

e. limiting use of labor-saving tools and equipment . . . . (______)

f. agitating for tariff protection . . . . (______)

g. agitating for limitations on immigration . . . . . (______)

---

a. D **b.** S **c.** D **d.** S **e.** D **f.** D **g.** S

9. The four panels of Figure 29-1 illustrate the four ways that unions can try to increase the wage paid to their members. List the four ways below, and identify which of the four panels is the most appropriate representation of each. The original demand and supply curves in each panel are designated *DD* and *SS*; the modified curves created by the union activity are designated *D′D′* and *S′S′* where appropriate.

a. __________________________; Panel (______)

b. __________________________; Panel (______)

c. __________________________; Panel (______)

d. __________________________; Panel (______)

Notice that employment falls in two of the cases and that employment increases in the other two cases.

---

a. restrict supply; (**d**) **b.** raise the standard wage; (**a**) **c.** increase productivity; (**c**) **d.** remove exploitation; (**c**)

10. Two of the means by which unions increase wages also produce larger levels of employment. They are:

____

and __________________________________.

For a given increase in the quantity or labor demanded at every wage, the effect on wages is largest when the supply of labor is *(elastic / inelastic)*. The effect on wages is also largest when the derived demand for labor is *(elastic / inelastic)*.

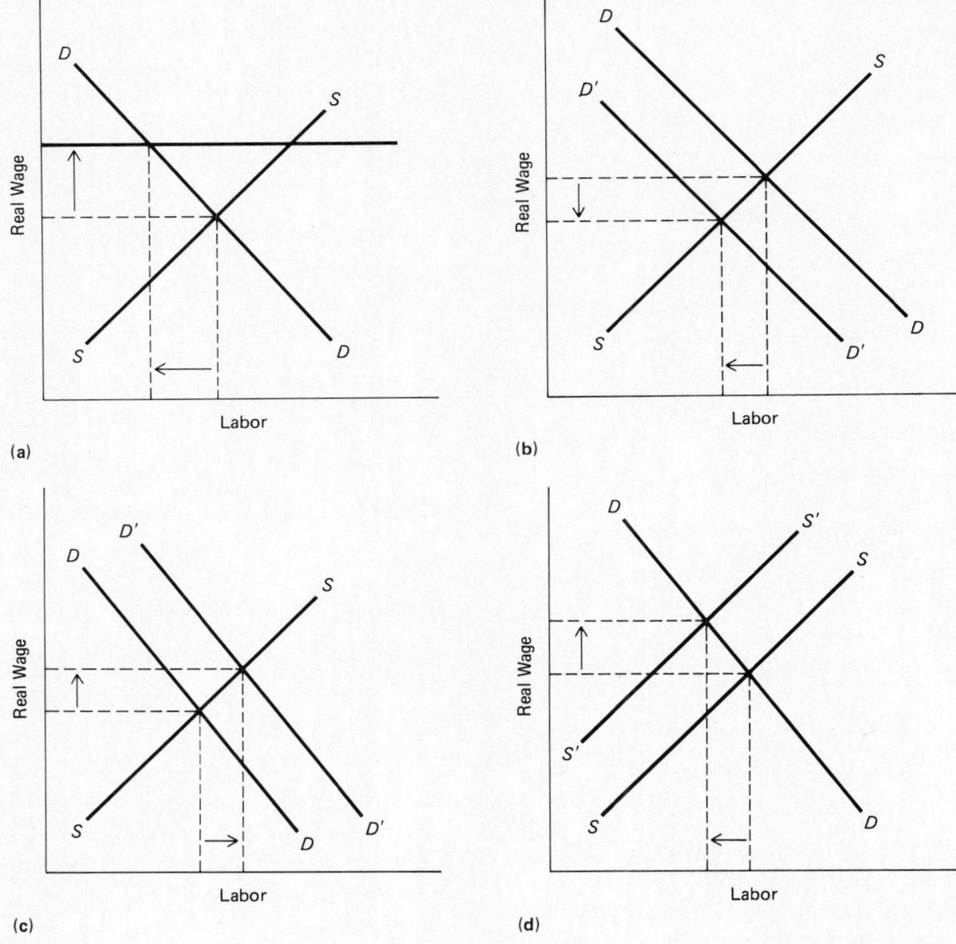

Figure 29-1

The other two means by which unions increase wages can cause employment to fall. They are:

____

and ______________________________ .

The employment effect of either means is largest when the derived demand for labor is *(elastic / inelastic)*. The elasticity of supply affects only the reduced-employment effect of which alternative?

____

In the other case, the elasticity of supply affects the level of *un*employment, instead.

____

increase productivity; remove (reduce) exploitation; inelastic; inelastic; restrict supply; increase standard wage; elastic; restrict supply

QUIZ: Multiple Choice

1. Which of the following statements is accurate?

(1) The membership roles of unions totalled across the United States include approximately 19 million names.

(2) Less than 5 percent of the people employed in each and every manufacturing industry in the United States work under an arrangement negotiated by a union, whether or not they are union members.

(3) Union membership has leveled off recently, after growing for over 50 years.

(4) Union wages tend to be about 50 percent higher than nonunion wages, but the share of GNP devoted to labor has remained remarkably constant over the past 60 years.

(5) All of the above.

2. The term "industrial union" means:

(1) the same thing as a trade union.

(2) a trade union in manufacturing, as opposed to the service trades or agriculture.

(3) a union with members in the same craft throughout industry.

(4) a union whose membership is drawn from all or nearly all the workers in a given industry.

(5) an organization of employers in an industry.

3. Collective bargaining agreements are usually negotiated by:

(1) the federation of national unions.

(2) the local union, but increasingly with the assistance of the federation.
(3) the local union, but increasingly with the assistance of the national union.
(4) the national union, but increasingly with the assistance of the federation.
(5) the national union, but increasingly with the assistance of the local union.

4. According the U.S. federal law, around the year 1910:
(1) labor organizations were considered legal, provided their purpose or activity could not be construed as an attempt to raise wages.
(2) all efforts on the part of labor to organize collectively (i.e., form unions) were still illegal.
(3) labor organizations were considered legal, provided their activity did not involve a conspiracy in restraint of trade or a monopolistic restraint of trade.
(4) all efforts on the part of labor to increase wages, whether they involved union organization or not, were still illegal.
(5) all nonviolent collective bargaining activity was already entirely legal.

5. "Exclusive bargaining agent" refers to:
(1) the craft union principle early adopted by the AFL, whereby each union had complete jurisdiction over workers in its class, and two unions could not conflict in attempting to organize the same workers.
(2) the union recognized by the National Labor Relations Board as exclusively entitled to represent all workers within the group concerned in bargaining with management.
(3) a provision in the Taft-Hartley Act which restrains the union from attempting to bargain on behalf of non-members.
(4) the official who is designated by the union to negotiate with management on behalf of its members.
(5) none of these.

6. One of the important principles by which Samuel Gompers ran the AFL was that:
(1) labor must learn to live within a capitalistic system and realize that it was unrealistic to expect "more and still more."
(2) wherever possible, member national unions should be organized by industry rather than by craft.
(3) although greater emphasis should be placed on business unionism, pro-union government intervention in collective bargaining was to be sought through political action.
(4) the autonomy of each member union with respect to its craft specialty must be clearly recognized.
(5) although labor must learn to live with capitalism, in the long run, effective business unionism would lay the basis for a philosophy of political action.

7. The act generally considered the most important piece of legislation in American labor history, in the sense of marking a real turning point in that history, is:
(1) the Landrum-Griffin Act (1959).
(2) the Wagner Act (1935).
(3) the Sherman Act (1890).
(4) the Fair Labor Standards Act (1938).
(5) the Walsh-Healy Act (1935).

8. One of the duties of the National Labor Relations Board is to:
(1) issue injunctions where needed to prevent strikes in "essential" industries.
(2) exclude unions from legal complaints about "unfair union labor practices."
(3) see that the provision of the Taft-Hartley Act prohibiting the union shop is enforced.
(4) enforce the federal minimum-wage law with respect to interstate commerce.
(5) hold elections to see which union is entitled to act as collective bargaining agent for workers in a plant.

9. If the President wants to suspend a strike that seems to endanger the nation's welfare, he or she:
(1) may apply the "essential industry" provision of the Wagner Act.
(2) may apply the "restraint of trade" provision of the Clayton Act.
(3) may apply the "court injunction" provision of the Taft-Hartley Act.
(4) may apply the "national emergency" provision of the Landrum-Griffin Act.
(5) must simply use the prestige of his office to prevent it, since there is no provision in any federal act which gives him any explicit power toward suspension.

10. Over the past 60 years, the share of GNP devoted to paying labor has:
(1) grown slightly.
(2) more than doubled.
(3) fallen.
(4) been halved.
(5) remained roughly constant.

11. The Taft-Hartley Act (1947), among other things:
(1) prohibited nonwage payments to union representatives by employers.
(2) made the "closed shop" illegal.
(3) was for many years used by the courts to curb union formation and activity.
(4) removed labor unions from the charge of being a "conspiracy in restraint of trade."
(5) charged the National Labor Relations Board with the duty of making sure that employers did not engage in "unfair labor practices."

12. Had question 11 referred to the Clayton Act (1914), which alternative would have been correct?
(1).
(2).

(3).
(4).
(5).

13. Had question 11 referred to the Wagner Act (1935), which alternative would have been correct?
(1).
(2).
(3).
(4).
(5).

14. Had question 11 referred to the Sherman Act (1890), which alternative would have been correct?
(1).
(2).
(3).
(4).
(5).

15. Which of the following is evidence of imperfection in the general labor market?
(1) Wage stickiness.
(2) Wage policies in major corporations and small businesses alike.
(3) Periods of prolonged unemployment.
(4) All of the above.
(5) Numbers (1) and (2) only.

16. Given the initial conditions in a labor market characterized by the demand and supply curves shown in Figure 29-2, which of the following is the likely effect of union action that restricts the supply of qualified labor?

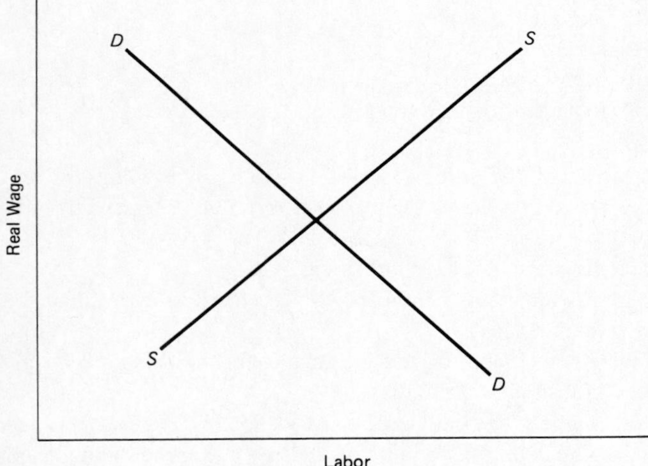

Figure 29-2

(1) Wages up and employment down.
(2) Wages down and employment up.
(3) Wages down and employment down.
(4) Wages up and employment up.
(5) Cannot tell.

17. Which answer to question 16 would have been correct if the question had referred to an action that would increase the productivity of labor?
(1).
(2).
(3).
(4).
(5).

18. Which answer to question 16 would have been correct if the question had referred to an action that would increase the standard wage paid by management?
(1).
(2).
(3).
(4).
(5).

SUGGESTED ANSWERS TO QUESTIONS IN THE TEXT: Chapter 29

1. The structure follows a chart like the one in Figure TQ29-1: Note that collections of local unions are organized into *N* national unions which are assembled into a federation of national unions. Monopoly power can be obtained by organizing all the people who can offer specific labor skills to employers into a national union of "________ workers."

2. The Clayton Act (1914) reversed the antitrust implications of applying the Sherman Act to labor activity. The Railway (1926) and Norris-LaGuardia (1932) acts protected union activity in collective bargaining and striking until the Wagner Act created the NLRB (among other things) in 1935. The Fair Labor Standards Act followed in 1938. The pendulum started to swing the other way with the Taft-Hartley Act of 1947 (national well-being, "cooling-off" period, no closed shops, union liability for the actions of agents, etc.). (Fill in some of the gaps in content.)

3. Opinion, but support it on the basis of a tradeoff between individual well-being and societal well-being. If you argue against striking, what instrument should be allowed in its stead?

4. Consider Figure TQ29-2. Panel **(a)** represents the union labor market; *DD* and *SS* are initial derived demand and supply curves, respectively. Panel **(b)** represents the unskilled, nonunion labor market; *dd* and *ss* are initial derived demand and supply curves, respectively. Assume initial equilibrium at E^* and e^*.

Now let a minimum-wage law be passed at w_{min}. Employment in the unskilled market falls to l', with corresponding unemployment equal to $l^- - l'$). A contraction in the demand for unskilled workers could easily increase the derived demand

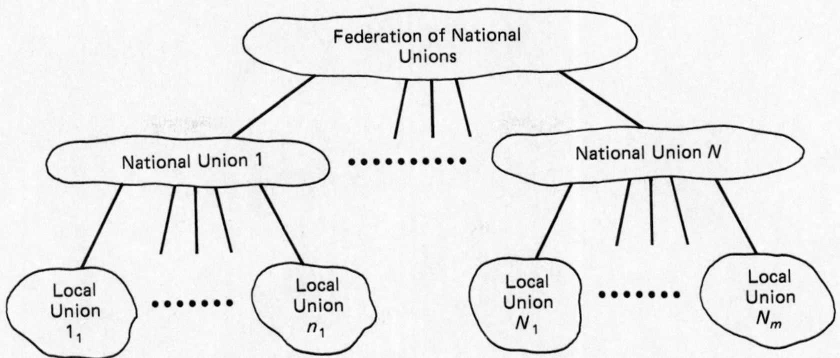

Figure TQ 29-1

for skilled labor from DD to $D'D'$. Wages and employment in the union market could thus increase at the expense of increased unemployment among the unskilled.

5. Cooperative elements come from mutually consistent goals—increased productivity, increased product demand, etc. Antagonistic elements come from objectives that run counter to one another—keeping costs down versus high wage settlements, flexibility in hiring versus job security, etc. A good arbitrator should be able to recognize cooperative elements and exploit them in overcoming antagonistic ones. Depends on the person?

6. Your own opinion. Remember, though, the philosophy of modern antitrust case law—behavior with power is more important than access to power.

7. **a.** Decreased productivity means lower derived demand, especially if nonunion bricklayers are available.
b. Decreased derived demand from reduced product demand (lower marginal revenue).
c. Increased supply for certain services.
d. Increased derived demand from greater power in the product market (higher marginal revenue).
e. Excess supply in the steelworker market.

8. The regulated monopolist. There is more room for increasing the standard wage and derived demand (*MR* and *MP* components) without costing jobs because of the inelastic demand. Would have to deal with an entire competitive industry (to do otherwise would be to drive union shops out of business and make room for nonunion shops). Restricting supply of labor doesn't seem to apply here.

9. Restrict supply on a supply-and-demand graph. Incomes of the professions increase if demand is wage inelastic in the relevant region.

10. **a.** M is equilibrium if the marginal cost of labor (higher than the paid wage for the monopsonist because all labor is paid a higher wage if one person is attracted by a higher wage) intersects DD above M.
b. Wage increases, as does employment, as the firm becomes a price (wage) taker, with rr representing the marginal cost of labor. E is the outcome—an efficient one at which MRP equals society's MC of labor.

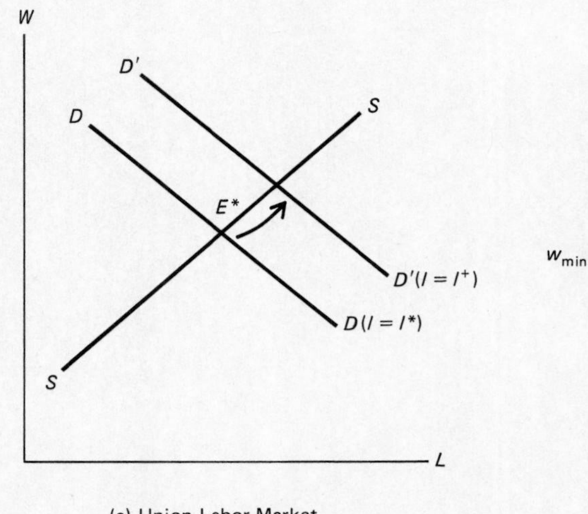

(a) Union Labor Market

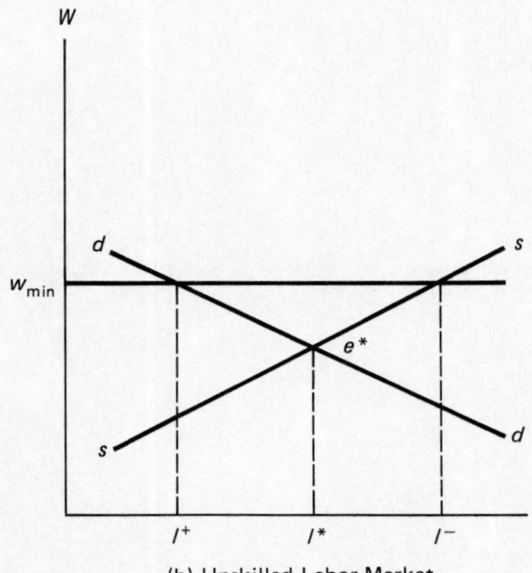

(b) Unskilled Labor Market

Figure TQ29-2

CHAPTER 30

CAPITAL, INTEREST, AND PROFITS

Preceding chapters have outlined how the rents earned by resources and the wages earned by labor are determined. It is now time to study the determination of the return to capital. Of the three major categories of inputs, this determination is the most complicated. The return to capital depends upon many factors, economic and psychological, that lie well beyond the straightforward intersection of a derived demand curve and a simple supply curve. The return to capital depends upon the willingness of people to forgo present consumption to finance increased consumption in the future. It depends upon the uncertainties inherent in forecasting the future, and the aversion of people to the risks that those uncertainties create. It depends, in a more fundamental way, upon the macroeconomic policies of the federal government and the central bank. The list goes on. For our purposes here, though, only the simplest of theories will be explored. Brief mention of these and other complications will be made, but the focus of the chapter is the naive, simple view of the workings of the capital market.

This rather extreme caveat notwithstanding, your work in Chapter 30 will produce substantial insight into one of the most critical topics of contemporary research. Having completed the chapter, in fact, you will have accomplished the following objectives.

LEARNING OBJECTIVES

1. Define precisely what economists mean when they speak of physical capital (structure, equipment, inventories, etc.), and understand why capital is not a primary factor of production.

2. Define the rate of return on capital, and relate it to the notion of an interest rate.

3. Explain the notion of present value and its importance in evaluating the potential profitability of a capital project. Record a formula for the present value of a perpetual asset which generates a constant return, and trace the sensitivity of present value to changes in the interest rate.

4. Explain the major factors that determine (*a*) the derived demand for capital and (*b*) the supply of capital in the classical theory. Relate the theory to some of its major qualifications: (*a*) technological change, (*b*) uncertainty and risk, (*c*) present and future inflation, and (*d*) macroeconomic shocks and policies.

5. State the relationship between the real rate of interest, the nominal rate of interest, and the rate of inflation. Explain why the classical theory of capital investment uses the real rate of interest as its price variable.

6. Define profit in a statistical sense, and explain the roles of (*a*) implicit rents, interest payments, and wages; (*b*) rewards for risk taking; and (*c*) monopoly rents in determining profit.

7. Explain the three types of risk involved in profit (default, pure, and innovation). Differentiate between natural scarcities, contrived scarcities, and innovation rents as parts of monopoly profit.

Economists make an explicit distinction between *financial assets* (money saved through some financial vehicle) and *physical assets* (real capital embodied in a stock of structures, equipment, inventories, etc.). Understanding this distinction is essential if one is going to understand how capital markets work to determine the rate of interest, otherwise known as the price of capital. We begin, therefore, by reviewing the definitions and economic roles of these two distinct assets.

The simplest view of financial capital is a picture of money—money which can be borrowed or lent. When you lend a quantity of money for a length of time, though, you usually expect to receive more than that quantity in return; i.e., you expect, and in fact have probably so contracted, to be paid something above and beyond the loan principal sometime in the future. Suppose, for example, that you were to agree today to lend somebody \$100 for a period of 1 year. You would do so only with the clear understanding that he or she would pay you more than $100, say, $110, in exactly 1 year's time. The extra $10 tacked onto the $100 principal repayment is interest, and its translates in this simple case directly into an interest *rate* of 10 percent. To borrow money at this 10 percent interest rate means that it costs 10 cents per year for every dollar borrowed.

Clearly then, the interest rate is, in a very real sense, simply the price that must be paid by someone who wants to use money for a specified period of time. It is, moreover, a price that is determined at least in part by the operation of a market for loanable funds. There are demanders in this market (those wanting to borrow money and who are willing to pay for that privilege), and there are suppliers (those with funds available for lending at a price). Whether lenders receive 5 percent per year, or 10 percent, or 15 percent depends upon the relative strengths of these two sets of economic actors.

The interest rate actually observed can, of course, depend on a large number of factors that are not easily captured in a simple supply-and-demand framework. The quoted rate might, for example, depend upon the degree of risk associated with a loan—the likelihood, as viewed by the lender, that the borrower might default on his or her obligation to repay. In general, the higher the risk, the higher the price—the higher the interest rate. If inflation were rampant, then the purchasing power of the money to be returned at a later date would be diminished, and that should affect the price at which people would be willing to make loans; the higher the anticipated rate of inflation, the higher the price—again, the higher the interest rate.

Supply and demand are, nonetheless, at work here. We have seen that (potential) lenders work to generate the supply side—the source of financial capital. But what of the demand side? The answer lies with those who want to invest in physical capital. Why? Because time is also a critical element in such investment.

If investors could somehow press a "dump" button on a piece of physical capital and make it instantaneously yield its entire flow of productive services in one enormous heap, then it would no longer be a capital good. It would, instead, be a consumption good. They could pay for the "consumption capital," press the "dump" button, and sell its total product all in the same time period; *and* they would not have to borrow any money to finance the operation (unless their product market turned out to be weaker than they had expected).

By way of contrast, the essence of physical capital is that it does not come equipped with a "dump" button; capital "pays off" slowly. Despite this inherent delayed return, though, investors have to pay relatively quickly for any physical investment that they might want to undertake. In considering their investment options, therefore, they are forced to consider borrowing money to finance their plans, so they are forced to consider the price of that money. In short, they become part of the demand side of a financial market simply by contemplating investment opportunities in physical capital.

1. Consider an asset that will cost you $100, right now, to construct. If you construct it, there will be no payoff for 2 years. But 2 years from now, this asset will pay you $121—nothing before that, and nothing after. This $121 is free of any incidental costs or expenses; it is the net return on your $100 outlay. The $121 return is safe; there is no uncertainty about its arrival.

This capital asset has an annual rate of return of 10 percent. Ten percent is the annual interest rate at which a loan of $100 will just "grow," with annual compounding of interest, into $121 in 2 years. At the end of year 1, the principal amount of $100 will earn $10 interest. This interest is left to become extra principal for year 2, so that in the second year the loan is $110, not $100. At the end of year 2, the interest for that year is $11. So the total repayment at the end of year 2 will be $121—$110 principal plus $11 interest.

a. Two dollar figures are involved: in the example, a cost figure of $100 today and a revenue figure of $121 just 2 years from today. An interest rate (10 percent annually in the example) "matches up" the two differing dollar figures. So the rate of return of a capital asset is expressed as *(a dollar figure / an interest rate)*.

b. If you had to borrow $100 to construct the asset of part **a**, and could borrow this money at a cost of 5 percent annually, would you do so? *(yes / no)*.

c. Would you borrow the money at 9 percent annually? *(yes / no)*. At 11 percent annually? *(yes / no)*.

---

a. an interest rate **b.** yes (for you would be ahead of the game financially even after paying your interest) **c.** yes [for the same reason (remember that there is no uncertainty about your $121 return)]; no (you would be out of pocket after paying interest)

2. Suppose you have money available to lend, or to use in the purchase of some revenue-yielding asset. The market interest rate is 10 percent annually. The borrowers in this market are of such good credit standing that the risk of any borrower's defaulting on his or her loan is virtually nonexistent.

The owner of an asset such as that described in question 1 (i.e., guaranteeing a single return of $121 at the end of 2 years) offers to sell it to you.

a. If this asset could be bought for $90, would you buy it? *(yes / no)*. If you did, the interest rate you would be getting on your outlay would be *(less than 10 percent / 10 percent / more than 10 percent)*.

b. If the asset could be bought for $100, then it would be *(an unusually good buy / an unusually poor buy / as good as, but no better than, other available alternatives)*.

c. Would you pay $102 for this asset? *(yes / no)*. If you did, the interest rate you would be getting on your outlay would be *(less than 10 percent / 10 percent / more than 10 percent)*.

---

a. yes; more than 10 percent (actually 16 percent per year on the $90 that returns $121 in 2 years) **b.** as good as, but no better than, other available alternatives **c.** no; less than 10 percent

3. **a.** Suppose that the market rate of interest were 4 percent annually, not 10 percent. Would you then buy the asset of question 1 for $102, if you had the opportunity? *(yes / no)*. If you did, the rate of return that you would be earning would be *(less than 4 percent / 4 percent / more than 4 percent)*.

b. Actually, with a market interest rate of 4 percent annually (i.e., if the return generally available for "investing" money capital is 4 percent per year), the market price of this asset would stand at about $112 (more precisely, $111.85). Why? (Pick one.)

(1) Because $112 is the amount which, if lent out for 2 years at 4 percent annually, would "grow" to $121.

(2) Because the interest return or net productivity of this asset is 10 percent regardless of the amount of money laid out to build or buy it.

---

a. yes; more than 4 percent **b.** **(1)** (This asset's rate of return is 10 percent *only* if it can be bought or build for $100.)

To repeat: An asset's rate of return is an interest rate. You need two pieces of information if you are asked to compute an asset's rate of return:

1. The amount it would cost to build or buy this asset now
2. The amounts of future *net* revenue that it is expected to bring in, and the expected dates of their arrival. (*Net* revenue means revenue after allowing for any costs incurred in using the asset or collecting the revenue.)

Given this information, there is always one interest rate that indicates the rate of return.

Question 3 looked at a related question: What is the maximum amount you should pay for a given asset? What is its present value? To reply, again you need two pieces of information:

1. As before, the amounts and dates of the future net revenue the asset is expected to bring in
2. The *market* interest rate

From this information, you can compute the asset's present value. In question 3, then, the asset yielding $121 just 2 years from now has a present value of $100 if the market interest rate is 10 percent. Its present value is about $112 if the market rate is 4 percent.

4. Suppose that you find that an asset's present value is different from its actual construction cost. What then? Suppose, in particular, that its actual cost is less than its present value. It *(would / would not)* then be profitable to borrow money to construct it. Why? This asset's rate of return would be *(less than / equal to / greater than)* the rate of interest.

If, on the other hand, its present value were less than its construction cost, then the asset *(would / would not)* be worth building. The market value of such an asset would be *(less than / equal to / greater than)* its construction cost, and its rate of return would be *(less than / equal to / greater than)* the rate of interest.

---

would; greater than; would not; less than; less than

5. **a.** Suppose now that you own a piece of land which brings you net rental income (after allowing for maintenance cost, etc.) of $5000 yearly, and that you expect this annual rental to continue well into the future. The present value of this land would be (pick one):

(1) $5000.

(2) the sum of all expected future receipts of $5000.

(3) the sum of all expected future annual receipts, each "discounted" down to a present-value figure by means of the market interest rate.

b. Suppose the asset in part **a** is expected to yield $5000 each year into the indefinite future so that it represents a "perpetual-income stream." Each $5000 can then be thought of as the interest yield on a loan which has no maturity date (date for repayment of principal).

What is the amount of principal that would have to be involved if its interest yield is $5000 annually and the interest rate is 4 percent annually? . . . . . $________

c. There is a simple formula for computing the capitalized value of such perpetual-income assets. Write it down, and make sure the formula works for the case of part **b**.

---

d. Is this formula consistent with the rule that capitalized values are reckoned as the sum of the discounted values of all expected future revenues? (Pick one.)

(1) No—the perpetuity case has to be handled by means of a different formula, because of the infinite number of expected future revenue items.

(2) Yes—in this special case of a constant net return into the indefinite future.

---

a. **(3)** **b.** 125,000 **c.** $V = \$N/i$, or $125,500 = $5000/0.04 **d.** **(2)**

6. This means, then, that if market interest rates rise, the present value of any sum expected at some date in the future will *(rise / remain unchanged / fall)*; and if the market interest rate should fall, an asset's present value (assuming no change in its expected future receipts) must *(rise / remain unchanged / fall)*.

---

fall; rise

All this discussion of present value leads directly to the problem of determining the interest rate. (*Interest*, remember, is the income received by those who supply money capital to borrowers.) We must begin by thinking of the interest rate as a rate determined by the demand for loanable money and the supply of such money, but talk of "supply and demand" is empty unless we probe for the factors lying *behind* the demand curve and *behind* the supply curve. We have already suggested that business firms with investment projects (the building of capital goods) to undertake are the demanders of financial capital. Their decisions to borrow will be influenced by the level of the interest rate because some projects will be worth undertaking at low interest rates and not worth undertaking at high ones. Why? Because the rate of return of such projects (and remember that this return is expressed as an interest rate) will be below a high market interest rate and above a low market interest rate.

In sum, computations of rates of return must lie behind the demand curve for loanable money. The suppliers of such money are largely those who have saved (or who are handling the money which other people have saved and entrusted to them). From here, we work our way into the classical, and simplified, version of capital and interest theory. Figures 30-1 through 30-3 illustrate this theory. On all three diagrams, the real interest rate (a percentage figure per annum) is measured vertically, with zero interest at bottom.

Figure 30-1 corresponds to the text's Figure 30-2. It is assumed in this case that all capital goods are exactly alike, so that we can add them together in physical units and get a meaningful total, just as we can add dollar figures together. The *SS* line in Figure 30-1 indicates the economy's *total* stock of capital at some particular period of time. It stands for some figure such as 400 units of capital. *SS* is vertical because the present capital stock is 400 units no matter whether the current interest rate is 2 percent, 10 percent, or any other figure.

The *DD* curve is the "demand" of business firms for such capital goods. It intersects *SS* at point *E*, indicating an interest rate of i_S. To grasp the meaning of the *DD* curve, suppose that i_s indicates an interest rate of 8 percent. Then *DD* intersects *SS* at the 8 percent level, because the firms estimate that the last (or marginal) units of that 400-unit capital stock have a rate of return of 8 percent. This estimate is based on the cost of producing more capital goods and on the present value of the estimated net revenues that those capital goods will bring in.

7. To further grasp what *DD* means and why it intersects *SS* where it does, suppose that the situation is a little different. With the capital stock at 400, business firms are optimistic about the payoff of capital goods. Specifically, they think that the last units of a 400-unit stock have a net productivity of 10 percent. Then, if the interest rate is not 10 percent but 8 percent, they will want to have *(more than 400 / just 400 / less than 400)* units of capital. Why? Because the rate of return of the next unit of capital would be greater than the 8 percent cost of borrowing. The interest rate must be 10 percent before their disposition to use capital goods is limited to 400. That is to say, *if* business firms were more optimistic about the net productivity of capital, then the *DD* curve in Figure 30-1 would lie (pick one):

(1) farther to the right than is now indicated.

(2) just where it is now.

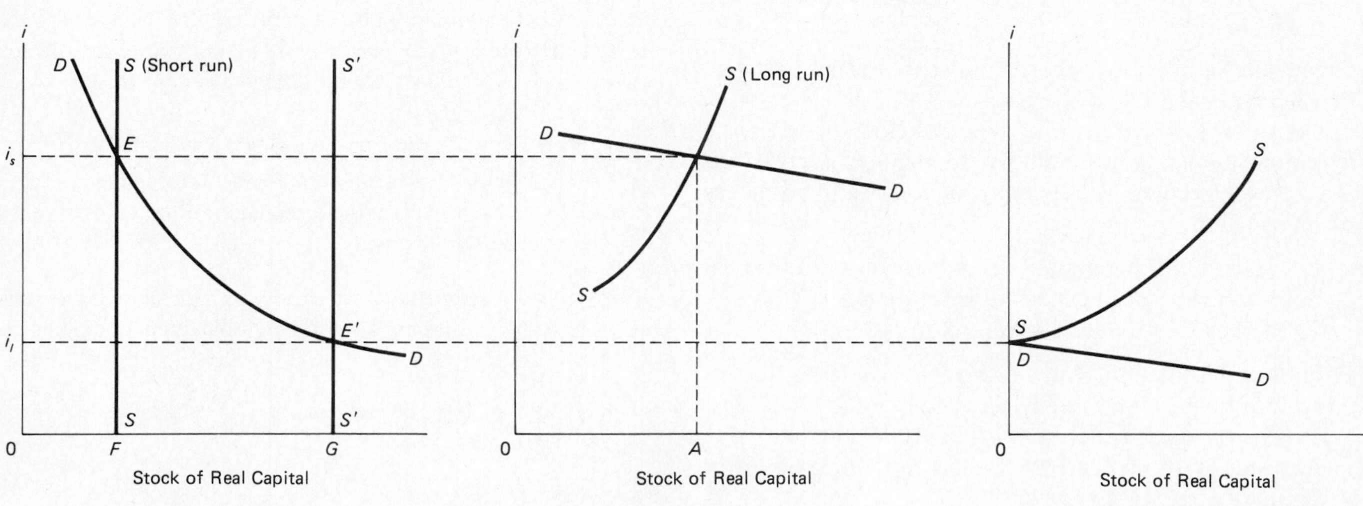

Figure 30-1

Figure 30-2

Figure 30-3

(3) farther to the left than is now indicated.

It would intersect the SS curve at a point indicating *(less than 8 percent / 8 percent / more than 8 percent).*

---

more than 400; **(1)**; more than 8 percent

8. Given the existing stock of capital and its rate of return as indicated in Figure 30-1, the interest rate in this economy, at this period time in its history, is i_s. The people in this economy are, however, still saving money. Moreover, in the classical view of the world, people save *because* of the interest rate, and they are willing to lend this saved money to business-firm borrowers. The *SS* curve in Figure 30-2 illustrates this situation. Its southwest-to-northeast direction illustrates the assumption that people would save and lend more if the interest rate were increased.

There is also a *demand* for this money. Business firms are willing to pay 8 percent on borrowed money because there are still some projects on which new capital goods (additions to the present total stock) would have a rate of return equal to 8 percent. Of course, large additions to the capital stock would lower its rate of return because of diminishing returns, but that comes later. For the time being, business firms are willing to borrow (in each period of time) the amount of money indicated by *OA* in Figure 30-2 at 8 percent because they think there is still useful employment for this amount of money at this rate. *DD* in Figure 30-2 is close to being flat at rates even a little above 8 percent, because it is assumed that there are few would-be borrowers who see projects with a payoff in excess of 8 percent. But if the rate were to drop a bit below 8 percent, that might produce a substantial increase in the quantity of money capital demanded (i.e., demand might be highly elastic with respect to interest-rate changes, if there are plenty of unexploited projects with rates of return just slightly below 8 percent).

a. *OA* in Figure 30-2 indicates, per period of time (pick one):

(1) the number of units of capital to be added to the capital stock.

(2) nothing whatever with respect to the capital stock.

(3) money that will be spent on construction of new units to be added to the capital stock.

b. As time goes by, then, the stock of capital goods will *(fall / remain constant / increase)*. In terms of Figure 30-1, the vertical *SS* curve will *(move to the left / remain unchanged / move to the right, from F toward G)*, and the interest rate will *(fall / remain constant / increase).*

This rightward movement of *SS* means that more and more homogeneous capital units are being built. The law of diminishing returns then applies (as long as there are no technological changes or large population influxes), and it causes the rate of return to capital to fall. Business firms will no longer pay 8 percent for money because there are no capital projects left that return 8 percent. In terms of Figure 30-2, the *DD* curve should *(fall / rise).*

This shift in *DD* lowers the equilibrium interest rate and thereby depresses the public's disposition to save. At rates below i_s, in particular, the amount saved (and loaned) falls so much that, at a sufficiently low rate, saving collapses to zero. This point of all consumption is shown in Figure 30-3 because *SS* cuts the vertical axis at i_l.

c. That is to say, after a sufficiently long period of time and a sufficient increase in the capital stock, the process of capital accumulation comes to an end. In terms of Figure 30-1, the economy's capital stock has then increased to the level indicated by ______, and the interest rate is ______.

In terms of Figure 30-3, the *DD* curve begins at interest rate i_l because (pick one):

(1) there are no more projects worth undertaking at i_l, only those at rates below that level.

(2) people will supply money only at rates below i_l.

---

a. (3) b. increase; move to the right, from *F* toward *G*; fall; fall **c.** *OG*; i_l; **(1)**

9. Questions 7 and 8 have reviewed the classical theory of capital and interest in terms of demand and supply curves. But (to repeat) a proper grasp of the theory requires that we look *behind* these curves. The fundamental element behind the demand-for-money curve is the

______________________________.

The corresponding element behind the supply curve is the

____

---

rate of return to physical capital; willingness of public to save rather than consume part of its income

10. A number of qualifications must be attached to the classical theory of capital and interest if that theory is to accord with contemporary reality.

a. For example, it is doubtful that people's consumption-saving decisions are greatly influenced by the level of the interest rate. At least, those decisions do not seem to be altered by moderate changes in the interest that they earn by saving.

Suppose (1) that the decision to save out of income is quite unresponsive to any change in the interest rate, and (2) that whatever amount people do save they are willing to lend out at any positive interest rate. In Figure 30-2, this would affect the *(DD / SS)* curve; it would, in fact, become *(vertical / horizontal / a diagonal line).*

However, the second of the assumptions listed above is probably unsound. While the amount people save may be unresponsive to interest-rate changes, the amount they lend probably is responsive. (This draws us back to the demand for money discussed in Chapter 16). That is, at lower interest rates, they will lend *(more / less)*. The *SS* curve shown in Figure 30-2 *(indicates / does not indicate)* such an attitude.

b. If real and money incomes gradually rise over time, people can and do save more money out of their incomes. This affects the *(DD / SS)* curve in Figure 30-2; this type of income effect would shift that curve to the *(right / left)*.

c. If you try to compute the income accruing from any proposed capital project, you must look into the future, and that future is always uncertain. You must, nonetheless, make your best guess about the future when you are thinking about borrowing money to finance a project. In the process of deciding whether or not to undertake the project, therefore, you must recognize that your best guess might turn out to be overly optimistic. As a result, the estimated rate of return used in the decision should be *(reduced below / hiked above)* your best guess to reflect a hedge against the uncertainty. It is a conservative measure to *(cut down / increase)* your revenue estimates to allow for uncertainty, and this makes it *(more / less)* likely that you will decide to undertake the project.

d. Estimates of likely rates of return are influenced also by a quite different factor: the climate of optimism or pessimism. If business firms, looking into the uncertain future with respect to projected capital plans, suddenly become more pessimistic, this will shift the *(DD / SS)* curve in Figure 30-2 to the *(right / left)*.

Similarly, if lenders, trying to decide whether or not borrowers will really make good on their borrowing obligations, suddenly become more pessimistic on this score, this will shift the *(DD / SS)* curve in Figure 30-2 to the *(right / left)*.

e. The rate of return to capital may be altered by technological change. We would ordinarily expect such changes to *(increase / decrease)* capital's return. In Figure 30-2, this sort of technological change would shift the *(DD / SS)* curve to the *(right / left)*.

Continuing this line of reasoning in the context of Figure 30-4, suppose that short-run equilibrium is initially at point E with S_1S_1 representing the initial short-run supply of capital, S_LS_L representing the long-run supply of capital, and DD representing the initial demand for capital. Suppose, for the sake of argument, that every increase in the supply of capital over time is accompanied by a technological advance that preserves the rate of interest. The long-run equilibrium rate of interest would then be ________ percent instead of ________ percent, and the long-run equilibrium stock of capital would be *(higher / lower)* than it would have been otherwise. Point *(E_1 / E^* / E^{**})* would represent this long-run equilibrium. Draw a demand curve in Figure 30-4 that supports this equilibrium. With the technological change, then, capital *(deepening / widening)* would continue further despite the higher long-run rate of interest.

It is interesting to note that this is apparently what has been happening in the United States. Despite the tendency illustrated in Figure 30-2 for interest rates to *(rise / remain constant / fall)* over time, interest rates in the United States have tended to *(rise / remain constant / fall)* over much of our recent history (at least through 1979, but that is another story left for parts **f** and **g** of this question).

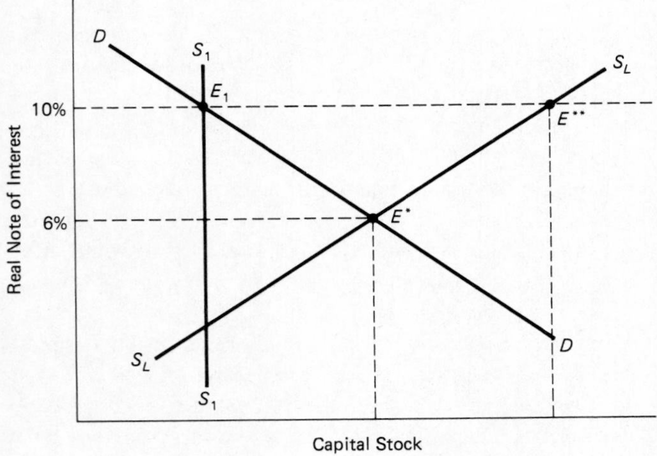

Figure 30-4

f. Inflation plays an important role in the determination of interest rates. Investment and lending decisions depend, in particular, upon the *(natural / real / nominal)* rate of interest. The equation that relates nominal and real rates is

Nominal rate = real rate + ____________________

This equation explains why, in the face of 18 percent nominal interest rates and 16 percent inflation, investors can behave as if the interest rate were really 2 percent.

g. Macroeconomic policy also plays a critical role in the investment decision. If, for example, tight monetary policy were to cause a recession, saving would *(rise / fall)* with GNP and the short-run supply curve in Figure 30-1 would *(shift to the right / rotate to a line with a positive slope / shift to the left)*. Meanwhile, business conditions would dampen the optimism of investors that capital projects would earn high returns and therefore *(shift the demand curve to the right / rotate the demand curve toward the vertical / shift the demand curve to the left)*. The net effect on investment would then be *(a reduction / an increase)* and the interest rate would *(fall / remain constant / rise)*.

h. Lenders also face uncertainties when they lend money. The result is their requiring risk premiums in the interest rates that they charge derived from:

(1) ____________________

(2) ____________________

---

a. *SS*; vertical; less; indicates **b.** *SS*; right **c.** reduced below; cut down; less **d.** *DD*; left; *SS*; left **e.** increase; *DD*; right; 10; 6; higher; E^{**}; (Draw a downward-sloping demand curve through E^{**}); deepening; fall; remain constant **f.** real; rate of inflation **g.** fall; shift to the left; shift the demand curve to the left; a reduction; any of the three, depending upon the relative sizes of the shifts **h. (1)** the risk of default **(2)** their own aversion to risk

We now turn our attention to the concept of profit. Classical economic theory identified three general types of inputs: land (resources), labor, and capital. If that is all there is to it, where does profit fit into the picture? The remaining questions will focus on this query.

11. a. Suppose that you run a roadside fruit and vegetable stand, situated on your own land. Typically, you will describe your net income as "profit." But part of that income should properly be considered as *(rent / interest)* earned by your land, and another part as *(wages / profit)* for the labor you have supplied.

Similarly, it is possible to think of at least part of a corporation's earnings as interest on money which the shareholders put up.

If you are self-employed, those parts of your income which you call "profit" but which can fit into one of the other three categories may also be called *("implicit" / "unearned" / "surplus")* wages, interest, or *(income / rent / surplus)*.

b. Economists are usually persuaded that it is impossible to translate *all* profit into factor earnings of the other three types, except in the very special situation of *(monopoly / perfect competition / imperfect competition)*, where everything has worked itself out to a full equilibrium level. In that situation, which in consequence is characterized by *(extremely settled and stable conditions / changing conditions / self-employment of all factors / no obligation to learn economics)*, there can be implicit wages, interest, or rent, but there will be no "pure economic profit."

---

a. rent; wages; "implicit"; rent **b.** perfect competition; extremely settled and stable conditions

If, in situations other than perfect competition, there is some part of profit which cannot be converted into implicit wages, implicit rent, or implicit interest, then it is necessary to answer the question: What useful function is performed or undertaken by the individual who receives a profit? Profit is the reward for doing what? There are, in response to this rather fundamental question, many different viewpoints.

12. a. One, associated at its inception with economist Frank Knight, views profit as the return for dealing with unavoidable *(scarcity / competition among self-employed factors / entrepreneurship / uncertainty)*. Profit, or at least part of profit, is the reward society gives to those who shoulder the burden of uncertainty successfully. The only circumstances in which the profit-or-loss uncertainty would not exist would be those of perfect competition, but the conditions of perfect competition are *(a goal we should strive for / unlikely to be attained / quite unattainable)*.

Three types of risk caused by this uncertainty were identified by Knight. List them in the following blanks:

(1) ____________________

(2) ____________________

(3) ____________________

b. The positive side to the risk of trying to exploit a new technology or other innovation is the monopoly power that success can bring. The power to control the price and the size of the market might be fleeting, but it is nonetheless real. In his work, Joseph Schumpeter argued that innovation lay at the very heart of productive capitalism, and that it was the real justification for a "profits system." He felt that most of the gains in real income that have accrued under capitalism have come, not from more careful allocation of a given stock of resources, but from the creation of new goods and new productive techniques.

Innovation, in the Schumpeterian view, is a risky and uncertain business, and the majority of would-be innovators *(fail / succeed)*. In this Schumpeterian view, situations of monopoly and of innovation are *(inextricably mixed / completely separate)*. A firm may be in a monopolistic position, but that position may have resulted entirely from successful innovation. Schumpeter thought we should be cautious in our monopoly-opposing public policies; he was afraid that too-harsh policies might destroy the very incentive to innovate on which truly significant gains in real income depend. Schumpeter thought that most monopoly situations acquired through innovation are in due course toppled by other successful innovations originating elsewhere—producing what he called "the process of creative destruction."

---

a. uncertainty; quite unattainable **(1)** pure risk **(2)** risk of bankruptcy or default **(3)** risk of innovation and/or enterprise **b.** fail; inextricably mixed

13. a. In a second major view, based on the absence of perfect competition, profit is considered unnecessary and undesirable; it is a ____________________ return resulting from a "____________________ scarcity."

b. The point is that when a good is offered for sale by a monopoly firm, price will be *(higher / lower)* and output will be *(higher than / lower than / the same as)* it would be under conditions of *(perfect competition / no competition)*.

---

a. monopoly; contrived **b.** higher; lower than; perfect competition

14. The monopoly view of profits is complicated by the fact that a genuine "monopoly return" may at the same time be a legitimate rent or interest return. Suppose that the original monopolist has an asset which for some reason is protected against competitive inroads and so is earning a large monopoly return. This monopolist sells this asset at its full capitalized value (i.e., the value established by its total discounted future earnings). The purchaser must charge *(the same price as / a higher price than / a lower price than)* the original monopolist did in order to receive *(the normal competitive return / a monopoly return)* on the money thus invested.

---

the same price as; the normal competitive return

To summarize, then, many sources of profits have been identified in the preceding questions. One source embraces the implicit rents, wages, and interest payments collected by an entrepreneur or a major corporation in the course of doing business. The second source identifies profits as reward for bearing risk—risk associated with falling flat on your face (default), risk associated with the business cycle as you see it, and risk associated with undertaking an innovative project. Finally, profit can be the return to monopoly power, derived from natural scarcities, temporary scarcities produced by innovation, or contrived scarcities. Some of these sources are laudable, but others are the cause for some concern.

QUIZ: Multiple Choice

1. Four of the following five statements more or less concur with Frank Knight's theory of profits. One statement runs *counter* to Knight's views. Which one?
(1) Successful innovation cannot be regarded as a valid instance of profit arising out of the acceptance of uncertainty.
(2) The operation of an insurance company cannot be regarded as a valid instance of the acceptance of risk.
(3) If profit is considered the reward for assuming risk, then the net total of profit in any given year might be a negative figure.
(4) Profit is a necessary component in national income if people by and large dislike risk and are prepared to pay in order to avoid risk.
(5) Profit, or a large part of it, is society's reward to those who shoulder the burden of uncertainty.

2. An asset's present value is:
(1) its original cost plus an estimate of maintenance expense throughout its lifetime.
(2) the same thing as its original cost.
(3) the sum of all its discounted net earnings.
(4) the sum of all its net earnings, without discounting.
(5) the rate of interest at which the asset would just become worth buying or building.

3. If the rate of return of any capital asset were to be computed, several items of information would be needed. Which among the following would *not* be required?
(1) The original cost of purchasing or constructing the asset.
(2) The means of financing the original purchase.
(3) The estimated maintenance or operating cost that must be incurred in order to keep the asset in satisfactory operating (revenue-earning) condition throughout its life.
(4) The estimated revenue that the asset will produce throughout its lifetime.
(5) The degree of "riskiness" surrounding estimated revenue, i.e., the degree of uncertainty as to whether revenues in the estimated amounts will really appear or not.

4. According to the classical theory, which of the following accurately describes the role played by the law of diminishing returns in the determination of interest rates?
(1) As capital goods accumulate relative to supplies of land and labor, the rate of return of new additions to the capital stock must fall.
(2) The cost of producing additional capital goods must necessarily increase (in the absence of innovation).
(3) A steady increase in the output of whatever consumer good a particular capital good produces must lower the price of that consumer good and thus lower the return to that capital good.
(4) It explains why innovation cannot continually check the long-run tendency of the interest rate of fall.
(5) It must be used if the rate of return of any capital good is to be computed.

5. In classical investment theory, the rate of interest is determined by:
(1) the estimated rate of return to capital.
(2) the extent to which the public wishes to use the income it receives for consumption.
(3) both the estimated rate of return to capital and the extent to which the public wishes to use the income it receives for consumption.
(4) the estimated rate of return to capital and the size of the capital stock.
(5) the estimated rate of return to capital and the rate of technological development.

6. Classical investment theory held that there should be:
(1) a tendency toward a long-run equilibrium in which the market interest rate would be zero.
(2) a tendency toward a long-run equilibrium in which gross investment would be constantly falling.
(3) a tendency toward a long-run equilibrium in which net investment would be maintained at a steady and nonzero rate.
(4) a tendency toward a long-run equilibrium in which saving out of income would be zero.
(5) no tendency toward any sort of long-run equilibrium.

7. The classical theory described in question 6 neglected the fact that:
(1) the amount saved out of income might be influenced by the interest rate.

(2) it is necessary to discount future items of income in order to establish their present value.
(3) while the interest rate may approach zero, it cannot actually reach zero.
(4) technological change might continually increase the rate of return to capital.
(5) people are typically impatient to consume now, rather than accumulate for future consumption.

8. A certain asset is expected to yield a steady net income (i.e., after allowing for all costs or expenses) of $100 annually from now until eternity. If the market rate of interest is 8 percent per annum, the market value of this asset ought to be:
(1) $800.
(2) $1250.
(3) $8000.
(4) $10,000.
(5) infinity.

9. If market interest rates generally fall, then the present value of any capital asset should:
(1) fall, since lower interest rates indicate that revenue amounts accruing at any future date are now given a higher present value.
(2) fall, since lower interest rates indicate that revenue amounts accruing at any future date are now given a lower present value.
(3) remain unchanged, unless relevant cost or revenue factors thereby changed.
(4) rise, because lower interest rates indicate that revenue amounts accruing at any future date are now given a lower present value.
(5) rise, because lower interest rates indicate that revenue amounts accruing at any future date are now given a higher present value.

10. Which alternative in question 9 would be correct had the question referred to the asset's rate of return instead of its present value?
(1).
(2).
(3).
(4).
(5).

11. In a period of deflation (i.e., of generally falling prices), the "real" rate of interest obtained by any lender:
(1) will exceed the nominal rate.
(2) will become a negative figure.
(3) will fall below the stated rate, although not to the extent of becoming a negative figure.
(4) will become a meaningless of incalculable figure.
(5) will exceed the rate of unemployment.

12. The rate of return to any capital good could reasonably be described as:
(1) that particular rate of interest at which the capital good would just be worth buying or building, i.e., the rate of interest for which the present value of anticipated revenues would just be matched by costs.
(2) the dollar amount of profit that would accrue if that capital good were bought or built.
(3) the same thing as the market rate of interest.
(4) the physical increase in output (as distinct from the money value) that would accrue if that capital good were bought or built.
(5) the percentage figure obtained by adding up all net revenues that would accrue from the capital good and dividing this total by its cost.

13. If business firms generally become more optimistic regarding the revenues that would accrue from the investment projects that they are planning, then the computed rate of return to that capital:
(1) will increase, since revenues enter into the computation of the rate of return.
(2) will decrease, since the rate of return is an interest rate, and the interest rate goes inversely to the value of the investment project.
(3) will not change, since the rate of return is governed by technical considerations, not be expected revenues.
(4) will probably fall, although there is a special case in which it would rise.
(5) may do any of the above, since the effect of a change in expected revenues upon the rate of return is unpredictable.

14. In the view of Frank H. Knight, "profit" should be regarded primarily as:
(1) the return received by an entrepreneur who face a downward-sloping demand curve for the product in question, and who seeks maximum profit in pricing that product.
(2) essentially a random distribution of profit among business firms—i.e., a distribution settled by chance, over which no firm has any control.
(3) the return received for activity in which some element of uncertainty is involved, so that loss is a possible outcome of this activity.
(4) only the return received by someone who engages in a particular form of uncertainty-involving activity, namely, innovation.
(5) none of the preceding descriptions.

15. One of the following would be a poor example of profit earned by the "uncertainty" definition of profit; namely, income earned by:
(1) a firm which gambles successfully on the introduction of a new product.
(2) a speculator in wheat.
(3) a firm now operating at a profit after a long investment of time and money in developing new cost-saving machinery for its production line.

(4) an insurance company which protects its policyholders against the risk of property damage by fire.
(5) a farmer who successfully grows a crop on land hitherto considered impossible or unsatisfactory for that crop.

16. A contrived scarcity is to be expected whenever:
(1) the seller of a product faces a horizontal demand curve.
(2) the seller of a product faces a downward-sloping demand curve.
(3) the entrepreneur undertaking the activity in question faces more than a usual degree of risk or uncertainty.
(4) profit can be considered an implicit factor return.
(5) heavy taxes are imposed in such a way as to discourage the undertaking of risky projects.

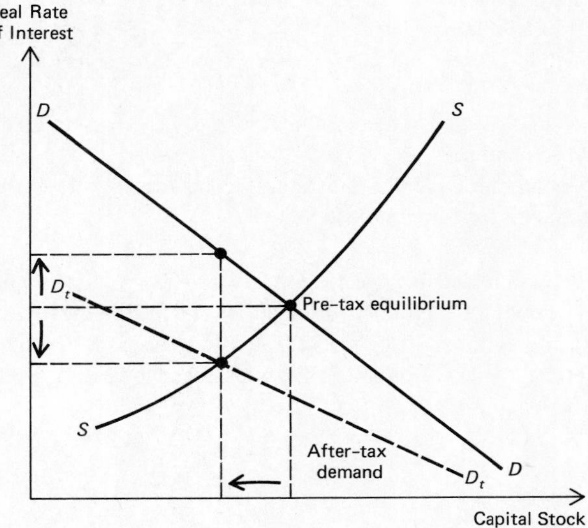

Figure TQ30-1

SUGGESTED ANSWERS TO QUESTIONS IN THE TEXT: Chapter 30

1. Think of any production process that proceeds in steps; there are, e.g., a lot of intermediate products in an automobile.

2. Consider a piece of capital. Its net dollar return per year per dollar invested is its rate of return. Its rental price would be the price charged by an owner to someone who wanted to use it for a period of time, say, a year. The rate of interest is the price of using money for a period of time, say, a year. If capital markets work perfectly, these are all the same in equilibrium.

3. **a.** Interest rate up because the derived demand curve shifts up; move along supply curve.
b. Interest rate up because the supply curve shifts in; move along demand curve.
c. Interest rate received by lenders down, but rate of return to capital (before taxes are paid) up. See Figure TQ30-1.

4. "Implicit" refers to returns earned by unpaid or owned labor, land, or capital. They can exist independently of other sources: risk, uncertainty, monopoly rents.

5. **a.** Zero pure economic profit here, so it must be normal return paid to capital.
b. Reward for risk (default during downturns; also pure risk because the cycles are unavoidable).
c. Reward for risk (innovation; also some monopoly rent for a short time).
d. Implicit rent paid for the land.

6. Innovation might increase the interest rate in the short run, but it would decline as the supply shifted out—new capital embodying the new technology. High government debt brings the long-run *SS* curve in, making the long-run interest rate higher and reducing the rate of capital accumulation even in the short run.

7. Play with the $PV = \$N/i$ formula. It comes from an infinite geometric series.

APPENDIX: 30

Advanced Analysis of Capital and Interest

Chapter 30 has covered, among other things, the classical model of interest-rate determination; historically, its origins are attributed to Irving Fisher. This appendix now tends to some of the qualifications to that model in a little more detail. The notion of society's impatience to consume will be conceptualized more formally. The rate of interest will be unmasked for what it is—the terms of trade between current consumption and future consumption. And the formula for present value will be extended to include assets of arbitrary annual return of fixed duration. Having worked through the appendix, therefore, you will have accomplished the following objectives.

LEARNING OBJECTIVES

1. Note explicitly that the interest rate is determined by the interaction of two forces: productivity on the demand side of the capital market and impatience to consume (subjective time preference) on the supply side.

2. Conceptualize the rate of interest as the terms of trade; i.e., see that it represents the rate at which present consumption can be turned into future consumption.

3. Note the possibility that the real rate of interest could be negative (if people were sufficiently impatient to consume and/or technology offered little for the tradeoff of present consumption into future consumption) even though the nominal rate of interest can never fall below the nominal return to holding currency (0 percent).

4. Recognize that the present value of an asset with a stream of net returns ($\$N_1$) into a foreseeable future of t years will, given interest rate i, equal

$$V = \frac{\$N_1}{(1+i)} + \frac{\$N_2}{(1+i)^2} + \ldots + \frac{\$N_t}{(1+i)^t}$$

and understand how to use this formula to rank potential investment projects.

1. Draw a demand curve for capital on a separate piece of paper; it is *(downward- / upward-)*sloping because it is a derived demand curve and the marginal revenue product of capital *(declines / increases)* with the quantity of capital employed. It is this type of curve, of course, that reflects the net productivity of capital. Can you, on the basis of this curve alone, determine the equilibrium rate of interest? ________. If you can, what is it? ________ percent.

Now draw on a *separate* graph either a long-run or a short-run supply curve for capital. It is this curve that reflects the willingness of people to save for the future—the inverse of their impatience for presence consumption. Can you, on the basis of this curve alone, determine the equilibrium rate of interest? ________. If you can, what is it? ________ percent.

You could not, of course, pick out an equilibrium rate of interest in either of these two exercises in futility. Only when the two components interact so that supply plays off against demand can an equilibrium be achieved.

---

downward-; declines; no; undetermined; no; again undetermined

2. The three panels of Figure 30A-1 display three alternative Fisher diagrams. Panel *(a / b / c)* depicts the production-possibility frontier in which technology offers society the most advantageous transfer of present consumption into future consumption. Conversely, panel *(a / b / c)* indicates a frontier in which deferring consumption into the future earns the least in terms of future consumption.

Now consider the indifference curves that also appear in the three panels of Figure 30A-1; they are identical across the three graphs. Panel *(a / b / c)* illustrates the situation in which additions to future consumption are the largest. It also illustrates the situation in which the rate of interest, represented by the slope of line *(OA / DEF / OB)* is the highest. Recalling your answers in the first paragraph of this question, therefore, it is clear that the case in which technology provides the best tradeoff into future consumption inspires the *(largest / smallest)* quantity of saving for future consumption supported by the *(lowest / highest)* rate of interest.

Conversely, when the tradeoff into future consumption is worst, in panel ________, the indifference curve that maximizes welfare indicates the *(smallest / largest)* deferment into future consumption and the *(smallest / largest)* rate of interest.

The rate of interest, therefore, is an accurate reflection of *(society's aversion to risk / the tradeoff rate between present consumption and future consumption / society's inherent rate of return)*.

(**b**); (**c**); (**b**); *DEF*; largest; highest; (**c**); smallest; smallest; the tradeoff rate between present consumption and future consumption

3. Now consider the opposite side of the Fisher graph—the indifference curve. Suppose, given panel **(b)** of Figure 30A-1, for example, that people became more impatient to consume; i.e., suppose that their subjective time preference rose. The indifference curves representing this new impatience would be *(steeper than / the same as / flatter than)* the one drawn in panel **(b)** because people would have to receive *(more / the same amount / less)* in future consumption to be compensated for any reduction in present consumption. The new equilibrium point would occur *(above point E / exactly at point E / below point E)* on the indicated PPF, indicating a(n) *(higher / unchanged / lower)* interest rate. As a result, present consumption would *(rise / remain the same / fall)* as future consumption *(rose / remained the same / fell)*.

---

steeper than; more; below point *E*; higher; rise; fell

4. Classical economists often regarded the interest rate as the device by which people choose between present and future consumption. If the rate is 5 percent per annum, and you have $100, you may choose between $100 consumption today or $105 consumption a year from now. Or you may pick $50 today and $52.50 next year, or any such intermediate combination. The point is that you save or you lend to transfer consumption from year to year or from one year to the next. It follows from this reasoning that a different interest rate would produce a different consumption-saving distribution.

In the classical view, there is a long-run interest-rate "floor," established when the rate falls enough that people feel the extra return is not worth waiting for. But if saving persists regardless of the interest rate level, will that rate drift down toward zero?

For two reasons, any such tendency seems unlikely. First, technological innovation should persistently *(increase / decrease)* the rate of return of new capital projects. Second, the lending process is always haunted by some uncertainty or risk that the money loaned will not come back, or will not come back in full. So if there is an interest-rate floor, it will be set by refusal to *(save / lend)* anything at rates at or below this floor.

increase; lend

5. a. You must decide whether asset A or asset B has the higher market value. Asset A promises to make four income payments of $1225 each at the end of years 1, 2, 3, and 4. Asset B promises to make five payments of $1000 each at the end of years 1, 2, 3, 4, and 5. The confidence with which payments can be expected is the same in both. The valuation rule to follow is to choose the asset which (pick one):

(1) has higher total income payments, regardless of the date on which these accrue.

(2) pays income for the longer period of time.

(3) pays off more quickly.

(4) yields the higher capitalized value—determined by discounting all income items by means of the market interest rate and summing all such discounted values.

b. Thus (to repeat something already said in the chapter), do not try to value assets by what they would cost, or did cost, to construct. Value them instead in terms of the future net revenues they are expected to bring in, and *discount* these revenues.

The basic discounting formula is simple. Take any one item of expected future revenue, $\$N_t$. It is due to arrive *t* years from now. The market interest rate, expressed as a fraction (e.g., 5 percent = 5/100) is *i*. The present value of that expected future revenue item is $\$N_t/(1-i)^t$. The present values of assets A and B accordingly depend on the market interest rate. The higher

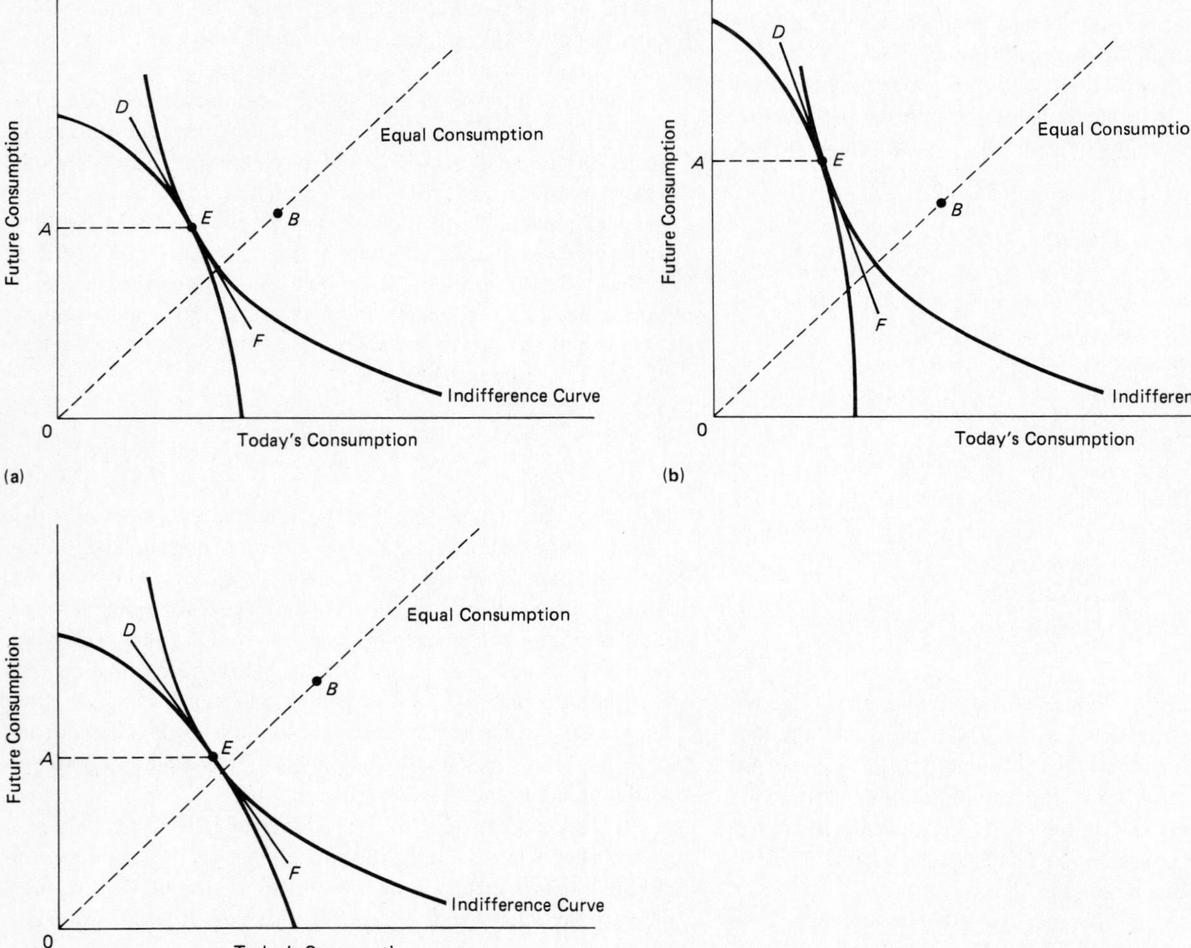

Figure 30A-1

this rate, the sharper the discounting knife. The further away in time any revenue item is, the more deeply it cuts. So the higher the interest rate, the more probable that asset *(A / B)* will have the higher capitalized (discounted) value.

---

a. (4) b. A (A and B have equal capitalized values when the interest rate is approximately 4 ½ percent annually. At any lower rate, B has the higher value; at any higher rate, A has.)

6. Classical capital and interest theory suggests that as an economy grows and matures, interest rates will (over the long run) gradually fall. As they do, the economy will gradually take up more "roundabout" methods of production. (If you are hungry, you want things in a hurry; if you are rich, you can afford to wait.) One example of a roundabout method would be a process involving a capital good which costs a lot to build and lasts for 50 to 100 years. You must wait a long time before you get the full payoff from your real capital investment.

Now consider the primitive example of roundaboutness. Two alternative methods of producing 1 unit of some finished product exist. Both require the input of some labor *now*; then you must wait until the finished product arrives or matures. Specifically,

Method A: 7 labor units now, then wait 2 years

Method B: 5 labor units now, then wait 3 years

Here, method B is the more roundabout: the waiting period is longer. Which method would be more attractive to producers? That depends on the interest rate.

Start with the case in which the market interest rate is 40 percent per year. Let the finished product be worth $10. Since this product accrues in the future (either 2 years or 3 years away), you must discount this $10 to get its *present* value. Discounted from 2 years ahead (see the formula in question **5b**) at the 40 percent rate, $10 is reduced to $5.11; discounted for 3 years, to $3.65.

Suppose labor costs 73 cents per unit. It makes no difference whether you use method A (hire 7 units of labor now at 73 cents each, total cost $5.11, then wait 2 years) or method B (5 units of labor now, total cost $3.65, then wait 3 years). Either way, your payoff will be $10, and the return of your investment will be 40 percent—just the market rate.

Now suppose that market rate is only 20 percent annually. Given the same input and output prices as before, both method A and method B would now be highly attractive. In both instances, their net productivity would still be 40 percent—twice the new market rate of return.

But now raise the cost of the investment, which in our example means increasing the price of labor. Method A, which requires more labor than method B, will cease to be profitable (cease to earn the market rate of return), while method B is still profitable. At 20 percent interest, $10 discounts down to $6.95 for 2 years, $5.79 for 3 years. Let labor's price be $1 rather than 73 cents. It *(would still / would not)* pay to spend $7 (method A) to get a return with a present value of $6.95. It *(would still / would not)* pay to spend $5 (method B) to get a return with a present value of $5.79.

This illustrates the classical argument: a gradual fall in interest rates will prompt society to move from the less roundabout method (A) to the more roundabout one (B).

---

would not; would still

QUIZ: Multiple Choice

1. Equilibrium interest rates are determined:
(1) by the interaction of the rate of return to capital and the risk aversion of individual lenders.
(2) by the interaction of the (lack of) impatience of society to consume and the risk aversion of potential investors.
(3) primarily by the federal government in its role in stabilizing macroeconomic variables.
(4) by the interaction of the rate of return to capital and the (lack of) impatience of society to consume.
(5) none of the above.

2. The Fisher diagram can be used to illustrate:
(1) how an increase in the impatience of society to consume can raise the interest rate.
(2) how an increase in the technological tradeoff that turns forgone present consumption into future consumption can increase the rate of interest.
(3) that a negative real interest rate is possible.
(4) that the construction of the production-possibility frontier can be used to explore the market for capital.
(5) all of the above.

3. If the market rate of interest rises, other things equal, the present value of any given capital asset should:
(1) rise, and the more the asset's expected revenues extend far into the future, the more it will rise.
(2) rise, and the more the asset's expected revenues accrue in the immediate rather than the remote future, the more it will rise.
(3) fall, and the more the asset's expected revenues extend far into the future, the more it will fall.
(4) fall, and the more the asset's expected revenues accrue in the immediate rather than the remote future, the more it will fall.
(5) not be changed at all.

4. Which alternative in question 3 would be correct had that question referred to the capital asset's rate of return rather than its present value (other factors remaining unchanged)?
(1).
(2).
(3).

(4).
(5).

5. Those who invest in any new capital good always face some degree of uncertainty about future revenues which that good might return. If investors are the least bit averse to risk, the effect of this uncertainty factor is:

(1) fully recognized in the classical account of capital and interest.
(2) to set an effective maximum level for the market interest rate.
(3) to make the task of establishing an easy monetary policy an easier one.
(4) to make the task of establishing a tight monetary policy a more difficult one.
(5) to set a positive minimum level for the nominal market interest rate.

6. The present discounted value of $500 payable 1 year from now, at a market interest rate of 9 percent annually, is:
(1) $545.
(2) $500.
(3) a little more than $455, but less than $500.
(4) $455.
(5) a little less than $455.

7. Implicit in any discussion of capital and interest is a rule for the proper method of determining the worth, or value, of any asset. This rule instructs us to:
(1) value assets according to original cost of construction or purchase, deducting from this cost figure an appropriate depreciation figure to arrive at present value.
(2) value assets according to the net revenue they are expected to yield in the future, capitalized value being the sum of all such expected future revenues.
(3) value assets according to the discounted sum of the net revenue that they are expected to yield in the future.
(4) determine the dollar figure which represents the net productivity of the asset and then discount that net productivity figure by means of the interest rate, should such a procedure be necessary.
(5) do none of the preceding.

SUGGESTED ANSWERS TO QUESTIONS IN THE TEXT: Appendix to Chapter 30

1. The bequest makes the marginal utility of future consumption financed by present saving fall; it makes sense, therefore, to increase the time preference of present consumption over future (deferred) consumption. The steak offer could be rational, in the extreme.

2. The same technology means that the *PPF*s start out the same in the Fisher diagrams. Think of things that can influence the indifference curves. Impatience does so directly. Also think of things that distort the *PPF*s. Inflation might, if the *PPF*s are denominated in currency terms, because it makes future consumption more expensive.

3. The general present-value equation, reads: with $1/(1 + i) = K$,

$$V = \frac{\$N}{(1+i)} + \frac{\$N}{(1+i)^2} + \cdots$$
$$= \$NK + \$NK^2 + \cdots$$
$$= \$NK(1 + K + K^2 + \cdots)$$
$$= \$NK/(1 - K) = \$NK/\{1 - [1/(1+i)]\}$$
$$= \$N\frac{1/(1+i)}{(1+i-1)/(1+i)} = \$N/i$$

4. Interest-rate changes affect the present value of net returns in the most distant future the most. Why? Because the power of the denominator is higher, so any increase in the value being raised to the power is enlarged. For example, doubling the interest rate affects $[1/(1+i)]^{10}$ more than it does $[1/(1+i)]^2$.

5. Move the shapes of the *PPF* and the indifference curves around so that their tangency is flat; then see what might cause those changes—see answer 2 above.

CHAPTER 31 ___
MARKETS AND ECONOMIC EFFICIENCY

Part Six of the text will lead you through some of the thorniest topics of economic analysis. It begins in Chapter 31 with a discussion of the efficiency properties of an economic system that determines all prices and wages simultaneously. Previous chapters have shown that individual competitive markets lead to efficient solutions of the production question when they are allowed to operate in isolation; i.e., under the partial-equilibrium assumption that all other prices and quantities in the surrounding economy are fixed and unchanging. But what about a general-equilibrium system in which the effects of production decisions in one market on the pricing and production decisions in another market are explicitly considered and allowed to feed back into the original decision? Can anything be said about efficiency, or lack thereof, in such a general-equilibrium setting?

In addition to gleaning some understanding of the qualifications that must be placed upon an economy to ensure that the answer to the last question is "Yes, efficiency is achieved," your work in this chapter will allow you to accomplish the following objectives.

LEARNING OBJECTIVES

1. Review the seven microeconomic steps, covered in previous chapters, with which competitive markets solve the simultaneous questions of *what*, *how*, and *for whom*.

2. Describe the circular pattern of interdependence between product and input markets, showing clearly the role played by households and businesses.

3. Describe in detail how the myopic actions of individuals and firms in a perfectly competitive economy would lead to the equality of marginal (social) cost, marginal utility, and price for *every* good at *every* firm and for *every* individual; i.e., illustrate the origins of the "first theorem of welfare economics" (which states that competitive economies achieve allocative efficiency).

4. List the conditions that must be satisfied before the existence of a competitive general equilibrium can be demonstrated, and illustrate the resulting efficiency in terms of a utility-possibility frontier.

5. Show how each of the qualifications listed in objective 4 leads to concern about the ability of the invisible hand to promote efficiency under a laissez-faire economic policy.

6. Describe the distributional-equity potential of perfectly competitive market economies.

Microeconomic analysis is, in its simplest form, conducted in partial equilibrium. Individuals maximize utility *given* limited income, product prices, and a pattern of tastes. Firms maximize profits *given* technology, some type of demand structure, and input prices. The next step toward generalization is to allow all individuals and firms to interact simultaneously to determine an entire set of prices and quantities that clear a multitude of prices. It is a step toward understanding the interdependence of markets of all sorts (input markets with input markets, product markets with product markets, and input markets with product markets), but it is more than that. It is an analysis that speaks to the conditions which guarantee that, given a Pareto notion of efficiency (an economic structure is efficient if nobody can be made better off without hurting somebody else; i.e., there is no "free" surplus to be had), all the market interactions achieve efficiency. Looking at the flip side, then, it is an analysis that identifies economic circumstances that undermine efficiency. And it is an analysis that does not forget its heart; it worries about equity and its association with efficiency.

1. a. In the spaces provided, list the seven steps with which an economy solves its *what*, *how*, and *for whom* questions.

Indicate, as well, what is held constant in the usual partial-equilibrium analysis of each step.

(1) ______________________________

(2) ______________________________

(3) ______________________________

(4) ______________________________

(5) ______________________________

(6) ______________________________

(7) ______________________________

These issues, all involving the behavior of single markets, households, or firms, are all subjects of partial-equilibrium analysis. They have, thus far, been explored under the assumption that *(all other people are equal / all other things are equal / all government policies are equal).*

b. It is not possible simply to build a general-equilibrium model of an entire economy by "tacking" partial-equilibrium models of individual sectors or markets onto each other. If, for example, there were only three goods in an economy, X, Y, and Z, you could not lump supply-demand analyses of the three goods together and expect to produce an accurate picture of the entire economy. Why not? The reason lies in the "other things being equal" approach of partial-equilibrium models.

The demand curve for good X, for example, would be drawn as a function of the price of X given the assumption that all the other factors that might influence the demand for X (e.g., incomes, the price of Y, etc.) were held constant. But that need not be the case. If the price of Y were to change, or the level of consumers' incomes were to change, then the demand curve for X might shift to a new position.

Consider a specific illustration with two commodities: butter and margarine. Suppose that the markets for both were initially in equilibrium. Now let a technical development sharply reduce the cost of producing margarine. What would happen? In terms of supply and demand, we would expect to see the supply curve for margarine shift *(down / up)*, thereby establishing a new and *(higher / lower)* equilibrium price for margarine. The demand curve for butter, unaffected up to this point, was drawn *given the initial price of margarine*. Since the two goods are substitutes, though, the adjustment in the price of margarine just noted should make the demand curve for butter shift *(to the left / to the right)*, thereby producing a new and *(higher / lower)* price for butter. The demand curve for margarine, unaffected up to this point, was drawn given *the initial price of butter*, so the process would continue until some final, mutually compatible pair of prices was achieved.

The point of all this is simply that using ordinary supply-and-demand models to examine the economic consequence of some change in economic circumstance deliberately ignores the impact which that change might have on the equilibrium prices and quantities of other goods. Moreover, it deliberately ignores the feedback effects that changes in those equilibria might have on the original market. Sometimes the omissions make no difference, but sometimes they do.

---

a. (1) Competitive supply and demand schedules determine equilibrium in individual markets given other prices and incomes. **(2)** Marginal utility analysis determines individual demand curves given other prices and income. **(3)** Marginal cost curves determine competitive supply curves given technology reflected by production functions and the prices of inputs. **(4)** Firms operate to maximize profits given marginal revenue product curves (revenue side) and marginal cost curves (cost side). **(5)** Marginal revenue products determine derived curves for inputs given other input employment levels and output prices. **(6)** Supply schedules for inputs interact with derived demand curves to determine input prices, holding everything else fixed. **(7)** Factor prices are major determinants of the distribution of income, holding resource endowments fixed, all other things are equal **b.** down; lower; to the left; lower

2. a. General-equilibrium theory is cast within the special case of perfect competition because (more than one may be correct):

(1) it has special significance with respect to the "best" use of a given but limited stock of resources or inputs.

(2) with only a few monopoly exceptions, the structure of the real-life American economy corresponds reasonably well to the requirements of perfect competition.

(3) the American economy is highly "competitive" in many senses even though it does not completely satisfy the structural requirements of pure competition. This prompts some economists to think that analysis built as though perfect competition applied can still give useful results (in some cases) when applied to the American economy.

b. Perfect competition has special significance from a "welfare" standpoint. If we take as given the stock of resources, the conditions of their ownership, and the state of technology, then the set of prices which would emerge under perfect competition would yield (pick one):

(1) the most efficient allocation of all such resources among their various possible allocations.

(2) the most desirable distribution of income among the people who make up the population in question.

c. Table 31-1 is intended to illustrate the meaning of "efficient resource allocation." It assumes that the economy produces only three goods, X, Y, and Z. A general equilibrium has been reached with the quantities recorded on line 1 being supported in that equilibrium by the prices recorded on line 3.

Table 31-1

	X	Y	Z
1. Total quantities of goods produced and bought	3,000	4,000	5,000
2. Marginal utilities of goods for a typical consumer	100	50	200
3. Price of good	$2	$1	$4
4. Marginal cost of good	$2	$1	$4

Given the X, Y, and Z prices on line 3, the "typical consumer" *(has / has not / may or may not have)* reached his or her maximum-satisfaction position. Why? Because the ratios of marginal utility to price are all equal to ________.

If supplying firms operate under conditions of perfect competition, then, with prices as on line 3 and marginal costs as on line 4, they *(have / have not)* reached maximum-profit positions. Why? Because the prices of all three goods equal their ____________________.

Note the general-equilibrium quality of this situation. Consumers reach maximum-satisfaction positions by juggling their X, Y, and Z purchases. Producers adjust the level of their marginal cost by varying the quantity of X, Y, and Z that they produce and sell. The quantities on line 1 and the prices on line 3 must be such that they simultaneously satisfy *both* consumers and producers. The situation must be one in which neither consumers nor producers can see any advantage in any change of position.

The significant property of this situation is indicated by comparing line 2 with line 4. Here, prices are an accurate indication of marginal costs. And marginal cost is a money indicator of the Real cost of getting another unit of X, Y, or Z.

Complete your understanding of this equilibrium by computing the marginal rate of substitution (*MRS*) and marginal rate of transformation (*MRT*) for each of the three possible pairings of X, Y, and Z. Record your answers in Table 31-2. For X and Y taken together, the (*MRS*) equals ________, and *MRT* equals ________, and the corresponding ratio of prices equals ________. Note the similar equality for X and Z taken together and Y and Z taken together.

d. Now suppose that all the figures—save one—in Table 31-1 are unchanged. Good X in this new case is produced under conditions of imperfect competition. This means that each producer of X will equate marginal cost with the *(price of X / marginal revenue from X)*. In imperfect competition, marginal revenue is *(the same as / greater than / less than)* price. The price of X is still $2; but its marginal revenue to producers is, say, $1. The *MC* figure for X on line 4 above must then be $1. All other figures are unchanged, and general equilibrium prevails. Note that the producers of X, by equating *MR* and *MC*, produce and sell a quantity of X which is *(the same as / less than / more than)* the quantity they would have produced by equating *MC* with price.

In this new case, consumers are still at equilibrium. But the prices they must pay are no longer a true indicator of real underlying marginal cost. Why? Because X's *MC* is $1, not $2.

Here there is a contrived scarcity of X which buyers must accept as though it were a real scarcity; i.e., as though it really cost $2 in real resources to produce 1 more unit of X. It is evident that if the price of X were to fall to $1, a new general equilibrium would have to be worked out, with new X, Y, and Z prices and quantities. And it can be shown—although it is not easy to show—that the new X, Y, and Z quantities would represent a slight gain in the community's welfare.

To see the potential for this gain, note that the *MRS* between X and Y is still ________ and the *MRS* between X and Z is still ________. Nonetheless, the true *MRT* between X and Y is now ________, and between X and Z it is ________. If $1 of resources were released from the production of Y and devoted to the production of X, then the production of Y would fall by 1 unit while the production of X could rise by ________ unit. Utility would *(rise / fall)* by ________ units as a direct result of the change in Y, but it would *(rise / fall)* by ________ units with the associated change in X. The net effect would be *(an increase / a reduction)* in total welfare (utility) of ________ units.

---

a. (1) and **(3)** **b. (1)** **c.** has; 2; have; marginal costs; row 2: *MRS* = 1/4, *MRT* = 1/4; row 3: *MRS* = 1/2, *MRT* = 1/2; 2; 2; 2 **d.** marginal revenue from X; less than; less than; 2; 1/2; 1; 1/4; 1; fall; 50; rise; 100; an increase; 50 (*Hint:* Remember, *MRS* equals a ratio of marginal utilities, and *MRT* equals a ratio of marginal cost.)

Table 31-2

	MU_x	MU_y	MU_z	*MRS*	MC_x	MC_y	MC_z	*MRT*
1. X and Y	100	50	________	2	$2	$1	________	2
2. Y and Z	________	50	200		________	$1	$4	________
3. X and Z	100	________	200		$2	________	$4	________

3. Kenneth Arrow and Gerard Debreu, both of whom have won Nobel Prizes, were among the first to prove the existence of competitive general equilibrium. Their proof depended upon a long list of qualifications. List at least five in the spaces provided, and state *in parentheses* which competitive condition would have been violated it this qualification had been ignored.

a. ______

b. ______

c. ______

d. ______

e. ______

a. no increasing returns to scale (Otherwise, positive profits and prices in excess of marginal cost would emerge.) **b.** no externalities (Otherwise, the prices of some goods would not match their true social costs.) **c.** flexible wages and prices (Otherwise, unemployed resources would be possible.) **d.** no uninsurable risk (Otherwise, inefficient losses might occur.) **e.** no monopolies or other types of imperfect competition (Otherwise, prices in excess of marginal cost would be forthcoming.) (See the footnote to the section entitled "Detailed Analysis of General Equilibrium.")

4. The previous question began a list of qualifications that undermine the application of the efficiency virtues of the competitive general equilibrium to support a laissez-faire policy recommendation. This question will build on that list. Indicate in the spaces provided below the inefficiencies caused by each of the following circumstances:

a. monopoly or monopolistic competition: ______

b. unrestrained water and/or air pollution: ______

c. discrimination against blacks in labor markets: ______

d. settlements that prevent wage responses to slack demand: ______

e. monopoly power in a labor union: ______

f. government regulation that prevents competition: ______

a. prices too high, output too low, wages and input prices distorted **b.** output too high because marginal cost too low, price too low, input prices distorted **c.** unequal pay for equal work, prices distorted, income distribution distorted **d.** unemployed resources during recession, prices stay too high **e.** wages too high, prices too high, output too low, other input prices distorted **f.** government-created monopolies—see answer **a.**

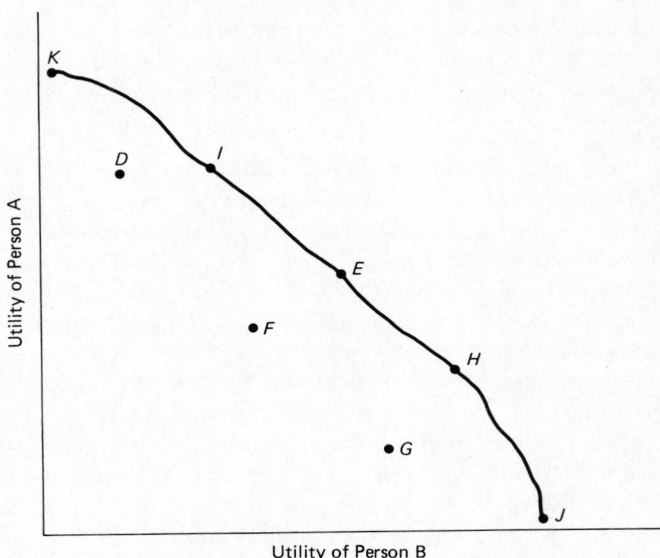

Figure 31-1

5. Figure 31-1 displays several points relative to a utility-possibility frontier. Record in the spaces below which point(s) illustrate the effects of the following circumstances relative to a Pareto-efficient allocation indicated by point *E*.

a. an unethical distribution of income . . . . (______)

b. unemployed resources . . . . (______)

c. wage discrimination against individual A . . . . (______)

d. unrestrained pollution in the production of a good consumed exclusively by B that hurts only A . . . . (______)

a. *J, K* (though some may object to *H* and *I*, as well) **b.** *D, F, G* **c.** *G* **d.** *G* (The answers to the last two are not *H* or *J* because both involve inefficiencies that allow the possibility of improving the utilities of both A and B; the answers cannot, therefore, be on the frontier.)

Welfare economics has nothing necessarily to do with improving the status of the poor. It refers only to that branch of economics in which the words "better" and "worse" are used, i.e., in which it is said that some situation A is more desirable than some alternative situation B.

The statement that A is preferable to B requires some value scale. Since individual preference scales differ, this makes welfare economics a difficult and dangerous area. However, the following statement seems fair: situation A is preferable to B if, in the course of a change from B to A, some people would be made better off while nobody would be made worse off. In the vernacular of economics, A is a Pareto improvement over B.

Unfortunately, there are probably not too many of these convenient nobody-worse-off changes. The next step in welfare economics is to find situations in which there are losers as well as gainers—but the predicted gain of the gainers exceeds the predicted loss of the losers. In this circumstance, the gainers could "bribe" the losers to make the change; or the gainers could be taxed by a sufficient amount to compensate the losers and still have some part of their gains left.

6. It is in this sense that the equilibrium of perfect competition is declared to be "efficient." When this equilibrium is reached, it is impossible to find any alternative attainable combination of goods and services in which those who gain by the change could *(fully / less than fully)* compensate the losers and still be better off.

Note particularly that this is ultimately a matter of the "efficient" allocation of a given and limited resource stock—limited in the particular sense that it cannot yield enough output to satisfy everybody's demands for everything he or she would like to have. Perfect competition achieve's allocative efficiency; i.e., it allocates the stock of resources so that the combination of goods and services produced meets the requirement set out in the preceding paragraph. With a competitive equilibrium, there are *no* Pareto improvements.

This "efficiency" definition is acceptable only insofar as the assumptions underlying perfect-competition theory are acceptable. The theory assumes that there *(are / are no)* significant economies of large-scale operations. There *(are / are no)* external diseconomies. (There is an external diseconomy if a plant pollutes the air or water and is not required to bear the cost which this pollution imposes.) The distribution of income, equal or unequal, is *(declared to be the most appropriate / accepted without comment on its desirability)*. The stock of resources is assumed to be *(fixed / increased)*, and the state of technology is assumed to be *(given / improving)*.

---

fully; are no; accepted without comment on its desirability; fixed; given

QUIZ: Multiple Choice

1. In general equilibrium and in a situation of perfect competition:
(1) for each consumer, the marginal utility of each good consumed is equal to the price of that good.
(2) for each consumer, marginal utilities of all goods consumed are proportional to the marginal costs of those goods.
(3) the marginal physical product of each input is equal to the price of that input.
(4) the marginal revenue product of each input is equal to the price of the finished good it produces.
(5) the ratio of total expenditure on any good to its price equals marginal utility.

2. The profit-maximizing motive in perfect competition differs from the profit-maximizing motive in imperfect competition in which of the following respects?
(1) The perfect competitor tries to equate price and average cost, which does *not* lead to maximum profit.
(2) The perfect competitor tries to equate price and marginal cost, which does *not* lead to maximum profit.
(3) The perfect competitor tries to equate marginal revenue and marginal cost, which does *not* lead to maximum profit.
(4) The imperfect competitor tries to equate price and marginal cost, which leads to a larger profit than the equating of marginal revenue and marginal cost.
(5) In none of these ways, because the firms in both situations are equally interested in earning as much profit as possible.

3. The theory of perfect competition, according to most economists:
(1) gives a reasonably accurate description of real performance, even though it cannot be used to evaluate the efficiency of that performance.
(2) describes real performance in rough outline despite competitive imperfections, and is most important for appraising the efficiency of that performance.
(3) is most important for appraising the efficiency of real performance, even though it is not even approximately correct in describing that performance.
(4) bears almost no resemblance to real performance, and cannot be used to evaluate its efficiency, but is most important because its material is a lead into the theory of imperfect competition.
(5) with relatively minor monopoly exceptions, gives a closely accurate outline of real performance, and can be used to identify the monopoly exceptions.

4. Four of the following five alternatives state conditions which must be satisfied if the equilibrium conditions of all-around perfect competition are to be satisfied. One alternative states a condition not so required; i.e., one would not necessarily be the result of perfect competition. Which one?
(1) Price is equal to average cost.
(2) For each individual, and for each good he or she consumes,

the ratio between marginal utility and price is the same for all such goods.
(3) Price is equal to marginal cost.
(4) There is no significant inequality in the distribution of income among individuals.
(5) Price is equal to minimum average cost.

5. Four of the following five alternatives state conditions which indicate that the conditions of all-around perfect competition are not satisfied. One alternative states a condition which must be satisfied to meet the requirements of perfect competition. Which one?
(1) Market prices are steady in the sense of being unresponsive to short-run changes in demand or in supply.
(2) Price is equal to average cost but not to marginal cost.
(3) Different wage rates are paid in different geographical locations for work whose requirements are exactly the same in both locations.
(4) Product differentiation yields a price that equals average cost, but not minimum-attainable average cost.
(5) Marginal cost is equal to average cost.

6. The theory of perfect competition began by recognizing two facts: resources are scarce, and the price system is a mechanism for allocating the use or employment of those resources. From here, the theory gradually developed a set of rules which, if satisfied, would indicate that the scarce resources were being utilized efficiently. These rules were stated with special regard for one kind of influence that might drive results away from the perfectly competitive equilibrium. That disrupting influence was:
(1) laissez-faire pricing activity.
(2) activity over time.
(3) interdependence among the inputs employed.
(4) the presence of monopoly or of monopoly elements.
(5) space, or geographical differences.

7. Perfect-competition theory's equilibrium requirements, as indicated in question 6, set out rules for an efficient allocation of scarce resources. Yet the result, even with these rules fully satisfied, may not be "optimal," to the extent that:
(1) price is equal to marginal cost.
(2) external economies or diseconomies are present.
(3) the economy is led to specialize in the production of only a few goods.
(4) price is equal to average cost.
(5) it is possible to substitute one input or resource in place of another.

SUGGESTED ANSWERS TO QUESTIONS IN THE TEXT: Chapter 31

1. Couch your answer around the circular diagram. Refer to the appropriate chapters if you have trouble with any of the seven steps.

2. No increasing returns to scale (natural monopolies like utilities, etc.); no externalities (like pollution or bees, etc.); flexible wages and prices (no long-term fixed contracts, etc.); no uninsurable risks [nuclear power plants (?)]; no imperfect competition (from whatever source).

3. First theorem: General equilibrium in a perfectly competitive market system achieves allocative efficiency. Second theorem: Given any situation of allocative efficiency, there exists a distribution of resources for which that system is in a competitive equilibrium.

a. Allocative efficiency can be supported by any distribution of resources and thus income.

b. Allocative efficiency will not correct unequal distributions of resources.

c. Refers to the first theorem.

d. This is the first theorem.

e. Apply the second theorem.

4. Imperfect competition may put the economy below the *PPF* (i.e., it may not achieve allocative efficiency), but the economy may grow faster given the Schumpeterian hypothesis, which holds that monopoly power generates the profit required for innovation. If that is true, then the economy may become better off over the long run. Consult Figure TQ31-1. There, a competitive economy grows from PPF_1 to PPF_2 over a period of time; specifically , it moves from E_1 on PPF_1 to E_2 on PPF_2. By comparison, an economy with a growth-amplifying monopolist moves from ppf^1 to ppf^2. Operating below both, such an economy could move from e^1 to e^2 with e^2 dominating E_2 (consumption of both goods is higher at e^2 than at E_2).

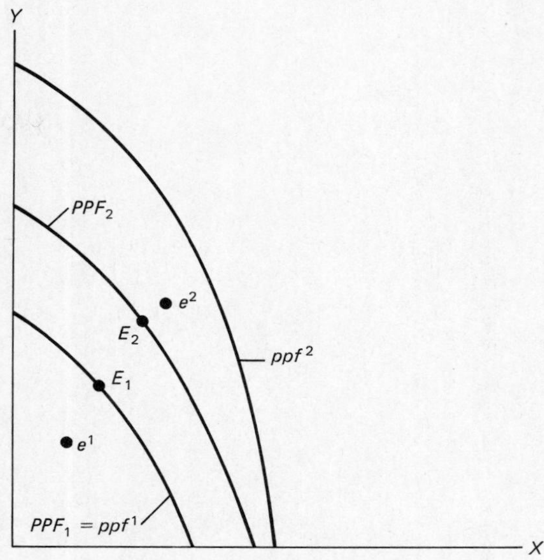

Figure TQ31-1

5. Given $Y = 2X$ and $X = Y - 25$, substitution generates $X = 2X - 25$, so $X^* = 25$ and $Y^* = 50$. Given two [*N*] independent equations, you can generally solve for two [*N*] variables.

6. Any point on a *PPF* achieved by a socialistic economy is a point of allocative efficiency, and it can (by the second theorem) be supported as a competitive equilibrium with the appropriate redistribution of resources (income). Ponder how to do that. What might be the incentive effects? Can socialism, with all its administrative needs, get to the frontier? Does the theorem hold for points below the frontier?

CHAPTER 32

ECONOMIC ROLE OF GOVERNMENT

Government has, in most advanced industrial countries, been growing in dramatic fashion over the past few decades. Government spending has climbed, both in absolute terms and in terms of a proportion of GNP. Taxation has been growing, as well. So have income-support programs and regulatory intervention into both the marketplace in specific and society in general. The size of government has, in fact, turned into one of *the* political issues of the 1980s in the United States, the United Kingdom, and elsewher[illegible] the democratic world.

Chapter 3[illegible] a two-chapter discussion of the economic issue[illegible]rround this growth. Section A of this chapter pr[illegible] begin the process, a brief chronicle of its rece[illegible]. A second section introduces you to an avenu[illegible]retical analysis, bearing the suggestive name of [illegible]hoice," that brings the old study of "political e[illegible] up to date. Finally, the analysis developed i[illegible]cond section is applied to the problem of econo[illegible]nality in section C. The general notion of publi[illegible] and bads) is reviewed there before a specific poll[illegible]mple crystallizes the role of government in that [illegible] market failure.

[illegible] emphasized from the beginning, though, that th[illegible]lity of "government failure" is not precluded. T[illegible], and do, exist governmental policies that do [illegible]m than good; and care needs to be taken that [illegible]ential is recognized and the specific cases are [illegible]lentified.

Proceeding through this first of two chapters, then, you will be able to accomplish the following objectives on the route to a preliminary understanding of how contemporary economic analysis deals with government activity.

LEARNING OBJECTIVES

1. Chronicle the changes in government spending, taxation, and regulatory activity over the past few decades, particularly in the United States. Contrast the growth in spending and taxation with the decline of regulation over the past 10 years or so.

2. List, explain, and provide examples of the four major functions that government must consider: provide and maintain a legal system, conduct stabilizing macroeconomic policy, work to allocate resources with maximum efficiency, and conduct programs of income redistribution.

3. Understand the genesis of "public choice": the need to determine whether government is organized in a way that allows it to achieve its objectives.

4. Identify various voting rules (unanimity, majority rule, supermajority rule) and the difficulties that might arise in their implementation. Explore their differences and similarities with the aid of a utility-possibility frontier.

5. Note the possibility that majority voting can cycle with no unambiguous outcome; explain why this potential places enormous power in the hands of those who control the decision rules and the public agenda.

6. State Arrow's impossibility theorem (which holds that no majority voting scheme exists which will guarantee efficiency, respect individual preferences, and generate outcomes that are not dependent upon the ordering of the voting agenda). Construct an example showing how this theorem works.

7. Define the notion of externality. Relate it to the notion of a public good (bad). Analyze the inefficiency of, e.g., a pollution externality, and describe how various control mechanisms might work to ameliorate its social damage.

You are already familiar with a wide range of decisions through which government influences the everyday lives of people, businesses, and other economic agents across the nation and around the world. Parts Two and Three of the text concentrated on the macro policies of government, for example. These are stabilization policies that are typically directed at macro variables like unemployment and inflation; nonetheless, they make it more or less difficult to buy a house, sell a car, or pay for college. Parts Four and Five reviewed the myriad of roles that government can play on a micro level, and found no less significant activity. Regulation and antitrust action are but two items of a long list of micro-based roles that government has assumed. The point of the next two chapters is not to reiterate; it is, instead, to investigate the norms against which these activities are measured and the way decisions about their directions are made in a democratic society.

1. Since World War I, the size of government, measured in terms of expenditures, taxation, and/or regulation has *(remained remarkably stable / fallen slightly since World War II after growing rapidly between wars / grown dramatically).* Compared with spending amounting to slightly more that 10 percent of GNP prior to World War I, the sum of budgets across all levels of government in the United States had, by the 1980s, *(fallen back to 10 percent of GNP after peaking during the Carter administration at 21 percent / grown steadily to nearly 25 percent of GNP / stabilized at approximately 35 percent of GNP).*

Over the same period of time, tax revenues collected by all levels of government have *(kept pace with / grown at a slightly slower pace than / grown at a slightly faster pace than)* expenditures, with enormous shortfalls coming during *(the Great Depression / World War II / the Reagan years).* Nonetheless, tax revenues are still perhaps *(5 / 50 / 500)* percent larger now than they were at the turn of the century.

b. Regulatory activity, started perhaps in *(1913 / 1887 / 1778)* with the formation of the *(Federal Reserve System / Department of Agriculture / Interstate Commerce Commission)*, reached its high point during the *(Nixon / Carter / Reagan)* administration. The ability of the U.S. government to regulate some of the activities of some of its citizens is justified by reference to the U.S. Constitution. Specifically, interpretation of a phrase about *(avoiding taxation with representation / equal protection under the law / securing the public interest)* had led to social and economic regulation of all kinds. List at least four industries that have faced significant regulation over the past half-century.

(1) ______________________

(2) ______________________

(3) ______________________

(4) ______________________

---

a. grown dramatically; stabilized at approximately 35 percent of GNP; grown at a slightly slower pace than; all three; 500 **b.** 1887; Interstate Commerce Commission; Carter; securing the public interest; **(1)** through **(4)** any of the following: airlines; trucking; water traffic; utilities of all sorts; banking; pipelines; oil and gas

2. It is extremely interesting to note that the size of the government in a nation's economy seems to depend upon the size of that economy; measured as a proportion of GNP, poor, less developed countries show a tendency to tax and spend *(less than / more than / about the same as)* advanced countries. Circle the country in each of the following pairs whose government spends more as a fraction of GNP.

a. United States / Nicaragua

b. United States / United Kingdom

c. United States / France

d. United States / Japan

e. United States / West Germany

f. United States / Sweden

g. India / Switzerland

h. Sri Lanka / Netherlands

Notice that the United States, despite all the political furor about the size of the American government, ranks far from the top among developed countries in this ordering. In absolute terms, the size of the American government is enormous, of course; but relative to GNP, its size is considerably more modest.

---

less than **a.** United States **b.** United Kingdom **c.** France **d.** United States **e.** West Germany **f.** Sweden **g.** Switzerland **h.** Netherlands (Consult Figure 32-2 to confirm these answers.)

3. Government can serve four distinct functions in a mixed economy. List them in the spaces provided:

a. ______________________

b. ______________________

c. ______________________

d. ______________________

Each of the following activities falls into at least one of the four categories that you just identified; indicate which in the spaces provided.

(1) Cutting taxes to reduce unemployment:

____

(2) Specifying that the manufacturer is liable for any harm caused by his product:

____

(3) Placing a tax on a steel producer's pollution:

____

(4) Legislating that it is illegal to discriminate on the basis of sex:

____

(5) Enacting an income policy that penalizes larger-than-specified wage increases:

____

(6) Enacting a program of aid to families with dependent children:

____

(7) Enacting day-care help to allow women to work:

____

(8) Writing laws that allow triple damages to be awarded in cases of gross and wanton negligence:

____

a. Prescribe legal framework **b.** work toward macroeconomic stability **c.** allocate resources efficiently **d.** allocate resources equitably **(1)** macro stabilization **(2)** legal framework **(3)** promote efficiency **(4)** legal, efficiency, and equity objectives **(5)** macro stabilization **(6)** promote equity **(7)** promote equity and efficiency **(8)** legal framework

Much of the material that has been presented in previous chapters has indicated what governments that want to do certain things "ought to do" to accomplish their goals. Public choice analyzes whether in fact they do what they ought to. Do they work to promote efficiency and equity, for example, or do they do the opposite even when their truly espoused goals are efficiency and equity? Are there barriers preventing governments from achieving their goals built into the way they operate—the rules of their games? If so, are there any general principles to be discovered to help break down those barriers?

Voting procedures define the rules of the decision-making game in the United States. We elect representatives who make decisions on our behalf and who want to continue to do so. These representatives therefore have an incentive to behave in a manner that will maximize their chances of (re)election. This behavior generates a supply of government activity, if you will, that is matched in the political arena against a demand for government activity generated by the voters. Two of the primary purposes of public-choice theory applied to the United States are therefore (1) to analyze the workings of this "political marketplace" and (2) to evaluate the properties of its likely set of outcomes. The next few questions will review your brief introduction to that endeavor.

4. Figure 32-1 provides three reproductions of the same utility-possibility frontier. Movement from point *E* in a specific direction can be used to illustrate the result of a Pareto-improving government activity; shade in the area that captures all possible Pareto-improving points relative to point *E* in panel **(a)**. A second area captures all points that would signify a redistribution of resources from individual A to individual B; shade in the area capturing all such points in panel **(b)**. A third area signifies government failure so that government activity would leave both A and B worse off. Shade in the area that captures all these points in panel **(c)**.

Of the three panels that you now have before you, panel *(a / b / c)* indicates with its shaded area all the possible outcomes that might arise from a unanimous voting rule. Why? Because both A and B would have to approve the activity, and that would happen only if the utilities of both A and B were increased. To illustrate the area of potential outcomes under majority rule (under the additional assumption that there are more type B people than there are type A people), you would need to combine the shaded areas of panels ________ and ________ .

Unanimity, as a voting rule, has its drawbacks. For one thing, any one individual can block a decision that can enhance

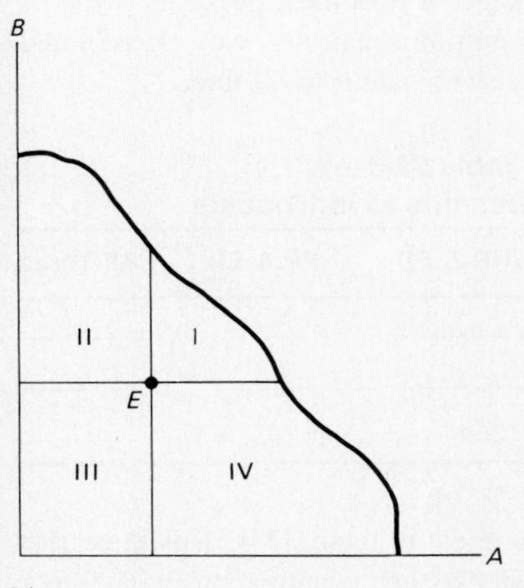

(a)

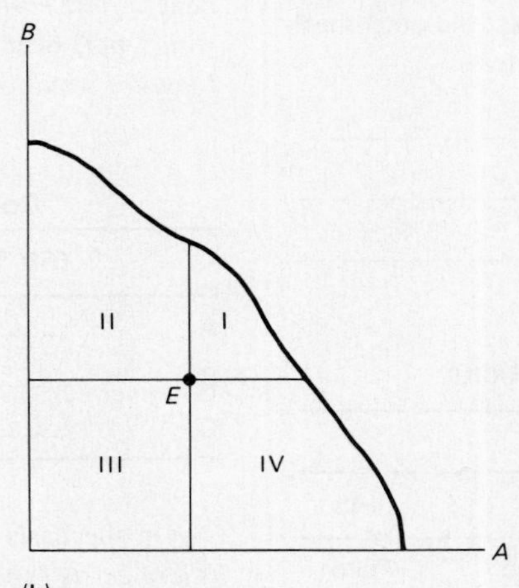

(b)

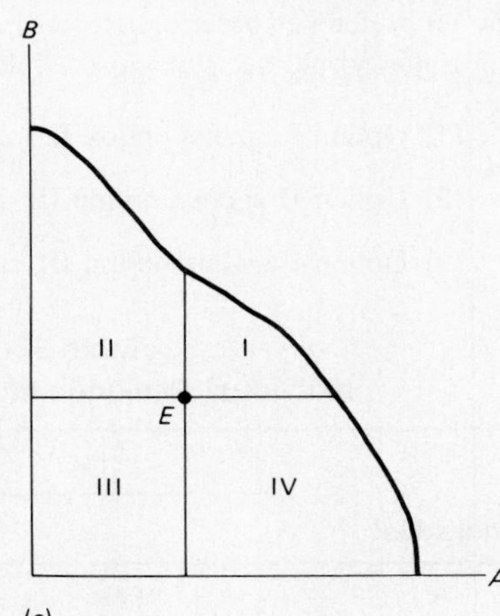

(c)

Figure 32-1

the welfare of everyone else. That means that unanimity can produce only *(a Pareto-improving / an income-transferring / an expansionary)* government policy. In addition to being enormously cumbersome, therefore, unanimity would lead to the potential extortion of most of the gains of any policy by a clever skeptic from the population at large. Because anyone could play that game, unanimity would, more probably, lead to *(a flurry of small actions / no action / the abandonment of government of any kind)*—a *(maintenance / shattering)* of the status quo.

Majority rule, on the other hand, is not necessarily more efficient, but it is certainly more manageable. To avoid the potential tyranny of the majority, though, some important issues require majorities of *(greater than 50 percent / less than 50 percent)* to pass. Although it is subject to the pressures of special-interest groups in its most pragmatic form, majority rule seems to work fairly well in most circumstances.

---

shade in area I; shade in area II; shade in area III; (a); (a); (b); a Pareto-improving; no action; maintenance; greater than 50 percent

Public-choice theory has extensively investigated the workings of majority rule, and its conclusions are not as reassuring as those gained from casual observation. For one thing, the result of a process involving majority rule need not be efficient. For another, there exists the possibility that a sequence of majority-rule referenda will cycle endlessly. That is the import of the Arrow impossibility theorem: there exists no majority-rule scheme that guarantees (1) efficiency, (2) respect of individual preferences, and (3) the independence of the result from the order of the agenda. Cycling, in particular, means that whoever controls the agenda controls the outcome. The next question explores this theorem.

5. a. Consider, first of all, the preferences of three people indicated in Table 32-1. Assume that, in voting between two options, each person votes for the option that ranks higher in his or her preference ordering. Record, in the blanks, the outcomes of majority-rule decisions in the following contests:

(1) Option I against option II ________________

(2) Option II against option III ________________

(3) Option I against option III ________________

Table 32-1
Individual Rankings of Three Options

Individual	Options I	Options II	Options III
A	First	Second	Third
B	Second	Third	First
C	Third	First	Second

b. Now suppose that the Rules Committee of the Process decides that option II will run off against the winner of an initial vote between I and III. The eventual winner will be option *(I / II / III)*. If option I were to run off against the winner of a vote-off between II and III, then the winner would be option *(I / II / III)*. And finally, allowing option III to run off against the winner of a I-to-II contest would produce option *(I / II / III)* as a winner. There would, in fact, be *(no / a single)* unambiguous winner until the agenda—the order of the voting decisions—were specified. This is an example of the impossibility theorem that contributed to Arrow's winning a Nobel Prize in economics.

c. Suppose, now, that individual preferences were formed on the basis of the net benefits indicated in Table 32-2. Regardless of the order of the vote, *(RR / FP / EI / SQ)* would win in pairwise contests of one project against another despite the fact that social welfare would be increased by passage of *(any of the three programs / only FP and EI / only FP and RR / only RR and EI / only EI / only RR / only FP)*.

Table 32-2
Net Benefits to Individuals

Individual	Railroad (RR)	Farm Program (FP)	Earthquake Insurance (EI)	Status Quo (SQ)
A	100	−15	−10	0
B	−20	100	−25	0
C	−20	−10	40	0

d. Consider the possibility of combining programs to accommodate the intensity of the preferences reflected in Table 32-2. Record, in Table 32-3, the net benefits of the indicated combined programs. Record, in columns (1) through (3) of Table 32-4, the preferred combined program based on the net benefits of Table 32-3 for the three indicated pairwise elections. Note, in column (4), the winner and, in column (5), the combined net benefit of the winning package. Any of these packages *(would / would not)* beat the status quo in a majority-wins election and *(would / would not)* beat a combination of all three.

Table 32-3
Combined Benefits to Individuals

	(RR & FP)	(RR & EI)	(FP & EI)	All Three
A	______	______	______	______
B	______	______	______	______
C	______	______	______	______

On the basis of your entries in Table 32-4, it is clear that *(there exists / there does not exist)* an unambiguous winner to a sequence of pairwise elections. This is true despite the fact that *(the status quo / passage of all three proposals / passage of any two of three proposals)* maximizes the increase in net welfare.

Table 32-4
Pairwise Preferences

Election	Individual A (1)	Individual B (2)	Individual C (3)	Winner (4)	Net Benefit (5)
(RR & FP) vs. (RR & EI)	______	______	______	______	______
(RR & FP) vs. (FP & EI)	______	______	______	______	______
(RR & EI) vs. (FP & EI)	______	______	______	______	______

In fact, among the three two-project combinations, *(FP & EI / RR & FP / RR & EI)* generates the largest increase in net welfare.

---

a. (1) I wins (A and B vote for I, while C votes for II.) **(2)** II wins (A and C vote for II, while B votes for III.) **(3)** III wins (B and C vote for III, while A votes for I.)
b. II (Running I vs. III first means that III wins the first round and then runs against II in the second round and loses.); I (Running II vs. III first means that II wins the first round and then runs against I in the second round and loses.); III (Running I against II first means that I wins the first round and then runs against III in the second round and loses.); no
c. SQ; any of the three programs
d. Table 32-3:

RR & FP	RR & EI	FP & EI	All Three
85	90	−25	75
80	−45	75	55
−30	20	30	10

Table 32-4:

A	B	C	Winner	Net Benefit
RR & EI	RR & FP	RR & EI	RR & EI	65
RR & FP	RR & FP	FP & EI	RR & FP	135
RR & EI	FP & EI	FP & EI	FP & EI	80

would; would not; there does not exist (Cycling occurs just as above in part **a**.); passage of all three proposals; RR & FP

6. Within the political system of the United States, there can be found a variety of problems that inhibit the workings of the pure majority-rule system envisioned by the public-choice theorists. For one thing, while there is a one-person, one-vote rule, money *(does / does not)* matter. It can cost $1 million to run for Congress, and that money can come from across the country if the district is targeted by a large Political Action Committee (PAC) or a special-interest group or two. Jesse Helms spent over $17 million to run for reelection to the Senate in 1984—almost $400 per registered voter. For another, the activities of special-interest group lobbying can produce unrepresentative government. Government "by the people and for the people" or the "best government that money can buy"?—that is the question. The U.S. government tends, in addition, to be *(shortsighted / longsighted)* because the longest term is *(2 / 4 / 6)* years for a U.S. *(congressmember / President / senator)*. This time limitation has a tendency to produce a *(high- / medium- / low-)*consumption economy aimed at making sure that the *(short / medium / long)* term is prosperous. It is little wonder, therefore, that fiscal policy is directed at employment and monetary policy is directed at unemployment (to see why, refer to Chapter 17).

---

does; shortsighted; 6; senator; high-; short

7. Turn, now, to the notion of an **externality**. An externality is present when the benefits (positive externality) and/or costs (negative externality) spill over into the lives of other people without their paying or being compensated. Public goods represent the extreme case of externality on the positive side; pollution, on the negative side.

Consider the economic consequences of a negative externality—the emission of heavy, toxic smoke from a factory chimney. No matter how disagreeable it might be to those who work or live nearby, the factory's owners might feel no obligation to clean up their act until public pressure, usually in the form of legislation, forces them to do so. A more recent example is acid rain. Many manufacturers, especially those involved in metal processing, emit sulfur dioxide and nitrogen oxide from their chimneys. These chemicals combine with moisture in the atmosphere to form sulfuric and nitric acid. The acidity of falling rain and snow is thereby increased, creating more acidic lakes and rivers in which fish cannot reproduce. Moreover, there may be long-term impacts on human health from these and other chemical emissions.

Presence of these sorts of externalities *(weakens / strengthens)* the case for laissez-faire. That case has assumed that the private market system, if fully competitive, would yield (in the form of market prices) an exact balance of costs and benefits. Insofar as externalities exist (and insofar as they are growing more widespread), the market system *(will still / cannot)* furnish an accurate or adequate measure of costs.

---

weakens; cannot

8. a. Figure 32-2 represents a simplification of Figure 32-6 in the text; the marginal social and private damages of pollution are assumed to be constant. The numbers recorded in Figure 32-2 can be used to explore the four mechanisms with which a pollution externality of the type illustrated can handled. Two

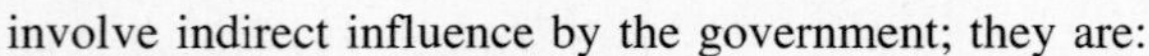

involve indirect influence by the government; they are:

(1) ________________

(2) ________________

Two more would result from direct collective action; they are:

(3) ________________

(4) ________________

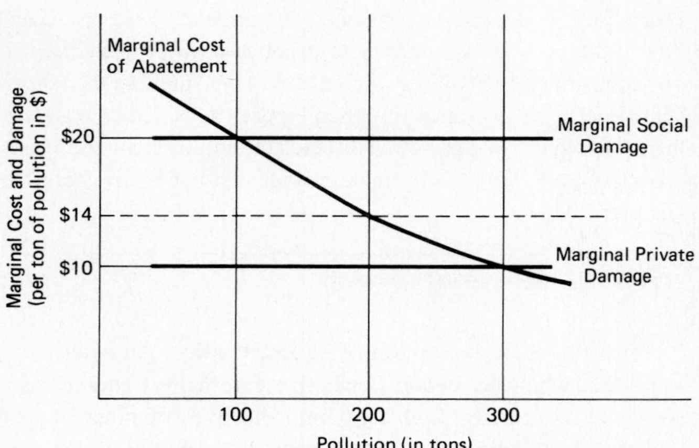

Figure 32-2

Given the curves defined in Figure 32-2, one of these actions is required because the privately determined level of pollution would be ________ tons, at which the marginal cost of abatement equals *(the marginal social damage caused by the pollution / zero / the marginal private damage caused by the pollution)*. That quantity *(exceeds / equals / is smaller than)* the efficient level of pollution—________ tons defined by the equality of the marginal cost of abatement and *(the marginal social damage caused by the pollution / zero / the marginal private damage caused by the pollution)*.

b. Suppose, first of all, that those hurt by the pollution offered to pay the polluter $4 for every unit of pollution not emitted. In that case, the marginal private damage caused by the pollution would *(climb by $4 / remain the same / fall by $4)* because each unit emitted would mean a loss of $4 in potential compensation. The result would be, on the basis of the private decision of the polluter, ________ tons of pollution. It would cost those paying the "bribe" $________ , but that would *(exceed / fall short of)* the reduction in extra social cost of $________ that they would otherwise incur. The end result *(would / would not)* be optimal, but it *(would / would not)* represent an improvement.

Second, the possibility exists that government would hold the polluter liable for the full extent of the social damage that his or her pollution produced. If it were 100 percent certain that these damages would be imposed, than the marginal social damage curve *(would / would not)* become the marginal private damage curve, and the optimal level of pollution *(would / would not)* be achieved. If the probability of assessing damages were not 100 percent, then there *(would / would not)* be some improvements as long as the chances of the polluter's being held liable were not 0 percent. (This last point is tricky until you think about it. Think about it.)

Direct control is, of course, an option. Were the government interested in setting a standard above which the polluter could not stray, then it would set a maximum level of pollution at ________ tons. Alternatively, a tax of $________ per ton could achieve the same result. The polluter, if it were left to him or her, would prefer the *(standard / tax)*, because that would allow the free emission of ________ tons of pollution.

a. (1) Promoting negotiation given property rights **(2)** setting liability rules **(3)** setting standards **(4)** setting pollution taxes; 300; the marginal private damage caused by the pollution; exceeds; 100; the marginal social damage caused by the pollution **b.** climb by $4; 200; 400 ($4 times the 100 tons of pollution *not* emitted); fall short of; 1000; would not; would; would; would; would; 100; 10; standard; 100

9. Recalling that public goods are enjoyed by everyone, consider the two demand curves for some public good *G* represented in the two panels of Figure 32-3. If 10 units of *G* were offered, then the two people represented here would, together, be willing to pay $________, $________ from individual A and $________ from individual B. This suggests that each person should *(necessarily pay an equal proportion / pay according to the marginal benefit that he or she would receive as indicated by the individual demand curves / pay according to how much he or she earns in income and how much property he or she owns)*.

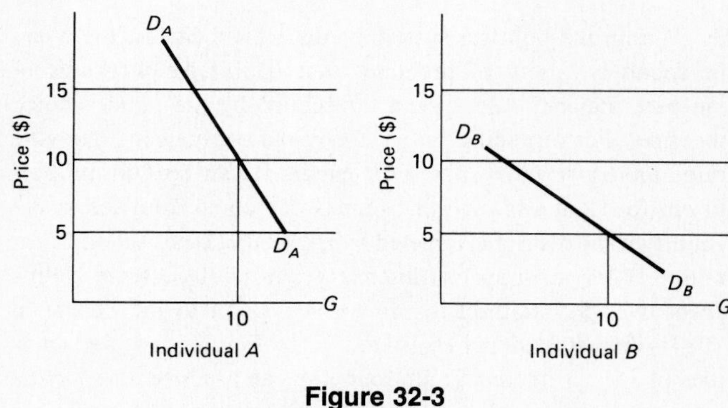

Figure 32-3

15; 10; 5; pay according to the marginal benefit that he or she would receive as indicated by the individual demand curves

QUIZ: Multiple Choice

1. Which of the following statements is an accurate description of the history of government spending in the United States?
(1) The cost of government at all levels climbed from nearly 10 percent of GNP in 1913 to slightly less than 25 percent in the late 1980s.
(2) The cost of government at all levels climbed from 25 percent of GNP in 1913 to 35 percent in the late 1980s.
(3) The cost of government at all levels climbed from approximately 10 percent of GNP in 1913 to nearly 35 percent in the late 1980s.
(4) The cost of the federal government in the United States climbed from 10 percent of GNP in 1913 to more than 30 percent of GNP in the late 1980s.
(5) None of the above.

2. Taxation in the United States:
(1) has grown at a rate that far exceeds the rate of growth of government spending.
(2) has grown at a rate that, until 1981, roughly matched the rate of growth of government spending.
(3) has fallen in size in terms of a fraction of GNP since 1939, but has climbed in absolute terms.
(4) has risen dramatically in the 1980s in an effort to balance the federal budget.
(5) none of the above.

3. The initial source of regulatory activity in the United States was a clause in the Constitution that made a point of:
(1) no taxation without representation.
(2) securing the public interest.
(3) guaranteeing equal pay for equal work.
(4) guaranteeing freedom of speech against inferior products.
(5) anticipating the Equal Rights Amendment.

4. Regulatory activity in the United States:
(1) began with the formation of the Interstate Commerce Commission in 1913 and reached a peak during the Reagan administration.
(2) began with the formation of the Interstate Commerce Commission in 1887 and reached a peak during the Carter administration.
(3) began with the advent of the Federal Reserve System to regulate banks and peaked with the deregulation of trucking during the Reagan administration.
(4) began with the formation of the Interstate Commerce Commission in 1887 and died with the deregulation of airlines during the Reagan administration.
(5) none of the above.

5. Regulation grew in the United States as it became clear that a laissez-faire policy was vulnerable to:
(1) pockets of poverty that are exploited by the more fortunate.
(2) the business cycle that buffeted the economic lives of nearly every citizen.
(3) inefficient and unfair discrimination on the basis of sex, race, and other factors.
(4) the flagrant abuse of the environment.
(5) all of the above.

6. Government can play a number of roles in a mixed economy. These potential roles include:
(1) prescribing a legal framework that defines "the rules of the game."
(2) reallocating resources to accomplish greater efficiency in the face of, say, monopoly or pollution.
(3) effecting macrostabilization by prudent exercise of fiscal, monetary, and other policies.
(4) reallocating resources to accomplish greater equity.
(5) all of the above.

7. Referring to the utility-possibility frontier depicted in Figure 32-4 a move that would illustrate a government failure might move an economy from a point like *A* to:
(1) a point like *B*.
(2) a point like *C*.
(3) a point like *D*.
(4) a point like *E*.
(5) none of the above.

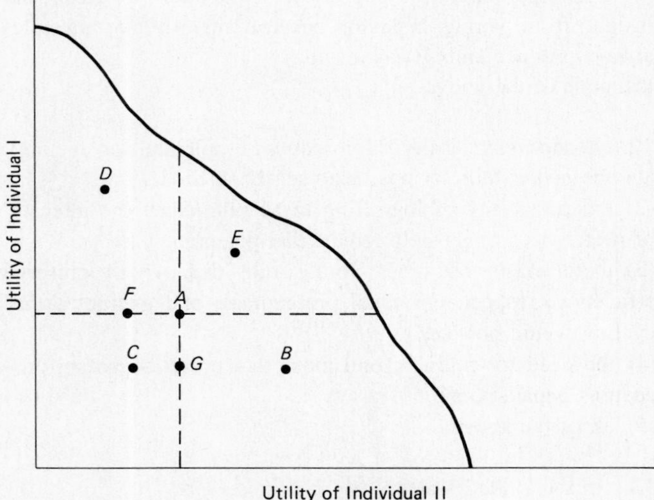

Figure 32-4

8. Referring again to Figure 32-4, a transfer of resources from individual I to II, might move an economy from a point like A to:
(1) a point like *B*.
(2) a point like *C*.
(3) a point like *D*.
(4) a point like *E*.
(5) none of the above.

9. In Figure 32-4, a move that would have been approved by a unanimous voting rule would move an economy from a point like *A* to:
(1) a point like *B*.
(2) a point like *C*.
(3) a point like *D*.
(4) a point like *F*.
(5) none of the above.

10. One last time on Figure 32-4, a move that would have been approved by a majority voting rule given more people of type I than type II, might move an economy from a point like *A* to:
(1) a point like *B*.
(2) a point like *C*.
(3) a point like *D*.
(4) a point like *F*.
(5) a point like *G*.

11. The Arrow impossibility theorem states that:
(1) it is impossible for people to agree, so a unanimous voting rule is necessarily a prescription for paralysis.
(2) it is impossible for a majority-rule system to last because of the tyranny that would necessarily be imposed by the majority.
(3) It is impossible for any voting rule to be analyzed because of the imponderables of the human mind.
(4) it is impossible for public-choice theorists to glean any insight from voting behavior because majority voting rules always produce ambiguous results.
(5) none of the above.

12. Whenever majority rule produces a potential for cycling:
(1) the power falls to those who set the agenda.
(2) the possibility of logrolling to accommodate the intensity of preferences might help reduce that potential.
(3) there exists no other voting rule that would preserve efficiency, respect individual preferences, and guarantee that cycling would not occur.
(4) the need for rules beyond those that prescribe voting procedures is paramount.
(5) all of the above.

13. In the United States:
(1) there is a one-person, one-vote-rule, but money and special interests are nonetheless powerful.
(2) the inherent democracy of one person, one vote overpowers all other factors in determining the outcome of any decision.
(3) the bureaucratic imperative is diminished by the watchdog arm of the U.S. Congress.
(4) the long time horizon of most politicians causes problems in maintaining short-term prosperity.
(5) all of the above.

14. A public good is one in which:
(1) the cost of exclusion is low and the marginal cost of one more consumer is low.
(2) the cost of exclusion is high and the marginal cost of one more consumer is low.
(3) the cost of exclusion is low and the marginal cost of one more consumer is high.
(4) the cost of exclusion is high and marginal cost of one more consumer is high.
(5) the cost of exclusion and the marginal cost of consumption are irrelevant.

15. Public goods and public bads:
(1) are just mirror images of themselves, with the effect of their provision extending beyond the producer.
(2) can both be analyzed as externalities—one positive and one negative.
(3) are subject to the same types of governmental intervention because a market for neither exists.
(4) are hard to evaluate because their utility or harm extends beyond the confines of one individual.
(5) are all of the above.

16. Referring now to Figure 32-5, the efficient level of emissions is indicated by:
(1) point *A*.
(2) point *B*.
(3) point *C*.
(4) point *D*.
(5) none of the above.

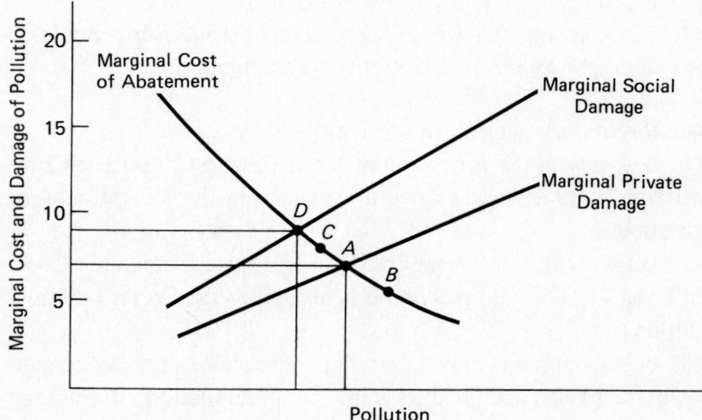

Figure 32-5

17. Referring a second time to Figure 32-5, the level of emissions that would emerge in response to a $2-per-unit emissions tax is indicated by:
(1) point *A*.
(2) point *B*.
(3) point *C*.

(4) point D.
(5) none of the above.

18. If half of the population of 10,000 were willing to pay $10 for the provision of a park and the rest were not willing to contribute a dime, then an expenditure of:
(1) $50,000 would match the town's demand price for parkland.
(2) a price less that $25,000 would reflect the town's collective demand for parkland.
(3) some amount of money for parkland would be appropriate only if one more person wanted to contribute to guarantee a majority of more than 50 percent.
(4) a price in excess of $50,000 would certainly reflect the town's true demand for parkland.
(5) none of the above.

19. The Coase result states that:
(1) negotiation would always solve an externality problem if only government would get out of the way.
(2) the potential exists for negotiation to diminish the magnitude of an externality if property rights are well defined and negotiation costs are not too severe.
(3) negotiation must be forgone in lieu of direct governmental intervention whenever an externality problem becomes too severe.
(4) negotiation will always generate an efficient solution as long as costs are not too high and property rights are clearly defined.
(5) none of the above.

SUGGESTED ANSWERS TO QUESTIONS IN THE TEXT: Chapter 32

1. Think about your experiences with all levels of government. The Reagan administration focused on cutting back the size of government, so there are a lot of examples in those 8 years of things that government no longer does; look at the budgets for those years for clues. Regulation peaked in the middle of the 1970s, so there are more examples during that period.

2. It is difficult for the share to change much because programs have so much momentum. Think about the bureaucratic imperative, the long-term expenditure profile of defense projects, the short time frame of political decision makers, the fiscal stimulus of government spending, etc. The share will have a hard time falling. Given the public's fear of deficits, though, it will probably have a hard time increasing, too.

3. Think about the marginal cost of one more person enjoying a public good (for a private good, it is the price) and also about the cost of provision relative to the marginal benefit that any one person (or small group of people) might receive (for a private good in a competitive market, it is the price, as well). Think also about how public goods might be financed given *(a)* the collective expenditure of money for provision and *(b)* the low marginal cost of utilization. Taxation by ability to pay or benefit received? Which approximates a market allocation?

4. It depends, at the very least, upon whether or not the radical doctrines are accepted into the mainstream.

5. His statement relates to government's role in providing public goods and handling externalities; i.e., the role of government in promoting efficiency. It does not speak to some of the other roles of government: promoting appropriate redistribution of resources, conducting appropriate stabilization measure, and creating appropriate legal frameworks. Believers in all sizes of government could adopt it, though, by defining their own views of what individuals are capable of doing "for themselves."

6. People with different preferences can sort themselves out by deciding where to live on the basis of the menu of public goods offered by various towns at various cost. Towns then try to meet the expectations of their citizens. Think about public education as you ponder this question.

7. **a.** Direct controls are possible, because the mills are clearly identified and located. Taxes might work, as well. Negotiation is not likely because property rights are not well defined; even if they were, the townsfolk might be difficult to organize into a cohesive negotiating unit. Liability rules could also work, but they would be expensive to enforce given the uncertainties of identifying the specific sources of environmental damage.
b. Liability rules work best because the cause is easily attributable. Direct control might be technologically possible (devices that prevent you from starting your car if you are drunk). The situation might not be serious enough if only bushes are hit; if people are hit, answer **(e)** would apply.
c. Direct control, as in answer **a**.
d. Probably not serious enough to warrant action, since smoke dissipates quickly outdoors in the fall.
e. Same as answer **b**. Perhaps control could be extended to revoking the licenses of repeated DWI drivers and of drivers involved in fatalities.
f. Same as answer **e**. Should the licenses be suspended to recognize the recklessness of youth?

8. Market allocations are supported by all *given prices of other goods and the distribution of income*, because everyone has as much as he or she wants—some more and some less, but all have the personally correct amount. There is always debate over how much national defense should be "purchased," because everyone gets the same amount. All moves made under unanimity are Pareto-improving.

9. Proceed with caution. Make your cases on the basis of cost, benefit, and likelihood of success; avoid government failure.

10. At point P, marginal *private* damage equals the marginal cost of abatement; it therefore defines the laissez-faire level of emissions. Point E is the efficient outcome because marginal *social* damage equals the marginal cost of abatement.

a. A direct control limiting emissions to 100 tons would achieve point *E*.

b. A tax of approximately $15 per ton would bring the marginal private damage of emission, including the pecuniary cost of the tax, into intersection with the marginal cost of abatement at point *E*.

c. A liability law that held the polluter accountable for the damage above and beyond private damage would make the marginal private damage curve match the marginal social damage curve; the private point of emission would thus become *E*.

d. The public should be willing to subsidize the difference between marginal social damages and marginal private damages. That potential subsidy therefore becomes an opportunity cost of emission, so the effective marginal private damage curve again moves up to match the marginal social damage curve.

CHAPTER 33
ECONOMIC ROLE OF GOVERNMENT: EXPENDITURE AND TAXATION

Chapter 32 provided some insight into the theory behind any analysis of the role of government in a mixed economy; Chapter 33 now turns your attention to the actual roles assumed by governments at all levels in the American economy. The first section reviews the major expenditure patterns of federal, state, and local governments that define the American system of fiscal federalism. It is a system based primarily on the degree of spillover, or externality, in government programs: local governments tend to take care of local public goods with limited spillover beyond their boundaries; the federal government tends to take care of national public goods whose external effects span the country; and state governments handle programs in between.

The second section provides similar coverage for taxation in the context of a general discussion of the principles upon which our tax policies are constructed and evaluated. Toward the end of the chapter, additional theory is provided to introduce you to the notion of incidence—the economist's attempt to answer the complicated question: "Who pays this here tax, anyway?" This theory leads naturally to consideration of the distribution of the overall net burden (imputed tax liability net of returned benefit) of our tax, transfer, and public expenditure system. Of particular interest here is the legacy of the fiscal revolution of the Reagan administration.

Having completed your work on this chapter, then, you will have accomplished the following objectives.

LEARNING OBJECTIVES

1. Describe the nature of the patterns of expenditure by local, state, and federal governments in the United States, and outline the recent evolution of those patterns into what we see today.

2. Relate, on the basis of these patterns, the construction of an efficient system of "fiscal federalism" and the blurring that necessarily occurs along the boundaries of the different levels of government.

3. Describe the conflicting principles of taxation—a benefit approach and an ability-to-pay approach—and the compromise between the two that has been accomplished in the United States.

4. Note specifically the difference between progressive and regressive taxation, and apply this distinction to differentiate the characters of various taxes employed in the United States.

5. Describe the character and importance of *(a)* individual income taxes, *(b)* sales taxes, *(c)* excise taxes, *(d)* payroll taxes, *(e)* corporate income taxes, and *(f)* property taxes in the United States.

6. List briefly the sources of erosion in the base of the federal income tax.

7. Outline the four pillars of the Reagan revolution: *(a)* a retreat from Keynesian demand management in favor of reliance on private enterprise; *(b)* a budgetary emphasis on defense at the expense of civilian programs, with little concern for the potential damage of large deficits; *(c)* a reduction in the regulatory burden facing American business; and *(d)* a general reduction in the tax burden facing many American citizens.

8. Discuss efficiency as an issue in the design of a tax system and relate it to *(a)* the Laffer curve, *(b)* the integration of the corporate income tax into the individual income tax, and *(c)* the flat tax proposal.

9. Define the term "tax incidence," and explain why and how a tax might not fall on the economic agent identified in the tax codes.

10. Describe the procedure and the results of the Brookings study that concluded that the pattern of expenditure in the United States turns a mildly progressive tax structure into a fairly progressive fiscal structure.

The United States has, over the years, adopted a pattern of fiscal federalism that assigns various expenditure programs to the levels of government whose jurisdictions most closely match the geographical boundaries of their spillover effects. As a result, we see the federal government providing and managing programs like national defense, space exploration, and foreign affairs. We see local governments taking care of things like police protection, fire protection, public education, and other "local public goods." Finally, we see state governments administering highway, port, and welfare programs. Frequently the money required to support these programs at state and local levels flows down from the federal government, but the administration of the programs is conducted at the lowest possible level.

It should, of course, be noted that this structure is in a constant state of flux. The boundaries between governments and the spillover effects of programs are typically hard to define, and programs are forever being transferred from one level of government to another. Moreover, the growth in federal support for state and local administration of various programs was brought to an abrupt halt in the first years of the Reagan administration. What happens next is anybody's guess; and it will affect almost everybody's life.

1. For the fiscal year 1989, annual expenditure by the U.S. federal government was estimated to be $*(600 / 735 / 925 / 1070)* billion. This is a total that exceeded the 1980 level of expenditure by nearly $550 billion.

The largest single item within this total for 1989 was *(interest on the public debt / national defense and international affairs / education, labor, and development / income security including social security)*. The expenditure for this item amounted to $*(500 / 400 / 300)* billion. It should be noted that income security was, in 1980, the largest component; a change in federal priorities toward defense expenditure *(is / is not)* therefore suggested by even a cursory glance at expenditure patterns.

1070; national defense and international affairs; $300; is

Some idea of the enormous increase in the size and importance of the federal government within the past few generations is to be gleaned by noting that in 1939, just before World War II, (1) total expenditure for national security was around $1 billion annually; (2) the federal social security program did not exist at all; and (3) other federal expenditures for health and welfare were of trivial importance. In sum, the federal government and its operations meant almost nothing in the everyday life of most people prior to the Second World War.

World War II changed all that. Ordinary citizens were then required to pay income taxes, to complete income-tax forms (a privilege previously reserved for the rich), and to meet a host of federal restrictions. Wartime rationing was temporary, but widespread federal taxation was not.

2. Development of the social security system has proven far and away the most important factor accounting for growth in federal government outlays and collections since World War II. The demand for wider coverage has grown. Social security benefits, and deductions from wages and salaries to cover those benefits, have increased steadily. Social security is not only the second biggest item in the federal budget today; it is but one item in a collection of "welfare security" programs that has increased most spectacularly over the middle term. In 1970, total expenditure for "health, labor, welfare, and education" (i.e., expenditure for income security plus outlays for some of the other items listed in Table 33-1 of the text) came to $62.9 billion; in 1973, $99.1 billion; in 1976, $161.4 billion. For income security *alone*, the fiscal 1989 figure was $129 billion. That is down from 1980, but expenditure for income security has nonetheless *(almost doubled / doubled / just about tripled)* since 1970.

This postwar rise in welfare expenditures might have been offset (at least in part) by a decline in spending on national security after World War II, but this spending category did not fall as most people expected and hoped it would. Instead, "the cold war" began, and it was fought through the preparation of newly developed and horrendously expensive nuclear weapons. Beginning in the 1950s, and continuing thereafter, the total of spending on national defense persisted at levels that would have been literally incredible by the standards of 1939.

In recent years, this national-defense spending has, by comparison with items like income security and health, accelerated again after being relatively stable during the 1970s. The Vietnam war pushed it upward (although not by any spectacular amount). The expenditure total has risen since then, but the increases through 1981 probably reflected as much the impact of inflation as they did a larger fraction of real national product being directed toward weapons of war. Since 1981, though, the growth has been explosive, both in real terms and as a fraction of GNP.

---

doubled

Turning now to the revenue side of governments' ledger sheets, we will quickly see that two questions dominate any discussion of taxation: *"Who should pay?"* and *"How do we know if the person who should pay is, in fact, actually paying?"* Much of the remainder of this chapter deals with these two fundamental queries.

Suppose, for example, that the benefits to be derived from some public project will accrue entirely to an identifiable group of people from within the population. It might then be reasonable to assert that the tax revenues required to finance that project should be collected from the people who benefit; e.g., taxes for the construction of roads might be collected solely from the people who use the road.

The welfare gains resulting from most public projects are, however, too diffuse to allow simple application of this "benefit principle." In most cases of public finance, therefore, policymakers must wrestle with the question of fairness and equity: How can society define a fair and equitable basis for distributing the burden of taxation? More specifically, how should the burden of financing government through taxes be distributed among the rich and the poor? What about the middle class? The debate on these issues is a never-ending one. One side argues that the rich should carry most or all of the burden simply because they are rich, and can afford it, while the poor cannot. The opposition insists that "making money" is at least one of the incentives for personal initiative and effort. They argue that accepting the "soak-the-rich" philosophy may create a tax system that discourages incentive and encourages the most talented and inventive members of the population to move someplace where the tax laws are less severe.

In purely technical terms, the issues are summed up in the terms **progressive taxes** and **regressive taxes**. A progressive tax thrusts most of its burden on people of above-average income. A regressive tax bears more heavily on poorer people. A tax is not, however, progressive simply because it collects more money from a rich individual than from a poor one. To establish whether a tax is regressive or progressive, you must (1) find the amount of tax typically paid at various income levels within the population and (2) express this tax paid as a percentage of income. If these percentage figures rise as income rises—that is, if as income rises, the percentage of income paid in tax rises also—then the tax is progressive. If the percentage figures go down as you move to higher income levels, then the tax is regressive. If the percentage figure is pretty much the same at all income levels, then the tax in neither progressive nor regressive; it is **proportional**.

3. In order to know whether a tax is progressive or regressive, it is *(essential / not strictly essential)* to know how much money it typically collects from individuals at different levels of income.

One existing U.S. tax is easily classified within this progressive-regressive distinction; namely, the ______________ tax. This tax is *(progressive / regressive)*, even after the Tax Reform Act of 1986.

---

essential; personal income; progressive

4. a. A tax levied as 1 percent on the first $5000 of income, 2 percent on the next $5000, 3 percent on the next $5000, and so on, would be *(progressive / proportional / regressive)*.

b. A tax of 10 percent on all income except the first $1000—that $1000 being exempt from tax—would be *(progressive / proportional / regressive)*.

c. If it is true that (among cigarette smokers) people with a yearly income of $8000 typically buy four packs of cigarettes per week, whereas those with an income of $16,000 typically buy six packs per week, then an excise tax of 10 cents per pack would be a *(progressive / proportional / regressive)* tax.

---

a. progressive **b.** progressive (This one is sneaky. The tax is *almost* proportional; but the tax, expressed as a percentage of income, goes up as income goes up.) **c.** regressive (The tax of, e.g., 40 cents weekly is a higher fraction of $8000 than 60 cents is of $16,000.)

5. a. The *benefit* approach to taxation argues that the distribution of tax levies between citizen A and citizen B should be in proportion to the benefit each receives from the expenditures of government—a "pay for what you get" principle. Which of the following (one or both) may be considered a valid criticism of this principle?

(1) It assumes the particular tax in question can be linked to a particular type of expenditure. If a government's expenditures are large and varied, this is often difficult to determine.

(2) Even if a particular tax can somehow be linked to a particular type of spending (e.g., federal government spending on national defense), it is difficult to decide, in quantity terms, how much benefit rich citizen A derives from it in comparison with poor citizen B.

b. An alternative principle is that tax payments constitute a sacrifice by citizens and that the distribution of sacrifices should match people's "ability to pay." It isn't altogether easy to establish what "ability to pay" really means, but one interpretation is that (pick one):

(1) every citizen should pay an equal amount of money in taxes, thus equalizing sacrifices.

(2) taxes should be levied and collected in strict proportion to the amount of income received by citizens.

(3) the tax system should be constructed so that the government collects its revenue from those who have the money.

---

a. both **(1)** and **(2)** **b.** **(3)**

6. The ability-to-pay approach raises two distinct issues of equity. The first, simply put, asserts that equals should pay equal taxes. This is identified in the literature as *(horizontal / vertical / reasonable)* equity. As simple as that assertion appears, it buries the fundamental question of how to determine when two people are equals. Are, for example, two people earning $30,000 per year equal if one of them has incurred $8000 in medical expenses? The tax codes say no. Medical expenses above 3 percent of adjusted gross income were deductible in 1988 (unless the taxpayer took the "standard deduction"), so the person who faced the medical problem could be taxed on the basis of an income of $34,400 rather than $30,000.

The second equity issue involves the taxation of unequals; it is captured under the general rubric of *(horizontal / vertical / redistributive)* equity. This is the more controversial issue because of the (dis)incentive effects of income taxation.

---

horizontal; vertical

7. A tax imposed directly on an individual—i.e., whose amount payable is calculated by some factor such as size of income or value of certain of that person's assets—is designated as *(a direct / an indirect)* tax. A tax levied on a transaction, most commonly on the purchase and sale of a commodity, is *(a direct / an indirect)* tax. Some taxes, such as the corporate income tax, do not fall neatly into either the direct or indirect category.

Problems of determining real incidence are usually more difficult with *(direct / indirect)* taxes.

---

a direct; an indirect; indirect

8. a. Disregarding social security taxes, the two taxes which yield the most revenue for the federal government, ranked in order of their revenue importance, are:

(1) ______________________

(2) ______________________

b. The most important tax at the level of state government is the ______________ tax; the most important tax at the level of local government is the ______________ tax.

c. The single most important expenditure item at the state and local government level is ______________ .

---

a. (1) personal income tax **(2)** corporation income tax **b.** sales; property **c.** education

9. The difference between a **sales tax** and an **excise tax** is this: if the tax applies to all items sold, omitting only items specifically named in the law as exempt, it is *(a sales / an excise)* tax. If, on the other hand, the tax applies *only* to commodities or services names in the law (e.g., liquor, cigarettes), it is *(a sales / an excise)* tax.

---

a sales; an excise

10. A **value-added tax** is a tax imposed on each producing firm, on the value added to goods at that stage of production. If a textile firm buys $4000 of yarn and other raw materials, and employs labor to weave these materials into cloth which it sells for $10,000, then the value which it added to its beginning materials was $*(4000 / 6000 / 10,000 / 14,000)*, and that is the amount on which the tax is levied.

Suppose another firm—a garment manufacturing firm—bought all of this cloth and paid the full $10,000 for it. It paid a further $2000 for all its other raw materials, such as thread. It sold the resulting output of garments for $20,000. Then the value added by this firm would be $*(2000 / 4000 / 6000 / 8000 / 10,000 / 20,000)*.

6000; 8000

11. The **marginal** tax rate on income means the fraction or percent *(of the last dollar of income that must be paid in tax / obtained by comparing total tax against total income)*. Alternatively, it is the extra amount of tax you would have to pay if you received an extra $1 in income (expressed as a percentage). If the personal-income-tax system is progressive (as it is in the United States and most other countries), this percentage figure will be higher than the *average* tax rate, which is the percent *(of the last dollar of income that must be paid in tax / obtained by comparing total tax against total income)*. That is, as the income level goes up, the marginal tax rate *(goes up / goes down / remains the same)*.

---

of the last dollar of income that must be paid in tax; obtained by comparing total tax against total income; goes up

12. It is frequently not an easy matter to determine whether a tax is progressive or regressive. The corporation income tax is a case in point; it takes a little thought to evaluate how this tax distributes its burden.

According to the Tax Reform Act of 1986, the marginal tax rates applied to corporate profits are:

Level of Profit	Marginal Tax Rate, %
Under $50,000	15
$50,000–$75,000	25
$75,000–$100,000	34
$100,000–$335,000	39
above $335,000	34

The bulge between $100,000 and $335,000 represents a technical correction for a tax break offered to small firms. It is therefore fair to represent the tax for large firms as very nearly proportional. In assessing its nature, then, you might be tempted by say that the tax is very mildly progressive.

Focusing only on the rate schedule is, however, the wrong way to think about the character of the corporation income tax. If corporations were living people, things would be different; but they are *not* living people. Not being human, they do not feel the tax. Those who do feel it are a corporation's owners: the *(bondholders / shareholders)*. The tax is levied on earnings which belong to them.

It is important here to grasp just how our reasoning is going. A corporation doesn't usually pay out all of its profit in dividends to stockholders. Part of that profit is typically "ploughed back" to expand its operations. Nevertheless, in principle, all profit belongs to the shareholder-owners.

Disregarding the different percentages applicable below $335,000 the tax is proportional in the sense that its marginal rate applied to profit is 34 percent regardless of whether you own 1 share or 10,000 shares. Remember that in taxation the term "proportional" is intended to mean a tax which takes the same percent of income at every income level, right across the entire population. The critical point here is that only a fraction of the population owns corporation stock, so the tax is a tax on a particular segment of the population.

Suppose that all corporation stock is owned by poor people. (Never mind the fact that if they owned all that stock, they wouldn't be poor!) As a tax on the incomes of the poor, the corporation tax would then be a *(progressive / regressive)* one. Alternatively, suppose all the stock is owned by rich people. That would make the tax *(progressive / regressive)*.

The facts are that some people in the lower income brackets own a little stock; many in the middle brackets do; but the great bulk of corporate stock is owned by people with above-average incomes. The corporation tax is (subject to the one vital qualification discussed in question 17), on balance, *(progressive / regressive)*.

---

shareholders; regressive; progressive; progressive

13. Some people complain that the corporation income tax imposes a burden of double taxation on stockholders. They mean that the dividends paid to stockholders out of after-tax corporate income *(are / are not)* subject to the personal income tax. Insofar as this specific double-taxation argument is valid, it applies *(to all corporate profit / only to that part of corporate profit which is paid out as dividends / only to that part of profit which is retained and undistributed)*.

---

are; only to that part of corporate profit which is paid out as dividends.

14. The base of the individual income tax is eroded by a number of factors. First of all, the Tax Reform Act of 1986 allows (after 1990) personal exemptions of $*(500 / 1000 / 2000)* for each person claimed on a tax return. In addition, many sources of income receive preferential treatment through what are known as tax expenditures. List at least five of these tax expenditures in the spaces provided below:

a. ____________________

b. ____________________

c. ____________________

d. ____________________

e. ____________________

The net effect of these tax expenditures is to *(increase / leave unaffected / decrease)* the effective progressivity of the U.S. personal income tax.

2000; **a.** through **e.** any of the following: tax exempt mortgage interest (on primary residences), social security benefits (up to a point), implicit homeowner rents, retirement-account contributions made by employers and (to some degree) by employees, employer contributions for medical insurance, state and local tax payments (excluding sales taxes), capital-gains carryovers at death (There are others, as well; see Table 33-5 in the text.); decrease

15. The Reagan administration worked throughout its entire tenure to change the role of government in nearly every arena of its activity. Indicate, in the spaces provided, whether the indicated role or variable increased (I), decreased (D), or stayed roughly the same (S) during the Reagan years in comparison with the previous two decades.

a. regulatory activity . . . . (______)

b. highest personal-income-tax rate . . . . (______)

c. highest corporation-income-tax rate . . . . (______)

d. federal deficits as a percentage of GNP . . . . (______)

e. defense spending . . . . (______)

f. spending on civilian social programs . . . . . . (______)

g. Keynesian-style management of aggregate demand . . . . (______)

h. unemployment rate (average) . . . . (______)

i. total federal tax liability for wealthiest 10 percent of the population . . . . (______)

j. total federal tax liability of poorest 10 percent of the population . . . . (______)

---

a. D **b.** D [reduced from 50 percent to 33 percent (28 percent for highest incomes)] **c.** D [reduced from 46 percent to 39 percent (34 percent for highest incomes)] **d.** I (increased from 1.1 percent to 4.2 percent) **e.** I **f.** S (for middle-class income-support programs) and I (for lower-class welfare-support programs) **g.** D (reliance on private enterprise) **h.** I (from 5.6 percent to 7.7 percent) **i.** I (grew by 3 percent) **j.** D (fell by 15 percent)

16. The Laffer curve, as a theoretical construction, simply notes the potential for high income-tax rates to eventually *(encourage people to work more / encourage people to invest less / encourage people to work less)*. Figure 33-1 provides an illustration of such a curve. The 25 percent tax cut instituted by the Reagan administration in 1981 was based on the belief that the economy was being taxed to a point like *(A / B / C)* so that revenues would actually climb with the reduction. That theory *(did / did not)* seem to work. On the basis of empirical work by Don Fullerton, in fact, it is most likely that the economy is being taxed to a point like *(A / B / C)*.

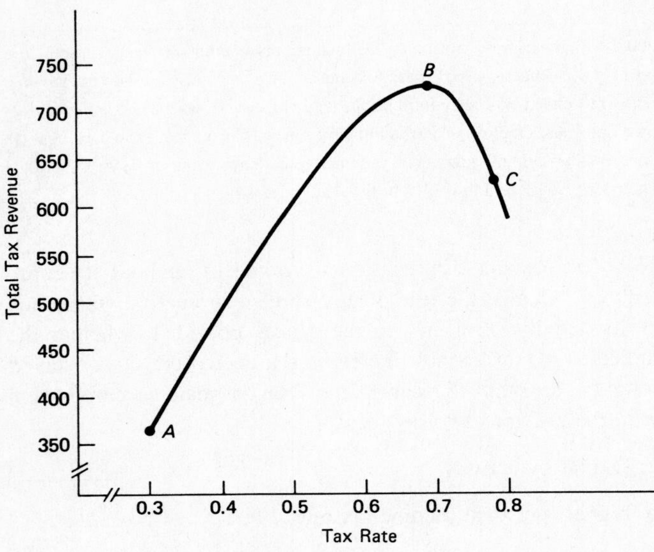

Figure 33-1

A second type of reform of the individual income tax, known as the flat tax proposal, has been advanced in both liberal and conservative quarters. It is estimated that the entire system as it now stands could be replaced by a proportional tax that takes *(10 / 20 / 30)* cents of every dollar earned by every American worker. Concern has been raised, however, that this amounts to *(an even larger transfer of the burden of the tax from the poor to the rich / a transfer of the burden from the rich to the poor / no transfer of the burden at all)*. Since a strict flat tax would allow no deductions, in its purest form, there might also be an enormous *(increase / decrease)* in the value of property in the United States because mortgage interest payments would no longer be deductible.

---

encourage people to work less; *C*; did not; *A*; 20; a transfer of the burden from the rich to the poor; decrease

17. Suppose that the maximum corporation-income-tax rate was raised from 39 to, say, 55 percent; but let corporations respond to this tax by raising their prices just enough that their after-tax profit is unchanged. If so, this is an instance of **tax shifting**, and the *incidence* of the extra tax falls on the *(corporations / corporations' customers)*. This possibility raises the interesting potential that most of the corporate tax, possibly even all of it, is not paid out of shareholders' incomes at all; it might be passed on to other people via higher prices. If a corporation's customers happened to consist almost entirely of people in the lower half of the income range, and if it did manage to shift the tax via higher prices, this would make the tax (with respect to this particular corporation, anyhow) *(progressive / regressive)*.

Conceivably, the tax might be shifted in another way. Corporations, when this tax is loaded upon them, might just possibly manage to *(lower / raise)* the prices they pay for their inputs, such as labor. There is a fair amount of evidence to suggest that at least part of the corporate tax is shifted via higher prices for the goods corporations sell, but the evidence is not all in. The issue is still being debated and explored.

The words "shifting" and "incidence" are important with respect to taxes; study their meaning. The government may require you to pay a certain tax; but you do not really pay it if, through the device of charging a higher price or paying a lower price, you make the tax come out of someone else's pocket. You have shifted the tax; and the true incidence of the tax is on the person out of whose pocket the money really comes.

Problems of tax incidence can become extremely complicated; it may be difficult to establish what the facts really are. Business firm or individual A may manage to shift part or all of a tax on to B; B in turn may shift some part of it to C—and so on. The one tax which has almost no incidence problem is the ______________________________ tax.

---

corporations' customers; regressive; lower; personal income

18. Suppose that there are 100 people in an economy, and suppose that they can be ordered according to their incomes so that each earns $1000 more per year than the next lowest person. That is to say, suppose that person 1 earns $1000, person 2 earns $2000, and so on, up to person 100, who earns $100,000 per year. Let each pay 10 percent of that income in taxes, and let the revenue collected by the tax be divided equally among the first 50 people.

Figure 33-2 illustrates this structure. Line __________ illustrates the tax program, line ________ illustrates the transfer program, and line ________ illustrates the overall program in the same way that the curves on Figure 33-6 of the text portray the actual distribution of the net burden of the present U.S. structure. Is the overall program progressive? ________. Is the tax structure progressive? ________. Is the transfer program progressive? ________.

Now let the 10 percent tax rate apply only to income above $10,000 so that people 1 through 10 pay no taxes but share in the transfer program. New lines are required to portray this new

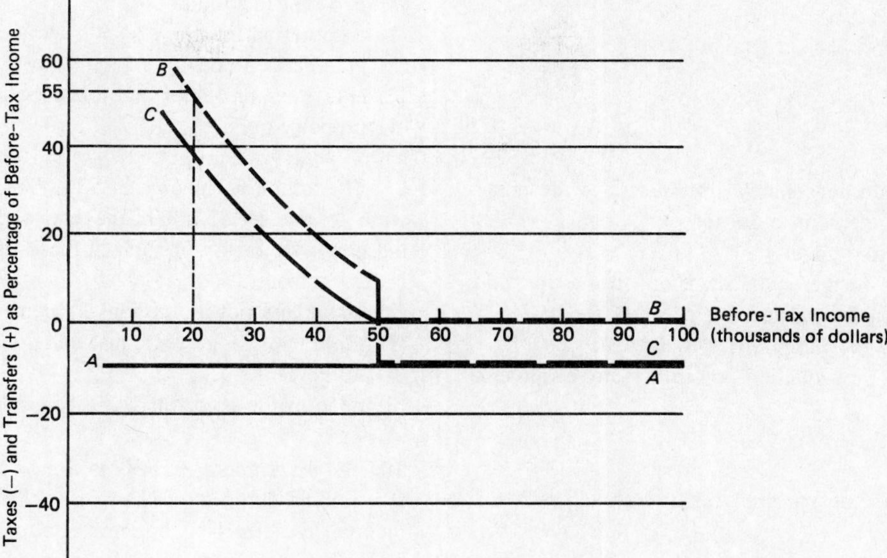

Figure 33-2

structure; they are recorded in Figure 33-3. Line ______ now portrays the tax structure, line ______ portrays the new transfer schedule, and line ______ portrays the overall program. Is the transfer program now more progressive? ______. Is the tax system now more progressive? ______. Is the overall program now more progressive? ______.

AA; *BB*; *CC*; yes; no (It is proportional.); yes; *AA*; *BB*; *CC*; no (It is unchanged.); yes; yes

QUIZ: Multiple Choice

1. The largest single money item in the U.S. federal government budget is currently:
(1) energy, science, and environment.
(2) national defense and international affairs.
(3) interest on the public debt.
(4) general government (including justice).
(5) income security.

2. Any highway that is built by the government and made available toll-free to the public furnishes an example of:

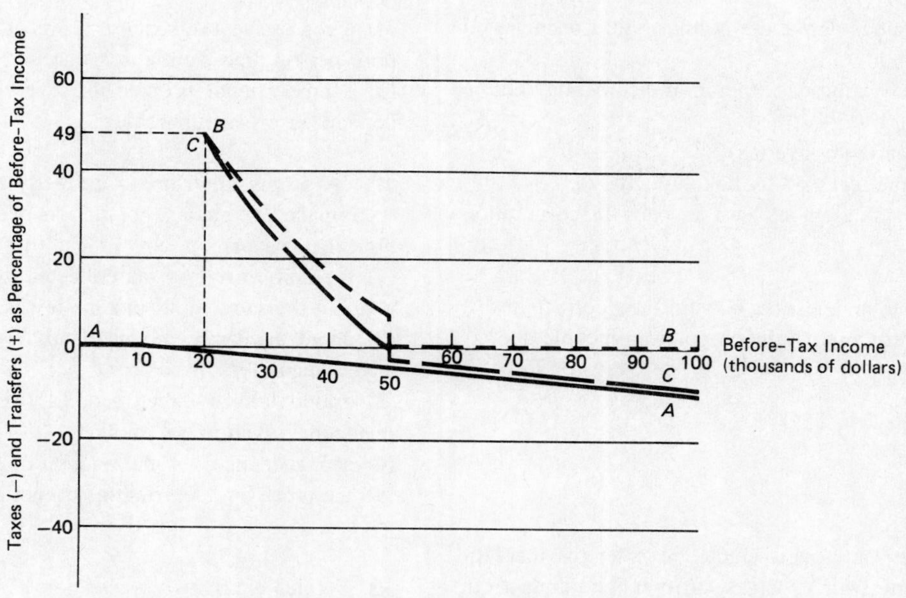

Figure 33-3

(1) private consumption.
(2) a transfer expenditure.
(3) a welfare expenditure.
(4) monetary policy.
(5) none of the above.

3. A government might reasonably introduce a widespread program of transfer payments in order to:
(1) create a surplus in its budget.
(2) effect some change in the social decision on the question of *for whom* goods are to be produced.
(3) provide more social consumption.
(4) move the economy's production-possibility curve outward and to the right.
(5) reduce inflation.

4. The corporation income (profits) tax is defined as a tax levied on:
(1) only the dividends paid to stockholders.
(2) the value added to production by each corporation.
(3) the corporation's total net sales.
(4) additions to corporate retained earnings.
(5) dividends paid plus undistributed profits.

5. One type of income not subject to taxation at all under U.S. income-tax law is:
(1) income in the form of dividends from stock owned.
(2) income in the form of interest on corporation bonds owned.
(3) real income in the form of housing services from a house occupied by its owner.
(4) real income (i.e., any income not in the form of direct money payment of any and all kinds.
(5) income in the form of capital gains.

6. An argument made in favor of the corporation income tax is that:
(1) it taxes only earnings above the normal return on invested capital.
(2) without it, some fraction of corporation income may not be currently taxed at all.
(3) on balance, it is a regressive tax.
(4) it taxes the income received by bondholders.
(5) it means double taxation (at least in part) of corporation earnings.

7. Which alternative in question 6 would be correct had it referred to an argument against the corporation income tax?
(1).
(2).
(3).
(4).
(5).

8. The tax yielding the largest annual revenue for the federal government (disregarding social security withholdings from wages and salaries) is the:
(1) personal income tax.
(2) corporation income tax.
(3) value-added tax.
(4) excise tax on liquor and tobacco.
(5) property tax.

9. The tax on an income of $20,000 is $4000. If this income were to rise to $22,000, the tax would rise to $4800. The marginal rate of tax implicit in these figures is:
(1) 20 percent.
(2) about (but not more than) 21 percent.
(3) more than 21 percent, just under 22 percent.
(4) 40 percent.
(5) none of the preceding.

10. A government introduces a new and very regressive tax. If a Lorenz curve is used to show the distribution of after-tax income, the effect of this new tax upon the Lorenz curve will be to (Lorenz curves were defined in Chapter 26):
(1) push the curve up to a new and higher level.
(2) cause it to bulge farther away from the diagonal line.
(3) cause it to move closer to the diagonal line.
(4) leave the curve unchanged.
(5) perhaps do any of the above—impossible to tell from the information given.

11. A general sales tax, without any exempted commodities, is considered to be:
(1) a progressive tax because it applies to luxuries as well as necessities.
(2) a regressive tax because wealthy people spend a smaller percentage of their total incomes on taxed commodities, and hence the proportion of tax payments to income is greater for poor people.
(3) a progressive tax because wealthy people spend more than poor people.
(4) a regressive tax because more money is collected from a poor person than from a rich one.
(5) a proportional tax because everybody pays the same tax percentage on each purchase.

12. A proportional tax is correctly defined as one in which (taking the tax-paying population overall, or in terms of the typical taxpayer):
(1) the ratio of money tax collected to money income received is about the same at all income levels.
(2) about the same amount of tax money is collected per taxpayer, regardless of taxpayer incomes.
(3) as one turns to higher incomes, one finds that the percentage of income taken in tax falls.
(4) at higher incomes, the amount of money taken in tax rises.
(5) the preceding descriptions do not apply (i.e., none of them is correct.

13. Which alternative in question 12 would be correct had that question referred to the correct definition of a progressive tax?

(1).
(2).
(3).
(4).
(5).

14. Which alternative in question 12 would be correct had that question referred to the correct definition of a regressive tax?
(1).
(2).
(3).
(4).
(5).

15. The incidence of a tax is:
(1) its tendency to fluctuate in total amount collected, as between boom and recession periods.
(2) its relative importance in the budget of the government involved.
(3) the extent to which payment can be avoided through one or more "loopholes."
(4) its burden, in the sense of identifying the people whose real incomes are actually reduced by that tax.
(5) the effect to which its imposition is likely to induce those who must pay it to work less, in an effort to avoid part of such payment.

16. How do the tax systems of state and local governments in the United States compare with the federal system?
(1) They are both more progressive.
(2) They are both more regressive.
(3) The state system is more progressive than the federal; the local system less so.
(4) The local system is more progressive than the federal; the state system less so.
(5) None of the preceding statements is correct.

17. The largest single tax expenditure in the existing federal personal-income-tax law concerns:
(1) the exclusion of pension contributions.
(2) illegal tax evasion by the self-employed.
(3) depletion allowances for crude-oil holdings.
(4) nontaxation of income in the form of services from owner-occupied homes.
(5) income from securities that by law are tax-exempt.

SUGGESTED ANSWERS TO QUESTIONS IN THE TEXT: Chapter 33

1. Progressive federal taxes: personal income tax, death and estate taxes, corporation income tax. Roughly proportional (though mildly regressive due to maximum liabilities): payroll (social security) tax. Regressive: excise taxes, highway tolls, customs duties.

Trading income tax for consumption tax would likely be a move toward regressive taxation, since poorer people spend larger percentages of their incomes; in response to this observation, some argue that the consumption tax rate could be progressive. A universal sales tax could not incorporate such rate flexibility, though, and *would* be more regressive.

2. Economic equivalence may exist, but smoking is worse for people than eating bread. Taxes can be used as financial disincentives aimed at discouraging people from doing certain things, but their effect can be regressive unless accompanied by lump-sum rebates of the income forgone in paying the taxes. This would preserve the substitution effect of increasing the price of (e.g.) cigarettes, but it would eliminate the income effect.

For example, consider a $2-per-pack tax on cigarettes accompanied by a pledge to reimburse the money as a lump-sum credit against the personal income tax. The substitution effect would still discourage smoking, but the credit would dramatically reduce the loss in real income.

3. Argue your own point of view, but remember the objectives of taxation and the criteria with which they are judged.

4. Progressive rates eliminate the question of regressivity. The effect on saving should be positive because money saved would not be taxed and interest earned on saving would not be taxed *until the money was used to purchase something*. For most, then, this would be a tax-delaying ploy, much like the old individual retirement accounts. They did not stimulate as much saving as originally forecast, but their stiumlus may have been overwhelmed by other changes in economic cicumstances.

This is a good question for indifference-curve analysis, with utility depending upon consumption over two periods and the potential to consume in excess of income in the second period by saving in the first period.

5. Correlation does not imply causality. To analyze the experience correctly, you need a model that captures causality, a complete description of the tax cuts and how they were distributed, and some historical context to evaluate the impacts of changes in other economic variables.

6. Think of taxes that are the sticks of disincentive, designed to discourage certain sorts of behavior. Pollution taxes are fine examples. Strong lobby groups generally oppose these taxes because they would not be requred if the targeted behaviors were not privately profitable. Even when the advocates of social welfare carry the day, lobbyists oppose taxes and favor direct controls. That way their clients get to do some of what they want for free.

Consider, for example, the sulfur polluter. Let 100 tons per week be the targeted level of emission. With a standard, the polluter gets the first 100 tons free. With a tax designed to elicit 100 tons (say, $10 per ton), the polluter must pay $1000.

7. Average tax rates based on AGI: 0, 1.5, 6, 9, 15, and 19 percent. Marginal tax rates based on the indicated jumps in AGI: 3, 11, 11, 20, 21 percent. The tax is progressive on the basis of the adjusted gross income.

Average tax rates based on TI: 0, 15, 15, 15, 21, and 24 percent. Marginal tax rates based on the indicated jumps in TI: 15, 15, 15, 25, and 25 percent.

8. Taking 20 percent of taxable income, the tax liabilities for the six incomes given are $0, $200, $1600, $6000, $14,000, and $80,000. As a percentage of AGI, these tax payments are 0, 2, 8, 12, 14, and 16 percent. This is less progressive.

9. Post-tax wages: $10, $9, $8, and so on, down to $0. Pre-tax earnings are $10 times the number of hours worked; tax revenues are $0, $200, $3900, $5700, $7400, $9000, $10,200, $11,200, $10,400, $5400, and $0. The Laffer curve plots tax revenue against tax rate; it seems to peak at 70 percent.

10. This is a thought question for which there are many answers. Some initial thoughts follow:

a. Global—subsidize its production and distribution.

b. National/global—effluent charges or standards [with compensation (?)].

c. National—provision.

d. Local—regulation [based on national or international standards to maintain competitive position (?)].

e. Private.

f. Global—absolute standards or ban them [substitutes exist (?)].

CHAPTER 34
POVERTY, EQUALITY, AND EFFICIENCY

Americans seem to be driven by two distinct motives as they work to shape their society. Americans want, on the one hand, to have a chance to live the "American dream"—to work hard, to work honest, perhaps to be lucky, but somehow to wind up a success in life. They want the opportunity to become wealthy, or at least to get ahead, and they do not think it fair or appropriate for economic or social policy to get in the way.

Americans also want to provide some measure of equity across the land. They are bound by the very wording of the Constitution to try to provide equal opportunity for all people. They have not always been very successful in that effort, though, and they have tried to compensate. The social fabric of the United States is filled with programs that try to help those individuals and families who have not been fortunate enough to ride opportunity to a position of economic security.

As noble as these two goals are, it is one of the major lessons of economics that they frequently get in each other's way. The very programs that provide some measure of protection for the disadvantaged cost money to run; they therefore require tax revenues to operate, and taxation makes the American dream more difficult. The programs, themselves, are often accused of generating disincentives among the disadvantaged against attempting to get ahead. The whole business is summarized in what Arthur Okun called "the big tradeoff." It is the classic tradeoff between equity and efficiency.

Chapter 34 reviews this tradeoff in theoretical as well as in practical terms. It begins with a section that defines poverty and identifies its sources in contemporary America. A second section then proceeds to explore the Okun thought experiment of the "leaky bucket"—the conceptual construction that allows the equity-efficiency tradeoff to be clearly delineated. Antipoverty programs currently in place in the United States are described briefly before they are confronted by one of the most provocative questions of contemporary debate: "Have they done more harm than good?" Charles Murray has recently published a study in which he argues that the answer to this question is a definite "Yes," but his view is widely disputed by other writers. His hypothesis does, in any case, add a new dimension of urgency to the search for alternatives to the plethora of antipoverty programs now offered by government. The chapter closes with a discussion of the strengths and weaknesses of one such alternative—the negative income tax.

Having completed your work in this chapter, you will have accomplished the objectives listed below. The major lesson of the chapter is not, however, recorded explicitly in that list; it is, instead, implicit in the debate over the effectiveness of antipoverty programs. The objectives make it clear that the debate hinges on the theoretical tradeoff between equity and efficiency, but the fundamental lesson of the chapter is that the debate must be conducted in the context of the practical, political world of interdependent government decision making.

The trend in government during the Reagan administration was, for example, toward a reduction in the size of antipoverty programs. The purported rationale for these reductions was couched in terms of a tightening of qualifying requirements to make certain that only the truly needy were receiving benefits; but was that really what was going on? The reductions were also consistent with the objectives of the supply-side tax cuts and the increased reliance on the private sector that were the cornerstones of the Reagan presidency. A more honest rationale for cutting welfare programs might have been couched in terms of a belief that the government had strayed too far toward promoting equity at the expense of economic efficiency. Some in the Reagan administration might have thought that the leaks in Okun's bucket were too large to tolerate. Others might have really believed that Murray was right. Still others might have thought that the programs were unnecessary.

LEARNING OBJECTIVES

1. Define poverty in the United States and discuss its various sources (differences in property wealth, ability, education, and training; discrimination; and inequality of opportunity).

2. Describe the incidence of poverty in the United States in the late 1980s, and explain the recent increases in the number of poor people.

3. Contrast three notions of equity (equality of political rights, opportunity, and outcome), and use Arthur Okun's notion of a leaky bucket to delineate the costs of providing increased equality.

4. Record a list of the major welfare programs still in place in the late 1980s (food stamps and child nutrition; AFDC; aid to the needy aged, blind, and disabled; Medicaid; housing assistance; etc.). Note the comparative expense of running each. Understand how qualifying standards might impose very high effective marginal tax rates on the working poor.

5. Define two views of poverty (poverty resulting from social and economic circumstances over which the poor have no control and poverty resulting from maladaptive behavior) and trace the implications of both for government activity.

6. Outline Murray's arguments in support of his conjecture that welfare programs have hurt more than they have helped; outline the arguments of those who counter Murray and claim that we have not been losing ground.

7. Critically analyze the notion of substituting a negative income tax for the plethora of welfare programs currently in place.

Classical economists believed that the distribution of income was determined by economic law and that nothing could change it. Wages, rents, and profits were all determined in the marketplace, they thought, and any attempt to alter the distribution that emerged from that determination would be futile. A majority of Americans in the 1960s would, however, have nothing to do with that conclusion. Before he died, President John Kennedy announced a "war on poverty" as part of the New Frontier; his dreams were embodied in the Great Society programs of the Johnson presidency. To what end? The percentage of American families living below the poverty line fell from 22 percent in 1960 to 11 percent in 1970. The percentage was still roughly 11 percent in 1980, but it climbed to something in excess of 15 percent by 1982. The percentage stood at 14 percent in 1988. Poverty is still a problem in the United States; and it is, at least in absolute terms, still growing.

1. The poverty line is determined by computing *(a maximum poverty index / a minimum-subsistence income / an average American's food budget)*. Social workers provide some information for the computation, and their numbers are corroborated by multiplying a subsistence food budget by *(2 / 3 / 4)*. Why? Because families at the lower end of the income scale typically spend *(one-quarter / one-third / one-half)* of their incomes on food. In 1962, the poverty-line income for a family of four was $3100; in 1988, the same benchmark income was $*(7800 / 9600 / 10,600 / 12,000)*.

---

a minimum-subsistence income; 3; one-third; 12,000

2. Name five causes of income inequality, listing first the factor specified as responsible for the greated disparities in income.

a. ______________________________

b. ______________________________

c. ______________________________

d. ______________________________

e. ______________________________

---

a. differences in property wealth **b.** differences in personal ability **c.** differences in education and opportunity **d.** class barriers to opportunity **e.** differences in age and health.

There are limits to the income which superior talent or energy can earn. A popular television personality may earn huge sums annually, but the income is limited by the number of performances he or she is physically capable of giving. Moreover, earnings may dwindle if popularity fades or old age begins to set in.

Property income is not subject to equivalent restraints. Ownership of stocks and bonds may demand comparatively little supervisory effort. If you have somehow made a good start in security ownership, you may reinvest your earnings and watch them grow. Moreover, unless checked by death or inheritance taxes, property and its income can be passed on to your children in ways that talent and energy cannot.

3. Table 34-1 records the incidence of poverty in some of the major demographic groups of the United States in 1982 and 1985. The percentages all *(rise / stay the same / fall)* during that 3-year period, but this is more reflective of recovery from deep recession than it is of winning the war on poverty. The number of people in or close to poverty has, in fact, *(risen / stayed the same / fallen)* since 1982.

Families headed by women rank *(first on / second on / third on)* the list, with ________ pecent of their numbers falling below the poverty line. Blacks rank *(second / first / fourth)*, with ________ percent. Perhaps most tragically, children under the age of 6 rank *(above / the same as / below)* the overall average with _______ percent—more than 1 child in every 5 in the richest country in the world.

Table 34-1
Incidence of Poverty in Different Groups, 1982 and 1985

Population Group	Percent of Group in Poverty 1982	1985
White	12.0	11.4
Black	35.6	31.3
Hispanic	29.9	29.0
Children under 6	23.8	21.5
Elderly	14.6	12.6
Married couples	7.6	6.7
Families headed by women	40.6	34.0
Total	15.0	14.0

Referring now to Figure 34-1, note that the average income of the bottom one-fifth of the population (ranked by income) has climbed _______ percent since 1930 from $_______ (real 1984 dollars) to $_______. As a percentage of national income, however, the income earned by the lowest 20 percent of the population *(fell / remained roughly the same / rose)*, to stand at *(2 / 5 / 10)* percent in 1984. Through the lowest 20 percent, therefore, 60 years of history has *(shifted the Lorenz curve in toward the 45° line / done nothing to the Lorenz curve / shifted the Lorenz curve away from the 45° line)*, indicating *(a trend toward greater equality / no trend toward greater equality / a trend toward less equality)*, in the lower incomes. Put another way, the average income of the lowest 20 percent of the population has climbed only because *(total income has fallen / total income has remained the same / total income has risen)*. Note: Lorenz curves were introduced in Chapter 26.

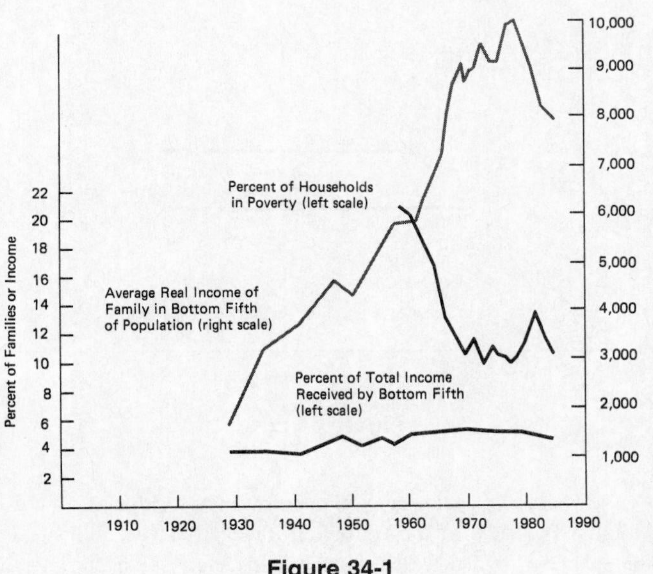

Figure 34-1

fall; risen; first on; 34 (in 1985, down from 40.6 percent in 1982); second; 31.3 (again down from the recession's 35.6 percent, but less significantly); above; 21.5 (down slightly from 23.8 percent); 130; 3000; 7000; remained roughly the same; 5; done nothing to the Lorenz curve; no trend toward greater equality; total income has risen

4. Figure 34-2(a) can be used to illustrate the **disincentive** or **leaky-bucket** consequence of income redistribution. The horizontal and vertical axes measure, respectively (to the same scale), the incomes of the upper half and the lower half of the population.

This diagram has a 45° line emerging from the origin. If there were complete equality in income distribution (if each individual received exactly the same income as every other individual), then the words "upper half" and "lower half" would be meaningless. Alternatively, the so-called upper half *(any half)* of the population would receive exactly the same total income as the so-called lower half. The distribution between them would have to be represented by some point (such as *E*) on this 45° line. (Remember, the scales on the two axes are the same.)

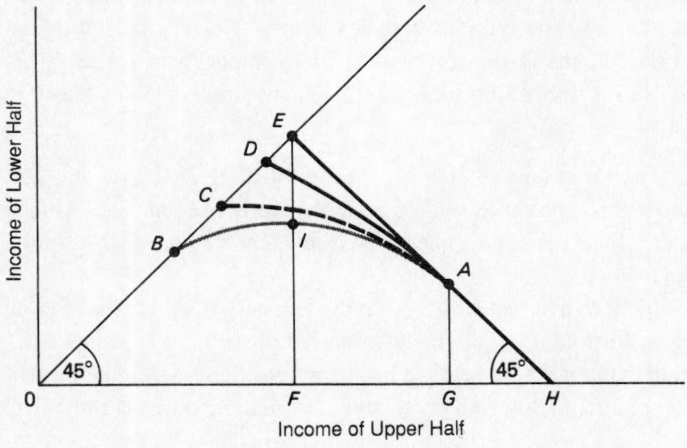

Figure 34-2(a)

a. In fact, incomes are not equally distributed. On this diagram, then, the point indicating the distribution between the two halves must lie *(to the right of and below / to the left of and above)* the 45° line. (Somehow, it always seems to work out that the upper half gets more income than the lower half.)

Suppose that total income received by both halves is *OH*, divided between an upper-half total of *OG* and a lower-half total of *GH*. Let us (temporarily) record this total and its division on the horizontal axis. However, this axis is reserved for upper-half income receivers, and they will probably object to this trespass by those lower-half people on their territory. So draw a 45° line from point *H*, extending up to the other 45° line. Point *E* is where the two lines meet. On *EH*, pick point *A* such that *AG* is equal to *GH*.

Now we have things sorted out as they should be. *OG* (measured horizontally) is the upper-half income total. *AG* (measured vertically) is the lower-half total. Point *A* indicates the distribution of income between the two halves.

Any movement toward greater equality of income distribution would mean a move away from *A (toward / and also away from) E*. Suppose there is such a movement, with absolutely no disincentive, or leaky-bucket, effect. That is, the population's entire income total is *(reduced / not reduced at all)*. On the diagram, this redistribution movement will follow the straight line *EH*, from *A* toward *E*.

b. It is usually argued that any movement directed toward greated equality of income distribution would have at least some disincentive consequences; i.e., there would be at least a small leak in the bucket. Suppose this redistribution is tackled by means of heavier progressive income taxation. The extra taxes thus collected from higher-income people would be passed on to lower-income groups via a **negative income tax** or some other such transfer-payment device. Insofar as people try to avoid heavier taxation by working shorter hours, or in other ways earning less money income, the total of real GNP will *(fall / rise)*. The path of redistribution will no longer run along the straight line *EH*. Starting at A, it will drift *(above / below) EH*. The total of real income will become *(less / more)* than it was at point *A*. The more sweeping the intended income redistribution (i.e., the farther the planned movement from *A* toward *E*) the *(less / more)* pronounced this disincentive effect is likely to be.

c. The three curved lines in Figure 34-2(a), *DA, CA,* and *BA*, show three possible sets of disincentive consequences. Among them, the smallest disincentive effect is indicated by *(DA / CA / BA)*.

Notice that line *CA* is approximately flat in the region close to point *C*. This means that if redistribution toward complete equality were pressed hard enough, there would be a sufficient drop in total GNP so that the real income of the lower half, in absolute terms, would *(increase only slightly / not increase at all / decrease)*. In *relative* terms, though, the *share* of the lower half would *(still increase / remain constant / decrease)*.

d. The most drastic disincentive effect is illustrated by line *BA*. If redistribution effects are such that total income follows this path, the lower-income half of the population will at first (as the movement from *A* toward *B* commences) experience a moderate *(increase / decrease)* in real income. Soon, however, the real income of this lower half of the population will *(increase / decline)* in absolute terms.

If the likely redistribution path is as indicated by *DA*, society may well decide that some movement from *A* toward *D* is worthwhile: the sacrifice of total real income is justified by the resulting greater equality. But if the probable path of redistribution is indicated by *BA*, or even by *CA*, the cost in terms of total real income sacrificed is greater, and society must put a higher priority on income equality if either of these two paths is to be followed, even for a short distance away from *A*.

---

a. to the right of and below; toward; not reduced at all **b.** fall; below; less; more **c.** *DA*; not increase at all; still increase (The upper half getting less means that total income is falling even though the income received by the lower half is constant. The *fractional share* of the lower half must therefore rise as the denominator—total income—falls.) **d.** increase; decline

5. [A question applying the leaky-bucket construction of Figure 34-2(a).] John Rawls, an economic philosopher of considerable reputation, suggested a welfare objective that would attempt to maximize the utility of a society's least well-off citizen. A mapping of the indifference curves associated with this objective in the geometry of Figure 34-2(a) is provided in Figure 34-2(b). Notice that as you move along line *JK* from point *J* to point *K*, society's welfare is unaffected even though the income of the upper half climbs. Why? Because the least well-off people—the lower half of the income distribution—receive nothing. To maximize society's welfare, therefore, the Rawls criteria would require that you simply push horizontal welfare lines as high as possible given some sort of feasibility constraint.

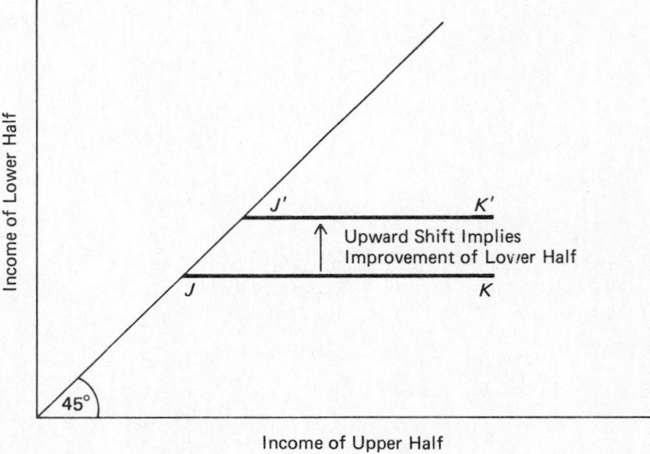

Figure 34-2(b)

Now use the leaky-bucket lines of Figure 34-2(a) as constraints. For each of the following tradeoff curves, indicate in the spaces provided which point would be chosen according to the Rawls criteria.

a. *AE* . . . . (________)

b. *AD* . . . . (________)

c. *AC* . . . . (________)

d. *AB* . . . . (________)

It is apparent, from this exercise, that the Rawls prescription mandates complete equity only when the leaks are *(not too big / enormous)* and the tradeoff schedules are not *(too curved / too straight)*. It is an objective function that, for at least one example, qualifies precisely what might be meant by "equity, but not at any cost."

---

a. *E* **b.** *D* **c.** *C* (barely) **d.** *I*; not too big; too curved

How big are the leaks? What are their sources? First, there are the administrative costs of running welfare and tax-redistribution programs. Although these costs might be enormous in absolute terms in an economy as large as America's, they do not mount up very quickly relative to the magnitudes of the programs actually administered.

Second, there is the potential for welfare programs to create disincentives to work. Jerry Hausman of MIT has determined that these effects are potentially significant, but his work is disputed by many others who find that, for example, the elasticity of the supply of labor to changes in the wage rate is quite small.

Third, there is the potential for progressive taxation to retard saving and investment and thus growth. Okun, himself, discounted this worry by noting that saving and investment accounted for 16 precent of GNP in 1929 and 16 percent of GNP in 1973; 1929 was before the imposition of the full force of the progressive income tax, and 1973 was at the height of the American welfare state. In response to the tax incentives with which the Reagan program tried to stimulate investment and saving, incidently, the combined total of saving and investment actually fell to 13 percent of GNP.

Finally, there are potentially harmful changes in attitude and behavior that might be fostered by a progressive tax and welfare state. More people might cheat on their taxes, or lay around and not work, and so on. These costs are hard to measure, and their jury is still out.

The opposite side of the argument can lead one to suggest that the tradeoff between equity and efficiency is overstated to the extreme. What if the drive toward equality opened opportunities to extraordinarily productive people who would have otherwise been shut out? What if programs that provided health care and nutrition for poor families actually broke the cycle of poverty, thereby increasing productivity and efficiency? Would not, then, operating the welfare state and incurring its expense be an investment in expanded human capital for the future?

6. **a.** List the following welfare-transfer programs in the order of their importance in the federal budget of 1988: Medicare; Medicaid; social security; unemployment insurance; food stamps and child nutrition; housing; aid to families with dependent children; and aid to the aged, blind, and disabled.

(1) ________________________________

(2) ________________________________

(3) ________________________________

(4) ________________________________

(5) ________________________________

(6) ________________________________

(7) ________________________________

(8) ________________________________

b. The total amount budgeted for these programs in 1988 was $________ billion. This is a large amount of money, but it should be noted that only $________ billion (________ percent of the total budget) is spent on programs designed to benefit the poor directly, with $________ billion devoted to increasing poor families' incomes. This percentage is *(up / the same / down)* from the last pre-Reagan budget of 1980.

---

a. **(1)** social security **(2)** Medicare **(3)** Medicaid **(4)** food stamps and child nutrition **(5)** unemployment insurance **(6)** housing **(7)** aid to the aged, blind, and disabled **(8)** aid to families with dependent children **b.** 397.5; 87.3; 8.5; 23; down (from 8.8 percent in 1980, but up from 7.7 percent in 1984)

Charles Murray used the strong disincentives of high effective marginal tax rates facing poor families participating in federal antipoverty programs to support his position that the entire system be scrapped. While many of his other arguments in support of his suggestion have been criticized as falling victim to the *post hoc, ergo propter hoc* fallacy, the potential for such high rates is easily illustrated.

7. Consider a welfare system organized around the following rules of qualification:

1. Basic welfare support is $4000; $0.50 is deducted from that amount for every dollar earned up to $8000.
2. $3000 in food stamps is available for $1000 provided outside earnings do not exceed $2500.
3. $2500 in housing subsidy is granted, but that amount is reduced by $0.50 for every dollar earned over $2000.
4. $1000 per child in supplemental income is available to families with dependent children and outside incomes that do not exceed $3999.

Fill in the blanks of Table 34-2 to reflect the benefits received by each of four different families according to these rules.

Table 34-2

	Family A	Family B	Family C	Family D
1. Basic welfare	______	______	______	______
2. Food stamps	______	______	______	______
3. Housing subsidy	______	______	______	______
4. AFDC	______	______	______	______
5. Outside income	______	______	______	______
6. Total	______	______	______	______
7. Marginal tax rates:				
Last dollar earned	______	______	______	______
Next dollar earned	______	______	______	______

Assume that each family takes advantage of all four programs to the fullest extent possible (not, in reality, a good assumption). Family A has one child and no private outside income. Family B has no children and a private income of $2,000 Family C has two children and an outside income of $2500. Family D has two children and an outside income of $4000.

Family A: basic welfare = $4000; food stamps = $2000 ($3000 net the cost of $1000 taken from basic welfare); housing subsidy = $2500; AFDC = $1000 (for the one child); outside income = $0; total = $9500; marginal tax rates: last dollar—not applicable (There is no "last dollar."), next dollar = 50% (the $0.50 in basic welfare lost on that dollar)
Family B: basic welfare = $3000 [$4000 - 0.5($2000)]; food stamps = $2000; housing subsidy = 2500; AFDC = $0; outside income = $2000; total = $9500; marginal tax rates: last dollar = 50% (the $0.50 lost in basic welfare), next dollar = 100% ($0.50 in housing subsidy lost, too)
Family C: basic welfare = $2750; food stamps = $2000; housing subsidy = $2250; AFDC = $2000; outside income = $2500; total = $11,500; marginal tax rates: last dollar = 100% (both welfare and housing reduced at $0.50 per dollar), next dollar = 200,100% (lost $2000 in net food-stamp payment for that $1 that is not even kept)
Family D: basic welfare = $2000; food stamps = $0 (exceed limit); housing subsidy = $1500; AFDC = $0 (just exceed limit); outside income = $4000; total = $7500; marginal tax rates: last dollar = 200,100% (lost $2000 in AFDC with the last dollar), next dollar = 100% (both welfare and housing reduced at $0.50 per dollar)

8. Record the points made by critics to counter each of the following claims used by Charles Murray in supporting his suggestion that the present welfare system be dismantled and not replaced.

a. Poverty has increased over the past two decades during growth of governmental antipoverty activity. ______________

____

____

____

b. Among black and poor teenage populations, the proportion of individuals with jobs has declined over the past two decades.

____

____

____

____

c. SAT scores point to a widening gap between black and white students over the past 2 years. ______________

____

____

____

d. Welfare programs tend to cause families to break up and women to have more children. ______________

____

____

____

e. Welfare programs provide enormous disincentives to work, so welfare dependency is trasmitted from generation to generation. ______________

____

____

____

a. Slow economic growth and high general unemployment during recession are better explanations. **b.** Other factors (high overall unemployment, changing school patterns, regional migration, smaller army) explain more of this decline than the existence of welfare programs. **c.** The relative performance of black students on SATs increased during that time. **d.** The evidence does not show either of these trends. **e.** Recent evidence shows that recipients are working and that low percentages of welfare-dependent children are ending up on welfare as adults.

9. One feature of the negative tax proposal is important because it gives it a resemblance to the ordinary tax system. Suppose you receive $3000 annually from the government as a negative income tax. Through personal effort, you then manage to increase your own earnings by $3000. The consequence will be that your negative tax payment *(ceases entirely / remains at $3000 / is reduced by some intermediate figure such as $1500)*. That is, your total income (negative tax plus earnings) *(goes up / goes down / is unchanged)*. Hence, there *(is an / is not any)* incentive to increase total receipts built into the system. In this, it *(differs from / is the same as)* most other welfare programs.

is reduced by some intermediate figure such as $1500; goes up; is an; differs from

10. Table 34-3 identifies four different families by their potential earnings. This final question will investigate the parameters of a negative income tax system designed to guarantee a minimum income of $15,000.

a. Suppose initially that all four families work to their fullest potential; their resulting incomes are recorded in row 2 of Table 34-3. If all four are to receive an initial grant of $15,000, then a self-sufficient tax system must raise a total of $______ to be distributed in equal parts. It the tax on earned income (income excluding the $15,000 grants) is to be proportional, then the marginal tax rate must be ______ percent. Now complete rows 3 through 6 by computing for each family the taxes paid, total after-tax earned income, the total after-tax income including the transfer, and the average tax rate. This negative income tax is, on average, *(progressive / proportional / regressive)*. Plot the initial, pre-tax distribution of income in Figure 34-3, and label the point *A*; plot the after-tax distribution of income in the same figure, and label this second point *B*. The after-tax distribution of income is *(more equal / less equal)* than before.

Table 34-3

	Family A	Family B	Family C	Family D	Total
1. Potential earnings	$10,000	$30,000	$60,000	$80,000	$180,000
2. Earned income	$10,000	$30,000	$60,000	$80,000	$180,000
3. Taxes	$3,333	______	______	______	______
4. After-tax earned income	$6,667	______	______	______	______
5. Total income	$21,667	______	______	______	______
6. Average tax rate	20%	______	______	______	______
7. Earned income	______	______	______	______	______
8. Taxes	______	______	______	______	______
9. After-tax earned income	______	______	______	______	______
10. Total income	______	______	______	______	______

b. Now suppose that the families suffer disincentives to work in the face of proportional taxation so that the income they earn equals their potential divided by $(1 + t)$, where $t \times 100$ percent is the tax rate. The tax rate that must now be imposed is 50 percent. Why? Because the requisite $60,000 must equal $t \times 100$ percent of the total potential income of $180,000 divided by $(1 + t)$. Note that

$$\$60,000 = 0.5 \times [\$180,000/(1 + 0.5)] = 0.5 \times \$120,000$$

Complete rows 7 through 10 in Table 34-3 given the 50 percent tax rate and the work disincentive. Plot the resulting distribution of income of Figure 34-3; label this final distribution point *C*. The distribution of income is now *(even more equal / even less equal)*, but the four families are sharing a smaller pie. Still, the two poorest families are *(better / worse)* off than without the negative income tax.

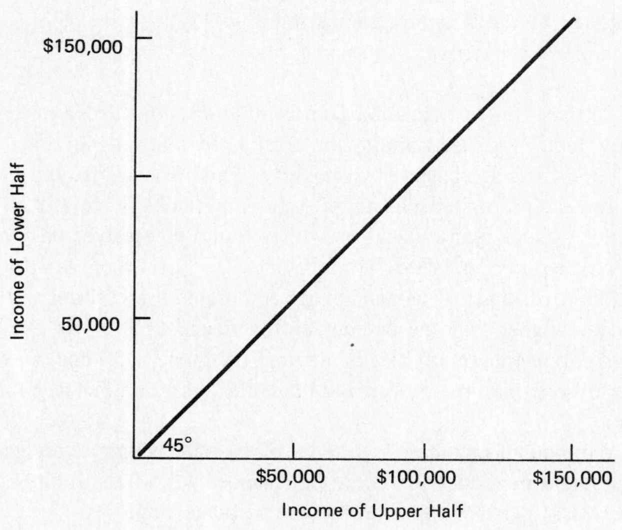

Figure 34-3

a. 60,000; 33.3 [(60/180) × 100%] Reading across the rows: 3: $10,000, $20,000, $26,667, $60,000; 4: $20,000, $40,000, $53,333, $120,000; 5: $35,000, $55,000, $68,333, $180,000; 6: 28.6%, 36.4%, 39.0%, 33.3% progressive; more equal (lying along a straight line through point *A* with slope equal to -1).
b. Reading across the rows: 7: $6667, $20,000, $40,000, $53,333, $120,000; 8: $3333, $10,000, $20,000, $26,667, $60,000; 9: $3333, $10,000, $20,000, $26,667, $60,000; 10: $18,333, $25,000, $35,000, $41,667, $120,000
even more equal; better (Point *C* is located below the *AB* line.)

QUIZ: Multiple Choice

1. The poverty line, computed to reflect a minimum-subsistence income:
(1) has grown from $3100 in 1962 to over $12,000 by the late 1980s.
(2) has been nearly stable in real terms over the 25 year internal between 1962 and 1987.
(3) is roughly 3 times the minimum-subsistence food budget.
(4) has seen its food component climb to approximately $4000 by 1988.
(5) all of the above.

2. The war on poverty, initiated by President John Kennedy embodied in the Great Society of Lyndon Johnson:
(1) managed to reduce the percentage of American people below the poverty line from 22 percent in 1962 to 15 percent in 1971; it remains at 15 percent today.
(2) managed to cut the percentage of Americans below the poverty line from 22 percent in 1962 to 11 percent by 1970; it remained at 11 percent until 1981, when it started a climb back above 15 percent.
(3) had little or no effect on the percentage of Americans below the poverty line and thus warranted cancellation by the Reagan administration.
(4) had a small effect on lowering the percentage of people below the poverty line until participation requirements were tightened by the Reagan administration in 1982.
(5) none of the above.

3. Differences in education and training are considered to be major factors in determining the likelihood that an individual will find himself or herself in poverty. This link is reflected in the correlation of statistics about American blacks in the 1980s. While twice as many blacks as whites found themselves below the poverty line in 1985:
(1) the percentage of whites having completed high school was 8 points higher than the percentage for blacks.
(2) the percentage of blacks having completed college was roughly one-half the percentage of whites who completed college.
(3) the median income of white families, with which a college or professional education could be financed for white children, was nearly twice the median income of black families.
(4) the median formal schooling experience of white men over 25 years of age was almost a full year longer than it was for black men of the same generation.
(5) all of the above are accurate statements which support the correlation of education and training to poverty.

4. Which of the following is not a reason that might explain the incidence of poverty in contemporary America?
(1) Differences in education and training.
(2) The existence of noncompeting groups.
(3) Differences in economic environment, including the distribution of wealth.
(4) The asymmetric effect of recession on demographic groups.
(5) Difference in ability among all people.

5. The average income of the lowest 20 percent of the population has increased by more than 130 percent since 1929:
(1) so the need for antipoverty programs is a myth.
(2) but the percentage of total income that represents has held steady at 5 pecent.
(3) but almost all that growth is explained by growth in total GNP.
(4) choices (2) and (3) only.
(5) none of the above.

6. Of all children living in the United States in 1988, less than:
(1) 1 in 10 were living below the poverty line.
(2) 1 in 20 were living below the poverty line.
(3) 1 in 5 were living below the poverty line.
(4) 1 percent were living below the poverty line.
(5) 1 million were living below the poverty line.

7. A poor family's employment earnings are supplemented by a negative income tax—in the amount, say, of $4000. Under this tax proposal, if family employment earnings were to rise by $1000, the income received from the negative tax would typically:
(1) fall by $1000.
(2) fall by more than $1000.
(3) fall by some amount less than $1000.
(4) fall by $4000.
(5) rise by some amount such as $500.

8. Referring to Figure 34-4, let point *A* represent some initial distribution of income between the indicated upper half and the lower half. Which point represents the equal distribution of income if there were no leaks in the bucket?
(1) *A*.
(2) *B*.
(3) *C*.
(4) *D*.
(5) *E*.

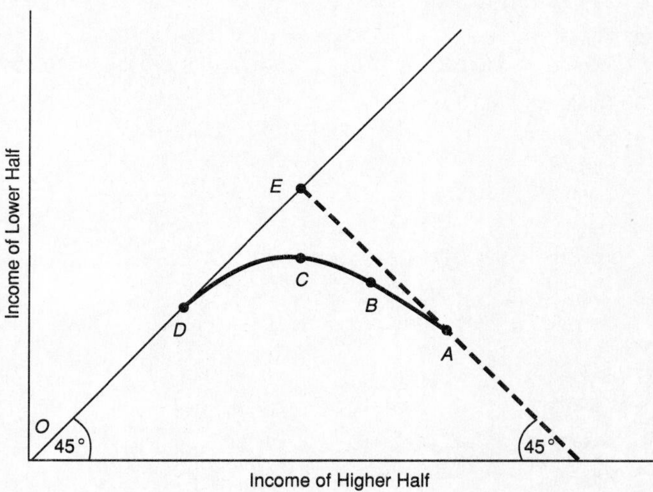

Figure 34-4

9. Which answer to question 8 would have been correct if it had asked for the point that would represent equality given the leaks that produce curve *ABCD*?
(1).
(2).

(3).
(4).
(5).

10. Which answer to question 8 would have been correct if it had asked for the point that would be selected if society chose on the basis of Rawlsian objective criteria?

(1).
(2).
(3).
(4).
(5).

11. Which of the following is not likely to be a significant source of "leaks" in the equity-efficiency tradeoff?
(1) The administrative costs of running a welfare-income-redistribution program.
(2) The work disincentives of the progressive income tax.
(3) The disincentives against saving and investment produced by the progressive income tax.
(4) A change in attitude that makes cheating on taxes more acceptable.
(5) All of the above could be significant, thought there is little evidence to support choice (3).

12. Which of the following was the largest item in the 1988 budget targeted directly at helping the poor?
(1) Medicaid.
(2) Aid to families with dependent children.
(3) Food stamps and child nutrition.
(4) Aid to the aged, blind, and disabled.
(5) Housing assistance.

13. Despite its importance in explaining the incidence of poverty, spending on programs that support the education and training of the poor fell from 1981 to 1984, as did most of the spending targeted directly at helping the poor:
(1) by less than 1 percent.
(2) by about 5 percent.
(3) by nearly 8 percent.
(4) by almost 15 percent.
(5) by more than 25 percent.

14. One serious problem with the current structure of the U.S. welfare state is:
(1) the inability of government to get all those eligible for a program to apply.
(2) the inability to make absolutely sure that anybody who is not eligible does not enter a program.
(3) the workings of the eligibility requirement that give the poor the country's highest effective marginal income-tax rates.
(4) the migration of the poor to states with high benefits.
(5) all of the above are serious problems with the current state of affairs.

15. "Inefficiency" in income redistribution means: (1) the reduction in total output caused by those unfavorably affected by redistribution and by their decision to pay less in income tax by working less.
(2) the administrative costs of redistribution and the burden it places on federal workers.
(3) the lesser skills of the gainers from redistribution.
(4) the total amount of income transferred from upper-income to lower-income groups.
(5) the resulting reduction in total taxes collected by the government.

SUGGESTED ANSWERS TO QUESTIONS IN THE TEXT: Chapter 34

1. State your own view. Couch your answer in terms of what you now know about capitalism (in its pure form, e.g., given the workings of the first theorem of welfare economics, and/or in its practical form), on the one hand, and the debate concerning the effectiveness of current programs (as they are designed to function and/or as they actually function), on the other. George McGovern proposed a negative income tax during the presidential campaign of 1972. Does that make any difference in the way you answer the question?

2. The three types of equity are equality of political rights, equality of economic opportunity, and equality of economic outcome. State your view, again, but make sure that you specify precisely the type of equity you are addressing. Remember that you can conceptualize the inefficiency associated with programs designed to promote equity in terms of Okun's leaky bucket and graphs like Figure 34-4. Are the graphs the same for each type, or is the tradeoff for one type more severe than the tradeoff for another? Why? So what?

3. One more time, express your own view. Remember that you now have a battery of economic tools and concepts to apply to issues like this. Use them. Personally, I have liked the negative income tax idea since 1972.

4. The efficiency argument in support of income grants is shown most clearly in indifference-curve analysis of the type presented in appendix 19. An income grant moves a budget constraint out in parallel across the entire quadrant; the consumption of all goods can increase. Grants in kind achieve the same parallel shift, but only to the extent that people want the goods specified in the grant; the consumption of all goods may not be able to be increased.

To see this, consult Figure TQ34-1. There, line *AB* is a budget constraint between food and other goods without any welfare program; the individual in question has just $300 to allocate between the two each month. A program that gives this person $180 in food stamps each month shifts the budget constraint to schedule *A′CB*; the quantity of other goods possible is still bound by $300, but the maximum amount of food possible is now $480. Were the program simply to give the person $180, the resulting budget constraint would be *A′B′*—a straight line

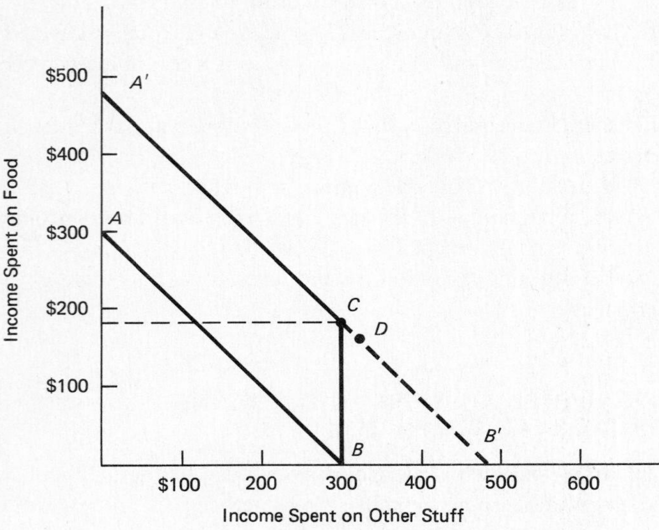

Figure TQ34-1

extending past point C to show that the maximum amount of other goods possible increased to $480.

Where is the increased efficiency? Suppose that this person were typical and wanted to spend one-third of his income on food. Given the income grant and a resulting income of $480, he would want to spend $160 on food and $320 on other goods (point D). With the food stamps, he would be constrained to purchase $180 of food and only $300 of other goods. His utility would therefore be lower with food stamps than with an income grant.

5. The equation of the tax is

$$T = -B + tY,$$

where T represents tax liability, B represents the benefit payment, Y represents income, and t represents the tax rate (in percentage terms, $t \times 100$ percent). With $t = 0.5$ and $B = \$4500$, breakeven occurs when

$$T = 0 = -\$4500 + 0.5Y$$

i.e., when

$$Y = \$4500/0.5 = \$9000$$

This conforms with Table 34-4 in the text. For $B = \$2700$, solving for t such that $9000 is the breakeven income means solving

$$0 = -\$2700 + t(\$9000);$$

i.e., the appropriate tax is $\$2700/\$9000 = 0.3$ (30 percent). For $B = \$7200$, the same procedure produces a tax of 0.8 (80 percent). For $B = \$9000$, the tax is 1 (100 percent).

6. To compute what happens generation by generation, multiply the fractions listed in the table by the fraction of the population on welfare and off. For example, start with 50 percent on and 50 percent off. The first line of the table states that 90 percent of those off stay off while 10 percent go on; the second line shows that 60 percent of those on go off while 40 percent of those on stay on. So, after one generation, the fraction off welfare is

$$[(.90 \times .50) + (.60 \times .50)] = [.45 + .30] = .75$$

Meanwhile, the fraction on is

$$[(.10 \times .50) + (.40 \times .50)] = [.05 + .25] = .25 = 1 - .75$$

Equilibrium, meanwhile, is some fraction Z off welfare that is not changed by the transition probabilities. The equilibrium Z must therefore solve

$$[(.90 \times Z) + (.60 \times Z)] = Z;$$

i.e., $Z = (.60/.70) = .857$. As a result, $(1 - Z) = .143$ stay on welfare, and that satisfies the mirror equation

$$\{[.10 \times (1 - Z)] + [.40 \times (1 - Z)]\} = (1 - Z)$$

With the second line changed to (.80, .20), the equilibrium Z is $(.80/.90) = .889$. Getting 95 percent of the way to that new equilibrium from the old means getting the fraction off welfare to .887, and that takes at least two generations.

CHAPTER 35
THE WINDS OF CHANGE: ALTERNATIVE ECONOMIC SYSTEMS

Your attention has thus far been focused on the modern mainstream view of how a mixed economy like that of the United States works to solve the fundamental economic questions of *how*, *what*, and *for whom*. Your introduction to this type of structure is almost complete. Chapter 35 focuses on the economic alternatives to mixed capitalism, and has been included at this point for two important reasons.

First of all, the profession did not arrive at its current state overnight. The mainstream view espoused by many economists in mixed economies is the product of an evolutionary process that has proceeded slowly over the course of more than two centuries. You should be aware of at least the broad outline of that evolution. Second, not all the world's economies operate in a fashion that is best described by the mixed structure envisioned by mainstream economic thought in the United States. Over 2.5 billion people across the world live in societies whose economic structures are based on the principles of Marxism or socialism. You should also be aware of the major differences that these structures impose on the workings of those economic structures.

The general objectives of this chapter are therefore easily defined; simply put, they prescribe your being exposed to different ways of looking for answers to the same fundamental questions. With your horizons thus broadened, you should have accomplished the following more specific objectives.

LEARNING OBJECTIVES

1. Explain Adam Smith's argument in support of laissez-faire: the market provides a self-regulating natural order even over the actions of people who are essentially self-motivated. Also note why Smith's book, *The Wealth of Nations*, was so well received by the business classes who were happy to see intellectual justification of their purposes.

2. Delineate the rationale behind David Ricardo's forecast that rents would rise as land became the bottleneck to economic growth. Also explain his expectation that the future would make the capitalists the captains of economic order even as the world fell into a state of pervasive poverty. Given the gloom and doom, why were his ideas so popular with both the capitalists and the socialists?

3. Summarize the major contributions which the neoclassical school made to classical theory by recognizing consumer preferences and the demand side of a market. Also recognize the major objections raised by this school to the laissez-faire recommendations of the classicists.

4. Place the Keynesian revolution into its historical context, and describe the modern mainstream view of macroeconomic theory in terms of its historical antecedents.

5. Explain each of the major modern critiques of mainstream economic thought: the libertarian view of the Chicago School, the passive policy view of the rational-expectations school, the Galbraithian view of modern capitalism, the lessons of the Japanese experience, and the New Left prescriptions of the radical economists.

6. Distinguish carefully between *(a)* pure market economy, *(b)* Marxism, *(c)* modern socialism, and *(d)* Soviet communism. Use your experience and understanding of current events to place modern economies in their appropriate position in this spectrum.

7. Define what Marx meant by "the exploitation of labor by capital" and by "surplus value." Explain why Marx felt that capitalism was inevitably headed for a crisis generated by a failure of the purchasing power of labor to match the total value of goods produced.

8. Describe the Soviet economic structure, and compare its performance with the major developed economies of the West. Outline both the intent and the effect of the Gorbachev reforms.

Adam Smith's *The Wealth of Nations* occupies a unique place in the esteem of economists, less because it argued in favor of laissez-faire and more because it was the first coherent account of the working of a market system. Much of what is found in Chapters 2 and 3 of the text derives from Adam Smith: the law of scarcity, the role of prices, the need for competition, and the consequences of monopoly. Smith's argument is sometimes incomplete, sometimes confused, sometimes contradictory, but these are the inevitable shortcomings of a pioneer work of immense scope.

Two further points about the classical economists deserve mention. First, their work developed out of a lively and perceptive interest in contemporary issues. *The Wealth of Nations* is a frontal attack on the then-influential mercantilist philosophy of governmental interference in trade matters. Malthus and Ricardo dealt at length with issues arising from the Napoleonic Wars, notably war-induced price inflation and tariff protection. When Napoleon's power play ended and normal shipping was resumed, the British food-growing aristocracy found itself exposed to new competition from America and elsewhere. The English landowners contrived an increase in the grain tariff—the famous Corn Laws. Subsequently, and largely in consequence of the influential writings of the classical economists, the Corn Law rates were reduced and, in 1846, abolished.

Second, there is just enough unanimity of viewpoint among the English classical economists to warrant grouping them together as a school, and no more. Malthus and Ricardo conducted a lengthy correspondence on innumerable issues. Almost always, they disagreed. (These disagreements did nothing to destroy a touchingly warm and enduring friendship which terminated only with Ricardo's death at the age of 51.) For example, most of the classical economists accepted, at least in rough outline, Say's Law of full-employment purchasing power. Malthus did not, although he could not build an alternative theory. It was more than 100 years later that Keynes did construct such a theory.

1. The most prominent members of the early English "classical school" of economists were:

Adam Smith (1723–1790)
Thomas Robert Malthus (1766–1834)
David Ricardo (1772–1823)

Match these names with the following descriptions:

a. Sought, as a major part of his work, to discover the "laws of distribution"—i.e., the economic laws by means of which the national product was divided between three classes: laborers, landowners, and entrepreneurs (manufacturers and merchants): ____________________.

b. Enunciated the doctrine of laissez-faire, which held that government should not interfere with human activity except in special areas such as the maintenance of law, police duties, and national defense: ____________________.

c. Although best known today for his theory of population growth, he dealt, in fact, with a wide range of contemporary economic problems: ____________________.

d. Developed the hypothesis that, in the long run, land was the crucially scarce economic factor, so that economic growth would result in a continuing increase in the rental price per acre received by owners of land (note that although one of the three economists cited is particularly associated with this hypothesis, it is implicit also in the reasoning of another of the three): ____________________.

e. Set out the doctrine of self-regulating "natural order" of human affairs, and used the **invisible-hand** concept to illustrate this doctrine: each individual, pursuing his own self-interest within a market system, is "led by an invisible hand to promote an end which was no part of his intention": ____________________.

f. Relied heavily on the law of diminishing returns in his analysis (note that two of the three economists did so): ____________________ and ____________________.

a. Ricardo **b.** Smith **c.** Malthus **d.** Ricardo (or Malthus) **e.** Smith **f.** Malthus; Ricardo

2. The English classical economists had, so to speak, roughed out the general shape of economic analysis. Thereafter, one group—the neoclassical economists, still predominantly English until the early twentieth century—undertook to correct, to refine, and to enlarge classical ideas. Another group—Marx and his followers—attempted a more fundamental revision.

The classical account, perhaps because it felt impelled to emphasize the basic scarcity of productive factors (Chapter 2), had stressed *supply* factors as the principal ingredient within commodity prices. Demand elements were not given much consideration. It is almost as though all classical supply curves were *(horizontal / vertical)*, so that any shift in the demand curve *(would / could not)* change the price.

This classical supply-side account vacillated between a labor theory of value and a cost-of-production theory. (The latter asserts that the price of a commodity must be explained in terms of the expenditures on labor, land, and capital required for its production.) Both labor and cost-of-production theories may seem plausible at first; on closer inspection, though, they have proved to be after-the-event explanations.

Marx worked to solve this problem by adding his own notion of *surplus* value to the more widely held labor theory of value.

Prices, Marx argued, *would* be equal to labor value in a properly functioning society. In a capitalist society, however, prices *would not* achieve this fundamental equality. The labor theory of value was, thereby transformed into more of a description of "what should be" than a description of "what is."

By way of contrast, the neoclassical economists stuck (or tried to stick, at any rate) to descriptions of "what is." They recognized that labor cost, and costs of production generally, have a major part to play in price determination. At the same time, however, they added the element which had earlier been neglected, namely: ____________________. The outcome—and here the work of Alfred Marshall (1842–1924) was most important—was the demand-curve and supply-curve approach of Chapters 4 and 18.

Demand and supply curves are graphs; therefore they have a mathematical background, whether that background is recognized or not. Economics was becoming more mathematical. The neoclassical introduction of "marginalist" concepts (marginal utility in Chapter 19, marginal cost and revenue in Chapters 22 through 24, marginal product in Chapter 21) illustrates the point. If you have had training in calculus, you will recognize that "marginal" signifies the taking of a partial derivative.

It was as part of this more mathematical trend that the theory of general equilibrium (Chapter 31) was developed. Major figures were ____________________, ____________________, and ____________________.

---

horizontal; could not; demand; Leon Walras; Stanley Jevons; Wilfred Pareto

3. In the twentieth century, the major development in economics has been the development of Keynesian analysis, already discussed at length earlier in the text. Bitterly resented upon its introduction because it seemed to upset so many traditional beliefs, this analysis warns that the market system cannot be left to its own devices with assurance that a full-employment equilibrium will result in developed societies relying heavily on investment spending. In brief, Keynesian analysis banished *(the law of scarcity / the law of supply and demand / Say's Law / the law of diminishing returns)*.

Say's Law

4. a. The Chicago School of economists, including ____________________, ____________________, ____________________, ____________________, and Milton Friedman, generally feels that markets *(work / don't work)* and that government intervention is *(necessary and beneficial / unnecessary and detrimental)*. The rational-expectations macroeconomics of the Chicago and Minnesota schools, covered in the appendix to Chapter 16, is simply a logical extension of this line of reasoning—a line of reasoning that traces its origins directly back to the *(invisible hand of Adam Smith / the lament of diminishing productivity of Malthus and Ricardo / the spending multipliers of Keynes)*. Lest anyone think that it abides only in the halls of academia, it should be emphasized that the Economic Report of the President prepared for President *(Nixon / Carter / Reagan)* by the Council of Economic Advisers in *(1972 / 1978 / 1982)* endorsed almost the entire philosophical picture of the Chicago School.

b. A second critique, made popular by John Kenneth Galbraith, also holds that mainstream theory is out of touch with reality. Circle each of the following statements that accurately reiterates either one of the contentions of the Galbraithian view or a commonly held opinion of his work.

(1) His theory is basically Marxist both in its origins and its conclusions.

(2) His work is more a criticism of existing theory than an outline of an identifiable and testable alternative theory.

(3) His argument presents a serious challenge to Keynesian economics.

(4) His reasoning is in large part a synthesis of other people's ideas; his role has been to merge these ideas and to present them in unusually persuasive fashion.

(5) Big business is not necessarily bad, though not necessarily good, either.

(6) Consumers are not the masters of their own fates; they are manipulated by advertising and salespeople to the point of not always knowing precisely what is in their best interest.

(7) The public sector seems to be starved for resources, while the private sector squanders enormous wealth that could otherwise be used to improve the welfare of all.

c. Radical economists come at the world from the New Left. They espouse many types of government intervention; list at least four in the spaces provided.

(1) ____

(2) ____

(3) ____

(4) ____

---

a. Frank Knight; Henry Simons; Friedrich Hayek; work; unnecessary and detrimental; invisible hand of Adam Smith; Reagan; 1982 **b. (2)**; **(4)**; **(5)**; **(6)**; **(7)** **c. (1)** Markets need democratic planning **(2)** Price controls are needed to free resources **(3)** Industrial policies are necessary **(4)** Greater equity is essential.

The term **socialism** has been applied to a variety of political and economic movements. It is generally agreed that the characteristic common to most of these movements is a belief that the privilege of unlimited ownership of private property is not an inalienable right. In particular, socialists challenge the right of private ownership of productive resources in the form of land and capital goods.

While the origins of socialist thought can be traced back to the Greeks, the socialist movement developed its real momentum in the eighteenth and nineteenth centuries. The Industrial Revolution profoundly altered European economic and social conditions. It brought immense wealth to some members of the new entrepreneur class. It brought degradation and misery to many workers employed in the new industries. To people of conscience, it seemed that in the new economy, the cards were stacked against anyone unlucky enough to be forced to try and earn his or her living from labor alone. Members of this "proletariat" class would inevitably be exploited by a small group of employers exercising power acquired through ownership of productive inputs other than labor.

However unanimous socialists may have been on the indignities of the new industrial society, they were far from agreement on the proper method of reform. The anarchists believed in total abolition of the state; later, anarchism came to be associated with the view that capitalism (and the state) could be overthrown only by violent means. In contrast, the "utopian" socialists hoped to reform society by establishing as seeds within that society small communal groups whose behavior would be governed by "high-minded" rules.

Karl Marx regarded these utopian projects as fatuous diversions of the reform effort. He insisted on a socialism that would be "practical" in the essential sense of being based on a *scientific* analysis of human society. In 1848, to express these views, he and Friedrich Engels published *The Communist Manifesto*.

Marxism's intellectual foundation is "dialectical materialism," an adaptation of Hegel's "dialectical idealism." This Marxian system describes human history in terms of movement and change. Each stage of development within that history contains some inner contradiction which is the seed of its own destruction. Change is the process by which one contradiction is removed, only to produce another. The fundamental assumption in Marxism, as stated in *The Communist Manifesto*, is that "the history of all hitherto-existing society is the history of class struggles." In this history, the ruling class exploits one or more other classes. Feudalism was one stage in human history, in which the ruling class consisted of landowning nobility. The inner contradiction within this system led to its overthrow by capitalism. According to Marx, the bourgeois ruling class of capitalists would in due course be overthrown by the proletarian laboring class. Marx though this would be the final stage of the class struggle, since the overthrow of capitalism would result in a classless society.

To enlarge his argument that capitalism carries within it an inner contradiction leading to its own destruction, Marx developed his theory of surplus value.

5. a. Karl Marx's principal work was his three-volume *Das Kapital*. Referring particularly to opinion among rebels and dissenters, *Das Kapital* is *(no longer / still)* considered Marx's major contribution to reform.

b. Marx's forecasts in this work included the following: the real wage of laborers would *(rise / fall)*; the "reverse army of the unemployed" would *(increase / decrease)* in number; the rate of capitalist profit would *(rise / fall)*; business cycles would *(grow / diminish)* in intensity; the capitalism system would collapse by reason of *(an excess / a deficiency)* of purchasing power.

Thus, far, these forecasts *(have / have not)* been vindicated.

c. Interest in Marx is today turning toward other aspects of his thought. Two ideas in particular are emphasized. Record them in the spaces provided below.

(1) ____________________

(2) ____________________

____

a. no longer **b.** fall; increase; fall; grow; a deficiency; have not **c. (1)** alienation **(2)** the economic interpretation of history (the view that behavior is shaped by material interests, or in more Marxian terms, by the conditions of production)

6. Circle the statements which accurately characterize the state of the Soviet Union prior to Gorbachev. Put stars next to the statements which identify the intent of some of the Gorbachev reforms.

a. The state relinquishing some of its ownership of the land.

b. The state owns almost all capital equipment.

c. Consumer goods are given money prices, and workers choose among these consumer goods according to these prices; the wages of workers are paid in money.

d. Central planners once were plagued with the problem of a widespread piling up of consumer goods which could not be sold; now this problem is much less acute.

e. Workers have, in general, no choice at to the geographic area in which they may work.

f. Workers have very little choice as to the occupation they would like to enter.

g. Planners use prices to support and achieve their planning goals.

h. There are no important differences in wages or salaries; i.e., there are no significant departures from equality of income distribution.

i. Inequalities of income distribution exist to reflect political influence rather than special competence or skill in some occupation.

j. In the decision of what goods to produce, top priority is given to investment projects and defense production, consumer goods being produced to the extent possible after these requirements have been satisfied.

k. Industrial workers are now given a fair degree of freedom to bargain collectively with plant managers on wages and other terms of employment.

l. Industrial plants operate by being given a quota of output which they are expected to meet or exceed.

m. The quota system is presently used only to allocate productive resources, while consumer goods sell at competitive prices because markets are allowed to function to some degree.

n. Enterprise managers are rewarded for achieving quantity targets, and this system breeds poor quality, hoarding, and reluctance to take risks and pursue innovations.

o. Prices change frequently without warning because planning is an imprecise science.

p. Political control of economic planning has moved gradually, but steadily, away from centralization and toward decentralization.

q. Material balances help planners keep track of thousands of different goods and factors of production.

r. The state levies a tax on the sale of goods at each production stage, so that consumer-goods prices considerably exceed wages paid to produce those goods.

s. Marxist concepts with respect to value are still employed with respect to relative prices set on consumer goods and on investment goods.

Circle: **b**; **c**; **g**; **j**; **l**; **n**; **q**; **r** Star: **a**, **p** and, tentatively, **m** [*Note*: Things are changing so quickly in the Soviet Union that these answers may be out of date as you read this.]

7. Circle the statement which make accurate comparisons between the United States, the Soviet Union, and other economies.

a. The Soviet Union's rate of growth in GNP since World War II has exceeded that of all Western countries.

b. As the Soviet Union's output grows and in consequence turns more toward services, it is estimated that her rate of growth will increase, since services do not involve the same heavy investment in capital equipment.

c. GNP in the Soviet Union is currently little more than one-half of U.S. GNP.

d. The Soviet Union has been able to imitate technologies already developed elsewhere. This fact has made it somewhat easier for her to maintain a high GNP growth rate.

e. The long-term rate of growth in real GNP in the United States is fractionally above 5 percent annually.

f. The Soviet Union devotes a larger fraction of her GNP to military expenditure than the United States does.

g. Experience with GNP figures since World War II furnishes no clear answer to the question of whether collectivist societies or decentralized societies are better adapted to rapid rates of growth.

---

c; **d**; **f**; **g**

QUIZ: Multiple Choice

1. The concept of a "natural order" is associated in economics particularly with the name of:
(1) John Maynard Keynes.
(2) Leon Walras.
(3) Adam Smith.
(4) Karl Marx.
(5) Alfred Marshall.

2. Which of the five economists cited in question 1 was the author of the statement, "People of the same trade seldom meet together, even for merriment and diversion, but the conversation ends in a conspiracy against the public or in some contrivance to raise price"?
(1).
(2).
(3).
(4).
(5).

3. An important part of David Ricardo's argument held that:
(1) the income or payment received by each productive factor or input would be governed by that factor's marginal productivity.
(2) economists relied to excess on the deductive process and neglected the requirement of verifying their conclusions empirically.
(3) supply and cost factors alone could not explain price or value, since demand was a factor of equal importance.
(4) the rate of business profit was bound to fall.
(5) profits would fall even as labor's wage fell.

4. Which alternative in question 3 would be correct, had that

question referred to Karl Marx (and to capitalist society) rather than to David Ricardo?
(1).
(2).
(3).
(4).
(5).

5. The contemporary economist whose name is most prominently associated with the principle of laissez-faire earlier advocated by Adam Smith is:
(1) Milton Friedman.
(2) Thomas Kuhn.
(3) Robert Solow.
(4) John G. Gurley.
(5) John Kenneth Galbraith.

6. The law of diminishing returns played a prominent part in:
(1) Leon Walras' theory of general equilibrium.
(2) the mercantilist theory of tariff protection.
(3) Adam Smith's principle of the invisible hand.
(4) David Ricardo's theory of income distribution.
(5) Karl Marx's theory of the business cycle.

7. The contributions of neoclassical theory to the advancement of economic analysis included:
(1) the development of a mathematical theory of general equilibrium and in the process brought marginalist concepts into use.
(2) the development of an econometric procedure to measure the significance of economic variables.
(3) the reversal of the classical emphasis on deduction, insisting that economists verify empirically the hypotheses on which they relied.
(4) a non-Marxist account of how the economy might reach an equilibrium which was substantially below the level of full resource employment.
(5) the first clear account of the significance of the law of scarcity on the supply side of the market.

8. The "economic interpretation of history" doctrine set out by Marx and Engels maintains that:
(1) the distribution of income by class is governed by the iron law of marginal productivity.
(2) the driving force behind entrepreneurial behavior is the maximization of money profit.
(3) each class has its own economic interest, and beliefs and behavior are dictated by such economic interest.
(4) an authoritarian leader, thrown up by world revolution, is an imperative before any change in the conditions of production can be accomplished.
(5) the inescapable scarcity of land must lead to the progressive impoverishment of the growing body of laborers who must work on that land.

9. Marx's argument was that the output which requires labor effort is given a price which exceeds the money wage paid that labor. The verdict of neoclassical economic theory on this argument is that it:
(1) may have some validity in labor-intensive production, but not in capital-intensive production.
(2) is entirely false.
(3) is correct, since inputs other than labor contribute to production.
(4) may have some validity as to capital-intensive production, but not as to labor-intensive production.
(5) is meaningless, since demand is a more powerful factor in price determination than is labor cost.

10. Marx's approach to the economic problem of values was that:
(1) the emphasis of the classical economists upon values was a distraction, the important thing being the exploitation of labor.
(2) the important thing is relative values, the valuation of one commodity against another.
(3) surplus value has to be measured altogether differently from labor value.
(4) there has to be an absolute measure of value, the measure being labor value.
(5) in capitalist societies, prices bear no consistent relationship to values whatsoever.

11. Socialism, as depicted in Great Britain, and Soviet communism differ in which respect?
(1) Since World War II, the emphasis on public ownership of industry has been somewhat moderated in communism but not in socialism.
(2) Significant inequalities of income are accepted as necessary in socialist thinking but not in communist.
(3) Socialism accepts and encourages the trade-union movement; communism does not.
(4) Significant inequalities of income are accepted as necessary in communist thinking but not in socialist.
(5) None of the above.

12. In the Soviet Union, the decision of what to produce is made:
(1) first on total consumer-goods production, then defense, with the residual in total output being devoted to capital goods.
(2) principally through a pricing system, except for defense and defense-related production.
(3) according to a system of national priorities, among which any of consumer goods, capital goods, or defense may rank highest at any particular time.
(4) by the central authority, but there is no clear evidence as to the priority system.
(5) on defense and capital-goods production first, with consumer goods being caught in the residual in total output.

13. The distribution of income and privilege within the Soviet Union today is best described by which of the following?
(1) There are neither significant class distinctions nor differences of privilege; the only significant differences in income take the form of merit bonuses for exceeding production quotas.
(2) There are significant class distinctions, but these are based almost entirely on occupation, not on income, since differences in income and in privilege are minor.
(3) The income distribution is polarized, with a few party members enjoying high income and privilege; the remainder of the population receives low and approximately equal incomes.
(4) There are marked social classes and differences of privilege, and there is considerable inequality in income; party members may receive substantial incomes derived from property ownership.
(5) There are marked social classes and differences of privilege, and there is considerable inequality in income distribution between classes even though no significant amount of income is attributable to ownership of capital goods or other such property.

14. The Soviet government acquires much of the revenues needed for its operation through:
(1) levying an income tax, although it is not a progressive income tax.
(2) levying a turnover tax applied on goods at each stage of production.
(3) payments made by each industrial plant in proportion to cost of plant construction, much as a Western company might pay interest on a bond issue.
(4) levying taxes on privately owned property.
(5) levying a progressive income tax.

15. The best available estimates suggest that the U.S.S.R.'s total real GNP (compared with that of the United States):
(1) is slightly over one-half, but its per capita GNP is less than one-half.
(2) is approximately equal, and its per capita GNP is slightly higher.
(3) is about one-third and its per capita GNP is perhaps less than one-quarter.
(4) has by now risen slightly above that of the United States, although its per capita GNP is still only about five-sixths.
(5) simply cannot be compared with that of the United States, because commodities consumed in the two countries are so different as to make comparisons meaningless.

SUGGESTED ANSWERS TO QUESTIONS IN THE TEXT: Chapter 35

1. The market system supports laissez-faire capitalism; it was most closely approximated in nineteenth-century Britain. Marxism predicts the laws of motion of capitalism from the exploitation of labor through an ultimate proletarian victory—the last phase in social history; it influenced thinking in Europe, the Soviet Union, the Peoples' Republic of China, and many parts of the developing world. Socialism calls for government ownership of the means of production, vigorous planning, and movement toward a welfare state; having evolved from a call for violence, it can represent one extreme in the market-command spectrum along which most mixed, developed economies find themselves. Soviet communism arose in Russia in 1917; the state owns (most of) the land and the capital and operates according to plans that are constructed down to the micro level. The Gorbachev reforms are moving the system toward more decentralization.

2. The market-system solution to the questions is the topic of most of the text—dollar votes and profit incentives. The general planning answers generated in the Soviet Union are outlined according to each question in the chapter.

3. Old thinkers would like little of the text—market prices, profit incentives, dollar votes, and all that. Contemporary thinkers would find it all very interesting as they search around in the reform process for thoughts that might work for them.

4. Succinctly, the libertarian argument is "If it is good for people, then they will do it on their own and the market will help them." There will be no lousy drugs, for example, because people will not buy lousy drugs. When constructing opposing arguments, think about externality effects and the information that people have when they buy things. What is good for one might not be good for all taken together (e.g., pollution, inflation, the fallacy of composition). Even harm that is apparently self-contained, like excessive injuries incurred by someone not wearing a seatbelt in a car crash, can have wider social costs (lost productivity, higher insurance rates generally, etc.). These are not academic arguments; there are libertarians running in many congressional and senatorial races across the United States in every even-numbered year.

5. In general, the libertarian argument is that government attempts to solve a problem are ineffective, create other problems elsewhere, or both. Express your own views about Freidman's opposition to social security, flood insurance, food and drug quality regulation, free public schooling, the licensing of doctors, the establishment and maintenance of national parks, etc. Again, consider information, externality, and common effects.

The fundamental issue is this: Is economic freedom a social objective to be pursued universally, or should it be considered on a case-by-case basis? Even if it has not been assigned, read *Capitalism and Freedom* sometime soon—with a critical, questioning eye—while your recollection of this economics course is fresh. You may end up agreeing with all, none, or some of what Friedman argues; that is for you to decide. One thing is certain, though, you will *certainly* be a better citizen for having pondered the questions that it raises.

6. The United States is better at (*b*) and (*d*); the Soviet Union, probably at (*a*) and (*c*). You may want to question whether Soviet full employment is really pervasive underemployment and whether administered prices hold inflation by removing all the informational content of those prices. You may want to worry about consumer tastes dictated by a distribution of income that may or may not be appropriately equitable.

7. Prices and profits indicate relative scarcity and provide incentives for firms to meet the demands of others. Remember dollar votes. In the Soviet Union, planned quantities based on planned objectives dictate quotas for firms and enterprises. Increasingly, though, the incentive structure for managers includes profit in addition to quantity relative to target. *Peristroika* is struggling to bring price signals and profit incentives to bear on the Soviet economy, as effectively as possible within the constraints of continued planning from within government. Decentralization is happening, but not to the degree that is displayed by the mixed market system of the United States.

8. As is clear from Figure TQ35-1, *MU* does not equal *MC* unless the quantity target is carefully chosen. In the figure, X_m is the correct quantity with $MU = MC$. If, for example, X_p were selected as the total supply, then X_p would be supplied, sold at $P_p > P_m$, and the marginal utility generated by consuming or employing X_p would exceed the marginal cost of producing X_p. Welfare would be improved, in terms of consumer plus producer surplus, by an amount equal to the area of triangle *ABE* if output were to increase to X_m and price were to fall to P_m. The output of some other good would have to fall, but that leads to the general-equilibrium solution to the entire planning problem.

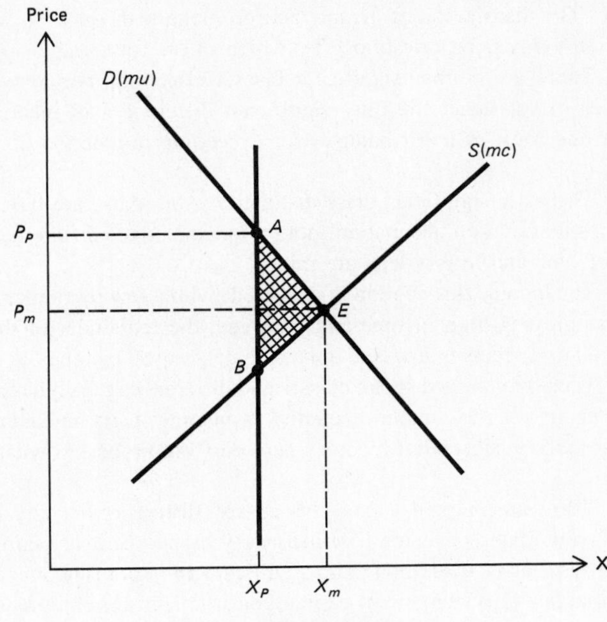

Figure TQ35-1

CHAPTER 36

ECONOMIC GROWTH: THEORY AND EVIDENCE

Most of your introduction to economics has thus far focused on short- to medium-term changes in economic conditions associated with the business cycle. These fluctuations are important, to be sure, for anyone whose job is in jeopardy during a recession or whose variable-rate mortgage payments are out of control during an inflationary boom. Viewed in the context of long-term patterns of growth, however, they are dwarfed by trends that have persisted over time periods measured in decades.

Chapter 36 looks at the American economy from a different perspective. It introduces the long-term view of economic growth by tracing the history of the American economy in broad terms over the past 90 years; it also ponders the processes by which the American standard of living has improved so dramatically and by which the stock of American capital has grown so large. These are not merely topics of academic curiousity. They are the topics that are important when policymakers and economic theorists question, for example, the sources of the recent slowdown in American productivity and search for remedies that can revitalize our economic growth. They are also the topics that need to be understood if we are to be able to assist developing economies in their attempts to improve the lots of their citizens. That is the message of Chapter 37.

Having completed your work in this chapter, you will have prepared for that application by accomplishing the following objectives.

LEARNING OBJECTIVES

1. Trace the evolution of thought about economic growth from the Marxian stages of history and the Smith-Malthus applications of diminishing returns through the neoclassical theory developed in large measure by Robert Solow.

2. Define capital deepening and explain why it tends to increase the real wage paid to labor and reduce the return earned by capital. Understand how and why, in the absence of technological change, reductions in the return to capital can bring capital deepening to a halt in a long-run steady state characterized by a constant capital-labor ratio, stable wages, and a stable return to capital.

3. Explain how and why technological change can push a factor-price frontier out, thereby illustrating how a relatively high return to capital can be maintained even as continued capital deepening drives the capital-labor ratio upward.

4. Summarize briefly the trends in aggregate U.S. statistics that describe the pattern of growth since 1900: (*a*) the annual growth rate of labor and employment has been consistently smaller than the annual growth rate of capital (indicated by a tripling of labor since 1980 and an eightfold increase in the capital stock); (*b*) the real wage paid to labor has increased; (*c*) the share of GNP paid to labor has increased only slightly; (*d*) the return earned by capital, while volatile, has been essentially trendless; (*e*) the capital-output ratio fell from 1900 through roughly 1950, and has remained fairly constant ever since; (*f*) the savings rate and the investment-output ratio has held stable, for the most part, except for deficit-induced contraction in the 1980s; and (*g*) GNP has been increasing, on average, at an annual rate between 3 percent and 4 percent.

5. Record the equations of growth accounting, and use that accounting to identify the major sources of growth in per capita output in the United States: increases in inputs [capital (15 percent contribution), labor (19 percent), and land (0 percent)] and increases in factor productivity [derived from education (19 percent) and other sources (47 percent)].

6. Note the decline in American productivity that has persisted since it appeared in the 1970s, and record the potential changes in investment, research support, employment, and arms control that might reverse the decline and stimulate growth in potential GNP.

The perspective of Chapter 36 is admittedly long-term, and the analysis might appear at first blush to be a bit more complex than usual. You should, nonetheless, quickly become comfortable with the approach once you realize that it is based firmly in the fundamentals of modern microeconomics presented in previous chapters. Long-term growth is, in fact, explained almost exclusively in terms of the interplay between diminishing marginal productivity and technological change.

Each new stage in this interplay affects the distribution of income between labor and capital. The point of this chapter, therefore, is to outline how, as a result of the interaction between diminishing returns and technological progress, (1) the economy's output grows, and (2) the income distribution between labor and capital is affected.

The fundamental point to be understood here is that input proportions can change even as economic growth occurs. How can that be? Diminishing returns can apply even when the supplies of all inputs are increasing if they are not increasing at the same rate. Consider the usual production function depending upon capital and labor. The input with the slower rate of growth (usually thought to be labor in a developed economy) can, for purposes of studying growth, be considered to be the (relatively) fixed input, while the other is viewed as the (relatively) variable input. Since the payment offered to the variable input (capital, in this simple illustration) depends upon its marginal product and that marginal product should decline as the supply of capital increases relative to labor, diminishing returns works against the well-being of the owners of capital. In the extreme, in fact, diminishing returns might drive the marginal product of the capital to zero so that the competitive return earned by capital would also move to zero. It is, of course, unlikely that this circumstance would come to pass; investment is likely to stop increasing the capital stock well before the zero-payment level is reached. Nonetheless, a zero return to capital is a logical, static extreme—the point of departure of Schumpeter's theory of growth and innovation noted in the appendix.

Early discussions of economic growth were, in fact, conducted mainly in terms of land (the fixed input) and labor (the variable input). With the emphasis on diminishing returns, it was inevitable that economists like Malthus should conclude that labor's future looked gloomy. In more recent discussions, labor has been the fixed input and capital the variable one (because the stock of capital is growing faster than population). Now the shoe is on the other foot. Capital, it would seem, is the input that is vulnerable to the ravages of diminishing returns; but capital has another card to play: technological progress. The diminishing-returns effect which continually works against the return to the owners of capital is more or less continually being offset (or more than offset) by technological advance. The first few questions explore this offset potential.

1. In Figure 36-1, the solid line *OP* is the ordinary diminishing-returns diagram. (Disregard for the present the two broken lines *OQ* and *OR*.) *OP* shows how output of good Q increases as more and more of variable input A is added to a *fixed* quantity of another input, B. The line is straight from *O* to *H*. This means that until the A quantity reaches *OD*, the marginal product of A is *(increasing / constant / decreasing)*. Thereafter it is *(increasing / constant / decreasing)*. This marginal product is measured by the slope of the line; so marginal product reaches zero when the line is *(flat / vertical)*; i.e., when A's quantity reaches *(OD / OE / OF / OG)*.

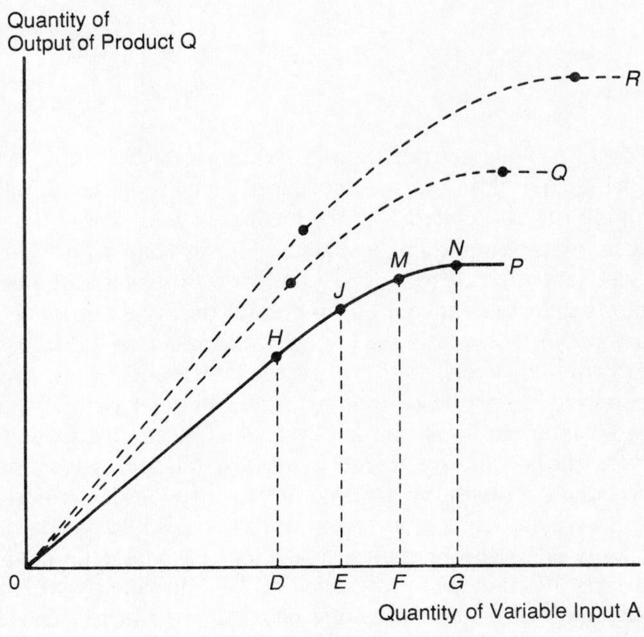

Figure 36-1

constant; decreasing; flat; *OG*

2. In very early attempts to construct economic theory (e.g., in Adam Smith), the discussion was often carried on as though production were exclusively a matter of labor cost (thus, the *labor* cost of hunting animals for food). With only one input to consider, there could not be any conflict over the division of the output. Soon, however, it became evident (and this drew major emphasis in the works of Malthus and Ricardo) that land was likewise a productive input, and one scarce or limited in supply. Moreover, there was no comparable limit to the size of population that might ultimately appear. "The law of diminishing returns" evolved, bringing along the need to ponder the distribution of output between the two input categories.

a. In the Malthus-Ricardo approach to diminishing returns, *(land / labor / capital)* was the fixed input, and *(land / labor / capital)* was the variable one. Malthus felt that a final "equilibrium" would be reached when labor had *(increased / decreased)* sufficiently to make the wage per worker just equal to the minimum-subsistence level.

b. This wage per worker would be labor's *(marginal / total)* product. The remainder of total product, after these wages were paid, would go to landowners. In Figure 36-1 terms, the Malthusian equilibrium would be reached with labor at a total *(of OG / necessarily less than OG, say, OE or OF)* and with total output *(NG / JE or MF)*.

---

a. land; labor; increased **b.** marginal; necessarily less than *OG*, say *OE* or *OF*; *JE* or *MF*

3. a. The two ingredients in Malthus-Ricardo diminishing-returns analysis were land and labor, with labor the vaiiable and increasing element. In modern growth theory, the participants have changed. The fixed input is considered to be *(land / labor / capital)*. The variable input is *(land / labor / capital)*. When *this* variable input is increased relative to the fixed input, the condition is described by economists as a (*widening / deepening / maintenance*) of capital.

b. If the stock of capital (i.e., machinery, tools, and other such equipment) is gradually increased over time, we would expect to see that increase accompanied by at least some technological improvement, i.e., the appearance of different and more efficient capital goods. Suppose, for the sake of illustration, though, that we assume that this type of technological change is absent. An increase in capital with labor or population fixed—or more generally, an increase in the ratio of total capital to total labor—would lead to *(an increase / a decrease)* in the return to each unit of capital (the profit rate or interest rate) and *(an increase / a decrease)* in the wage paid to labor.

---

a. labor; capital; deepening **b.** a decrease; an increase

4. Consider the process indicated in question 3 in more detail. Designate the variable input capital as *K*, the fixed input labor as *L*, and quantity of total output as *Q*. Then, with no technological progress, the following results are to be expected as *K* is increased relative to *L*:

a. The *capital-labor ratio K/L (increases / decreases)*.

b. The *capital-output ratio K/Q* will *(increase / decrease)*. When the law of diminishing returns is operating, any increase in the variable input yields an increase in output *Q* that is *(less than / exactly / more than)* proportionate to the *K* increase.

c. As the *K/L* ratio increases, the interest or profit rate (price of *K* per unit) *(increases / decreases)* and the wage rate (price of *L*) *(increases / decreases)*.

d. The fractional or percentage share of total output going to *K* owners *(must increase / might increase / must decrease)*.

---

a. increases **b.** increase; less than **c.** decreases; increase **d.** might increase

5. Figure 36-2 portrays some geometry that can vividly illustrate the points of question 4. Capital deepening, in the absence of technological progress, would move an economy from a point like *A* in panel **(a)** to a point like *(B / C / D)*. Looking then at panel **(b)**, we see that the resulting *(higher / lower)* wage must be associated with a move from point *a* to a point like *(b / c / d)* of interest. The effect on the share of GNP going to capital is therefore *(necessarily positive / necessarily negative / ambiguous)* because the increase in the capital stock *(is /*

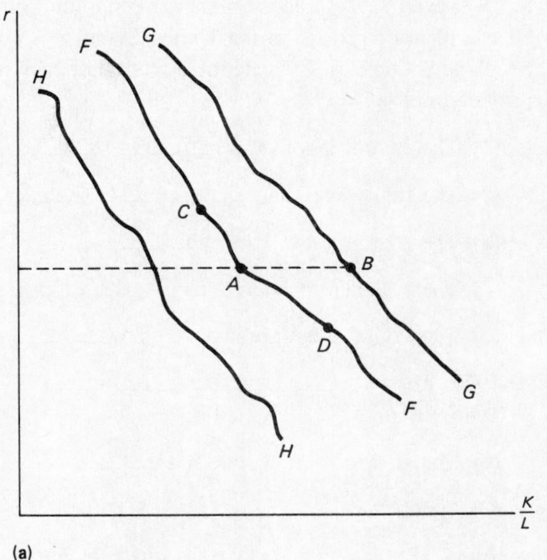

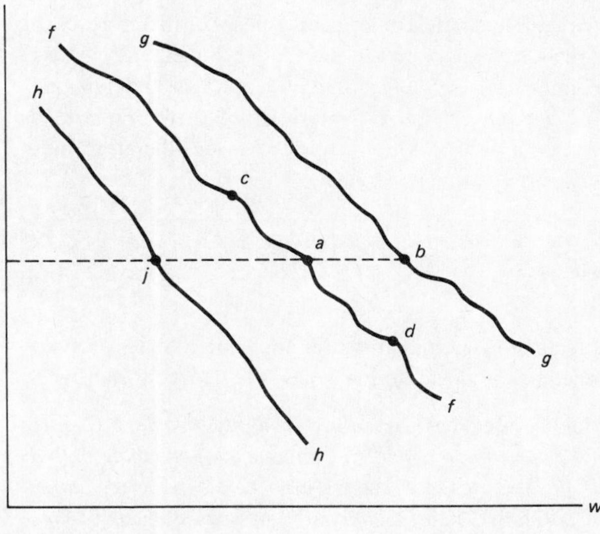

Figure 36-2

might be) canceled by the *(increase / reduction)* in the rate of profit. Because of diminishing returns, though, the ratio of capital to GNP must *(rise / fall)*.

D; higher; *d*; a reduction; ambiguous; might be; reduction; fall

6. a. In the United States, over the past century, the stock of capital has grown more or less steadily and has grown more rapidly than population or the labor force. To this extent, then, it is appropriate to apply the reasoning of questions 3 through 5. But what about technological progress, which improves the performance of *K* (capital), and which was specifically ruled out in those questions? In terms of Figure 36-1 (where the variable input is now *K*), technological progress lifts the output curve from *OP* to *OQ* and from *OQ* to *OR*. [The black dots on the *OQ* and *OR* lines mark the points at which curvature begins (the line begins to "bend over")—i.e., the point at which the influence of diminishing returns first begins to set in.] Thus even though *K* is increasing, the shift in position of the total product curve means that the marginal product of *K* will *(increase / decrease)*. The rate of interest or profit (per unit of capital) will thus *(fall / rise)* relative to labor's wage rate.

b. Combining the two effects (diminishing returns and technological progress), we see that the increase in the capital stock *(raises / lowers)* total output. Technological progress *(raises / lowers)* total output. The increase in the capital stock (disregarding technological progress) *(raises / lowers)* the demand for labor. Hence we would expect labor's wage or price to *(increase / decrease)*. Moving against this trend is technological progress, which *(increases / decreases)* the interest or profit rate and tends to *(increase / decrease)* the demand for labor.

c. The same general effect can be noted in Figure 36-2. Curve *(FF / GG / HH)* shows what happens when progress increases the performance of capital in panel **(a)**. The net effect on the ratio of wages to interest rates *(can / cannot)* therefore be in either direction. Experience in the United States has, in fact, displayed *(climbing / falling / steady)* real wages and *(climbing / falling / steady)* real interest rates; a move from point *a* on curve *ff* in panel **(b)** to a point like *(j / b / d)* therefore most accurately portrays that experience.

a. increase; rise **b.** raises; raises; raises; increase; increases; decrease **c.** *GG*; can; climbing; steady; *b*

7. The facts of economic growth in the United States are to be summarized below. Refer to Figure 36-3 to deduce the answers.

a. The labor force has *(remained roughly constant / nearly doubled / approximately tripled / increased more than sixfold)* since 1900. The stock of capital has, meanwhile, *(remained roughly constant / nearly doubled / increased nearly fourfold / increased approximately eightfold / increased by more than elevenfold)*. That is to say, the capital stock, in proportion to the labor force, has *(increased / decreased)* by a factor of approximately *(1 / 2 / 3 / 6)*. There *(has / has not)* been a *(small / significant)* deepening of capital.

b. Disregarding technological change, if both capital and labor had increased eightfold, then we would have expected to see output increase by a factor of 8. With labor only tripled, though, we would expect to see output increase by *(more / less)* than 8 times its value in 1900. In fact, output has increased by a factor of approximately *(3 / 8 / 11)*. This means that the ratio of the capital stock to annual output has *(increased / remained about constant / decreased slightly)*. Things *(have / have not)* worked out as the simple law of diminishing returns would indicate, the reason evidently being *(that the law has been incorrectly set out / the effects of technological change / the higher real wage paid to labor)*.

c. The actual capital-output (*K/Q*) ratio in the United States is at present about *(1 year / 3 times K / 3 years / 5 times L)*.

d. Real wages *(have risen / have fallen / show no clear trend either up or down)*. The interest or profit rate—the "price of capital"—*(has risen / has fallen / shows no clear trend either up or down)*.

e. Output per worker-hour, or *Q/L*, has *(risen / remained constant / fallen)*. The increase in the wage rate *(has significantly exceeded / has been approximately equal to / has fallen behind)* the *(increase / decrease)* in output per worker-hour.

a. approximately tripled; increased approximately eightfold; increased; 3; has; significant **b.** less 8; decreased slightly; have not; the effects of technological change **c.** 3 years (that is, the value of the capital stock is reckoned as approximately equal to the value of 3 years' output.) **d.** have risen; shows no clear trend either up or down **e.** risen; has been approximately equal to (though slightly higher); increase

8. a. Seven basic trends in major economic variables have been typical of growth in the United States as well as in most developed countries. Indicate the direction of each in the spaces provided below.

(1) The capital-labor ratio has ____________________.

(2) The real wage has ____________________.

(3) The share paid to labor has ____________________.

(4) The real rate of interest has ____________________.

(5) The capital-output ratio has ____________________ since 1950 after ____________________ from 1920 through 1945.

(6) The savings-output ratio has ____________________.

(7) Output has ____________________.

b. Trend **(6)**, combined with a small level of net foreign investment, implies that the investment-output ratio has *(risen / remained steady / fallen)*. Trends **(1)** and **(2)** are consistent

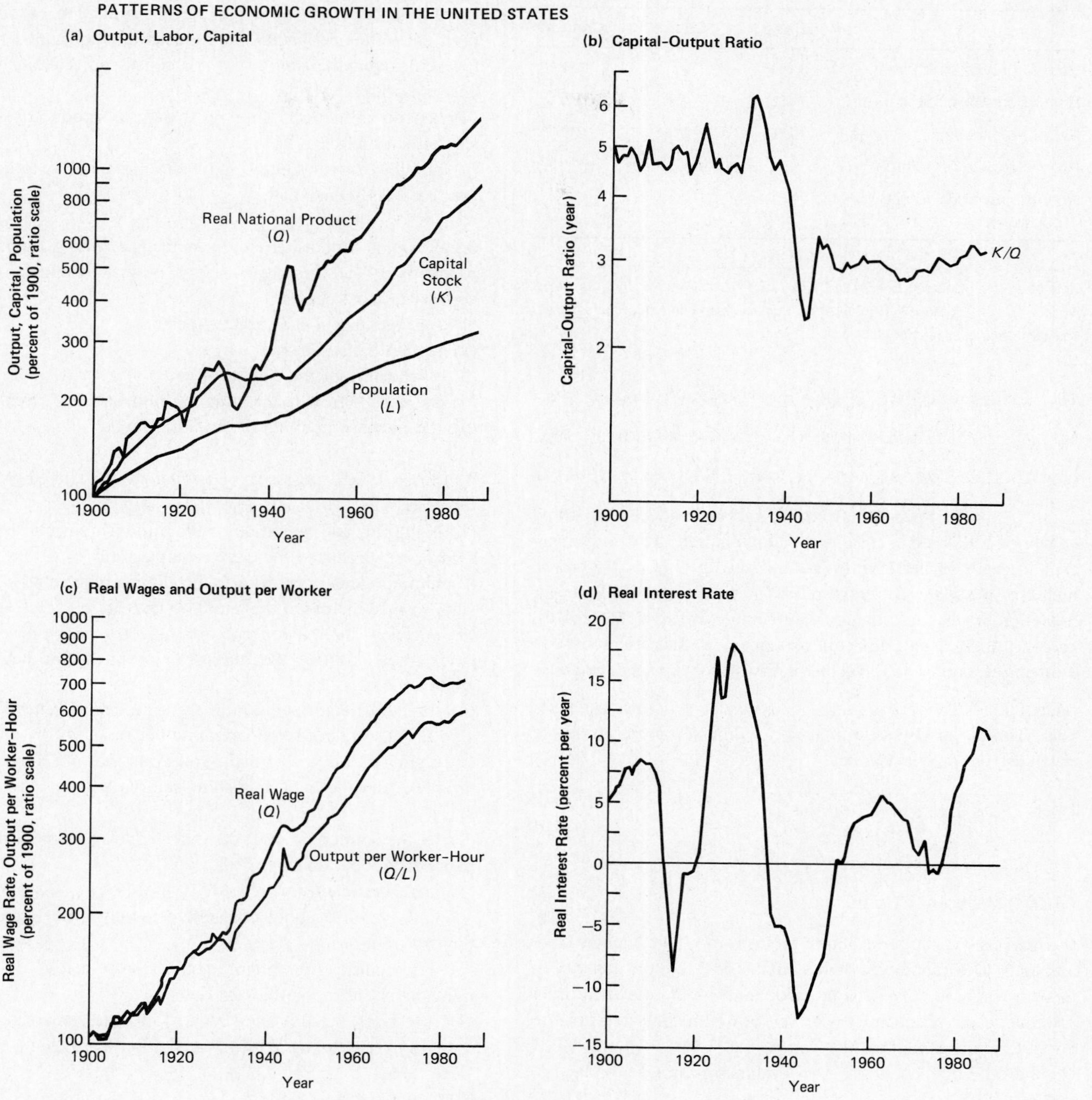

PATTERNS OF ECONOMIC GROWTH IN THE UNITED STATES

(a) Output, Labor, Capital

(b) Capital-Output Ratio

(c) Real Wages and Output per Worker

(d) Real Interest Rate

Figure 36-3

with the neoclassical model of growth *(only when technological change is introduced / even without technological change)*. Trend **(3)** is a coincidence of nature and is not the theoretical implication of any part of the model. Trends **(4)** and **(5)** *(do / do not)* depend on technological change because no progress would always combine with a deepening capital stock to predict *(higher / lower)* real interest rates and *(higher / lower)* capital-output ratios.

---

a. (1) risen **(2)** risen **(3)** risen (very slightly) **(4)** been trendless **(5)** been constant; falling **(6)** been stable **(7)** increased (at 3 to 4 percent per year) **b.** remained steady; even without technological change; do; lower; higher

9. Complete the following table on the basis of the growth-accounting procedures presented in the text.

	Case I	Case II	Case III
Rate of growth of labor	1%	0%	1%
Rate of growth of capital	4%	4%	5%
Rate of technological change	2%	2%	2%
Rate of growth of output	______	______	______
Rate of growth of output per worker	______	______	______

Rate of growth of output: I: 3 3/4%; II: 3%; III 4% Rate of growth of output per worker: I: 2 3/4%; II: 3%; III: 3%[*Note:* Percent change in (K/L equals percent change in K minus percent change in L.]

10. Labor productivity in the United States fell from an average of ______ percent per year from 1948 through 1973 (and ______ percent per year from 1948 through 1965) to ______ percent per year from 1973 through 1983. According to work by Edward Denison, the combination of *(a)* a 20 percent increase in net investment and saving, *(b)* a 20 percent increase in support for research as a fraction of GNP, *(c)* a reduction in the natural rate in unemployment by almost 20 percent, and *(d)* an arms-control agreement that released government resources to investment could be expected to cause potential GNP to grow ______ percentage points faster per year. This is, of course, *(an easy / a difficult)* prescription for reversing the recent decline.

2; 2.5; 0; 0.64; a difficult

QUIZ: Multiple Choice

1. Suppose agricultural output requires only two inputs, labor and land. The quantity of land available is fixed; the quantity of labor is variable. Then, as labor quantity is increased in order to increase output quantity, the law of diminishing returns will begin to operate, and:
(1) the ratio of labor to land will increase; the ratio of land to output will fall.
(2) both the labor-land ratio and the land-output ratio will fall.
(3) both the labor-land ratio and the land-output ratio will increase.
(4) the labor-land ratio will fall, and the land-output ratio will not change.
(5) the labor-land ratio will increase, but the land-output ratio will not change.

2. In the simple labor theory of value, demand for goods plays the following role. It:
(1) interacts with supply to determine price, as in any other case.
(2) dominates over supply in the determination of price, but does not influence quantities produced and consumed.
(3) settles quantities produced and consumed, but has no influence on price.
(4) has no influence either on quantities produced and consumed or on price.
(5) dominates over supply both as to price and as to quantities produced and consumed.

3. The most important single factor accounting for increased productivity and growth in the American economy thus far appears to have been:
(1) a deepening of the capital stock.
(2) technological change.
(3) a widening of the capital stock.
(4) the use of growth-encouraging monetary and fiscal policy.
(5) the increase in skills of the labor force.

4. Since 1900, the stock of capital in the United States has increased:
(1) eightfold, and operation of the diminishing-returns law has significantly reduced the capital-output ratio.
(2) tenfold, and operation of the diminishing-returns law has significantly increased the capital-output ratio.
(3) only by an amount proportionate to the increase in the labor force, so that the diminishing-returns law has had no application.
(4) threefold, and operation of the diminishing-returns law has significantly reduced the capital-output ratio.
(5) eightfold, but the capital-output ratio has not increased significantly despite the diminishing-returns law.

5. In the United States the share of wages and salaries in national production since 1900:
(1) has significantly increased.
(2) has remained about constant, showing only a very slight upward trend.
(3) has significantly fallen, except for a period during and immediately after World War II.
(4) rose fairly steadily until about 1930 and remained constant until 1945 (excluding World War II), but has fallen perceptibly since then.
(5) is not correctly described by any of the above.

6. If the amount of capital employed is increased, if the amount of labor and other inputs stays approximately fixed, and if the capital-output ratio remains constant, then:
(1) the capital-labor ratio must have fallen.
(2) the price of capital must have fallen.
(3) the law of diminishing returns has been in operation.
(4) technological improvements would explain this result.
(5) total output must have fallen.

7. If the capital-output ratio increases, then it should follow that:

(1) the real wage of labor must fall if there has been no technological change, but not otherwise.
(2) the real wage of labor must fall, regardless of the extent of technological change.
(3) the total stock of capital must have decreased, or at best remained constant.
(4) the real rate of interest or profit must fall if there has been no technological change, but not otherwise.
(5) the real rate of interest or profit must fall, regardless of the extent of technological change.

8. A deepening of capital must, in the absence of technological change, eventually:
(1) increase the capital-output ratio.
(2) decrease the capital-output ratio.
(3) increase output more than proportionately to the increase in capital.
(4) increase output in proportion to the increase in capital.
(5) increase the share of capital-owners in the total of output.

9. According to the law of diminishing returns, if land is the fixed input and labor the variable input, then as the quantity of output is increased:
(1) the relative share of labor in total product must fall.
(2) the price of land must fall.
(3) the share of labor in total product or output must rise.
(4) land's percentage share in total product or output must rise.
(5) none of the above is necessarily correct.

10. "Deepening of capital" means:
(1) an increase in the stock of capital relative to the size of the labor force.
(2) the introduction of new capital goods which embody technological change.
(3) a change in either productivity or amount of capital which increases the share of capital-owners in total product.
(4) an increase in the productivity of capital which reduces, or at least does not increase, the total of the capital stock.
(5) none of the above.

11. If capital is considered the variable input, then in the operation of the law of diminishing returns (without technological change), as output is increased:
(1) the share of capital-owners in total output must increase.
(2) the capital-output ratio must decrease.
(3) the share of capital-owners in total output must decrease.
(4) the capital-output ratio must increase.
(5) the capital-output ratio must, by definition, remain constant.

12. If a nation's capital-output ratio gradually increases over time despite capital deepening:
(1) the share of capital-owners in total output is increasing.
(2) the diminishing-returns stage has not yet been reached with respect to capital.
(3) the marginal physical product of capital must have reached zero.
(4) technological progress must be improving the productivity of capital.
(5) the law of diminishing returns is operating with respect to capital's productivity.

SUGGESTED ANSWERS TO QUESTIONS IN THE TEXT: Chapter 36

1. They missed things like technological change. Catalogue the historical ones as in the text. Recently published forecasts are seldom as long term as the growth scenarios considered here and might therefore focus on the business cycle. Looking into the twenty-first century, though, we see that technological change is still hard to call. So, too, are energy futures, environmental concerns, and international tensions. As you read the forecasts, try to uncover their driving assumptions, and question whether or not changing those assumptions might make any difference.

2. Consult the Denison estimates in Table 36-3 of the text and the sources of growth identified in Table 36-1. Science and invention are, though, catchwords for the sources of technological change; they make investment more attractive and capital more productive.

3. Run diminishing returns to capital to its logical conclusion.

4. Year-to-year fluctuation is still to be expected. The long-term trends are, however, insulated from all but the most severe shocks. The Great Depression seems to have affected the long-term capital-output ratio, for example, but little else. If we have gotten better at avoiding large swings across the business cycle, then perhaps we have made it less likely that the aggregate long-term trends will change.

5. The formula holds that

$$\%\text{ growth in } Q = 0.75(\%\text{ growth in } L) + 0.25(\%\text{ growth in } K) + TC$$

So,

$$(0.75 \times 1\%) + (0.25 \times 4\%) + 1.5\% = 3.25\%$$

A 1-point reduction in the growth rate of L would cause a 0.75-point reduction in the growth rate of Q. A 1-point increase in the growth rate of K would cause a 0.25-point increase in the growth rate of Q. If labor and capital had equal shares, then the weights in the equation would be 0.5 for both the rate of growth of L and the rate of growth of K. To get the rate of growth per worker, subtract the trace of growth of L from the rate of growth of Q.

6. Both changes would leave the slope of the *PPF* unchanged but would move it out from the origin twice as far.

7. **a.** Increase both; Denison numbers suggest increasing the growth rate by 0.16 percentage point.
b. Increase both; Denison numbers suggest that an increase in R&D of 0.5 percent of GNP should increase the rate

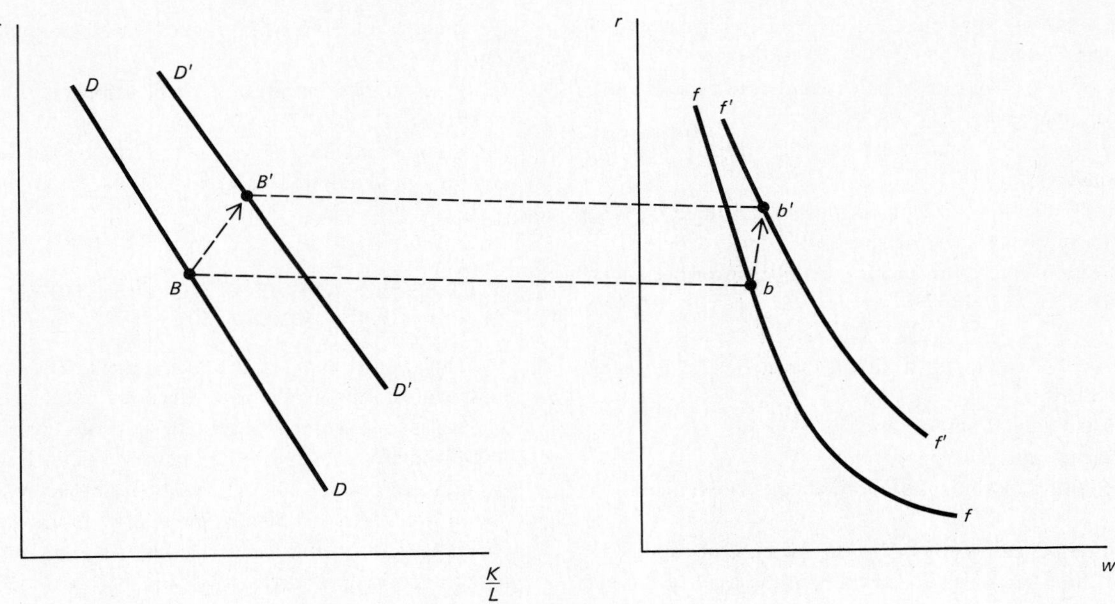

Figure TQ36-1

of growth by more than 0.18 percentage point. Given the 3-to-1 social rate of return, the reduction in investment that would be used to finance the subsidy would reduce the growth rate by something slightly more than 0.06 percentage point.

c. Denison suggests that arms control would spur growth; increases in defense spending should therefore reduce growth. The multiplier effect is not sufficient to produce enough private investment to overcome the reduction in public investment.

d. Increase the growth rate by the same proportion as lowering the natural rate of unemployment; i.e., 0.2 percentage point.

e. Increase the growth rate by increasing labor productivity by education; human capital, if it matches physical capital in effect on GNP, might thereby spur a 0.08-percentage-point increase in the growth rate.

8. Refer to the Smith-Malthus predictions. If technological change was the panacea, then it still is. Suggest things that will spur change. By the way, with the rate of change in technology since 1973, who can believe the pessimist?

9. *DD* shifts out with *ff*, but perhaps to points like B' and b' indicated in Figure TQ36-1; r increases and w falls. The horse analogy does not necessarily apply because people can be retrained to do other things; they are also required to run the robots—at least so far!

APPENDIX: 36
Modern Economic-Growth Theories

Chapter 36 introduces the analysis of economic growth in its simplest form. Growth is, however, not a simple phenomenon, and models of its properties can quickly become extremely complex. The point of this appendix is not to record the differential equations that reflect some of the advance modeling of economic growth. It is, instead, included to give the interested reader some flavor of the difficulty involved in conceptualizing what we mean, in precise terms, by economic growth and how we can use modeling to discover what drives it and what can shut it down.

Having completed your work in this short appendix, you will have accomplished the following objectives.

LEARNING OBJECTIVES

1. Relate the Schumpeter reliance on innovation in explaining how economic growth overcomes the Smith-Malthus constraint of diminishing marginal productivity.

2. Understand the significance of the natural rate of growth, the rate of growth of the labor supply measured in efficiency units. Denoting the natural rate of growth by g, relate g to the savings rate s which supports balanced growth by satisfying the equation $s = g \times (K/Q)$.

3. Explain how a balanced, neoclassical growth model explains the seven basic trends in the economic growth of the United States over the past 90 years or so.

4. Define the Leontief input-output table, and explain how it is useful in helping economic planners explore the means by which they might alter the structures of their economies.

Economic-growth analysis often begins by drawing on the Ricardo-Mill idea of the stationary state. Many classical economists thought that nations would grow until they reached final "stationary-state" condition. Thereafter, there would be no further growth, at least in the stock of capital. When this final state was reached, the economy's stock of capital goods might be very large, but there would be no *net* investment.

1. Joseph Schumpeter was prominent among the critics of this stationary-state idea. He argued that any such tendency is repeatedly offset by the work of crazy and not-so-crazy inventors who want to do things differently and better. There is an important distinction to be made here. The inventor is one who thinks up a new idea, but there is a huge gap between that new idea and the new (or improved) and commercially successful product in which the idea finds its expression. Schumpeter called the individual who bridges (or tries to bridge) that gap the *(speculator / economist / innovator)*.

In Schumpeter's view, if you want to understand what "capitalism" has meant, and how it has really behaved over the past 100 or 150 years, you must look at the process of technological change. Inventors invent, and innovators seek to profit from invention. Some innovators have succeeded; very few have succeeded spectacularly. Most of them have (with less publicity) gone broke; but the lure of winning the grand prize in the innovation lottery remains undiminished.

Normally, innovators go to the money capital markets, seeking to raise the financing that they need. They therefore bid *(up / down)* the interest rate and *(encourage / discourage)* saving out of income to finance their new projects. Repeated innovations can, in this way, keep pushing the economy into bursts of capital accumulation and growth and can maintain interest rates above the zero-level logical extreme.

---

innovator (or entrepreneur); up; encourage

Much of this appendix deals with the notion of the natural rate of growth described in **Harrod-Domar growth models**. These models tackle one broad question: Can an economy maintain a reasonably steady rate of growth without drifting either too far into recession or too far into inflationary boom? The answer turns out to be yes, but only if the rate of increase of the capital stock, the rate of saving, and the rate of increase in the effective labor supply all mesh properly.

To see how that meshing might be accomplished, let the rate of growth of labor, measured in efficiency units L^* so that it includes both population growth *and* "labor-augmenting" technological change, be represented by g. To keep the capital stock K in balance with labor, then, K must grow at the same rate g; intended investment I must therefore be given by $I = gK$. To maintain full employment, though, intended saving must equal intended investment. With s representing the proportion of output Q that people want to save, the full-employment condition requires that $sQ = I$. Reading across these two equations, then, we have $sQ = gK$ or $s = g \times (Q/K)$.

A numerical example can illustrate the rationale behind balanced growth more concretely. Consider an economy in which $K/Q = 3\frac{1}{3}$. Let L^* grow at 3 percent per year so that we want both K and Q to grow at 3 percent to stay on the natural-rate-of-growth path. This calls for net investment and thus an equal amount of saving to finance that investment. How much saving and investment? One may at first be tempted to say 3 percent of Q, but that is wrong. The capital-output ratio says that *that* amount of new capital goods would fall short of producing an additional 3 percent of Q. It tells us that 10 units of I are needed for 3 additional units of Q. Putting 10 percent of Q into investment will yield just a 3 percent increase in Q annually. (It will also increase K by just 3 percent. The value of total K is $3\frac{1}{3}$ times Q. So 10 percent of Q equals 3 percent of K.)

2. a. In brief, given any effective labor-force growth rate g, we must multiply g by the capital-output ratio K/Q in order to determine the required rate of saving s out of income. With a K/Q ratio of $3\frac{1}{3}$ and a labor-force growth rate of 3 percent annually, 10 percent of income must be saved and invested to keep this economy on its natural-rate-of-growth path. If, instead, L^* grew at an annual rate of 4 percent (with the same K/Q ratio), then the required s-value would be approximately *(8.5 / 10.0 / 13.3 / 15.0 / 16.7)* percent. If the L^* growth rate were 5 percent, then the required s-value would become *(8.5 / 10.0 / 13.3 / 15.0 / 16.7)* percent.

b. If saving *does* take place at the percentage rate required, we have **balanced growth**: the saving rate is balanced against the labor-force growth rate. Using the 3 percent L^* growth figure, if saving *is* 10 percent of Q, then output will grow annually at *(3 / 10)* percent. Allowing for population increase as part of growth in L^*, output per capital will increase *(by 3 percent / by 10 percent / by the rate of labor-augmenting technological change)*. The capital-labor proportion K/L^* will *(rise / remain constant / fall)*.

c. If saving falls short of that required by population growth, then the ratio K/L^* will *(rise / remain constant / fall)*, and the result will be *(unemployment / inflation)* by reason of an *(excess / insufficiency)* of capital goods.

---

a. 13.3; 16.7 **b.** 3; by the rate of labor-augmenting technological change; remain constant **c.** fall; unemployment; insufficiency

3. **a.** In actual fact, as was pointed out earlier in the chapter, the ratio of capital stock to population in the United States has *(risen / fallen / remained constant)* since 1900. This suggests that the path followed has not been that of balanced growth, but note carefully that population statistics specifically exclude technological change. Even if the K/L ratio rises, as it has in the United States, it is *(impossible / still possible)* for the ratio K/L^* to remain constant.

b. In the United States since 1900, the division of GNP between K owners and L owners has *(shifted in favor of K owners / shifted in favor of L owners / remained approximately constant)*. Further, the capital-output ratio K/Q has *(increased significantly / decreased significantly / remained approximately constant)*, particularly since 1950. These two facts *(correspond / do not correspond)* to balanced growth.

c. In the United States, the real wage per unit of L has *(risen / remained constant)*. In balanced growth, the wage per unit of L^* *(rises / falls / remains constant)*. The actual rise in the U.S. wage per unit of L *(can be / cannot be)* consistent with balanced growth. (Remember that L is smaller than L^*, so an unchanged per capital income for each L^* unit will mean a higher per capita income for each L unit.)

---

a. risen; still possible **b.** remained approximately constant; remained approximately constant; correspond **c.** risen; remains constant; can be

The **Leontief input-output system** is not at all concerned, as Harrod-Domar models are, with "aggregate growth." Although it involves some interest in the matter of growth, the Leontief construction is "microeconomic" in the particular sense that it deals with the individual products which collectively make up GNP and with the individual inputs required for manufacture of these finished products.

Suppose that GNP is composed of just three types of finished goods: X, Y, and Z. Suppose further that (for whatever reason) this problem is posed: we need a 5 percent increase in X output and a 15 percent increase in Y output, and we can afford to reduce Z output by 10 percent. Overall, what would these output changes call for in the way of extra productive inputs needed? This is the type of question the Leontief system is constructed to answer. As its base, it uses statistical material covering production in past years.

It is appropriate to illustrate the nature of the Leontief system through the example of a three-good GNP. In real life, though, things are rather more complicated. Within any actual GNP, there are thousands upon thousands of different items. Even a computer-aided system cannot take full account of them all. The most appropriate simplification is to lump products together by industry, thus making *the industry* the microeconomic unit. Even a quite modest plan of division yields several hundred industries for a Leontief system to digest.

Typically, the output of any one industry goes in two directions. Part of that output may be a finished consumer good for households, but part (or all) may go to other industries as inputs. Fuel oil is an output used by families for home heating. It is also an input used by firms for their manufacturing needs. A Leontief table is built to record this fact. Each industry gets a line (technically, a *row*), showing where its output went. On the X-industry line, so much of X output went to the Y industry as a raw-material input; so much to the Z industry for similar use; and finally, so much of X to households for consumption purposes. This arrangement of rows, one for each industry, means that each industry also gets a *column* (a vertical listing) showing the inputs it got from other industries—the raw materials it needed to produce its own finished product. At the bottom of each column is a figure showing that particular industry's total *labor* input.

The Leontief system probes for total input-output needs: the total L per unit of X, total Y per unit of X, total Z per unit of X, and so on. Each such input-output figure (e.g., 10 L units per X unit) is assumed to be fixed. If the Leontief system has developed these "input-output coefficients" correctly, then it can indicate the requirements for any given increase in output.

4. Suppose, working in a three-good Leontief system describing the production requirements of goods X, Y, and Z, that you are interested in determining how to generate a 10 percent increase in the net final product of X with no change in the net final outputs of either Y or Z. Assume that Y and Z are needed as inputs in the production of X. As a result, more of these commodities will have to be turned out even though there is to be no increase in their final outputs. Even the production of X might have to increase by more than 10 percent if X is needed as an input in the production of Y or Z.

The Leontief system will accordingly report that your desired 10 percent increase in net final X output would require so many extra units of X, so many of Y, so many of Z, and so much extra L. We would expect the L requirement to be *(less than / the same as / greater than)* the extra L needed directly in the X industry. The rise in Y production will *(increase "final consumption" of Y / be fully absorbed as inputs for other industries)*. The same is true of Z production. Of the increase in Y production, *(all will go directly to the X industry / some may go, for example, to the Z industry, hence only indirectly to the X industry)*.

---

greater than; be fully absorbed as inputs for other industries; some may go, for example, to the Z industry, hence only indirectly to the X industry

QUIZ: Multiple Choice

1. A deepening of capital can be expected to reduce the rate of interest or profit unless:
(1) the capital-output ratio remains constant.
(2) the capital-output ratio increases.
(3) the capital-labor ratio increases.
(4) the capital-labor ratio decreases.
(5) output remains constant.

2. If saving and investment take place in the amounts indicated by the natural rate of growth, then:
(1) the ratio of capital to labor in production will rise.
(2) the ratio of capital to output will rise.
(3) the rate of profit or interest will rise.
(4) the share of labor-owners in GNP will rise relative to the share of capital-owners.
(5) none of the above is correct.

3. If an economy is actually growing at the natural rate, then:
(1) the capital-output ratio will increase, but at a rate less than the natural rate of growth.
(2) technological change will be taking place at a steady rate, and the rate of return on capital will be maintained at a steady level by this technological change.
(3) there will be an increase in the stock of capital but no deepening of capital.
(4) there will be a deepening of capital but no increase in the stock of capital.
(5) none of the above is correct.

4. "Balanced growth," as the term is used in Harrod-Domar models, involved essentially a balance between:
(1) saving and investment.
(2) investment and the capital-output ratio.
(3) total capital and total labor.
(4) investment and the distribution of income between capital and labor.
(5) saving and population growth.

5. The principal concern in maintaining a natural-growth path lies in determining the:
(1) rate of increase in the labor force needed to just match the scheduled increase in investment spending.
(2) rate of saving needed to just balance against the rate of increase in the labor force.
(3) rate of interest that will attract a volume of investment just sufficient to maintain full employment.
(4) maximum rate of growth in output that is possible without setting off inflationary price increases.
(5) rate of investment spending needed to just balance against the fraction of income which the public wishes to save.

6. The results attributed to capital deepening (without technological change) are those produced by:
(1) the law of diminished returns.
(2) a fixed capital-output ratio.
(3) balanced growth.
(4) the warranted rate of growth.
(5) a decrease in the K/L ratio.

7. A Leontief input-output system records, with respect to the total output of any one industry:
(1) only that part going to households, since to include the part going to other industries would be double counting.
(2) only that part going to other industries, since its purpose is to record input-output relationships.
(3) that part going to households and the part going to other industries as well, but the latter on a value-added basis to avoid double counting.
(4) both the part going to households and the part going to other industries, in full.
(5) none of the above, since for industries it records inputs, not outputs.

SUGGESTED ANSWERS TO QUESTIONS IN THE TEXT: Appendix to Chapter 36

1. Each coefficient in the input-output matrix indicates a quantity of one good used in the production of another. Reading across a row for an industry indicates output—where product that is produced is employed or consumed. Reading down a column for the same industry (the second place that it is recorded) indicates inputs—the input requirements of that industry.

2. The equations that must be solved are

$$250 + (1/2)M = A$$

and

$$1750 + (1/3)A = M$$

The resulting input-output matrix is shown below.

	Agriculture	Manufacturing	Household Labor	Gross (output)
Agriculture	—	1,100	250	1,350
Manufacturing	450	—	1,750	2,200
Household labor	900	1,100	2,000	—
Gross (inputs)	1,350	2,200	—	—

Notice that the Household Labor column shows the requisite 250 in agriculture and 1750 in manufacturing. Notice, too, that the same 2000 in labor input is assumed. Finally, the input proportions for agriculture and manufacturing are satisfied.

3. The growth rate g = savings rate/K-Q ratio = 0.09/3 = 0.03; thus, 3 percent per year is the natural rate.

4. Capitalism, without innovation, would grow to drive the return to capital to zero.

CHAPTER 37 THE ECONOMICS OF DEVELOPING COUNTRIES

Twenty percent of the world's population, more than 1 billion people, live at or below the subsistence level. Only about 25 percent of the world's population earn the equivalent of $3,000 per year or more. Nonetheless, the average per capita income of people living in the advanced market economies of North America and Western Europe exceeds $14,000 per year. A list of alarming statistics like this can be extended almost indefinitely, but the point is clear. There exists, across the globe, a disparity in standards of living that boggles the mind; and it is this observation that raises a litany of questions which could turn out to be *the* critical questions for survival through the twenty-first century. What, first of all, could possibly be the source of this disparity? Second, what can be done by the developing countries to correct it? And finally, is there anything that the developed world can do to help? Without some attempt to answer these questions, the growing gap between the wealthy and poor nations of the world could foster economic, political, and military conflict that could wreak havoc across the planet.

These are the questions raised in Chapter 37. For our purposes, though, they will turn out to be, to one degree or another, almost unanswerable, and the text is modest in advancing solutions and answers only in their most general form. The focus of the chapter is, instead, to ponder the ability of economic analysis to provide insight into possible answers. Only if we understand the sources of inequity can we begin to work to correct it, and only if we sort out false strategies from productive strategies will progress be made. The major objective of the chapter is, therefore, an understanding of the dimension of the problem. As you develop that understanding, you will also achieve the following more specific objectives.

LEARNING OBJECTIVES

1. Outline the modern theory of population through its four distinct stages (preindustrial with high birth and death rates, early development with diminishing death rates, later development with further reductions in death rates and diminishing birth rates, and maturity with low birth and death rates). Record its implications for economic growth, and relate it to its Malthusian antecedent.

2. Identify the four "wheels of development" (human resources, natural resources, capital formation, and technology), and explain the problems faced by less developed countries in getting any one of them "rolling uphill."

3. Describe the vicious circle of underdevelopment, and identify the means by which it might be broken. Relate how the applicability of these means depends upon the circumstance of the less developed country being considered (e.g., resource rich or resource poor, high population or low population, etc.).

4. Explain (*a*) the takeoff theory of development, (*b*) the backward hypothesis applied to economic development, and (*c*) the balanced-growth theory of development. Indicate the path of development that each implies, and contrast each to the reality described by Simon Kuznets.

5. Explain several strategies for economic development, including emphasis on export goods, emphasis on import-competing goods, technology borrowing, etc.), and indicate the potential pitfalls associated with each. Explain the value of diversification.

The world's less developed countries are characterized by per capita income levels that are well below the worldwide average. Associated with low incomes are, moreover, human problems like poor health, widespread illiteracy, poor housing, poor diets, and demoralizing underemployment. Question 1 asks you to refer to Table 37-1 to record quantitative measures of these problems.

1. Compared with the high-income market economies, countries on the bottom of the development scale display the following characteristics:

Table 37-1
Important Indicators for Different Groups of Countries

Country Group	Population: Level 1985 (millions)	Population: Growth 1965–1985 (% per year)	GNP 1985 ($ billions)	Per Capita GNP 1985 ($)	Adult Literacy 1980 (%)	Life Expectancy at Birth (years)	Percent of Employment in Agriculture 1980 (% of labor force)
Low-income economies (e.g., China, India)	2,439	2.2	659	270	52	60	72
Middle-income economies (e.g., Brazil, Philippines, South Korea)	1,242	2.4	1,602	1,290	65	62	43
High-income oil exporters (e.g., Saudi Arabia, Libya)	18	5.0	180	9,800	32	63	35
European non-reporting, non-member economies (e.g., U.S.S.R, GDR)	363	1.0	2,258	5,900	99	69	22
High-income market economies (e.g., U.S.A., West Germany, Japan)	737	0.8	8,708	11,810	99	76	7

Countries are grouped by the World Bank into five major categories. In each, two or three important countries are listed. Note how well the indicators are correlated across most of the groups, with low-income economies having low per capita incomes, low literacy and life expectancy, and a very large fraction of the labor force in agriculture. (Source: World Bank, *World Development Report, 1987.*)

a. Population growth rates that are *(twice as high / about the same / almost 3 times as high).*

b. Per capita levels of GNP that are *(about 50 percent lower / about 90 percent lower / over 90 percent lower).*

c. Adult literacy rates that are *(25 percent lower / nearly 50 percent lower / over 75 percent lower).*

d. Life expectancies that are approximately *20 percent lower / 33 percent lower / 50 percent lower.*

e. Employment participation rates in agriculture that are *(5 times higher / 8 times higher / over 10 times higher).*

---

a. almost 3 times as high **b.** over 90 percent lower **c.** nearly 50 percent lower **d.** 20 percent lower **e.** over 10 times higher

2. Compared with the Malthusian view of population growth that predicted *(gradual / geometric / logarithmic)* growth in population and *(increasing / constant / decreasing)* growth in food production, modern population theorists espouse a transition model of growth and development. They identify four stages in the transition; list them in order in the spaces provided:

As countries proceed through the transitions, history suggests that high birth and death rates give way first to lower *(death / birth)* rates and second to correspondingly lower *(death / birth)* rates before converging to a final stage of *(growing / stable / declining)* populations. During the second stage, though, the birth rate *(exceeds / falls short of)* the death rate and the population can be expected to *(climb / fall / remain stable).*

---

geometric; decreasing; **a.** preindustrial stage **b.** early development stage **c.** later development stage **d.** maturity; death; birth; stable; exceeds; climb

3. The characteristics of a modern developed economy are well understood. A country in this category has a large supply of capital goods per capita. Members of its population accept the principle of division of labor, and they are trained in skills adapted to that principle. Money is almost universally employed in place of barter, and money is used for the hiring of labor.

There is an active "entrepreneur class," and the making of money is not frowned upon or treated with scorn. There are well-organized money and credit markets. There is general acceptance of the authority and trustworthiness of a central government which passes laws, imposes taxes, and enforces execution of private contracts. The laws are in general obeyed and any taxes are generally paid. The developed economy accomplishes new things because of its entrepreneur class, its use of the money market mechanism, and its refusal to accept unquestioningly the dictates of tradition or custom as to how things should be done. As a result, it produces high material living standards for its members and a greatly increased life expectancy.

Since the characteristics described are common to all developed societies, it is agreed that they explain the higher material living standards and increased life expectancy. The problem remains of *how* these characteristics were acquired. This is the central problem for planners in less developed societies. It is also agreed that most citizens of these less developed nations want the benefits of development. "The theory of development" is therefore charged with the task of explaining how the characteristics of developed societies emerged and how they can be fostered elsewhere.

a. Some of these explanations have emphasized wholly, or in the main, one single factor—for example, geography. Here the view is usually that a cool, temperate climate is conducive to vigorous activity and hence to growth. Most economists *(accept/ accept with qualification / reject)* the view that geography is a vital consideration.

b. Another factor emphasized is culture. Most economists *(accept / accept with qualification / reject)* the view that some cultures have properties which impede growth.

Two questions are raised by the problem of cultures that seemingly oppose economic development: (1) Can established culture patterns be altered by planners for development? (2) Even if they can be broken, should they be? There is a partial answer to the first of these questions. What appear on the surface to be well-established culture patterns sometimes break up quite easily, and without evidence of any great distress appearing among the people involved. A more positive answer exists for the second question. No country can avoid the worldwide impact of economic development, so that proposals to "protect" an established culture are becoming less popular. In their place are suggestions about how to integrate the essentials of a unique culture into a modern economy.

---

a. reject **b.** accept

4. **a.** Max Weber did not agree that all determining forces in history were economic in origin. He felt that cultural elements were of at least equal importance, and that in Europe's economic development, religion had been a critical element. The name given to summarize Weber's views here is: ______________ .

b. Many economists speak of the preconditions for economic growth—a kind of foundation that must be laid before any significant growth can begin. In general terms, this means the development of a reasonably well-knit and cooperative society, the establishment of tolerable stability in that society, and the acceptance of some degree of central authority.

We can be a bit more specific as to these preconditions. They find expression in **external economies**. These are economies which facilitate production (and so reduce cost) for the individual firm, but are outside the control of any such firm (hence "external"). They would include such things as development in transportation facilities, health measures to improve the productivity of labor, and establishment of a system of law which makes contracts enforceable. The point about such external economies is that an individual firm *(can / cannot)* undertake them. They *(must / can, but need not necessarily)* be undertaken by government. Any individual firm which tackled such an external-economy project would find *(it worthless / that most of the benefit accrued to other firms who bore no part of its cost)*.

---

a. the "Protestant ethic" **b.** cannot; must; that most of the benefit accrued to other firms who bore no part of its cost

5. Economists have identified four economic fundamentals which drive economic development: population, natural resources, capital formation, and technology.

a. Focusing for a moment on natural resources, which of the following statements or questions accurately describe a resources-related issue? (Circle as many as apply to the role of natural resources in development.)

(1) Many less developed countries appear to be resource-poor. How then are they to develop?

(2) Land reform is necessary for development in many countries, since land is not being used to the best advantage because individual holdings are too small.

(3) Land reform is necessary for development in many countries, since land is not being used to the best advantage because individual holdings are too large.

b. Turning now to capital formation, identify the statements that accurately record a development issue.

(1) Less developed nations find it very difficult to save (to refrain from consumption) to free resources for investment activity.

(2) The social customs in some less developed countries are such that rich people prefer to hoard their savings or use them in nonproductive ways; they are not used to finance investment projects that would raise the national product.

(3) The desire for development and the example of the developed nations have noticeably increased the amount of saving out of income in many less developed countries.

(4) In many poor countries, investment expenditure tends to go heavily into housing, an investment form which does not have the highest priority in development.

(5) The amount of private lending for financing investment activity by citizens in developed areas to those in less developed areas is greater than it was in the nineteenth century, both absolutely and relatively.

c. Finally, repeat the process one more time for the role of technology.

(1) Less developed countries have the advantage that imitation of techniques already worked out is easier than the development of new and sometimes sophisticated techniques.

(2) Efforts by developed countries to export advanced "technological know-how" are frequently unsuccessful.

(3) Some advanced technologies are "capital-saving," and these are likely to be particularly well suited to adoption in less developed countries.

---

a. **(1)**; (2); **(3)**; **b.** **(1)**; **(2)**; **(4)**; **c.** **(1)**; **(2)**; **(3)**

6. Figure 37-1 illustrates the vicious cycle of underdevelopment. Identify the boxes of the cycle in the spaces provided.

A: ______________________

B: ______________________

C: Low productivity

D: ______________________

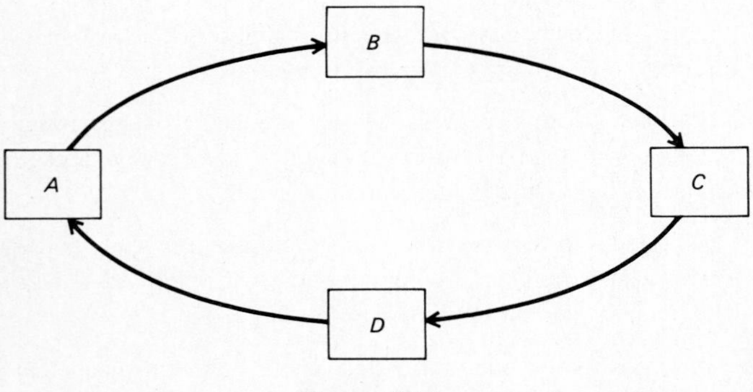

Figure 37-1

A: low saving and investment; *B:* low rate of capital accumulation; *D:* low average income

7. a. Higher savings will be useless and productive investment will not take place in any country unless it has a class of vigorous, creative ______________.

b. Sometimes it is said that the recurring problem with which a developed country must cope during recession is that of *(too much / too little)* saving and hence *(too little / too much)* demand for goods. By contrast, the problem of the less developed country is that of *(too much / too little)* saving and hence *(too little / too much)* demand for goods.

---

a. entrepreneurs **b.** too much; too little; too little; too much

8. Figure 37-2 displays the growth trends of three different countries (denoted I, II, and III) that are implied by the three different and modern theories of development. One is the takeoff theory, which envisions a leading sector catching fire, creating profits, encouraging investment, increasing the capital stock, increasing wages and incomes, and generally providing the initial momentum for consistent growth. The second is the backward hypothesis that suggests that developing countries have it easier today than they did a century ago because technology and markets already exist. The third contemplates a balanced-growth approach that is slow but steady once it starts. Label each panel with the theory that it portrays. The work of Simon Kuznets, for which he won a Nobel Prize, suggests that ______________ is the most accurate description of historical development trajectories.

A: balanced growth; *B:* takeoff theory; *C:* backward hypothesis; balanced growth.

9. Strategies for development must confront at least three general questions. First of all, is it more worthwhile to concentrate on industry or agriculture in initiating growth? Investment in industry might provide a few high-paying jobs, but investment in agriculture might support industrialization by *(increasing the productivity of city workers / increasing the productivity of the farms and thereby releasing labor for industrial jobs / creating large agricultural surpluses that can replace imports)*.

Second, it is important to decide whether or not to promote exports to generate growth supported by the worldwide marketplace or to protect import-competing industries to generate growth in domestic markets. Care should be taken in considering the second alternative because protection can *(increase / decrease)* domestic prices, *(increase / decrease)* real incomes, and *(stimulate / retard)* investment at home and from abroad.

Finally, many developing countries find themselves overspecialized and vulnerable to the whims of the world market for their good. The key to avoiding this difficulty is ______________. The question is how to do that.

---

increasing the productivity of the farms and thereby releasing labor for industrial jobs; increase; decrease; retard; diversification

10. **a.** One particularly troubling problem that beset the developing countries of the world in the late 1970s and 1980s was the debt crisis. Borrowing by developing countries from pri-

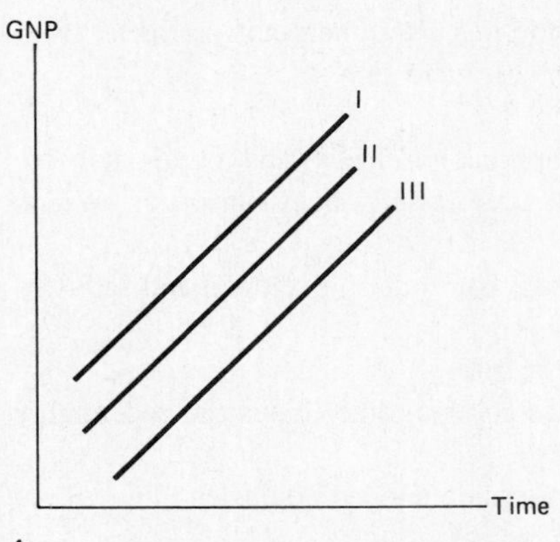

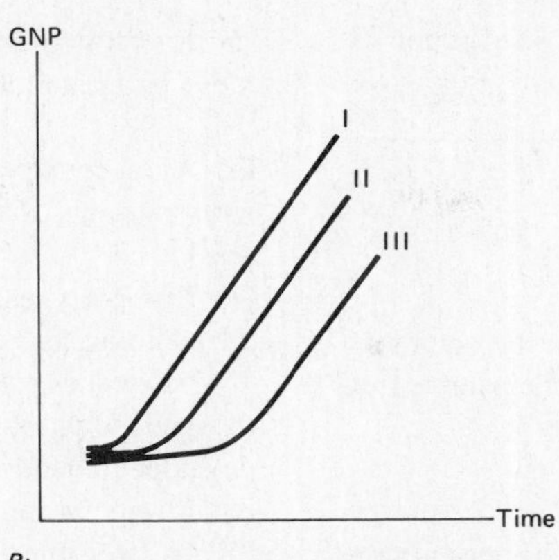

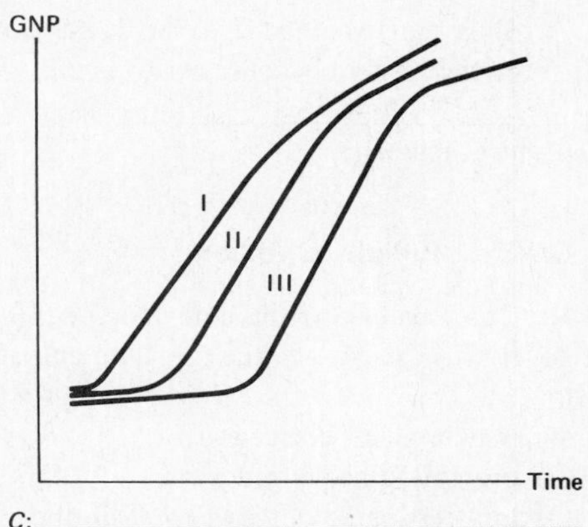

Figure 37-2

vate banks had grown by $*(25 / 500 / 1000)* billion from 1972 to 1983, and these debts were denominated in dollars. Many countries, particularly in Central and South America, began to have trouble meeting their debt obligations in the early 1980s because (pick as many as apply):

(1) American interest rates were so high.

(2) the value of the dollar was so high.

(3) the price of oil had climbed so high in the late 1970s that higher-than-expected debt was required.

(4) the crisis added risk premiums to the interest rates charged by private banks, particularly on refinancing agreements.

(5) the price of oil stopped rising so that the revenues that were expected to cover the debt were lower than anticipated.

b. The crisis seems to be under control, at least to some degree, but any disturbance that causes massive default *(could / could not)* create a major, worldwide banking crisis. To bail defaulting countries out with grants and income transfers would, however, dramatically increase the world's money supply and could therefore cause significant worldwide *(deflation / inflation)*.

---

a. 500; all apply; **b.** could; inflation

11. A less developed country is undertaking a large-scale development program and asks you to supply information on the following points. (Under each point, circle the number which you think furnishes the most likely answer.)

a. Change in population to be expected:

(1) Both the birth rate and the death rate are likely to remain high for some time.

(2) Both the birth rate and the death rate are likely to remain low for some time.

(3) Both the birth rate and the death rate are likely to fall substantially in the next few years.

(4) The death rate is likely to fall, and the birth rate to remain at its present high level for some time.

b. Capital-formation policy:

(1) In view of the post–World War II experience, primary reliance can be placed on borrowing and aid from abroad.

(2) The primary problem will be better allocation of existing saving rather than increasing total saving.

(3) Historical experience suggests that the percentage of national product put into personal saving and into capital formation will have to be increased.

(4) "Borrowing technology" will enable development at existing levels of saving.

c. Investment allocation:

(1) The government should make sure that it is undertaking adequate investment in social overhead capital with external economies.

(2) Private entrepreneurs can be relied upon to properly allocate available saving.

(3) Although inflation tends ultimately to discourage saving, it also tends to better allocate available saving.

(4) Modern technology makes heavy use of capital in production and hence should be avoided.

d. Change in foreign trade:

(1) Imports are likely to fall as domestic manufactures replace foreign manufactures.

(2) Imports are likely to rise because of the need for foreign capital goods, and possibly for food and fuel.

(3) Exports of primary products should be pushed, since this is where comparative advantage must lie.

(4) Exports should fall as the demand of developed countries for raw materials continues to decline.

---

a. (4) **b.** (3) **c.** (1) **d.** (2)

QUIZ: Multiple Choice

1. One area of economic development in which the country's government must take the initiative and also participate relates to:
(1) maintaining balanced growth.
(2) promoting heavy industry.
(3) transferring resources needed in the shift from agricultural predominance to industrial predominance.
(4) providing social overhead capital.
(5) none of the above, because there are no areas in which such government involvement is always needed.

2. The main reason population growth has spurted ahead so rapidly in many less developed countries in recent years is that:
(1) birth rates have increased sharply with improvements in nutrition.
(2) great strides have been made in keeping older people alive an extra 5 or 10 years.
(3) infant mortality and mortality due to epidemics have been drastically lowered.
(4) large-scale immigration has occurred into many countries since World War II.
(5) birth rates have risen markedly as the natural result of widespread reductions in the customary age of marriage.

3. Four of the following five statements identify a problem of economic development. One does not. Which one?
(1) Developing economies often have reasonable prospects of looking to "increasing returns to scale" as they expand their total output.
(2) Ordinarily, individual firms cannot undertake investment in social overhead capital, no matter how important such projects may be.
(3) Entrepreneurship and innovation are vital for the success of any developing economy.
(4) The principle of protecting import-competing industries is not necessarily a wise one for a developing nation to follow.
(5) In a probable majority of the less developed nations, excess saving is a significant problem.

4. "Disguised unemployment" refers to a situation in which:
(1) deficiencies in population statistics give a faulty picture of the labor force that is actually available.
(2) workers who actually are effectively self-employed claim to be in need of work.
(3) a country, having reached a certain stage in development, finds difficulty in recruiting workers for industrial jobs because of their reluctance to leave traditional occupations.
(4) demand for finished consumer goods is insufficient.
(5) for most (or all) of the year, the marginal productivity of labor in agriculture is actually very low.

5. As a country develops economically and builds its own industry, one of the following usually does not occur. Which one?
(1) It imports less and less from other developed and industrialized countries.
(2) Its total exports tend to rise.
(3) It imports more and more from other industrialized, highly developed countries.
(4) It imports more from less developed countries.
(5) Its total imports tend to rise.

6. "Social overhead capital" is:
(1) the money investment required before any return is obtainable from a particular natural resource.
(2) a particular form of external economy.
(3) investment in those projects considered to have the highest net productivity.
(4) projects which must be financed by the nation itself, as distinct from those financed by external aid.
(5) any capital investment the amount of which does not vary as the quantity of national output is increased.

7. An absolute precondition for growth is the:
(1) development of some excess of income over consumption.
(2) creation of a surplus labor force for employment in manufacturing.
(3) discovery and exploitation of some internal economies.
(4) cultural acceptance of free enterprise principles of economic behavior.
(5) development of manufacturing to the point where it can begin to supplant agriculture.

8. Four of the following five statements identify a problem of economic development. One does not. Which one?
(1) In some less developed countries, considerable investment takes place, but goes into items that are of low priority or even are undesirable from the standpoint of national economic development.
(2) The development of adequate social overhead capital is usually essential if there is to be much economic development.
(3) In history, political revolutions have often taken place *after* some economic progress has been achieved.
(4) Most of the less developed countries are known to have substantial unexploited natural resources, if only the capital needed to bring them into effective use were available.
(5) In poor countries, especially rural ones, often a large part of the labor pool does almost nothing because there is nothing for it to do.

9. Less developed countries have lower per capita incomes than developed countries. Over the past several decades, that gap has been:

(1) diminishing between the "free enterprise" less developed countries, widening with respect to the socialist-oriented ones.
(2) almost incapable of measurement because of differences in cultures, tastes, and climates.
(3) perceptibly diminishing, evidently as the result of foreign-aid programs.
(4) diminishing with respect to those countries which have concentrated their investment upon social overhead capital.
(5) essentially stable, and in some areas may even be widening.

SUGGESTED ANSWERS TO QUESTIONS IN THE TEXT: Chapter 37

1. Low-income countries: early development (high birth and death rates).
Middle-income countries: later development (lower birth and death rates).
High-income countries: maturity (low birth and death rates).

2. Higher populations generate congestion and increase the need for more services. However, more people to choose from can increase the likelihood of finding extraordinary individuals. Think of finding the tall trees in a forest. The more acreage you survey, the more tall trees you will find, provided that you do not run out of good forest and have to survey over the tops of mountains.

3. Tell your story. Think of mouths to feed, sources of family income, the opportunity cost of children with respect to multi-job family units, etc.

4. The geometric series grows at a constant rate β; the arithmetic series grows at a declining rate that converges to zero.

5. The growth rate of the food-population ratio is equal to the growth rate of food minus the growth rate of population. This can be less than zero if food grows slower than population.

6. No, with increasing or decreasing frequency depending upon the national mood. Madonna's "Material Girl" would not have been a hit during the New Frontier and New Society days of the 1960s.

7. Human resources, natural resources, capital, and technology. The oil-rich countries got rich by exploiting their resource base into international currency with which they could finance internal capital investment and technology adoption. Bangladesh has a real problem, particularly if the Indian Ocean rises.

8. Consider the strategies outlined at the end of the chapter. Invest in capital that makes the farms more productive to release some time and people (e.g.).

9. Now, there is an increased opportunity for better education to increase the productivity of the human resources; perhaps a relatively depleted resource stock; more capital available in international markets, and more technology to adopt.

10. **a.** Let $s_k = g_k = TC = 0$. Then

$$g_q = s_L g_L < g_L$$

if $s_L < 1$, as can be expected. This is the Malthus model.
b. Let s_L approach 0; the Chapter 36 equation then holds. Malthus misses the things identified there.
c. Is technological change nearing zero? Are conservation and substitution effectively slowing the rate of depletion of natural resources? How many resources are there for which there is *no* possible substitute? (Think no further than chemicals and elements that living things *absolutely* require.) Will technology solve the resource problem by bringing the planets to us? How productive can we be in space? What will be the effect of our global experiment in climate change?

CHAPTER 38

INTERNATIONAL TRADE AND THE THEORY OF COMPARATIVE ADVANTAGE

Chapter 38 begins a three-chapter excursion into the fundamentals of international economics—the issues surrounding the conduct of international trade and finance. The first two chapters introduce the real factors involved in trade and describe how differences in resource endowments, tastes, and technology can generate the potential for gleaning substantial welfare benefits from trade abroad. The problems associated with that trade and the restraint of its proliferation by tariffs and quotas are thus central to the discussion. Chapter 39, in fact, focuses on these issues almost exclusively. In the meantime, the end of Chapter 38 presents a brief survey of how international trade accounts are kept. The details of the monetary mechanisms that support international trade, including exchange-rate determination and other current issues of international finance, occupy Chapter 40.

The details of international economics are extremely complex, and an introductory course can only scratch their surface. Nonetheless, the fundamental welfare implications of international and interregional trade are easily presented and understood. Chapter 38 starts the presentation and puts you on the way to achieving this general learning objective. In the process, you will also achieve the following more specific objectives.

LEARNING OBJECTIVES

1. Distinguish between absolute advantage and comparative advantage, the latter being defined in terms of the relative expense of producing a commodity; a country generally has a comparative advantage in goods which it can produce, relative to other tradeable commodities, less expensively.

2. Explain, using a simple two-commodity model, how a country can increase its real income by specializing (for the purpose of export) in the commodity in which it has a comparative advantage and importing the commodity in which it has a comparative disadvantage.

3. Understand that the Ricardo model in which exploiting comparative advantage is shown to improve welfare is a classical, cost-based, full-employment model. Without the perfect markets that ensure full employment, the transitions required to take full advantage of the potential gains from specialization and trade can be costly, pushing an economy below its production-possibility frontier.

4. Explain why, assuming no transportation costs, the establishment of an international equilibrium price ratio common to both (all) trading partners is essentially a supply-demand problem of the sort studied in previous chapters.

5. Outline the basic accounting procedure with which the world keeps track of its international accounts. Define, in that outline, the four components of balance-of-payments accounting: current account, capital account, changes in official reserves, and statistical discrepancy. Note, as well, that a credit is recorded any time a transaction produces foreign currency and that a debit is recorded any time a transaction expends foreign currency.

6. Trace the usual evolution from young, debtor nation to mature, creditor nation. Show that the United States moved through that evolution to a new category—a mature nation whose low saving has made it a debtor nation.

The fundamental result of Chapter 38 is that foreign trade can improve welfare (i.e., the standard of living) of most nations, even if they are the most productive in producing everything. There are, of course, political problems that frequently stand in the way of countries' exploiting this potential: problems of reciprocal trade restriction in the face of "unfair" trading practices by trading partners; problems of national security and overreliance on foreign suppliers of critical commodities; and so on. There can, moreover, exist problems caused by the multiplicity of currencies across the world. Still, the welfare result that produces the potential gains from trade is robust and widely known. Chapter 38 produces it for you in the simple context of the Ricardo model, and the *Study*

Guide explores it further. The numbers are different here, for the sake of variety and to avoid "puppeting" answers; but the point is the same: international trade has the potential to improve the welfare of everyone involved by expanding the consumption possibilities of everyone involved.

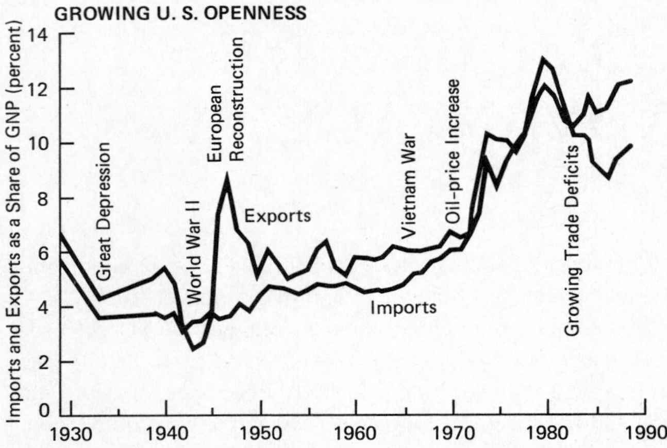

Figure 38-1 America has become more exposed to the winds of international competition. Like all major industrial countries, the United States has opened its borders to greater amounts of foreign trade over the last half-century. The greatest growth of the dollar value of imports came with the rise of oil prices and with the foreign penetration of American consumer markets. (Source: U.S. Department of commerce.)

1. As shown in Figure 38-1, the trend in the United States over the past half-century has been to *(open / close)* its economy to foreign trade. The usual measure of openness, the ratio of ________________ and/or ________________ to GNP has, in fact, *(risen / fallen)* to _______ percent. This is a percentage that is, however, *(higher / lower)* than the _______ percent that characterizes most of the economies of Europe.

It is important to note that although the simple Ricardo model implies complete specialization by bilateral trading partners, reality seldom achieves that extreme condition. The pattern of trade *(in fact shows that / does, however, show that)* the United States *(frequently / never)* imports and exports the same general commodity within the same year.

---

open; imports; exports; risen; 10; lower; 50; in fact shows that; frequently

If the United States has no domestic sources of tin, then surely it must import the tin it needs. What is not so obvious is why the United States, or any other country, should import a commodity which it *could* and does produce. The basic message of this chapter is that a nation should import some goods which it is capable of producing at home if it wants to use its resources to the best advantage. Each country should move toward specializing in the production of those commodities it is best equipped to make, given its own resources, *and given those available to other countries*. It should export part of what it has produced, receiving in exchange other goods (imports) which it is less well equipped to make.

The "model" used in this chapter is intended to drive home this point in the simplest possible form. Based on the model, most of the chapter concentrates on a critical review of some *wrong* ideas about international trade. One such incorrect idea holds that when a highly efficient country can outproduce another country in every line of activity, then profitable trade between them is impossible. Part of David Ricardo's great contribution to this subject was to show that even if a country is relatively inefficient in all lines of production, this predicament shows up in a lower living standard at home and not in an impossible bargaining position in international trade. The efficient and inefficient countries can still trade to mutual advantage, provided there are some differences in their *relative* costs of producing different goods.

Before trying to understand why certain ideas about international trade are mistaken ideas, you must grasp the basic **comparative-advantage** idea: why, in real-income terms, it pays each nation to specialize in production, to export, and to import. The first group of questions below builds toward an elaboration of comparative advantage by beginning with a nation's situation before it engages in foreign trade. The idea is first to identify the country's before-trade real-income position, and then to show how foreign trade, when it begins, can increase real income.

The same simplifying assumptions are employed as in the text chapter. There are only two countries: "America" and "Europe." Only two commodities are involved: food (F) and clothing (C). All costs of producing F or C can be measured in hours of labor. For some reason or reasons, such as differences in climate or in skills, the yields from an hour of labor, in the making of both F or C, differ across international boundaries. (The specific productivity figures used here are different from those employed in the text chapter.)

2. The quantities of F and of C yielded by 1 hour of labor effort in America and in Europe are as follows:

Yield of 1 Labor-Hour	Units of *F*	Units of *C*
In America	20	6
In Europe	10	8

They translate into the following input requirement data:

	Minutes of Labor Required to Produce	
	1 Unit of *F*	1 Unit of *C*
In America	3	10
In Europe	6	7.5

Assuming that "1 hour of labor effort" means the same thing in both countries, these figures indicate that, for some reason, America is more productive in *(F / both F and C / C / neither F nor C)*. Europe is more productive in *(F / both F and C / C / neither F nor C)*.

In an 8-hour day, a worker in America can produce either $8 \times 20 = 160$ units of *F* or *(10 / 48 / 64 / 80)* units of *C*. In Europe, in an 8-hour day, a worker can produce either 64 units of *C* or *(10 / 48 / 64 / 80 / 160)* units of *F*.

F; C; 48, 80

3. a. This chapter assumes that all costs of producing either commodity in either country are solely labor costs and that all revenue from sale of the commodity goes to that labor. Hence, if the market price of a unit of *F* in America is $1, the hourly wage earned by an American worker producing *F* will be $*(0.05 / 0.10 / 1 / 10 / 20)*.

If, instead, *F*'s price in America were to be $0.05 (5 cents), the corresponding hourly wage for an *F*-worker would be $(0.05 / 0.10 / 1 / 10 / 20).

Similarly, if *C*'s price per unit in America were to be $2, the hourly wage of a *C*-worker would be $*(0.30 / 0.60 / 2 / 10 / 12)*.

b. If in Europe the price per unit of *F* is £1, the hourly wage of an *F*-worker there will be £*(1 / 4 / 6 / 8 / 10)*. If *C*'s price in Europe is £1, the corresponding hourly *C*-wage will be £*(1 / 4 / 6 / 8 / 10)*.

a. 20 ($1 per unit times 20 units per hour; labor is the only factor that is paid.); 1; 12 **b.** 10; 8

4. a. Suppose that, for some unspecified reason, the prices of *F* and *C* in America were both $1. A worker, free to choose either occupation, would earn more by going into *(F / C)* production. Specifically, in *F* production earnings per hour would be $*(1 / 6 / 8 / 10 / 20)*, and in *C* production $*(1 / 6 / 8 / 10 / 20)*.

Given freedom of labor to enter either occupation (and with no other preference between them), the prices noted above (both $1) *(could / could not)* characterize an "equilibrium" situation in America. If such prices did prevail—say the government tried to enforce them by law—then ultimately *(only F would / only C would / both F and C would continue to)* be produced.

b. In Europe, if the prices of both *F* and *C* were somehow £10, then (again assuming no barrier to movement between occupations) *(all workers would move into F / all workers would move into C / such prices would not affect F and C)* production.

c. The point here is that unless the prices of *F* and *C* stand in the proper relation to one another, the entire resource supply (here, the entire labor force) will shift away from production of the "underpriced" commodity. If in America the price of *F* were $3, then, if both *F* and *C* are to continue to be produced, *C*'s price must be $*(1 / 3 / 8 / 10 / 12)*. If *C*'s price in America were $2, then *F*'s price should be $*(0.30 / 0.60 / 1 / 1.50 / 2)*. Prices of $2.40 for *F* and $9 for *C* *(would / would not)* constitute an equilibrium relation.

Relative prices are what matter here. In America, the ratio between p_F and p_C must be *(1:1 / 3:10 / 5:10 / 10:3)* because that pair of figures matches the underlying ratio of production costs, measured in labor time needed to produce 1 unit of each commodity. (The absolute level of prices will be governed by such factors as the quantity of money circulating within the country.)

If prices of *F* and *C* somehow got stuck at $2.40 and $9, respectively, workers would move away from *(F / C)* production and into *(F / C)* production.

d. In Europe the same requirement holds, except that the relationship must match productive conditions there. If the price of *F* in Europe were £4, then, for an equilibrium in which both commodities were produced, the price of *C* would have to be £*(1 / 2 / 3 / 4 / 5 / 6)*. More generally, Europe's ratio p_F/p_C must be *(3:10 / 5:10 / 4:5 / 5:4)*.

a. *F*; 20; 6; could not; only *F* would **b.** all workers would move into *F* **c.** 10; .60; would not, 3:10, *F*; *C* **d.** 5; 4:5

The questions thus far have assumed that there is no international trade between America and Europe. Now assume that the opportunity of such trading suddenly materializes. For simplicity, the costs of shipping goods from one region to the other are assumed to be so small that they can be considered zero. The prices of *F* and of *C* in America are, respectively, 60 cents and $2.

5. a. You are a shrewd American entrepreneur. To be more specific, you have $9 in cash, and you are the first to notice that *F*'s price in Europe is £4 and *C*'s price is £5. Given such prices, how can you convert your $9 into $24? Describe the necessary operations in four steps; the first step is provided to get you on your way.

(1) Buy 15 *F* for $9.

(2) ______________________

(3) ______________________

(4) ______________________

b. If you were an entrepreneur in Europe with a nest egg of £15 and a similar desire to improve your financial standing, what would you do, and what would the result be?

(1) ____________________

(2) ____________________

(3) ____________________

(4) ____________________

---

a. **(2)** Sell the 15 *F* in Europe for £60. **(3)** Buy 12 *C* for £60. **(4)** Sell the 12 *C* in America for $24. **b.** **(1)** Buy 3 *C* for £15. **(2)** Sell the 3 *C* in America for $6. **(3)** Buy 10 *F* for $6. **(4)** Sell the 10 *F* in Europe for £40.

6. **a.** As a result of this difference in price ratios between the two countries, the two commodities will accordingly begin to move internationally. Specifically (pick two alternatives), *(F moves from America to Europe / F moves from Europe to America / F moves in both directions / C moves from America to Europe / C moves from Europe to America / C moves in both directions)*.

A quick rule of thumb for determining what country will export which commodity in such circumstances is this: Write down the two before-trade price ratios as fractions, and take the smaller of the two, noting the country to which it belongs. (In question 5, the p_F/p_C fractions would be 3/10 and 8/10; America's 3/10 is the smaller.) The numerator of that fraction indicates that country's export commodity. (The numerator is 3, and that 3 pertains to food price; so America will export food.) The other country will export the other commodity.

b. Had America's *F* and *C* prices been 30 cents and $1, respectively, rather than 60 cents and $2, the results described in part a *(would / would not)* have changed. Had Europe's *F* and *C* prices been £8 and £10, respectively, rather than £4 and £5, this *(would / would not)* have changed the results described.

---

a. *F* moves from America to Europe; *C* moves from Europe to America
b. would not; would not

7. **a.** In America (and in Europe), open trade disrupts the pre-trade domestic "equilibrium." For example, in the United States, trade supplements domestic supplies of *C*. Thus *C*'s price should *(rise / remain unchanged / fall)*. This in turn means that the ratio p_F/p_C will *(rise / remain unchanged / fall)*.

b. We know from questions 3 and 4 that if America's ratio p_F/p_C is anything other than 3:10 (or 0.3), workers will leave the "underpriced" occupation. In this case, workers will move from *(F / C)* to *(F / C)* production, and that is good. Why? Because America's new export trade means that more workers are needed in the production of American exports—commodity *F*.

c. In Europe, which imports what America exports, there will *(be a / not be any)* corresponding change in domestic prices. There, the ratio p_F/p_C will *(rise / remain unchanged / fall)*. The price of *F* will fall, as imports of this commodity arrive from America. The price of *C* will rise, since there is a new demand for *C* from those exporting it to America. Workers will leave *(F / C)* production, moving instead to production of Europe's export—commodity *C*.

---

a. fall; rise **b.** *C*; *F* **c.** be a; fall; *F*

8. **a.** The before-trade price ratios were 3:10 in America and 4:5 (or 8:10) in Europe. Clearly, such different ratios allow you to make a financial killing, when trade opens up, by going through the trading process of question 5. The profit you make would be one of "arbitrage." These arbitrage profit opportunities will not last. They are in fact a symptom of disequilibrium. As question 7 indicated, when goods begin to move in volume between the two countries, prices are affected. Specifically (to repeat question 7), America's before-trade p_F/p_C of 3:10 will *(rise / fall)* and Europe's ratio of 4:5 (or 8:10) will *(rise / fall)*. That is, the two ratios move *(closer together / farther apart)*.

Suppose that America's ratio rises from 3:10 to 4:10, and Europe's falls from 8:10 to 7:10. There is *(no longer / still)* an arbitrage profit to be made; it persists so long as any difference at all persists between the two ratios. But as more and more people discover this opportunity, the trade volume keeps increasing. This increase in turn pushes the two ratios even *(closer together / farther apart)*. In the case here assumed, that of literally zero transport cost, the two ratios must finally meet at a common figure, the same in both countries. A possible common figure would be 5:10. (It would be any figure between 3:10 and 8:10, but leave the matter of determination of the exact common ratio for a later question.)

b. When this common ratio is reached, your chances of getting right quickly are ended; the arbitrage opportunity vanishes. Does this mean that international trade will stop? Not at all; it means only that the trade volume will stop increasing. Therefore, a good producer in America gets the same return whether the output is sold in America or in Europe; the same is true of a clothing producer in Europe. An international equilibrium is established, comparable to the separate equilibria formerly prevailing in the two countries. The new equilibrium is one in which America produces only food, Europe only clothing.

If the trade volume were somehow greatly disrupted (say, by serious and persisting shipping difficulties), the price ratios in the two countries might *(still remain at a common figure / draw apart again)*. Introduce some transportation cost, and the two price ratios would continue to differ by just enough to reflect that transportation cost and not by enough to allow for any enduring arbitrage profit.

---

a. rise; fall; closer together; still; closer together **b.** draw apart again

9. The result of this international exchange is that both countries enjoy an increase in real income. Specializing in *F* production, America will have available for consumption more of *F* that it did before, and more of *C* also. The same holds for Europe, which concentrates on *C* production.

This point is illustrated by looking at the labor cost to America of the two methods of getting C—domestic production or export-import.

America can produce 6 units of C per hour; thus each unit costs 10 minutes of labor time. What will that unit cost if C is obtained by producing F, exporting it, and bringing back C in exchange?

Assume, as in question 8, that the international price ratio, p_F/p_C, is 5:10. That is, a unit of clothing costs twice as much as a unit of food; or in barter terms, $2F$ exchange for $1C$. America can produce 20 units of F in 1 hour. If this is sent to Europe (with transport cost still assumed zero), America can get *(5 / 6 / 10 / 20 / 40)* units of C in exchange. Since 1 hour of labor effort was involved, each of those C units costs *(5 / 6 / 10 / 20 / 40)* minutes of labor. This is *(not as good as / better than)* obtaining C through domestic production.

International trade thereby produces for America a result equivalent to development of a new technology greatly improving labor productivity in the C industry. The same is true for Europe, but for the F industry instead of the C industry.

(The introduction of transportation cost would again somewhat reduce this real-income gain. If transportation costs were sufficiently high, there would be no point in trade, and no real-income gain.)

10; 6; better than

10. The points of questions 2 through 9 can all be illustrated graphically. Take the input requirements listed in question 2 as given, and suppose that Europe and America are both endowed with 10 hours of labor (not very realistic, to be sure, but a convenient number around which to build some illustrative geometry). Suppose further that both countries start in the absence of any trade by dividing their labor resources equally between F and C.

a. Draw, in panel (**a**) of Figure 38-2, the production-possibility frontier for America, and identify the initial production mix as point A. Draw the corresponding frontier for Europe in panel (**b**) and identify the initial production mix as point B. The slope of the American frontier, equaling ________ in magnitude, represents the relative domestic price ratio of food to clothing in the United States. The corresponding slope of the European frontier, equaling ________ in magnitude, is similarly the relative domestic price ratio in Europe. Let's begin with America, which produces ________ units of F and ________ units of C; Europe begins producing ________ units of F and ________ of C. Total production of C is ________ units; total production of F is ________ units.

b. Suppose now, for the sake of argument, that America chooses to specialize in F in trade with Europe at the European domestic price ratio to generate its desired consumption of C. Draw a budget constraint indicating the possible points of consumption given this strategy. If America were to continue to consume the original 30 units of C, then she could increase her consumption of F from 100 units to ________ units by selling ________ units of F for 30 units of C. Welfare in America, assuming a smooth transition from a 50-50 labor split to 100 percent concentration in the production of F, would therefore necessarily *(fall / stay the same / rise)*.

c. Now play the same game from the other side of the Atlantic. Assume that Europe decides to specialize completely in the production of C and buys as much F as is desirable given the American price ratio. Draw the appropriate budget constraint in panel (**b**). If Europe were still interested in consuming 40 units of C, it could increase its consumption of F from 50 units to ________ units by selling 40 units of C for ________units of F. European welfare would, in this second case, also *(climb / remain the same / fall)*, making the same assumption of continued full employment.

d. The world production frontier can now be constructed. Suppose, first of all, that both countries specialize in F; production of F would equal ________ units in America and ________ units in Europe, for a total of ________ units; total production of C would then equal ________ units. Plot this combination in panel (**c**) and label it point D.

Now reverse the specializations of both countries. Total F production would then equal ________ units with C production, climbing to a maximum of ________ units. Plot this point and label it E.

Halfway between these extremes are two intermediate cases of mixed specialization. If Europe specialized in C and America specialized in F, then ________ units of F would be produced with ________ units of C. Denote this point G and plot it in panel (**c**), as well. If the specializations were reversed, though, ________ units of F would be produced by Europe and ________ units of C would be produced in America. This point, plotted and labelled H in panel (**c**), *(would / would not)* be on the frontier because production levels of *(F / C / neither F nor C / both F and C)* are lower at H than at G.

The world frontier is now at hand. A straight line connecting points D and G would correspond to specialization by *(America / Europe)* in the production of *(F / C)* and some intermediate combination of F and C production in *(America / Europe)*. Similarly, points along a line connecting points G and E would correspond to specialization in *(America / Europe)* in the production of *(F / C)* and some intermediate combination in *(America / Europe)*. (Note that the frontier you just drew looks like the frontier shown in text Figure 38-3).

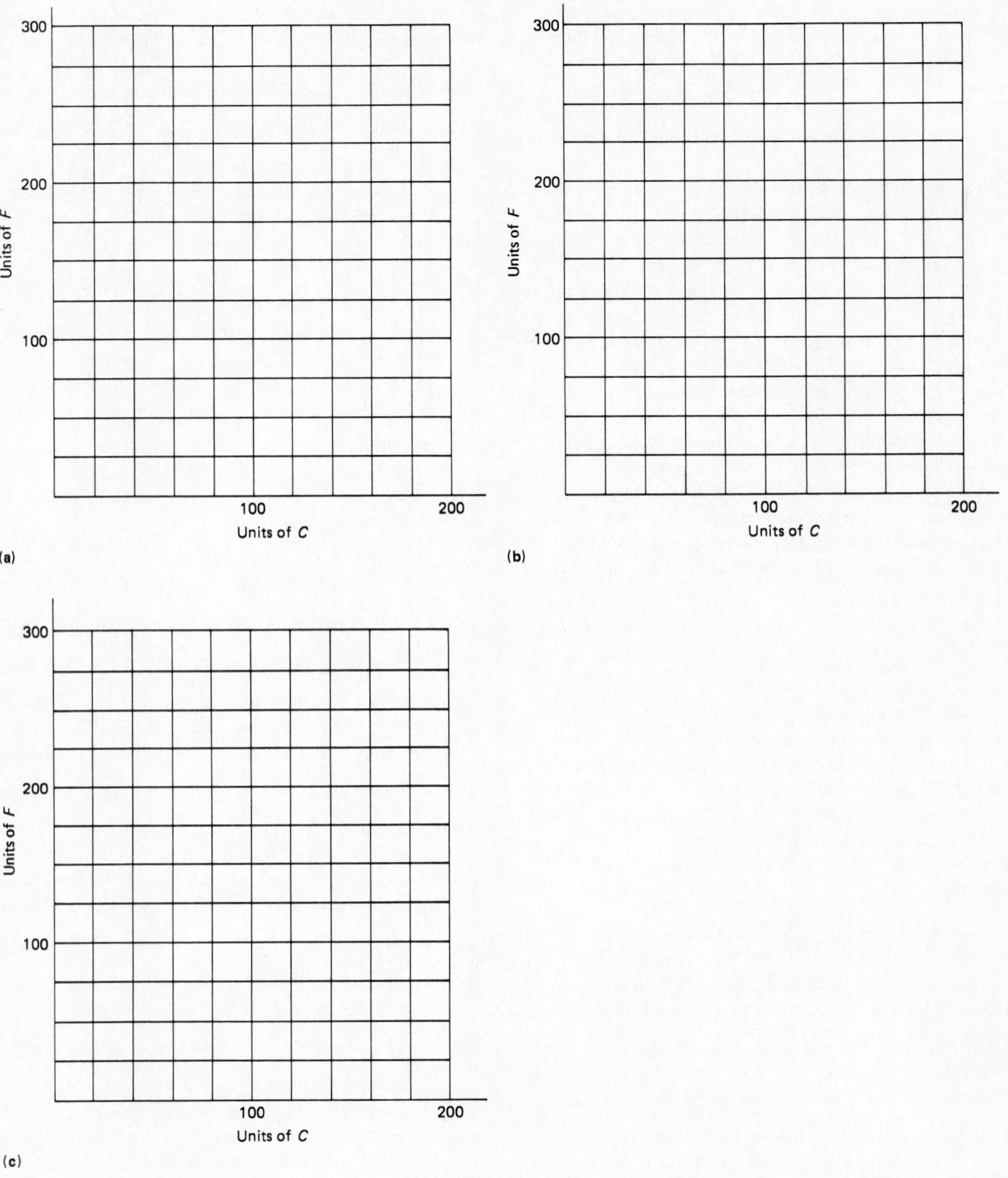

Figure 38-2

e. Finally, plot the pre-trade initial production combination; it *(is / is not)* on the frontier. The point chosen by free trade outlined above would be *(D / E / G / H)*. It *(would / would not)* be on the frontier and it would, for both countries, be superior to the initial, pre-trade position.

---

a. Panel (**a**): straight line from (C = 0; F = 200) to (C = 60; F = 0); A = (C = 30; F = 100); Panel (**b**): straight line from (C = 0; F = 100) to (C = 80; F = 0); B = (C = 40; F = 50); 10/3; 5/4; 100; 30; 50; 40; 70; 150 **b.** straight line from (C = 0; F = 200) to (C = 250 [= 200 F × Europe price ratio of (10/8)]; F = 0); 162.5; 37.5; rise **c.** straight line from (C = 0; F = 266 2/3) to (C = 80; F = 0); 133.3; 133.3; climb **d.** 200; 100; 300; 0 [point D is C = 0; F = 300]; 0; 140 [point E is C = 140; F = 0]; 200; 80 [point G is C = 80; F = 200]; 100; 60 [point H is C = 60; F = 100]; would not; both F and C; America; F; Europe; Europe; C; America **d.** (F = 150; C = 70); is not; E; would

The preceding questions have concentrated on an example in which Europe and America both held absolute advantages in the production of one good; America was more productive in food and Europe was more productive in clothing. The theory of comparative advantage stresses, however, that an even distribution of absolute advantage is not necessary for trade to be mutually beneficial. The next few questions will concentrate on this possibility—the real power of the Ricardo result.

11. Change the productivity figures. Double America's yield per labor-hour in the production of both commodities (leaving the figures for Europe unchanged). Thus, the tables in question 2 become:

Yield of 1 Labor-Hour	Units of *F*	Units of C
In America	40	12
In Europe	10	8

	Minutes of Labor Required to Produce	
	1 Unit of *F*	1 Unit of *C*
In America	1.5	5
In Europe	6	7.5

The critical difference is that American labor is now assumed more productive than European labor in the production of *both* commodities. We do not ask what background factors would result in such differences. We simply accept the fact that there is now a "high-productivity" country and a "low-productivity" country so that we may ask the Ricardo question: Is trade that would be profitable to both participants possible in such circumstances?

In America's previous pre-trade situation (questions 2 through 4), its ratio p_F/p_C was 3:10. In the new situation—still pre-trade—that ratio will be *(higher / unchanged / lower)*. (The two absolute prices may of course be different.)

Question 5 examined the trading opportunity arising out of the opening up of international trade. With the changed productivity figures introduced in this present question, this trading opportunity will *(no longer exist / be exactly as it was before)*. Why? Because domestic, pre-trade prices are unchanged. The dimensions of the transactions identified in question 5 might have changed, but the *directions* have not.

unchanged; be exactly as it was before (Relative prices have not changed.)

12. Let America be endowed with 5 hours of labor and Europe be endowed with 10; suppose that the production possibilities of both countries are accurately described by the tables recorded in question 11. Plot, in panels (**a**), (**b**), and (**c**) of Figure 38-3 the production-possibility frontier of America, or Europe, and the world, respectively.

Indicate in panel (**c**) the point toward which free trade would lead the two countries, if they would only trade with one another at some price ratio between 10:3 and 5:4. At that point, world production of F would equal ______ units and world production of C would equal ______ units because Europe would specialize in producing *(F / C)*, exporting *(F / C)*, and importing *(F / C)*; America would do the reverse.

They are identical to those of question 10. point G at the corner; 200; 80; C; C; F

13. The point, then, is that a low-productivity country should still be capable of dealing profitably with a high-productivity country; both should gain in real income from international trade. The cost of low productivity is a low per capita income within that country, not an inability to cope with international exchanges. The essential factor upon which an opening up of trade (and profitable trade) *does* depend is a difference in the pre-trade price ratio between the two countries.

a. Below are three sets of pre-trade price figures (each quite different from anything used earlier). In the right-hand column, indicate the proper conclusion by this code:

1. America would export F, Europe C.
2. America would export C, Europe F.
3. No opportunity for any trading gain here.

America		Europe		
P of *F* in $	*P* of *C* in $	*P* of *F* in £	*P* of *C* in £	Answer
1	2	3	4	
1	2	3	6	
1	2	3	8	

(To answer, use the question 5 technique—which between-country transfer of goods would earn you a profit?—or the rule of thumb suggested in question 6.)

b. All the foregoing may indicate why it was thought necessary to introduce such terms as *absolute advantage* (or disadvantage) and *comparative advantage* (or disadvantage). America would have an *absolute* advantage over Europe in the production of some good if she could produce that commodity at less real cost (which in this chapter means simply labor cost) than Europe can. (If America needs 1 hour to produce 1 unit of F, and Europe

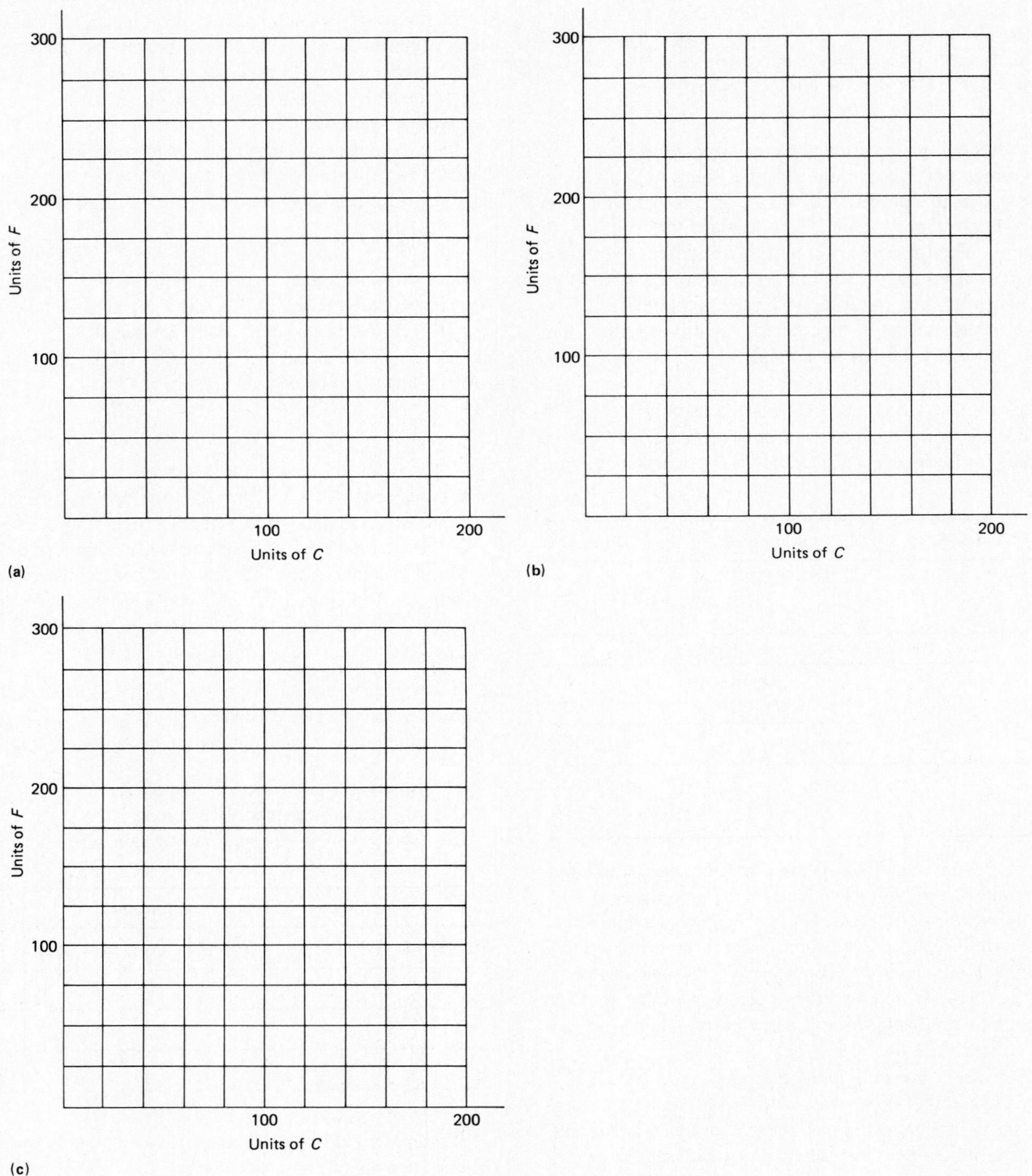

Figure 38-3

needs 1½ hours, the America has the absolute advantage with respect to *F*).

Look back at the question 11 tables. They indicate that America has the absolute advantage in *(F alone / both F and C / C alone)*. Nonetheless, this circumstance should not prevent Europe from exporting good *C*. Regardless of her absolute disadvantage, Europe still has a comparative advantage in production of good *(F / C)*. (In terms of question 11 data, America is decidedly the high-productivity country. Yet, in comparative terms, its productivity shows up less prominently with respect to good *C*.)

In two-country, two-commodity examples like the ones used

here, it is necessary to examine and compare the prices of both commodities *(in that one country alone / in both countries)* to determine who has a comparative advantage in what.

---

a. 1; 3; 2 **b.** both *F* and *C*; *C*; in both countries

14. At what exact level will the common, post-trade price ratio be established? This is essentially a supply-and-demand question. The trade process described earlier is just an exchange of one good for another. Indeed, for purposes of understanding how the common intermediate ratio is reached, it's easiest to think of this trade as simple barter. The exact quantities exchanged are settled by working out a barter rate which both countries find, in terms of the amounts exchanged, satisfactory.

Start with the same pair of pre-trade p_F/p_C ratios used earlier: 3:10 in America, 4:5 (or 8:10) in Europe. If the price of *F* in America is, say, \$3, then the price of *C* is \$10. One unit of *C* costs 3⅓ times as much as 1 unit of *F*. In barter terms, it takes 10 units of *F* to match 3 units of *C*. Similarly, Europe's 4:5 p_F/p_C ratio means that *(4 of F equals 5 of C / 5 of F equals 4 of C)*.

When trade opens up, these two pre-trade ratios (recall questions 7 and 8) are pushed closer together. Consider any intermediate ratio picked at random—say, 1:2. At that ratio, there will be a particular quantity of *F* which America would wish to export, and a corresponding quantity of *C* it would want to import. If the desired *F*-export quantity were 100 units daily, then the quantity of *C* that America would want in exchange (remember, the 1:2 ratio is expressed in p_F/p_C terms, as before) would be *(50 / 100 / 150 / 200 / 250)* units daily. At that same 1:2 ratio, there are particular quantities of *C* and *F* which Europe would wish to export and import daily, respectively, but these quantities may not match the American ones. If they did not, then 1:2 would not be an "equilibrium" international price ratio.

The intermediate and common ratio finally established is one at which the two countries' wishes (in terms of *F* and *C* quantities as exchanged) *do* match. The better the barter terms America is offered—the more then old 3:10 ratio moves upward—the *(more / less)* it will want to exchange. Europe, by contrast, will want to trade more extensively, the more that its pre-trade ratio of 4:5 moves *(up / down)*. Somewhere between the two differing pre-trade price ratios, there should be a common price ratio that is mutually satisfactory.

---

5 of *F* equals 4 of *C*; 50; more; down

15. The principal basis for mutually profitable international trade is a difference in relative production costs and prices. The case in which a country imports a commodity which it cannot produce at all is simply an illustration of the extreme case of such differences-in-production-cost trade. It does not matter what factors account for these relative cost differences (e.g., climate, differences in labor education and skill, differences in capital equipment); they must simply emerge in the form of differences in relative prices.

Differences in "factor endowments" are usually cited as the principal source of such differences in relative production costs and prices (although this explanation is of the kind which may raise as many questions as it answers). Two other possible sources of mutually beneficial international trade are frequently identified. They are:

a. ______________________________

b. ______________________________

---

a. decreasing cost (*Note:* In this case, we can assume that the pre-trade cost ratio between commodities *F* and *C* is the same in country A as in country E. Given decreasing costs, though, if country A specializes in production of *F*, this may lower the per-unit cost of producing *F*. Here, trade is still based on a difference in costs, but it can be a difference which emerges only *after* trade has begun.) **b.** differences in tastes between the two countries

16. The Ricardo analysis depends upon an implicit assumption of full employment. That is to say, when a country moves from producing a mix of goods to specializing more heavily in a few goods, resources must flow freely from the production of one good to the other. Remember that Ricardo was a classical economist, and note that this is nothing more than the classical assumption of perfectly functioning markets. Labor *(must be / need not be)* included in this flow—labor which may or may not like the idea. If it does not, then serious opposition to free trade can arise, as labor asks its government for *(unemployment compensation / protection from foreign competition)*. Even though total welfare might improve with trade, it therefore is possible that some individuals would be forced to endure short-term pain sufficient to lobby against it. There could, moreover, be a long-term loss to some if the distribution of relative wages were to shift with the move toward specialization.

All is not barter and roses in the world of multilateral trade. The world is full of currencies and floating exchange rates that complicate international transactions almost beyond belief. The costs of foreign business offices, foreign exchange hedging, and insurance certainty lead to the conclusion that the Ricardo assumption of zero transportation (read transactions) cost is far from reality. Profit margins have to be large to make international trade worth the effort.

---

must be; protection from foreign competition

17. A country's balance of payments is the official record of all its transactions with foreign countries for some specified period of time—usually 1 year. There are four main categories; list them in the spaces provided.

a. ______________________________

b. ______________________________

c. ______________________________

d. ______________________________

The key to entries in any of these categories is the effect that the transaction has on domestic holdings of foreign currencies. If a transaction generates foreign currency, then it is recorded as a *(debit / credit)*; if it costs currency because a foreign citizen (or institution) requires payment in his or her (or its) own currency, then it is a *(debit / credit)*.

a. current account **b.** capital account **c.** statistical discrepancy **d.** changes in official reserves; credit; debit

18. A less developed nation is typically one which borrows abroad to the full extent of its line of credit. A mature, developed nation is typically one which lends to other countries. As a nation develops over a long time period, it may change from borrower to lender, and this shift will affect its balance-of-payments position. The sequence outlined below—*young debtor, mature debtor, new creditor, mature creditor*—is an attempt to describe the likely balance-of-payments changes involved. In the 1980s, the United States moved from mature creditor into a new category. Greatly diminished saving caused heavy U.S. borrowing and turned the world's biggest creditor into the world's biggest debtor.

a. A less developed nation is likely to try to build up its stock of capital goods through sales of its IOUs to more developed countries. On its balance of payments, these security sales will be recorded as a *(credit / debit)*. The import of capital equipment or other goods purchased with security-sale proceeds will appear on the "merchandise" line as a *(credit / debit)*. This country has *(a favorable / an unfavorable)* balance of trade. These facts make it a "young debtor" nation.

b. As time passes, this country ceases to borrow, or borrows in smaller quantities. It still pays interest and dividends on earlier years of bond and stock financing, but its exporting capacity has increased. It now shows a surplus of merchandise exports over imports, or an excess of *(credits over debits / debits over credits)*. This *(favorable / unfavorable)* balance of trade is matched, or approximately so, by a surplus of debits on the investment income line of the balance of payments. The "mature debtor" stage has been reached.

c. Further down the road, this country may begin not only to repay its own earlier borrowings but also to lend to other countries itself. This means a surplus of *(credits over debits / debits over credits)* in the balance-of-payments capital account. If this is matched, or approximately so, by a surplus of merchandise exports over imports, the "new creditor" stage has been reached.

d. Ultimately, the "mature creditor" stage may be attained. Such a country may still be lending capital abroad, but its inflow of interest and dividend payments is more than sufficient to offset this lending. On the balance-of-payments merchandise account, therefore, there is a surplus of *(credits over debits / debits over credits)* and the balance of trade is *(favorable / unfavorable)*. This balance is supported by the *(debit / credit)* balance on the investment income account.

a. credit; debit; an unfavorable **b.** credits over debits; favorable **c.** debits over credits **d.** debits over credits; unfavorable; credit

QUIZ: Multiple Choice

1. In terms of comparative advantage, the most correct explanation of why bananas are imported instead of being grown commercially in the United States is that:
(1) bananas cannot be produced in the temperate zones.
(2) it would take a great deal of effort to produce bananas in the United States.
(3) bananas can be produced with less effort in other countries than they can in the United States.
(4) U.S. resources are better employed in producing other commodities, and tropical-country resources are better employed in banana production than in other things.
(5) the United States climate does not lend itself to banana production.

2. David Ricardo's theory of comparative advantage is intended to show that trade between two countries will be mutually beneficial. One assumption made in this analysis, to which some objection might be raised on the ground that it influences and perhaps alters the conclusions reached, is that:
(1) comparative advantage, not absolute advantage, is the important element in trade.
(2) each country, in consequence of such trade, will specialize in the commodity it exports.
(3) full employment is at all times maintained in both countries.
(4) no tariffs exist in either of the two countries.
(5) the pre-trade ratio of prices within each country has no part to play in the determination of trade flows.

3. Before international trade begins, a country will have an equilibrium ratio of prices (determined by relative production costs in the classical Ricardo model) between any two commodities. If trade with another country begins, involving these commodities, this price ratio will ordinarily be altered:
(1) only if a change in production costs results within the country.
(2) in all cases (excepting only the one where the volume of international trade proves to be too small to affect it).
(3) only in cases where the volume of international trade is small.
(4) not at all, since it is an equilibrium relationship.
(5) only in cases where the volume of international trade is exceedingly large.

4. The following table records the output of labor (assumed to be the only input involved) in production of wine and of cloth in two countries, A and B.

Production per Hour	A	B
Yards of cloth	5	15
Liters of wine	10	20

Comparing the two countries and contemplating trade between them on the basis of production advantages, it would be correct to say that country A has:
(1) an absolute advantage in cloth production.
(2) an absolute advantage in wine production.
(3) a comparative advantage in cloth production.
(4) a comparative advantage in wine production.
(5) a comparative advantage in neither commodity.

5. Initially, there is no trade between the two countries of question 4; each lives in isolation. In country A, the currency unit is the "donaro"; in country B, it is the "gelt." The prices of cloth in A and B in their pre-trade situations are, respectively, 20 donaros and 60 gelts. For an equilibrium in which each country continues to produce both commodities, the corresponding wine prices would have to be:
(1) 5 donaros, 20 gelts.
(2) 40 donaros, 45 gelts.
(3) 10 donaros, 45 gelts.
(4) 10 donaros, 80 gelts.
(5) 40 donaros, 80 gelts.

6. If trading opportunities were to be opened up, given the data of questions 4 and 5 (international transport cost assumed to be zero or negligible), then we should expect country B to:
(1) import wine.
(2) export wine.
(3) import both commodities.
(4) export both commodities.
(5) neither export nor import, since her productive situation is such that there is no prospect of profitable trade with country A.

7. Before the trading opportunity of question 6 emerged, each country had its own price ratio, reflecting domestic production costs. If trade develops between countries A and B, this ratio—specifically, the ratio of the price of wine to the price of cloth—will:
(1) rise in country A, fall in country B.
(2) fall in country A, rise in country B.
(3) rise in both.
(4) fall in both.
(5) not change in either country, except perhaps during a short transitional period before equilibrium is reestablished.

8. When international trade has become established, in the circumstances of questions 4 through 7, and a new equilibrium has been reached, the ratio of cloth price to wine price (transport cost still assumed zero) might reasonably be:
(1) 1.2 in both countries.
(2) 1.8 in A; 1.5 in B.
(3) 1.6 in both countries.
(4) 2.1 in A; 1.3 in B.
(5) 2.3 in both countries.

9. Given the price ratio or ratios set out in question 8, if we know that the total of cloth exports is 500 yards daily, then the daily wine exports must be:
(1) 600 liters from A.
(2) 600 liters from B.
(3) 800 liters from A.
(4) 800 liters from B.
(5) 1150 liters from A.

10. The gain from trade can be illustrated by the position of the wine-importing country. Question 4 shows hourly output of wine if that wine is produced at home. If the country specializes in cloth production and gets its wine via imports, then—at the price ratio of question 8, transport cost still assumed zero—the number of liters of wine resulting from 1 hour's labor is:
(1) 16.
(2) 20.
(3) 24.
(4) 28.
(5) 32.

11. Differences in comparative production costs are usually cited as the principal basis for international trade. Another (and different) possible source of such exchanges is:
(1) differences in climates.
(2) fixed foreign exchange rates.
(3) differences in transport costs.
(4) differences in labor skills.
(5) economies of mass production.

12. Trade between countries of comparable size with different standards of living will be:
(1) profitable to the country of lower living standards at the expense of the one of higher standards.
(2) profitable to both as long as price ratios differ in the two countries, but of no profit to either once a common price ratio has been established.
(3) profitable in some degree to both, even after a common price ratio has been established.
(4) unprofitable to both because one country would be at an absolute disadvantage in all products.
(5) profitable to the country of higher living standards at the expense of the one of lower living standards.

13. A "favorable balance of trade" means:
(1) an excess of merchandise exports and other current account credits over merchandise imports and other current account debits.
(2) an excess of foreign currency received by the home country over domestic currency received by foreigners.
(3) an excess of merchandise exports over merchandise imports.
(4) an excess of total credits over total debits in the entire balance of payments.
(5) a situation in which the value of total imports exceeds the value of total exports.

14. The five transactions listed below are all entries to be made on the U.S. balance of payments. For balance-of-payments

purposes, four of the five are fundamentally similar. Which one is different?
(1) The Federal Reserve Bank of New York receives gold from the Bank of England.
(2) An American tourist on vacation spends francs in Paris.
(3) A South American government sells long-term bonds in New York.
(4) A British shipping firm is paid to carry an American export commodity abroad.
(5) An American investor receives a dividend check from a West German steel company.

15. A mature debtor nation is one whose balance of trade is:
(1) unfavorable, the import surplus being paid for by borrowing.
(2) unfavorable, thanks to the interest which is received from abroad.
(3) favorable, the interest on past borrowing being paid out of the surplus of exports.
(4) favorable, being made so by interest received from abroad.
(5) not correctly identified by any of these descriptions.

SUGGESTED ANSWERS TO QUESTIONS IN THE TEXT: Chapter 38

1. Not necessarily; it may be simply a statement of absolute advantage. Importing a good in which a country has an absolute advantage does not guarantee that welfare would improve.

2. **a.** Incorrect; it is a statement that the north has an absolute advantage in everything, but Mexico would help both itself and the north if it could export things in which it nonetheless has a comparative advantage (at least after factor markets adjust).
b. Correct; the point of Ricardo.
c. Incorrect; trade can increase aggregate income, though it may redistribute it.
d. Correct if it said the balance of payments, including not only the current account but also the capital account, changes in reserves, and any discrepancy.
e. Sure! Do what you do well.

3. Graph the following table:

Food:	0	50	100	150	200
Clothing:	150	112.5	75	37.5	0

4. With (1,2; 2,4), relative prices are 1-to-2 in both countries; neither has a comparative advantage, and neither can expand its consumption frontier through trade.

5. The gains come from specialization. Should Korea end up with the same technology as the United States, trade will disappear. The Korean standard of living will improve, but the American standard of living will decline with the decline in relative comparative advantage. Yes, there is a lesson here . . .

6. Those countries have the largest relative comparative advantages, and they are not diminished by international price adjustments as they enter the international market. Why not? Because their demand increment is too small to drive the price of the goods that they import up, and their supply increment is too small to drive the price of their exports down.

7. Newly discovered and unexploited land and resources should support relatively inexpensive food and resource supplies.

8. Refer to the definitions in the chapter. Remember that the flow of foreign currency determines whether a transaction is a credit or a debit. "Invisibles" are reflections of transactions for which there is no physical piece of material or commodity.

9. Again, apply the definitions, taking careful note of current and capital accounts. Remember that the overall balance of payments must balance.

10. Oil exports cause the current account surplus. The country can use the money to purchase foreign assets—debits in the capital account. Then, when it gets around to internal investment, it sells some of those assets to purchase the material required to supply the investment projects. The materials shipments turn the current account toward deficit; the sale of foreign assets produces foreign currency—credits that move the capital account toward surplus.

11. The table should read:

	Credit	Debit	Net
I. Current	$250	$250	$ 0
II. Capital	40	−50	−10
III. Stat. discrepancy			−20
IV. Official settlements			30

12. The first statement is the Ricardo result. Growth of competitors need not cause the standard of living in a trading country to decline. Growth that diminishes diversity can, however.

13. Countries balance only their multilateral accounts. The U.S. deficit against Japan showed Japanese comparative advantage in goods traded between the two countries; but the overall net to zero meant that other goods were traded by both countries around the world. The United States showed a comparative advantage vis-à-vis the rest of the world in those goods; Japan, a comparative disadvantage. Moving to a system that required bilateral balance would destroy this flexibility, reduce efficiency, and diminish the international gains from trade.

14. Consult Figure TQ38-1. The D_aD_a curve starts with a horizontal section at 10/3; this shows the domestic condition in America without trade. At a certain level of consumption C, though, the price (in units of food per unit of clothing) supporting the indicated quantity demanded begins to fall. The S_eS_e curve starts with a horizontal section at 10/8; this shows the domestic condition in Europe without trade. At a certain level, the price (in units of food per unit of clothing) supporting the

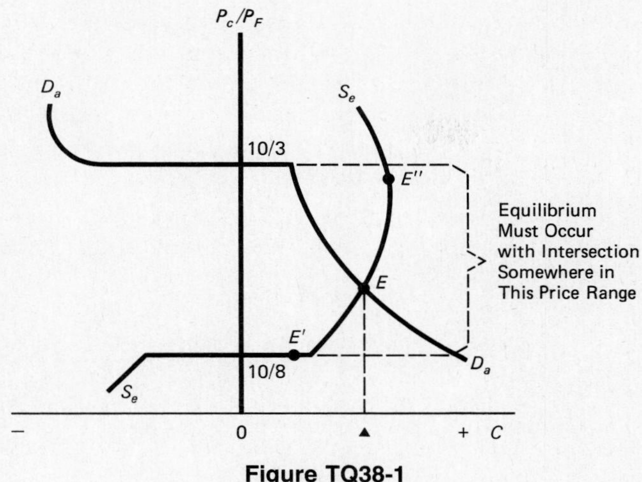

Figure TQ38-1

indicated quantity supplied begins to rise. Equilibrium occurs at point *E*, with the corresponding quantity of clothing imported by America.

A weak demand would make the D_aD_a curve more vertical, with equilibrium likely to occur somewhere like point E' on the horizontal portion of the S_eS_e curve; the quantity demanded by America would have been so small that it would have no effect on the international price of clothing—a price determined in Europe at 10/8. If the demand for clothing were large, then equilibrium would occur somewhere like E'' with the price close to 10/3. The geometry shows that intersection in any of these cases can occur at a price no higher than 10/3 and no lower than 10/8.

CHAPTER 39
PROTECTIONISM AND FREE TRADE

The case for free trade has been made. The comparative-advantage results of Chapter 38 were produced in a simplified environment, to be sure, but they are strong and robust. It is now time to turn the coin over to look at its opposite side. If, in particular, free trade is so beneficial, then why do we see so many barriers to free trade in the real world?

To answer this question, it is essential to see how trade barriers work. Only then can their effects be delineated and their merits evaluated. Chapter 39 tends to this task in its initial sections. With the effects of protection firmly in hand, the various arguments for and against protection are then critically reviewed. Having completed your work on this chapter, therefore, you will have accomplished the following objectives.

LEARNING OBJECTIVES

1. Use supply-and-demand analysis to outline the economic effects of protection. Show, first of all, that opening trade in a good drives its domestic price toward equality with its world price. Then show that a tariff can be expected to generate welfare losses by *(a)* promoting inefficient domestic production and *(b)* causing uneconomical reductions in domestic consumption even as it *(c)* generates some extra revenue for the government (unless it is prohibitive).

2. Outline a few non-economic arguments for trade restriction (protecting national interest, preserving national or regional culture, etc.), and evaluate their validity.

3. Outline a few traditional, false economic arguments for trade restriction (pursuing favorable terms of trade in a mercantilistic spirit, reacting to special-interest lobbying, protecting domestic employment from cheap foreign labor, retaliating against the trade barriers of others, etc.), and indicate how they fall short.

4. Outline a few dynamic economic arguments for trade restriction (exploiting power over terms of trade with optimal tariffs in the absence of retaliation, protecting infant industries, preserving employment in special cases, etc.), and explain when they might apply.

5. List a few non-tariff barriers to trade that have been employed by the United States in the past few years (escape clauses, antidumping tariffs, etc.), and explain how they work.

Three principal reasons, often working together, explain the rationale behind most of the actual or proposed restraints of foreign trade:

1. A country fears unemployment and regards import competition as a potential source of that unemployment.
2. A country is short of foreign exchange reserves and sees increased tariffs as a potential source of new revenue.
3. The groups within a country who would benefit most directly from protection bring political pressure to bear for its imposition.

Much of this chapter will explore the validity of these reasons, but we must always be aware that they must be evaluated in the context of national economies which also have a multitude of nontrade policy options available.

In a period of heavy unemployment, for example, it is hard to preach comparative advantage and free trade to legislators and businesspeople. They will argue that a reduction in imports would raise domestic employment, and so they might advocate an increase in protective tariffs. Such an attempt to "export unemployment" could, of course, be negated when other countries retaliate with similar tariff increases, but it would be wrong to insist that import restrictions can never reduce unemployment or raise GNP. The proper objection is that use of fiscal and monetary policies, as discussed in Parts Two and Three of the text, is far more effective. Moreover, these policies avoid the dubious ethics of trying to foist off your unemployment onto other nations; hence they do not incur the danger of retaliation.

Given reasonable assurance that unemployment can be handled by methods other than tariff or quota protection, then, many people in large, developed countries find it fairly easy to accept the free-trade principle; but people living in less developed countries tend to be more hesitant. They look at the world's most prosperous nations and they hope in due course their own country will enjoy equally high standards of production and income. They wonder if some restriction on the import of particular goods may not be needed in order to widen production and employment opportunities and to foster their nation's industrial growth.

To evaluate the validity of these basic motives behind trade protection, it is essential to understand precisely how a tariff works. The first few questions explore their operation in a simple supply-and-demand model.

1. Consult Figure 39-1. Curve *SS* drawn there represents a domestic supply curve for some good X; if X is a competitive industry, *SS* represents the horizontal sum of the marginal cost curves of many firms. Curve *DD* represents domestic demand for the same good. It is implicitly assumed that consumers do not care where the good was made; they simply want to buy the indicated quantities at the indicated prices.

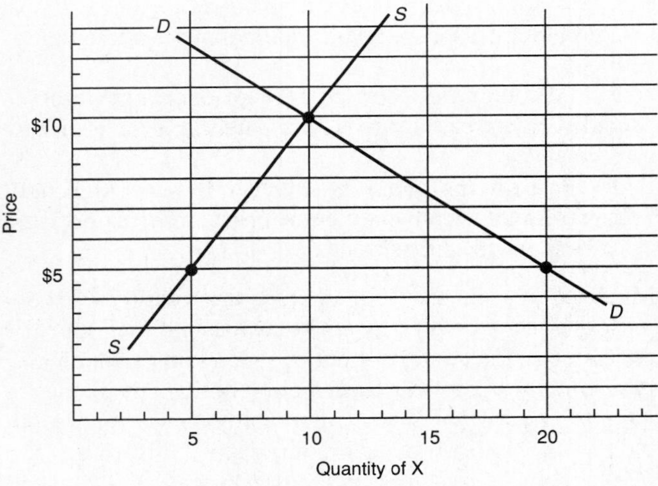

Figure 39-1

a. The market-clearing price in the absence of trade is $________; ________ units of X are demanded and supplied domestically at that price. If the world price of $5 were allowed to prevail, though, ________ units of X would be demanded, ________ units would be supplied domestically, and ________ units would be imported.

b. Now suppose that the domestic government has been convinced somehow to restrict imports by 50 percent. A tariff of $________ per unit imported would do the trick, but it would raise the domestic price to $________. At that price, ________ units would be demanded, ________ units would be supplied domestically, and ________ units would be imported. The effect of the tariff, therefore, is to *(raise / lower)* the price of X, *(raise / lower)* domestic production and employment, and *(raise / lower)* imports.

c. Given the tariff of part **b**, the government would collect $________ in revenue; this is revenue that would be collected above and beyond the revenue that it collected from its domestic tax base. The higher domestic price would, however, promote *(less / more)* efficient production at home, and thereby produce an efficiency *(loss / gain)* of $________. The marginal cost of producing X at home would, quite simply, increase to a level 50 percent higher than the marginal cost incurred by the rest of the world. The domestic economy would, in other words, be wasting resources in the production of X that would have been employed more efficiently somewhere else. Consumer surplus would, moreover, be *(reduced / increased)* by $________. Total spending on X would, in fact, climb in the case drawn, so that income effects on the demand for other goods across the economy should be expected.

d. If the government chose to impose a quota rather than a tariff, then it would award licenses to import up to ________ units of X. If these licenses were given away, then importers would earn excess profits of $________ by buying X abroad and selling X domestically. If the government auctioned the licenses, though, the total revenue generated by the auction would be $________.

e. If there were no tariff, but if it cost $2.50 per unit to transport X from the world marketplace into the domestic economy, then your answers to part **b** *(would / would not)* be altered. The revenue in part **c** identified as going to the government *(would / would not)* simply go to the transport company.

---

a. 10; 10; 20; 5; 15 **b.** 2.50; 7.50; 15; 7.5; 7.5; raise; raise; lower **c.** 18.75; less; loss; 3.12 (= ½ × $2.50 × 2.5); reduced; 6.25 (= ½ × $2.50 × 5) **d.** 7.5; 18.75; 18.75 **e.** would not; would

2. Often it is argued that a high tariff (*a*) brings revenue for the government and (*b*) protects the domestic industry against competition. There is an inconsistency in using both of these arguments. Why?

____

____

Revenue can fall as protection increases. In the extreme, for example, a tariff sufficiently high to keep out all imports brings in zero revenue.

3. Several non-economic arguments for tariff protection have been advanced. One suggests that protection is necessary to preserve national security. The nation here is that foreign sources of supply are unreliable, and that domestic production of certain strategic goods should be guaranteed even if it is inefficient. Protection, if it is awarded in response to this reasoning, should *(be total / be large enough to satisfy only minimum and essential consumption needs / be permanent and growing)*. If the commodity is a raw material, then perhaps

____________________ sufficient emergency supplies would be more efficient. If the commodity is a production good, then

internal protection by ____________________ would be better than external protection by trade restraint.

Second, some argue that protection is needed to preserve a way of life—a culture or a unique characteristic of an economy.

____________________ is again a more reasonable alternative than tariff protection.

be large enough to satisfy only minimum and essential consumption needs; storing; subsidy; Subsidy

4. a. The **mercantilist** approach to international trade argued that a nation should try to have *(exports / imports)* in excess of *(exports / imports)*—hence the phrase "favorable balance of trade." The surplus so obtained would be used to acquire *(merchandise / gold)*. The mercantilist position was thus strongly disposed toward *(protectionism / free trade)*. It was a convenient argument for many *(producer / consumer)* groups seeking protection against foreign competition.

The underlying mercantilist philosophy was that a nation ought to apply the same principles of prudence appropriate for a family. It is prudent for a family to try to save part of its income. The nation, mercantilists said, is just the family on a larger scale. And they equated saving, at the national level, with the accumulation of gold.

The argument is not totally fallacious. Any nation will find it desirable to have reserves of gold (or foreign exchange) to cope with changing events which may produce balance-of-payments deficits. Even at the family level, though, the argument for "prudence" is wrong if interpreted as meaning that all families must hoard their money. Saving which is not allowed to flow into investment spending leads only to depression and to a fall in saving (remember the paradox of thrift).

b. It would be quite *(possible / impossible)* for every nation to practice mercantilism successfully, since it is *(possible / impossible)* for every nation to have a surplus of exports. A general attempt to practice this philosophy, by trying to expand exports and restrict imports, would lead to a major *(rise / fall)* in *(exports / imports / both exports and imports)*.

a. exports; imports; gold; protectionism; producer **b.** impossible; impossible; fall; both exports and imports

5. a. In a country such as the United States, a protariff argument sometimes put forward is that American producers cannot compete against "cheap foreign labor." The free-trade response to this argument is that (pick one):

(1) cheap labor is simply a particular illustration of international cost differences on which mutually profitable trade can, on the principle of comparative advantage, be based.

(2) protection from cheap labor is sometimes a valid reason to impose a tariff, but it has often been used to excess.

(3) the proper remedy is a subsidy or quota, not a tariff, when cheap foreign labor threatens a domestic industry.

b. If the United States were to impose a tariff on imported industrial goods, it would reduce U.S. exports of, say, agricultural goods if (pick one):

(1) but only if, foreign nations retaliate with a countertariff against such agricultural goods.

(2) foreign earnings of American dollars are reduced by this tariff to the point that other nations can no longer buy the agricultural goods, regardless of the imposition or nonimposition of a countertariff.

c. The "escape clause" provision in U.S. tariff legislation comes into play when import volume harms a domestic producer. A tariff imposed according to this clause is (pick one):

(1) valid where national security is involved.

(2) unfounded on economic grounds because the industry ought to be exposed to that competition even to the point of possible extinction.

d. If another country harms us by erecting a tariff against our goods, our own position *(will / will not)* normally be improved if we impose a retaliatory tariff.

e. If a country happens to be economically powerful, and also important in international trade, it may find that a moderate tariff improves its real-income position, due to a change in the

____________________.

a. (1) b. (2) c. (2) d. will not **e.** terms of trade

6. a. The "national-survival" argument for tariff protection for a particular industry may be valid, but it should be viewed with some skepticism. Why? Because it has so often been used by special-interest groups to support self-indulgent protection. Where concern for national survival (particularly in wartime) does seem to warrant protection for some domestic industry, the best remedy is a *(quota / tariff / subsidy)*.

b. There may also be a valid argument for imposition of tariffs in the case of the *(less developed / richer)* nations, because such tariffs *(may be one of the few sources of revenue for government that are administratively feasible / are almost the only effective means of protecting domestic employment in time of recession).*

c. The "infant-industry" argument is one often invoked within the less developed nations. It holds that domestic industry needs protection when it is young, inexperienced, and unable to stand up to the competition of mature foreign producers. Economists generally agree that the infant-industry argument (circle one):

(1) has at least some validity in principle, although in practice many industries have proved to be perpetual infants, never able to survive without protection.

(2) has no validity at all, since international trade is founded on natural cost advantages.

Tariff arguments such as the infant-industry suggestion move us from the realm of static economic analysis to that of dynamic analysis. (Chapter 38, on comparative advantage, is a good example of static analysis. Such material puts its emphasis upon equilibrium and the properties of equilibrium positions. Dynamic analysis deals with changes—e.g., with growth—and with the process of change.) In general, economic arguments for protection are probably stronger in *(static / dynamic)* analysis.

---

a. subsidy **b.** less developed; may be one of the few sources of revenue for government that are administratively feasible **c.** **(1)**; dynamic

7. Much has been made recently of domestic-content legislation for American-built automobiles. Under this idea, a fixed percentage of the parts used to produce a car built in the United States would have to be built in the United States. It is argued by labor that this would protect American jobs and increase employment in the United States. This question will explore the validity of that claim under the (reasonable) assumption that domestic-content restrictions would limit the quantity of parts imported from abroad (if that were not the case, why bother?).

Let some good Y be produced from some combination of inputs including both labor and good X of question 1. Content legislation would amount to placing a quota on imports of X, so Figure 39-1 shows that the price of X should *(rise / fall)* and quantities demanded should *(rise / fall)*. At the same time, though, domestic production of X should *(climb / fall)* and domestic employment in that industry should *(climb / fall).*

It is now clear that the marginal cost of producing good Y should *(increase / decrease)*; illustrate this effect assuming perfect competition in Figure 39-2 by drawing a new supply curve for Y. The price of Y must therefore *(climb / fall)*, the output of Y must correspondingly *(climb / fall)* as the economy moves along the *(demand curve / old supply curve / new supply curve)*, and employment in the production of Y must follow suit—it must *(climb / fall)*, as well.

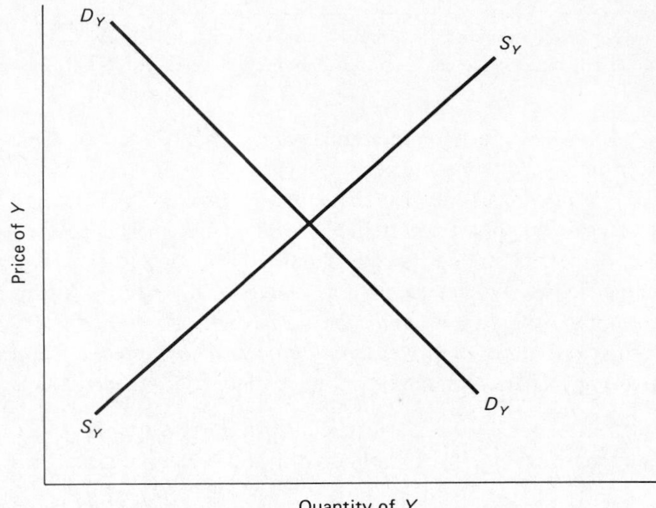

Figure 39-2

The result, if you add things up, is ambiguous. The claim that domestic-content legislation will help the employment picture in the United States is premature. Its employment effect will depend upon the elasticity of demand for automobiles (good Y), and it is by no means certain that it will be positive.

---

rise; fall; climb; climb; increase; new supply curve: above and to the left of S_YS_Y; climb; fall; demand curve; fall

QUIZ: Multiple Choice

1. One argument for tariffs contends that they should be imposed to help a domestic producer to compete when the level of foreign wages is significantly below the level of domestic wages. This argument:
(1) is conceded by most economists to be correct, although sometimes exaggerated in order to justify some level of tariff protection.
(2) is fallacious because there are almost no instances in which there is any real difference between the level of foreign and domestic wages.
(3) ignores the fact that differences in relative costs constitute the principal basis for international trade.
(4) may be correct with respect to money wages at home and abroad, but is not correct with respect to real wages.
(5) is not correctly described by any of the preceding.

2. Country A imposes a new tariff on country B's products. Country B is considering a retaliatory tariff on A's goods. On economic grounds, B should:
(1) reject the idea of a tariff increase.
(2) make the retaliatory tariff less than A's tariff.
(3) make the retaliatory tariff more than A's tariff.

(4) impose the retaliatory tariff only if B is in a situation of full employment.
(5) adjust the price of its currency relative to B's currency.

3. The policy of the mercantilists with respect to foreign trade held that:
(1) imports should exceed exports—i.e., the country should "get more than it gives"—in order to increase real income at home as much as possible.
(2) exports should exceed imports in order to bring in gold.
(3) since this trade represented commerce, it should be encouraged to the greatest possible degree—i.e., there should be free trade.
(4) exports should be kept in balance with imports, and at the lowest possible level of both.
(5) trade in agricultural products was more important than trade in industrial goods.

4. The principal reason high-wage American labor should not require tariff protection from lower-paid foreign labor is:
(1) no American labor would be thrown out of work even if there were no tariffs.
(2) the high per-worker-hour productivity of American labor in many industries is an offset to the lower cost of foreign labor.
(3) American consumers tend to buy American-made goods in preference to foreign-made goods.
(4) a high-wage American industry can be presumed to have a comparative advantage over foreign competitors.
(5) none of the preceding reasons.

5. The argument by workers in a protected industry in the United States that free trade would worsen the income position of American labor is:
(1) not valid even for workers in that industry after allowance is made for the improvement in real income afforded by cheaper imports.
(2) not valid even for workers in that industry after allowance is made for the employment effect of increased exports.
(3) valid for workers in that industry but probably not valid for American labor as a whole.
(4) valid for workers in that industry and probably valid for American labor as a whole.
(5) probably valid for workers in that industry but unquestionably invalid for American labor as a whole.

6. From a purely economic point of view, the best level at which to set a tariff (under static assumptions) is:
(1) the prohibitive point.
(2) the amount needed to bring the level of foreign costs up to the level of domestic costs.
(3) zero.
(4) a level sufficiently low so that it is not likely to invite retaliation by other countries.
(5) the level at which revenues from the tariff will be at a maximum.

7. One argument for tariff protection contends that a tariff would improve the terms of trade in dealing with other nations. This argument:
(1) is a refinement of the mercantilist argument that a nation's exports should exceeds its imports.
(2) may be valid if the tariff-imposing country is a relatively large one and the tariff is a relatively small one.
(3) is a refined version of the infant-industry arguments, hence has no validity.
(4) may be valid if the tariff-imposing country is unimportant in world trade for the commodity or commodities involved.
(5) may be valid if it is applied to all the country's imports, without or almost without exception.

8. It may be argued that a tariff should be imposed on a commodity if that commodity is considered essential to material well-being and/or if it is suspected that the foreign suppliers thereof might use their supply control for purposes of political blackmail. Most economists hold that:
(1) the tariff is justified if the commodity is deemed really essential.
(2) a subsidy would be preferable to a tariff if the commodity is deemed really essential.
(3) the best remedy for threats of political blackmail is to insist on all-around free trade.
(4) although the imposition of a tariff might be used as a threat, political moves should be met by political countermoves (even to the threat of war), not by economic moves.
(5) its domestic production should be nationalized if the commodity is deemed really essential.

9. If we reduce the flow of import goods by imposing heavy tariffs, our exports are likely to be affected in which of the following ways?
(1) They will likely be reduced when other countries retaliate by imposing tariffs against those exports (as is likely), but not otherwise.
(2) There is little reason to expect that they will be affected at all, since retaliatory tariffs have usually proved ineffective.
(3) They will likely be increased, since other countries will find it necessary to buy more from us to compensate for the higher cost of the goods they sell us.
(4) They will likely be increased if the tariff raises the level of employment and national product at home, but not otherwise.
(5) They are likely to be reduced in all or almost all circumstances.

10. A valid counter to the argument that a tariff results in increased money wages in the protected industry is that:
(1) workers in that industry will in all probability suffer a loss in real wages.
(2) workers in other industries will suffer a loss in real wages.
(3) the increase in money wages in the protected industry will cause unemployment.

(4) tariffs cannot increase money wages in any industry.
(5) any increase in real wages is likely to lead to inflation.

11. Arguments cited in favor of a protective tariff frequently note that tariffs *(a)* protect domestic industry against foreign competition and *(b)* bring revenue to the government. In response to these arguments, it may be said that:
(1) the tariff reduces rather than increases the sales of the domestic industry.
(2) if the industry in question enjoys an absolute advantage in production, it stands in no need of such a tariff.
(3) the emphasis on government revenue may lead to a tariff per unit much higher than the domestic industry needs for protection.
(4) an effective tariff will actually bring in no government revenue at all.
(5) none of these statements is correct.

12. A difference between a tariff on an imported good and a quota on the same good is that:
(1) a quota can never be made to yield revenue for the government, whereas a tariff can.
(2) a tariff can never be made to yield revenue for the government, whereas a quota can.
(3) a quota can be used to shut off all, or virtually all, the inflow of the imported good, whereas a tariff cannot.
(4) a tariff can be used to shut off all, or virtually all, the inflow of the imported good, whereas a quota cannot.
(5) a quantity-equivalent quota will generate the same revenue only if import rights are auctioned.

SUGGESTED ANSWERS TO QUESTIONS IN THE TEXT: Chapter 39

1. You are on your own. Think of the difference between static and dynamic arguments, long-run and short-run effects, and the likelihood of retaliation to your proposal. Also, state carefully your objective in supporting protection, and look at the pros and cons carefully. Are you talking about protection in a small country or a large country? Finally, how do you feel about "beggar-thy-neighbor" effects that (e.g.) effectively "export" things like unemployment?

2. The same as above, with particular circumstances more clearly defined. Investigate both (either) industry and (or) its foreign competition. Think of the role of technological change. Note, as well, that all Japanese TVs except SONYs are now being made in Korea or Singapore. What does that tell you about the Japanese understanding of comparative advantage?

3. The infant-industry argument, in its proper context, is one of potential comparative advantage: "If we protect this industry, we will soon have a comparative advantage in its product, which will improve our standard of living." They still exist in manufacturing industries around the world (e.g., electronics).

4. You must argue whether or not this is really protection. It seems to be, even though it can be applied only after injury has been felt; if no injury has been felt, why would anyone have suggested protection, anyway?

5. For trading partners, there must be at least two goods. There must, therefore, be two versions of text Figure 39-3 with two loss triangles each; $2 \times 2 = 4$.

6. **a.** This is an optimal-tariff argument, with the country having power over the terms of trade.
b. This is a short-run argument, and it might better be solved by domestic monetary or industrial policy. Maybe this domestic market should disappear?
c. This is a non-economic reason that illustrates the multiplicity of objectives in trade policy.
d. This one is awful, ignoring the notion of comparative advantage.

7. The terms-of-trade effect is shown by increases in national incomes for both America and Japan when high tariffs are imposed without retaliation. If each country responds to this with no worry about what the other country will do, they will both impose high tariffs and end up in the box on the lower-right part of the matrix—the worst position. Cooperation through free trade in the upper-left box is better than that, and the sum of the incomes of both countries is maximized there.

8. Special interests argue hard and are often heard; they can therefore benefit even as they harm society as a whole. This pressure may materialize in support of protection for textiles and sugar because we produce textiles and sugar; there are domestic interest groups for these products. This pressure will not be applied in bananas or coffee because domestic banana and coffee industries do not exist.

9. Everything is exactly the same, except that the revenue goes to the importers who buy or produce at the world price and sell at the higher domestic import price. When auctioned, these surpluses will be bid away and will flow to the government.

10. This is a national defense argument. With inelastic supply, though, the tariff is borne entirely by the supplier.

CHAPTER 40

EXCHANGE RATES AND THE INTERNATIONAL FINANCIAL SYSTEM

This concluding chapter focuses attention on the workings of the international financial system. Coverage begins with one essential fact of life: there exists, in the world today, a multiplicity of currencies that all function as money in one place or another. To conduct transactions on an international level is therefore to deal in foreign exchange markets. Flowing immediately from this fact of life is the necessity for the world community to prescribe some sort of standard of monetary exchange that sets down the rules of the game. Be it the gold standard and its fixed exchange-rate regime, the marketplace and its pure flexible exchange-rate regime, or the intermediate managed float mechanism and its goal to minimize inefficient exchange-rate variability, the rules of the game must be clearly understood by all the players. The first part of Chapter 40 reviews these issues.

The second and final part provides a description of the evolution of the international financial system from the Bretton Woods agreement of 1945 to the managed float regime of the 1980s. It sets the context for a critical review of the major issues of contemporary international finance. Significant here, of course, is the impact of recent wide swings in the value of the dollar on the United States and the rest of the world.

These are all complicated topics that draw on your understanding of much of what has gone before. Micro concepts are exercised as well as macro concepts. Having completed your work on this chapter, therefore, not only will you have accomplished the following objectives, but also you will have accomplished an integrated review of many of the fundamentals of economic analysis.

LEARNING OBJECTIVES

1. Define precisely what is meant when someone quotes an exchange rate, and describe the supply-and-demand framework through which exchange rates are determined.

2. Differentiate between devaluation and revaluation in a fixed exchange-rate system; do the same between depreciation and appreciation in a flexible exchange-rate system.

3. Contrast the fixed exchange-rate system of the gold standard with the pure floating of a flexible exchange-rate system. Describe the intermediate managed float that characterizes the contemporary international system.

4. Outline the worldwide effects of an overvaluation in the currency of a large economy like that of the United States and the various means by which an overvaluation might be corrected under a fixed-rate system (gold flows), a flexible system (market forces), and a managed system (official intervention). Explain why protectionism frequently accompanies overvaluation by noting that overvalued currencies make for relatively expensive exports.

5. Sketch a brief chronology of the evolution of the international financial system from the Bretton Woods fixed-rate system that was created following World War II through today's managed float system.

6. Describe how the wide swings in the value of the U.S. dollar (down in the 1970s, up in the early 1980s, then down in the mid-1980s) have been caused by and have been the causes of major worldwide economic events.

7. Differentiate between the forced discipline of a fixed exchange-rate system and the market-imposed discipline of a flexible exchange-rate system.

The chapter begins with a thorough description of how equilibrium exchange rates are determined; it is a direct application of supply-and-demand analysis in which the only tricky part is identifying the determinants of supply and demand.

1. a. The earliest exchanges in human history were barters—goods exchanging for goods. These were succeeded by what we ordinarily call "money transactions"—those everyday swaps in which goods were exchanged for money. When we investigate international transactions, though, we are discussing transactions in which one money exchanges for another money. In a sense, therefore, we are back to barter again. If we refer to the exchange market between dollars and pounds, we can speak equally well of the price of the pound sterling in *(dollars / pounds sterling)* and of the price of the dollar in *(dollars / pounds sterling)*.

b. Suppose, for example, that the rate of exchange between U.S. dollars and British pounds sterling is £1 = \$2. This means that (pick one or both):

(1) the price of the pound sterling is \$2.

(2) the price of the dollar is £0.50, or one-half a pound sterling.

c. As a further consequence of the money-for-money property of foreign exchange transactions, note that the participants can be identified as "demanders" or as "suppliers" only by identifying which of the two monies is being bought and sold. If you want to buy pounds sterling, you think of yourself as a demander of pounds, but it would be equally correct to describe yourself as a *(supplier of pounds / demander of dollars / supplier of dollars)*.

---

a. dollars; pounds sterling **b.** **(1)** and **(2)** **c.** supplier of dollars

Left to its own devices, a foreign exchange rate will move up and down under the pressure of changes in supply and demand. The exchange rate is a price; it is subject to the same influences as any other price. However, governments rarely leave the foreign prices of their own currencies entirely free to *float*. To a greater or lesser degree, they try to manage foreign exchange rates. Any nation heavily engaged in exporting and importing finds the price which its currency can command on the foreign exchange markets to be a matter of the highest importance.

Until 1971, most governments tried to keep the prices of their own currencies in foreign monies fixed, or very nearly so. Fixed rates were altered only under the strongest pressure for change. The great advantage of a fixed exchange rate was that everyone knew exactly what a foreign purchase would cost and what a foreign sale would bring in domestic money. Occasional calls for a return to a fixed-rate system (commonly heard among bankers and business firms especially) are further bolstered by long memories of the days when nations relied on a particular technique for maintaining fixed rates: **the gold standard**. A country went on the gold standard by declaring that gold was the basis or standard for its currency unit. Thus the United States might have said that the gold "content" of its dollar was 1/100 of an ounce, but it had to back this statement by a declared willingness to buy or to sell gold freely at \$100 per ounce.

2. Taking the viewpoint of the United States for illustrative purposes, most international transactions fall into two categories: (*a*) export and exportlike items whose effect is to bring foreign money to the United States and (*b*) imports and importlike items whose effect is to send American money abroad. If the total money volume in category (*a*) exceeds that in (*b*), then under a fixed exchange-rate system, U.S. reserves tend to increase. Under a floating-rate system, the same excess of (*a*) over (*b*) tends to drive up the U.S. dollar price, expressed in any foreign money.

Assume a floating-rate system. For each of the following, indicate whether its effect would be to increase (I) or to decrease (D) the dollar's price in foreign-currency terms. Use the supply-demand framework illustrated in Figure 40-1.

a. American demand for imports increases. . . . . . *(I / D)*

b. Foreign demand for U.S. goods decreases. . . . . . *(I / D)*

c. A recession in the United States results in falling GNP, employment, and imports. . . . . *(I / D)*

d. The rate of inflation in foreign countries is more rapid than that in the United States. . . . . *(I / D)*

e. Americans decide to invest less abroad—i.e., their demand for foreign assets decreases. . . . . *(I / D)*

f. Foreign firms increase their dividend payments, and some of the shareholders are Americans. . . . . *(I / D)*

g. Foreigners decide to hold fewer U.S. dollars. . . . *(I / D)*

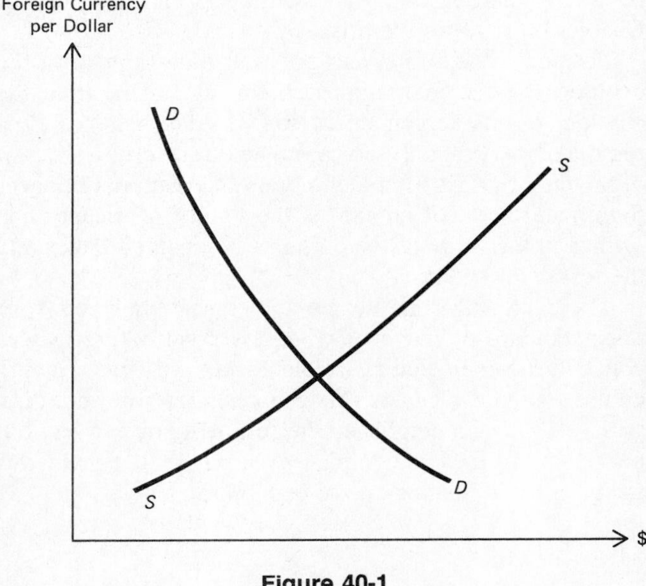

Figure 40-1

---

a. D (increases supply of dollars) **b.** D (reduces demand for dollars) **c.** I (reduces supply of dollars) **d.** I (increases demand for dollars) **e.** I (reduces supply of dollars) **f.** I (increases demand for dollars) **g.** D (increases supply of dollars or reduces demand)

3. Below is a demand schedule for francs, at various dollars-and-cents prices. Convert it into a supply schedule for dollars, at various franc prices. [NOTE: Although this is not a simple problem, it is an interesting one. A "straight-line" demand schedule results in a supply schedule of quite unexpected shape. Convert in this way: if the price of 1 franc is 90 cents, then 1 franc = 90 cents, and so $1 = 100/0.90 francs (i.e., the price of $1 is about 1.1 francs). The schedule below says that when the price of the franc is 90 cents, 100 francs will be demanded; i.e., $90 will be supplied to buy them. In sum, when the dollars price is 1.1 francs, $90 will be supplied. Work out other points on the supply schedule similarly.] Plot both curves in Figure 40-2.

P of Franc (in $)	*Q* of Francs Demanded	*P* of Dollar (in Francs)	*Q* of Dollars Supplied
$1.00	0	______	______
0.90	100	______	______
0.80	200	______	______
0.70	300	______	______
0.60	400	______	______
0.50	500	______	______
0.40	600	______	______
0.30	700	______	______
0.20	800	______	______
0.10	900	______	______

(fr. 1.00, 0), (fr. 1.11, 90), (fr. 1.25, 160), (fr. 1.43, 210), (fr. 1.67, 240), (fr. 2.00, 250), (fr. 2.50, 240), (fr. 3.33, 210), (fr. 5.00, 160), (fr. 10.00, 90)

4. The exchange rate between U.S. dollars and French francs is a floating one. What effect, if any, is each of the following events likely to have on the price of the franc in dollars? Put (U) in the space if the effect should be to push the price of the franc (in dollars) up; (D) if down; (N) if there is no reason why the price of the franc should be affected.

a. French corporations have a large interest payment to make, in dollars, to American bondholders. . . . . (______)

b. French corporations have a large interest payment to make, in francs, to American bondholders. . . . . (______)

c. France emerges from a recession, and with this increase in incomes, the French people want to buy more American merchandise. . . . . (______)

d. American residents decide to buy French bonds. (______)

e. The French government ships gold to the United States. . . . . (______)

f. French corporations sell bonds to Americans, borrowing in dollars and in New York because the interest rate is lower there. The proceeds of the bond issue are to be spent on French labor and materials. . . . . (______)

g. Foreign exchange speculators decide that the price of the dollar in francs is going to fall. . . . . (______)

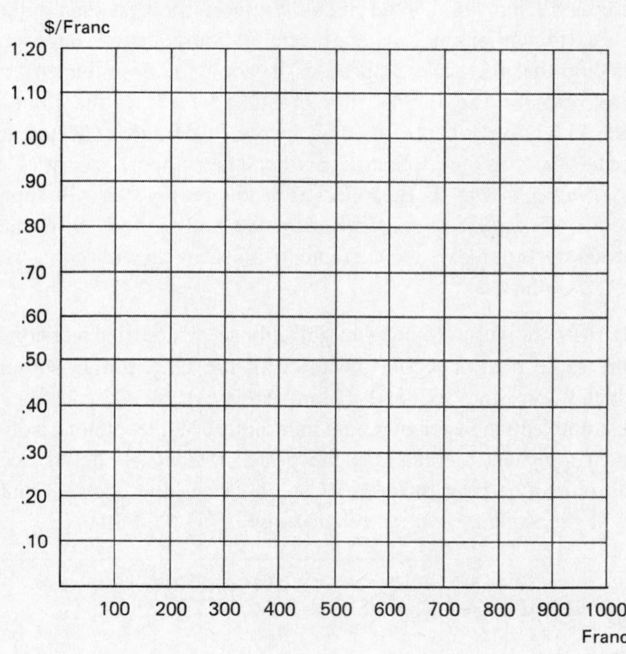

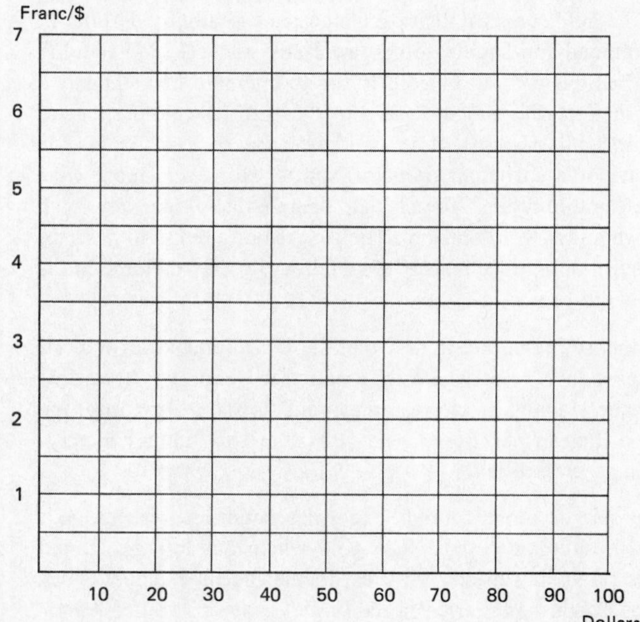

Figure 40-2

h. The taste of American gourmets for French wine is replaced by a taste for California wine. . . . . (______)

i. The French government decides that American movies are immoral and refuses to admit them into France. . . (______)

j. An American citizen sends a package of merchandise to her French relatives as a gift. . . . . (______)

k. An American citizen sends a remittance of dollars to his French relatives as a gift. . . . . (______)

l. A French bank, in possession of a dollar bank account, decides to convert these dollars into gold. . . . . . (______)

m. A French bank, in possession of a dollar bank account, decides to convert these dollars into francs. . . . . (______)

---

a. D **b.** D **c.** D **d.** U **e.** N **f.** U **g.** U **h.** D **i.** U **j.** N **k.** U **l.** N **m.** U

5. Suppose that a widespread taste for Scotch whiskey develops in the United States. This means an increase in demand for *(dollars / pounds sterling)*. If the United States were on the gold standard, and if this demand increase were sufficiently large, then there would be a flow of gold *(away from / toward)* the United States. If this demand increase persisted without countering effect for a long time, the United States might be drained of its entire stock of *(gold / Scotch whiskey)*.

---

pounds sterling; away from; gold

6. The gold standard kept exchange rates steady by definition, but demand-and-supply forces were still at work. Why didn't some nations run out of gold trying to maintain that standard?

A nation did, indeed, have to "go off" the gold standard if it lost all or most of its gold because of a major rise in imports or a sufficient drop in exports. However, there were some "equilibrating" forces that operated to brake any such overwhelming gold outflow. The first major attempt to describe an equilibrating mechanism was laid out by David Hume in the eighteenth century.

a. Suppose, as in question 5, that the U.S. demand for imports increases to a point where imports exceed exports. According to Hume's analysis, the resulting gold flow *(out of / into)* the United States *(increases / decreases)* the U.S. money supply, causing the price level to *(rise / fall)*.

b. In one or more foreign exporting countries, the *(same / reverse)* situation occurs. The gold which has left the United States flows into these countries, increasing their money stock and so causing their prices to be *(higher / lower)*. Since American prices have gone down while foreign prices have gone up, *(more / fewer)* American goods will be bought by foreigners, while Americans will tend to buy *(more / fewer)* foreign goods. That is, in America, exports will *(rise / fall)*, imports will *(rise / fall)*, and the rise in the U.S. imports which began the process is offset.

---

a. out of; decreases; fall **b.** reverse; higher; more; fewer; rise; fall

In rough outline, for sufficiently large movements, Hume's analysis may have some validity. But today there is almost no link between a nation's total gold stock and its total money supply. Moreover, Hume's analysis relies heavily on the quantity theory of money and its assumption of full employment. Both of these caveats leave the Hume analysis wanting as a description of modern-day responses to current account imbalance.

7. Although the old international gold standard and Bretton Woods system are both gone today, their influence persists, particularly in two important respects. First, nations still consider their gold stocks as reserves for settling international balances. (But now they tend to regard gold as an "emergency" reserve; they do not part with gold unless events force them to do so. Here, the United States was one of the last to yield. Until 1971, America stood ready to give gold to any nation which had accumulated dollars and wanted them swapped for gold; today, it will no longer do so.)

Second, the desire for relative stability in exchange rates persists. The gold standard is not the only possible mechanism to this end. You can hold the price of your currency steady by simply maintaining a sufficiently large inventory of foreign monies.

a. Canada, for example, relies heavily on exports to, and imports from, the United States. Suppose the Canadian authorities (to whom the exchange rate is consequently important) decide that for trading purposes it would be desirable to keep the price of the U.S. dollar at \$(Can.)1.15. If the price of the U.S. dollar begins to drift below this figure, Canada will enter the foreign exchange market and support the price by *(selling / buying)* U.S. dollars. For this purpose, it will supply (sell) *(Canadian / American)* dollars. And if the U.S. dollar's price starts to move above \$(Can.)1.15, Canada will *(buy / sell)* U.S. dollars.

b. Alternatively, Canada might choose a modified version of the same plan, keeping the price of the U.S. dollar within a "band" of, say, \$(Can.)1.12 and \$(Can.)1.18. Of course, she cannot keep the exchange rate indefinitely at a level not justified by supply and demand. If the price of the U.S. dollar keeps chronically trying to push \$(Can.)1.18, in due course Canada will *(accumulate too many / run out of)* U.S. dollars.

---

a. buying; Canadian; sell **b.** run out of (Use supply-and-demand geometry to see that these answers are correct.)

8. a. The word **devaluation** goes back to the gold-standard days in which the currency unit allegedly had a "gold content," and gold consequently had an "official price" per ounce. Devaluation meant a government-decreed *(reduction / increase)* in that gold content—i.e., *(a reduction / an increase)* in the official price. President Roosevelt's 1933 declaration that the dollar's gold content would be reduced from 1/21 to 1/35 of an ounce would *(be / not be)* an instance of devaluation. With the dissolution of the gold standard, "devaluations" no longer take place. The U.S. government may still sell gold from time to time, but there is nothing "official" about the price it obtains.

b. Depreciation (in the foreign exchange markets) means a change in the price of a currency relative to other monies. It occurs when the price of the currency falls. Suppose that the price of the Canadian dollar is 90 U.S. cents. If this price were to drop to 85 U.S. cents, then the Canadian dollar would be worth, in U.S. funds, *(more / less)*; this would be an instance of depreciation. If the price were to rise from 90 to 95 U.S. cents, this would be *(depreciation / appreciation)* of the Canadian dollar.

c. Any depreciation of a foreign currency (relative to the U.S. dollar) makes that foreign country's goods appear *(cheaper / dearer)* to Americans. To residents in that other country, in terms of their own currency, American goods appear *(cheaper / dearer)*. When a country's currency is depreciated, therefore, this move tends to *(increase / decrease)* the volume of its exports and to *(increase / decrease)* the volume of its imports.

---

a. reduction; an increase; be **b.** less; appreciation **c.** cheaper; dearer; increase; decrease

9. At the close of World War II, the Western nations created two new international agencies: the International Monetary Fund (IMF) and the World Bank.

The intended goal behind the IMF's formation was this: there were to be, so far as possible, stable exchange rates. But no nation would have to push itself deliberately into recession or depression just to maintain a steady international value for its currency. Each participating nation deposited with the IMF a supply of its own currency (and, in some cases, gold). These deposits established a "lending pool," from which any nation could borrow if temporarily losing reserves as a consequence of maintaining a fixed rate. It was of course understood that persisting reserve losses indicated some form of "fundamental disequilibrium" which could not be sustained by continual borrowing. A nation could devalue its currency value by up to 10 percent if it wished. Further devaluation required "consultation with the fund"—in effect, international approval.

Over the course of time, it became evident that the IMF's "lending pool" of national currencies—dollars, pounds sterling, francs, etc.—was *(insufficient / excessive)* and in need of *(reduction / supplement)*. A new "international money"—although one to be used only in settlements between governments or central banks—was created. Its name was ________ ________________________________.

The prime movers behind this new money were those who felt that gold should be eliminated (or its status reduced, at least) as an international reserve. Thus an alternative and more colloquial name for these SDRs was "____________________." These SDRs are created just as commercial banks create money through their lending activity. The maximum amount of their creation each year is settled by vote of IMF members. The extent to which any nation can draw SDRs is governed by its quota participation in the IMF.

---

insufficient; supplement; Special Drawing Rights; paper gold

10. a. The World Bank's task, in brief, is to channel money from the richer nations to less developed ones. In slightly more detail, the bank's function is to *(make short-term loans / make long-term loans / provide foreign exchange for balance-of-payments shortages)* to the world's poorer countries. It provides funds for a less developed nation *(even if that nation can / only if that nation cannot)* borrow privately at a reasonable interest rate.

The World Bank can make loans (pick one):

(1) only from its capital, subscribed by member nations.

(2) from its capital, or by floating bond issues with principal and interest payments guaranteed by member nations.

b. In its early years, the bank was rather *(liberal / conservative)* in its loan policies, but when Robert McNamara became its president (in 1968), it *(expanded / curtailed)* the scope of its activity. McNamara's plan for the World Bank in the 1980s was to focus especially upon the *(more rapidly developing / poorest)* nations.

---

a. make long-term loans; only if that nation cannot; **(2)** **b.** conservative; expanded; poorest

11. One of the most significant problems of international finance in the early 1980s was the overvalued U.S. dollar, estimated by some to have been *(10 / 25 / 50)* percent overvalued from 1981 into 1984. The scenario that produced this overvaluation begins with the *(tight / loose)* monetary policy and *(stimulative / contractionary)* fiscal policy under the Reagan administration that drove real interest rates in the United States *(up / down)*. Foreign investment therefore flowed *(into / out of)* the United States, *(increasing / decreasing)* the demand for dollars and thus causing the dollar to *(appreciate / depreciate)* in money markets all around the world. United States exports thus became *(more / less)* expensive while foreign imports into the United States become *(more / less)* costly. Net exports *(expanded / contracted)* by nearly *($50 billion / $140 billion / $250 billion)*, as a result, and created an enormous *(deficit / surplus)* in the current account. This discrepancy was, though, almost canceled by a *(deficit / surplus)* in the capital account, so the overvaluation persisted and drove interest rates abroad *(up / down)*. The result was a tendency for foreign economies to move into *(recession / boom)* and for *(depressed / overextended)* export- and import-competing industries in the United States to call for *(free trade / protection and subsidy)*.

Under fixed exchange rates, the only way to relieve overvaluation is to endure a *(recession / boom)* to generate *(higher / lower)* domestic prices. Under flexible exchange rates, the correction is supposed to be automatic, but it can be retarded by capital account flows. Under a managed float of the type now in place, the government of the United States can help things along by *(selling / buying)* dollars in the world marketplace. The Reagan administration *(pursued this policy vigorously / claimed that the dollar was not overvalued and undertook little official intervention)*. The result was America's conversion into the worlds largest *(creditor / debtor)* nation and a plunge in the value of the dollar after 1985.

50; tight; stimulative; up; into; increasing; appreciate; more; less; contracted; $140 billion; deficit; surplus; up; recession; depressed; protection and subsidy; recession; lower; selling; claimed that the dollar was not overvalued and undertook little official intervention; debtor

QUIZ: Multiple Choice

1. If we say that a country's currency has been devalued, we mean that:
(1) it has gone off the gold standard.
(2) the domestic purchasing power of its currency unit has fallen.
(3) its government has increased the price it will pay for gold.
(4) it is experiencing an unfavorable balance of trade.
(5) the prices of at least some foreign currencies, as expressed in that country's domestic currency, have fallen.

2. To be fully on the gold standard, the government of a country must:
(1) set a fixed price at which it is prepared to buy or sell gold in any quantity without restriction.
(2) be prepared to buy or sell gold at any time without restriction, but at a price which it is free to vary from day to day as it chooses, provided the same price (or almost the same price) applies to both purchases and sales.
(3) be prepared to buy gold in any quantity without restriction at a fixed price, but not necessarily to sell it.
(4) be prepared to sell gold in any quantity without restriction, but not necessarily to buy it.
(5) maintain a fixed gold content in its money unit, but not necessarily be prepared to buy or sell gold at any fixed price or without restriction.

3. In a stable exchange-rate situation, if the price of the French franc is 25 U.S. cents and the price of the U.S. dollar is 600 Italian lire, then the price of the French franc in Italian lire must be:
(1) 90 lire.
(2) 150 lire.
(3) 200 lire.
(4) 300 lire.
(5) 600 lire.

4. The exports of country A to country B increase substantially. Both A and B operate on the gold standard. According to David Hume's gold-flow mechanism:
(1) A's domestic price level will fall; B's domestic price level may or may not change.
(2) A's price level may or may not change, but B's will fall.
(3) A's price level will rise, B's will fall.
(4) A's price level will fall; B's will rise.
(5) none of the above will happen.

5. If the exchange rate between Swiss francs and U.S. dollars changes from Sfr. 4 to the dollar to Sfr. 3 to the dollar, the franc's price has:
(1) risen from 25 cents to 33 cents, and the dollar has appreciated relative to the franc.
(2) fallen from 33 to 25 cents, and the dollar has depreciated relative to the franc.
(3) risen from 25 to 33 cents, and the dollar has been devalued relative to the franc.
(4) risen from 25 to 33 cents, and the dollar has depreciated relative to the franc.
(5) fallen from 33 to 25 cents, and the dollar has appreciated relative to the franc.

6. If American corporations make large dividend payments (in dollars) to foreigners:
(1) the effect on the price of the U.S. dollar, if any, will be to depreciate it.
(2) the effect on the price of the U.S. dollar, if any, will be to appreciate it.
(3) gold will tend to flow into the United States to compensate for the U.S. money going abroad.
(4) imports into the United States will tend to increase to compensate for the U.S. money going abroad.
(5) none of the above will be true.

7. If the exchange rate between Canadian and U.S. dollars is a floating one, and if the demand for Canadian dollars increases, then:
(1) the supply of Canadian dollars has decreased or will decrease.
(2) the price of the Canadian dollar in U.S. currency will fall.
(3) the supply of U.S. dollars has decreased.
(4) the price of the U.S. dollar in Canadian currency will fall.
(5) the U.S. dollar has been devalued.

8. A substantial fall in the price of the dollar in foreign currencies (e.g., the price of the dollar in francs) could be expected to affect physical quantities of exports from the United States and imports into the United States in which of the following ways?

(1) It would increase both exports and imports.
(2) It would increase exports, decrease imports.
(3) It would decrease both exports and imports.
(4) It would decrease exports, increase imports.
(5) It would have no perceptible effect on either imports or exports.

9. If a country depreciates the foreign exchange value of its currency, the results will typically be that:
(1) its imports will seem cheaper (from the viewpoint of its own citizens), and its exports will seem more expensive (from the viewpoint of foreigners.)
(2) its imports will seem more expensive (from the viewpoint of its own citizens), and its exports will seem cheaper (from the viewpoint of foreigners.)
(3) both its imports and its exports will seem cheaper (from the viewpoint of both its own citizens and foreigners.)
(4) both its imports and its exports will seem more expensive (from the viewpoint of both its own citizens and foreigners.)
(5) none of the above, since there is no reason why the prices of either imports or exports should be affected.

10. If GNP falls in the United States, and exchange rates are floating:
(1) imports will tend to decrease and the price of the U.S. dollar to increase.
(2) imports will tend to decrease and the price of the U.S. dollar to decrease.
(3) imports will tend to increase and the price of the U.S. dollar to increase.
(4) imports will tend to increase and the price of the U.S. dollar to decrease.
(5) none of the preceding statements will be true.

11. The principal task assigned to the International Monetary Fund at the time of its organization was to:
(1) serve as a partial substitute for the gold standard in maintaining stable exchange rates.
(2) try to maintain a high level of employment within member countries, so as to avoid any danger of competitive depreciation policies in the foreign exchange markets.
(3) make loans to private companies in any country where the funds could not otherwise be borrowed at any reasonable interest rate.
(4) facilitate the development of free trade "regions" similar to the European Common Market.
(5) coordinate the views of the larger and more developed nations concerning exchange-rate and trade problems.

12. It could also be said that the principal task assigned to the International Monetary Fund was to:
(1) act as the world's banker in matters of both short-term and long-term credit.
(2) make direct long-term loans to less developed nations when necessary, so as to assist in their economic development.
(3) control international credit sufficiently to enable member nations to maintain their price levels at reasonably non-inflationary levels.
(4) help bridge short-run disequilibrium in any member nation's balance of payments.
(5) work toward the gradual reduction of tariffs and elimination of protectionist policies among nations.

13. Which alternative in question 12 would be correct had that question referred to the World Bank, not to the International Monetary Fund?
(1).
(2).
(3).
(4).
(5).

14. A disturbance in its balance of payments may cause any nation to lose gold or foreign exchange reserves. This danger of loss is most acute whenever that nation:
(1) increases its exports.
(2) seeks to maintain a flexible exchange rate.
(3) seeks to maintain a fixed exchange rate.
(4) increases its borrowing from other nations.
(5) experiences a drop in GNP—i.e., whenever any recession or depression occurs.

15. A "managed float" means:
(1) an increase in the protectionist policies by some device other than a tariff increase.
(2) refusal by a nation to allow its currency to appreciate even though its reserves are large and increasing.
(3) a beggar-my-neighbor policy.
(4) introduction of a split exchange rate—a fixed rate for some transactions, a floating rate for others.
(5) periodic intervention by a central bank to check excessive fluctuation in an otherwise-floating exchange rate.

SUGGESTED ANSWERS TO QUESTIONS IN THE TEXT: Chapter 40

1. These are all definitions. Their significance is derived from our experience with them.

2. $1 = 0.54 pounds = 5.72 francs = 126.74 yen = 740.74 won = 1.69 marks.

3. Under a fixed system, all of them need fixed conversion rates. Under a floating system, they are required as needed to stabilize exchange rates given their degree of acceptability. A commodity like gold, for which supply and demand beyond financial markets determines a price and thus a conversion rate, can become less accepted.

4. The demand for pounds comes from Americans who are supplying dollars at a rate equal to the (dollar-per-pound) exchange rate times the quantity of pounds demanded at that rate. The supply of pounds comes from Britons who are demanding dollars at a rate equal to the exchange rate times the quantity of pounds supplied. Draw a graph with equilibrium at £/$ = 0.67.

5. It is a reflection of the need to protect against the disorder of excessive volatility. Volatility disrupts all sorts of markets, causes people to put too much effort into hedging, and may reduce the efficiency of international trade by inserting a "risk-premium" sort of transactions cost.

6. A crawling peg allows some flexibility, but puts a limit on volatility.

7. **a.** Increases the yen/$ exchange rate by intervening above the equilibrium. Why get 150 to the dollar when the government will give you 160?
b. Supply of dollars falls, and the yen/$ exchange rate climbs.
c. The demand for yen climbs, and so does the yen/$ exchange rate.
d. The supply curve of yen shifts out, so the yen/$ exchange rate falls.

8. Intervention by selling marks when the exchange rate tries to push about 1.60 marks per dollar and by buying when the exchange rate tries to fall below $1.50.

9. Move the supply curves around.

10. An increase in the sale of oil should increase the demand for currency and thus push up the exchange rate. In anticipation of this, speculators may purchase the currency early, increasing its price early, and making other exports prematurely expensive.

11. Increases in the value of the dollar make exports more expensive. So do higher wage costs and reduced productivity. If prices = (1 + markup) × (wage/productivity index), the relative inflation rate must have been smaller in the United States. It was.

12. Parts **a**, **b**, **d**, and **e** are straightforward. Relative prices move according to monetary theory under fixed rates; they move with the exchange rate otherwise.

13. All things equal, trade should bring prices to equivalent positions throughout the world; the exchange rate is the means to that end. If prices are higher for one country than they should be, then the demand for its exports will fall, the demand for its currency will fall, and its currency will depreciate. By the way, congratulations for reaching the end of the book.

ANSWERS TO QUIZ QUESTIONS: Multiple Choice

Chapter 2

1. (4) Definition.
2. (4) These questions are independent of the type of economic system employed.
3. (4) If there is no substitution possible between commodities, then there is no choice to exercise.
4. (3) The definition applies to all circumstances.
5. (2) The *PPF* is the "choice set" of the *what* decision.
6. (1) Refer to #5.
7. (5) Definition.
8. (4) Point *D* shows the largest value against the food axis.
9. (2) Shift to line 1 shows potential for more clothing but not more food.
10. (5) Shift to line 2 shows potential for more food but not more clothing.
11. (3) Shift to line 3 shows potential for more of both food and clothing.
12. (1) Only *A* shows smaller increments of wheat as labor employment climbs.
13. (3) Definition.
14. (2) Not on *PPF* means production of all goods can increase simultaneously; resources must be being wasted.
15. (1) Connecting the points is concave only for $X = 280$ and $Y = 270$.
16. (3) You net $1750 at home and $50 in France; the difference is opportunity cost.

Chapter 3

1. (1) Definition.
2. (5) Developing countries are typically too strapped to be able to forgo present consumption.
3. (2) The least-cost incentive answers *how*; specialization may be one way of cutting costs.
4. (3) The present consumption–future consumption choice.
5. (5) None of the listed factors is "productive."
6. (3) A problem and an opportunity.
7. (2) Definition.
8. (2) Definition applied to deferred consumption.
9. (5) Capital "deepening" means growth in the mix of production opportunities.
10. (1) Definition.
11. (3) Definition.
12. (2) Definition.
13. (5) Capital is deferred consumption.
14. (5) This suggests a role for government
15. (1) Directly, but usually affects "all of the above."

Chapter 4

1. (4) Definition.
2. (4) Definition.
3. (1) This is the income effect.
4. (1) Only panel (a) shows any quantity being associated with one given price.
5. (2) Only panel (b) specifies a given quantity for any price.
6. (1) The store is committed to a constant price per unit.
7. (5) Demand curves assume fixed incomes; changing incomes mean at least two curves.
8. (4) Higher prices imply higher quantities supplied; only panel (d) shows the required positive slope.
9. (3) Only panel (c) shows the requisite negative slope.
10. (5) Only (3) identifies a change that might cause a shift, but it goes in the wrong direction.
11. (2) Only (2) does not identify a change in an "other things being equal" type of variable for demand.
12. (5) The price of X must change if you are tracing out a demand curve for X.
13. (2) Higher costs of production contract supply.
14. (5) It is explained by an upward shift in demand.
15. (2) Supply contraction means a leftward shift in demand.
16. (3) Higher demand for pork means a rightward shift in demand.
17. (1) Excess supply puts downward pressure on price; one result is a reduction in the quantity supplied.
18. (3) Definition.

Chapter 5

1. (5) Taken together, the answers are a start to a definition.

2. (3) Variation in GNP has diminished significantly since 1946, so the mandated intervention has had some success.
3. (4) The first two influence aggregate demand; the last is targeted directly at price volatility.
4. (5) Higher exports translate into higher aggregate demand, so there is a potential effect on employment, price stability, and the GNP gap. The trade balance is affected directly by definition.
5. (1) Pushing unemployment too low can overheat an economy and cause inflation. All the others can be seen to be compatible either by accounting [e.g., (2)—low unemployment means high income, the potential for high investment, and high growth] or by manipulating the *AD* and *AS* curves [e.g., (5)—rapid growth in *AD* matching growth in potential GNP maintains constant prices].
6. (3) Higher output prices inspire increased production until input prices have enough time to react.
7. (2) Only prices adjust to changes in *AD* in the long run.
8. (4) Definition—they are determined by an economy.
9. (3) Potential GNP is determined by the technological link between the sum of resources available and the output.
10. (1) *AD* shifting right, moving equilibrium up along *AS*.
11. (2) Oil-price increases shift the *AS* curve up; they can be accommodated by increases in *AD* so that the intersection of the new curves occurs above the old output, indicating higher prices.
12. (4) Higher interest rates caused investment and consumption to fall—two components of *AD*.

Chapter 6

1. (3) Definition.
2. (4) Housing services are part of the sum of goods and services produced in a year.
3. (5) Subtract the cost of materials, because they are part of the value added elsewhere.
4. (4) Depreciation can make net investment negative, but not gross investment. The only subtraction possible in the computation of gross investment is a reduction in inventories.
5. (3) The value added in producing iron is net of the value of the ore input.
6. (3) The computation of profits includes deductions for indirect taxes paid in the price of inputs and bond interest.
7. (2) Transfer payments represent money given to people in exchange for nothing that contributes to GNP.
8. (1) Depreciation is already deducted in NNP. The other items are part of the translation from national income to the amount of income subject to the discretion of individuals.
9. (1) GNP must capture all goods and services, regardless of who purchased them.
10. (4) Definition.
11. (1) The answer solves $(120/100)X = 360$ for X; $X = 300$.
12. (5) Adding government expenditures and total wages would be to intermingle the product-flow approach and the earnings-cost approach to national-income accounting.

Chapter 7

1. (4) Definition.
2. (5) Investment depends upon expectations and real interest rates.
3. (1) $DI = C + S$, so $MPC + MPS = 1$.
4. (2) Definition.
5. (1) Definition.
6. (5) Definition.
7. (2) Definition.
8. (3) Definition.
9. (4) Definition.
10. (2) Consumption climbing for any level of *DI* means that the entire function shifts up.
11. (1) Figure 7-6 shows a straight-line consumption function, so the slope (i.e., *MPC*) is constant; Figure 7-7 shows a declining slope, so *MPC* falls as *DI* climbs.
12. (3) $S = DI - C$; so in terms of lengths, $S = OK - KM = PM$.
13. (5) $S = DI - C$, again and still.
14. (2) Move along *CC*.
15. (4) Definition.
16. (4) *MPC* falls with income.
17. (1) $MPC =$ slope $= (\$6000 - \$2000)/(\$6000 - \$0) = 2/3$.
18. (2) Both are part of aggregate demand. Investment depends on expectations and real interest rates; consumption, on disposable income.

Chapter 8

1. (5) Excessively sticky wages and prices imply a horizontal aggregate supply curve below potential GNP, at least in the short run.
2. (5) Immediate wage and price response to disequilibrium means that GNP is determined by potential GNP.
3. (5) Each means either that wages are inflexible in the short run or that unemployment is not personally expensive.
4. (2) The increase in investment would signal an increase in aggregate demand, and so an increase in GNP; higher GNP would also mean higher consumption.
5. (4) At any income, with *C* larger, $S =$ GNP $- C$ must be smaller.
6. (5) The formula for the multiplier is $1/(1 - MPC)$; it equals $1/0.2 = 5$ in this case.
7. (5) GNP will eventually fall by an amount equal to the multiplier times the original decline in *I*.
8. (1) Changes in *C* caused by changes in GNP are movements along an existing consumption function; changes for reasons other than changes in GNP shift the entire function and have their own multiplier effects. (This is a hard question. Use some graph paper to see that this answer is correct.)
9. (3) Aggregate demand falling brings GNP down, as well, by the multiplier effect; smaller GNP means smaller saving.
10. (5) It shows $C =$ GNP, which characterizes equilibrium only if the other components of aggregate demand are zero.

11. (1) $S > I$ occurs to the right of equilibrium.
12. (5) $(C + I) >$ GNP to the left of equilibrium.
13. (4) Definition.
14. (2) Move down the consumption function and the savings schedule.
15. (4) With $G = X = 0$, equilibrium is characterized simply by GNP $= C + I$.
16. (2) Even without G and X (or assuming that they are equal to zero), aggregate demand $= (C + I) >$ GNP. The economy is out of equilibrium, and its level of economic activity is too high; GNP will fall.
17. (4) The multiplier is $1/0.3 = 3.33$; equilibrium GNP should climb by $(10/3) \times \$6$ billion $= \$20$ billion.
18. (4) To make $C = \$170$ conform with GNP $= \$200$ *and* $MPC = 0.75$, the consumption function must be $C = 20 + 0.75$ GNP. Saving must therefore be given by $S = -20 + 0.25$ GNP; saving will therefore equal investment at \$20 when GNP $= \$160$. Alternatively, note that $C + I$ is \$10 short when GNP $= \$200$. To move from full employment to equilibrium, therefore, would require a reduction in investment of \$10, from \$30 to the reported \$20. With $MPC = 0.75$, the multiplier is 4, and GNP would fall \$40 below the \$200; i.e., it would equal \$160. As soon as you see the multiplier of 4, though, you know that the answer is less than \$190.
19. (2) See answer 18.
20. (3) Otherwise, prices might change and diminish the multiplier.

Chapter 9

1. (5) Of the years cited in the answers, actual GNP exceeded potential GNP in 1961 and 1982; potential exceeded actual in 1965, 1968, and 1973.
2. (5) Definition.
3. (3) Movement up along the positive slope of the *AS* curve.
4. (2) The consumption function shifts down.
5. (4) The spending multiplier is $1/0.25 = 4$.
6. (3) The tax multiplier is $0.75/0.25 = 3$.
7. (5) The spending multiplier is now $1/(0.25 + 0.25) = 2$.
8. (5) Depreciation would cause exports (x) to *fall* by \$2 billion; the multiplier is still 2.
9. (5) The paradox of thrift.
10. (1) Given the classical model with its vertical aggregate supply curve, no real variables change.
11. (5) Definition.
12. (5) Total saving must equal investment.
13. (1) Tax changes have smaller effects on GNP than spending changes.
14. (2) The multiplier is $1/0.4 = 2.5$.
15. (4) The tax multiplier is equal to the *PMC* multiplied by the spending multiplier, and $MPC < 1$.
16. (3) Planned inventories fall to the left of equilibrium; real values increase if actual GNP is less than potential GNP.
17. (5) The paradox applies unless the aggregate supply curve is vertical.
18. (3) More saving leaves GNP unaffected, but perhaps produces lower interest rates.
19. (1) For these and other reasons.

Chapter 10

1. (4) Declined from 2.9 percent per year to 2.4 percent per year.
2. (3) The business cycle is driven by changes in *AD*; thus, anything that changes *AD* can contribute to the cycle.
3. (2) Dividing 9 percent by 2 results in a change in unemployment of 4.5 percentage points.
4. (5) The supply-side approach was built on three pillars: retreat from Keynesian demand management, supply-side incentives, and large tax cuts.
5. (5) Recession means that unemployment climbs, so compensation expenditures increase.
6. (2) The recession of 1982–1983 was the deepest since the Great Depression.
7. (5) Vietnam War expenditures not financed by taxes caused inflationary boom.
8. (5) Definition.
9. (4) Employment stability in Europe is maintained to some degree by a buffer of imported (temporary immigrant) labor.
10. (2) Thus the focus of the acceleration principle.
11. (4) Definition.
12. (1) The Keynesian interaction.
13. (2) Gross investment net of depreciation adds to the capital stock.
14. (3) Definition.
15. (3) Thus the volatility of investment.

Chapter 11

1. (5) All the answers make sense even without a knowledge of history.
2. (2) Stores of value should not fluctuate in value.
3. (1) Definition.
4. (3) Definition.
5. (5) And many others, these days.
6. (1) Definition.
7. (5) Definition; you can only count money once in the summing of M_1.
8. (1) Definition; M_1 is the sum of currency and demand deposits.
9. (4) There is a need for all of these functions.
10. (4) Transactions demand is positively correlated with nominal GNP.
11. (2) Assets demand is negatively correlated with the interest rate.
12. (5) Definition.
13. (1) They are set high so that the monetary authorities know that banks are operating close to the required ratios.
14. (5) The point of the money multiplier.

15. (2) Loans are made possible by the fractional-reserve system; the money multiplier tells how many loans are possible for any given increase in reserves.
16. (2) Bank X could count on only the $10,000 deposit; against a 25 percent required reserve ratio, it could thus lend at least $0.75 \times \$10,000 = \$7500$.
17. (4) The multiplier is $1/0.25 = 4$; $40,000 in new demand deposits can be supported by $10,000 in reserves and $30,000 in new loans.
18. (3) The multiplier would be slightly smaller.
19. (4) Same reasoning as in answer 17.
20. (3) Apply the reasoning of answer 16; $0.8 \times \$10,000 = \$8000$.
21. (2) Same reasoning as in answer 16.
22. (1) Bank Y would have to contract loans by an equal amount.
23. (5) $\$15/0.3 = \$50$.
24. (4) Definition.
25. (4) The two caveats to the money-multiplier formula are listed; high ratios guard against banks' holding excess reserves.

Chapter 11 Appendix

1. (3) From over 40 percent to under 25 percent.
2. (1) Lots of people own "little pieces" of corporate America, but most of corporate America is owned by a few.
3. (5) The informational content of prices is instantaneous, according to the theory; other movement is noise.
4. (4) Definition.
5. (3) Quantity demanded increases at every (relevant) price.
6. (1) Investing retained earnings instead of paying dividends should make the company, and thus the stock, more valuable.
7. (2) Fewer actors in the market means that there is less diversity of opinion, and swings can be enlarged.
8. (4) Margin calls require dollars, and selling stock was the only available source of (fewer and fewer) dollars and (more and more) margin calls.

Chapter 12

1. (5) Definition.
2. (4) Versus liabilities including capital accounts, Federal Reserve notes, and deposits by banks and the Treasury.
3. (2) Stimulative Fed policy lowers interest rates and thus stimulates borrowing for consumption and investment.
4. (3) Major changes, like changes in the required reserve ratio, are exceptional.
5. (1) Definition.
6. (1) Higher discount rates signal tighter monetary policy.
7. (4) An open-market purchase increases bank reserves and the Fed's holdings of securities.
8. (5) The Federal Reserve note liability will fall by $10, but the Fed's deposit liability will increase by $10.
9. (3) It is more of a signal, since use of the discount window is restrained, at most.
10. (2) The sale of securities represents a tightening of monetary policy.
11. (1) The purchase of securities is expansionary and increases bank reserves; and some of those reserves will be held in deposit at the Fed.
12. (2) Large excess reserves mean that a contraction of reserves could be accommodated by a shrinking of the excess with no effect on the (bank) money supply (i.e., no multiplier effect).
13. (3) Definition.
14. (1) The Fed would be buying securities, thereby increasing the demand for those securities and their prices; their returns would, correspondingly, fall.
15. (5) Selling securities removes reserves and thus should work to reduce the money supply.
16. (4) An increase in the discount rate signals tighter money. It must be, therefore, that the Fed is worried about inflation and will try to drive interest rates up. The resulting lower aggregate demand is bad for business, so stock prices should fall. Bond prices are inversely related to the interest rate.
17. (5) It is independent, more or less.
18. (5) Each answer describes part of the consequence.

Chapter 13

1. (3) Amounting to 35 percent of average annual GNP over the period.
2. (1) Losing a job ranks behind only the death of a spouse and going to jail in terms of personal stress.
3. (2) Definition.
4. (3) Definition.
5. (3) If the percentage (of the labor force) getting discouraged is greater than the percentage becoming unemployed, then the rate can fall.
6. (2) If wages fall, then any increased unemployment is voluntary.
7. (5) All the answers describe stylized facts about unemployment.
8. (3) Definition.
9. (2) Definition.
10. (1) Definition.
11. (5) Definition—conceptually and in practice.

Chapter 14

1. (5) Definition.
2. (1) Substitution out of an increasingly expensive commodity could reduce that commodity's weight.
3. (5) It could have been anything, depending upon the index for the other components of the CPI, medical expenses are included, though.
4. (1) The up-and-down movement of the inflation *rate* has diminished in scale since World War II, just like the amplitude of the business cycle.
5. (5) Definition and experience.
6. (3) Though inflation was high in Israel.

7. (2) It is associated with increasing GNP if driven by increased aggregate demand, and falling GNP if created by upward shocks to aggregate supply.
8. (1) Wealth goes from lenders to borrowers, who pay loans back with currency of diminished purchasing power.
9. (5) All the answers identify hedges against the potential that currency will carry less value in purchasing power.
10. (4) Wealth is transferred between people who are caught in the right and wrong positions; owners of goods or assets whose prices suddenly increase relative to others are the winners; owners of the other goods and assets are the losers. Efficiency would be improved if people were prepared (had anticipated) and if relative prices were not distorted (were balanced).
11. (2) Orchestrated recession is a possible anti-inflationary policy.
12. (1) This is the only answer that works in the correct direction—diminishing exposure to inflation. All the others increase exposure.

Chapter 15

1. (3) Definition.
2. (1) Definition.
3. (2) Definition.
4. (5) Expected inflation works into each of the listed variables.
5. (2) Both curves shift as cost increases match the increased demand.
6. (5) Stagflation involves higher prices and lower GNP (higher unemployment); demand push inflation is associated with higher GNP.
7. (2) A shift down to a lower short run Phillips curve.
8. (4) Applied definitions.
9. (1) Okun's second empirical observation; reducing inflation by one point requires unemployment 2 points higher for a year.
10. (1) Inflation being reduced by increased unemployment.
11. (1) Movement along the higher short run Phillips curve.
12. (3) A shift to a lower curve with lower inertial inflation.
13. (4) Movement along the lower short run Phillips curve.
14. (5) Definition.
15. (2) Indexing works to institutionalize inertial inflation making it harder to lower.

Chapter 16

1. (4) Transactions demand varies directly with nominal income.
2. (2) Assets demand varies inversely with nominal interest rates.
3. (5) Panel **(b)** of Figure 16-2.
4. (5) Lower borrowing costs bring marginal investment projects into the realm of expected profitability.
5. (3) Definitions.
6. (2) Internal financing still turns on the rate of interest (opportunity cost), but less directly. More inelastic demand for money or more elastic investment demand would actually increase the effectiveness of monetary policy; play with Figure 16-2 to see why.
7. (5) Tight money means higher interest rates and lower investment for any level of GNP; the investment schedule shifts down.
8. (1) The Fed would be buying government securities, thus increasing their demand, increasing their prices, and lowering their returns.
9. (5) Tight money is contractionary, but may correspond to an equilibrium.
10. (3) This short-circuits the connection to increase aggregate demand through increased investment.
11. (5) Another short circuit of the same connection.
12. (4) This is a contractionary policy; interest rates should climb as security prices fall, and the assets demand for money should decline.
13. (1) Both policies should be expansionary; spending could easily exceed revenue, in that case, while the Fed buys securities.
14. (3) New bonds and existing bonds pay the same return so that they can be competitive with one another in the securities markets.
15. (1) Even if real rates are constant, nominal rates can fall as their inflation component shrinks.
16. (2) Definition; $M \times V = P \times$ real GNP, with real GNP given by potential real GNP and the velocity V constant. Prices therefore move proportionately with the money supply.
17. (5) All follow from their views of private stability, market price flexibility, and money growth as the determinant of output growth.
18. (5) The monetarist experiment showed that money affects aggregate demand, but combating inflation with tight money is expensive in terms of output and employment, at least in the short run.

Chapter 16 Appendix

1. (4) Pretty much definition.
2. (1) Directly from flexibility in wages.
3. (3) Directly from the rationality assumption; people incorporate future tax payments into their computation of current disposable income.
4. (3) Unstable, if sloped, so that it cannot be exploited by policy.
5. (2) Because of the instability, any attempt to move along a short-run curve causes the curve to shift.
6. (1) People would see that real wages had not climbed, and nobody who was voluntarily unemployed (the only kind of unemployment allowed) would take a job.
7. (5) Collectively, these answers cover the purported impotence of discretionary policy.
8. (3) Flexible prices and/or rational expectations would have provoked behavior that would have mitigated against prolonged recession.
9. (5) Inflexible prices and wages give some power to discre-

tionary policy, but can coexist with the expectations hypothesis.

Chapter 17

1. (1) Definition; structural deficits reflect deliberate changes in policy.
2. (3) Definition; cyclical deficits reflect the business cycle.
3. (3) A change in defense spending is a discretionary adjustment in fiscal policy.
4. (5) Tax revenues grow automatically with GNP given a progressive tax structure; both deficits fall.
5. (5) Open-market operations are part of monetary policy.
6. (4) Tax cuts, a defense-spending surge, moderate domestic-spending cuts, and the monetarist experiment market in 1981 and 1982.
7. (3) Stagnant economies need some stimulus; only this answer includes only stimulus.
8. (3) The idea was to create stimulus through monetary policy while tightening fiscal policy to create low interest rates and high growth.
9. (2) Also, deficits tend to grow over time while growth slows in response to rising interest rates.
10. (5) And many more.
11. (3) The key is that the money supply, when held constant, must sum in equilibrium to the total of assets demand and transactions demand.
12. (4) Vertical aggregate supply means that GNP is invariant to changes in aggregate demand; the crowding out must therefore be complete.
13. (1) The empirical work suggests a 50 percent crowding out in the short run.
14. (4) The empirical work suggests an eventual 100 percent crowding out.
15. (5) None lead to the conclusion that the budget *must* be balanced.
16. (1) It would, as well, be increasingly difficult to maintain balance in the non-interest component of the budget as interest payments consumed increasingly large fractions of GNP.

Chapter 17 Appendix

1. (5) Definition and history.
2. (2) Definition; it is negatively sloped because investment is negatively correlated with the interest rate.
3. (4) Definition and construction.
4. (2) For any interest rate, the transactions demand for money would have to grow.
5. (1) The sale of bonds restricts the money supply; the opposite of question 4.
6. (4) Stimulative fiscal policy increases aggregate demand for any *r*; to preserve equilibrium, GNP must rise.
7. (2) Stimulative monetary policy, effectively raising the money supply.
8. (2) *IS* curve shifts left with a contractionary change in fiscal policy.
9. (4) *LM* curve shifts right with an expansionary monetary policy.
10. (3) Shift *LM* curve left; *IS* curve right.
11. (4) Definition linked with vertical aggregate supply curve.
12. (3) Move against a vertical *LM* curve.
13. (1) Because there would have been no effect without the change in the money supply.
14. (2) Shown with *IS* and *LM* curves of some slope; both moving right.

Chapter 18

1. (5) Revenue fixed means that the percentage change in quantity equals the percentage change in price.
2. (4) Definition.
3. (2) Definition.
4. (3) Definition.
5. (5) Higher incomes implies that demand shifts up; equilibrium moves along the supply curve.
6. (1) Revenue up with price down means that the percentage increase in quantity exceeded 10 percent.
7. (3) $E_D = 5\%/10\% = 0.5 < 1$.
8. (2) Definition.
9. (4) With some price elasticity in supply and demand, tax is shared. Graph it.
10. (1) The tax means that supply changes; equilibrium moves along the demand curve. Graph it.
11. (1) Definition.
12. (1) Definition.
13. (4) Definition.
14. (1) Definition.
15. (3) Definition.
16. (5) Unit elasticity throughout is a rectangular hyperbola with revenue constant; formula: $P = k \times Q^{-1}$ or $P \times Q = k$.
17. (2) Longer term means that the price elasticity of supply climbs; the price increase is therefore smaller. Graph it.
18. (2) Definition.
19. (4) Failure means a contraction in supply; quantity falls along the demand curve. Graph it.
20. (1) Contract supply; graph it.
21. (4) Definition of responsiveness.
22. (1) Only answer that maintains constant ratio of percentage changes *and* correct slope; (2) is unitary elasticity for demand.

Chapter 19

1. (4) Definition.
2. (1) Definition.
3. (2) Definition.
4. (5) The ratio of marginal utilities to prices must be equal.
5. (1) An increase in the price of a substitute or a decline in the price of a complement causes the quantity demanded to increase *for each and every* price; i.e., demand shifts up.

6. (3) $MU_A/P_A = 30/0.7 = 45 > 40 = 20/0.5 = MU_B/P_B$.
7. (2) Definition.
8. (5) Definition.
9. (4) $MU_X/1.5 = MU_Y/P_Y = 30/1 = 30$ means that $MU_X = 45$.
10. (5) You need marginal utility numbers, not total utility.
11. (1) Definition.
12. (1) $MU = 0$ means that more consumption does not cause total utility to increase further; total utility must have peaked.
13. (2) Marginal utility falling for all goods means that consumption in all of them must be higher.
14. (2) Definition.

Chapter 19 Appendix

1. (5) Definition.
2. (4) Definition.
3. (4) Only the process here leads to the requisite tangency.
4. (5) Definition.
5. (5) Definition.

Chapter 20

1. (2) Definition.
2. (1) Debt service (interest payment) is a contractual obligation regardless of circumstance.
3. (5) Unlike the other things listed, dividends need not be paid.
4. (2) Investment banks are intermediaries between corporations and potential shareholders.
5. (2) Preferred stocks have fixed yields like bonds, but not paying dividends does not signal bankruptcy.
6. (4) Definition.
7. (1) Debt service is still a contractual obligation.
8. (1) Definition.
9. (2) And so was formed the Harvard Business School.
10. (5) The investment house must do its homework!
11. (3) Dividend payments are optional; interest payments are not.
12. (2) A step might be skipped, though.
13. (3) Depreciation is an accounting device to finance replacement capital.
14. (2) Personal taxes apply only to accrued income.
15. (1) Revenue net of business expense and interest is subject to the corporate tax.

Chapter 20 Appendix

1. (3) Think goodwill and inventories.
2. (3) Interest payments are a current expense.
3. (2) Depreciation should not exceed 100% of the cost of the machine. What does that do in inflationary times?
4. (2) Definition.
5. (1) To neglect depreciation is to ignore the future.
6. (3) Definition.
7. (4) Net worth at the end of 1988 was $30,000; at the end of 1989, $40,000. Thus, a $10,000 increase. Coupled with dividends of $15,000, total profits must have been $25,000.
8. (4) Definition.
9. (2) Profits are either distributed as dividends or held as retained earnings.
10. (3) Definition.
11. (4) Accelerated depreciation allows a firm to deduct a larger percentage of investment cost from revenue; profits and tax liability therefore fall.
12. (3) Net worth rose by $150,000 [($550,000 − $200,000) − ($600,000 − $400,000)] financed by $100,000 in stock sales and profit; profit must have contributed $50,000. Combine that with dividends of $50,000 to get total profit after taxes.

Chapter 21

1. (3) Definition.
2. (5) Diminishing returns can coexist with increasing, decreasing, and/or constant returns to scale; they measure different things.
3. (4) $MP < AP$ means that the contribution of the last unit employed is smaller than the previous average; that addition must therefore bring the average down.
4. (1) $AP = [TP(K = 3;\ L = 4)]/4 = 52/4 = 13$.
5. (4) $TP(K = 2;\ L = 5) = 40$, while $TP(K = 3;\ L = 5) = 62$. The MP of the third unit of K must therefore be $(62 - 40)/1 = 22$.
6. (5) Production displays diminishing returns throughout with respect to both K and L.
7. (3) *IRS*, because twice the inputs yield more than twice the output.
8. (4) $TP(K = 2;\ L = 3) = 27$, so $TP(K = 2 \times 2;\ L = 2 \times 3)$ must equal 2×27.
9. (5) Answers 2, 3, and 4 are short-run responses, but anything possible in the short run is possible in the long run, too.
10. (3) Total productivity up an average of 1.5 percent per year since 1900, but only 0.5 percent per year since 1970.
11. (4) Technological progress means productivity up and output higher for any level of employment; the new curve must be higher and steeper (try to draw it always above and flatter).

Chapter 22

1. (4) Definition.
2. (4) Definition.
3. (5) Change in fixed cost does not affect variable cost; marginal cost thus unaffected.
4. (3) $MC = \$10$ while $AC(1000) = \$4.90$ and $AC(999) = \$4.88$.
5. (1) Definition.
6. (4) If $MC > AC$, then AC rising; if $MC < AC$, then AC falling. At minimum where AC is flat, MC must therefore equal MC.

7. (1) $MC > AC$ means incremental cost is larger than previous average, so average *must* climb.
8. (4) Only constant AC means constant MC, so AC must change. Rise or fall depends upon whether MC is larger or smaller.
9. (1) Definition.
10. (4) The least-cost rule.
11. (4) Definition. Need input prices to judge efficiency and/or compute costs.
12. (4) Definition.
13. (5) Definition.
14. (2) Definition.
15. (2) $MP_A/P_A = 60/4 = 15 < MP_B/P_B = 40/2 = 20$; costs not minimized means profits not maximized.
16. (3) Equal MP/P ratios give minimum cost but not necessarily maximum profits.

Chapter 22 Appendix

1. (3) Definition.
2. (4) Definition.
3. (4) Definition.
4. (2) Equal-cost line satisfies $C = P_X X + P_Y Y$ for two goods X and Y. With the vertical axis, that is $Y = -(P_X/P_Y)X + (C/P_Y)$
5. (1) L-shaped isoproduct curve; increasing 1 input causes *no* change in output.
6. (1) B intercept fixed and A intercept higher means P_A falling and P_B fixed.
7. (5) Both intercepts out means either cost up or *both* prices down.
8. (4) A intercept fixed and B intercept lower means P_B rising and P_A fixed.
9. (5) Definition.
10. (3) Definition.
11. (3) Definitions.
12. (2) Fixed proportions mean single combination of inputs exists for each output.

Chapter 23

1. (4) Definition; produce where MC is rising.
2. (2) Specifically, the part above the shutdown point where $AVC > MC$.
3. (4) Need information about MC, AC is not sufficient to judge profits.
4. (5) MC of unit 2001 is $\$19,010 - \$19,000 = \$10 = P$.
5. (4) Is it covering variable cost? Don't know.
6. (2) It is now covering variable cost.
7. (5) Necessarily wants to set MC equal to P.
8. (3) Entry or exit drives pure economic profit to zero, and P to minimum AC.
9. (5) Need price information to set $MC = P$.
10. (1) Tax raises AC up along unaffected MC; output must climb along same MC.
11. (1) It is in long-run equilibrium.
12. (2) Output maximizes profit, so $P = MC = \$10$; output $=$ TR/P $= \$5000/\$10 = \$500$.
13. (4) $AC = \$8$ and $AVC = \$5$, so $AFC = \$3$. $FC = \$3 \times 500 = \$1500$.
14. (4) P exceeds AC by \$2 for each unit; profit $= \$2 \times 500 = \$1000$.
15. (1) Definition.
16. (3) Check if $P = MC$. $P = \$7$ and $MC = TC(201) - TC(200) = (\$5 \times 201) - (\$4.99 \times 200) = \$7$. Yes.
17. (1) Need MC to climb toward \$1.90; so output must rise.
18. (5) Decreasing costs undermine perfect competition.
19. (5) MC unaffected, so $P = MC$ at the same output and price.
20. (2) Tax causes minimum AC to climb; equilibrium price therefore climbs with the quantity demanded falling.
21. (5) Definition.
22. (3) Direction of output change depends upon whether $P > MC$, $P = MC$, or $P < MC$.
23. (1) $P > MC$ means that output must climb to get MC to move up toward P.
24. (3) Price will fall to minimum AC where $MC = AC$; quantity demanded rises along demand curve.
25. (4) Decreasing costs breed imperfect competition.

Chapter 23 Appendix

1. (2) Definition of perfectly elastic.
2. (3) Definition of perfectly elastic.
3. (1) Pure rent implies perfectly inelastic supply.
4. (1) Definition.
5. (3) Constant cost implies perfectly elastic supply.
6. (1) Tax increases constant (average and marginal) cost by the full \$1, so price goes up by that \$1, too.
7. (3) Definition.
8. (4) Definition.
9. (2) Definition.
10. (1) Rent implies perfectly inelastic supply, so quantity cannot change.
11. (1) Definition.
12. (1) Rent implies fixed supply and thus fixed price paid by demanders regardless of tax; tax is thus paid entirely by suppliers.
13. (1) Diminishing returns is one reason for positively sloped supply curves.
14. (1) Diminishing returns at work for other inputs, but not to the extent of fixing wheat output.

Chapter 24

1. (5) Definition.
2. (3) Roughly 38 percent, at least in the mid-1970s.
3. (1) $P > MR > MC$ means that output must increase to bring MC up toward either P (perfect competition) or MR (imperfect competition).
4. (3) Each unit of increased sales increases revenue by exactly the price of the good sold.
5. (1) Definition.

6. (3) Definition.
7. (3) For a monopolist, $MC = MR$ and $MR < P$.
8. (5) Definition.
9. (1) Definition.
10. (3) $MR > P$ would mean that the sale of 1 more unit would allow the price of all the previously demanded units to *increase*.
11. (2) Minimum $AC = MC = \$1.75 < \$2.00 = MR$. Output should be increased (to move MC up toward MR), and thus price should fall.
12. (5) Need MR information to tell anything.
13. (1) Definition.
14. (2) The rule for perfect competition is $P = MC$; $P > MC$ means output should increase. For the imperfect competitor, though, need information about MR.
15. (4) $P < MC$ means that the competitor should cut back. Since $MR < P$ ($< MC$) along a demand curve, so should the monopolist.
16. (3) Economies of scale are major sources of market power.
17. (1) $MR > 0$ ($=0$; < 0) mean that TR increases (stays the same; falls) as Q increases and P falls; so the percentage increase in Q must be larger (equal to, smaller) than the percentage reduction in price.
18. (5) Horizontal demand means no power over price.

Chapter 25

1. (5) The answers trace out the characteristics of highly concentrated markets.
2. (2) Definition; focus on the word "legal."
3. (4) Definition.
4. (1) Predatory pricing is illegal.
5. (2) Think Saudi Arabia, which is generally the "swing" producer for the agreed-to price.
6. (3) Lots of close substitutes.
7. (5) Lots of producers of identical products.
8. (5) A dominant firm without a cost advantage would be unable to quote a price that would prevent the competitive fringe from making excessive profits, attracting other firms, and driving the price below its minimum average cost.
9. (4) The monopolistic competition long-run equilibrium shows $P = AC >$ min AC.
10. (1) Knowledge of MC should be better, since it is its own production process.
11. (1) Definition of the hypothesis.
12. (5) A restatement of the modern view of market intervention.
13. (3) Definition.
14. (2) Definition.
15. (2) It has the greatest potential to breed anticompetitive behavior.
16. (2) Clayton Act (as amended) bans tying contracts, price discrimination, interlocking directorates, and *mergers formed by acquiring common stock of competitors*.
17. (4) The Federal Trade Commission Act (as amended) outlaws unfair methods of competition as well as unfair or deceptive practices.
18. (1) The Sherman Act (as amended) bans monopolizing trade, conspiring to monopolize trade, and *conspiring to restrain trade among several states or foreign nations*.

Chapter 26

1. (5) All the statements are accurate descriptions of historical experience.
2. (2) Definition.
3. (4) The 45° line specifies that percentage of people = percentage of income at all levels.
4. (3) A line running along the horizontal axis until it reached 100 percent of the people, then climbing vertically to 100 percent of the income.
5. (3) The proportion of income received by the lowest 20 percent of the people was, e.g., 4.7 percent in the mid-1970s and 4.2 percent in the late 1980s.
6. (2) Up from \$42,000 in 1984.
7. (4) \$260, up from \$255 in 1984.
8. (3) Experience.
9. (1) Definition.
10. (2) Definition.
11. (4) Start with perfect equality: the lowest 20 percent get 20 percent of the income. Introducing any inequality means that the people that lose, relatively, must be in the bottom 20 percent of the population, and their cumulative percentage must fall below the original 20 percent of the income.
12. (2) The distributions do not match, so there must be something else going on as well.
13. (4) The greater disparity in the distribution of wealth is striking in the light of similar distributions of income.

Chapter 27

1. (3) Definition.
2. (3) Definition.
3. (5) Definition.
4. (3) $MRP = MR \times MP = P$.
5. (5) $MRP = P$.
6. (1) Monopoly power means that the price of output > MR, so $MRP_A < P_A$.
7. (1) Again, monopoly power means that the price of output > MR; only \$1 conforms to this fact.
8. (3) Given perfect competition, the price of output $= MR$, so here, $MRP_A = P_A$.
9. (4) The single good serves as the "numeraire"; it is as if the price of output is \$1.
10. (3) Definition, given constant returns to scale.
11. (3) Definition.
12. (1) "Many alternative uses" means that the rental price *received* by suppliers is fixed; the entire tax is thus borne by the tobacco growers, even if they rent the land.

13. (1) A leftward shift of demand means that price falls—by more than it would if quantity could fall, too.
14. (2) Apply the definition of opportunity cost.
15. (4) Apply the definition of opportunity cost.
16. (1) Land with fixed supply allows high demand to be translated into a high price.
17. (1) Definition; price signals reflect social cost.
18. (3) If more than one use exists, then the supply for any *one* user or group of users is not inelastic.
19. (5) Definition.
20. (2) Definition.

Chapter 28

1. (2) Competition tends to equalize prices (wages, here).
2. (1) Definition.
3. (5) Anything that affects the quantity of labor supplied.
4. (3) Definition.
5. (3) The "reserve army" of unemployed workers was Marx's explanation of the same idea.
6. (3) Inelastic product demand supports inelastic derived demand for labor.
7. (4) Definition.
8. (3) Definition.
9. (5) Definition; the fallacy ignores possible creation of new jobs.
10. (1) Precisely when the need to create new job opportunities was most severe.
11. (3) D_1D_1 and D_2D_2 both intersect *SS* in its backward-bending, negatively sloped region—the region dominated by the income effect in which lower wages decrease leisure.
12. (2) Quantity of labor supplied is unaffected; the two effects must cancel to achieve this, since they *always* push in opposite directions.
13. (1) Lower wage implies substitution toward leisure (its opportunity cost is down) that dominates income effect.
14. (1) Direction does not matter; here, substitution out of leisure dominates.
15. (5) Definition of rent applied to people.
16. (2) Real wages rose from 1.5 [= 600/400] to 1.8 [= 540/300].

Chapter 29

1. (1) Union membership has fallen recently to 19 million—roughly one-sixth of the labor force.
2. (4) Definition—the genesis of the CIO.
3. (3) The local unions represent workers most directly; they do, however, gain support from their ties to national unions and federations of national unions.
4. (3) Unions were subject to the Sherman Antitrust Act, which banned any activity that served to restrain trade.
5. (2) Definition (legal) from the Wagner Act.
6. (4) Gompers believed in federalism (of which this question speaks), voluntarism, and business unionism.
7. (2) The Wagner Act (National Labor Relations Act) established the right of workers to organize and bargain collectively.
8. (5) The NLRB, established before Taft-Hartley, validates the appropriate bargaining unit by election.
9. (3) The creation of the limited "cooling-off period."
10. (5) Supporting an aggregate production with a constant share of roughly 80 percent.
11. (2) Taft-Hartley, in general, started the pendulum moving away from legislative sanction of increased union power.
12. (4) The Clayton Act removed unions from the preview of the Sherman Antitrust Act.
13. (5) The "high-water" benchmark of pro-union legislation.
14. (3) Prior to the 1914 Clayton Act, unions fell under the Sherman notion of "restraint of trade" by interpretation, not intent.
15. (4) Imperfections limit the market response to excess supply or excess demand.
16. (1) Shift supply curve up.
17. (4) Shift supply curve up.
18. (1) Draw a horizontal line above the *DD-SS* intersection; read new (employment, wage) pair from the *DD* curve.

Chapter 30

1. (1) Innovation is one of the primary sources of uncertainty in Knight's theory of profit.
2. (3) Definition; highlight the word "net."
3. (2) The cost should include the cost of financing, if any; knowing the means associated with that cost is irrelevant.
4. (1) Definition—influencing the derived demand for capital.
5. (3) You need both sides of the market—demand (derived demand depending upon the rate of return) and supply (willingness to defer consumption).
6. (4) Definition—diminishing returns pushing rates so low that saving falls to zero.
7. (4) Technological change can push the demand out even as short-run supply shifts out to maintain a higher interest rate.
8. (2) Market value = present value = \$100/0.08 = \$1250.
9. (5) Just look at the $PV = \$N/i$ formula. Lower i means higher *PV* because future installments of $\$N$ are not discounted as strenuously.
10. (3) The rate of return depends on cost and revenue stream; a lower interest rate increases the likelihood that the assets in question might be constructed. (Remember, it will be considered if the rate of return exceeds the interest rate.)
11. (1) Real rate + inflation rate = nominal rate; if the inflation rate is negative, then real > nominal.
12. (1) Investors consider undertaking capital projects when their rates of return exceed (or just equal) the market rate of interest; otherwise, they can do better by lending their money to someone at the market rate.

13. (1) Definition.
14. (3) Profit was the justifiable reward for those who took risks, according to Knight; without those rewards, why would anyone take any risk at all?
15. (4) Insurance companies spread risk.
16. (2) Definition.

Chapter 30 Appendix

1. (4) Rate of return determines the demand side; rate of time preference determines the supply side.
2. (5) More impatience makes the indifference curves steeper. Improved technology makes the *PPF* steeper. Tangency with slope between 0 and -1 shows a negative interest rate.
3. (3) The interest rate appears in the denominators of the components of present value, with higher powers for more distant future returns.
4. (5) Higher interest rates simply make assets of given rates of return relatively less attractive (so investment falls).
5. (5) Rates can fall only to the point at which holding currency becomes the dominant investment strategy.
6. (3) According to the formula for present value, $V = \$500/(1.09) \approx \$459$.
7. (3) Definition.

Chapter 31

1. (2) $MU = P = MC$.
2. (5) The profit motive can move perfect competitors and imperfect competitors alike; profits are maximized by producing the output at which MR ($=P$ in perfect competition) $=MC$.
3. (2) The competitive model provides a benchmark of efficiency against which other situations can be evaluated.
4. (4) Given any distribution of resources, and thus income, there exists a set of prices that will support competitive equilibrium.
5. (5) In long-run competitive equilibrium, $P = MC =$ minimum AC.
6. (4) Power over price distorts competitive equilibrium because $P > MC$.
7. (2) Definition.

Chapter 32

1. (3) The sum of the budgets of *all* governments in the United States have climbed from 10 percent of GNP prior to World War I to 35 percent now.
2. (2) Tax receipts nearly kept pace until the tax cuts of the 1980s.
3. (2) The only reference available that might apply is "securing the public interest."
4. (2) The ICC was the first (1887); regulation peaked in the mid-to-late 1970s.
5. (5) Each choice identifies a role for government, and regulation is one possible tool.
6. (5) The general list is provided among the answers.
7. (2) The utilities of both people fall only in moving from A to C.
8. (1) The utility of II increases as the utility of I falls only in moving from A to B.
9. (4) Unanimity requires that the utilities of both people increase—a condition met only in moving from A to E.
10. (3) Majority approval requires that people of type I see their utilities increase—a condition met only by point D.
11. (5) Arrow proved that there exists no majority voting scheme that guarantees efficiency, respects individual preferences, and produces outcomes independent of agenda.
12. (5) All are consequences.
13. (1) Refer to your own experience; mine is indicated.
14. (2) The public nature of the good suggests that it is difficult to exclude; the fact that many can enjoy a public good simultaneously suggests that the cost of one more person (i.e., marginal cost) is small.
15. (5) Both have all the characteristics of externalities.
16. (4) Marginal social damage equals marginal cost of abatement at point D.
17. (3) The difference between marginal private cost and marginal abatement cost must be \$2; it is too large for \$2 at point D and just about right at C.
18. (1) Add the amount each would pay for the community demand curve.
19. (2) Some people stretch the result to *always*; most economists do not believe in the result that much, but admit to *may*.

Chapter 33

1. (2) Defense has been particularly emphasized in the budgets of the Reagan administration.
2. (5) It is an example of the government providing a public good—in this case, physical infrastructure.
3. (2) Transfer payments increase the incomes of some people at the expense of the incomes of others.
4. (5) Corporate income is the sum of dividends paid and retained earnings.
5. (3) All explicit money income is subject to the personal-income-tax structure; some implicit income is (employer-subsidized mortgages) and some is not (housing services to homeowners).
6. (2) Money earned and retained would not be subject to any tax (save for capital gains, when realized) were it not for the corporation income tax.
7. (5) The personal income tax is applied to dividends generated by corporate income that has already been taxed.
8. (1) The federal government has long relied most heavily on the personal income tax.
9. (4) The increase in income is \$2000. The increase in tax liability is \$800. The marginal rate is thus $(800/200) \times 100\% = 40\%$.

10. (2) Regressive taxes increase inequality in the distribution of (after-tax) income.
11. (2) The reason is given in the answer; answer (4) is a tautology.
12. (1) Definition.
13. (5) Definition.
14. (3) Definition.
15. (4) Definition.
16. (2) Property taxes (local governments) and sales taxes (state governments) tend to be regressive, particularly when compared with the personal income tax that is designed to be at least mildly progressive and the corporation income tax that is effectively progressive if it is not shifted.
17. (1) $52.8 billion in 1988.

Chapter 34

1. (5) All the statements are accurate.
2. (2) It reached 15 percent in 1984 before falling slightly to 14 percent in 1988.
3. (5) All the statements are accurate; consult Tables 34-1 and 34-2.
4. (4) Recession has, recently, been fair—hitting most demographic groups equally.
5. (4) Poverty still exists, even though those in the poorest 20 percent of the population have seen their incomes grow in line with GNP.
6. (3) The exact percentage is 21.5 percent.
7. (3) The notion behind the negative income tax is that the marginal tax rate applied to the income earned by the working poor is small.
8. (5) No leaks means moving along the 45° line *AE*; equality occurs on the 45° line *OE*.
9. (4) Equality occurs on the 45° line *OE*.
10. (3) Remember, question 5 set forth Rawlsian indifference curves that are horizontal—the higher, the better.
11. (5) All are subjects for continued investigation.
12. (1) Medicaid was highest, followed by food stamps.
13. (5) Part of the Reagan agenda and reliance on the private sector.
14. (5) And all are subjects of criticism and concern.
15. (1) Work disincentives imply inefficiency.

Chapter 35

1. (3) The self-regulating natural order that Smith asserted would be provided by a freely operating market system.
2. (3) It was competitive markets to which Smith referred.
3. (5) Land would be the bottleneck of continued economic growth; profit falls while wage maintains a subsistence level.
4. (4) A decline in the rate of business profit would be the source of increased pressure on payment to labor that would lead to the proletarian revolt and ultimate victory.
5. (1) Milton Friedman has argued vigorously against many forms of government intervention in markets and society.
6. (4) Diminishing returns applied to land would make the capitalists more important.
7. (1) The notion of marginalism extended to all factors of production ultimately led to the development of a general-equilibrium view of economic systems.
8. (3) Those other inputs must be paid out of the price that the product commands in the market.
9. (3) The Clark theory of distribution (e.g.).
10. (4) The labor theory of value described what should be.
11. (3) There are other differences, of course, but their distinctly different treatment of unionism is important.
12. (5) Consumer-goods shortages have plagued the Soviet Union for years.
13. (3) The Gorbachev reforms may change this to some degree.
14. (2) There are no income taxes in the Soviet Union.
15. (1) 52 percent and 44 percent, respectively, in 1985.

Chapter 36

1. (1) Output increases, though at a decreasing rate, with increases in labor, so the ratio of land, which is fixed, to output must fall.
2. (3) Prices are determined by labor costs.
3. (2) Technological change explains why diminishing returns have not set in.
4. (5) Again, the result of counterbalancing technological change.
5. (2) At about 75 percent of GNP.
6. (4) No decline in the capital-output ratio indicates no diminishing returns; technological change must be the reason.
7. (5) Technological progress, if present, is reflected in the capital-output ratio. Since that ratio is falling, technology is not keeping pace with diminishing returns; the return to capital is given by its declining marginal product.
8. (1) Diminishing returns must eventually set in.
9. (5) It all depends on the rate of technological change; any of the answers *might* be right, but none is *necessarily* right.
10. (1) Definition.
11. (4) The incremental increases in output decline with larger amounts of capital, so the capital-output ratio must fall.
12. (5) Diminishing returns is the only answer that *must* apply.

Chapter 36 Appendix

1. (1) A constant capital-output ratio means that diminishing returns have not come to bear.
2. (5) All of those things will remain stable.
3. (3) The capital-labor ratio holds.
4. (5) Definition.
5. (5) To maintain full employment, planned investment must equal intended saving.
6. (1) Definition.

7. (4) Noted by reading across a row; input needs are shown in columns.

Chapter 37

1. (4) Providing, essentially, public goods that promote development but for which there is insufficient gain to rely on private provision.
2. (3) They have moved into the "early development" demographic stage with continued high birth rates and reduced death rates.
3. (5) Insufficient saving is one problem.
4. (5) People have work, but their productivity is minimal; in a developed economy, they would be called underemployed.
5. (1) Imports rise as its markets open and its needs increase (e.g., for the capital that embodies the technology that the country is "borrowing").
6. (2) Definition.
7. (1) Saving required to finance the necessary investment.
8. (4) Some do, but many do not.
9. (5) There has been some widening since the early 1980s.

Chapter 38

1. (4) All the other answers speak to absolute advantage; trade patterns are determined by comparative advantage.
2. (3) The Ricardo analysis is classical, assuming swift market adjustment to the changes created by trade.
3. (2) The demand for exported goods climbs, creating upward pressure on their prices; the demand for imported goods falls, tending to push their prices down.
4. (4) In A, each yard of cloth takes 12 minutes to produce; each liter of wine, 6 minutes. In B, each yard takes 4 minutes; each liter, 3 minutes. The wine-to-cloth ratio in A is thus 1:2; in B, it is 3:4. A therefore has a comparative advantage in wine even though B has absolute advantages in both goods.
5. (3) The prices of wine must preserve the 1:2 and 3:4 cost ratios in the Ricardo classical model.
6. (1) Country A has the comparative advantage in wine.
7. (1) It will move somewhere between 1:2 and 3:4.
8. (3) Without transportation costs, it must be the same in both countries. The wine-to-cloth price ratio must be between 0.5 and 0.75, so the cloth-to-wine ratio must be between 1.33 and 2.
9. (3) Each yard of cloth is worth 1.6 liters of wine; so 800 liters (500×1.6) must be exchanged—exported from A.
10. (3) B is the wine-importing country. Each hour devoted to wine there produces 20 liters; devoted to cloth, that hour could product 15 yards which, given a 1.6 price-of-cloth-to-wine ratio, could be translated into 24 liters of wine.
11. (5) Decreasing costs (economies of scale) can produce gains from trade only after trade is begun and they can be exploited.
12. (3) This is the point of the Ricardo model; comparative advantage matters.
13. (4) Definition.
14. (5) Only this answer would be recorded as a credit because it produces foreign currency; all of the others are debit transactions because they expand foreign currency.
15. (3) Definition.

Chapter 39

1. (3) It ignores the theory of comparative advantage.
2. (1) The second tariff would make country B even worse off.
3. (2) The parallel view to personal saving, the mercantile position cannot be maintained by all countries.
4. (2) Higher productivity should give the United States a comparative advantage in some goods, but not necessarily an absolute advantage in all (any) goods.
5. (3) Protection makes domestic prices higher.
6. (3) Under static conditions, general welfare is maximized in long-run, full-employment, free-trade equilibrium.
7. (2) The optimal-tariff idea depends upon a country's ability to move the terms of trade without retaliation; its trading partner must, therefore, be small *and* the volume of its trade must have influence over the world price.
8. (2) Subsidy provides the effective encouragement without the price effects and the direct threat of retaliation.
9. (5) With other countries' exports reduced by our large tariffs, their ability to import *our exports* will be diminished if they are to maintain a reasonable trade balance even without retaliation.
10. (2) Protection increases domestic prices, and thus reduces domestic real income.
11. (3) Effective protection and revenue maximization are two different goals; they need not lead to the same policy.
12. (5) The right to import 1 unit will be sold for exactly the tariff in an auction.

Chapter 40

1. (3) Definition.
2. (1) Definition.
3. (2) Four francs buy $1, which buys 600 lire; 1 franc must therefore buy 600/4 = 150 lire.
4. (3) B must pay for the exports with gold, increasing the money supply and prices in A and reducing both in B.
5. (4) Four francs to the dollar makes the price of 1 franc $0.25; three to the dollar, $0.33.
6. (1) Increase the supply of dollars.
7. (4) An increase in the demand for Canadian dollars increases the supply of U.S. dollars.
8. (2) Depreciation in the dollar makes U.S. exports less expensive and imports from abroad more expensive.
9. (2) Depreciation of a domestic currency makes imports more expensive at home and exports less expensive abroad.

10. (1) A decline in economic activity in the United States causes imports to shrink, the demand for foreign currency to fall, and thus the price of the dollar to fall.

11. (1) New rules were defined for maintaining exchange-rate levels.

12. (4) Some short-term, rate-sustaining borrowing was allowed.

13. (2) The World Bank was created to help developing countries with long-term loans.

14. (3) Without fixed rates, the exchange rate can move to ameliorate a balance-of-trade problem.

15. (5) Definition.